3-2-1 Code It!

Fourth Edition

Michelle A. Green
MPS, RHIA, FAHIMA, CPC

3-2-1 Code It!

Fourth Edition

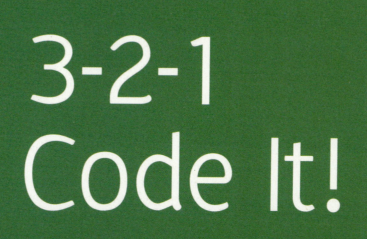

Michelle A. Green

MPS, RHIA, FAHIMA, CPC

DELMAR
CENGAGE Learning

3-2-1 Code It! Fourth Edition
Michelle A. Green, MPS, RHIA, FAHIMA, CPC

Vice President, Careers & Computing: Dave Garza

Publisher, Health Care: Stephen Helba

Director, Development - Careers & Computing: Marah Bellegarde

Product Development Manager, Careers: Juliet Steiner

Associate Acquisitions Editor: Jadin B. Kavanaugh

Product Manager: Amy Wetsel

Editorial Assistant: Courtney Cozzy

Brand Manager: Wendy Mapstone

Market Development Manager: Nancy Bradshaw

Senior Production Director: Wendy A. Troeger

Production Manager: Andrew Crouth

Senior Content Project Manager: Kara A. DiCaterino

Senior Art Director: Jack Pendleton

Technology Project Manager: Patricia Allen

Media Editor: William Overocker

Cover image(s): www.Shutterstock.com

For product information and technology assistance, contact us at
Cengage Learning Customer & Sales Support, 1-800-354-9706

For permission to use material from this text or product, submit all requests online at **www.cengage.com/permissions**.
Further permissions questions can be e-mailed to **permissionrequest@cengage.com**

ExamView® and ExamView Pro® are registered trademarks of FSCreations, Inc. Windows is a registered trademark of the Microsoft Corporation used herein under license. Macintosh and Power Macintosh are registered trademarks of Apple Computer, Inc. Used herein under license.

© 2014 Cengage Learning. All Rights Reserved. Cengage Learning WebTutor™ is a trademark of Cengage Learning.

Library of Congress Control Number: 2012951823

ISBN-13: 978-1-285-42289-3

ISBN-10: 1-285-42289-9

Delmar
Executive Woods
5 Maxwell Drive
Clifton Park, NY 12065
USA

Cengage Learning is a leading provider of customized learning solutions with office locations around the globe, including Singapore, the United Kingdom, Australia, Mexico, Brazil, and Japan. Locate your local office at: **www.cengage.com/global**

Cengage Learning products are represented in Canada by Nelson Education, Ltd.

To learn more about Delmar, visit **www.cengage.com/delmar**

Purchase any of our products at your local book store or at our preferred online store **www.cengagebrain.com**

The 2013 versions of CPT, ICD-9-CM, ICD-10-CM, and ICD-10-PCS were used in preparation of this product.

CPT copyright 2012 American Medical Association. All rights reserved. CPT is a registered trademark of the American Medical Association. Applicable FARS/DFARS Restrictions Apply to Government Use. Fee schedules, relative value units, conversion factors and/or related components are not assigned by the AMA, are not part of CPT, and the AMA is not recommending their use. The AMA does not directly or indirectly practice medicine or dispense medical services. The AMA assumes no liability for data contained or not contained herein.

Printed in the United States of America
1 2 3 4 5 6 7 17 16 15 14 13

Table of Contents

List of Tables

Preface

Introduction

Accurate coding is crucial to the successful operation of any health care facility or provider's office because reported codes determine the amount of reimbursement received. The annual (and sometimes more frequent) revision of coding guidelines and payer requirements serve to challenge coders. Those responsible for assigning and reporting codes in any health care setting require thorough instruction in the use of the ICD-9-CM (or ICD-10-CM/PCS), CPT, and HCPCS level II coding systems. Students who are completing formal coursework as part of an academic program and experienced coders who are already employed in the health care field will find that *3-2-1 Code It!* provides the required information in a clear and comprehensive manner.

ICD-10 Alert:

Effective October 1, 2014, ICD-10-CM and ICD-10-PCS (abbreviated as ICD-10-CM/PCS) replaces ICD-9-CM. ICD-10-CM and ICD-10-PCS content has been incorporated into Chapters 2–6 of this textbook.

Due to the comprehensive nature of the *3-2-1 Code It!* textbook, instructors may choose to cover its content in more than one course.

- Chapters 1 through 7 could be taught in an ICD-9-CM, ICD-10-CM/PCS and HCPCS level II coding course.

- Chapters 8 through 18 could be taught in a CPT coding course.

- Chapter 19 could be included as required reading in an insurance and reimbursement course, either as an introductory or summary chapter.

Instructors for medical assistant (MA) and medical office administration (MOA) programs may choose to cover the following chapters only in their coding course(s):

- Chapters 2 through 4 and 6 through 7 in an ICD-9-CM, ICD-10-CM and HCPCS Level II coding course. (ICD-10-PCS is not used for outpatient or physician office coding.)

Note:

Delmar Cengage Learning distributes an Educational ICD-9-CM and HCPCS Level II code book for OptumInsight. Contact your Delmar sales representative to adopt for your course.

- Chapters 8 through 9, selected sections of 11 through 15, and 16 through 18 in a CPT coding course.

Note:

Your academic program's community of interest (e.g., employers of graduates) will determine which sections of Chapters 11 through 15 (CPT Surgery) should be covered in your CPT coding course. Likewise, if your graduates obtain employment assigning and submitting CPT Anesthesia codes, your course should include Chapter 10. If your graduates do not assign radiology or pathology/laboratory codes during their employment, Chapters 16 and 17 can be excluded from your CPT coding course.

Instructors can refer to the Instructor's Manual for sample course syllabi that organize textbook content into one or two courses. For example, the syllabus for a one-semester course includes content from *3-2-1 Code It!* appropriate for an introductory course.

ICD-10 Alert:

During academic terms starting Fall 2013 and Spring 2014, ICD-10-CM and ICD-10-PCS (abbreviated as ICD-10-CM/PCS) coding manuals will replace the ICD-9-CM coding manual. Until then academic programs should teach both ICD-9-CM and ICD-10-CM/PCS coding, and require student to learn how to code using all of the coding manuals.

The *3-2-1 Code It!* text requires users to have access to paper-based coding manuals (ICD-9-CM, ICD-10-CM, ICD-10-PCS, HCPCS level II, CDT, and CPT) because they are used as references when coding rules are explained and for completing exercises and reviews in each chapter. To provide students with experience using encoder software, a 59-day trial of OptumInsight's www.EncoderPro.com is provided. Students should not activate the 59-day trial until instructed to do so by faculty. Students should use paper-based coding manuals to learn how to assign codes. Then, www.EncoderPro.com software can be used to assign codes for exercises as assigned by your instructor.

Note:

HCPCS level II previously included dental codes (D codes), which are copyrighted by the American Dental Association. Effective 2012, purchase of a separate Current Dental Terminology (CDT) coding manual is required to assign dental codes to procedure and service statements in Chapter 7 of the textbook and its ancillary products.

The intended use of *3-2-1 Code It!* is for:

- Academic programs in coding and reimbursement, health information management, medical assisting, medical office administration, and so on.

- In-service education programs in health care facilities (e.g., physicians' offices, hospitals, nursing facilities, home health agencies, hospices, and so on), health insurance companies, quality improvement organizations, and so on.

- Individuals who want to use it for self-instruction to learn how to code or to update their coding skills.

- Health care professionals who need a comprehensive coding reference to assist them in accurately assigning codes.

It is recommended that students complete the following course work before they begin and/or during the same time they are learning concepts presented in *3-2-1 Code It!*.

- Essentials of health information management

- Medical terminology

- Anatomy and physiology

- Essentials of pharmacology

- Human diseases/pathophysiology

Organization of This Textbook

This textbook is organized into 19 chapters and 3 appendices.

- Chapter 1 includes an overview of coding systems used to report inpatient and outpatient diagnoses and procedures and services to health plans. It also focuses on coding career opportunities in health care, the importance of joining professional organizations and obtaining coding credentials, the impact of networking with other coding professionals, and the development of opportunities for career advancement.

Note:

Content about long-term care, home health care, and hospice coding is located at the textbook's Premium Website at www.cengagebrain.com.

- Chapters 2 through 3 cover general ICD-9-CM and ICD-10-CM/PCS coding concepts and provide coding practice. Chapter 3 covers ICD-9-CM official coding guidelines and includes ICD-10 coding alerts. (ICD-10-CM official coding guidelines are located at the textbook's online Student Companion).

- Chapters 5 and 6 are specific to inpatient and outpatient coding concepts, respectively. Inpatient coding concepts apply to acute care hospitals, and the chapter included ICD-9-CM and ICD-10-PCS official coding guidelines. Outpatient coding concepts covered include the physicians' office, and hospital emergency and outpatient departments. ICD-9-CM and ICD-10-CM/PCS chapters are sequenced before HCPCS/CPT chapters in this textbook because diagnosis codes are reported to justify the medical necessity of procedures and/or services provided.

- Chapter 7 covers the HCPCS level II national coding system, which was developed by the Centers for Medicare & Medicaid Services.

- Chapters 8 through 18 cover CPT coding concepts. Each CPT section has its own chapter, except for the Surgery section, which requires five separate chapters.

- Chapter 19 contains a detailed discussion of insurance and reimbursement concepts. (For comprehensive coverage of third-party payers and reimbursement methodologies, refer to Delmar, Cengage Learning's *Understanding Health Insurance: A Guide to Billing and Reimbursement,* by Michelle A. Green and JoAnn C. Rowell.)

- Appendix I contains the E/M CodeBuilder, which can also be downloaded from the Premium Website site at www.cengagebrain.com and printed for use with Chapter 9 cases to select evaluation and management (E/M) service codes.

- Appendix II (located on the Premium Website) contains the *Official ICD-10-CM Guidelines for Coding and Reporting* because they are too lengthy to be included in Chapter 4 of this textbook. However ICD-10-CM coding examples and exercises are included in Chapter 4 of this textbook (and its supplementary products). In the next edition of *3-2-1 Code It!,* the *Official ICD-10-CM Guidelines for Coding and Reporting* will replace the *Official ICD-9-CM Guidelines for Coding and Reporting* in Chapter 4.

- Appendix III contains a *Coding Practice Using www.EncoderPro.com* assignment, which allows students to become familiar with the use of an encoder (after having learned how to code using paper-based coding manuals). The answer key to the coding practice is also included in Appendix III.

Features of the Textbook

Each textbook chapter contains the following elements:

- Introduction
- Exercises
- Internet links
- Summary
- Study checklist
- Review

Textbook features include:

- Key terms and learning objectives located at the beginning of each chapter to help organize the material
- Boldfaced terms throughout each chapter to assist students in learning the technical vocabulary associated with coding systems
- Coding tips and notes that highlight important concepts presented in each chapter
- Exercises after each chapter section that reinforce content presented
- *ICD-10 Alert!* items in Chapters 1 through 6 to facilitate the transition to ICD-10-CM and ICD-10-PCS
- Multiple choice and coding practice reviews that allow for mastery of coding concepts.

- OptumInsight's www.EncoderPro.com 59-day trial online software that automates the ICD-9-CM, ICD-10-CM, ICD-10-PCS, CPT, and HCPCS level II coding manuals. ICD-10-CM and ICD-10-PCS crosswalks for ICD-9-CM codes are also included.

- StudyWARE™ software with multiple-choice, fill-in-the-blank, matching, and true/false quizzes for each chapter; hangman, crossword puzzles, and concentration activities for each chapter; and intermediate/advanced coding cases. The StudyWARE™ is located on the Premium Website. To access, follow the instructions on the Printed Access Card located in this textbook.

StudyWARE™ Coding Cases

Images Case #	Patient Name	Type of Facility	Medical Service	3–2–1 Code It! Chapter(s)
1	Edward Barry II	Outpatient – Emergency Dept	Endocrine, Nutritional and Metabolic, Immunity	6, 7, 9
2	Jason DuPonte	Outpatient – Emergency Dept	Respiratory	6, 9, 12
3	Lisa Shutman	Outpatient – Emergency Dept	Musculoskeletal and Connective Tissue	6, 9, 18
4	Kathy Monahan	Inpatient – Hospital	Digestive	5
5	Cecil Gibb	Outpatient – Physician's Office	Metabolic Circulatory	6, 9
6	Jerry White	Outpatient – Physician's Office	Musculoskeletal Injury	6, 9
7	Sophia Dunkie	Outpatient – Physician's Office	Digestive/Mental	6, 9
8	Roger Manowitz	Outpatient – Physician's Office	Circulatory	6, 9, 18
9	John O'Reilly	Outpatient – Physician's Office	Circulatory	6, 9
10	Albert Rodgers	Outpatient – Physician's Office	Infectious	6, 9
11	George Hoover	Outpatient – Physician's Office	Injury – Integumentary/Resp	6, 9
12	Kevin Caldwell	Outpatient – Physician's Office	Injury – Integumentary/Resp	6, 9
13	Brittany Banes	Outpatient – Physician's Office	Digestive – Metabolic	6, 9
14	Regina Roman	Outpatient – Physician's Office	Respiratory	6, 9
15	James Underwood	Inpatient – Hospital	Circulatory	5
16	Sophia Romanski	Inpatient – Nursing Facility	Nervous, Metabolic, Circulatory	5
17	Eileen Weaver	Inpatient – Hospital	Nervous	5
18	Scott Groves	Inpatient – Hospital	Injury – Musculoskeletal	5
19	Maria DeGust	Inpatient – Hospital	Congenital	5
20	Megan Pompadores	Inpatient – Hospital	Neoplasms	5
Video Case #	Patient Name	Type of Facility	Medical Service	3–2–1 Code It! Chapter(s)
21	Richard McEwen	Outpatient – Emergency Dept	Respiratory System	6, 7, 9, 18
22	Wilbur Glendale	Outpatient – Physician's Office	Circulatory	6, 7, 9, 18
23	John Welsh	Outpatient – Emergency Dept	Injury	6, 7, 9, 16, 18
24	Rodney Hutchinson	Outpatient – Emergency Dept	Nervous System	6, 7, 9, 16, 18
25	Mary Ballard	Outpatient – Physician's Office	Poisoning	6, 7, 9, 17, 18
26	Tony Marcotto	Hospital – Inpatient	Respiratory System	5
27	Jarrid Foust	Outpatient – Emergency Dept	Injury	6, 7, 9, 12, 16
28	Kyle Stevenson	Hospital – Inpatient	Musculoskeletal, Respiratory	5
29	Brad Ferrington	Outpatient – Physician's Office	Musculoskeletal	6, 7, 9

(continues)

StudyWARE™ Coding Cases (*continued*)

Video Case #	Patient Name	Type of Facility	Medical Service	3–2–1 Code It! Chapter(s)
30	Sheila Thompson	Outpatient – Physician's Office	Circulatory	6, 9
31	Patrick Donovan	Hospital – Inpatient	Circulatory	5
32	Sarah McDavies	Outpatient – Pediatric Critical Care Patient Transport Services	Circulatory	6, 9
33	Loretta Michaels	Outpatient – Ambulatory Surgery	Musculoskeletal	6, 7, 12
34	Cleveland Parks	Hospital – Inpatient	Circulatory	5
35	Eduardo Jimenez	Outpatient – Ambulatory Surgery	Cardiovascular	6, 13, 16
36	Mary Shelby	Outpatient – Physician's Office	Ophthalmology	6, 7, 9, 15, 18
37	Nina Lash	Outpatient – Physician's Office	Cardiology	6, 9, 18
38	Herb Smith	Outpatient – Physician's Office	Orthopedics	6, 9, 16
39	William Barrett	Outpatient – Emergency Department	Injury and Poisoning	6, 7, 9, 18
40	Nick Green	Outpatient – Observation Care	Pediatrics	6, 9
41	Sally Straight	Hospital – Inpatient	Gynecology	5
42	Karen Powley	Outpatient – Emergency Department	Cardiology	6, 9, 18
43	Marcia Cleary	Outpatient – Emergency Department	Gastroenterology	6, 9
44	Terry Stewart	Hospital – Inpatient	Integumentary	5
45	Valerie Carpella	Hospital – Inpatient	Orthopedics	5

New to Edition

- The textbook and its ancillaries have been updated to include the latest ICD-9-CM, ICD-10-CM, ICD-10-PCS, CPT, and HCPCS level II code sets, conventions, and guidelines.

- ICD-10-CM and ICD-10-PCS content has been updated within Chapters 2 through 6 to facilitate teaching students both ICD-9-CM and ICD-10-CM/PCS.

- Coding exercises and reviews in Chapters 2 through 6 have been updated, and ICD-10-CM/PCS codes have been updated in the *Instructor's Manual to Accompany 3-2-1 Code It!* using a side-by-side format (next to ICD-9-CM codes).

- ICD-10-CM and ICD-10-PCS answer keys have been updated at the Instructor Resources section of the textbook's Premium Website (www.cengagebrain.com).

- Chapter 1 includes new content about ICD-9-CM as a legacy classification system (and a new workbook assignment about this concept was also created). Computer-assisted coding (CAC) content was also updated in Chapter 1, and the corresponding workbook chapter contains a revised assignment to assist students in their understanding of CAC concepts.

- Chapter 2 contains updated content about medical necessity as well as the ICD-10-CM index to diseases and injuries, ICD-10-CM tabular list of diseases and injuries, ICD-10-PCS index, and ICD-10-PCS tables. The ICD-10-CM and ICD-10-PCS content, with examples, is included side-by-side with ICD-9-CM content to allow educators and students to view differences and similarities among the classification systems. Exercises and the chapter review include updated questions about ICD-10-CM and ICD-10-PCS coding.

- Chapter 3 includes updated content about coding conventions in ICD-9-CM and ICD-10-CM/PCS in a side-by-side format, and examples allow educators and students to compare the use of conventions in the classification systems. Exercises and the chapter review were updated to include both ICD-9-CM and ICD-10-CM/PCS coding practice.

- Chapter 4 includes updated content about the ICD-9-CM *Official Guidelines for Coding and Reporting*, and examples have been updated to include new ICD-9-CM codes. *ICD-10 Alerts!* have been embedded within ICD-9-CM coding guidelines to indicate the *ICD-10-CM Official Guidelines for Coding and Reporting* that remain similar (to ICD-9-CM's) as well as those that are brand new. Examples, exercises, and the chapter review include both ICD-9-CM and ICD-10-CM codes.

- Chapter 5 includes updated content about inpatient diagnosis coding guidelines as well as updated sections about inpatient procedure coding guidelines, ICD-9-CM procedure coding, and ICD-10-PCS procedure coding. Examples, exercises, and the chapter review were updated to include both ICD-9-CM and ICD-10-CM/PCS coding.

- Chapter 6 contains updated content about ICD-9-CM diagnosis coding as well as updated content about ICD-10-CM (diagnosis) coding. Examples, exercises, and the chapter review were updated to include both ICD-9-CM and ICD-10-CM coding.

- Chapter 7 contains updated content about HCPCS level II coding, including a note about the new copyright enforcement of *Current Dental Terminology* (CDT) codes by the American Dental Association (ADA). As such, HCPCS level II coding manuals no longer contain the dental "D" codes, and purchase of the CDT coding manual from the ADA is now required. Content about "D" codes is still included in Chapter 7, along with a coding exercise; however, schools that do not require students to purchase the separate CDT coding manual should skip that coding exercise.

- Chapter 8 contains updated introductory content about CPT coding.

- Chapter 9 contains updated content about CPT's Evaluation and Management (E/M) section, including revised definitions for new and established patients and revised direct and indirect services content.

- Chapter 10 contains updated content about CPT's Anesthesia section, including clarification about when a teaching anesthesiologist must be present during the administration of anesthesia.

- Chapters 11 through 15 contain updated content about CPT's Surgery section, including new figures throughout.

- Chapter 16 contains updated content about CPT's Radiology section.

- Chapter 17 contains updated content about CPT's Pathology and Laboratory section.

- Chapter 18 contains updated content about CPT's Medicine section.

- Chapter 19 contains updated content about insurance and reimbursement.

- Appendix I contains an E/M CodeBuilder (also available on the Premium Website), which can be used with Chapter 9 to assign evaluation and management codes.

- Appendix II (located on the Premium Website) contains the updated *ICD-10-CM Official Guidelines for Coding and Reporting*. (Chapter 4 contains the *ICD-9-CM Official Guidelines for Coding and Reporting*, with *ICD-10 Alerts!* to bring attention to similarities and differences between the coding systems.)

- Appendix III contains inpatient and outpatient coding assignments, requiring the use of www.EncoderPro.com. The updated ICD-9-CM, ICD-10-CM/PCS, CPT, and HCPCS Level II answer keys are included in Appendix III.

Supplements

The following supplements accompany this text:

- Instructor's manual
- Student workbook
- Instructor Resources CD-ROM

- Premium Website at www.cengagebrain.com
- CourseMate™ at www.cengagebrain.com
- WebTUTOR™ Course Cartridges for Angel and Blackboard

Instructor's Manual

(ISBN: 978-1-285-42291-6)

The Instructor's Manual contains six sections:

- Section I—Instructor's Resources
- Section II—Answer Keys to Textbook Chapter Exercises and Reviews

- Section III—Chapter Exams and Answer Keys to Chapter Exams
- Section IV—Answer Keys to Workbook Assignments and Reviews
- Section V—Answer Key to Coding Patient Records (Workbook Appendices A–D)
- Section VI—Answer Key to Mock Certified Professional Coder (CPC) Certification Examination (Workbook Appendix E)
- Section VII—Answer Key to Mock Certified Coding Specialist—Physician-based (CCS-P) Certification Examination (Workbook Appendix F)
- Section VIII—Answer Key to Mock Certified Coding Specialist (CCS) Certification Examination (Workbook Appendix G)

Student Workbook

(ISBN: 978-1-285-42290-9)

The workbook follows the chapter organization of the text and contains application-based assignments, including numerous diagnosis/procedure statements and case studies so that students can practice coding. Each assignment contains a list of objectives, an overview of content relating to the assignment, and instructions for completing the assignment. The last assignment in each workbook chapter contains review questions in multiple-choice format to emulate credentialing exam questions. The workbook also contains actual patient records and mock CPC, CCS-P, and CCS certification examinations.

Instructor Resources CD-ROM

(ISBN: 978-1-285-42292-3)

Spend less time planning and more time teaching with Delmar Cengage Learning's Instructor Resources to Accompany the Fourth Edition of *3-2-1 Code It!* As an instructor, you will find this CD-ROM offers invaluable assistance by giving you access to all of your resources, anywhere and at any time.

Features of the Instructor Resources CD-ROM include:

- The Instructor's Manual in Adobe's PDF format, which contains class preparation information, sample syllabi, and complete answer keys for each chapter of the book.
- The computerized test bank in ExamView® makes generating tests and quizzes a snap. With approximately 2,000 questions, including ICD-10-CM/PCS questions, you can create customized assessments for your students with the click of a button.
- Customizable instructor support slide presentations in PowerPoint® format focus on key points for each chapter.
- *2013 Insurance Billing & Coding Curriculum Guide* helps you plan your course using *3-2-1 Code It!* and other coding resources.

Premium Website

Additional textbook resources for students and instructors can be found online by following the instructions that follow.

Student Resources on the Premium Website

Some resources located on the Premium Website to accompany *3-2-1 Code It!* are free, whereas others (such as StudyWARE™) will require passcode entry. To access passcode-protected content, follow the instructions on the printed access card bound into this textbook. Student resources include:

- StudyWARE™ chapter content including games, flashcards, quizzes, and coding cases (passcode required to access)
- Revisions to textbook and workbook due to coding changes as they become available.
- E/M Codebuilder (also found in Appendix I of the textbook).
- Textbook Appendix II: ICD-10-CM Draft Official Guidelines for Coding and Reporting 2012

- Electronic patient records (also found in Appendices A–D of the workbook).
- Extra content about related coding topics, including long-term care, home health care, and hospice coding, and alternate care coding systems.

Instructor Resources at the Premium Website

All instructor resources can be accessed by going to www.cengagebrain.com to create a unique user login. Contact your sales representative for more information. Online instructor resources at the Instructor Companion site are password-protected and include the following:

- All resources found on the Instructor Resources CD-ROM, including test bank, presentations in PowerPoint®, electronic Instructor's Manual, and more coding answer keys for electronic patient records (Section V of the Instructor's Manual).
- Revisions to textbook, workbook, and instructor supplements due to coding changes as they become available.
- Insurance, coding, and billing curriculum guide with content mapped to certification exams.
- Conversion grids mapping the 4th edition to the 3rd edition and to competing texts to make adapting your course to *3-2-1 Code It!* a snap.
- Access to all free student supplements, including StudyWARE™, additional textbook content, etc.

CourseMate™

New to this Edition! CourseMate helps students make the grade, with several components: (1) an interactive eBook, with highlighting, note taking, and search capabilities; (2) interactive learning tools including Quizzes, Flash Cards, Videos, Games, and Presentations; and (3) Engagement Tracker, a first-of-its-kind tool that monitors student engagement in the course. To access CourseMate, visit www.CengageBrain.com. At the CengageBrain.com homepage, search for *3-2-1 Code It! Fourth Edition* (978-1-285-42289-3) using the search box at the top of the page. This will take you to the product page where all of the textbook's additional resources, including CourseMate, can be found.

WebTUTOR™ Course Cartridges

Note:

> WebTUTOR™ is designed to accompany *3-2-1 Code It!,* by Michelle A. Green. Its purpose is to help students organize their study of the textbook material, reinforce their learning, test their mastery of the content, and improve their performance on exams. WebTUTOR™ is intended to complement the textbook and course delivery. It is not intended as a substitute for either.

WebTUTOR™ is an Internet-based course management and delivery system designed to accompany the text. Its content is available for use in Blackboard® and Angel. Available to supplement on-campus course delivery or as the course management platform for an online course, WebTUTOR™ contains the following:

- Video clips
- Online quizzes for each chapter
- Discussion topics and learning links
- Online glossary
- Answer keys to textbook exercises and reviews
- Instructor presentations in PowerPoint®
- Testbank
- Communication tools, including a course calendar, chat, e-mail, and threaded discussions

To learn more, visit http://webtutor.cengage.com.

About the Author

Michelle A. Green, MPS, RHIA, FAHIMA, CPC, SUNY Distinguished Teaching Professor, Alfred State College, Alfred, New York, has been a full-time college professor since 1984. She taught traditional classroom-based courses until 2000, when she transitioned all of the health information management and coding courses to an Internet-based format. Prior to 1984, she worked as a director of health information management at two acute care hospitals in Florida's Tampa Bay area. Both positions required her to assign codes to inpatient cases. Upon becoming employed as a college professor, she routinely spent the semester breaks coding for a number of health care facilities so that she could further develop her inpatient and outpatient coding skills.

A Note About CPT Coding Manual Editions

Every attempt is made to make the material within this textbook and its ancillary products (e.g., workbook, instructor's manual) as current as possible by updating to CPT 2013 just prior to publication.

Note:

In January 2014, CPT, ICD-9-CM, ICD-10-CM, ICD-10-PCS, and HCPCS level II coding updates to the workbook and ancillary products will be posted on the Premium Website.

Reviewers

Technical Reviewer

Mary Jo Bowie, MS, RHIA, RHIT
Instructor
Health Information Technology
Broome Community College
Binghamton, New York

Acknowledgements

To my son, Eric, for keeping me "on task" by asking, "How much did you get finished in the chapter today, Mom?" Thank you for supporting my need to pursue my passion for teaching and writing.

To my students, located throughout the world! You always ask me the toughest coding questions, and you also make me want to find the answers. You are truly critical thinkers!

To my technical reviewer, Mary Jo Bowie, thank you for keeping me on task and making the revision process fun!

To my product manager, Amy Wetsel, for her invaluable support, patience, and guidance.

To Rhonda Dearborn, Executive Editor, for challenging me to do my best work and always believing I will succeed.

To my mom, Alice B. Bartholomew, for her unending support and assistance.

A special thank you to Mr. Odum, my tenth-grade high school English teacher who originally instilled in me the confidence to become a writer. He said he knew I could do it, and that made me believe it too.

Special appreciation is expressed to OptumInsight publishing group for granting permission to reprint selected images, tables, and pages from:

- *Coder's Desk Reference for Diagnoses*
- *Coders Desk Reference for Procedures*
- *Coding & Payment Guide for Anesthesia Services*
- *HCPCS Level II Professional and Expert versions*
- *ICD-10-CM Professional*
- *ICD-10-PCS Professional*

Michelle A. Green, MPS, RHIA, FAHIMA, CPC

Feedback

Contact the author at delmarauthor@yahoo.com with questions, suggestions, or comments about the text or its supplements. Please realize that the publisher (www.cengage.com) authorizes the release of the Instructor's Manual (with coding answers) to educators only. The publisher also posts AAPC CEU exams on the Premium Website.

How to Use This Text

Chapter Outline

- Career as a Coder
- Professional Associations and Discussion Boards
- Coding Overview
- Documentation as Basis for Coding
- Health Data Collection

Chapter Objectives

At the conclusion of this chapter, the student should be able to:

- Define key terms.
- Explain coding career opportunities and the coding credentialing process.
- Identify professional associations and describe the benefits of membership.
- Clarify student responsibilities during a coding internship.
- Identify coding systems used for reimbursement, and indicate the relationship between patient record documentation and accurate coding.

Key Terms

application service provider (ASP)	code	document imaging	health care provider
Assessment (A)	coder	documentation	health data collection
assumption coding	coding	downcoding	Health Insurance Portability and Accountability Act of 1996 (HIPAA)
automated case abstracting software	coding system	electronic health record (EHR)	health insurance specialist
automated record	computer-assisted coding (CAC)	electronic medical record (EMR)	health plan
Centers for Medicare & Medicaid Services (CMS)	concurrent coding	encoding	hospitalist
claims examiner	continuity of care	HCPCS level II	hybrid record
classification system	Current Procedural Terminology (CPT)	HCPCS national codes	indexed
clearinghouse	database	health care clearinghouse	initial plan
CMS-1450	demographic data	Healthcare Common Procedure Coding System (HCPCS)	integrated record
CMS-1500	diagnostic/management plan		
	discharge note		

Introduction

This chapter provides an overview of coding systems used to report inpatient and outpatient diagnoses and procedures and services to health plans. It also focuses on coding career opportunities in health care, the importance of joining professional associations and obtaining coding credentials, the impact of networking with other coding professionals, and the development of opportunities for career advancement.

Note:

This chapter does not require the use of ICD-9-CM (or ICD-10-CM/PCS), CPT, or HCPCS level II coding manuals. However, later chapters in this textbook do require them (because learning how to code is easier when you use paper-based coding manuals). A 59-day trial of www.EncoderPro.com software is included with this textbook. Do not install the software until directed to do so by your instructor.

HIPAA Alert!

HIPAA regulations for electronic transactions require providers and payers (including MACs) to adhere to the *Official Guidelines for Coding and Reporting*. Thus, a violation of the coding guidelines is a HIPAA violation. Unfortunately, some payers do not appear to be aware of or understand this HIPAA provision. Payers should be informed of the provision in the HIPAA regulation that references the use of coding guidelines. If payers deny claims because certain codes are reported as principal diagnosis (e.g., V57), contact your regional CMS office or the HIPAA enforcement office (at CMS) to alert them about the HIPAA violation.

Chapter Outline and Key Terms

The **Chapter Outline** organizes the chapter material at a glance. The **Key Terms** list represents new vocabulary in each chapter. Each term is highlighted in color in the chapter, where it is also defined and used in context. A complete definition of each term appears in the Glossary at the end of the textbook.

Objectives

The **Objectives** list the outcomes expected of the learner after a careful study of the chapter. Read the objectives before reading the chapter content. When you complete the chapter, read the objectives again to see if you can say for each one, "Yes, I know that." If you cannot say this about an objective, go back to the appropriate content and reread. These outcomes are critical to a successful career as an insurance specialist.

Introduction

The **Introduction** provides a brief overview about major topics covered in the chapter. The introduction (and the objectives) provide a framework for your study of the content.

Notes

Notes appear throughout the text and serve to bring important points to your attention. The notes clarify content, refer you to reference material, provide more background for selected topics, or emphasize exceptions to rules.

HIPAA Alerts

The **HIPAA Alert** feature highlights issues related to the privacy and security of personal health information.

Coding Tip:

Report HCPCS level II modifiers (-FA through -F9 and -TA through -T9) with codes for procedures performed on a patient's fingernails and toenails.

Coding Tips

The **Coding Tips** feature provides recommendations and hints for selecting codes and for the correct use of the coding manuals.

EXAMPLE 1: The provider documented congestive heart failure on the face sheet of the patient record. On review of progress notes that document the patient's response to treatment, the coder finds documentation of *acute and chronic diastolic and systolic congestive heart failure* in the discharge progress note.

Examples

Examples appear throughout the text to promote understanding of presented concepts.

ICD-10 Alert!

Effective October 1, 2014, ICD-10-CM and ICD-10-PCS (abbreviated as ICD-10-CM/PCS) will replace ICD-9-CM.

ICD-10 Alert!

The **ICD-10 Alert!** feature focuses on the differences and similarities between ICD-9-CM and ICD-10-CM/PCS.

Internet Links

AHA Central Office Go to *http://www.ahacentraloffice.org* to review resources available at the AHA Central Office Web site. The American Hospital Association's (AHA) Central Office serves as the official U.S. clearinghouse for proper use of ICD-9-CM (or ICD-10-CM/PCS),

Internet Links

Internet Links are provided to encourage you to expand your knowledge at various state and federal government agency, commercial, and organization sites.

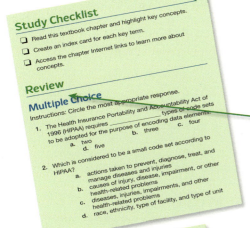

Study Checklist

The **Study Checklist** appears toward the end of each chapter and directs you to other learning and application aids. Completing each of the items in the checklist will help you to gain confidence in your understanding of the key concepts and in your ability to apply them correctly.

Review

Each chapter **Review** includes multiple-choice questions and coding practice cases that will test your understanding of chapter content and critical thinking ability.

Exercises

Exercises reinforce chapter content.

Summary

The **Summary** at the end of each chapter recaps the key points of the chapter. The summary also serves as a review aid when preparing for tests.

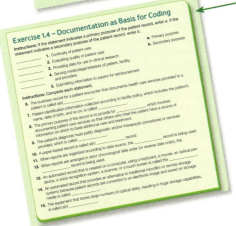

Summary

A coder is expected to master the use of coding systems, coding principles and rules, government regulations, and third-party payer requirements to ensure that all diagnoses, services, and procedures documented in patient records are accurately coded for reimbursement, research, and statistical purposes. To prepare for entry into the profession, students are encouraged to join a professional association. They usually pay a reduced membership fee and receive most of the same benefits as active members. The benefits of joining a professional association include eligibility for scholarships and grants, opportunity to network with members, free publications, reduced certification exam fees, and Web site access for members only.

How to Use StudyWARE™

The StudyWARE™ software helps you learn terms and concepts presented in the *3-2-1 Code It!* textbook. As you study each chapter in the text, be sure to complete the activities for the corresponding content areas in StudyWARE™. Use StudyWARE™ as your own private tutor to help you learn the material in your *3-2-1 Code It!* textbook.

Getting started is easy. Access the software by going to www.cengagebrain.com and using the passcode printed on the tear-out card in this textbook. When you first access the software, enter your first and last name so the software can store your quiz results. Then choose a content area from the menu to take a quiz, complete one of the activities, or complete coding cases.

Menus

You can access any of the menus from wherever you are in the program. The menus include Chapter Quizzes and Activities, Coding Cases, and Scores.

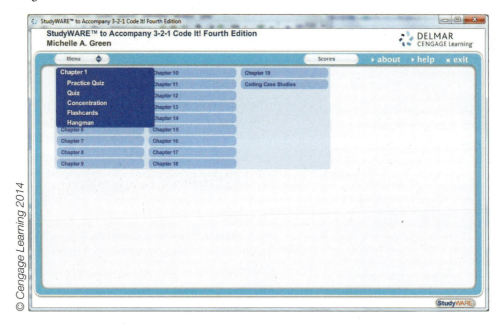

© Cengage Learning 2014

Quizzes

Quizzes include multiple-choice, true-false, and fill-in-the-blank questions. You can take the quizzes in both Practice Mode and Quiz Mode.

- Use Practice Mode to improve your mastery of the material. You have multiple tries to get the answers correct. Instant feedback tells you whether you're right or wrong and helps you learn quickly by explaining why an answer was correct or incorrect.

- Use Quiz Mode when you are ready to test yourself and keep a record of your scores. In Quiz Mode, you have one try to get the answers right, but you can take each quiz as many times as you want.

- You can view your last scores for each quiz and print out your results to submit to your instructor.

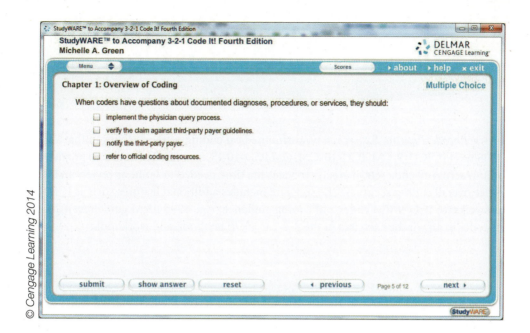

Activities

Activities include hangman, crossword puzzles, and concentration. Have fun while increasing your knowledge!

Coding Cases

Coding cases were created at intermediate and advanced levels, and they include images and videos. View the StudyWARE™ Coding Cases table in the preface of this book to locate corresponding textbook chapter(s) so you know when to complete the coding cases.

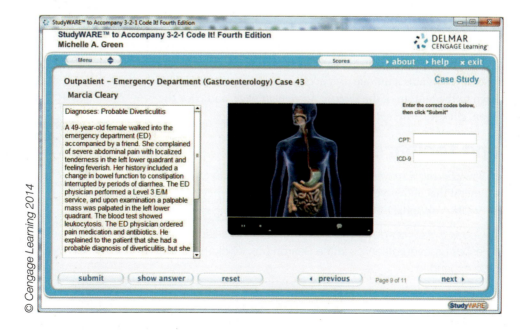

How to Use *EncoderPro.com Expert* Online Encoder Software

OptumInsight's *www.EncoderPro.com Expert* is a powerful medical coding software solution that allows you to locate CPT, HCPCS level II, ICD-9-CM, ICD-10-CM, and ICD-10-PCS codes. The software provides users with fast searching capabilities across all code sets, it greatly reduces the time needed to build or review an insurance claim, and it helps improve overall coding accuracy. The software includes additional features such as ICD-10-CM and ICD-10-PCS crosswalks for ICD-9-CM codes and coding guidance (e.g., 1995 E&M guidelines). This software can be used to assign codes to any of the exercises in the *3-2-1 Code It!* textbook and workbook.

 Note:

Appendix II of this textbook contains a Coding Practice Using www.EncoderPro.com assignment, which allows students to become familiar with the use of an encoder (after having learned how to code using paper-based coding manuals). All software images used in this section are copyrighted by OptumInsight. All Rights Reserved.

EncoderPro.com Video-based Autodemo

View OptumInsight's online *EncoderPro.com* video-based Autodemo at www.optumcoding.com by scrolling your mouse over Products and eSolutions, and clicking on the eSolution Online Demos link. Then, click on the *EncoderPro.com* link to start the Autodemo, which is approximately five minutes in length. The EncoderPro.com features are described and using the encoder to locate a code is demonstrated.

 Note:

Be sure to check with your instructor before beginning your free trial because it will expire 59 days after your initial login.

How to Access the Free Trial of *www.EncoderPro.com*

Information about how to access your 59-day trial of *www.EncoderPro.com* (Expert version) is included on the printed tear-out card located in the back cover of this textbook, and the card contains a unique user access code and password. Once you log in, scroll down to the bottom of the *License Agreement* page, and click the *I Accept* link. Then, click the *I Accept* link on the *Terms of Use* page.

Menus and Toolbars

OptumInsight's *www.EncoderPro.com* contains a black toolbar with an *All Codes Sets* drop- down menu that allows you to select the CPT, HCPCS (level II), ICD-9-CM Vol. 1, ICD-9-CM Vol. 3, ICD-10-CM, or ICD-10-PCS coding system.

Permission to reprint granted by OptumInsight, Inc.

- Use the *All Codes Sets* drop-down menu on the far left to select a coding system. Then, enter a condition (e.g., diabetes) or procedure/service in the Search box. Click the *Search* button to view tabular list results, which can be expanded.

All Code Sets drop down menu → All Code Sets

Coding drop down menu → Coding ▾   Policy Lookup

Enter name of condition or procedure/service

Click Search button

EncoderPro.com EXPERT   [ ]   Search

Permission to reprint granted by OptumInsight, Inc.

- Use the *Coding* drop-down menu (located below the *All Code Sets* drop-down menu) to view features of each coding system (e.g., new codes, reinstated codes, neoplasm table, and so on).

Software Features

The Expert version of OptumInsight's *www.EncoderPro.com* contains the following features:

- *CodeLogic™ Search Technology,* which allows simultaneous code search across the CPT, HCPCS (level II), ICD-9-CM Vol. 1, ICD-9-CM Vol. 3, ICD-10-CM, and ICD-10-PCS code sets. Search results can display all four code sets or can be limited to one code set.

- *Search Terms*, which allow entry of up to four search terms, acronyms, and/or abbreviations that results in the ability to narrow down results when initiating a search. An automatic spell-check feature ensures that valid terms are entered.

- *Code Detail,* which is a comprehensive reference page for each CPT and HCPCS level II code with access to modifiers, CCI edits, and cross-coding data. CPT and HCPCS level II codes are organized by section and subsection. For ICD-9-CM or ICD-10-CM codes, excludes and includes notes as well as "code first" and "code also" references are displayed.

- *Code-Specific Edits and Information for ICD-9-CM or ICD-10-CM*, which allows you to view instructional notes, AHA coding clinic references, and annotations for the selected ICD-9-CM or ICD-10-CM code.

- *Code-Specific Edits and Information for CPT*, which allows you to view lay descriptions, CPT® Assistant references, AMA guidelines, and modifiers for the selected CPT code. You can also view primary CPT procedure codes (for add-on codes), surgical and anesthesia crosscodes, Medicare Physician Fee Schedule information, and the unbundle edits from Medicare's Correct Coding Initiative.

- *Code-Specific Edits and Information for HCPCS (level II)*, which allows you to view annotations, section notes, modifiers, and coverage instruction references from the Pub-100 References for the selected HCPCS code.

- *Color Codes*, which allows you to look up all codes with their color codes in sorted lists.

- *User Notes*, which allows organizations to establish *global notes* based on for company-wide rules. Individuals can also add and edit comments to codes, and each code with a User Note attached is flagged for quick reference.

- *Claim Compliance*, which allows you to check claim charge detail for coding compliancy so any billing errors can be edited as needed.

Features of *www.EncoderPro.com Expert*

OptumInsight's *www.EncoderPro.com Expert* includes the following software features:

- CPT color codes that identify add-on codes, modifier -51 exempt status, age- and gender-specific codes, etc.

Permission to reprint granted by OptumInsight, Inc.

- HCPCS level II color codes that identify new or revised codes or those that contain special coverage instructions, policy flags, etc.

Permission to reprint granted by OptumInsight, Inc.

- ICD-9-CM volume 1 (diagnosis) or ICD-10-CM color codes that identify codes that require additional characters are age- and gender-specific, etc.

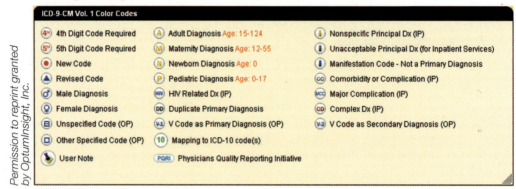

Permission to reprint granted by OptumInsight, Inc.

- ICD-9-CM volume 3 (procedure) color codes that identify codes that require third and fourth digits, are gender-specific, etc.

Permission to reprint granted by OptumInsight, Inc.

- User notes, notepad, HCPCS level II notes, and lay descriptions

Permission to reprint granted by OptumInsight, Inc.

- ICD-10-CM code mapping (to ICD-9-CM disease codes)

Permission to reprint granted by OptumInsight, Inc.

- CPT and HCPCS level II modifiers

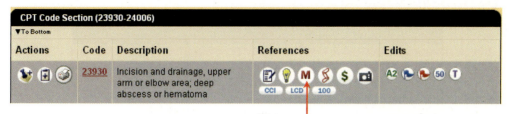

Permission to reprint granted by OptumInsight, Inc.

- LCD and NCD coverage determinations and medical necessity edits, CCI unbundle edits, and Medicare Pub-100 references

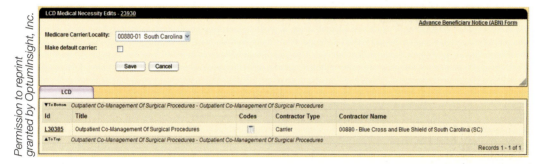

- Surgical crosscodes for:

  - CPT to ICD-9-CM Vol. 3 and ICD-10-PCS

  - HCPCS level II to ICD-9-CM Vol. 3 and ICD-10-PCS

  - ICD-9-CM Vol. 3 and ICD-10-PCS to CPT and HCPCS level II

  - CPT to CPT Anesthesia

- Modifier crosswalk

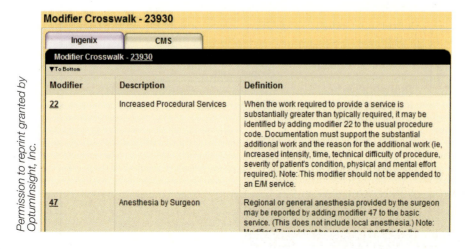

- Medicare physician fee schedule dialog box and fee calculation by locality

Payment Information - 23930

Medicare Fee

Medicare Carrier/Locality

00880-01 South Carolina

Make default Medicare Carrier/Locality ☐

Conversion Factor 36.8729

-- OR --

% of Medicare 100.0

[Calculate]

	National	Global (Locality)	26	TC
Facility:	$208.33	$195.39	n/a	n/a
Non-Facility:	$329.64	$311.12	n/a	n/a

RVUs - Nonfacility

	National	Global (Locality)	26	TC
Work RVU:	2.9900	2.9900	n/a	n/a
PE RVU:	5.5000	5.2470	n/a	n/a
Malpractice RVU:	0.4500	0.2007	n/a	n/a
Total RVU:	8.9400	8.4377	n/a	n/a

Conversion Factor: 36.8729

RVUs - Facility

	National	Global (Locality)	26	TC
Work RVU:	2.9900	2.9900	n/a	n/a
PE RVU:	2.2100	2.1083	n/a	n/a
Malpractice RVU:	0.4500	0.2007	n/a	n/a
Total RVU:	5.6500	5.2990	n/a	n/a

Conversion Factor: 36.8729

Global Information

	Global-Split
Preoperative %:	10
Intraoperative %:	80
Postoperative %:	10
Global Period (days):	010

Medicare Rules

Physician Service
Multiple Surgery Reduction
Bilateral Procedure Allowed
Assist-at-Surgery Not Allowed

- Compliance edit

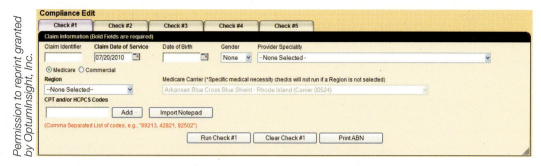

Permission to reprint granted by OptumInsight, Inc.

- Medically Unlikely Edit (MUE) reports

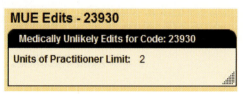

Permission to reprint granted by OptumInsight, Inc.

- Claims batch editor

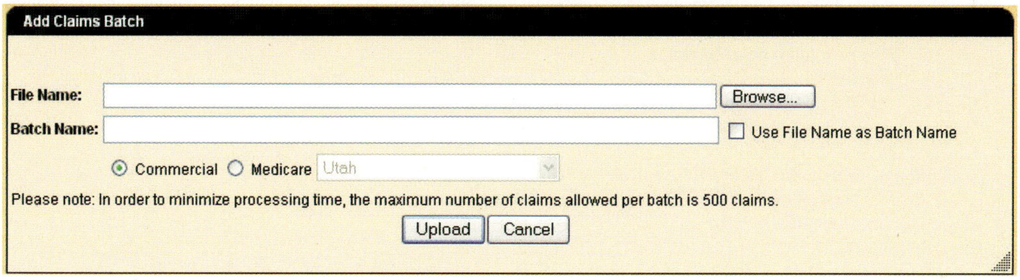

Permission to reprint granted by OptumInsight, Inc.

OptumInsight's *www.EncoderPro.com* Tutorial

Instructions: Use this tutorial to learn how to use Ingenix's *www.EncoderPro.com* software.

Note:

Be sure to check with your instructor before beginning your free trial because it will expire 59 days after your initial login.

Step 1 Log in to *www.EncoderPro.com* by entering the unique user access code and password (located on the printed tear-out card inside the front cover of this textbook).

Step 2 Scroll down to the bottom of the **License Agreement** page, and click the **I Accept** link.

Step 3 Then, click the **I Accept** link on the **Terms of Use** page.

Step 4 Locate the black toolbar that contains the **All Code Sets** drop-down list, which allows you to select a coding system. Refer to the image below, which identifies the location of the black toolbar on the software page.

Permission to reprint granted by OptumInsight, Inc.

Step 5 • You will use *www.EncoderPro.com* to automate the process of locating ICD-10-CM codes for:

  ○ Hypertension

  ○ Myocardial Infarction

• Select ICD-10-CM from the **All Code Sets** drop-down menu.

• Click in the empty search box, located to the right of the **ICD-10-CM** menu item.

• Enter HYPERTENSION as the condition search term. (You can enter as hypertension or Hypertension, too.)

• Click the **Search** button.

Permission to reprint granted by OptumInsight, Inc.

Step 6 • Search results for HYPERTENSION include category code I10.

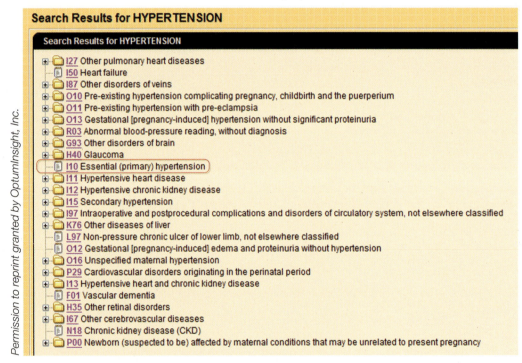

Permission to reprint granted by OptumInsight, Inc.

• Click on code I10 to view the tabular listing entry for the code.

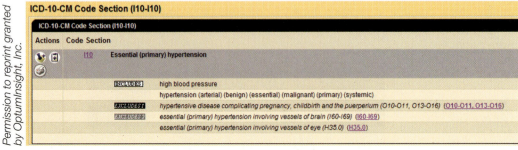

Permission to reprint granted by OptumInsight, Inc.

Step 7 • Now you try it! The physician documents "angina pectoris" as the patient's diagnosis.

• Enter **ANGINA** in the search box. Notice that many **Search Results** display. This condition requires more advanced coding skills than "hypertension," which means the *www.EncoderPro.com* index feature should be used to locate the code(s).

Step 8 • Scroll your mouse over the **Coding** drop-down menu, then scroll your mouse over the ICD-10-CM index menu item, and select **Index to Diseases**.

• Enter ANGINA to the right of the **Term starts with**: empty box.

• Click **Find**.

• Click on the **Angina Pectoris I20.9** link.

• Notice that **Myocardial Infarction** displays on the right side of the page.

• Click on code **I20.9** to display the tabular list entry.

• When you click on code **I20.9** again, *code information* displays.

PART I

Coding Overview

Overview of Coding

Chapter Outline

Career as a Coder

Professional Associations and Discussion
    Boards

Coding Overview

Documentation as Basis for Coding

Health Data Collection

Chapter Objectives

At the conclusion of this chapter, the student should be able to:

- Define key terms.
- Explain coding career opportunities and the coding credentialing process.
- Identify professional associations and describe the benefits of membership.
- Clarify student responsibilities during a coding internship.
- Identify coding systems used for reimbursement, and indicate the relationship between patient record documentation and accurate coding.

Key Terms

application service
    provider (ASP)

Assessment (A)

assumption coding

automated case
    abstracting software

automated record

Centers for Medicare &
    Medicaid Services
    (CMS)

claims examiner

classification system

clearinghouse

CMS-1450

CMS-1500

code

coder

coding

coding system

computer-assisted
    coding (CAC)

concurrent coding

continuity of care

Current Procedural
    Terminology (CPT)

database

demographic data

diagnostic/management
    plan

discharge note

document imaging

documentation

downcoding

electronic health
    record (EHR)

electronic medical
    record (EMR)

encoding

HCPCS level II

HCPCS national codes

health care
    clearinghouse

Healthcare Common
    Procedure Coding
    System (HCPCS)

health care provider

health data collection

Health Insurance
    Portability and
    Accountability Act
    of 1996 (HIPAA)

health insurance
    specialist

health plan

hospitalist

hybrid record

indexed

initial plan

integrated record

International Classification of Diseases, Ninth Revision, Clinical Modification (ICD-9-CM)

International Classification of Diseases, Tenth Revision, Clinical Modification (ICD-10-CM)

International Classification of Diseases, Tenth Revision, Clinical Modification/ Procedure Coding System (ICD-10-CM/PCS)

International Classification of Diseases, Tenth Revision, Procedure Coding System (ICD-10-PCS)

internship

internship supervisor

jamming

jukebox

listserv

manual record

medical assistant

medical coding process

medical management software

medical necessity

medical nomenclature

medical record

Objective (O)

online discussion board

optical disk imaging

overcoding

patient education plan

patient record

physician query process

Plan (P)

problem list

problem-oriented record (POR)

progress notes

provider

resident physician

scanner

sectionalized record

source-oriented record (SOR)

specialty coders

Subjective (S)

teaching hospital

teaching physician

therapeutic plan

third-party administrator (TPA)

third-party payer

transfer note

UB-04

unbundling

upcoding

Introduction

This chapter provides an overview of coding systems used to report inpatient and outpatient diagnoses and procedures and services to health plans. It also focuses on coding career opportunities in health care, the importance of joining professional associations and obtaining coding credentials, the impact of networking with other coding professionals, and the development of opportunities for career advancement.

Note:

This chapter does not require the use of ICD-9-CM (or ICD-10-CM/PCS), CPT, or HCPCS level II coding manuals. However, later chapters in this textbook do require them (because learning how to code is easier when you use paper-based coding manuals). A 59-day trial of www.EncoderPro.com software is included with this textbook. Do not install the software until directed to do so by your instructor.

Note:

The following additional content is located on the Premium Website at www.cengagebrain.com:

• Documentation Requirements for Teaching Physician 2012
• History of Medical Classification and Coding Systems
• Alternate Healthcare Coding Systems

Career as a Coder

A **coder** acquires a working knowledge of coding systems (e.g., CPT, HCPCS level II, and ICD-9-CM or ICD-10-CM/PCS), coding principles and rules, government regulations, and third-party payer requirements to ensure that all diagnoses (conditions), services (e.g., office visits), and procedures (e.g., surgery, X-rays) documented in patient records are coded accurately for reimbursement, research, and statistical purposes. Excellent interpersonal skills are required of coders because they communicate with providers about documentation and compliance issues related to the appropriate assignment of diagnosis and procedure/service codes.

Note:

Although graduates of medical assistant and medical office administration programs typically do not become employed as full-time coders, they often are responsible for the coding function in a physician's office or medical clinic. This chapter provides the following resources for students pursuing any health-related academic program that includes coding as a job function:

- Professional associations that offer coding and other certification exams
- Internet-based discussion boards that cover coding and other topics
- Impact of HIPAA federal legislation on coding and reimbursement
- Coding references and other resources that facilitate accurate coding
- Physician query process as a way to prevent assumption coding
- Manual and automated patient record formats and health data collection

Training

Training methods for those interested in pursuing a coding career include college-based programs that contain coursework in medical terminology, anatomy and physiology, health information management, pathophysiology, pharmacology, ICD-9-CM (or ICD-10-CM/PCS) and HCPCS/CPT coding, and reimbursement methodologies. Many college programs also require students to complete a nonpaid internship (e.g., 240 hours) at a health care facility. Professional associations (e.g., the American Health Information Management Association) offer noncredit-based coding training, usually as distance learning (e.g., Internet-based), and some health care facilities develop internal programs to retrain health professionals (e.g., nurses) who are interested in a career change.

Note:

Refer to the *Documentation Requirements for Teaching Physicians 2012* document, which is located on the Premium Website at www.cengagebrain.com.

Note:

Pharmacology plays a significant role in accurate and complete coding. Coders review the medication administration record (MAR) to locate medications administered that impact diagnosis coding. For example, upon review of the MAR the coder notices that the patient received a course of Librium (chlordiazepoxide) during inpatient hospitalization. Librium is classified as an antianxiety medication, but it can be also used to counteract alcohol withdrawal symptoms. If the latter is the reason that the patient received the Librium (based on physician documentation), the coder can assign an appropriate alcohol dependence diagnosis code as well as alcohol detoxification procedure codes.

Coding Internship

The coding **internship** benefits the student and the facility that accepts the student for placement. Students receive on-the-job experience prior to graduation, and the internship assists them in obtaining permanent employment. Facilities benefit from the opportunity to participate in and improve the formal education process. Quite often, students who complete professional practice experiences (or internships) are later employed by the facility at which they completed the internship.

The **internship supervisor** is the person to whom the student reports at the site. Students are often required to submit a professional résumé to the internship supervisor and to schedule an interview prior to being accepted for placement. While this experience can be intimidating, it is excellent practice for the interview process that the student will undergo prior to obtaining permanent employment. Students should research the résumé writing and interview technique services available from the college's career services office. This office will review résumés and will provide interview tips. (Some even videotape mock interviews for students.)

The internship is on-the-job training even though it is nonpaid, and students should expect to provide proof of immunizations (available from a physician) and possibly undergo a preemployment physical examination and participate in facility-wide and department-specific orientations. In addition, because of the focus on privacy and security of patient information, the facility will likely require students to sign a nondisclosure agreement (to protect patient confidentiality), which is kept on file at the college and by the professional practice site.

Note:

Breach of patient confidentiality can result in termination from the internship site, failure of the internship course, and even possible suspension and/or expulsion from your academic program. Make sure you check out your academic program's requirements regarding this issue.

During the internship, students are expected to report to work on time. Students who cannot attend the internship on a particular day (or who arrive late) should contact their internship supervisor or program faculty, whoever is designated for that purpose. Students are also required to make up any lost time. Because the internship is a simulated job experience, students are to be well groomed and should dress professionally. Students should show interest in all aspects of the experience, develop good working relationships with coworkers, and react appropriately to criticism and direction. If any concerns arise during the internship, students should discuss them with their internship supervisor and/or program faculty.

Credentials

The American Health Information Management Association (AHIMA) and the American Academy of Professional Coders (AAPC) offer certification in coding. Credentials available from AHIMA include the following:

- Certified Coding Associate (CCA)
- Certified Coding Specialist (CCS)
- Certified Coding Specialist—Physician-based (CCS-P)

The AAPC offers the following core certification exams:

- Certified Professional Coder (CPC)
- Certified Professional Coder, Apprentice status (CPC-A)
- Certified Professional Coder—Hospital (CPC-H)
- Certified Professional Coder—Hospital, Apprentice status (CPC-H-A)
- Certified Professional Coder—Payer (CPC-P)
- Certified Interventional Radiology Cardiovascular Coder (CIRCC)
- Certified Professional Medical Auditor (CPMA)
- Certified Professional Compliance Officer (CPCO)
- Certified Professional Practice Manager (CPPM)

The AAPC also offers specialty certifications in response to a demand for **specialty coders** who have obtained advanced training in medical specialties and who are skilled in compliance and reimbursement areas, such as the Ambulatory Surgical Center (ASC) credential.

The American Medical Billing Association (AMBA) offers the Certified Medical Reimbursement Specialist (CMRS) exam, which recognizes the competency of members who have met high standards of proficiency. According to AMBA, Certified Medical Reimbursement Specialists (CMRS) are skilled in facilitating the claims reimbursement process from the time a service is rendered by a health care provider until the balance is paid. The CMRS is knowledgeable in ICD, CPT, and HCPCS level II coding; medical terminology; insurance claims and billing; appeals and denials; fraud and abuse; Health Insurance Portability and Accountability Act (HIPAA) regulations; Office of Inspector General (OIG) compliance; information and Internet technology; and reimbursement methodologies.

Note:

The AAPC continues to investigate further expansion of its body of certifications to prepare coders for proficiency in medical and surgical specialty coding. Technological advancements and changes in outpatient and inpatient prospective payment system regulations, such as Medicare severity diagnosis-related groups (MS-DRGs), create a compliance risk that has to be carefully monitored. Specialty coders have the expertise to monitor such areas, impacting the facility's coding and reimbursement process. Specialty coders typically perform the following tasks:

- Analyze provider documentation for accuracy, completeness, and timeliness
- Maintain and update chargemasters and/or encounter forms
- Meet with coding staff members to educate them about revised rules and regulations
- Review patient charges to ensure accuracy in reported codes and modifiers, and enter billing edits
- Write letters of appeals to address third-party payer reimbursement denials

The type of setting in which you seek employment will indicate which credential(s) you should pursue. Inpatient and/or outpatient coders obtain CCS certification, and physician office coders choose the CCS-P and/or CPC credential. Outpatient coders also have the option of selecting the CPC-H credential. Insurance specialists who work for health care facilities and third-party payers obtain the CCS-P. Those who have not met requirements for field experience as a coder can seek apprentice-level certification as a CCA, CPC-A, or CPC-H-A. (Once certified, both professional associations require maintenance of the credential through continuing education [CE] recertification per two-year cycle.)

Employment Opportunities

Coders can obtain employment in a variety of settings, including clinics, consulting firms, government agencies, hospitals, insurance companies, nursing facilities, home health agencies, hospices, and physicians' offices. Coders also have the opportunity to work at home for employers who partner with an Internet-based **application service provider (ASP)** (e.g., eWebCoding by ChartOne), which is a third-party entity that manages and distributes software-based services and solutions to customers across a wide area network (WAN) (computers that are far apart and are connected by telephone lines) from a central data center.

OTHER PROFESSIONS RELATED TO THE CODER

One profession that is closely related to a coder is that of a **health insurance specialist** (or **claims examiner**). When employed by third-party payers, these specialists review health-related claims to determine whether the costs are reasonable and medically necessary based on the patient's diagnosis. This process involves verification of the claim against third-party payer guidelines to authorize appropriate payment or to refer the claim to an investigator for a more thorough review.

Another profession that is closely related to a coder is the **medical assistant**. When employed by a provider, this person performs administrative and clinical tasks to keep the office and clinic running smoothly. Medical assistants who specialize in administrative aspects of the profession answer telephones, greet patients, update and file patient medical records, complete insurance claims, process correspondence, schedule appointments, arrange for hospital admission and laboratory services, and manage billing and bookkeeping.

When employed by a physician's office, health insurance specialists and medical assistants perform medical billing, coding, record keeping, and other medical office administrative duties. Health insurance specialists (or claims examiners) and medical assistants receive formal training in college-based programs or at vocational schools. They also receive on-the-job training.

- Health insurance specialists (or claims examiners) and medical assistants often become certified as a CCS or a CCS-P (through the AHIMA) or as a CPC-P (through the AAPC).

- The health insurance specialist also has the option of becoming credentialed by the:
  - Medical Association of Billers (MAB) as a Certified Medical Billing Specialist (CMBS)
  - National Electronic Billers Alliance (NEBA) as a Certified Healthcare Reimbursement Specialist (CHRS)

- Health insurance specialists can participate in the International Claim Association (ICA) program of education. The ICA offers Associate, Life and Health Claims (ALHC) and Fellow, Life and Health Claims (FLHC) examinations to claims examiners in the life and health insurance industries.

- Medical assistants often become credentialed as a Certified Medical Assistant (CMA) through the American Association of Medical Assistants (AAMA) or as a Registered Medical Assistant (RMA) through the American Medical Technologists (AMT).

Health insurance specialists (or claims examiners) and medical assistants obtain employment in clinics, health care clearinghouses, health care facility billing departments, insurance companies, and physicians' offices and with third-party administrators (TPAs). When employed by clearing houses, insurance companies, or TPAs, they often have the opportunity to work at home, where they process and verify health care claims using an Internet-based application server provider (ASP).

Exercise 1.1 – Career as a Coder

Instructions: Match the description with its career. Answers may be assigned more than once.

_____ 1. Answers telephones, greets patients, and updates and files patient medical records

_____ 2. Communicates with providers about documentation and compliance issues related to code assignment

_____ 3. Reviews claims for third-party payers to determine whether costs are reasonable and medically necessary

_____ 4. Schedules hospital admission and laboratory services

_____ 5. Verifies claims against third-party payer guidelines to authorize appropriate payments

a. Coder

b. Health insurance specialist

c. Medical assistant

(continues)

Exercise 1.1 (continued)

Instructions: Match the type of certification exam with the professional association that offers it.

_____	**6.** Certified Coding Specialist (CCS)	**a.** AAPC
_____	**7.** Certified Medical Reimbursement Specialist (CMRS)	**b.** NEBA
_____	**8.** Certified Professional Coder (CPC)	**c.** AHIMA
_____	**9.** Certified Healthcare Reimbursement Specialist (CHRS)	**d.** ICA
_____	**10.** Fellow, Life and vHealth Claims (FLHC)	**e.** AMBA

Professional Associations and Discussion Boards

Students are often able to join a professional association (Table 1-1) for a reduced membership fee and receive most of the same benefits as active members (who pay much more!). Benefits of joining a professional association include the following:

- Eligibility for scholarships and grants
- Opportunity to network with members (internship and job placement)
- Free publications (e.g., professional journals)
- Reduced certification exam fees
- Website access for members only

Table 1-1 Professional Associations

Career	Professional Association
Coder	American Academy of Professional Coders (AAPC)
	American Health Information Management Association (AHIMA)
Health Insurance Specialist	International Claim Association (ICA)
	Alliance of Claims Assistance Professionals (ACAP)
	American Medical Billing Association (AMBA)
	Medical Association of Billers (MAB)
Medical Assistant	American Association of Medical Assistants (AAMA)
	American Medical Technologists (AMT)

© Cengage Learning 2014

Table 1-2 Internet-Based Discussion Boards (Listservs)

Name of Discussion Board	Website
AHIMA communities of practice	AHIMA members can log in at http://www.ahima.org
Coders forum	Go to http://www.advanceforhim.com and select "Forums" from the "Community" dropdown menu.
Hospital outpatient coders	Go to http://list.nih.gov and click on the Browse link. Click on the OP-PPS-L (Outpatient Prospective Payment System List) link.
Medicare Part B claims coding, billing, and reimbursement challenges	Go to http://www.partbnews.com, click on the Community link, click on the Forums link, and click on the Medicare Part-B link.
Physician office lab billing, reimbursement, and compliance challenges	Go to http://www.partbnews.com, click on the Community link, click on the Forums link, and click on the Physician Office Laboratory link.

© Cengage Learning 2014

Exercise 1.2 – Professional Associations and Discussion Boards

Instructions: Match the professional association with the type of professional. Answers may be assigned more than once.

_____ **1.** AAMA	**a.** Coder
_____ **2.** AAPC	**b.** Health insurance specialist
_____ **3.** ACAP	**c.** Medical assistant
_____ **4.** AHIMA	
_____ **5.** AMT	

Attending professional association conferences and meetings provides opportunities to network with professionals. Another way to network is to join an **online discussion board** (or **listserv**) (Table 1-2), which is an Internet-based or e-mail discussion forum that covers a variety of topics and issues.

Coding Overview

Coding systems and medical nomenclatures are used by health care facilities, health care providers, and third-party payers to collect, store, and process data for a variety of purposes (e.g., health care reimbursement). A **coding system** (or **classification system**) organizes a medical nomenclature according to similar conditions, diseases, procedures, and services, and it contains codes for each. (ICD-9-CM and ICD-10-CM arranges these elements into appropriate chapters and sections.) A **medical nomenclature** is a vocabulary of clinical and medical terms (e.g., arthritis, gastritis, pneumonia) used by health care providers to document patient care. A **code** includes numeric and alphanumeric characters that are reported to health plans for health care reimbursement, to external agencies (e.g., state departments of health) for data collection, and internally (acute care hospital) for education and research. **Coding** is the assignment of codes to diagnoses, services, and procedures based on patient record documentation.

EXAMPLE 1: CODING SYSTEMS:

- The *International Classification of Diseases, Ninth Revision, Clinical Modification* **(ICD-9-CM)** was adopted in 1979 to classify diagnoses (Volumes 1 and 2) and procedures (Volume 3). All health care facilities assign ICD-9-CM codes to report diagnoses; hospitals also report ICD-9-CM procedure codes for inpatient procedures and services. The *International Classification of Diseases, Tenth Revision, Clinical Modification* **(ICD-10-CM)** (and ICD-10-PCS) will replace ICD-9-CM.

- The *International Classification of Diseases, Tenth Revision, Procedure Coding System* **(ICD-10-PCS)** was

Note:

You are already familiar with a well-known coding system called the United States Postal Service ZIP Code system, which classifies addresses as numbers (e.g., 12345-9876)

ICD-10 Alert!

Effective October 1, 2014, ICD-10-CM and ICD-10-PCS (abbreviated as ICD-10-CM/PCS) will replace ICD-9-CM.

Note:

International Classification of Diseases, Tenth Revision, Clinical Modification/ Procedure Coding System, (ICD-10-CM/PCS) is the shortened name the Centers for Medicare and Medicaid Services uses to identify both classification systems.

developed by the National Center for Health Statistics (NCHS) to replace Volume 3 of ICD-9-CM; it will be used to classify inpatient procedures and services.

- The *Current Procedural Terminology (CPT)* was originally published by the American Medical Association (AMA) in 1966. Subsequent editions were published about every five years until the late 1980s, when the AMA began publishing annual revisions. CPT classifies procedures and services, and it is used by physicians and outpatient health care settings (e.g., the hospital ambulatory surgery department) to assign CPT codes for reporting procedures and services on health insurance claims. CPT is considered level I of the Healthcare Common Procedure Coding System (HCPCS).

- The **Healthcare Common Procedure Coding System (HCPCS)** also includes level II (national) codes, called **HCPCS level II** (or **HCPCS national codes**), which are managed by the **Centers for Medicare & Medicaid Services (CMS)**, an administrative agency in the federal Department of Health and Human Services (DHHS). HCPCS level II classifies medical equipment, injectable drugs, transportation services, and other services not classified in CPT. Physicians and ambulatory care settings use HCPCS level II to report procedures and services.

> **Note:**
>
> HCPCS level III local codes were discontinued in 2004. They had been managed by Medicare carriers and fiscal intermediaries (FIs). You might come across the legendary use of HCPCS level III local codes in health care facility or insurance company databases.

EXAMPLE 2: MEDICAL NOMENCLATURES:

- The *Systematized Nomenclature of Medicine (SNOMED)* was originally developed by the College of American Pathologists (CAP) in 1974 and is cross-referenced to the ICD-9-CM. It can also be considered a classification system because it contains codes for activities within the patient record (e.g., medical diagnoses, procedures, nursing diagnoses, nursing procedures, patient signs and symptoms, occupational history, and causes and etiologies of diseases).

- The current revision, of SNOMED, created in 2002, is called *SNOMED Clinical Terms* (or SNOMED CT); it includes comprehensive coverage of diseases, clinical findings, therapies, procedures, and outcomes. It combines the content and structure of a previous revision of SNOMED with medical nomenclatures titled the United Kingdom's *National Health Service's Clinical Terms Version 3* (formerly called *Read Codes*, developed in the early 1980s by Dr. James Read to record and retrieve primary care data in a computer).

The **Health Insurance Portability and Accountability Act of 1996 (HIPAA)** is federal legislation that amended the Internal Revenue Code of 1986 to:

- improve portability and continuity of health insurance coverage in the group and individual markets;
- combat waste, fraud, and abuse in health insurance and health care delivery;
- promote the use of medical savings accounts;
- improve access to long-term care services and coverage;
- simplify the administration of health insurance by creating unique identifiers for providers, health plans, employers, and individuals;
- create standards for electronic health information transactions; and
- create privacy and security standards for health information.

To facilitate the creation of standards for electronic health information transactions, HIPAA requires two types of code sets to be adopted for the purpose of encoding data elements (e.g., procedure and service codes). **Encoding** is the process of standardizing data by assigning numeric values (codes or numbers) to text or other information (e.g., diagnosis and gender).

Large code sets encode:

- diseases, injuries, impairments, other health-related problems, and their manifestations;
- causes of injury, disease, impairment, or other health-related problems;

- actions taken to prevent, diagnose, treat, or manage diseases, injuries, and impairments; and

- substances, equipment, supplies, or other items used to perform these actions.

Small code sets encode:

- race/ethnicity;

- type of facility; and

- type of unit.

EXAMPLE:

- **SMALL CODE SET:** A patient's gender is assigned a 1 if male, a 2 if female, or a 3 if undetermined.

- **LARGE CODE SET:** The diagnosis "essential hypertension" is assigned ICD-9-CM code 401.9 (or ICD-10-CM code I10).

HIPAA also requires the following specific code sets to be adopted for use by clearinghouses, health plans, and providers:

- *International Classification of Diseases, Ninth Revision, Clinical Modification* (ICD-9-CM), or ICD-10-CM/PCS

- *Current Procedural Terminology* (CPT)

- HCPCS level II (national codes)

- *Current Dental Terminology* (CDT)

- National Drug Codes (NDC)

 A **clearinghouse** (or **health care clearinghouse**) is a public or private entity (e.g., billing service) that processes or facilitates the processing of health information and claims from a nonstandard to a standard format. A **health plan** (or **third-party payer**) (e.g., Blue Cross/Blue Shield, a commercial insurance company) is an insurance company that establishes a contract to reimburse health care facilities and patients for procedures and services provided. A **provider** (or **health care provider**) is a physician or another health care professional (e.g., a nurse practitioner or physician assistant) who performs procedures or provides services to patients. Adopting HIPAA's standard code sets has improved data quality and simplified claims submission for health care providers who routinely deal with multiple third-party payers. The code sets have also simplified claims processing for health plans. Health plans that do not accept standard code sets are required to modify their systems to accept all valid codes or to contract with a health care clearinghouse that does accept standard code sets.

> **Note:**
>
> A health care clearinghouse is not a **third-party administrator (TPA)**, which is an entity that processes health care claims and performs related business functions for a health plan. The TPA might contract with a health care clearinghouse to standardize data for claims processing.

Coding References

Professional organizations that are recognized as national authorities on CPT, HCPCS, and ICD-9-CM (or ICD-10-CM/PCS) coding publish references and resources that are invaluable to coders. To ensure the development of excellent coding skills, make sure you become familiar with and use the following references and resources:

- *AHA Coding Clinic for ICD-9-CM* and *AHA Coding Clinic for HCPCS,* quarterly newsletters published by the American Hospital Association and recognized by the CMS as official coding resources

- *Conditions of Participation* (CoP) and *Conditions for Coverage* (CfC), Medicare regulations published by CMS

- *CPT Assistant* and *HCPCS Assistant,* monthly newsletters published by the AMA and recognized by CMS as official coding resources

- *National Correct Coding Initiatives* (NCCI), code edit pairs that cannot be used in the same claim (developed by CMS and published by the federal government's National Technical Information Service [NTIS])

- Compliance program guidance documents, guidelines published by the DHHS OIG

- *ICD-9-CM Official Guidelines for Coding and Reporting,* guidelines provided by CMS and the NCHS to be used as a companion document to the official version of the ICD-9-CM (CMS and the NCHS also publish ICD-10-CM and ICD-10-PCS official guidelines for coding and reporting)

- *Outpatient Code Editor with Ambulatory Payment Classification,* software developed by CMS, distributed by NTIS, and used by hospitals to edit outpatient claims to help identify possible CPT/HCPCS coding errors and assign Ambulatory Payment Classifications (APCs) that are used to generate reimbursement

Note:

- Official coding policy is published in the *AHA Coding Clinic for ICD-9-CM* and *AHA Coding Clinic for HCPCS,* in the AMA's *CPT Assistant,* and as National Correct Coding Initiative (NCCI) edits.

- The AAPC and AHIMA publish coding newsletters, journals, and so on, but such publications do not contain official coding policy.

- It is likely that the AHA will also publish official coding resources for ICD-10-CM/PCS.

Incorporating the use of the above references and resources assists coders in avoiding the following abusive and fraudulent (dishonest and illegal) coding practices:

- **Unbundling**: Reporting multiple codes to increase reimbursement when a single combination code should be reported.

- **Upcoding**: Reporting codes that are not supported by documentation in the patient record for the purpose of increasing reimbursement.

- **Overcoding**: Reporting codes for signs and symptoms in addition to the established diagnosis code.

- **Jamming**: Routinely assigning an unspecified ICD-9-CM or ICD-10-CM disease code instead of reviewing the coding manual to select the appropriate code number.

- **Downcoding**: Routinely assigning lower-level CPT codes as a convenience instead of reviewing patient record documentation and the coding manual to determine the proper code to be reported.

Medical Coding Process

The **medical coding process** requires the review of patient record documentation to identify diagnoses, procedures, and services for the purpose of assigning ICD-9-CM (or ICD-10-CM/PCS), HCPCS level II, and/or CPT codes. Each health care entity (e.g., hospital, medical clinic, physician office) implements a unique medical coding process, which requires adherence to the following:

- Code of ethics
- Steps to accurate coding
- Avoid assumption coding
- Physician query process
- Coding compliance program

Code of Ethics

Professional associations establish a *code of ethics* to help members understand how to differentiate between "right" and "wrong" and apply that understanding to decision making. The AAPC publishes code of ethics, and AHIMA publishes standards of ethical coding; both serve as guidelines for ethical coding conduct, and they demonstrate a commitment to coding integrity.

Steps to Accurate Coding

Regardless of health care setting, the *steps to accurate coding* begin with a review of the entire patient record (manual or electronic) before selecting diagnoses, procedures, and services to which codes are assigned. Depending on the setting, coders perform retrospective coding, concurrent coding, or a combination of both.

Retrospective coding is the review of records to assign codes after the patient is discharged from the health care facility (e.g., hospital inpatient) or released from same-day outpatient care (e.g., hospital outpatient surgery unit). It is most commonly associated with inpatient hospital stays because accurate coding requires verification of diagnoses and procedures by reviewing completed face sheets, discharge summaries, operative reports, pathology reports, and progress notes in the patient records.

Concurrent coding is the review of records and/or use of encounter forms and chargemasters to assign codes during an inpatient stay (e.g., hospital) or an outpatient encounter (e.g., hospital outpatient visit for laboratory testing or X-rays, physician office visit). It is typically performed for outpatient encounters because encounter forms (e.g., physician office) and chargemasters (e.g., hospital emergency department visit, hospital outpatient visit for laboratory testing, etc.) are completed in "real time" by health care providers as part of the charge-capture process.

- *Encounter forms* are used to record encounter data about office procedures and services provided to patients.

- *Chargemasters* contain a computer-generated list of procedures, services, and supplies and corresponding revenue codes along with charges for each.

Note:

Information about encounter forms and chargemasters is located in Chapter 19 of this textbook, along with samples of each.

EHR RESULTS IN GREATER IMPLEMENTATION OF CONCURRENT CODING

Concurrent coding was introduced for inpatient coding just after the inpatient prospective payment system (using diagnosis-related groups) was implemented October 1, 1983. Coders from the health information department worked part of the day on nursing units, accessing paper-based manual medical records to begin the process of assigning codes to diagnosis and procedures. On discharge of the patient from the hospital, the coders performed a final review of the patient record to ensure accuracy of reported codes. Because the paper-based manual patient record can be handled by just one individual at a time, coders "competed" with nurses, physicians, and other health care providers for access to the record. As a result, concurrent coding as a process was discontinued in some facilities because it was inefficient.

Today, implementation of the electronic health record (EHR) has resulted in a resurgence of concurrent coding practices because coders (still located in the health information department) access patient records in an electronic format. They no longer "compete" with other health care providers for access to the record and, as a result, efficiency associated with

the concurrent coding concept has been realized. In practice, coders remain at their work stations in the health information department (and *remote coders* use their at-home work stations) to access patient EHRs to begin the discharge coding process. Rising health care costs created an impetus for concurrent coding processes because it is a much faster method for coders to review and verify the accuracy of codes on discharge of inpatients based on concurrent coding work performed (according to an established schedule) up until the date of discharge. For tertiary-care facilities that provide complex health care (e.g., transplant surgery) and quaternary-care facilities that provide highly specialized care (e.g., experimental medicine), both of which are also characterized as providing high-cost care (e.g., $500,000 transplant surgery), having the ability to submit codes for reimbursement purposes within hours (instead of days) of inpatient discharge significantly and positively impacts their accounts receivables (and their "bottom line"). In addition, community-based hospitals that submit claims averaging $50,000 or higher also realize the benefits of concurrent coding.

According to the American Hospital Association's *Coding Clinic for ICD-9-CM* (May/June 1984), "The importance of understanding and following the basic ICD-9-CM [and ICD-10-CM/PCS] coding principles cannot be overemphasized in the training of coders and in quality control activities undertaken to improve the accuracy of data reported for internal and external hospital use. The measures for coding accuracy include (a) adherence to ICD-9-CM [and ICD-10-CM/PCS] coding principles and instructions, (b) attention to specificity in code selection where indicated by physician documentation in the medical record [patient record], (c) grasp of medical terminology, and (d) absence of clerical-type errors, such as those due to carelessness in reading or in transposing numbers. Auditing of coded diagnostic and procedural information for accuracy should not be confused with the review for relevancy in sequencing of the codes at hand. They are separate tasks linked together in the data reporting process."

The underlined statement in the above quote is significant because it means that coders are expected to review the *entire* record when assigning codes to diagnoses and procedures documented on the face sheet and in the discharge summary. Thus, coders should review the face sheet, discharge summary, and other documentation (e.g., progress notes, operative reports, pathology reports, laboratory data, and so on) to assign the most specific codes possible.

Remember! Coders must avoid assumption coding, and when a problem with documentation quality is noted (e.g., conflicting diagnostic statements on the discharge summary, face sheet, and elsewhere in the record) the physician query process is initiated (discussed below).

> **EXAMPLE 1:** The provider documented *congestive heart failure* on the face sheet of the patient record. On review of progress notes that document the patient's response to treatment, the coder finds documentation of *acute and chronic diastolic and systolic congestive heart failure* in the discharge progress note. Instead of reporting a code for *congestive heart failure*, report the more specific code for *acute and chronic diastolic and systolic congestive heart failure*.

> **EXAMPLE 2:** The provider documented *malnutrition* on the discharge summary in the patient record. On review of progress notes, the coder finds documentation of *moderate malnutrition*. Instead of reporting the nonspecific code for *malnutrition,* report the more specific code for *moderate malnutrition*.

Avoid Assumption Coding

Coders are prohibited from performing **assumption coding**, which is the assignment of codes based on assuming, from a review of clinical evidence in the patient's record, that the patient has certain diagnoses or received certain procedures/services even though the provider did not specifically document those diagnoses or procedures/services. According to the *Compliance Program Guidance for Third-Party Medical Billing Companies*, published by the Department of Health and Human Services' Office of Inspector General, assumption coding creates risk for fraud and abuse because the coder assumes certain facts about a patient's condition or procedures/services although the physician has not specifically documented the level of detail to which the coder assigns codes. (Coders can avoid fraudulent assumption coding by implementing the physician query process discussed in the following section.)

> **EXAMPLE:** An elderly patient is admitted to the hospital for treatment of a fractured femur. Upon examination, the physician documents that the skin around the fractured femur site has split open. X-ray of the left femur reveals a displaced fracture of the shaft. The patient underwent fracture reduction and full-leg casting. The physician documents *open Type I fracture of shaft, left femur* as the final diagnosis.

The coder assigns code 821.11 (S72.302B) for the *open Type I fracture of shaft, left femur*, which is correct. The coder assigns code 79.25 (0QS90ZZ) for the *fracture reduction and full leg casting procedure,* which is incorrect because its code description is *open reduction (reposition) of fracture without internal fixation (no device), femur (shaft)*. Although the patient has an open fracture, the physician did *not* perform an open reduction procedure. (An open reduction involves making a surgical incision to align displaced bones, and it may require external fixation to heal properly.) In this case, the coder incorrectly "assumed" that an open reduction was performed because the patient's open fracture was treated. The code that should be assigned for this procedure is

79.05 (0QS9XZZ) because its code description is *closed reduction of fracture without internal fixation, femur.* (A closed reduction involves casting the affected limb to stabilize the fracture for healing, and it might also require the physician to pull back two ends of bone that are touching each other and/or to correct any wide angles.)

Physician Query Process

When coders have questions about documented diagnoses or procedures/services, they use a **physician query process** to contact the responsible physician to request clarification about documentation and the code(s) to be assigned.

Note:

The query should *not* lead the physician to a desired outcome.

- A *leading query* would be phrased as, *"Is the patient's anemia due to blood loss?"* and leads the physician to add due to blood loss to the anemia diagnosis for more specific code assignment and possible increased reimbursement.

- A *nonleading query* would be phrased as, *"Can the cause of the patient's anemia be specified? The history documents symptoms of fatigue, headaches, inflamed tongue, and lightheadedness. The CBC reveals low hemoglobin levels."* This query allows the physician to determine whether the anemia can be qualified according to type.

The following guidelines should be followed when activating the physician query process:

- Establish a policy to indicate when a coder should generate a physician query, such as when documentation in the patient's record fails to meet one of the following five criteria (according to AHIMA's 2008 practice brief entitled, *Managing an Effective Query Process*):

  ○ *Legibility* (e.g., illegible handwritten patient record entries)

  ○ *Completeness* (e.g., abnormal test results but clinical significance of results is not documented)

  ○ *Clarity* (e.g., signs and symptoms are present in the patient record, but a definitive diagnosis is not documented)

  ○ *Consistency* (e.g., discrepancy among two or more treating providers regarding a diagnosis, such as a patient who presents with shortness of breath and the consulting physician pneumonia as the cause while the attending physician documents congestive heart failure as the cause)

  ○ *Precision* (e.g., clinical documentation indicates a more specific diagnosis than is documented, such as a sputum culture that indicates bacterial pneumonia and the diagnosis does not indicate the cause of the pneumonia)

Note:

The EHR allows for development of an automated physician query process, which is used by utilization managers (or case managers), clinical documentation improvement specialists, and coders to obtain clarification about patient record documentation. Integrating the automated physician query process with the EHR allows physicians to more easily receive and reply to queries, which results in better and timely responses from physicians.

- Query the physician when the following are noted by the coder and when provider documentation in the patient record is not present (according to AHIMA's 2008 practice brief entitled, *Managing an Effective Query Process*):

  ○ Clinical indicators of a diagnosis (e.g., lab, X-ray) but the diagnosis is not documented

  ○ Clinical evidence for a higher degree of specificity or severity (e.g., progress notes) but specificity or severity is not documented in the diagnosis

- Cause-and-effect relationship between two conditions or an organism but the relationship is not documented in the diagnosis (e.g., due to, with)

- An underlying cause when a patient is admitted with symptoms (e.g., shortness of breath is documented instead of diagnosed pneumonia)

- Treatment is documented without a corresponding diagnosis for medical necessity (e.g., antibiotics for a secondary diagnosis of UTI, which is not documented as a diagnosis)

- Lack of present on admission (POA) indicator status (e.g., history did not indicate diagnoses that were present on admission, such as chronic asthma) (The POA indicator status is discussed in textbook Chapter 19.)

- Determine whether the query will be generated concurrently (during inpatient hospitalization) or retrospectively (after patient discharge).

- Designate an individual who will serve as the physician's contact during the physician query process (e.g., coding supervisor, utilization manager). Remember that the coder's role is to assign codes based on documentation and that asking for clarification is appropriate, but making an assumption about codes to be assigned is considered fraud. That means that coders should ask physicians open-ended questions to avoid leading the physicians by indicating a preference for a particular response. Coders do not make clinical assumptions—that is the sole responsibility of the physician.

> **Note:**
>
> *Utilization managers (or case managers)* are responsible for coordinating inpatient care to ensure the appropriate utilization of resources, delivery of health care services, and timely discharge or transfer. They usually have a bachelor's degree (e.g., nursing), professional licensure (e.g., RN), and clinical practice experience. Utilization managers work closely with physicians on a daily basis, and they are a logical choice to facilitate the physician query process. In this role, they serve as the liaison for coders (and physicians) by helping coders write appropriate queries and clarifying queries for physicians so that responses are timely and complete.

Use a query form (Figure 1-1), not scrap paper, to document the coder's query and the physician's response. If the completed query form is filed in the patient's record, determine whether it is considered an official part of the record and subject to disclosure by those requesting copies of records or whether it is an administrative form that is not subject to disclosure. The query form could also be stored in an administrative file in the coding supervisor's office and the information resulting from the query documented kept in the patient record by the physician (e.g., an addendum to the discharge summary). The length of time that the completed query form is retained is determined by each health care organization.

> **EXAMPLE:** A patient is admitted with severe dyspnea (shortness of breath), chest pain, and fever. Upon physical examination, the physician documents rhonchi (gurgling sound in the lungs), wheezing, and rales (clicking, bubbling, or rattling sounds in the lungs). Laboratory data during the hospitalization include a culture and sensitivity report of sputum that documents the presence of gram-negative bacteria. A review of the physician orders reveals documentation of appropriate medications to treat *pneumonia due to gram-negative bacteria.* The medication administration record (MAR) documents administration of the medications, and the physician progress notes document the patient's positive response to medications (and resolution of the pneumonia). The physician documents *viral pneumonia* as the final diagnosis.

Depending on the health care facility's coding policy and procedure, the coder has two options.

1. If the coding policy and procedure allow coders to use the entire patient record as the basis of assigning codes to final diagnoses and procedures, because documentation in the record supports a final diagnosis of *pneumonia due to gram-negative bacteria* (instead of viral pneumonia), the coder would assign the code for that condition.

2. If the coding policy and procedure require coders to generate a *physician query* when the final diagnosis (on the face sheet or in the discharge summary) differs from documentation found in the patient record, the coder would submit the following query to the physician, which allows the physician an opportunity to

PHYSICIAN QUERY FORM

Patient Name: _____   Date: _____
Admission Date: _____   Coder: _____
Patient Number: _____   Email Address: _____
                                         Office Number: _____

Dear Dr. _____ ,

The diagnosis or procedure of _____ requires more specific information in order to assign the most accurate and complete code. The following information is documented in the _____ .

_____
_____
_____
_____
_____

I have the following question(s) about this record:

_____
_____
_____
_____
_____

Please respond to this question in the space below, and also document an amendment in the patient record (if appropriate):

_____
_____
_____
_____
_____
_____

© Cengage Learning 2014

Figure 1-1 Sample physician query form

correct the documented final diagnosis if warranted. In this case, the physician changed *viral pneumonia* to *pneumonia due to gram-negative bacteria* (using the proper procedure for amending the patient record).

EXAMPLE: PHYSICIAN QUERY: To: Dr. Smith, The final diagnosis documented on this case is viral pneumonia. A review of laboratory results indicates gram-negative bacteria. Would you reply to (1) confirm the original final diagnosis of viral pneumonia or to (2) document a different final diagnosis? Thank you for your attention to this query.

—Michelle G.

The assignment of a code to pneumonia due to *gram-negative bacteria* results in reimbursement of about $3,500, and the assignment of a code to *viral pneumonia* results in reimbursement of about $2,500. Not querying the physician would have resulted in a loss of $1,000 to the facility.

This case also includes documentation of signs and symptoms, which are due to the pneumonia. Thus, the coder would *not* assign codes to symptoms of dyspnea, chest pain, fever or signs of rhonchi, wheezing, and rales.

Clinical Documentation Improvement Program

The purpose of a *clinical documentation improvement (CDI) program* is to help health care facilities comply with government programs (e.g., RAC audits, ARRA/HITECH) and other initiatives (Joint Commission accreditation) with the goal of improving health care quality. As part of a CDI program, the CDI specialist initiates concurrent and retrospective reviews of inpatient records to identify conflicting, incomplete, or nonspecific provider documentation. Concurrent reviews are performed on patient care units (to access paper-based patient records) or remotely (to access EHRs). The goal of the CDI program is to that patient diagnoses and procedures are supported by ICD-9-CM (or ICD-10-CM/PCS) codes, and CDI specialists use a physician query form to communicate with physicians (and other health care providers) with the intended result of improving documentation, coding, reimbursement, and severity of illness (SOI) and risk of mortality (ROM) classifications. CDI programs are usually associated with acute health care facilities; however, they are also implemented on alternate health care settings (e.g., acute rehabilitation facility, skilled nursing facility). A *clinical documentation improvement (CDI) specialist* is responsible for performing inpatient record reviews for the purpose of:

- implementing documentation clarification and specificity processes (as part of the physician query process);

- using and interpreting clinical documentation improvement statistics;

- conducting research and providing education to improve clinical documentation; and

- ensuring compliance with initiatives that serve to improve of the quality of health care, which include:

  - complying with fraud and abuse regulations;

  - enforcing privacy and security of patient information; and

  - monitoring *health information exchange (HIE)*.

Coding Compliance Program

A *coding compliance program* ensures that the assignment of codes to diagnoses, procedures, and services follows established coding guidelines, such as those published by the Centers for Medicare and Medicaid Services (CMS). Health care organizations write *policies* (guiding principles that indicate "what to do") and *procedures* (processes that indicate "how to do it") to assist in implementing the coding compliance stages of detection, correction, prevention, verification, and comparison.

- *Detection* is the process of identifying potential coding compliance problems. For example, a coder notices that some patient records contain insufficient or incomplete documentation, which adversely impacts coding specificity. The coder brings these records to the attention of the coding compliance officer (e.g., coding supervisor), who implements the next stage of the coding compliance program.

- *Correction* is based on the review of patient records that contain potential coding compliance problems, during which specific compliance issues are identified and problem-solving methods are used to implement necessary improvements (corrections). For example, the coding compliance officer conducts a careful review of the patient records that contain insufficient or incomplete documentation. She determines that all of them are the responsibility of a physician new to the practice, and she prepares educational material specific to documentation issues noted during her review of the patient records.

- *Prevention* involves educating coders and providers so as to prevent coding compliance problems from recurring. For example, the coding compliance officer schedules a meeting with the physician responsible for insufficient or incomplete documentation, and educates the physician about the specific areas of insufficient or incomplete documentation that adversely impact medical coding. This meeting is conducted in a nonconfrontational manner, with education and correction as its goals.

- *Verification* provides an "audit trail" that the detection, correction, and prevention functions of the coding compliance program are being actively performed. For example, the coding compliance officer maintains a file that contains the following:

  - Original codes assigned based on insufficient and incomplete documentation

  - Educational materials prepared specific to the documentation issues

  - Minutes of the educational meeting with the responsible physician

  - Final codes assigned based on sufficient and complete documentation

  - Remittance advice from third-party payer, which contains adjudication (decision about reimbursement, including possible claims denial)

- *Comparison* requires the analysis of internal coding patterns over specified periods of time (e.g., quarterly) as well as the analysis of external coding patterns by using external benchmarks (trends). For example, the coding compliance officer reviews reports of quarterly medical audits to determine whether the new physician's documentation has improved. Such reports contain the results of claims submission, which indicate the number of claims denials based on nonspecific codes submitted as a result of insufficient and incomplete documentation. In addition, the coding compliance officer obtains benchmark data (reports) from third-party payers and compares the coding practices in her facility with those of similar providers; if reimbursement to similar providers is significantly higher (or lower) than that paid to her provider, she initiates the *detection* process in an attempt to identify related coding compliance problems.

An effective coding compliance program monitors coding processes for completeness, reliability, validity, and timeliness.

- *Completeness* ensures that codes are assigned to all *reportable* diagnoses, procedures, and services documented in the patient record. For example, coders review the entire patient record to assign the most specific codes possible.

- *Reliability* allows for the same results to be consistently achieved. For example, when the same patient record is coded by different coding professionals, they assign identical diagnosis and procedure/service codes.

- *Validity* confirms that assigned codes accurately reflect the patient's diagnoses, procedures, and services. For example, coders do *not* assign codes to diagnoses that were not medically managed or treated during an encounter.

- *Timeliness* means that patient records are coded in accordance with established policies and procedures to ensure timely reimbursement.

Computer Assisted Coding

Computer assisted coding (CAC) uses computer software to automatically generate medical codes by "reading" transcribed clinical documentation provided by health care practitioners (Figure 1-2 and Figure 1-3).

Exercise 1.3 – Coding Overview

Instructions: Match the code set description with its type. Answers may be assigned more than once.

_____ **1.** Race, ethnicity, type of facility, and type of unit

_____ **2.** Substances, equipment, supplies, or other items

_____ **3.** Actions taken to prevent, diagnose, treat, or manage diseases, injuries, and impairments

_____ **4.** Causes of injury, disease, impairment, or other health-related problems

_____ **5.** Diseases, injuries, impairments, other health-related problems, and their manifestations

a. Large code set

b. Small code set

Instructions: If the title in the first column is a coding system, enter *a*; if the title is a medical nomenclature, enter *b*.

_____ **6.** SNOMED

_____ **7.** *National Health Service's Clinical Terms Version 3*

_____ **8.** ICD-9-CM

_____ **9.** HCPCS level II

_____ **10.** *Read Codes*

a. Coding system

b. Medical nomenclature

CAC uses "natural language processing" theories to generate codes that are reviewed and validated by coders for reporting on third-party payer claims. Similar to the medical editor's role in ensuring the accuracy of reports produced from speech recognition technology, the coder's role changes from that of data entry to validation/audit. The coder reviews and approves the CAC-assigned codes, improving efficiency and offering expanded career opportunities for enthusiastic coders.

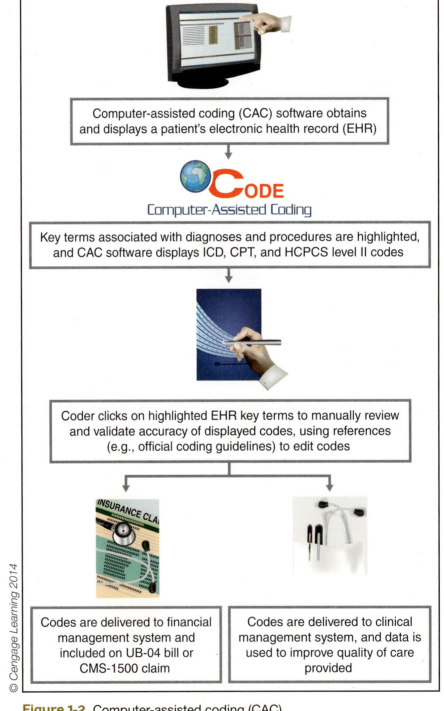

Figure 1-2 Computer-assisted coding (CAC)

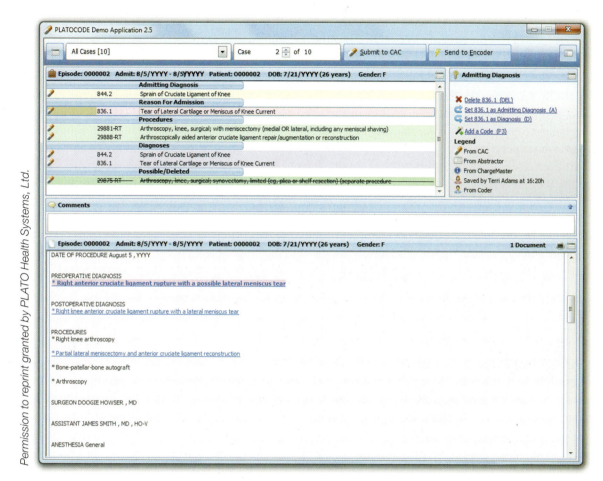

Permission to reprint granted by PLATO Health Systems, Ltd.

Figure 1-3 Sample screen from PLATOCODE computer-assisted coding software

Documentation as Basis for Coding

Health care providers are responsible for documenting and authenticating legible, complete, and timely patient records in accordance with federal regulations (e.g., Medicare CoP) and accrediting agency standards (e.g., The Joint Commission). The provider is also responsible for correcting or altering errors in patient record documentation.

A **patient record** (or **medical record**) is the business record for a patient encounter (inpatient or outpatient) that documents health care services provided to a patient. It stores patient demographic data and documentation that supports diagnoses, and justifies treatment. It also contains the results of treatment provided. (**Demographic data** is patient identification information that is collected according to facility policy and includes information such as the patient's name, date of birth, mother's maiden name, and Social Security number.) The primary purpose of the record is to provide for **continuity of care**, which involves documenting patient care services so that others who treat the patient have a source of information on which to base additional care and treatment. The record also serves as a communication tool for physicians and other patient care professionals. It assists in planning individual patient care and documenting a patient's illness and treatment. Secondary purposes of the record do not relate directly to patient care and include:

- Evaluating the quality of patient care
- Providing data for use in clinical research, epidemiology studies, education, public policy making, facilities planning, and health care statistics
- Providing information to third-party payers for reimbursement
- Serving the medicolegal interests of the patient, facility, and providers of care

Documentation includes dictated and transcribed, typed or handwritten, and computer-generated notes and reports recorded in the patient's records by a health care professional. Documentation must be dated and authenticated (with a legible signature or electronic authentication).

In a teaching hospital, documentation must identify what service was furnished, how the teaching physician participated in providing the service, and whether the teaching physician was physically present when care was provided. A **teaching hospital** is engaged in an approved graduate medical education (GME) residency program in medicine, osteopathy, dentistry, or podiatry. A **teaching physician** is a physician (other than another resident physician) who supervises residents during patient care. A **resident physician** is an individual who participates in an approved GME program. A **hospitalist** is a physician whose practice emphasizes providing care for hospital inpatients. They are often internists (e.g., internal medicine specialists) who handle a patient's entire admission process, including examining the patient, reviewing patient history and medications, writing admission orders, counseling the patient, and performing other tasks that would have required the primary care physician to travel to the hospital to coordinate the inpatient admission. Similar to the concept of emergency physicians practicing in the hospital's emergency department, hospitalists are based in the hospital and provide inpatient care. Thus, their practice is location-based instead of organ-centered (e.g., neurology) or age-centered (e.g., gerontology).

Medical Necessity

Documentation in the patient record serves as the basis for coding. The information in the record must support codes submitted on claims for third-party payer reimbursement processing. The patient's diagnosis must also justify diagnostic and/or therapeutic procedures or services provided. This is called **medical necessity** and requires providers to document services or supplies that are proper and needed for the diagnosis or treatment of a medical condition; provided for the diagnosis, direct care, and treatment of a medical condition; consistent with standards of good medical practice in the local area; and not mainly for the convenience of the physician or health care facility.

It is important to remember the familiar phrase "If it wasn't documented, it wasn't done." The patient record serves as a medicolegal document and a business record. If a provider performs a service but doesn't document it, the patient (or third-party payer) can refuse to pay for that service, resulting in lost revenue for the provider. In addition, because the patient record serves as an excellent defense of the quality of care administered to a patient, missing documentation can result in problems if the record has to be admitted as evidence in a court of law.

EXAMPLE 1: MISSING PATIENT RECORD DOCUMENTATION: A representative from XYZ Insurance Company reviewed 100 outpatient claims submitted by the Medical Center to ensure that all services billed were documented in the patient records. Upon reconciliation of claims with patient record documentation, the representative denied payment for 13 services (totaling $14,000) because reports of the services billed were not found in the patient records. The facility must pay back the $14,000 it received from the payer as reimbursement for the claims submitted.

EXAMPLE 2: MEDICAL NECESSITY: The patient underwent an X-ray of his right knee, and the provider documented "severe right shoulder pain" in the record. The coder assigned a CPT code to the "right knee X-ray" and an ICD code to the "right shoulder pain." In this example, the third-party payer will deny reimbursement for the submitted claim because the *reason* for the X-ray (shoulder pain) does not match the *type* of X-ray performed. For medical necessity, the provider should have documented a diagnosis such as "right knee pain."

Patient Record Formats ●

Health care facilities and physicians' offices usually maintain either manual or automated records, and sometimes maintain a hybrid record. A **manual record** is paper-based, while an **automated record** uses computer technology. A **hybrid record** consists of both paper-based and computer-generated documents, which means the facility or office creates and stores some patient reports as paper-based records (e.g., handwritten progress notes, physician orders, and graphic charts) and some documents using a computer (e.g., transcribed reports and automated laboratory results). A variety of formats are used to maintain manual records, which include the source-oriented record (SOR), problem-oriented record (POR), and integrated record. Automated record formats include the electronic health record (EHR) (or computer-based patient record, CPR), electronic medical record (EMR), and optical disk imaging. Hybrid records use a combination format, such as the POR for paper-based reports and EMR for computer-stored reports.

Manual Record Formats

Source-oriented record (SOR) (or **sectionalized record**) reports are organized according to documentation (or data) source (e.g., ancillary, medical, and nursing). Each documentation (or data) source is located in a labeled section.

The **problem-oriented record (POR)** systematic method of documentation consists of four components:

- Database
- Problem list
- Initial plan
- Progress notes

Note:

The Premium Website contains electronic records that, if printed, generate paper-based records. When viewed on a computer monitor, they are considered to be a sort of EHR. True EHRs are generated by multiple providers using specialized software, and results are stored electronically in a format that is easily retrievable and viewable by users.

The POR **database** contains patient information collected on each patient, including the following:

- Chief complaint
- Present conditions and diagnoses
- Social data
- Past, personal, medical, and social history
- Review of systems
- Physical examination
- Baseline laboratory data

The POR **problem list** serves as a table of contents for the patient record because it is filed at the beginning of the record and contains a numbered list of the patient's problems, which helps to index documentation throughout the record. The POR **initial plan** contains the strategy for managing patient care and any actions taken to investigate the patient's condition and to treat and educate the patient. The initial plan consists of three categories:

- **Diagnostic/management plans**: Plans to learn more about the patient's condition and the management of the conditions.
- **Therapeutic plans**: Specific medications, goals, procedures, therapies, and treatments used to treat the patient.
- **Patient education plans**: Plans to educate the patient about conditions for which the patient is being treated.

The POR **progress notes** are documented for each problem assigned to the patient, using the SOAP structure:

- **Subjective (S)**: Patient's statement about how he or she feels, including symptomatic information (e.g., "I have a headache").
- **Objective (O)**: Observations about the patient, such as physical findings, or lab or X-ray results (e.g., chest X-ray negative).
- **Assessment (A)**: Judgment, opinion, or evaluation made by the health care provider (e.g., acute headache).
- **Plan (P)**: Diagnostic, therapeutic, and education plans to resolve the problems (e.g., patient to take Tylenol as needed for pain).

A **discharge note** is documented in the progress notes section of the POR to summarize the patient's care, treatment, response to care, and condition on discharge—documentation of all problems is included. A **transfer note** is documented when a patient is being transferred to another facility. It summarizes the reason for admission, current diagnoses and medical information, and reason for transfer.

Integrated record reports are arranged in strict chronological date order (or in reverse date order), which allows for observation of how the patient is progressing according to test results and how the patient responds to treatment based on test results. Many facilities integrate only physician and ancillary services (e.g., physical therapy) progress notes, which require entries to be identified by appropriate authentication (e.g., complete signature of the professional documenting the note as Mary Smith, RRT, registered respiratory therapist).

Automated Record Formats

The **electronic health record (EHR)** is a collection of patient information documented by a number of providers at different facilities regarding one patient. It is a multidisciplinary (many specialties) and multi-enterprise (many facilities) approach to record keeping because it has the ability to link patient information created at different locations according to a unique patient identifier (or identification number). The EHR provides access to complete and accurate health problems, status, and treatment data; it contains alerts (e.g., of drug interaction) and reminders (e.g., prescription renewal notice) for health care providers. According to the *Journal of Contemporary Dental Practice*, February 15, 2002, some professionals prefer to "use *electronic* instead of the earlier term *computer-based* because *electronic* better describes the medium in which the patient record is managed."

The **electronic medical record (EMR)** is created on a computer, using a keyboard, a mouse, an optical pen device, a voice recognition system, a scanner, or a touch screen. Records are created using vendor software, which also assists in provider decision making (e.g., alerts, reminders, clinical decision support systems, and links to medical knowledge). Numerous vendors offer EMR software, mostly to physician office practices that require practice management solutions (e.g., appointment scheduling, claims processing, clinical notes, patient registration).

Optical disk imaging (or **document imaging**) provides an alternative to traditional microfilm or remote (off-site) storage systems because patient records are converted to an electronic image and saved on storage media (e.g., optical disks). Optical disk imaging uses laser technology to create the image, and a **scanner** is used to capture paper record images onto the storage media (e.g., optical disk). It allows for rapid automated retrieval of records. Although labor-intensive, optical disk imaging serves as an interim measure for facilities that want to move away from paper-based medical records toward development of an EHR. For optical disk imaging, the paper record must be prepared for scanning (e.g., removal of staples and separation of pages) so documents can pass through the scanner properly. The paper record is inserted into a document feeder (similar to that on a copy machine) that is attached to the scanner, and each report is pulled through the scanner so the image is saved to optical disk. Each scanned page is **indexed**, which means it is identified according to a unique identification number (e.g., patient record number). A unique feature is that documents for the same patient do *not* have to be scanned at the same time. Because each scanned page is indexed, the complete patient record can be retrieved even when a patient's reports are scanned at a later time. A **jukebox** stores large numbers of optical disks, resulting in huge storage capabilities (e.g., gigabytes of data). Optical disk imaging systems can also be networked, or connected, to other computer equipment in the facility, such as transcription systems and diagnostic imaging systems, which allows other data and documents to be added to the optical disk imaging system, thus creating a complete patient record.

DOCUMENTATION CLONING IS AN EMR/EHR CONCERN

Office of Inspector General Work Plan, Fiscal Year 2012. (Permission to reuse in accordance with http://oig.hhs.gov content reuse and linking policy.)

Medicare administrative contractors have noted an increased frequency of electronic medical records (EMRs) and electronic health records (EHRs) that contain identical documentation across services. This may be the result of *documentation cloning*, which involves using the EMR/EHR to bring information from previous patient encounters forward to the current encounter without updating that information. As a result, questions about the validity of services have been raised and they are supported by Office of Inspector General (OIG) statistics that indicate Medicare paid $25 billion (or 19 percent of all Medicare Part B payments) for evaluation and management services in 2009. The OIG work plan includes the review of multiple E/M services for the same providers and Medicare beneficiaries to identify EMR/EHR documentation practices associated with potentially improper payments.

Exercise 1.4 – Documentation as Basis for Coding

Instructions: If the statement in the first column indicates a primary purpose of the patient record, enter *a*. If the statement indicates a secondary purpose of the patient record, enter *b*.

_____ **1.** Continuity of patient care

_____ **2.** Evaluating quality of patient care

_____ **3.** Providing data for use in clinical research

_____ **4.** Serving medicolegal interests of patient, facility, and providers

_____ **5.** Submitting information to payers for reimbursement

a. Primary purpose

b. Secondary purpose

Instructions: Complete each statement.

6. The business record for a patient encounter that documents health care services provided to a patient is called a(n) _____.

7. Patient identification information collected according to facility policy, which includes the patient's name, date of birth, and so on, is called _____.

8. The primary purpose of the record is to provide for _____, which involves documenting patient care services so that others who treat the patient have a source of information on which to base additional care and treatment.

9. The patient's diagnosis must justify diagnostic and/or therapeutic procedures or services provided, which is called _____.

10. A paper-based record is called a(n) _____ record.

11. When reports are organized according to data source, the _____ record is being used.

12. When reports are arranged in strict chronological date order (or reverse date order), the _____ record is being used.

13. An automated record that is created on a computer, using a keyboard, a mouse, an optical pen device, a voice recognition system, a scanner, or a touch screen is called the _____.

14. An automated record that provides an alternative to traditional microfilm or remote storage systems because patient records are converted to an electronic image and saved on storage media is called _____.

15. The equipment that stores large numbers of optical disks, resulting in huge storage capabilities, is called a(n) _____.

Health Data Collection

Health data collection is performed by health care facilities and providers for the purpose of administrative planning, submitting statistics to state and federal government agencies (and other organizations), and reporting health claims data to third-party payers.

Reporting Hospital Data

Hospitals and other health care facilities use **automated case abstracting software** to collect and report inpatient and outpatient data for statistical analysis and reimbursement purposes. Data is entered in an abstracting software program (Figure 1-4), and the facility's billing department imports it to the **UB-04** (or **CMS-1450**) claim (Figure 1-5) for submission to third-party payers. The facility's information technology department generates

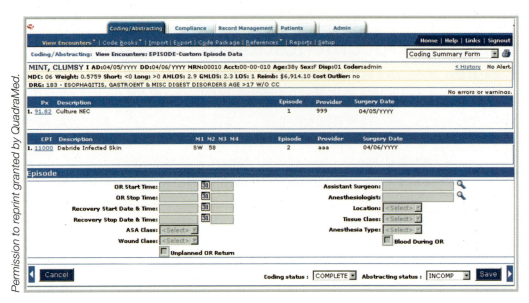

Permission to reprint granted by QuadraMed.

Figure 1-4 Sample data entry screen

reports (e.g., procedure index) (Figure 1-6), which are used for statistical analysis. The UB-04 (or CMS-1450) is a standard claim (uniform bill) submitted by health care institutions to payers for inpatient and outpatient services. (The UB-04 is based on the UB-92, which was developed in 1992 and discontinued in 2007. There was also a UB-82, which was developed in 1982 and discontinued when the UB-92 was implemented.)

> **EXAMPLE:** Procedure indexes, profit/loss statements, and patient satisfaction surveys are used by health care planning and forecasting committees to determine the types of procedures performed at its facilities and the costs associated with providing such services. As a result of report analysis, procedures that contribute to the facility's profits and losses can be determined; in addition, some services may be expanded while others are eliminated.

Reporting Physician Office Data

Computerized physicians' offices use medical management software to enter claims data and either electronically submit CMS-1500 claims data to third-party payers or print paper-based CMS-1500 claims that are mailed or faxed to clearinghouses or payers for processing. The **CMS-1500** is a standard claim submitted by physicians' offices to third-party payers. **Medical management software** (e.g., Affinity by QuadraMed, HealthQuest by McKesson Information Solutions, The Medical Manager, and Soft-Aid Medical Office Suite) is a combination of practice management and medical billing software that automates the daily workflow and procedures of a physician's office or clinic. The software automates the following functions:

- Appointment scheduling (e.g., initial and follow-up appointments) (Figure 1-7)

- Claims processing (e.g., CMS-1500 claims processing) (Figure 1-8)

- Patient invoicing (e.g., automated billing) (Figure 1-9)

- Patient management (e.g., patient registration) (Figure 1-10)

- Report generation (e.g., accounts receivable aging report) (Figure 1-11)

Medical assistants and insurance specialists use medical management software to collect data for reimbursement purposes by locating patient information, inputting ICD-9-CM (or ICD-10-CM/PCS) and CPT/HCPCS codes for diagnoses and procedures/services, and generating and processing CMS-1500 claims. Medical management software generates claims for a variety of medical specialties, and claims can be printed and mailed to clearinghouses, TPAs, or third-party payers for processing. The software also allows for submission of HIPAA-compliant electronic claims to clearinghouses, TPAs, or third-party payers.

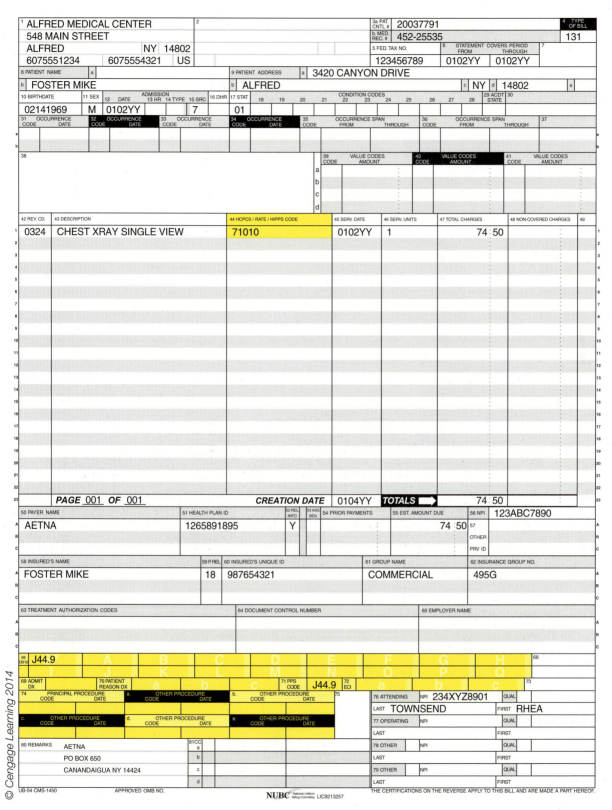

Figure 1-5 UB-04 claim containing sample patient data with highlighted form locators that contain ICD-9-CM (or ICD-10-CM/PCS) and CPT codes

Alfred State Medical Center

Procedure Index

| Reporting Period | 0301YYYY-0301YYYY | | | Date Prepared | 03-02-YYYY |

Page 1 of 5

Principal Procedure	Secondary Procedures	Attending Physician	Age	Gender	Payer	Patient Number
CLOSED BIOPSY OF BRAIN 01.13		248	42	F	01	562359
CRANIOTOMY NOS 01.24		235	56	F	03	231587
01.24		326	27	M	02	239854
01.24		236	08	F	05	562198
01.24		236	88	M	05	615789
DEBRIDEMENT OF SKULL NOS 01.25		326	43	M	03	653218

© Cengage Learning 2014

Figure 1-6 Sample procedure index

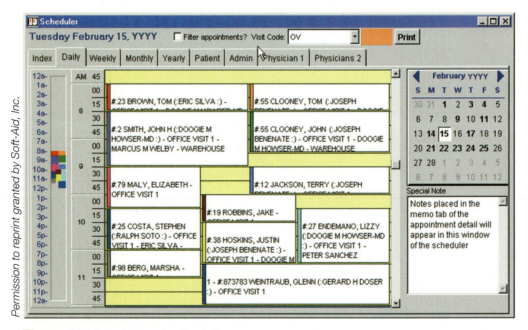

Permission to reprint granted by Soft-Aid, Inc.

Figure 1-7 Appointment scheduling screen

When records are reviewed to select ICD-9-CM (or ICD-10-CM/PCS), CPT, and HCPCS codes for reporting to third-party payers, documentation in the patient record serves as the basis for coding. Coders are responsible for reviewing patient records to select the appropriate diagnoses and procedures/services to which codes are assigned. Information in the record must support the codes submitted on claims for third-party payer reimbursement processing. The patient's diagnosis must justify diagnostic or therapeutic procedures or services provided (medical necessity), and the provider must document services or supplies that:

- are proper and needed for the diagnosis or treatment of a medical condition;

- are provided for the diagnosis, direct care, and treatment of a medical condition;

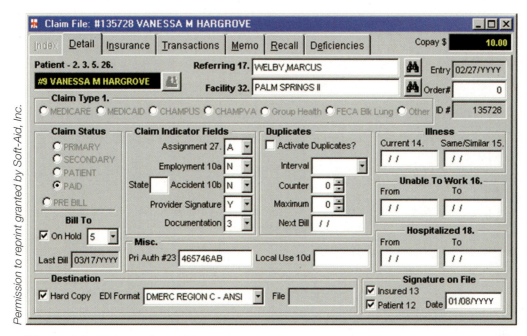

Figure 1-8 Claims processing screen

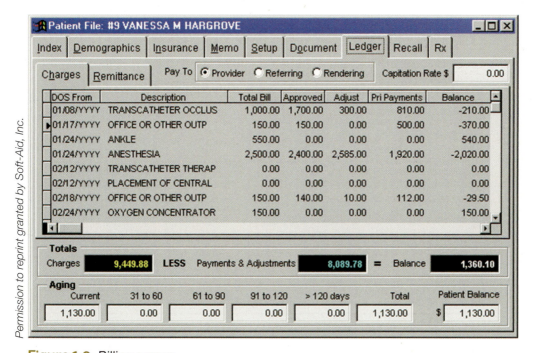

Figure 1-9 Billing screen

- meet the standards of good medical practice in the local area; and

- are not mainly for the convenience of the physician or health care facility.

Claims can be denied if the medical necessity of procedures or services is not established. Each procedure or service reported on the CMS-1500 claim must be linked to a condition that justifies the necessity for performing that procedure or providing that service. If the procedures or services delivered are determined to be unreasonable and unnecessary, the claim is denied. On the UB-04 claim, procedures/services are not linked; however, payers often request copies of patient records to review documentation to verify diagnoses, procedures, and services reported on the claim.

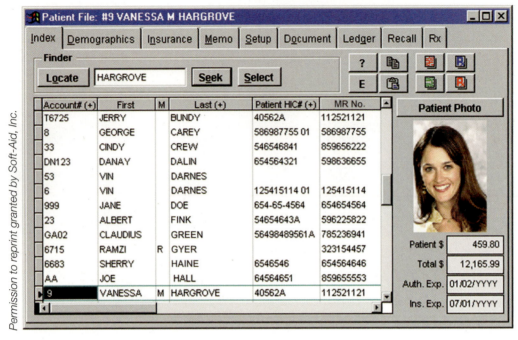

Figure 1-10 Patient registration screen

1500 A/R Aging All						Options	
SOFTAID DEMO DATA						Entry Date 03/01/YYYY to 03/05/YYYY	
03/19/YYYY 16:11:34							

Status Carrier Code	Claim ID	Last Bill	Current	31 to 60	61 to 90	91 to 120	>120
CLAIM STATUS: PRIMARY							
AETNA OF CALIFORNIA – AETNA5						510 382-8563	
PETERS, GEORGE 58698775501	135741	03/05/YYYY	160.00	0.00	0.00	0.00	0.00
AETNA OF CALIFORNIA			160.00	0.00	0.00	0.00	0.00
HOME HEALTH AGENCY - AG						958 855-4454	
PETERS, GEORGE 58698775501	135740	03/05/YYYY	60.00	0.00	0.00	0.00	0.00
HOME HEALTH AGENCY			60.00	0.00	0.00	0.00	0.00
BLUE CROSS BLUE SHIELD OF FLOR - BCBS						305 336-3727	
PETERS, GEORGE 58698775501	135735	03/01/YYYY	160.00	0.00	0.00	0.00	0.00
PETERS, GEORGE 58698775501	135736	03/01/YYYY	240.00	0.00	0.00	0.00	0.00
PETERS, GEORGE 58698775501	135738	03/10/YYYY	80.00	0.00	0.00	0.00	0.00
PETERS, GEORGE 58698775501	135739	03/04/YYYY	113.00	0.00	0.00	0.00	0.00
BLUE CROSS BLUE SHIELD OF FLOR			593.00	0.00	0.00	0.00	0.00
TOTAL: PRIMARY			813.00	0.00	0.00	0.00	0.00
CLAIM STATUS: SECONDARY							
MEDICAID - MCD							
PETERS, GEORGE 58698775501	135737	03/03/YYYY	1,580.00	0.00	0.00	0.00	0.00
MEDICAID			1,580.00	0.00	0.00	0.00	0.00
TOTAL: SECONDARY			1,580.00	0.00	0.00	0.00	0.00

Current	31 to 60	61 to 90	91 to 120	>120	Grand Total
2,393.000	0.00	0.00	0.00	0.00	2,393.00
100.00%	0.00%	0.00%	0.00%	0.00%	

Figure 1-11 Accounts receivable aging report

Exercise 1.5 – Health Data Collection

Instructions: Complete each statement.

1. Appointment scheduling and claims processing are processes associated with _____ software.

2. Hospital coders and abstractors use automated _____ software to collect and report inpatient and outpatient data for statistical analysis and reimbursement purposes.

3. Physicians' offices submit data to third-party payers on the _____ claim.

4. Hospitals submit data to third-party payers on the _____ claim.

5. Claims are denied if _____ of procedures or services is not established.

Summary

A coder is expected to master the use of coding systems, coding principles and rules, government regulations, and third-party payer requirements to ensure that all diagnoses, services, and procedures documented in patient records are accurately coded for reimbursement, research, and statistical purposes. To prepare for entry into the profession, students are encouraged to join a professional association. They usually pay a reduced membership fee and receive most of the same benefits as active members. The benefits of joining a professional association include eligibility for scholarships and grants, opportunity to network with members, free publications, reduced certification exam fees, and website access for members only.

Coding systems and medical nomenclatures are used by health care facilities, health care providers, and third-party payers to collect, store, and process data for a variety of purposes. A coding system organizes a medical nomenclature according to similar conditions, diseases, procedures, and services; it contains codes for each. A medical nomenclature is a vocabulary of clinical and medical terms used by health care providers to document patient care. Codes include numeric and alphanumeric characters that are reported to health plans for health care reimbursement and to external agencies for data collection and internally for education and research. Coding is the assignment of codes to diagnoses, services, and procedures based on patient record documentation.

Health care providers are responsible for documenting and authenticating legible, complete, and timely patient records in accordance with federal regulations and accrediting agency standards. The provider is also responsible for correcting or altering errors in patient record documentation. Health data collection is performed by health care facilities to do administrative planning, to submit statistics to state and federal government agencies, and to report health claims data to third-party payers for reimbursement purposes.

Internet Links

AHA Central Office Go to: *www.ahacentraloffice.org* to review resources available at the AHA Central Office website. The American Hospital Association's (AHA) Central Office serves as the official U.S. clearinghouse for proper use of ICD-9-CM (or ICD-10-CM/PCS), HCPCS level I (CPT), and HCPCS level II codes for hospitals, physicians, and other health professionals.

American Academy of Professional Coders (AAPC): *www.aapc.com*

American Association of Medical Assistants (AAMA): *www.aama-ntl.org*

American Health Information Management Association (AHIMA): *www.ahima.org*

American Institute for Chartered Property Casualty Underwriter and Insurance Institute of America (AICPCU/IIA): *www.aicpcu.org*

American Medical Billing Association (AMBA): Go to *www.ambanet.net* and click on the American Medical Billing Association link.

American Medical Technologists (AMT): *www.amt1.com*

Decision Health electronic newsletters: *ezines.decisionhealth.com*

LexiCode Corp: Go to *www.LexiCode.com* and click on the Remote Coding Services link.

Medical Association of Billers (MAB): *www.physicianswebsites.com*

PlatoCode: Go to *www.platocode.com* and explore "computer assisted coding" (CAC).

Study Checklist

- ❏ Read this textbook chapter and highlight key concepts.
- ❏ Create an index card for each key term.
- ❏ Access the chapter Internet links to learn more about concepts.
- ❏ Complete the chapter review, verifying answers with your instructor.
- ❏ Complete WebTutor assignments and take online quizzes.
- ❏ Complete Workbook chapter, verifying answers with your instructor.
- ❏ Go to *www.cengagebrain.com* to access StudyWARE™ on the Premium Website. Login instructions are located in this textbook's Preface and on the Printed Access Card.
- ❏ Form a study group with classmates to discuss chapter concepts in preparation for an exam.

Review

Multiple Choice

Instructions: Circle the most appropriate response.

1. The Health Insurance Portability and Accountability Act of 1996 (HIPAA) requires _____ types of code sets to be adopted for the purpose of encoding data elements.
   - a. two
   - b. three
   - c. four
   - d. five

2. Which is considered to be a small code set according to HIPAA?
   - a. actions taken to prevent, diagnose, treat, and manage diseases and injuries
   - b. causes of injury, disease, impairment, or other health-related problems
   - c. diseases, injuries, impairments, and other health-related problems
   - d. race, ethnicity, type of facility, and type of unit

3. Which is a code set adopted by HIPAA for use by clearinghouses, health plans, and providers?
   - a. ABC codes
   - b. CMIT
   - c. NDC
   - d. SNOMED

4. The purpose of adopting standard code sets was to:
   - a. establish a medical nomenclature to standardize HIPAA data submissions.
   - b. improve data quality and simplify claims submission for providers.
   - c. increase costs associated with processing health insurance claims.
   - d. regulate health care clearinghouses and third-party administrators.

5. According to HIPAA, health plans that do not accept standard code sets are required to modify their systems to accept all valid codes or to contract with a(n):
   a. electronic data interchange.
   b. health care clearinghouse.
   c. insurance company.
   d. third-party administrator.

6. Which is a vocabulary of clinical terms used by health care providers to document patient care?
   a. classification system
   b. demographic data
   c. medical nomenclature
   d. *Nosologia Methodica*

7. The requirement that the patient's diagnoses justify diagnostic and/or therapeutic procedures or services provided is called:
   a. continuity of care.
   b. facilities planning.
   c. medical necessity.
   d. policy making.

8. Which is the business record for a patient encounter (inpatient or outpatient) that documents health care services provided to a patient?
   a. demographic data
   b. financial record
   c. jukebox
   d. medical record

9. The primary purpose of the record is _____, which involves documenting patient care services so that others who treat the patient have a source of information on which to base additional care and treatment.
   a. continuity of care
   b. medical necessity
   c. medicolegal
   d. quality of care

10. Which is a secondary purpose of the medical record, that does not relate directly to patient care?
    a. clinical research
    b. continuity of care
    c. discharge note
    d. hybrid record

11. Which type of medical record format stores documentation in labeled sections?
    a. integrated record
    b. problem-oriented record
    c. source-oriented record
    d. SOAP notes

12. A progress note contains diagnoses of muscle strain and weakness. This statement would be located in the portion of the _____ POR progress note.
    a. Assessment
    b. Objective
    c. Plan
    d. Subjective

13. A progress note contains documentation that the patient is to be followed up with in the physician's office two weeks after discharge from the hospital. This statement would be located in the _____ portion of the POR progress note.
    a. Assessment
    b. Objective
    c. Plan
    d. Subjective

14. A progress note contains documentation that the EKG showed elevated T-wave changes. This statement would be located in the _____ portion of the POR progress note.
    a. Assessment
    b. Objective
    c. Plan
    d. Subjective

15. Which is documented in the progress note section of the POR to summarize the patient's care, treatment, response to care, and condition on discharge?
    a. demographic data
    b. discharge note
    c. medical necessity
    d. transfer note

16. Which is used to capture paper record images onto the storage media?
    a. EHR
    b. EMR
    c. jukebox
    d. scanner

17. To provide the maximum benefit to students, internships are typically _____ work experiences that are arranged by academic program faculty.
    a. elective
    b. nonpaid
    c. optional
    d. voluntary

18. To whom does the student report at the professional practice experience (or internship) site?
    a. supervisor   b. patient   c. physician   d. program faculty

19. Which is a benefit of joining a professional association?
    a. free certification examination fees
    b. opportunities to network with other members
    c. reduced benefits as compared with nonmembers
    d. website–only access to professional journals

20. Which processes health care claims and performs related business functions for a health plan?
    a. health care clearinghouse   c. third-party administrator
    b. health care provider   d. third-party payer

PART II

ICD-9-CM, ICD-10-CM, and ICD-10-PCS Coding Systems

Introduction to ICD-9-CM and ICD-10-CM/PCS Coding

Chapter Outline

Chapter Objectives

At the conclusion of this chapter, the student should be able to:

- Define key terms.
- Explain the organization of the ICD-9-CM Tabular List of Diseases, Index to Diseases, and Index to Procedures and Tabular List of Procedures.
- Explain the organization of the ICD-10-CM Tabular List of Diseases and Injuries and Index to Diseases and Injuries.
- Explain the organization of the ICD-10-PCS Index and Tables.
- List and describe the official guidelines for coding and reporting ICD-9-CM and ICD-10-CM/PCS codes.
- Interpret ICD-9-CM and ICD-10-CM/PCS guidelines for coding and reporting.
- Apply guidelines for coding and reporting when assigning ICD-9-CM and ICD-10-CM/PCS codes.
- Describe ICD-9-CM as a legacy coding system, including the use of general equivalency mappings (GEMs).

Key Terms

benign

category code

Classification of Drugs by AHFS List

Classification of Industrial Accidents According to Agency

cooperating parties for the ICD-9-CM

cooperating parties for the ICD-10-CM/PCS

E code (ICD-9-CM)

encoder

encounter

essential modifier

etiology

Introduction

There are two related classifications of diseases with similar titles. The
International Classification of Diseases (ICD) is published
by the World Health Organization (WHO) and is used to classify
mortality (death) data from death certificates. WHO published the
tenth revision of ICD in 1994 with a new name, *International Statistical
Classification of Diseases and Related Health Problems*, and reorganized
its 3-digit categories. (Although the name of the publication was
changed, the familiar abbreviation ICD was kept.)

The *International Classification of Diseases, Ninth Revision, Clinical
Modification* (ICD-9-CM) (Figure 2-1) was developed in the United
States and is used to code and classify **morbidity** (disease) data from
inpatient and outpatient records, including physician office records.
ICD-9-CM is a closed classification system that is used in the United
States to classify diagnoses (Volumes 1 and 2) and procedures (Volume 3),
which means that ICD-9-CM provides just one place to classify
each condition and procedure. Conditions that occur infrequently
are grouped together as "other" or "not elsewhere classified" codes;
unspecified diagnoses are also classified separately. Occasionally,
both groups are combined in one code. All health care settings use
ICD-9-CM to report diagnoses, while hospitals use ICD-9-CM
procedure codes to report inpatient procedures and services.

Overview of ICD-9-CM
and ICD-10-CM/PCS

ICD-9-CM is a clinical modification of the WHO's *International
Classification of Diseases, Ninth Revision* (ICD-9). ICD-10-CM is also a
clinical modification of WHO's *International Classification of Diseases,
Tenth Revision* (ICD-10). The term *clinical* is used to emphasize the
modification's intent. This means that the coding system serves as a

ICD-10 Alert!

Provider offices and health care
facilities (e.g., hospitals) will use
ICD-10-CM to code diagnoses.
Hospitals will use ICD-10-PCS
to code inpatient procedures.
(Provider offices and outpatient
health care settings will
continue to use CPT and HCPCS
level II to code procedures and
services.)

The *International Classification
of Diseases, Tenth Revision,
Clinical Modification* (ICD-10-CM)
is used to code and classify
disease data from inpatient
and outpatient records. The
*International Classification
of Diseases, Tenth Revision,
Procedure Classification
System* (ICD-10-PCS) is used
to code and classify procedure
data from inpatient records
only. (ICD-10-CM and ICD-10-
PCS are abbreviated as
ICD-10-CM/PCS.)

An overview of ICD-10-CM
and ICD-10-PCS is included in
this chapter, and ICD-10-CM
alerts are provided throughout
this chapter (as well as
Chapters 3 through 6) to assist
in the transition to the new
coding system.

Permission to reprint granted by Optuminsight, Inc.

Figure 2-1 ICD-9-CM coding manuals

useful tool in the classification of morbidity data for indexing of patient records, reviewing quality of care, and compiling basic health statistics. Used to describe the clinical picture of the patient, ICD-9-CM and ICD-10-CM codes are more precise than those needed for statistical groupings and trends analysis.

ICD-9-CM

ICD-9-CM was adopted in 1979 as the official classification system for assigning codes to diagnoses (all health care settings) and procedures (inpatient hospital care). The ICD-9-CM was originally published as three volumes:

- Volume 1 (Tabular List of Diseases)

- Volume 2 (Index to Diseases)

- Volume 3 (Index to Procedures and Tabular List of Procedures)

ICD-10-CM and ICD-10-PCS (ICD-10-CM/PCS)

The *International Classification of Diseases, Tenth Revision, Clinical Modification* (ICD-10-CM) and the *International Classification of Diseases, Tenth Revision, Procedure Coding System* (ICD-10-PCS), also abbreviated as ICD-10-CM/PCS, will replace ICD-9-CM. ICD-10-CM/PCS includes many more codes and applies to more users than ICD-9-CM because it is designed to collect data on every type of health care encounter (e.g., inpatient, outpatient, hospice, home health care, and long-term care). ICD-10-CM/PCS also enhances accurate payment for services rendered and facilitates evaluation of medical processes and outcomes. The term *clinical* emphasizes the modification's intent, which is to:

- Describe the clinical picture of the patient, which means the codes must be more precise than those needed only for statistical groupings and trend analysis.

- Serve as a useful tool in the area of classification of morbidity data for indexing of medical records, medical care review, and ambulatory and other medical care programs, as well as for basic health statistics.

    ICD-10-CM is the diagnosis classification system developed by the Centers for Disease Control and Prevention (CD) for use in *all* U.S. health care treatment settings. ICD-10-CM codes require

> ## Note:
>
> The Centers for Medicare & Medicaid Services (CMS) shortens the name of the classification systems to *International Classification of Diseases, 10th Edition, Clinical Modification/Procedure Coding System*, abbreviating it as ICD-10-CM/PCS.

up to 7 characters, are entirely alphanumeric, and have new coding conventions (e.g., Excludes1 and Excludes2 notes). (The format of ICD-10-CM is very similar to ICD-9-CM Volumes 1 and 2 in that both coding systems use a disease index to initially locate codes for conditions and a tabular list to verify codes).

ICD-10-CM and ICD-10-PCS (or ICD-10-CM/PCS) (Figure 2-2) incorporate much greater specificity and clinical information, resulting in:

- Decreased need to include supporting documentation with claims.
- Enhanced ability to conduct public health surveillance.
- Improved ability to measure healthcare services.
- Increased sensitivity when refining grouping and reimbursement methodologies.

ICD-10-CM/PCS also includes updated medical terminology and classification of diseases, provides codes to allow comparison of mortality and morbidity data, and provides better data for:

- Conducting research.
- Designing payment systems.
- Identifying fraud and abuse.
- Making clinical decisions.
- Measuring care furnished to patients.

Note:

The International Classification of Diseases, *Ninth Edition, Clinical Modification (ICD-9-CM)* does not provide the necessary detail about patients' medical conditions or procedures performed on hospitalized inpatients. ICD-9-CM is over 30 years old, has outdated and obsolete terminology, uses outdated codes that produce inaccurate and limited data, and is inconsistent with current medical practice. It cannot accurately describe diagnoses or inpatient procedures of care delivered in the 21st century.

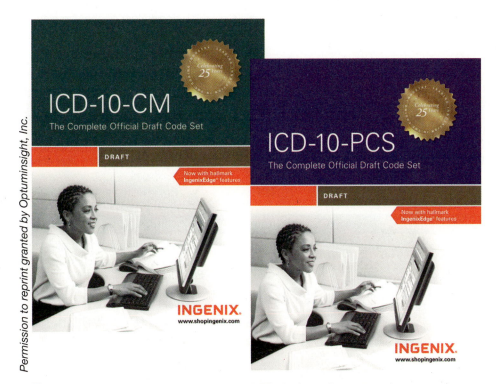

Permission to reprint granted by Optuminsight, Inc.

Figure 2-2 ICD-10-CM and ICD-10-PCS draft coding manuals

- Processing claims.

- Tracking public health.

To prepare for implementation of ICD-10-CM/PCS, health care professionals should assess their coding staff to determine whether they require education and training to:

- Apply anatomy and physiology, medical terminology, pathophysiology, and pharmacology concepts.

- Apply official coding guidelines to assign ICD-10-CM/PCS codes to diagnoses and procedures.

- Effectively communicate with members of the medical staff (e.g., physician query).

- Interpret patient record documentation (e.g., identify conditions associated with medications administered).

- Interpret patient record documentation requirements (e.g., authentication, use of abbreviations).

 ICD-10-PCS is an entirely new procedure classification system developed by the CMS for use in the United States for inpatient hospital settings *only*, and it replaces Volume 3 of ICD-9-CM. ICD-10-PCS uses a multiaxial 7-character alphanumeric code structure (e.g., 047K04Z) that provides a unique code for all substantially different procedures. It also allows new procedures to be easily incorporated as new codes. ICD-10-PCS more than 87,000 7-character alphanumeric procedure codes. (ICD-9-CM has about 4,000 3- or 4-digit numeric procedure codes.)

ICD-10-CM far exceeds ICD-9-CM in the number of codes provided, having been expanded to (1) include health-related conditions, (2) provide much greater specificity at the sixth digit level, and (3) add a seventh digit extension (for some codes). Assigning the sixth and seventh characters when available for ICD-10-CM codes is mandatory because they report information documented in the patient record.

> **Note:**
>
> In ICD-10-PCS, *multiaxial* means the codes contain independent characters, with each axis retaining its meaning across broad ranges of codes (to the extent possible). (There is no decimal used in ICD-10-PCS codes). ICD-9-CM procedure codes contain 3–4 digits, including a decimal (e.g., 39.50).

EXAMPLE 1: The diagnosis is stage III pressure ulcer of the right lower back. In ICD-9-CM, two separate codes are reported for location and stage, but laterality (e.g., right sidedness) cannot be classified. In ICD-10-CM, a combination code is reported, and the right side (laterality) is classified.

```
ICD-9-CM:   707.03, 707.23
ICD-10-CM:  L89.133
```

ICD-9-CM Tabular List of Diseases	ICD-10-CM Tabular List of Diseases and Injuries

707.0 Pressure ulcer
    Bed sore
    Decubitus ulcer
    Plaster ulcer
    Use additional code to identify
      pressure ulcer stage (707.20–707.25)
	L89.13 Pressure ulcer of right lower back
	    L89.131 Pressure ulcer of right lower back, stage I
	      Healing pressure ulcer of right lower back, stage I
	      Pressure pre-ulcer skin changes limited to persistent focal edema, right lower back

ICD-9-CM Tabular List of Diseases	**ICD-10-CM Tabular List of Diseases and Injuries**

707.03 Lower back
      Coccyx
      Sacrum
707.2 Pressure ulcer stages
    Code first site of pressure ulcer (707.00–707.09)
    707.23 Pressure ulcer stage III
      Healing pressure ulcer, stage III
      Pressure ulcer with full thickness skin loss involving damage or necrosis of subcutaneous tissue
	L89.132 Pressure ulcer of right lower back, stage II
	    Healing pressure ulcer of right lower back, stage II
	    Pressure ulcer with abrasion, blister, partial thickness skin loss involving epidermis and/or dermis, right lower back
	L89.133 Pressure ulcer of right lower back, stage III
	    Healing pressure ulcer of right lower back, stage III
	    Pressure ulcer with full thickness skin loss involving damage or necrosis of subcutaneous tissue, right lower back

ICD-9-CM contains just 15 codes to classify pressure ulcers according to location and depth. ICD-10-CM contains greater specificity because 125 codes are available to classify pressure ulcers according to location, depth, and laterality.

EXAMPLE 2: The diagnosis is "mechanical breakdown of femoral arterial graft." In ICD-9-CM, just one code is available for any mechanical complication of a vascular graft. In ICD-10-CM, a combination code is reported, and the right side is classified.

ICD-9-CM: 996.1

ICD-10-CM: T82.312A

In ICD-9-CM, just one code classifies mechanical complications of vascular grafts. ICD-10-CM contains a greatly expanded number of codes because over 150 codes are available to classify of mechanical complications of vascular grafts according to type of complication, type of graft (which also indicates the location of the graft).

ICD-9-CM Tabular List of Diseases	ICD-10-CM Tabular List of Diseases

996.1 Mechanical complication of other vascular device, implant, or graft
Mechanical complications involving:
aortic (bifurcation) graft (replacement)
arteriovenous:
dialysis catheter
fistula } surgically created
shunt
balloon (counterpulsation) device, intra-aortic
carotid artery bypass graft
femoral-popliteal bypass graft
umbrella device, vena cava
EXCLUDES: atherosclerosis of biological graft (440.30–440.32)
embolism (occlusion NOS) (thrombus) of (biological) (synthetic) graft (996.74)
peritoneal dialysis catheter (996.56)
	The appropriate 7th character is to be added to each code from category T82.
	A initial encounter
	D subsequent encounter
	S sequela
	T82.3 Mechanical complication of other vascular grafts
	  T82.31 Breakdown (mechanical) of other vascular grafts
	    T82.310 Breakdown (mechanical) of aortic (bifurcation) graft (replacement)
	    T82.311 Breakdown (mechanical) of carotid arterial graft (bypass)
	    T82.312 Breakdown (mechanical) of femoral arterial graft (bypass)
	    T82.318 Breakdown (mechanical) of other vascular grafts
	    T82.319 Breakdown (mechanical) of unspecified vascular grafts

Coding Manuals

Many publishers produce their own versions of ICD-9-CM and ICD-10-CM/PCS, and ICD-9-CM hospital (Volumes 1, 2, and 3) and ICD-9-CM outpatient (Volumes 1 and 2) versions of the coding manuals are available. ICD-9-CM is now published as a single volume coding manual, with the Index to Diseases (Volume 2) located in front of the Tabular List of Diseases (Volume 1). (The Index to Procedures and Tabular List of Procedures, Volume 3, are located after the Tabular List of Diseases in that order.) Companies also publish **encoders**, which automate the coding process. Computerized or Web-based software is used instead of coding books, and the coder uses the software's Search feature to locate and verify codes.

Updating ICD-9-CM and ICD-10-CM/PCS 🟢

The National Center for Health Statistics (NCHS) and the Centers for Medicare and Medicaid Services (CMS) are the U.S. Department of Health & Human Services (DHHS) agencies comprise the **ICD-9-CM Coordination and Maintenance Committee**, which is responsible for overseeing all changes and modifications to ICD-9-CM.

The NCHS works with the WHO to coordinate official disease classification activities for ICD-9-CM (Volume 1—Tabular List of Diseases and Volume 2—Index to Diseases). Activities include the use, interpretation, and periodic revision of the classification system. CMS is responsible for annually updating the ICD-9-CM procedure classification (Volume 3—Index to Procedures and Tabular List of Procedures).

The **Medicare Prescription Drug, Improvement, and Modernization Act (MMA)** requires all code sets (e.g., ICD-9-CM, ICD-10-CM/PCS) to be valid at the time services are provided. This means that midyear (April 1) and end-of-year (October 1) coding updates must be implemented immediately so accurate codes are reported on claims.

It is crucial that updated coding manuals be purchased and/or billing systems be updated with coding changes so that billing delays (e.g., due to waiting for new coding manuals to arrive) and claims rejections are avoided. If outdated codes are submitted on claims, providers and health care facilities will incur administrative costs associated with resubmitting corrected claims and delayed reimbursement for services provided.

ICD-10 Alert!

ICD-10-CM is also published as a single-volume coding manual, with the Index to Diseases and Injuries located in front of the Tabular List of Diseases and Injuries. ICD-10-PCS is published as a separate single-volume coding manual, with the Index to Procedures located in front of the Tables. The two classification systems are commonly abbreviated as ICD-10-CM/PCS.

- Coders should consider using updateable coding manuals (Figure 2-3), which publishers offer as a subscription service. These coding manuals are usually stored in a 3-ring binder so that coders can remove outdated pages and add newly printed pages provided by the publisher.

- Another option is to purchase encoder software, which publishers also offer as a subscription service. Coders routinely download the most up-to-date encoder software, which contains edits for new, revised, and discontinued codes. An encoder (Figure 2-4) automates the coding process using computerized or Web-based software; instead of manually looking up conditions (or procedures) in the coding manual index, the coder uses the software's search feature to locate and verify diagnosis and procedure codes.

- Automating the medical coding process is the goal of *computer-assisted coding (CAC)*, which uses a natural language processing engine to "read" patient records and generate ICD-9-CM, ICD-10-CM/PCS, and HCPCS/CPT codes. Because of this process, coders become coding auditors (or coding editors), responsible for ensuring the accuracy of codes reported to payers. (CAC can be compared to speech recognition technology that has transitioned the role of medical transcriptionists in certain fields, such as radiology, to that of medical editors.)

ICD-10 Alert!

The *ICD-9-CM Coordination and Maintenance Committee* will be renamed the **ICD-10-CM/PCS Coordination and Maintenance Committee** once ICD-10-CM and ICD-10-PCS are implemented. The new Committee is expected to follow the same procedures used by the current Committee for consideration of new codes and revisions to existing codes. In addition, the Committee will discuss issues such as mappings to the prior coding system and the need to continue updating these mappings for a minimum of three years after the implementation date for ICD-10-CM and ICD-10-PCS.

The ICD-9-CM Coordination and Maintenance Committee currently has jurisdiction over any action impacting the code sets. At the September 2010 meeting, a *partial freeze of the ICD-9-CM, ICD-10-CM, and ICD-10-PCS code* sets prior to implementation of ICD-10-CM/PCS was approved.

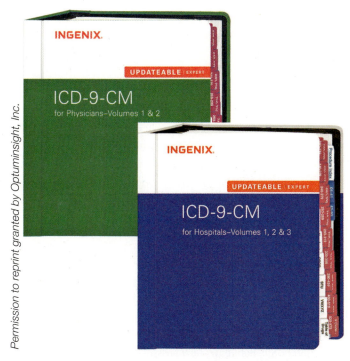

Permission to reprint granted by Optuminsight, Inc.

Figure 2-3 Updateable ICD-9-CM coding manuals

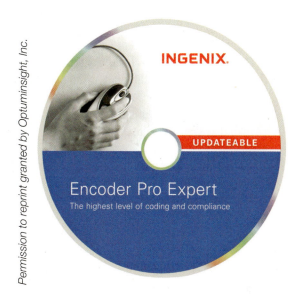

Permission to reprint granted by Optuminsight, Inc.

Figure 2-4 Encoder Pro Expert software

HISTORY OF THE INTERNATIONAL CLASSIFICATION OF DISEASES (ICD)

The WHO's original intent for ICD was that it would serve as a statistical tool for the international collection and exchange of mortality (death) data. A subsequent revision was expanded to accommodate data collection for morbidity (disease) statistics. The seventh revision (ICD-7), published by WHO in 1955, was clinically modified for use in the United States after a joint study was conducted to evaluate the efficiency of indexing hospital diseases (cataloging diseases and procedures by code number). The study participants included the American Hospital Association (AHA) and the American Association of Medical Record Librarians (AAMRL) (now called the American Health Information Management Association, or AHIMA). Results of that study led to the 1959 publication of the International Classification of Diseases, Adapted for Indexing Hospital Records (ICDA), by the federal Public Health Service. The ICDA uniformly modified ICD-7, and it gave the United States a way to classify patient operations and treatments.

An eighth edition of ICD (ICD-8), published by WHO in 1965, lacked the depth of clinical data required for America's emerging health care delivery system. In 1968, two widely accepted modifications were published in the United States: the Eighth Revision of the International Classification of Diseases, Adapted for Use in the United States (ICDA-8), and the Hospital Adaptation of ICDA (H-ICDA).

Hospitals used either of these two systems until 1979, when ICD-9-CM was implemented. The ninth revision of the ICD (ICD-9), published by WHO in 1975, once again prompted the development of a clinical modification. This time the incentive resulted from a process initiated in 1977 by the National Center for Health Statistics (NCHS) for hospital indexing and the retrieval of case data for clinical studies. After more than 30 years since its adoption in the United States, ICD has proven to be indispensable to anyone interested in payment schedules for the delivery of health care services to patients.

(continues)

HISTORY OF THE INTERNATIONAL CLASSIFICATION OF DISEASES (ICD) (*continued*)

The WHO published ICD-10 in 1994 with a new name (*International Statistical Classification of Diseases and Related Health Problems*) and reorganized its 3-digit categories. Although the title was amended to clarify content and purpose and to reflect development of codes and descriptions beyond diseases and injuries, the familiar abbreviation "ICD" was kept.

ICD-10 contains clinical detail, expands information about previously classified diseases, and classifies diseases discovered since the last revision. ICD-10 also incorporates organizational changes and new features, but its format and conventions remain largely unchanged. Chapter titles, organization and includes notes are similar to ICD-9. The greatest difference is that the new codes are alphanumeric, new excludes1 and excludes2 notes were added, and there is more detail in ICD-10-CM than in ICD-9-CM.

A number of other countries have already adopted ICD-10, including United Kingdom (1995), France (1997), Australia (1998), Germany (2000), and Canada (2001). ICD-10-CM and ICD-10-PCS provides significant improvements through greater detailed information and the ability to expand in order to capture additional advancements in clinical medicine. The change from ICD-9-CM to the NCHS-developed ICD-10-CM and the CMS-developed ICD-10-PCS (Procedure Coding System) will be in effect on October 1, 2014. Information about each coding system is included below, and ICD-10 alerts appear throughout the remainder of this chapter (and in Chapters 3 through 6 of this textbook) to assist with the transition to the new classification system.

Mandatory Reporting of ICD-9-CM and ICD-10-CM Codes

The Medicare Catastrophic Coverage Act of 1988 mandated the reporting of ICD-9-CM diagnosis codes on Medicare claims; and in subsequent years, private third-party payers adopted similar requirements for claims submission.

Reporting ICD-9-CM and ICD-10-CM codes on submitted claims (Figure 2-5A and Figure 2-5B) ensures the medical necessity of procedures and services provided to patients during an encounter. An **encounter** is a face-to-face contact between a patient and a health care provider (e.g., physician, nurse practitioner) who assesses and treats the patient's condition. Medicare defines medical necessity as "the determination that a service or procedure rendered is reasonable and necessary for the diagnosis or treatment of an illness or injury."

ICD-10 Alert!

The Administrative Simplification subtitle of the Health Insurance Portability and Accountability Act of 1996 (HIPAA) mandated the adoption of code set standards in the Transactions and Code Sets final rule published in the *Federal Register*. The final rule modifies the standard medical data code sets for coding diagnoses and inpatient hospital procedures by concurrently adopting the International Classification of Diseases, 10th Revision, Clinical Modification (ICD-10-CM) for diagnosis coding (including the Official ICD-10-CM Guidelines for Coding and Reporting, as maintained and distributed by the U.S. Department of Health and Human Services) and the International Classification of Diseases, 10th Revision, Procedure Coding System (ICD–10–PCS) for inpatient hospital procedure coding (including the *Official ICD-10-PCS Guidelines for Coding and Reporting*, as maintained and distributed by the HHS).

Medical Necessity

Today's concept of medical necessity determines the extent to which individuals with health conditions receive health care services. (The concept was introduced in the 1970s when health insurance contracts intended to exclude care, such as voluntary hospitalizations prescribed primarily for the convenience of the provider or patient.) *Medical necessity* is the measure of whether a health care procedure or service is appropriate for the diagnosis and/or treatment of a condition. This decision-making process is based on the payer's contractual language and the treating

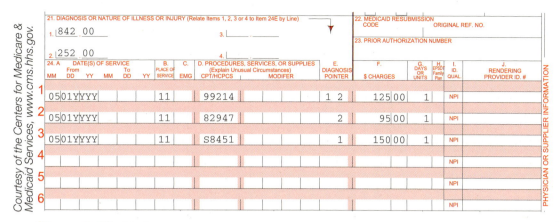

Figure 2-5A CMS-1500 claim Blocks 21 (ICD-9-CM codes) and 24F, which illustrate medical necessity of procedures and services

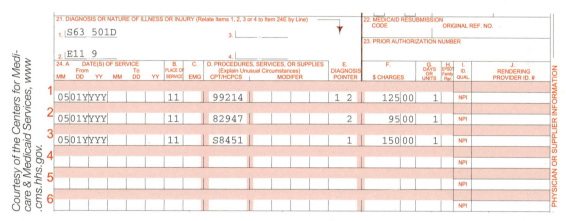

Figure 2-5B CMS-1500 claim Blocks 21 (ICD-10-CM codes) and 24F, which illustrate medical necessity of procedures and services. (ICD-10-CM's E codes classify endocrine, nutritional and metabolic diseases, *not* external causes of morbidity.)

provider's documentation. Generally, the following criteria are used to determine medical necessity:

Note:

Cost-effective does not necessarily mean least expensive.

- *Purpose:* The procedure or service is performed to treat a medical condition.

- *Scope:* The most appropriate level of service is provided, taking into consideration potential benefit and harm to the patient.

- *Evidence:* The treatment is known to be effective in improving health outcomes.

- *Value:* The treatment is cost-effective for this condition when compared to alternative treatments, including no treatment.

EXAMPLE: A 70-year-old male patient with type 1 diabetes mellitus is treated at the physician's office for severe wrist pain resulting from a fall. When the physician asks the patient whether he has been regularly taking his insulin and checking his blood glucose levels, the patient says that most of the time he takes his insulin and sometimes he forgets to check his blood glucose levels. The physician orders a blood glucose test to be done in the office, which reveals elevated blood glucose levels. The physician provides counseling and education to the patient about the importance of taking his daily insulin and checking his blood glucose levels. The physician also orders an X-ray of the wrist, which proves to be negative for a fracture. The physician provides the patient with a wrist brace and instructs the patient to follow up in the office within four weeks.

The insurance specialist reports ICD-9-CM (or ICD-10-CM) codes for type 1 diabetes mellitus and sprained wrist along with HCPCS/CPT codes for an office visit, blood glucose lab test, and the wrist brace. If the only diagnosis reported on the claim (Figure 2-5A and Figure 2-5B) was a sprained wrist, the blood glucose lab test would be rejected for payment by the insurance company as an unnecessary medical procedure.

Exercise 2.1 – Overview of ICD-9-CM and ICD-10-CM/PCS

Instructions: Complete each statement.

1. ICD-9-CM was adopted in _____ as the official classification system for assigning codes to diagnoses and procedures, and ICD-10-CM/PCS will be adopted on _____ to replace ICD-9-CM.

2. The ICD-9-CM Coordination and Maintenance Committee will be renamed the _____ Coordination and Maintenance Committee once the use of ICD-9-CM is discontinued.

3. The U.S. Department of Health & Human Services agencies responsible for overseeing all changes and modifications to ICD-9-CM are _____ and _____.

4. The _____ requires all code sets to be valid at the time services are provided, which means that midyear (April 1) and end-of-year (October 1) coding updates must be implemented immediately so accurate codes are reported on claims.

5. Updateable coding manuals, which publishers offer as an annual _____ service, are popular because coders can remove outdated pages and insert updated pages into the binders.

6. The coding process is automated when computerized or Web-based _____ software is used instead of coding books to locate codes manually; the coder uses the software's search feature to locate and verify codes.

7. The reporting of ICD-9-CM diagnosis codes on Medicare claims was originally mandated by the _____ while mandated reporting of ICD-10-CM/PCS codes was mandated by _____.

8. Reporting ICD-9-CM codes on submitted claims ensures the _____ of procedures and services provided to patients during an encounter, which is defined as "the determination that a service or procedure rendered is reasonable and necessary for the diagnosis or treatment of an illness or injury."

9. A patient is seen in the office for the following conditions: chest pain, chronic hypertension, and controlled diabetes mellitus. The provider orders a blood glucose level, chest X-ray, and EKG. For medical necessity, the chest X-ray would be linked to the _____.

10. A patient is seen in the hospital emergency department for treatment of multiple lacerations; the patient also complains of dizziness and a severe headache that is unrelieved by pain medications. The emergency department physician orders a brain scan and performs extensive suturing. For medical necessity, the suturing would be linked to the _____.

ICD-9-CM Tabular List of Diseases and ICD-10-CM Tabular List of Diseases and Injuries

The ICD-9-CM **Tabular List of Diseases** (Table 2-1A) arranges codes and descriptions in numerical order: it contains 17 chapters, 2 supplemental classifications, and 4 appendices. Chapters in ICD-9-CM classify diseases and injuries according to specific body systems as well as **etiology** (cause of disease).

Note:

> Appendix B, Glossary of Mental Disorders, was permanently removed from ICD-9-CM in 2004, because the glossary can be found in the *Diagnostic and Statistical Manual of Mental Disorders* (DSM), which is published by the American Psychiatric Association (APA).

Table 2-1A ICD-9-CM Tabular List of Diseases

ICD-9-CM Chapters	
Chapter 1	Infectious and Parasitic Diseases (001–139)
Chapter 2	Neoplasms (140–239)
Chapter 3	Endocrine, Nutritional and Metabolic Disorders, and Immunity Disorders (240–279)
Chapter 4	Diseases of the Blood and Blood-forming Organs (280–289)
Chapter 5	Mental Disorders (290–319)
Chapter 6	Diseases of the Nervous System and Sense Organs (320–389)
Chapter 7	Diseases of the Circulatory System (390–459)
Chapter 8	Diseases of the Respiratory System (460–519)
Chapter 9	Diseases of the Digestive System (520–579)
Chapter 10	Diseases of the Genitourinary System (580–629)
Chapter 11	Complications of Pregnancy, Childbirth, and the Puerperium (630–677)
Chapter 12	Diseases of the Skin and Subcutaneous Tissue (680–709)
Chapter 13	Diseases of the Musculoskeletal System and Connective Tissue (710–739)
Chapter 14	Congenital Anomalies (740–759)
Chapter 15	Certain Conditions Originating in the Perinatal Period (760–779)
Chapter 16	Symptoms, Signs, and Ill-defined Conditions (780–799)
Chapter 17	Injury and Poisoning (800–999)
Supplementary Classifications	
V codes	Supplemental Classification of Factors Influencing Health Status and Contact with Health Services (V01–V91)
E codes	Supplementary Classification of External Causes of Injury and Poisoning (E800–E999)

(continues)

Table 2-1A (*continued*)

Appendices	
Appendix A	Morphology of Neoplasms (M codes)
Appendix B	The Glossary of Mental Disorders was permanently removed from ICD-9-CM effective October 1, 2004, because the glossary can be found in the *Diagnostic and Statistical Manual of Mental Disorders* (DSM). (Your ICD-9-CM coding manual may contain a page that directs you to the DSM for the glossary.)
Appendix C	Classification of Drugs by American Hospital Formulary Service List Number and Their ICD-9-CM Equivalents
Appendix D	Classification of Industrial Accidents According to Agency
Appendix E	List of 3-Digit Categories

The ICD-10-CM **Tabular List of Diseases and Injuries** (Table 2-1B) contains 21 chapters (compared with 17 chapters and 2 supplementary classifications for V and E codes in the ICD-9-CM Tabular List of Diseases). (ICD-10, created by WHO, has 22 chapters; ICD-10-CM excludes the chapter entitled Codes for Special Purposes, U00–U99.)

ICD-10 Alert!

The ICD-10-CM Tabular List of Diseases and Injuries arranges codes and descriptors in alphanumeric order within 21 separate chapters according to body system or nature of injury and disease. The supplemental classifications in ICD-9-CM (E codes and V codes) are incorporated into the ICD-10-CM tabular list as individual chapters:

- Chapter 20 (External Causes of Morbidity)
- Chapter 21 (Factors Influencing Health Status and Contact with Health Services)

At this time, it is unknown whether ICD-10-CM (or ICD-10-PCS) will contain appendices.

Format and Structure of ICD-9-CM

ICD-9-CM disease and injury codes consist of 3 digits, but some are followed by a decimal point and one or two additional digits. (ICD-9-CM procedure codes consist of two digits followed by a decimal point and one or two additional digits.) Each ICD-9-CM tabular list is organized according to code number, with chapters (and Tabular List of Diseases supplemental classifications) organized as follows (Figure 2-6A):

Note:

ICD-9-CM and ICD-10-CM index entries provide direction to codes (not page numbers) in the tabular lists. ICD-10-PCS index entries provide direction to codes (not page numbers) in the tables.

- Major topic headings (or **sections**) are printed in bold uppercase letters and followed by groups of ICD-9-CM 3-digit disease categories within a chapter (e.g., 410–414). (The ICD-9-CM Tabular List of Procedures does not contain major topic headings within chapters.)

- **Category codes** are 3-digit ICD-9-CM disease codes within a major topic heading (or section) (e.g., 410) (or two-digit ICD-9-CM procedure code numbers, such as 01).

- **Subcategory codes** are 4-digit ICD-9-CM disease codes within a category that contain a decimal (e.g., 410.0) (or 3-digit ICD-9-CM procedure codes that contain a decimal, such as 01.2).

- **Subclassification codes** are 5-digit ICD-9-CM disease codes within a subcategory that contain a decimal (e.g., 410.00) (or 4-digit ICD-9-CM procedure codes, such as 01.21).

Table 2-1B ICD-10-CM Tabular List of Diseases and Injuries

Chapter Number	Range of Codes	Chapter Title
Chapter 1	A00–B99	Certain Infectious and Parasitic Diseases
Chapter 2	C00–D49	Neoplasms
Chapter 3	D50–D89	Diseases of the Blood and Blood-forming Organs and Certain Disorders Involving the Immune Mechanism
Chapter 4	E00–E90	Endocrine, Nutritional, and Metabolic Diseases
Chapter 5	F01–F99	Mental, Behavioral, and Neurodevelopmental Disorders
Chapter 6	G00–G99	Diseases of the Nervous System
Chapter 7	H00–H59	Diseases of the Eye and Adnexa
Chapter 8	H60–H95	Diseases of the Ear and Mastoid Process
Chapter 9	I00–I99	Diseases of the Circulatory System
Chapter 10	J00–J99	Diseases of the Respiratory System
Chapter 11	K00–K95	Diseases of the Digestive System
Chapter 12	L00–L99	Diseases of the Skin and Subcutaneous Tissue
Chapter 13	M00–M99	Diseases of the Musculoskeletal System and Connective Tissue
Chapter 14	N00–N99	Diseases of the Genitourinary System
Chapter 15	O00–O9A	Pregnancy, Childbirth, and the Puerperium
Chapter 16	P00–P96	Certain Conditions Originating in the Perinatal Period
Chapter 17	Q00–Q99	Congenital Malformations, Deformations, and Chromosomal Abnormalities
Chapter 18	R00–R99	Symptoms, Signs, and Abnormal Clinical and Laboratory Findings, Not Elsewhere Classified
Chapter 19	S00–T88	Injury, Poisoning, and Certain Other Consequences of External Causes
Chapter 20	V00–Y99	External Causes of Morbidity
Chapter 21	Z00–Z99	Factors Influencing Health Status and Contact with Health Services

ICD-10 Alert!

The ICD-10-CM Tabular List of Diseases (Figure 2-6B) uses an indented format for ease of reference and contains category codes, subcategory codes, and codes.

- *Category codes* contain 3 characters (e.g., H40, which has further subdivisions). A 3-character category code that has no further subdivision is equivalent to a code (e.g., H36).

- *Subcategory codes* contain 4 characters (e.g., H40.0), 5 characters (e.g., H40.10), or 6 characters (e.g,. T36.0x1).

- *Codes* may contain 3 characters (e.g., I10) 4 characters (e.g., O36.4), 5 characters (e.g., O36.60), 6 characters (e.g., O36.891) or 7 characters (e.g., O40.1xx0, where "x" serves as

(continues)

ICD-10 Alert! *(continued)*

5th and 6th character placeholders to allow for future expansion). (There is no reference to the term "subclassification" in ICD-10-CM.)

For reporting purposes (e.g., CMS-1500, UB-04), only complete codes are permitted.

- Category and subcategory codes that require additional characters are invalid if the 4th, 5th, 6th and/or 7th character(s) are absent.

- Codes that have applicable 7th characters are invalid if the "x" placeholder(s) and/or the 7th character are missing.

- When a 7th character exists for a code, the character must be entered in the 7th data field even when "x" placeholder(s) are also needed.

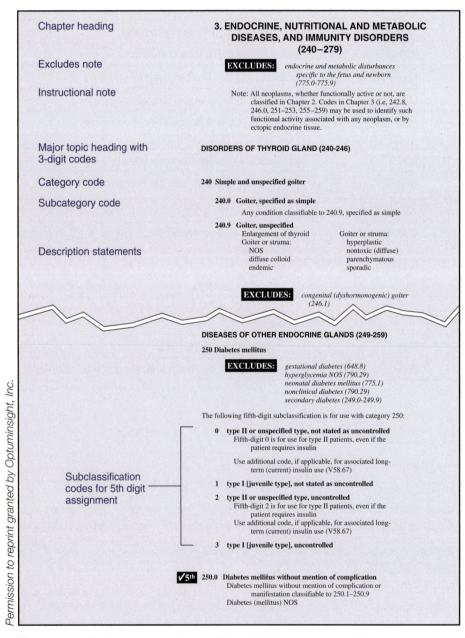

Figure 2-6A Sample page from ICD-9-CM Tabular List of Diseases

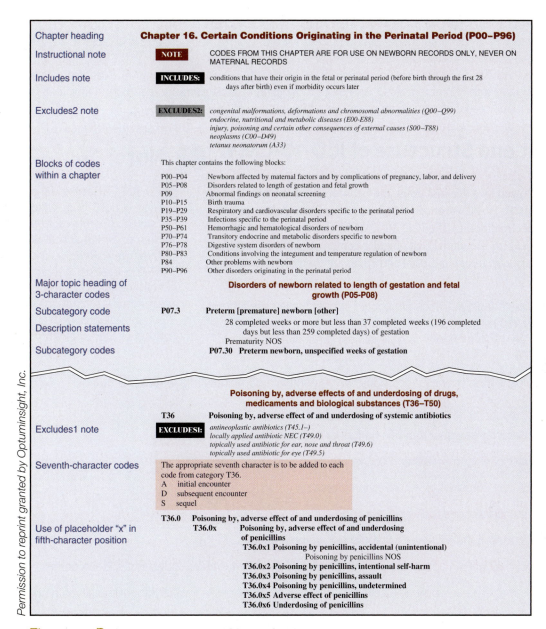

Figure 2-6B Sample page from ICD-10-CM Tabular List of Diseases and Injuries

EXAMPLE 1: ICD-9-CM CATEGORY, SUBCATEGORY, AND SUBCLASSIFICATION CODES: Go to Figure 2-6A, refer to the DISORDERS OF THYROID GLAND (240–246) section, and locate category code (240) and subcategory codes (240.0 and 240.9). Then, refer to the DISEASES OF OTHER ENDOCRINE GLANDS (249–259) section, and locate category code (250), subcategory code (250.0), and the list of fifth-digit subclassification codes to be used with category code 250.

EXAMPLE 2: ICD-10-CM CATEGORY AND SUBCATEGORY CODES: Go to Figure 2-6B, refer to the "Disorders of newborn related to length of gestation and fetal growth (P05–P08) section," and locate the 4-character subcategory code (P07.3) and the 5–character subcategory codes (P07.30, P07.31, and P07.32).

EXAMPLE 3: ICD-10-CM 6-CHARACTER AND 7-CHARACTER CODES: Go to Figure 2-6B, refer to the "Poisoning by, adverse effects of and underdosing of drugs, medicaments and biological substances (T36–T50) section," and locate the 6-character subcategory codes (T36.0x1, T36.0x2, T36.0x3, T36.0x4, and T36.0x5), which also contain "x" as a placeholder to allow for future expansion. Then, locate the seventh characters (A, D, and S), one of which is to be added to each code from category T36 (depending on status of encounter or whether the condition is a sequela).

Format and Structure of ICD-10-CM

ICD-10-CM disease and injury codes consist of 3 characters, but most are followed by a decimal point and between 1 and 4 additional characters. (ICD-10-PCS procedure codes contain 7 characters, and there is no decimal point.) The ICD-10-CM Tabular List of Diseases is a chronological (or sequential) list of codes contained within chapters based on body system or condition, and codes are then organized within:

- Major topic headings, which are printed in bold uppercase letters and followed by groups of ICD-10-CM 3-character disease categories within a chapter (e.g., Intestinal Infectious Diseases, A00–A09).

> **Note:**
>
> ICD-10-PCS Tables are organized into sections (e.g., medical and surgical, obstetrics, imaging), each of which contains a code table. Refer to the *ICD-10-PCS Indexes and Tables* heading later in this chapter for more information about the organization and structure of the ICD-10-PCS coding system.

- Categories, subcategories, and codes, which contain a combination of letters and numbers.

  ○ All categories contain 3 characters (e.g., A09).

  ○ A 3-character category that has no further subdivision is a valid code.

  ○ Subcategories contain either 4 or 5 characters.

  ○ Codes may contain 4, 5, 6, or 7 characters.

    ■ The final level of subdivision is a code.

    ■ All codes in the ICD-10-CM tabular list are boldfaced.

  ○ Codes that have an applicable seventh character are referred to as codes (not subcategories).

  ○ Codes that have an applicable seventh character are considered invalid without the seventh character.

  EXAMPLE: Code T36.0x1A requires "x" as a placeholder in the 5th-character position. Thus, reporting the code as T36.01A (without the "x" placeholder in the 5th-character position) is an invalid code, which is incorrect if reported and results in a denied claim for third-party payer reimbursement.

ICD-9-CM V Codes

The **V codes** supplementary classification (Figure 2-7A) is located in the ICD-9-CM Tabular List of Diseases, and these codes are reported for patient encounters when a circumstance other than disease or injury is documented (e.g., annual physical examination). V codes are different from other ICD-9-CM codes in that they report conditions other than a disease or an injury that may influence the patient's health status. V codes also further clarify the reason for a patient's encounter, and they should be used to report additional factors associated with a patient receiving care for illnesses or injuries classifiable to categories 001–999 in ICD-9-CM. Reporting V codes is beneficial to a payer's evaluation of the medical necessity of a reported procedure or service (e.g., personal history of malignant neoplasm, surgical aftercare).

ICD-10 Alert!

ICD-9-CM's Factors Influencing Health Status (V codes) (Figure 2-7B) are incorporated into the core ICD-10-CM classification system as Factors Influencing Health Status and Contact with Health Services (Chapter 21) (Z codes). The codes are no longer located in a supplementary classification.

Z codes are located in the last chapter of the ICD-10-CM tabular list (similar to the location of V codes in the ICD-9-CM tabular list), and they are reported for patient encounters when a circumstance other than disease or injury is documented (e.g., well child visit).

"Z codes rhymes with V codes." This mnemonic is intended to assist with memory, making it easier to remember where the Chapter 21, *Factors Influencing Health Status and Contact with Health Services*, codes are located.

V Codes

PERSONS WITHOUT REPORTED DIAGNOSIS ENCOUNTERED DURING EXAMINATION AND INVESTIGATION OF INDIVIDUALS AND POPULATIONS (V70–V82)

Note: Nonspecific abnormal findings disclosed at the time of these examinations are classifiable to categories 790–796.

V70 General medical examination

Use additional code(s) to identify any special screening examination(s) performed (V73.0–V82.9)

V70.0 Routine general medical examination at a health care facility

Health checkup

> **EXCLUDES:** *health checkup of infant or child over 28 days old (V20.2)*
> *health supervision of newborn 8 to 28 days old (V20.32)*
> *health supervision of newborn under 8 days old (V20.31)*
> *pre-procedural general physical examination (V72.83)*

V70.1 General psychiatric examination, requested by the authority

V70.2 General psychiatric examination, other and unspecified

Permission to reprint granted by Optuminsight, Inc.

Figure 2-7A Sample page of V codes in ICD-9-CM tabular list

Z Codes

Chapter 21. Factors Influencing Health Status and Contact With Health Services (Z00–Z99)

NOTE Z codes represent reasons for encounters. A corresponding procedure code must accompany a Z code if a procedure is performed. Categories Z00–Z99 are provided for occasions when circumstances other than a disease, injury or external cause classifiable to categories A00–Y89 are recorded as "diagnoses" or "problems". This can arise in two main ways:

(a) When a person who may or may not be sick encounters the health services for some specific purpose, such as to receive limited care or service for a current condition, to donate an organ or tissue, to receive prophylactic vaccination (immunization), or to discuss a problem which is in itself not a disease or injury.

(b) When some circumstance or problem is present which influences the person's health status but is not in itself a current illness or injury.

This chapter contains the following blocks:

Z00–Z13	Persons encountering health services for examination
Z14–Z15	Genetic carrier and genetic susceptibility to disease
Z16	Resistance to antimicrobial drugs
Z17	Estrogen receptor status
Z18	Retained foreign body fragments
Z20–Z28	Persons with potential health hazards related to communicable diseases
Z30–Z39	Persons encountering health services in circumstances related to reproduction
Z40–Z53	Encounters for other specific health care
Z55–Z65	Persons with potential health hazards related to socioeconomic and psychosocial circumstances
Z66	Do not resuscitate status
Z67	Blood type
Z68	Body mass index (BMI)
Z69–Z76	Persons encountering health services in other circumstances
Z77–Z99	Persons with potential health hazards related to family and personal history and certain conditions influencing health status

Persons encountering health services for examinations (Z00–Z13)

NOTE Nonspecific abnormal findings disclosed at the time of these examinations are classified to categories R70–R94.

EXCLUDES1: *examinations related to pregnancy and reproduction (Z30–Z36, Z39.–)*

Z00 Encounter for general examination without complaint, suspected or reported diagnosis

> **EXCLUDES1:** *encounter for examination for administrative purposes (Z02.–)*

> **EXCLUDES2:** *encounter for pre-procedural examinations (Z01.81–)*
> *special screening examinations (Z11–Z13)*

Z00.0 Encounter for general adult medical examination

Encounter for adult periodic examination (annual) (physical) and any associated laboratory and radiologic examinations

> **EXCLUDES1:** *encounter for examination of sign or symptom—code to sign or symptom*
> *general health check-up of infant or child Z00.12.–)*

Z00.00 Encounter for general adult medical examination without abnormal findings

Encounter for adult health check-up NOS

Z00.01 Encounter for general adult medical examination with abnormal findings

Use additional code to identify abnormal findings

Permission to reprint granted by Optuminsight, Inc.

Figure 2-7B Sample page of Z codes in ICD-10-CM tabular list

Coding Tip:

- ICD-9-CM V codes (and ICD-10-CM Z codes) are always reported as diagnosis codes. They are not reported as procedure codes, although some ICD-9-CM V codes (and ICD-10-CM Z codes) classify situations associated with procedures (e.g., canceled procedure ICD-9-CM V64 or Z53 category codes).

- Although indexed in the ICD-9-CM Index to Diseases (and ICD-10-CM Index to Diseases and Injuries), it can be challenging to locate main terms. Consider using main terms from the list below to locate the codes:

  - Admission
  - Aftercare
  - Attention to
  - Contact
  - Counseling
  - Donor
  - Encounter
  - Examination
  - Exposure to
  - Fitting
  - Follow-up
  - History
  - Newborn
  - Observation
  - Outcome of delivery
  - Problem
  - Screening
  - Status
  - Test
  - Therapy
  - Vaccination

ICD-9-CM E Codes

The ICD-9-CM **E codes** supplementary classification (Figure 2-8) is located in the Tabular List of Diseases; they describe external causes of injury, poisoning, or other adverse reactions affecting a patient's health. ICD-9-CM E codes and ICD-10-CM external cause codes (that begin with V-Y) are also reported for environmental events,

E Codes

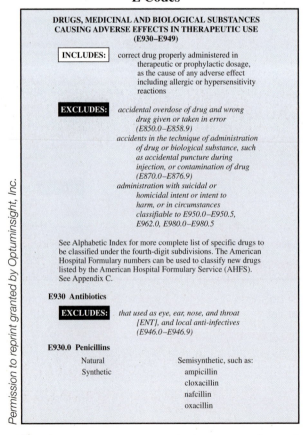

Permission to reprint granted by Optuminsight, Inc.

Figure 2-8 Sample page of E codes in ICD-9-CM tabular list

industrial accidents, injuries inflicted by criminal activity, and so on. While assigning the codes does not directly impact reimbursement to the provider, reporting them can expedite insurance claims processing because the circumstances related to an injury are indicated.

> **EXAMPLE:** A patient fell off the toilet in the downstairs bathroom of her single-family house during an attempt to coax her cat to come down from the top of a cabinet. It apparently worked because the cat jumped off the cabinet and landed on the patient. However, the patient was so surprised that she screamed and fell off the toilet onto the floor. The patient landed on her left arm due to the fall and experienced extremely sharp pain. She was evaluated in the emergency department where she was diagnosed with a closed nondisplaced comminuted fracture of the shaft of the humerus, left. She received treatment and was discharged home to follow-up with her primary care physician in the office.
>
> For ICD-9-CM, report the injury (fracture) (812.20), cause of injury (fall) (E884.6), and place of injury (home) (E849.0).
>
> For ICD-10-CM, report the injury (fracture) (S42.355A), cause of injury (fall) (W18.11xA), and place of injury (bathroom of patient's home) (Y92.010). ICD-10-CM's level of specificity results in different codes for other locations in the patient's home (e.g., bathroom). For ICD-10-CM code W18.11xA (fall from toilet), the 7th character (A) indicates she received initial treatment.
>
> The ICD-9-CM and ICD-10-CM place of injury codes for this case indicate that the patient's health insurance policy should be billed, not a liability or workers' compensation policy. If the place of injury had been at a grocery store or other place of business, the business's liability insurance would be billed instead of the patient's health insurance.

ICD-9-CM Appendix A—Morphology of Neoplasms (M codes)

The **Morphology of Neoplasms (M codes)** (Figure 2-9) are found in Appendix A of ICD-9-CM, which contains a reference to the WHO publication entitled *International Classification of Diseases for Oncology* (ICD-O). Appendix A also interprets the meaning of each digit of the morphology code number. **Morphology** indicates the tissue type of a neoplasm (e.g., adenocarcinoma and sarcoma); and they are reported to state cancer registries. **Neoplasms** are new growths, or tumors, in which cell reproduction is out of control.

A basic knowledge of morphology coding can be helpful to a coder because the name of the neoplasm documented in the patient's record does not always indicate whether the neoplasm is **benign** (not cancerous) or **malignant** (cancerous). Referring to the morphology entry in the ICD-9-CM Index to Diseases helps determine which column in the neoplasm table should be referenced to select the correct code.

ICD-10 Alert!

In ICD-10-CM, *External Causes of Injury, Poisoning, or Other Adverse Reactions Affecting a Patient's Health* are incorporated into ICD-10-CM's tabular list as Chapter 19 (S00–T98). (The codes are no longer located in a supplementary classification as they were in ICD-9-CM.)

ICD-10 Alert!

Provider offices will report morphology codes (M codes) in addition to ICD-10-CM neoplasm codes. (Refer to chapter 4 of this textbook for information about ICD-10-CM morphology coding.)

- ICD-10-CM Chapter 2 classifies neoplasms primarily by site (topography), with broad groupings for behavior, malignant, *in situ,* benign, etc. The ICD-10-CM Table of Neoplasms in its Index to Diseases and Injuries, is used to identify the correct topography code.

- Morphology codes* for most of ICD-10-CM's Chapter 2 (Neoplasms) codes do not include histologic type. Thus, a comprehensive separate set of morphology codes are used from the *International Classification of Diseases for Oncology* (ICD-O).

*In a few cases, such as for malignant melanoma and certain neuroendocrine tumors, the morphology (histologic type) is included in the ICD-10-CM category and code.

Appendix A: Morphology of Neoplasms

MORPHOLOGY OF NEOPLASMS

The World Health Organization has published an adaptation of the International Classification of Diseases for oncology (ICD-O). It contains a coded nomenclature for the morphology of neoplasms, which is reproduced here for those who wish to use it in conjunction with Chapter 2 of the International Classification of Diseases, 9th Revision, Clinical Modification.

The morphology code numbers consist of five digits; the first four identify the histological type of the neoplasm and the fifth indicates its behavior. The one-digit behavior code is as follows:

/0   Benign

/1   Uncertain whether benign or malignant
Borderline malignancy

/2   Carcinoma in situ
Intraepithelial
Noninfiltrating
Noninvasive

/3   Malignant, primary site

/6   Malignant, metastatic site
Secondary site

/9   Malignant, uncertain whether primary or metastatic site

In the nomenclature below, the morphology code numbers include the behavior code appropriate to the histological type of neoplasm, but this behavior code should be changed if other reported information makes this necessary. For example, "chordoma (M9370/3)" is assumed to be malignant; the term "benign chordoma" should be coded M9370/0. Similarly, "superficial spreading adenocarcinoma (M8143/3)" described as "noninvasive" should be coded M8143/2 and "melanoma (M8720/3)" described as "secondary" should be coded M8720/6.

The following table shows the correspondence between the morphology code and the different sections of Chapter 2:

Morphology Code Histology/Behavior			ICD-9-CM Chapter 2
Any	0	210-229	Benign neoplasms
M8000-M8004	1	239	Neoplasms of unspecified nature
M8010+	1	235-238	Neoplasms of uncertain behavior
Any	2	230-234	Carcinoma in situ
Any	3	140-195 200-208	Malignant neoplasms, stated or presumed to be primary
Any	6	196-198	Malignant neoplasms, stated or presumed to be secondary

The ICD-O behavior digit /9 is inapplicable in an ICD context, since all malignant neoplasms are presumed to be primary (/3) or secondary (/6) according to other information on the medical record.

Only the first-listed term of the full ICD-O morphology nomenclature appears against each code number in the list below. The ICD-9-CM Alphabetical Index (Volume 2), however, includes all the ICD-O synonyms as well as a number of other morphological names still likely to be encountered on medical records but omitted from ICD-O as outdated or otherwise undesirable. A coding difficulty sometimes arises where a morphological diagnosis contains two qualifying adjectives that have different code numbers. An example is "transitional cell epidermoid carcinoma." "Transitional cell carcinoma NOS" is M8120/3 and "epidermoid carcinoma NOS" is M8070/3. In such circumstances, the higher number (M8120/3 in this example) should be used, as it is usually more specific.

CODED NOMENCLATURE FOR MORPHOLOGY OF NEOPLASMS

M8000   Neoplasms NOS

M8000/0	Neoplasm, benign
M8000/1	Neoplasm, uncertain whether benign or malignant
M8000/3	Neoplasm, malignant
M8000/6	Neoplasm, metastatic
M8000/9	Neoplasm, malignant, uncertain whether primary or metastatic
M8001/0	Tumor cells, benign
M8001/1	Tumor cells, uncertain whether benign or malignant
M8001/3	Tumor cells, malignant
M8002/3	Malignant tumor, small cell type
M8003/3	Malignant tumor, giant cell type
M8004/3	Malignant tumor, fusiform cell type

M801-M804   Epithelial neoplasms NOS

M8010/0	Epithelial tumor, benign
M8010/2	Carcinoma in situ NOS
M8010/3	Carcinoma NOS
M8010/6	Carcinoma, metastatic NOS
M8010/9	Carcinomatosis
M8011/0	Epithelioma, benign
M8011/3	Epithelioma, malignant
M8012/3	Large cell carcinoma NOS
M8020/3	Carcinoma, undifferentiated type NOS
M8021/3	Carcinoma, anaplastic type NOS
M8022/3	Pleomorphic carcinoma
M8030/3	Giant cell and spindle cell carcinoma
M8031/3	Giant cell carcinoma
M8032/3	Spindle cell carcinoma
M8033/3	Pseudosarcomatous carcinoma
M8034/3	Polygonal cell carcinoma
M8035/3	Spheroidal cell carcinoma
M8040/1	Tumorlet
M8041/3	Small cell carcinoma NOS
M8042/3	Oat cell carcinoma
M8043/3	Small cell carcinoma, fusiform cell type

Figure 2-9 ICD-9-CM Appendix A: Morphology of Neoplasms (partial)

Morphology codes contain five digits preceded by the letter M and range from M8000/0 to M9970/2. The first four digits (e.g., M8000) indicate the specific histologic term. The fifth digit, after the slash is a behavior code, which indicates whether a tumor is malignant, benign, *in situ*, or uncertain whether malignant or benign. In addition, a separate one-digit code is assigned for histologic grading to indicate differentiation.

EXAMPLE: The patient's record documents adenocarcinoma of the breast. The Index to Diseases entry for adenocarcinoma instructs the coder to "*see also* Neoplasm by site, malignant." This index entry directs the coder to the Neoplasm Table, and the code selected from one of the first three columns depends

Note:

It is best to assign codes for neoplasms when the pathology report is available for review in the patient's record. (If the responsible physician documents a diagnosis other than that recorded on the pathology report, query the physician about the discrepancy so an accurate code is assigned.)

on whether the cancer is primary, secondary, or *in situ* (make sure you review the pathology report for documentation of the type of adenocarcinoma).

The index entry for adenocarcinoma also contains the morphology code, M8140/31, which is reported to the state's cancer registry. When you refer to code M8140/31 in Appendix A of ICD-9-CM, you'll see that its description is Adenocarcinoma, NOS, malignant, primary site, well-differentiated. (The /3 indicates "malignant, primary site," per the instructions at the beginning of Appendix A. The /_1 indicates well-differentiated.)

ICD-9-CM Appendix B—Glossary of Mental Disorders

The Glossary of Mental Disorders, previously found in Appendix B of ICD-9-CM, was permanently removed as of October 1, 2004. The glossary can be found in the DSM, which is published by the APA.

ICD-9-CM Appendix C—Classification of Drugs by AHFS List

The **Classification of Drugs by AHFS List** (Figure 2-10) is located in Appendix C of ICD-9-CM, and it contains the American Hospital Formulary Services (AHFS) List number and its ICD-9-CM equivalent code number (Table 2-2). Appendix C is organized in numerical order according to AHFS List number, and the List is published under the direction of the American Society of Hospital Pharmacists.

EXAMPLE: The patient record documents the patient's reaction to substance 4:00. By referring to ICD-9-CM Appendix C, the coder can determine that 4:00 refers to antihistamine drugs. The coder then refers to the Table of Drugs and Chemicals in the ICD-9-CM Index to Diseases and locates antihistamine (found in alphabetical order) to assign the codes.

The AHFS List can also be referenced within the Table of Drugs and Chemicals by looking up the main term *Drug*. Because providers infrequently document the AHFS List number, it *may be* easier for coders to remember to reference the appendix.

ICD-9-CM Appendix D—Classification of Industrial Accidents According to Agency

The **Classification of Industrial Accidents According to Agency** (Figure 2-11) is located in Appendix D of ICD-9-CM, and it is based on employment injury statistics adopted by the Tenth International Conference of Labor Statisticians. Because it may be difficult to locate the E codes entry in the ICD-9-CM Index to External Causes, coders may find Appendix D more helpful in identifying, for example, the category of equipment for an external cause of injury.

EXAMPLE: The patient was using a combine on his farm when it stopped working. While he was repairing the machine, he sustained a 10-centimeter skin laceration of the right arm when a malfunctioning blade cut his arm.

While the E codes for "accident, caused by, combine" can be easily located in the Index to External Causes, if the coder doesn't know what a combine reaper is, the location of the accident cannot be properly coded. By referencing Appendix D, the coder can determine that a combine reaper is categorized as agricultural machines.

Thus, the coder can assign the location E codes as "Accident, occurring (at), farm." The coder can also report the injury (skin laceration) (884.0), cause of injury (combine agricultural machine) (E919.0), and place of injury (farm) (E849.1).

ICD-9-CM Appendix E—List of 3-Digit Categories

The **List of 3-Digit Categories** (Figure 2-12) is located in Appendix E of ICD-9-CM, and it contains a list of 3-digit category disease codes organized beneath section headings.

CLASSIFICATION OF DRUGS BY AMERICAN HOSPITAL FORMULARY SERVICE LIST NUMBER AND THEIR ICD-9-CM EQUIVALENTS

The coding of adverse effects of drugs is keyed to the continually revised Hospital Formulary of the American Hospital Formulary Service (AHFS) published under the direction of the American Society of Hospital Pharmacists.

The following section gives the ICD-9-CM diagnosis code for each AHFS list.

AHFS List Code		ICD-9-CM Diagnosis Code
4:00	ANTIHISTAMINE DRUGS	963.0
8:00	ANTI-INFECTIVE AGENTS	
8:04	Amebacides	961.5
	hydroxyquinoline derivatives	961.3
	arsenical anti-infectives	961.1
8:08	Anthelmintics	961.6
	quinoline derivatives	961.3
8:12.04	Antifungal Antibiotics	960.1
	nonantibiotics	961.9
8:12.06	Cephalosporins	960.5
8:12.08	Chloramphenicol	960.2
8:12.12	The Erythromycins	960.3
8:12.16	The Penicillins	960.0
8:12.20	The Streptomycins	960.6
8:12.24	The Tetracycline	960.4
8:12.28	Other Antibiotics	960.8
	antimycobacterial antibiotics	960.6
	macrolides	960.3
8:16	Antituberculars	961.8
	antibiotics	960.6
8:18	Antivirals	961.7
8:20	Plasmodicides (antimalarials)	961.4
8:24	Sulfonamides	961.0
8:26	The Sulfones	961.8
8:28	Treponemicides	961.2
8:32	Trichomonacides	961.5
	hydroxyquinoline derivatives	961.3
	nitrofuran derivatives	961.9
8:36	Urinary Germicides	961.9
	quinoline derivatives	961.3
8:40	Other Anti-Infectives	961.9
10:00	ANTINEOPLASTIC AGENTS	963.1
	antibiotics	960.7
	progestogens	962.2
12:00	AUTONOMIC DRUGS	
12:04	Parasympathomimetic (Chollinergic) Agents	971.0
12:08	Parasympatholytic (Cholinergic Blocking) Agents	971.1
12:12	Sympathomimetic (Adrenergic) Agents	971.2
12:16	Sympatholytic (Adrenergic Blocking) Agents	971.3
12:20	Skeletal Muscle Relaxants	975.2
	central nervous system muscle-tone depressants	968.0
16:00	BLOOD DERIVATIVES	964.7

Appendix C: Claslsification of Drugs by AHFS List

Figure 2-10 ICD-9-CM Appendix C: Classification of Drugs by AHFS List (partial)

CLASSIFICATION OF INDUSTRIAL ACCIDENTS ACCORDING TO AGENCY

Annex B to the Resolution concerning Statistics of Employment Injuriesadopted by the Tenth International Conference of Labor Statisticians on 12 October 1962

1 MACHINES

11	Prime-Movers, except Electrical Motors
111	Steam engines
112	Internal combustion engines
119	Others
12	Transmission Machinery
121	Transmission shafts
122	Transmission belts, cables, pulleys, pinions, chains, gears
129	Others
13	Metalworking Machines
131	Power presses
132	Lathes
133	Milling machines
134	Abrasive wheels
135	Mechanical shears
136	Forging machines
137	Rolling-mills
139	Others
14	Wood and Assimilated Machines
141	Circular saws
142	Other saws
143	Molding machines
144	Overhand planes
149	Others
15	Agricultural Machines
151	Reapers (including combine reapers)
152	Threshers
159	Others
16	Mining Machinery
161	Under-cutters
169	Others
19	Other Machines Not Elsewhere Classified
191	Earth-moving machines, excavating and scraping machines, except means of transport
192	Spinning, weaving and other textile machines
193	Machines for the manufacture of foodstuffs and beverages
194	Machines for the manufacture of paper
195	Printing machines
199	Others

2 MEANS OF TRANSPORT AND LIFTING EQUIPMENT

21	Lifting Machines and Appliances
211	Cranes
212	Lifts and elevators
213	Winches
214	Pulley blocks
219	Others
22	Means of Rail Transport
221	Inter-urban railways
222	Rail transport in mines, tunnels, quarries, industrial establishments, docks, etc.
229	Others
23	Other Wheeled Means of Transport, Excluding Rail Transport
231	Tractors
232	Lorries
233	Trucks
234	Motor vehicles, not elsewhere classified
235	Animal-drawn vehicles
236	Hand-drawn vehicles
239	Others
24	Means of Air Transport
25	Means of Water Transport
251	Motorized means of water transport
252	Non-motorized means of water transport
26	Other Means of Transport
261	Cable-cars
262	Mechanical conveyors, except cable-cars
269	Others

Appendix D: Industrial Accidents According to Agency

Figure 2-11 ICD-9-CM Appendix D: Industrial Accidents According to Agency (partial)

Table 2-2 ICD-9-CM Groupings of the AHFS List (Partial)

4:00	Antihistamine drugs
8:00	Anti-infective drugs
10:00	Antineoplastic agents
12:00	Autonomic drugs
16:00	Blood derivatives
20:00	Blood formation and coagulation

LIST OF THREE-DIGIT CATEGORIES

1. INFECTIOUS AND PARASITIC DISEASES

Intestinal infectious diseases (001-009)
001 Cholera
002 Typhoid and paratyphoid fevers
003 Other salmonella infections
004 Shigellosis
005 Other food poisoning (bacterial)
006 Amebiasis
007 Other protozoal intestinal diseases
008 Intestinal infections due to other organisms
009 Ill-defined intestinal infections

Tuberculosis (010-018)
010 Primary tuberculous infection
011 Pulmonary tuberculosis
012 Other respiratory tuberculosis
013 Tuberculosis of meninges and central   nervous system
014 Tuberculosis of intestines, peritoneum, and mesenteric glands
015 Tuberculosis of bones and joints
016 Tuberculosis of genitourinary system
017 Tuberculosis of other organs
018 Miliary tuberculosis

Zoonotic bacterial diseases (020-027)
020 Plague
021 Tularemia
022 Anthrax
023 Brucellosis
024 Glanders
025 Melioidosis
026 Rat-bite fever
027 Other zoonotic bacterial diseases

Permission to reprint granted by Optuminsight, Inc.

Appendix E: List of Three-Digit Categories

Figure 2-12 ICD-9-CM Appendix E: List of 3-Digit Categories (partial)

EXAMPLE: Acute rheumatic fever (390–392)
390   Rheumatic fever without mention of heart involvement
391   Rheumatic fever with heart involvement
392   Rheumatic chorea

Exercise 2.2 – ICD-9-CM Tabular List of Diseases and ICD-1O-CM Tabular List of Diseases and Injuries

Instructions: Complete each statement.

1. The ICD-9-CM _____ arranges codes and descriptions in numerical order, and it contains 17 chapters that classify diseases and injuries, 2 supplemental classifications, and 4 appendices.

2. The Glossary of Mental Disorders Appendix, previously found in _____ of ICD-9-CM , permanently removed from ICD-9-CM as of October 1, 2004 because its content can be found in the _____, published by the APA.

(continues)

Exercise 2.2 (*continued*)

3. The codes that are reported for patient encounters when a circumstance other than disease or injury is documented are called _____.

4. The supplementary classification located in the ICD-9-CM Tabular List of Diseases that describes external causes of injury, poisoning, or other adverse reactions affecting a patient's health contain _____.

5. Appendix A of ICD-9-CM contains _____, which are reported to state cancer registries.

6. New growths, or tumors, in which cell reproduction is out of control, are called _____.

7. Tumors are often classified as _____ (not cancerous) or _____ (cancerous).

8. Appendix C of ICD-9-CM, which contains the American Hospital Formulary Services List number and its ICD-9-CM equivalent code number, is titled _____.

9. Appendix D of ICD-9-CM contains the _____, which is based on employment injury statistics adopted by the Tenth International Conference of Labor Statisticians.

10. Appendix E of ICD-9-CM contains the _____, which are organized beneath section headings.

ICD-9-CM Index to Diseases and ICD-10-CM Index to Diseases and Injuries ●

The ICD-9-CM **Index to Diseases** (Figure 2-13A) is an alphabetical listing of main terms or conditions printed in boldfaced type that may be expressed as nouns, adjectives, or eponyms. The ICD-9-CM index contains three sections (Table 2-3A):

- Index to Diseases, which includes two official tables that make it easier to code hypertension and neoplasms. (Some publishers print special editions of ICD-9-CM manuals that contain additional tables to simplify the search for the correct code of other complex conditions.)

- Table of Drugs and Chemicals, which is an alphabetic index of medicinal, chemical, and biological substances that result in poisonings (and associated external causes) and external causes of adverse effects.

- Alphabetic Index to External Causes of Injury and Poisoning, which is a separate index that is often forgotten; it is helpful to mark it with a tab as a reminder of its usefulness.

Letter-by-letter alphabetization is used throughout the ICD-9-CM Index to Diseases (and the ICD-9-CM Index to Procedures), which means single spaces and hyphens are ignored.

ICD-10 Alert!

The ICD-10-CM *Index to Diseases and Injuries* (Figure 2-13B) is an alphabetical list of terms and their corresponding codes. Main terms are printed in boldfaced type, and subterms and qualifiers are indented below main terms. The ICD-10-CM index is subdivided into two parts (Table 2-3B):

- Index to Diseases and Injuries, which includes a Neoplasm Table and a Table of Drugs and Chemicals

- Index to External Causes (of morbidity)

EXAMPLE: LETTER BY LETTER ALPHABETIZATION (ICD-9-CM INDEX TO DISEASES)

Beer-drinkers' heart (disease) 425.5

Bee sting (with allergic or anaphylactic shock) 989.5

Begbie's disease (exophthalmic goiter) 242.0

Because the space between *bee* and *sting* is ignored, *bee sting* (beesting) is sequenced alphabetically <u>after</u> *beer-drinkers'* heart (disease).

Abnormal, abnormality

A

AAT (alpha-1 antitrypsin) deficiency 273.4
AAV (disease) (illness) (infection) — *see*
  Human immunodeficiencyvirus (disease)
  (illness) (infection)
Abactio — *see* Abortion, induced
Abactus venter — *see* Abortion, induced
Abarognosis 781.99
Abasia (-astasia) 307.9
  atactica 781.3
  choreic 781.3
  hysterical 300.11
  paroxysmal trepidant 781.3
  spastic 781.3
  trembling 781.3
  trepidans 781.3
Abderhalden-Kaufmann-Lignac syndrome
  (cystinosis) 270.0
Abdomen, abdominal — *see also* condition
  accordion 306.4
  acute 789.0
  angina 557.1
  burst 868.00
  convulsive equivalent (*see also* Epilepsy) 345.5
  heart 746.87
  muscle deficiency syndrome 756.79
  obstipum 756.79
Abdominalgia 789.0
  periodic 277.31
Abduction contracture, hip or other joint — *see*
  Contraction, joint
Abercrombie's syndrome (amyloid degeneration)
  277.39
Aberrant (congenital) — *see also* Malposition,
  congenital
  adrenal gland 759.1
  blood vessel NEC 747.60
    arteriovenous NEC 747.60
    cerebrovascular 747.81
    gastrointestinal 747.61
    lower limb 747.64
    renal 747.62
    spinal 747.82
    upper limb 747.63
  breast 757.6

Permission to reprint granted by Optuminsight, Inc.

Figure 2-13A ICD-9-CM Index to
Diseases (partial)

ICD-10-CM Index to Diseases and Injuries

A

Aarskog's syndrome Q87.1
Abandonment - *see* Maltreatment
Abasia (-astasia) (hysterical) F44.4
Abderhalden-Kaufmann-Lignac syndrome
  (cystinosis) E72.04
Abdomen, abdominal — *see also* condition
  acute R10.0
  angina K55.1
  muscle deficiency syndrome Q79.4
Abdominalgia - *see* Pain, abdominal
Abduction contracture, hip or other joint —
  see Contraction, joint
Aberrant(congenital) — (*see also* Malposition,
  congenital)
  adrenal gland Q89.1
  artery (peripheral) Q27.8
    basilar NEC Q28.1
    cerebral Q28.3
    coronary Q24.5
    digestive system Q27.8
    eye Q15.8
    lower limb Q27.8
    precerebral Q28.1
    pulmonary Q25.7
    renal Q27.2
    retina Q14.1
    specified site NEC Q27.8
    subclavian Q27.8
    upper limb Q27.8
    vertebral Q28.1
  breast Q83.8
  endocrine gland NEC Q89.2
  hepatic duct Q44.5
  pancreas Q45.3
  parathyroid gland Q89.2
  pituitary gland Q89.2
  sebaceous glands, mucous membrane,
    mouth, congenital Q38.6
  spleen Q89.09
  subclavian artery Q27.8
  thymus (gland) Q89.2
  thyroid gland Q89.2
  vein (peripheral) NEC Q27.8
    cerebral Q28.3

Permission to reprint granted by Optuminsight, Inc.

Figure 2-13B ICD-10-CM Index to
Diseases and Injuries (partial)

Table 2-3A ICD-9-CM Index to Diseases (Volume 2)

Section 1
Index to Diseases (contains two tables)
Hypertension Table
Neoplasm Table
Section 2
Table of Drugs and Chemicals
Section 3
Alphabetic Index to External Causes of Injury and Poisoning

Table 2-3B ICD-10-CM Index to Diseases and Injuries

© Cengage Learning 2014

Index to Diseases and Injuries (contains two tables)
Neoplasm Table
Table of Drugs and Chemicals
Index to External Causes (of morbidity)

ICD-10 Alert!

Main terms in the ICD-10-CM Index to Diseases and Injuries (and the ICD-10-PCS Index to Procedures) are listed in alphabetical order, which means hyphens within main terms are ignored, but a single space within a main term is not ignored. (This differs from the letter-by-letter alphabetization used throughout the ICD-9-CM Index to Diseases.) A code listed next to a main term in the ICD-10-CM index is referred to as a "default code." The default code represents the code for the condition most commonly associated with the main term, or it may represent an unspecified code for the condition. (The ICD-10-CM Tabular List of Diseases and Injuries must always be referenced so that the most accurate and complete code is assigned.) If a condition is documented in a medical record (for example, appendicitis) without any additional information, such as acute or chronic, the default code should be assigned (after reviewing the ICD-10-CM Tabular List of Diseases and Injuries).

EXAMPLE: ALPHABETIZATION (ICD-10-CM INDEX TO DISEASES AND INJURIES)

`Catatonic`

`Cat-scratch`

The hyphen in "Cat-scratch" is ignored, resulting in sequencing of that main term after "Catatonic."

`Bee sting` (with allergic or anaphylactic shock)—*see* Toxicity, venom, arthropod, bee

`Beer-drinkers' heart` (disease) I42.6

`Begbie's disease` (exophthalmic goiter)—*see* Hyperthyroidism, with, goiter

The space between "bee" and "sting" is considered, resulting in that main term being sequenced above "Beer-drinkers' heart (disease)"

"With" references immediately follow the main term to which they refer. When multiple subterms are present, they are indented under *with* and are listed in alphabetical order.

EXAMPLE 1: USE OF "WITH" IN ICD-9-CM INDEX TO DISEASES

```
Asthma, asthmatic (bronchial)(catarrh)(spasmodic) 493.9
  with
    chronic obstructive pulmonary disease (COPD) 493.2
    hay fever 493.0
    rhinitis 493.0
  allergic 493.9
    stated cause (external allergen) 493.0
  atopic 493.0
  cardiac (see also Failure, ventricular, left) 428.1
```

EXAMPLE 2: USE OF "WITH" IN ICD-10-CM INDEX TO DISEASES AND INJURIES

```
Asthma, asthmatic (bronchial) (catarrh) (spasmodic) J45.909
  with
    chronic obstructive bronchitis J44.9
      with
        acute lower respiratory infection J44.0
        exacerbation (acute) J44.1
    chronic obstructive pulmonary disease J44.9
      with
        acute lower respiratory infection J44.0
        exacerbation (acute) J44.1
        exacerbation (acute) J45.901
    hay fever - see Asthma, allergic extrinsic
    rhinitis, allergic - see Asthma, allergic extrinsic
    status asthmaticus J45.902
  allergic extrinsic J45.909
    with
      exacerbation (acute) J45.901
      status asthmaticus J45.902
  atopic - see Asthma, allergic extrinsic
  cardiac - see Failure, ventricular, left
```

Make sure you have an excellent understanding of alphabetization rules so you can quickly and easily locate main terms and subterms in the ICD-9-CM, ICD-10-CM and ICD-10-PCS indexes.

When Arabic and Roman numerals and numerical words appear below a main term or subterm, they are listed in numerical order, not in alphabetical order.

EXAMPLE 1: The cranial nerves are listed in numerical order below main term *Disorder*, subterm *nerve*, and second qualifier *cranial* in the ICD-9-CM Index to Diseases:

```
Disorder
  nerve
    cranial 352.9
      first 352.0
      second 377.49
      third
        partial 378.51
        total 378.52
      fourth 378.53
```

EXAMPLE 2: In the ICD-10-CM Index to Diseases and Injuries, the cranial nerves are listed in alphabetic order below the main term *Disorder*, subterm *nerve*, and second qualifier *cranial*.

```
Disorder
  nerve G58.9
    cranial G52.9
      eighth - see subcategory H93.3
      eleventh G52.8
      fifth G50.9
      first G52.0
      fourth NEC — see Strabismus, paralytic, fourth nerve
      multiple G52.7
      ninth G52.1
      second NEC — see Disorder, nerve, optic
      seventh NEC G51.8
      sixth NEC - see Strabismus, paralytic, sixth nerve
```

```
specified NEC G52.8
tenth G52.2
third NEC — see Strabismus, paralytic, third nerve
twelfth G52.3
```

Main Terms, Subterms, and Qualifiers

ICD-9-CM, ICD-10-CM and ICD-10-PCS index **main terms** (e.g., conditions) are printed in boldfaced type and are followed by the code number. Main terms may or may not be followed by a listing of parenthetical terms, which serve as nonessential modifiers of the main term. **Nonessential modifiers** are qualifying words contained in parentheses after the main term that do not have to be included in the diagnostic or procedural statement for the code number listed after the parentheses to be assigned.

Subterms (or **essential modifiers**) qualify the main term by listing alternative sites, etiology, or clinical status. A subterm is indented two spaces under the main term. Second qualifiers are indented two spaces under a subterm, and third qualifiers are indented two spaces under a second qualifier (Figure 2-14A and Figure 2-14B).

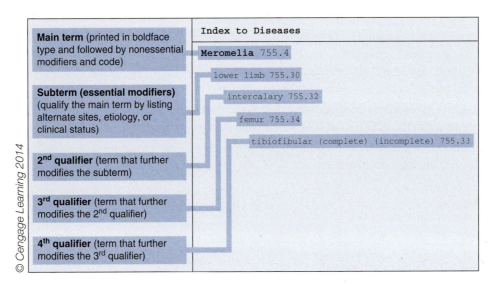

Figure 2-14A Display of main terms, subterms (nonessential modifiers), and qualifiers in the ICD-9-CM Index to Diseases

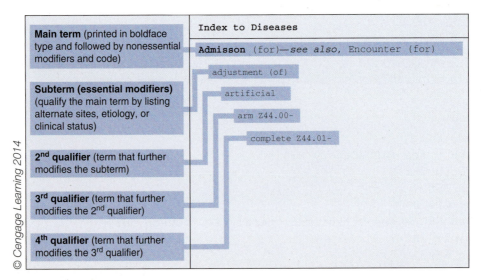

Figure 2-14B Display of main terms, subterms (nonessential modifiers), and qualifiers in the ICD-10-CM Index to Diseases and Injuries

Care must be taken when moving from the bottom of one column to the top of the next column or when turning to the next page of the index. The main term will be repeated and followed by —*continued*. When moving from one column to another, watch carefully to determine whether the subterm has changed or new second or third qualifiers appear.

EXAMPLE 1: CONTINUATION OF TERMS IN ICD-9-CM INDEX TO DISEASES: ICD-9-CM Index to Diseases entries are organized according to main terms, subterms, second qualifiers, and third qualifiers. Refer to the index entry for "stricture, artery, cerebral, congenital (747.81)" and note the indented subterm and qualifiers. Notice that when the main term continues at the top of a column (or on the next page of the Index to Diseases), the word — *continued* appears after the main term and subterms and qualifiers are indented below the main term.

Start of Main Term in Index to Diseases		Continuation of Main Term (Next Page)	
Main term:	`Stricture` —*see also* `Stenosis`	Main Term:	`Stricture` —*continued*
Continuation line:	`799.89`	Subterm:	`lacrimal`
Subterm:	`artery 447.1`	Second qualifier:	`canaliculi 375.53`
Second qualifier:	`cerebral 437.0`	Third qualifier:	`congenital 743.65`
Third qualifier:	`congenital 747.81`		

EXAMPLE 2: CONTINUATION OF TERMS IN ICD-10-CM INDEX TO DISEASES AND INJURIES: ICD-10-CM Index to Diseases and Injuries entries are organized according to main terms, subterms, second qualifiers, and third qualifiers. Refer to the index entry for "stricture, aqueduct of Sylvius, with spina bifida, acquired (G91.1)," and note the indented subterm and qualifiers. Notice that when the main term continues at the top of a column (or on the next page of the Index to Diseases and Injuries), the word —*continued* appears after the main term and subterms and qualifiers are indented below the main term.

Start of Main Term in Index to Diseases		Continuation of Main Term (Next Page)	
Main term:	`Stricture` —*see also* `Stenosis`	Main Term:	`Stricture` —*continued*
Subterm:	`aqueduct of Sylvius (congenital) Q03.0`	Subterm:	`urethra`
Second qualifier:	`with spina bifida` —*see* `Spina bifida,`	Second qualifier:	`postprocedural`
Continuation line:	`by site, with hydrocephalus`	Third qualifier:	`female N99.12`
Third qualifier:	`acquired G91.1`	Third qualifier:	`male N99.114`

Basic Steps for Using the Index to Diseases

It is important to remember that you should never code directly from the Index to Diseases. After locating a code in the index, go to that code in the Tabular List of Diseases to find important instructions (e.g., includes notes and excludes note) and to verify the code selected. Instructions may require the assignment of additional codes or indicate conditions that are classified elsewhere.

STEP 1   Locate the main term in the Index to Diseases (Volume 2).

Begin the coding process in the ICD-9-CM Index to Diseases by locating the condition's boldfaced main term and then reviewing the subterms listed below the main term to locate the proper disorder.

EXAMPLE: The underlined terms in the following conditions are main terms:

```
Allergens investigation

Auditory agnosia secondary to organic lesion

Intussusception, ileocolic

Status (post) angioplasty
```

STEP 2   If the instructional phase —*see condition* is found after the main term, a descriptive term (an adjective) or the anatomic site has been referenced instead of the disorder or the disease (the condition) documented in the diagnostic statement.

EXAMPLE: The provider's diagnostic statement is "upper respiratory infection." In the ICD-9-CM (or ICD-10-CM) Index to Diseases, look up the phrase *upper respiratory*. Notice that the term —*see condition* appears next to the phrase *upper respiratory*. This instruction directs you to the condition, which is "infection."

STEP 3   When the condition in the diagnostic statement is not easily found in the index, use the main terms below to locate the code. (V codes main terms are on page 47.)

Abnormal	Findings	Neoplasm
Anomaly	Foreign body	Obstruction
Complication	Infection	Pregnancy
Delivery	Injury	Puerperal
Disease	Late effects	Syndrome
Disorder	Lesion	Wound

Note:

To locate a code that describes an external cause of injury, refer to the separate Index to External Causes, which is located after the Table of Drugs and Chemicals at the back of the Index to Diseases.

Exercise 2.3 – ICD-9-CM Index to Diseases and ICD-10-CM Index to Diseases and Injuries

Instructions: Complete each statement.

1. The alphabetical listing of main terms or conditions printed in boldfaced type that may be expressed as nouns, adjectives, or eponyms is called the ICD-9-CM _____.

2. The _____ contains adverse effects and poisonings associated with medicinal, chemical, and biological substances.

3. Spaces between words and single hyphens between words are ignored when locating main terms in the ICD-9-CM indexes, which means the _____ style of alphabetization is used.

4. For the following list of main terms found in the ICD-9-CM Index to Diseases, main term _____ is not in letter-by-letter alphabetical order. (In the ICD-10-CM Index to Diseases and Injuries, the following list of main terms are in alphabetical order.)

    ```
    Lathyrism

    Launois' syndrome

    Launois-Cleret syndrome
    ```

5. When numerical characters and words appear under a main term or subterm, they are listed in _____ order.

6. Main terms are printed in _____ type and are followed by the code number.

7. Qualifying words that are contained in parentheses after the main term, which do not have to be included in the diagnostic statement for the code number listed after the parentheses to be assigned, are called _____.

8. Subterms are considered _____, and they qualify the main term by listing alternative sites, etiology, or clinical status.

9. The provider documents "acute asthmatic attack." The main term in the ICD-9-CM or ICD-10-CM index is _____.

10. The provider documents "history of affective psychosis." The main term in the ICD-9-CM or ICD-10-CM index is _____.

Instructions: First reorder the list of terms below according to letter-by-letter alphabetization as used in the ICD-9-CM Index to Diseases. Then, reorder the same list according to alphabetical order as used in the ICD-10-CM Index to Diseases and Injuries.

ICD-9-CM	**ICD-10-CM**	
_____	_____	**11.** Hazard-Crile tumor
_____	_____	**12.** Hay
_____	_____	**13.** Headache
_____	_____	**14.** Head
_____	_____	**15.** Haygarth's nodosities

ICD-9-CM Index to Procedures and Tabular List of Procedures ●

The ICD-9-CM **Index to Procedures and Tabular List of Procedures** (Volume 3) (Table 2-4) is included in the hospital version of commercial ICD-9-CM coding manuals as a combined alphabetical index (Figure 2-15) and tabular list of inpatient procedures and services (Figure 2-16). The tabular list is organized by code number (and Index to Procedures entries include codes, not page numbers), with each chapter and supplemental classification organized into sections (groups of two-digit categories). Procedure codes consist of two digits, followed by a decimal point and one or two additional digits.

The ICD-9-CM Index to Procedures is an alphabetical listing of main terms or procedures printed in boldfaced type that may be expressed as nouns, adjectives, or eponyms. The index uses letter-by-letter alphabetization, which means single spaces and hyphens are ignored. "With" and "without" references

Table 2-4 ICD-9-CM Index to Procedures and Tabular List of Procedures (Volume 3)

Section I	
Index to Procedures	
Section II	
Tabular List of Procedures (17 chapters)	
Chapter 00	Procedures and Interventions, Not Elsewhere Classified (00)
Chapter 1	Operations on the Nervous System (01–05)
Chapter 2	Operations on the Endocrine System (06–07)
Chapter 3	Operations on the Eye (08–16)
Chapter 3A	Other Miscellaneous Diagnostic and Therapeutic Procedures
Chapter 4	Operations on the Ear (18–20)
Chapter 5	Operations on the Nose, Mouth, and Pharynx (21–29)
Chapter 6	Operations on the Respiratory System (30–34)
Chapter 7	Operations on the Cardiovascular System (35–39)
Chapter 8	Operations on the Hemic and Lymphatic Systems (40–41)
Chapter 9	Operations on the Digestive System (42–54)
Chapter 10	Operations on the Urinary System (55–59)
Chapter 11	Operations on the Male Genital Organs (60–64)
Chapter 12	Operations on the Female Genital Organs (65–71)
Chapter 13	Obstetrical Procedures (72–75)
Chapter 14	Operations on the Musculoskeletal System (76–84)
Chapter 15	Operations on the Integumentary System (85–86)
Chapter 16	Miscellaneous Diagnostic and Therapeutic Procedures (87–99)

immediately follow the main term to which they refer. Other connecting terms (e.g., *by, for,* and *to*) are usually listed in alphabetical order. When multiple subterms are present, they are indented under *with* and are listed in alphabetical order. When Arabic and Roman numerals and numerical words appear below a main term or subterm, they are listed in numerical order, not in alphabetical order. Main terms are printed in boldfaced type followed by the code number, and they may or may not be followed by a listing of parenthetical terms. Subterms (or essential

ICD-10 Alert!

ICD-10-PCS replaces Volume 3 (procedures) of ICD-9-CM. ICD-10-PCS is used by hospitals to report inpatient procedures. Provider offices and outpatient settings will continue to use CPT and HCPCS level II to report procedures and services.

UAE

U

UAE (uterine artery embolization), NOS 68.25
  with coils 68.24
  particulate agent (gelatin sponge)(gelfoam)
    (microspheres)(polyvinyl alcohol) (PVA)
    (spherical embolics) 68.25
Uchida operation (tubal ligation with or without
    fimbriectomy) 66.32
UFR (uroflowmetry) 89.24
Ultrafiltration 99.78
  hemodiafiltration 39.95
  hemodialysis (kidney) 39.95
  removal, plasma water 99.78
  therapeutic plasmapheresis 99.71
Ultrasonography
  abdomen 88.76
  aortic arch 88.73
  biliary tract 88.74
  breast 88.73
  deep vein thrombosis 88.77
  digestive system 88.74
  eye 95.13
  head and neck 88.71
  heart (intravascular) 88.72
  intestine 88.74
  intravascular - *see* Ultrasound, intravascular (IVUS)
  lung 88.73
  midline shift, brain 88.71
  multiple sites 88.79
  peripheral vascular system 88.77
  retroperitoneum 88.76

Figure 2-15 ICD-9-CM Index to Procedures (partial)

modifiers) (e.g., anatomic site) qualify the main term and are indented two spaces under the main term. Secondary qualifying conditions are indented two spaces under a subterm.

Note:

- Hospital outpatient departments and health care providers' offices assign Current Procedural Terminology (CPT) and the Healthcare Common Procedure Coding System (HCPCS) level II national codes, covered later in this textbook.

- HCPCS level III local codes were eliminated December 31, 2003, because they may have duplicated national codes, may have identified brand names rather than product categories, and/or may have varied in use from locality to locality. This decision was also based on the Health Insurance Portability and Accountability Act (HIPAA) requirement to adopt standards for coding systems used for reporting health care transactions.

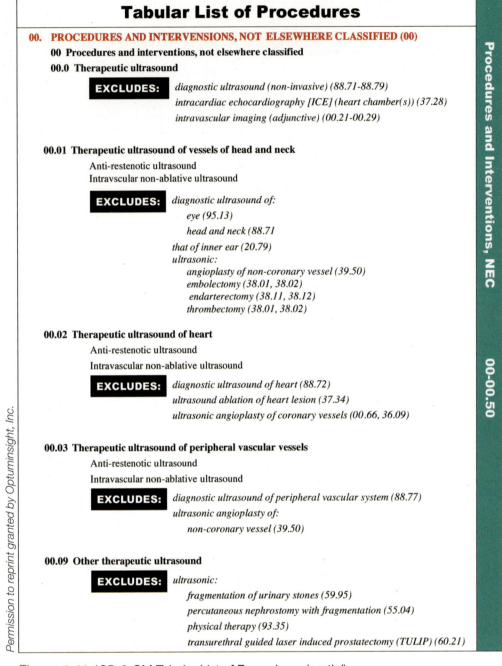

Permission to reprint granted by Optuminsight, Inc.

Figure 2-16 ICD-9-CM Tabular List of Procedures (partial)

Basic Steps for Using the Index to Procedures

It is important to remember that you should never code directly from the Index to Procedures. After locating a code in the index, go to that code in the Tabular List of Procedures for important instructions (e.g., includes notes and excludes note) and to verify the code selected. Instructions may require the assignment of additional codes or indicate procedures that are classified elsewhere.

STEP 1   Locate the main term in the Index to Procedures (Volume 3).

Begin the coding process in the ICD-9-CM Index to Procedures by locating the procedure's boldfaced main term and then reviewing the subterms listed below the main term to locate the proper procedure.

EXAMPLE: The underlined terms in the following procedures are main terms:

- Medical <u>interview</u>

- Artificial <u>rupture</u> of membranes for surgical induction of labor

- Intracranial <u>angiotomy</u>

STEP 2   If the term —*omit* code is found after the main term or a subterm, do not assign a code to the operative approach because it is considered an integral part of the procedure. In addition, do not assign codes for operative closures or the administration of anesthesia.

EXAMPLE: The Index to Procedures instructs the coder to—*omit code* for an operative approach into the abdominal wall when a definitive procedure is performed.

Incision (and drainage)

with
    exploration—*see* Exploration
    removal of foreign body—*see* Removal, foreign body
abdominal wall 54.0
    as operative approach—*omit code*

> **Note:**
>
> The operative approach (e.g., laparotomy) is coded when an opening into a body cavity is followed only by a diagnostic procedure, such as a biopsy.

STEP 3   When the procedure in the statement is not easily found in the index, use the main terms below to locate the code:

Application	Insertion	Resection
Closure	Operation	Revision
Correction	Procedure	Suture
Destruction	Release	Test
Division	Removal	Therapy
Incision	Repair	Transfer

Exercise 2.4 – ICD-9-CM Index to Procedures and Tabular List of Procedures

Instructions: Complete each statement.

1. The hospital version of commercial ICD-9-CM coding manuals includes the _____ as a combined alphabetical index and numerical listing of inpatient procedures and services.

2. Hospital outpatient departments and health care providers' offices use the _____, which is published by the American Medical Association (AMA), along with the _____.

(continues)

Exercise 2.4 (continued)

3. HCPCS level III local codes were eliminated _____ because they may have duplicated national codes, may have identified brand names rather than product categories, and/or may have varied in use from locality to locality.

4. The ICD-9-CM Index to Procedures and Tabular List of Procedures contain _____ sections.

5. The ICD-9-CM Tabular List of Procedures contains _____ chapters.

ICD-10-PCS Index and Tables

The International Classification of Diseases, 10th Revision, Procedure Coding System (ICD-10-PCS) is an entirely new procedure classification system developed by the Centers for Medicare & Medicaid Services (CMS) for use in the United States for inpatient hospital settings *only*, and will replace Volume 3 of ICD-9-CM. ICD-10-PCS uses a multiaxial 7-character alphanumeric code structure (e.g., 047K04Z) that provides a unique code for all substantially different procedures. It also allows new procedures to be easily incorporated as new codes. ICD-10-PCS contains more than 87,000 7-character alphanumeric procedure codes. (ICD-9-CM has about 4,000 3- or 4-digit numeric procedure codes.)

Development of ICD-10-PCS

The development of ICD-10-PCS incorporates four major attributes:

- *Completeness.* There are unique codes for all substantially different procedures.

- *Expandability.* As new procedures are developed, the structure of ICD-10-PCS allows them to be easily incorporated as unique codes.

- *Multiaxial.* ICD-10-PCS codes consist of independent characters, with each individual axis retaining its meaning across broad ranges of codes to the extent possible.

  EXAMPLE: The Medical and Surgical Section axes include:

  1. Section (medical and surgical)
  2. Body system (e.g., heart and great vessels)
  3. Root operation (e.g., dilation)
  4. Body part (e.g., skin)
  5. Approach (e.g., open)
  6. Device (e.g., drainage device)
  7. Qualifier (e.g., anterior)

Note:

ICD-9-CM, Volume 3, has been used in the United States for reporting inpatient procedures since 1979. Its structure has not allowed new procedures associated with rapidly changing technology to be effectively incorporated as new codes. In 1992, CMS funded a project to design a replacement and after review of the preliminary design, in 1995 a 3-year contract was awarded to 3M Health Information Systems to complete development of the replacement system. ICD-10-PCS was completed in 1998, and it has been updated annually to add codes for new procedures, devices, and technologies.

Note:

In Volume 3 of ICD-9-CM, sometimes the same code classified procedures performed on different body types, with different approaches, or of different types (e.g., ICD-9-CM code 22.01 classifies puncture of nasal sinus for aspiration or lavage).

Note:

In Volume 3 of ICD-9-CM, there is no room to classify new procedures associated with rapidly changes technology.

However, the Imaging Section axes include:

1. Section (imaging)
2. Body system (e.g., respiratory system)
3. Root type (e.g., fluoroscopy)
4. Body part (e.g., lungs, right)
5. Contract (e.g., low osmolar)
6. Qualifier (e.g., laser)
7. Qualifier (e.g., intraoperative)

- *Standardized terminology.* ICD-10-PCS includes definitions of the terminology used, and while the meaning of specific words varies in common usage, each term is assigned a specific meaning.

Development of ICD-10-PCS followed the below-listed general principles:

- *Diagnostic information is not included in procedure code descriptions.* Instead, ICD-10-CM diagnosis codes classify diseases, disorders, injuries, signs, symptoms, external causes, and so on.

Note:

ICD-10-PCS uses a "build-a-code" approach to classify procedures, which means one character is assigned to each of 7 axes (multiaxial) (e.g., code 02700ZZ is assigned for open dilation of one coronary artery).

Note:

ICD-10-PCS requires detailed knowledge of medical terminology and anatomy and physiology, and its unique vocabulary also requires mastery.

- *"Not otherwise specified" (NOS) options are not provided.* A minimal level of specificity is required for each component of the procedure. (Volume 3 of ICD-9-CM often provided a "not otherwise specified" code option.)

- *Use of "not elsewhere classified" (NEC) is limited.* ICD-10-PCS specifies all significant components of a procedure, generally eliminating the need for an NEC code option. Some NEC options are included in ICD-10-PCS where necessary (e.g., "other device" because new devices are frequently developed). (Volume 3 of ICD-9-CM often provides a "not elsewhere classified" code option.)

- *Level of specificity is enhanced.* All procedures currently performed can be assigned a specific code in ICD-10-PCS. The frequency (or infrequency) with which a procedure is performed is *not* a consideration. Thus, a unique code is classified for each variation of a procedure performed. For example, in Volume 3 of ICD-9-CM code 64.5 is assigned for "operations for sex transformation, not elsewhere classified." In ICD-10-PCS, eight different codes classify male or female intersex surgery.

Structure of ICD-10-PCS Codes

ICD-10-PCS has a 7-character alphanumeric code structure, and the code assigned is the result of a build-a-code process instead of verifying codes in a tabular list of codes (after locating the procedure name in an index).

- Each character contains up to 34 possible values (because characters in positions 2–7 can have different meanings in different sections).

    EXAMPLE: In the Medical and Surgical Section of ICD-10-PCS, the character in position 1 is the number 0 (for Medical and Surgical Section). The character in position 2 refers to body system (e.g., central nervous system, peripheral nervous system, and so on).

    In the Physical Rehabilitation and Diagnostic Audiology Section, the character in position 1 is the letter F (for Physical Rehabilitation and Diagnostic Audiology Section). The character in position 2 refers to "section qualifier" (e.g., rehabilitation or diagnostic audiology).

- Each value represents a specific option for the general character definition.

EXAMPLE: In the Administration Section of ICD-10-PCS, the character in position 2 refers to body system, and it contains just two values:

○ Circulatory system, assigned number 0.

○ Indwelling device, assigned letter C.

○ Physiological systems and anatomical regions, assigned letter E.

• The 10 digits 0–9 and the 24 letters A–H, J–N, and P–Z may be used in each of the 7 characters, depending on the documented procedure. *The letters O and I are not used so as to avoid confusion with the digits 0 and 1.*

• A code is built by selecting a specific value for each of the 7 characters (Table 2-5). Thus, a step-by-step "build-a-code" approach is used when assigning ICD-10-PCS procedure codes. As such, a number or a letter is assigned to *each* of the 7 characters of an ICD-10-PCS code based on documentation of the procedure performed.

Note:

In ICD-10-PCS, the term "procedure" refers to the complete specification of the 7 characters that comprise a complete code. The first character of the 7-character procedure code always specifies the section. Then, depending on the ICD-10-PCS section in which a procedure is classified, the values of characters 2–7 may vary. However, the values of characters 2–7 within a particular section remain the same.

ICD-10-PCS procedures are first divided into sections (Table 2-5, column 1), which identify the general type of procedure (e.g., medical and surgical, obstetrics, imaging, and so on). *The first character of the 7-character procedure code always specifies the section.* While the characters 2–7 have the same meaning within a section, they may have different meanings in different sections (Table 2-5, columns 2–7). Within all sections, the third character specifies either the root operation or the root type (of procedure performed). Characters 4–7 provide additional information (e.g., body part, approach, and so on) that formulate the procedure code.

Then, depending on the ICD-10-PCS section in which a procedure is classified, the values of characters 2–7 may vary (Table 2-5, columns 2–7). However, the values of characters 2–7 *within a particular section* remain the same.

Format of ICD-10-PCS Coding Manual

The ICD-10-PCS coding manual contains three separate parts:

• Index

• Tables

Some publishers include appendices to assist in accurate ICD-10-PCS coding. For example, Ingenix includes the following appendices in its coding manual:

• Appendix A (Root Operations Definitions)

• Appendix B (Comparison of Medical and Surgical Root Operations)

• Appendix C (Body Part Key)

• Appendix D (Type and Type Qualifier Definitions for Sections B–H)

• Appendix E (Components of the Medical and Surgical Approach Definitions)

• Appendix F (Character Meanings)

Build-a-Code Using ICD-10-PCS

The ICD-10-PCS index allows the first 3–5 values, and sometimes all 7 characters, of a 7-character procedure code to be located

Note:

Some ICD-10-PCS tables are extensive, and coders must continue on to the next page of the coding manual to build an accurate code. (Coders say "a table bleeds onto the next page" to describe this.)

Table 2-5 Value Assigned to Each Character in a 7-Character ICD-10-PCS Code

Character 1	Character 2	Character 3	Character 4	Character 5	Character 6	Character 7
Medical and Surgical Section	Body system	Root operation	Body part	Approach	Device	Qualifier
Obstetrics Section	Body system	Root operation	Body part	Approach	Device	Qualifier
Placement Section	Body system	Root operation	Body system/ Region	Approach	Device	Qualifier
Administration Section	Body system	Root operation	Body system/ Region	Approach	Substance	Qualifier
Measurement and Monitoring Section	Body system	Root operation	Body system	Approach	Function/ Device	Qualifier
Extracorporeal Assistance and Performance Section	Body system	Root operation	Body system	Duration	Function	Qualifier
Extracorporeal Therapies Section	Body system	Root operation	Body system	Duration	Qualifier	Qualifier
Osteopathic Section	Body system	Root operation	Body region	Approach	Method	Qualifier
Other Procedures Section	Body system	Root operation	Body region	Approach	Method	Qualifier
Chiropractic Section	Body system	Root operation	Body region	Approach	Method	Qualifier
Imaging Section	Body system	Root type	Body part	Contrast	Qualifier	Qualifier
Nuclear Medicine Section	Body system	Root type	Body part	Radionuclide	Qualifier	Qualifier
Radiation Oncology Section	Body system	Root type	Body part	Modality qualifier	Isotope	Qualifier
Physical Rehabilitation and Diagnostic Audiology Section	Section qualifier	Root type	Body system/ Region	Type qualifier	Equipment	Qualifier
Mental Health Section	Body system	Root type	Qualifier	Qualifier	Qualifier	Qualifier
Substance Abuse Treatment Section	Body system	Root type	Qualifier	Qualifier	Qualifier	Qualifier

alphabetically according to general type of procedure (e.g., excision), commonly used medical terms (e.g., appendectomy), or body part (e.g., adductor brevis muscle). The first 3–5 values of a 7-character procedure code as listed in the index entry directs the coder to a specific location in the ICD-10-PCS tables, which must be used to construct a complete and valid 7-character code. (Sometimes the coder is directed to a different main term by the instructional note *see*, which is located next to a main term.)

Each ICD-10-PCS table identifies the first three values of the 7-character code (e.g., 027). Thus, locating the first three values of the 7-character code in the index allows the corresponding table to be located. The table is then used to determine the complete code by specifying the last four values, which is based on documentation of the procedure performed. ICD-10-PCS tables contain rows that specify the valid combinations of code values. Within a *body system* (or *section qualifier*, for the Physical Rehabilitation and Diagnostic Section Audiology Section), the

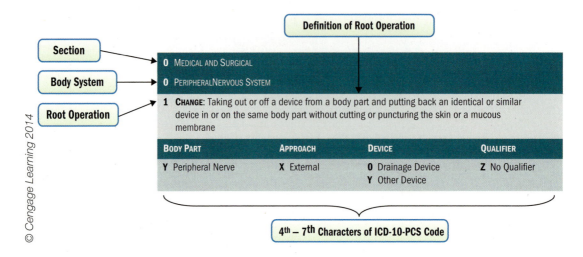

three rows of text above each table specify values for characters 1–3 of an ICD-10-PCS code. The fourth row labels characters 4–7 of a possible code. Subsequent rows in the table specify valid combinations of values for characters 4–7.

EXAMPLE: The patient underwent an *open procedure of the spinal canal to insertion a subarachnoid-peritoneal shunt using synthetic substitute for the purpose of decreasing cerebrospinal fluid levels via bypass (using the shunt) to the peritoneal cavity,* which is assigned ICD-10-PCS code 001U0J6. Refer to the highlighted items below to *build-a-code*.

STEP 1   After identifying the name of the procedure performed in the operative report, locate the main term in the ICD-10-PCS Index.

Index
Shortening
—*see* Excision
—*see* Repair
—*see* Reposition
Shunt creation—*see* Bypass

STEP 2   After following any instructional notes (e.g., *see*) present after a main term, locate the appropriate main term, subterm, and qualifier to identify the first 3 (or 4–5) values of a 7-character code.

Index
Bypass
Canal, Spinal 001U0
Cavity
Cranial 0W110J
Pelvic 0W1J

STEP 3   Locate the ICD-10-PCS table that corresponds to the first 3 values of a 7-character code, and review the procedure performed to assign a character to each position in the complete 7-character code.

0 Medical and Surgical			
0 Central Nervous System			
1 Bypass: Altering the route of passage of the contents of a tubular body part			
Body Part Character 4	Approach Character 6	Device Character 6	Qualifier Character 7
6 Cerebral Ventricle	0 Open	7 Autologous Tissue Substitute J Synthetic Substitute K Nonautologous Tissue Substitute	0 Nasopharynx 1 Mastoid Sinus 2 Atrium 3 Blood Vessel 4 Pleural Cavity 5 Intestine 6 Peritoneal Cavity 7 Urinary Tract 8 Bone Marrow B Cerebral Cisterns
U Spinal Canal	0 Open	7 Autologous Tissue Substitute J Synthetic Substitute K Nonautologous Tissue Substitute	4 Pleural Cavity 6 Peritoneal Cavity 7 Urinary Tract 9 Fallopian Tube

© Cengage Learning 2014

Exercise 2.5 – ICD-10-PCS Index and Tables

Instructions: Complete each statement.

1. The complete name for ICD-10-PCS is _____.
2. ICD-10-PCS is an entirely new procedure classification system developed by CMS for use in the USA for _____ settings only.
3. ICD-10-PCS uses a multiaxial _____ alphanumeric code structure that provides a unique code for all substantially different procedures.
4. The multiaxial approach used by ICD-10-PCS means that _____.
5. Refer to Table 2-5, and list each axis associated with the Imaging Section: _____.
6. Refer to Table 2-5, and list each axis associated with the Mental Health Section: _____.
7. Refer to Table 2-5, and list each axis associated with the Medical and Surgical Section: _____.
8. Based on your answers to numbers 5–7 (above), complete the following statement: Depending on the ICD-10-PCS section in which a procedure is classified, _____. However, the values of characters 2–7 within a particular section _____.
9. List the two parts of the ICD-10-PCS coding manual: _____.
10. Refer to pages 67 and 68 and use the build-a-code method to assign an ICD-10-PCS code for a *open procedure of the spinal canal to insertion a subarachnoid-pleural shunt using autologous tissue substitute for the purpose of decreasing cerebrospinal fluid levels via bypass (using the shunt) to the peritoneal cavity*: _____

Official ICD-9-CM and ICD-10-CM/PCS Guidelines for Coding and Reporting

The CMS and the NCHS are two agencies in the DHHS that prepare guidelines for coding and reporting using the ICD-9-CM. These guidelines, which have been approved by the four organizations that comprise the **cooperating parties for the ICD-9-CM**, should be used as a companion document when coding from ICD-9-CM. The organizations include the American Hospital Association (AHA), American Health Information Management Association (AHIMA), CMS, and NCHS.

The **Official ICD-9-CM Guidelines for Coding and Reporting** (and the **Official ICD-10-CM Guidelines for Coding and Reporting** and the **Official ICD-10-PCS Guidelines for Coding and Reporting**) are rules that were developed to accompany and complement the official conventions and instructions provided in the classification system. They are based on coding and sequencing instructions in the classification system, but provide additional instruction. Adherence to these guidelines when assigning diagnosis and procedure codes is required under HIPAA. ICD-9-CM (and ICD-10-CM) diagnosis codes (Volumes 1 and 2) were adopted under HIPAA for all health care settings. ICD-9-CM Volume 3 (and ICD-10-PCS) procedure codes were adopted for inpatient procedures reported by hospitals. A joint effort between the health care provider and the coder is essential to achieve complete and accurate documentation, code assignment, and reporting of diagnoses and procedures. The importance of consistent, complete documentation in the medical record cannot be overemphasized because without such documentation, accurate coding cannot be achieved. Make sure you review the entire medical record to determine the specific reason for the encounter and the conditions treated.

The guidelines use the term *encounter* to indicate all health care settings, including inpatient hospital admissions. The term *provider* is used throughout the guidelines to refer to physicians or any qualified health care

ICD-10 Alert!

The **cooperating parties for the ICD-10-CM/PCS** will continue to include AHIMA, AMA, CMS, and NCHS.

Note:

Official coding advice (e.g., interpretation of ICD-9-CM coding principles) is developed by the four cooperating parties for ICD-9-CM and is published in the Coding Clinic for ICD-9-CM by the central office of the AHA. (It is likely that the AHA will also publish official coding advice for ICD-10-CM/PCS.)

Exercise 2.6 – Official Guidelines for Coding and Reporting

Instructions: Complete each statement.

1. The guidelines for coding and reporting using ICD-9-CM (or ICD-10-CM/PCS) have been approved by the four organizations that comprise the _____.

2. The abbreviations for the four organizations that develop and approve the coding guidelines are _____, _____, _____, and _____.

3. Adherence to the coding guidelines when assigning ICD-9-CM (or ICD-10-CM/PCS) diagnosis and procedure codes is required by _____ legislation.

4. The guidelines use the term _____ to indicate all health care settings, including inpatient hospital admissions.

5. The term _____ is used throughout the guidelines to refer to physicians or any qualified health care practitioners who are legally accountable for establishing the patient's diagnosis.

practitioners who are legally accountable for establishing the patient's diagnosis. The guidelines are organized as follows:

- Structure and coding conventions (refer to Chapter 3)
- Chapter-specific ICD-9-CM (or ICD-10-CM) coding guidelines (refer to Chapter 4)
- Selection of principal and additional diagnoses and procedures for inpatient settings (refer to Chapter 5)
- Outpatient coding and reporting (refer to Chapter 6)

ICD-9-CM LEGACY CODING SYSTEM

When the ICD-10-CM and ICD-10-PCS coding systems are implemented, the *International Classification of Diseases, Ninth Revision, Clinical Modification* (ICD-9-CM) will become a **legacy coding system** (or **legacy classification system**), which means it will be used to as archive data but will no longer be supported or updated by the ICD-9-CM Coordination and Maintenance Committee. However, because ICD-9-CM has been used since 1979 in the United States to classify inpatient and outpatient/ physician office diagnoses (Volumes 1 and 2) and inpatient procedures (Volume 3), *general equivalency mappings (GEMs)* (discussed below) will be annually published by the National Center for Health Statistics (NCHS) and Centers for Medicare & Medicaid Services (CMS).

Note:

Existing coders will be considered ICD-9-CM coding experts when ICD-10-CM (and ICD-10-PCS) are implemented on October 1, 2014. That means new coders will *not* be required to learn ICD-9-CM in detail.

ICD-9-CM is over 30 years old, has outdated and obsolete terminology, uses outdated codes that produce inaccurate and limited data, and is inconsistent with current medical practice. It cannot accurately describe diagnoses or inpatient procedures of care delivered in the 21st century. ICD-9-CM does not provide the necessary detail about patients' medical conditions or procedures performed on hospitalized inpatients; thus, effective October 1, 2014, provider offices and health care facilities (e.g., hospitals) will use ICD-10-CM to code diagnoses. (Hospitals will use ICD-10-PCS to code inpatient procedures. Provider offices and outpatient health care settings will continue to use CPT and HCPCS level II to code procedures and services.)

General Equivalency Mappings (GEMs)

NCHS and CMS annually publish **general equivalence mappings (GEMs)**, which are translation dictionaries or crosswalks of codes that can be used to roughly identify ICD-10-CM codes for their ICD-9-CM equivalent codes (and vice versa). (GEMs published by the NCHS and CMS do not contain code descriptions; however, other publishers include code descriptions to facilitate code translation.) GEMs facilitate the location of corresponding diagnosis codes between two code sets. In some areas of the classification, the correlation between codes is close and since the two code sets share the conventions of organization and formatting common to both revisions of ICD, translating between them is straightforward.

EXAMPLE 1: There is straightforward correspondence between the two code sets for infectious diseases, neoplasms, eye diseases, and ear diseases.

ICD-9-CM to ICD-10-CM General Equivalency Mapping	
ICD-9-CM DIAGNOSIS CODE AND DESCRIPTION	ICD-10-CM DIAGNOSIS CODE AND DESCRIPTION
003.21 Salmonella meningitis	A02.21 Salmonella meningitis
205.01 Acute myeloid leukemia in remission	C92.01 Acute myeloid leukemia, in remission

EXAMPLE 2: In other areas of the two code sets, such as obstetrics, entire chapters are organized according to a different axis of classification and translating between them offers a series of possible codes that must be verified in the appropriate tabular list (ICD-9-CM or ICD-10-CM) or table of codes (ICD-10-PCS) to identify the correct code. (Think about translating the English language into Chinese or any other foreign language, and you will see the problems inherent in such translation.)

ICD-9-CM to ICD-10-CM General Equivalency Mapping	
ICD-9-CM DIAGNOSIS CODE AND DESCRIPTION	ICD-10-CM DIAGNOSIS CODE AND DESCRIPTION
649.50 Spotting complicating pregnancy, unspecified as to episode of care or not applicable	026.851 Spotting complicating pregnancy, first trimester
	026.852 Spotting complicating pregnancy, second trimester
	026.853 Spotting complicating pregnancy, third trimester
	026.859 Spotting complicating pregnancy, unspecified trimester

EXAMPLE 3: Procedures located in ICD-9-CM Volume 3 that correspond to ICD-10-PCS codes are contained within its general equivalent mapping.

ICD-9-CM to ICD-10-PCS General Equivalency Mapping	
ICD-9-CM PROCEDURE CODE AND DESCRIPTION	ICD-10-CM PROCEDURE CODE AND DESCRIPTION
47.11 Laparoscopic incidental appendectomy	0DTJ4ZZ Laparoscopic appendectomy

© Cengage Learning 2014

Partial Code Freeze

CMS implemented a *partial code freeze* because continuous updates and changes to existing (ICD-9-CM) and new (ICD-10-CM and ICD-10-PCS) code sets have the potential to make the transition to ICD-10-CM/PCS difficult.

- Regular code updates to ICD-9-CM, ICD-10-CM, and ICD-10-PCS were discontinued October 1, 2011.

- *Limited* code updates will be made to all code sets to capture new technology and new diseases only beginning October 1, 2012.

- All code updates to ICD-9-CM will discontinue effective October 1, 2014 because that classification system will no longer be a HIPAA standard.

- Regular code updates to ICD-10-CM and ICD-10-PCS will resume effective October 1, 2014 because those classifications become the HIPAA standard.

Exercise 2.7–ICD-9-CM LEGACY CODING SYSTEM

Instructions: Complete each statement.

1. Effective October 1, 2013, when ICD-10-CM and ICD-10-PCS are implemented, the *International Classification of Diseases, Ninth Revision, Clinical Modification* (ICD-9-CM) will become a _____.

© Cengage Learning 2014

2. The NCHS and CMS will publish _____ to facilitate the location of corresponding diagnosis codes between ICD-9-CM and ICD-10-CM.

3. ICD-9-CM was the classification (or coding) system used since _____ in the United States to classify inpatient and outpatient/physician office diagnoses (Volumes 1 and 2) and inpatient procedures (Volume 3).

4. Because ICD-9-CM is over 30 years old, it contains _____, uses outdated codes that produce inaccurate and limited data, and is inconsistent with current medical practice.

5. CMS implemented a _____ because continuous updates and changes to existing (ICD-9-CM) and new (ICD-10-CM and ICD-10-PCS) code sets have the potential to make the transition to ICD-10-CM/PCS difficult.

6. When an ICD-9-CM code maps to a single ICD-10-CM code, review of the tabular list to validate the code is optional. (TRUE or FALSE)

Instructions: Use the diagnosis GEM depicted in the table below to complete each statement.

ICD-9-CM to ICD-10-CM General Equivalency Mapping	
ICD-9-CM DIAGNOSIS CODE AND DESCRIPTION	ICD-10-CM DIAGNOSIS CODE AND DESCRIPTION
078.81 Epidemic vertigo	A88.1 Epidemic vertigo
078.82 Epidemic vomiting syndrome	R11.11 Vomiting without nausea
078.88 Other specified diseases due to *Chlamydiae*	A74.89 Other chlamydial diseases
078.89 Other specified diseases due to viruses	A96.2 Lassa fever
	A98.3 Marburg virus disease
	A98.4 Ebola virus disease
	B33.8 Other specified viral diseases

7. ICD-9-CM code 078.81 maps to ICD-10-CM code(s) _____.
8. ICD-9-CM code 078.89 maps to ICD-10-CM code(s) _____.
9. ICD-10-CM code A74.89 maps to ICD-9-CM code(s) _____.
10. ICD-10-CM code B33.8 maps to ICD-9-CM code(s) _____.

Summary

ICD-9-CM is a clinical modification of the World Health Organization's *International Classification of Diseases, Ninth Revision* (ICD-9). The ICD-9-CM Tabular List of Diseases contains 17 chapters, 2 supplemental classifications, and 4 appendices. The chapters classify diseases and injuries according to specific body systems as well as etiology. The ICD-9-CM Index to Diseases (Volume 2) is an alphabetical listing of main terms or conditions printed in boldfaced type that may be expressed as nouns, adjectives, or eponyms. ICD-9-CM Volume 2 contains an Index of Diseases, Table of Drugs and Chemicals, and Alphabetic Index to External Causes of Injury and Poisoning. The ICD-9-CM Index to Procedures and Tabular List of Procedures are included in the hospital version of commercial ICD-9-CM coding manuals.

The *International Classification of Diseases, 10th Revision, Clinical Modification* (ICD-10-CM) and the *International Classification of Diseases, 10th Revision, Procedure Coding System* (ICD-10-PCS), also abbreviated as ICD-10-CM/PCS, will replace ICD-9-CM. ICD-10-CM/PCS includes many more codes and applies to more users than ICD-9-CM because it is designed to collect data on every type of health care encounter (e.g., inpatient, outpatient, hospice, home health care, and long-term care). The ICD-10-CM tabular list of diseases and injuries contains 21 chapters (compared with 17 chapters and 2 supplementary classifications for V and E codes in the ICD-9-CM tabular list of diseases). The ICD-10-CM tabular list of diseases and injuries is a chronological list of codes contained within chapters based on body system or condition, and codes are then organized within major topic headings, categories, subcategories, and codes. ICD-10-CM disease and injury codes consist of three characters, but most are followed by a decimal point and between one and four additional characters. ICD-10-CM Index to Diseases and Injuries entries are organized according to main terms, subterms, second qualifiers, and third qualifiers.

The *International Classification of Diseases, 10th Revision, Procedure Coding System* (ICD-10-PCS) is an entirely new procedure classification system developed by the Centers for Medicare & Medicaid Services (CMS) for use in the United States for inpatient hospital settings *only*, and will replace Volume 3 of ICD-9-CM. ICD-10-PCS uses a multiaxial 7-character alphanumeric code structure (e.g., 047K04Z) that provides a unique code for all substantially different procedures. It also allows new procedures to be easily incorporated as new codes. ICD-10-PCS contains more than 87,000 seven-character alphanumeric procedure codes. (ICD-9-CM has about 4,000 three- or four-digit numeric procedure codes.)

Medical necessity is the measure of whether a health care procedure or service is appropriate for the diagnosis and/or treatment of a condition. This decision-making process is based on the payer's contractual language and the treating provider's documentation. Generally, the following criteria are used to determine medical necessity: purpose, scope, evidence, and value.

The DHHS agencies CMS and NCHS prepare guidelines for coding and reporting using the ICD-9-CM and ICD-10-CM/PCS. The guidelines are approved by the four organizations that comprise the cooperating parties for the ICD-9-CM and ICD-10-CM/PCS. The organizations include the AHA, AHIMA, CMS, and NCHS. The guidelines should be used as a companion document when coding from ICD-9-CM or ICD-10-CM/PCS. The guidelines are rules that were developed to accompany and complement the official conventions and instructions provided in ICD-9-CM. They are based on coding and sequencing instructions in ICD-9-CM and ICD-10-CM/PCS, but provide additional instruction. Adherence to these guidelines when assigning ICD-9-CM or ICD-10-CM/PCS diagnosis and procedure codes is required under HIPAA.

ICD-9-CM diagnosis codes (Volumes 1 and 2) have been adopted under HIPAA for all health care settings, and ICD-9-CM Volume 3 procedure codes have been adopted for inpatient procedures reported by hospitals. (ICD-10-CM/PCS will replace ICD-9-CM.) A joint effort between the health care provider and the coder is essential to achieving complete and accurate documentation, code assignment, and reporting of diagnoses and procedures. Consistent, complete documentation in the patient record is crucial because without such documentation, accurate codes cannot be assigned. In addition, the entire patient record must be reviewed to determine the specific reason for the encounter and the conditions treated so that appropriate codes are assigned.

When the ICD-10-CM (and ICD-10-PCS) coding systems are implemented, ICD-9-CM will become a *legacy coding system (or legacy classification system),* which means it will be used as archive data but it will no longer be supported or updated. *General equivalency mappings (GEMs),* which are translation dictionaries or crosswalks of codes that can be used to roughly identify ICD-10-CM codes for their ICD-9-CM equivalent codes (and vice versa), will be annually published by NCHS and CMS.

Internet Links

AHA Central Office: *www.ahacentraloffice.org*

***Federal Register* Listserv:** At *listserv.access.gpo.gov*, click on the online mailing list archives link, click on the FEDREGTOC-L link, and click on the Join or leave the list (or change settings) link to register to receive the daily *Federal Register* table of contents via e-mail. The document contains the Centers for Medicare and Medicaid Services final rule about implementation of ICD-10-CM and ICD-10-PCS.

ICD-9-CM encoder (free): *www.icd9coding.com*

ICD-9-CM encoders (subscription-based): *www.codecorrect.com www.encoderpro.com* (free trial available)

ICD-9-CM and ICD-10 searchable indexes and tabular lists (free or sample use): *icd9cm.chrisendres.com www.findacode.com*

ICD-9-CM and ICD-10-CM/PCS updates: Go to *www.cdc.gov*, click on the More Data & Statistics link, click on the Disease Classification link, and click on any of the ICD links.

ICD-10-CM/PCS: Go to *www.cms.gov*, click on Medicare, click on ICD-10, and click on links in the first column to locate coding manual PDF files, general equivalency mappings (GEMs), and more.

Ingenix ICD-10 Prepared: Go to *www.icd10prepared.com* to locate ICD-10 blogs, FAQs, coding scenarios, and more.

Official version of ICD-9-CM and ICD-10-CM/PCS from the U.S. Government Bookstore: *bookstore .gpo.gov*

Study Checklist

❏ Read this textbook chapter and highlight key concepts.

❏ Create an index card for each key term.

❏ Access the chapter Internet links to learn more about concepts.

❏ Complete the chapter review, verifying answers with your instructor.

❏ Complete WebTutor assignments and take online quizzes.

❏ Complete Workbook chapter, verifying answers with your instructor.

❏ Go to *www.cengagebrain.com* to access StudyWARE™ and the Premium Website. Login instructions are located in this textbook's Preface and on the Printed Access Card.

❏ Form a study group with classmates to discuss chapter concepts in preparation for an exam.

Review

Multiple Choice

Instructions: Circle the most appropriate response.

1. When ICD-9-CM is published as a single coding manual that contains multiple volumes, in which order are the volumes sequenced?
   a. Index to Diseases, Tabular List of Diseases, and Index to Procedures and Tabular List of Procedures
   b. Tabular List of Diseases and Index to Diseases, Index to Procedures, Tabular List of Procedures, and Index to Procedures
   c. Tabular List of Diseases, Index to Diseases, Index to Procedures, and Tabular List of Procedures
   d. Tabular List of Diseases, Index to Diseases, Tabular List of Procedures, and Index to Procedures

2. Which entities work together to coordinate official ICD-9-CM (or ICD-10-CM) disease classification activities?
   a. National Center for Health Statistics (NCHS) and the Centers for Medicare and Medicaid Services (CMS)
   b. National Center for Health Statistics (NCHS) with the World Health Organization (WHO)
   c. U.S. Department of Health & Human Services (DHHS)
   d. World Health Organization (WHO)

3. Which ICD-9-CM resource would provide assistance regarding interpreting tumor tissue type?
   a. Appendix A   b. Appendix C   c. Appendix D   d. Appendix E

4. *Outcome of delivery, follow-up, history*, and *vaccination* are examples of ICD-9-CM:
   a. essential modifiers used to locate V codes.
   b. main terms used to locate E codes.
   c. main terms used to locate V codes.
   d. subterms used to locate E codes.

5. The hypertension table is located in the ICD-9-CM:
   a. Volume 1, Tabular List of Diseases.
   b. Volume 1, Appendices.
   c. Volume 2, Index to Diseases.
   d. Volume 3, Tabular List of Procedures and Index to Procedures.

6. Review the Index to Diseases entry for main term *Contusion*, and locate subterm "arm" below it. Which ICD-9-CM code is assigned to the second qualifier?
   a. 923.03   b. 923.09   c. 923.9   d. 924.9

7. The ICD-9-CM (or ICD-10-PCS) Index to Procedures and Tabular List of Procedures are used to classify _____ procedures and services.
   a. emergency department
   b. inpatient
   c. outpatient
   d. physician office

8. Current Procedural Terminology (CPT) is published by the:
   a. American Medical Association (AMA).
   b. Centers for Medicare and Medicaid Services (CMS).
   c. National Center for Health Statistics (NCHS).
   d. World Health Organization (WHO).

9. HIPAA requires ICD-9-CM (or ICD-10-CM) _____ codes to be adopted for use by all health care settings and ICD-9-CM (or ICD-10-PCS) _____ codes to be adopted for use by acute care hospitals for the purpose of classifying inpatient care.
   a. all, all
   b. all, procedure
   c. diagnosis, procedure
   d. procedure, diagnosis

10. Adhering to official coding guidelines is:
    a. at the discretion of a health care facility's operating procedures.
    b. mandated by the cooperating parties.
    c. not necessary if the facility has a 90 percent or higher coding accuracy rate.
    d. required by the Health Insurance Portability and Accountability Act.

Matching

Instructions: Match the format in Column 2 with each line of the ICD-9-CM Tabular List of Diseases entry in Column 1.

Tabular List of Diseases Entry

_____ 11. DISEASES OF THE NERVOUS SYSTEM
AND SENSE ORGANS (320-389)

_____ 12. DISEASES OF THE EAR AND MASTOID
PROCESS (380-389)

_____ 13.   380 Disorders of external ear

_____ 14.   380.0 Perichondritis and
chondritis of pinna

_____ 15.   380.00 Perichondritis of pinna,
unspecified

Format

a. Category code
b. Chapter title
c. Section title
d. Subcategory code
e. Subclassification code

Coding Practice

Instructions: Underline the main term and assign the appropriate ICD-9-CM (or ICD-10-CM/PCS) code. (Adobe *.pdf files of the ICD-10-CM and ICD-10-PCS coding manuals can be found at http://www.cms.gov.)

ICD-9-CM and ICD-10-CM Index to Diseases (and Injuries) and Tabular List of Diseases (and Injuries)

ICD-9-CM	ICD-10-CM	
_____	_____	16. Abdominal hernia
_____	_____	17. Abnormal nonfasting glucose tolerance test
_____	_____	18. Acute otitis media
_____	_____	19. Hyperplasia of endometrium
_____	_____	20. Fracture, right humerus (initial encounter)
_____	_____	21. Congenital fibrocystic disease of the lung
_____	_____	22. Degenerative arthritis
_____	_____	23. Fibrocystic disease of right and left breasts
_____	_____	24. Hereditary epistaxis
_____	_____	25. Personal history of cancer

ICD-9-CM Index to Procedures and Tabular List of Procedures and ICD-10-PCS Index and Tables

ICD-9-CM	ICD-10-PCS	
_____	_____	26. Open biopsy, left axillary lymph node
_____	_____	27. Open cholecystectomy, total
_____	_____	28. Cystoscopy
_____	_____	29. Exploratory laparotomy, open
_____	_____	30. Intravenous right pyelogram
_____	_____	31. Incidental appendectomy (open)
_____	_____	32. Open biopsy of left frontal nasal sinus
_____	_____	33. Percutaneous biopsy of prostate
_____	_____	34. Right frontal craniotomy (open approach)
_____	_____	35. Transurethral biopsy of bladder

ICD-9-CM and ICD-10-CM/PCS Coding Conventions

Chapter Outline

Format and Typeface
Eponyms
Abbreviations
Punctuation
Boxed Notes
Tables
Includes Notes
Excludes Notes

Inclusion Terms
Other, Other Specified, and Unspecified Codes
Etiology and Manifestation Rules
And
Due to
In
With
Cross-References

Chapter Objectives

At the conclusion of this chapter, the student should be able to:

- Define key terms.
- List ICD-9-CM and ICD-10-CM/PCS coding conventions.
- Explain ICD-9-CM and ICD-10-CM/PCS coding conventions.
- Interpret ICD-9-CM and ICD-10-CM/PCS coding conventions to assign codes accurately.

Key Terms

coding conventions
  abbreviations
    NEC (not elsewhere classifiable)
    NOS (not otherwise specified)
  and
  boxed note
  cross-references
    see
    see also
    see category

see condition
due to
eponym
etiology and manifestation rules
  code first underlying disease
  code, if applicable, any causal condition first
  in diseases classified elsewhere
  use additional code

excludes note (ICD-9-CM)
Excludes1 note (ICD-10-CM)
Excludes2 note (ICD-10-CM)
format
in
includes note
inclusion term
other and other specified

punctuation
  colon
  parentheses
  slanted brackets
  square brackets
unspecified code
with
manifestation
modifier
tables
trust the index

Introduction •

The ICD-9-CM, ICD-10-CM, and ICD-10-PCS coding conventions (rules) can usually be found at the beginning of any ICD-9-CM, ICD-10-CM or ICD-10-PCS coding manual. Coders are required to reference this material when reviewing case scenarios (and patient records) to assign ICD-9-CM, ICD-10-CM, and ICD-10-PCS codes. It is also helpful to coders when health care providers become familiar with coding conventions (and guidelines). When a coder initiates a physician query, an understanding of coding conventions and guidelines helps ensure the assignment of accurate codes for certain conditions and diagnoses.

Coding conventions for ICD-9-CM, ICD-10-CM, and ICD-10-PCS are general rules used in the classification, and they are independent of the coding guidelines (covered in Chapters 2, 4, 5, and 6 of this textbook). The conventions are incorporated into ICD-9-CM, ICD-10-CM, and ICD-10-PCS as instructional notes, and they include the following:

> ● **Note:**
>
> When reviewing examples and completing exercises and review questions in this chapter, use your ICD-9-CM coding manual to locate disease and procedure index entries and verify codes in the tabular lists.

- Format and typeface
- Eponyms
- Abbreviations
- Punctuation
- Boxed notes
- Tables

- Includes and excludes notes and inclusion terms
- Other, other specified, and unspecified codes
- Etiology and manifestation rules
- And

- Due to
- In
- With
- Cross-references, including, *see*, *see also*, *see* category, and *see* condition

Format and Typeface

Each ICD-9-CM, ICD-10-CM, and ICD-10-PCS index uses an indented **format** for ease in reference (Figure 3-1). All ICD-9-CM and ICD-10-CM Index to Diseases subterms associated with an index entry's main term are indented two spaces, with any 2nd and 3rd qualifiers associated with the main term further indented by two and four spaces, respectively. In addition, if an index entry requires more than one line, the additional text is printed on the next line and indented five spaces.

Boldface type is used for main term entries in the alphabetic index and all codes and descriptions in the tabular list. Italicized type is used for all exclusion notes and to identify manifestation codes, which are codes that should not be reported as the first-listed (principal) diagnoses.

EXAMPLE 1: ICD-9-CM INDEX TO DISEASES—INDENTED FORMAT: Locate main term *ulcer* in the ICD-9-CM Index to Diseases, and notice that subterm *aphthous (oral) (recurrent) 528.2* is indented 2 spaces below the "U" of main term *ulcer*. Then, notice that second qualifier *genital organ(s)* is further indented two spaces.

EXAMPLE 2: ICD-10-CM INDEX TO DISEASES AND INJURIES—INDENTED FORMAT: Locate main term *ulcer* in the ICD-10-CM Index to Diseases and Injuries, and notice that subterm *aphthous (oral) (recurrent) K12.0* is indented 2 spaces below the "U" of main term *ulcer*. Then, notice that second qualifier *genital organ(s)* is further indented two spaces.

Additional terms are indented below the term to which they are linked in the ICD-9-CM and ICD-10-CM tabular lists; and if a definition or disease requires more than one line, that text is printed on the next line and indented five spaces.

EXAMPLE 1: ICD-9-CM TABULAR LIST OF DISEASES—INDENTED FORMAT: Locate code *528.2 Oral Aphthae* in the ICD-9-CM Tabular List of Diseases, and notice that its synonyms (e.g., canker sore) and the *excludes* note is indented.

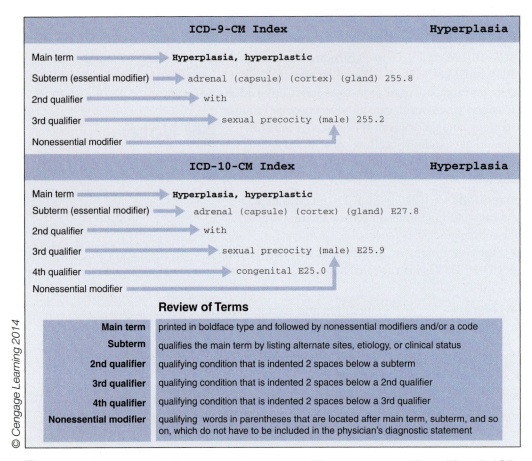

Figure 3-1 Display of main terms, subterms, qualifiers, nonessential modifiers in ICD-9-CM Index to Diseases and ICD-10-CM Index to Diseases and Injuries.

EXAMPLE 2: ICD-10-CM TABULAR LIST OF DISEASES—INDENTED FORMAT: Locate code *K12.0 Recurrent Oral Aphthae* in the ICD-10-CM Tabular List of Diseases, and notice that its synonyms (e.g., Bednar's aphthae) are indented.

The indented format is also found in the ICD-9-CM Index to Procedures and Tabular List of Procedures (Volume 3) and the ICD-10-PCS index.

EXAMPLE 1: ICD-9-CM INDEX TO PROCEDURES— INDENTED FORMAT: Locate main term *Laparoscopy* in the ICD-9-CM Index to Procedures, and notice that subterm *with* is indented two spaces below main term *Laparoscopy* and that 2nd qualifier *biopsy* is indented two spaces below subterm *with*.

EXAMPLE 2: ICD-10-PCS INDEX TO PROCEDURES— INDENTED FORMAT: Locate main term *Laparotomy* in the ICD-10-PCS Index to Procedures, and notice that subterm *Drainage* is indented two spaces below the "L" of *Laparotomy*.

EXAMPLE 3: ICD-9-CM TABULAR LIST OF PROCEDURES— INDENTED FORMAT: Locate code *54.24 Closed (percutaneous) (needle) biopsy of intra-abdominal mass* in the ICD-9-CM Tabular List of Procedures, and notice that its synonyms and excludes note are indented.

Note:

The indented format is not used in the ICD-10-PCS tables. Locate Table 001 (on the first page of the Medical and Surgical Section, Central Nervous System 001–00X), and notice that indenting is not used in the ICD-10-PCS Tables. (ICD-10-PCS Tables are organized entirely differently as compared with ICD-9-CM's Tabular List of Procedures. Each page of Tables contains rows that specify the valid combinations of code values.)

Exercise 3.1 – Format

Instructions: Assign the ICD code(s) to each statement below. Make sure that you appropriately interpret the use of the indented format in the ICD-9-CM, ICD-10-CM, and ICD-10-PCS indexes.

ICD-9-CM　　　**ICD-10-CM/PCS**

_____ _____ **1.** Acariasis infestation

_____ _____ **2.** Acquired pilaris pityriasis

_____ _____ **3.** Admission for adjustment of artificial leg

_____ _____ **4.** Adjustment disorder with anxiety

_____ _____ **5.** Anorexia nervosa

_____ _____ **6.** High forceps delivery

_____ _____ **7.** Laser interstitial thermal therapy (LITT) destruction, left breast tissue, with MRI guidance

_____ _____ **8.** Termination of pregnancy (by) dilation and curettage

_____ _____ **9.** Heart transplantation, allogenic

_____ _____ **10.** Ultrasonography, abdomen

● ICD-10 Alert!

ICD-10-CM Official Guidelines for Coding and Reporting _include the following new coding conventions related to its format and structure:_

- **Format and structure.** The ICD-10-CM Tabular List contains categories, subcategories, and codes. Characters for categories, subcategories and codes may be either a letter or a number. All categories are 3 characters. A three-character category that has no further subdivision is equivalent to a code. Subcategories are either 4 or 5 characters. Codes may be 3, 4, 5, 6 or 7 characters. That is, each level of subdivision after a category is a subcategory. The final level of subdivision is a code. Codes that have applicable 7th characters are still referred to as codes, not subcategories. A code that has an applicable 7th character is considered invalid without the 7th character. The ICD-10-CM uses an indented format for ease in reference.

- **Use of codes for reporting purposes.** For reporting purposes, only codes are permissible (not categories or subcategories), and any applicable 7th character is required.

- **Placeholder character.** The ICD-10-CM utilizes a placeholder character "X". The "X" is used as a placeholder at certain codes to allow for future expansion. An example of this is at the poisoning, adverse effect and underdosing codes, categories T36–T50. Where a placeholder exists, the "X" must be used in order for the code to be considered a valid code.

- **Seventh characters.** Certain ICD-10-CM categories contain applicable 7th characters, which are required for all codes within the category (or as notes in the tabular list instruct). The 7th character must always be located in the 7th-character data field. If a code that requires a 7th character is not 6 characters in length, the placeholder "X" is entered to fill in the empty character(s) (e.g., M48.46xS, reporting sequelae of fracture for previous fatigue fracture of lumbar vertebrae; an additional code is assigned to the sequelae, such as pain).

(continues)

ICD-10 Alert! (continued)

ICD-10-PCS Official Guidelines for Coding and Reporting include the following new coding conventions related to its format and structure:

- ICD-10-PCS codes are 7 characters in length. Each code contains 7 characters, and each character is an axis of classification that specifies information about the procedure performed. Within a defined code range, a character specifies the same type of information in that axis of classification. For example, in the SAMPLE ICD-10-PCS TABLE at the end of this ICD-10 Alert!, the fifth axis of classification specifies an open or percutaneous approach.

- An axis of classification is used. One of 34 possible values is assigned to each axis of classification in the ICD-10-PCS 7-character code. They include numbers 0 through 9 and letters of the alphabet (except for letters I and O because they are easily confused with numbers 1 and 0). The number of unique values used in an axis of classification differs as needed. For example, in the SAMPLE ICD-10-PCS TABLE at the end of this ICD-10 Alert!, just two different values specify the approach. (In ICD-10-PCS, up to seven values are used to specify the approach, depending on the axis of classification.)

- Valid values for an axis of classification can be added as needed. For example, in the SAMPLE ICD-10-PCS TABLE at the end of this ICD-10 Alert!, values for up to three different devices can be assigned to the axis of classification, but if a new device is invented for the purpose of performing procedures on subcutaneous tissue and fascia via insertion, there is room to add a new device value (number or letter) to that axis of classification.

- The meaning of any single value is a combination of its axis of classification and any preceding values on which it may be dependent. For example, in the SAMPLE ICD-10-PCS TABLE at the end of this ICD-10 Alert!, Section 0 refers to "Medical and Surgical," value J refers to "subcutaneous tissue and fascia," and value H refers to "insertion."

- As ICD-10-PCS is expanded to become increasingly more detailed, adding more values will depend on preceding values for their meaning. For example, in the SAMPLE ICD-10-PCS TABLE at the end of this ICD-10 Alert!, it would not make sense to add a device value for use of a Stryker saw to the axis of classification (because a Stryker saw is used on bone, not subcutaneous tissue and fascia).

- The purpose of the alphabetic index is to locate the appropriate table that contains all information necessary to construct a procedure code. For example, the ICD-10-PCS index often contains just the first 3 or 4 characters of a code; thus the ICD-10-PCS Tables must be consulted to report a valid code (so that the remaining 3 characters needed to create a 7-character code can be assigned).

- It is not required that the ICD-10-PCS index be referenced first, before proceeding to the tables to complete the code. A valid code may be selected directly from the ICD-10-PCS tables.

- All 7 characters must be specified to report a valid ICD-10-PCS code. If documentation is incomplete for coding purposes, the physician should be queried to obtain necessary information.

- Within an ICD-10-PCS table, valid codes include all combinations of choices in character fields 4–7 that are contained in the same row of the table. For example, in the SAMPLE ICD-10-PCS TABLE at the end of this ICD-10 Alert!, 0JHT3VZ is a valid code, but 0JHW3VZ is not a valid code. And, when used in a code description means "and/or". For example, in the SAMPLE ICD-10-PCS TABLE at the end of this ICD-10 Alert!, Subcutaneous Tissue and Fascia means "subcutaneous tissue and/or fascia".

- "And," when used in a code description, means "and/or." For example, "Lower Arm and Wrist Muscle" means lower arm and/or wrist muscle.

- Many of the terms used to construct ICD-10-PCS codes are defined within the classification system. It is the coder's responsibility to interpret documentation in the patient record, and the physician is not expected to use the terms classified in ICD-10-PCS code descriptions. This also means that the coder is not required to query a physician when the correlation between patient record documentation and the defined ICD-10-PCS terms is clear.

  ○ For example, when the physician documents "placing" or "introducing" a radioactive element into subcutaneous fascia of the right upper extremity, the coder can independently correlate "placing" and "introducing" to the root operation "Insertion" without querying the physician for clarification.

○ For example, when the physician documents "partial resection" the coder can independently correlate "partial resection" to root operation Excision without querying the physician for clarification.

SAMPLE ICD-10-PCS TABLE			
SECTION	0	Medical and Surgical	
BODY SYSTEM	J	Subcutaneous Tissue and Fascia	
OPERATION	H	*Insertion*: putting in a nonbiological appliance that monitors, assists, performs, or prevents a physiological function but does not physically take the place of a body part	
Body Part	**Approach**	**Device**	**Qualifier**
S Subcutaneous Tissue and Fascia, Head and Neck	0 Open	1 Radioactive Element	Z No Qualifier
V Subcutaneous Tissue and Fascia, Upper Extremity	3 Percutaneous	3 Infusion Device	
W Subcutaneous Tissue and Fascia, Lower Extremity			
T Subcutaneous Tissue and Fascia, Trunk	0 Open 3 Percutaneous	1 Radioactive Element 3 Infusion Device V Infusion Pump	Z No Qualifier

Courtesy of the Centers for Medicare & Medicaid Services, www.cms.hhs.gov

Eponyms

Eponyms are diseases or syndromes that are named for people. They are listed in appropriate alphabetical sequence as main terms in the ICD-9-CM and ICD-10-CM Index to Diseases and the ICD-9-CM Index to Procedures. They are also listed as subterms below main terms *Disease, Syndrome,* and *Operation* in the index. A description of the disease, syndrome, or procedure is usually included in parentheses following the eponym. (Both tabular lists usually list the eponym in the code description.)

ICD-10 Alert!

There are no eponyms (e.g., Billroth procedure) or common procedure terms (e.g., appendectomy) in ICD-10-PCS.

EXAMPLE 1: ICD-9-CM INDEX TO DISEASES—EPONYM: The Index to Diseases entry for *Barlow's syndrome* can be located in alphabetical order or under main term *Syndrome*. (Although the Tabular List of Diseases entry for code 424.0 does not list *Barlow's syndrome*, other eponyms are routinely listed in the tabular list.)

EXAMPLE 2: ICD-10-CM INDEX TO DISEASES—EPONYM: The Index to Diseases and Injuries entry for *Barlow's syndrome* can be located in alphabetic order. However, it can be located under main term *Disease*. (Although the Tabular List of Diseases entry for code E54 does not list Barlow's syndrome, other eponyms are routinely listed in the tabular list.)

EXAMPLE 3: ICD-9-CM INDEX TO PROCEDURES—EPONYM: The Index to Procedures entry for *Billroth I operation* can be located in alphabetical order or under main term *Operation*. (The Tabular List of Procedures entry for code 43.6 also lists *Billroth I operation*.)

Exercise 3.2 – Eponyms

Instructions: Assign the ICD code(s) to each statement below. Make sure that you appropriately interpret the use of eponyms in the ICD-9-CM disease and procedure indexes and the ICD-10-CM disease index. (There are no eponyms in ICD-10-PCS, which means you will not enter ICD-10-PCS codes in 6–10.)

ICD-9-CM	ICD-10-CM	
_____	_____	**1.** Costen's complex
_____	_____	**2.** Madelung's deformity
_____	_____	**3.** Coats' disease
_____	_____	**4.** Kaschin-Beck disease
_____	_____	**5.** Meniere's disease, right ear
_____	n/a	**6.** Mediterranean tick fever
_____	n/a	**7.** Caldwell-Luc operation
_____	n/a	**8.** Roux-Goldthwait operation
_____	n/a	**9.** Masters two-step stress test
_____	n/a	**10.** Millin-Read operation

Abbreviations

The ICD-9-CM and ICD-10-CM indexes and tabular lists contain **abbreviations** to save space. The abbreviation **NEC (not elsewhere classifiable)** means "other" or "other specified" and identifies codes that are to be assigned when information needed to assign a more specific code cannot be located in the code book. When a specific code is not available in the index for a condition, the coder is directed to the "other specified" code in the tabular lists.

> **ICD-10 Alert!**
>
> The NEC abbreviation does not appear in the ICD-10-PCS Index or Tables.

EXAMPLE 1: ICD-9-CM INDEX TO DISEASES—NEC ABBREVIATON: The Index to Diseases entry for *impediment, speech* contains the NEC abbreviation in front of code 784.5, which means a more specific code cannot be assigned in the code book. When verifying code 784.5 in the Tabular List of Diseases, notice that the code description is *Other speech disturbance* and that the NEC abbreviation does not appear in the code description. A fifth digit is also required, so code 784.59 is assigned.

EXAMPLE 2: ICD-9-CM TABULAR LIST OF DISEASES—NEC ABBREVIATION: Locate code 008.67 in the tabular list, and notice that the NEC abbreviation is included in the code description.

EXAMPLE 3: ICD-9-CM INDEX TO PROCEDURES—NEC ABBREVIATION: The Index to Procedures entry for *installation, genitourinary* contains the NEC abbreviation in front of code 96.49, which means a more specific code cannot be assigned in the code book. When verifying code 96.49 in the Tabular List of Procedures, notice that the code description is *Other genitourinary instillation.* The NEC abbreviation does not appear in the code description. Thus, code 96.49 is assigned to *genitourinary instillation* because the Index to Procedures NEC abbreviation directs the coder to that code.

EXAMPLE 4: ICD-10-CM INDEX TO DISEASES AND INJURIES—NEC ABBREVIATION: The Index to Diseases and Injuries entry for *aberrant, artery, basilar* contains the NEC abbreviation in front of code Q28.1, which means a more specific code cannot be assigned in the code book. When verifying code Q28.1 in the Tabular List of Diseases and Injuries, notice that the code description is *Other malformations of precerebral vessels* and that the NEC abbreviation does not appear in the code description. Code Q28.1 is assigned to *aberrant basilar artery* because the Index to Diseases NEC abbreviation directs the coder to that code.

EXAMPLE 5: ICD-10-CM TABULAR LIST OF DISEASES AND INJURIES—NEC ABBREVIATION:

Locate code Q28.8 in the tabular list, and notice that the NEC abbreviation is included next to *Congenital aneurysm, specified site NEC* below the code description.

 The ICD-9-CM tabular lists and ICD-10-CM index and tabular list contain the abbreviation **NOS (not otherwise specified)**, which is the equivalent of "unspecified." It identifies codes that are to be assigned when information needed to assign a more specific code cannot be obtained from the provider. Because selecting a code from the index based on limited documentation results in the coder being directed to an "unspecified" code in the tabular list, the coder should contact the physician to request that additional documentation be provided so that a more specific diagnosis and/or procedure code can be assigned. A review of the patient record to assign a more specific code is also an important part of the coding process (e.g., laboratory data, radiology reports, operative report, pathology report).

EXAMPLE 1: ICD-9-CM TABULAR LIST OF DISEASES—
NOS ABBREVIATION: Locate code 008.00 in the Tabular List of Diseases, notice the NOS abbreviation appears after *E. coli enteritis*.

EXAMPLE 2: ICD-9-CM TABULAR LIST
OF PROCEDURES—NOS ABBREVIATION: The Index to Procedures entry for *gastric bypass* directs the coder to 44.39, which is an *unspecified* code number. Notice the indented subterms; the provider should specify the type of *gastric bypass* so that a more specific code can be assigned. When verifying code 44.39 in the Tabular List of Procedures, notice that the code description is *Other gastroenterostomy* and that the NOS abbreviation appears next to the *Gastrojejunostomy without gastrectomy* entry in the code description.

EXAMPLE 3: ICD-10-CM INDEX TO DISEASES AND INJURIES—NOS ABBREVIATION: The index entry for *Bronchomycosis NOS B49 [J99]* directs the coder to B49, which is an *unspecified* code number.

EXAMPLE 4: ICD-10-CM TABULAR LIST OF DISEASES AND INJURIES—NOS ABBREVIATION:
Locate code A03.9 in the tabular list, and notice the NOS abbreviation appears after *dysentery*.

Note:

It is appropriate to ask the physician for clarification about a diagnosis if the patient's record contains documentation (e.g., laboratory data) to support the assignment of a more specific code.

ICD-10 Alert!

The NOS abbreviation does not appear in the ICD-10-PCS Index or Tables.

Exercise 3.3 – Abbreviations

Instructions: Assign the ICD code(s) to each statement below. Make sure that you appropriately interpret the use of abbreviations in the ICD-9-CM disease and procedure indexes and the ICD-10-CM disease index. (The NEC and NOS abbreviations are not used in ICD-10-PCS, which means you will not enter ICD-10-PCS codes in items 6–10.)

ICD-9-CM	ICD-10-CM	
_____	_____	**1.** Purpura
_____	_____	**2.** Femoral hernia

(continues)

Exercise 3.3 *(continued)*

ICD-9-CM	ICD-10-CM	
_____	_____	**3.** ST elevation myocardial infarction, anterior wall
_____	_____	**4.** Hyperinsulinism
_____	_____	**5.** Laceration, right eyeball (initial encounter)
_____	n/a	**6.** Punch biopsy of cervix
_____	n/a	**7.** Bilateral orchidectomy
_____	n/a	**8.** Upper arm reattachment
_____	n/a	**9.** Irrigation of bronchus
_____	n/a	**10.** Surgical removal of tooth

Punctuation

ICD-9-CM and ICD-10-CM include the following **punctuation**:

- Slanted brackets
- Square brackets
- Parentheses
- Colons

Slanted brackets are used in the ICD-9-CM Index to Diseases to identify manifestation codes. In the ICD-10-CM Index to Diseases and Injuries, square brackets are used to identify manifestation codes. A **manifestation** is a condition that occurs as the result of another condition, and manifestation codes are always reported as secondary codes. The code and description may or may not appear in italics in the tabular list. When code descriptions are not italicized in the tabular list, make sure you sequence the codes according to the sequence in the index entry.

 EXAMPLE 1: ICD-9-CM INDEX TO DISEASES—SLANTED BRACKETS (and Tabular List of Diseases code and description that is italicized): The Index to Diseases entry for *neuritis, amyloid, any site* indicates that two codes should be reported: 277.39 and 357.4. Because code 357.4 appears in slanted brackets, it is reported as a secondary code. Then, when verifying codes 277.39 and 357.4 in the Tabular List of Diseases, notice that the description for code 277.39 does not instruct you to assign code 357.4. However, the description for code 357.4 is italicized and includes a *Code first underlying disease,* as: instruction that prompts you to report code 277.39 first. Therefore, report code 277.39 followed by code 357.4.

EXAMPLE 2: ICD-9-CM INDEX TO DISEASES—SLANTED BRACKETS (and Tabular List of Diseases code and description that is not italicized): The Index to Diseases entry for *scleritis tuberculous* indicates that two codes should be reported: 017.3 and 379.09. Because code 379.09 appears in slanted brackets, it is reported as a secondary code. When verifying codes 017.3 and 379.09 in the Tabular List of Diseases, notice that the code and description for 379.09 are not italicized and that

ICD-10 Alert!

Square brackets enclose manifestation codes in the ICD-10-CM Index to Diseases and Injuries (instead of slanted brackets as used in the ICD-9-CM Index to Diseases).

Note:

When reporting manifestation codes, do not enclose them in slanted brackets.

CORRECT: 277.39
      357.4
INCORRECT: 277.39
      [357.4]

there is no instruction to *code first underlying disease*. However, subcategory code 017.3 instructs you to *use additional code to identify manifestation* . . .; and in this case, the code for episcleritis (379.09) is assigned as the secondary code. (Subcategory code 017.3 requires the assignment of a fifth digit, which is located under the section heading *Tuberculosis 010—018* in the Tabular List of Diseases).

When the index entry for a condition contains two codes, one of which is in slanted italics, and the tabular list does not italicize the code and description, you must *trust the index* and sequence the codes according to the index entry. (The *trust the index* concept is further discussed later in this chapter.)

Square brackets are used in the ICD-9-CM and ICD-10-CM tabular lists to enclose abbreviations, synonyms, alternative wording, or explanatory phrases. Square brackets are also used to identify manifestation codes in the ICD-10-CM Index to Diseases and Injuries.

EXAMPLE 1: ICD-9-CM TABULAR LIST OF DISEASES—SQUARE BRACKETS: In the description for code subcategory 493.2, the abbreviation for *chronic obstructive pulmonary disease* is included in square brackets as [COPD].

EXAMPLE 2: ICD-9-CM TABULAR LIST OF PROCEDURES—SQUARE BRACKETS: In the description for code 35.5, *extracorporeal circulation* and *heart-lung machine* are included in square brackets as synonyms for *cardiopulmonary bypass*.

EXAMPLE 3: ICD-10-CM INDEX TO DISEASES AND INJURIES—SQUARE BRACKETS: The index entry for *Amyloid heart (disease) E85.4 [I43]* indicates that two codes should be reported: E85.4 and I43. Because code I43 appears in square brackets, it is reported as a secondary code. When verifying code I43 in the tabular list, notice that its description is italicized and a *Code first underlying disease, such as*: instruction is provided, prompting you to report code I43 as the second code.

The index entry for *Abnormal, electrocardiogram [ECG] [EKG] R94.31* encloses abbreviations in square brackets.

EXAMPLE 4: ICD-10-CM TABULAR LIST OF DISEASES AND INJURIES—SQUARE BRACKETS: Code I45.89 uses square brackets to enclosed the abbreviation for atrioventricular as [AV].

Parentheses are used in both the ICD-9-CM and ICD-10-CM indexes and tabular lists and ICD-10-PCS index to enclose nonessential modifiers, which are supplementary words that may be present in or absent from the physician's statement of a disease or procedure without affecting the code number to which it is assigned.

ICD-10 Alert!

There is limited use of punctuation in the ICD-10-PCS Index and Tables.

EXAMPLE 1: ICD-9-CM INDEX TO DISEASES—PARENTHESES: The terms located in parentheses after the main term *Galactosemia* are nonessential modifiers that may be present in or absent from the provider's diagnostic statement. This means that code 271.1 is assigned for any of the following diagnostic statements:

- Galactosemia
- Classic galactosemia
- Congenital galactosemia

EXAMPLE 2: ICD-9-CM TABULAR LIST OF DISEASES—PARENTHESES: The terms located in parentheses after the inclusion terms located below 4- and 5-digit codes are nonessential modifiers that may be present in or absent from the provider's diagnostic statement. This means that code 002.0 is assigned for any of the following diagnostic statements:

- Typhoid
- Typhoid fever
- Typhoid infection

The bracketed phrase *any site* next to *Typhoid (fever) (infection)* under code 002.0 is an explanatory phrase for code 002.0 because typhoid fever is a contagious infection caused by the *Salmonella typhi* bacterium that affects the whole body.

EXAMPLE 3: ICD-9-CM INDEX TO PROCEDURES—PARENTHESES: The terms located in parentheses after the main term *Injection* and subterm *anti-D* may be present in or absent from the provider's diagnostic statement. This means that code 99.11 is assigned for any of the following procedural statements:

- Injection of anti-D globulin into muscle (or vein)

- Intravenous injection of anti-D globulin

- Intramuscular injection of anti-D globulin

- Local injection of anti-D globulin

- Systemic injection of anti-D globulin

- Injection of anti-D globulin

- Injection of Rhesus anti-D globulin

EXAMPLE 4: ICD-9-CM TABULAR LIST OF PROCEDURES—PARENTHESES: When you verify code 99.11 in the Tabular List of Procedures, the term in parentheses, (Rhesus), may be present in or absent from the provider's procedural statement.

EXAMPLE 5: ICD-10-CM INDEX TO DISEASES AND INJURIES—PARENTHESES: Index entry *abasia (-astasia) (hysterical) F44.4* contains two nonessential modifiers in parentheses, which means that the terms may be present or absent from the provider's diagnostic statement.

EXAMPLE 6: ICD-10-CM TABULAR LIST OF DISEASES AND INJURIES—PARENTHESES: Code I47.9 contains a nonessential modifier, (-Hoffman), in parentheses, which means that the term may be present or absent from the provider's diagnostic statement.

EXAMPLE 7: ICD-10-PCS INDEX—PARENTHESES: Index entry *acromion (process)* contains a nonessential modifier in parentheses, which means the term may be present or absent from the provider's procedural statement.

A **colon** is used after an incomplete term or phrase in the ICD-9-CM and ICD-10-CM/PCS indexes and tabular lists after an incomplete term that needs one or more of the **modifiers** (additional terms) following the colon to make it assignable to a given category.

EXAMPLE 1: ICD-9-CM TABULAR LIST OF DISEASES—COLON: The Tabular List of Diseases entry for code 455.5 contains a colon after the phrase *External hemorrhoids*: along with additional terms (modifiers) that must be included in the provider's diagnostic statement. (If the provider had documented *external hemorrhoids* without mentioning the bleeding, code 455.3 would be assigned instead.)

EXAMPLE 2: ICD-9-CM TABULAR LIST OF PROCEDURES—COLON: The Tabular List of Procedures entry for code 88.79 contains a colon after the phrase *Ultrasonography of*: along with additional terms (modifiers) that must be included in the provider's procedural statement. If the provider had documented ultrasonography (without mentioning total body) the provider would have to be contacted to determine the type of ultrasonography.

EXAMPLE 3: ICD-10-CM INDEX TO DISEASES AND INJURIES—COLON: The 2nd qualifier "with gestation of:" (located after index main term *Immaturity* and subterm *extreme*) requires the number of weeks gestation to be documented in the patient record so that a specific code can be selected.

Exercise 3.4 – Punctuation

Instructions: Assign the ICD code(s) to each statement below. Make sure that you appropriately interpret the use of punctuation in the ICD-9-CM disease and procedure indexes and tabular lists and the ICD-10-CM disease index and tabular list. (Except for the limited use of parentheses and square brackets to enclose terms, punctuation is not used in ICD-10-PCS, which means you will not enter ICD-10-PCS codes in items 6–10.)

ICD-9-CM	ICD-10-CM	
_____	_____	1. Creutzfeldt-Jakob syndrome with dementia, without behavioral disturbance
_____	_____	2. Malaria with hepatitis
_____	_____	3. Dimorphous leprosy
_____	_____	4. Acute pyogenic thyroiditis
_____	_____	5. Neuritis due to beriberi
_____	n/a	6. Percutaneous transluminal coronary angioplasty
_____	n/a	7. Cranial puncture, subdural tap
_____	n/a	8. Endometrial ablation
_____	n/a	9. Alveoloplasty
_____	n/a	10. Arteriography of basilar artery

Boxed Notes

Certain main terms in the ICD-9-CM indexes are followed by **boxed notes**, which define terms, provide coding instruction, and list fifth-digit subclassifications for those categories that use the same fifth digits. Index to Procedures boxed notes provide coding instruction and list fourth-digit subclassifications for those categories that use the same fourth digits.

 ICD-10 Alert!

The boxed notes coding convention is not used in ICD-10-CM or ICD-10-PCS.

Note:

- ICD-9-CM diagnosis category codes contain 3 digits, and subcategory codes contain 4 digits.
- ICD-9-CM procedure category codes contain just 2 digits, and subcategory codes contain just 3 digits.

EXAMPLE: ICD-9-CM INDEX TO DISEASES—BOXED NOTE:

- The Index to Diseases main term "Adenoma" contains a boxed note that provides coding instruction.
- The Index to Diseases main term "Cholelithiasis" contains a boxed note that lists fifth-digit subclassifications.
- The Index to Procedures main term "Examination (for), microscopic (specimen) (of)" contains a boxed note that lists fourth-digit subclassifications.
- The Index to Procedures main term "Renotransplantation" contains a boxed note that provides coding instruction.

Exercise 3.5 – Boxed Notes

Instructions: Assign the code(s) to each statement. Make sure you interpret the content of boxed notes in the ICD-9-CM Index to Diseases and Index to Procedures. (The boxed notes coding convention is not used in ICD-10-CM or ICD-10-PCS.)

ICD-9-CM

_____ 1. Traumatic brain hemorrhage with no loss of consciousness

_____ 2. Multiple open wounds to arms

_____ 3. Single episode of mild involutional affective psychosis

_____ 4. Chronic periostitis with chronic osteomyelitis of the lower leg

_____ 5. Recurrent bleeding peptic ulcer

_____ 6. Infected blister

_____ 7. Cellular blue nevus on calf

_____ 8. Toxicology examination of urine specimen

_____ 9. Anterior spinal fusion of C4-C6

_____ 10. Laparoscopic lysis of abdominal adhesions

Tables

The ICD-9-CM and ICD-10-CM indexes include **tables**, which organize subterms, 2nd qualifiers, and 3rd qualifiers and their codes in columns and rows to make it easier to select the proper code. ICD-10-PCS also uses tables, but not in its index; instead of a tabular list of codes, ICD-10-PCS uses tables that are used to assign procedure codes.

ICD-9-CM organizes the following main terms in tables, and they are located in alphabetic order in the Index to Diseases with the exception of the Table of Drugs and Chemicals, which is located at the end of the index (before the Index to External Causes):

- Hypertension
- Neoplasms
- Drugs and chemicals

ICD-10-CM organizes the following main terms in tables, which are located at the end of the Index to Diseases and Injuries (before the Index to External Causes):

- Neoplasms
- Drugs and chemicals

The *Table of Neoplasms* is an alphabetic index of anatomic sites for which there are six possible code numbers according to whether the neoplasm in question is malignant, benign, *in situ*, of uncertain behavior, or of unspecified nature. The description of the neoplasm will often indicate which of the six columns is appropriate (e.g., malignant melanoma of skin, benign fibroadenoma of breast, carcinoma *in situ* of cervix uteri).

The table of drugs and chemicals in ICD-9-CM includes a code for the substance administered or taken (when considered a poisoning) and four columns of external causes of injury (ICD-9-CM E code) to indicate the reason (e.g., suicide attempt). The table also includes one column of external causes of injury codes to indicate that a substance was taken for therapeutic use (and that an adverse reaction occurred). This external cause of injury code is *never* reported with codes in the other five columns of the table for a specific substance. Instead, it is reported with the adverse effect of a substance taken for therapeutic use (e.g., stomach ache due to proper administration of aspirin).

The table of drugs and chemicals in ICD-10-CM is an alphabetic index of medicinal, chemical, and biological substances that result in poisonings and adverse effects. The first column of the table lists generic names of drugs and chemicals (although some publishers have added brand names) with six columns for *Poisoning: Accidental (Unintentional)* (poisoning that results from an inadvertent overdose, wrong substance administered/taken, or intoxication that includes combining prescription drugs with nonprescription drugs or alcohol); *Poisoning: Intentional Self-harm* (poisoning that results from a deliberate overdose, such as a suicide attempt, of substance(s) administered/taken or intoxication that includes purposely combining prescription drugs with nonprescription drugs or alcohol); *Poisoning: Assault* (poisoning inflicted by another person who intended to kill or injure the patient); *Poisoning: Undetermined* (subcategory used if the patient record does not document whether the poisoning was intentional or accidental); *Adverse Effect* (development of a pathologic condition that results from a drug or chemical substance that was properly administered or taken); and *Underdosing* (taking less of a medication than is prescribed by a provider or a manufacturer's instruction).

Note:

- Tables appear only in the ICD-9-CM Index to Diseases and ICD-10-CM Index to Diseases and Injuries, and their use is further discussed in Chapters 4–6 of this textbook. ICD-10-PCS also uses tables to facilitate the assignment of procedure codes, but the tables do not appear in the ICD-10-PCS index.

- Consider using a yellow highlighter to mark the Therapeutic Use column on each page of the ICD-9-CM table of drugs and chemicals (to change the appearance of that column). The highlighted columns will remind you not to report an E code for a substance administered for therapeutic use with a code from one of the other five columns.

EXAMPLE: ICD-9-CM INDEX TO DISEASES—TABLE: A portion of the ICD-9-CM Index to Diseases entry for "Hypertension."

	Malignant	Benign	Unspecified
Hypertension, hypertensive (arterial) (arteriolar) (crisis) (degeneration) (disease) (essential) (fluctuating) (idiopathic) (intermittent) (labile) (low renin) (orthostatic) (paroxysmal) (primary) (systemic) (uncontrolled) (vascular)	401.0	401.1	401.9
with			
heart involvement (conditions classifiable to 429.0–429.3, 429.8, 429.9 due to hypertension) (see also Hypertension, heart)	402.00	402.10	402.90

© Cengage Learning 2014

Exercise 3.6 – Tables

Instructions: Assign the ICD code(s) to each statement below. Make sure that you appropriately interpret the use of tables in the ICD-9-CM and ICD-10-CM disease indexes. The hypertension table does not appear in ICD-10-CM, which means you will not assign ICD-10-CM codes to items 8–10 below. Tables are not used in the ICD-9-CM Index to Procedures or the ICD-10-PCS Index.

ICD-9-CM   ICD-10-CM

_____   _____   **1.** Ethmoid tumor

_____   _____   **2.** Basal cell carcinoma, skin of external cheek

(*continues*)

Exercise 3.6 (continued)

ICD-9-CM	ICD-10-CM	
_____	_____	**3.** Carcinoma of liver
_____	_____	**4.** Prostate cancer
_____	_____	**5.** Poisoning due to inhalation of paint fumes (initial encounter)
_____	_____	**6.** Circulatory collapse due to therapeutic use of magnesium sulfate (oral) (initial encounter)
_____	_____	**7.** Accidental overdose of antidepressants (initial encounter)
_____	n/a	**8.** Malignant idiopathic hypertension
_____	n/a	**9.** Secondary hypertension
_____	n/a	**10.** Benign hypertension due to renal stenosis

Includes Notes

An **includes note** appears in the ICD-9-CM and ICD-10-CM tabular lists below certain categories to further define, clarify, or give examples of the content of a code category.

EXAMPLE 1: ICD-9-CM TABULAR LIST OF DISEASES—INCLUDES NOTE: The *includes note* located below category code *387 Otosclerosis* in the Tabular List of Diseases indicates that *otospongiosis* is classified to that same category. This means that the provider could document *otosclerosis* or *otospongiosis*, and a code from category 387 would be assigned.

EXAMPLE 2: ICD-9-CM TABULAR LIST OF PROCEDURES—INCLUDES NOTE: The *includes note* below subcategory code *35.5 Repair of atrial and ventricular septa with prosthesis* in the Tabular List of Procedures indicates that *repair of septa with synthetic implant or patch* is classified to code 35.5. This means the physician could document *repair of atrial and ventricular septa with synthetic implant or patch* or *repair of septa with synthetic implant or patch,* and code 35.5 would be assigned.

EXAMPLE 3: ICD-10-CM TABULAR LIST OF DISEASES AND INJURIES—INCLUDES NOTE: The *includes note* located below category code *H80 Otosclerosis* in the Tabular List of Diseases and Injuries indicates that *otospongiosis* is classified to that same category. This means that the provider could document *otosclerosis* or *otospongiosis,* and a code from category H80 would be assigned.

Exercise 3.7 – Includes Notes

Instructions: Assign the ICD code(s) to each statement below. Make sure you appropriately interpret the use of includes notes in the ICD-9-CM disease and procedure tabular lists and the ICD-10-CM disease tabular list. (Includes notes are not used in ICD-10-PCS, which means you will not assign ICD-10-PCS codes to items 6–10 below.)

ICD-9-CM	ICD-10-CM	
_____	_____	**1.** Meningoencephalitis
_____	_____	**2.** Nephrosclerosis

ICD-9-CM	ICD-10-CM	
_____	_____	**3.** Anastomotic ulcer
_____	_____	**4.** Hypertensive vascular degeneration
_____	_____	**5.** Acute lymphangitis
_____	n/a	**6.** Malstrom's vacuum extraction with episiotomy (Extraction, Products of Conception in ICD-10-PCS) (Episiotomy in ICD-10-PCS)
_____	n/a	**7.** Open reduction and fixation of left zygomatic fracture
_____	n/a	**8.** Open arthrodesis of C1-C2 (cervical spine) anterior column using anterior approach with internal fixation device
_____	n/a	**9.** Impedence phlebography with venipuncture for injection of contrast material, chest
_____	n/a	**10.** Repair of right retinal defect

Excludes Notes

An **excludes note** appears below an ICD-9-CM Tabular List of Diseases or Tabular List of Procedures code to direct the coder to another location in the tabular list to classify conditions (or procedures) that are excluded from the code. Depending on the coding instructions, codes for excluded conditions (or procedures) may or may not be reported with the code from which the condition (or procedure) is excluded. Make sure you carefully review coding instructions before assigning codes.

EXAMPLE 1: ICD-9-CM TABULAR LIST OF DISEASES—EXCLUDES NOTE (excluded code that *may be reported with the code for which the condition is excluded*): When fractures of different bones are assigned different codes, multiple codes may be reported if appropriate documentation is present in the patient record. The provider documented that the patient has a *closed fracture of femur, left,* which is a fracture of an unspecified part of the femur. The patient also has a *closed fracture of hip (femur neck), left* (820.8). The *excludes* note below code 821.00 in the tabular list indicates that code 820.8 is assigned if a fracture of the *hip NOS* is documented.

```
821 Fracture of other and unspecified parts of femur
      821.0 Shaft or unspecified part of femur, closed
            821.00 Unspecified part of femur
                  Thigh    Upper leg
                  EXCLUDES hip NOS (820.8)
      821.01 Shaft
```

EXAMPLE 2: ICD-9-CM TABULAR LIST OF DISEASES— EXCLUDES NOTE (excluded code that *may* not be reported with the code for which the condition is excluded): A code for a congenital condition that is excluded from the code for an acquired type of the same condition may not be reported together. If the provider documents *congenital deformities of the feet* assign code 754.70. Do not also assign a code from 736.70 through 736.79.

 ICD-10 Alert!

ICD-10-PCS does not use excludes notes.

ICD-10 Alert!

The ICD-10-CM Tabular List of Diseases and Injuries contains two types of excludes notes. Each note has a different definition for use. However, they are similar in that they both indicate that codes excluded from each other are independent of each other.

An **Excludes1 note** *is a pure excludes. It means "not coded here" and indicates mutually exclusive codes, in other words—two conditions that cannot be reported together.*

 EXAMPLE 1: ICD-10-CM EXCLUDES1 NOTE: Locate ICD-10-CM code **Q03 Congenital hydrocephalus**, and find the Excludes1 note for *acquired hydrocephalus (G91.-)*. Hydrocephalus diagnosed in a newborn is assigned a code from Q03.0–Q03.9. For hydrocephalus that develops later in life, a code from G91.0–G91.9 is assigned. A congenital form of a disease is not reported with an acquired form of the same condition. Thus, the excluded code is never reported with the code located above the Excludes1 note.

 EXAMPLE 2: ICD-10-CM EXCLUDES1 NOTE: Locate ICD-10-CM code *E10 Type 1 diabetes mellitus,* and find the Excludes1 note for *type 2 diabetes mellitus (E11.-)*. Type 1 diabetes mellitus is classified to a code from E10.1x–E10.9. Thus, a code for type 2 diabetes mellitus (E11.0x–E11.9) would never be assigned with a code for type 1 diabetes mellitus.

Note:

The ICD-9-CM excludes note were difficult to interpret because instructions were not provided regarding the assignment of one or more codes. ICD-10-CM's excludes notes clarify the required assignment of one code (Excludes1) versus the permitted assignment of two (or more) codes (Excludes2).

Coding Tip:

An Excludes1 note instructs you to assign one code or the other.

Coding Tip:

An Excludes2 note instructs you to assign more than one code when medical documentation supports all conditions.

An **Excludes2 note** *means* not included *here and indicates that although the excluded condition is not classified as part of the condition it is excluded from, a patient may be diagnosed with all conditions at the same time. Therefore, when an Excludes2 note appears under a code, it may be acceptable to assign both the code and the excluded code(s) together* if supported by the medical documentation.

EXAMPLE: ICD-10-CM EXCLUDES2 NOTE: Locate ICD-10-CM **code M19.14 Post-traumatic osteoarthritis**, hand and find the Excludes2 note for post-traumatic osteoarthritis of first carpometacarpal joint (M18.2-, M18.3-). The Excludes2 note means that because a patient can be diagnosed with both "post-traumatic osteoarthritis of the hand" and "post-traumatic osteoarthritis of the first carpometacarpal joint," it is acceptable to assign codes to both conditions if supported by medical documentation.

Exercise 3.8 – Excludes Notes (ICD-9-CM) and Excludes1 and Excludes2 Notes (ICD-10-CM)

Instructions: Assign the ICD code(s) to each statement below. Make sure you appropriately interpret the use of excludes notes in the ICD-9-CM Tabular List of Diseases for items 1–5. Then, appropriately interpret the use of Excludes1 and Excludes2 notes in the ICD-10-CM Tabular List of Diseases and Injuries for items 1–10. (Excludes notes are not used in ICD-9-CM, Volume 3, or ICD-10-PCS.)

ICD-9-CM	ICD-10-CM	
_____	_____	**1.** Cardiovascular disease of native coronary artery
_____	_____	**2.** Arteritis
_____	_____	**3.** Absence of menstruation
_____	_____	**4.** Herpetiformis dermatosis
_____	_____	**5.** Dextrocardia
n/a	_____	**6.** Meningeal tuberculoma. Tuberculoma of brain and spinal cord.
n/a	_____	**7.** Malignant neoplasm of dorsal surface of base of tongue (Neoplasm table).
n/a	_____	**8.** Sucrase-isomaltase deficiency. Congenital lactose deficiency.
n/a	_____	**9.** Psychotic disorder with hallucinations. Paranoid schizophrenia.
n/a	_____	**10.** Hemorrhage from the throat. Hemoptysis.

Inclusion Terms

Lists of inclusion terms are included below certain codes in the ICD-9-CM and ICD-10-CM tabular lists. The **inclusion terms** indicate some of the conditions for which that code number may be assigned. They may be synonyms with the code title, or, in the case of "other specified" codes, the terms may also provide a list of various conditions included within a classification code. The list of inclusion terms in the tabular lists are not exhaustive. Each index may provide additional terms that may also be assigned to a given code.

 Note:

Although inclusion terms are *not* technically associated with the ICD-9-CM and ICD-10-CM indexes, the indexes contain many more terms that do not appear in the tabular lists.

The ICD-9-CM and ICD-10-CM indexes are important supplements to the tabular lists because they contain many diagnostic terms that do not appear in the tabular lists. The inclusion terms listed below codes in the tabular lists are not meant to be exhaustive, and additional terms found only in the indexes may also be assigned to a code. This concept is called **trust the index**.

EXAMPLE 1: ICD-9-CM TABULAR LIST OF DISEASES—INCLUSION TERMS (synonyms):
The following inclusion terms are located in the Tabular List of Diseases for the diagnosis code 724.2, Lumbago:

- Low back pain

- Low back syndrome

- Lumbalgia

    This means the provider can document any one of the above conditions, and code 724.2 is assigned.

EXAMPLE 2: ICD-9-CM TABULAR LIST OF DISEASES—INCLUSION TERMS (conditions classified to "other" subcategory codes): If the provider documents *polyalgia* as the patient's condition, assign code 729.99 even though the code description indicates it is an *other and unspecified* code.

EXAMPLE 3: ICD-9-CM INDEX TO DISEASES AND TABULAR LIST OF DISEASES—TRUST THE INDEX: Locate the index entry for *cysticercosis, mammary 123.1.* Then, go to the tabular list to verify code 123.1 where you will notice that *mammary cysticercosis* is not listed as an inclusion term. The coder has to *trust the index* and assign code 123.1 for the documented condition.

EXAMPLE 4: ICD-9-CM TABULAR LIST OF PROCEDURES—INCLUSION TERMS: When the physician documents *heat therapy,* the Index to Procedures lists code 93.35 and the Tabular List of Procedures contains several inclusion terms below the code. Refer to Tabular List of Procedures entry 93.35 and notice that the physician could have documented any one of the inclusion terms instead of *heat therapy* and code 93.35 would still be assigned.

EXAMPLE 5: ICD-10-CM TABULAR LIST OF DISEASES AND INJURIES—INCLUSION TERMS: The following inclusion terms are located in the Tabular List of Diseases and Injuries for diagnosis code M54.5, Low back pain:

- Loin pain

- Lumbago NOS

EXAMPLE 6: ICD-10-CM TABULAR LIST OF DISEASES AND INJURIES—INCLUSION TERMS (conditions classified to "other specified" subcategory codes): If the provider documents *polyalgia* as the patient's condition, assign code M79.89 even though the code description indicates it is an *other specified* code.

EXAMPLE 7: ICD-10-CM INDEX TO DISEASES AND INJURIES AND TABULAR LIST OF DISEASES AND INJURIES—*TRUST THE INDEX*: Locate the index entry for *infection, fish tapeworm, larval B70.1.* Then, go to the tabular list to verify code B70.1 where you will notice that *infection due to fish tapeworm, larval* is not listed as an inclusion term. The coder has to *trust the index* and assign code B70.1 for the documented condition.

ICD-10 Alert!

ICD-10-PCS does not contain inclusion terms.

Exercise 3.9 – Inclusion Terms

Instructions: Assign the ICD code(s) to each statement below. Make sure that you appropriately interpret the use of inclusion terms in the ICD-9-CM disease and procedure tabular lists and the ICD-10-CM disease tabular list. (Inclusion terms are not used in ICD-10-PCS, which means you will not assign ICD-10-PCS codes to items 6–10 below.)

ICD-9-CM	ICD-10-CM	
_____	_____	**1.** Acute amebic dysentery
_____	_____	**2.** Disseminated blastomycosis
_____	_____	**3.** Megakaryocytic (thrombocytic) leukemia, acute
_____	_____	**4.** GM2 gangliosidosis, juvenile
_____	_____	**5.** Congenital toxoplasmosis
_____	n/a	**6.** Nasal polypectomy
_____	n/a	**7.** Intrapericardial poudrage
_____	n/a	**8.** Transcervical fetal oxygen saturation monitoring (intrapartum)
_____	n/a	**9.** Radio-cobalt B12 Schilling test
_____	n/a	**10.** Classic infrafascial SEMM hysterectomy (abdominal)

Other, Other Specified, and Unspecified Codes

When **other and other specified** appear in a code description, the codes are assigned when patient record documentation provides detail for which a specific code does not exist in ICD-9-CM or ICD-10-CM. The ICD-9-CM and ICD-10-CM tabular list "other and other specified codes" usually contain a fourth and/or fifth digit of 8 and/or 9. ICD-9-CM and ICD-10-CM index entries that contain the abbreviation NEC are classified to "other" codes in the tabular lists. These index entries represent specific disease entities for which no specific code exists in the tabular list, so the term is included within an "other" code.

> **ICD-10 Alert!**
>
> The *other and unspecified* coding convention does not appear in ICD-10-PCS.

Unspecified codes are assigned because patient record documentation is insufficient to assign a more specific code. ICD-9-CM and ICD-10-CM tabular list codes designated as "unspecified" usually contain a fourth digit of 9 and/or a fifth digit of 0. (Before assigning an unspecified code, ask the provider to document additional information so that a more specific code can be reported.) When an ICD-9-CM or ICD-10-CM tabular list category does not contain an unspecified code, the "other specified" code may represent both "other and unspecified" [In ICD-10-CM, "other and unspecified" category and subcategory codes require assignment of extra digit(s) to classify the condition.]

When the index directs the coder to an "other, other specified, or unspecified code" in the tabular list, it is important to review the record carefully (or ask the physician for clarification of documentation) to determine if a more specific code can be assigned. This is referred to as "moving up the ladder" of codes in the tabular list.

EXAMPLE 1: ICD-9-CM TABULAR LIST OF DISEASES—OTHER, OTHER SPECIFIED, AND UNSPECIFIED CODES: Refer to the tabular list entries for the following:

- Code 285.8 is an *other specified* code.
- Code 285.9 is an *unspecified* code.
- Code 286.9 is an *other and unspecified* code.

EXAMPLE 2: ICD-10-CM TABULAR LIST OF DISEASES AND INJURIES—OTHER, OTHER SPECIFIED, AND UNSPECIFIED CODES:

- D64.89 is an *other specified* code.
- D64.9 is an *unspecified* code.
- I70.9 is an *other and unspecified* code.

Exercise 3.10 – Other, Other Specified, and Unspecified Codes

Instructions: Assign the ICD code(s) to each statement below. Make sure that you appropriately interpret the use of "other, other specified, and unspecified codes" in the ICD-9-CM disease and procedure tabular lists and the ICD-10-CM tabular list. (Inclusion terms are not used in ICD-10-PCS, which means you will not assign ICD-10-PCS codes to items 6–10 below.)

ICD-9-CM	ICD-10-CM	
_____	_____	**1.** Intussusception of appendix
_____	_____	**2.** Ectopic pregnancy, week #6
_____	_____	**3.** Hepatorenal syndrome following delivery (postpartum condition)
_____	_____	**4.** Arterial atheroembolism
_____	_____	**5.** Glaucoma

(continues)

Exercise 3.10 (continued)

ICD-9-CM	ICD-10-CM	
_____	____n/a____	**6.** Cataract extraction, left eye
_____	____n/a____	**7.** Cholecystogram
_____	____n/a____	**8.** Oxygen by nasal cannula
_____	____n/a____	**9.** Abdominal appendectomy
_____	____n/a____	**10.** Removal of impacted tooth

Etiology and Manifestation Rules

Etiology and manifestation rules include the following notes in the ICD-9-CM Tabular List of Diseases and the ICD-10-CM Tabular List of Diseases and Injuries:

- Code first underlying disease
- Code, if applicable, any causal condition first
- Use additional code
- In diseases classified elsewhere

To classify certain conditions completely, codes must be assigned to the underlying *etiology* (cause or origin of disease) and multiple body system manifestations (resulting symptoms or conditions) due to the underlying etiology. For such conditions, the underlying condition is sequenced first, followed by the manifestation. Wherever an etiology and manifestation combination of codes exists, the tabular list etiology code contains a **use additional code** note and the manifestation code contains a **code first underlying disease** note. These instructional notes assist coders in the proper sequencing of the codes: etiology code followed by manifestation code. In most cases, the manifestation code will have in its title an **in diseases classified elsewhere** note, which indicates that the manifestation codes are a component of the etiology/manifestation coding convention. A manifestation code that does not contain *in diseases classified elsewhere* in its title will contain a "use additional code" note. (Make sure you sequence the manifestation code after the etiology code.)

 The instruction to **code, if applicable, any causal condition first** requires the causal condition to be sequenced first if present. A *causal condition* is a disease (e.g., diabetes mellitus) that manifests (or results in) another condition (e.g., diabetic cataracts). If no causal condition is documented, the code that contains the instruction (*code, if applicable, any causal condition first*) may be reported without the causal condition code. (This differs from the instruction to *code first underlying condition*, which does not allow for the code that contains the instruction to be reported without first sequencing the underlying condition.)

 Note:

Some publishers of ICD-9-CM coding manuals include the phrase *use additional code, if desired* (instead of use additional code). This phrasing resulted when ICD-9 was translated into English from its original French because the polite phrase s'il vous plaît *(if you please)* was included in the instruction. If you encounter the phrase *use additional code, if desired* in a coding manual, remember that assigning the additional code is not only desirable, it's mandatory.

Note:

Manifestation codes that include the instruction code *first underlying condition* are never reported first on health insurance claims. They must be reported in conjunction with an underlying condition (etiology) code, and they must be listed after the underlying condition code.

Etiology/manifestation conditions are listed together in the ICD-9-CM Index to Diseases; the etiology code is listed first, followed by the manifestation codes in slanted brackets. (The manifestation code listed in slanted brackets is always sequenced second.)

 EXAMPLE 1: ICD-9-CM INDEX TO DISEASES AND TABULAR LIST OF DISEASES—ETIOLOGY/ MANIFESTATION CODES: For diagnostic statement *idiopathic pulmonary hemosiderosis,* two codes are assigned: 275.09 and 516.1. The index entry lists code 275.09 in front of code 516.1, which is in slanted brackets, which is the manifestation code and is reported second. Notice that the tabular list entry for 275.09 does not instruct you to *use additional code* for idiopathic pulmonary hemosiderosis. However, code 516.1 does contain the *code first underlying disease* note, instructing you to report code 275.09 first.

EXAMPLE 2: ICD-9-CM TABULAR LIST OF DISEASES— USE ADDITIONAL CODE: The patient is diagnosed with *benign hypertrophy of the prostate with urinary obstruction and stress incontinence.* Locate category code 600 in the tabular list and notice that the *use additional code to identify urinary incontinence (788.30–788.39)* note instructs the coder to report an additional code. Therefore, assign codes 600.01 and 788.32.

EXAMPLE 3: ICD-9-CM TABULAR LIST OF DISEASES— CODE, IF APPLICABLE, ANY CAUSAL CONDITION FIRST: A patient who has acute alcoholism (303.00) was recently seen in the office, complaining of urinary incontinence. The physician determined that the condition was nonorganic in origin and was most likely the result of the patient being too inebriated to realize he had urinated while unconscious. Code 307.6 is assigned to urinary incontinence that is of nonorganic origin. (Code 788.30 is assigned to urinary incontinence that is organic in nature (e.g., due to urethritis, 597.80).

EXAMPLE 4: ICD-10-CM INDEX TO DISEASES AND INJURIES AND TABULAR LIST OF DISEASES AND INJURIES—ETIOLOGY/MANIFESTATION CODES: Diagnostic statement *idiopathic pulmonary hemosiderosis* includes two codes in the ICD-10-CM index: E83.1 [J84.03]. Code J84.03 is listed in brackets in the index, which indicates it is the manifestation code and is reported second. The ICD-10-CM tabular list entry for J84.03 is in italics, and it contains a *code first underlying disease* note.

EXAMPLE 5: ICD-10-CM TABULAR LIST OF DISEASES AND INJURIES—USE ADDITIONAL CODE: The patient is diagnosed with *benign hypertrophy of the prostate with urge and stress incontinence.* Locate subcategory code N40.1 in the ICD-10-CM tabular list, and notice that the *use additional code…* note instructs you to report an additional code. Therefore, assign codes N40.1 and N39.46. Next, notice that category code N39.4 in the tabular list includes a *code also any associated overactive bladder (N32.81)* note. Because the diagnostic statement (above) does not include *overactive bladder,* do not assign code N32.81.

EXAMPLE 6: ICD-10-CM TABULAR LIST OF DISEASES AND INJURIES—CODE, IF APPLICABLE, ANY CAUSAL CONDITION FIRST: A patient with an alcohol addiction (F10.20) was seen in the office,

Note:

- "Code first underlying disease" and "use additional code" notes are used to classify certain codes that are not part of an etiology/ manifestation combination.
- ICD-9-CM index codes that are contained in slanted brackets are manifestation codes.
- ICD-10-CM index codes that are contained in brackets are manifestation codes

ICD-10 Alert!

Etiology/manifestation conditions are listed together in the ICD-10-CM Index to Diseases and Injuries with the etiology code listed first and the manifestation code located in brackets (*not* slanted brackets). However, the ICD-10-CM Tabular List of Diseases and Injuries continues to use italics for manifestation codes and descriptions.

It is likely that slanted brackets were discontinued in ICD-10-CM because any code located in brackets is a manifestation code (which is sequenced second).

complaining of urinary incontinence. The physician determined that the condition was nonorganic in origin and most likely the result of the patient being too inebriated to realize he had urinated while unconscious. Code F98.0 is assigned to urinary incontinence that is of nonorganic origin. (Code R32 is assigned to urinary incontinence that is organic in nature [e.g., due to urethritis, N34.2].)

Exercise 3.11 – Etiology and Manifestation Rules

Instructions: Assign the ICD code(s) to each statement below. Make sure you appropriately interpret the use of etiology and manifestation codes in the ICD-9-CM and ICD-10-CM disease indexes and tabular lists. (Etiology and manifestation codes are not used in ICD-10-PCS.)

ICD-9-CM   ICD-10-CM

_____ _____   **1.** Tetanic cataract in hypoparathyroidism

_____ _____   **2.** Cardiac sarcoidosis

_____ _____   **3.** Uremic pericarditis

_____ _____   **4.** Congenital syphilitic peritonitis

_____ _____   **5.** Typhoid osteomyelitis

And

When the word **and** appears in category titles and code descriptions in the ICD-9-CM Tabular List of Diseases, ICD-9-CM Tabular List of Procedures, ICD-10-CM Tabular List of Diseases and Injuries, ICD-10-PCS Index to Procedures, and ICD-10-PCS Tables, it is interpreted as meaning *and/or*.

EXAMPLE 1: ICD-9-CM TABULAR LIST OF DISEASES—AND: Category code 464 (Acute laryngitis and tracheitis) means that codes are reported for conditions of the larynx, trachea, or larynx and trachea.

EXAMPLE 2: ICD-9-CM TABULAR LIST OF PROCEDURES—AND: Category code 28 (Operations on tonsils and adenoids) means that codes are reported for procedures performed on tonsils, adenoids, or the tonsils and adenoids. Code 28.11 (Biopsy of tonsils and adenoids) is reported for the biopsy of tonsils, biopsy of adenoids, or biopsy of tonsils and adenoids.

EXAMPLE 3: ICD-10-PCS TABLES—AND: In section 0 (Medical and Surgical), value N (Head and Facial Bones), codes are assigned for procedures performed on head bones, facial bones, or head and facial bones.

Exercise 3.12 – And

Instructions: Assign the code(s) to each statement. Make sure you appropriately interpret the use of the word and in the ICD-9-CM Tabular List of Diseases and Tabular List of Procedures, the ICD-10-CM Tabular List of Diseases and Injuries, and the ICD-10-PCS Index and Tables.

ICD-9-CM   ICD-10-CM/PCS

_____ _____   **1.** Venereal disease of the rectum due to chlamydia

_____ _____   **2.** Malignant neoplasm of costal cartilage

ICD-9-CM	ICD-10-CM/PCS	
_____	_____	**3.** Acromegaly
_____	_____	**4.** Parietoalveolar pneumopathy
_____	_____	**5.** Carcinoma *in situ* of scalp (Neoplasm)
_____	_____	**6.** Ultrasonography of head
_____	_____	**7.** Insertion of oropharyngeal (mouth and throat) airway
_____	_____	**8.** Open division of muscle, left upper arm
_____	_____	**9.** Repair of skin, right hand
_____	_____	**10.** Open biopsy, tonsils

Due To

The subterm **due to** is located in the ICD-9-CM Index to Diseases and the ICD-10-CM Index to Diseases and Injuries in alphabetical order to indicate the presence of a cause-and-effect (or causal) relationship between two conditions. When the index includes *due to* as a subterm, the code is assigned only if the physician documented the causal relationship between two conditions, such as meningitis due to adenovirus. It's possible that a patient could have meningitis along with an unrelated adenovirus at the same time. (The *due to* phrase is included in tabular list code descriptions, but it is not a coding instruction.)

 ICD-10 Alert!

The "due to" instruction does not appear in ICD-10-PCS Index (or in the ICD-9-CM Index to Procedures).

> **Note:**
>
> The ICD-9-CM Index to Diseases includes subterm *in* and the ICD-10-CM disease index includes subterm *in* (*due to*) to indicate the presence of a cause-and-effect (or causal) relationship between two conditions.

ICD-9-CM and ICD-10-CM occasionally presume a causal relationship between two conditions. This means that the physician is not required to document *due to* in the diagnostic statement, such as when the patient has hypertension and renal failure. This condition is coded as hypertensive renal failure, which is interpreted as hypertension due to renal failure. (Chapter 4 of this textbook contains further discussion about causal relationships that are presumed by ICD-9-CM and ICD-10-CM.)

EXAMPLE 1: ICD-9-CM INDEX TO DISEASES—DUE TO: When the physician documents *pneumonitis due to inhalation of regurgitated food,* a causal relationship exists and code 507.0 is assigned.

EXAMPLE 2: ICD-10-CM INDEX TO DISEASES AND INJURIES—DUE TO: When the physician documents *pneumonitis due to inhalation of regurgitated food*, a causal relationship exists and code J69.0 is assigned.

EXAMPLE 3: ICD-10-CM INDEX TO DISEASES AND INJURIES—IN (DUE TO): When the physician documents *anemia in moderate chronic kidney disease*, a causal relationship exists, and codes N18.3 and D63.1 are assigned.

Exercise 3.13 – Due To

Instructions: Assign the ICD code(s) to each statement below. Make sure that you appropriately interpret the use of due to in the ICD-9-CM and ICD-10-CM disease indexes. (The due to instruction does not appear in the ICD-9-CM Index to Procedures or ICD-10-PCS Index.)

ICD-9-CM	ICD-10-CM	
_____	_____	**1.** Cirrhosis due to Wilson's disease
_____	_____	**2.** Bubo due to *Haemophilus ducreyi*
_____	_____	**3.** Carnitine deficiency due to hemodialysis
_____	_____	**4.** Hypothyroidism due to irradiation therapy
_____	_____	**5.** Airway obstruction due to laryngospasm

In

When the word **in** appears in the ICD-9-CM and ICD-10-CM disease indexes, it is located in alphabetical order below the main term. To assign a code from the list of qualifiers below the word *in*, the physician must document both conditions in the patient's record. ICD-9-CM and ICD-10-CM classify certain conditions as if there were a cause-and-effect relationship present because they occur together much of the time (e.g., pneumonia in Q fever).

ICD-10 Alert!

The "in" instruction does not appear in ICD-10-PCS (or the ICD-9-CM Index to Procedures).

> **EXAMPLE 1: ICD-9-CM INDEX TO DISEASES—IN:** Locate main term *pneumonia* in the Index to Diseases and notice that the word *in* appears in alphabetical order above a list of 2nd qualifiers. To assign a code from the list, the physician must document a relationship between both conditions, such as *pneumonia in measles* (or *postpneumonia measles*) to which combination code 055.1 would be assigned. (Other conditions that occur together may require the assignment of multiple codes, one for the etiology and another for the manifestation.)

> **EXAMPLE 2: ICD-10-CM INDEX TO DISEASES AND INJURIES—IN:** Locate main term *pneumonia* in the index, and notice that the word *in* appears in alphabetical order above a list of second qualifiers. To assign a code from the list, the physician must document a relationship between both conditions, such as *pneumonia in measles* (or *postpneumonia measles*) to which combination code B05.2 is. (Other conditions that occur together may require the assignment of multiple codes, one for the etiology and another for the manifestation.)

Exercise 3.14 – In

Instructions: Assign the code(s) to each statement. Make sure you interpret the use of the word in appropriately in the ICD-9-CM and ICD-10-CM disease indexes. (The in subterm does not appear in the ICD-9-CM Index to Procedures or ICD-10-PCS.)

ICD-9-CM	ICD-10-CM	
_____	_____	**1.** Bicornis uterus in pregnancy, week #12

ICD-9-CM	ICD-10-CM	
_____	_____	**2.** Adenocarcinoma in adenomatous polyposis coli
_____	_____	**3.** Uterine fibroid tumor in pregnancy (antepartum, second trimester, week #14)
_____	_____	**4.** Keratoconjunctivitis in exanthema
_____	_____	**5.** Nephrosis in epidemic hemorrhagic fever

With

When the word **with** appears in the ICD-9-CM Index to Diseases or Index to Procedures (or the ICD-10-CM Index to Diseases and Injuries), it is located immediately below the main term, not in alphabetical order. To assign a code from the list of qualifiers below the word *with*, the physician must document the presence of both conditions (or procedures) in the patient's record.

 ICD-10 Alert!

Subterm *with* occasionally appears in the ICD-10-PCS Index.

Note:

The word *with* is interpreted to mean "associated with" or "due to" when it appears in a code title, the index, or an instructional note in the tabular list. When the word *with* is included in disease and procedure code descriptions in the ICD-9-CM and ICD-10-CM tabular lists, the physician must document both conditions (or procedures) for the code to be assigned.

EXAMPLE 1: ICD-9-CM INDEX TO DISEASES—WITH: Locate main term *measles* in the Index to Diseases and notice that the word *with* appears above a list of 2nd qualifiers. To assign a code from the list, the physician must document both conditions, such as *measles with keratitis* (055.71). The physician could also document *measles with keratitis* as:

- Measles with mention of keratitis

- Measles associated with keratitis

- Measles and keratitis

EXAMPLE 2: ICD-9-CM INDEX TO PROCEDURES—WITH: Locate main term *excision* in the index, subterm *adenoids (tag)*, and notice that the word *with* appears in the phrase *with tonsillectomy*. To assign code 28.3, the physician must document both procedures, such as *tonsillectomy with excision of adenoids*.

EXAMPLE 3: ICD-10-CM INDEX TO DISEASES AND INJURIES—WITH: Locate main term *measles* in the index, and notice that the word *with* appears above a list of second qualifiers. To assign a code from the list, the physician must document both conditions, such as *measles with keratitis* (B05.81). The physician could also document:

- Measles keratitis

- Measles associated with keratitis

- Measles and keratitis

Exercise 3.15 – With

Instructions: Assign the code(s) to each statement. Make sure you interpret the use of subterm with appropriately in the ICD-9-CM, ICD-10-CM and ICD-10-PCS indexes. (The in subterm does not appear in ICD-10-PCS.)

ICD-9-CM   **ICD-10-CM**

_____   _____   **1.** Appendicitis with perforation

_____   _____   **2.** Thyrotoxicosis with uninodular adenomatous goiter

_____   _____   **3.** Traumatic hemothorax with pneumothorax (initial encounter)

_____   _____   **4.** Adjustment disorder with anxiety

_____   _____   **5.** Skull agenesis with anencephalus (or anencephaly)

_____   _____n/a_____   **6.** Open repair of anterior abdominal wall hernia with synthetic substitute

_____   _____n/a_____   **7.** Correction of coarctation of aorta with anastomosis

_____   _____n/a_____   **8.** Destruction of fallopian tube with ligation

_____   _____n/a_____   **9.** Extraocular muscle operation with revision

_____   _____n/a_____   **10.** Removal of halo traction with synchronous replacement

Cross-References

The Index to Diseases and Index to Procedures ICD-9-CM, ICD-10-CM and ICD-10-PCS indexes include **cross-references,** which instruct the coder to refer to another entry in the index (e.g., *see, see also, see* condition) or to the tabular list (e.g., *see* category) to assign the correct code.

- The *see* instruction after a main term directs the coder to refer to another term in the ICD-9-CM, ICD-10-CM, and ICD-10-PCS indexes to locate the code. The coder must go to the referenced main term to locate the correct code.

- The *see also* instruction is located after a main term or subterm in the ICD-9-CM and ICD-10-CM indexes and directs the coder to another main term (or subterm) that may provide additional useful index entries. The see also instruction does not have to be followed if the original main term (or subterm) provides the correct code.

- The *see category* instruction directs the coder to the ICD-9-CM or ICD-10-CM tabular list, where a code can be selected from the options provided there.

- The *see condition* instruction directs the coder to the main term for a condition, found in the ICD-9-CM or ICD-10-CM disease index.

EXAMPLE 1: ICD-9-CM INDEX TO DISEASES—*SEE* AND *SEE ALSO:* Locate main term *Laceration* in the Index to Diseases and notice that the *see* instruction for subterm *blood vessel* directs the coder to another location in the index where the correct code number can be found.

The *see also* instruction is optional if the correct code can be located below the main term (e.g., laceration of esophagus, 530.89). If the correct code cannot be located, the *see also* instruction directs the coder to another location in the index (e.g., there is no code for *laceration of skin,* so refer to *wound, open, skin NEC* to assign code 879.8.).

EXAMPLE 2: ICD-9-CM INDEX TO PROCEDURES— *SEE* AND *SEE ALSO*: Locate main term *removal* in the Index to Procedures and notice that the *see* instruction for *removal, abscess* directs the coder to another location in the index where the correct code number can be found.

The *see also* instruction for main term *removal* is optional if the correct code can be located below this main term (e.g., Removal, Abrams bar, 34.01). If the correct code cannot be located, the *see also* instruction directs the coder to another location in the index (e.g., there is no code for *removal, adrenal gland,* so refer to *excision, adrenal gland* to assign code 07.22.).

EXAMPLE 3: ICD-9-CM INDEX TO DISEASES— *SEE* CATEGORY AND *SEE* CONDITION: The *see* category instruction for Index to Diseases main term *Late effect(s), phlebitis or thrombophlebitis of intracranial venous sinuses* is mandatory and directs the coder to go to the Tabular List of Diseases category 326 to assign the code.

The *see* condition instruction for main term *remote effect of cancer* is mandatory because no codes are listed. The coder is instructed to identify the condition (e.g., pain, dizziness, anemia) in the patient record and locate it in the index.

EXAMPLE 4: ICD-10-CM INDEX TO DISEASES AND INJURIES— *SEE:* Locate main term *Laceration* and subterm *blood vessel* in the ICD-10-CM index. Notice that a cross-reference directs you to "See Injury, blood vessel," which is at a different location in the index where the code can be found.

EXAMPLE 5: ICD-10-CM INDEX TO DISEASES AND INJURIES— *SEE ALSO:* The *see also* instruction is optional if the correct code can be located below the main term (e.g., laceration of lower back, S31.010). If the correct code cannot be located, the *see also* cross-reference directs the coder to a different location in the index where the code can be found.

EXAMPLE 6: ICD-10-CM INDEX TO DISEASES AND INJURIES— *SEE* CATEGORY: Locate main term *pyelitis,* subterm *with,* and second qualifier *calculus* in the ICD-10-CM index. Notice that a cross-reference directs you to *see* category N20. To assign the correct code, review category N20 in the tabular list to select the appropriate fourth digit.

EXAMPLE 7: ICD-10-CM INDEX TO DISEASES AND INJURIES— *SEE* CONDITION: Locate main term *Accidental* in the ICD-10-CM index, and notice that a cross-reference directs you to *see* condition, which means the patient record needs to be reviewed to determine the condition (e.g., fracture).

EXAMPLE 8: ICD-10-PCS INDEX— *SEE:* Locate main term *abdominal esophagus* in the ICD-10-PCS index, and notice that a cross-reference directs you to "*see* Esophagus, Lower," which is at a different location in the index where the code can be found.

Exercise 3.16 – Cross-References

Instructions: Assign the code(s) to each statement. Make sure you appropriately interpret the use of cross-reference terms in the ICD-9-CM, ICD-10-CM, and ICD-10-PCS indexes. Cross-reference see (but not see also) is used in the ICD-10-PCS Index, so there is just one ICD-10-PCS procedure to code in number 6.

ICD-9-CM   ICD-10-CM/PCS

_____   _____   **1.** Abnormal acid–base balance

_____   _____   **2.** Toxicosis

_____   _____   **3.** Strangulated gangrenous abdominal hernia

(*continues*)

Exercise 3.16 (continued)

ICD-9-CM   **ICD-10-CM/PCS**

ICD-9-CM	ICD-10-CM/PCS		
_____	_____	**4.**	Undescended testis
_____	_____	**5.**	Proteinuria complicating pregnancy
_____	_____	**6.**	Advancement graft, skin of abdomen (split-thickness)
_____	n/a	**7.**	Plasty of peripheral blood vessel
_____	n/a	**8.**	Removal of thrombus with endarterectomy
_____	n/a	**9.**	Fracture repair with insertion of bone growth stimulator
_____	n/a	**10.**	Halsted operation

ICD-10 Alert!

The following ICD-10-CM coding conventions are new to its official coding guidelines:

- *Code Also note:* In ICD-10-CM, a *code also* note provides instruction that two codes may be required to fully describe a condition, but this note does not provide sequencing direction.

- *Default Codes:* In ICD-10-CM, a code listed next to a main term in the ICD-10-CM index is referred to as a default code. The default code represents that condition that is most commonly associated with the main term, or is the unspecified code for the condition. If a condition is documented in a patient record (e.g., appendicitis) without any additional information, such as acute or chronic, the default code should be assigned.

- *Syndromes:* In ICD-10-CM, coders should follow the alphabetic index guidance when assigning codes to syndromes. In the absence of index guidance, assign codes for the documented manifestations of the syndrome.

Summary

Coding conventions are general rules used in the classification, independent of official coding guidelines. An indented format is used for ease in reference in the ICD-9-CM, ICD-10-CM, and ICD-10-PCS indexes.

Eponyms are diseases or syndromes that are named for people, and they appear in ICD-9-CM and ICD-10-CM. Abbreviations include NEC and NOS, and they appear in ICD-9-CM and ICD-10-CM. Punctuation includes parentheses, slanted brackets (ICD-9-CM only), square brackets, and colons. Certain main terms in the ICD-9-CM disease index are followed by boxed notes, which contain special instructions. The ICD-9-CM disease index also contains the following tables: hypertension, neoplasm, and the table of drugs and chemicals. The ICD-10-CM index contains a neoplasm table and a table of drugs and chemicals. The ICD-10-PCS index does not contain tables; however, instead of a tabular list of codes, ICD-10-PCS contains tables (discussed in Chapter 5). The ICD-9-CM and ICD-10-CM tabular lists contain includes notes, excludes notes, and inclusion terms.

"Other" and "other specified" codes are assigned when patient record documentation provides detail for which a specific code does not exist in ICD-9-CM or ICD-10-CM. "Unspecified" codes are assigned because patient record documentation is insufficient for the assignment of a more specific code. Etiology and manifestation codes contain the following notes in the ICD-9-CM and ICD-10-CM disease tabular lists: code first underlying disease; code, if applicable, any causal condition first; use additional code; and in diseases classified elsewhere. When the word *and* appears in category titles and code descriptions in the ICD-9-CM and ICD-10-CM disease indexes tabular lists, it is interpreted as meaning "and/or." The instruction *due to* is located in the ICD-9-CM and ICD-10-CM as a subterm (in alphabetical order) to indicate the presence of a cause-and-effect relationship between two conditions. The word *in* as it appears in the ICD-9-CM and ICD-10-CM disease indexes is located in alphabetical order below the main term. The word *with* appears in the ICD-9-CM, ICD-10-CM, and ICD-10-PCS indexes immediately below the main term, and it is not in alphabetical order. Cross-reference terms in the ICD-9-CM, ICD-10-CM, and ICD-10-PCS indexes instruct the coder to refer to another entry in the index or, in ICD-9-CM and ICD-10-CM, to go directly to the tabular list to assign the correct code.

Internet Links

ICD-9-CM and ICD-10-CM/PCS updates: Go to **www.cdc.gov**, click on the More Data & Statistics link, click on the Disease Classification link, and click on any of the ICD links.

JustCoding News free e-newsletter: Go to **www.justcoding.com**, and click on the "Sign up for free *JustCoding News*" link.

Official version of ICD-9-CM and ICD-10-CM/PCS from the U.S. Government Bookstore: **bookstore.gpo.gov**

Study Checklist

- ❏ Read this chapter and highlight key concepts.
- ❏ Create an index card for each key term.
- ❏ Access the chapter Internet links to learn more about concepts.
- ❏ Complete the chapter review, verifying answers with your instructor.
- ❏ Complete WebTutor assignments and take online quizzes.
- ❏ Complete Workbook chapter, verifying answers with your instructor.
- ❏ Go to **www.cengagebrain.com** to access StudyWARE™ and the Premium Website. Login instructions are located in the Preface and on the Printed Access Card.
- ❏ Form a study group with classmates to discuss chapter concepts in preparation for an exam.

Review

Matching I

Instructions: Match the format in Column 2 with each line of the ICD-9-CM Index to Diseases entry in Column 1.

ICD-9-CM Index to Diseases Entries	Format
_____ 1. `Ulcer, ulcerated, ulcerating, Ulceration,`	a. 2nd qualifier
_____ 2. `     ulcerative 707.9`	b. 3rd qualifier
_____ 3. `aphthous (oral)(recurrent) 528.2`	c Continuation line
_____ 4. `   genital organ(s)`	d. Main term
_____ 5. `     female 616.50`	e. Subterm

Matching II

Instructions: Match the format in Column 2 with the underlined term or phrase in the ICD-9-CM Index to Procedures entries in Column 1.

ICD-9-CM Index to Procedures

Format

_____ 6. **Venotomy 38.00**
    Abdominal 38.07

a. 2nd qualifier

b. 3rd qualifier

_____ 7. **Baffes operation** (interatrial
    transposition of venous return) 35.91

c. Continuation line

d. Main term

_____ 8. **Destruction**
    fallopian tube 66.39
      with
        crushing (and ligation) 66.31

e. Subterm

_____ 9. **Gingivectomy 24.31**

_____ 10. **Thrombectomy** 38.00
    abdominal
      artery 38.06

Matching III

Instructions: Match the format in Column 2 with each line of the ICD-10-CM Index to Diseases and Injuries entries in Column 1.

ICD-10-CM Index to Diseases and Injuries

Format

_____ 11. **Abnormal, abnormality, abnormalities**—_see_

a. 2nd qualifier

_____ 12.   _also_ Anomaly

b. 3rd qualifier

_____ 13.   chromosome, chromosomal Q99.9

c. Continuation line

_____ 14.   sex Q99.8

d. Main term

_____ 15.   female phenotype Q97.9

e. Subterm

Multiple Choice

Instructions: Circle the most appropriate response.

16. If an index entry is too long to fit on one line, additional text is:
    a. edited so that the content fits onto just one line.
    b. located on the next line, flush with the preceding line.
    c. moved to the next line and indented two spaces.
    d. printed on a second line and indented five spaces.

17. A coder locates a code in the disease index, which contains the abbreviation NEC. Upon verification of the code in the tabular, the coder assigns that code. Which coding convention explains this code assignment?
    a. Information needed to assign a more specific code has not been obtained from the provider.
    b. The coder is directed to an "other specified" code by the index when a specific code is not available in the tabular list.
    c. Use of a more general code is indicated when the coder is unsure about information contained in documentation.
    d. Whenever a specific code is not available in the index for a condition, the coder is directed to the "other specified" code in the tabular list.

18. When the ICD-9-CM or ICD-10-CM disease tabular list contains the abbreviation NOS, which coding convention explains the code assignment?
    a. If the coder is not sure about the information contained in the documentation, use of a more general code is indicated.
    b. Information needed to assign a more specific code has not been obtained from the provider.
    c. The coder is directed to an "other specified" code by the index when a specific code is not available in the tabular list.
    d. Whenever a specific code is not available in the index for a condition, the coder is directed to the "other specified" code in the tabular list.

19. The use of a colon in the ICD-9-CM or ICD-10-CM disease tabular list:
    a. identifies the use of manifestation codes, which are to be sequenced second.
    b. indicates that one or more additional terms are to be included in the diagnostic statement to classify a condition or procedure.
    c. means that the words following the colon may be present in or absent from the provider's diagnostic statement.
    d. suggests the use of synonyms, alternative wording, or explanatory phrases.

20. *Includes* notes appear:
    a. below an ICD-9-CM or ICD-10-CM code in the disease tabular list.
    b. after main terms in the ICD-9-CM or ICD-10-CM disease index.
    c. above an ICD-9-CM or ICD-10-CM code in the disease tabular list.
    d. underneath essential modifiers in the ICD-9-CM or ICD-10-CM disease index.

21. *Excludes* notes appear in the:
    a. ICD-9-CM, ICD-10-CM and ICD-10-PCS indexes.
    b. ICD-9-CM and ICD-10-CM disease index and tabular list.
    c. ICD-9-CM and ICD-10-CM tabular lists.
    d. ICD-9-CM and ICD-10-CM disease indexes and ICD-9-CM procedure index.

22. "Trust the index" is ICD-9-CM and ICD-10-CM concept that is used when:
    a. a subterm located in the disease index is not listed in the disease tabular list.
    b. additional information was not obtained from the provider.
    c. insufficient documentation prevents the assignment of a more specific code.
    d. the coder is directed to the "other specified" code in the disease tabular list.

23. Unspecified codes:
    a. are classified as "other" codes in ICD-9-CM and ICD-10-CM disease tabular lists.
    b. contain the NEC abbreviation in the ICD-9-CM and ICD-10-CM disease indexes.
    c. result when a code is not found in the ICD-9-CM and ICD-10-CM disease indexes for a specified condition.
    d. usually contain a fourth digit of 9 and a fifth digit of 0.

24. Etiology codes:
    a. are designated in the ICD-9-CM disease index by slanted brackets.
    b. classify a condition that occurs as the result of another condition.
    c. contain a *use additional code* instruction in the tabular list.
    d. must be sequenced second as the underlying condition code.

25. The *see also* instruction in the ICD-9-CM and ICD-10-CM disease indexes follows a subterm and refers the coder to another main term that:
    a. allows for assignment of a secondary code.
    b. contains the code that is to be assigned.
    c. may provide additional useful index entries.
    d. must be followed to assign the correct code.

26. The physician documents "curly toe, left 5th toe" in the patient's record (downward flexion of toe with twisting underneath the adjacent toe). (Refer to the following ICD-9-CM Index to Diseases and Tabular List of Diseases entries.) Since there is no index entry for "curly toe," the coder reviews index entries for "deformity, toe" and identifies 735.8. Upon review of the tabular list entry for 735.8, the coder assigns the code.

Note:

The portion of the coding manual needed to answer each question is provided to simulate coding questions included on the Registered Health Information Administrator (RHIA) and Registered Health Information Technician (RHIT) certification exams.

ICD-9-CM INDEX TO DISEASES

```
Deformity — Continued
  toe (acquired) 735.9
    congenital 755.66
    specified NEC 735.8
```

ICD-9-CM TABULAR LIST OF DISEASES

```
735 Acquired deformities of toe
        EXCLUDES  congenital (754.60–754.69, 755.65–755.66)
    735.0 Hallux valgus (acquired)
    735.1 Hallux varus (acquired)
    735.2 Hallux rigidus
    735.3 Hallux malleus
    735.4 Other hammer toe (acquired)
    735.5 Claw toe (acquired)
    735.8 Other acquired deformities of toe
    735.9 Unspecified acquired deformity of toe
```

Code 735.8 is correct because the NEC abbreviation in the index represents "other specified," which means:
  a. a nonspecific condition is documented, no index entry exists, and the coder is directed to assign an "unspecified" code.
  b. a specific code is not available for a condition and the index directs the coder to assign an "other specified" code.
  c. supplementary words are present or absent in the documented condition (e.g., non-essential modifiers) and no code is assigned.
  d. terms are excluded from a code (e.g., essential modifiers) and the documented condition is to be coded elsewhere.

27. The surgeon documented "hysterectomy" as the surgery performed on a 59-year-old female. (Refer to the following ICD-9-CM Index to Procedures and Tabular List of Procedures entries.) The index entry for "hysterectomy" directed the coder to 68.9 in the tabular list, which contains the NOS abbreviation.

ICD-9-CM INDEX TO PROCEDURES

```
Hysterectomy 68.9
```

31. The physician documents "otosclerosis" on the patient's record. The coder locates code 387.9 in the ICD-9-CM Index to Diseases and verifies it in the ICD-9-CM Tabular List of Diseases. (Refer to the following ICD-9-CM Tabular List of Diseases entry.)

ICD-9-CM TABULAR LIST OF DISEASES

387 Otosclerosis

    INCLUDES   Otospongiosis

    387.0 Otosclerosis involving oval window, nonobliterative

    387.1 Otosclerosis involving oval window, obliterative

    387.2 Cochlear otosclerosis

        Otosclerosis involving:

          otic capsule

          round window

    387.8 Other otosclerosis

    387.9 Otosclerosis, unspecified

Upon review of the tabular list, the coder notices additional codes for otosclerosis, including 387.2, which contains a colon that is interpreted to mean that the:

    a. coder should ask the physician to add "otic capsule" to the diagnostic statement so 387.2 can be coded.

    b. condition "otic capsule" is associated with codes 387.0, 387.1, and 387.2; so code 387.0 should be assigned.

    c. phrase *otic capsule* can be present or absent from the diagnosis because it is a non-essential modifier.

    d. physician must include the phrase *otic capsule* or *round capsule* in the diagnostic statement if 387.2 is to be assigned.

32. How is the excludes note in the following ICD-9-CM Tabular List of Diseases entry interpreted?

ICD-9-CM TABULAR LIST OF DISEASES

493.2 Chronic obstructive asthma

    Asthma with chronic obstructive pulmonary disease

        [COPD]

    Chronic asthmatic bronchitis

    EXCLUDES *acute bronchitis (466.0)*

          Chronic obstructive bronchitis (491.20–491.22)

---

    a. Code 466.0 is assigned if the physician documents "acute bronchitis" instead of "chronic bronchitis."

    b. Codes 493.2 and 466.0 are assigned if the physician documents "asthma with chronic bronchitis."

    c. If the physician documents acute bronchitis, codes 466.0 and 493.2 are assigned by the coder.

    d. The abbreviation located in square brackets is considered a nonessential modifier and is assigned code 466.0.

33. The physician performed a repair of the atrial and ventricular septa and inserted a prosthesis (e.g., mesh). Upon review of the following ICD-9-CM Tabular List of Procedures code description for 35.5, how is the *includes note* interpreted?

> **ICD-9-CM TABULAR LIST OF PROCEDURES**
>
> **35.5 Repair of atrial and ventricular septa with prosthesis**
>   **INCLUDES**   repair of septa with synthetic implant
>   or patch
>   Code also cardiopulmonary bypass [extracorporeal
>   circulation] [heart-lung machine] (39.61)

    a. ICD-9-CM code 39.61 should be assigned instead of code 35.5.
    b. Code 35.5 classifies "repair of septa with synthetic implant or patch."
    c. The coder should ask the physician for clarification of the procedure.
    d. The coder should refer to code 39.61 for additional instructions.

34. The physician documented the diagnostic statement "benign hypertrophy of the prostate." How are the inclusion terms below code 600.0 in the following ICD-9-CM Tabular List of Diseases entry interpreted?

> **ICD-9-CM TABULAR LIST OF DISEASES**
>
> **600 Hyperplasia of prostate**
> **INCLUDES**   enlarged prostate
>   **600.0 Hypertrophy (benign) of prostate**
>   Benign prostatic hypertrophy
>   Enlargement of prostate
>   Smooth enlarged prostate
>   Soft enlarged prostate

    a. All of the conditions below 600.0 are synonyms for "hypertrophy (benign) of prostate," and any of them could be documented.
    b. If one of the conditions below 600.0 is not included from the diagnostic statement, assign a code from 788.30 through 788.39 instead.
    c. The conditions below 600.0 are essential modifiers, and they must be included in the diagnostic statement for the code to be assigned.
    d. The inclusion terms are always listed below 2-digit category codes and above the 4- and 5-digit codes to which they are assigned.

35. The coder located 345.9 in the ICD-9-CM Index to Diseases for the diagnosis "epilepsy." Upon verifying the code in the ICD-9-CM Tabular List of Diseases, the coder noticed that the term *idiopathic* does not appear in the code description. (Refer to the following ICD-9-CM Index to Diseases and Tabular List of Diseases entries.)

> **ICD-9-CM INDEX TO DISEASES**
>
> **Epilepsy, epileptic** (idiopathic) 345.9

How should the coder interpret the missing term from the tabular list?

    a. Because *idiopathic* is located in parentheses, it is an essential modifier and must be in the diagnostic statement so code 345.9 can be assigned.

    b. Since *idiopathic* is not included in the diagnostic statement or in the code description, the coder should assign code 780.3 instead of 345.9.

    c. The coder should contact the physician to request clarification about the diagnostic statement so that code 345.9 can be assigned to the case.

    d. This is a case of trust the index, which means that terms in the index may not appear in the tabular list; so assigning code 345.9 is acceptable.

 Note:

ICD-10-CM and ICD-10-PCS coding manual entries that are needed to answer each question are provided to simulate coding questions included on the RHIA and RHIT certification exams.

36. Two weeks ago, the patient was riding her bicycle when she fell and scraped her right knee on the gravel road. She had her mother look at it, and after washing it with warm soap and water and pouring some hydrogen peroxide on the abrasion, the patient returned to riding her bicycle. Today the patient is due to complaints of tenderness and pain of her right knee. Upon examination, it was determined that small pebbles are embedded below the skin's surface. The pebbles were successfully removed, the wound was wrapped, and the patient was discharged home. The discharge diagnosis is retained stones, skin of right knee. (Refer to the following ICD-10-CM Index to Diseases and Injuries entry.)

ICD-10-CM INDEX TO DISEASES AND INJURIES

Retained *—see* Retention

Retention, retained

    foreign body *—see also* Foreign body,

        retained

      current trauma *—code as* Foreign body,

      by site or type

Upon review of the ICD-10-CM Index to Diseases and Injuries entry, the coder locates main term *Retained* and notes the "*see* Retention" instruction, which means the coder should:

    a. Generate a physician query to ask the physician to document a more specific diagnosis.

    b. Go to main term *Retention* in the ICD-10-CM index to begin locating the code.

    c. Locate the main term in the ICD-9-CM disease index, and use the GEM to assign the ICD-10-CM code.

    d. Review the ICD-10-CM Tabular List of Diseases and Injuries to locate the code.

37. A patient was installing a new roof on his house using a nail gun when he got distracted by someone calling his name from the sidewalk. He proceeded to nail the fleshy skin between his left thumb and forefinger to the roof. He was able to pull the flesh free, but the nail remained embedded in his skin. The nail was removed, the wound irrigated and bandaged, and the patient discharged home with a diagnosis of puncture wound with nail (from nail gun) located the in skin and soft tissue between left thumb and forefinger. (Refer to the following ICD-10-CM Index to Diseases and Injuries entry.)

ICD-10-CM INDEX TO DISEASES AND INJURIES

```
Foreign body
  in
    puncture wound —see Puncture, by site,
      with foreign body
    soft tissue (residual) M79.5
Puncture
  hand S61.439
    with
      foreign body S61.449
    finger —see Puncture, finger
    left S61.432
      with
        foreign body S461.422
    right S61.431
      with
        foreign body S61.441
```

The coder locates ICD-10-CM Index to Diseases and Injuries main term *Foreign body* and follows the instructional note to "*See* Puncture, by site"; this means the coder should:

    a. Assign code M79.5 after verifying it in the tabular list.
    b. Follow the cross-reference *see* Puncture, finger.
    c. Look up code S61.439 in the diseases tabular list.
    d. Verify code S61.442 in the tabular list, and assign it.

38. Three months ago, the 17-year-old patient broke up with his girlfriend, and she assaulated him by sticking him in the right eye with a plastic straw. Luckily, she missed the eyeball and embedded the straw in the soft tissue of the outer right eye. The patient presents today with pain and swelling of the right eye, and upon examination a tiny piece of plastic is found to have embedded in the soft tissue. The foreign body was removed, the wound irrigated, and the patient discharged home with a prescription for an antibiotic. (Refer to the following ICD-10-CM Tabular List of Diseases and Injuries entry.)

> **H05.5 Retained (old) foreign body following penetrating wound of orbit**
>
> Retrobulbar foreign body
>
> **Use additional** code to identify the type of retained foreign body (Z18.-)
>
> **EXCLUDES1** *current penetrating wound of orbit (S05.4-)*
>
> **EXCLUDES2** *retained foreign body of eyelid (H02.81-)*
>
> *retained intraocular foreign body (H44.6-, H44.7-)*
>
> **H05.50** Retained (old) foreign body following penetrating wound of unspecified orbit
>
> **H05.51** Retained (old) foreign body following penetrating wound of right orbit
>
> **H05.52** Retained (old) foreign body following penetrating wound of left orbit
>
> **H05.53** Retained (old) foreign body following penetrating wound of bilateral orbits

In addition to external causes of morbidity codes W45.8xxA and Y07.04, and factors influencing health status and contact with health services code Z18.2, select the appropriate disease and injury code.

    a. H02.81–
    b. H05.50
    c. H05.51
    d. S05.4–

39. The patient underwent an angiotripsy procedure of the right brachial artery. Review the following ICD-10-PCS Index entry, and select the appropriate cross-reference.

> **ICD-10-PCS Index**
>
> **Angiotripsy**
>
>   -*See* Occlusion, Upper Arteries 03L
>
>   -*See* Occlusion, Upper Veins 05L

    a. *See* Occlusion, Upper Arteries 03L
    b. *See* Occlusion, Upper Veins 05L

40. The patient underwent replacement of a spinal cord drainage device. Review the following ICD-10-PCS Table entry, and using the build-a-code approach, which ICD-10-PCS code would be assigned?

ICD-10-PCS Table

Central Nervous System 001-00X

0	Medical and Surgical
0	Central Nervous System
2	Change:

Change: Taking out or off a device from a body part and putting back an identical or similar device in or on the same body part without cutting or puncturing the skin or a mucous membrane

Body Part Character 4	Approach Character 5	Device Character 6	Qualifier Character 7
0 Brain	X External	0 Drainage Device	Z No Qualifier
E Cranial Nerve		Y Other Device	
U Spinal Canal			

a. 0020X0Z   b. 002EX0Z   c. 002UX0Z   d. 002UXYZ

ICD-9-CM and ICD-10-CM Coding Guidelines

Chapter Outline

ICD-9-CM and ICD-10-CM Official Guidelines
  for Coding and Reporting
General ICD-9-CM and ICD-10-CM Diagnosis
  Coding Guidelines
ICD-9-CM Chapter-Specific Diagnosis Coding
  Guidelines with ICD-10 Alerts

> **Note:**
>
> The ICD-9-CM Volume 3 and ICD-10-PCS procedure coding guidelines are located in Chapter 5 because they impact inpatient hospital coding only.

Chapter Objectives

At the conclusion of this chapter, the student should be able to:

- Define key terms.
- Explain HIPAA's impact on the adherence to *ICD-9-CM Official Guidelines for Coding and Reporting* and *ICD-10-CM Official Guidelines for Coding and Reporting*.
- Describe the content of each section of the *ICD-9-CM Official Guidelines for Coding and Reporting* and the *ICD-10-CM Official Guidelines for Coding and Reporting* (see Appendix II located on the Premium Website at www.cengagebrain.com).
- Apply general ICD-9-CM and ICD-10-CM coding guidelines when assigning codes to diagnoses.
- Apply chapter-specific ICD-9-CM and ICD-10-CM coding guidelines when assigning codes to diagnoses.

Key Terms

aircraft
benign
benign hypertension
carcinoma (Ca) *in situ*
closed fracture

combination code
commercial transport
  aircraft
compound fracture
contiguous sites

driver
fracture
late effect
lexicon
malignant hypertension

malunion
metastatic cancer
motor vehicle
motor vehicle
  accident

motor vehicle nontraffic accident

motor vehicle traffic accident

motorcycle

motorcyclist

multiple codes

nonunion

off-road motor vehicle

open fracture

opportunistic infection

other road vehicle

overlapping sites

passenger

pedal cycle

pedal cyclist

pedestrian

pedestrian conveyance

perinatal period

primary malignancy

public highway

railroad

railway

railway accident

railway train

railway vehicle

residual condition

roadway

secondary malignancy

simple fracture

small boat

streetcar

trafficway

transport accident

type 1 diabetes mellitus

type 2 diabetes mellitus

uncertain behavior

unspecified hypertension

unspecified nature

watercraft

Introduction

This chapter includes an interpretation of the following coding guidelines, which are published in the *ICD-9-CM Official Guidelines for Coding and Reporting* (or *ICD-10-CM Official Guidelines for Coding and Reporting*):

- General ICD-9-CM (or ICD-10-CM) diagnosis coding guidelines

- ICD-9-CM chapter-specific diagnosis coding guidelines (with ICD-10 Alerts!)

The coding guidelines are to be used as a companion to the official version of the ICD-9-CM (or ICD-10-CM) coding manual, which contains coding conventions to ensure accurate coding.

ICD-9-CM (or ICD-10-CM) disease codes describe causes of illness or clinical symptoms exhibited by the patient, and codes assigned must be supported by documentation in the patient's record. Third-party payers require that claims submitted for reimbursement demonstrate medical necessity for treatment, which means that a diagnosis code must be reported for each procedure or service code included on the claim. (ICD-9-CM Volume 3 and ICD-10-PCS procedure codes describe procedures performed for the inpatient treatment of illness and injury. HCPCS level II and CPT codes are reported on outpatient claims, and these coding systems are discussed in Chapters 7–18.)

Note:

When reviewing examples and completing exercises and review questions in this chapter, use your ICD-9-CM (or ICD-10-CM) coding manual to locate disease and procedure index entries and to verify them in the tabular list.

Note:

ICD-9-CM and ICD-10-PCS procedure coding guidelines apply to inpatient hospitalizations only, and the guidelines are discussed in Chapter 5.

Note:

The following additional content is located on the Premium Website at www.cengagebrain.com:

- *Alternate Healthcare Facilities and Coding Guidelines*
- *HIV-Related Conditions and Opportunistic Infections*
- *ICD-10-CM Official Guidelines for Coding and Reporting 2012*

ICD-10 Alert!

- ICD-10-CM chapter-specific coding guidelines are highlighted in Appendix II located on the Premium Website because they are too lengthy to incorporate into this chapter.
- ICD-10-CM coding examples are included in the appropriate sections of this chapter to allow for comparison with ICD-9-CM coding examples.
- Although ICD-10-CM codes are alphanumerical (when compared with mostly numerical ICD-9-CM codes), the coding guidelines are similar. ICD-10 Alerts! are included throughout this chapter to identify differences and similarities between ICD-9-CM and ICD-10-CM coding guidelines.
- The *Instructor's Manual to Accompany 3-2-1 Code It!* contains both ICD-9-CM and ICD-10-CM codes for each chapter exercise and the review.

ICD-9-CM and ICD-10-CM Official Guidelines for Coding and Reporting

The Centers for Medicare & Medicaid Services (CMS) and the National Center for Health Statistics (NCHS) are the agencies in the U.S. Department of Health & Human Services (DHHS) that provide official guidelines for coding and reporting using ICD-9-CM and ICD-10-CM. The *Official Guidelines for Coding and Reporting* are approved by the four organizations that make up the cooperating parties. They include the American Hospital Association (AHA), American Health Information Management Association (AHIMA), CMS, and NCHS. The guidelines are a set of rules developed to accompany and complement the official conventions and instructions provided within ICD-9-CM (or ICD-10-CM). They are based on the coding and sequencing instructions in ICD-9-CM (or ICD-10-CM) and provide additional instruction. The health care provider is responsible for complete and accurate patient record documentation, and the coder is responsible for providing complete and accurate code assignment and reporting diagnoses and procedures. The guidelines were developed to assist both health care providers and coders in identifying diagnoses and procedures that are to be reported. Coders should review the entire patient record to determine the reason for an encounter and the conditions treated.

HIPAA Alert!

Adherence to the *Official Guidelines for Coding and Reporting* when assigning ICD-9-CM diagnosis and procedure codes is required under the Health Insurance Portability and Accountability Act (HIPAA). ICD-9-CM diagnosis codes (Volumes I and II) were adopted under HIPAA for all health care settings, and ICD-9-CM procedure codes (Volume III) were adopted for inpatient procedures reported by hospitals. ICD-10-CM and ICD-10-PCS (abbreviated as ICD-10-CM/PCS) will replace ICD-9-CM.

Note:

The structure and conventions of ICD-9-CM, ICD-10-CM, and ICD-10-PCS are discussed in Chapter 3. ICD-9-CM and ICD-10-CM general coding guidelines and ICD-9-CM chapter-specific coding guidelines are discussed later in this chapter. ICD-10-CM chapter-specific coding guidelines are highlighted in Appendix II located on the Premium Website. ICD-10 Alerts! appear in this chapter to clarify similarities and differences between ICD-9-CM and ICD-10-CM chapter-specific coding guidelines.

The *Official Guidelines for Coding and Reporting* are organized into four sections and one appendix:

- Section I includes the structure and conventions of the classification and general guidelines that apply to the entire classification and chapter-specific guidelines that correspond to the chapters as they are arranged in the classification.

- Section II includes guidelines for selection of the principal diagnosis for nonoutpatient settings. (Nonoutpatient settings include acute care hospitals, long-term care facilities, home health care agencies, nursing homes, and so on.)

- Section III includes guidelines for reporting additional diagnoses (e.g., coexisting conditions, complications) in nonoutpatient settings.

- Section IV includes guidelines for outpatient diagnosis coding and reporting.

- Appendix I of the CMS official coding guidelines includes present on admission (POA) reporting guidelines. (POA reporting is discussed in Chapter 19.)

The *Official Guidelines for Coding and Reporting* contain rules that accompany and complement the official conventions and instructions provided within ICD-9-CM (or ICD-10-CM); they are based on coding and sequencing instructions in the coding manual. A joint effort between the health care provider and the coder is essential to achieving complete and accurate documentation, code assignment, and reporting of diagnoses and procedures. The coding guidelines were developed to assist both the health care provider and the coder in identifying diagnoses and procedures that are to be reported. The importance of consistent, complete documentation in the medical record is crucial because without such documentation, accurate coding cannot be achieved. In addition, the entire record must be reviewed to determine the specific reason for the encounter and the conditions treated. (The term *encounter* is used in the coding guidelines for all heath care settings, including inpatient hospital admissions. The term *provider* is used in the coding guidelines to mean physician or any qualified health care practitioner who is legally accountable for establishing the patient's diagnosis.)

Note:

Selection of principal diagnosis (and principal procedure) is discussed in Chapter 5.

Note:

Reporting additional diagnoses (e.g., comorbidities and complications) (and secondary procedures) for inpatient care is discussed in Chapter 5.

ICD-10 Alert!

The ICD-10-CM coding guidelines do *not* include POA reporting guidelines (Appendix I of the ICD-9-CM coding guidelines).

Note:

Outpatient diagnosis coding and reporting guidelines, which include selection of the first-listed diagnosis (formerly called the primary diagnosis) and secondary diagnoses, are discussed in Chapter 6.

Note:

Present on admission (POA) reporting guidelines are discussed in Chapter 19.

ICD-10 Alert!

The ICD-10-PCS (and ICD-9-CM Volume III) procedure coding guidelines are located in Chapter 5.

HIPAA Alert!

The HIPAA regulations for electronic transactions require providers and third-party payers, including Medicare administrative contractors (MACs), to adhere to the *Official Guidelines for Coding and Reporting*. Thus, a violation of the coding guidelines is technically a HIPAA violation. Because some third-party payers and MACs do not appear to be aware of (or understand) this HIPAA provision, to obtain appropriate reimbursement for submitted ICD-9-CM or ICD-10-CM/PCS codes, you may need to point out specific provisions in the regulation that reference the coding guidelines. For example, the V57 codes in ICD-9-CM (or Z51 codes in ICD-10-CM) can be reported as a first-listed code for outpatient care. However, some third-party payers and MACs deny claims that report V57 (or Z51) codes. In that case, you will need to contact your regional CMS office or the HIPAA enforcement office (which is located at CMS) for resolution. Third-party payers and MACs should not be allowed to violate the *Official Guidelines for Coding and Reporting* because that means they are violating HIPAA provisions!

Exercise 4.1 – ICD-9-CM and ICD-10-CM Official Guidelines for Coding and Reporting

Instructions: Complete each statement.

1. The *Official Guidelines for Coding and Reporting* contains guidelines developed by the _____ to accompany and complement the official conventions and instructions provided within ICD-9-CM or ICD-10-CM.

2. Coding guidelines use the term _____ for all heath care settings, including inpatient hospital admissions.

3. Coding guidelines use the term _____ to mean physician or any qualified health care practitioner who is legally accountable for establishing the patient's diagnosis.

4. The _____ regulations for electronic transactions require providers and third-party payers, including Medicare administrative contractors (MACs), to adhere to the *Official Guidelines for Coding and Reporting*.

5. Section I of the *Official Guidelines for Coding and Reporting* includes the _____ of the classification and general guidelines that apply to the entire classification and chapter-specific guidelines that correspond to the chapters as they are arranged in the classification.

6. Section II of the *Official Guidelines for Coding and Reporting* includes guidelines for selection of the _____ for nonoutpatient settings.

7. Section III of the *Official Guidelines for Coding and Reporting* includes guidelines for reporting _____ in nonoutpatient settings.

8. Inpatient care requires the reporting of additional diagnoses, which are called _____.

9. Section IV is of the *Official Guidelines for Coding and Reporting* covers _____.

10. Appendix I of the *ICD-9-CM Official Guidelines for Coding and Reporting* covers _____.

General ICD-9-CM and ICD-10-CM Diagnosis Coding Guidelines

The *International Classification of Diseases (ICD)* was originally created to track diseases for statistical reporting purposes. Its origin is based on the Bertillon *International Statistical Classification of Causes of Death*, which was revised by the American Public Health Association (APHA) every 10 years. In 1948, the World Health

Organization (WHO) assumed responsibility for revisions and the official name of the classification system was changed to the *International Classification of Diseases*. The NCHS created the clinical modification (CM) of ICD-9, and ICD-9-CM was implemented in 1979. Although ICD-9-CM contains additional clinical information, its 3-digit codes and their sequence correlate to the ICD-9 system developed by the WHO.

The general coding guidelines are followed when assigning ICD-9-CM diagnosis codes for inpatient, outpatient and physician office settings:

Locating a Code in ICD-9-CM or ICD-10-CM— Use of Both Index and Tabular List

Use both the disease index and the disease tabular list when locating and assigning codes because relying on just the index or tabular list results in coding errors and less specificity when selecting codes.

Locate Each Term in the Alphabetic Index

Locate each term in the ICD-9-CM or ICD-10-CM disease index first, and verify the code selected in the disease tabular list. Make sure you read and are guided by coding conventions (e.g., instructional notations such as NOS and NEC) that appear in either the index or the tabular list.

ICD-10 Alert!

ICD-10-CM and ICD-10-PCS will replace ICD-9-CM. ICD-10-CM contains additional clinical information, as compared with ICD-9-CM Volumes I and II, but its 3-character codes and their sequence correlate to the ICD-10 system developed by the WHO. ICD-10-PCS is used to report procedure codes, and its content is included in Chapter 5.

Note:

Before assigning codes, review the explanation and examples of ICD-9-CM and ICD-10-CM/PCS coding conventions in Chapter 3.

ICD-10 Alert!

Use *both* the ICD-10-CM index and tabular list because the ICD-10-CM index does not always provide the complete code. Selection of the complete code, including laterality (e.g., bilateral, right side, left side) and any applicable seventh character is done using the tabular list. A dash (-) at the end of a code in the index indicates that additional character(s) are required. Even if a dash is *not* included at the index entry, refer to the tabular list to verify whether additional character(s) are required.

EXAMPLE 1: The ICD-9-CM Index to Diseases entry for *diabetes mellitus* lists code 250.0. Upon verification in the Tabular List of Diseases, the coder should note that a fifth-digit subclassification code is needed.

EXAMPLE 2: The ICD-10-CM Index to Diseases and Injuries entry for *diabetes mellitus* lists code E11.9, as verified in the tabular list.

Level of Detail in Coding

Pay attention to the level of detail when assigning codes because diagnosis codes are to be reported using the highest number of digits or characters available.

Note:

ICD-9-CM disease codes contain three, four, or five digits. Codes with three digits are category codes, which may be further subdivided by assigning fourth and/or fifth digits to provide greater detail. A three-digit code is reported only if it is not further subdivided. Where fourth-digit subcategories and/or fifth-digit subclassifications are provided, they must be assigned. A code is invalid if it has not been coded to the complete number of digits required for that code.

ICD-10-CM codes contain three, four, five, six, or seven characters. Codes with three characters are category codes, which may be further subdivided by assigning up to four additional characters to provide greater detail.

Codes with four, five, or six characters that require additional character(s) are subcategory codes. Codes that do *not* require additional character(s) are simply called *codes*. (It might be helpful to think of such *codes* as *complete codes*.) The concept of *subclassification codes* is not used in ICD-10-CM. A three-character code is reported only if it is not further subdivided. Where fourth through seventh characters are provided, they must be assigned. A code is invalid if it has not been coded to the complete number of characters required for that code.

EXAMPLE 1: ICD-9-CM diagnosis code 410 (acute myocardial infarction) requires the assignment of a fourth-digit subcategory to describe the location of the infarction and a fifth digit to identify the episode of care. It is incorrect to report a category 410 code without the fourth *and* fifth digits. Thus, you would assign code 410.01 to a patient diagnosed with an anterolateral myocardial infarction who received initial treatment, for example, at an acute care hospital.

EXAMPLE 2: ICD-10-CM code M1a (chronic gout) requires the assignment of a fourth, fifth, sixth, and seventh character to complete the code. It is incorrect to report a category M1a code without the fourth through seventh characters. Thus, you would assign code M1a.0110 to a patient diagnosed with idiopathic chronic gout of the right shoulder, without tophus.

Code or Codes from 001.0 through V91.99 (ICD-9-CM) and A00.00 through T88.9, Z00–Z99.8 (ICD-10-CM)

Appropriate codes from ICD-9-CM (001.0 through V91.99) and ICD-10-CM (A00.0 through T88.9, Z00–Z99.8) are reported to identify diagnoses, symptoms, conditions, problems, complaints, or other reason(s) for the encounter.

The selection of ICD-9-CM codes 001.0 through 999.9 (or ICD-10-CM codes A00.0 through T88.9) frequently will be used to describe the reason for the encounter (instead of an ICD-9-CM V code or an ICD-10-CM Z code). Make sure you verify these codes in the disease tabular list.

ICD-10 Alert!

Codes V00 through Y99 are reported for external causes of morbidity. (In ICD-9-CM, E codes are reported for external causes of morbidity.)

Signs and Symptoms

Codes that describe symptoms and signs are reported when a related definitive diagnosis has not been established (or confirmed) by the provider.

Note:

ICD-9-CM Chapter 16 (Symptoms, Signs, and Ill-Defined Conditions, 780–799) contains many, but not all, of these codes. Some symptoms, signs, and ill-defined condition codes are found in other ICD-9-CM chapters. (e.g., stomach pain, 536.8). ICD-10-CM Chapter 18 (Symptoms, Signs and Abnormal Clinical and Laboratory Findings, Not Elsewhere Classified) contains many, but not all codes for signs and symptoms. Some codes are found in other ICD-10-CM chapters (e.g., acute neoplasm-related pain, G89.3).

EXAMPLE: The patient is seen at a physician's office for an initial visit, complaining of pain and limited range of motion of her right pinky finger knuckle. The physician examines the joint and notices a solid mass. He orders an X-ray to rule out ganglion. Upon the follow-up visit, the X-ray results reveal no arthritis or stalklike growth. The diagnosis is ganglion cyst (Figure 4-1), little finger knuckle joint, right. The patient is scheduled for outpatient surgery to remove the ganglion.

For the initial visit, assign ICD-9-CM codes for the pain (719.44), limited range of motion (719.54), and mass of the little finger knuckle joint (719.64). Assign ICD-10-CM codes for pain (M79.644), limited range of motion (M25.641), and mass of the little finger knuckle joint (R22.31).

For the follow-up visit, assign ICD-9-CM code 727.41 to the ganglion cyst, little finger knuckle joint, right. The ICD-10-CM code is M67.441. Code 727.41 (or M67.441) is reported as a definitive diagnosis, which means signs and symptoms codes for pain, limited range of motion, or mass of the little finger knuckle joint are *not* reported on the claim for the follow-up visit.

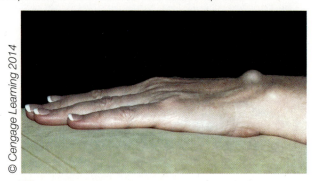

Figure 4-1 Ganglion cyst

Conditions That Are an Integral Part of a Disease Process

Signs and symptoms that are associated with a disease process should *not* be assigned as additional codes (unless otherwise instructed by ICD-9-CM or ICD-10-CM) because they are included in the disease process.

EXAMPLE: The patient is seen at the hospital's emergency department (ED) with a complaint of shortness of breath. A chest X-ray reveals pneumonia (Figure 4-2), and the ED physician prescribes an antibiotic.

Assign ICD-9-CM code 486 (or ICD-10-CM code J18.9) to the pneumonia, and do not assign a code for the shortness of breath because it is a symptom of pneumonia.

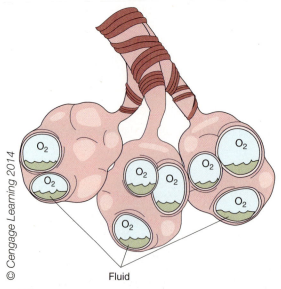

Fluid

Figure 4-2 Pneumonia: alveoli filling with fluid

Conditions That Are *Not* an Integral Part of a Disease Process

Conditions that are not considered an integral part of a disease process, such as additional signs and symptoms that may not be associated routinely with a disease process, should be coded when present (e.g., severe headache for which treatment or medical management is provided is coded when the patient is diagnosed with pneumonia).

> **EXAMPLE:** The patient is seen at the physician's office for follow-up care of her controlled hypertension. During the visit, she tells the physician that she has been experiencing some insomnia. The physician discussed possible reasons for the insomnia with the patient, who admitted to being under extreme stress recently. The patient was reluctant to take over-the-counter or prescription medications for the insomnia, and the physician suggested alternative solutions. The physician also instructed the patient to return in two weeks for follow-up of the insomnia.
>
> Assign ICD-9-CM code 401.9 (or ICD-10-CM code I10) to the hypertension. In addition, assign ICD-9-CM code 780.52 (or ICD-10-CM code G47.00) to the insomnia because it is not a symptom of hypertension and it was medically managed during the visit.

Multiple Coding for a Single Condition

The etiology/manifestation coding convention requires that two codes be reported to completely describe a single condition that affects multiple body systems.

> **EXAMPLE:** The diagnosis amyloid neuritis requires ICD-9-CM codes 277.39 and 357.4 to be assigned, in that order. ICD-10-CM codes E85.1 and G63 are reported in that order. (Remember: italicized codes in the tabular list are never sequenced first.)

In addition, other single conditions require more than one code to be reported, such as those associated with "use additional code" notes found in the tabular list. These codes are not part of

> **Note:**
>
> Multiple codes also may need to be reported for ICD-9-CM late effects (or ICD-10-CM *sequela*), complications, and obstetrical cases to describe more fully the patient's conditions. (Refer to specific guidelines below for further instruction.)

an etiology/manifestation pair where a secondary code is useful to describe a condition fully. The sequencing rule for "use additional code" is the same as the etiology/manifestation pair in that a secondary code should be reported.

> **EXAMPLE:** For infections not included in ICD-9-CM Chapter 1, a secondary code from category 041 (bacterial infection in conditions classified elsewhere and of unspecified site) may be required to identify the bacterial organism causing the infection. A "use additional code" note will usually be found at the infectious disease code, indicating the need to report the organism code as a secondary code. For a diagnosis of urinary tract infection due to *Escherichia coli,* report codes ICD-9-CM 599.0 and 041.4 (or ICD-10-CM codes N39.0 and B96.2), in that order.

"Code first" notes are also located below certain ICD-9-CM and ICD-10-CM codes in the tabular lists that are not specifically manifestation codes but may be due to an underlying cause. When a "code first" note is present *and* an underlying condition is documented in the patient record, the underlying condition is reported first.

> **EXAMPLE:** The physician documents rheumatic pneumonia in the patient's record. Upon review of the index and tabular list, assign ICD-9-CM codes 390 and 517.1 (or ICD-10-CM codes I00 and J17) for the condition, in that order.

"Code, if applicable, any causal condition first" notes in the ICD-9-CM and ICD-10-CM tabular lists indicate that this code may be assigned as a first-listed or principal diagnosis when the causal condition is unknown or not applicable. If a causal condition is known, the code for that condition should be reported as the first-listed or principal diagnosis.

> **EXAMPLE:** The patient is diagnosed with urinary incontinence and congenital ureterocele. Assign ICD-9-CM codes 753.23 and 788.30 (or ICD-10-CM codes Q62.31 and R32, although generating a physician query could result in a more specific urinary incontinence code), in that order.

Acute and Chronic Conditions

If the same condition is described as both acute (or subacute) and chronic and separate subentries exist in the disease index at the same indentation level, code both and sequence the acute (or subacute) code first.

> **EXAMPLE:** The diagnoses acute gastritis and chronic gastritis are assigned ICD-9-CM codes 535.00 and 535.10, in that order. (Fifth-digit 0 is assigned because the diagnostic statement does not include mention of hemorrhage.) ICD-10-CM codes K29.00 and K29.50 are assigned in that order.

> ## Note:
>
> Multiple codes may be needed for ICD-9-CM late effects (or ICD-10-CM *sequela*), complication codes and obstetric codes to more fully describe a condition. Coding guidelines for these conditions are discussed later in this chapter.

Combination Code

Assign combination codes when available and multiple codes as needed. A **combination code** is a single code that is used to classify two diagnoses (or procedures), a diagnosis with an associated secondary process (manifestation), or a diagnosis with an associated complication. Combination codes are located by referring to subterm entries in the disease index and by reading "includes" and "excludes" notes in the disease tabular list. Assign two or more **multiple codes** to completely classify the elements of a complex diagnosis statement. Diagnosis statements contain words or phrases such as *due to, incidental to, secondary to*, and *with*. Make sure you carefully review tabular list entries, which provide guidance regarding the assignment of multiple codes.

Make sure you assign only the combination code when that code fully identifies the diagnostic conditions involved or when the index so directs. Do not report multiple codes when ICD-9-CM or ICD-10-CM provides a combination code that clearly identifies all of the elements documented in the diagnosis. When a combination code lacks necessary specificity in describing the manifestation or a complication, an additional code should be reported as a secondary code.

> **EXAMPLE 1: COMBINATION CODE:** Assign ICD-9-CM combination code 574.00 (or ICD-10-CM code K80.00) to the diagnosis acute cholecystitis and cholelithiasis because the code description includes both conditions. (The fifth-digit subclassification 0 is assigned to each code because there is no mention of obstruction in the diagnostic statement.)

> **EXAMPLE 2: MULTIPLE CODES:** The diagnosis trigonitis due to *Escherichia coli* is assigned ICD-9-CM multiple codes 595.3 and 041.49 (and ICD-10-CM codes N30.30 and B96.20), in that order.

Late Effects (*Sequela*)

A **late effect** is the **residual condition** (long-term condition produced) (or *sequela*) that develops after the acute phase of an illness or injury has ended. *There is no time limit on when a late effect or residual code can be reported.*

- In ICD-9-CM, the Index to Diseases main term is *Late effect*.

- In the ICD-10-CM Index to Diseases and Injuries, the main term is *Sequela (of)* and it includes a "—*see also* condition" instruction because in the tabular list, seventh-character "S" is added to condition codes for which sequela (residual conditions) are treated.

The residual effect may be apparent early (e.g., hemiparesis or neurogenic bladder due to cerebrovascular accident and painful scar contracture following severe burns), or it may occur months or years later (e.g., traumatic arthritis of the elbow due to previous fracture of lower end of humerus). Coding late effects usually requires two codes to be reported, as follows:

- The residual condition or nature of the late effect is reported first.

- The late effect code is reported second.

An exception to reporting two codes for residuals due to late effects is made when:

- The residual effect is not documented, which means the cause of the late effect is coded alone, such as *sequela of poliomyelitis*, which is assigned ICD-9-CM code 138 or ICD-10-CM code B91.

- A late effect code is not classified in ICD-9-CM or ICD-10-CM, but the condition is described as being a late effect, which means the residual is coded alone, such as *contracture of right hip following partial hip replacement*, which is assigned ICD-9-CM code 718.45 or ICD-10-CM code M24.551.

- The late effect code has been expanded at the ICD-9-CM fourth- and/or fifth-digit levels or the ICD-10-CM fourth-, fifth-, or sixth-character levels to include the residual condition or the classification instructs otherwise. The code for the acute phase of an illness or injury that led to the late effect is never used with a code for the late effect. For example, a combination code is assigned to aphasia due to CVA in ICD-9-CM (438.11) or ICD-10-CM (I69.920).

Note:

- The code for the acute phase of an illness or injury that led to the late effect is never reported with a code for the late effect (because treatment for the acute phase has ended).

- Do not confuse late effects with complications that are associated with current acute illness or injuries and usually develop from problems that occur during the course of medical or surgical care (e.g., postoperative wound infection).

- Multiple codes are assigned to classify a late effect when no combination code exists, such as "headaches due to intracranial injury without loss of consciousness that occurred several years ago" for which ICD-9-CM codes 784.0 and 907.0 (or ICD-10-CM codes G44.1 and S06.9x0S) are both assigned. (In ICD-10-CM, late effect of injuries are classified by assigning an S as the seventh character of the injury code.)

- A combination code is assigned to classify a late effect when it is exists, such as "nondominant left-sided paralysis due to previous CVA" for which ICD-9-CM code 438.52 or ICD-10-CM I69.864 only is assigned.

EXAMPLE: The patient was in an automobile accident last year and sustained fractures of the left femur and right tibia, which healed without incident. The patient presents today with stiffness of the left hip and numbness of the left leg. Assign codes to the stiffness of the left hip (719.55 or M25.652); numbness of the left leg (782.0 or R20.0); and late effect of fracture, femur (905.4 or S72.92xS).

ICD-10 Alert!

See Appendix II located on the Premium Website to review guidelines about sequelae codes and code extensions, including:

- *Section I.C.9. Sequelae of cerebrovascular disease*
- *Section I.C.15. Sequelae of complication of pregnancy, childbirth, and the puerperium*
- *Section I.C.19. Code extensions*

Impending or Threatened Condition

Code any condition described at the time of encounter/visit as "impending" or "threatened" as follows:

- If the condition did occur, code as confirmed diagnosis.

- If the condition did not occur, reference the disease index to determine if the condition has a subentry term for "impending" or "threatened" and also reference main term entries for "impending" and "threatened."

- If subterms for "impending" or "threatened" are listed, assign the listed code.

Note:

Coding impending or threatened conditions applies to inpatient cases only.

- If subterms for "impending" or "threatened" are not listed, code the existing underlying condition(s), and *not* the condition described as "impending" or "threatened."

  EXAMPLE: The patient is treated for impending myocardial infarction (MI) and is assigned ICD-9-CM code 411.1 or ICD-10-CM code I20.0 because the MI diagnosis has not been confirmed.

Reporting Same Diagnosis Code More Than Once

Each unique ICD-9-CM or ICD-10-CM diagnosis code is reported only once for an encounter. This applies to bilateral conditions *when there are no distinct ICD-10-CM codes identifying laterality* or two different conditions that are classified to the same ICD-9-CM or ICD-10-CM diagnosis code.

EXAMPLE 1: On March 14, the patient was diagnosed with bilateral lung abscesses. Even though both lungs contain abscesses, assign ICD-9-CM code 513.0 or ICD-10-CM code J85.2 only once.

EXAMPLE 2: The patient was diagnosed with septic colitis and catarrhal dysentery. Both conditions are classified to ICD-9-CM code 009.0 or ICD-10-CM code A09 and reported only once.

Admissions/Encounters for Rehabilitation (ICD-9-CM Only)

When the purpose for the admission/encounter is rehabilitation, sequence the appropriate V code from category V57 (Care involving use of rehabilitation procedures) as the principal diagnosis (for inpatient treatment) or first-listed diagnosis (for outpatient treatment). The code for the condition for which the service is being performed is also reported as an additional diagnosis.

Because just one code from category V57 is reported, code V57.89 (Other specified rehabilitation procedures) is assigned when more than one type of rehabilitation is performed during a single encounter. (Appropriate procedure codes are also reported to identify each type of rehabilitation therapy performed.)

EXAMPLE: The patient underwent outpatient speech therapy for dysphasia, the result of a cerebrovascular accident from two months ago. Report disease codes V57.3 and 438.12, in that order.

Laterality (ICD-10-CM Only)

For bilateral sites, the final character of relevant ICD-10-CM codes indicates laterality. An unspecified code is also included in ICD-10-CM should documentation of the affected side be missing from the patient record. If there is no bilateral code provided in ICD-10-CM *and the condition is documented as bilateral*, assign two separate codes for the left and right side.

EXAMPLE:

- *Bilateral contusion of fallopian tubes* is assigned ICD-10-CM code S37.522.
- *Presence of bilateral finger-joint replacement* is assigned ICD-10-CM code Z96.693, while Z96.691 is assigned for the *right finger-joint* and Z96.692 for the *left finger-joint*.

Documentation for Body Mass Index (BMI) and Pressure Ulcer Stages

The assignment of body mass index (BMI) and pressure ulcer stage codes may be based on documentation from clinicians who are not the patient's provider (e.g., physician, other qualified healthcare practitioner legally accountable for establishing the patient's diagnosis) *because such information is typically documented by other clinicians involved in the care of the patient* (e.g., dietitians document BMI, nurses document pressure ulcer stages). However, associated diagnosis (e.g., overweight, obesity, pressure ulcer) must be documented by the patient's provider. If conflicting documentation is evident in the patient record, either from the same clinician or different clinicians, query the patient's attending provider for clarification.

BMI and pressure ulcer stage codes are reported only as secondary diagnoses. As with all other secondary diagnosis codes, BMI and pressure ulcer stage codes are assigned only when they meet the definition of a reportable additional diagnosis.

EXAMPLE: On May 10, the patient's BMI of 39.4 was documented by the medical center's dietician. The 40-year-old patient has an established diagnosis of morbid obesity. Report ICD-9-CM codes 278.01 and V85.39 (or ICD-10-CM codes E66.01 and Z68.39), in that order.

Syndromes

Follow the alphabetic index guidance when coding syndromes. In the absence of index guidance, assign codes for the documented manifestations of the syndrome.

Documentation of Complications of Care

The assignment of codes is based upon documentation of a relationship between a condition and the procedure or service provided, which also applies to complications of care (regardless of the ICD-9-CM or ICD-10-CM chapter in which the code is located). Not all conditions that occur during or following medical care or surgery are classified as complications. There must be a cause-and-effect relationship between the condition and procedure or service provided along with documentation that the condition is a complication. If a complication is not clearly documented, query the provider for clarification.

Exercise 4.2 – General ICD-9-CM and ICD-10-CM Diagnosis Coding Guidelines

Instructions: Indicate whether the statement is true (T) or false (F).

_____ **1.** The ICD-9-CM Index to Diseases entry for main term *Burn* is 949.0. The boxed note below the code indicates that a fifth-digit subclassification is required for this code.

_____ **2.** When reviewing ICD-9-CM Index to Disease entries, if the code listed contains a fifth-digit subclassification, it is unnecessary to verify the code in the ICD-10-CM Tabular List of Diseases.

_____ **3.** Upon verification of codes in the ICD-9-CM Tabular List of Diseases, when fifth-digit subclassifications are provided, they must be assigned.

_____ **4.** Certain V codes in ICD-9-CM can be reported as a first-listed code for outpatient care.

_____ **5.** Codes that describe symptoms and signs are always reported with established diagnoses.

_____ **6.** Some symptoms, signs, and ill-defined condition codes are found in ICD-10-CM chapters other than Chapter 18, Symptoms, Signs, and Abnormal Clinical and Laboratory Findings, Not Elsewhere Classified (R00.0-R99).

_____ **7.** Signs and symptoms that are integral to the disease process should be assigned as additional codes because they are included in the disease process.

_____ **8.** Conditions that are not considered an integral part of a disease process, such as additional signs and symptoms that may not be associated routinely with a disease process, should be coded when present.

_____ **9.** Etiology/manifestation conditions often require that two codes be reported to completely describe a single condition that affects multiple body systems.

_____ **10.** If the same condition is described as acute (or subacute) *and* chronic, always assign a combination code.

(continues)

Exercise 4.2 (continued)

_____ 11. One multiple code can be assigned as a single code to classify two entirely different conditions.

_____ 12. Combination codes are located by referring to subterm entries in the disease index and by reading "includes" and "excludes" notes in the tabular list.

_____ 13. A late effect is the condition produced after the acute phase of an illness or injury has ended.

_____ 14. Residual conditions are coded as such only if they occur at least one year after the previous condition has resolved.

_____ 15. Conditions described at the time of visit as "impending" or "threatened" are always coded as if the condition is confirmed, regardless of the type of patient encounter.

ICD-9-CM Chapter-Specific Diagnosis Coding Guidelines with ICD-10 Alerts

In addition to coding conventions and general coding guidelines, the _Official Guidelines for Coding and Reporting_ contain chapter-specific coding guidelines that clarify the assignment of disease codes. Unless otherwise indicated in an individual chapter-specific guideline, the chapter-specific guidelines apply to all health care settings. Some of the guidelines include the following terms, which apply to the reporting of inpatient and outpatient diagnoses (covered in this chapter and Chapters 5 and 6). The terms are briefly defined below to clarify their use in the chapter-specific guidelines.

- _Principal diagnosis_: Reported for inpatient care, it is "that condition established after study to be chiefly responsible for occasioning the admission of the patient to the hospital for care."

- _Secondary diagnoses_: Additional conditions affect patient care in terms of requiring clinical evaluation, therapeutic treatment, diagnostic procedures, extended length of hospital stay, or increased nursing care and/or monitoring.

- _First-listed diagnosis_: Reported for outpatient care instead of the principal diagnosis, it is the diagnosis, condition, problem, or other reason for an encounter/visit documented in the medical record to be chiefly responsible for the services provided. (The first-listed diagnosis was previously called the _primary diagnosis_.)

ICD-9-CM CHAPTER-SPECIFIC CODING GUIDELINES

To locate the ICD-9-CM chapter-specific coding guidelines online, go to _http://www.cms.gov_ and click on the Medicare link, click on the ICD-9-CM link below the Coding heading, and then scroll down and click on the ICD-9-CM Official Coding Guidelines link. The _ICD-9-CM Official Coding Guidelines_ will open as an Adobe PDF file.

The _ICD-9-CM Official Guidelines for Coding and Reporting_ publication includes a table of contents that organizes the chapter-specific guidelines according to the chapters in the ICD-9-CM classification system

(Table 4-1A). Although the CMS and NCHS have not created chapter-specific guidelines for every ICD-9-CM chapter, the title of each ICD-9-CM chapter is included in the table of contents with the statement "Reserved for future guideline expansion." Refer to the chapter-specific guidelines when assigning ICD-9-CM diagnosis codes. (This section defines terminology associated with each ICD-9-CM chapter, interprets official chapter-specific coding guidelines, and includes exercises for coding practice.)

Table 4-1A Portion of Chapter-Specific Coding Guidelines Table of Contents from *ICD-9-CM Official Guidelines for Coding and Reporting*

C.	Chapter-Specific Coding Guidelines	
1.	Chapter 1: Infectious and Parasitic Diseases (001–139)	12
a.	Human Immunodeficiency Virus (HIV) Infections.	12
b.	Septicemia, Systemic Inflammatory Response Syndrome (SIRS), Sepsis, Severe Sepsis, and Septic Shock	16
2.	Chapter 2: Neoplasms (140–239)	21
a.	Treatment directed at the malignancy	23
b.	Treatment of secondary site	23
c.	Coding and sequencing of complications	24
d.	Primary malignancy previously excised	24
e.	Admissions/encounters involving chemotherapy, immunotherapy, and radiation therapy	25
f.	Admission/encounter to determine extent of malignancy	26

Note:

There are no official chapter-specific coding guidelines for ICD-9-CM procedures. Go to Chapter 5 to locate content about ICD-9-CM procedure coding *and* ICD-10-PCS coding.

ICD-10-CM CHAPTER-SPECIFIC CODING GUIDELINES

ICD-10-CM chapter-specific coding guidelines are highlighted in Appendix II located on the Premium Website as well as online at **http://www.cms.gov** by clicking on the *Medicare* link, clicking on the *ICD-10* link (below the Coding heading), clicking on the *2012 ICD-10-CM and GEMs* link, and scrolling down and clicking on the *2012 ICD-10-CM Official Coding Guidelines* [PDF, *343KB*] link. (The *ICD-10-CM Official Coding Guidelines* will open as an Adobe PDF file.)

The *ICD-10-CM Official Guidelines for Coding and Reporting* includes a table of contents that organizes the chapter-specific guidelines according to chapters in the ICD-10-CM classification system (Table 4-1B). Refer to the complete ICD-10-CM chapter-specific coding guidelines (Appendix II located on the Premium Website) when assigning ICD-10-CM codes. This section of Chapter 4 includes *ICD-10 Alerts!* that highlight the similarities and differences between ICD-9-CM and ICD-10-CM coding guidelines.

ICD-9-CM Chapter 1: Infectious and Parasitic Diseases (001–139)

The Infectious and Parasitic Diseases chapter of ICD-9-CM classifies communicable diseases as well as diseases of unknown origin. The following organisms (Table 4-2) are classified in ICD-9-CM and ICD-10-CM Chapter 1, which impact different body organs and systems:

- Bacteria
- Chlamydia
- Fungi
- Helminth

- Mycoplasmas
- Protozoans
- Rickettsias
- Viruses

ICD-10 Alert!

In ICD-10-CM, *Certain Parasitic and Infectious Diseases (A00–B99)* are also located in Chapter 1.

Table 4-1B Portion of Chapter-Specific Coding Guidelines Table of Contents from *ICD-9-CM Official Guidelines for Coding and Reporting*

ICD-10 Alert!

ICD-10-CM's Chapter 1: Certain Infectious and Parasitic Diseases (A00–B99) also classifies communicable diseases as well as diseases of unknown origin. *Refer to Appendix II located on the Premium Website for chapter-specific coding guidelines.*

Table 4-2 Organisms

Organism	Definition
Bacteria	• Single-celled organisms that in certain conditions cause illnesses such as strep throat, most ear infections, and bacterial pneumonia • Some bacteria are considered helpful (for example, intestinal *Escherichia coli*).
Chlamydia	• Infection caused by a parasitic bacteria called *Chlamydia trachomatis* • Affects male and female genitals
Fungi	• Opportunistic pathogens such as aspergillus, candida, and cryptococcus that cause infections in immunocompromised people such as cancer patients, transplant recipients, and people with AIDS • Pathogens such as endemic mycoses, histoplasmosis, coccidioidomycosis, and superficial mycoses that cause infections in healthy people
Helminth	• Parasitic worms that usually lodge in the intestines • Include roundworm, pinworm, trichinella spiralis (causes thrichinosis), tapeworm, and fluke
Mycoplasmas	• Surface parasites of the human respiratory and urogenital tracts • Mainly affect children aged 5 to 9 years • Spread by close personal contact • Have a long incubation period

(continues)

Table 4-2 *(continued)*

Organism	Definition
Protozoans	• Single-celled organisms (e.g., amoeba) that cause parasitic diseases in people with AIDS: • Toxoplasmosis • Cryptosporidiosis • *Pneumocystis carinii* pneumonia (PCP) is thought to be caused by protozoans (but might be caused by fungi); PCP is now known as *Pneumocystis jiroveci* pneumonia.
Rickettsias	• Intracellular parasites that grow and reproduce only in living cells of their host • Named for U.S. pathologist Howard T. Ricketts, who died of typhus in 1910 while investigating the spread of the disease • Typhus fever is caused by *Rickettsia prowazekii* when transmitted to humans by lice. • Rocky Mountain spotted fever is a rickettsial disease transmitted to humans by ticks.
Viruses	• Submicroscopic parasites that cause disease • Contain DNA or RNA, are surrounded by protein, and use host cells to replicate • Include varicella (chickenpox virus), cold viruses, hepatitis viruses, herpes viruses, and human immunodeficiency virus (HIV)

© Cengage Learning 2014

🟢 Refer to tabular list code descriptions to locate ICD-9-CM fourth and/or fifth digits or ICD-10-CM fourth, fifth, sixth, and seventh characters that further classify infectious and parasitic diseases according to anatomic site.

The ICD-9-CM "Supplemental Classification of Factors Influencing Health Status and Contact with Health Services" contains a section titled "Persons with Potential Health Hazards Related to Communicable Diseases" (V01–V06) that classifies the following:

- Contact with or exposure to communicable diseases (V01)
- Carrier or suspected carriers of infectious diseases (V02)
- Need for prophylactic vaccination and inoculation against bacterial, viral, and single and combination diseases (V03–V06)

In addition, the section titled "Persons with Need for Isolation, Other Potential Health Hazards and Prophylactic Measures" (V07–V09) classifies the following:

- Need for isolation and other prophylactic or treatment measures (V07)
- Asymptomatic human immunodeficiency virus (HIV) infection status (V08)
- Infection with drug-resistant microorganisms (V09)

🟢 **Coding Tip:**

Infections are also classified in other ICD-9-CM and ICD-10-CM chapters, such as *Diseases of the Respiratory System*.

🟢 **ICD-10 Alert!**

In ICD-10-CM, *Factors Influencing Health Status and Contact With Health Services [Z00–Z99]* are located in Chapter 21, and *Persons with potential health hazards related to communicable diseases* are classified to codes Z20–Z28. ICD-9-CM's V codes have become ICD-10-CM's Z codes, included in a chapter instead of a supplemental classification.

Human Immunodeficiency Virus (HIV)

HIV is a virus that attacks the body's immune system, which provides protection against infections and disease; however, people's immune systems have no clear way to protect them from HIV. Individuals infected with HIV are unable to ward off microorganisms that do not usually make a healthy person sick. Although those infected with HIV may exhibit no symptoms for 10 or more years, because the HIV-positive patient's immune system has been weakened by the virus, these microorganisms ultimately cause life-threatening infections and cancers. To determine whether a patient is considered HIV-positive, review the patient record to locate the following phrases:

- Has HIV disease
- Has HIV infection
- HIV infected
- HIV-positive

When the above phrases are included in the patient's record, the person has HIV in his or her body and can spread the virus to other people. HIV spreads when infected blood, breast milk, semen, or vaginal fluid enters the bloodstream of another person through:

- Break in the skin (e.g., abrasion, laceration, or other open wound)
- Direct entry into a blood vessel
- Mucous linings (e.g., eyes, mouth nose, penis, rectum, or vagina)

Acquired immune deficiency syndrome (AIDS) is a late stage of HIV disease, and it is considered the most severe manifestation of HIV. The Centers for Disease Control and Prevention (CDC) includes a list of opportunistic infections and cancers that, in an HIV-positive patient, establishes the diagnosis of AIDS. Although medications help HIV-positive and AIDS patients live longer, healthier lives, there is no cure. (An **opportunistic infection** takes advantage of the body's weakened defenses.)

When a patient is treated for an HIV-related condition, report ICD-9-CM code 042 (or ICD-10-CM code B20) first on the health insurance claim and assign (and report) additional diagnosis codes for all documented HIV-related conditions and opportunistic infections, such as candidiasis or Kaposi's sarcoma (Figure 4-3).

> **Note:**
>
> HIV is not spread through saliva (spit), nor is it spread by casual contact (e.g., coughing, eating or drinking from common utensils, hugging, shaking hands, sneezing, or using restrooms and drinking fountains).

> **Note:**
>
> A list of HIV-related conditions and opportunistic infections and definitions can be found on the Premium Website for *3-2-1 Code It!* at www.cengagebrain.com.

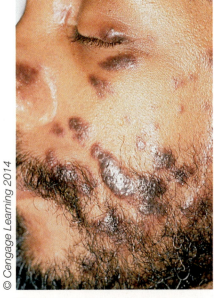

© Cengage Learning 2014

Figure 4-3 Kaposi's sarcoma

ICD-9-CM CHAPTER-SPECIFIC CODING GUIDELINES WITH ICD-10 ALERTS!

 ICD-10 Alert!

- In ICD-10-CM, *Certain Infectious and Parasitic Diseases (A00–B99)* are also located in Chapter 1, and the ICD-9-CM coding guidelines with *ICD-10 Alerts!* are included below.

- ICD-10-CM and ICD-9-CM coding guidelines about *Human Immunodeficiency Virus (HIV) Infections* are similar.

- Sections I.C.1.b., Infectious Agents as the Cause of Diseases Classified to Other Chapters, and I.C.1.c., *Infections Resistant to Antibiotics,* are brand new to the ICD-10-CM coding guidelines.

- Section I.C.1.d., *Sepsis, Severe Sepsis, and Septic Shock,* of the ICD-10-CM coding guidelines include major revisions.

- *Go to Appendix II located on the Premium Website to review Section I.C.1., Chapter 1: Certain Infectious and Parasitic Diseases (A00–B99), of the ICD-10-CM coding guidelines.*

Chapter 1: Infectious and Parasitic Diseases (001–139)

a. **Human Immunodeficiency Virus (HIV) infections**

1) **Code only confirmed cases**

Code only confirmed cases of HIV infection/illness. This is an exception to the hospital inpatient guideline Section II, H. In this context, "confirmation" does not require documentation of positive serology or culture for HIV; the provider's diagnostic statement that the patient is HIV-positive, or has an HIV-related illness is sufficient.

EXAMPLE: A 38-year-old symptomatic HIV-positive female patient was seen in follow-up at the office, for resolved *Pneumocystis carinii* pneumonia (PCP). Lab tests today reveal CBC hemoglobin of 9.0, hematocrit 27, and normal WBC differential and platelets. Hepatitis A, B, and C tests negative. CMV test negative. Rapid plasma reagin test negative. Decreased reticulocytes of 0.3 noted. Normal peripheral smear. Parvovirus B19 antibody test negative. Comprehensive metabolic panel was normal. CD4 test revealed somewhat depressed T helper cell level of 460. Viral load is 22,000. Erythropoietin level elevated at 120 milliunits per milliliter. Patient was started on medications of nevirapine plus Combivir.

In this example, the provider's statement of a "symptomatic HIV-positive female patient" is sufficient to assign ICD-9-CM code 042 (or ICD-10-CM code B20) for HIV infection. Because the PCP is resolved, a code to that HIV-related condition is not assigned.

2) **Selection and sequencing of HIV codes**

(a) **Patient admitted for HIV-related condition**

If a patient is admitted for an HIV-related condition, the principal diagnosis should be 042, followed by additional diagnosis codes for all reported HIV-related conditions.

EXAMPLE 1: A 42-year-old HIV-positive male underwent treatment for septic arthritis of the left shoulder. Culture and sensitivity lab test revealed *Klebsiella pneumoniae* as the bacterial agent. When reviewing the ICD-9-CM code for septic arthritis of the left shoulder, note the Tabular List of Diseases instruction below subcategory code 711.0, which states, "Use additional code to identify infectious organism (041.0–041.8)." Because septic arthritis is considered an opportunistic infection in an HIV-positive patient, sequence the HIV code (042) first and then the opportunistic infection codes (711.01 and 041.3). (ICD-10-CM codes include B20, M00.812, and B96.1)

(continues)

ICD-9-CM CHAPTER-SPECIFIC CODING GUIDELINES WITH ICD-10 ALERTS! (*continued*)

(b)  **Patient with HIV disease admitted for unrelated condition**

If a patient with HIV disease is admitted for an unrelated condition (such as a traumatic injury), the code for the unrelated condition (e.g., the nature of injury code) should be the principal diagnosis. Other diagnoses would be 042 followed by additional diagnosis codes for all reported HIV-related conditions.

EXAMPLE: A 53-year-old female patient with symptomatic HIV disease undergoes treatment for a closed left wrist fracture. In this example, a fracture is not considered an opportunistic infection or disease in an HIV-positive patient and it is considered a condition unrelated to HIV status. Therefore, sequence the closed left wrist fracture code (814.00) and then the HIV code (042). (ICD-10-CM codes include S62.102A and B20. If HIV-related symptoms had been documented and medically managed, you would assign codes for each of them.)

> **ICD-10 Alert!**
>
> The ICD-10-CM code for HIV is B20.

(c) **Whether the patient is newly diagnosed**

Whether the patient is newly diagnosed or has had previous admissions/encounters for HIV conditions is irrelevant to the sequencing decision.

(d) 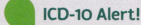 **Asymptomatic human immunodeficiency virus**

V08, Asymptomatic human immunodeficiency virus [HIV] infection, is to be applied when the patient without any documentation of symptoms is listed as being "HIV positive," "known HIV," "HIV test positive," or similar terminology. Do not use this code if the term *AIDS* is used or if the patient is treated for any HIV-related illness or is described as having any condition(s) resulting from his/her HIV-positive status; use 042 in these cases.

> **ICD-10 Alert!**
>
> The ICD-10-CM code for asymptomatic HIV infection is Z21, and the ICD-10-CM code for HIV is B20.

EXAMPLE: A 42-year-old female HIV-positive asymptomatic patient undergoes routine CD4 testing to determine current levels. In this example, even though the patient is HIV-positive, she is also asymptomatic, which means that there are no documented symptoms. Therefore, assign ICD-9-CM code V08 (or ICD-10-CM code Z21) for asymptomatic HIV status. *Do not assign ICD-9-CM code 042 (or ICD-10-CM code B20), which is assigned to patients diagnosed as HIV-positive who are treated for HIV-related illness(es) or to patients described as having AIDS.*

(e) **Patients with inconclusive HIV serology**

Patients with inconclusive HIV serology, but no definitive diagnosis or manifestations of the illness, may be assigned code 795.71, Inconclusive HIV test.

EXAMPLE: A 52-year-old asymptomatic male patient was seen in the office after having undergone HIV testing, the results of which proved inconclusive. Patient is scheduled for repeat HIV test. In this example, assign ICD-9-CM code 795.71 (or ICD-10-CM code R75) for inconclusive HIV test code V73.89 (or ICD-10-CM code Z11.4) for "screening for HIV status" because the patient is being seen to determine his HIV status. If HIV counseling was provided during the encounter, code V65.44 (or ICD-10-CM code Z71.7) would also be assigned. If the patient was determined to be in a high-risk group for HIV, such as *high risk bisexual behavior*, ICD-9-CM code V69.2 (or ICD-10-CM code Z72.53) would also be assigned.

> **ICD-10 Alert!**
>
> The ICD-10-CM code for:
> - HIV is B20.
> - Inconclusive laboratory evidence of HIV is R75.
> - Asymptomatic HIV infection is Z21.

(f) Previously diagnosed HIV-related illness

Patients with any known prior diagnosis of an HIV-related illness should be coded to 042. Once a patient has developed an HIV-related illness, the patient should always be assigned code 042 on every subsequent admission/encounter. Patients previously diagnosed with any HIV illness (042) should never be assigned to 795.71 or V08.

EXAMPLE: A 29-year-old female HIV-positive patient was seen in the office to undergo routine CD4 testing. She has a past history of having been treated for HIV wasting syndrome and Hodgkin's disease. The patient is currently asymptomatic. In this example, because the patient has known prior diagnoses of HIV-related illnesses, assign ICD-9-CM code 042 (or ICD-10-CM code B20) for HIV disease. *Although the patient is currently asymptomatic, according to official coding guidelines, it is incorrect to assign ICD-9-CM code 795.71 (or ICD-10-CM code R75) for inconclusive HIV test or ICD-9-CM code V08 (or ICD-10-CM code Z21) asymptomatic HIV status.*

(g) HIV infection in pregnancy, childbirth, and the puerperium

During pregnancy, childbirth or the puerperium, a patient admitted (or presenting for a health care encounter) because of an HIV-related illness should receive a principal diagnosis code of 647.6x. Other specified infectious and parasitic diseases in the mother classifiable elsewhere, but complicating the pregnancy, childbirth, or the puerperium, followed by 042 and the code(s) for the HIV-related illness(es). Codes from Chapter 15 (of ICD-9-CM) always take sequencing priority. Patients with asymptomatic HIV infection status admitted (or presenting for a health care encounter) during pregnancy, childbirth, or the puerperium should be assigned codes 647.6x and V08 (or ICD-10-CM codes O98.7- and Z21).

> **ICD-10 Alert!**
>
> The ICD-10-CM code for other maternal viral disease complicating pregnancy, childbirth, or the puerperium is O98.7-.

EXAMPLE: A 33-year-old HIV-positive patient in her second trimester received inpatient treatment for cytomegalovirus (CMV) disease. The patient was discharged to follow up with Dr. Jones regarding the CMV, and she will continue to receive prenatal care from Dr. Miller. When a pregnant patient is admitted for an HIV-related illness, assign ICD-9-CM code 647.63 (or ICD-10-CM code O98.512) for "other maternal viral disease complicating pregnancy, childbirth, or the puerperium." (ICD-9-CM fifth-digit 3 is assigned because this hospitalization treated an antepartum condition.) Then, assign ICD-9-CM code 042 (or ICD-10-CM code B20) for HIV disease and code 078.5 (or ICD-10-CM code B25.9) for the HIV-related condition of CMV.

When this patient is admitted for delivery, even if she has an asymptomatic HIV infection status upon admission, assign ICD-9-CM codes 647.61 and 042 (or ICD-10-CM codes O98.72 and B20) (because she was admitted during her antepartum period for treatment of an HIV-related condition). (The case of an HIV-positive patient who delivers and who has not been treated for an HIV-related condition in the past is assigned ICD-9-CM codes 647.61 and V08 or ICD-10-CM codes O98.72 and Z21.) (An outcome of delivery code is also assigned.)

> **ICD-10 Alert!**
>
> • The ICD-10-CM code for encounter for screening for HIV is Z11.4, and the ICD-10-CM code for encounter for HIV counseling is Z71.7.
>
> • If test results are positive, see previous guidelines and assign ICD-10-CM codes as appropriate.

(h) Encounters for testing for HIV

If a patient is being seen to determine his/her HIV status, use code V73.89, Screening for other specified viral disease. Use code V69.8, Other problems related to lifestyle, as a secondary code if an asymptomatic patient

(continues)

ICD-9-CM CHAPTER-SPECIFIC CODING GUIDELINES WITH ICD-10 ALERTS! (*continued*)

is in a known high-risk group for HIV. Should a patient with signs or symptoms or illness, or a confirmed HIV-related diagnosis be tested for HIV, code the signs and symptoms or the diagnosis. An additional code V65.44 may be used if counseling is provided during the encounter for the test.

When a patient returns to be informed of his/her HIV test results use code V65.44, HIV counseling, if the results of the test are negative. If the results are positive but the patient is asymptomatic, use code V08, Asymptomatic HIV infection. If the results are positive and the patient is symptomatic use code 042, HIV infection, with codes for the HIV-related symptoms or diagnosis. The HIV counseling code may also be used if counseling is provided for patients with positive test results.

b. **Septicemia, Systemic Inflammatory Response Syndrome (SIRS), Sepsis, Severe Sepsis, and Septic Shock**
1) **SIRS, septicemia, and sepsis**
   (a) The terms *septicemia* and *sepsis* are often used interchangeably by providers; however, they are not considered synonymous terms. The following descriptions are provided for reference but do not preclude querying the provider for clarification about terms used in the documentation:

ICD-10 Alert!

- *Section I.C.1.b., Infectious Agents as the cause of diseases classified to other chapters, and Section I.C.1.c., Infections resistant to antibiotics, do not appear in the ICD-9-CM coding guidelines. They are new ICD-10-CM coding guidelines.*

- *Section I.C.1.d., Sepsis, Severe Sepsis, and Septic Shock, of the ICD-10-CM coding guidelines contains major revisions. For example, ICD-10-CM eliminated nonspecific term Urosepsis from its index, and the ICD-10-CM coding guideline states that a provider who documents that term must be queried for clarification.*

- *The classification of Systemic inflammatory response syndrome (SIRS) was relocated to ICD-10-CM Chapter 18, Symptoms, Signs, and Abnormal Clinical and Laboratory Findings, Not Elsewhere Classified (R00–R99). In ICD-9-CM, SIRS is classified to Chapter 17, Injury and Poisoning (800–999).*

- *Go to Appendix II located on the Premium Website to review the Sections I.C.1.b, I.C.1.c, and I.C.1.d. of the ICD-10-CM coding guidelines.*

   (i) Septicemia generally refers to a systemic disease associated with the presence of pathological microorganisms or toxins in the blood, which can include bacteria, viruses, fungi, or other organisms.
   (ii) Systemic inflammatory response syndrome (SIRS) generally refers to the systemic response to infection, trauma/burns, or other insult (such as cancer) with symptoms including fever, tachycardia, tachypnea, and leukocytosis.
   (iii) Sepsis generally refers to SIRS due to infection.
   (iv) Severe sepsis generally refers to sepsis with associated acute organ dysfunction.
   (b) **The coding of SIRS, sepsis and severe sepsis**
      The coding of SIRS, sepsis, and severe sepsis requires a minimum of two codes: a code for the underlying cause (such as infection or trauma) and a code from subcategory 995.9 Systemic inflammatory response syndrome (SIRS).
      (i) The code for the underlying cause (such as infection or trauma) must be sequenced before the code from subcategory 995.9 Systemic inflammatory response syndrome (SIRS).
      (ii) Sepsis and severe sepsis require a code for the systemic infection (038.xx, 112.5, etc.) and either code 995.91, Sepsis, or 995.92, Severe sepsis. If the causal organism is not documented, assign code 038.9, Unspecified septicemia.

(iii) Severe sepsis requires additional code(s) for the associated acute organ dysfunction(s).

(iv) If a patient has sepsis with multiple organ dysfunctions, follow the instructions for coding severe sepsis.

(v) Either the term *sepsis* or SIRS must be documented to assign a code from subcategory 995.9.

(vi) *See Section I.C.17.g, Injury and poisoning, for information regarding systemic inflammatory response syndrome (SIRS) due to trauma/burns and other noninfectious processes.*

(c) Due to the complex nature of sepsis and severe sepsis, some cases may require querying the provider prior to assignment of the codes.

2) **Sequencing sepsis and severe sepsis**

(a) **Sepsis and severe sepsis as principal diagnosis**

If sepsis or severe sepsis is present on admission, and meets the definition of principal diagnosis, the systemic infection code (e.g., 038.xx, 112.5, etc.) should be assigned as the principal diagnosis, followed by code 995.91, Sepsis, or 995.92, Severe sepsis, as required by the sequencing rules in the Tabular List. Codes from subcategory 995.9 can never be assigned as a principal diagnosis. A code should also be assigned for any localized infection, if present.

If the sepsis or severe sepsis is due to a postprocedural infection, see Section I.C.1.b.10 for guidelines related to sepsis due to postprocedural infection.

(b) **Sepsis and severe sepsis as secondary diagnoses**

When sepsis or severe sepsis develops during the encounter (it was not present on admission), the systemic infection code and code 995.91 or 995.92 should be assigned as secondary diagnoses.

(c) ● **Documentation unclear as to whether sepsis or severe sepsis is present on admission**

Sepsis or severe sepsis may be present on admission, but the diagnosis may not be confirmed until sometime after admission. If the documentation is not clear whether the sepsis or severe sepsis was present on admission, the provider should be queried.

3) **Sepsis/SIRS with localized infection**

If the reason for admission is both sepsis, severe sepsis, or SIRS and a localized infection, such as pneumonia or cellulitis, a code for the systemic infection (038.xx, 112.5, etc.) should be assigned first, then code 995.91 or 995.92, followed by the code for the localized infection. If the patient is admitted with a localized infection, such as pneumonia, and sepsis/SIRS doesn't develop until after admission, see guideline I.C.1.b.2b.

If the localized infection is postprocedural, see Section I.C.1.b.10 for guidelines related to sepsis due to postprocedural infection.

> ● **Note:**
>
> The term *urosepsis* is a nonspecific term. If that is the only term documented, only code 599.0 should be assigned based on the default for the term in the ICD-9-CM index, in addition to the code for the causal organism, if known.

4) **Bacterial sepsis, and septicemia**

In most cases, it will be a code from category 038, Septicemia, that will be used in conjunction with a code from subcategory 995.9 such as the following:

(a) **Streptococcal sepsis**

If the documentation in the record states streptococcal sepsis, codes 038.0, Streptococcal septicemia, and code 995.91 should be used, in that sequence.

(b) **Streptococcal septicemia**

If the documentation states streptococcal septicemia, only code 038.0 should be assigned; however, the provider should be queried whether the patient has sepsis, an infection with SIRS.

5) **Acute organ dysfunction that is not clearly associated with the sepsis**

If a patient has sepsis and an acute organ dysfunction, but the medical record documentation indicates that the acute organ dysfunction is related to a medical condition other than the sepsis, do not assign code

(continues)

ICD-9-CM CHAPTER-SPECIFIC CODING GUIDELINES WITH ICD-10 ALERTS! (*continued*)

995.92, Severe sepsis. An acute organ dysfunction must be associated with the sepsis in order to assign the severe sepsis code. If the documentation is not clear as to whether an acute organ dysfunction is related to the sepsis or another medical condition, query the provider.

6) **Septic shock**

(a) **Sequencing of septic shock**

Septic shock generally refers to circulatory failure associated with severe sepsis, and, therefore, it represents a type of acute organ dysfunction.

For cases of septic shock, the code for the systemic infection should be sequenced first, followed by codes 995.92, Severe sepsis, and 785.52, Septic shock or 998.02, Postoperative septic shock. Any additional codes for other acute organ dysfunctions should also be assigned. As noted in the sequencing instructions in the Tabular List, the code for septic shock cannot be assigned as a principal diagnosis.

(b) **Septic shock without documentation of severe sepsis**

Since septic shock indicates the presence of severe sepsis, code 995.92, Severe sepsis, can be assigned with code 785.52, Septic shock, or code 998.02 Postoperative shock, septic, even if the term *severe sepsis* is not documented in the record.

7) **Sepsis and septic shock complicating abortion and pregnancy**

Sepsis and septic shock complicating abortion, ectopic pregnancy, and molar pregnancy are classified to category codes in Chapter 11 (630–639). *See Section I.C.11.i.7 for information on the coding of puerperal sepsis.*

8) **Negative or inconclusive blood cultures**

Negative or inconclusive blood cultures do not preclude a diagnosis of septicemia or sepsis in patients with clinical evidence of the condition; however, the provider should be queried.

9) **Newborn sepsis**

See Section I.C.15.j for information on the coding of newborn sepsis.

10) **Sepsis due to a postprocedural infection**

(a) **Documentation of causal relationship**

As with all postprocedural complications, code assignment is based on the provider's documentation of the relationship between the infection and the procedure.

(b) **Sepsis due to postprocedural infection**

In cases of postprocedural sepsis, the complication code, such as code 998.59, Other postoperative infection, or 674.3x, Other complications of obstetrical surgical wounds, should be coded first, followed by the appropriate sepsis codes (systemic infection code and either code 995.91 or 995.92). An additional code(s) for any acute organ dysfunction should also be assigned for cases of severe sepsis. *See Section I.C.1.b.6 if the sepsis or severe sepsis results in postprocedural septic shock.*

(c) **Postprocedural infection and postprocedural septic shock**

In cases where a postprocedural infection has occurred and has resulted in severe sepsis and postprocedural septic shock, the code for the precipitating complication such as code 998.59, Other postoperative infection, or 674.3x, Other complications of obstetrical surgical wounds should be coded first followed by the appropriate sepsis codes (systemic infection code and code 995.92). Code 998.02, Postoperative septic shock, should be assigned as an additional code. In cases of severe sepsis, an additional code(s) for any acute organ dysfunction should also be assigned.

11) **External cause of injury codes with SIRS**

Refer to Section I.C.19.a.7 for instruction on the use of external cause of injury codes with codes for SIRS resulting from trauma.

12) **Sepsis and severe sepsis associated with noninfectious process**

In some cases, a noninfectious process, such as trauma, may lead to an infection that can result in sepsis or severe sepsis. If sepsis or severe sepsis is documented as associated with a noninfectious condition, such as a burn or serious injury, and this condition meets the definition for principal diagnosis, the code for the noninfectious condition should be sequenced first, followed by the code for the systemic infection and either code 995.91, Sepsis, or 995.92, Severe sepsis. Additional codes for any associated acute organ dysfunction(s) should also be assigned for cases of severe sepsis. If the sepsis or severe sepsis meets the definition of principal diagnosis, the systemic infection and sepsis codes should be sequenced before the noninfectious condition. When both the associated noninfectious condition and the sepsis or severe sepsis meet the definition of principal diagnosis, either may be assigned as principal diagnosis.

See Section I.C.1.b.2.a for guidelines pertaining to sepsis or severe sepsis as the principal diagnosis.

Only one code from subcategory 995.9 should be assigned. Therefore, when a noninfectious condition leads to an infection resulting in sepsis or severe sepsis, assign either code 995.91 or 995.92. Do not additionally assign code 995.93, Systemic inflammatory response syndrome due to noninfectious process without acute organ dysfunction, or 995.94, Systemic inflammatory response syndrome with acute organ dysfunction.

See Section I.C.17.g for information on the coding of SIRS due to trauma/burns or other noninfectious disease processes.

c. Methicillin-Resistant *Staphylococcus aureus* (MRSA) conditions
1) Selection and sequencing of MRSA codes
(a) Combination codes for MRSA infection

When a patient is diagnosed with an infection that is due to methicillin-resistant *Staphylococcus aureus* (MRSA), and that infection has a combination code that includes the causal organism (e.g., septicemia, pneumonia) assign the appropriate code for the condition (e.g., code 038.12, Methicillin-resistant *Staphylococcus aureus* septicemia or code 482.42, Methicillin-resistant pneumonia due to *Staphylococcus aureus*). Do not assign code 041.12, Methicillin-resistant *Staphylococcus aureus*, as an additional code because the code includes the type of infection and the MRSA organism. Do not assign a code from subcategory V09.0, Infection with microorganisms resistant to penicillins, as an additional diagnosis.

See Section C.1.b.1 for instructions on coding and sequencing of septicemia.

(b) Other codes for MRSA infection

When there is documentation of a current infection (e.g., wound infection, stitch abscess, urinary tract infection) due to MRSA, and that infection does not have a combination code that includes the causal organism, select the appropriate code to identify the condition along with code 041.12, Methicillin-resistant *Staphylococcus aureus*, for the MRSA infection. Do not assign a code from subcategory V09.0, Infection with microorganisms resistant to penicillins.

(c) Methicillin-susceptible *Staphylococcus aureus* (MSSA) and MRSA colonization

The condition or state of being colonized or carrying MSSA or MRSA is called colonization or carriage, while an individual person is described as being colonized or being a carrier.

Colonization means that MSSA or MSRA is present on or in the body without necessarily causing illness. A positive MRSA colonization test might be documented by the provider as "MRSA screen positive" or "MRSA nasal swab positive."

Assign code V02.54, Carrier or suspected carrier, Methicillin-resistant *Staphylococcus aureus*, for patients documented as having MRSA colonization. Assign code V02.53, Carrier or suspected carrier, Methicillin-susceptible *Staphylococcus aureus*, for patient documented as having MSSA colonization. Colonization is not necessarily indicative of a disease process or as the cause of a specific condition the patient may have unless documented as such by the provider.

Code V02.59, Other specified bacterial diseases, should be assigned for other types of staphylococcal colonization (e.g., *S. epidermidis*, *S. saprophyticus*). Code V02.59 should not be assigned for colonization with any type of *Staphylococcus aureus* (MRSA, MSSA).

(d) MRSA colonization and infection

If a patient is documented as having both MRSA colonization and infection during a hospital admission, code V02.54, Carrier or suspected carrier, Methicillin-resistant *Staphylococcus aureus*, and a code for the MRSA infection may both be assigned.

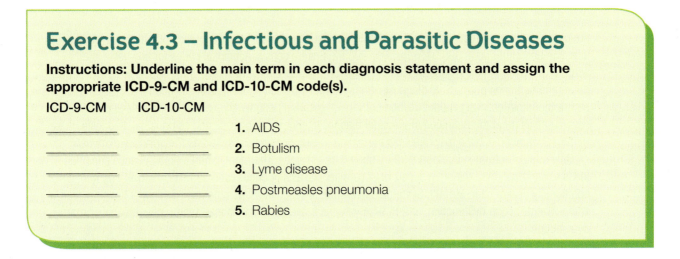

Exercise 4.3 – Infectious and Parasitic Diseases

Instructions: Underline the main term in each diagnosis statement and assign the appropriate ICD-9-CM and ICD-10-CM code(s).

ICD-9-CM   ICD-10-CM

_____   _____   1. AIDS

_____   _____   2. Botulism

_____   _____   3. Lyme disease

_____   _____   4. Postmeasles pneumonia

_____   _____   5. Rabies

ICD-9-CM Chapter 2: Neoplasms (140–239)

Neoplasms are new growths or tumors in which cell reproduction is out of control, and they are classified according to appearance and growth pattern (Figure 4-4). For coding purposes, the provider should specify whether the tumor is benign (noncancerous, nonmalignant, or noninvasive) or malignant (cancerous, invasive, or capable of spreading to other parts of the body). It is highly advisable that neoplasms be coded directly from the pathology report (generated by a hospital's or stand-alone laboratory's pathology department and mailed to the provider's office); however, until the diagnostic statement specifies whether the neoplasm is benign or malignant, coders should code the patient's sign (e.g., breast lump) or report a subcategory code from the Unspecified Nature column of the documented site using the neoplasm table in the disease index.

ICD-10 Alert!

In *ICD-10-CM*, Neoplasms (C00-D49) are also located in Chapter 2.

Note:

Functionally active malignant neoplasms behave like their surrounding tissue, such as a thyroid tumor that secretes thyroxine and causes hyperthyroidism.

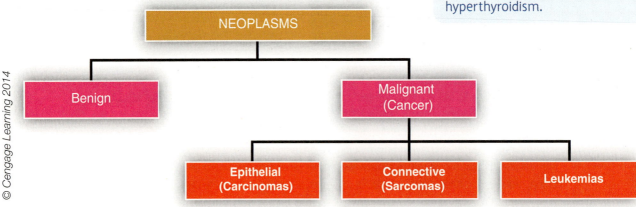

© Cengage Learning 2014

Figure 4-4 Classification of neoplasms

Another term associated with neoplasms is *lesion*, which is defined as "any discontinuity of tissue (e.g., skin or organ) that may or may not be malignant." Index to Disease entries for *lesion* contain subterms according to anatomic site (e.g., organs or tissue), and the term *lesion* should be referenced if the diagnostic statement does not confirm a malignancy. In addition, the following conditions are examples of benign lesions and are listed as separate Index to Disease entries:

- Adenosis
- Cys
- Dysplasia
- Mass (unless the word *neoplasm* is included in the diagnostic statement)
- Polyp

Do not reference the neoplasm table to assign codes for the above conditions. Instead, first locate the specific term in the disease index; then locate the subterm for the specific organ or body area. When the specific organ or body area is not listed as subterm, follow the instructions provided (e.g., *see*, *see also*, or *see* category).

EXAMPLE: The provider documents "liver mass" as the final diagnosis because the pathology report of examined tissue is not yet available. A "mass" is not a "neoplasm." Therefore, locate main term *Mass* in the disease index and look for subterm *liver*. Notice that in the ICD-9-CM index there is no subterm for *liver*. However, this is an instruction that states "Mass—specified organ NEC—see Disease of specified organ or site." Locate main term *Disease* and subterm *liver* to identify 573.9; and after verifying 573.9 (unspecified disorder of liver) in the Tabular List of Diseases, report 573.8 (other specified disorders of liver) instead because *mass* is documented. (When pathology report results are available, assign a more appropriate code.)

In the ICD-10-CM index, locate main term *Mass* and subterm *liver* to assign R16.0 (after verifying it in the tabular list).

The ICD-9-CM and ICD-10-CM neoplasm tables (Figure 4-5A and Figure 4-5B) is indexed by anatomic site and contains four cellular classifications: malignant, benign, uncertain behavior, and unspecified nature.

	Malignant			Benign	Uncertain Behavior	Unspecified Nature
	Primary	Secondary	Ca in situ			
Neoplasm, neoplastic	199.1	199.1	234.9	229.9	238.9	239.9

Notes — 1. The list below gives the code numbers for neoplasms by anatomic site. For each site there are six possible code numbers according to whether the neoplasm in question is malignant, benign, in situ, of uncertain behavior, or of unspecified nature. The description of the neoplasm will often indicate which of the six columns is appropriate, e.g., malignant melanoma of skin, benign fibroadenoma of breast, carcinoma in situ of cervix uteri.

Where such descriptors are not present, the remainder of the Index should be consulted where guidance is given to the appropriate column for each morphologica (histological) variety listed; e.g., Mesonephroma — see Neoplasm, malignant; Embryoma — see also Neoplasm, uncertain behavior; Disease, Bowen's — see Neoplasm, skin, in situ. However, the guidance in the Index can be overridden if one of the descriptors mentioned above is present; e.g., malignant adenoma of colon is coded to 153.9 and not to 211.3 as the adjective "malignant" overrides the Index entry "Adenoma — see also Neoplasm, benign."

2. Sites marked with the sign * (e.g., face NEC*) should be classified to malignant neoplasm of skin of these sites if the variety of neoplasm is a squamous cell carcinoma or an epidermal carcinoma, and to benign neoplasm of skin of these sites if the variety of neoplasm is a papilloma (any type).

	Primary	Secondary	Ca in situ	Benign	Uncertain Behavior	Unspecified Nature
abdomen, abdominal	195.2	198.89	234.8	229.8	238.8	239.8
cavity	195.2	198.89	234.8	229.8	238.8	239.8
organ	195.2	198.89	234.8	229.8	238.8	239.8
viscera	195.2	198.89	234.8	229.8	238.8	239.8
wall	173.5	198.2	232.5	216.5	238.2	239.2
basal cell carcinoma	173.51	—	—	—	—	—
connective tissue	171.5	198.89	—	215.5	237.1	239.2
specified type NEC	173.59	—	—	—	—	—
squamous cell carcinoma	173.52	—	—	—	—	—
abdominopelvic	195.8	198.89	234.8	229.8	238.8	239.8
accessory sinus – see Neoplasm, sinus						
acoustic nerve	192.0	198.4	—	225.1	237.9	239.7
acromion (process)	170.4	198.5	—	213.4	238.0	239.2

Figure 4-5A ICD-9-CM neoplasm table (partial)

	Malignant Primary	Malignant Secondary	Ca *in situ*	Benign	Uncertain Behavior	Unspecified Nature
Neoplasm, neoplastic	C80	C79.9	D09.9	D36.9	D48.9	D49.9

> Notes — 1. The list below gives the code numbers for neoplasms by anatomic al site. For each site there are six possible code numbers according to whether the neoplasm in question is malignant, benign, *in situ* of uncertain behavior, or of unspecified nature. The description of the neoplasm will often indicate which of the six columns is appropriate; e.g., malignant melanoma of skin, benign fibroadenoma of breast, carcinoma *in situ* of cervix uteri.
>
> Where such descriptors are not present, the remainder of the Index should be consulted where guidance is given to the appropriate column for each morphologic (histological) variety listed; e.g., Mesonephroma—*s*   Neoplasm, malignant; Embryoma—*s   s*   Neoplasm, uncertain behavior; Disease, Bowen's—*s*   Neoplasm, skin, *in situ*. However, the guidance in the Index can be overridden if one of the descriptors mentioned above is present; e.g., malignant adenoma of colon is coded to C18.9 and not to D12.6 as the adjective "malignant" overrides the Index entry "Adenoma—*s   s*   Neoplasm, benign."
>
> 2. Sites marked with the sign * (e.g., face NEC*) should be classified to malignant neoplasm of skin of these sites if the variety of neoplasm is a squamous cell carcinoma or an epidermoid carcinoma and to benign neoplasm of skin of these sites if the variety of neoplasm is a papilloma (any type).

	Malignant Primary	Malignant Secondary	Ca *in situ*	Benign	Uncertain Behavior	Unspecified Nature
abdomen, abdominal	C76.2	C79.8-	D09.8	D36.7	D48.7	D49.89
cavity	C76.2	C79.8-	D09.8	D36.7	D48.7	D49.89
organ	C76.2	C79.8-	D09.8	D36.7	D48.7	D49.89
viscera	C76.2	C79.8-	D09.8	D36.7	D48.7	D49.89
wall	C44.99	C79.2	D04.5	D23.5	D48.5	D49.2
connective tissue	C49.4	C79.8-	—	D21.4	D48.1	D49.2
skin	C44.509					
basal cell carcinoma	C44.519	—	—	—	—	—
specified type NEC	C44.599	—	—	—	—	—
squamous cell carcinoma	C44.529	—	—	—	—	—

Figure 4-5B ICD-10-CM neoplasm table (partial)

The malignant classification is subdivided into three divisions: primary, secondary, and carcinoma *in situ*. The six neoplasm classifications are defined as follows:

- 🔵 **Primary malignancy**: Original tumor site.

- **Secondary malignancy** (or **metastatic cancer**): Tumor that has metastasized, or spread, to a secondary site either adjacent to the primary site or to a remote region of the body.

- **Carcinoma (Ca) *in situ***: Malignant tumor that is localized, circumscribed, encapsulated, and noninvasive, but has not spread to deeper or adjacent tissues or organs.

- **Benign:** Noninvasive, nonspreading, nonmalignant tumor.

- **Uncertain behavior**: Subsequent morphology or behavior that cannot be predicted based on the submitted specimen; the tissue appears to be in transition, and the pathologist cannot establish a definitive diagnosis.

🔵 **Note:**

Malignant tumors are considered primary unless otherwise documented as metastatic or secondary.

Coding Tip:

To assign a code from the Uncertain Behavior column, the pathology report must specifically indicate the "uncertain behavior" of the neoplasm.

- **Unspecified nature**: A neoplasm is identified, but the results of pathology examination are not available; thus, there is no indication as to histology or nature of the tumor.

Coding Tip:

Assign a code from the Unspecified Nature column when the neoplasm was destroyed or removed and a tissue biopsy was performed and results are pending.

To use the neoplasm table, first identify the classification and then locate the site of the neoplasm. Some diagnostic statements specifically document "neoplasm" classification, while others do not provide a clue. If the diagnostic statement classifies the neoplasm, the coder can refer directly to the neoplasm table in the disease index to assign the proper code (after verifying the code in the tabular list).

When the diagnostic statement does not classify the neoplasm, the coder must refer to the disease index entry for the condition documented (instead of the neoplasm table) (e.g., lipoma). That entry either will contain a code number that can be verified in the tabular list or will refer the coder to the proper neoplasm table entry under which the code can be located.

EXAMPLE: DIAGNOSTIC STATEMENTS AND ICD-9-CM/ICD-10-PCS INDEX ENTRIES: For non-Hodgkin's lymphoma, go to main term *Lymphoma* in the ICD-9-CM disease index and verify code 202.8 in the tabular list to add the fifth digit for the anatomic site. Go to main term *Lymphoma* in the ICD-10-CM index, subterm *non-Hodgkin*, and verify code C85.9 in the tabular list to assign the fifth digit for the anatomic site.

For adrenal gland adenolymphoma, go to main term *Adenolymphoma* in the ICD-9-CM disease index and follow the instruction to *see Neoplasm, by site, benign*. Locate code 227.0 for Neoplasm, adrenal (cortex) (gland) (medulla) in the Neoplasm table, and verify it in the tabular list. Go to main term *Adenolymphoma* in the ICD-10-CM index, and follow the instruction to *see Neoplasm, benign*, and verify code D35.00 in the tabular list.

ICD-9-CM Index Entries	ICD-10-CM Index Entries
Lymphoma	**Lymphoma**
non-Hodgkin's type NEC (M9591/3) 202.8	non-Hodgkin (*see also* Lymphoma, by type) C85.9
Adenolymphoma (M8561/0)	**Adenolymphoma**
specified site—*see* Neoplasm, by site, benign	specified site—*see* Neoplasm, benign, by site
unspecified 210.2	unspecified site D11.9

Coding Tip:

Assigning codes from the neoplasm table is a two-step process. First, classify the neoplasm by its behavior (e.g., malignant or secondary); then classify the neoplasm by its anatomic site (e.g., acoustic nerve). To classify the neoplasm's behavior, review the provider's diagnostic statement (e.g., carcinoma of the throat) and locate the term *carcinoma* in the disease index. The entry will classify the behavior, directing you to the proper column in the neoplasm table. (If the neoplasm is malignant, you still need to determine primary, secondary, or *in situ* based on documentation in the patient's record.)

Primary and Secondary Malignancies

A malignancy is coded as a primary site if the diagnostic statement documents:

- Metastatic *from* a site
- Spread *from* a site
- *Primary neoplasm* of a site
- A malignancy for which no specific classification is documented
- A *recurrent* tumor

EXAMPLE 1: For "carcinoma of cervical lymph nodes, metastatic from the breast," the primary site is female breast and the secondary site is cervical lymph nodes.

EXAMPLE 2: For "oat cell carcinoma of the lung with spread to the brain," the primary site is lung and the secondary site is brain.

Coding Tip:

The sequencing of neoplasm codes depends on the reason for the encounter. Review the patient's record to determine whether the primary or secondary cancer site is being treated or medically managed.

- If the primary site is being treated or medically managed during the encounter, report that code first, followed by code(s) for secondary site(s) if present.
- If the secondary site is being treated or medically managed, report that code first, followed by a code for the primary site.

Secondary malignancies are metastatic and indicate that a primary cancer has spread (metastasized) to another part of the body. Cancer described as *metastatic from* a site is *primary of* that site. Assign one code to the primary neoplasm and a second code to the secondary neoplasm of the specified site (if secondary site is known) or unspecified site (if secondary site is unknown). (Remember that sequencing of codes depends on which site is being treated.)

 Note:

In each example, ICD-10-CM codes appear in parentheses after ICD-9-CM codes.

EXAMPLE 1: For "metastatic carcinoma from female breast to lung," assign two codes:

- Primary malignant neoplasm of female breast (174.9) (C50.919)
- Secondary neoplasm of lung (197.0) (C78.00)

EXAMPLE 2: For "metastatic carcinoma from female breast," assign two codes:

- Primary malignant neoplasm of female breast (174.9) (C50.919)
- Secondary neoplasm of unspecified site (199.1) (C79.9)

Cancer described as *metastatic to* a site is considered *secondary of* that site. Assign one code to the secondary site and a second code to the specified primary site (if primary site is known) or unspecified site (if primary site is unknown).

EXAMPLE 1: For "metastatic carcinoma from liver to lung," assign two codes:

- Primary malignant neoplasm of liver (155.0) (C22.0)
- Secondary neoplasm of lung (197.0) (C78.00)

EXAMPLE 2: For "metastatic carcinoma to lung," assign two codes:

- Primary malignant neoplasm of unspecified site (199.1) (C80.1)
- Secondary neoplasm of lung (197.0) (C78.00)

When anatomic sites are documented as *metastatic*, assign *secondary* neoplasm code(s) to those sites and assign an *unspecified site* code to the primary malignant neoplasm.

EXAMPLE 1: For "metastatic renal cell carcinoma of lung," assign two codes:

- Primary renal cell carcinoma, right side (189.0) (C64.1)
- Secondary neoplasm of lung (197.0) (C78.00)

EXAMPLE 2: For "metastatic osteosarcoma of brain," assign two codes:

- Primary malignant neoplasm of bone (170.9) (C41.90)
- Secondary neoplasm of brain (198.3) (C79.31)

EXAMPLE 3: For "metastatic melanoma of lung and liver," assign three codes:

- Primary malignant melanoma of unspecified site (172.9) (C43.9)
- Secondary neoplasm of lung (197.0) (C78.00)
- Secondary neoplasm of liver (197.7) (C78.7)

EXAMPLE 4: For "metastatic adenocarcinoma of prostate and vertebra," assign three codes:

- Primary adenocarcinoma of unspecified site (199.1) (C80.1)
- Secondary neoplasm of prostate (198.82) (C79.82)
- Secondary neoplasm of vertebra (198.5) (C79.51)

If the diagnostic statement does not specify whether the neoplasm site is primary or secondary, code the site as *primary*, except for the following sites, which are considered *secondary* sites (unless the physician specifies that they are primary):

> **Note:**
>
> Lung is not included in the list of secondary sites. Therefore, lung cancer is coded as a primary site (unless the physician specifies that it is a secondary site).

- Bone
- Brain
- Diaphragm
- Heart
- Liver
- Lymph nodes
- Mediastinum
- Meninges
- Peritoneum
- Pleura
- Retroperitoneum
- Spinal cord
- Neoplasms classifiable to ICD-9-CM category 195 (or ICD-10-CM category C76)

EXAMPLE 1: For "breast cancer," assign one code:

- Primary malignant neoplasm of left female breast (174.9) (C50.912)

EXAMPLE 2: For "brain cancer," assign two codes:

- Primary malignant neoplasm of unspecified site (199.1) (C80.1)
- Secondary neoplasm of brain (198.3) (C79.31)

EXAMPLE 3: For "metastatic cancer of hip," assign two codes:

- Primary malignant neoplasm of unspecified site (199.1) (C80.1)
- Secondary neoplasm of left hip (198.89) (C79.51)

Anatomic Site Is Not Documented

If the cancer diagnosis does not contain documentation of the anatomic site but the term *metastatic* is documented, assign codes for "unspecified site" for both the primary and secondary sites.

EXAMPLE: For "metastatic chromophobe adenocarcinoma," assign two codes:

- Secondary neoplasm of unspecified site (199.1) (C79.9)
- Primary chromophobe adenocarcinoma of unspecified site (194.3) (C75.1)

Primary Malignant Site Is No Longer Present

If the primary site of malignancy is no longer present and no further treatment is directed to the site, do not assign the code for primary of unspecified site. Instead, classify the previous primary site by assigning the appropriate code from category V10, "Personal history of malignant neoplasm."

EXAMPLE: For "metastatic carcinoma to right lung from right female breast (left radical mastectomy performed last year)," assign two codes:

- Secondary neoplasm of right lung (197.0) (C78.01)
- Personal history of malignant neoplasm of right female breast (V10.3) (Z85.3)

Inoperable Primary Site with Metastasis

When the primary neoplasm site is considered inoperable and is not treated, assign a code for the metastatic site first.

> **EXAMPLE:** For "carcinoma of fundus of stomach (inoperable) with metastasis to liver," assign two codes:

- Secondary malignant neoplasm of liver (197.7) (C78.7)
- Malignant neoplasm of fundus of stomach (151.3) (C16.1)

Contiguous or Overlapping Sites

Contiguous sites (or **overlapping sites**) occur when the origin of the tumor (primary site) involves two adjacent sites. Neoplasms with overlapping site boundaries are classified to the fourth-digit subcategory .8, "Other."

> **EXAMPLE:** For "cancer of the jejunum and ileum," go to the entry for "intestine, small, contiguous sites" in the ICD-9-CM neoplasm table. Locate code 152.8 in the Malignant—Primary column and verify the code in the tabular list. In the ICD-10-CM Neoplasm table, locate "intestine, small, overlapping lesion" and verify code C17.8 in the tabular list.

Reexcision of Tumors

A reexcision of a tumor occurs when the pathology report recommends that the surgeon perform a second excision to widen the margins of the original tumor site. The reexcision is performed to ensure that all tumor cells have been removed and that a clear border (margin) of normal tissue surrounds the excised specimen. Use the diagnostic statement found in the report of the original excision to code the reason for the reexcision. The pathology report for the reexcision may not specify a malignancy at that time, but the patient is still under treatment for the original neoplasm.

 Coding Tip:

1. Read all notes in the neoplasm table that apply to the condition you are coding.
2. Never assign a code directly from the neoplasm table or index.
3. Report only those codes that represent the current status of the neoplasm.
4. Assign a neoplasm code if the tumor has been excised and the patient is still undergoing radiation or chemotherapy treatment.
5. Assign an ICD-9-CM V code (or ICD-10-CM Z code) if the tumor is no longer present or if the patient is not receiving treatment but is returning for follow-up care (e.g., personal history of a malignancy).
6. The classification documented on a pathology report overrides the morphology classification entry in the Index to Diseases. (Additional information about the assignment of morphology codes can be found on the Premium Website.)

ICD-9-CM CHAPTER-SPECIFIC CODING GUIDELINES WITH ICD-10 ALERTS!

ICD-10 Alert!

- In ICD-10-CM, *Neoplasms [C00-D49]* are also located in Chapter 2, and the ICD-9-CM coding guidelines with *ICD-10 Alerts!* are included below.
- Many of the ICD-10-CM and ICD-9-CM *Neoplasms* coding guidelines are similar; however, ICD-10-CM's coding guidelines contain new Sections I.C.2.i. through I.C.2.q., including:
  - i. Malignancy in two or more noncontiguous sites.

j. Disseminated malignant neoplasm, unspecified.

k. Malignant neoplasm without specification of site.

l. Sequencing of neoplasm codes.

m. Current malignancy versus personal history of malignancy.

n. Leukemia, Multiple Myeloma, and Malignant Plasma Cell Neoplasms in remission versus personal history.

o. Aftercare following surgery for neoplasm.

p. Follow-up care for completed treatment of a malignancy.

q. Prophylactic organ removal for prevention of malignancy.

- *Go to Appendix II located on the Premium Website to review Section I.C.2., Chapter 2: Neoplasms (C00-C49), of the ICD-10-CM coding guidelines.*

Chapter 2: Neoplasms (140–239)

General guidelines

Chapter 2 of the ICD-9-CM contains the codes for most benign and all malignant neoplasms. Certain benign neoplasms, such as prostatic adenomas, may be found in the specific body system chapters. To properly code a neoplasm, it is necessary to determine from the record if the neoplasm is benign, *in situ*, malignant, or of uncertain histologic behavior. If malignant, any secondary (metastatic) sites should also be determined.

The neoplasm table in the Alphabetic Index should be referenced first. However, if the histological term is documented, that term should be referenced first, rather than going immediately to the neoplasm table, in order to determine which column in the neoplasm table is appropriate. For example, if the documentation indicates "adenoma," refer to the term in the Alphabetic Index to review the entries under this term and the instructional note to "see also neoplasm, by site, benign." The table provides the proper code based on the type of neoplasm and the site. It is important to select the proper column in the table that corresponds to the type of neoplasm. The tabular should then be referenced to verify that the correct code has been selected from the table and that a more specific site code does not exist.

Note: See the Supplemental Classification of Factors Influencing Health Status and Contact with Health Services—History (of) coding guidelines for information about reporting V codes for genetic susceptibility to cancer.

ICD-10 Alert!

In ICD-10-CM, Chapter 21, *Factors Influencing Health Status and Contact with Health Services (Z00–Z99)* contains information about Z15.0 codes for *genetic susceptibility* to cancer.

a. ### Treatment directed at the malignancy

If the treatment is directed at the malignancy, designate the malignancy as the principal diagnosis.

The only exception to this guideline is if a patient admission/encounter is solely for the administration of chemotherapy, immunotherapy, or radiation therapy, assign the appropriate V51.- code as the first-listed or principal diagnosis, and the diagnosis or problem for which the service is being performed as a secondary diagnosis.

b. ### Treatment of secondary site

When a patient is admitted because of a primary neoplasm with metastasis and treatment is directed toward the secondary site only, the secondary neoplasm is designated as the principal diagnosis even though the primary malignancy is still present.

ICD-10 Alert!

The ICD-10-CM code for the administration of chemotherapy, immunotherapy, or radiation therapy is Z51.-.

(continues)

ICD-9-CM CHAPTER-SPECIFIC CODING GUIDELINES WITH ICD-10 ALERTS! (*continued*)

c. Coding and sequencing of complications

Coding and sequencing of complications associated with the malignancies or with the therapy thereof are subject to the following guidelines:

1) Anemia associated with malignancy

When admission/encounter is for management of an anemia associated with the malignancy, and the treatment is only for anemia, the appropriate anemia code (such as code 285.22, Anemia in neoplastic disease) is designated as the principal diagnosis and is followed by the appropriate code(s) for the malignancy.

Code 285.22 may also be used as a secondary code if the patient suffers from anemia and is being treated for the malignancy.

If anemia in neoplastic disease and anemia due to antineoplastic chemotherapy are both documented, assign codes for both conditions.

2) Anemia associated with chemotherapy, immunotherapy, and radiation therapy

 ICD-10 Alert!

The ICD-10-CM coding guideline for *anemia associated with malignancy* was revised and requires sequencing of the cancer code first. The coding guideline states, "When admission/encounter is for management of an anemia associated with the malignancy, and the treatment is only for anemia, the appropriate code for the malignancy is sequenced as the principal or first-listed diagnosis followed by code D63.0, Anemia in neoplastic disease."

When the admission/encounter is for management of an anemia associated with chemotherapy, immunotherapy, or radiotherapy, and the only treatment is for the anemia, the anemia is sequenced first. The appropriate neoplasm code should be assigned as an additional code.

 ICD-10 Alert!

The ICD-10-CM coding guideline for *anemia associated with chemotherapy, immunotherapy, and radiation therapy* was revised so as to address adverse effects only. The coding guideline states, "When the admission/encounter is for management of an anemia associated with an adverse effect of chemotherapy, immunotherapy or radiotherapy and the only treatment is for the anemia, the appropriate adverse effect code should be sequenced first, followed by the appropriate codes for the anemia and neoplasm."

3) Management of dehydration due to the malignancy

When the admission/encounter is for management of dehydration due to the malignancy or the therapy, or a combination of both, and only the dehydration is being treated (intravenous rehydration), the dehydration is sequenced first, followed by the code(s) for the malignancy.

4) Treatment of a complication resulting from a surgical procedure

When the admission/encounter is for treatment of a complication resulting from a surgical procedure, designate the complication as the principal or first-listed, diagnosis if treatment is directed at resolving the complication.

 **ICD-10 Alert!**

The ICD-10-CM category for *personal history of primary and secondary malignant neoplasm is Z85.*

d. 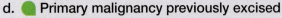 Primary malignancy previously excised

When a primary malignancy has been previously excised or eradicated from its site and there is no further treatment directed to that site and there is no evidence of any existing primary malignancy, a code from category V10, Personal history of malignant neoplasm, should be used to indicate the former site of the malignancy. Any mention of extension, invasion, or metastasis to another site is coded as a secondary malignant neoplasm to that site. The secondary site may be the principal or first-listed, with the V10 code used as a secondary code.

e. **Admissions/Encounters involving chemotherapy, immunotherapy and, radiation therapy**

1) **Episode of care involves surgical removal of neoplasm**

When an episode of care involves the surgical removal of a neoplasm, primary or secondary site, followed by adjunct chemotherapy or radiation treatment during the same episode of care, the neoplasm code should be assigned as principal or first-listed diagnosis, using codes in the 140–198 series or, where appropriate, in the 200–203 series.

> **ICD-10 Alert!**
>
> Use codes in the ICD-10-CM *C00-D49* series or, where appropriate, in the C83–C90 series.

2) **Patient admission/encounter solely for administration of chemotherapy, immunotherapy, and radiation therapy**

If a patient admission/encounter is solely for the administration of chemotherapy, immunotherapy, or radiation therapy, assign code V58.0, Encounter for radiation therapy; V58.11, Encounter for antineoplastic chemotherapy; or V58.12, Encounter for antineoplastic immunotherapy as the first-listed or principal diagnosis. If a patient receives more than one of these therapies during the same admission, more than one of these codes may be assigned, in any sequence.

The malignancy for which the therapy is being administered should be assigned as a secondary diagnosis.

> **ICD-10 Alert!**
>
> The ICD-10-CM code for encounter for antineoplastic:
> - Radiation therapy is Z51.0.
> - Chemotherapy is Z51.11.
> - Immunotherapy is Z51.12.

3) **Patient admitted for radiotherapy/chemotherapy and immunotherapy and develops complications**

When a patient is admitted for the purpose of radiotherapy/chemotherapy and immunotherapy and develops complications such as uncontrolled nausea and vomiting or dehydration, the principal or first-listed diagnosis is V58.0, Encounter for radiotherapy; V58.1v1, Encounter for antineoplastic chemotherapy; or V58.12, Encounter for antineoplastic immunotherapy, followed by any codes for the complications.

See Section 18.d.7. for additional information regarding aftercare V codes.

> **ICD-10 Alert!**
>
> In the ICD-10-CM coding guidelines, the instruction regarding aftercare codes was removed. However, ICD-10-CM still classifies aftercare codes in Chapter 21, *Factors Influencing Health Status and Contact with Health Services [Z00–Z99].*

f. **Admission/encounter to determine extent of malignancy**

When the reason for admission/encounter is to determine the extent of the malignancy, or for a procedure such as paracentesis or thoracentesis, the primary malignancy or appropriate metastatic site is designated as the principal or first-listed diagnosis, even though chemotherapy or radiotherapy is administered.

g. **Symptoms, signs, and ill-defined conditions listed in Chapter 16 associated with neoplasms**

Symptoms, signs, and ill-defined conditions listed in Chapter 16 characteristic of, or associated with, an existing primary or secondary site malignancy cannot be used to replace the malignancy as principal or

(continues)

ICD-9-CM CHAPTER-SPECIFIC CODING GUIDELINES WITH ICD-10 ALERTS! (*continued*)

first-listed diagnosis, regardless of the number of admissions or encounters for treatment and care of the neoplasm.

See Section 18.d.14, Encounter for prophylactic organ removal.

 ICD-10 Alert!

- *Symptoms, Signs and Abnormal Clinical and Laboratory Findings, Not Elsewhere Classified (R00-R99) are located in Chapter 18 of ICD-10-CM.*
- Encounters for prophylactic organ removal are classified in ICD-10-CM's Chapter 21, *Factors Influencing Health Status and Contact with Health Services.*

h. **Admission/encounter for pain control/management**

See Section I.C.6.a.5 for information on coding admission/encounter for pain control/management.

 ICD-10 Alert!

- In the ICD-10-CM coding guidelines, go to Section I.C.6.b. in *Chapter 6: Diseases of Nervous System and Sense Organs (G00-G99)* for information about coding an admission/encounter for pain control/management.
- *Go to Appendix II located on the Premium Website to review Sections I.C.2.i. through I.C.2.q of the ICD-10-CM coding guidelines.*

i. **Malignant neoplasm associated with transplanted organ**

A malignant neoplasm of a transplanted organ should be coded as a transplant complication. Assign first the appropriate code from subcategory 996.8, Complications of transplanted organ, followed by code 199.2, Malignant neoplasm associated with transplanted organ. Use an additional code for the specific malignancy.

ICD-10 Alert!

The ICD-10-CM code for:
- Complications of transplanted organ is T86.-.
- Malignant neoplasm associated with transplanted organ is C80.2.

Exercise 4.4 – Neoplasms

Instructions: Underline the main term in each diagnosis statement and assign the appropriate ICD-9-CM and ICD-10-CM code(s).

ICD-9-CM	ICD-10-CM	
_____	_____	**1.** Carcinoma *in situ*, cervix uteri (neoplasm)
_____	_____	**2.** Choriocarcinoma (female patient)
_____	_____	**3.** Hemangioma
_____	_____	**4.** Kaposi's sarcoma
_____	_____	**5.** Lipoma, skin of abdomen

ICD-9-CM Chapter 3: Endocrine, Nutritional and Metabolic Diseases, and Immunity Disorders (240–279)

The endocrine system includes specialized organs and body tissues that produce, secrete, and store hormones. Hormones regulate the body's development, control the function of various tissues, support reproduction, and regulate metabolism. Hormones from the endocrine system are secreted into the blood, where proteins keep them intact and regulate their release. Other changes in the body also influence hormone secretions.

> **EXAMPLE 1: NORMAL HORMONE FUNCTION:** Parathyroid hormone causes the body to increase the level of calcium in blood. As calcium levels rise, the secretion of parathyroid hormone decreases.

> **EXAMPLE 2: HORMONE FUNCTION DURING ILLNESS:** During illness, the adrenal glands increase the secretions of certain hormones to help the body overcome the stress of illness. The normal regulation of hormone secretion is suspended, allowing for a tolerance of higher levels of hormone in the blood until the illness is resolved.

> **ICD-10 Alert!**
>
> In ICD-10-CM, Endocrine, *Nutritional, and Metabolic Diseases (E00-E89)* are located in Chapter 4.

> **ICD-10 Alert!**
>
> In ICD-10-CM, Chapter 3 contains *Diseases of the Blood and Blood-forming Organs and Certain Disorders Involving the Immune Mechanism (D50–D89)*.

Nutritional deficiencies in ICD-9-CM Chapter 3 cover deficiencies in vitamins, minerals, and protein-calorie malnutrition. Deficiencies of anemia are classified to ICD-9-CM Chapter 4, Disease of the Blood and Blood-Forming Organs. Metabolic diseases in ICD-9-CM Chapter 3 cover a wide range of diseases, including problems with amino-acid and carbohydrate transport; lipoid metabolism; plasma protein metabolism; gout; mineral metabolism; and fluid, electrolyte, and acid-base imbalances. Cystic fibrosis, porphyrin, purine and pyrimidine metabolism, and obesity are also classified.

Coding Diabetes Mellitus

The ICD-9-CM code descriptions for diabetes mellitus were edited effective October 1, 2004, to remove the parenthetical phrases of *(adult onset)*, *(noninsulin dependent diabetes mellitus)*, and *(insulin dependent diabetes mellitus)*. In their place, instruction has been provided for coders to select a fifth digit for type 1, type 2, or unspecified type. To assign the fifth digit for type 1 diabetes mellitus, the provider must document it in the patient record. With **type 1 diabetes mellitus**, the patient's body is *unable to produce insulin*; with **type 2 diabetes mellitus**, the patient's body is *unable to properly use insulin produced.*

> **Coding Tip:**
>
> If the patient's record documents the administration of insulin, do not assume that the patient is a type 1 diabetic. The provider must document "type 1" to assign that code.

Once you've identified whether the patient is type 1 or type 2, review the patient record to determine whether the patient's diabetes mellitus is controlled or uncontrolled. If the provider did not document either status, assign fifth digits 0 or 1. Next, make sure you review the patient record to identify any disease complications (e.g., ketoacidosis or ophthalmologic manifestations), which are assigned fourth digits 0–9. Don't forget to assign a code to documented manifestations (e.g., diabetic cataract) and make sure you sequence the diabetes mellitus code first.

> **Coding Tip:**
>
> - Report code V58.67, Long-term (current) insulin use, as an other (additional) diagnosis code for type 2 patients who use insulin.
> - For a diagnosis of "pre-diabetes," assign code 790.29.

ICD-9-CM CHAPTER-SPECIFIC CODING GUIDELINES WITH ICD-10 ALERTS!

 ICD-10 Alert!

- In ICD-10-CM, *Endocrine, Nutritional, and Metabolic Diseases (E00–E89)* are located in Chapter 4, and the ICD-9-CM coding guidelines with ICD-10 Alerts! are included below.
- *Go to Appendix II located on the Premium Website to review Section I.C.4., Chapter 4: Endocrine, Nutritional, and Metabolic Diseases (E00–E89), of the ICD-10-CM coding guidelines.*

Chapter 3: Endocrine, Nutritional, and Metabolic Diseases and Immunity Disorders (240–279)

a. **Diabetes mellitus**

Codes under category 250, Diabetes mellitus, identify complications/manifestations associated with diabetes mellitus. A fifth digit is required for all category 250 codes to identify the type of diabetes mellitus and whether the diabetes is controlled or uncontrolled.

1) **Fifth digits for category 250:**

The following are the fifth digits for the codes under category 250:

0   type 2 or unspecified type, not stated as uncontrolled
1   type 1, [juvenile type], not stated as uncontrolled
2   type 2 or unspecified type, uncontrolled
3   type 1, [juvenile type], uncontrolled

The age of a patient is not the sole determining factor, though most type 1 diabetics develop the condition before reaching puberty. For this reason, type 1 diabetes mellitus is also referred to as juvenile diabetes.

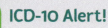 **ICD-10 Alert!**

If the type of diabetes mellitus is not documented in the medical record the default code from category E11 (*Type 2 diabetes mellitus*) is selected.

2) **Type of diabetes mellitus not documented**

If the type of diabetes mellitus is not documented in the medical record, the default is type 2.

3) **Diabetes mellitus and the use of insulin**

All type 1 diabetics must use insulin to replace what their bodies do not produce. However, the use of insulin does not mean that a patient is a type 1 diabetic. Some patients with type 2 diabetes mellitus are unable to control their blood sugar through diet and oral medication alone and do require insulin. If the documentation in a medical record does not indicate the type of diabetes but does indicate that the patient uses insulin, the appropriate fifth digit for type 2 must be used. For type 2 patients who routinely use insulin, code V58.67, Long-term (current) use of insulin, should also be assigned to indicate that the patient uses insulin. Code V58.67 should not be assigned if insulin is given temporarily to bring a type 2 patient's blood sugar under control during an encounter.

ICD-10 Alert!

If the documentation in a medical record does not indicate the type of diabetes but does indicate that the patient uses insulin, code E11, *Type 2 diabetes mellitus,* should be assigned for type 2 patients who routinely use insulin. Code Z79.4, *Long-term (current) use of insulin,* should also be assigned to indicate that the patient uses insulin. Code Z79.4 should *not* be assigned when insulin is administered temporarily to bring a type 2 patient's blood sugar under control during an encounter.

4) **Assigning and sequencing diabetes codes and associated conditions**

When assigning codes for diabetes and its associated conditions, the code(s) from category 250 must be sequenced before the codes for the associated conditions. The diabetes codes and the secondary codes that correspond to them are paired codes that follow the etiology/manifestation convention of the classification.

Assign as many codes from category 250 as needed to identify all of the associated conditions that the patient has. The corresponding secondary codes are listed under each of the diabetes codes.

(a) Diabetic retinopathy/diabetic macular edema

Diabetic macular edema, code 362.07, is only present with diabetic retinopathy. Another code from subcategory 362.0, Diabetic retinopathy, must be used with code 362.07. Codes under subcategory 362.0 are diabetes manifestation codes, so they must be used following the appropriate diabetes code.

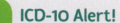

> **ICD-10 Alert!**
>
> *Go to Appendix II located on the Premium Website to review Section I.C.15, Diabetes mellitus in pregnancy and Section I.C.15. Gestational [pregnancy induced] diabetes, of the ICD-10-CM coding guidelines.*

5) ● **Diabetes mellitus in pregnancy and gestational diabetes**

(a) For diabetes mellitus complicating pregnancy, see Section I.c.11.c.f, Diabetes mellitus in pregnancy.

(b) For gestational diabetes, see Section I.C.11.g, Gestational diabetes.

6) **Insulin pump malfunction**

(a) Underdose of insulin due to insulin pump failure

An underdose of insulin due to an insulin pump failure should be assigned 996.57, Mechanical complication due to insulin pump, as the principal or first-listed code, followed by the appropriate diabetes mellitus code based on documentation.

> **ICD-10 Alert!**
>
> An underdose of insulin due to an insulin pump failure should be assigned to a code from subcategory T85.6, *Mechanical complication of other specified internal and external prosthetic devices, implants and grafts* [assigning a fifth digit to specify type of pump malfunction], as the principal or first-listed code. Then, code T38.3x6-, *Underdosing of insulin and oral hypoglycemic [antidiabetic] drugs* is reported. Additional codes for the type of diabetes mellitus and any associated complications due to the underdosing should also be assigned.

(b) Overdose of insulin due to insulin pump failure

The principal or first-listed code for an encounter due to an insulin pump malfunction resulting in an overdose of insulin should also be 996.57, Mechanical complication due to insulin pump, followed by code 962.3, Poisoning by insulins and antidiabetic agents, and the appropriate diabetes mellitus code based on documentation.

> **ICD-10 Alert!**
>
> The principal or first-listed code for an encounter due to an insulin pump malfunction resulting in an overdose of insulin, should also be T85.6-, *Mechanical complication of other specified internal and external prosthetic devices, implants and grafts,* followed by code T38.3x1-, *Poisoning by insulin and oral hypoglycemic [antidiabetic] drugs, accidental [unintentional].*

7) **Secondary diabetes mellitus**

Codes under category 249, Secondary diabetes mellitus, identify complications/manifestations associated with secondary diabetes mellitus. Secondary diabetes is always caused by another condition or event (e.g., cystic fibrosis, malignant neoplasm of pancreas, pancreatectomy, adverse effect of drug, or poisoning).

(a) Fifth digits for category 249

A fifth digit is required for all category 249 codes to identify whether the diabetes is controlled or uncontrolled.

(continues)

ICD-9-CM CHAPTER-SPECIFIC CODING GUIDELINES WITH ICD-10 ALERTS! (*continued*)

 ICD-10 Alert!

Codes in category E08, *Diabetes mellitus due to underlying condition,* and category E09, *Drug or chemical induced diabetes mellitus,* identify complications/manifestations associated with secondary diabetes mellitus.

(b) **Secondary diabetes mellitus and the use of insulin**

For patients who routinely use insulin, code V58.67, Long-term (current) use of insulin, should also be assigned. Code V58.67 should not be assigned if insulin is given temporarily to bring a patient's blood sugar under control during an encounter.

ICD-10 Alert!

The ICD-10-CM code for *long-term (current) use of insulin* is Z79.4.

(c) **Assigning and sequencing secondary diabetes codes and associated conditions**

When assigning codes for secondary diabetes and its associated conditions (e.g., renal manifestations), the code(s) from category 249 must be sequenced before the codes for the associated conditions. The secondary diabetes codes and the diabetic manifestation codes that correspond to them are paired codes that follow the etiology/manifestation convention of the classification. Assign as many codes from category 249 as needed to identify all of the associated conditions that the patient has. The corresponding codes for the associated conditions are listed under each of the secondary diabetes codes. For example, secondary diabetes with diabetic nephrosis is assigned to code 249.40, followed by 581.81.

(d) **Assigning and sequencing secondary diabetes codes and its causes**

The sequencing of the secondary diabetes codes in relationship to codes for the cause of the diabetes is based on the reason for the encounter, applicable ICD-9-CM sequencing conventions, and chapter-specific guidelines.

If a patient is seen for treatment of the secondary diabetes or one of its associated conditions, a code from category 249 is sequenced as the principal or first-listed diagnosis, with the cause of the secondary diabetes (e.g., cystic fibrosis) sequenced as an additional diagnosis.

If, however, the patient is seen for the treatment of the condition causing the secondary diabetes (e.g., malignant neoplasm of pancreas), the code for the cause of the secondary diabetes should be sequenced as the principal or first-listed diagnosis followed by a code from category 249.

 ICD-10 Alert!

The sequencing of the secondary diabetes codes in relationship to codes for the cause of the diabetes is based on tabular list instructions for categories E08 and E09. For example, for category E08, *Diabetes mellitus due to underlying condition,* code first the underlying condition. And, for category E09, *Drug or chemical induced diabetes mellitus,* code first the drug or chemical (T36–T65).

(i) **Secondary diabetes mellitus due to pancreatectomy**

For postpancreatectomy diabetes mellitus (lack of insulin due to the surgical removal of all or part of the pancreas), assign code 251.3, Postsurgical hypoinsulinemia. A code from subcategory 249 should not be assigned for secondary diabetes mellitus due to pancreatectomy. Code also any diabetic manifestations (e.g., diabetic nephrosis 581.81).

(ii) **Secondary diabetes due to drugs**

Secondary diabetes may be caused by an adverse effect of correctly administered medications, poisoning, or late effect of poisoning.

ICD-10 Alert!

For postpancreatectomy diabetes mellitus (lack of insulin due to the surgical removal of all or part of the pancreas), assign code E89.1, *Postsurgical hypoinsulinemia.* Assign a code from category E08, *Diabetes mellitus due to underlying condition,* and code Z79.4, *Other acquired absence of organ,* as additional codes.

> *See Section I.C.17.e for coding of adverse effects and poisoning, and section 19 for E code reporting.*

 ICD-10 Alert!

Go to Appendix II located on the Premium Website to review Section I.C.19.e, Coding of Adverse Effects and Poisoning, and section I.C.20, External Cause Code Reporting, of the ICD-10-CM coding guidelines.

Exercise 4.5 – Endocrine, Nutritional and Metabolic Diseases, and Immunity Disorders

Instructions: Underline the main term in each diagnosis statement and assign the appropriate ICD-9-CM and ICD-10-CM code(s).

ICD-9-CM	ICD-10-CM	
_____	_____	**1.** Diabetes mellitus, type 1, uncontrolled
_____	_____	**2.** Diabetes mellitus, type 2
_____	_____	**3.** Hyperprolactinemia
_____	_____	**4.** Morbid obesity
_____	_____	**5.** Polycystic ovaries

ICD-9-CM Chapter 4: Diseases of the Blood and Blood-Forming Organs (280–289)

Diseases and disorders of blood and blood-forming (hemopoietic) organs include anemias, coagulation defects, purpura and other hemorrhagic condions, diseases of white blood cells, and other diseases of blood and blood-forming organs. Bone marrow is the principal site for hemopoietic cell proliferation and differentiation. One of the largest organs in the human body, hemopoietic tissue is responsible for producing erythrocytes (red blood cells), neutrophils, eosinophils, basophils, monocytes, platelets, and lymphocytes.

Anemia refers to a lower-than-normal erythrocyte count or level of hemoglobin in the circulating blood. A clinical sign rather than a diagnostic entity, anemia can be classified by three morphological variations of the erythrocyte: size (volume), hemoglobin content, and shape. These variations give clinicians clues to the specific type of anemia. In laboratory blood tests, erythrocyte size is gauged by estimating the volume of red cells in the circulating blood.

ICD-10 Alert!

In ICD-10-CM, *Diseases of the Blood and Blood-forming Organs and Certain Disorders Involving the Immune Mechanism (D50–D89)* are located in Chapter 3.

- Red cell volume (or mean corpuscular volume) is estimated by dividing the patient's hematocrit (percentage of red blood cells in whole blood) by the red blood cell count (RBC). Normal values are normocytic, abnormally low values are microcytic, and abnormally high values are macrocytic.

- Hemoglobin content refers to the average amount of hemoglobin in each red blood cell. This value, called the mean cell hemoglobin, is calculated by dividing the patient's hemoglobin by the number of red blood cells. Normal values are normochromic, less-than-normal values are hypochromic, and greater-than-normal values are hyperchromic.

- Shape is determined by microscopy. Normally, red blood cells have a smooth, concave shape. Erythrocytes with irregular shapes are called poikilocytes, a general term meaning "abnormally shaped." Terms referring to specific abnormal cell shapes include *acanthocytes, leptocytes, nucleated erythrocytes, macro-ovalocytes, schistocytes, helmet cells, teardrop cells, sickle cells*, and *target cells*.

Once the cell morphology is determined, the anemia can be further classified based on certain physiologic and pathologic criteria.

EXAMPLE: Constitutional aplastic anemia (ICD-9-CM code 284.09 or ICD-10-CM code D61.09) is classified physiologically as an anemia of hypoproliferation and pathologically as inborn error of heredity.

The term *coagulation defect* refers to deficiencies or disorders of hemostasis. A complicated process involving substances in the injured tissues, formed elements of blood (platelets and monocytes), and the coagulation proteins, coagulation requires the production of thrombin, a substance that stabilizes the platelet plug and forms the fibrin clot. Together they mechanically block the extravasation of blood from ruptured vessels. The coagulation process can be interrupted by a genetic or disease-caused protein deficiency, by an increase in the catabolism of coagulation proteins, or by antibodies directed against the coagulation proteins. Many proteins are involved in coagulation, many of which are identified by the term *factor* followed by a Roman numeral. The appropriate Roman numeral followed by the suffix *a* indicates the activated form of a coagulation factor.

EXAMPLE: When protein Factor II (prothrombin) is activated by the enzyme thrombin, it is designated Factor IIa.

The term *purpura* refers to a condition characterized by hemorrhage, or extravasation of blood, into the tissues, producing bruises and small red patches on the skin. Purpura may be associated with thrombocytopenia or can occur in a nonthrombocytopenic form. Thrombocytopenia is a decrease of the number of platelets in the circulating blood and may be primary (hereditary or idiopathic) or secondary to a known cause.

 Coding Tip:

Excluded from ICD-9-CM Chapter 4, Diseases of the Blood and Blood-Forming Organs (280–289), is "anemia complicating pregnancy and the puerperium," which is classified to category 648.

 ICD-10 Alert!

In ICD-10-CM, *Anemia complicating pregnancy, childbirth and the puerperium* is classified to subcategory O99.0 (ICD-10-CM Chapter 15, *Pregnancy, Childbirth, and the Puerperium*).

Diseases of white blood cells refer to increases, decreases, or genetic or idiopathic anomalies of white blood cells not associated with malignant disease classified to categories 200–208, *Malignant Neoplasm of Lymphatic and Hematopoietic and Related Tissue.*

 ICD-10 Alert!

In ICD-10-CM, *Malignant Neoplasms of Lymphoid, Hematopoietic and Related Tissue* are classified in categories C81–C96 (ICD-10-CM Chapter 2, Neoplasms).

ICD-9-CM CHAPTER-SPECIFIC CODING GUIDELINES WITH ICD-10 ALERTS!

● Chapter 4: Diseases of the Blood and Blood-Forming Organs (280–289)

a. Anemia of chronic disease

Subcategory 285.2, Anemia in chronic illness, has codes for anemia in chronic kidney disease, code 285.21; anemia in neoplastic disease, code 285.22; and anemia in other chronic illness, code 285.29. These codes can be used as the principal/first-listed code if the reason for the encounter is to treat the anemia. They may also be used as secondary codes if treatment of the anemia is a component of an encounter, but not the primary reason for the encounter. When using a code from subcategory 285 it is also necessary to use the code for the chronic condition causing the anemia.

1) Anemia in chronic kidney disease

When assigning code 285.21, Anemia in chronic kidney disease, it is also necessary to assign a code from category 585, Chronic kidney disease, to indicate the stage of chronic kidney disease.

See Section I.C.10.a, Chronic kidney disease (CKD).

2) Anemia in neoplastic disease

When assigning code 285.22, Anemia in neoplastic disease, it is also necessary to assign the neoplasm code that is responsible for the anemia. Code 285.22 is used of anemia that is due to the malignancy, not for anemia due to antineoplastic chemotherapy. Assign the appropriate code for anemia due to antineoplastic chemotherapy.

See Section I.C.2.c.1, Anemia associated with malignancy.
See Section I.C.2.c.2, Anemia associated with chemotherapy, immunotherapy, and radiation therapy.

● ICD-10 Alert!

- There are no ICD-10 Alerts! among the ICD-9-CM coding guidelines (below) because there are no ICD-10-CM official coding guidelines for codes D50-D89. (The ICD-10-CM index and tabular list provide clear direction to appropriate codes.)

- Go to Appendix II located on the Premium Website to review Section I.C.3., Chapter 3: Diseases of the Blood and Blood-forming Organs and Certain Disorders Involving the Immune Mechanism (D50-D89), of the ICD-10-CM coding guidelines. Notice the "Reserved for future guideline expansion" phrase, which means space has been allowed for including future guidelines.

Exercise 4.6 – Diseases of the Blood and Blood-Forming Organs

Instructions: Underline the main term in each diagnosis statement and assign the appropriate ICD-9-CM and ICD-10-CM code(s).

ICD-9-CM   ICD-10-CM

_____   _____   **1.** Acquired polycythemia

_____   _____   **2.** Acute posthemorrhagic anemia

_____   _____   **3.** Agranulocytosis

_____   _____   **4.** Chronic simple anemia

_____   _____   **5.** Chronic congestive splenomegaly

ICD-9-CM Chapter 5: Mental Disorders (290–319)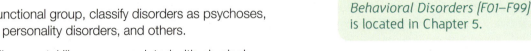

The WHO offers the following guidelines that apply to this chapter:

- When classifying behavioral disorders, organically based illnesses are reported before functional illnesses.

- Within a functional group, classify disorders as psychoses, neuroses, personality disorders, and others.

- When coding mental illnesses associated with physical conditions, assign as many codes as necessary to fully describe the clinical picture.

ICD-10 Alert!

In ICD-10-CM, *Mental and Behavioral Disorders [F01–F99]* is located in Chapter 5.

Note:

There are no official ICD-9-CM coding guidelines for mental disorders (290–319).

ICD-10 Alert!

- In ICD-10-CM, *Mental and Behavioral Disorders [F01–F99]* are located in Chapter 5 and a portion of the new ICD-10-CM coding guideline is located below:

  a. **Pain disorders related to psychological factors**
  Assign code F45.41, for pain that is exclusively related to psychological disorders. As indicated by the Excludes1 note under the category G89, a code from category G89 should not be assigned with code F45.41. Code F45.4, Pain disorders related to psychological factors, should be used with a code from category G89, Pain, not elsewhere classified, if there is documentation of a psychological component for a patient with acute or chronic pain.

- *Go to Appendix II located on the Premium Website to review Section I.C.5., Chapter 5: Mental and Behavioral Disorders [F01–F99], of the ICD-10-CM coding guidelines.*

Exercise 4.7 – Mental Disorders

Instructions: Underline the main term in each diagnosis statement and assign the appropriate ICD-9-CM and ICD-10-CM code(s).

ICD-9-CM	ICD-10-CM	
_____	_____	1. Alzheimer's disease
_____	_____	2. Chronic paranoid schizophrenia
_____	_____	3. Alcoholic delirium tremens
_____	_____	4. Episodic cocaine abuse
_____	_____	5. Major depressive disorder, recurrent episode

ICD-9-CM Chapter 6: Diseases of the Nervous System and Sense Organs (320–389)

This ICD-9-CM chapter classifies diseases and disorders of the nervous system, including the meninges (covering for the brain and spinal cord), central nervous system (brain and spinal cord), and peripheral nervous system (nerves that relay signals between the central nervous system and the organs of the body). This ICD-9-CM chapter also classifies conditions affecting the eye and ear.

 ICD-10 Alert!

> The ICD-10-CM coding manual includes three separate chapters for Diseases of Nervous System (G00–G99) (Chapter 6), *Diseases of the Eye and Adnexa (H00–H59)* (Chapter 7), and Diseases of the *Ear and Mastoid Process (H60–H95)* (Chapter 8).

ICD-9-CM CHAPTER-SPECIFIC CODING GUIDELINES WITH ICD-10 ALERTS!

 ICD-10 Alert!

- In ICD-10-CM, Diseases of Nervous System (G00–G99) are located in Chapter 6, *Diseases of the Eye and Adnexa (H00–H59)* are located in Chapter 7, Diseases of the Ear and Mastoid Process (H60–H95) are located in Chapter 8, and ICD-9-CM coding guidelines with *ICD-10 Alerts!* are included below.

- Go to Appendix II located on the Premium Website to review Section I.C.6., Chapter 6: Diseases of Nervous System, Section I.C.7., *Chapter 7: Diseases of the Eye and Adnexa*, and Section I.C.8., Chapter 8: *Diseases of the Ear and Mastoid Process*, of the ICD-10-CM coding guidelines.

Chapter 6: Diseases of Nervous System and Sense Organs (320–389)

 ICD-10 Alert!

> There is a new ICD-10-CM coding guideline for category G81, as follows:
>
> a. Dominant/nondominant side
>
> Codes from category G81, *Hemiplegia and hemiparesis,* and subcategories, G83.1, *Monoplegia of lower limb,* G83.2, *Monoplegia of upper limb,* and G83.3, *Monoplegia, unspecified,* identify whether the dominant or nondominant side is affected. Should this information not be available in the record, and the classification system does not indicate a default, the default should be dominant. For ambidextrous patients, the default should also be dominant.

(continues)

ICD-9-CM CHAPTER-SPECIFIC CODING GUIDELINES WITH ICD-10 ALERTS! (*continued*)

a. Pain–Category 338
1) General coding information

Codes in category 338 may be used in conjunction with codes from other categories and chapters to provide more detail about acute or chronic pain and neoplasm-related pain, unless otherwise indicated below.

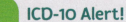 If the pain is not specified as acute or chronic, do not assign codes from category 338, except for postthoracotomy pain, postoperative pain, neoplasm-related pain, or central pain syndrome.

A code from subcategories 338.1 and 338.2 should not be assigned if the underlying (definitive) diagnosis is known, unless the reason for the encounter is pain control/management and not management of the underlying condition.

ICD-10 Alert!

The ICD-10-CM code for *pain, not elsewhere classified,* is G89, which applies whenever you see ICD-9-CM category code 338 in the official guidelines below.

(a) Category 338 Codes as principal or first-listed diagnosis

Category 338 codes are acceptable as principal diagnosis or the first-listed code:

- When pain control or pain management is the reason for the admission/encounter (e.g., a patient with displaced intervertebral disc, nerve impingement, and severe back pain presents for injection of steroid into the spinal canal). The underlying cause of the pain should be reported as an additional diagnosis, if known.

ICD-10 Alert!

The ICD-10-CM subcategory for *acute pain, not elsewhere classified,* is G89.1, and the subcategory for *chronic pain, not elsewhere classified,* is G89.2.

- When an admission or encounter is for a procedure aimed at treating the underlying condition (e.g., spinal fusion, kyphoplasty), a code for the underlying condition (e.g., vertebral fracture, spinal stenosis) should be assigned as the principal diagnosis. No code from category 338 should be assigned.

- When a patient is admitted for the insertion of a neurostimulator for pain control, assign the appropriate pain code as the principal or first-listed diagnosis. When an admission or encounter is for a procedure aimed at treating the underlying condition and a neurostimulator is inserted for pain control during the same admission/encounter, a code for the underlying condition should be assigned as the principal diagnosis and the appropriate pain code should be assigned as a secondary diagnosis.

(b) Use of category 338 codes in conjunction with site-specific pain codes
(i) Assigning category 338 codes and site-specific pain codes

Codes from category 338 may be used in conjunction with codes that identify the site of pain (including codes from Chapter 16) if the category 338 code provides additional information. For example, if the code describes the site of the pain but does not fully describe whether the pain is acute or chronic, both codes should be assigned.

(ii) Sequencing of category 338 codes with site-specific pain codes

The sequencing of category 338 codes with site-specific pain codes (including Chapter 16 codes), is dependent on the circumstances of the encounter/admission as follows:

ICD-10 Alert!

The ICD-10-CM code for *acute pain due to trauma* is G89.11, and the code for *cervicalgia* is M54.2.

- If the encounter is for pain control or pain management, assign the code from category 338 followed by the code identifying the specific site of pain (e.g., encounter for pain management for acute neck pain from trauma is assigned code 338.11, Acute pain due to trauma, followed by code 723.1, Cervicalgia, to identify the site of pain).

- If the encounter is for any reason other than pain control or pain management and a related definitive diagnosis has not been established (confirmed) by the provider, assign the code for the specific site of pain first, followed by the appropriate code from category 338.

2) **Pain due to devices, implants, and grafts**

Pain associated with devices, implants, or grafts left in a surgical site (for example, painful hip prosthesis) is assigned to the appropriate code(s) found in Chapter 17, Injury and Poisoning. Use additional code(s) from category 338 to identify acute or chronic pain due to presence of the device, implant, or graft (338.18–338.19 or 338.28–338.29).

3) **Postoperative pain**

Post-thoracotomy pain and other postoperative pain are classified to subcategories 338.1 and 338.2, depending on whether the pain is acute or chronic. The default for post-thoracotomy and other postoperative

ICD-10 Alert!

The ICD-10-CM official coding guideline for *pain due to devices, implants, and grafts* was relocated to Section I.C.19 to associate it with ICD-10-CM's Chapter 19, *Injury, Poisoning and Certain Other Consequences of External Causes [S00-T98]* where *complications of surgical and medical care, not elsewhere classified* are assigned codes T80–T88.

pain not specified as acute or chronic is the code for the acute form.

ICD-10 Alert!

The ICD-10-CM subcategory for *acute pain, not elsewhere classified,* is G89.1, and the subcategory for *chronic pain, not elsewhere classified,* is G89.2.

Routine or expected postoperative pain immediately after surgery should not be coded.

(a) **Postoperative pain not associated with specific postoperative complication**

Postoperative pain not associated with a specific postoperative complication is assigned to the appropriate postoperative pain code in category 338.

(b) **Postoperative pain associated with specific postoperative complication**

Postoperative pain associated with a specific postoperative complication (such as painful wire sutures) is assigned to the appropriate code(s) found in Chapter 17, Injury and Poisoning. If appropriate, use additional code(s) from category 338 to identify acute or chronic pain (338.18 or 338.28). If pain control/management is the reason for the encounter, a code from category 338 should be assigned as the principal or first-listed diagnosis in accordance with Section I.C.6.a.1.a above.

(c) **Postoperative pain as principal or first-listed diagnosis**

Postoperative pain may be reported as the principal or first-listed diagnosis when the stated reason for the

ICD-10 Alert!

The ICD-10-CM codes for *postoperative pain* include G89.12, G89.18 G89.22, and G89.28.

ICD-10 Alert!

Content about *postoperative pain as principal or first-listed diagnosis* was removed from the ICD-10-CM official coding guidelines.

(continues)

ICD-9-CM CHAPTER-SPECIFIC CODING GUIDELINES WITH ICD-10 ALERTS! (*continued*)

admission/encounter is documented as postoperative pain control/management.

(d) Postoperative pain as secondary diagnosis

Postoperative pain may be reported as a secondary diagnosis code when a patient presents for outpatient surgery and develops an unusual or inordinate amount of postoperative pain.

The provider's documentation should be used to guide the coding of postoperative pain, as well as Section III. Reporting Additional Diagnoses, and Section IV. Diagnostic Coding and Reporting in the Outpatient Setting.

See Section II.I.2 (of the official guidelines) for information on sequencing of diagnoses for patients admitted to hospital inpatient care following postoperative observation.

See Section II.J (of the official guidelines) for information on sequencing of diagnoses for patients admitted to hospital inpatient care from outpatient surgery.

See Section IV.A.2 (of the official guidelines) for information on sequencing of diagnoses for patients admitted for observation.

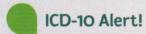 **ICD-10 Alert!**

Content about the *postoperative pain as secondary diagnosis* was removed from the ICD-10-CM official coding guidelines

4) Chronic pain

Chronic pain is classified to subcategory 338.2. There is no time frame defining when pain becomes chronic pain. The provider's documentation should be used to guide the use of these codes.

ICD-10 Alert!

The ICD-10-CM code for chronic pain *is G89.2.*

5) Neoplasm-related pain

Code 338.3 is assigned to pain documented as being related, associated with or due to cancer, primary or secondary malignancy, or tumor. This code is assigned regardless of whether the pain is acute or chronic.

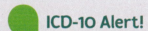 **ICD-10 Alert!**

The ICD-10-CM code for *neoplasm-related pain* is G89.3. Coders are also directed to Section I.C.2 of the ICD-10-CM official coding guidelines for instructions on the *sequencing of neoplasms for all other stated reasons for the admission/encounter (except for pain control/pain management).*

This code may be assigned as the principal or first-listed code when the stated reason for the admission/encounter is documented as pain control/pain management. The underlying neoplasm should be reported as an additional diagnosis.

When the reason for the admission/encounter is management of the neoplasm and the pain associated with the neoplasm is also documented, code 338.3 may be assigned as an additional diagnosis.

See Section I.C.2.a. through 2.g. for instructions on the sequencing of neoplasms for all other stated reasons for the admission/encounter (except pain control/pain management).

6) Chronic pain syndrome

This condition is different from the term *chronic pain*, and therefore this code should be used only when the provider has specifically documented this condition.

b. Glaucoma

1) Glaucoma

For types of glaucoma classified to subcategories 365.1–365.6, an additional code should be assigned from subcategory 365.7, Glaucoma stage, to identify the glaucoma stage. Codes from 365.7, Glaucoma stage, may not be assigned as a principal or first-listed diagnosis.

2) **Bilateral glaucoma with same stage**

When a patient has bilateral glaucoma and both are documented as being the same type and stage, report only the code for the type of glaucoma and one code for the stage.

3) **Bilateral glaucoma stage with different stages**

When a patient has bilateral glaucoma and each eye is documented as having a different stage, assign one code for the type of glaucoma and one code for the highest glaucoma stage.

4) **Bilateral glaucoma with different types and different stages**

When a patient has bilateral glaucoma and each eye is documented as having a different type and a different stage, assign one code for each type of glaucoma and one code for the highest glaucoma stage.

5) **Patient admitted with glaucoma and stage evolves during the admission**

If a patient is admitted with glaucoma and the stage progresses during the admission, assign the code for highest stage documented.

6) **Indeterminate stage glaucoma**

Assignment of code 365.74, Indeterminate stage glaucoma, should be based on the clinical documentation. Code 365.74 is used for glaucomas whose stage cannot be clinically determined. This code should not be confused with code 365.70, Glaucoma stage, unspecified. Code 365.70 should be assigned when there is no documentation regarding the stage of the glaucoma.

 ICD-10 Alert!

- Coders are also directed to Section I.C.5 of the ICD-10-CM official coding guidelines for instructions about *pain disorders related to psychological factors.*

- There are no official coding guidelines for Sections I.C.7., *Chapter 7: Diseases of the Eye and Adnexa, and I.C.8., Chapter 8: Diseases of the Ear and Mastoid Process.* However, the phrase *"Reserved for future guideline expansion"* appears below each chapter heading in the official guidelines to allow space for future guidelines.

Exercise 4.8 – Diseases of the Nervous System and Sense Organs

Instructions: Underline the main term in each diagnosis statement and assign the appropriate ICD-9-CM and ICD-10-CM code(s).

ICD-9-CM	ICD-10-CM	
_____	_____	**1.** Acute swimmers' ear, right
_____	_____	**2.** Bell's palsy
_____	_____	**3.** Diplopia
_____	_____	**4.** Congenital quadriplegia
_____	_____	**5.** Intraspinal abscess

ICD-9-CM Chapter 7: Diseases of the Circulatory System (390–459)

Coding diseases of the circulatory system can be complex for several reasons, some of which follow:

ICD-10 Alert!

In ICD-10-CM, *Diseases of the Circulatory System (I00–I99)* is located in Chapter 9.

- Interrelationship of conditions
- Specificity of coding guidelines
- Varied medical **lexicon** (glossary) used to describe circulatory conditions

Hypertension/Hypertensive Table

The ICD-9-CM hypertension/hypertensive table (of which Figure 4-6 shows a partial listing) contains a complete listing of hypertension codes and other conditions associated with it.

ICD-10 Alert!

- The hypertension table and the terms *benign* and *malignant* (associated with hypertension) were eliminated from ICD-10-CM. (Providers rarely classified hypertension as benign or malignant, which meant ICD-9-CM code 401.9, unspecified hypertension, was usually assigned.) ICD-10-CM classifies *essential (primary) hypertension* as code I10.

- ICD-10-CM categories I11–I15 classify hypertension due to other conditions and secondary hypertension.

- The word *hypertension* is a main term in the ICD-10-CM index, with subterms and qualifiers facilitating its classification.

- *Use additional code* instructions are located in the ICD-10-CM tabular list, facilitating complete coding.

- Malignant: A severe form of hypertension with vascular damage and a diastolic pressure reading of 140 mmHg (millimeters of mercury) or greater (hypertension is out of control, or there was a rapid change from a benign state for a prolonged period)

- Benign: Mild and/or controlled hypertension, with no damage to the patient's vascular system or organs

- Unspecified: No notation of benign or malignant status is found in the diagnosis or in the patient's chart

	Malignant	Benign	Unspecified
Hypertension, hypertensive (arterial) (arteriolar) (crisis) (degeneration) (disease) (essential) (fluctuating) (idiopathic) (intermittent) (labile) (low renin) (orthostatic) (paroxysmal) (primary) (systemic) (uncontrolled) (vascular) ...	401.0	401.1	401.9
with			
chronic kidney disease			
stage I through stage IV, or unspecified	403.00	403.10	403.90
stage V or end stage renal disease	403.01	403.11	403.91
heart involvement (conditions classifiable to 429.0–429.3, 429.8, 429.9			
due to hypertension) (*see also* Hypertension, heart)	402.00	402.10	402.90
with kidney involvement – see Hypertension, cardiorenal			
renal involvement (only conditions classifiable to 585, 586, 587)			
(excludes conditions classifiable to 584)			
(*see also* Hypertension, kidney)	403.00	403.10	403.90
with heart involvement – *see* Hypertension, cardiorenal			
failure (and sclerosis) (*see also* Hypertension, kidney)	403.01	403.11	403.91
sclerosis without failure (*see also* Hypertension, kidney)	403.00	403.10	403.90
accelerated (*see also* Hypertension, type, malignant)	401.0	—	—
antepartum – *see* Hypertension complicating pregnancy,			
childbirth, or the puerperium			

Figure 4-6 ICD-9-CM hypertension/hypertensive table (partial)

Coding Tip:

- The ICD-9-CM hypertension/hypertensive table uses all three levels of indentations when the word *with* is included in the diagnostic statement. Make sure you review the subterms carefully. You may have to assign two codes when *with* separates two conditions in the diagnostic statement.

- When the provider does not document the type of hypertension (for example, benign or malignant), assign the subcategory code for "unspecified." Do not assume that "hypertension" is "benign" just because the provider has not indicated that it is a malignant type. **Benign hypertension** is of prolonged or chronic duration, and it is likely that the patient's hypertension has been controlled by medication. **Malignant hypertension** is an accelerated, severe hypertensive disorder with progressive cardiovascular damage and a poor prognosis; it is characterized by rapidly rising blood pressure greater than 140 diastolic. Patients diagnosed with malignant hypertension are usually hospitalized. **Unspecified hypertension** is an ICD-9-CM subcategory assigned when the provider does not document benign or malignant type, likely because the provider has the mistaken impression that a "benign" condition is limited or minor in nature.

- Always review the Tabular List of Diseases before assigning a code for hypertension/hypertensive conditions.

- Secondary hypertension is a unique and separate condition listed on the table. When secondary hypertension is documented, the hypertension was caused by another primary condition (e.g., cancer).

- Assign the fourth digit 9 sparingly. Most insurance companies insist on conditions being coded to the highest degree of specificity known at the time of the encounter. They may not accept 401.9 Hypertension, unspecified, except during the first few weeks of treatment for hypertension. After that point, the physician usually knows whether the patient has benign (controlled by medication) or malignant (out-of-control) hypertension. If "benign" or "malignant" is not specified in the diagnosis, ask the physician to document the type of hypertension.

ICD-9-CM CHAPTER-SPECIFIC CODING GUIDELINES WITH ICD-10 ALERTS!

 ICD-10 Alert!

In ICD-10-CM, *Diseases of the Circulatory System (I00–I99)* is located in Chapter 9, and ICD-9-CM coding guidelines with *ICD-10 Alerts!* are included below.

Chapter 7: Diseases of the Circulatory System (390–459)

a. Hypertension
   Hypertension table
       The hypertension table, found under the main term *Hypertension* in the Index to Diseases, contains a complete listing of all conditions due to or associated with hypertension and classifies them according to malignant, benign, and unspecified.

ICD-10 Alert!

There is no hypertension table in ICD-10-CM. However, Section I.C.9 of the ICD-10-CM official coding guidelines includes content about hypertension.

(continues)

ICD-9-CM CHAPTER-SPECIFIC CODING GUIDELINES WITH ICD-10 ALERTS! (*continued*)

1) **Hypertension, essential, or NOS**

Assign hypertension (arterial)(essential)(primary)(systemic)(NOS) to category code 401 with the appropriate fourth digit to indicate malignant (.0), benign (.1), or unspecified (.9). Do not use either .0 malignant or .1 benign unless medical record documentation supports such a designation.

2) **Hypertension with heart disease**

Heart conditions (425.8, 429.0–429.3, 429.8, 429.9) are assigned to a code from category 402 when a causal relationship is stated (due to hypertension) or implied (hypertensive). Use an additional code from category 428 to identify the type of heart failure in those patients with heart failure. More than one code from category 428 may be assigned if the patient has systolic or diastolic failure and congestive heart failure (Figure 4-7). The same heart conditions (425.8, 429.0–429.3, 429.8, 429.9) with hypertension, but without a stated casual relationship, are coded separately. Sequence according to the circumstances of the admission/encounter.

ICD-10 Alert!

Content about *hypertension, essential, or NOS* was removed from the ICD-10-CM official coding guidelines because just one code is now assigned (I10). However, content about *hypertension with other conditions* and *secondary hypertension* remains.

ICD-10 Alert!

The ICD-10-CM codes for heart conditions are I50.- and I51.4–I51.9.

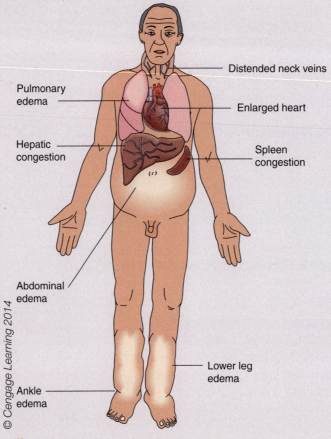

Figure 4-7 Signs of congestive heart failure

© Cengage Learning 2014

3) Hypertensive chronic kidney disease

Assign codes from category 403, Hypertensive kidney disease, when conditions classified to category 585 or code 587 are present with hypertension. Unlike hypertension with heart disease, ICD-9-CM presumes a cause-and-effect relationship and classifies renal failure with hypertension as hypertensive kidney disease.

Fifth digits for category 403 should be assigned as follows:

0   with CKD stage I through stage IV, or unspecified.

1   with CKD stage V or end-stage renal disease. The appropriate code from category 585, Chronic kidney disease, should be used as a secondary code with a code from category 403 to identify the stage of chronic kidney disease.

See Section I.C.10.a for information about the coding of chronic kidney disease.

4) Hypertensive heart and chronic kidney disease

Assign codes from combination category 404, Hypertensive heart and kidney disease, when both hypertensive kidney disease and hypertensive heart disease are stated in the diagnosis. Assume a relationship between the hypertension and the kidney disease, whether or not the condition is so designated. Assign an additional code from category 428 to identify the type of heart failure. More than one code from category 428 may be assigned if the patient has systolic or diastolic failure and congestive heart failure.

ICD-10 Alert!

- The ICD-10-CM category for hypertensive chronic kidney disease is I12.

- Coders are directed to Section I.C.14, *Chronic kidney disease,* in the ICD-10-CM official coding guidelines for additional clarification.

- Coders are also directed to assign an additional code for the acute renal failure when a patient has hypertensive chronic kidney disease and acute renal failure.

Fifth digits for category 404 should be assigned as follows:

0   without heart failure and with chronic kidney disease (CKD) stage I through stage IV, or unspecified

1   with heart failure and with CKD stage I through stage IV, or unspecified

2   without heart failure and with CKD stage V or end-stage renal disease

3   with heart failure and with CKD stage V or end-stage renal disease

The appropriate code from category 585, Chronic kidney disease, should be used as a secondary code with a code from category 404 to identify the stage of kidney disease.

ICD-10 Alert!

- The ICD-10-CM category for *hypertensive heart and chronic kidney disease* is I13.

- The ICD-10-CM category for heart failure is I50.

- The ICD-10-CM category for Chronic kidney disease is N18.

- Coders are directed to Section I.C.14, Chronic kidney disease, in the ICD-10-CM official coding guidelines for additional clarification.

- Coders are also directed to assign a code for the acute renal failure when a patient has both acute renal failure and chronic kidney disease.

See Section I.C.10.a for information on the coding of chronic kidney disease.

(continues)

ICD-9-CM CHAPTER-SPECIFIC CODING GUIDELINES WITH ICD-10 ALERTS! (*continued*)

5) **Hypertensive cerebrovascular disease**

First assign codes from 430–438, Cerebrovascular disease, then the appropriate hypertension code from categories 401–405.

ICD-10 Alert!

The ICD-10-CM categories for hypertensive cerebrovascular disease are I60–I69.

6) **Hypertensive retinopathy**

Two codes are necessary to identify the condition. First assign the code from subcategory 362.11, Hypertensive retinopathy, then the appropriate code from categories 401–405 to indicate the type of hypertension.

ICD-10 Alert!

The ICD-10-CM code for *hypertensive retinopathy* is H35.0 (with appropriate fifth and sixth characters), and the code for *essential (primary) hypertension* is I10.

7) **Hypertension, secondary**

Two codes are required: one to identify the underlying etiology and one from category 405 to identify the hypertension. Sequencing of codes is determined by the reason for admission/encounter.

ICD-10 Alert!

The ICD-10-CM category for *secondary hypertension* is I15.

8) **Hypertension, transient**

Assign code 796.2, Elevated blood pressure reading without diagnosis of hypertension, unless patient has an established diagnosis of hypertension. Assign code 642.3x for transient hypertension of pregnancy.

ICD-10 Alert!

The ICD-10-CM code for *elevated blood pressure is R03.0,* the subcategory for *gestational hypertension without significant proteinuria* is O13, and the subcategory for gestational hypertension with significant proteinuria is O14.

9) **Hypertension, controlled**

Assign appropriate code from categories 401–405. This diagnostic statement usually refers to an existing state of hypertension under control by therapy.

ICD-10 Alert!

The *hypertension, controlled* content was revised in the ICD-10-CM official coding guidelines to state, controlled hypertension *usually refers to an existing state of hypertension under control by therapy. Assign code I10.*

10) **Hypertension, uncontrolled**

Uncontrolled hypertension may refer to untreated hypertension or hypertension not responding to current therapeutic regimen. In either case, assign the appropriate code from categories 401–405 to designate the stage and type of hypertension. Code to the type of hypertension.

ICD-10 Alert!

The *hypertension, uncontrolled* content was revised in the ICD-10-CM official coding guidelines to state, *Uncontrolled hypertension may refer to untreated hypertension or hypertension not responding to current therapeutic regimen. In either case, assign code I10.*

11) Elevated blood pressure

For a statement of elevated blood pressure without further specificity, assign code 796.2, Elevated blood pressure reading without diagnosis of hypertension, rather than a code from category 401.

ICD-10 Alert!

The *elevated blood pressure* content was removed from the ICD-10-CM official coding guidelines, and a new guideline about *atherosclerotic coronary artery disease and angina* was added.

b. Cerebral infarction/stroke/cerebrovascular accident (CVA)

The terms stroke and CVA are often used interchangeably to refer to a cerebral infarction. The terms stroke, CVA, and cerebral infarction NOS are all indexed to the default code 434.91, Cerebral artery occlusion, unspecified, with infarction. Additional code(s) should be assigned for any neurologic deficits associated with the acute CVA, regardless of whether or not the neurologic deficit resolves prior to discharge. *(See Section I.C.18.d.3 for information on coding status post administration of tPA in a different facility within the last 24 hours.)*

ICD-10 Alert!

The *cerebral infarction/stroke/cerebrovascular accident (CVA)* content was removed from the ICD-10-CM official coding guidelines. Each of these is a main term in the ICD-10-CM index, listing code I63.9. *Old CVA (without sequelae)* is classified as Z86.73.

c. Postoperative cerebrovascular accident

A cerebrovascular hemorrhage or infarction that occurs as a result of medical intervention is coded to 997.02, Iatrogenic cerebrovascular infarction or hemorrhage. Medical record documentation should clearly specify the cause-and-effect relationship between the medical intervention and the cerebrovascular accident in order to assign this code. A secondary code from the code range 430–432 or from a code from subcategories 433 or 434 with a fifth digit of 1 should also be used to identify the type of hemorrhage or infarct. This guideline conforms to the "use additional code" note instruction at category 997. Code 436, Acute, but ill-defined, cerebrovascular disease, should not be used as a secondary code with code 997.02.

ICD-10 Alert!

The ICD-9-CM *postoperative cerebrovascular accident* was revised as *intraoperative and postprocedural cerebrovascular accident,* and content states that patient record documentation must clearly specify the cause-and- effect relationship between the medical intervention and the cerebrovascular accident to assign a code from category I97.

(continues)

ICD-9-CM CHAPTER-SPECIFIC CODING GUIDELINES WITH ICD-10 ALERTS! (*continued*)

d. **Late effects of cerebrovascular disease**

1) **Category 438, late effects of cerebrovascular disease**

   Category 438 is used to indicate conditions classifiable to categories 430–437 as the causes of late effects (neurologic deficits), themselves classified elsewhere. These "late effects" include neurologic deficits that persist after initial onset of conditions classifiable to 430–437. The neurologic deficits caused by cerebrovascular disease may be present from the onset or may arise at any time after the onset of the condition classifiable to 430–437. Codes in category 438 are only for use for late effects of cerebrovascular disease, not for neurologic deficits associated with an acute CVA.

2) **Codes from category 438 with codes from 430–437**

   Codes from category 438 may be assigned on a health care record with codes from 430–437, if the patient has a current CVA and deficits from an old CVA.

3) **Code V12.54**

   Assign code V12.54, Transient ischemic attack (TIA), and cerebral infarction without residual deficits (and not a code from category 438) as an additional code for history of cerebrovascular disease when no neurologic deficits are present.

ICD-10 Alert!

The ICD-9-CM *late effects of cerebrovascular disease* coding guideline was renamed *sequelae of cerebrovascular disease* in the ICD-10-CM official coding guidelines. The ICD-10-CM category for *sequelae of cerebrovascular disease* is I69, and the guideline states that a code from category I69 may be assigned with codes from categories I60-I67 *if the patient has a current CVA and sequelae from an old CVA.* ICD-10-CM code Z86.73 classifies *personal history of transient ischemic attack (TIA).*

e. **Acute myocardial infarction (AMI)**

1) **ST elevation myocardial infarction (STEMI) and non-ST elevation myocardial infarction (NSTEMI)**

   The ICD-9-CM codes for acute myocardial infarction (AMI) identify the site, such as anterolateral wall or true posterior wall. Subcategories 410.0–410.6 and 410.8 are used for STEMI. Subcategory 410.7, Subendocardial infarction, is used for NSTEMI and nontransmural myocardial infarctions.

ICD-10 Alert!

The ICD-10-CM subcategories for *ST elevation myocardial infarction (STEMI)* are I21.0–I21.3. Code I21.4 is assigned to *non-ST elevation myocardial infarction (MI)* and *nontransmural MI.*

2) **Acute myocardial infarction, unspecified**

   Subcategory 410.9 is the default for the unspecified term acute myocardial infarction. If only STEMI or transmural myocardial infarction without the site is documented, query the provider as to the site, or assign a code from subcategory 410.9.

ICD-10 Alert!

The ICD-10-CM code for *ST elevation myocardial infarction of unspecified site* is I21.3.

3) **AMI documented as nontransmural or subendocardial but site provided**

    If an AMI is documented as nontransmural or subendocardial, but the site is provided, it is still coded as a subendocardial AMI. If NSTEMI evolves to STEMI, assign the STEMI code. If STEMI converts to NSTEMI due to thrombolytic therapy, it is still coded as STEMI.

 ICD-10 Alert!

The ICD-10-CM official coding guidelines provides direction to Section I.C.21.3 for information about coding the *status post administration of tPA in a different facility within the last 24 hours.*

Exercise 4.9 – Diseases of the Circulatory System

Instructions: Underline the main term in each diagnosis statement and assign the appropriate ICD-9-CM and ICD-10-CM code(s).

ICD-9-CM   ICD-10-CM

_____   _____   **1.** Acute ST elevation myocardial infarction, inferolateral wall, initial episode of care

_____   _____   **2.** Acute rheumatic endocarditis

_____   _____   **3.** Aphasia, late effect of cerebrovascular disease

_____   _____   **4.** Benign hypertension

_____   _____   **5.** Mitral and aortic valve insufficiency

ICD-9-CM Chapter 8: Diseases of the Respiratory System (460–519)

Chapter 8, Diseases of the Respiratory System (460–519), classifies diseases and disorders of the nose (external and nasal cavity), sinuses (frontal, ethmoid, sphenoid, and maxillary), pharynx (nasopharynx and oropharynx), larynx (true and false vocal cords and glottis), trachea, bronchi (left, right, main, and carina), and lungs (intrapulmonary bronchi, bronchioli, lobes, alveoli, and pleura). This complex of organs is responsible for pulmonary ventilation and the exchange of oxygen and carbon dioxide between the lungs and ambient air. The organs of the respiratory system also perform nonrespiratory functions such as warming and moisturizing the air passing into the lungs, providing airflow for the larynx and vocal cords for speech, and releasing excess body heat in the process of thermoregulation for homeostasis. The lungs also perform important metabolic and embolic filtering functions.

⬤ ICD-10 Alert!

In ICD-10-CM, *Diseases of the Respiratory System (J00–J99)* is located in Chapter 10.

Chronic Obstructive Pulmonary Disease (COPD)

To classify COPD correctly, refer to main term *Obstruction, obstructed or obstructive* in the ICD-9-CM Index to Diseases, subterm *lung*, and second qualifier *chronic* to locate code 496.

- When verifying code 496 in the Tabular List of Diseases, note the instruction that "This code is not to be used with any code from categories 491–493." This means that code 496 is not reported with a code from categories 491–493 during the same encounter.

- COPD is considered a nonspecific condition. Therefore, the patient's record should be reviewed to locate documentation of a more specific condition. For example, acute exacerbation of obstructive chronic bronchitis is assigned code 491.21. (Codes from categories 490–495 classify more specific lung conditions.)

ICD-10 Alert!

The ICD-10-CM code for COPD is J44.9, and the instruction that "This code is not to be used with any code from categories..." was eliminated from the ICD-10-CM coding manual.

Pneumonia

Pneumonia is classified in this chapter according to infectious agent. For bronchitis and other infections, first code the infection and then report the infective agent classified in Chapter 1, Infectious and Parasitic Diseases.

ICD-9-CM CHAPTER-SPECIFIC CODING GUIDELINES WITH ICD-10 ALERTS!

ICD-10 Alert!

In ICD-10-CM, *Diseases of the Respiratory System (J00–J99)* is located in Chapter 10, and ICD-9-CM coding guidelines with *ICD-10 Alerts!* are included below.

Chapter 8: Diseases of the Respiratory System (460–519)

a. **Chronic obstructive pulmonary disease [COPD] and asthma**

1) **Conditions that comprise COPD and asthma**

   The conditions that comprise COPD are obstructive chronic bronchitis, subcategory 491.2, and emphysema, category 492. All asthma codes are under category 493, Asthma. Code 496, Chronic airway obstruction, not elsewhere classified, is a nonspecific code that should be used only when the documentation in a medical record does not specify the type of COPD being treated.

   ICD-10 Alert!

   The content about *conditions that comprise COPD* and *asthma* was removed from the ICD-10-CM official coding guidelines.

2) **Acute exacerbation of chronic obstructive bronchitis and asthma**

   The codes for chronic obstructive bronchitis and asthma distinguish between uncomplicated cases and those in acute exacerbation. An acute exacerbation is a worsening or a decompensation of a chronic condition. An acute exacerbation is not equivalent to an infection superimposed on a chronic condition, although an exacerbation may be triggered by an infection.

3) **Overlapping nature of the conditions that comprise COPD and asthma**

   Due to the overlapping nature of the conditions that make up COPD and asthma, there are many variations in the way these conditions are documented. Code selection must be based on the terms as documented. When selecting the correct code for the documented type of COPD and asthma, it is essential to first review the index, and then verify the code in the tabular list. There are

   ICD-10 Alert!

   The content about *overlapping nature of the conditions that comprise COPD* and *asthma* was removed from the ICD-10-CM official coding guidelines.

many instructional notes under the different COPD subcategories and codes. It is important that all such notes be reviewed to ensure correct code assignment.

4) **Acute exacerbation of asthma and status asthmaticus**

An acute exacerbation of asthma is an increased severity of the asthma symptoms, such as wheezing and shortness of breath. Status asthmaticus refers to a patient's failure to respond to therapy administered during an asthmatic episode and is a life-threatening complication that requires emergency care. If status asthmaticus is documented by the provider with any type of COPD or with acute bronchitis, the status asthmaticus should be sequenced first. It supersedes any type of COPD, including that with acute exacerbation or acute bronchitis. It is inappropriate to assign an asthma code with fifth digit 2, with acute exacerbation, together with an asthma code with fifth digit 1, with status asthmaticus. Only the fifth digit 1 should be assigned.

> **ICD-10 Alert!**
>
> The content about *acute exacerbation of asthma and status asthmaticus* was removed from the ICD-10-CM official coding guidelines.

b. **Chronic obstructive pulmonary disease [COPD] and bronchitis**

1) **Acute bronchitis with COPD**

Acute bronchitis, code 466.0, is due to an infectious organism. When acute bronchitis is documented with COPD, code 491.22, Obstructive chronic bronchitis with acute bronchitis, should be assigned. It is not necessary to also assign code 466.0. If a medical record documents acute bronchitis with COPD with acute exacerbation, only code 491.22 should be assigned. The acute bronchitis included in code 491.22 supersedes the acute exacerbation. If a medical record documents COPD with acute exacerbation without mention of acute bronchitis, only code 491.21 should be assigned.

> **ICD-10 Alert!**
>
> The content about *chronic obstructive disease [COPD] and bronchitis* was removed from the ICD- 10-CM official coding guidelines.

c. **Acute respiratory failure**

1) **Acute respiratory failure as principal diagnosis**

Code 518.81, Acute respiratory failure, may be assigned as a principal diagnosis when it is the condition established after study to be chiefly responsible for occasioning the admission to the hospital and the selection is supported by the Alphabetic Index and Tabular List. However, chapter-specific coding guidelines (such as obstetrics, poisoning, HIV, newborn) that provide sequencing direction take precedence.

> **ICD-10 Alert!**
>
> The ICD-10-CM code for *acute respiratory failure* is J96.0. ICD-10-CM also includes code J96.2 for *acute and chronic respiratory failure.* Either can be reported as the principal diagnosis code except when ICD-10-CM chapter-specific coding guidelines (e.g., HIV, newborn, obstetrics, poisoning) that provide sequencing direction take precedence.

2) **Acute respiratory failure as secondary diagnosis**

Respiratory failure may be listed as a secondary diagnosis if it occurs after admission, or if it is present on admission but does not meet the definition of principal diagnosis.

(continues)

ICD-9-CM CHAPTER-SPECIFIC CODING GUIDELINES WITH ICD-10 ALERTS! (*continued*)

3) **Sequencing of acute respiratory failure and another acute condition**

When a patient is admitted with respiratory failure and another acute condition (e.g., myocardial infarction, cerebrovascular accident, aspiration pneumonia), the principal diagnosis will not be the same in every situation. This applies whether the other acute condition is a respiratory or nonrespiratory condition. Selection of the principal diagnosis will be dependent on the circumstances of admission. If both the respiratory failure and the other acute condition are equally responsible for occasioning the admission to the hospital and there are no chapter-specific sequencing rules, the guideline regarding two or more diagnoses that equally meet the definition for principal diagnosis (Section II, C. of the coding guidelines) may be applied in these situations.

If the documentation is not clear as to whether acute respiratory failure and another condition are equally responsible for occasioning the admission, query the provider for clarification.

d. **Influenza due to identified avian influenza virus (avian influenza)**

Code only confirmed cases of avian influenza (codes 488.01-488.02, 488.09, Influenza due to identified avian influenza virus), 2009 H1N1 influenza virus (codes 488.11-488.12, 488.19), or novel influenza A (codes 488.81-488.82, 488.89, Influenza due to identified novel influenza A virus). This is an exception to the hospital inpatient guideline Section II, H. (Uncertain Diagnosis).

In this context, "confirmation" does not require documentation of positive laboratory testing specific for avian, 2009 H1N1 or novel influenza A virus. However, coding should be based on the provider's diagnostic statement that the patient has avian influenza, 2009 H1N1 influenza, or novel influenza A.

If the provider records "suspected" or "possible" or "probable" avian, 2009 H1N1, or novel influenza A, the appropriate influenza code from category 487, Influenza should be assigned. A code from category 488, Influenza due to certain identified influenza viruses, should not be assigned.

 ICD-10 Alert!

The ICD-10-CM subcategory for *influenza due to identified avian influenza virus* is J09.0, the code for *novel H1N1 or swine flu* is J09.0, and the category for *influenza due to other influenza virus* is J10.

Exercise 4.10–Diseases of the Respiratory System

Instructions: Underline the main term in each diagnosis statement and assign the appropriate ICD-9-CM and ICD-10-CM code(s).

ICD-9-CM   ICD-10-CM

_____   _____   **1.** Acute frontal sinusitis

_____   _____   **2.** Allergic rhinitis due to pollen

_____   _____   **3.** Chronic obstructive pulmonary disease

_____   _____   **4.** Atelectasis

_____   _____   **5.** Croup

ICD-9-CM Chapter 9: Diseases of the Digestive System (520–579)

Chapter 9, Diseases of the Digestive System (520–579), classifies diseases and disorders of all of the organs along the alimentary tract (or digestive tract), which is the long, muscular tube that begins at the mouth and ends at the anus. Major digestive organs include the pharynx, esophagus, stomach, and intestines. Accessory, or secondary, organs include the salivary and parotid glands; jaw; teeth; and supporting structures of the teeth, tongue, liver, gallbladder and biliary tract, pancreas, and peritoneum. Structures that support the digestive process from outside this continuous tube are also included in this system: gallbladder, pancreas, and liver. (These organs provide secretions that are critical to food absorption and use by the body.)

Diseases and disorders that interfere with the digestive function are classified in this ICD-9-CM chapter, along with diseases and disorders that affect the organs of the digestive tract, although they may have no direct affect on digestion.

> **EXAMPLE:** The following are examples of diseases that interfere with the digestive function, and they are classified in ICD-9-CM Chapter 9.

- Dental caries (tooth decay), assigned ICD-9-CM code 521.00 (or ICD-10-CM code K02.9), has a direct effect on digestion because the disease process interferes with mastication, the mechanical breakdown of food by chewing.

- Portal hypertension, assigned ICD-9-CM code 572.3 (or ICD-10-CM code K76.6), is high blood pressure in the liver's portal circulatory system. Although it does not directly affect digestion, portal hypertension is included because it represents a disease of a digestive system organ. Portal hypertension has no apparent effect on the digestive process until the disease has progressed to the point that the liver can no longer perform its function as a digestive organ. (Portal hypertension can be caused by cirrhosis of the liver and other conditions that cause obstruction to the portal vein, such as cancer.)

ICD-10 Alert!

In ICD-10-CM, *Diseases of the Digestive System (K00–K94)* are located in Chapter 11.

Note:

There are no official ICD-9-CM or ICD-10-CM coding guidelines for diseases of the digestive system. However, Section I.C.11 of the ICD-10-CM official coding guidelines includes the phrase "Reserved for future guideline expansion" to make room for future guidelines.

Exercise 4.11 – Diseases of the Digestive System

Instructions: Underline the main term in each diagnosis statement and assign the appropriate ICD-9-CM and ICD-10-CM code(s).

ICD-9-CM	ICD-10-CM	
_____	_____	**1.** Crohn disease
_____	_____	**2.** Canker sore
_____	_____	**3.** Acute gastrojejunal ulcer, with perforation
_____	_____	**4.** Gastroesophageal reflux
_____	_____	**5.** Inguinal hernia

ICD-9-CM Chapter 10: Diseases of the Genitourinary System (580–629)

Chapter 10, Diseases of the Genitourinary System (580–629), classifies diseases and disorders of the kidney, ureter, bladder, urethra, prostate, male genital organs, female and male breast, and female genital organs.

> **ICD-10 Alert!**
>
> The ICD-10-CM category for *chronic kidney disease* are N18, and subcategory codes N18.1–N18.5 classify stages I–V.

Chronic Kidney Disease (CKD)

Category code 585 describes "chronic kidney disease (CKD)" (formerly called "chronic renal failure). Subcategory codes 585.1–585.9 describe "chronic kidney disease" according to stage except code 585.6 (classifies "end-stage renal disease") and code 585.9 (classifies "chronic kidney disease, unspecified").

Coding Tip:

- Chapter 10, Diseases of the *Genitourinary System (580–629)*, excludes hypertensive kidney disease, which is classified in ICD-9-CM category 403 (or ICD-10-CM category N18)

- Signs and symptoms of genitourinary system disorders that may describe the emerging nature of the patient's condition are classified in category 788, which includes codes specific to incontinence of urine, painful or frequent urination, and kidney pain.

ICD-10 Alert!

The signs and symptoms of genitourinary system disorders are classified in ICD-10-CM Chapter 10, *Diseases of the Genitourinary System (N00–N99)*, as well as Chapter 18, *Symptoms, Signs and Abnormal Clinical and Laboratory Findings, Not Elsewhere Classified (R00–R99)*.

- Some genitourinary diseases are linked by family history, which are classified in ICD-9-CM categories V16–V19 (or ICD-10-CM categories Z80–Z84).

ICD-9-CM CHAPTER-SPECIFIC CODING GUIDELINES WITH ICD-10 ALERTS!

ICD-10 Alert!

In ICD-10-CM, *Diseases of the Genitourinary System* is located in Chapter 14, and ICD-9-CM coding guidelines with *ICD-10 Alerts!* are included below.

Chapter 10: Diseases of the Genitourinary System (580–629)

a. Chronic kidney disease

1) Stages of chronic kidney disease (CKD)

The ICD-9-CM classifies CKD based on severity. The severity of CKD is designated by stages I–V. Stage II, code 585.2, equates to mild CKD; stage III, code 585.3, equates to moderate CKD; and stage IV, code 585.4, equates to severe CKD. Code 585.6, End-stage renal disease (ESRD), is assigned when the provider has documented end-stage renal disease (ESRD).

If both a stage of CKD and ESRD are documented, assign code 585.6 only.

ICD-10 Alert!

ICD-10-CM code N18.2 (Stage II) equates to mild CKD, code N18.3 (Stage III) equates to moderate CKD, and code N18.4 (Stage IV) equates to severe CKD. Code N18.6, *End-stage renal disease (ESRD)*, is assigned when the provider has documented end-stage-renal disease (ESRD). If both a stage of CKD and ESRD are documented, assign code N18.6 only.

2) **Chronic kidney disease and kidney transplant status**

Patients who have undergone kidney transplant may still have some form of CKD because the kidney transplant may not fully restore kidney function. Therefore, the presence of CKD alone does not constitute a transplant complication. Assign the appropriate 585 code for the patient's stage of CKD and code V42.0. If a transplant complication such as failure or rejection is documented, see Section I.C.17.f(1)(b) for information on coding complications of a kidney transplant. If the documentation is unclear as to whether the patient has a complication of the transplant, query the provider.

ICD-10 Alert!

Review ICD-10-CM category code N18 code for the patient's stage of CKD, and assign code Z94.0 for *kidney transplant status*. Go to Appendix II located on the Premium Website to review ICD-10-CM coding guidelines Section I.C.19.g for information on coding complications of a kidney transplant.

3) **Chronic kidney disease (CKD) with other conditions**

Patients with CKD may also suffer from other serious conditions, most commonly diabetes mellitus and hypertension. The sequencing of the CKD code in relationship to codes for other contributing conditions is based on the conventions in the tabular list.

See Section I.C.3.a.4 for sequencing instructions for diabetes.
See Section I.C.4.a.1 for anemia in CKD.
See Section I.C.7.a.3 for hypertensive kidney disease.
See Section I.C.17.f.1.b Transplant complications, for instructions on coding of documented rejection or failure.

ICD-10 Alert!

Go to Appendix II located on the Premium Website to review ICD-10-CM coding guidelines Section I.C.9., Hypertensive chronic kidney disease, and Section I.C.19., Chronic kidney disease and kidney transplant complications.

Exercise 4.12 – Diseases of the Genitourinary System

Instructions: Underline the main term in each diagnosis statement and assign the appropriate ICD-9-CM and ICD-10-CM code(s).

ICD-9-CM   ICD-10-CM

_____   _____   **1.** Abscess of epididymis

_____   _____   **2.** Chronic cystic mastitis, right breast

_____   _____   **3.** Chronic prostatitis

_____   _____   **4.** Diverticulitis of bladder

_____   _____   **5.** Excessive menstruation

ICD-9-CM Chapter 11: Complications of Pregnancy, Childbirth, and the Puerperium (630–677)

> **ICD-10 Alert!**
>
> In ICD-10-CM, *Pregnancy, Childbirth, and the Puerperium (O00–O9A)* are located in Chapter 15.

Chapter 11, Complications of Pregnancy, Childbirth, and the Puerperium (630–677), classifies diseases and disorders that occur during pregnancy, childbirth, and the six weeks immediately following childbirth. All obstetrical discharges require a code from ICD-9-CM Chapter 11 (or ICD-10-CM Chapter 15), and these codes are never reported on the baby's record.

- When the physician's documentation indicates that the pregnancy is incidental to the encounter, assign ICD-9-CM code V22.2 (normal pregnancy, pregnant state incidental) (or ICD-10-CM code Z33.1, Pregnant state, incidental).

- When an obstetrical patient's encounter is related to her pregnancy, sequence ICD-9-CM code(s) 630–677 (or ICD-10-CM codes O00–O99) first, followed by codes for secondary conditions.

- When the obstetrical patient delivers, assign an outcome of delivery ICD-9-CM codes V27.0–V27.9 (or ICD-10-CM codes Z37.1–Z37.9) as a secondary code.

Ectopic and Molar Pregnancy (630–633)

When an ectopic or molar pregnancy occurs during a pregnancy admission, assign a code from ICD-9-CM category 630–633 (or ICD-10-CM category O00–O02). However, when complications of molar and ectopic pregnancies occur, assigned a code from ICD-9-CM category 639 (Complications following abortion and ectopic and molar pregnancies) or ICD-10-CM category O08 (Complications following ectopic and molar pregnancy).

EXAMPLE 1: Tubal abortion with pelvic sepsis, without intrauterine pregnancy. ICD-9-CM codes 633.10 and 639.0 (or ICD-10-CM O00.1 and O08.0) are assigned.

EXAMPLE 2: Pelvic infection following ectopic pregnancy. ICD-9-CM code 639.0 (or ICD-10-CM code O08.0) is assigned.

Pregnancy with Abortive Outcome (634–639)

Codes 634–638 require the assignment of a fifth digit to identify the abortive stage:

- Unspecified (0)
- Complete (2)
- Incomplete (1)

(Fourth-digit subcategories for codes 634–638 refer to the presence or absence of complications associated with the "other pregnancy with abortive outcome.")

When retained products of conception follow a spontaneous or legally induced abortion, assign a code from subcategory 634.0–635.9 and select fifth digit 1 to indicate the "incomplete" stage.

When fetal complications are documented as a causal factor in an abortion, two codes are assigned:

> **ICD-10 Alert!**
>
> There are no fifth characters for ICD-10-CM categories O02–O04.

- One code for the abortion (ICD-9-CM codes 634–638 or ICD-10-CM codes O03–O08)

- A second code for the fetal complication (ICD-9-CM codes 655–656 or ICD-10-CM codes O35–O36)

Complications Mainly Related to Pregnancy (640–648)

An abortion that results in a live birth is assigned ICD-9-CM code 644.21 (Early onset of delivery) (or a code from ICD-10-CM subcategory O60.1). If the abortion was induced, a procedure code for "termination of pregnancy" is assigned along with a code from ICD-9-CM category V27 (Outcome of delivery) (or ICD-10-CM code Z33.2, Encounter for elective termination of pregnancy).

When a patient experiences a delivery and an antepartum or a postpartum condition during the same encounter, assign two separate codes. (The ICD-9-CM fifth digit for each code may be different.)

EXAMPLE: Patient is discharged from the hospital with the diagnoses of "ablatio placenta, pregnancy at term, third trimester, delivered" and "delayed postpartum bleed." ICD-9-CM codes 641.21 and 666.22 are assigned (or ICD-10-CM codes O45.93 and O72.2). (Also report the appropriate code from ICD-9-CM category V27 or ICD-10-CM category Z37.)

Normal Delivery and Other Indications for Care in Pregnancy, Labor, and Delivery (650–659)

ICD-9-CM code 650 (or ICD-10-CM code O80) is assigned for a normal delivery, which required minimal or no assistance. An episiotomy is permitted, but fetal manipulation (e.g., use of forceps) is not permitted. In addition, code 650 (or O80) is never reported with any other code in range 630–676 (or O00–O99).

Complications Occurring Mainly in the Course of Labor and Delivery (660–669)

ICD-9-CM codes 660–669 require the assignment of a fifth digit to indicate the current episode of care:

- Unspecified as to episode of care or not applicable (0)
- Delivered, with or without mention of antepartum condition (1)
- Delivered, with mention of postpartum complication (2)
- Antepartum condition or complication (3)
- Postpartum condition or complication (4)

ICD-10 Alert!

ICD-10-CM does not require the *episode of care* fifth digits to categories O60–O82.

EXAMPLE: Patient was treated for failed trial of labor, undelivered. ICD-9-CM code 660.63 (or ICD-10-CM code O66.40) is assigned.

Complications of the Puerperium (670–677)

Codes 670–677 also require the assignment of a fifth digit to indicate the current episode of care:

- Unspecified as to episode of care or not applicable (0)
- Delivered, with or without mention of antepartum condition (1)
- Delivered, with mention of postpartum complication (2)
- Antepartum condition or complication (3)
- Postpartum condition or complication (4)

ICD-10 Alert!

ICD-10-CM does not require the *episode of care* fifth digits to categories O85–O92.

EXAMPLE: Patient admitted to the hospital for treatment of deep vein thrombosis, postpartum. The patient delivered a liveborn male infant three weeks ago. ICD-9-CM code 671.44 (or ICD-10-CM codes O87.1 and I82.40) is assigned.

ICD-9-CM CHAPTER-SPECIFIC CODING GUIDELINES WITH ICD-10 ALERTS!

 ICD-10 Alert!

In ICD-10-CM, *Pregnancy, Childbirth, and the Puerperium* are located in Chapter 15, and ICD-9-CM coding guidelines with *ICD-10 Alerts!* are included below.

(continues)

ICD-9-CM CHAPTER-SPECIFIC CODING GUIDELINES WITH ICD-10 ALERTS! (*continued*)

Chapter 11: Complications of Pregnancy, Childbirth, and the Puerperium (630–677)

a. General rules for obstetric cases

1) **Codes from Chapter 11 and sequencing priority**

Obstetric cases require codes from Chapter 11, codes in the range 630–677, Complications of pregnancy, childbirth, and the puerperium. Chapter 11 codes have sequencing priority over codes from other chapters. Additional codes from other chapters may be used in conjunction with Chapter 11 codes to further specify conditions. Should the provider document that the pregnancy is incidental to the encounter, code V22.2 should be used in place of any Chapter 11 codes. It is the provider's responsibility to state that the condition being treated is not affecting the pregnancy.

> **ICD-10 Alert!**
>
> In ICD-10-CM, categories O00–O9a are located in Chapter 15, *Pregnancy, Childbirth, and the Puerperium,* and code Z33.1 classifies *Pregnant state, incidental.*

2) **Chapter 11 codes used only on the maternal record**

Chapter 11 codes are to be used only on the maternal record, never on the record of the newborn.

> **ICD-10 Alert!**
>
> In ICD-10-CM, Chapter 15 codes are used only on the maternal record.

3) **Chapter 11 fifth digits**

Categories 640–648, 651–676 have required fifth digits, which indicate whether the encounter is antepartum, postpartum, and whether a delivery has also occurred.

> **ICD-10 Alert!**
>
> The *Chapter 11 fifth digits* content was eliminated from the ICD-10-CM official coding guidelines.

4) **Fifth digits, appropriate for each code**

The fifth digits, which are appropriate for each code number, are listed in brackets under each code. The fifth digits on each code should all be consistent with each other. That is, should a delivery occur, all of the fifth digits should indicate the delivery.

 ICD-10 Alert!

- The *fifth digits, appropriate for each code,* was eliminated from the ICD-10-CM official coding guidelines.

- *Go to Appendix II located on the Premium Website to review ICD-10-CM coding guidelines in Sections I.C.15.a.3 through I.C.15.a.5.*

b. Selection of OB principal or first-listed diagnosis

1) **Routine outpatient prenatal visits**

For routine outpatient prenatal visits when no complications are present, codes V22.0, Supervision of normal first pregnancy, and V22.1, Supervision of other normal pregnancy, should be used as the first-listed diagnoses. These codes should not be used in conjunction with Chapter 11 codes.

 ICD-10 Alert!

In ICD-10-CM, category Z34 classifies *encounter for supervision of normal pregnancy,* and ICD-10-CM's Chapter 15 codes may also be assigned

2) **Prenatal outpatient visits for high-risk patients**

For prenatal outpatient visits for patients with highrisk pregnancies, a code from category V23, Supervision of high-risk pregnancy, should be used as the principal or first-listed diagnosis. Secondary Chapter 11 codes may be used in conjunction with these codes if appropriate.

> **ICD-10 Alert!**
>
> In ICD-10-CM, category O09 classifies *supervision of high risk pregnancy,* and ICD-10-CM's Chapter 15 codes may also be assigned.

3) **Episodes when no delivery occurs**

In episodes when no delivery occurs, the principal diagnosis should correspond to the principal complication of the pregnancy, which necessitated the encounter. Should more than one complication exist, all of which are treated or monitored, any of the complications codes may be sequenced first.

4) **When a delivery occurs**

When a delivery occurs, the principal diagnosis should correspond to the main circumstances or complication of the delivery. In cases of cesarean delivery, the selection of the principal diagnosis should be the condition established after study that was responsible for the patient's admission. If the patient was admitted with a condition that resulted in the performance of a cesarean procedure, that condition should be selected as the principal diagnosis. If the reason for the admission/encounter was unrelated to the condition resulting in the cesarean delivery, the condition related to the reason for the admission/encounter should be selected as the principal diagnosis, even if a cesarean was performed.

5) **Outcome of delivery**

An outcome of delivery code, V27.0–V27.9, should be included on every maternal record when a delivery has occurred. These codes are not to be used on subsequent records or on the newborn record.

 ICD-10 Alert!

- In ICD-10-CM, category Z37 classifies outcome of delivery.

- *Go to Appendix II located on the Premium Website to review ICD-10-CM coding guidelines in Sections I.C.15.c and I.C.15.d.*

c. **Fetal conditions affecting the management of the mother**

1) **Codes from category 655 and 656**

Codes from categories 655, Known or suspected fetal abnormality affecting management of the mother, and 656, Other known or suspected fetal and placental problems affecting the management of the mother, are assigned only when the fetal condition is actually responsible for modifying the management of the mother (i.e., by requiring diagnostic studies, additional observation, special care, or termination of pregnancy). The fact that the fetal condition exists does not justify assigning a code from this series to the mother's record.

 ICD-10 Alert!

In ICD-10-CM, category O35 classifies *maternal care for known or suspected fetal abnormality and damage,* and category O36 classifies *maternal care for other fetal problems.*

(continues)

ICD-9-CM CHAPTER-SPECIFIC CODING GUIDELINES WITH ICD-10 ALERTS! (*continued*)

1) *In utero* surgery

In cases when surgery is performed on the fetus, a diagnosis code from category 655, Known or suspected fetal abnormalities affecting management of the mother, should be assigned identifying the fetal condition. Procedure code 75.36, Correction of fetal defect, should be assigned on the hospital inpatient record.

No code from Chapter 15, the perinatal codes, should be used on the mother's record to identify fetal conditions. Surgery performed *in utero* on a fetus is still to be coded as an obstetric encounter.

ICD-10 Alert!

In ICD-10-CM, category O35 classifies *maternal care for known or suspected fetal abnormality,* and no code from Chapter 15, *certain conditions originating in the perinatal period,* are assigned.

d. HIV infection in pregnancy, childbirth and the puerperium

During pregnancy, childbirth, or the puerperium, a patient admitted because of an HIV-related illness should receive a principal diagnosis of 647.6x, Other specified infectious and parasitic diseases in the mother classifiable elsewhere, but complicating the pregnancy, childbirth or the puerperium, followed by 042 and the code(s) for the HIV-related illness(es).

Patients with asymptomatic HIV-infection status admitted during pregnancy, childbirth, or the puerperium should receive codes of 647.6x and V08.

ICD-10 Alert!

In ICD-10-CM, subcategory O98.7 classifies *human immunodeficiency [HIV] disease complicating pregnancy,* and category Z21 classifies *asymptomatic human immunodeficiency virus [HIV] infection status.*

e. Current conditions complicating pregnancy

Assign a code from subcategory 648.x for patients who have current conditions when the condition affects the management of the pregnancy, childbirth, or puerperium. Use additional secondary codes from other chapters to identify the conditions, as appropriate.

ICD-10 Alert!

The *Current conditions complicating pregnancy* content was eliminated from the ICD-10-CM official coding guidelines.

f. Diabetes mellitus in pregnancy

Diabetes mellitus is a significant complicating factor in pregnancy. Pregnant women who are diabetic should be assigned code 648.0x, Diabetes mellitus complicating pregnancy, and a secondary code from category 250, Diabetes mellitus, to identify the type of diabetes.

Code V58.67, Long-term (current) use of insulin, should also be assigned if the diabetes mellitus is being treated with insulin.

ICD-10 Alert!

- In ICD-10-CM, category O24 classifies diabetes mellitus in pregnancy, childbirth, and the puerperium, and appropriate diabetes code(s) (E08-E13) from Chapter 4 are also assigned.

- In ICD-10-CM, code Z79.4 classifies long-term (current) use of insulin.

g. Gestational diabetes

Gestational diabetes can occur during the second and third trimesters of pregnancy in women who were not diabetic prior to pregnancy. Gestational diabetes can cause complications in the pregnancy similar to those of preexisting diabetes mellitus. It also puts the woman at greater risk of developing diabetes after the pregnancy. Gestational diabetes is coded to 648.8x, Abnormal glucose tolerance. Codes 648.0x and 648.8x should never be used together on the same record.

Code V58.67, Long-term (current) use of insulin, should also be assigned if the gestational diabetes is being treated with insulin.

ICD-10 Alert!

- In ICD-10-CM, subcategory O24.4 classifies *gestational diabetes mellitus,* and the subcategory includes diet-controlled and insulin-controlled.

- No other code from category O24 is assigned with subcategory O24.4.

- Code Z79.4 classifies *long-term (current) use of insulin,* and it is not assigned with subcategory O24.4.

- Subcategory O99.81 classifies *abnormal glucose complicating pregnancy, childbirth, and the puerperium.*

- *Go to Appendix II located on the Premium Website to review ICD-10-CM coding guidelines in Sections I.C.15.j through I.C.15.m.*

h. **Normal delivery, code 650**
   1) **Normal delivery**
      Code 650 is for use in cases when a woman is admitted for a full-term normal delivery and delivers a single healthy infant without any complications antepartum, during the delivery, or postpartum during the delivery episode. Code 650 is always a principal diagnosis. It is not to be used if any other code from Chapter 11 is needed to describe a current complication of the antenatal, delivery, or perinatal period. Additional codes from other chapters may be used with code 650 if they are not related to or are in any way complicating the pregnancy.

ICD-10 Alert!

In ICD-10-CM, code O80 classifies a *normal delivery,* and it is not assigned with any other codes from Chapter 15. Additional codes from other ICD-10-CM chapters may be assigned with code O80.

   2) **Normal delivery with resolved antepartum complication**
      Code 650 may be used if the patient had a complication at some point during her pregnancy but the complication is not present at the time of the admission for delivery.
   3) **V27.0, Single liveborn, outcome of delivery**
      V27.0, Single liveborn, is the only outcome of delivery code appropriate for use with 650.

ICD-10 Alert!

In the ICD-10-CM official coding guidelines, *V27.0, single liveborn, outcome of delivery* was retitled *outcome of delivery for O80.* The guideline states, *Z37.0, single livebirth, is the only outcome of delivery code appropriate for use with O80.*

i. **The postpartum and peripartum periods**
   1) **Postpartum and peripartum periods**
      The postpartum period begins immediately after delivery and continues for six weeks following delivery. The peripartum period is defined as the last month of pregnancy to five months postpartum.
   2) **Postpartum complication**
      A postpartum complication is any complication occurring within the 6-week period.

(continues)

ICD-9-CM CHAPTER-SPECIFIC CODING GUIDELINES WITH ICD-10 ALERTS! (*continued*)

3) Pregnancy-related complications after 6-week period

Chapter 11 codes may also be used to describe pregnancy-related complications after the 6-week period, should the provider document that a condition is pregnancy-related.

> **ICD-10 Alert!**
>
> In ICD-10-CM, Chapter 15 codes may also be used to describe pregnancy-related complications after the 6-week period.

4) Postpartum complications occurring during the same admission as delivery

Postpartum complications that occur during the same admission as the delivery are identified with a fifth digit of 2. Subsequent admissions/encounters for postpartum complications should be identified with a fifth digit of 4.

> **ICD-10 Alert!**
>
> In the ICD-10-CM official coding guidelines, content about *postpartum complications occurring during the same admission as delivery* was eliminated.

5) Admission for routine postpartum care following delivery outside hospital

When the mother delivers outside the hospital prior to admission and is admitted for routine postpartum care and no complications are noted, code V24.0, Postpartum care and examination immediately after delivery, should be assigned as the principal diagnosis.

> **ICD-10 Alert!**
>
> In ICD-10-CM, code Z39.0 classifies *encounter for care and examination of mother immediately after delivery.*

6) Admission following delivery outside hospital with postpartum conditions

A delivery diagnosis code should not be used for a woman who has delivered prior to admission to the hospital. Any postpartum conditions and/or postpartum procedures should be coded.

7) Puerperal sepsis

Code 670.2x, Puerperal sepsis, should be assigned with a secondary code to identify the causal organism (e.g., for a bacterial infection, assign a code from category 041, Bacterial infections in conditions classified elsewhere and of unspecified site). A code from category 038, Septicemia, should not be used for puerperal sepsis. Do not assign code 995.91, Sepsis, as code 670.2x describes the sepsis. If applicable, use additional codes to identify severe sepsis (995.92) and any associated acute organ dysfunction.

> **ICD-10 Alert!**
>
> In the ICD-10-CM official coding guidelines, *normal delivery with resolved antepartum complication* was retitled *uncomplicated delivery with resolved antepartum complication.*

j. Code 677, Late effect of complication of pregnancy

1) Code 677

Code 677, Late effect of complication of pregnancy, childbirth, and the puerperium, is for use in those cases when an initial complication of a pregnancy develops sequelae, requiring care or treatment at a future date.

> **ICD-10 Alert!**
>
> In the ICD-10-CM official coding guidelines, content about *admission following delivery outside hospital with postpartum conditions and* puerperal sepsis *were eliminated.*
>
> *Go to Appendix II located on the Premium Website to review the ICD-10-CM coding guideline in Section I.C.15.o.5.*

2) After the initial postpartum period

This code may be used at any time after the initial postpartum period.

3) Sequencing of Code 677

This code, like all late effect codes, is to be sequenced following the code describing the sequelae of the complication.

k. **Abortions**

1) **Fifth digits required for abortion categories**

Fifth digits are required for abortion categories 634–637. Fifth digit assignment is based on the status of the patient at the beginning (or start) of the encounter. Fifth digit 1, incomplete, indicates that all of the products of conception have not been expelled from the uterus. Fifth digit 2, complete, indicates that all products of conception have been expelled from the uterus prior to the episode of care.

> **ICD-10 Alert!**
>
> In ICD-10-CM, code O94 classifies *sequelae of complication of pregnancy, childbirth, and the puerperium.*

2) Code from categories 640–649 and 651–659

A code from categories 640–649 and 651–659 may be used as additional codes with an abortion code to indicate the complication leading to the abortion. Fifth digit 3 is assigned with codes from these categories when used with an abortion code because the other fifth digits will not apply. Codes from the 660–669 series are not to be used for complications of abortion.

3) Code 639 for complications

Code 639 is to be used for all complications following abortion. Code 639 cannot be assigned with codes from categories 634–638.

> **ICD-10 Alert!**
>
> In the ICD-10-CM official coding guidelines, content about *fifth digits required for abortion categories (ICD-9-CM categories 640–649 and 651–659,* and *code 639 for complications)* were eliminated.

4) Abortion with liveborn fetus

When an attempted termination of pregnancy results in a liveborn fetus, assign code 644.21, Early onset of delivery, with an appropriate code from category V27, Outcome of delivery. The procedure code for the attempted termination of pregnancy should also be assigned.

> **ICD-10 Alert!**
>
> In ICD-10-CM subcategory O60.1 classifies *preterm labor with preterm delivery,* and category Z37 classifies *outcome of delivery.*

5) Retained products of conception following an abortion

Subsequent admissions for retained products of conception following a spontaneous or legally induced abortion are assigned the appropriate code from category 634, Spontaneous abortion, or 635, Legally induced abortion, with a fifth digit of 1 (incomplete). This advice is appropriate even when the patient was discharged previously with a discharge diagnosis of complete abortion.

> **ICD-10 Alert!**
>
> In ICD-10-CM, category O03 classifies *spontaneous abortion* and code Z33.2 classifies *encounter for elective termination of pregnancy.*

ICD-9-CM Chapter 12: Diseases of the Skin and Subcutaneous Tissue (680–709)

Chapter 12, Diseases of the Skin and Subcutaneous Tissue (ICD-9-CM categories 680–709 or ICD-10-CM categories L00-L99), classifies diseases and disorders of the epidermis, dermis, subcutaneous tissue, nails, sebaceous glands, sweat glands, and hair and hair follicles.

 **ICD-10 Alert!**

In ICD-10-CM, Diseases of the Skin and Subcutaneous Tissues *(L00–L99)* are located in *Chapter 12.*

Exercise 4.13 – Complications of Pregnancy, Childbirth, and the Puerperium

Instructions: Underline the main term in each diagnosis statement and assign the appropriate ICD-9-CM and ICD-10-CM code(s).

ICD-9-CM	ICD-10-CM	
_____	_____	**1.** Amnionitis
_____	_____	**2.** Engorgement of female breasts (postpartum)
_____	_____	**3.** Gestational hypertension, third trimester (antepartum)
_____	_____	**4.** Incoordinate uterine contractions, delivered
_____	_____	**5.** Laceration of cervix (postpartum complication)

ICD-9-CM CHAPTER-SPECIFIC CODING GUIDELINES WITH ICD-10 ALERTS!

ICD-10 Alert!

In ICD-10-CM, *Diseases of the Skin and Subcutaneous Tissues* are located in Chapter 12, and ICD-9-CM coding guidelines with *ICD-10 Alerts!* are included below.

Chapter 12: Diseases Skin and Subcutaneous Tissue (680–709)

a. Pressure ulcer stage codes
  1) Pressure ulcer stages
     Two codes are needed to completely describe a pressure ulcer: A code from subcategory 707.0, Pressure ulcer, to identify the site of the pressure ulcer and a code from subcategory 707.2, Pressure ulcer stages.
     The codes in subcategory 707.2, Pressure ulcer stages, are to be used as an additional diagnosis with a code(s) from subcategory 707.0, Pressure ulcer. Codes from 707.2, Pressure ulcer stages, may not be assigned as a principal or first-listed diagnosis. The pressure ulcer stage codes should be used only with pressure ulcers and not with other types of ulcers (e.g., stasis ulcer).
     The ICD-9-CM classifies pressure ulcer stages based on severity, which is designated by stages I–IV and unstageable.

ICD-10 Alert!

In ICD-10-CM, category L89 classifies *pressure ulcers,* which identify both site and stage. Stages are based on severity, and they are designated as stages 1–4, unspecified stage, or unstageable. Assign as many codes from category L89 as needed to identify all the pressure ulcers (e.g., different sites and stages) the patient has, if applicable.

2) **Unstageable pressure ulcers**

Assignment of code 707.25, Pressure ulcer, unstageable, should be based on the clinical documentation. Code 707.25 is used for pressure ulcers whose stage cannot be clinically determined (e.g., the ulcer is covered by eschar or has been treated with a skin or muscle graft) and pressure ulcers that are documented as deep tissue injury but not documented as due to trauma. This code should not be confused with code 707.20, Pressure ulcer, stage unspecified. Code 707.20 should be assigned when there is no documentation regarding the stage of the pressure ulcer.

 ICD-10 Alert!

The ICD-10-CM code for *unstageable pressure ulcer* (L89.–0) is based on clinical documentation. This code should not be confused with the code for *pressure ulcer, stage unspecified* (L89.–9), which is assigned when the provider has not documented the stage. (Ideally, the provider should be queried about the stage so a specific code can be assigned.)

3) **Documented pressure ulcer stage**

Assignment of the pressure ulcer stage code should be guided by clinical documentation of the stage or documentation of the terms found in the index. For clinical terms describing the stage that are not found in the index, and there is no documentation of the stage, the provider should be queried.

4) **Bilateral pressure ulcers with same stage**

When a patient has bilateral pressure ulcers (e.g., both buttocks) and both pressure ulcers are documented as being the same stage, only the code for the site and one code for the stage should be reported.

5) **Bilateral pressure ulcers with different stages**

When a patient has bilateral pressure ulcers at the same site (e.g., both buttocks) and each pressure ulcer is documented as being at a different stage, assign one code for the site and the appropriate codes for the pressure ulcer stage.

6) **Multiple pressure ulcers of different sites and stages**

When a patient has multiple pressure ulcers at different sites (e.g., buttock, heel, shoulder) and each pressure ulcer is documented as being at different stages (e.g., stage 3 and stage 4), assign the appropriate codes for each different site and a code for each different pressure ulcer stage.

ICD-10 Alert!

In the ICD-10-CM official coding guidelines, content about *bilateral pressure ulcers with same stage, bilateral pressure ulcers with different stages,* and *multiple pressure ulcers of different sites and stages* were eliminated.

7) **Patients admitted with pressure ulcers documented as healed**

No code is assigned if the documentation states that the pressure ulcer is completely healed.

8) **Patients admitted with pressure ulcers documented as healing**

Pressure ulcers described as healing should be assigned the appropriate pressure ulcer stage code based on the documentation in the medical record. If the documentation does not provide information about the stage of the healing pressure ulcer, assign code 707.20, Pressure ulcer stage, unspecified.

If the documentation is unclear as to whether the patient has a current (new) pressure ulcer or if the patient is being treated for a healing pressure ulcer, query the provider.

(continues)

ICD-9-CM CHAPTER-SPECIFIC CODING GUIDELINES WITH ICD-10 ALERTS! (*continued*)

9) **Patient admitted with pressure ulcer evolving into another stage during the admission**
   If a patient is admitted with a pressure ulcer at one stage and it progresses to a higher stage, assign the code for highest stage reported for that site.

Exercise 4.14 – Diseases of the Skin and Subcutaneous Tissue

Instructions: Underline the main term in each diagnosis statement and assign the appropriate ICD-9-CM and ICD-10-CM code(s).

ICD-9-CM	ICD-10-CM	
_____	_____	**1.** Alopecia areata
_____	_____	**2.** Carbuncle, left foot
_____	_____	**3.** Decubitus ulcer
_____	_____	**4.** Impetigo
_____	_____	**5.** Keloid

ICD-9-CM Chapter 13: Diseases of the Musculoskeletal and Connective Tissue (710–739)

Chapter 13, Diseases of the Musculoskeletal and Connective Tissue (ICD-9-CM categories 710–739 or ICD-10-CM categories M00–M99), classifies diseases and disorders of the bones, muscles, cartilage, fascia, ligaments, synovia, tendons, and bursa. Connective tissue disorders classified to Chapter 13 are those affecting primarily the musculoskeletal system. Injuries and certain congenital disorders of the musculoskeletal system are classified elsewhere. Many codes for the manifestation of musculoskeletal diseases due to specified infections and other diseases and disorders classified elsewhere are included in this chapter.

Also included are many codes describing the residuals of previous diseases, disorders, and injuries classified as late effects. These codes often can be identified by the term *acquired* in the description.

Localized osteoarthrosis is classified as primary or secondary. Primary osteoarthritis (or polyarticular degenerative arthritis) has an unknown etiology (cause), which means it is idiopathic. It affects apophyseal joints (joints with nodular or bony eminence) of the hips, knees, spine, and small joints of the hands and feet. Secondary osteoarthritis (or monarticular arthritis) is caused by external or internal injuries (for example, acute or chronic trauma) or disease processes and is confined to the joints of one area. Disease processes include endocrine, infectious, metabolic, and neuropathic disease, as well as disease processes that alter the normal structure and function of hyaline cartilage (e.g., chondrocalcinosis, gout, and Paget's disease).

> **ICD-10 Alert!**
>
> In ICD-10-CM, *Diseases of the Musculoskeletal System and Connective Tissue (M00–M99)* are located in Chapter 13.

> **EXAMPLE:** A patient is diagnosed with degenerative joint disease, bilateral knees. Assign ICD-9-CM code 715.36 (Osteoarthrosis, localized, not specified whether primary or secondary, for bilateral degenerative joint disease, knee) or ICD-10-CM code M17.0 (Bilateral osteoarthritis of knee).

ICD-9-CM CHAPTER-SPECIFIC CODING GUIDELINES WITH ICD-10 ALERTS!

ICD-10 Alert!

In ICD-10-CM, Diseases of the Musculoskeletal System and Connective Tissue are located in Chapter 13, and ICD-9-CM coding guidelines with ICD-10 Alerts! are included below.

Chapter 13: Diseases of Musculoskeletal and Connective Tissue (710–739)

ICD-10 Alert!

Go to Appendix II located on the Premium Website to review ICD-10-CM coding guidelines in Section I.C.13, Chapter 13: Diseases of Musculoskeletal and Connective Tissue (M00–M99).

a. Coding of pathologic fractures
1) Acute fractures vs. aftercare
Pathologic fractures are reported using subcategory 733.1, when the fracture is newly diagnosed. Subcategory 733.1 may be used while the patient is receiving active treatment for the fracture. Examples of active treatment are: surgical treatment, emergency department encounter, evaluation and treatment by a new physician.

ICD-10 Alert!

In ICD-10-CM, subcategory M80 classifies pathological fractures, and a seventh character is required to classify the type of encounter.

Fractures are coded using the aftercare codes (subcategories V54.0, V54.2, V54.8 or V54.9) for encounters after the patient has completed active treatment of the fracture and is receiving routine care for the fracture during the healing or recovery phase. Examples of fracture aftercare are: cast change or removal, removal of external or internal fixation device, medication adjustment, and follow-up visits following fracture treatment.

ICD-10 Alert!

In ICD-10-CM, assign the appropriate fracture code with seventh-character D to classify aftercare provided to patients who have completed active treatment of the fracture and who are receiving routine care for the fracture during the healing or recovery phase. [This differs from the assignment of ICD-9-CM's V codes for aftercare.]

Care for complications of surgical treatment for fracture repairs during the healing or recovery phase should be coded with the appropriate complication codes.

Care of complications of fractures, such as malunion and nonunion, should be reported with the appropriate codes.

See Section I.C.17.b for information on the coding of traumatic fractures.

Exercise 4.15 – Diseases of the Musculoskeletal and Connective Tissue

Instructions: Underline the main term in each diagnosis statement and assign the appropriate ICD-9-CM and ICD-10-CM code(s).

ICD-9-CM	ICD-10-CM	
_____	_____	**1.** Arthralgia, hand, lower leg, and ankle
_____	_____	**2.** Claw foot, left (acquired)
_____	_____	**3.** Contracture of joint, pelvic region
_____	_____	**4.** Kissing spine
_____	_____	**5.** Muscle spasm

ICD-9-CM Chapter 14: Congenital Anomalies (740–759)

Chapter 14, Congenital Anomalies (ICD-9-CM categories 740–759 or ICD-10-CM categories (Q00-Q99), classifies all conditions according to a principal or defining defect rather than to the cause, except for chromosome abnormalities. Congenital anomalies may be the result of genetic factors (chromosomes), teratogens (agents causing physical defects in the embryo), or both. The anomalies may be apparent at

ICD-10 Alert!

In ICD-10-CM, *Congenital Malformations, Deformations and Chromosomal Abnormalities (Q00–Q99)* are located in Chapter 17.

birth or hidden and identified sometime after birth. Whatever the cause, congenital anomalies can be attributed to nearly 50 percent of deaths to full-term newborn infants. Regardless of origin, dysmorphology (clinical structural abnormality) is generally the primary indication of a congenital anomaly; in many cases, a syndrome may be classified according to a single anatomic anomaly rather than a complex of symptoms.

> **EXAMPLE:** Apert's syndrome (or acrocephalosyndactyly) is a group of congenital syndromes that include peaking at the head due to premature closure of skull sutures and fusion or webbing of digits. Apert's syndrome is a single anatomic anomaly of a multicomplex syndrome, which can include fusion in the hands *and* facial anomalies. ICD-9-CM code 755.55 (or ICD-10-CM Q87.0) is assigned.

ICD-9-CM (and ICD-10-CM) do not differentiate between intrinsic abnormalities (defects related to the fetus) or extrinsic abnormalities (defects that are the result of intrauterine problems). ICD-9-CM (and ICD-10-CM) do make a distinction in the classification of an anomaly as compared to a deformity. An anomaly is a malformation caused by abnormal fetal development (e.g., transposition of great vessels, or spina bifida). A deformity is an alteration in structure caused by an extrinsic force, such as intrauterine compression. The force may cause a disruption in a normal fetal structure, including congenital amputations from amniotic bands. In some cases, assigning two codes is necessary to describe the condition.

> **EXAMPLE:** Thalidomide phocomelia results from influence of the drug thalidomide on the developing fetus during the perinatal period. It is a congenital birth defect in which the hands and feet are attached to abbreviated arms and legs, respectively. To classify this condition, multiple codes are assigned:
>
> - 755.2x (or ICD-10-CM code Q71.-): Reduction deformities of upper limb (replace x with type of deformity)
> - 755.3x (or ICD-10-CM code Q72.8-): Reduction deformities of lower limb (replace x with type of deformity)
> - 760.79 (or ICD-10-CM code P04.-): Other (noxious influences affecting fetus or newborn via placenta or milk)
>
> Codes 755.2x and/or 755.3x (or Q71.- and Q72.8-) classify the limb deformities. Code 760.79 (or P04.-) classifies the transmission of the drug across the placenta, which resulted in the limb deformities.

ICD-9-CM CHAPTER-SPECIFIC CODING GUIDELINES WITH ICD-10 ALERTS!

 ICD-10 Alert!

In ICD-10-CM, *Congenital Malformations, Deformations and Chromosomal Abnormalities* are located in Chapter 17, and ICD-9-CM coding guidelines with *ICD-10 Alerts!* are included below.

Chapter 14: Congenital Anomalies (740–759)

a. Codes in categories 740–759, Congenital Anomalies

Assign an appropriate code(s) from categories 740–759, Congenital Anomalies, when an anomaly is documented. A congenital anomaly may be the principal/first-listed diagnosis on a record or a secondary diagnosis.

 ICD-10 Alert!

ICD-10-CM categories Q00–Q99 classify *congenital malformations, deformations, and chromosomal abnormalities.*

When a congenital anomaly does not have a unique code assignment, assign additional code(s) for any manifestations that may be present. When the code assignment specifically identifies the congenital anomaly, manifestations that are an inherent component of the anomaly should not be coded separately. Additional codes should be assigned for manifestations that are not an inherent component.

Codes from Chapter 14 (or ICD-10-CM Chapter 17) may be used throughout the life of the patient. If a congenital anomaly has been corrected, a personal history code should be used to identify the history of the anomaly. Although present at birth, a congenital anomaly may not be identified until later in life. Whenever the condition is diagnosed by the physician, it is appropriate to assign a code from codes 740–759.

For the birth admission, the appropriate code from category V30, Liveborn infants, (or ICD-10-CM category Z38, liveborn infants) according to type of birth, should be sequenced as the principal diagnosis, followed by any congenital anomaly codes, 740–759 (or ICD-10-CM categories Q00–Q89).

Exercise 4.16–Congenital Anomalies

Instructions: Underline the main term in each diagnosis statement and assign the appropriate ICD-9-CM and ICD-10-CM code(s).

ICD-9-CM   ICD-10-CM

_____   _____   **1.** Anomalies of aortic arch

_____   _____   **2.** Congenital heart block

_____   _____   **3.** Congenital hydrocephalus

_____   _____   **4.** Cystic eyeball, congenital

_____   _____   **5.** Fissure of tongue, congenital

ICD-9-CM Chapter 15: Certain Conditions Originating in the Perinatal Period (760–779)

Chapter 15, Certain Conditions Originating in the Perinatal Period (760–779) (or ICD-10-CM Chapter 16, Certain Conditions Originating in the Perinatal Period (P00–P96), classifies conditions that begin during the perinatal period even if death or morbidity occurs later. The **perinatal period** is the interval of time occurring before, during, and up to 28 days following birth. These codes classify causes of morbidity and mortality in the fetus or newborn. Additional codes can be assigned from other ICD-9-CM (or ICD-10-CM) chapters to further specify the newborn's condition.

ICD-10 Alert!

In ICD-10-CM, *Certain Conditions Originating in the Perinatal Period (P00–P96)* are located in Chapter 16.

Coding Tip:

Codes from ICD-9-CM Chapter 15 (or ICD-10-CM Chapter 16) are never reported for the mother's episode of care.

ICD-9-CM CHAPTER-SPECIFIC CODING GUIDELINES WITH ICD-10 ALERTS!

ICD-10 Alert!

In ICD-10-CM, *Certain Conditions Originating in the Perinatal Period* are located in Chapter 16, and ICD-9-CM coding guidelines with *ICD-10 Alerts!* are included below.

Chapter 15: Certain Conditions Originating in the Perinatal Period (760–779)

For coding and reporting purposes, the perinatal period is defined as "before birth through the 28th day following birth." The following guidelines are provided for reporting purposes. Hospitals may record other diagnoses as needed for internal data use.

a. General perinatal rules
  1) Chapter 15 codes
     They are *never* for use on the maternal record. Codes from Chapter 11 *(or ICD-10-CM Chapter 15)*, the obstetrics chapter, are never permitted on the newborn record. Chapter 15 *(or ICD-10-CM Chapter 16)* codes may be used throughout the life of the patient if the condition is still present.
  2) Sequencing of perinatal codes
     Generally, codes from Chapter 15 *(or ICD-10-CM Chapter 16)* should be sequenced as the principal/first-listed diagnosis on the newborn record, with the exception of the appropriate V30 code *(or ICD-10-CM Z38 code)* for the birth episode, followed by codes from any other chapter that provide additional detail. The "use additional code" note at the beginning of the chapter supports this guideline. If the index does not provide a specific code for a perinatal condition, assign code 779.89, Other specified conditions originating in the perinatal period, followed by the code from another chapter that specifies the condition. Codes for signs and symptoms may be assigned when a definitive diagnosis has not been established.
  3) Birth process or community-acquired conditions
     If a newborn has a condition that may be either due to the birth process or community-acquired and the documentation does not indicate which it is, the default is "due to the birth process" and the code from Chapter 15 *(or ICD-10-CM Chapter 16)* should be used. If the condition is "community-acquired," a code from Chapter 15 *(or ICD-10-CM Chapter 16)* should not be assigned.

ICD-10 Alert!

ICD-10-CM official coding guidelines (perinatal) include the following revised/new titles:

- Use of Chapter 16 codes
- Principal diagnosis for birth record
- Use of codes from other chapters with codes from Chapter 16
- Use of Chapter 16 codes after the perinatal period

4) Code all clinically significant conditions

All clinically significant conditions noted on routine newborn examination should be coded. A condition is clinically significant if it requires:

- Clinical evaluation
- Therapeutic treatment
- Diagnostic procedures

- Extended length of hospital stay
- Increased nursing care and/or monitoring
- Implications for future health care needs

Note: The perinatal guidelines listed above are the same as the general coding guidelines for "additional diagnoses" except for the final point regarding implications for future health care needs. Codes should be assigned for conditions that have been specified by the provider as having implications for future health care needs. Codes from the perinatal chapter should not be assigned unless the provider has established a definitive diagnosis.

b. Use of codes V30–V39

When coding the birth of an infant, assign a code from categories V30–V39, according to the type of birth. A code from this series is assigned as a principal diagnosis, and assigned only once to a newborn at the time of birth.

c. Newborn transfers

If the newborn is transferred to another institution, the V30 series is not used at the receiving hospital.

d. Use of category V29

1) Assigning a code from category V29

Assign a code from category V29, Observation and evaluation of newborns and infants for suspected conditions not found, to identify those instances when a healthy newborn is evaluated for a suspected condition that is determined, after study, not to be present. Do not use a code from category V29 when the patient has identified signs or symptoms of a suspected problem; in such cases, code the sign or symptom.

A code from category V29 may also be assigned as a principal code for readmissions or encounters when the V30 code no longer applies. Codes from category V29 are for use only for healthy newborns and infants for which no condition after study is found to be present.

2) V29 code on a birth record

A V29 code is to be used as a secondary code after the V30, Outcome of delivery, code.

ICD-10 Alert!

The ICD-10-CM official guidelines have eliminated content about *use of codes V30–V39.*

ICD-10 Alert!

The ICD-10-CM official guidelines have eliminated content about newborn transfers.

ICD-10 Alert!

The ICD-10-CM official guidelines have eliminated content about assigning a code from category V29 and V29 code on a birth record.

(continues)

ICD-9-CM CHAPTER-SPECIFIC CODING GUIDELINES WITH ICD-10 ALERTS! (*continued*)

e. ● **Use of other V codes on perinatal records**

V codes other than V30 and V29 may be assigned on a perinatal or newborn record code. The codes may be used as a principal or first-listed diagnosis for specific types of encounters or for readmissions or encounters when the V30 code no longer applies.

See Chapter 18 official guidelines for information regarding the assignment of V codes.

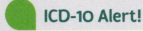

ICD-10 Alert!

The ICD-10-CM official guidelines have eliminated content about *use of other V codes on perinatal records.*

f. ● **Maternal causes of perinatal morbidity**

Codes from categories 760–763, Maternal causes of perinatal morbidity and mortality, are assigned only when the maternal condition has actually affected the fetus or newborn. The fact that the mother has an associated medical condition or experiences some complication of pregnancy, labor, or delivery does not justify the routine assignment of codes from these categories to the newborn record.

ICD-10 Alert!

The ICD-10-CM official guidelines have eliminated content about *maternal causes of perinatal morbidity.*

g. ● **Congenital anomalies in newborns**

For the birth admission, the appropriate code from category V30, Liveborn infants according to type of birth, should be used, followed by any congenital anomaly codes, categories 740–759. Use additional secondary codes from other chapters to specify conditions associated with the anomaly, if applicable.

See Chapter 14 official guidelines for information on the coding of congenital anomalies.

ICD-10 Alert!

The ICD-10-CM official guidelines have eliminated content about *congenital anomalies in newborns.*

h. **Coding additional perinatal diagnoses**

1) **Assigning codes for conditions that require treatment**

Assign codes for conditions that require treatment or further investigation, prolong the length of stay, or require resource utilization.

2) **Codes for conditions specified as having implications for future health care needs**

Assign codes for conditions that have been specified by the provider as having implications for future health care needs.

Note: This guideline should not be used for adult patients.

3) ● **Codes for newborn conditions originating in the perinatal period**

Assign a code for newborn conditions originating in the perinatal period (categories 760–779), as well as complications arising during the current episode of care classified in other chapters, only if the diagnoses have been documented by the responsible provider at the time of transfer or discharge as having affected the fetus or newborn.

i. **Prematurity and fetal growth retardation**

Providers utilize different criteria in determining prematurity. A code for prematurity should not be assigned unless it is documented. The fifth-digit assignment for codes from category 764 and sub-categories 765.0 and 765.1 should be based on the recorded birth weight and estimated gestational age.

A code from subcategory 765.2, Weeks of gestation, should be assigned as an additional code with category 764 and codes from 765.0 and 765.1 to specify weeks of gestation as documented by the provider in the record.

ICD-10 Alert!

The ICD-10-CM official guidelines have eliminated content about *codes for newborn conditions origination in the perinatal period.*

ICD-10 Alert!

- In ICD-10-CM, category P05 classifies *disorders of newborn related to slow fetal growth and fetal malnutrition,* category P07 classifies *disorders of newborn related to short gestation and low birth weight,* not elsewhere classified, and assignment of codes should be based on the recorded birth weight and estimated gestational age. Codes from category P05 should not be assigned with codes from category P07. When both birth weight and gestational age are available, two codes from category P07 should be assigned, with the code for birth weight sequenced before the code for gestational age.

- *Go to Appendix II located on the Premium Website to review ICD-10-CM coding guidelines in Section I.C.16.e,* Low birth weight and Immaturity Status.

j. Newborn sepsis

Code 771.81, Septicemia [sepsis] of newborn, should be assigned with a secondary code from category 041, Bacterial infections in conditions classified elsewhere and of unspecified site, to identify the organism. A code from category 038, Septicemia, should not be used on a newborn record. Do not assign code 995.91, Sepsis, as code 771.81 describes the sepsis. If applicable, use additional code to identify severe sepsis (995.92) and any associated dysfunction.

ICD-10 Alert!

Go to Appendix II located on the Premium Website to review ICD-10-CM coding guidelines in Sections I.C.16.f, Bacterial Sepsis of Newborn, and I.C.16.g., Stillbirth.

Exercise 4.17 – Certain Conditions Originating in the Perinatal Period

Instructions: Underline the main term in each diagnosis statement and assign the appropriate ICD-9-CM and ICD-10-CM code(s).

ICD-9-CM	ICD-10-CM	
_____	_____	**1.** Cyanotic attacks of newborn
_____	_____	**2.** Exceptionally large baby
_____	_____	**3.** Facial palsy, newborn
_____	_____	**4.** Feeding problems in newborn
_____	_____	**5.** Fetal blood loss

ICD-9-CM Chapter 16: Signs, Symptoms, and Ill-Defined Conditions (780–799)

Chapter 16, Signs, Symptoms and Ill-Defined Conditions (780–799) (or ICD-10-CM Chapter 17, Symptoms, signs, and abnormal clinical and laboratory findings, not elsewhere classified, R00–R99), includes symptoms, signs, and abnormal results of laboratory or other investigative procedures, as well as ill-defined conditions for which there are no other, more specific diagnoses classifiable elsewhere. In general, codes from this chapter are used to report symptoms, signs, and ill-defined conditions that point with equal suspicion to two or more diagnoses or represent important problems in medical care that may affect management of the patient. In addition, this chapter classifies abnormal findings that are reported without a corresponding definitive diagnosis. Codes for such findings can be located in the alphabetical index under the following terms:

ICD-10 Alert!

In ICD-10-CM, *Symptoms, Signs and Abnormal Clinical and Laboratory Findings, Not Elsewhere Classified (R00–R99)* are located in Chapter 18.

- Abnormal, abnormality, abnormalities
- Decrease, decreased
- Elevation
- Findings, abnormal, without diagnosis

Codes from this chapter also are used to report symptoms and signs that existed on initial encounter but proved to be transient and without a specified cause. Also included are provisional diagnoses for patients who fail to return for further investigation, cases referred elsewhere for further investigation before being diagnosed, and cases in which a more definitive diagnosis was not available for other reasons. Do not assign a code from ICD-9-CM categories 780–799 (or (or ICD-10-CM categories R00-R99) when the symptoms, signs, and abnormal findings pertain to a definitive diagnosis.

EXAMPLE: Do not assign ICD-9-CM code 789.00 (or ICD-10-CM code R10.9) for abdominal pain ICD-9-CM code 789.00 (or ICD-10-CM code R10.9) or ICD-9-CM code 789.40 (or ICD-10-CM code R19.30) for abdominal rigidity when a patient is diagnosed with acute appendicitis. Such signs and symptoms are associated with acute appendicitis, and they add no value to the patient's coding profile when assigned as other (additional) diagnosis codes.

Coders may assign codes from ICD-9-CM Chapter 16 (or ICD-10-CM Chapter 18) to report symptoms, signs, and abnormal findings that pertain to a particular clinical diagnosis if the findings represent important problems in medical care. Such problems are useful to record because they may affect length of stay or level of nursing care and/or monitoring. Such problems also may require additional diagnostic or clinical evaluation or may affect treatment plans. In these cases, list the definitive condition as the principal diagnosis, and the symptoms secondarily. List as a secondary diagnosis any symptoms, signs, and abnormal findings that are not integral to the principal diagnosis but provide important clinical information.

EXAMPLE: For a patient admitted with uncontrolled type 1 diabetes mellitus and acute urinary retention, report both ICD-9-CM codes 250.03 (or ICD-10-CM code E10.65) and 788.20 (or R33.9). Acute urinary retention is not integral to uncontrolled type 1 diabetes mellitus, and it is an indication for catheterization or surgery. (In ICD-10-CM, "uncontrolled" is reported as "with hyperglycemia.") Acute urinary retention can also be viewed as an "important medical problem" when patient record documentation indicates the need for clinical evaluation or diagnostic procedures to rule out pathology other than benign prostatic hypertrophy as the etiology. Therapeutic treatment (e.g., catheterization prior to surgery) includes increased nursing care and/or monitoring, such as catheter care or extended length of hospital stay.

Report as the principal diagnosis any symptoms, signs, and abnormal findings that, after study, *cannot be attributed to a definitive diagnosis classifiable to another ICD-9-CM (or ICD-10-CM) chapter.*

EXAMPLE: Patient was admitted with right lower quadrant abdominal pain. Pelvic ultrasound was negative. Assign ICD-9-CM code 789.03 (or ICD-10-CM code R10.31) because the provider did not document a definitive diagnosis.

Also report as the principal diagnosis any symptom, sign, or abnormal finding that is associated with contrasting or comparative diagnoses (e.g., sign or symptom associated with two or more suspected or possible diagnoses). Report the contrasting or comparative diagnoses as other (additional) diagnosis codes.

EXAMPLE: Patient was admitted for treatment of severe chest pain. Provider documented severe chest pain due to acute myocardial infarction (AMI) versus hiatal hernia. Assign ICD-9-CM code 786.50 (or ICD-10-CM code R07.9) (chest pain) as the principal diagnosis. Assign codes 410.90 (MI) (or ICD-10-CM code I21.3) and ICD-9-CM code 553.3 (or ICD-10-CM code K44.9) (hiatal hernia) as other (additional) diagnosis codes.

Note:

There are no official ICD-9-CM coding guidelines for signs, symptoms, and ill-defined conditions (780–799)

Exercise 4.18 – Signs, Symptoms, and Ill-Defined Conditions

Instructions: Underline the main term in each diagnosis statement and assign the appropriate ICD-9-CM and ICD-10-CM code(s).

ICD-9-CM	ICD-10-CM	
_____	_____	1. Abnormal reflex
_____	_____	2. Ataxia
_____	_____	3. Elevated prostate specific antigen
_____	_____	4. Failure to thrive (child)
_____	_____	5. Elevated blood pressure reading

ICD-9-CM Chapter 17: Injury and Poisoning (800–999)

Chapter 17, Injury and Poisoning (800–999), (or ICD-10-CM Chapter 19, Injury, Poisoning and Certain Other Consequences of External Causes, S00–T98) classifies the following:

- Injuries
- Fractures
- Burns
- Adverse effects, poisonings, and toxic effects

Separate codes are assigned for each injury except when a combination code is provided in ICD-9-CM. When multiple codes are assigned, the code for the most serious injury is sequenced first (as determined by the provider and based on treatment provided).

Fractures

A **fracture** is a break in a bone resulting from two possible causes:

- Direct or indirect application of undue force against the bone (injury)
- Pathologic changes resulting in spontaneous fractures (disease process)

ICD-10 Alert!

In ICD-10-CM, *Injury, Poisoning and Certain Other Consequences of External Causes (S00–T98)* are located in Chapter 19.

Coding Tip:

Injury and poisoning codes are not assigned for normal, healing surgical wounds or to identify complications of surgical wounds. (To classify complications of surgical wounds, refer to main term *Complication* in the ICD-9-CM Index to Diseases.)

The provider always determines whether a fracture is open or closed, which is one of the first determinations made. A **closed fracture** (or **simple fracture**) is contained beneath the skin and has intact ligaments and skin, while an **open fracture** or **compound fracture**) indicates an associated open wound.

Coding Tip:

ICD-9-CM Chapter 17 (or ICD-10-CM Chapter 19) does not contain codes for the **malunion** (or **nonunion**) of fractured bones, which is the failure of the ends of a fractured bone to heal (unite). Such codes are located in Chapter 13, In ICD-10-CM, malunion and nonunion of fractured bones are classified in Chapter 19 by adding a seventh character (e.g., S72.001k, S72.001p).

The following terms typically describe closed fractures:

- Comminuted fracture: A splintering of the fractured bone.

- Depressed fracture: Portion of the skull broken and driven inward from a forceful blow.

- Fissured fracture: Fracture that does not split the bone.

- Greenstick fracture: Occurs in children; the bone is somewhat bent and partially broken.

- Impacted fracture: One fractured bone end wedged into another.

- Linear fracture: Fracture that is in a straight line.

- Slipped epiphysis: Separation of the growth plate, which is the growing end of the bone, or epiphysis, from the shaft of the bone; occurs in children and young adults who still have active epiphyses.

- Spiral fracture: Fracture resembles a helix or has a corkscrew shape.

Coding Tip:

If there is no documentation in the patient record as to whether a fracture is open or closed, the fracture is coded as closed.

An open fracture is classified as a compound fracture because it contains a wound that leads to the fracture or has broken bone ends protruding through the skin. There is a very high risk of infection with open fractures because the tissues are exposed to contaminants (toxins). There may be foreign bodies (or missiles) embedded in the tissues that must be removed during surgery, and puncture wounds may also be present.

Open and closed fractures may both be described as "complicated," which means a bone fragment has injured an internal organ.

EXAMPLE: The ribs may injure the lungs, liver, and spleen, depending on the nature and direction of the force causing the fracture.

Burns

Burns (ICD-9-CM categories 940–949 or ICD-10-CM categories T20-T32) (Figure 4-7) are classified according to the following:

- Depth

  - First-degree (erythema)

  - Second-degree (blistering)

  - Third-degree (full-thickness involvement)

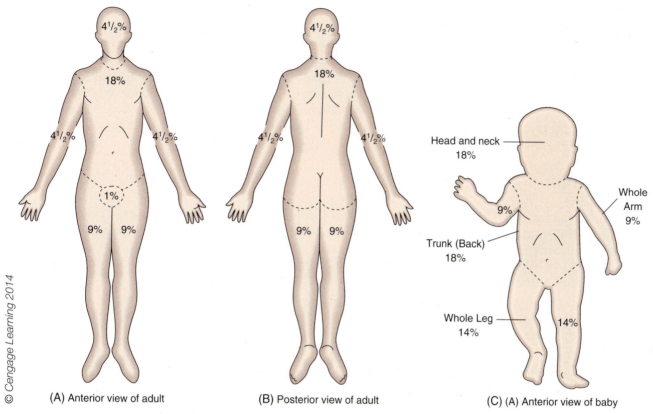

(A) Anterior view of adult   (B) Posterior view of adult   (C) (A) Anterior view of baby

Figure 4-8 The rule of nines is used to calculate the percentage of body surface affected by burns (ICD-9-CM category 948 or ICD-10-CM category T32). (Percentage assignments are modified to accommodate infants and children who have proportionately larger heads than adults or for patients who have large buttocks, thighs, or abdomen.)

- Extent (percentage of body surface involved) (Figure 4-8)
- Agent (e.g., chemicals, fire, sun) (assigned an E code)

Adverse Effects, Poisonings, and Toxic Effects

Certain drugs, medicinal substances, and biological substances (or combinations of them) may cause toxic reactions. Such drug toxicity is classified in ICD-9-CM as:

- Adverse effects (or adverse reaction): Appearance of a pathologic condition caused by ingestion or exposure to a chemical substance properly administered or taken.

- Poisonings: Occur as the result of an overdose, wrong substance administered or taken; or intoxication, which involves combining prescribed drugs with nonprescribed drugs or alcohol.

- Toxic effects: When a harmful substance is ingested or comes in contact with a person.

Coding Tip:

To locate the code for an adverse effect, go to main term *Effect, adverse* in the ICD-9-CM (or ICD-10-CM) Index to Diseases, and locate the appropriate subterm (e.g., drugs and medicinals). Or, go to main term *Reaction*, and locate the appropriate subterm(s) (e.g., *adverse food, allergic, Arthus, drug NEC, food adverse NEC, insulin*). Then, assign the appropriate E code from the Table of Drugs and Chemicals, Therapeutic Use column.

Coding Tip:

To locate the code for a poisoning or topic effect, go to the Table of Drugs and Chemicals, review the first column to locate the drug, alcohol, or harmful substance, and assign the code listed below the Poisoning column. Then, determine the circumstances for the poisoning or toxic effect (e.g., accident, suicide attempt, assault, undetermined), and assign the code from that column. If more than one substance is documented as causing the poisoning or toxic effect, assign codes from the Tables of Drugs and Chemicals for *each* substance.

Coding Tip:

- The term *intoxication* often indicates that ethyl alcohol (e.g., beer, wine) was involved (i.e., alcohol intoxication) or that an accumulation effect of a medication in the patient's bloodstream occurred (e.g., Coumadin intoxication). When this occurs, assign a code from the appropriate Poisoning column of the ICD-9-CM (or ICD-10-CM) Table of Drugs and Chemicals along with the appropriate external cause code. In this situation, intoxication means "poisoning."

- When an accumulation effect of a medication occurs, assign the manifestation code first (e.g., dizziness) and an external cause code from the ICD-9-CM Therapeutic Use column (e.g., Coumadin) (or ICD-10-CM Adverse Effect column) in the Table of Drugs and Chemicals.

- External cause codes are used to explain the cause of the poisoning or the adverse effect. They are not diagnoses, but external causes or results of injury. Therefore, ICD-9-CM E codes (or ICD-10-CM V or Y codes) are always reported as secondary codes.

Refer to the Table of Drugs and Chemicals in the ICD-9-CM index (Figure 4-9A) or in the ICD-10-CM index (Figure 4-9B) when assigning codes for adverse effects, poisonings, and toxic effects.

For adverse effects, first code the result or manifestation of the adverse effect (e.g., arrhythmia, vomiting, headache, or dizziness) by referring to the appropriate entry in the ICD-9-CM Index to Diseases. Then code the chemical substance by referring to the Therapeutic Use column of the Table of Drugs and Chemicals (highlighted in yellow in Figure 4-9A). If more than one substance is documented as causing the adverse effect, assign codes from the Tables of Drugs and Chemicals for *each* substance.

> **EXAMPLE:** Gastritis due to prescribed tetracycline. In this statement, gastritis (535.50) is the adverse effect (or manifestation) of the properly administered drug tetracycline (E930.4). ICD-10-CM codes are reported as T36.4x5A (adverse effect of tetracycline) and K29.70 (gastritis), in that order.

ICD-10 Alert!

For underdosing, first code the medical condition for which the (underdosing) drug was prescribed by referring to the appropriate entry in the ICD-10-CM index. Then, code the chemical substance by referring to the Underdosing column in the Table of Drugs and Chemicals (highlighted in yellow in Figure 4-9B). (*Underdosing* refers to taking less of a medication than is prescribed by a provider or a manufacturer's instruction.)

For poisonings and toxic effects, in ICD-9-CM first code the poisoning by referring to the Poisoning column of the Table of Drugs and Chemicals. Next, code the result or manifestation of the poisoning or toxic effect (e.g., coma). Then code the external cause (E code) (e.g., accident, or suicide) by referring to the appropriate column in the table. If more than one substance is documented as causing the poisoning or toxic effect, assign codes from the Tables of Drugs and Chemicals for *each* substance. (Never assign a code from the Therapeutic Use column in the table.)

Substance	Poisoning	External Cause (E Code)				
		Accident	Therapeutic Use	Suicide Attempt	Assault	Undetermined
1-propanol	980.3	E860.4	—	E950.9	E962.1	E980.9
2-propanol	980.2	E860.3	—	E950.9	E962.1	E980.9
2, 4-D (dichlorophenoxyacetic acid)	989.4	E863.5	—	E950.6	E962.1	E980.7
2, 4-toluene diisocyanate	983.0	E864.0	—	E950.7	E962.1	E980.6
2, 4, 5-T (trichlorophenoxyacetic acid)	989.2	E863.5	—	E950.6	E962.1	E980.7
14-hydroxydihydromorphinone	965.09	E850.2	E935.2	E950.0	E962.0	E980.0
ABOB	961.7	E857	E931.7	E950.4	E962.0	E980.4
Abrus (seed)	988.2	E865.3	—	E950.9	E962.1	E980.9
Absinthe	980.0	E860.1	—	E950.9	E962.1	E980.9
beverage	980.0	E860.0	—	E950.9	E962.1	E980.9
Acenocoumarin, acenocoumarol	964.2	E858.2	E934.2	E950.4	E962.0	E980.4
Acepromazine	969.1	E853.0	E939.1	E950.3	E962.0	E980.3
Acetal	982.8	E862.4	—	E950.9	E962.1	E980.9
Acetaldehyde (vapor)	987.8	E869.8	—	E952.8	E962.2	E982.8
liquid	989.89	E866.8	—	E950.9	E962.1	E980.9
Acetaminophen	965.4	E850.4	E935.4	E950.0	E962.0	E980.0
Acetaminosalol	965.1	E850.3	E935.3	E950.0	E962.0	E980.0
Acetanilid(e)	965.4	E850.4	E935.4	E950.0	E962.0	E980.0
Acetarsol, acetarsone	961.1	E857	E931.1	E950.4	E962.0	E980.4
Acetazolamide	974.2	E858.5	E944.2	E950.4	E962.0	E980.4
Acetic						
acid	983.1	E864.1	—	E950.7	E962.1	E980.6
with sodium acetate (ointment)	976.3	E858.7	E946.3	E950.4	E962.0	E980.4
irrigating solution	974.5	E858.5	E944.5	E950.4	E962.0	E980.4
lotion	976.2	E858.7	E946.2	E950.4	E962.0	E980.4
anhydride	983.1	E864.1	—	E950.7	E962.1	E980.6
ether (vapor)	982.8	E862.4	—	E950.9	E962.1	E980.9

Figure 4-9A ICD-9-CM Table of Drugs and Chemicals (partial)

Substance	Poisoning, Accidental (unintentional)	Poisoning, Intentional Self-harm	Poisoning, Assault	Poisoning, Undetermined	Adverse Effect	Under-dosing
1-propanol	T51.3x1	T51.3x2	T51.3x3	T51.3x4	—	—
2-propanol	T51.2x1	T51.2x2	T51.2x3	T51.2x4	—	—
2, 4-D (dichloro-phenoxyacetic acid)	T60.3x1	T60.3x2	T60.3x3	T60.3x4	—	—
2, 4-toluene diisocyanate	T65.0x1	T65.0x2	T65.0x3	T65.0x4	—	—
2, 4, 5-T (trichloro-phenoxyacetic acid)	T60.1x1	T60.1x2	T60.1x3	T60.1x4	—	—
14-hydroxydihydromorphinone	T40.2x1	T40.2x2	T40.2x3	T40.2x4	T40.2x5	T40.2x6
ABOB	T37.5x1	T37.5x2	T37.5x3	T37.5x4	T37.5x5	T37.5x6
Abrine	T62.2x1	T62.2x2	T62.2x3	T62.2x4	—	—
Abrus (seed)	T62.2x1	T62.2x2	T62.2x3	T62.2x4	—	—
Absinthe	T51.0x1	T51.0x2	T51.0x3	T51.0x4	—	—
beverage	T51.0x1	T51.0x2	T51.0x3	T51.0x4	—	—
Acaricide	T60.8x1	T60.8x2	T60.8x3	T60.8x4	—	—
Acebutolol	T44.7x1	T44.7x2	T44.7x3	T44.7x4	T44.7x5	T44.7x6
Acecarbromal	T42.6x1	T42.6x2	T42.6x3	T42.6x4	T42.6x5	T42.6x6
Aceclidine	T44.1x1	T44.1x2	T44.1x3	T44.1x4	T44.1x5	T44.1x6
Acedapsone	T37.0x1	T37.0x2	T37.0x3	T37.0x4	T37.0x5	T37.0x6
Acefylline piperazine	T48.6x1	T48.6x2	T48.6x3	T48.6x4	T48.6x5	T48.6x6

Figure 4-9B ICD-10-CM Table of Drugs and Chemicals (partial)

For poisonings and toxic effects in ICD-10-CM, go to the appropriate Poisoning column of the Table of Drugs and Chemicals to assign the code. If more than one substance is documented as causing the poisoning or toxic effect, assign codes from the Tables of Drugs and Chemicals for *each* substance. Next code the result or manifestation of the poisoning or toxic effect (e.g., coma). (A separate external cause code is not assigned.)

EXAMPLE: Accidental (unintentional) overdose of tetracycline resulting in severe vomiting. In this statement, the ICD-9-CM poisoning code is listed first (960.4), followed by the manifestation (vomiting) (787.03) and the accidental overdose E code (E856). ICD-10-CM codes are reported as T36.4x1A (unintentional accidental poisoning by tetracycline) and R11.2 (vomiting), in that order.

> **Coding Tip:**
>
> The ICD-9-CM (and ICD-10-CM) Table of Drugs and Chemicals contains a listing of the generic names of the drugs or chemicals. (Some publishers are now adding brand names to the list of drugs and chemicals.)

ICD-9-CM CHAPTER-SPECIFIC CODING GUIDELINES WITH ICD-10 ALERTS!

 ICD-10 Alert!

In ICD-10-CM, *Injury, Poisoning and Certain Other Consequences of External Causes* are located in Chapter 19, and ICD-9-CM coding guidelines with *ICD-10 Alerts!* are included below.

Chapter 17: Injury and Poisoning (800–999)

ICD-10 Alert!

Go to Appendix II located on the Premium Website to review ICD-10-CM coding guidelines in Section I.C.19., which contains a new coding guideline about code extensions.

a. Coding of injuries

When coding injuries, assign separate codes for each injury unless a combination code is provided, in which case the combination code is assigned. Multiple-injury codes are provided in ICD-9-CM, but should not be assigned unless information for a more specific code is not available. These traumatic injury codes are not to be used for normal, healing surgical wounds or to identify complications of surgical wounds.

The code for the most serious injury, as determined by the provider and the focus of treatment, is sequenced first.

1) Superficial injuries

Superficial injuries such as abrasions or contusions are not coded when associated with more severe injuries of the same site.

2) Primary injury with damage to nerves/blood vessels

When a primary injury results in minor damage to peripheral nerves or blood vessels, the primary injury is sequenced first with additional code(s) from categories 950–957, Injury to nerves and spinal cord, and/or 900–904, Injury to blood vessels. When the primary injury is to the blood vessels or nerves, that injury should be sequenced first.

 ICD-10 Alert!

In ICD-10-CM, the primary injury is also sequenced first with additional code(s) for injuries to nerves and spinal cord (such as category S04), and/or injury to blood vessels (such as category S15).

b. Coding of traumatic fractures

The principles of multiple coding of injuries should be followed in coding fractures. Fractures of specified sites are coded individually by site in accordance with both the provisions within categories 800–829 and the level of detail furnished by medical record content. Combination categories for multiple fractures are provided for use when there is insufficient detail in the medical record (such as trauma cases transferred to another hospital), when the reporting form limits the number of codes that can be used in reporting pertinent clinical data, or when there is insufficient specificity at the fourth-digit or fifth-digit level. More specific guidelines are as follows:

1) Acute fractures vs. aftercare

ICD-10 Alert!

In ICD-10-CM fractures of specified sites are coded individually by site in accordance with both the provisions within categories S02, S12, S22, S32, S42, S49, S52, S59, S62, S72, S79, S82, S89, S92 and the level of detail furnished by medical record content. A fracture not indicated as open or closed should be coded to closed. A fracture not indicated whether displaced or not displaced should be coded to displaced. *Additional ICD-10-CM coding guidelines in guidelines are in Appendix II located on the Premium Website in Section I.C.19.c.1., initial versus subsequent encounter for fractures, and I.C.19.c.2., multiple fractures sequencing.*

Traumatic fractures are coded using the acute fracture codes (800–829) while the patient is receiving active treatment for the fracture. Examples of active treatment are: surgical treatment, emergency department encounter, and evaluation and treatment by a new physician.

Fractures are coded using the aftercare codes (subcategories V54.0, V54.1, V54.8, or V54.9) for encounters after the patient has completed active treatment of the fracture and is receiving routine care for the fracture during the healing or recovery phase. Examples of fracture aftercare are: cast change or removal, removal of external or internal fixation device, medication adjustment, and follow-up visits following fracture treatment.

Care for complications of surgical treatment for fracture repairs during the healing or recovery phase should be coded with the appropriate complication codes.

Care of complications of fractures, such as malunion and nonunion, should be reported with the appropriate codes.

Pathologic fractures are not coded in the 800–829 range, but instead are assigned to subcategory 733.1. *See Section I.C.13.a for additional information.*

2) Multiple fractures of same limb

Multiple fractures of same limb classifiable to the same three-digit or four-digit category are coded to that category.

3) Multiple unilateral or bilateral fractures of same bone

Multiple unilateral or bilateral fractures of same bone(s) but classified to different fourth-digit subdivisions (bone part) within the same three-digit category are coded individually by site.

4) Multiple fracture categories 819 and 828

Multiple fracture categories 819 and 828 classify bilateral fractures of both upper limbs (819) and both lower limbs (828), but without any detail at the fourth-digit level other than open and closed type of fractures.

5) Multiple fractures sequencing

Multiple fractures are sequenced in accordance with the severity of the fracture. The provider should be asked to list the fracture diagnoses in order of severity.

(continues)

ICD-9-CM CHAPTER-SPECIFIC CODING GUIDELINES WITH ICD-10 ALERTS! (*continued*)

c. Coding of burns

 ICD-10 Alert!

Go to Appendix II located on the Premium Website to review ICD-10-CM coding guidelines in Section I.C.19.d., which includes extensively revised coding guidelines about the coding of burns and corrosions. ICD-10-CM distinguishes between burns and corrosions; however, the guidelines are the same for burns and corrosions.

- Burn codes classify thermal burns, except sunburns, which come from a heat source (e.g., fire, hot appliance), electricity, and radiation.
- Corrosions are burns due to chemicals.

Current burns (940–948) are classified by depth, by extent, and by agent (E code). Burns are classified by depth as first-degree (erythema), second-degree (blistering), and third-degree (full-thickness involvement).

1) Sequencing of burn and related condition codes

Sequence first the code that reflects the highest degree of burn when more than one burn is present.

(a) When the reason for the admission or encounter is for treatment of external multiple burns, sequence first the code that reflects the burn of the highest degree.

(b) When a patient has both internal and external burns, the circumstances of admission govern the selection of the principal diagnosis or first-listed diagnosis.

(c) When a patient is admitted for burn injuries and other related conditions such as smoke inhalation and/or respiratory failure, the circumstances of admission govern the selection of the principal or first-listed diagnosis.

2) Burns of the same local site

Classify burns of the same local site (three-digit category level, 940–947) but of different degrees to the subcategory identifying the highest degree recorded in the diagnosis.

3) Nonhealing burns

Nonhealing burns are coded as acute burns.
Necrosis of burned skin should be coded as a nonhealed burn.

4) Code 958.3, Posttraumatic wound infection

Assign code 958.3, Posttraumatic wound infection, not elsewhere classified, as an additional code for any documented infected burn site.

5) Assign separate codes for each burn site

When coding burns, assign separate codes for each burn site. Category 946, Burns of multiple specified sites, should be used only if the location of the burns is not documented. Category 949, Burn, unspecified, is extremely vague and should rarely be used.

6) Assign codes from category 948, Burns

Burns should be classified according to extent of body surface involved when the site of the burn is not specified or when there is a need for additional data. It is advisable to use category 948 as additional coding when needed to provide data for evaluating burn mortality, such as that needed by burn units. It is also advisable to use category 948 as an additional code for reporting purposes when there is mention of a third-degree burn involving 20 percent or more of the body surface. In assigning a code from category 948:

- Fourth-digit codes are used to identify the percentage of total body surface involved in a burn (all degree).
- Fifth digits are assigned to identify the percentage of body surface involved in a third-degree burn.

- Fifth digit zero (0) is assigned when less than 10 percent or when no body surface is involved in a third-degree burn.

- Category 948 is based on the classic "rule of nines" in estimating body surface involved: head and neck are assigned 9 percent; each arm, 9 percent; each leg, 18 percent; the anterior trunk, 18 percent; posterior trunk, 18 percent; and genitalia, 1 percent. Providers may change these percentage assignments where necessary to accommodate infants and children who have proportionately larger heads than adults and patients who have large buttocks, thighs, or abdomen that involves burns.

7) Encounters for treatment of late effects of burns

Encounters for the treatment of the late effects of burns (i.e., scars or joint contractures) should be coded to the residual condition (sequela) followed by the appropriate late effect code (906.5–906.9). A late effect E code may also be used, if desired.

8) Sequelae with a late effect code and current burn

When appropriate, both a sequela with a late effect code and a current burn code may be assigned on the same record (when both a current burn and sequelae of an old burn exist).

d. Coding of debridement of wound, infection, or burn

Excisional debridement involves surgical removal or cutting away, as opposed to a mechanical (brushing, scrubbing, or washing) debridement. For coding purposes, excisional debridement is assigned to code 86.22. Nonexcisional debridement is assigned to code 86.28.

e. Adverse effects, poisoning and toxic effects

ICD-10 Alert!

ICD-10-CM categories T36–T65 are combination codes that classify substances related to adverse effects, poisonings, toxic effects and underdosing, and the external cause. A code from categories T36–T65 is sequenced first, followed by the code(s) that specify the nature of the adverse effect, poisoning, or toxic effect. However, this sequencing instruction does not apply to underdosing codes, which are never assigned as principal or first-listed codes. Instead, first report a code for the medical condition for which the drug is prescribed and also report the underdosing code from the Table of Drugs and Chemicals.

The properties of certain drugs, medicinal and biological substances, or combinations of such substances, may cause toxic reactions. The occurrence of drug toxicity is classified in ICD-9-CM as follows:

1) Adverse effect

When the drug was correctly prescribed and properly administered, code the reaction and the appropriate code from the E930–E949 series. Codes from the E930–E949 series must be used to identify the causative substance for adverse effects of drugs or medicinal or biological substances correctly prescribed and properly administered. The effect, such as tachycardia, delirium, gastrointestinal hemorrhaging, vomiting, hypokalemia, hepatitis, renal failure, or respiratory failure, is coded and followed by the appropriate code from the E930–E949 series.

Adverse effects of therapeutic substances correctly prescribed and properly administered (toxicity, synergistic reaction, side effect, and idiosyncratic reaction) may be due to (1) differences among patients, such as age, sex, disease, and genetic factors, and (2) drug-related factors, such as type of drug, route of administration, duration of therapy, dosage, and bioavailability.

2) Poisoning

(a) Error was made in drug prescription

Errors made in drug prescription or in the administration of the drug by provider, nurse, patient, or other person use the appropriate poisoning code from the 960–979 series.

(continues)

ICD-9-CM CHAPTER-SPECIFIC CODING GUIDELINES WITH ICD-10 ALERTS! (continued)

(b) Overdose of a drug intentionally taken

If an overdose of a drug was intentionally taken or administered and resulted in drug toxicity, it would be coded as a poisoning (960–979 series).

(c) Nonprescribed drug taken with correctly prescribed and properly administered drug

If a nonprescribed drug or medicinal agent was taken in combination with a correctly prescribed and properly administered drug, any drug toxicity or other reaction resulting from the interaction of the two drugs would be classified as a poisoning.

(d) Interaction of drug(s) and alcohol

When a reaction results from the interaction of a drug(s) and alcohol, this would be classified as poisoning.

(e) Sequencing of poisoning

When coding a poisoning or reaction to the improper use of a medication (e.g., wrong dose, wrong substance, or wrong route of administration), the poisoning code is sequenced first, followed by a code for the manifestation. If there is also a diagnosis of drug abuse or dependence to the substance, the abuse or dependence is coded as an additional code. *See Section I.C.3.a.6.b. if poisoning is the result of insulin pump malfunctions and see Section I.C.19 for general use of E codes.*

ICD-10 Alert!

Go to Appendix II located on the Premium Website to review ICD-10-CM coding guidelines in Section I.C.e.5.c., which includes the new guideline about underdosing, which refers to taking less of a medication than is prescribed by a provider or a manufacturer's instruction. ICD-10-CM categories T36-T50 (with fifth or sixth character 6) classify underdosing, but they are never assigned as the principal or first-listed codes. The medical condition is reported first, followed by the underdosing code. In addition, noncompliance codes Z91.12- and Z91.13- or complication of care codes Y63.61 and Y63.8-Y63.9 are reported with an underdosing code to indicate intent, if known.

3) Toxic effects

(a) Toxic effect codes

When a harmful substance is ingested or comes in contact with a person, this is classified as a toxic effect. The toxic effect codes are in categories 980–989.

ICD-10 Alert!

In ICD-10-CM, toxic effect codes are classified in categories T51–T65.

(b) Sequencing toxic effect codes

A toxic effect code should be sequenced first, followed by the code(s) that identify the result of the toxic effect.

(c) External cause codes for toxic effects

An external cause code from categories E860–E869 for accidental exposure, codes E950.6 or E950.7 for intentional self-harm, category E962 for assault, or categories E980–E982 for undetermined should also be assigned to indicate intent.

f. **Complications of care**
1) **Complications of care**
(a) **Documentation of complications of care**
See Section I.B.18. for information on documentation of complications of care.
(b) **Use additional code to identify nature of complication**
An additional code identifying the complication should be assigned with codes in categories 996-999, Complications of Surgical and Medical Care NEC, when the additional code provides greater specificity as to the nature of the condition. If the complication code fully describes the condition, no additional code is necessary.

ICD-10 Alert!

Go to Appendix II located on the Premium Website to review ICD-10-CM coding guidelines in Section I.C.19.g.2., which contains a new coding guideline about pain due to medical devices.

2) **Transplant complications**

ICD-10 Alert!

Go to Appendix II located on the Premium Website to review ICD-10-CM coding guidelines in Section I.C.19.g.3., which contains revised coding guidelines about transplant complications.

(a) **Transplant complications other than kidney**
Codes under subcategory 996.8, Complications of transplanted organ, are for use for both complications and rejection of transplanted organs. A transplant complication code is only assigned if the complication affects the function of the transplanted organ. Two codes are required to fully describe a transplant complication: the appropriate code from subcategory 996.8 and a secondary code that identifies the complication.

Preexisting conditions or conditions that develop after the transplant are not coded as complications unless they affect the function of the transplanted organs.
See Section I.C.18.d.3 for transplant organ removal status
See Section I.C.2.i for malignant neoplasm associated with transplanted organ.
(b) **Kidney transplant complications**
Patients who have undergone kidney transplant may still have some form of chronic kidney disease (CKD) because the kidney transplant may not fully restore kidney function. Code 996.81 should be assigned for documented complications of a kidney transplant, such as transplant failure or rejection or other transplant complication. Code 996.81 should not be assigned for post kidney transplant patients who have chronic kidney disease (CKD) unless a transplant complication such as transplant failure or rejection is documented. If the documentation is unclear as to whether the patient has a complication of the transplant, query the provider.

Conditions that affect the function of the transplanted kidney, other than CKD, should be assigned code 996.81, Complications of transplanted organ, Kidney, and a secondary code that identifies the complication.

For patients with CKD following a kidney transplant, but who do not have a complication such as failure or rejection, see Section I.C.10.a.2, Chronic kidney disease and kidney transplant status.
3) **Ventilator-associated pneumonia**
(a) **Documentation of ventilator-associated pneumonia**
As with all procedural or postprocedural complications, code assignment is based on the provider's documentation of the relationship between the condition and the procedure.

(continues)

ICD-9-CM CHAPTER-SPECIFIC CODING GUIDELINES WITH ICD-10 ALERTS! (*continued*)

Code 997.31, Ventilator-associated pneumonia, should be assigned only when the provider has documented ventilator-associated pneumonia (VAP). An additional code to identify the organism (e.g., *Pseudomonas aeruginosa*, code 041.7) should also be assigned. Do not assign an additional code from categories 480–484 to identify the type of pneumonia.

ICD-10 Alert!

Go to Appendix II located on the Premium Website to review ICD-10-CM coding guidelines in Section I.C.19.g.6., which contains revised coding guideline about ventilatory-associated pneumonia.

Code 997.31 should not be assigned for cases where the patient has pneumonia and is on a mechanical ventilator but the provider has not specifically stated that the pneumonia is ventilator-associated pneumonia.

If the documentation is unclear as to whether the patient has a pneumonia that is a complication attributable to the mechanical ventilator, query the provider.

(b) **Patient admitted with pneumonia and develops VAP**

A patient may be admitted with one type of pneumonia (e.g., code 481, *Pneumococcal pneumonia*) and subsequently develop VAP. In this instance, the principal diagnosis would be the appropriate code from categories 480–484 for the pneumonia diagnosed at the time of admission. Code 997.31, Ventilator-associated pneumonia, would be assigned as an additional diagnosis when the provider has also documented the presence of ventilator-associated pneumonia.

g. **SIRS due to noninfectious process**

ICD-10 Alert!

In the ICD-10-CM official coding guidelines, content about SIRS due to noninfectious process was relocated to Section I.C.1.d.6., Chapter 1: Certain Infectious and Parasitic Diseases (A00–B99).

The systemic inflammatory response syndrome (SIRS) can develop as a result of certain noninfectious disease processes, such as trauma, malignant neoplasm, or pancreatitis. When SIRS is documented with a noninfectious condition, and no subsequent infection is documented, the code for the underlying condition, such as an injury, should be assigned, followed by code 995.93, Systemic inflammatory response syndrome due to noninfectious process without acute organ dysfunction, or 995.94, Systemic inflammatory response syndrome due to noninfectious process with acute organ dysfunction. If an acute organ dysfunction is documented, the appropriate code(s) for the associated acute organ dysfunction(s) should be assigned in addition to code 995.94. If acute organ dysfunction is documented, but it cannot be determined if the acute organ dysfunction is associated with SIRS or due to another condition (e.g., directly due to the trauma), the provider should be queried.

When the noninfectious condition has led to an infection that results in SIRS, *see* Section 1.b.12 for the guideline for sepsis and severe sepsis associated with a noninfectious process.

Exercise 4.19 – Injury and Poisoning

Instructions: Underline the main term in each diagnosis statement and assign the appropriate ICD-9-CM and ICD-10-CM code(s).

ICD-9-CM	ICD-10-CM	
_____	_____	1. Closed fracture mandible, subcondylar (initial encounter)
_____	_____	2. Closed dislocation of clavicle (initial encounter)
_____	_____	3. Concussion with brief loss of consciousness (30 minutes) (initial encounter)
_____	_____	4. Foot burn, blisters, epidermal loss (second-degree) (initial encounter)
_____	_____	5. Heart laceration without penetration of heart chambers (initial encounter)
_____	_____	6. Hives resulting from penicillin taken as prescribed (initial encounter)
_____	_____	7. Coma due to overdose of barbiturates during an attempted suicide (initial encounter)
_____	_____	8. Adverse reaction to pertussis vaccine (initial encounter)
_____	_____	9. Cardiac arrhythmia due to interaction of prescribed ephedrine and alcohol intoxication (accident) (initial encounter)
_____	_____	10. Stupor due to overdose of Nytol (accident) (initial encounter)

ICD-9-CM Supplementary Classification of Factors Influencing Health Status and Contact with Health Services (V01–V89)

The Supplementary Classification of Factors Influencing Health Status and Contact with Health Services (V01–V89) classifies occasions when circumstances *other than* a disease or an injury classifiable to ICD-9-CM categories 001–999 (or ICD-10-CM categories A00-Y99) are recorded as "diagnoses" or "problems."

ICD-10 Alert!

In ICD-10-CM, *Factors Influencing Health Status and Contact with Health Services [Z00–Z99]* are located in Chapter 21.

This can arise when:

- A person who is not currently sick encounters the health services for some specific purpose, such as to act as a donor of an organ or tissue, to receive prophylactic vaccination, or to discuss a problem that is in itself not a disease or an injury. This will be a fairly rare occurrence among hospital inpatients, but will be relatively more common among hospital outpatients and patients of family practitioners, health clinics, etc.

- A person with a known disease or injury, whether it is current or resolving, encounters the health care system for a specific treatment of that disease or injury (e.g., dialysis for renal disease, chemotherapy for malignancy, or a cast change).

- Some circumstance or problem is present that influences the person's health status but is not in itself a current illness or injury. Such factors may be elicited during population surveys, when the person may or may not be currently sick, or may be recorded as an additional factor to be borne in mind when the person is receiving care for some current illness or injury classifiable to ICD-9-CM categories 001–999 (or ICD-10-CM categories A00-Y99).

Coding Tip:

Certain V codes in ICD-9-CM (or Z codes in ICD-10-CM) can be reported as a first-listed or additional diagnosis for outpatient care.

 In the last situation, the ICD-9-CM V code (or ICD-10-CM Z code) should be assigned as an other (additional) code and is not selected as the principal diagnosis for inpatient cases or the first-listed diagnosis for outpatient cases. For example, such circumstances include personal history of certain diseases or a person with an artificial heart valve *in situ*.

Coding Tip:

Refer to ICD-9-CM (or ICD-10-CM) index main terms to begin the process of assigning an ICD-9-CM V code (or ICD-10-CM Z code). Common main terms include:

Admission	Donor	Outcome of delivery
Aftercare	Encounter for	Pregnancy
Attention to	Examination	Procedure (surgical) not done
Carrier (suspected) of	Exposure	Prophylactic
Checking	Fitting	Removal
Checkup	Follow-up	Resistance, resistant
Closure	History, family	Routine postpartum follow-up
Contact	History (personal) of	Screening
Contraception, contraceptive	Maladjustment	Status
Counseling	Newborn	Test(s)
Dialysis	Observation	Vaccination

Categories V01–V06

Report codes from categories V01–V06 when patients have potential health hazards related to communicable diseases. Assign codes from category:

- V01 when patients have been exposed to communicable diseases but have not been diagnosed.

- V02 when patients have been identified as or are suspected of being infectious disease carriers.

- V03–V06 when patients are seeking immunization against disease.

Categories V07–V09

Report codes from categories V07–V09 for people with need for isolation, other potential health hazards, and prophylactic measures. Assign codes from category:

- V07 when patients are placed in an isolation area or receive prophylactic measures (e.g., prophylactic fluoride administration by a dentist).

- V08 when patients have asymptomatic HIV-infection status.

- V09 when patients' infections are drug-resistant. Report category V09 codes as secondary diagnoses.

Coding Tip:

Do not report code V08 if the patient is diagnosed with AIDS (042), exposure to HIV (V01.79), or nonspecific serologic evidence of HIV (795.71).

ICD-10 Alert!

ICD-10-CM Chapter 21 contains the following blocks of codes:

- Z00–Z13 Persons encountering health services for examination and investigation
- Z14–Z15 Genetic carrier and genetic susceptibility to disease
- Z16 Resistance to antimicrobial drugs
- Z17 Estrogen receptor status
- Z18 Retained foreign body fragments
- Z20–Z28 Persons with potential health hazards related to communicable diseases
- Z30–Z39 Persons encountering health services in circumstances related to reproduction
- Z40–Z53 Encounters for other specific health care
- AZ55–Z65 Persons with potential health hazards related to socioeconomic and psychosocial circumstances
- Z66 Do not resuscitate [DNR] status
- Z67 Blood type
- Z68 Body mass index (BMI)
- Z69–Z76 Persons encountering health services in other circumstances
- Z77–Z99 Persons with potential health hazards related to family and personal history and certain conditions influencing health status

Categories V10–V19

Report codes from categories V10–V19 for people with potential health hazards related to personal and family history. Assign codes from category:

- V10–V15 when patients have a personal history of malignant neoplasm, disease, allergy, or hazard to health or having undergone certain surgeries.
- V16–V19 when patients have a family history of malignant neoplasm or other diseases/conditions.

Categories V20–V29

Report codes from categories V20–V29 for people encountering health services in circumstances related to reproduction and development. Assign codes from category:

- V20–V21 when patients are seen for well-baby or well-child office visits. If documentation supports treatment of a condition during the well-baby/child visit, report a code for the condition in addition to a code from category V20–V21.
- V22–V23 when patients are seen during pregnancy, whether normal or high-risk.
- V24 when patients are treated after having given birth.
- V25–V26 when patients are seen for contraceptive or procreative management.

Coding Tip:

- Codes from categories V10–V15 are reported when the patient's condition no longer exists.
- Verify history of codes in the tabular list before reporting. Also do not confuse personal history of with family history of codes.

-  V27 to classify outcome of delivery (on the mother's claim).
- V28 when patients are screened during pregnancy.
- V29 when newborns are observed/evaluated but no condition is diagnosed.

Coding Tip:

V27.x is never reported as the first code on the insurance claim. Codes from 650–659 are reported first.

Categories V30–V39

Report codes from categories V30–V39 for liveborn infants according to type of birth. The code is reported as the principal diagnosis *on the baby's insurance claim.* If documented, make sure you report additional codes for congenital, perinatal, and other conditions as secondary diagnoses.

Categories V40–V49

Report codes from categories V40–V49 for people with a condition influencing their health status. Assign codes from category:

- V40–V49 when patients have not been diagnosed but have conditions that influence their health status. These codes are reported when a patient has an ongoing condition that may influence health care (e.g., cardiac pacemaker, V45.01).

Categories V50–V59

Report codes from categories V50–V59 for people encountering health services for specific procedures and aftercare. Make sure you report aftercare visit codes (V51–V58) as the first-listed or principal diagnosis when the patients require care (including planned care) after treatment of an illness or injury is completed. (Do not assign V51–V58 codes for treatment of an acute illness or injury.) When reporting codes from category V56–V57, code the associated condition (e.g., renal failure) as a secondary diagnosis. Assign codes from category:

- V50 when patients undergo elective surgery. (Most payers will not provide reimbursement.)
- V51 when patients undergo plastic surgery following injury (e.g., reconstructive surgery for healed third-degree burns or a breast implant following mastectomy).
- V52–V54 when patients are fitted for a prosthesis or an implant or the device is adjusted or removed.
- V55 when patients receive attention to an artificial opening, such as colostomy cleansing.
- V56 when patients undergo dialysis and dialysis catheter care. When reporting V56.xx, code also the associated condition (e.g., renal failure).
- V57 when patients undergo rehabilitation procedures. When reporting V57.xx, code also the associated condition (e.g., dysphasia).
- V58 when patients receive other treatment or aftercare. Code V58.12 is reported for the use of drugs (e.g., high-dose interleukin 2 or IL-2) that stimulate the body's immune system to produce cancer-killing cells. (Chemotherapy administration procedure codes are also assigned.)
- V59 when an individual donates an organ or tissue. Do *not* report codes from category V59 on the organ recipient's insurance claim.

  EXAMPLE: Patient is diagnosed with breast cancer, undergoes mastectomy, and is admitted for chemotherapy. Report ICD-9-CM code V58.11 (or ICD-10-CM code Z51.11) as the first-listed diagnosis and the appropriate breast cancer code as the secondary diagnosis.

Categories V60–V69

Report codes from categories V60–V69 for people encountering health services in other circumstances. Make sure you check with the payer to determine whether services reported with codes from categories V60–V69 will be reimbursed. Assign codes from category V60–V69 when individuals are seen for reasons other than those due to illness or injury.

  EXAMPLE 1: A 5-year-old male patient was seen for an annual well-child visit, during which the provider planned to administer the Menactra meningococcal vaccine. The mother refused to allow the vaccine to be administered to her child because she had read an article about an alert being issued by government agencies that five cases of Guillain-Barré syndrome (GBS) had been diagnosed following administration of the Menactra meningococcal vaccine. Assign codes V20.2 (Routine infant or child health check) (or a code from ICD-10-CM subcategory Z00.12) and V64.05 (Vaccination not carried out because of caregiver refusal) (or a code from ICD-10-CM subcategory Z28.2). (The provider should document the vaccine refusal and reason in the patient's record.)

EXAMPLE 2: Patient pretends to be in pain so a narcotic will be prescribed, and the provider is alerted to the pretense by another provider. Assign code V65.2 (or ICD-10-CM code Z76.5)

EXAMPLE 3: Patient is admitted to the hospital for palliative care during a terminal phase of an illness. Report V66.7 (or ICD-10-CM code Z51.5) as the secondary code. Report the underlying disease process (e.g., cancer, end-stage renal disease) as the first-listed or principal diagnosis code.

 EXAMPLE 4: Patient with a history of colon cancer, removed two years ago, is seen for follow-up examination to determine whether there is recurrence. Report codes V67.09 and V10.05 (or ICD-10-CM codes Z09 and Z85.030 or Z85.038).

> **Coding Tip:**
>
> V67 follow-up examination codes are reported as the first-listed or principal diagnosis when a patient requires surveillance after treatment of an illness or injury is completed.

Categories V70–V91

Report codes from categories V70–V91 for people without reported diagnosis encountered during examination and investigation of individuals and populations. Assign codes from category:

- V70 when patients are seen for routine examination (e.g., annual physical examination). When documentation supports treatment of conditions during a routine examination, make sure you assign ICD codes as secondary diagnoses.

- V71 when patients are observed and evaluated for suspected conditions that are ruled out. Category V71 codes are reported when, after study, *a suspected condition is not found*. Therefore, before reporting a code from category V71, review the record to determine whether a sign or symptom can be coded instead. If a code from category V71 is assigned, report it as a first-listed or principal diagnosis code only.

- V72–V82 when patients undergo special investigations, examinations, or screenings.

- V83 when patients have genetic carrier status.

- V84 when patients have genetic susceptibility to disease.

- V85 when patients have their body mass index documented.

- V86 when patients have estrogen receptor status documented.

- V87 when patients have other specified personal exposure and history that presents a hazard to their health.

- V88 when patients underwent surgery to have organs or other tissue removed.

- V89 when patients have other suspected conditions not found.

- V90 when patients have a retained foreign body.

- V91 to classify multiple gestation placenta status.

EXAMPLE 1: Patient undergoes outpatient chest X-ray as part of routine physical examination. The patient has no signs or symptoms. Report code V72.5 (or ICD-10-CM code Z01.89) as the first-listed diagnosis.

EXAMPLE 2: Patient has extensive family history of ovarian cancer (e.g., mother, aunts, and sisters) (V16.41) (or ICD-10-CM code Z80.41) and elects to undergo screening as a preventive measure (V76.46) (or ICD-10-CM code Z12.73).

ICD-9-CM CHAPTER-SPECIFIC CODING GUIDELINES WITH ICD-10 ALERTS!

 ICD-10 Alert!

In ICD-10-CM, *Factors Influencing Health Status and Contact with Health Services* are located in Chapter 21, and ICD-9-CM coding guidelines with *ICD-10 Alerts!* are included below.

Supplemental Classification of Factors Influencing Health Status and Contact with Health Services (V01–V91)

 ICD-10 Alert!

Go to Appendix II located on the Premium Website to review ICD-10-CM coding guidelines in Section I.C.21., Factors Influencing Health Status and Contact with Health Services [Z00–Z99], which contain extensive revisions to the official coding guidelines.

NOTE: The chapter-specific guidelines provide additional information about the use of V codes for specified encounters.

a. Introduction

ICD-9-CM provides codes to deal with encounters for circumstances other than a disease or an injury. The Supplementary Classification of Factors Influencing Health Status and Contact with Health Services (V01.0–V91.99) is provided to deal with occasions when circumstances other than a disease or an injury (codes 001–999) are recorded as a diagnosis or problem. There are four primary circumstances for the use of V codes:

1) A person who is not currently sick encounters the health services for some specific reason, such as to act as an organ donor, to receive prophylactic care (such as inoculations or health screenings), or to receive counseling on health-related issues.

2) A person with a resolving disease or injury, or a chronic, long-term condition requiring continuous care, encounters the health care system for specific aftercare of that disease or injury (e.g., dialysis for renal disease, chemotherapy for malignancy, or a cast change). A diagnosis/symptom code should be used whenever a current, acute diagnosis is being treated or a sign or symptom is being studied.

3) Circumstances or problems influence a person's health status but are not in themselves a current illness or injury.

4) Newborns, to indicate birth status

b. V codes use in any health care setting

V codes are for use in any health care setting. V codes may be used as either a first-listed (principal diagnosis code in the inpatient setting) or secondary code, depending on the circumstances of the encounter. Certain V codes may only be used as first-listed; others, only as secondary codes.

See Section I.C.18.e, V Codes That May Only Be Principal/First-Listed Diagnosis.

c. V codes indicate a reason for an encounter

They are not procedure codes. A corresponding procedure code must accompany a V code to describe the procedure performed.

d. Categories of V codes

1) Contact/Exposure

Category V01 indicates contact with or exposure to communicable diseases. These codes are for patients who do not show any sign or symptom of a disease but have been exposed to it by close personal contact with an infected individual or are in an area where a disease is epidemic. These codes may be used as a first-listed code to explain an encounter for testing, or, more commonly, as a secondary code to identify a potential risk.

Codes V15.84–V15.86 describe contact with or (suspected) exposure to asbestos, potentially hazardous body fluids, and lead.

Subcategories V87.0–V87.3 describe contact with or (suspected) exposure to hazardous metals, aromatic compounds, other potentially hazardous chemicals, and other potentially hazardous substances.

2) Inoculations and vaccinations

Categories V03–V06 are for encounters for inoculations and vaccinations. They indicate that a patient is being seen to receive a prophylactic inoculation against a disease. The injection itself must be represented by the appropriate procedure code. A code from V03–V06 may be used as a secondary code if the inoculation is given as a routine part of preventive health care, such as a well-baby visit.

3) Status

Status codes indicate that a patient is either a carrier of a disease, has the sequela or residual of a past disease or condition, or has another factor influencing a person's health status. This includes things such as the presence of prosthetic or mechanical devices resulting from past treatment. A status code is informative because the status may affect the course of treatment and its outcome. A status code is distinct from a history code. The history code indicates that the patient no longer has the condition.

A status code should not be used with a diagnosis code from one of the body system chapters *if the diagnosis code includes the information provided by the status code*. For example, code V42.1, Heart transplant status, should not be used with code 996.83, Complications of transplanted heart. The status code does not provide additional information about complications the patient experienced. The complication code indicates that the patient is a heart transplant patient.

The status V codes/categories are:

V02	Carrier or suspected carrier of infectious diseases
	Carrier status indicates that a person harbors the specific organisms of a disease without manifest symptoms and is capable of transmitting the infection.
V07.5X	Use of agents affecting estrogen receptors and estrogen level
	This code indicates when a patient is receiving a drug that affects estrogen receptors and estrogen levels for prevention of cancer
V08	Asymptomatic HIV infection status
	This code indicates that a patient has tested positive for HIV but has manifested no signs or symptoms of the disease.
V09	Infection with drug-resistant microorganisms
	This category indicates that a patient has an infection that is resistant to drug treatment. Sequence the infection code first.
V21	Constitutional states in development
V22.2	Pregnant state, incidental
	This code is a secondary code only for use when the pregnancy is in no way complicating the reason for visit. Otherwise, a code from the obstetric chapter is required.
V26.5x	Sterilization status
V42	Organ or tissue replaced by transplant
V43	Organ or tissue replaced by other means
V44	Artificial opening status
V45	Other postsurgical states
	Assign code V45.87, Transplant organ removal status, to indicate that a transplanted organ has been previously removed. This code should not be assigned for the encounter in which the transplanted organ is removed. The complication necessitating removal of the transplant organ should be assigned for that encounter.

(continues)

ICD-9-CM CHAPTER-SPECIFIC CODING GUIDELINES WITH ICD-10 ALERTS! (continued)

See Section 17.f.2. for information on the coding of organ transplant complications.

Assign code V45.88, Status post administration of tPA (rtPA) in a different facility within the last 24 hours prior to admission to the current facility, as a secondary diagnosis when a patient is received by transfer into a facility and documentation indicates they were administered tissue plasminogen activator (tPA) within the last 24 hours prior to admission to the current facility.

This guideline applies even if the patient is still receiving the tPA at the time he or she are received into the current facility.

The appropriate code for the condition for which the tPA was administered (such as cerebrovascular disease or myocardial infarction) should be assigned first.

Code V45.88 is applicable only to the receiving facility record and not to the transferring facility record.

V46	Other dependence on machines
V49.6	Upper limb amputation status
V49.7	Lower limb amputation status

NOTE: Categories V42–V46, and subcategories V49.6, V49.7 are for use only if there are no complications or malfunctions of the organ or tissue replaced, the amputation site, or the equipment on which the patient is dependent.

V49.81	Asymptomatic postmenopausal status (age-related) (natural)
V49.82	Dental sealant status
V49.83	Awaiting organ transplant status
V49.86	Do not resuscitate status

This code may be used when it is documented by the provider that a patient is on do not resuscitate status at any time during the stay.

V49.87   Physical restraint status

This code may be used when it is documented by the provider that a patient has been put in restraints during the current encounter. Please note that this code should not be reported when it is documented by the provider that a patient is temporarily restrained during a procedure.

V58.6x   Long-term (current) drug use

Codes from this subcategory indicate a patient's continuous use of a prescribed drug (including such things as aspirin therapy) for the long-term treatment of a condition or for prophylactic use. It is not for use for patients who have addictions to drugs.

This subcategory is not for use of medications for detoxification or maintenance programs to prevent withdrawal symptoms in patients with drug dependence (e.g., methadone maintenance for opiate dependence). Assign the appropriate code for the drug dependence instead.

Assign a code from subcategory V58.6, Long-term (current) drug use, if the patient is receiving a medication for an extended period as a prophylactic measure (such as for the prevention of deep vein thrombosis) or as treatment of a chronic condition (such as arthritis) or a disease requiring a lengthy course of treatment (such as cancer). Do not assign a code from subcategory V58.6 for medication being administered for a brief period of time to treat an acute illness or injury (such as a course of antibiotics to treat acute bronchitis).

V83   Genetic carrier status

Genetic carrier status indicates that a person carries a gene associated with a particular disease, which may be passed to offspring who may develop that disease. The person does not have the disease and is not at risk of developing the disease.

V84   Genetic susceptibility status

Genetic susceptibility indicates that a person has a gene that increases the risk of that person developing the disease.

Codes from category V84, Genetic susceptibility to disease, should not be used as principal or first-listed codes. If the patient has the condition to which he/she is susceptible, and that condition is the reason for the encounter, the code for the current condition should be sequenced first. If the patient is being seen for follow-up after completed treatment for this condition, and the condition no longer exists, a follow-up code should be sequenced first, followed by the appropriate personal history and genetic susceptibility codes. If the purpose of the encounter is genetic counseling associated with procreative management, a code from subcategory V26.3, Genetic counseling and testing, should be assigned as the first-listed code, followed by a code from category V84.

Additional codes should be assigned for any applicable family or personal history. *See Section I.C.18.d.14. for information on prophylactic organ removal due to a genetic susceptibility.*

V86   Estrogen receptor status
V88   Acquired absence of other organs and tissue
V90   Retained foreign body

4) History (of)

There are two types of history V codes, personal and family. Personal history codes explain a patient's past medical condition that no longer exists and is not receiving any treatment but that has the potential for recurrence and, therefore, may require continued monitoring. The exceptions to this general rule are category V14, Personal history of allergy to medicinal agents, and subcategory V15.0, Allergy, other than to medicinal agents. A person who has had an allergic episode to a substance or food in the past should always be considered allergic to the substance.

Family history codes are for use when a patient has a family member who has had a particular disease that causes the patient to be at higher risk of also contracting the disease.

Personal history codes may be used in conjunction with follow-up codes and family history codes may be used in conjunction with screening codes to explain the need for a test or procedure. History codes are also acceptable on any medical record regardless of the reason for visit. A history of an illness, even if no longer present, is important information that may alter the type of treatment ordered.

The history V code categories are:

V10   Personal history of malignant neoplasm
V12   Personal history of certain other diseases
V13   Personal history of other diseases

Except: V13.4, Personal history of arthritis, and subcategory V13.6, Personal history of congenital (corrected) malformations. These conditions are lifelong, so they are not true history codes.

V14   Personal history of allergy to medicinal agents
V15   Other personal history presenting hazards to health

Except: V15.7, Personal history of contraception; ; V15.84, Contact with and (suspected) exposure to asbestos; V15.85, Contact with and (suspected) exposure to potentially hazardous body fluids; V15.86, Contact with and (suspected) exposure to lead.

V16   Family history of malignant neoplasm
V17   Family history of certain chronic disabling diseases
V18   Family history of certain other specific diseases
V19   Family history of other conditions
V87   Other specified personal exposures and history presenting hazards to health

(continues)

ICD-9-CM CHAPTER-SPECIFIC CODING GUIDELINES WITH ICD-10 ALERTS! (*continued*)

Except: Subcategories V87.0, Contact with and (suspected) exposure to hazardous metals; V87.1, Contact with and (suspected) exposure to hazardous aromatic compounds; V87.2, Contact with and (suspected) exposure to other potentially hazardous chemicals; and V87.3, Contact with and (suspected) exposure to other potentially hazardous substances.

5) **Screening**

Screening is the testing for disease or disease precursors in seemingly well individuals so that early detection and treatment can be provided for those who test positive for the disease. Screenings that are recommended for many subgroups in a population include: routine mammograms for women over 40, a fecal occult blood test for everyone over 50, an amniocentesis to rule out a fetal anomaly for pregnant women over 35, because the incidence of breast cancer and colon cancer in these subgroups is higher than in the general population, as is the incidence of Down syndrome in older mothers.

The testing of a person to rule out or confirm a suspected diagnosis because the patient has some sign or symptom is a diagnostic examination, not a screening. In these cases, the sign or symptom is used to explain the reason for the test.

A screening code may be a first-listed code if the reason for the visit is specifically the screening exam. It may also be used as an additional code if the screening is done during an office visit for other health problems. A screening code is not necessary if the screening is inherent to a routine examination, such as a Pap smear done during a routine pelvic examination.

Should a condition be discovered during the screening, the code for the condition may be assigned as an additional diagnosis.

The V code indicates that a screening exam is planned. A procedure code is required to confirm that the screening was performed.

The screening V code categories:

V28	Antenatal screening
V73–V82	Special screening examinations

6) **Observation**

There are three observation V code categories. They are for use in very limited circumstances when a person is being observed for a suspected condition that is ruled out. The observation codes are not for use if an injury or illness or any signs or symptoms related to the suspected condition are present. In such cases, the diagnosis/symptom code is used with the corresponding E code to identify any external cause.

The observation codes are to be used as principal diagnosis only. The only exception to this is when the principal diagnosis is required to be a code from the V30, Liveborn infant, category. Then the V29 observation code is sequenced after the V30 code. Additional codes may be used in addition to the observation code but only if they are unrelated to the suspected condition being observed.

Codes from subcategory V89.0, Suspected maternal and fetal conditions not found, may be used either as a first listed or as an additional code assignment depending on the case. They are for use in very limited circumstances on a maternal record when an encounter is for a suspected maternal or fetal condition that is ruled out during that encounter (for example, a maternal or fetal condition may be suspected due to an abnormal test result). These codes should not be used when the condition is confirmed. In those cases, the confirmed condition should be coded. In addition, these codes are not for use if an illness or any signs or symptoms related to the suspected condition or problem are present. In such cases the diagnosis/symptom code is used.

Additional codes may be used in addition to the code from subcategory V89.0, but only if they are unrelated to the suspected condition being evaluated.

Codes from subcategory V89.0 may not be used for encounters for antenatal screening of mother. *See Section I.C.18.d, Screening.*

For encounters for suspected fetal condition that are inconclusive following testing and evaluation, assign the appropriate code from category 655, 656, 657 or 658.

The observation V code categories:

V29	Observation and evaluation of newborns for suspected condition not found
	For the birth encounter, a code from category V30 should be sequenced before the V29 code.
V71	Observation and evaluation for suspected condition not found
V89	Suspected maternal and fetal conditions not found

7) Aftercare

Aftercare visit codes cover situations when the initial treatment of a disease or an injury has been performed and the patient requires continued care during the healing or recovery phase, or for the long-term consequences of the disease. The aftercare V code should not be used if treatment is directed at a current, acute disease or injury; the diagnosis code is to be used in these cases. Exceptions to this rule are codes V58.0, Radiotherapy, and codes from subcategory V58.1, Encounter for chemotherapy and immunotherapy for neoplastic conditions. These codes are to be first-listed, followed by the diagnosis code when a patient's encounter is solely to receive radiation therapy or chemotherapy for the treatment of a neoplasm. Should a patient receive both chemotherapy and radiation therapy during the same encounter, code V58.0 and V58.1 may be used together on a record with either one being sequenced first.

The aftercare codes are generally first-listed to explain the specific reason for the encounter. An aftercare code may be used as an additional code when some type of aftercare is provided in addition to the reason for admission and no diagnosis code is applicable. An example of this would be the closure of a colostomy during an encounter for treatment of another condition.

Aftercare codes should be used in conjunction with any other aftercare codes or other diagnosis codes to provide better detail on the specifics of an aftercare encounter visit, unless otherwise directed by the classification. The sequencing of multiple aftercare codes is discretionary.

Certain aftercare V code categories need a secondary diagnosis code to describe the resolving condition or sequela; for others, the condition is inherent in the code title.

Additional V code aftercare category terms include fitting and adjustment and attention to artificial openings.

Status V codes may be used with aftercare V codes to indicate the nature of the aftercare. For example, code V45.81, Aortocoronary bypass status, may be used with code V58.73, Aftercare following surgery of the circulatory system, NEC, to indicate the surgery for which the aftercare is being performed. Also, a transplant status code may be used following code V58.44, Aftercare following organ transplant, to identify the organ transplanted. A status code should not be used when the aftercare code indicates the type of status, such as using V55.0, Attention to tracheostomy with V44.0, Tracheostomy status.

The aftercare V category/codes:

V51.0	Encounter for breast reconstruction following mastectomy
V52	Fitting and adjustment of prosthetic device and implant
V53	Fitting and adjustment of other device
V54	Other orthopedic aftercare
V55	Attention to artificial openings
V56	Encounter for dialysis and dialysis catheter care
V57	Care involving the use of rehabilitation procedures
V58.0	Radiotherapy
V58.11	Encounter for antineoplastic chemotherapy
V58.12	Encounter for antineoplastic immunotherapy
V58.3x	Attention to dressings and sutures
V58.41	Encounter for planned postoperative wound closure
V58.42	Aftercare, surgery, neoplasm
V58.43	Aftercare, surgery, trauma
V58.44	Aftercare involving organ transplant

(continues)

ICD-9-CM CHAPTER-SPECIFIC CODING GUIDELINES WITH ICD-10 ALERTS! (*continued*)

V58.49	Other specified aftercare following surgery
V58.7x	Aftercare following surgery
V58.81	Fitting and adjustment of vascular catheter
V58.82	Fitting and adjustment of nonvascular catheter
V58.83	Monitoring therapeutic drug
V58.89	Other specified aftercare

8) Follow-up

The follow-up codes are used to explain continuing surveillance following completed treatment of a disease, condition, or injury. They imply that the condition has been fully treated and no longer exists. They should not be confused with aftercare codes that explain current treatment for a healing condition or its sequela. Follow-up codes may be used in conjunction with history codes to provide the full picture of the healed condition and its treatment. The follow-up code is sequenced first, followed by the history code.

A follow-up code may be used to explain repeated visits. Should a condition be found to have recurred on the follow-up visit, the diagnosis code should be used in place of the follow-up code.

The follow-up V code categories:

V24	Postpartum care and evaluation
V67	Follow-up examination

9) Donor

Category V59 is the donor codes. They are used for living individuals who are donating blood or other body tissue. These codes are only for individuals donating for others, not for self-donations. They are not for use to identify cadaveric donations.

10) Counseling

Counseling V codes are used when a patient or family member receives assistance in the aftermath of an illness or injury, or when support is required in coping with family or social problems. They are not necessary for use in conjunction with a diagnosis code when the counseling component of care is considered integral to standard treatment.

The counseling V categories/codes:

V25.0	General counseling and advice for contraceptive management
V26.3	Genetic counseling
V26.4	General counseling and advice for procreative management
V61.x	Other family circumstances
V65.1	Person consulted on behalf of another person
V65.3	Dietary surveillance and counseling
V65.4	Other counseling, not elsewhere classified

11) Obstetrics and related conditions

See ICD-9-CM Chapter 11–Obstetrics coding guidelines for further instruction on the use of these codes.

V codes for pregnancy are for use in those circumstances when none of the problems or complications included in the codes from the Obstetrics chapter exist (a routine prenatal visit or postpartum care). Codes V22.0, Supervision of normal first pregnancy, and V22.1, Supervision of other normal pregnancy, are always first-listed and are not to be used with any other code from the OB chapter.

The outcome of delivery, category V27, should be included on all maternal delivery records. It is always a secondary code.

V codes for family planning (contraceptive) or procreative management and counseling should be included on an obstetric record either during the pregnancy or the postpartum stage, if applicable.

Obstetrics and related conditions V code categories:

V22	Normal pregnancy

V23	Supervision of high-risk pregnancy
	Except: V23.2, Pregnancy with history of abortion. Code 646.3, Habitual aborter, from the OB chapter is required to indicate a history of abortion during a pregnancy.
V24	Postpartum care and evaluation
V25	Encounter for contraceptive management
	Except V25.0x (*See Section I.C.18.d.11, Counseling coding guidelines.*)
V26	Procreative management
	Except V26.5x, Sterilization status, V26.3 and V26.4 (*See Section I.C.18.d.11, Counseling.*)
V27	Outcome of delivery
V28	Antenatal screening (*See Section I.C.18.d.6, Screening.*)
V91	Multiple gestation placenta status

12) Newborn, infant, and child

See ICD-9-CM Chapter 15 Newborn (Perinatal) coding guidelines for further instruction on the use of these codes.

Newborn V code categories:

V20	Health supervision of infant or child
V29	Observation and evaluation of newborns for suspected condition not found (*See Section I.C.18.d.7, Observation.*)
V30–V39	Liveborn infant according to type of birth

13) Routine and administrative examinations

The V codes allow for the description of encounters for routine examinations, such as a general checkup, or examinations for administrative purposes, such as a pre-employment physical. The codes are for use as first-listed codes only and are not to be used if the examination is for diagnosis of a suspected condition or for treatment purposes. In such cases, the diagnosis code is used. During a routine exam, should a diagnosis or condition be discovered, it should be coded as an additional code. Preexisting and chronic conditions and history codes may also be included as additional codes as long as the examination is for administrative purposes and not focused on any particular condition.

Preoperative examination and pre-procedural laboratory examination V codes are for use only in those situations when a patient is being cleared for a procedure or surgery and no treatment is given.

The V codes categories/code for routine and administrative examinations:

V20.2	Routine infant or child health check
	Any injections given should have a corresponding procedure code.
V70	General medical examination
V72	Special investigations and examinations

Codes V72.5 and V72.62 may be used if the reason for the patient encounter is for routine laboratory/radiology testing in the absence of any signs, symptoms, or associated diagnosis. If routine testing is performed during the same encounter as a test to evaluate a sign, symptom, or diagnosis, it is appropriate to assign both the V code and the code describing the reason for the nonroutine test.

14) Miscellaneous V codes

The miscellaneous V codes capture a number of other health care encounters that do not fall into one of the other categories. Some of these codes identify the reason for the encounter, others are for use as additional codes that provide useful information on circumstances that may affect a patient's care and treatment.

Prophylactic organ removal

For encounters specifically for prophylactic removal of breasts, ovaries, or another organ due to a genetic susceptibility to cancer or a family history of cancer, the principal or first-listed code should be a code from subcategory V50.4, Prophylactic organ removal, followed by the appropriate genetic susceptibility code and the appropriate family history code. If the patient has a malignancy of one site and is having prophylactic removal at another site to prevent either a new primary malignancy or metastatic

(*continues*)

ICD-9-CM CHAPTER-SPECIFIC CODING GUIDELINES WITH ICD-10 ALERTS! (*continued*)

disease, a code for the malignancy should also be assigned in addition to a code from subcategory V50.4. A V50.4 code should not be assigned if the patient is having organ removal for treatment of a malignancy, such as the removal of the testes for the treatment of prostate cancer.

Miscellaneous V code categories/codes:

V07	Need for isolation and other prophylactic or treatment measures
	Except V07.5 Use of agents affecting estrogen receptors and estrogen levels
V50	Elective surgery for purposes other than remedying health states
V40.31	Wandering in diseases classified elsewhere
V58.5	Orthodontics
V60	Housing, household, and economic circumstances
V62	Other psychosocial circumstances
V63	Unavailability of other medical facilities for care
V64	Persons encountering health services for specific procedures, not carried out
V66	Convalescence and palliative care
V68	Encounters for administrative purposes
V69	Problems related to lifestyle

15) Nonspecific V codes

Certain V codes are so nonspecific, or potentially redundant with other codes in the classification, that there can be little justification for their use in the inpatient setting. Their use in the outpatient setting should be limited to those instances when there is no further documentation to permit more precise coding. Otherwise, any sign or symptom or any other reason for visit that is captured in another code should be used.

Nonspecific V code categories/codes:

V11	Personal history of mental disorder
	A code from the mental disorders chapter, with an in remission fifth digit, should be used.
V13.4	Personal history of arthritis
V13.6	Personal history of congenital malformations
V15.7	Personal history of contraception
V23.2	Pregnancy with history of abortion
V40	Mental and behavioral problems
	Exception: V40.31 Wandering in diseases classified elsewhere
V41	Problems with special senses and other special functions
V47	Other problems with internal organs
V48	Problems with head, neck, and trunk
V49	Problems with limbs and other problems

	Exceptions:	V49.6	Upper limb amputation status
		V49.7	Lower limb amputation status
		V49.81	Asymptomatic postmenopausal status (age-related) (natural)
		V49.82	Dental sealant status
		V49.83	Awaiting organ transplant status
		V49.86	Do not resuscitate status
		V49.87	Physical restraints status

V51.8	Other aftercare involving the use of plastic surgery
V58.2	Blood transfusion, without reported diagnosis
V58.9	Unspecified aftercare

See Sections IV.K and IV.L of the Outpatient coding guidelines.

e. V Codes That May Only Be Principal/First-Listed Diagnosis

The list of V codes/categories below may only be reported as the principal/first-listed diagnosis, except when there are multiple encounters on the same day and the medical records for the encounters are combined or when there is more than one V code that meets the definition of principal diagnosis (e.g., a patient is admitted to home healthcare for both aftercare and rehabilitation and they equally meet the definition of principal diagnosis). These codes should not be reported if they do not meet the definition of principal or first-listed diagnosis.

See Section II and Section IV.A for information on selection of principal and first-listed diagnosis.

See Section II.C for information on two or more diagnoses that equally meet the definition for principal diagnosis.

V20.x	Health supervision of infant or child
V22.0	Supervision of normal first pregnancy
V22.1	Supervision of other normal pregnancy
V24.x	Postpartum care and examination
V26.81	Encounter for assisted reproductive fertility procedure cycle
V26.82	Encounter for fertility preservation procedure
V30.x	Single liveborn
V31.x	Twin, mate liveborn
V32.x	Twin, mate stillborn
V33.x	Twin, unspecified
V34.x	Other multiple, mates all liveborn
V35.x	Other multiple, mates all stillborn
V36.x	Other multiple, mates live- and stillborn
V37.x	Other multiple, unspecified
V39.x	Unspecified
V46.12	Encounter for respirator dependence during power failure
V46.13	Encounter for weaning from respirator [ventilator]
V51.0	Encounter for breast reconstruction following mastectomy
V56.0	Extracorporeal dialysis
V57.x	Care involving use of rehabilitation procedures
V58.0	Radiotherapy
V58.11	Encounter for antineoplastic chemotherapy
V58.12	Encounter for antineoplastic immunotherapy
V59.x	Donors
V66.0	Convalescence and palliative care following surgery
V66.1	Convalescence and palliative care following radiotherapy
V66.2	Convalescence and palliative care following chemotherapy
V66.3	Convalescence and palliative care following psychotherapy and other treatment for mental disorder
V66.4	Convalescence and palliative care following treatment of fracture
V66.5	Convalescence and palliative care following other treatment
V66.6	Convalescence and palliative care following combined treatment
V66.9	Unspecified convalescence
V68.x	Encounters for administrative purposes
V70.0	Routine general medical examination at a health care facility
V70.1	General psychiatric examination, requested by the authority
V70.2	General psychiatric examination, other and unspecified
V70.3	Other medical examination for administrative purposes
V70.4	Examination for medicolegal reasons
V70.5	Health examination of defined subpopulations
V70.6	Health examination in population surveys
V70.8	Other specified general medical examinations
V70.9	Unspecified general medical examination
V71.x	Observation and evaluation for suspected conditions not found

Exercise 4.20 – Factors Influencing Health Status and Contact with Health Services

Instructions: Underline the main term in each diagnosis statement and assign the appropriate ICD-9-CM and ICD-10-CM code(s).

ICD-9-CM   ICD-10-CM

_____   _____   **1.** Bone marrow donor

_____   _____   **2.** Chemotherapy encounter

_____   _____   **3.** Examination for summer camp

_____   _____   **4.** Exposure to smallpox

_____   _____   **5.** Family history of stroke

ICD-9-CM Supplemental Classification of External Causes of Injury and Poisoning (E000–E999)

Supplemental Classification of External Causes of Injury and Poisoning (E000–E999) classifies environmental events, circumstances, and conditions as the cause of injury, poisoning, and other adverse effects. When an E code is assigned, it is reported in addition to a code from ICD-9-CM Chapters 1–17 to indicate the nature of the condition. Certain other conditions that may be stated due to external causes are also classified in ICD-9-CM Chapters 1–17. For these, the E code is assigned as an additional code to provide more detail.

ICD-10 Alert!

In ICD-10-CM, *External Causes of Morbidity (V00–Y99)* are located in Chapter 21.

Coding Tip:

- Refer to ICD-9-CM Index to External Causes (or ICD-10-CM Index to External Causes) main terms to begin the process of assigning an E code. Common main terms include:
  - Accident
  - Effect(s) (adverse) of
  - Injury, injured
  - Misadventure(s) to patient(s) during surgical or medical care
- The list of 3-digit categories in the Supplementary Classification of External Causes of Injury and Poisoning section of Appendix E (List of Three-Digit Categories, located after the ICD-9-CM Tabular List of Diseases) can also prove helpful in locating main terms in the Index to External Causes.
- Before assigning an E code (or ICD-10-CM Z code), review the notes located at the beginning of the Supplementary Classification of External Causes of Injury and Poisoning in the ICD-9-CM Tabular List of Diseases (or Chapter 21 in ICD-10-CM).

Machinery Accidents (E919)

Machinery accidents (other than those connected with transport) are classifiable to category E919, in which the fourth digit allows a broad classification of the type of machinery involved. If a more detailed classification of type

ICD-10 Alert!

In ICD-10-CM, the following blocks of codes are located in Chapter 21, *External Causes of Morbidity (V00–Y99):*

- V00–X58 (Accidents)
- V00–V99 (Transport accidents)
- V00–V09 (Pedestrian injured in transport accident)
- V10–V19 (Pedal cyclist injured in transport accident)
- V20–V29 (Motorcycle rider injured in transport accident)
- V30–V39 (Occupant of three-wheeled motor vehicle injured in transport accident)
- V40–V49 (Car occupant injured in transport accident)
- V50–V59 (Occupant of pick-up truck or van injured in transport accident)
- V60–V69 (Occupant of heavy transport vehicle injured in transport accident)
- V70–V79 (Bus occupant injured in transport accident)
- V80–V89 (Other land transport accidents)
- V90–V94 (Water transport accidents)
- V95–V97 (Air and space transport accidents)
- V98–V99 (Other and unspecified transport accidents)
- W00–X58 (Other external causes of accidental injury)
- W00–W19 (Slipping, tripping, stumbling, and falls)
- W20–W49 (Exposure to inanimate mechanical forces)
- W50–W64 (Exposure to animate mechanical forces)
- W65–W74 (Accidental non-transport drowning and submersion)
- W85–W99 (Exposure to electric current, radiation, and extreme ambient air temperature and pressure)
- X00–X08 (Exposure to smoke, fire, and flames)
- X10–X19 (Contact with heat and hot substances)
- X30–X39 (Exposure to forces of nature)
- X52, X58 (Accidental exposure to other specified factors)
- X71–X83 (Intentional self-harm)
- X92–Y08 (Assault)
- Y21–Y33 (Event of undetermined intent)
- Y35–Y38 (Legal intervention, operations of war, military operations, and terrorism)
- Y62–Y84 (Complications of medical and surgical care)
- Y62–Y69 (Misadventures to patients during surgical and medical care)
- Y70–Y82 (Medical devices associated with adverse incidents in diagnostic and therapeutic use)
- Y83–Y84 (Surgical and other medical procedures as the cause of abnormal reaction of the patient, or of later complication, without mention of misadventure at the time of the procedure)
- Y90–Y99 (Supplementary factors related to causes of morbidity classified elsewhere)

of machinery is required, refer to the "Classification of Industrial Accidents according to Agency," which is prepared by the International Labor Office and is located in Appendix D of the ICD-9-CM coding manual.

Late Effects of Accidents and Other External Causes (E929, E959, E969, E977, E989, and E999)

A *late effect* is a condition reported as such or sequelae that may occur any time after the injury. An E code is reported in addition to the condition code (from ICD-9-CM Chapters 1–17) to indicate late effect status. Category codes for late effects of injuries include:

- Late effects of accidental injury (E929).
- Late effects of self-inflicted injury (E959).
- Late effects of injury purposely inflicted by other person (E969).

- Late effects of injuries due to legal intervention (E977).

- Late effects of injury, undetermined whether accidentally or purposely inflicted (E989).

- Late effect of injury due to war operations and terrorism (E999).

Transport Accidents (E800–E848)

A **transport accident** (E800–E848) is any accident involving a device designed primarily for, or being used at the time primarily for, conveying people or goods from one place to another. When classifying transport accidents that involve more than one method of transport, report codes in the following order of precedence:

- Aircraft and spacecraft (E840–E845)
- Railway (E800–E807)
- Watercraft (E830–E838)
- Other road vehicles (E826–E829)
- Motor vehicles (E810–E825)

Accidents that involve agricultural and construction machines (e.g., tractors, cranes, and bulldozers) are regarded as transport accidents only when these vehicles are under their own power on a highway. Otherwise, the vehicles are regarded as machinery. Vehicles that can travel on land *or* water (e.g., hovercraft and other amphibious vehicles) are regarded as watercraft when on the water, as motor vehicles when on the highway, and as off-road motor vehicles when on land but off the highway.

A **railway accident** is a transport accident involving a railway train or another railway vehicle operated on rails, whether in motion or not. Excluded from this rule are accidents that occur in railway repair shops, in railway roundhouses, or on turntables, or on railway premises, but not involving a train or another railway vehicle. A **railway train** (or **railway vehicle**) is any device with or without cars coupled to it that is designed for traffic on a railway. Railway trains and vehicles include: interurban electric cars (operated chiefly on its own right-of-way, not open to other traffic), interurban streetcars (operated chiefly on its own right-of-way, not open to other traffic), railway trains (any power, such as diesel, electric, or steam), funiculars, monorails or two-rails (subterranean or elevated), and other vehicles designed to run on a railway track. (Excluded from this rule are interurban electric cars (e.g., streetcars) specified to be operating on a right-of-way that forms part of the public street or highway.) A **railway** (or **railroad**) is a right-of-way designed for traffic on rails that is used by carriages or wagons transporting passengers or freight and by other rolling stock and that is not open to other public vehicular traffic.

A **motor vehicle accident** is a transport accident involving a motor vehicle, and it is classified as a motor vehicle traffic accident or as a motor vehicle nontraffic accident according to whether the accident occurs on a public highway or elsewhere. Excluded from this rule are injuries or damages due to cataclysm and the time when a motor vehicle, not under its own power, is being loaded on or unloaded from another conveyance. A **motor vehicle traffic accident** is any motor vehicle accident occurring on a public highway (e.g., originating, terminating, or involving a vehicle partially on the highway). A motor vehicle accident is assumed to have occurred on the highway unless another place is specified, except in the case of accidents involving only off-road motor vehicles, which are classified as nontraffic accidents unless the contrary is stated. A **motor vehicle nontraffic accident** is any motor vehicle accident that occurs entirely in any place other than a public highway.

A **public highway** (**trafficway**) or street is the entire width between property lines (or other boundary lines) of every way or place of which any part is open to the use of the public for purposes of vehicular traffic as a matter of right or custom. A **roadway** is that part of the public highway designed, improved, and ordinarily used for vehicular travel. Public highway and roadway E codes include approaches (public) to docks, public buildings, and stations. (The following are not classified as public highways and roadways: private driveways; parking lots; ramps; and roads on airfields, farms, industrial premises, mines, private grounds, and quarries.)

A **motor vehicle** is any mechanically or electrically powered device not operated on rails upon which any person or property may be transported or drawn upon a highway. Any object such as a trailer, coaster, sled, or wagon being towed by a motor vehicle is considered a part of the motor vehicle. Motor vehicles and objects include automobiles (any type); buses; construction machinery, farm and industrial machinery, steam roller, tractor, army tank, highway grader, or similar vehicle on wheels or treads while in transport under own power; fire engines (motorized); motorcycles; motorized bicycles (mopeds) or scooters; trolley buses not operating on rails; trucks; and vans. The following devices are not considered motor vehicles because they are used solely to move people or materials within the confines of a building and its premises: building elevators, coal cars in a mine, electric baggage or mail trucks used solely within a railroad station, electric trucks used solely within an industrial plant, and moving overhead cranes.

A **motorcycle** is a two-wheeled motor vehicle having one or two riding saddles and sometimes having a third wheel for the support of a sidecar. The sidecar is considered part of the motorcycle. The following motorized vehicles are also classified by ICD-9-CM as motorcycles: motorized bicycles, mopeds, scooters, and tricycles.

An **off-road motor vehicle** is a motor vehicle of special design that enables it to negotiate rough or soft terrain or snow. Special design includes high construction, special wheels and tires, driven by treads, or support on a cushion of air. The following are classified by ICD-9-CM as off-road motor vehicles: all-terrain vehicles (ATVs), army tanks, hovercrafts (on land or swamp), and snowmobiles.

A **driver** of a motor vehicle is the occupant of the motor vehicle operating it or intending to operate it. A **motorcyclist** is the driver of a motorcycle. Other authorized occupants of a motor vehicle are **passengers**.

An **other road vehicle** is any device (except a motor vehicle and pedestrian conveyance) in, on, or by which any person or property may be transported on a highway. Examples include animals carrying a person or goods, animal-drawn vehicles, animals harnessed to conveyances, bicycles (pedal cycle), streetcars, and tricycles (pedal).

A **streetcar** is a device that is designed and used primarily for transporting people within a municipality, that runs on rails, that is usually subject to normal traffic control signals, and that operates principally on a right-of-way that forms part of the traffic way. A trailer being towed by a streetcar is considered a part of the streetcar. Examples include interurban or intraurban electric car or streetcar when specified to be operating on a street or public highway, trams, and trolleys.

A **pedal cycle** is any road transport vehicle operated solely by pedals that includes bicycles, pedal cycles, and tricycles. A **pedal cyclist** is any person riding on a pedal cycle or in a sidecar attached to such a vehicle.

Note:

A pedal cycle is not a motorized bicycle.

A **pedestrian conveyance** is any human-powered device by which a pedestrian may move other than by walking or by which a walking person may move another pedestrian. Examples include baby carriages, coaster wagons, ice skates, perambulators, pushcarts, pushchairs, roller skates, scooters, skateboards, skis, sleds, and wheelchairs. A **pedestrian** is any person involved in an accident who was not at the time of the accident riding in or on a motor vehicle, railroad train, streetcar, or animal-drawn or other vehicle or on a bicycle or animal. Examples include a person changing the tire of vehicle, being in or operating a pedestrian conveyance, or making an adjustment to the motor vehicle on foot.

A **watercraft** is any device for transporting passengers or goods on the water. A **small boat** is any watercraft propelled by paddle, oars, or small motor, with a passenger capacity of fewer than ten. Examples of small boats include canoes, cobles, dinghies, punts, rafts, rowboats, rowing shells, sculls, skiffs, and small motorboats. (Small boats exclude barges, lifeboats used after abandoning ship, rafts anchored and/or being used as a diving platform, and yachts.)

An **aircraft** is any device for transporting passengers or goods in the air and includes airplanes, balloons, bombers, dirigibles, (hang) gliders, military aircraft, and parachutes. A **commercial transport aircraft** is any device for collective passenger or freight transportation by air, whether run on commercial lines for profit or by government authorities, with the exception of military craft.

Terrorism

Category E979 terrorism codes are assigned as secondary codes when patients sustain injuries resulting from the unlawful use of force or violence for the purpose of intimidating or coercing a government, the civilian population, or any segment thereof in furtherance of political or social objectives. Code E979.9 is assigned for the secondary effects of terrorism (e.g., post-traumatic stress disorder, which patients often exhibit after the initial terrorist attack).

Coding Tip:

Code E999.1 is assigned as a secondary code for the late effect of an injury due to terrorism. A late effect is the residual effect of the injury. For example, paralysis is the late effect of severing of the spinal cord due to a bomb blast.

ICD-9-CM CHAPTER-SPECIFIC CODING GUIDELINES WITH ICD-10 ALERTS!

 ICD-10 Alert!

In ICD-10-CM, External Causes of Morbidity *are located in Chapter 21, and ICD-9-CM coding guidelines with ICD-10 Alerts! are included below.*

Supplemental Classification of External Causes of Injury and Poisoning (E800–E999)

These guidelines are provided for those who are currently collecting E codes in order that there be standardization in the process. If your institution plans to begin collecting E codes, these guidelines are to be applied. The use of E codes is supplemental to the application of ICD-9-CM diagnosis codes. E codes are never to be recorded as principal diagnoses (first-listed in non-inpatient setting) and are not required for reporting to the Centers for Medicare and Medicaid Services (CMS).

External causes of injury and poisoning codes (categories E000 and E800–E999) are intended to provide data for injury research and evaluation of injury prevention strategies. Activity codes (categories E001–E030) are intended to be used to describe the activity of a person seeking care for injuries as well as other health conditions, when the injury or other health condition resulted from an activity or the activity contributed to a condition.

ICD-10 Alert!

Go to Appendix II located on the Premium Website to review ICD-10-CM coding guidelines in Section I.C.20., which contains revised official coding guidelines for external causes of morbidity.

E codes capture how the injury, poisoning, or adverse effect happened (cause), the intent (unintentional or accidental; or intentional, such as suicide or assault), the person's status (e.g. civilian, military), the associated activity and the place where the event occurred.

Some major categories of E codes include:

- Transport accidents

- Poisoning and adverse effects of drugs, medicinal substances, and biologicals

- Accidental falls

- Accidents caused by fire and flames

- Accidents due to natural and environmental factors

- Late effects of accidents, assaults, or self-injury

- Assaults or purposely inflicted injury

- Suicide or self-inflicted injury

These guidelines apply for the coding and collection of E codes from records in hospitals, outpatient clinics, emergency departments, other ambulatory care settings and provider offices, and nonacute care settings, except when other specific guidelines apply.

a. **General E code coding guidelines**
   1) **Used with any code in the range of 001–V91**
      An E code from categories E800–E999 may be used with any code in the range of 001–V91, which indicates an injury, a poisoning, or an adverse effect due to an external cause.
      An activity E code (categories E001–E030) may be used with any code in the range of 001–V91 that indicates an injury, or other health condition that resulted from an activity, or the activity contributed to a condition.

2) **Assign the appropriate E code for all initial treatments**

Assign the appropriate E code for the initial encounter of an injury, a poisoning, or an adverse effect of drugs, not for subsequent treatment.

3) **Use the full range of E codes**

Use the full range of E codes to completely describe the cause, the intent, and the place of occurrence, if applicable, for all injuries, poisonings, and adverse effects of drugs.

4) **Assign as many E codes as necessary**

Assign as many E codes (E800–E999) as necessary to fully explain each cause.

5) **Select of the appropriate E code**

The selection of the appropriate E code is guided by the Index to External Causes, which is located after the alphabetical Index to Diseases and by inclusion and exclusion notes in the tabular list.

6) **E code can never be a principal diagnosis**

An E code can never be a principal (first-listed) diagnosis.

7) **External cause code(s) with systemic inflammatory response syndrome (SIRS)**

An external cause code is not appropriate with a code from subcategory 995.9, unless the patient also has another condition for which an E code would be appropriate (such as an injury, poisoning, or adverse effect of drugs.)

8) **Multiple cause E code coding guidelines**

More than one E code is required to fully describe the external cause of an illness, injury or poisoning. The assignment of E codes should be sequenced in the following priority:

If two or more events cause separate injuries, an E code should be assigned for each cause. The first-listed E code will be selected in the following order:

- E codes for child and adult abuse take priority over all other E codes.

- *See Section I.C.19.e., Child and Adult abuse guidelines.*

- E codes for terrorism events take priority over all other E codes except child and adult abuse.

- E codes for cataclysmic events take priority over all other E codes except child and adult abuse and terrorism.

- E codes for transport accidents take priority over all other E codes except cataclysmic events, child and adult abuse and terrorism.

- Activity and external cause status codes are assigned following all causal (intent) E codes.

- The first-listed E code should correspond to the cause of the most serious diagnosis due to an assault, accident, or self-harm, following the order of hierarchy listed above.

9) **If the reporting format limits the number of E codes**

If the reporting format limits the number of E codes that can be used in reporting clinical data, report the code for the cause/intent most related to the principal diagnosis. If the format permits capture of additional E codes, the cause/intent, including medical misadventures, of the additional events should be reported rather than the codes for place, activity or external status.

b. **Place of occurrence guideline**

Use an additional code from category E849 to indicate the place of occurrence for injuries and poisonings. The place of occurrence describes the place where the event occurred and not the patient's activity at the time of the event.

Do not use E849.9 if the place of occurrence is not stated.

c. **Adverse effects of drugs, medicinal and biological substances guidelines**

1) Do not code directly from the Table of Drugs and Chemicals. Always refer back to the tabular list.
2) Use as many codes as necessary to completely describe all drugs, medicinal or biological substances.

(continues)

ICD-9-CM CHAPTER-SPECIFIC CODING GUIDELINES WITH ICD-10 ALERTS! (*continued*)

If the reporting format limits the number of E codes, and there are different fourth-digit codes in the same three-digit category, use the code for "Other specified" of that category of drugs, medicinal or biological substances. If there is no "Other specified" code in that category, use the appropriate "Unspecified" code in that category.

If the reporting format limits the number of E codes, and the codes are in different three-digit categories, assign the appropriate E code for other multiple drugs and medicinal substances.

3) If the same E code would describe the causative agent for more than one adverse reaction, assign the code only once.

4) If two or more drugs, medicinal or biological substances are reported, code each individually unless the combination code is listed in the Table of Drugs and Chemicals. In that case, assign the E code for the combination.

5) When a reaction results from the interaction of a drug(s) and alcohol, use poisoning codes and E codes for both.

6) Codes from the E930–E949 series must be used to identify the causative substance for an adverse effect of drug, medicinal and biological substances, correctly prescribed and properly administered. The effect, such as tachycardia, delirium, gastrointestinal hemorrhaging, vomiting, hypokalemia, hepatitis, renal failure, or respiratory failure, is coded and followed by the appropriate code from the E930–E949 series.

d. Child and adult abuse guideline
1) Intentional injury
When the cause of an injury or neglect is intentional child or adult abuse, the first-listed E code should be assigned from categories E960–E968, Homicide and injury purposely inflicted by other persons (except category E967). An E code from category E967, Child and adult battering and other maltreatment, should be added as an additional code to identify the perpetrator, if known.

2) Accidental intent
In cases of neglect when the intent is determined to be accidental, E code E904.0, Abandonment or neglect of infant and helpless person, should be the first-listed E code.

e. Unknown or suspected intent guideline
1) If the intent (accident, self-harm, assault) of the cause of an injury or poisoning is unknown or unspecified, code the intent as undetermined E980–E989.

2) If the intent (accident, self-harm, assault) of the cause of an injury or poisoning is questionable, probable, or suspected, code the intent as undetermined E980–E989.

f. Undetermined cause
When the intent of an injury or poisoning is known but the cause is unknown, use codes E928.9, Unspecified accident; E958.9, Suicide and self-inflicted injury by unspecified means; and E968.9, Assault by unspecified means.

These E codes should rarely be used, as the documentation in the medical record, in both the inpatient/ outpatient and other settings, should normally provide sufficient detail to determine the cause of the injury.

g. Late effects of external cause guidelines
1) Late effect E codes
Late effect E codes exist for injuries and poisonings but not for adverse effects of drugs, misadventures, and surgical complications.

2) Late effect E codes (E929, E959, E969, E977, E989, or E999.1)
A late effect E code (E929, E959, E969, E977, E989, or E999.1) should be used with any report of a late effect or sequela resulting from a previous injury or poisoning (905–909).

3) Late effect E code with a related current injury
A late effect E code should never be used with a "related current nature of injury" code.

4) Use of late effect E codes for subsequent visits

Use a late effect E code for subsequent visits when a late effect of the initial injury or poisoning is being treated. There is no late effect E code for adverse effects of drugs. Do not use a late effect E code for subsequent visits for follow-up care (e.g., to assess healing, to receive rehabilitative therapy) of the injury or poisoning when no late effect of the injury has been documented.

h. Misadventures and complications of care guidelines

1) Code range E870–E876

Assign a code in the range of E870–E876 if misadventures are stated by the provider.

2) Code range E878–E879

Assign a code in the range of E878–E879 if the provider attributes an abnormal reaction or later complication to a surgical or medical procedure, but does not mention misadventure at the time of the procedure as the cause of the reaction.

i. Terrorism guidelines

1) Cause of injury identified by the federal government (Federal Bureau of Investigation [FBI]) as terrorism

When the cause of an injury is identified by the FBI as terrorism, the first-listed E code should be a code from category E979, Terrorism. The definition of terrorism employed by the FBI is found in the inclusion note at E979. The terrorism E code is the only E code that should be assigned. Additional E codes from the assault categories should not be assigned.

2) Cause of an injury is suspected to be the result of terrorism

When the cause of an injury is suspected to be the result of terrorism, a code from category E979 should not be assigned. Assign a code in the range of E codes based on circumstances on the documentation of intent and mechanism.

3) Code E979.9, Terrorism, secondary effects

Assign code E979.9, Terrorism, secondary effects, for conditions occurring subsequent to the terrorist event. This code should not be assigned for conditions that are due to the initial terrorist act.

4) Statistical tabulation of terrorism codes

For statistical purposes, these codes will be tabulated within the category for assault, expanding the current category from E960–E969 to include E979 and E999.1.

j. Activity Code Guidelines

Assign a code from category E001–E030 to describe the activity that caused or contributed to the injury or other health condition.

Unlike other E codes, activity E codes may be assigned to indicate a health condition (not just injuries) resulted from an activity, or the activity contributed to the condition.

The activity codes are not applicable to poisonings, adverse effects, misadventures, or late effects. Do not assign E030, Unspecified activity, if the activity is not stated.

k. External cause status

A code from category E000, External cause status, should be assigned whenever any other E code is assigned for an encounter, including an Activity E code, except for the events noted below. Assign a code from category E000, External cause status, to indicate the work status of the person at the time the event occurred. The status code indicates whether the event occurred during military activity, whether a non-military person was at work, or whether an individual including a student or volunteer was involved in a non-work activity at the time of the causal event.

A code from E000, External cause status, should be assigned, when applicable, with other external cause codes, such as transport accidents and falls. The external cause status codes are not applicable to poisonings, adverse effects, misadventures, or late effects.

Do not assign a code from category E000 if no other E codes (cause, activity) are applicable for the encounter.

Do not assign code E000.9, Unspecified external cause status, if the status is not stated.

Exercise 4.21 – External Causes of Injury and Poisoning

Instructions: Underline the main term in each diagnosis statement and assign the appropriate ICD-9-CM E code(s) and ICD-10-CM external cause V through X.

ICD-9-CM	ICD-10-CM	
_____	_____	1. Fall from skateboard at public park
_____	_____	2. Burning bedclothes resulting from cooking in kitchen of mobile home
_____	_____	3. Explosion in watercraft
_____	_____	4. Fall from ladder
_____	_____	5. Foot injury taking place on baseball field (accident)

Summary

The National Center for Health Statistics (NCHS) created the clinical modification (CM) of ICD-9, and ICD-9-CM was implemented in 1979. Although ICD-9-CM contains additional clinical information, its three-digit codes and their sequence correlate to the ICD-9 system developed by the World Health Organization (WHO). The ICD-9-CM Tabular List of Procedures is a modification of the WHO's *ICD-9 Classification of Procedures in Medicine* (ICPM), *Fascicle V—Surgical Procedures*. The structure of the ICD-9-CM Tabular List of Procedures is based on anatomy rather than surgical specialty, and it contains numeric codes only (no alphabetical characters are used).

The Centers for Medicare & Medicaid Services (CMS) and the NCHS are the agencies in the U.S. Department of Health and Human Services (DHHS) that provide official guidelines for coding and reporting using the *International Classification of Diseases, Ninth Revision, Clinical Modification* (ICD-9-CM). The *ICD-9-CM Official Guidelines for Coding and Reporting* (and *ICD-10-CM Official Guidelines for Coding and Reporting*), as approved by the four organizations that make up the cooperating parties (the AHA, AHIMA, CMS, and NCHS), are used as a companion document to the official version of the ICD-9-CM or ICD-10-CM. The guidelines are a set of rules developed to accompany and complement the official conventions and instructions provided within ICD-9-CM or ICD-10-CM. They are based on the coding and sequencing instructions in ICD-9-CM or ICD-10-CM and provide additional instruction.

In addition to coding conventions and general coding guidelines, the *Official Guidelines for Coding and Reporting* contains chapter-specific coding guidelines that clarify the assignment of ICD-9-CM or ICD-10-CM disease codes. Unless otherwise indicated in an individual chapter-specific guideline, the ICD-9-CM or ICD-10-CM chapter-specific guidelines apply to all health care settings.

Internet Links

ICD-9-CM and ICD-10-CM/PCS updates: Go to *www.cdc.gov* click on the *Data & Statistics* link, click on the *Disease Classification* link, and click on any of the ICD links.

ICD-9-CM Official Guidelines for Coding and Reporting: Go to *www.cdc.gov.* Click on the letter *I*, next to the A–Z Index heading. Click on the *ICD-9-CM (ICD-9-CM (International Classification of Diseases, Ninth Revision, Clinical Modification)* link. Scroll to the bottom of the page, and click on the *Guidelines* link.

Click on the *ICD-9-CM Guidelines* link. (To view the guidelines, download free *Adobe Reader* software from *www.adobe.com.*)

ICD-10-CM Official Guidelines for Coding and Reporting: Go to *www.cdc.gov.* Click on the letter I, next to the A-Z Index heading. Then click on the ICD-10-CM (International Classification of Diseases, 10th Revision, Clinical Modification) link. Scroll down and click on the *ICD-10-CM Guidelines* link.

MedLine Plus Interactive Tutorials (for diseases and procedures): Go to *www.nlm.nih.gov.* Click on the Medline Plus link, and click on Videos and Cool Tools; then click on the Interactive Tutorials link.

Study Checklist

❑ Read this chapter and highlight key concepts.

❑ Create an index card for each key term.

❑ Access the chapter Internet links to learn more about concepts.

❑ Complete the chapter review, verifying answers with your instructor.

❑ Complete WebTutor assignments and take online quizzes.

❑ Complete Workbook chapter, verifying answers with your instructor.

❑ Go to *www.cengagebrain.com* to access StudyWARE™ and the Premium Website. Login instructions are located in the Preface and on the Printed Access Card.

❑ Form a study group with classmates to discuss chapter concepts in preparation for an exam.

Review

Multiple Choice I—ICD-9-CM

Instructions: Circle the most appropriate response after locating the code(s) using ICD-9-CM.

1. Gram-negative septicemia due to *E. coli*.
   - **a.** 038.3
   - **b.** 038.40
   - **c.** 038.42
   - **d.** 038.9

2. Metastatic carcinoma from the lung.
   - **a.** 162.9, 199.1
   - **b.** 199.1, 239.1
   - **c.** 239.9, 162.9
   - **d.** 239.9, 199.1

3. Diabetes mellitus with iritis.
   - **a.** 250.00, 364.3
   - **b.** 250.50, 364.42
   - **c.** 364.3, 250.00
   - **d.** 364.3, 250.50

4. Pancytopenia.
   - **a.** 284.09
   - **b.** 284.19
   - **c.** 285.9, 288.00, 287.5
   - **d.** 288.00, 287.5, 285.9

5. Delirium tremens due to chronic continuous alcoholism.
   - **a.** 291.0, 303.90
   - **b.** 291.0, 303.91
   - **c.** 291.1, 303.91
   - **d.** 781.0, 303.90

6. Hemiparesis due to old spinal cord injury.
   - **a.** 342.80, 952.9
   - **b.** 342.90, 907.2
   - **c.** 342.90, 952.9
   - **d.** 907.3, 342.90

7. Cerebral thrombosis with transient hemiplegia, which resolved by discharge.
   - **a.** 434.00
   - **b.** 434.00, 438.20
   - **c.** 434.00, 438.9
   - **d.** 438.20, 434.00

8. Male patient admitted for sterilization procedure.
   a. E872.8   b. V25.2   c. V25.9   d. V26.5

9. Diverticulitis of the colon with hemorrhage.
   a. 562.01   b. 562.03   c. 562.12   d. 562.13

10. Acute prostatitis due to streptococcus.
   a. 041.00, 601.0   b. 041.09, 601.0   c. 601.0, 041.00   d. 601.00, 041.09

11. Spontaneous delivery of full-term pregnancy (single liveborn).
   a. 650, V27.0   b. 650.0, V27.0   c. 650, V27.9   d. V27.0, 650.0

12. Hard corn of right little toe.
   a. 700   b. 700, 735.8   c. 735.8   d. 735.9

13. Herniated cervical intervertebral disc. No evidence of myelopathy.
   a. 721.0   b. 721.1   c. 722.0   d. 722.10

14. Congenital dislocation of hip.
   a. 754.30   b. 754.31   c. 835.00   d. 835.10

15. Five-hour-old infant, premature at 30 weeks, spontaneous birth, transferred from general hospital to tertiary care hospital's neonatal intensive care unit. Final diagnosis at tertiary hospital is male newborn with respiratory distress syndrome due to prematurity.
   a. 765.25, 770.89   c. 769, 765.10, 765.25
   b. 765.10, 765.25, 769   d. 770.89, 765.10

16. Abnormal mammogram.
   a. 793.99   b. 793.8   c. 793.80   d. 793.89

17. First- and second-degree burns of forearm and third-degree burns of back. Burn injuries sustained at warehouse where patient is employed.
   a. 942.34, 943.21, 943.11   c. 942.34, 943.21, E899, E849.3
   b. 942.34, 943.21, 943.11,   d. 943.11, 943.21, 942.34, E849.0
      E849.3, E899

18. Patient with Stage IV chronic kidney disease underwent hemodialysis.
   a. 586.4, V56.0   b. V56.0   c. V56.0, 585.4   d. V56.0, 586

19. Acute nasopharyngitis.
   a. 460   b. 462   c. 472.1   d. 472.2

20. Family history of sudden cardiac death (SCD).
   a. V12.53   b. V13.81   c. V17.3   d. V17.41

Multiple Choice II—ICD-10-CM

Instructions: Circle the most appropriate response after locating the code(s) using ICD-10-CM.

21. Gram-negative septicemia due to *E. coli*.
   a. A41.4   b. A41.50   c. A41.51   d. A41.9

22. Metastatic carcinoma from the lung.
   a. C34.90, C79.9   b. C79.9, D49.1   c. D49.9, C34.90   d. D49.9, C80

23. Type 2 diabetes mellitus with iritis.
   a. E08.39   b. E09.39   c. E10.39   d. E11.39

24. Anemia, neutropenia, and thrombocytopenia.
   a. D61.09   c. D64.9, D70.9, D69.6
   b. D61.9   d. P61.4, D70.4, D69.3

25. Alcohol-induced delirium tremens.
  a. F10.121, F10.20 b. F10.231   c. F10.96, F10.26 d. G25.1, F10.20

26. Hemiparesis due to old spinal cord injury, lumbar region.
  a. G81.90, S34.01xS   c. G81.90, S34.109S
  b. G81.90, S30.91xS   d. G81.90, S34.119S

27. Cerebral thrombosis.
  a. I66.09   b. I66.19   c. I66.29   d. I66.9

28. Male patient admitted for ligation of vas deferens sterilization procedure.
  a. Z30.2   b. Z31.0   c. Z31.42   d. Z31.89

29. Diverticulitis of the colon with hemorrhage.
  a. K57.20   b. K57.21   c. K57.32   d. K57.33

30. Acute prostatitis due to streptococci.
  a. N41.00, B95.5 b. N41.01, B95.5 c. N41.8, B95.5 d. N41.9, B95.5

31. Spontaneous delivery of full-term pregnancy (single liveborn).
  a. O80, Z37.0 b. O82, Z37.0 c. Z34.00, Z37.0 d. Z34.90, Z38.00

32. Hard corn of right little toe.
  a. L84   b. M20.5x1   c. M20.61   d. M21.271

33. Herniated cervical intervertebral disc. No evidence of myelopathy.
  a. M50.00   b. M50.10   c. M50.20   d. M50.30

34. Congenital partial dislocation of the hip.
  a. Q65.1   b. Q65.2   c. Q65.4   d. Q65.5

35. Liveborn infant, born in taxi cab and then admitted for evaluation. Discharged in excellent condition.
  a. Z38.00   b. Z38.01   c. Z38.1   d. Z38.2

36. Abnormal mammogram.
  a. R92.0   b. R92.1   c. R92.2   d. R92.8

37. First- and second-degree burns of right forearm.
  a. T22.019   b. T22.011   c. T22.111, T22.211 d. T22.211

38. Stage IV chronic kidney disease (CKD) patient undergoes outpatient renal dialysis.
  a. N18.4   b. N18.6, Z49.31 c. N18.9, Z91.15 d. N19, Z99.2

39. Acute nasopharyngitis.
  a. J00   b. J02.9   c. J31.1   d. J31.2

40. Family history of sudden cardiac death (SCD).
  a. Z82.41   b. Z82.49   c. Z86.74   d. Z87.898

Coding Practice—Diseases

Instructions: Underline the main term in each diagnosis statement and assign the appropriate ICD-9-CM (or ICD-10-CM) code(s).

_____ 41. Classical hemophilia

_____ 42. Fitting of cardiac pacemaker

_____ 43. Gray syndrome from chloramphenicol administration in newborn as prescribed (initial encounter)

_____ 44. Injury by shotgun, undetermined whether accidental or intentional (shooting) (initial encounter)

_____ 45. Irritable bowel syndrome

_____ 46. Malignant neoplasm, right breast (female)

_____ 47. Medial dislocation of tibia, proximal end, open (initial encounter)

_____ 48. Motor vehicle traffic accident involving a collision with a pedestrian (initial encounter)

_____ 49. Multiple personality

_____ 50. Nausea with vomiting

_____ 51. Personal history of penicillin allergy

_____ 52. Pneumonia due to streptococcus, group B

_____ 53. Polyarticular juvenile rheumatoid arthritis, acute

_____ 54. Polycystic kidney, autosomal recessive

_____ 55. Postsurgical hypothyroidism

_____ 56. Pulmonary arteriosclerosis

_____ 57. Sand flea infestation

_____ 58. Spontaneous abortion, complicated by excessive hemorrhage, complete

_____ 59. Preterm labor with preterm delivery of twins, third trimester

_____ 60. Uterine prolapse, first degree

ICD-9-CM and ICD-10-CM/PCS Hospital Inpatient Coding

Chapter Outline

Acute Care Facilities (Hospitals)

Inpatient Diagnosis Coding Guidelines

Inpatient Procedure Coding Guidelines

ICD-9-CM Procedure Coding

ICD-10-PCS Procedure Coding

Chapter Objectives

At the conclusion of this chapter, the student should be able to:

- Define key terms.
- List and explain differences among acute care inpatient settings.
- Interpret inpatient diagnosis and procedure coding and reporting guidelines.
- Assign ICD-9-CM and ICD-10-CM/PCS diagnosis and/or procedure codes for acute care inpatient cases.

Key Terms

acute care facility (ACF)

acute care hospital

admitting diagnosis

ancillary service

axis of classification (ICD-10-PCS)

bed count

bed size

behavioral health care hospital

comorbidity

complication

critical access hospital (CAH)

general hospital

Index (ICD-10-PCS)

inpatient

long-term acute care hospital (LTACH)

long-term hospital

maximizing reimbursement

multiaxial structure (ICD-10-PCS)

multihospital system

newborn patient

optimizing reimbursement

other (additional) diagnosis

other significant procedure

principal diagnosis

principal procedure

rehabilitation hospital

secondary procedure

short-term hospital

single hospital

specialty hospital

subacute care patient

swing bed

Tables (ICD-10-PCS)

Uniform Hospital Discharge Data Set (UHDDS)

value (ICD-10-PCS)

Introduction

This chapter defines inpatient acute care settings and includes an interpretation of the guidelines for sequencing diagnosis (and procedures, as required by some third-party payers) published in the *CMS ICD-9-CM Official Guidelines for Coding and Reporting*, *ICD-10-CM Official Guidelines for Coding and Reporting*, and *ICD-10-PCS Coding Guidelines*.

Coding guidelines discussed in this chapter are to be used as a companion to the official version of the ICD-9-CM, ICD-10-CM, and ICD-10-PCS, which contain coding conventions to ensure accurate coding. ICD-9-CM or ICD-10-CM and ICD-10-PCS (abbreviated as ICD-10-CM/PCS) codes are assigned to inpatient cases to collect statistical data for education and research, determine third-party payer reimbursement, and facilitate health care financial planning. Once codes are assigned to an inpatient case, patient-demographic data and codes are entered manually onto paper-based abstract forms (for keyboarding by the facility's information technology (IT) department) or directly into an automated case abstracting-software, using a data entry screen (Figure 5-1).

Once entered into the facility's database, the codes are transmitted to the facility's billing department, which generates the outpatient UB-04 claim for submission to third-party payers (to obtain reimbursement). (Inpatient reimbursement systems are discussed in Chapter 19). As a result of data entry, the facility's IT department has the capability of producing disease, procedure and service, and physician indexes from abstracted data. Indexes are used to retrieve patient

Note:

The following additional content is located on the Premium Website at www .cengagebrain.com:

- *ICD-10-PCS Root Operations, Definitions, and Examples.*
- *Inpatient Coding Tutorial.*

Note:

Students enrolled in medical assistant and medical office administration programs may notice that their instructor skips this chapter.

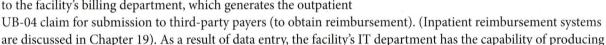

Figure 5-1 Inpatient abstracting screen generated from PC-based software

records for quality management purposes; and the IT department can generate summary data from the computer system for education, research, and statistical purposes. Statistical data allow the facility to conduct financial planning to determine which facility services to expand or deactivate.

When assigning codes, coders carefully review patient records to locate conditions, diseases, procedures, and services to which codes are assigned. Coders are prohibited from assigning codes when the provider does not specifically document those diagnoses or procedures/services. This is called assumption coding, and it is considered fraud because the coder assumes certain facts about a patient's condition or procedures/services although the physician has not specifically documented the level of detail to which the coder assigns codes.

- When patient record documentation appears to support the assignment of a specific code but the provider has not completely documented the diagnosis or procedure on the record's face sheet or discharge summary, the coder should query the physician to determine whether the more specific code should be assigned. (Refer to Chapter 1 for more information about the physician query process.)

- *Reviewing the patient record to assign a more specific code to a documented diagnosis is appropriate.* For example, when a physician documents "fracture of femur," the coder reviews the X-ray report to assign a specific code for the fracture site (e.g., shaft of femur). In addition, codes may be assigned if they are based on other physician (e.g., consultant, resident, or anesthesiologist) documentation as long as there is no conflicting documentation from the attending physician.

- It is appropriate to base the assignment of codes on patient record documentation by any physician involved in the care and treatment of a patient. A physician query is unnecessary if a physician involved in the care and treatment of the patient documents a diagnosis and no conflicting documentation by another physician exists. However, if documentation by two or more physicians conflicts, query the attending physician.

Hospital inpatient cases usually have multiple diagnoses and procedures documented; and once codes are assigned, the coder sequences diagnoses according to principal diagnosis and other (additional) diagnoses as defined by the UHDDS. (Implementation of MS-DRGs resulted in CMS discontinuing the practice of requiring the sequencing of the principal procedure and significant other, or secondary, procedures. However, some third-party payers might still require it.) The **Uniform Hospital Discharge Data Set (UHDDS)** was established by the federal government to define data collected for inpatient hospitalizations (e.g., age, gender, race, patient's residence, length of stay (LOS), diagnoses and procedures, physicians, patient disposition, and payment sources).

Note:

Nursing facilities (NFs) are required to report the Minimum Data Set (MDS) for all residents regardless of age, diagnosis, LOS, or payment category. *The Minimum Data Set (MDS)* includes screening elements (e.g., demographic data, ICD-9-CM or ICD-10-CM codes, cognitive patterns, and communicating/hearing patterns) used for the comprehensive assessment of nursing facility residents. Nursing facilities (NFs) use the Resident Assessment Validation and Entry (RAVEN) data entry system to report MDS data, which standardize communication about resident problems and conditions and facilitates quality monitoring and improvement. (More information about skilled nursing coding can be found on the Premium Website at www.cengagebrain.com.)

Acute Care Facilities (Hospitals) ●●●

An **acute care facility (ACF)** is a hospital that provides health care services to patients who have serious, sudden, or acute illnesses or injuries and/or who need certain surgeries. ACFs provide a full range of health care services including

Note:

Inpatient health care settings include:

- Acute care facilities (hospitals).
- Behavioral health care facilities.
- Hospice inpatient care.
- Long-term care facilities.

ancillary services, emergency and critical care, surgery, and obstetrics (labor and delivery). **Ancillary services** are diagnostic and therapeutic services provided to inpatients and outpatients (e.g., laboratory, physical therapy). Most hospital inpatient stays are short (fewer than 30 days), although some patients may stay for a longer time if medically necessary. Because each inpatient day is expensive, a utilization or case manager closely monitors patient care to determine whether acute health care services are required.

Note:

Content about other than acute care inpatient settings (e.g., hospice) is located on the Premium Website at www.cengagebrain.com.

Hospitals have an organized medical and professional staff, and inpatient beds are available 24 hours per day. The primary function of hospitals is to provide inpatient medical, nursing, and other health-related services to patients for surgical and nonsurgical conditions; hospitals usually provide some outpatient services as well. Hospitals are categorized as (1) **single hospitals** (hospitals are self-contained and not part of larger organizations) and (2) **multihospital systems** (where two or more hospitals are owned, managed, or leased by a single organization; these may include acute, long-term, pediatric, rehabilitation, or psychiatric care facilities).

Another consideration when discussing hospital organization is to identify the *population served by a health care facility*, which means that health care is provided to specific groups of people in that some hospitals specialize in the treatment of children (e.g., pediatric hospitals) while others have special units (e.g., burn unit). The hospital **bed size** (or **bed count**) is the total number of inpatient beds for which the facility is licensed by the state; the hospital must be equipped and staffed to care for these patient admissions. The hospital's average LOS determines classification as a:

- **Short-term hospital** (or **acute care hospital**): Average LOS of 4–5 days and a total LOS of fewer than 25 days.

- **Long-term hospital** (or long-term acute care hospital or LTACH): Average LOS is more than 25 days.

  EXAMPLE: Patient was admitted 4/5/YYYY and discharged on 4/10/YYYY. To calculate the LOS, count the day of admission but not the day of discharge. This patient's LOS is 5 days.

Hospitals are also categorized by type:

- **Critical access hospitals (CAHs)** are located more than 35 miles from any hospital or another CAH, or they are state-certified as being a necessary provider of health care to area residents. (The requirement is reduced to 15 miles in areas where only secondary roads are available or in mountainous terrains.) CAHs must provide emergency services 24 hours per day and maintain no more than 15 inpatient beds (except swing-bed facilities, which can have up to 25 inpatient beds if no more than 15 are used at any one time for acute care). Inpatients are restricted to 96-hour stays unless a longer period is required due to inclement weather or the development of another emergency condition. (A **swing bed** allows a rural hospital to admit a nonacute care patient.)

Note:

Do not confuse LTACHs with long-term care facilities (LTCFs) (e.g., nursing facilities) that provide a range of services including custodial, intermediate, rehabilitative, and skilled nursing care.

- **General hospitals** provide emergency care, perform general surgery, and admit patients for a range of problems from fractures to heart disease based on licensing by the state.

- **Long-term acute care hospitals (LTACH)** provide care designed specifically for patients who need functional restoration and/or rehabilitation and medical management for an average of 3 to 6 weeks.

- **Specialty hospitals** concentrate on a particular population of patients (e.g., children) or disease (e.g., cancer).

- **Rehabilitation hospitals** admit patients who are diagnosed with trauma (e.g., car accident) or disease (e.g., stroke) and need to learn how to function.

- **Behavioral health care hospitals** specialize in treating individuals with mental health diagnoses.

Hospital patients who receive care while residing in the facility are categorized as inpatients, newborn patients, and subacute care patients.

- **Inpatients** stay overnight in the facility for 24 or more hours and are provided with room and board and nursing services.

- **Newborn patients** receive infant care upon birth, and if necessary they receive neonatal intensive care (either within the hospital or as the result of transfer to another hospital).

 Note:

Hospital outpatients, ambulatory surgery patients, emergency care patients, and observation care patients are discussed in Chapter 6.

- **Subacute care patients** receive specialized long-term acute care such as chemotherapy, injury rehabilitation, ventilator (breathing machine) support, wound care, and other types of health care services provided to seriously ill patients. Subacute care facilities look like *mini-intensive care units*, and they usually do not offer the full range of health care services available in acute care facilities (e.g., emergency departments [EDs], obstetrics, and surgery). Subacute care costs less than acute care, and patients are often transferred directly from an intensive care unit. Medicare will reimburse subacute care facilities if care provided is appropriate and medically necessary.

Exercise 5.1 – Acute Care Facilities (Hospitals)

Instructions: Complete each statement.

1. The type of hospital that provides health care services to patients who have serious, sudden, or acute illnesses or injuries and/or who need certain surgeries is called a(n) _____.

2. Diagnostic and therapeutic services provided to inpatients and outpatients (e.g., laboratory, physical therapy) are called _____.

3. Hospitals that are self-contained and not part of larger organizations are called _____; while two or more hospitals owned, managed, or leased by a single organization are called _____.

4. The total number of inpatient beds for which a facility is licensed by the state is called the hospital _____.

5–6. A hospital's average length of stay (LOS) determines whether the hospital is classified as

(5.) _____ (average LOS of 4–5 days and a total LOS of fewer than 25 days) or

(6.) _____ (average LOS is more than 25 days).

7. A patient was admitted on May 30 and discharged on June 3 of the same year. The LOS is calculated as _____ days.

8. A swing bed allows a rural hospital to admit a(n) _____ care patient.

9. Patients who are diagnosed with trauma or disease and who need to learn how to function are usually admitted to _____ hospitals.

10. Physicians who spend most of their time in a hospital setting admitting patients to their inpatient services (from local primary care providers) are called _____.

Inpatient Diagnosis Coding Guidelines

The circumstances of inpatient admission govern the sequencing of diagnoses. UHDDS definitions have always been used by acute care hospitals to report inpatient data elements in a standardized manner. Since the creation of the UHDDS in 1985, the application of the UHDDS definitions has been expanded to include all nonoutpatient settings (e.g., acute care, short-term, long-term, and psychiatric hospitals; home health agencies; rehabilitation facilities; and skilled nursing facilities and nursing homes).

Circumstances associated with an inpatient admission govern the sequencing of the following diagnoses:

- Admitting diagnosis
- Principal diagnosis
- Other (additional) diagnoses (or secondary diagnoses, which include comorbidities and complications)

Coding Tip:

Inpatient and outpatient health care settings require different diagnosis definitions (e.g., principal diagnosis versus first-listed diagnosis) because of the time frame available for patient care and treatment. The first-listed diagnosis, reported as an ICD-9-CM or ICD-10-CM code for outpatient and physician office care, is defined in Chapter 6.

 The attending physician doesn't document final diagnoses until an inpatient is discharged from the hospital; and by that time, a definitive diagnosis has usually been established. Because inpatient coding guidelines prohibit the coding of signs and symptoms when a definitive diagnosis has been established, signs and symptoms are seldom documented as the principal diagnosis on inpatient charts. In addition, qualified diagnoses can be coded as principal and other diagnoses for hospital inpatients because physicians use hospital resources to treat the patient for these types of conditions and because hospital reimbursement is based on the utilization and consumption of resources. (In the outpatient setting, the physician usually does not have time to establish a definitive diagnosis during one encounter. Thus, signs and symptoms are often reported as the first-listed diagnosis for third-party payer reimbursement purposes.)

Note:

The attending physician is responsible for documenting the list of diagnoses in the patient record (e.g., face sheet, discharge summary, or final progress note).

Admitting Diagnosis

The **admitting diagnosis** is the provisional or tentative diagnosis upon which initial patient care is based. It is obtained from the patient's attending physician by the admissions office staff, who enter it in a field on the inpatient face sheet. The admitting diagnosis is often a sign (e.g., fever, cough, rash) or symptom (chest pain, sore throat, numbness). One admitting diagnosis ICD code is reported on the UB-04.

Principal Diagnosis

The **principal diagnosis** is defined in the UHDDS as "that condition established after study to be chiefly responsible for occasioning the admission of the patient to the hospital for care." The most important part of the definition is the phrase *after study*, which directs the coder to review all patient record documentation associated with an inpatient hospitalization to determine the clinical reason for the admission. The circumstances of admission that impact selection of the principal

Note:

When determining principal diagnosis, ICD-9-CM or ICD-10-CM coding conventions take precedence over official coding guidelines.

diagnosis include the chief complaint and the patient's signs and symptoms on admission, which are documented on the history and physical examination. In addition, the entire patient record is reviewed to determine which condition was *established after study*; this means that the coder reviews ancillary test results (e.g., laboratory, X-ray) and other reports (e.g., operative report, pathology report) to select the principal diagnosis. If selection of the principal diagnosis is unclear, the physician should be queried and the outcome of the query corroborated with supporting documentation in the patient record. One principal diagnosis code is reported on the UB-04.

HIPAA Alert!

HIPAA regulations for electronic transactions require providers and payers (including MACs) to adhere to the *Official Guidelines for Coding and Reporting*. Thus, a violation of the coding guidelines is a HIPAA violation. Unfortunately, some payers do not appear to be aware of or understand this HIPAA provision. Payers should be informed of the provision in the HIPAA regulation that references the use of coding guidelines. If payers deny claims because certain codes are reported as principal diagnosis (e.g., V57), contact your regional CMS office or the HIPAA enforcement office (at CMS) to alert them about the HIPAA violation.

EXAMPLE: A 51-year-old male patient presented to the ED, complaining of ringing in his ears, dizziness, blurred vision, confusion, and difficulty walking. Upon evaluation by the ED physician, the patient stated that these symptoms started suddenly just two hours ago. Past history revealed that the patient takes medication for hypercholesterolemia and hypertension. The patient used to smoke two packs of cigarettes daily until 5 years ago, when he quit. Physical examination revealed blood pressure of 175/110. When asked, the patient stated that he had been taking his hypertension medication as prescribed.

Patient underwent carotid ultrasound to evaluate the blood flow of the carotid arteries, and results indicated the need for carotid angiogram to measure blockage of the carotid arteries. The ED physician transferred the case to a cardiologist, who performed a bilateral carotid angiogram that revealed 90% blockage of the right carotid artery and 20% blockage of the left carotid artery. The patient was admitted to the hospital and scheduled for carotid angioplasty with insertion of carotid stent in the morning, which was performed uneventfully. Final diagnoses were documented as carotid artery occlusion, hypertension, hypercholesterolemia, and impending stroke. Procedures performed included carotid ultrasound, carotid angiogram, and carotid angioplasty.

In this example, the principal diagnosis is the carotid artery occlusion (433.10). Other diagnoses (or secondary diagnoses) include impending stroke (435.9), hypertension (401.9), and hypercholesterolemia (272.0). Do not assign codes to the symptoms of ringing in his ears, dizziness, blurred vision, confusion, and difficulty walking because they are associated with the carotid artery occlusion and impending stroke. Signs and symptoms are often documented in the patient's record, but they are not coded if they are considered part of an established diagnosis.

ICD-10 Alert!

The principal diagnosis is the carotid artery occlusion (I65.29). Other diagnoses (or secondary diagnoses) include impending stroke (G45.9), hypertension (I10), and hypercholesterolemia (E78.0).

Codes for Symptoms, Signs, and Ill-Defined Conditions

Codes for symptoms, signs, and ill-defined conditions from ICD-9-CM Chapter 16 or ICD-10-CM Chapter 18 are not to be reported as the principal diagnosis when a related definitive diagnosis has been established.

EXAMPLE: The patient is admitted as a hospital inpatient after having been treated in the ED for chest pain and a positive electrocardiogram (EKG), which revealed anterolateral MI. The patient underwent cardiac catheterization (Figure 5-2) during hospitalization and subsequent quadruple coronary artery bypass graft surgery. The principal diagnosis for this case is acute anterolateral MI, first episode. The chest pain is not assigned a code because it is a symptom of the MI.

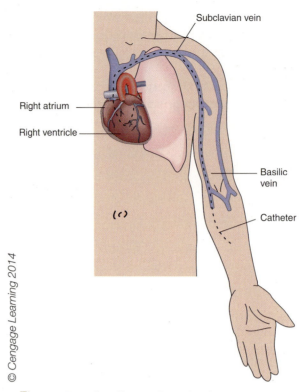

Figure 5-2 Cardiac catheterization

Two or More Interrelated Conditions, Each Potentially Meeting the Definition for Principal Diagnosis

When two or more interrelated conditions (e.g., diseases located in the same ICD-9-CM or ICD-10-CM chapter, manifestations associated with a certain disease) potentially meet the definition of principal diagnosis, either condition may be sequenced first unless the circumstances of the admission, the therapy provided, or the Tabular List of Diseases or Index to Diseases indicates otherwise.

EXAMPLE: A patient is admitted as a hospital inpatient with chest pain, fever, and shortness of breath. Chest X-ray reveals exacerbated CHF. Physical examination reveals acute bronchitis. The patient's prior history and current EKG findings are consistent with unstable angina (Figure 5-3). All three conditions were treated with medications, and all three diagnoses equally meet the criteria for the definition of principal diagnosis. The coder can code and sequence any one of the three diagnoses as the principal diagnosis.

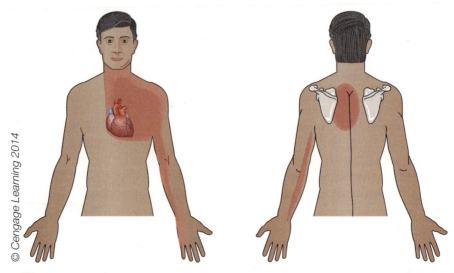

Figure 5-3 Patterns of angina

As an alternative scenario, this patient underwent coronary arteriography that revealed coronary artery disease and 95% blockage of two prominent arterial branches. Subsequently, the patient was taken to the operating room for percutaneous transluminal coronary angioplasty (PTCA). In this scenario, the coronary arteriography diagnostic work-up and PTCA treatment criteria clearly distinguish coronary artery disease, identified as the etiology (cause) of the patient's unstable angina, as the principal diagnosis.

Two or More Diagnoses That Equally Meet the Definition for Principal Diagnosis

In the unusual instance when two or more diagnoses *equally* meet the criteria for principal diagnosis, as determined by one or more of the following, any one of the diagnoses may be reported as the principal diagnosis:

- Circumstances of admission

- Diagnostic work-up and/or therapy provided

- Alphabetic index, tabular list, or other coding guidelines do not provide sequencing direction

Determining which of several diagnoses to report as the principal diagnosis when multiple diagnoses equally meet the criteria for selection as the principal diagnosis is called **optimizing reimbursement**, and it is permitted under the PPS. (Trauma cases often result in several diagnoses, any one of which could be selected and reported as the principal diagnosis.) **Maximizing reimbursement** is not permitted because it involves (1) selecting and reporting as principal diagnosis the code that results in the highest level of reimbursement for the facility, whether that diagnosis meets the criteria for selection or not, or (2) assigning a higher-paying code (upcoding) to a diagnosis (or ICD-9-CM, ICD-10-PCS or CPT/HCPCS code to a procedure) even if patient record documentation does not support that code selection. (Under the IPPS, upcoding and maximizing reimbursement is called DRG creep.)

EXAMPLE 1: OPTIMIZING REIMBURSEMENT: The patient was admitted to the hospital after an automobile accident, initial evaluation was performed in the ED, and the patient was diagnosed with fractured left femur and fractured right humerus. Inpatient treatment included an open reduction internal fixation of the fractured left femur and open reduction internal fixation of the fractured right humerus. In this case, either the fractured left femur or the fractured right humerus could be reported as the principal diagnosis. The best practice would be to assign codes to each diagnosis and procedure, enter them into the diagnosis-related grouper, determine which would result in optimal reimbursement for the hospital, and report that code as the principal diagnosis.

EXAMPLE 2: MAXIMIZING REIMBURSEMENT AND UPCODING: The patient was admitted as a hospital inpatient for treatment of urosepsis, which is a urinary tract infection (UTI). (A secondary code is assigned to indicate the cause of the infection, such as *E. coli*). The DRG reimbursement rate is approximately $2,300. Using encoder and DRG grouper software, the coder may notice that the code for sepsis results in the higher DRG rate of approximately $6,400. If the code for sepsis is reported as principal diagnosis, this case would most likely be reviewed by the MAC and/or the quality improvement organization to verify accuracy of the reported code. Upon review, the error would be discovered and the hospital could be subject to sanctions (e.g., loss of Medicare participating provider status) and/or fines.

Two or More Comparative or Contrasting Conditions

In those rare instances when two or more contrasting or comparative diagnoses are documented as *either/or* (or similar terminology), they are coded as if the diagnoses were confirmed. The diagnoses are sequenced according to the circumstances of the admission. If no further determination can be made as to which diagnosis should be principal, either diagnosis may be sequenced first.

EXAMPLE: An elderly patient was treated for complaints of chest pain and shortness of breath, and the physician documented "acute asthma or acute pneumonia" on the patient's record. The patient died before diagnostic work-up could be initiated, and the family declined to have the patient undergo an autopsy. Assign an ICD-9-CM or ICD-10-CM code to both conditions, and either diagnosis may be sequenced as the principal diagnosis to optimize reimbursement.

Symptom(s) Followed by Contrasting/Comparative Diagnoses

When a symptom(s) is followed by contrasting/comparative diagnoses, the symptom code is sequenced first. All of the contrasting/comparative diagnoses should be coded as additional diagnoses.

EXAMPLE: An elderly male patient was admitted to the hospital for genitourinary evaluation due to complaints that he never feels the urge to urinate, but it seems as though his bladder never completely empties and small amounts of urine leak continuously. The physician explained to the patient that this condition is called "overflow incontinence," is seen in older males who have enlarged prostates, and can be the result of several underlying conditions. The physician documented the following diagnoses: rule out benign prostatic hyperplasia, rule out genitourinary neoplasm, rule out urinary stones, and rule out neurogenic bladder. Report the code for "overflow incontinence" followed by codes for each "rule out" diagnosis.

Original Treatment Plan Not Carried Out

Even though treatment may not have been carried out due to unforeseen circumstances, the condition which, after study, occasioned the admission to the hospital is sequenced as the principal diagnosis.

EXAMPLE: The patient was scheduled for surgery due to severe ureteritis. After administration of anesthesia, the patient was prepped for an endoscopic biopsy of the right ureter. The endoscope passed easily into the urinary bladder but was unable to advance to the right ureter due to ureteral blockage. The surgeon removed the endoscope, and the patient was taken to the recovery room.

In this example, the surgery was halted because after the cystourethroscope was advanced through the urinary bladder, it could not be advanced into the ureter. The principal diagnosis is ureteritis, and the significant other diagnosis is ureteral blockage.

Complications of Surgery and Other Medical Care

When an admission is for treatment of a complication resulting from surgery or other medical care, the complication code is sequenced as the principal diagnosis. If the complication is classified to the 996–999 series and the code lacks the necessary specificity in describing the complication, an additional code for the specific complication should be assigned.

EXAMPLE: A 54-year-old male patient was admitted to the hospital for severe stomach pain, nausea, vomiting, and fever of 102 degrees. The abdomen was rigid and distended. Past history revealed that two months ago the patient had undergone open cholecystectomy for cholecystitis with cholelithiasis. Laboratory tests revealed elevated white blood cell count. Patient was scheduled for exploratory laparotomy, which revealed the presence of abscessed stitches. Cultures taken were positive for *Staphylococcus aureus*.

In this example, the principal diagnosis is abscessed stitches, which is a complication of the open cholecystectomy. The significant other diagnoses include staphylococcal infection and postoperative status. The principal procedure is exploratory laparotomy, and the significant other procedure is reopening of recent laparotomy site.

Uncertain Diagnosis (or Qualified Diagnosis)

If the principal diagnosis documented at the time of discharge is qualified as probable, suspected, likely, questionable, possible, or still to be ruled out, code the condition as if it existed or was established. The basis for this guideline is the diagnostic work-up, arrangements for further work-up or observation, and initial therapeutic approach that correspond most closely with the established diagnosis.

 Note:

The *uncertain diagnosis* guideline applies only to diagnoses reported for inpatient admissions to acute, short-term, long-term, psychiatric, and rehabilitation *hospitals*. Other nonoutpatient health care settings (e.g., home health care, skilled nursing facilities, nursing homes) and all outpatient health care settings do not assign codes to uncertain diagnoses. They assign codes to signs and/or symptoms when a provider has not documented a definitive diagnosis.

EXAMPLE: A 24-year-old female was admitted due to fever of 102 degrees for a period of two days, as well as chills. The patient has a past history of having undergone a recent laparoscopic appendectomy, for which she was prescribed postoperative antibiotics. She had completed the prescription when she spiked a fever and started experiencing chills. Review of systems reveals complaints of painful urination for two days. The patient states that she has frequent UTIs. Although the urine culture was negative, it is likely that this patient has a UTI, which has to be treated aggressively given her postoperative status.

Patient received intravenous ciprofloxacin and aminoglycoside for a period of 72 hours, after which she improved and was discharged for follow-up in the office. She was prescribed an oral antibiotic to be continued 10 days after discharge. Final diagnosis is possible UTI. In this example, although the final diagnosis of possible UTI is uncertain (or qualified), it is the principal diagnosis. The other significant diagnosis is postoperative surgical status.

Admission from Observation Unit

Admission Following Medical Observation. When a patient is admitted to an observation unit for a medical condition that either worsens or does not improve and is subsequently admitted as an inpatient to the same hospital for this same medical condition, the principal diagnosis would be the medical condition that led to the hospital admission.

Admission Following Postoperative Observation. When a patient is admitted to an observation unit to monitor a condition (or complication) that develops following out patient surgery, and is subsequently admitted as an inpatient of the same hospital, hospitals should apply the Uniform Hospital Discharge Data Set (UHDDS) definition of principal diagnosis as "that condition established after study to be chiefly responsible for occasioning the admission of the patient to the hospital for care."

Admission from Outpatient Surgery

When a patient receives surgery in the hospital's outpatient surgery department and is subsequently admitted for continuing inpatient care at the same hospital, the following guidelines should be followed in selecting the principal diagnosis for the inpatient admission:

- If the reason for the inpatient admission is a complication, assign the complication as the principal diagnosis.

- If no complication, or other condition, is documented as the reason for the inpatient admission, assign the reason for the outpatient surgery as the principal diagnosis.

- If the reason for the inpatient admission is another condition unrelated to the surgery, assign the unrelated condition as the principal diagnosis.

Other (Additional) Diagnoses with Documentation That Supports Reporting ●

For reporting purposes, the definition for *other (additional) diagnoses* is interpreted as additional conditions that affect patient care by requiring one or more of the following:

- Clinical evaluation
- Therapeutic treatment
- Diagnostic procedures
- Extended length of hospital stay
- Increased nursing care and/or monitoring

The UHDDS defines **other (additional) diagnoses** as "all conditions that coexist at the time of admission, that develop subsequently, or that affect the treatment received and/or the length of stay." Diagnoses related to an earlier episode that have no bearing on the current hospital stay are not coded. Up to 17 secondary diagnoses are reported on a UB-04 claim. The UB-04 claim contains separate fields for entry of three external cause of effect ICD codes (in addition to the 17 secondary diagnosis codes).

Note:

Effective January 1, 2011, CMS expanded the number of other (additional) diagnoses reported from to 24. CMS is conducting an analysis of the entire claims processing system to determine the changes needed to process the additional ICD codes (e.g., increasing the number of diagnosis code fields required for electronic submission of UB-04 data). It is unknown whether the paper-based UB-04 claim will be similarly revised to expand the number of diagnosis code fields.

The Centers for Medicare & Medicaid Services (CMS) has developed a standard list of diagnoses that are recognized as comorbidities and/or complications (CC) for DRGs. When a CC is present as a secondary diagnosis, it can affect DRG assignment. A **comorbidity** is a condition that coexists at the time of admission (e.g., diabetes mellitus, hypertension, asthma), and a **complication** is a condition that occurs during the course of the inpatient hospital episode (e.g., fractured hip resulting from fall while gait training, postoperative infection, hospital-acquired staphylococcus infection).

Note:

The UHDDS definition for other *(additional) diagnoses* applies to inpatient diagnoses reported by acute care, short-term care, long-term care, behavioral health care, and rehabilitation hospitals.

DRGs with CC require a substantial increase in utilization of hospital resources, and the reimbursement for these DRGs reflects an increase in payment. While just one CC can change a *DRG without CC* to a *DRG with CC*, there are a number of stand-alone DRGs that are not affected by the presence or absence of CCs. For stand-alone DRGs, the DRG (and reimbursement amount) will change (and increase) only if the principal diagnosis is changed or a significant surgical procedure is reported.

EXAMPLE: An 86-year-old female was admitted to the hospital with complaints of severe shortness of breath, dyspnea, and chest pain. Upon evaluation, the attending physician determined that the patient has a history of intrinsic asthma and is currently experiencing acute exacerbation of that condition. The patient also has a past history of hypertension, for which she takes medication. Last year the patient was treated in the hospital's pain clinic on an outpatient basis for cluster headaches, which have not recurred. Patient received respiratory therapy and drug therapy for the asthma. The physician also ordered medications and patient education for the hypertension and blood pressure monitoring three times per nursing shift. The final diagnoses documented upon discharge include acute exacerbation of intrinsic asthma and hypertension.

In this example, the principal diagnosis is acute exacerbation of intrinsic asthma and the comorbidity (coexisting condition or other significant diagnosis) is hypertension. The hypertension increased nursing care and monitoring because medications were administered, patient teaching was performed, and the patient's blood pressure was taken three times per shift.

Coding Tip:

When other diagnoses are documented and no supporting documentation can be found in the patient record, make sure you query the physician to determine whether the diagnosis is to be coded and reported. For example, when a patient is admitted for treatment of an acute condition (e.g., trauma, illness) and the physician notes positive findings on the physical examination (e.g., tendonitis) that are not treated during the hospitalization, do not code the positive findings because they do not impact the episode of care.

Previous Conditions Stated as a Diagnosis

If the provider has documented a diagnosis in the list of diagnoses on the discharge summary or the face sheet in the patient record, it should ordinarily be coded. However, some providers document diagnoses for resolved conditions or chronic diagnoses and status-post procedures from previous admissions that have no bearing on the current inpatient stay. Such conditions are not coded and reported for reimbursement purposes. However, family and personal history codes are reported as secondary codes *if* the historical condition or family history impacts current care or influences the patient's treatment.

EXAMPLE: A 92-year-old female patient was admitted as a hospital inpatient for acute MI of the anterolateral wall. The patient's history is negative for cardiovascular or respiratory complaints, and she states that she has not had an MI in the past. The patient does have a past history of localized uterine adenocarcinoma 20 years ago, for which she underwent vaginal hysterectomy. The final diagnosis is acute anterolateral wall MI, initial episode of care.

In this example, the principal diagnosis is acute anterolateral wall MI, initial episode of care. The localized uterine adenocarcinoma is not assigned a neoplasm code from ICD-9-CM or ICD-10-CM Chapter 2. Instead, it is appropriate to assign a code for history of uterine cancer.

Abnormal Findings

Abnormal findings (e.g., ancillary tests such as laboratory, X-ray, pathologic, and other diagnostic results) are not coded and reported unless the provider documents their clinical significance. If the ancillary test findings are outside the normal range and the attending provider has ordered other tests to evaluate the condition or prescribed treatment, it is appropriate to ask the provider whether the abnormal finding should be added.

 Note:

In the outpatient setting, the provider interprets diagnostic test results, and codes are assigned for such encounters.

EXAMPLE: A 49-year-old male patient was admitted as a hospital inpatient for acute pneumonia due to *Staphylococcus aureus*, which was evaluated and successfully treated. During hospitalization, the patient underwent an EKG that was interpreted by the cardiologist as being normal. The EKG report did document abnormal T-wave changes.

In this example, the principal diagnosis is acute pneumonia due to *Staphylococcus aureus*. The coder should query the physician to determine if a code should be assigned to "abnormal T-wave changes" as documented on the EKG. It is likely that the coder will be told by the physician that such changes are commonly associated with EKGs performed on anxious patients and that this male patient was quite ill, which could cause anxiety.

Note:

The "uncertain diagnosis" is applicable only to inpatient admissions to short-term, acute, long-term care, and psychiatric hospitals. ("uncertain diagnosis" is also called "qualified diagnosis.")

Uncertain Diagnosis (as Other/Additional Diagnosis)

If the diagnosis documented at the time of discharge is qualified as "probable," "suspected," "likely," "questionable," "possible," or "still to be ruled out" or other similar terms indicating uncertainty, code the condition as if it existed or was established. The basis for these guidelines are the diagnostic work-up, arrangements for further work-up or observation, and initial therapeutic approach that correspond most closely with the established diagnosis.

Inpatient Procedure Coding Guidelines

Depending on state reporting requirements, when the circumstances of inpatient admission govern the sequencing of procedure codes, UHDDS definitions are used to report inpatient data elements in a standardized manner. Circumstances associated with an inpatient admission govern the sequencing of:

- Principal procedure.

- Significant other procedures (or secondary procedures).

EXAMPLE: New York State's (NYS) *Statewide Planning and Research Cooperative System (SPARCS)* is a comprehensive data reporting system that was established in 1979 in cooperation with the

Exercise 5.2 – Inpatient Diagnosis Coding Guidelines

Instructions: Match the case scenario with the sequencing guideline.

_____   1. Patient undergoes appendectomy and develops postoperative wound infection.

_____   2. Patient admitted with acute asthma and acute CHF, both of which were treated.

_____   3. Patient admitted with chest pain and shortness of breath due to either pneumonia or pneumonitis.

_____   4. Patient admitted and treated for acute gastroenteritis has extremely low potassium level. (Physician query initiated.)

_____   5. Patient admitted with acute gastroenteritis versus acute gastric ulcer; patient treated symptomatically.

_____   6. Elderly patient admitted with recent history of confusion, forgetfulness, and combative behavior. Senile dementia due to Alzheimer's disease.

_____   7. Patient admitted for treatment of acute MI and receives medication and patient education for previously diagnosed insulin-dependent diabetes mellitus.

_____   8. Patient admitted with right lower quadrant pain and elevated fever. Possible ectopic pregnancy. Possible acute appendicitis.

_____   9. Patient admitted for treatment of fractured hip; has a past history of cholecystitis with cholecystectomy one year ago.

_____   10. Patient with a diagnosis of multiparity, admitted for elective sterilization, was found to have elevated temperature, and surgery was canceled.

a. Abnormal findings

b. Complications of surgery and other medical care

c. Original treatment plan not carried out

d. Other (additional) diagnoses reported

e. Previous conditions stated as diagnoses

f. Symptom(s) followed by contrasting/comparative diagnoses

g. Two or more comparative or contrasting conditions coded as if the diagnosis is confirmed

h. Two or more diagnoses equally meeting definition for principal diagnosis

i. Two or more interrelated conditions equally meeting definition of principal diagnosis

j. Uncertain, or qualified, diagnosis

health care industry and state government. Initially created to collect information on discharges from hospitals, SPARCS now collects patient-level detail on patient characteristics, diagnoses and treatments, services, and charges for every NYS hospital discharge, ambulatory surgery patient, and emergency department admission. SPARCS created *output data dictionaries*, which include definitions, codes and values, and edit applications for inpatient and outpatient *output data elements*. For electronic claims purposes, SPARCS requires reporting of the principal procedure and significant other procedures. The SPARCS outpatient data dictionary's definition of these terms is based on the federal government's UHDDS definition.

Coding Tip:

Inpatient procedures are classified using ICD-9-CM Volume 3 *or* ICD-10-PCS. Outpatient and physician office settings report CPT and HCPCS level II codes for procedure/ services (discussed in Chapters 7–18.)

Note:

When CMS implemented MS-DRGs (discussed in Chapter 19), they discontinued the practice of sequencing procedure codes for reimbursement purposes. Instead, all operating room procedures performed that are surgical in nature, carry a procedural risk, carry an anesthetic risk, or require specialized training are assigned ICD-9-CM or ICD-10-PCS codes and reported. Nonsurgical procedures and minor surgical procedures that are not usually performed in an operating room are not treated as operating procedures by MS-DRGs. However, a few nonoperating room procedures that impact the assignment of MS-DRGs for certain principal diagnoses *are* reported (e.g., extracorporeal shock wave lithotripsy for patients with a principal diagnosis of urinary stones).

Principal Procedure and Other Significant Procedures

When required for reimbursement purposes, the principal procedure is sequenced first, followed by other significant procedure(s) (when more than one procedure is reported on an inpatient claim). The **principal procedure** is:

- Performed for definitive treatment rather than for diagnostic or exploratory purposes.
- Necessary to treat a complication.
- Most closely related to the principal diagnosis.

Other significant procedures (or **secondary procedures**):

- Are surgical in nature (e.g., incision, excision, amputation).
- Carry a procedural (or operative) risk.
- Carry an anesthetic risk.
- Require highly trained personnel.
- Require special facilities or equipment.

One principal procedure is reported on a paper-based UB-04 claim, and up to five significant procedures can be reported on the same paper-based UB-04 claim. Similarly, one principal procedure is reported on an electronic claim, but up to 14 significant procedures can be reported on the same electronic claim.

Effective January 1, 2011, CMS expanded the number of other (secondary) significant procedure codes reported to 24. CMS is conducting an analysis of the entire claims processing system to determine the changes needed to report the additional ICD procedure codes (e.g., increasing the number of procedure code fields required for electronic submission of UB-04 data). *It is unknown whether the paper-based UB-04 claim will be similarly revised to expand the number of procedure code (and date) fields.*

EXAMPLE: A 64-year-old male patient presented to the ED complaining of ringing in his ears, dizziness, blurred vision, confusion, and difficulty walking. Upon evaluation by the ED physician, the patient stated that these symptoms started about 24 hours ago. Past history revealed that the patient takes medication for hypercholesterolemia and hypertension. Physical examination revealed blood pressure of 180/115. When asked, the patient stated that he had been taking his hypertension medication as prescribed. Patient underwent carotid ultrasound to evaluate the blood flow of the carotid arteries, and results indicated the need for carotid angiogram to measure blockage of the carotid arteries.

The ED physician transferred the case to a cardiologist, who admitted the patient to the hospital and performed a bilateral carotid angiogram. Angiogram revealed 92% blockage of the right carotid artery and 24% blockage of the left carotid artery. The patient was admitted to the hospital and scheduled for carotid angioplasty with insertion of carotid stent in the morning, which was performed uneventfully. Final diagnoses were documented as carotid artery occlusion, hypertension, hypercholesterolemia, and impending stroke. Procedures performed included carotid ultrasound, carotid angiogram, and carotid angioplasty.

In this example, the principal procedure is carotid angioplasty, Other significant procedures include insertion of carotid stent and carotid angiogram. (The carotid ultrasound is not categorized as an operating room procedure and is not reported.)

Exercise 5.3 – Inpatient Procedure Coding Guidelines

Instructions: Complete each statement.

1. Depending on state reporting requirements, when the circumstances of inpatient admission govern the sequencing of procedure codes, _____ are used to report inpatient data elements in a standardized manner.

2. Inpatient procedures are classified using _____ or _____.

3. Outpatient and physician office settings report _____ and _____ codes for procedure and services.

4. When CMS implemented _____, they discontinued the practice of sequencing procedure codes for reimbursement purposes.

5. When required for reimbursement purposes, the principal procedure is sequenced _____.

6. The principal procedure is defined as being: _____.

7. Other significant procedures (or secondary procedures) are defined as: _____.

8. A paper-based UB-04 claim allows for the reporting of _____ principal procedure(s) and _____ significant procedure(s).

9. An electronic inpatient claim allows for reporting of _____ principal procedure(s) and up to _____ significant procedures.

10. Effective January 2011, CMS expanded the number of other (secondary) significant procedure codes that can be reported to _____.

ICD-9-CM Procedure Coding

The ICD-9-CM Tabular List of Procedures is a modification of the WHO publication *ICD-9 Classification of Procedures in Medicine (ICPM), Fascicle V—Surgical Procedures*. Whenever feasible, the three-digit subcategories that range from 01.0 to 86.9 are maintained in ICD-9-CM Volume 3 as they appear in the WHO publication. Nonsurgical procedures (e.g., diagnostic procedures) are classified separately in the ICD-9-CM Tabular List of Procedures as categories 87–99 whenever feasible, and category 00 was added to classify additional procedures and interventions that are *not elsewhere classified* in ICD-9-CM Volume 3.

 ICD-10 Alert!

The *International Classification of Diseases, 10th Revision, Procedure Classification System* (ICD-10-PCS) will replace ICD-9-CM, Volume 3. Hospitals will use ICD-10-PCS to code and classify procedure data from inpatient records only. (Provider offices and outpatient healthcare settings will continue to use CPT and HCPCS level II to code procedures and services.)

The structure of the ICD-9-CM Tabular List of Procedures is based on anatomy rather than surgical specialty, and it contains numeric codes only (no alphabetical characters are used).

The following general coding guidelines are followed when assigning ICD-9-CM procedure codes for inpatient settings:

1. The ICD-9-CM procedure classification is published in its own volume (Volume 3) and contains both an Index to Procedures and a Tabular List of Procedures. All of the ICD-9-CM Tabular List of Procedures chapters are organized as body systems, except for the following three chapters:

    • Chapter 00 – Procedures and Interventions, Not Elsewhere Classified

    • Chapter 13 – Obstetrical Procedures

    • Chapter 16 – Miscellaneous Diagnostic and Therapeutic Procedures

    The ICD-9-CM coding system was developed in the 1970s and implemented in 1979. Since then, many of the Tabular List of Procedures chapters have become full, making it difficult to create new codes. Once a category is full, similar procedures are combined under one code and/or new codes are located in another chapter of the tabular list.

    CMS examined ICD-9-CM to identify available codes that could be assigned to new procedures and technologies. Chapter 00 (codes 00.00 through 00.99) and Chapter 17 (codes 17.00 through 17.99) were available. As of October 2002, CMS has been using Chapter 00 to assign codes to identify new technology. New codes are added to the appropriate section of ICD-9-CM as a first priority; when no codes are available in appropriate chapters, new codes are created using the next available code number in Chapter 00. Prior to 2001, procedures were grouped exclusively by body system, except for Chapters 13 and 16, and similar procedures were assigned to the same two-digit category. This new method of assigning new codes means that Chapter 00 contains an assorted group of procedures and interventions that affect all body systems.

    Chapter 17 (codes 17.00 through 17.99) in the ICD-9-CM Tabular List of Procedures will be created when available codes in Chapter 00 have been exhausted. Thus far, no codes have been assigned to ICD-9-CM Chapter 17, which does not yet appear in published versions of the Tabular List of Procedures.

2. The coding conventions that appear in ICD-9-CM Index to Procedures and Tabular List of Procedures are similar to those used in the ICD-9-CM Index to Diseases, Index to External Causes and Injuries, and Tabular List of Diseases. (ICD-9-CM coding conventions are discussed in Chapter 3.)

3. Use both the ICD-9-CM Index to Procedures and the Tabular List of Procedures when locating and assigning codes because relying on just the index or tabular list results in coding errors and less specificity when selecting codes.

     EXAMPLE: The ICD-9-CM Index to Procedures entry for "microscopic examination" lists code 91.9. Verify code 91.9 in the Tabular List of Procedures and notice that a fourth-digit subclassification code is assigned to identify the type of examination.

    > **Note:**
    >
    > Surgical procedures indexed as eponyms are listed under main term *Operation* and then the eponym (e.g., *Operation*, Billroth I) in addition to the type of procedure (e.g., gastrectomy, Billroth I).

4. ICD-9-CM Index to Procedures main terms are organized in alphabetical order according to type of procedure (e.g., excision), common name of the procedure (e.g., gastrectomy), and eponyms (e.g., Billroth I operation).

    To find procedure codes for the removal of an organ, go to main term *Excision* or *Resection* and locate the appropriate subterm (e.g., *adenoids* or *bronchus*). When a lesion (pathologic change in tissue) has been removed from an organ, go to main term *Excision*, subterm *lesion* and locate the appropriate organ (e.g., skin) or site (e.g., peritoneum).

5. Locate each term in the ICD-9-CM Index to Procedures first, and verify the code selected in the Tabular List of Procedures. Make sure you read and are guided by coding conventions (e.g., instructional notations such as NOS) that appear in either the index or the tabular list.

6.   Pay attention to the level of detail when assigning ICD-9-CM codes because procedure codes are to be reported using the highest number of digits available.

Note:

Review the explanations and examples of ICD-9-CM coding conventions in Chapter 3.

ICD-9-CM procedure codes contain three or four digits. Codes with two digits are category codes, and they are further subdivided by assigning third and/or fourth digits to provide greater detail. A two-digit procedure is not reported because all of them are further subdivided. Where third-digit subcategories and/or fourth-digit subclassifications are provided, they must be assigned. A code is invalid if it has not been coded to the complete number of digits required for that code.

EXAMPLE: The ICD-9-CM Index to Procedures entry for "excision, lesion, larynx" lists code 30.09. Verify code 30.09 in the Tabular List of Procedures and note that a different fourth-digit subclassification code is assigned if the physician documented "marsupialization of a laryngeal cyst." (*Marsupialization* is a surgical procedure in which the interior of an unremovable cyst is laid open so that the cyst can be allowed to shrink gradually and spontaneously.)

7.   Appropriate codes from ICD-9-CM (00.0 through 99.99) are reported to identify procedures and services provided during an encounter. Make sure you carefully review the code description before assigning the code. Some procedure codes indicate whether a procedure was performed unilaterally or bilaterally. If the surgeon performed a procedure on both sides (e.g., joint replacement surgery of both knees), assign the code twice. If the surgeon performed a bilateral procedure and the code description indicates "bilateral," assign the code once.

8.   If the phrase *omit code* is found after the main term or a subterm, do not assign a code to the operative approach because it is considered an integral part of the procedure. In addition, do not assign codes for operative closures or the administration of anesthesia.

EXAMPLE: The Index to Procedures entry for "Incision (and drainage), abdominal wall, as operative approach" instructs the coder to *omit code* for an operative approach into the abdominal wall when a definitive procedure is performed.

The operative approach *is* coded when the procedure for creating an opening into a body cavity (e.g., exploratory laparotomy) is for diagnostic purposes only, *and a therapeutic procedure was not performed*.

9.   When the procedure in the statement is not easily found in the index, use the main terms below to locate the code.

ICD-9-CM Index to Procedures—Main Terms		
Application	Insertion	Resection
Closure	Operation	Revision
Correction	Procedure	Suture
Destruction	Release	Test
Division	Removal	Therapy
Incision	Repair	Transfer

© Cengage Learning 2014

10.   Assign combination codes when available and multiple codes as needed. A combination code is a single code that is used to classify two procedures. *Combination codes* are located by referring to subterm entries in the Index to Procedures and by reading "includes" and "excludes" notes in the Tabular List of Procedures. Assign two or more *multiple codes* to completely classify the elements of a complex procedure. Make sure you carefully review tabular list entries, which provide guidance regarding the assignment

of multiple codes. Make sure you assign only the combination code when that code fully identifies the procedure performed or when the index so directs. Do not report multiple codes when ICD-9-CM provides a combination code that clearly identifies all of the elements documented in the procedure.

EXAMPLE 1: ICD-9-CM COMBINATION CODE: Assign combination code 28.3 to the procedure "tonsillectomy and adenoidectomy" because the code description includes both procedures. Note that the description for code 28.2 is "tonsillectomy without adenoidectomy," while the description for code 28.6 is "adenoidectomy without tonsillectomy." It would be incorrect to assign 28.2 and 28.6 to a tonsillectomy and adenoidectomy procedure.

EXAMPLE 2: ICD-9-CM MULTIPLE CODES: Assign two codes (28.3 and 28.7) for a tonsillectomy and adenoidectomy case if the patient record includes documentation of "control of hemorrhage after tonsillectomy and adenoidectomy." The Index to Procedures entry for "Control, hemorrhage, tonsils (postoperative)" lists code 28.7, which should be verified in the Tabular List of Procedures. The word *and* in the code description is interpreted as "and/or." If the patient had undergone "tonsillectomy without adenoidectomy" (28.2) *or* "adenoidectomy without tonsillectomy" (28.6) and the patient record documented "control of hemorrhage after tonsillectomy and adenoidectomy," code 28.7 would be reported with either code 28.2 or 28.6, depending on the procedure performed.

11. When laparoscopic, thoracoscopic, or arthroscopic procedures are converted to open procedures (for which a lengthier surgical incision is made), assign only the open procedure code. An open procedure involves making an incision through skin, underlying tissues, and possibly muscle to access the affected body area that requires surgery (e.g., an abdominal hysterectomy). A closed procedure uses an endoscope to visualize an area (e.g., a colonoscopy), and instruments are passed through the scope to complete the procedure (e.g., a closed biopsy).

Coding Tip:

Assign the appropriate V code, listed below, as an additional diagnosis code when laparoscopic, thoracoscopic, or arthroscopic procedures are converted to open procedures.

- V64.41 (laparoscopic surgical procedure converted to open procedure)
- V64.42 (thoracoscopic surgical procedure converted to open procedure)
- V64.43 (arthroscopic surgical procedure converted to open procedure)

12. When coding endoscopic procedures, if the endoscope is passed through more than one body cavity, assign the code for the most distant site. For example, endoscopy of esophagus and stomach is coded as endoscopy of the stomach (gastroscopy, 44.13).

13. When coding biopsies, review the patient record to determine the type of biopsy performed, as follows:

- *Closed*: Performed percutaneously, or through the skin, by aspiration, bristle or brush, endoscope, or needle.

- *Open*: Performed after an incision has been made.

    The ICD-9-CM Tabular List of Procedures classifies most (closed) endoscopic biopsies as a combination code. However, if a combination code for an endoscopic biopsy (e.g., endoscopic biopsy of urethra) is not classified in the Tabular List of Procedures, assign two codes. The code for the endoscopic approach is reported first because it is considered the more significant procedure and creates more risk for the patient. Then the code for the biopsy is reported.

    For an open biopsy, it is understood that the incision is included in the description of the biopsy code (even though the code description might not actually state this). For example, a skin incision is made to perform a bone biopsy, but only the code for the bone biopsy is reported. It is understood that the surgeon had to make a skin incision to reach to the bone.

When a patient undergoes both a biopsy and subsequent removal of additional tissue (e.g., partial gastrectomy), assign two codes. Report the code for the more definitive procedure (e.g., partial gastrectomy) first, followed by the biopsy code.

When an aspiration, bristle or brush, or needle biopsy is performed during another open procedure, assign a closed biopsy code. For example, during surgery for a partial gastrectomy, the surgeon noticed that the liver was enlarged, so he performed a needle biopsy of the liver. Report the code for the partial gastrectomy first, followed by the code for closed biopsy of the liver.

When the surgeon performs an open or a closed biopsy, the pathologist evaluates a frozen section (to determine the presence of cancer), and the surgeon performs a procedure to remove malignant tissue, report the therapeutic procedure code (e.g., removal of malignant tissue) first and then the code for the biopsy.

14. When a scheduled procedure is canceled after the patient had been admitted to the facility and the patient had not been prepped for the surgical procedure, do not report a procedure code. A scheduled procedure that is halted after the patient has been prepped for surgery and/or during performance of surgery is considered an incomplete procedure. The following guidelines are to be followed when assigning codes for incomplete procedures:

- If the surgeon makes an incision to begin surgery and the surgery is halted, assign a code for the incision of the site (e.g., skin incision). Do not assign a code for the scheduled procedure because it was not performed.

EXAMPLE: CANCELLED SURGERY AFTER INCISION OF THE SITE: The patient was admitted for a partial gastrectomy due to perforated gastric ulcer. Just after the surgeon had made the abdominal incision, the anesthesiologist alerted the surgeon that the patient was experiencing respiratory distress. The surgeon closed the abdominal incision, and the patient was transferred to the intensive care unit. Assign procedure code 54.0 for incision of the abdominal wall. (Do not assign a procedure code for the partial gastrectomy because it was not performed.) Assign diagnosis code 531.50 for "perforated gastric ulcer" first and assign diagnosis code V64.1 as a secondary diagnosis for "surgical procedure not carried out because of contraindications."

- If an endoscopic approach does not result in the intended procedure (e.g., endoscopic biopsy of ureter, 56.33), assign a code for just the endoscopy (e.g., ureteroscopy, 56.31).

EXAMPLE: ENDOSCOPIC SURGERY THAT DOES NOT RESULT IN THE INTENDED PROCEDURE: The patient was scheduled for surgery due to severe ureteritis. After administration of anesthesia, the patient was prepped for an endoscopic biopsy of the right ureter. The endoscope passed easily into the urinary bladder but was unable to advance to the right ureter due to ureteral blockage. The surgeon removed the endoscope, and the patient was taken to the recovery room.

Assign procedure code 57.32 for "cystoscopy." (Do not assign a procedure code for the biopsy of the ureter because it was not performed.) Assign diagnosis code 593.89 for severe ureteritis first and assign diagnosis code V64.1 as a secondary diagnosis code to explain why the surgery was halted. Assign diagnosis code 593.4 as an additional secondary diagnosis for the ureteral blockage, which was noted during surgery (and resulted in halting of the procedure).

- If a cavity or an anatomical site was entered and the surgery was halted at that point, assign a code for the exploration of the cavity or site (e.g., exploration of abdominal cavity, or exploratory laparotomy, 54.11)

EXAMPLE: HALTED SURGERY AFTER CAVITY OR ANATOMIC SITE IS ENTERED: Patient was surgically prepped for lobectomy of liver due to liver thrombosis. A transabdominal incision was made and exploratory laparotomy performed. As the surgeon prepared to perform lobectomy of the liver, the surgical suite went dark due to a severe thunderstorm. The hospital's generators were activated, and the surgeon closed the transabdominal incision. The patient's surgery was rescheduled. Assign procedure code 54.11 for the exploratory laparotomy. (Do not assign a procedure code for the lobectomy of liver, which was not performed.) Assign diagnosis code 453.0 for "liver thrombosis" first and assign diagnosis code V64.3 as a secondary diagnosis to explain why the surgery was halted.

 **Note:**

Assign a code from the ICD-9-CM Tabular List of Diseases V64 category as an additional code to indicate a reason for the canceled surgery. Do *not* report a code from V64 as the first-listed diagnosis (outpatient) or principal diagnosis (inpatient); instead, report the reason for the scheduled surgery as the first diagnosis.

Exercise 5.4 – ICD-9-CM Procedure Coding

Instructions: Indicate whether the statement is true (T) or false (F).

_____ **1.** The ICD-9-CM procedure classification is published in Volumes 3 and 4, which contains an Index to Procedures and a Tabular List of Procedures, respectively.

_____ **2.** The coding conventions that appear in ICD-9-CM Index to Procedures and Tabular List of Procedures are different from those used in the Index to Diseases, Index to External Causes and Injuries, and Tabular List of Diseases.

_____ **3.** Coders must use both the ICD-9-CM Index to Procedures and the Tabular List of Procedures when locating and assigning codes because relying on just the index or tabular list results in coding errors and less specificity when selecting codes.

_____ **4.** Index to Procedures main terms are organized in alphabetical order according to type of procedure only.

_____ **5.** Before assigning a procedure code, locate the procedure in the ICD-9-CM Index to Procedures first and then verify it in the Tabular List of Procedures, paying close attention to coding conventions that appear in either the index or the tabular list.

_____ **6.** ICD-9-CM procedure codes contain a maximum of two digits before the decimal and two digits after the decimal.

_____ **7.** If a surgeon performs a procedure on both sides (e.g., bilateral hip replacement surgery), assign the ICD-9-CM code once and add a modifier to indicate that the procedure was performed bilaterally.

_____ **8.** The phrase *omit code* is located after an ICD-9-CM Index to Procedures main term or a subterm, and the coder should assign the code because it is considered an integral part of the procedure.

_____ **9.** ICD-9-CM combination codes are multiple codes assigned to classify two or more procedures.

_____ **10.** When laparoscopic, thoracoscopic, or arthroscopic procedures are converted to open procedures (for which a lengthier surgical incision is made), assign only the open ICD-9-CM procedure code.

Instructions: Underline the main term in each procedure statement, and assign the appropriate ICD-9-CM procedure code(s).

_____ **11.** Augmentation mammoplasty

_____ **12.** Closed aspiration biopsy of spleen

_____ **13.** Injection of neurolytic agent into sympathetic nerve

_____ **14.** Laparoscopic unilateral salpingo-oophorectomy

_____ **15.** Ligation and stripping of varicose veins, left leg

(continues)

Exercise 5.4 (continued)

_____ **16.** Open biopsy of prostate

_____ **17.** Operative esophagoscopy (by incision)

_____ **18.** Parathyroidectomy, complete

_____ **19.** Partial breech extraction with forceps to head

_____ **20.** Partial hip replacement

_____ **21.** Percutaneous nephrostomy with fragmentation

_____ **22.** Puncture of nasal sinus for aspiration

_____ **23.** Replacement of only cardiac resynchronization defibrillator pulse generator device

_____ **24.** Transposition of pterygium

_____ **25.** Type II tympanoplasty

ICD-10-PCS Procedure Coding

The *International Classification of Diseases, 10th Revision, Procedure Classification System* (ICD-10-PCS) will replace ICD-9-CM, Volume 3, for use by hospitals to code and classify procedure data from inpatient records only. ICD-10-PCS codes use a **multiaxial structure** for its 7-character alphanumeric codes, which means a value from each of 7 hierarchies (positions) is assigned to construct a code. As a result, unique codes are constructed for all substantially different procedures, and the multiaxial structure allows new procedures to be easily incorporated as new codes.

The ICD-10-PCS coding manual contains the following:

- Index

- Tables

ICD-10-PCS Index

The ICD-10-PCS **Index** (Figure 5-4) organizes main terms in alphabetic order, providing the first 3 or 4 characters (and sometimes all 7 characters) of a code as well as direction to a specific location in the Tables. The Index is used to access the Tables, and it mirrors the structure of the Tables so it follows a consistent pattern of organization and use of hierarchies. The Index is organized as an alphabetic lookup, and the two types of main terms used are:

- Based on the value of the third character, which is the *root operation* (e.g., bypass, excision, incision).

- Common procedure terms (e.g., appendectomy, cholecystectomy), which usually provide direction to a root operation main term.

Purpose of ICD-10-PCS Index

The purpose of the ICD-10-PCS Index is to locate the appropriate table that contains all information necessary to construct a procedure code. The ICD-10-PCS Tables must always be consulted to construct the most appropriate valid code. It is not possible to construct a procedure code by using just the alphabetic index.

ICD-10-PCS Index
A

Abdominal aortic plexus *see* Nerve, Abdominal Sympathetic
Abdominal esophagus *see* Esophagus, Lower
Abdominohysterectomy
    see Excision, Uterus 0UB9
    see Resection, Uterus 0UT9
Abdominoplasty
    see Alteration, Wall, Abdominal 0W0F
    see Repair, Wall, Abdominal 0WQF
    see Supplement, Wall, Abdominal 0WUF
Abductor hallucis muscle
    see Muscle, Foot, Right
    see Muscle, Foot, Left
AbioCorTotal Replacement Heart
    see Synthetic Substitute
Ablation *see* Destruction
Abortion
    Abortifacient 10A07ZX
    Laminaria 10A07ZW
    Products of Conception 10A0
    Vacuum 10A07Z6
Abrasion *see* Extraction
Accessory cephalic vein
    see Vein, Cephalic, Right
    see Vein, Cephalic, Left
Accessory obturator nerve *see* Nerve, Lumbar Plexus
Accessory phrenic nerve *see* Nerve, Phrenic
Accessory spleen *see* Spleen

Permission to reuse in accordance with http://www.cms.hhs.gov Content Reuse and Linking policy.

Figure 5-4 ICD-10-CM Index (partial)

Note:

- The ICD-10-PCS index contains a hierarchical alphabetic lookup for locating a table that includes supplemental procedure terms (e.g., appendectomy) that correspond to root operation options.

- It is *not* possible to construct an ICD-10-PCS procedure code from the index. The purpose of the index is to locate the appropriate table that contains all information necessary to construct a procedure code.

- Coders are *not* required to consult the index before proceeding to the tables to construct an ICD-10-PCS code. A valid code can be constructed directly from the tables (by locating the appropriate section, body system, and root operation table).

ICD-10-PCS Tables

ICD-10-PCS **Tables** (Figure 5-5) are used to construct a complete and valid code (using a build-a-code approach). *Tables* include terms (and definitions) and rows, which contain **values** that are characters (individual letters and numbers) assigned to each of seven unique hierarchies (positions) needed to construct a valid ICD-10-PCS code. The first three rows of each Table list values and descriptions of the first 3 characters of codes in that table; subsequent rows list values (and descriptions) for the fourth through seventh characters of the ICD-10-PCS code.

0	**Medical and Surgical**			
0	**Central Nervous System**			
1	**Bypass:**		Altering the route of passage of the contents of a tubular body part	

Body Part Character 4	Approach Character 5	Device Character 6	Qualifier Character 7
6 Cerebral Ventricle	0 Open 3 Percutaneous	7 Autologous Tissue Substitute J Synthetic Substitute K Nonautologous Tissue Substitute	0 Nasopharynx 1 Mastoid sinus 2 Atrium 3 Blood Vessel 4 Pleural Cavity 5 Intestine 6 Peritoneal Cavity 7 Urinary Tract 8 Bone Marrow B Cerebral Cisterns
U Spinal Canal	0 Open 3 Percutaneous	7 Autologous Tissue Substitute J Synthetic Substitute K Nonautologous Tissue Substitute	4 Pleural Cavity 6 Peritoneal Cavity 7 Urinary Tract 9 Fallopian Tube

Figure 5-5 ICD-10-PCS Table (sample)

EXAMPLE: Refer to Figure 5-5, and notice that the first three characters in the upper portion of the table are 001. This indicates that codes will be constructed for procedures in the Medical and Surgical *section*, Central Nervous System *body system*, and Bypass *root operation* (defined in the table). Use the table in Figure 5-5 to construct an ICD-10-PCS code for the procedural statement (below) by assigning assign the fourth through seventh character values for each element of the procedure.

After *open incision into the cerebral ventricle, a synthetic shunt was inserted to allow excess cerebrospinal fluid (CSF) to flow* (bypass) *into the peritoneal cavity* (to decrease CSF pressure). ICD-10-PCS code 00160J6 is constructed by assigning a character for each value of the 7-character code:

Section	Body System	Root Operation	Body Part	Approach	Device	Qualifier
Medical and Surgical	Central Nervous System	Bypass	Cerebral Ventricle	Open	Synthetic Substitute	Peritoneal Cavity
0	0	1	6	0	J	6

© Cengage Learning 2014

ICD-10-PCS tables are organized in sections (Figure 5-6) that identify the general type of procedure, and each of the 7 characters in a table has a specific meaning (Figure 5-7). Within a section, all character meanings remain constant. (The first character of the ICD-10-PCS procedure code *always* specifies the section.) Within an ICD-10-PCS table, valid values include all combinations of choices for the fourth through seventh characters that are contained in the same row of a table.

- The columns in ICD-10-PCS Tables contain values for the fourth through seventh characters.

- The rows in ICD-10-PCS Tables delineate valid combinations of values.

- Any combination of values not contained in a single row of the Tables is invalid.

Coding Tip:

Construct valid ICD-10-PCS codes using a *build-a-code* approach to assign values to each of the seven unique hierarchies (positions).

EXAMPLE: Refer to the portion of a Medical and Surgical section table below, and notice that 0JHT3VZ is a valid code, but 0JHW3VZ is not a valid code. The "V" in code 0JHW3VZ is not a valid value for sixth character device because it is associated with the subcutaneous tissue and fascia, trunk body part.

0	**Medical and Surgical**						
J	**Subcutaneous Tissue and Fascia**						
H	**Insertion:**	Putting in a nonbiological appliance that monitors, assists, performs, or prevents a physiological function but does not physically take the place of a body part					

Body Part Character 4		Approach Character 5		Device Character 6		Qualifier Character 7	
S	Subcutaneous Tissue and Fascia, Head and Neck	**0**	Open	**1**	Radioactive Element	**Z**	No Qualifier
V	Subcutaneous Tissue and Fascia, Upper Extremity	**3**	Percutaneous	**3**	Infusion Device		
W	Subcutaneous Tissue and Fascia, Lower Extremity						
T	Subcutaneous Tissue and Fascia, Trunk	**0**	Open	**1**	Radioactive Element	**Z**	No Qualifier
		3	Percutaneous	**3**	Infusion Device		
				V	Infusion Pump		

All 7 characters *must* contain valid values (selected from the appropriate table) to construct a valid ICD-10-PCS procedure code. If documentation is incomplete for coding purposes, query the physician for the necessary information. However, according to ICD-10-PCS coding guidelines, the coder is *not* required to query the physician when the correlation between documentation and defined ICD-10-PCS terms is clear (e.g., surgeon documents "partial resection" and coder determines that "partial resection" is root operation "excision").

- Columns in the ICD-10-PCS Tables contain values for characters 4 through 7.

- Rows in the ICD-10-PCS Tables delineate valid combinations of values.

- Any combination of values *not* contained in a single row of the ICD-10-PCS Tables is invalid (and results in construction of an invalid code if used).

ICD-10-PCS SECTIONS	
0	Medical and Surgical
1	Obstetrics
2	Placement
3	Administration
4	Measurement and Monitoring
5	Extracorporeal Assistance and Performance
6	Extracorporeal Therapies
7	Osteopathic
8	Other Procedures
9	Chiropractic
B	Imaging
C	Nuclear Medicine
D	Radiation Oncology
F	Physical Rehabilitation and Diagnostic Audiology
G	Mental Health
H	Substance Abuse Treatment

Figure 5-6 ICD-10-PCS sections

Section	Meaning of Each Character Within a Section						
	1st	2nd	3rd	4th	5th	6th	7th
Medical and Surgical	Section	Body system	Root operation	Body part	Approach	Device	Qualifier
Obstetrics	Section	Body system	Root operation	Body part	Approach	Device	Qualifier
Placement	Section	Body system	Root operation	Body system/ Region	Approach	Device	Qualifier
Administration	Section	Body system	Root operation	Body system/ Region	Approach	Substance	Qualifier
Measurement and Monitoring	Section	Body system	Root operation	Body system	Approach	Function/ Device	Qualifier
Extracorporeal Assistance and Performance	Section	Body system	Root operation	Body system	Duration	Function	Qualifier
Extracorporeal Therapies	Section	Body system	Root operation	Body system	Duration	Qualifier	Qualifier
Osteopathic	Section	Body system	Root operation	Body region	Approach	Method	Qualifier
Other Procedures	Section	Body system	Root operation	Body region	Approach	Method	Qualifier
Chiropractic	Section	Body system	Root operation	Body region	Approach	Method	Qualifier
Imaging	Section	Body system	Root type	Body part	Contrast	Qualifier	Qualifier
Nuclear Medicine	Section	Body system	Root type	Body part	Radionuclide	Qualifier	Qualifier
Radiation Oncology	Section	Body system	Root type	Body part	Modality qualifier	Isotope	Qualifier
Physical Rehabilitation and Diagnostic Audiology	Section	Section qualifier	Root type	Body system/ Region	Type qualifier	Equipment	Qualifier
Mental Health	Section	Body system	Root type	Qualifier	Qualifier	Qualifier	Qualifier
Substance Abuse Treatment	Section	Body system	Root type	Qualifier	Qualifier	Qualifier	Qualifier

Figure 5-7 Meaning of first through seventh characters within each ICD-10-PCS section

ICD-10-PCS inpatient coding guidelines are organized as follows:

- Structure
- Values
- Index
- Tables
- Medical and surgical section guidelines
- Obstetrics section guidelines

Structure of ICD-10-PCS Codes

ICD-10-PCS codes contain 7 characters. Each character is associated with an **axis of classification** (e.g., section, body part, root operation, and so on), which specifies information about the procedure performed. Within a defined code range, a character specifies the same type of information for that axis of classification.

All 7 characters must be specified to construct a valid code. If documentation is incomplete for coding purposes, query the physician queried for the necessary information to construct a valid code.

EXAMPLE: The fifth *axis of classification* specifies the approach in the Medical and Surgical section.

ICD-10-PCS Values

One of 34 possible *values* may be assigned to each axis of classification in the 7-character code. The values include numbers 0 through 9 and the alphabet (except for letters I and O because they are easily confused with numbers 1 and 0). The number of unique values used in an axis of classification differs as needed.

EXAMPLE: Where the fifth axis of classification specifies the Approach, seven different approach values are currently used to specify the approach.

Valid values for an axis of classification can be added (by the Centers for Medicare and Medicaid Services) as needed. This means that when a significantly distinct type of device is used during performance of a new procedure, a new device value can be added to the system.

EXAMPLE: There are currently no device values listed in the *Medical and Surgical* section, *Skin and Breast* body system, and *Repair* root operation. In the future, perhaps CMS will add *surgical glue* as a device. That means instead of selecting value Z for the device, the coder would select the appropriate value for surgical glue (or some other new device).

The meaning of any single value is based on its axis of classification *and* any preceding values on which it may be dependent.

EXAMPLE: A body part value in the *Medical and Surgical* section is *always* dependent on the body system value. Thus, body part value 0 in the *Central Nervous System* body system always classifies Brain, while body part value 0 in the *Peripheral Nervous System* body system always classifies Cervical Plexus.

As ICD-10-PCS expands to become increasingly more detailed, more values will depend on preceding values for their meaning.

EXAMPLE: In the *Medical and Surgical* section, *Lower Joints* body system, *Insertion* root operation, device value 3 refers to *Infusion Device*. In the *Medical and Surgical* section, *Lower Joints* body system, *Fusion* root operation, device value 3 refers to *Interbody Internal Fixation Device*.

ICD-10-PCS Coding Conventions

ICD-10-PCS contains just one coding convention.

And

When the word *and* is used in a code description, it means *and/or*.

EXAMPLE: The *Mouth and Throat* body system is interpreted as procedures performed on the mouth *and/or* throat.

Medical and Surgical Section Coding Guidelines

Coding guidelines associated with the *Medical and Surgical* section of ICD-10-PCS include:

- Body system
- Root operation
- Body part
- Approach
- Device

Body System—General Coding Guidelines

Procedure codes in the *General Anatomical Regions* body system are used *only when*:

- The procedure is performed on an anatomical region rather than a specific body part.

- Insufficient information is available to support the assignment of a value to a specific body part.

EXAMPLE: *Control of postoperative hemorrhage of the gastrointestinal tract, open approach*, procedure is performed. Index main term *Control postprocedural bleeding in*, and subterm *Gastrointestinal Tract* list values 0W3P. Go to ICD-10-PCS Table 0W3 to construct code 0W3P3ZZ.

Body systems designated as upper or lower contain body parts that are located above or below the diaphragm, respectively.

EXAMPLE: The jugular veins are located above the diaphragm (in the neck), and they are assigned values from the *Medical and Surgical* section and *Upper Veins* body system. The saphenous veins are located below the diaphragm (in the legs), and they are assigned values from the *Medical and Surgical* section and *Lower Veins* body system.

Root Operation—General Coding Guidelines

To determine the appropriate root operation, apply the *complete* definition and explanation of the root operation (located in the ICD-10-PCS Tables). The root operation is specified in the third character, and in the *Medical and Surgical* section of ICD-10-PCS, there are 31 different root operations. The root operation identifies the objective of the procedure, and each root operation has a precise definition (Table 5-1), which were created specifically for ICD-10-PCS and may differ from those found in medical dictionaries and other resources.

- Components of a procedure that are included in the root operation's definition and explanation are *not* coded separately.

  EXAMPLE: During an *open left knee joint replacement procedure using a synthetic substitute*, the original knee joint was resected. Index main term *Replacement*, subterm *Joint*, second qualifier *Knee*, third qualifier *Left* list values 0SRD0. Go to ICD-10-PCS Table 0SR to construct code 0SRD0JZ for the joint replacement procedure *only*. (The resection of the original joint is *not* assigned a separate code.)

- Procedural steps necessary to reach the operative site *and* to close the operative site are *not* coded separately.

  EXAMPLE: A laparotomy is performed to reach the site where an open liver biopsy (diagnostic) is carried out. Index main term *Biopsy* and its subterm provide a cross reference to —*see Excision, Diagnostic*. Index main term *Excision* and subterm *Liver* list values 0FB0. Go to ICD-10-PCS Table 0FB to construct code 0FB00ZX for the open liver biopsy *only*.

  - The Index cross reference for main term *Biopsy* included the term *Diagnostic*, which means seventh qualifier value X is assigned instead of Z.

  - The laparotomy is *not* coded separately.

Root Operation—Multiple Procedures

During the same operative episode, codes are constructed for multiple procedures performed *if* the:

- Same root operation (e.g., excision, replacement) is performed on different body parts, as defined by distinct values of the body part axis of classification.

  EXAMPLE: Two different ICD-10-PCS codes are constructed for a diagnostic excision (e.g., biopsy) of the liver and of the pancreas.

  - Index main term *Biopsy* and its subterm provide a cross reference to —*see Excision, Diagnostic*. Index main term *Excision* and subterm *Liver* list values 0FB0. Go to ICD-10-PCS Table 0FB to construct code 0FB00ZX for the liver biopsy.

  - Index main term *Excision* and subterm *Pancreas* list values 0FBG. Return to ICD-10-PCS Table 0FB to construct code 0FBG0ZX for the pancreatic biopsy.

  - The Index cross reference for main term *Biopsy* included the term *Diagnostic*, which means seventh qualifier value X is assigned instead of Z.

- Same root operation is repeated at different body sites that are included in the same body part axis of classification.

  EXAMPLE: Two ICD-10-PCS codes are constructed for *biopsy of the right sartorius muscle and right gracilis muscle*, both of which are classified to the *Upper Leg Muscle, Right* body part.

  - Index main term *Biopsy* and its subterm provide a cross reference to —*see Excision, Diagnostic*. Index main term *Excision*, subterm *Muscle*, second qualifier *Upper Leg*, and third qualifier *Right* list values 0KBQ. Got to ICD-10-PCS Table 0KB to construct both codes 0KBQ3ZX (right sartorius muscle) and 0KBQ3ZX (right gracilis muscle).

Table 5-1 Medical and Surgical Section Root Operations and Definitions

Root Operation	Definition
Alteration	Modifying the natural anatomic structure of a body part without affecting the function of the body part
Bypass	Altering the route of passage of the contents of a tubular body part
Change	Taking out or off a device from a body part and putting back an identical or similar device in or on the same body part
Control	Stopping, or attempting to stop, postprocedural bleeding
Creation	Making a new genital structure that does not take over the place of a body part
Destruction	Physical eradication of all or a portion of a body part by the direct use of energy, force, or a destructive agent
Detachment	Cutting off all or a portion of the upper or lower extremities
Dilation	Expanding an orifice or the lumen of a tubular body part
Division	Cutting into a body part without draining fluids and/or gases from the body part in order to separate or transect a body
Drainage	Taking or letting out fluids and/or gases from a body part
Excision	Cutting out or off, without replacement, a portion of a body part
Extirpation	Taking or cutting out solid matter from a body part
Extraction	Pulling or stripping out or off all or a portion of a body part by the use of force
Fragmentation	Breaking solid matter in a body part into pieces
Fusion	Joining together portions of an articular body part rendering the articular body part immobile
Insertion	Putting in a nonbiological appliance that monitors, assists, performs, or prevents a physiological function but does not physically take the place of a body part
Inspection	Visually and/or manually exploring a body part
Map	Locating the route of passage of electrical impulses and/or locating functional areas in a body part
Occlusion	Completely closing an orifice or lumen of a tubular body part
Reattachment	Putting back in or on all or a portion of a separated body part to its normal location or other suitable location
Release	Freeing a body part from an abnormal physical constraint
Removal	Taking out or off a device from a body part
Repair	Restoring, to the extent possible, a body part to its normal anatomic structure and function
Replacement	Putting in or on biological or synthetic material that physically takes the place and/or function of all or a portion of a body part
Reposition	Moving to its normal location or other suitable location all or a portion of a body part
Resection	Cutting out or off, without replacement, all of a body part
Restriction	Partially closing an orifice or lumen of a tubular body part
Revision	Correcting, to the extent possible, a malfunctioning or displaced device
Supplement	Putting in or on biological or synthetic material that physically reinforces and/or augments the function of a portion of a body part
Transfer	Moving, without taking out, all or a portion of a body part to another location to take over the function of all or a portion of a body part
Transplantation	Putting in or on all or a portion of a living body part taken from another individual or animal to physically take the place and/or function of all or a portion of a similar body part

- The codes are identical (and both are reported) because the biopsy was performed on two different muscles, which are considered two different body sites within the same *Upper Leg Muscle, Right,* body part axis of classification.

- The Index cross reference for main term *Biopsy* included the term *Diagnostic*, which means seventh qualifier value X is assigned instead of Z.

 Note:

> *Root operations and definitions were created specifically for ICD-10-PCS and may differ from those found in medical dictionaries and other resources.*

- Multiple root operations with distinct objectives are performed on the same body part.

  EXAMPLE: Two codes are constructed for *Endoscopic destruction of lesion, sigmoid colon*, and *bypass of sigmoid colon, open*.

  - Index main term *Destruction*, subterm *Colon*, and second qualifier *Sigmoid* list values 0D5N. Go to ICD-10-PCS Table to construct code 0D5N8ZZ.

  - Index main term *Bypass*, subterm *Colon*, and second qualifier *Sigmoid* list values 0D1N. Go to ICD-10-PCS Table 0D1 to construct code 0D1N0ZN.

- The intended root operation is attempted using one approach, but it is converted to a different approach.

  EXAMPLE: *Laparoscopic cholecystectomy converted to an open cholecystectomy* is assigned two codes: one for the percutaneous endoscopic *Inspection* root operation and a different code for the open *Resection* root operation.

  - Index main term *Inspection*, and subterm *Gallbladder* list values 0FJ4. Go to ICD-10-PCS Table 0FJ to construct code 0FJ44ZZ.

  - Index main term *Resection* and subterm *Gallbladder* list values 0FT4. Go to ICD-10-PCS Tables 0FT to construct code 0FT40ZZ.

Root Operation—Discontinued Procedures

- When the intended procedure is discontinued, code the procedure to the root operation performed.

  EXAMPLE: A planned *total abdominal hysterectomy was discontinued after resecting just the uterus, leaving the ovaries and fallopian tubes intact*, because there was no evidence of dysplasia. Index main term provides a cross reference to —*see Resection, Uterus 0UT9*. Go to ICD-10-PCS Table 0UT to construct code 0UT90ZZ. (If bilateral ovaries and fallopian tubes had also been resected, codes 0UT20ZZ and 0UT70ZZ would also be constructed.)

- When a procedure is discontinued before any other root operation is performed, assign a code to the *Inspection* root operation of the body part or anatomical region inspected.

  EXAMPLE: A planned *aortic valve replacement procedure was discontinued after initial thoracotomy, but before any incision was made into the heart muscle,* due to the patient becoming hemodynamically unstable. Index main term *Inspection* and subterm *Mediastinum* list values 0WJC. Go to ICD-10-PCS Table 0WJ to construct code 0WJC0ZZ.

  - Do not go to Index main term *Thoracotomy* because its cross reference is to —*see Drainage, Anatomical Regions, General 0W9*, which was not the procedure performed.

  - The coding guideline provides direction to locate Index main term *Inspection*, and the subterm is the body part or anatomical region that was inspected.

Root Operation—Biopsy Followed by More Definitive Treatment

If a diagnostic excision, extraction, or drainage procedure (biopsy) is followed by a more definitive procedure (e.g., destruction, excision, resection) *at the same procedure site*, assign separate codes for the biopsy and the more definitive treatment.

> **EXAMPLE:** For *open biopsy of left breast with left partial mastectomy*, assign a code for the biopsy *and* a separate code for the partial mastectomy.
>
> - Index main term *Biopsy* provides a cross reference to *—see Excision, Diagnostic*. Index main term *Excision*, subterm *Breast*, and second qualifier *Left* list values 0HBU. Go to ICD-10-PCS Table 0HB to construct code 0HBU0ZX. (The Index cross reference for main term *Biopsy* included the term *Diagnostic*, which means seventh qualifier value X is assigned instead of Z.)
>
> - Index main term *Mastectomy* provides a cross reference to *—see Resection, Skin and Breast 0HT*. Go to ICD-10-PCS Table 0HT to construct code 0HTU0ZZ.

Root Operation—Overlapping Body Layers

When root operations Excision, Repair, or Inspection are performed on overlapping layers of the musculoskeletal system, the body part specifying the *deepest layer* is coded.

> **EXAMPLE:** For an *open excisional debridement of the skin, subcutaneous tissue, and muscle, left foot*, assign just one code for the procedure performed on the *Muscle* body part (because muscle is the deepest layer). Index main term *Debridement* and subterm *Excisional* include cross reference *—see Excision*. Thus, Index main term *Excision*, subterm *Muscle*, second qualifier *Foot*, and third qualifier *Left* list values 0KBW. Go to ICD-10-PCS Table 0KB to construct code 0KBW0ZZ.

Root Operation—Bypass Procedures

Bypass procedures are coded by identifying the body part bypassed *from* and the body part bypassed *to*.

- The fourth character (body part) specifies the body part bypassed *from*.
- The seventh character qualifier specifies the body part bypassed *to*.

> **EXAMPLE:** For an *open bypass from stomach to jejunum*, stomach is the body part (fourth character) and jejunum is the qualifier (seventh character). Index main term *Bypass*, subterm *Stomach* list values DD16. Go to ICD-10-PCS Table 0D1 to construct code 0D160ZA.

Root Operation—Coronary Bypass Procedures

Coronary arteries are classified by number of distinct sites treated, *not* the number of coronary arteries or the anatomical name of a coronary artery (e.g., left anterior descending).

- The fourth character (body part) value classifies the number of coronary artery sites bypassed *to*.
- The seventh character qualifier classifies the vessel bypassed *from*.

 Coding Tip:

> Coronary artery bypass procedures are classified the *opposite* of other bypass procedures (as explained in the above *Root Operation—Bypass Procedures* coding guideline) because the fourth character body part classifies the number of coronary artery sites bypassed *to*, and the seventh character qualifier classifies the vessel bypassed *from*.

> **EXAMPLE:** For an *open aortocoronary artery bypass of left anterior descending coronary artery and obtuse marginal coronary artery, using synthetic substitute for each bypass*, the two coronary artery sites are the body part (fourth character) and aorta is the qualifier (seventh character). Index main term *Bypass*, subterm *Artery*, second qualifier *Coronary*, third qualifier *Two Sites* list values 0211. Go to ICD-10-PCS Table 021 to construct code 02110JW.

When multiple coronary artery sites are bypassed, a separate procedure code is assigned for each coronary artery site *that uses a different device and/or qualifier.*

> **EXAMPLE:** For an *open aortocoronary artery bypass and open right internal mammary coronary artery bypass using synthetic substitute for each bypass,* assign two codes because there are different seventh character qualifier values for the aorta and for the right internal mammary artery. Index main term *Bypass,* subterm *Artery,* second qualifier *Coronary,* and third qualifier *One Site* list values 0210. Go to ICD-10-PCS Table 021 to construct both codes 02100JW and 02100J8. (Index third qualifier *Two Sites* is *not* used because the seventh character qualifiers differ for each code.)

Root Operation—*Control* vs. More Definitive Root Operations

Root operation *Control* is defined as *stopping, or attempting to stop, postprocedural bleeding.* If an attempt to stop postprocedural bleeding is initially unsuccessful, and the procedure performed to stop the bleeding requires any of the following root operation, the ICD-10-PCS code is constructed using the indicated root operation (instead of the *Control* root operation):

- Bypass
- Detachment
- Excision
- Extraction
- Reposition
- Replacement
- Resection

> **EXAMPLE:** The ICD-10-PCS code for *open splenectomy to stop postprocedural bleeding* is constructed using the *Medical and Surgical* section, *Lymphatic and Hemic Systems* body system, and *Resection* root operation. Index main term *Splenectomy* contains a subterm cross reference to —*see Resection, Lymphatic and Hemic Systems,* which list values 07T. Go to ICD-10-PCS Table 07T to construct code 07TP0ZZ.
>
> - Although the objective of the procedure was to *stop postprocedural bleeding,* the *Control* root operation is not used because the spleen was resected.
>
> - If surgical cautery or sutures had been performed to stop postprocedural bleeding, the code would have be constructed using the *Control* root operation in the *Anatomical Regions, General* body system and *Medical and Surgical* system.

Root Operation—Excision vs. Resection

ICD-10-PCS contains specific body parts for anatomical subdivisions of a body part (e.g., lobes of the lungs or liver, regions of the intestine). The resection of a specific body part is coded whenever all of that body part is cut out or off (instead of coding an excision of a less specific body part).

> **EXAMPLE:** For an *open left upper lung lobectomy,* go to the *Resection* root operation and *Upper Lung Lobe, Left* body part (instead of the *Excision* root operation and *Lung, Left* body part). Index main term *Resection,* subterm *Lobe,* second qualifier *Upper Lobe,* and third qualifier *Left* list values 0BTG. Go to ICD-10-PCS Table 0BT to construct code 0BTG0ZZ.

Root Operation—Excision for Graft

When an autograft is obtained from a different body part in order to complete the objective of the procedure, a separate procedure is coded.

> **EXAMPLE:** For an *open aortocoronary bypass with open excision of right greater saphenous vein (for use as aortocoronary bypass graft material),* the *excision of saphenous vein* is assigned a separate code.
>
> - Index main term *Bypass,* subterm *Artery,* second qualifier *Coronary,* third qualifier *One Site* list values 0210. Go to ICD-10-PCS Table 021 to construct code 021009W.
>
> - Index main term *Excision,* subterm *Vein,* second qualifier *Greater Saphenous,* and third qualifier *Right* list values 06BP. Go to ICD-10-PCS Table 06B to construct code 06BP0ZZ.

Root Operation—Fusion Procedures of the Spine

The body part coded for a *spinal vertebral joint(s) rendered immobile by a spinal fusion procedure* is classified according to the level of the spine (e.g., thoracic). There are distinct body part values for a single vertebral joint and for multiple vertebral joints at each spinal level.

EXAMPLE: Go to ICD-10-PCS Table 0RG, and locate values 1, 2, and 4 for body parts *Cervical Vertebral Joint*, *Cervical Vertebral Joints, 2 or more*, and *Cervicothoracic Vertebral Joint*, respectively.

When multiple vertebral joints are fused, a separate procedure code is assigned for *each vertebral joint that uses a different device and/or qualifier.*

EXAMPLE: *Open fusion of lumbar vertebral joint, posterior approach, anterior column* and *open fusion of lumbar vertebral joint, posterior approach, posterior column* are each assigned separate codes. Index main term *Fusion*, and subterm *Lumbar Vertebral* list values 0SG0. Go to ICD-10-PCS Table 0SG to construct codes 0SG00ZJ and 0SG00Z1.

Combinations of devices and materials are often used on a vertebral joint to render the joint immobile. When combinations of devices are used on the *same* vertebral joint, the device value assigned to the procedure code is as follows:

- If an interbody fusion device is used to render the joint immobile (alone or containing other material like bone graft), refer to device value *Interbody Fusion Device*.

EXAMPLE: *Open fusion of two lumbar vertebral joints, posterior approach, posterior column, using a cage style interbody internal fusion device containing morsellized bone graft* is assigned a device value for *Interbody Internal Fusion Device*. Index main term *Fusion*, subterm *Lumbar Vertebral* 0SG02, and second qualifier *or more* list values 0SG1. Go to ICD-10-PCS Table 0SG to construct code 0SG10A1.

- If bone graft is the *only* device used to render the joint immobile, refer to device value *Nonautologous Tissue Substitute* or *Autologous Tissue Substitute*.

EXAMPLE: *Open fusion of the right elbow joint using bone graft material from a bone bank* is assigned a device value for *Nonautologous Tissue Substitute*. Index main term *Fusion*, subterm *Elbow*, and second qualifier *Right* list values 0RGL. Go to ICD-10-PCS Table 0RG to construct code 0RGL0KZ.

- If a mixture of autologous and nonautologous bone graft (with or without biological or synthetic extenders or binders) is used to render the joint immobile, refer to device value *Autologous Tissue Substitute*.

EXAMPLE: *Open fusion of the left temporomandibular joint using both autologous bone graft and bone bank bone graft* is assigned a device value for *Autologous Tissue Substitute*. Index main term *Fusion*, subterm *Temporomandibular*, and second qualifier *Left* list values 0RGD. Go to ICD-10-PCS Table 0RG to construct code 0RGD07Z.

 Coding Tip:

When an internal fixation device is used to render the joint immobile and an interbody fusion device is not used, refer to device value *Internal Fixation Device*.

EXAMPLE: Open fusion of the cervicothoracic vertebral joint, posterior approach, posterior column, using a bone dowel interbody fusion device mtade of cadaver bone and packed with a mixture of local morsellized bone and demineralized bone matrix is assigned a device value for *Interbody Fusion Device*. Index main term *Fusion*, and subterm *Cervicothoracic Vertebral* list values 0RG4. Go to ICD-10-PCS Table 0RG to construct code 0RG4031.

Root Operation—Inspection Procedures

Inspection of a body part(s) that is performed to achieve the objective of a procedure is *not* coded separately.

EXAMPLE: For *fiberoptic bronchoscopy with irrigation of bronchus*, code only the *irrigation of bronchus* procedure. Index main term *Irrigation*, and subterm *Respiratory Tract Cavity, Irrigating Substance* list values 3E1F. Go to ICD-10-PCS Table 3E1 to construct code 3E1F88Z.

- The bronchus is a part of the respiratory tract.

- Do *not* assign code 0BJ08ZZ for the bronchoscopy.

- When *multiple tubular body parts are inspected*, the most distal body part inspected is assigned a body part value.

   EXAMPLE: For *cystoureteroscopy with inspection of urethra, urinary bladder and ureters*, code only the inspection of the ureter (ureteroscopy) because it is distal to both the urethra and the urinary bladder. Index main term *Ureteroscopy* lists code 0TJ98ZZ. Go to ICD-10-PCS Table 0TJ to construct code 0TJ98ZZ (to verify its accuracy).

- When *multiple nontubular body parts in a region are inspected*, the body part that specifies the entire area inspected is assigned a body part value.

   EXAMPLE: Exploratory laparotomy with percutaneous endoscopic inspection of abdominal contents is assigned the *Peritoneal Cavity* body part value. Index main term *Laparotomy* provides a cross reference for *Exploratory —see Inspection, Cavity, Peritoneal 0WJG*. Go to ICD-10-PCS Table 0WJ to construct code 0WJG4ZZ.

- When both an inspection procedure and another procedure are performed on the same body part during the same operative episode, if the inspection procedure is performed using a different approach than the other procedure, the inspection procedure is coded separately.

   EXAMPLE: For *percutaneous endoscopic inspection of the duodenum and open biopsy of the duodenum*, two codes are assigned. (The duodenum is part of the lower intestinal tract.)

   - Index main term *Inspection*, subterm *Intestinal Tract*, and second qualifier *Lower* list values 0DJD. Go to ICD-10-PCS Table 0DJ to construct code 0DJD4ZZ.

   - Index main term *Biopsy* contains a cross reference to *—see Excision, Diagnostic*. Index main term *Excision*, and subterm *Duodenum* list values 0DB9. Go to ICD-10-PCS Table 0DB to construct code 0DB94ZX. (The Index cross reference for main term *Biopsy* included the term *Diagnostic*, which means seventh qualifier value X is assigned instead of Z.)

Root Operation—Occlusion vs. Restriction for Vessel Embolization Procedures

- When the objective of an embolization procedure is to completely close a vessel, a value for root operation *Occlusion* is assigned.

   EXAMPLE: *Percutaneous tumor embolization, left axillary artery,* is assigned a value for root operation *Occlusion* because the objective of the procedure is to cut off the blood supply to the vessel. Index main term *Embolization* includes a cross reference to *—see Occlusion*. Index main term *Occlusion*, subterm *Axillary*, and second qualifier *Left* list values 03L6. Go to ICD-10-PCS Table 03L to construct code 03L63ZZ.)

- When the objective of an embolization procedure is to narrow the lumen of a vessel, a value for root operation *Restriction* is assigned.

   EXAMPLE: *Clipping of right popliteal artery with intraluminal device, open,* is assigned a value for root operation *Restriction* because the objective of the procedure is to narrow the lumen of the vessel at the site of the aneurysm where it is abnormally wide (not to close off the vessel entirely). Index main term *Clipping, Aneurysm* includes a cross reference to *—see Restriction*. Index main term *Restriction*, subterm *Popliteal,* and second qualifier *Right* list values 04VM. Go to ICD-10-PCS Table 04V to construct code 04VM0DZ.

Root Operation—Release Procedures

In root operation *Release*, a value is assigned to the body part being freed, *not* to the tissue being manipulated or cut to free the body part.

   EXAMPLE: *Open lysis of ascending colon adhesions* is assigned a value for the *Ascending Colon* body part. Index main term *Lysis* includes a cross reference to *—see Release*. Index main term *Release*, subterm *Colon*, and second qualifier *Ascending* list values 0DNK. Go to ICD-10-PCS Table 0DN to construct code 0DNK0ZZ.

Root Operation—Release vs. Division

- When the sole objective of the procedure is to free a body part *without cutting into the body part*, a value is assigned to root operation *Release*.

   EXAMPLE: *Freeing of vagus nerve root from surrounding scar tissue via open approach to relieve pain* is coded to root operation *Release*. Index main term *Release*, subterm *Nerve*, and second qualifier *Vagus* list values 00NQ. Go to ICD-10-PCS Table 00N to construct code 00NQ0ZZ.

- When the sole objective of the procedure is to separate or transect a body part, a value is assigned to root operation *Division*.

   EXAMPLE: *Severing a vagus nerve root via open approach* to stop hiccups is coded to the root operation *Division*. Index main term *Division*, subterm *Nerve*, and second qualifier *Vagus* list values 008Q. Go to ICD-10-PCS Table 008 to construct code 008Q0ZZ.

Root Operation—Reposition for Fracture Treatment

The reduction of a displaced fracture is coded to root operation *Reposition*, and the application of a cast or splint in conjunction with the reposition procedure is *not* coded separately. Treatment of a nondisplaced fracture is coded to the procedure performed.

   EXAMPLE 1: *Open insertion of pin as an internal fixation device in a nondisplaced fracture of left fibula* is coded to root operation *Insertion of device in*. Index main term *Insertion of device in*, subterm *Fibula*, second qualifier *Left* list values 0QHK. Go to ICD-10-PCS Table 0QH to construct code 0QHK04Z.

   EXAMPLE 2: *Applying a cast to a nondisplaced right radial fracture* is coded to root operation *Immobilization* in the *Placement* section. Index main term *Casting* includes a cross reference to —*see Immobilization*. Index main term *Immobilization*, subterm *Arm*, and second qualifier *Lower* list values 2W3CX. Go to ICD-10-PCS Table 2W3 to construct code 2W3CX2Z.

Root Operation—Transplantation vs. Administration

- Inserting a mature and functioning living body part taken from another individual or animal is coded to root operation *Transplantation*.

   EXAMPLE: For *left kidney transplant, allogeneic*, Index main term *Transplantation*, subterm *Kidney*, and second qualifier *Left* list values 0TY10Z. Go to ICD-10-PCS Table 0TY to verify code 0TY10Z0.

- Inserting autologous or nonautologous cells is coded to the *Administration* section (and root operation *Transfusion*).

   EXAMPLE: *Percutaneous autologous bone marrow transplant via central venous line* is coded to the *Administration* section. Index main term *Bone marrow transplant* includes a cross reference to —*see Transfusion*. Index main term *Transfusion*, subterm *Vein*, second qualifier *Central*, and third qualifier *Blood, Whole* list values 3024. Go to ICD-10-PCS Table 302 to construct code 30243G0.

Body Part—General Guidelines

- When a procedure is performed on a portion of a body part that does not have a separate body part value, code the body part value corresponding to the whole body part.

   EXAMPLE: A procedure performed on the alveolar process of the mandible is assigned a value for body part *Mandible*. Index main term *Alveolar process of mandible* includes a cross reference to —*see Mandible, Left* or —*see Mandible, Right*.

- If the prefix *peri* is combined with a body part to identify the site of the procedure, the procedure is coded to the body part named.

   EXAMPLE: A procedure site identified as *perirenal* is assigned a value for the body part *Kidney*.

Body Part—Branches of Body Parts

Where a specific branch of a body part does not have its own body part value in ICD-10-PCS, the body part is coded to the closest proximal branch that has a specific body part value.

> **EXAMPLE:** A procedure performed on the *mandibular branch of the trigeminal nerve* is assigned a value for body part *Trigeminal Nerve*.

Body Part—Bilateral Body Part Values

Bilateral body part values are available for a limited number of body parts. If the identical procedure is performed on contralateral body parts, and a bilateral body part value exists for that body part, just one code is assigned using the bilateral body part value. If no bilateral body part value exists, each procedure is assigned a separate code using the appropriate body part value.

> **EXAMPLE 1:** An identical procedure performed on both fallopian tubes is assigned a value for body part *Fallopian Tube, Bilateral*.

> **EXAMPLE 2:** An identical procedure performed on both knee joints is assigned two different codes, which means assigning values for body part *Knee Joint, Right* and *Knee Joint, Left* to each code.

Body Part—Coronary Arteries

The coronary arteries are classified as a single body part that is further specified by number of sites treated and not by name or number of arteries. Separate body part values are used to specify the number of sites treated when the same procedure is performed on multiple sites in the coronary arteries.

> **EXAMPLE 1:** An angioplasty of two distinct sites in the left anterior descending coronary artery with placement of two stents is assigned a code as *Dilation of Coronary Arteries, Two Sites, with Intraluminal Device*.

> **EXAMPLE 2:** An angioplasty of two distinct sites in the left anterior descending coronary artery, one with stent placement and one without, is assigned two separate codes as *Dilation of Coronary Artery, One Site with Intraluminal Device*, and *Dilation of Coronary Artery, One Site with No Device*.

Body Part—Tendons, Ligaments, Bursae and Fascia Near a Joint

Procedures performed on tendons, ligaments, bursae, and fascia supporting a joint are coded to the body part in the respective body system that is the focus of the procedure. Procedures performed on joint structures themselves are coded to the body part in the joint body systems.

> **EXAMPLE 1:** *Repair of anterior cruciate ligament, left knee* is assigned a value from body part *Knee Bursae and Ligament* in the body system *Bursae and Ligaments*.

> **EXAMPLE 2:** A *knee arthroscopy with shaving of articular cartilage* is assigned a value from body part *Knee Joint* in body system *Lower Joints*.

Body Part—Skin, Subcutaneous Tissue and Fascia Overlying a Joint

When a procedure is performed on skin, subcutaneous tissue, or fascia overlying a joint, assign a value to body parts as indicated below:

- Shoulder is assigned a value for body part *Upper Arm*.

- Elbow is assigned a value for body part *Lower Arm*.

- Wrist is assigned a value for body part *Lower Arm*.

- Hip is assigned a value for body part *Upper Leg*.

- Knee is assigned a value for body part *Lower Leg*.

- Ankle is assigned a value for body part *Foot*.

Body Part—Fingers and Toes

When a body system does not contain a separate body part value for the fingers, procedures performed on the fingers are assigned value(s) for body part *Hand*. If a body system does not contain a separate body part value for the toes, procedures performed on the toes are assigned value(s) for body part *Foot*.

> **EXAMPLE:** *Excision of finger muscle* is assigned a value for body part *Hand Muscle* in body system *Muscles*.

Approach

The technique used to reach the site of the procedure is called the *approach*, and there are seven different approaches:

- *Open*: Cutting through the skin or mucous membrane and any other body layers necessary to expose the site of the procedure.

- *Percutaneous*: Entry, by puncture or minor incision, of instrumentation through the skin or mucous membrane and any other body layers necessary to reach the site of the procedure.

- *Percutaneous Endoscopic*: Entry, by puncture or minor incision, of instrumentation through the skin or mucous membrane and any other body layers necessary to reach and visualize the site of the procedure.

- *Via Natural or Artificial Opening*: Entry of instrumentation through a natural or artificial external opening to reach the site of the procedure.

- *Via Natural or Artificial Opening Endoscopic*: Entry of instrumentation through a natural or artificial external opening to reach and visualize the site of the procedure.

- *Via Natural or Artificial Opening Endoscopic with Percutaneous Endoscopic Assistance:* Entry of instrumentation through a natural or artificial external opening to reach and visualize the site of the procedure, and entry, by puncture or minor incision, of instrumentation through the skin or mucous membrane and any other body layers necessary to aid in the performance of the procedure.

- *External*: Procedures performed directly on the skin or mucous membrane and procedures performed indirectly by the application of external force through the skin or mucous membrane.

An approach also includes the following three components:

- *Access location*: For procedures performed on an internal body part, the access location specifies the external site through which the site of the procedure is reached. There are two general types of access locations:

  ○ Skin or mucous membranes, which can be cut or punctured to reach the procedure site.

  ○ External openings, which are natural (e.g., mouth) or artificial (e.g., colostomy stoma).

- *Method*: For procedures performed on an internal body part, the method specifies how the external access location is entered, including:

  ○ Open method, which specifies cutting through skin or mucous membrane and any other intervening body layers necessary to expose the site of the procedure.

  ○ Instrumentation method, which specifies the entry of instrumentation through an access location (e.g., puncture, minor incision, external opening) to the internal procedure site.

- *Type of instrumentation*: For procedures performed on an internal body part, instrumentation refers to specialized equipment used to perform the procedure (e.g., sigmoidoscope).

> **Note:**
>
> Punctures and minor incisions are not considered open approaches because they do not expose the site of the procedure.

Approach—Open Approach with Percutaneous Endoscopic Assistance

Procedures performed using the open approach with percutaneous endoscopic assistance are coded to the approach *Open*.

> **EXAMPLE:** *Laparoscopic-assisted sigmoidectomy* is assigned a value for approach *Open*.

Approach—External Approach

- Procedures performed within an orifice on structures that are visible without the aid of any instrumentation are coded to the approach *External*.

  EXAMPLE: *Resection of tonsils* is assigned a value for approach *External*.

- Procedures performed indirectly by the application of external force through the intervening body layers are coded to the approach *External*.

  EXAMPLE: Closed reduction of fracture is assigned a value for approach *External*.

Body Part—Percutaneous Procedure Via Device

Procedures performed percutaneously via a device placed for the procedure are coded to the approach *Percutaneous*.

  EXAMPLE: *Fragmentation of kidney stone performed via percutaneous nephrostomy* is assigned a value for approach *Percutaneous*.

Device

The sixth character device value is assigned for devices that remain after the procedure is completed. There are four general types of devices:

- Biological or synthetic material that takes the place of all or a portion of a body part (e.g., skin grafts and joint prosthesis)

- Biological or synthetic material that assists or prevents a physiological function (e.g., IUD)

- Therapeutic material that is not absorbed by, eliminated by, or incorporated into a body part (e.g., radioactive implant)

- Mechanical or electronic appliances used to assist, monitor, take the place of, or prevent a physiological function (e.g., cardiac pacemaker, orthopedic pins)

Device—General Guidelines

A device value is assigned *only if a device remains after the procedure is completed*. If no device remains, the *No Device* device value is assigned.

Materials such as sutures, ligatures, radiological markers and temporary postoperative wound drains are considered integral to the performance of a procedure; thus, they are not coded as devices.

Procedures performed on a device only, and not on a body part, are classified to root operations *Change*, *Irrigation*, *Removal*, or *Revision*, and they are coded to the procedure performed.

  EXAMPLE: *Irrigation of percutaneous nephrostomy tube* is classified to root operation *Irrigation*, *indwelling device* in the *Administration* section. Index main term *Irrigation*, subterm *Genitourinary Tract*, *Irrigating Substance* list values 3E1K. Go to ICD-10-PCS Table 3E1 construct code 3E1K38Z.

Device—Drainage Device

A separate procedure to insert a drainage device is assigned a value for root operation *Drainage* and a value for device *Drainage Device*.

  EXAMPLE: *Percutaneous insertion of peritoneal cavity drainage device*. Index main term *Drainage*, subterm *Cavity*, and second qualifier *Peritoneal* list values 0W9G. Go to ICD-10-PCS Table 0W9 to construct code 0W9G30Z.

Note:

Index main term *Insertion of device in*, subterm *Cavity*, and second qualifier *Peritoneal* list values 0WHG, which directs you to ICD-10-PCS Table 0WH. Table 0WH is not used to construct the code because drainage devices are not classified in the Device column.

Obstetrics Section Coding Guidelines

The Obstetrics section includes two additional root operations:

- *Abortion*: Artificially terminating a pregnancy.

- *Delivery*: Assisting the passage of the products of conception from the genital canal.

A cesarean section is *not* a separate root operation because the underlying objective is *Extraction* (i.e., pulling out all or a portion of a body part).

Obstetrics Section—Products of Conception

Procedures performed on the products of conception are coded to the *Obstetrics* section. Procedures performed on a pregnant female, other than those performed on the products of conception, are coded to the appropriate root operation in the *Medical and Surgical* section.

EXAMPLE 1: *Amniocentesis* is assigned a value from body part *Products of Conception* in the *Obstetrics* section.

EXAMPLE 2: *Repair of obstetric urethral laceration* is assigned a value from body part *Urethra* in the *Medical and Surgical* section.

Obstetrics Section—Procedures Following Delivery or Abortion

Procedures performed following a delivery or abortion for (1) curettage of the endometrium or (2) evacuation of retained products of conception are coded to the *Obstetrics* section, *Pregnancy* body system, *Extraction* root operation, and *Products of Conception, Retained* body part.

Diagnostic or therapeutic dilation and curettage performed during times *other than* the postpartum or post-abortion period are coded in the *Medical and Surgical* section, *Female Reproductive* body system, *Extraction* root operation, and *Endometrium* body part.

EXAMPLE 1: After delivery of a healthy male term infant, the patient underwent endometrial dilatation and curettage (D & C) to remove retained placenta. D & C code 10D17ZZ is constructed using values from the *Obstetrics* section, *Pregnancy* body system, *Extraction* root operation, and *Products of Conception, Retained* body part.

EXAMPLE 2: A 58-year-old patient underwent diagnostic D & C. Code 0UDB7ZX is constructed using values from the *Medical and Surgical* section, *Female Reproductive* body system, *Extraction* root operation, and *Endometrium* body part.

Placement Section

The Placement section includes five root operations:

- *Compression*: Putting pressure on a body region.

- *Dressing*: Putting material on a body region for protection.

- *Immobilization*: Limiting or preventing motion of an external body region.

- *Packing*: Putting material in a body region or orifice.
- *Traction*: Exerting a pulling force on a body region in a distal direction.

Administration Section

There Administration section includes three root operations:

- *Introduction*: Putting in or on a therapeutic, diagnostic, nutritional, physiological, or prophylactic substance except blood or blood products.
- *Irrigation*: Putting in or on a cleansing substance.
- *Transfusion*: Putting in blood or blood products.

Measurement and Monitoring Section

The Measurement and Monitoring section includes two root operations:

- *Measurement*: Determining the level of a physiological or physical function at a point in time.
- *Monitoring*: Determining the level of a physiological or physical function repetitively over a period of time.

Extracorporeal Assistance and Performance Section

The Extracorporeal Assistance and Performance section includes three root operations:

- *Assistance*: Taking over a portion of a physiological function by extracorporeal means.
- *Performance*: Completely taking over a physiological function by extracorporeal means.
- *Restoration*: Returning, or attempting to return, a physiological function to its natural state by extracorporeal means; this root operation contains a single procedure code that identifies *extracorporeal cardioversion.*

Extracorporeal Therapies Section

The Extracorporeal Therapies section includes 10 root operations:

- *Atmospheric Control*: Extracorporeal control of atmospheric pressure and composition.
- *Decompression*: Extracorporeal elimination of undissolved gas from body fluids; this root operation involves just one type of procedure, *treatment for decompression sickness* (or *the bends*) in a hyperbaric chamber.
- *Electromagnetic Therapy*: Extracorporeal treatment by electromagnetic rays.
- *Hyperthermia*: Extracorporeal raising of body temperature; *hyperthermia* describes both a temperature imbalance treatment and an adjunct radiation treatment for cancer; for temperature imbalance treatment, assign a code from the Extracorporeal Therapy section; for adjunct radiation treatment, assign a code from the Radiation Oncology section.
- *Hypothermia*: Extracorporeal lowering of body temperature.
- *Pheresis*: Extracorporeal separation of blood products; *pheresis has* two main purposes, the treatment of diseases when too much of a blood component is produced (e.g., leukemia) and the removal of a blood product (e.g., platelets) from a donor for transfusion into another patient.
- *Phototherapy*: Extracorporeal treatment by light rays; *phototherapy* involves using a machine that exposes blood to light rays outside the body, recirculates it, and then returns it to the body.
- *Shock Wave Therapy*: Extracorporeal treatment by shock waves.
- *Ultrasound Therapy*: Extracorporeal treatment by ultrasound.
- *Ultraviolet Light Therapy*: Extracorporeal treatment by ultraviolet light.

Osteopathic Section

The Osteopathic section includes just one root operation, *treatment*, which is the manual treatment to eliminate or alleviate somatic dysfunction and related disorders.

Other Procedures Section

The Other Procedures section has just one root operation, *other procedures*, which are methodologies that attempt to remediate or cure a disorder or disease.

Chiropractic Section

The Chiropractic section has just one root operation, *manipulation*, which is a manual procedure that involves a directed thrust to move a joint past the physiological range of motion, without exceeding the anatomical limit.

Imaging Section

The Imaging section includes five root types:

- *Computerized Tomography (CT Scan)*: Computer-reformatted digital display of multiplanar images developed from the capture of multiple exposures of external ionizing radiation.

- *Fluoroscopy*: Single plane or bi-plane real-time display of an image developed from the capture of external ionizing radiation on fluorescent screen. The image may also be stored by either digital or analog means.

- *Magnetic Resonance Imaging (MRI)*: Computer reformatted digital display of multiplanar images developed from the capture of radiofrequency signals emitted by nuclei in a body site excited within a magnetic field.

- *Plain Radiography*: Planar display of an image developed from the capture of external ionizing radiation on photographic or photoconductive plate.

- *Ultrasonography*: Real-time display of images of anatomy or flow information developed from the capture of reflected and attenuated high-frequency sound waves.

Nuclear Medicine Section

The Nuclear Medicine section includes 10 root types:

- *Nonimaging Uptake*: Introduction of radioactive materials into the body for measurements of organ function, from the detection of radioactive emissions.

- *Nonimaging Probe*: Introduction of radioactive materials into the body for the study of distribution and fate of certain substances by the detection of radioactive emissions; or alternatively, measurement of absorption of radioactive emissions from an external source.

- *Nonimaging Assay*: Introduction of radioactive materials into the body for the study of body fluids and blood elements, by the detection of radioactive emissions.

- *Planar Imaging*: Introduction of radioactive materials into the body for single-plane display of images developed from the capture of radioactive emissions.

- *Positron Emission Tomography (PET)*: Introduction of radioactive materials into the body for three-dimensional display of images developed from the simultaneous capture, 180 degrees apart, of radioactive emissions.

- *Systemic Therapy*: Introduction of unsealed radioactive materials into the body for treatment.

- *Tomographic (Tomo) Imaging*: Introduction of radioactive materials into the body for three dimensional display of images developed from the capture of radioactive emissions.

Radiation Oncology Section

The Radiation Oncology section includes root types that specify the general modalities used (e.g., beam radiation), and the modality qualifier specifies the radiation modality used (e.g., electrons, photons).

Physical Rehabilitation and Diagnostic Audiology Section

The Physical Rehabilitation and Diagnostic Audiology section includes four root types:

- *Assessment*: Includes a determination of the patient's diagnosis when appropriate, need for treatment, planning for treatment, periodic assessment, and documentation related to these activities.

- *Caregiver Training*: Educating caregiver with the skills and knowledge used to interact with and assist the patient.

- *Fitting(s)*: Design, fabrication, modification, selection, and/or application of splint, orthosis, prosthesis, hearing aids, and/or other rehabilitation device.

- *Treatment*: Use of specific activities or methods to develop, improve, and/or restore the performance of necessary functions, compensate for dysfunction and/or minimize debilitation.

Mental Health Section

The Mental Health section includes 24 types of mental health procedures:

Psychological Tests	
Developmental	Age-normed developmental status of cognitive, social, and adaptive behavior skills.
Intellectual and Psychoeducational	Intellectual abilities, academic achievement, and learning capabilities, including behavior and emotional factors affecting learning.
Neurobehavioral and Cognitive Status	Includes neurobehavioral status exam, interview(s), and observation for the clinical assessment of thinking, reasoning, and judgment, acquired knowledge, attention, memory, visual spatial abilities, language functions, and planning.
Neuropsychological	Thinking, reasoning and judgment, acquired knowledge, attention, memory, visual spatial abilities, language functions, planning.
Personality and Behavioral	Mood, emotion, behavior, social functioning, psychopathological conditions, personality traits, and characteristics.
Crisis Intervention	Includes defusing, debriefing, counseling, psychotherapy, and/or coordination of care with other providers or agencies.
Individual Psychotherapy	

 Note:

There are no official ICD-10-PCS definitions for the Individual Psychotherapy root type; however, your author has provided definitions.

Behavior	Primarily to modify behavior. Includes modeling and role playing, positive reinforcement of target behaviors, response cost, and training of self-management skills.
Cognitive/behavioral	Combining cognitive and behavioral treatment strategies to improve functioning. Maladaptive responses are examined to determine how cognitions relate to behavior patterns in response to an event. Uses learning principles and information-processing models.
Cognitive	Primarily to correct cognitive distortions and errors.
Interactive	Uses primarily physical aids and other forms of nonoral interaction with a patient who is physically, psychologically, or developmentally unable to use ordinary language for communication (e.g., the use of toys in symbolic play).

(continues)

Individual Psychotherapy (*continued*)	
Interpersonal	Helps an individual make changes in interpersonal behaviors to reduce psychological dysfunction. Includes exploratory techniques, encouragement of affective expression, clarification of patient statements, analysis of communication patterns, use of therapy relationship, and behavior change techniques.
Psychoanalysis	Methods of obtaining a detailed account of past and present mental and emotional experiences to determine the source and eliminate or diminish the undesirable effects of unconscious conflicts by making the individual aware of their existence, origin, and inappropriate expression in emotions and behavior.
Psychodynamic	Exploration of past and present emotional experiences to understand motives and drives using insight-oriented techniques (e.g., empathetic listening, clarifying self-defeating behavior patterns, and exploring adaptive alternatives) to reduce the undesirable effects of internal conflicts on emotions and behavior.
Psychophysiological	Monitoring and alternation of physiological processes to help the individual associate physiological reactions combined with cognitive and behavioral strategies to gain improved control of these processes to help the individual cope more effectively.
Supportive	Formation of therapeutic relationship primarily for providing emotional support to prevent further deterioration in functioning during periods of particular stress. Often used in conjunction with other therapeutic approaches.
Counseling	
Vocational	Exploration of vocational interest, aptitudes, and required adaptive behavior skills to develop and carry out a plan for achieving a successful vocational placement, enhancing work-related adjustment, and/or pursuing viable options in training education or preparation.
Family Psychotherapy	Remediation of emotional or behavioral problems presented by one or more family members when psychotherapy with more than one family member is indicated.
Electroconvulsive Therapy	Includes appropriate sedation and other preparation of the individual.
Biofeedback	Includes electroencephalogram (EEG), blood pressure, skin temperature or peripheral blood flow, electrocardiogram (ECG), electrooculogram, electromyogram (EMG), respirometry or capnometry, galvanic skin response (GSR) or electrodermal response (EDR), perineometry to monitor and regulate bowel or bladder activity, and electrogastrogram to monitor and regulate gastric motility.

Note:

There are no official ICD-10-PCS definitions for the remaining procedures (below); however, your author has provided definitions.

Hypnosis	State that resembles deep sleep, but is more active, in which an individual has little will of his own and acts in accordance with suggestions by the therapist.
Narcosynthesis	Psychological disorders are treated by guiding an individual toward resolution of emotional conflicts expressed while under the influence of a hypnotic drug.
Group Psychotherapy	Technique in which clients are treated together, with the group often contributing to the therapy.
Light Therapy	Treatment of mental disorders using light.
Medication Management	Management of prescription drug dosages through laboratory testing and other evaluation and management services.

Substance Abuse Treatment Section

The Substance Abuse Treatment section includes seven root types:

- *Detoxification Services*: Not a treatment modality but helps the patient stabilize physically and psychologically until the body becomes free of drugs and the effects of alcohol.

- *Individual Counseling*: Comprising several techniques, which apply various strategies to address drug addiction.

- *Group Counseling*: Provides structured group counseling sessions and healing power through the connection with others.

- *Family Counseling*: Provides support and education for family members of addicted individuals. Family member participation seen as critical to substance abuse treatment.

- *Individual Psychotherapy*: Includes behavior, cognitive/behavioral, cognitive, interactive, interpersonal, psychoanalysis, psychodynamic, psychophysiological, and supportive types.

- *Medication Management*: Management of prescription drug dosages through laboratory testing and other evaluation and management services.

- *Pharmacotherapy*: Management of mental disorders using pharmacological agents.

Exercise 5.5 – ICD-10-PCS Procedure Coding

Instructions: Indicate whether the statement is true (T) or false (F):

_____   **1.** ICD-10-CM uses a multiaxial structure for its 7-character alphanumeric codes.

_____   **2.** The ICD-10-PCS Index organizes main terms in numeric order, providing the first three or four characters (and sometimes all 7 characters).

_____   **3.** ICD-10-PCS Tables are used to construct a complete and valid procedure code.

_____   **4.** Values are individual letters and numbers assigned to each of seven unique hierarchies to construct a valid ICD-10-PCS code.

_____   **5.** ICD-10-PCS Tables are organized in chapters that identify the type of procedure.

_____   **6.** ICD-10-PCS contains an Index which includes all valid codes and complete text descriptions accompanying each code.

_____   **7.** Each character of an ICD-10-PCS code is associated with an axis of classification that specifies information about the condition diagnoses.

_____   **8.** The ICD-10-PCS Tables must always be consulted to construct the most appropriate valid code.

_____   **9.** It is possible to construct a procedure code by using just ICD-10-PCS Index.

_____   **10.** As ICD-10-PCS expands to become increasingly more detailed, more values will depend on preceding values for their meaning.

Instructions: Underline the main term in each procedure statement, and construct the appropriate ICD-10-PCS procedure code(s).

_____   **11.** Bilateral augmentation mammoplasty using synthetic substitute, open approach

_____   **12.** Percutaneous biopsy of spleen

_____   **13.** Injection of neurolytic agent (nerve block) into peripheral nerve

_____   **14.** Laparoscopic oophorectomy, left

_____   **15.** Open stripping of varicose veins, left lesser saphenous vein

_____ **16.** Open biopsy of prostate

_____ **17.** Operative esophagoscopy (by incision)

_____ **18.** Parathyroidectomy, complete

_____ **19.** Partial breech extraction with high forceps

_____ **20.** Partial left hip replacement, synthetic substitute

_____ **21.** Percutaneous nephrostomy with fragmentation of right kidney pelvis

_____ **22.** Puncture of bilateral ethmoid sinuses for aspiration

_____ **23.** Replacement of cardiac resynchronization defibrillator pulse generator device, heart, open approach

_____ **24.** Repair of pterygium of conjunctiva, left eye

_____ **25.** Left tympanoplasty

Exercise 5.6 – Coding Inpatient Diagnoses and Procedures

Instructions: Review each case scenario, and assign and properly sequence the ICD-9-CM diagnosis and procedure codes. Then, re-review each case scenario, and assign and properly sequence the ICD-10-CM diagnosis and ICD-10-PCS procedure codes. (Free Adobe.pdf files of the ICD-10-CM and ICD-10-PCS coding manuals are located at http://www.cms.gov.)

 Note:

> Do not assign procedure codes to ancillary tests (e.g., laboratory tests, X-rays) because they do not impact DRG assignment or the reimbursement amount for an inpatient case. (Some hospitals do assign codes to ancillary tests even though doing so does not impact the level of reimbursement received; therefore, you should be aware of this practice.)

1. Patient admitted for treatment of AIDS-related conditions and underwent diagnostic fiberoptic bronchoscopy with cell washings for specimen collection. Final diagnoses included AIDS-related *Pneumocystis carinii* and oral candidiasis.

_____

2. Patient admitted with slurred speech and weakness on the right side. Patient is right-handed. CT scan reveals carotid artery occlusion with cerebral infarction. Patient discharged to inpatient rehabilitation facility for continued treatment of dysphasia and hemiparesis.

_____

3. Patient was seen during an initial encounter after having sustained a closed fracture of the distal radius, left, due to a fall from the roof of his single-family house while cleaning gutters. X-ray of the left lower arm revealed nondisplaced fracture of distal radius with fracture fragments in good alignment. The physician determined that reduction was unnecessary, and a plaster splint was applied as a stabilizing device.

_____

4. Patient admitted for treatment of diabetic toe ulcer, left, with gangrene of the bone. The underlying cause was type 1 diabetic peripheral neuropathy. Patient underwent a complete left foot amputation.

_____

(continues)

Exercise 5.6 (*continued*)

5. Patient admitted following repeated temporal lobe seizures. History revealed that the patient had had 18 seizures within the past 24 hours. He has had seizures since the age of 16, previously well controlled with phenobarbital. Blood levels indicate an acceptable therapeutic level. During hospitalization, patient continued to seize at least hourly. Patient was immediately transferred to the neurology unit of tertiary care hospital due to localization-related intractable epilepsy with complex partial seizures.

Summary

Inpatient health care settings include acute care facilities (hospitals), behavioral health care facilities, hospice inpatient care, and long-term acute-care hospitals (LTACHs). The circumstances of inpatient admission always govern sequencing of diagnoses for DRG purposes. Upon implementation of MS-DRGs, CMS eliminated the requirement to sequence principal and secondary procedures. However, third-party payers might still require this practice. Uniform Hospital Discharge Data Set (UHDDS) definitions have always been used by acute care hospitals to report inpatient data elements in a standardized manner. Since the creation of the UHDDS in 1985, the application of the UHDDS definitions has been expanded to include all nonoutpatient settings (e.g., acute, short-term, long-term, and behavioral health care facilities; home health agencies; rehabilitation facilities; and skilled nursing facilities and nursing homes). (Content about home health, hospice, and skilled nursing facility care can be found on the Premium Website at www.cengagebrain.com.)

CMS publishes official ICD-9-CM, ICD-10-CM, and ICD-10-PCS guidelines for coding and reporting, which provide direction about assignment of diagnosis and procedure codes and the sequencing of diagnosis codes for reimbursement purposes. Depending on state reporting requirements, when the circumstances of inpatient admission govern the sequencing of procedure codes, UHDDS definitions are used to report inpatient data elements in a standardized manner. Circumstances associated with an inpatient admission govern the sequencing of principal procedure and significant other procedures (or secondary procedures).

Internet Links

CDC Topics A-Z: Go to *www.cdc.gov* and click on the A-Z Index link.

Decision Health free e-zines: *ezines.decisionhealth.com*

HCPro, Inc.: Go to *www.hcmarketplace.com*, and click on the Sign up for our FREE e-Newsletters link. Click on the box located in front of the *JustCoding News: Inpatient* (along with other e-Newsletters that interest you) to subscribe.

Maxim Health Information Services™: Go to *www.maximhealthinformationservices.com* to locate online *Coding Corner Newsletter and Ask a Coding Question* resources.

NYS DOH SPARCS: Go to *www.nyhealth.gov*, and click on the Statistics and Data link, and scroll down and click on the SPARCS link.

Virtual Hospital: *www.vh.org*

Virtual Pediatric Hospital: *www.virtualpediatrichospital.org*

Study Checklist

- ❏ Read this chapter and highlight key concepts.
- ❏ Create an index card for each key term.
- ❏ Access the chapter Internet links to learn more about concepts.
- ❏ Complete the chapter review, verifying answers with your instructor.
- ❏ Complete WebTutor assignments and take online quizzes.
- ❏ Complete Workbook chapter, verifying answers with your instructor.
- ❏ Go to **www.cengagebrain.com** to access StudyWARE™ and the Premium Website. Login instructions are located in the Preface and on the Printed Access Card.
- ❏ Form a study group with classmates to discuss chapter concepts in preparation for an exam.

Review

Multiple Choice I—ICD-9-CM

Instructions: Circle the most appropriate response.

1. Fever of unknown origin. Rule out tuberculosis. (Final diagnosis at time of inpatient hospital discharge.)
   a. 011.90   b. 780.60   c. 780.60, 011.90   d. 71.2

2. Primary pancreatic cancer.
   a. 157.1   b. 157.9   c. 196.2   d. 197.8

3. Graves disease with thyrotoxic crisis.
   a. 242.01   b. 242.0   c. 242.0, 242.9   d. 242.91

4. Acute posthemorrhagic anemia.
   a. 280.0   b. 285.1   c. 285.9, 459.0   d. 459.0, 285.9

5. Anorexia nervosa.
   a. 307.1   b. 307.50   c. 783.0   d. 783.3

6. Bilateral myringotomy with placement of tubes.
   a. 20.00   b. 20.01   c. 20.01, 20.01   d. 20.09, 20.01

7. CHF due to hypertension. Anterior wall MI, diagnosed on EKG (currently presenting no symptoms).
   a. 402.01, 428.0   c. 428.0, 401.9
   b. 402.91, 428.0, 412   d. 428.0, 401.9, 412

8. Endoscopic bronchoalveolar lavage (BAL).
   a. 33.23   b. 33.24   c. 33.99   d. 96.56

9. Repair of unilateral direct inguinal hernia.
   a. 53.00   b. 53.01   c. 53.11   d. 53.9

10. Extracorporeal shock wave lithotripsy of the right kidney.
    a. 98.5   b. 98.51   c. 98.52   d. 98.59

Multiple Choice II—ICD-10-CM/PCS

11. Classical cesarean section by hysterotomy.
    - a. 10207YZ
    - b. 10900ZC
    - c. 10A00ZZ
    - d. 10D00Z0

12. Excision of pilonidal abscess.
    - a. 0H98X0Z
    - b. 0H90X0Z
    - c. 0HB8XZZ
    - d. 0HC0XZZ

13. Open temporomandibular joint (TMJ) repair, right.
    - a. 0RQC0ZZ
    - b. 0MM00ZZ
    - c. 0C00X7Z
    - d. 0KQ00ZZ

14. Congenital hydrocephalus.
    - a. G91.0
    - b. G91.9
    - c. Q03.8
    - d. Q03.9

15. Transurethral cystoscopy for control of postoperative hemorrhage of bladder.
    - a. 0TJB8ZZ
    - b. 0W3R0ZZ
    - c. 0W3R8ZZ
    - d. 0WWR4YZ

16. Respiratory distress syndrome of newborn.
    - a. J80
    - b. P22.0
    - c. P27.8
    - d. P28.81

17. Stab wound (from knife) of thoracic aorta, repaired with synthetic graft.
    - a. S21.109A, X99.9xxA, 02UP0JZ
    - b. S31.000A, X99.9xxA, 02UW0KZ
    - c. S25.00xA, X99.1xxA, 02UW0JZ
    - d. S29.001A, X99.8xxA, 02UJ0JZ

18. Partial splenectomy.
    - a. 009F0ZX
    - b. 075P0ZZ
    - c. 07BP0ZZ
    - d. 07TP0ZZ

19. Needle biopsy of cerebral meninges.
    - a. 00B13ZX
    - b. 00B13ZZ
    - c. 00C13ZZ
    - d. 00D13ZZ

20. Complete substernal thyroidectomy.
    - a. 0GBG0ZX, 0GBH0ZX
    - b. 0GBH0ZZ
    - c. 0GPKX0Z
    - d. 0GTK0ZZ

Coding Practice—Hospital Inpatient Cases

Instructions: Review each case scenario, and assign and properly sequence the ICD-9-CM diagnosis and procedure codes. Then, assign and properly sequence the ICD-10-CM diagnosis and ICD-10-PCS procedure codes. (Adobe.pdf files of the ICD-10-CM and ICD-10-PCS coding manuals can be found at http://www.cms.gov.)

21. A 70-year-old female presented to the hospital with fever, myalgia, arthralgia, tachycardia, and dehydration and was believed to be septic. This patient has a history of hypertension, CHF, and migraines. Routine medications include Lasix 40 milligrams by mouth each morning, if needed, for significant pedal edema and Isordil 20 milligrams by mouth four times a day.

    A variety of studies were obtained to further delineate the source of her problem. Urine cultures were negative. Blood cultures grew *Escherichia coli*. The blood urea nitrogen level was 22, and a random glucose was 149. An anterior-posterior film of the chest taken at the same time showed acute pulmonary edema.

    The patient received intravenous fluids. The patient's routine medications were continued, and she received intravenous antibiotics. On the fourth day of her hospital stay, it was believed that the patient had reached maximal hospital benefit and was therefore switched to oral antibiotics and was discharged. The patient left the hospital in good condition.

    DISCHARGE DIAGNOSES: Septicemia. Dehydration. Positive blood culture, *Escherichia coli*. Acute pulmonary edema due to CHF. Hypertensive heart disease.

22. A 2-year-old male presented with fever, vomiting, and abdominal pain. The patient was severely dehydrated with a blood urea nitrogen level of 54, indicating acute renal failure. Blood cultures obtained grew *Staphylococcus aureus*. The patient was treated with a 10-day course of intravenous vancomycin. The patient also received intravenous fluids and had improved renal function. Upon admission, the patient was noted to have a rash on his buttocks and was treated with topical ointment. The patient improved and was discharged.

DISCHARGE DIAGNOSES: Septic shock. Acute renal failure, secondary to *Staphylococcus aureus* septicemia. Diaper rash. Dehydration.

---

23. A 70-year-old white female with pancreatic head carcinoma, confirmed by previous percutaneous fine-needle aspiration and determined to be unresectable. The patient was also found to have probable metastasis to the lower lobe of the left lung, and she was admitted now for resection of the lower lobe of the left lung. The patient had a history of hypothyroidism and diet-controlled diabetes.

During hospitalization, the patient was continued on Levoxyl, and a "no-concentrated-sweets diet" was ordered. The patient was taken to the operative suite, where a partial left lower lobe lung resection was performed. Pathology from this procedure revealed adenocarcinoma. The patient had an uneventful postoperative course and was discharged with an appointment to see the oncologist to discuss radiation and chemotherapy options.

DISCHARGE DIAGNOSES: Pancreatic adenocarcinoma metastatic to left lung. Hypothyroidism. Diet-controlled type 2 diabetes mellitus.

PROCEDURE: Left lower lung lobe resection.

---

24. A 94-year-old male was admitted to the hospital with a chief complaint of abdominal pain and loss of weight. The patient had a history of coronary artery disease and myocardial infarction. There is no history of coronary bypass surgery. The patient had a nebulizer at home and takes metoprolol. These medications were continued during the patient's stay. Physical examination revealed abdomen to be tender to palpation in the left mid and lower quadrants with some rebound. Bowel sounds were present, and there was no guarding. Blood pressure was normal. Pulse, respirations, and temperature were normal.

During hospitalization, EKG showed sinus rhythm with myocardial changes of ischemia. Sputum cytology was suggestive of adenocarcinoma, compatible with bronchoalveolar growth. Chest X-ray showed metastatic lesions and chronic obstructive lung disease in both lung fields. Barium enema showed adenocarcinoma of proximal sigmoid colon. Abdominal series showed no evidence of obstruction, but moderate dilation of his transverse colon was evident. Patient was seen in consultation, and it was decided to do as little as possible at this time due to the patient's age and lung conditions. The patient agreed with this approach and requested discharge to home to receive hospice care.

DISCHARGE DIAGNOSES: Carcinoma of sigmoid colon. Probable metastatic bronchogenic carcinoma. End-stage chronic obstructive lung disease. Coronary artery disease. Previous myocardial infarction.

---

25. After outpatient treatment was unsuccessful, a 62-year-old white female was admitted to the hospital for metatarsal amputation due to diabetic gangrene of the left foot. The patient had a 10-year history of type II diabetes mellitus, and her blood sugars had been controlled with Actos. Wound culture and sensitivity testing revealed *Pseudomonas aeruginosa* and *Escherichia coli*. The patient was treated with wide-spectrum antibiotics prior to surgery. On the fourth hospital day, the patient was taken to the operative suite and underwent complete amputation of the left great toe. The patient healed slowly and was discharged to home care.

DISCHARGE DIAGNOSIS: Type II diabetic peripheral angiopathy with gangrene, left great toe. Bacterial infection was due to *Pseudomonas aeruginosa* and *Escherichia coli*.

PROCEDURE: Complete amputation, metatarsal, left great toe.

---

26. This patient is a 43-year-old female with a long history of joint pain. Lately she had been feeling very tired and weak. She also has had intermittent abdominal pain with nausea and vomiting. Her joint exam showed tenderness of the knees. She denied any problems suggestive of hypothyroidism (myxedema). The patient's hematocrit was 27.6, serum iron was found to be decreased at 27, and thyroid functions were found to be markedly low. Upper GI series showed a 4-millimeter ulcer at the posterior wall of the duodenal bulb. The patient was transfused two units of packed red cells. She was started on ferrous sulfate 300 milligrams twice a day. She was also begun on Tagamet for the ulcer. Further questioning revealed that she had indeed been hypothyroid in the past and has been on thyroid medication until stopped by another physician. The patient was restarted on Synthroid .2 milligrams per day. She was discharged on the sixth hospital day.

DISCHARGE DIAGNOSES: Anemia due to myxedema. Acute duodenal ulcer.

---

27. This patient is a 14-year-old African-American male who was admitted due to sickle cell crisis and acute chest syndrome. His mother has sickle cell anemia, and his father has the sickle cell trait. Because of this, the patient was tested at birth; a blood sample was drawn, and it was sent to the laboratory for hemoglobin electrophoresis to obtain a definitive diagnosis. Unfortunately, the test was positive for sickle cell disease. The patient was given intravenous fluids and was started on Darvocet for pain management. When the Darvocet failed to keep his pain at an acceptable level, he was switched to Vicodin. The patient is to be discharged with follow-up in the pediatrician's office tomorrow.

DISCHARGE DIAGNOSES: Sickle cell disease with crisis and acute chest syndrome.

---

28. This unfortunate 34-year-old woman was diagnosed 6 months ago with breast cancer. At the time of diagnosis, she was also found to have metastases to the bone and the liver. Her oncologist has recommended that she undergo intensive chemotherapy before she has surgery to remove her breast tumor and liver tumor. She is currently undergoing this chemotherapy on an outpatient basis. She presented to the hospital with extreme fatigue. She stated that she feels light-headed and just generally does not feel well. Her blood work revealed her to have a hematocrit of 27.5, and her anemia is apparently due to her neoplastic disease. She received four units of packed red blood cells, and her hematocrit improved. At the time of discharge, hematocrit is 32.3; and the patient is discharged in improved condition. She is to follow up with her oncologist to determine if she needs to start undergoing Epogen injections.

DISCHARGE DIAGNOSES: Anemia in neoplastic disease. Carcinoma of the right breast with metastases to bone and liver.

---

29. A 31-year-old white male presented to the emergency room reportedly having taken 8 to 10 naproxen at home in a suicide attempt. He reported that he had been having trouble with his girlfriend, and he is unemployed. He had apparently become despondent over this and attempted to take his own life with his girlfriend's pills. The patient is admitted to the telemetry unit due to paroxysmal ventricular tachycardia. The patient was started on metaraminol for the tachycardia. Fortunately, the patient seemed to sustain no other ill effects from the naproxen. The mental health service was consulted, and an appointment was made for outpatient services. He was given Prozac to treat his depression. At this time, the patient does not appear to be a threat to himself or to others. He appears remorseful and denies any suicidal ideations. He was discharged in good condition.

DISCHARGE DIAGNOSES: Suicide attempt with naproxen. Paroxysmal ventricular tachycardia. Depression.

30. A 52-year-old male bus driver is admitted to receive a course of electroconvulsive therapy for his depressive symptomatology. This patient was seen approximately one year ago in consultation; and at that time, he was showing early evidence of involutional psychotic reaction. He has had several admissions since that time; and on each occasion, he had been drinking excessively. It appears that he attempts to use alcohol as a tranquilizer. During the first two days of his admission, he continued to show marked depressive symptomatology and he was started on electroconvulsive therapy. After treatment, he showed a mitigation of his depressive symptomatology. He was discharged home on Pertofrane 25 milligrams twice a day and was instructed to call for follow-up care. Condition on discharge was improved.

DISCHARGE DIAGNOSIS: Moderate involutional psychotic reaction, recurrent.

31. A 71-year-old male presented to the hospital with the chief complaint of increasing confusion. The patient has been wandering away from home and has displayed aggressive behavior to his family members. The patient is a known type 2 diabetic and is on Orinase 0.5 milligrams daily. He also uses an albuterol inhaler, two puffs, twice daily. The patient is thin and emaciated and has diminished breath sounds. During his period of hospitalization, the patient was uncooperative in all aspects. He refused food and medications. He was confused and seemed slightly paranoid. The family was consulted about the patient's worsening dementia, and the decision was made to transfer the patient to the state psychiatric hospital for care. The patient was transferred on the fifth hospital day.

DISCHARGE DIAGNOSES: Alzheimer's disease with senile dementia and increasing confusion. Emphysema. Type 2 diabetes mellitus, controlled.

32. An 84-year-old female was admitted to the hospital because of severe dizziness and weakness. The patient has had previous brain stem transient ischemic attacks and also has completed radiation for what was assumed to be cancer of the endometrium. The patient is currently receiving short-term chemotherapy for the endometrial carcinoma on an outpatient basis, and she was administered her chemotherapy during this inpatient stay. The patient had 3+ hyperreflexia and rotary nystagmus on admission. The urinalysis showed white blood cells and bacteria. Her urine culture grew *Klebsiella pneumoniae*. The patient was started on Velosef. Over the next several days, the dizziness cleared, but the patient continued to be quite weak. Gait training physical therapy was started, and she was eventually able to walk with her walker without assistance. Her reflexia had come back down to 1+, which is her usual state. The patient had no more nystagmus and was switched from heparin to Persantine. The patient was discharged home and was to be seen as an outpatient in one month.

DISCHARGE DIAGNOSES: Brain stem transient ischemic attack. Endometrial carcinoma. UTI due to *Klebsiella pneumoniae*.

33. This patient is a practical nurse who presented to the hospital because her blood pressure was 240/140 at home. Her blood pressure at admission was 220/120. This patient has had multiple strokes, and her first stroke was 5 years ago. This patient has a history of hypertension and atrial fibrillation. She was started on intravenous Aldomet, Dyazide, Catapres, and Lanoxin. Her blood pressure lowered to 190/98. On admission, her radial, brachial, popliteal, and femoral pulses were 2–4. The next day the femoral pulse was decreased to 1–4, and the posterior tibial pulses were not palpable. The leg on the left side was clammy and cold. There was minimal cyanosis over the heel of the left foot. Possible femoral and popliteal artery embolism had to be ruled out, and it was decided to transfer the patient.

    DISCHARGE DIAGNOSES: Hypertensive crisis. Possible bilateral iliofemoral emboli. Multiple previous CVAs resulting in hemiplegia on the nondominant left side and aphasia. Atrial fibrillation.

---

34. A 47-year-old male corrections officer presented to the emergency room with an acute onset of chest pain. The pain was described as a crushing pain and was accompanied with radiation of the pain into the jaw and diaphoresis. He does not have a history of previous myocardial infarction (MI). His risk factors include morbid obesity, hypertension, and hypercholesterolemia. The patient takes metoprolol and Lipitor. The cardiologist was consulted, and the patient was found to have an acute ST elevation anterior wall MI. The patient was admitted to the intensive care unit and was observed on telemetry. On the second day of hospitalization, the patient was thought to be stable for transfer. The patient was transferred for coronary angiography and possible angioplasty.

    DISCHARGE DIAGNOSES: Acute ST elevation anterior wall MI. Hypertension. Hypercholesterolemia. Morbid obesity.

---

35. A 16-month-old infant was admitted from the emergency room because of nausea and vomiting and some cough. She was felt to have acute bronchitis due to respiratory syncytial virus (RSV) with possible pneumonia. This child was hospitalized previously with meningitis but has had no other serious illnesses until the present time. She has no prior history of diabetes or tuberculosis. Her parents are alive and well. The physical examination revealed generalized sibilant rales. The patient's chest X-ray was normal. Pneumonia was ruled out. Her urinalysis was normal. Her hematocrit was 34. The low hematocrit was thought to be due to the persistent vomiting and lack of iron intake from her diet. The patient was given penicillin and Phenergan injections. She was also given nebulizer treatments every 6 hours on an as-needed basis. The patient was started on clear liquids, and she progressed to a general diet. After the first few days, the vomiting ceased. She was discharged with prescriptions for ferrous gluconate, ampicillin, and Phenergan.

    DISCHARGE DIAGNOSES: Acute bronchitis due to RSV. Nutritional anemia due to in adequate dietary iron intake. Nausea and vomiting.

---

36. The patient is a 77-year-old male admitted to the hospital due to shortness of breath and progressive chest pain. The patient has had evidence of acute bronchitis with discolored sputum for 5 days and, despite antibiotics, was not improving. With this, he developed an increasing need for nitroglycerin. During his hospitalization, the patient was treated with intravenous antibiotics, steroids, theophylline, and handheld nebulizer with Alupent. The patient improved with the cough clearing nicely. Unfortunately, several days prior to discharge, he developed severe precordial chest pain typical of his angina. This required three nitroglycerin plus morphine to stop the pain. The EKG showed significant ischemic distress, which cleared over the next few hours; and there was no evidence of damage by isoenzyme study. The patient was monitored on telemetry and increased his activity slowly. The patient improved and was discharged to home on Procardia 10 milligrams every other day, nitroglycerin patch 5 milligrams daily, Isordil 10 milligrams every other day, Lasix 40 milligrams daily, Theo-Dur 300

milligrams twice a day, prednisone in a decreasing dose, and Velosef 500 milligrams twice a day and is to be seen in the office in one week.

DISCHARGE DIAGNOSES: Respiratory distress secondary to chronic obstructive pulmonary disease with acute bronchitis. Arteriosclerotic cardiovascular disease, native coronary artery, with progressive angina. Mitral insufficiency.

---

37. This patient is a 62-year-old woman with a 15-year history of Parkinson's disease on Sinemet. She is otherwise in good health. She was admitted with progressive abdominal distension over the past 5 days. She had had no bowel movement for the week prior to admission. She had vomited several times with intermittent nausea. She was able to keep down liquids. Her physical examination showed a distended abdomen with tympanitic, high-pitched bowel sounds. The patient's rectal exam showed no areas of tenderness and no stool. Her admission EKG was within normal limits. The abdominal films showed gas-filled large and small bowel with air fluid levels in both. There was no evidence of free air. The impression was of distal colonic obstruction versus impaction with an incompetent ileocecal valve. She was admitted and treated conservatively with nasogastric suction and intravenous hydration. Her Parkinson's disease was medically managed. The abdominal distension became slowly but progressively worse. A Gastrografin enema was done, which revealed an intrinsic mass obstructing retrograde flow beyond the mid-sigmoid that was consistent in appearance with carcinoma of the mid-sigmoid colon. The distension of the colon had increased greatly, and she was taken to the operating room for transverse loop colostomy. The patient tolerated the procedure well. Her diet has been slowly advanced. The patient and her daughter are able to manage changing of the colostomy bag. She was discharged with follow-up arranged for sigmoid resection and return of the loop colostomy to the abdomen.

DISCHARGE DIAGNOSES: Intrinsic mass obstructing the mid-sigmoid region of the colon consistent with carcinoma. Parkinson's disease.

PROCEDURES: Loop colostomy, sigmoid colon, via open transverse incision.

---

38. This patient was admitted to the hospital due to severe low back pain and a great amount of indigestion. She has had frequent episodes of abdominal pain in the past, but this is more severe and has failed to respond to therapy as an outpatient. She is known to have chronic ulcer disease, esophageal hiatus hernia, and polyps of the gallbladder in addition to her osteoporosis and stenosis of the lumbar spine, all of which were medically managed during the inpatient stay. The physical examination revealed a 74-year-old white woman who appeared to be acutely and chronically ill. She had epigastric tenderness with no masses palpable. The patient's EKG was normal. An upper gastrointestinal series showed a small sliding hiatal hernia and a chronic duodenal ulcer with considerable evidence for an active ulcer. The gallbladder showed abnormal filling defects, which were consistent with polyps. The X-rays of the spine showed a great deal of osteoporosis and stenosis of the lumbar spine. The patient was given Demerol and Phenergan for the pain and was started on intravenous Prevacid. She was given Dalmane 30 milligrams at bedtime and a calcium supplement one time daily. She was started on a bland diet. The patient has slowly improved as far as the back pain. She is now up and about and is having less indigestion since therapy for the ulcer was begun. The patient is being discharged to be followed as an outpatient. She will continue on a bland diet and will be discharged on Prevacid, Carafate, a calcium substitute, and Darvocet.

DISCHARGE DIAGNOSES: Acute and chronic duodenal ulcer. Sliding esophageal hiatus hernia. Gallbladder polyps. Osteoporosis. Spinal stenosis of the lumbar region.

39. This patient is an 84-year-old female who was admitted to the hospital because of extreme weakness and inability to eat. The patient had been a resident of the nursing home when she suddenly developed progression of her symptoms of weakness. She refused to eat. Several days later she was not responding well. Laboratory studies done at that time revealed the hemoglobin to be 8.4 and her white count to be 14,700. There were significant abnormalities of her blood work that included a blood urea nitrogen level of 181, a sodium level of 149, a potassium level of 5.1, and glucose of 232. The patient was admitted to the hospital and hydrated with intravenous fluids. With that, her hemoglobin dropped to a low of 6. The patient was given a total of four units of packed red blood cells, and this brought her blood count up to 14.3. With appropriate hydration, there was a continual decline of her blood urea nitrogen level and improvement of her electrolytes. Despite this, she did not seem to be as strong as expected. We were trying to switch her from intravenous to oral medication. The next day it became apparent that despite the intravenous fluids and blood transfusions, the patient was not responding. Her blood urea nitrogen level was beginning to rise, and she was becoming less responsive. Her breathing began to slow, and she became completely unresponsive. At 1:10 A.M. of the next morning, she was pronounced dead.

DISCHARGE DIAGNOSES: Acute renal failure and dehydration. Anemia in end-stage renal disease.

---

40. This is a 62-year-old patient seen in the office because of urinary difficulty. The patient noticed that he had to strain when he had to urinate. He has been having this problem off and on during the past year. Also, sometimes he has to move his bowels when he urinates because of the strain. His urinary stream is very slow. He has no history of dysuria or hematuria. His past history reveals that he has high blood pressure, and he is taking medication for that with occasional Valium. He also has been complaining of some pain in the lower back at the area of the coccyx bone. On his physical examination, the abdomen was soft with no tenderness or mass palpable. He has normal external genitalia with a rectally grade III smooth prostate gland. The patient's urological work-up was done as an outpatient, and this showed an essentially normal upper urinary tract and enlarged prostate. He is admitted to the hospital for transurethral resection of the prostate. On the day of admission, under general anesthesia, transurethral resection of the prostate (via artificial opening) was performed. Postoperatively, the patient did well. When his catheter was removed, he was able to void well without any difficulty. The pathology report revealed benign prostatic hyperplasia. Because of a tender coccyx bone, he did have several X-rays, which were negative. The pain was improved by injecting Aristocort and Novocain into this area. The patient's hypertension medication was continued. The patient was discharged and will be seen in the office in 3 weeks.

DISCHARGE DIAGNOSES: Benign hyperplasia of the prostate with urinary obstruction and lower urinary tract symptoms. Coccygodynia. Hypertension.

PROCEDURE: Transurethral resection of the prostate.

---

41. The patient is a 35-year-old female who had been seen in the emergency room on a couple previous occasions. She also had been seen at the clinic and underwent pelvic examination with cervical culture. She appeared to be ill and was unable to take oral antibiotics. Therefore, she was admitted to the hospital for treatment. At admission, she appeared ill and toxic. Her chest X-ray was normal. A pelvic ultrasound showed a 3-centimeter bulge involving the left posterior uterus, which was thought to be fibroid, and a 2-centimeter cyst in the left ovary. A pregnancy test was negative. Her urine culture and sensitivity showed no growth. A plain urinalysis was normal. She was started on ampicillin 500 milligrams intravenously every six hours, and she required Demerol for pain. It is believed that both the ovarian cyst and uterine fibroid were the cause of her pain. The intravenous therapy was continued until the next day, at which time it was stopped. The patient's condition improved, and she was discharged to be seen in follow-up for possible endometriosis.

DISCHARGE DIAGNOSES: Ovarian cyst. Degenerating fibroid with leiomyomata of the uterus. Possible endometriosis.

---

42. The patient is a 23-year-old white female, gravida 2, para 1, who has had no problems with her pregnancy until two days prior to admission. She began with some spotting, which progressed to heavier bleeding with cramping. The cramping became severe on the morning of admission; and she suddenly expelled the fetus, placenta, and everything at home. She did not save it. She began to bleed excessively then, and she presented herself to the emergency room. At that point, it was believed that she had had an incomplete abortion. At the time of admission, she was a well-developed, well-nourished white female in no apparent distress. Her vital signs are stable. She is afebrile. Her pertinent physical findings included a negative abdominal exam and a pelvic exam that revealed blood, clots, and mucus in the external cervical canal and in the vaginal vault. The bimanual exam was deferred until the time of surgery when sterile conditions could be met. She was taken to the operating room after her complete blood count and urinalysis showed nothing unusual. In the operating room, a dilatation and curettage was done without problem. Postoperatively, she has done fine. She has had no unusual vaginal bleeding. She has had no problem with ambulation to the bathroom. Her abdomen is soft and nontender this morning. She feels fine. She is discharged to home in good condition.

DISCHARGE DIAGNOSIS: Incomplete spontaneous abortion with excessive vaginal bleeding.

PROCEDURE: Dilatation and curettage to remove retained products of conception.

---

43. The patient is a 25-year-old white female, gravida 1, whose pregnancy has been benign. She had gone into spontaneous labor late in the evening and came to the obstetric unit at about 0230 hours. She was dilated a fingertip. She came to 50% effacement, and labor picked up every few minutes. By 8 o'clock in the morning, she was only 2 to 3 centimeters dilated. This continued until late in the afternoon. She was station minus 2 and had good contractions for several hours with no further progression of labor. Pelvimetry showed borderline cephalopelvic disproportion. It was finally decided to do a Cesarean section. She was taken to the operating room and underwent a low transverse cervical incision with delivery of a live female child. She had an essentially uneventful postoperative course. Her incision has been healing well, and her bowels have been moving. The abdomen is soft and nontender. The patient was anxious to go home and was discharged to home to be seen in the office for her 2-week postpartum check.

DISCHARGE DIAGNOSES: Borderline cephalopelvic disproportion with obstructed labor. Failure to progress at labor.

PROCEDURE: Cesarean section, low cervical.

---

44. A 35-year-old white male had a mass on his right wrist for quite some time. It had become tender and quite achy. It was, therefore, recommended that this be excised under axillary block anesthesia. Incidentally, he also had a mass of the skin of the nose and requested removal of the mass as well as sterilization by vasectomy to be done at the same time. The patient was admitted to undergo these surgeries under local anesthesia following excision of the ganglion cyst. His orthopedic examination at the time of admission revealed him to have a 1 × 2 centimeter fluctuant but fairly firm mass of the radial volar aspect of the right wrist, which was just proximal to the flexor crease. This was nonpulsatile. He also had what appeared to be a sebaceous cyst involving the skin on the tip of the nose. The patient's preoperative chest X-ray, complete blood count, and urinalysis were all within normal limits. An X-ray of the right wrist revealed no bony abnormality, but it did reveal a soft tissue mass on the lateral aspect of the wrist. The patient underwent the operative procedures described above, the first under axillary block and the other two under local anesthetic. The patient tolerated the procedures well and left the operating room in good condition. The pathology report revealed a ganglion cyst of the wrist and a sebaceous cyst of the nose. He was discharged the next day with instructions to return to the office for follow-up.

DISCHARGE DIAGNOSES: Ganglion cyst, right wrist. Sterilization. Sebaceous cyst, nose.

PROCEDURES: Excision, ganglion cyst, right wrist. Bilateral vasectomy, open approach. Excision, lesion, skin of nose.

---

45. This patient has had a decubitus gangrenous ulcer on the dorsum of his left heel that had not improved and was, in fact, getting worse. He was given intensive medical treatment as an outpatient; but the entire foot became more swollen and red, and he was brought to the hospital for more intensive therapy. Studies revealed a *Staphylococcus aureus* infection from the wound culture. He was treated for cellulitis with intravenous vancomycin and following surgery was placed on gentamicin and intravenous Vibramycin. These medications were effective in controlling his infection and improving the cellulitis. They were not, however, able to improve the ulcer. Whirlpool treatments and dressing changes also failed to improve the ulcer. It was ultimately decided that an above-the-knee amputation was necessary. After 5 days of intravenous antibiotics, the patient was taken to the operative suite, where it was determined that below-the-knee amputation of the left leg was appropriate; and that procedure was performed. He is now being transferred to a rehabilitation facility for continued care. His leg stump sutures will be removed as able, probably in about 2 weeks.

DISCHARGE DIAGNOSES: Gangrenous decubitus ulcer of the left heel, stage IV. *Staphylococcus aureus* infection.

PROCEDURE: Below-the-knee amputation, left leg.

---

46. A 62-year-old white female had been hospitalized 5 months previously with a subcapital fracture of the right hip. She underwent open reduction with internal fixation of the fracture. The fracture healed, but she continued to have difficulty with pain over the ends of the Gouffon pins. She was admitted for surgical removal of these pins. Postoperatively, her blood pressure dropped in the recovery room. This was treated with and responded to ephedrine. For the rest of her hospitalization, she had no further problems with her blood pressure. Her incision began to drain serous-type drainage. She was dangled on the side of her bed on her first postoperative day and was transferred out of bed and into the chair on her second postoperative day and subsequently started on physical therapy for gait training with a walker. Serous drainage persisted from the hip, and a culture of the wound from her right hip incision grew *Escherichia coli*. She was treated with cephalothin for this postoperative infection. She was ultimately discharged to home with care by the visiting nurse, who will do twice-a-week dressing changes.

DISCHARGE DIAGNOSES: Painful Gouffon pins of the right hip. Postoperative hypotension. Postoperative wound infection, right hip, with *Escherichia coli*. (Initial encounter.)

PROCEDURE: Removal of Gouffon pins, right hip.

---

47. A 64-year-old male was admitted to the hospital, complaining of right knee pain. X-rays revealed that he had degenerative arthritis of the right knee. His options were discussed with him. He decided to undergo a right total knee replacement with insertion of a molded polyethylene synthetic knee implant. He underwent the procedure without incident. Postoperatively, he has done well. He began with physical therapy, ambulating with a walker. He was afebrile; and his wound was clean, dry, and intact upon discharge. He was stable upon discharge. He will have a home health nurse come to his house to remove his staples in 2 weeks' time. He should continue to work on range of motion and strengthening of his right leg. He should ambulate with the assistance of a walker. The patient should call immediately if he notices any redness, pain, or swelling around his incision.

DISCHARGE DIAGNOSIS: Degenerative primary osteoarthritis of right knee.

PROCEDURE: Total knee replacement, right knee.

48. This child was delivered vaginally during this admission to a 24-year-old mother, gravida 2, para 2, with blood type A positive. The child was born at term (38 weeks) and had a birth weight of 2425 grams. The mother's pregnancy was uncomplicated, and delivery was by sterile spontaneous vaginal delivery without difficulties. The child was noted to have multiple congenital defects on birth. This child had multiple anomalies, including small for gestation age size, bilateral cleft lip and palate, prominent sternum, an accessory finger of the left hand (below the pinkie finger), and penile hypospadias; on X-ray, he had 11 ribs with hemivertebra at the T5 to T6 level. He also had dextroversion malrotation of the left kidney but no apparent cardiac anomalies. During the majority of his course, he was maintained on intravenous fluids and nutrition. Because of the child's multiple anomalies, bone marrow chromosomes were done. These were positive, showing trisomy 13 in all of the cells counted. Because of this, he also had consultation with the genetics service, which agreed with the diagnosis. The child also had evaluation by the cardiology service, which believed the child had kidney dextroversion malrotation but no structural heart disease. As mentioned, the child has trisomy 13, which is uniformly poor in terms of prognosis. The parents were informed of this, and they elected to do no heroic treatment or resuscitation for the child. The child stopped breathing and was pronounced dead later that same day. Autopsy was denied by the parents, and disposition has been arranged.

DISCHARGE DIAGNOSES: Trisomy 13. Term male. Small for dates. Cleft lip and palate, complete. Accessory finger, left hand. Hypospadias, penile. Eleven ribs. Hemivertebra. Dextroversion malrotation, left kidney.

---

49. This patient is a 17-year-old male who had a syncopal episode at his football practice that lasted approximately 2 minutes. The patient has a completely benign medical history. He is a well-developed, well-nourished teenager who is active in sports. Upon questioning, the patient admits to feeling dizzy during practices, with vague chest pain. He has been tired lately, but he attributes that to daily practices. The patient admits to shortness of breath. There is no family history of heart disease. The patient's EKG in the emergency room was abnormal. The patient was admitted, and a cardiology consult was ordered. Ultrasonography of the heart revealed the patient to have persistent truncus arteriosus. The findings were discussed with the patient's parents, and the decision was made to transfer the patient to the care of a pediatric cardiologist at the nearby Children's Hospital. The patient was transferred in stable condition.

DISCHARGE DIAGNOSES: Persistent truncus arteriosus. Syncope.

---

50. The patient is a premature female infant who was born during this admission to a 20-year-old woman who has a known drug problem. The patient was born by spontaneous vaginal delivery. The infant was born at 32 weeks' gestation and weighed 1760 grams. On the second day of admission, it was apparent that the infant was beginning to experience withdrawal symptoms. She was agitated and cried inconsolably. She required constant attention from the nursing staff. She was rocked almost continuously and bundled tightly in her blanket. The mother tested positive for cocaine, and the matter was turned over to social services. The infant is being discharged to foster care and will be seen in the office in the morning.

DISCHARGE DIAGNOSES: Premature female infant born by spontaneous vaginal delivery. Withdrawal symptoms due to mother's drug addiction.

---

51. The patient is a male infant who was born during this admission via Cesarean section. The day after delivery he appeared jaundiced. His blood was drawn, and he was found to have an elevated bilirubin level. The patient was treated with phototherapy and was discharged the next day with great improvement of his bilirubin level. He is scheduled to see the pediatrician in 2 days for a repeat bilirubin test.

DISCHARGE DIAGNOSES: Term male, born by Cesarean section. Hyperbilirubinemia.

PROCEDURE: Phototherapy of a newborn.

---

52. The patient is a 2-year-old male who was admitted to the hospital after a febrile seizure at home. He had been pulling at his ears and crying intermittently for 2 days prior to admission. At home, his temperature was 103.5 degrees. By the time he arrived in the emergency room, his fever had dropped to 102; and he was admitted for treatment. On examination, his ears looked red and had serous drainage. He was placed on phenobarbital elixir for seizures and amoxicillin 125 every 8 hours for acute otitis media. He responded well to this therapy; and by the end of the second day of hospitalization, his fever was down. He had a urine culture that did show some *Staphylococcus epidermis,* thought to be due to a contaminant. His throat culture showed normal flora. His hemaglobin was 11.1 with a white blood cell count of 10,800. His chest X-ray was normal. The patient was discharged on the amoxicillin and will be seen in 1 week for follow-up.

DISCHARGE DIAGNOSES: Febrile seizure with acute serous otitis media on the right.

53. This patient is an 18-year-old female who presented to the emergency room for severe right lower quadrant abdominal pain. She was given morphine in the emergency room, which did little to help the pain. A surgical consult was requested, and she was admitted to the hospital. Her pelvic and abdominal computed tomography scans were negative. They showed no abnormalities with her liver, spleen, kidneys, gallbladder, or ovaries. Her amylase, complete blood count, white blood cell count, and glucose were all within normal limits. Her urinalysis was completely normal. Despite these findings, the patient's abdominal pain continued. She was continued on morphine. She had no nausea or vomiting. Gynecology was consulted, and an intravaginal ultrasound ordered. This was also negative. By the third day of the patient's hospitalization, her pain began to abate. She was started on a liquid diet and quickly advanced to solid food. She was discharged to be followed up with her physician. A copy of all reports will be sent to his office.

DISCHARGE DIAGNOSIS: Right lower quadrant abdominal pain.

54. This patient is a 5-year-old female who presented to the ED one day after experiencing at home a coffee burn injury on her forearm, right and left legs, and vulva. She presented to this burn center for evaluation. The patient was admitted with a 7% total body surface area burn to her forearm, vulva, and right and left legs thigh area. The wounds were second-degree burns with no evidence of any full-thickness burn. She was taken to the operating room for an irrigation debridement as well as application of a burn dressing. The patient's hospital course was essentially uneventful. She had twice daily dressing changes, and her wounds were assessed daily. On hospital day four, she was thought ready to be discharged. The mother felt quite comfortable doing the dressing changes. Her pain was well controlled with medications. She remained afebrile. There was no evidence of any infection in any of her wounds. The patient is to continue Silvadene dressing changes twice a day. The mother is to call for any temperature higher than 101 degrees or pain uncontrolled by medication.

DISCHARGE DIAGNOSES: Second-degree burns to forearm, vulva, and right and left legs thigh area (7% total body surface area). (Initial encounter.)

55. A 22-year-old white male was involved in a motorcycle-truck accident and was admitted with open comminuted type IIIA fractures of the shaft of the left tibia and fibula; a closed Colles' fracture of the distal radius on the right arm; and a laceration of the tongue, which was approximately 1 inch in length. He was the driver of the motorcycle, and he lost control and hit a parked truck in a parking lot. The remainder of his physical and history was essentially noncontributory. He was started on lactated Ringers and D5% dextrose and given 1 gram of Kefzol. His tetanus immunization was up-to-date. The laboratory studies included an EKG that was read as abnormal with nonspecific myocardial changes in the inferolateral region, not felt to be significant or warranting further follow-up. His chest X-ray was grossly normal on admission. The cervical spine was normal. He was taken to the operating room, where he underwent an open reduction and internal fixation of the fractured tibia and fibula, casting of the right radial fracture, and suturing of the tongue laceration. The patient was treated for a full 10 days with intravenous Keflex. His wounds looked good. His post-reduction X-rays revealed good position of the right wrist and left leg fractures. He was discharged to follow-up in the office in 10 days. At that time, he will have an X-ray of the right wrist and left lower leg. He was given a prescription for Talwin 50 milligrams by mouth every four hours as needed for pain.

DISCHARGE DIAGNOSES: Traumatic open comminuted type IIIA fractures, left tibia shaft and fibula. Traumatic Colles' closed, distal radius, right. Laceration, tongue, approximately 1 inch in length. (Initial encounter.)

PROCEDURES: Open reduction, internal fixation, left tibia and fibula. Suture repair, tongue laceration.

CHAPTER 6

ICD-9-CM and ICD-10-CM Outpatient and Physician Office Coding

Chapter Outline

Outpatient Care

Diagnostic Coding and Reporting Guidelines for Outpatient Services: Hospital-Based and Physician Office

Coding Guidelines for Outpatient Diagnostic Tests

Note:

ICD-10-CM codes are also provided in this chapter.

Chapter Objectives

At the conclusion of this chapter, the student should be able to:

- Define key terms.
- List and explain differences among outpatient and physician office health care settings.
- Interpret outpatient diagnosis coding and reporting guidelines.
- Assign ICD-9-CM and ICD-10-CM diagnosis codes for outpatient and physician office care.

Key Terms

ambulatory care

ambulatory patient

ambulatory surgery patient

clinic outpatient

Coding Guidelines for Outpatient Diagnostic Tests

Diagnostic Coding and Reporting Guidelines for Outpatient Services: Hospital-Based and Physician Office

emergency care patient

first-listed diagnosis

observation patient

outpatient

outpatient care

preadmission testing (PAT)

primary care

primary care provider

qualified diagnosis

referred outpatient

triage

Uniform Ambulatory Care Data Set (UACDS)

Introduction

This chapter defines outpatient care settings and interprets the *Diagnostic Coding and Reporting Guidelines for Outpatient Services: Hospital-Based and Physician Office,* published in the CMS *Guidelines for Coding and Reporting Using ICD-9-CM.*

The Centers for Medicaid & Medicare Services (CMS) has also made available on its website Coding Guidelines for Outpatient Diagnostic Tests, which are also interpreted in this chapter. It is important to remember that coding guidelines are to be used as a companion to the official version of the *International Classification of Diseases, Ninth Revision, Clinical Modification* (ICD-9-CM), which contain coding conventions to ensure accurate coding.

ICD-9-CM or ICD-10-CM codes are assigned to outpatient and physician office diagnoses for health care financial planning, reimbursement, and statistical purposes. (Outpatient reimbursement systems are discussed in Chapter 19 after students have learned how to assign HCPCS level II and CPT codes to procedures and services. Patient demographic data and codes are reported to third-party payers on the CMS-1500 claim to generate reimbursement.

> **Note:**
>
> Outpatient health care settings, such as home health care and hospice, use the UB-04 claim instead of the CMS-1500 claim.

Coders review patient records to locate conditions and diseases to which ICD-9-CM or ICD-10-CM codes are assigned. Coders also assign HCPCS level II and CPT codes to procedures and services, (discussed in Chapters 7–18.) Similar to the inpatient coding process, outpatient coders may not assign codes to conditions and diseases when the provider does not specifically document the diagnoses or procedures/services. Such assumption coding is considered fraud, and the coder should query the physician to determine whether the documented diagnosis should be edited so a more specific code can be assigned. (Refer to Chapter 1 for more information about the physician query process.)

 Note:

> The **Uniform Ambulatory Care Data Set (UACDS)** was established by the federal government as a standard data set for ambulatory care facility records. Its goal is to improve data comparison for ambulatory and outpatient care settings.
>
> Home health agencies (HHAs) report data according to the Outcome and Assessment Information Set (OASIS), which is a core set of comprehensive assessment for adult home care patients that is used to:
>
> - Measure patient outcomes for Outcome-Based Quality Improvement (OBQI).
> - Conduct patient assessment, patient care planning, and internal HHA performance improvements.
> - Generate agency-level case mix reports that contain aggregate statistics about various patient characteristics such as demographic, health, or functional status at start of care.
>
> HHAs use Home Assessment and Validation and Entry (HAVEN) data entry software to report OASIS data.

Outpatient Care

Outpatient care (or **ambulatory care**) includes any health care service provided to a patient who is not admitted to a facility. Such care may be provided in a physician's office, a stand-alone health care facility, a hospital outpatient or emergency department (ED), or the patient's home.

Primary Care Services

Primary care includes both preventive and acute care services, which are often provided as outpatient care and are referred to as the *point of first contact.* Services are usually provided by a general practitioner or another health professional (e.g., nurse practitioner) who has first contact with a patient seeking medical treatment, including general dental, ophthalmic, and pharmaceutical services. These services are usually provided in an office setting where the care is continuous (e.g., quarterly office visits for a chronic condition) and comprehensive (e.g., preventive and medical care). The **primary care provider** manages and coordinates the patient's care, including referring the patient to a medical specialist (Table 6-1) for consultation and a second opinion. Primary care services include the following:

- Annual physical examinations
- Early detection of disease
- Family planning
- Health education
- Immunizations
- Treatment of minor illnesses and injuries
- Vision and hearing screening

Hospital Outpatient Services

Hospital outpatients include ambulatory patients, ambulatory surgery patients, emergency care patients, and observation care patients. The maximum length of stay of an outpatient is 23 hours, 59 minutes, and 59 seconds. **Ambulatory patients** (or **outpatients**) are treated and released the same day and do not stay overnight in the hospital. **Ambulatory surgery patients** undergo certain procedures that can be performed on an outpatient basis, with the patient treated and released the same day. An ambulatory surgery patient who requires a longer stay must be admitted to the facility as an inpatient. **Emergency care patients** are treated for urgent problems (e.g., trauma) and are either released the same day or admitted to the hospital as inpatients. **Observation patients** receive services furnished on a hospital's premises that are ordered by a physician (or another authorized individual), including use of a bed and periodic monitoring by nursing or other staff, and that are reasonable and necessary to evaluate the outpatient's condition or determine the need for possible admission as an inpatient.

Outpatient care allows patients to receive care in one day without the need for inpatient hospitalization. Care is provided in either a freestanding or a hospital-based facility and includes the following (Table 6-2):

- Ambulatory surgical centers (freestanding)
- Hospital-based outpatient department
- Hospital-based ED
- Hospital-based ambulatory surgery program
- Hospital-based partial hospitalization program
- Hospital-owned physician practice
- Hospital-owned satellite clinics
- Industrial health clinic
- Neighborhood health centers
- Physicians' offices
- Public health departments
- Satellite clinics
- Staff model health maintenance organizations (HMOs)
- Urgent care centers

Diagnostic Coding and Reporting Guidelines for Outpatient Services: Hospital-Based and Physician Office

The *Diagnostic Coding and Reporting Guidelines for Outpatient Services: Hospital-Based and Physician Office* were developed by the federal government and approved for use by hospitals and providers for coding and reporting hospital-based outpatient services and provider-based office visits. Although the guidelines were originally developed for use in submitting government claims, insurance companies have also adopted them (sometimes with variation).

Note:

Because variations may contradict the official coding guidelines, make sure you review each insurance company's coding guidelines.

Selection of First-Listed Condition

In the outpatient setting, the **first-listed diagnosis** is reported (instead of the inpatient setting's *principal diagnosis*); it is the diagnosis, condition, problem, or other reason for encounter/visit documented in the patient record to be chiefly responsible for the services provided. It is determined in accordance with ICD-9-CM (or ICD-10-CM) *coding conventions* (or rules) as well as general and disease-specific coding guidelines. Because diagnoses are often not established at the time of the patient's initial encounter or visit, two or more visits may be required before a diagnosis is confirmed.

An outpatient is a person treated in one of four settings:

- *Ambulatory surgery center*: Patient is released prior to a 24-hour stay and length of stay must be 23 hours, 59 minutes, and 59 seconds or less.

- *Health care provider's office* (e.g., physician)

- *Hospital clinic, ED, outpatient department, same-day surgery unit*: Length of stay must be 23 hours, 59 minutes, and 59 seconds or less.

- *Hospital observation status or hospital observation unit*: Patient's length of stay is 23 hours, 59 minutes, and 59 seconds or less unless documentation for additional observation is medically justified.

Note:

When reviewing the coding guidelines, remember that the terms encounter and visit are used interchangeably when describing outpatient and physician office services. In addition, you'll notice that some outpatient coding guidelines were previously discussed in the general coding guidelines.

Note:

The first-listed diagnosis on an outpatient chart reflects the reason for the encounter, which often is a sign or symptom. Physicians don't usually have time during one encounter to establish a definitive diagnosis. Thus, the first-listed diagnosis code indicates to third-party payers why the physician provided the services.

Note:

- The *first-listed diagnosis* was previously called the *primary diagnosis*.
- When determining the *first-listed diagnosis,* ICD-9-CM (or ICD-10-CM) coding conventions and general and disease-specific guidelines take precedence over the outpatient guidelines (e.g., etiology/manifestation coding convention).
- Chapter 5 contains the definition of an inpatient and a discussion of principal diagnosis, comorbidities, complications, principal procedure, and secondary procedures.

EXAMPLE: A patient received ED care for an injury to the right arm, which upon X-ray revealed closed displaced oblique fracture of the shaft of the right humerus (ICD-9-CM code 812.21) (ICD-10-CM code

S42.331A). While receiving treatment for the fracture, the physician also medically managed the patient's chronic obstructive asthma (ICD-9-CM code 493.20) (ICD-10-CM code J44.9).

The first-listed diagnosis code is 812.21 (ICD-9-CM) or S42.331A (ICD-10-CM), and the secondary diagnosis code is 493.20 (ICD-9-CM) or J44.9 (ICD-10-CM).

Note:

- *Outpatient Surgery:* When a patient presents for outpatient surgery, code the reason for the surgery as the first-listed diagnosis (reason for the encounter), even if the surgery is cancelled due to a contraindication (e.g., patient's blood pressure increases unexpectedly upon administration of anesthesia).
- *Observation Stay:* When a patient is admitted for observation for a medical condition, assign a code for the medical condition as the first-listed diagnosis.

  When a patient presents for outpatient surgery and develops complications requiring admission to observation, code the reason for the surgery as the first-listed diagnosis (reason for the encounter), followed by codes for the complications (e.g., respiratory distress) as secondary diagnoses.

ICD-9-CM Tabular List of Diseases (001.0 through V91.99) or ICD-10-CM Tabular List of Diseases (A00.0 through T88.9, Z00-Z99)

The appropriate code or codes from the ICD-9-CM Tabular List of Diseases (001.0 through V91.99) or ICD-10-CM Tabular List of Diseases (A00.0 through T88.9, Z00-Z99) must be used to identify diagnoses, symptoms, conditions, problems, complaints, or other reason(s) for the encounter/visit.

Accurate Reporting of ICD-9-CM or ICD-10-CM Diagnosis Codes

For accurate reporting of ICD-9-CM or ICD-10-CM diagnosis codes, the documentation should describe the patient's condition, using terminology that includes specific diagnoses as well as symptoms, problems, or reasons for the encounter. There are ICD-9-CM or ICD-10-CM codes to describe all of these.

Reason for Encounter (Selection of ICD-9-CM Codes 001.0 through 999.9)

ICD-9-CM codes 001.0 through 999.9 will frequently be used to describe the reason for the encounter. These codes are from the section of ICD-9-CM for the classification of diseases and injuries (e.g., infectious and parasitic diseases; neoplasms; and symptoms, signs, and ill-defined conditions).

Note:

Because all ICD-10-CM codes contain alphanumeric characters, the "reason for encounter" outpatient guideline does not apply to the ICD-10-CM classification system.

Codes That Describe Signs and Symptoms

Codes that describe symptoms and signs, as opposed to definitive diagnoses, are acceptable for reporting purposes when the physician has not documented an established diagnosis or confirmed diagnosis.

- ICD-9-CM Chapter 16 (Symptoms, Signs, and Ill-defined Conditions, 780.0–799.9) contains many, but not all, codes for symptoms.
- In ICD-10-CM, Chapter 18 (Symptoms, Signs, and Abnormal Clinical and Laboratory Findings Not Elsewhere Classified) (R00-R99) contain many, but not all codes for symptoms.

Some symptom codes are located in other ICD-9-CM or ICD-10-CM chapters, which can be found by properly using the ICD-9-CM Index to Diseases or ICD-10-CM Index to Diseases and Injuries.

Encounters for Circumstances Other than a Disease or Injury (V Codes)

ICD-9-CM and ICD-10-CM provides codes to deal with encounters for circumstances other than a disease or an injury.

- In ICD-9-CM, the Supplementary Classification of Factors Influencing Health Status and Contact with Health Services (V01.0–V91.88) is provided to deal with occasions when circumstances other than a disease or an injury are recorded as diagnoses or problems.

- In ICD-10-CM, Factors Influencing Health Status and Contact with Health Services (Z00-Z99) are provided to deal with occasions when circumstances other than a disease or injury are recorded as diagnosis or problems.

Level of Detail in Coding

ICD-9-CM diagnosis codes contain three, four, or five digits.

1. *ICD-9-CM codes with 3, 4, or 5 digits:* Disease codes with three digits are included in ICD-9-CM as the heading of a category of codes that may be further subdivided by the assignment of fourth and/or fifth digits, which provide greater specificity.

2. *Use of full number of digits required for a code:* A three-digit code is to be assigned only if it is not further subdivided. Where fourth-digit subcategories and/or fifth-digit subclassifications are provided, they must be assigned. A code is invalid if it has not been coded to the full number of digits required for that code.

ICD-10-CM diagnosis codes contain 3, 4, 5, 6, or 7 characters:

1. *ICD-10-CM codes with 3, 4, 5, 6, or 7 characters:* Disease codes with three characters are included in ICD-10-CM as the heading of a category of codes that may be further subdivided by the use of fourth, fifth, sixth, or seventh characters to provide greater specificity.

2. *Use of full number of characters required for a code:* A three-character code is to be assigned only if it cannot be further subdivided. A code is invalid if it has not been coded to the full number of characters required for that code, including the seventh character extension, if applicable.

ICD-9-CM or ICD-10-CM Code for the Diagnosis, Condition, Problem, or Other Reason for Encounter/Visit

Report first the ICD-9-CM or ICD-10-CM code for the diagnosis, condition, problem, or other reason for encounter/visit shown in the medical record to be chiefly responsible for the services provided. Then report additional codes that describe any coexisting conditions that were treated or medically managed or that influenced the treatment of the patient during the encounter. In some cases, the first-listed diagnosis may be a symptom when a diagnosis has not been established (confirmed) by the physician.

Uncertain Diagnoses

Do not code diagnoses documented as probable, suspected, questionable, rule out, or working diagnosis, or other similar terms indicating uncertainty, all of which are considered **qualified diagnoses**. Instead, code condition(s) to the highest degree of certainty for that encounter/visit, such as symptoms, signs, abnormal test results, or other reasons for the visit.

Note:

This differs from coding practices used by short-term, acute care, long-term, and psychiatric hospitals, where qualified diagnoses are coded and reported.

EXAMPLE:

For Qualified Diagnosis:	Code the Following Sign or Symptom:
Suspected pneumonia	Shortness of breath, wheezing
Questionable Raynaud's	Numbness of hands
Possible wrist fracture	Wrist pain and swelling
Rule out pneumonia	Influenza (flu)

Qualified or uncertain diagnoses are a necessary part of the hospital and office chart until a specific diagnosis can be determined. Although qualified diagnoses are routinely coded for hospital inpatient admissions and reported on the UB-04 claim, CMS *specifically prohibits the reporting of qualified diagnoses on the CMS-1500 claim submitted for outpatient care.* CMS regulations permit the reporting of patients' signs and/or symptoms instead of the qualified diagnoses.

An additional incentive for not coding qualified diagnoses resulted from the Missouri case of *Stafford v. Neurological Medicine Inc., 811 F. 2d 470 (8th Cir., 1987).* In this case, the diagnosis stated in the physician's office chart was *rule out brain tumor.* The claim submitted by the office listed the diagnosis code for *rule out brain tumor* although test results were available that proved a brain tumor did not exist. The physician assured the patient that although she had lung cancer, there was no metastasis to the brain. Some time after the insurance company received the provider's claim, it was inadvertently sent to the patient. When the patient received the claim, she was so devastated by the diagnosis that she committed suicide. Her husband sued and was awarded $200,000 on the basis of *negligent paperwork* because the physician's office had reported a *qualified or uncertain diagnosis.*

> **Note:**
> When assigning codes to physician services provide to inpatients, adhere to the outpatient "Uncertain Diagnosis" guideline (so that codes for signs and symptoms are reported instead of qualified diagnoses).

Chronic Diseases

Chronic diseases treated on an ongoing basis may be coded and reported as many times as the patient receives treatment and care for the condition(s).

Code All Documented Conditions That Coexist

Code all documented conditions that coexist at the time of the encounter/visit and that require or affect patient care, treatment, or management. Do not code conditions that were previously treated and no longer exist. However, history codes (ICD-9-CM categories V10–V19 or ICD-10-CM categories Z80–Z87) may be reported as secondary codes if the historical condition or family history has an impact on current care or influences treatment.

> **Note:**
> Third-party payers review claims for "family history of" codes to determine reimbursement eligibility. Some plans reimburse for conditions that may not normally be eligible for payment when family history of a related condition is documented in the patient's record and reported on the claim.

Patients Receiving Diagnostic Services Only

For patients receiving diagnostic services only during an encounter/ visit, report first the diagnosis, condition, problem, or other reason for encounter/visit that is documented in the medical record as being chiefly responsible for the outpatient services provided during the encounter/ visit. (This is the *first-listed diagnosis.*) Codes for other diagnoses (e.g., chronic conditions) may be reported as additional diagnoses.

> **Note:**
> This differs from the coding practice in the hospital inpatient setting regarding abnormal findings on test results, for which the physician may document a qualified diagnosis that is coded and reported.

For encounters for routine laboratory/radiology testing in the absence of any signs, symptoms, or associated diagnosis, assign V72.5 (Radiological exam, not elsewhere classified) and a code from subcategory V72.6 (Laboratory examination) (ICD-9-CM) or Z01.89 (ICD-10-CM). If routine testing is performed during the same encounter as a test to evaluate a sign, symptom, or diagnosis, it is appropriate to assign both the V code and the code describing the reason for the nonroutine test.

For outpatient encounters for diagnostic tests that have been interpreted by a physician and for which the final report is available at the time of coding, code any confirmed or definitive diagnoses documented in the interpretation. *Do not code related signs and symptoms as additional diagnoses.*

Patients Receiving Therapeutic Services Only

For patients receiving *therapeutic services only* during an encounter/visit, sequence first the diagnosis, condition, problem, or other reason for encounter/visit shown in the medical record to be chiefly responsible for the outpatient services provided during the encounter/visit.

Assign codes to other diagnoses (e.g., chronic conditions) that are treated or medically managed or that would affect the patient's receipt of therapeutic services during this encounter/visit.

The only exception to this rule is when the reason for admission/encounter is for chemotherapy, radiation therapy, or rehabilitation. For these services, the appropriate ICD-9-CM V code or ICD-10-CM Z code for the service is listed first and the diagnosis or problem for which the service is being performed is reported second.

Patients Receiving Preoperative Evaluations Only

For patients receiving *preoperative evaluations only,* assign and report first the appropriate code from ICD-9-CM subcategory V72.8 (other specified examinations) or ICD-10-CM subcategory Z01.81 (encounter for pre-procedural examinations), to describe the pre-op consultations.

Assign an additional code for the condition that describes the reason for the surgery. Also assign additional code(s) to any findings discovered during the preoperative evaluation.

Ambulatory Surgery (or Outpatient Surgery)

Note:

Preadmission testing (PAT) is routinely completed prior to an inpatient admission or outpatient surgery to facilitate the patient's treatment and reduce the length of stay. As an incentive to facilities that perform PAT, some payers provide higher reimbursement for PAT, making it important to assign codes properly.

For *ambulatory surgery* (or *outpatient surgery*), assign a code to the diagnosis for which the surgery was performed. If the postoperative diagnosis is different from the preoperative diagnosis when the diagnosis is confirmed, assign a code to the postoperative diagnosis instead (because it is more definitive).

Routine Outpatient Prenatal Visits

For routine outpatient prenatal visits when no complications are present:

- Report ICD-9-CM code V22.0 (Supervision of normal first pregnancy) *or* V22.1 (Supervision of other normal pregnancy) as the first-listed diagnosis. *Do not report either of these codes in combination with ICD-9-CM Chapter 11 codes.*

- Report a code from ICD-10-CM category Z34 (encounter for supervision of normal pregnancy) as the first-listed diagnosis. *Do not report this code in combination with ICD-10-CM Chapter 15 codes.*

For routine prenatal outpatient visits for patients with high-risk pregnancies, report an ICD-10-CM code from category O09 (supervision of high-risk pregnancy) as the first-listed diagnosis. A code from ICD-10-CM Chapter 15 may also be reported as a secondary diagnosis, if appropriate.

THE FOLLOWING GUIDELINES APPLY ONLY TO ICD-10-CM

Encounters for General Medical Examinations with Abnormal Findings

ICD-10-CM subcategories Z00.0 (encounters for general medical examinations) provide codes for with and without abnormal findings. When a general medical examination results in an abnormal finding, report the code for general medical examination with abnormal finding as the first-listed diagnosis. Then, report a secondary code for the abnormal finding.

Encounters for Routine Health Screenings

ICD-10-CM Z codes describe encounters for routine examinations (e.g., general check-up) or examinations for administrative purposes (e.g., pre-employment physical). Z codes are not to be reported *if the examination is for diagnosis of a suspected condition or for treatment purposes.* In such cases, report an ICD-10-CM diagnosis code.

- During a routine exam, if a diagnosis or condition is discovered, report it as an additional ICD-10-CM code.

- Pre-existing conditions, chronic conditions, and history codes may also be reported as additional ICD-10-CM codes if the examination performed is for administrative purposes and does not focus on any particular condition.

- Some ICD-10-CM codes for routine health examinations distinguish between "with" and "without" abnormal findings. Code assignment depends on the information that is known at the time the encounter is being coded.

  ○ If no abnormal findings were found during examination, but the encounter is being coded before test results are back, it is acceptable to assign the code for "without abnormal findings."

  ○ When assigning a code for "with abnormal findings," additional code(s) should be assigned to identify the specific abnormal finding(s).

- Pre-operative examination and pre-procedural laboratory examination Z codes are reported only for those situations when a patient is being cleared for a procedure or surgery *and no treatment is provided.*

Exercise 6.2 – Diagnostic Coding and Reporting Guidelines for Outpatient Services: Hospital-Based and Physician Office

Instructions: Underline the first-listed diagnosis in each statement.

1. The patient underwent office treatment for removal of a skin lesion from her face. She also received a renewed prescription for her chronic asthma.

2. Dr. Smith ordered a chest X-ray to rule out pneumonia; he also documented shortness of breath in the record.

3. Sally Jones fell out of her tree house and sustained a fractured humerus, which was treated in the emergency department (ED). While in the ED, the physician noted severe swelling of the arm.

4. Cindy Frasier was seen in the office, complaining of severe stomach pain and vomiting. The physician diagnosed gastroenteritis.

5. Tom Noble was treated in the outpatient department for urinary frequency. The physician documented probable cystitis in the record.

6. The patient was treated on an outpatient basis for both acute and chronic bronchitis, for which each was assigned an ICD-9-CM diagnosis code.

7. Eric Fischer was treated for back pain in the physician's office. The physician documented that Eric's previously diagnosed influenza had completely resolved.

8. Scott Taylor was seen for complaints of dizziness, shakiness, and fainting spells; his blood was drawn and sent to the lab to have a blood glucose level performed. Lab results revealed blood glucose level of 325, Scott was placed on oral insulin, and the physician documented diabetes mellitus in the record.

9. Tina Day had an encounter for outpatient chemotherapy for treatment of breast cancer.

10. Joe Daly's preoperative diagnosis was cholelithiasis, for which he underwent laparoscopic cholecystectomy. The postoperative diagnosis was acute cholecystitis with cholelithiasis.

Coding Guidelines for Outpatient Diagnostic Tests

The **Coding Guidelines for Outpatient Diagnostic Tests** (published in CMS Transmittal AB-01-144) includes instructions and examples that are to be used when assigning ICD-9-CM or ICD-10-CM codes for coding diagnostic test results. The instructions and examples provide guidance regarding the appropriate assignment of diagnosis codes to simplify coding for diagnostic tests, consistent with the Diagnostic Coding and Reporting Guidelines for Outpatient Services: Hospital-Based and Physician Office.

Determining the Appropriate First-Listed ICD-9-CM or ICD-10-CM Diagnosis Code for Diagnostic Tests Ordered Due to Signs and/or Symptoms

When a diagnosis is confirmed based on the results of the diagnostic test, the testing facility or the physician interpreting the test should assign a code to that diagnosis. The signs and/or symptoms that prompted the test to be ordered may be reported as additional diagnoses *only if they are not related or integral to the confirmed diagnosis.*

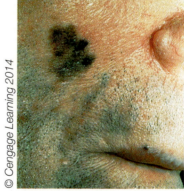

© Cengage Learning 2014

Figure 6-1 Malignant melanoma

> **EXAMPLE:** A surgical specimen is sent to a pathologist, with a diagnosis of mole. The pathologist personally reviews the slides made from the specimen and makes a diagnosis of malignant melanoma (Figure 6-1). The pathologist should report a diagnosis of malignant melanoma as the first-listed diagnosis.

When the diagnostic test did not confirm a diagnosis or was normal, the interpreting physician should code the sign(s) or symptom(s) that prompted the treating physician to order the diagnostic test.

> **EXAMPLE 1:** A patient is referred to a radiologist for a spine X-ray due to complaints of back pain. The radiologist performs the X-ray, and the results are normal. The radiologist should report a diagnosis of back pain because this was the reason for performing the spine X-ray.

> **EXAMPLE 2:** A patient is seen in the ED for chest pain. An electrocardiogram (EKG) is normal, and the final diagnosis is chest pain due to suspected gastroesophageal reflux disease (GERD). The patient is told to follow up with his primary care

Note:

Do not report qualified diagnoses on outpatient claims because they are considered unconfirmed. This is consistent with the outpatient coding guideline to code the diagnosis to the highest degree of certainty.

physician for further evaluation of the suspected GERD. The first-listed code for the EKG is chest pain because the EKG was normal and a definitive cause for the chest pain was not determined. (The suspected GERD is a qualified diagnosis, which is not reported on outpatient claims.)

When the results of the diagnostic test are normal or nondiagnostic *and the referring physician documents a qualified diagnosis* (e.g., probable, suspected, questionable, rule out, provisional, or working), the testing facility or interpreting physician should not code the qualified diagnosis. Rather, the testing facility or interpreting physician should report the sign(s) or symptom(s) that prompted the study.

EXAMPLE: A patient is referred to a radiologist for a chest X-ray with a diagnosis of rule out pneumonia. The radiologist performs the chest X-ray, and the results are normal. The radiologist should report the sign(s) or symptom(s) that prompted the test (e.g., cough).

Instruction to Determine the Reason for the Test

As specified in §4317(b) of the Balanced Budget Act (BBA), referring physicians are required to provide diagnostic information to the testing entity at the time the test is ordered. If the order is communicated via telephone, the treating physician *and* the testing facility must document the telephone call in their respective patient records.

 On the rare occasion when the interpreting physician does not have diagnostic information as to the reason for the test *and* the referring physician is unavailable to provide such information, it is appropriate to obtain the information directly from the patient or the patient's medical record if available. The source of the information (e.g., patient) pertaining to the reason for the test should be documented in the patient's medical record. However, an attempt should be made to confirm any information obtained from the patient by contacting the referring physician.

> **Note:**
>
> If the order is communicated via telephone, both the treating provider and the testing facility must document the telephone call in their respective patient's records.

EXAMPLE: A patient is referred to a radiologist for a gastrografin enema to rule out appendicitis. However, the referring physician does not provide the reason for the referral and is unavailable at the time of the study. The patient is queried and indicates that she saw the physician for abdominal pain and was referred to rule out appendicitis. The radiologist performs the X-ray, and the results are normal. The radiologist should report the abdominal pain as the first-listed diagnosis.

In the event that the physician's interpretation of the test result is unclear or ambiguously stated in the patient's medical record, either the primary care physician or the physician who performed the test should be contacted for clarification. This may result in the reporting of symptoms or a confirmed diagnosis.

If the test (e.g., lab test) has been performed and the results are available but the patient's physician has not yet reviewed them to render a diagnosis or there is no physician interpretation, code the symptom or the diagnosis provided by the referring physician.

In the event that the individual responsible for reporting the codes for the testing facility or the physician's office does not have the report of the physician interpretation at the time of billing, the individual responsible for reporting the codes for the testing facility or the physician's office should code what is known at the time of billing. Sometimes reports of the physician's interpretation of diagnostic tests are not available until several days later, which could result in delayed billing. Therefore, in such instances, the individual responsible for reporting the codes for the testing facility or the physician's office should code based on the available information/reports or on what is known at the time of billing.

Incidental Findings

Incidental findings should never be listed as the first-listed diagnosis. If documented, incidental findings may be reported as secondary diagnoses by the testing facility or the physician interpreting the diagnostic test.

EXAMPLE: A patient is referred to a radiologist for an abdominal ultrasound due to jaundice. After review of the ultrasound, the interpreting physician discovers that the patient has an aortic aneurysm.

The testing facility or the interpreting physician reports jaundice as the first-listed diagnosis and the aortic aneurysm as a secondary diagnosis because it is an incidental finding (and unrelated to the jaundice).

Unrelated/Coexisting Conditions/Diagnoses

Unrelated and coexisting conditions/diagnoses may be reported as additional diagnoses by the testing facility or the physician interpreting the diagnostic test.

> **EXAMPLE:** A patient is referred to a radiologist for a chest X-ray because of a cough. The result of the chest X-ray indicates that the patient has pneumonia. During the performance of the diagnostic test, it was determined that the patient has hypertension and diabetes mellitus. The testing facility or interpreting physician reports a first-listed diagnosis of pneumonia. The testing facility or the interpreting physician may also report the hypertension and diabetes mellitus as secondary diagnoses if those conditions were medically managed (e.g., patient education provided and prescriptions renewed).

Diagnostic Tests Ordered in the Absence of Signs and/or Symptoms (e.g., Screening Tests)

When a diagnostic test is ordered in the absence of signs/symptoms or other evidence of illness or injury, the testing facility or the physician interpreting the diagnostic test should report the screening code as the first-listed diagnosis. Any condition discovered during the screening should be reported as a secondary diagnosis.

Use of ICD-9-CM or ICD-10-CM to the Greatest Degree of Accuracy and Completeness

The testing facility or the interpreting physician should assign the ICD-9-CM or ICD-10-CM code that provides the highest degree of accuracy and completeness for the diagnosis resulting from the test or for the sign(s)/symptom(s) that prompted the ordering of the test. In the past, there has been some confusion about the meaning of *highest degree of specificity* and in *reporting the correct number of ICD-9-CM digits (up to 5) or ICD-10-CM characters (up to 7)*. In the context of coding, the highest degree of specificity refers to assigning the most precise ICD-9-CM or ICD-10-CM code that most completely explains the medical record's narrative description of the symptom or diagnosis.

> **EXAMPLE:** A chest X-ray reveals a primary lung cancer in the left lower lobe. The interpreting physician reports ICD-9-CM code 162.5 (or ICD-10-CM code C34.32) for malignancy of the left lower lobe, bronchus, or lung.

Exercise 6.3 – Coding Guidelines for Outpatient Diagnostic Tests

Instructions: Respond to the question for each case.

1. A patient is referred to a radiologist for an abdominal CT scan with a diagnosis of abdominal pain. The CT scan reveals the presence of an intra-abdominal abscess. What is the first-listed diagnosis?

_____

2. A patient is referred to a radiologist for a chest X-ray because of a persistent cough. The chest X-ray reveals a 3-cm peripheral pulmonary nodule. The patient's physician documents "persistent cough due to pulmonary nodule." What is the first-listed diagnosis?

_____

(continues)

Exercise 6.3 (continued)

3. A patient is referred to a radiologist for a chest X-ray because of wheezing. The X-ray is normal except for scoliosis and degenerative joint disease of the thoracic spine. What does the testing facility or interpreting physician report as the first-listed diagnosis?

_____

4. A patient is referred to a radiologist for magnetic resonance imaging (MRI) of the lumbar spine due to possible L4 radiculopathy. The MRI reveals degenerative joint disease at L1 and L2. What is reported as the first-listed diagnosis?

_____

5. A sputum specimen is sent to a pathologist, who confirms growth of streptococcus, type B. A diagnosis of pneumonia due to streptococcus, Group B is documented in the patient's medical record. What is reported as the first-listed diagnosis?

_____

Summary

Outpatient care includes any health care service provided to a patient who is not admitted to a facility. Such care may be provided in a physician's office, a stand-alone health care facility, a hospital outpatient or emergency department, or the patient's home. The CMS *Diagnostic Coding and Reporting Guidelines for Outpatient Services: Hospital-Based and Physician Office* were developed by the federal government and have been approved for use by hospitals and providers for coding and reporting hospital-based outpatient services and provider-based office visits. Although the guidelines were originally developed for use in submitting government claims, insurance companies have also adopted them (sometimes with variation). The CMS Coding Guidelines for Outpatient Diagnostic Tests includes instructions and examples that are to be used when assigning ICD-9-CM or ICD-10-CM codes for diagnostic test results. The instructions and examples provide guidance regarding the appropriate assignment of ICD-9-CM or ICD-10-CM diagnosis codes to simplify coding for diagnostic tests, consistent with the CMS *Diagnostic Coding and Reporting Guidelines for Outpatient Services: Hospital-Based and Physician Office*.

Internet Links

AHA Central Office: Go to *www.ahacentraloffice.com* to access coding resources.

APC Payment Insider Listserv (free): *www.decisionhealth.com/apc-enroll*

CDC Topics A–Z: Go to *www.cdc.gov* and click on the A–Z Index link.

Coding Pro Listserv (free): *www.decisionhealth.com/codingpro-l-enroll*

Encoder Pro: *www.EncoderPro.com*

HCPro, Inc.: Go to *www.hcmarketplace.com*, and click on the Sign up for our FREE e-Newsletters link. Click on the box located in front of the *JustCoding News: Outpatient* (along with other e-Newsletters that interest you) to subscribe.

ICD-9-CM encoder (free): *www.ICD9coding.com*

ICD-9-CM searchable indexes/tabular lists (free): *icd9cm.chrisendres.com* and *www.eicd.com*

Medical Information Bureau (MIB): *www.mib.com*

National Practitioner Data Bank (NPDB) and Healthcare Integrity and Protection Data Bank (HIPDB): *www.npdb-hipdb.com*

Web-based training courses (free from CMS): Go to *cms.meridianksi.com*, and click on the Web-Based Training Courses link.

Study Checklist

- ❏ Read this chapter and highlight key concepts.
- ❏ Create an index card for each key term.
- ❏ Access the chapter Internet links to learn more about concepts.
- ❏ Complete the chapter review, verifying answers with your instructor.
- ❏ Complete WebTutor assignments and take online quizzes.
- ❏ Complete Workbook chapter, verifying answers with your instructor.
- ❏ Go to *www.cengagebrain.com* to access StudyWARE™ and the Premium Website. Login instructions are located in the Preface and on the Printed Access Card.
- ❏ Form a study group with classmates to discuss chapter concepts in preparation for an exam.

Review

Multiple Choice

Instructions: Select the most appropriate response.

1. A patient was seen on an outpatient basis to have lab tests performed. The next day the patient underwent an outpatient procedure. Due to complications, he was admitted to the hospital. One week after discharge from the hospital, he was seen in the physician's office for a follow-up visit. Coding guidelines classify all of these visits as:
   - a. admissions.
   - b. appointments.
   - c. claims.
   - d. encounters.

2. A patient's record underwent review because the outpatient diagnosis about multiple injuries was unclear. Who is authorized to clarify the diagnosis?
   - a. health care provider
   - b. HIM supervisor
   - c. insurance company
   - d. outpatient coder

3. A patient is diagnosed with osteoarthritis, and the encounter is assigned code 715.9. When referring to the ICD-9-CM index and following tabular list entries, the code assignment of 715.9 was:

```
INDEX TO DISEASES
Osteoarthritis (see also Osteoarthrosis) 715.9
```

```
TABULAR LIST OF DISEASES
715     Osteoarthrosis and allied disorders
        Note: Localized, in the subcategories below, includes bilateral
              involvement of the same site.
           INCLUDES    arthritis or polyarthritis:
                           degenerative
                           hypertrophic
                           degenerative joint disease
                       osteoarthritis
```

EXCLUDES *Marie-Strumpell spondylitis (720.0)*

osteoarthrosis [osteoarthritis] of spine

(721.0–721.9)

The following fifth-digit subclassification is for use with category 715; valid digits are in [brackets] under each code. See list at beginning of chapter for definitions.

0 site unspecified

1 shoulder region

2 upper arm

3 forearm

4 hand

5 pelvic region and thigh

6 lower leg

7 ankle and foot

8 other specified sites

9 multiple sites

715.0 Osteoarthrosis, generalized

[0,4,9] Degenerative joint disease, involving multiple joints Primary hypertrophic osteoarthrosis

715.1 Osteoarthrosis, localized, primary

[0-8]   Localized osteoarthropathy, idiopathic

715.2 Osteoarthrosis, localized, secondary

[0-8]   Coxae malum senilis

715.3 Osteoarthrosis, localized, not specified whether primary or secondary

[0-8]   Otto's pelvis

715.8 Osteoarthrosis involving, or with mention of more than

[0,9] one site, but not specified as generalized

715.9 Osteoarthrosis, unspecified whether generalized or

[0-8] localized

   a. correct because 715.9 is listed in the index as the code for osteoarthritis.

   b. correct because no further information was available in the patient record to assign a more specific code.

   c. invalid because upon verifying 715.9 in the tabular list, the coder should have assigned a fifth digit.

   d. incorrect because the tabular list's excludes note directs the coder to assign a code from 721.0–721.9.

4. In ICD-10-CM, code Z85.02 (personal history of malignant neoplasm of stomach) is reported as a:

   a. complication diagnosis

   b. first-listed or additional diagnosis.

   c. primary diagnosis.

   d. secondary diagnosis.

5. When a definitive diagnosis has not been established or confirmed by the provider, which should be reported?

   a. codes that describe symptoms and signs

   b. none because code assignment must wait until a diagnosis is confirmed

   c. office visit only

   d. qualified diagnosis, such as rule out, possible, or suspected

6. When referring to the ICD-9-CM index and following tabular list entries, diverticulitis with diverticulosis (562.11) is an example of a(n) _____ code.

```
INDEX TO DISEASES
Diverticula, diverticulosis, diverticulum
(acute)(multiple)(perforated)(ruptured) 562.10
    with diverticulitis 562.11
```

```
TABULAR LIST OF DISEASES
562.1    Colon
         562.10 Diverticulosis of colon (without mention of hemorrhage)
                Diverticular disease (colon) without mention of
                   diverticulitis
                Diverticulosis NOS without mention of diverticulitis:
                   intestine (large) without mention of diverticulitis
         562.11 Diverticulitis of colon (without mention of hemorrhage)
                Diverticulitis (with diverticulosis):
                 NOS
                 colon
                 intestine (large)
         562.12 Diverticulosis of colon with hemorrhage
         562.13 Diverticulitis of colon with hemorrhage
```

    a. combination   b. history   c. late effect   d. multiple

7. When a bacterial organism is documented as the cause of a condition (e.g., UTI), it is:
   a. coded as either a first-listed or a secondary code.
   b. coded as a first-listed diagnosis only.
   c. reported as a secondary code, below the code for the condition.
   d. not coded because bacterial organisms are always classified in the disease code.

8. When determining the first-listed diagnosis, the ICD-9-CM and ICD-10-CM coding conventions and _____ guidelines take precedence over the official outpatient guidelines.
   a. drugs and adverse effects
   b. eponyms and procedure/surgical
   c. external cause of injury and poisoning
   d. general and disease-specific

9. For accurate reporting of ICD-9-CM and ICD-10-CM diagnosis codes:
   a. a definitive diagnosis must be documented by the physician who provides care to the patient.
   b. all diagnosis and condition codes must contain five digits (ICD-9-CM) or seven digits (ICD-10-CM).
   c. codes 001.0 through V91.99 (ICD-9-CM) or A00.0 through T88.9, Z00-Z99.89 (ICD-10-CM) are used to classify the encounter.
   d. definitive diagnoses in addition to all signs and symptoms are classified.

10. Which section of ICD-9-CM or ICD-10-CM would be referenced to assign codes that deal with encounters for circumstances other than a disease or an injury?
    a. Classification of Diseases and Injuries
    b. Morphology of Neoplasms
    c. Factors Influencing Health Status and Contact with Health Services
    d. Table of Drugs and Chemicals

11. An encounter is reported with codes for symptoms listed first, followed by an unrelated secondary condition. Thus, the condition was the reason the visit had:
   a. been confirmed, and a coexisting condition was treated or medically managed during the same encounter.
   b. been confirmed, and the patient also exhibited unrelated signs and symptoms during the same encounter.
   c. not been confirmed at the time of coding, and a coexisting condition was treated or medically managed during the same encounter.
   d. not been confirmed at the time of coding, and the patient also exhibited unrelated signs and symptoms during the same encounter.

12. A woman is examined for a routine prenatal visit, with no apparent complications. Which would be the reason for this encounter?
   a. complications of pregnancy and childbirth
   b. encounter for pregnancy test, result positive
   c. personal history of complications of pregnancy
   d. supervision of normal uncomplicated pregnancy

13. A physician ordered diagnostic tests based on a patient's signs and symptoms. A diagnosis was established by the primary care physician based on the results of the diagnostic tests. How should the signs and symptoms that prompted the ordering of the tests be reported?
   a. If signs/symptoms are not related or integral to the confirmed diagnosis, report them as additional diagnoses.
   b. If signs/symptoms are not related or integral to the confirmed diagnosis, report one of them as the first-listed diagnosis.
   c. If signs/symptoms are related or integral to the confirmed diagnosis, report them as additional diagnoses.
   d. No signs and/or symptoms are reported because a diagnosis was established based on results of diagnostic tests.

14. Referring physicians are required to provide diagnostic information to the testing entity at the time the test is ordered. If the order is communicated via telephone, what documentation is required?
   a. No documentation is required by the testing facility or the treating physician.
   b. The testing facility must document the telephone call in the patient record.
   c. The treating physician and the testing facility must document the telephone call in their respective patient records.
   d. The treating physician must document the telephone call in the patient record.

15. A patient is referred by a physician for diagnostic testing, no diagnostic information is available as to the reason for the test, and the referring physician is unavailable to provide such information. Is it appropriate to obtain this information from the patient?
   a. No, the patient should never be used as the source of information as to the reason for diagnostic testing.
   b. Yes, if an attempt is made to confirm any information obtained from the patient by contacting the referring physician.
   c. Yes, if the medical record documents that the information was obtained from the patient.
   d. Yes, if the medical record documents that the information was obtained from the patient and an attempt is made to confirm that information by contacting the referring physician.

16. The patient is seen in the office because of chronic asthma. Coding guidelines for chronic conditions state that such codes:
   a. are not to be reported if the condition is already being medically managed.
   b. may be reported as additional diagnosis only if medically managed.
   c. may be reported as first-listed if medically managed during the encounter.
   d. should never be reported on an outpatient claim.

17. A patient complains of nausea and abdominal pain and undergoes an endoscopy for suspected hiatal hernia. The test results were negative, so the physician instructed the patient to return next week to be tested for gastroesophageal reflux disease. To code this encounter to the highest degree of accuracy and completeness, which would be reported?
    a. gastroesophageal reflux disease
    b. hiatal hernia
    c. nausea and abdominal pain
    d. nausea and vomiting and gastroesophageal reflux disease

18. A patient is referred to a radiologist for a chest X-ray because of wheezing. The X-ray is normal except for degenerative joint disease of the thoracic spine. Which is reported as the first-listed diagnosis?
    a. chest X-ray
    b. degenerative joint disease
    c. thoracic spine
    d. wheezing

19. A patient is referred to a radiologist for a magnetic resonance imaging (MRI) of the lumbar spine, and the primary care physician documented L4 radiculopathy as the reason for the test. The MRI reveals degenerative joint disease at L1 and L2. Which is reported as the first-listed diagnosis?
    a. degenerative joint disease, L1 and L2
    b. lumbar spine
    c. magnetic resonance imaging (MRI)
    d. radiculopathy, L4

20. The patient is diagnosed with pneumonia. A sputum specimen is sent to a pathologist and growth of streptococcus, type B, is confirmed and documented in the patient's record. Use your ICD-9-CM coding manual to determine which code is reported for this diagnosis.
    a. 481   b. 482.32   c. 484.8   d. 486

Coding Practice

Instructions: Review each case scenario and assign and properly sequence the ICD-9-CM and ICD-10-CM diagnosis codes, including ICD-9-CM V- and E-codes and ICD-10-CM external cause codes, as appropriate.

Ambulatory Surgery Center (ASC)

21. SUBJECTIVE: 20-year-old female patient with past medical history significant for asthma underwent total thyroidectomy due to feelings of fatigue and weight gain for the past six months. OBJECTIVE: Thyroid function tests revealed that the patient was hypothyroid with a thyroid-stimulating hormone level of 110.2, free thyroxine index of 0.9, and total T3 of 0.41. The patient also has a palpable mass in the left lobe of the thyroid, and thyroid ultrasound revealed diffuse enlargement of the thyroid gland and microcalcifications. Thyroid lobes were biopsied bilaterally; and based on those results, the patient underwent total thyroidectomy. DIAGNOSIS: Hypothyroidism.

_____

22. SUBJECTIVE: 42-year-old female with past family history of gastric polyposis underwent upper gastrointestinal endoscopy, which revealed multiple gastric polyps in the fundus and body. OBJECTIVE: Biopsies of the gastric polyps were submitted for pathological examination. DIAGNOSIS: Multiple gastric polyps.

_____

23. This 35-year-old states that her menstrual periods have been regular, and she had been taking birth control pills until January of this year. Since that time, she has been using other methods of birth control that are unsatisfactory to her. She and her husband also desire tubal ligation for prevention of further pregnancies. PHYSICAL EXAMINATION reveals a grossly obese white female in no obvious distress; heart and lungs normal to auscultation; abdomen flat; on pressure, the cervix protrudes to the opening of the vaginal os; otherwise, the uterus was average size. Patient was taken to surgery and underwent laparoscopic bilateral tubal ligation. She was discharged in stable condition to be seen by Dr. Baker for follow-up care next week. DIAGNOSIS: Elective sterilization.

24. A 53-year-old male is admitted with a right inguinal hernia. Laboratory results were within normal limits. Right inguinal herniorrhaphy was performed, and the patient did well; there were no complications. He was discharged to be seen in the office in several days for suture removal. No specific diet or medication was prescribed. The patient was advised to avoid any strenuous activities. DIAGNOSIS: Right inguinal hernia.

25. This 31-year-old white female is admitted to the ambulatory surgery unit with chief complaint of multiparity. She states that she wants to undergo a sterilization procedure. She underwent laparoscopic tubal fulguration, bilateral. There are no familial diseases such as epilepsy, diabetes, bleeding tendency, tuberculosis, or heart attacks. She smokes a pack of cigarettes a day and takes no alcohol. She is married, but now separated. She has been in good health and has had no other problems. Her menses are every 28 days and last four days. No clots or pains. Her last period was January 1. She has two children living and well, ages 11 and 5. DIAGNOSIS: Multiparity.

Chiropractic Office

26. A 37-year-old contractor was lifting boards from his truck while on the job in the driveway at a singlefamily residence and began to experience acute burning pain in his neck. His symptoms persisted; and he was seen by his chiropractor, who checked the range of motion in his neck and noted restriction in lateral bending and rotation. Neurological screening revealed decreased sensation at the left thumb and first finger. Reflexes were normal (intact), but there was some muscle weakness in the arm. Patient underwent magnetic resonance imaging (MRI), which was negative, and received chiropractic treatment. DIAGNOSIS: Cervical disc syndrome.

27. A 15-year-old high school student was playing in a basketball game one evening; and when he went up for a rebound, he collided with another player. He felt his neck "wrench" backward, and he experienced immediate pain in both sides of his neck. That evening he felt pain and stiffness in his neck, and he had trouble turning his head. DIAGNOSIS: Acute cervical sprain. (Initial encounter.)

28. A 48-year-old online college professor who sits at a computer all day in her office at the college has been experiencing neck pain accompanied by soreness and stiffness in her upper back. She became concerned when she began to experience numbness and tingling in her left arm, especially at night. History reveals no weakness in her arms and minor arm pain. All neurological signs are normal, and the patient has full range of motion in her neck except for some restriction when she bends her head to the left. Tight and very tender muscles in the upper back and along both side of the neck are palpated. There are also joint restrictions in the middle back. Chiropractic treatment was provided. DIAGNOSIS: Cervical neck strain. Myalgia, upper back.

29. A 77-year-old former bank clerk experiences neck pain and seeks chiropractic treatment. Upon examination, all neurological signs are normal. There is restricted joint motion and tight muscles along both sides of the neck and into the upper and midback. Previous X-ray of the neck revealed osteoarthritis. The patient undergoes chiropractic treatment. DIAGNOSIS: Osteoarthritis, cervical spine.

30. A 25-year-old college student who had been in a recent car accident is seen for chiropractic treatment. She complains of neck stiffness, shoulder and back pain, and headaches. Neck X-rays are negative. Chiropractic treatment included adjustment and heat therapy. DIAGNOSIS: Neck sprain. (Initial encounter.)

Hospital Emergency Department

31. SUBJECTIVE: 15-year-old male patient with congenital cataracts and retinal detachments had experienced in the past an episode of orbital hemorrhage, which was treated. He arrived in the ED today after developing pain behind his right eye yesterday. OBJECTIVE: Physical examination revealed no redness of the eye. The left pupil is deviated medially with a steamy anterior chamber. This is the normal appearance, according to the mother. There was no sight in that eye. Funduscopic exam shows a pigmented retina in the right eye, but no evidence of hemorrhage or optic disc cupping. Schiotz tonometry showed a right orbital pressure of 21 and left orbital pressure of 0. There was no cervical lymphadenopathy. Tympanic membranes were clear. Chest was clear, and heart is regular rate and rhythm. There is full range of motion of the neck. No palpable temporal arteries; no abrasions or swelling. There has been no fever. ASSESSMENT: Headache, etiology unknown. PLAN: I called his primary care physician, who explained that this has been a problem in the past and that neurologically, the patient has been evaluated for this type of problem but nothing was ever found. He believed that the pressure of 21 was okay and that the patient could be discharged on some sort of analgesic. The patient is scheduled to be seen by him in two weeks. DIAGNOSIS: Headache.

32. SUBJECTIVE: 25-year-old male was working with a heavy sledgehammer on his personal property when he noted pain in his right shoulder area. The pain developed suddenly as he was swinging the hammer rather vigorously. The pain has persisted over the past three weeks. At certain times, it was somewhat better; but it became painful once again. The patient has continued working, which involves swinging this sledgehammer. OBJECTIVE: Physical examination reveals tenderness over the anterior joint line; there is no swelling or abnormal mass present. The rotator cuff does not seem involved, as the patient can tolerate extreme downward pressure on his elbows without any pain whatsoever. What really causes the patient's pain is bringing the arms apart when they are in the midline in front of his chest. Distal neurovascular status is intact. X-ray of the shoulder was negative. DIAGNOSIS: Pain, right shoulder. Probable strain, deltoid muscle, and possibly the deeper muscles of the anterior shoulder area. TREATMENT: The patient was given a prescription for Motrin 600 milligrams three times daily and advised to apply heat to the area once or twice each day. He is also to rest the arm as much as possible; however, he says he must work and will not take time off. He was told that this pain may last for a number of weeks before it resolves completely. He is to return to see Dr. Callus if there are any problems.

33. SUBJECTIVE: This 48-year-old man is a patient of mine who complains of midsternal chest pain but no radiation. This has occurred intermittently today since 10 P.M. and did not occur reliably with exertion. He has not been exerting himself too much, as he is a pastor at a Baptist church in Alfred. He complains of feeling quite warm, but has had no diaphoresis or shortness of breath. He previously had his gallbladder removed. He has been taking Inderal 40 milligrams four times each day, and he took Isordil sublingually with mixed results during the day today. He says that Tylenol will help somewhat with the pain in the midsternal area. OBJECTIVE: Physical examination reveals a mildly anxious middle-aged male in little distress. The neck is supple; carotids are two plus without bruits. Chest is symmetrical in expansion, and lungs show few abnormal sounds and some rales in the right base. Heart is regular rate and rhythm; S1 and S2 and 2/4; no murmurs, clicks, heaves, gallops, or rubs were appreciated. The abdomen is soft and nontender. There is a right upper quadrant surgical scar; no masses or organomegaly noted. EKG was done and read as normal. Chest X-ray shows slightly increased density at right lower lobe. He was given Mylanta without any change in his pain. DIAGNOSIS: Bronchitis and early pneumonia on the right.

34. SUBJECTIVE: This 22-year-old female was playing softball yesterday when she twisted her ankle while running to second base. She states that she developed pain in the ankle subsequent to this injury and has been on crutches prior to her arrival in the ED this morning. She denies any previous significant injuries to the ankle. OBJECTIVE: Physical examination reveals a healthy, cooperative 22-year-old female in no acute distress. There is tenderness about the left ankle. There is no ecchymoses or swelling present. There is tenderness beneath both malleoli and anteriorly across the ankle. X-rays of the ankle show no evidence of fracture. PLAN: The patient was instructed to be on crutches for 7 days and maintain complete nonweightbearing and then begin partial weightbearing. If she is uncomfortable, she is to return to using crutches for several more days before attempting weightbearing. She is to elevate the leg and use ice, and she was advised to be reevaluated if she is not able to walk comfortably in 7 to 10 days. DIAGNOSIS: Sprain, left ankle.

35. SUBJECTIVE: This is a 28-year-old female who was handed a knife by her husband, blade first; and she accidentally punctured her left ring finger on the blade. OBJECTIVE: Patient has a superficial puncture wound over the lateral aspect of the left fourth finger. The area has been cleansed well, and a bandage was applied. ASSESSMENT: Puncture wound, left ring finger. PLAN: Patient is to watch for any signs of infection and follow up with her primary care physician.

Hospital Outpatient Department

36. A 39-year-old female patient undergoes a screening electrocardiogram (EKG) as an outpatient. She has a family history of cardiovascular disease. EKG results were negative. The nonspecific T-wave changes illustrated on the EKG were explained to the patient as probably due to anxiety and positional changes.

37. A 42-year-old male patient diagnosed with systemic lupus erythematosus received a scheduled transfusion of erythrocytes and platelets in the ambulatory transfusion clinic.

38. A 54-year-old male previously diagnosed with arteriosclerotic heart disease (ASHD) underwent scheduled right and left cardiac catheterization as an outpatient. The patient has no past history of previous coronary artery bypass graft (CABG) surgery. Cardiac catheterization results revealed 40% blockage of the right coronary artery, 70% blockage of the left main coronary artery, and 80% blockage of the left anterior descending coronary artery. Surgical intervention options to treat the blockages were discussed with the patient, and the patient will be admitted in two days to undergo triple CABG.

39. A 62-year-old patient with known congestive heart failure was seen by the outpatient services at the heart failure clinic to receive lifestyle modification counseling about his diet and activities. He received instruction from the dietician about following a low-sodium, low-fat diet, and he was also counseled to avoid tobacco and heavy alcohol use. His current medications were reviewed, and his diuretic dosage was adjusted.

40. A 45-year-old patient was admitted as an outpatient to undergo scheduled hemodialysis. The patient was born with just one kidney, which failed when she was 30 years old. She previously underwent a kidney transplant, which also failed. Currently, dialysis is her only option as she awaits the availability of another kidney for transplant. The hemodialysis takes three hours and is uneventful.

Hospital Same Day Surgery

41. This 5-year-old white male is admitted with the chief complaint of recurrent bouts of tonsillitis and tonsils so large that foods get stuck in them and he chokes on it. He has had a sore throat now for 4 to 5 weeks, and this is the second time this year that this has happened. He has consulted Dr. Blair, and she advised that the patient undergo tonsillectomy and adenoidectomy (T&A). The patient has no ear problems, and he has not had strep throat that his father knows of. PAST MEDICAL HISTORY: He has had no operations, serious illnesses, or injuries. FAMILY HISTORY: He has had no familial diseases such as cancer, tuberculosis, epilepsy, diabetes, bleeding tendency, or heart attacks. SOCIAL HISTORY: The patient is in kindergarten. He lives with his parents and has no social problems. SYSTEMIC REVIEW: The father states that his son has been in good health and has had no other problems. PHYSICAL EXAMINATION: Reveals his tonsils to be huge. There is evidence that he had an anterior lymphadenopathy. LABORATORY STUDIES: Urinalysis negative. Bleeding time 1 minute 30 seconds. Partial prothrombin time 30 seconds. Hemoglobin 12.3 grams, hematocrit 37 volume percent, white blood count 6,500 with 34 polys. Chest X-ray normal. The patient was prepared for surgery and taken to the operating room where, under satisfactory general intratracheal anesthesia, T&A was performed. Following the operation, he had an uncomplicated postoperative recovery. He had no bleeding, he was afebrile, tonsillar fossa are clean, and he has had no anesthetic complications. DIAGNOSIS: Diseased and greatly hypertrophied tonsils and adenoids.

42. This is an 89-year-old white male who was apparently in good health except for pneumonia in 1938 and had never had any serious medical problems since then. For about a month prior to outpatient surgery, he developed urgency and frequency upon urination and marked nocturia every hour, followed finally by the passing of blood in the urine. He was seen in the emergency room (ER) last week due to passing blood in the urine every day for several days and having a great deal of difficulty voiding. ER treatment involved inserting a Foley catheter, from which 400 cc of grossly bloody urine was evacuated. PHYSICAL EXAMINATION: Reveals a degree of blindness due to cataracts. The testes are atrophic. Prostate is a grade II benign, enlarged gland. LABORATORY AND X-RAY FINDINGS: BUN 62, blood sugar 155, CO_2 14, creatinine 3.6. Urinalysis reveals many red blood cells per high-power field and WBC 4-6. Urine culture reveals innumerable enterococcus. Complete blood count reveals hemoglobin of 11.9 grams, hematocrit of 35. Blood gases reveal pH of 7.38, pCO_2 of 22.9, PO_2 of 91, HCO of 313. WBC of 12,200. EKG was negative. Drip infusion IVP revealed poorly functioning kidneys and one bladder diverticulum with elevation of the bladder floor consistent with a large prostate gland. Chest X-ray showed bilateral basal pulmonary infiltration and calcification of the thoracic aorta. Upper gastrointestinal and gallbladder series and small bowel series revealed small active ulcer crater of the lesser curvature of the pyloric canal. Patient underwent cystoscopy and retropubic prostatectomy. DIAGNOSES: Benign prostatic hypertrophy. Chronic renal insufficiency secondary to benign prostatic hypertrophy. Anemia. Prepyloric gastric ulcer. Urinary tract infection.

43. This 48-year-old male patient has had an anal fissure for several months and is complaining of pain and bleeding. This has not responded to conservative measures, and he is scheduled to undergo outpatient fissurectomy and hemorrhoidectomy. PHYSICAL EXAM reveals no other pertinent positive findings except the presence of obesity, anal fissure, and hemorrhoids. X-ray of the chest was unremarkable. Barium enema studies were unremarkable. EKG showed no abnormality. Lab results revealed blood sugar 92, BUN 14, normal electrolytes and normal enzymes. CBC and differential were normal. Urinalysis was essentially unremarkable. After adequate work-up, the patient was taken to surgery; and under endotracheal anesthesia, a fissurectomy, hemorrhoidectomy, and sphincterotomy were performed. Post-op, the patient was voiding and comfortable. The patient was prescribed Tylenol with Codeine, Metamucil, sitz baths, and limited activity. The patient will be followed in my office. DIAGNOSES: Anal fissure, hemorrhoids, obesity.

44. This 51-year-old white female has noticed a steady enlargement on the left side of the neck for the past year. A thyroid scan revealed a cold nodule in the right lobe, and carcinoma is to be ruled out. The patient also complains of some difficulty with pain in the neck and on swallowing. PHYSICAL EXAMINATION reveals a large mass in the left lobe of the thyroid and a questionable mass on the right side. The patient was taken to surgery, where at the time of exploration, both lobes of the thyroid were markedly enlarged and revealed multiple nodules. A total thyroidectomy was performed after identifying the parathyroid glands and protecting them. The patient was discharged and instructed to return for follow-up examination within 2 weeks. She was placed on Synthroid 0.15 daily and no other medication. DIAGNOSES: Nodular colloid goiter, left and right lobes of thyroid. Degenerating follicular adenoma, right lobe of thyroid.

45. Patient was diagnosed as missed abortion at 20 weeks' gestation. The patient was noted to have grown appreciably in the last month of her prenatal care, and it was noted that she had begun bleeding 3 days before being seen in the office yesterday. At the time of the office visit, she was passing clots. The cervix was dilated, and she was developing a foul-smelling discharge but no morbidity. She was scheduled for outpatient surgery, during which pregnancy was removed with curettage of the uterus; and the patient was discharged in satisfactory condition. Her hemoglobin was 13.8 gm, white blood cell count was normal differential. Pathology revealed products of conception and degenerated decidual and placental tissue. DIAGNOSIS: Incomplete abortion at 20 weeks' gestation; no fetus seen.

Physician Office

46. This 38-year-old man was accidentally poked in his left eye by his 9-month-old little girl yesterday when she came to visit him in his office on a college campus, where he teaches. He says that she was very excited about seeing him and when she reached up to be lifted into his arms, her finger accidentally poked him in the eye and her fingernail scratched his eyeball. He had to teach a class after he saw her, or he would have been in my office earlier. He states, "My eye is killing me!" Since that time, he has pain in his left eye and a lot of watering. He has had no changes in vision, no blurriness noted, and he is otherwise well. Physical examination shows the conjunctiva to be inflamed. Funduscopic examination is normal, and extraocular movements are intact. Stain with fluorescein shows positive corneal abrasion. I administered an ophthalmic topical analgesic to relieve his discomfort and Chloromycetin ointment to the eye to prevent infection. He was fitted with an eye patch, and he is to see me tomorrow for a recheck. DIAGOSIS: Corneal laceration.

47. This 15-year-old male was struck on the left leg by a stick yesterday, which created a puncture wound in the skin of his leg. The patient presents today with swelling and localized redness around the wound. Physical exam reveals a healthy and cooperative 15-year-old male in no acute distress with a small puncture-type wound approximately 5 millimeters in length on the anterior aspect of the left leg, just proximal to the knee. The wound is noted to have a small amount of induration, approximately 2 centimeters in diameter around the area with localized redness. There is no discomfort to motion of the knee. DIAGNOSIS: Puncture wound, left knee. (Initial encounter.) PLAN: The patient was instructed to use warm soaks to that knee several times each day and have it rechecked if it becomes worse. He will return or be seen sooner if the knee does not appear to improve. He was started on Keflex 500 milligrams four times daily.

48. This 34-year-old male, who has had a hydrocele in the past and had been seen and treated by Dr. Wise, returns now for continued pain and swelling in the hydrocele, which is causing poor sleep habits. Apparently, the patient has been given some kind of fluid pill for the discomfort. OBJECTIVE: Patient has a tender, swelling right scrotal region about the size of a grapefruit, which is very tense. ASSESSMENT: Right-sided hydrocele. PLAN: The patient is to wear tight, supportive underwear; take Tylenol #3 for pain; and see Dr. Wise for evaluation.

49. This man cut his left thumbnail and thumb with a powered hand saw today, which flapped back the lateral aspect of the thumb. The thumb was cleansed, numbed, and one stitch put through the nail, fixing the flap in place. He is current on his tetanus immunizations. He will return to the office to have the stitch removed in six to eight days unless he experiences symptoms, in which case he is to call the office to be seen. DIAGNOSIS: Laceration, thumbnail and thumb, left.

50. This 1-year-old little girl injured her hand while "playing the drum" by banging away at pots and pans on the floor of the kitchen while her mother was nearby preparing last evening's meal. The child slept fitfully last night, and this morning her left hand is somewhat swollen and painful to touch. X-ray was taken and is negative for fracture. I treated her with a sling, ice, and elevation, which will continue at home. She will be rechecked as needed. She left the office in good condition.

Stand-alone Radiology Center

51. A 50-year-old male patient underwent ultrasound of neck and ultrasound guided placement of internal jugular dialysis catheter. Indication for radiographic procedures is chronic renal failure and occluded dialysis access graft. Real-time ultrasound examination was done of the neck and showed patency of both internal jugular veins. Following sterile prep and drape and infiltration with local anesthetic, puncture was done of the lower aspect of the right internal jugular vein using a 21-gauge needle. Using Seldinger technique, the tract was dilated and a 14 French dialysis catheter was introduced and positioned within the right atrium. The catheter was secured with a silk suture and irrigated and the patient sent for dialysis.

52. Gallbladder cholecystogram shows moderate concentration of dye in the gallbladder, no evidence of stone, and moderate hypertrophic change of lumbar spine. Small intestinal pattern is normal below the level of the duodenum. Impression is hypertrophic gallbladder with no diagnostic evidence of stones.

53. Patient underwent upper gastrointestinal study due to severe stomach pain. Study reveals esophagus and stomach to be normal in appearance, and first portion of duodenum is normal. There is moderate deformity of the medial aspect of the second portion of the duodenum with moderate flattening of the mucosal pattern in this area, but without any definite evidence of ulceration. The duodenal loop is not significantly widened, but there does appear to be slight extrinsic pressure and probable stiffening of the medial wall of the second portion of the duodenum. IMPRESSION: Second portion of duodenum is consistent with residues of recurrent pancreatitis with probable exacerbation of the pancreatitis at this time. The possibility of neoplasm arising in the head of the pancreas is not excluded.

54. Patient underwent excretory urogram for complaints of urinary incontinence. Urogram revealed that both kidneys appear to concentrate Renografin media in a satisfactory manner. Renal collecting system on the left appears grossly normal. Visualized lateral contour of right kidney appears normal. Renal pelvis and ureters are of normal caliber. Urinary bladder is moderately distended, normal in contour, and shows some indentation on its dome, probably due to the adjacent uterus. There is moderate post-voiding residual. Impression is normal right and left calices, small post-voiding residual with indentation on dome of urinary bladder possibly due to an enlarged uterus.

55. Patient underwent opaque right knee arthrogram for severe pain and limited mobility. Following shaving and scrubbing of the knee in the usual manner, local anesthetic was infiltrated along the lateral approach to the patellofemoral joint. A needle was directed through the anesthetized tissue and into the joint with subsequent removal of 30 cc of pink-colored joint fluid. Then, 11 cc of Renografin 76 were injected and films taken in various projections. Fissures are demonstrated in the posterior segment of the medial meniscus. Cruciate ligaments and lateral meniscus appear intact. Impression is knee joint effusion and rupture of posterior segment of right medial meniscus. (Initial encounter.)

Stand-alone Urgent Care Center

56. SUBJECTIVE: A 45-year-old female was seen complaining of severe pain of the right knee and ankle after having been in a motorcycle accident earlier today. She has difficulty bearing weight on her right leg. OBJECTIVE: Multiple abrasions are noted on both forearms. Two lacerations are noted on the left elbow, approximately 2 centimeters in length. She has a sprain of the right knee, lower leg, and ankle. X-rays of the right knee, lower leg, and ankle were negative. Multiple views revealed no bony abnormality. There was slight soft tissue swelling over the lateral malleolus. TREATMENT: The lacerations on the left elbow were 1 inch long and 1/2 inch long. They were closed with interrupted 4-0 Prolene sutures after thorough cleansing. The abrasions were cleansed. She was given a tetanus toxoid booster, and a sterile dressing was applied. The patient is to be rechecked by her primary care physician in 48 hours. She left in good condition. DIAGNOSES: Multiple abrasions, arms and legs. Laceration, left elbow. Sprain, right knee, lower leg, and ankle.

57. The patient is a 41-year-old male seen for treatment of a scratch on the dorsum of his right hand that occurred about a week ago. It didn't seem to bother him, and he didn't think too much of it. He accidentally stepped on the edge of a piece of 2×4 wood and the opposite end raised up and struck his right hand about two days ago, and it stung a little bit and became a little swollen. It was rather tender today and looking a bit red. He was quite concerned because he has had blood poisoning once before with an infected hair follicle on his hand. I instructed him to come to the urgent care center for evaluation. The patient does have swelling and induration around the area where he had the original scratch. It is red and warm, but there is no streaking that I can see in the lymphatic channels. I think he is developing an infection there, or cellulitis. IMPRESSION: Cellulitis, right hand. (Initial encounter.) DISPOSITION: Hot soaks three or four times each day. Amoxil 250 milligrams three times each day for a week. If it should progressively worsen and become more swollen, the patient should call and have it checked again to be sure he isn't developing an abscess; otherwise, we'll give him a few days. If it hasn't cleared within 5 to 7 days, he is to let me know. The patient did have a borderline blood pressure reading; so I have advised him to contact my office, and we'll check the blood pressure reading to see what he's running because he does tend to get tense when he comes to the doctor's office or hospital. The blood pressure isn't high enough to require treatment at this point, but the patient has been advised to check in with my office to have it rechecked within 2 weeks.

58. This 44-year-old male presents with a chief complaint of back pain. HPI: 44-year-old gentleman states that he went fishing Wednesday. He did not fall or injure himself, but Thursday he was feeling quite bad with right flank pain radiating into the back of his leg and into the testicle. He stated that he had no change in the color of his urine and that the pain actually started to subside. Friday he had another recurrence of pain, and it gradually worsened and stayed with him. Today it was much worse, he was unable to work, and he came to the urgent care center for evaluation and treatment. The patient walks leaning to the right where his pain is. He has a significant amount of difficulty in hyperextension and also forward bending. It does not hurt him too much to bend to the right, but it hurts him quite a bit to bend to the left. He has a lot of tenderness in the sacroiliac region and also in the superior rim of the ilium and the sacrum. X-rays of the area appear normal to my eye. The radiology report is not back

at this time. PLAN: We will treat him with Tylenol with Codeine, two every four hours as needed, and Flexeril 10 milligrams three times a day. He should not work tomorrow or Monday, and perhaps he will be able to return to work on Tuesday. He was instructed to call the urgent care center if he gets any worse. He is instructed to schedule a follow-up visit in one week. He left the urgency care center in satisfactory condition. DIAGNOSIS: Sacroiliac inflammation.

59. This 15-year-old male presents to the urgent care center with the complaint of a cyst on his right cheek. Over the past two days, the patient has developed a reddened, tender mass on the right cheek, just lateral to the nose. Physical exam reveals an erythematous, tender mass approximately 7 millimeters in diameter on the right cheek. It is hard and tender, but does not seem to be fluctuant at this time. DIAGNOSIS: Infected sebaceous cyst, right cheek. PLAN: The patient was instructed to use warm soaks frequently, and he was given a prescription for tetracycline 250 milligrams four times daily. He was instructed to see Dr. Smith in two days. He is to return sooner if he has further difficulty.

60. This young lady was hit in her nose and mouth two days ago; she has had intermittent nosebleeds since that time. She is residing at the detention center here in the village and was brought to the urgent care center and examined. There was moderate swelling in the nose and quite a bit of edema and swelling in the nasal mucosa, but there is no active bleeding noted at the present time. No treatment was given other than Dimetapp one every 12 hours, and the patient was told to avoid taking aspirin. She is to take Tylenol and apply ice to her nose. The detention center staff person who accompanied the patient to the urgent care center was told to call if the patient experienced further problems.

PART III

Health Care Procedure Coding System (HCPCS), Level II National Coding System

HCPCS Level II National Coding System

Chapter Outline

Overview of HCPCS

HCPCS Level II National Codes

Assigning HCPCS Level II Codes

Determining Payer Responsibility

Chapter Objectives

At the conclusion of this chapter, the student should be able to:

- Define key terms.
- List the HCPCS levels and their components.
- Assign HCPCS level II procedure and services codes for outpatient care.
- Identify situations in which both HCPCS levels I and II codes are assigned.
- Assign claims to primary Medicare administrative contractors (MACs) or durable medical equipment MACs according to HCPCS level II code number.

Key Terms

advance beneficiary notice (ABN)

certificate of medical necessity (CMN)

DME MAC medical review policies

durable medical equipment, prosthetics, orthotics, and supplies (DMEPOS)

durable medical equipment, prosthetics, orthotics, and supplies (DMEPOS) dealer

HCPCS level I

HCPCS level II miscellaneous codes

HCPCS level II modifiers

HCPCS level II permanent national codes

HCPCS level II temporary codes

local coverage determinations (LCDs)

Medicare Carriers Manual (MCM)

Medicare National Coverage Determinations Manual

Medicare Pricing, Data Analysis, and Coding (PDAC) contractor

national coverage determinations (NCDs)

orthotics

prosthetics

transitional pass-through payment

Introduction

The HCPCS level II national coding system contains alphanumeric codes that were developed to complement the Current Procedural Terminology (CPT) coding system. HCPCS level II was introduced in 1983 after Medicare found that its payers used more than 100 different coding systems, making it difficult to analyze claims data. HCPCS furnishes health care providers and suppliers with a standardized language for reporting professional and nonphysician services, procedures, supplies, and equipment. (Most state Medicaid programs and many commercial payers also use the HCPCS level II coding system.)

> ## Note:
>
> When reviewing examples and completing exercises and review questions in this chapter, use your HCPCS Level II coding manual to locate index entries and to verify them in the tabular list.

> ## Note:
>
> Instruction about the HCPCS level II coding system is sequenced prior to CPT Chapters 8–18 in this textbook to familiarize students with HCPCS level II modifiers that must be added to CPT codes and HCPCS level II codes that must be reported with CPT codes. Examples. exercises, and review questions in Chapters 8–18 of this textbook require students to report HCPCS level II modifiers and codes, where appropriate.

Overview of HCPCS

Two levels of codes are associated with HCPCS, commonly referred to as HCPCS level I and II codes. Most of the procedures and services are reported using CPT (HCPCS level I) codes. However, CPT does not describe durable medical equipment, prosthetics, orthotics, supplies (DMEPOS), and certain other services. Therefore, the CMS developed HCPCS level II national codes to report DMEPOS and other services. (Medicare carriers previously developed HCPCS level III local codes, which were discontinued December 31, 2003. However, some third-party payers continue to use level III codes.)

HCPCS Level I

HCPCS level I includes the five-digit (and some five-character) CPT codes developed and published by the American Medical Association (AMA). The AMA is responsible for the annual update of this coding system and its two-digit modifiers. (CPT was defined in Chapter 1 of this textbook, and its content is covered is Chapters 8–18.)

HCPCS Level II

HCPCS level II (or HCPCS national codes) was created in the 1980s to describe common medical services and supplies not classified in CPT. HCPCS level II national codes are five characters in length, and they begin with the letters *A–V* followed by four numbers. The codes identify services performed by physician and nonphysician providers (e.g., nurse practitioners and speech therapists) and ambulance and durable medical equipment (DME) companies, which are called durable medical equipment, prosthetics, orthotics, and supplies (DMEPOS) dealers. *Durable medical equipment (DME)* is defined by Medicare as equipment that:

- Can withstand repeated use.

- Is primarily used to serve a medical purpose.

- Is used in the patient's home.

- Would not be used in the absence of illness or injury.

   Durable medical equipment, prosthetics, orthotics, and supplies (DMEPOS) include artificial limbs, braces, medications, surgical dressings, and wheelchairs. **Durable medical equipment, prosthetics, orthotics, and supplies (DMEPOS) dealers** supply patients with DME (e.g., canes, crutches, walkers, commode chairs, and blood-glucose monitors). DMEPOS claims are submitted to DME Medicare administrative contractors (MACs) (previously called durable medical equipment regional carriers, or DMERCs) that were awarded contracts by CMS. Each DME MAC covers a specific geographic region of the country and is responsible for processing DMEPOS claims for its specific region.

Note:

When claims are to be submitted to one of the four DME MACs, DMEPOS dealers that have coding questions should check with the **Medicare Pricing, Data Analysis, and Coding (PDAC) contractor** (formerly called the Statistical Analysis Durable Medical Equipment Regional Carrier, or SADMERC), which assists suppliers and manufacturers in determining HCPCS codes to be used. The PDAC has a toll-free help line for this purpose at (877) 735-1326.

When people refer to HCPCS codes, they are most likely referring to HCPCS level II national codes. CMS is responsible for the annual updates to HCPCS level II codes and the two-character alphanumeric modifiers. HCPCS level II national codes are further discussed in this chapter.

HCPCS Level III

Effective December 31, 2003, HCPCS level III local codes were no longer required. They had the same structure as level II codes, but were assigned by the local Medicare carrier (LMC) (now called MAC), which processes Medicare claims. Level III codes began with the letters *W, X, Y,* or *Z*. (Some third-party payers continue to use level III codes.)

Exercise 7.1 – Overview of HCPCS

Instructions: Complete each statement.

1. HCPCS level II codes are considered_____ codes.

2. HCPCS level II codes describe procedures, services, and_____.

3. CPT codes are included as HCPCS_____ codes.

4. HCPCS level II national codes are_____ characters in length.

5. HCPCS level II national codes begin with the letters_____.

HCPCS Level II National Codes

The HCPCS level II national coding system classifies similar medical products and services for the purpose of efficient claims processing. Each code contains a description, and the codes are used primarily for billing purposes. The codes describe the following:

- DME devices, accessories, supplies, and repairs; prosthetics; orthotics; and medical and surgical supplies

- Medications

- Provider services

- Temporary Medicare codes (e.g., Q codes)

- Other items and services (e.g., ambulance services)

    EXAMPLE: DMEPOS dealers report HCPCS level II national codes to identify equipment reported on claims submitted to private or public health insurers.

HCPCS is *not* a reimbursement methodology or payment system; it is important to understand that just because codes exist for certain products or services, coverage (e.g., payment) is not guaranteed. The HCPCS level II national coding system:

- Ensures uniform reporting of medical products or services on claims forms.

- Has code descriptors that identify similar products or services (instead of specific products or brand/trade names).

- Is not a reimbursement methodology for making coverage or payment determinations. (Each payer makes determinations on coverage and payment outside this coding process.)

Responsibility for HCPCS Level II National Codes

HCPCS level II national codes are developed and maintained by the HCPCS National Panel, which consists of representatives from the Blue Cross/Blue Shield Association (BCBSA), the Health Insurance Association of America (HIAA), and the CMS. HCPCS level II codes are revised annually, and the revised codes are implemented each January. (The revision involves adding and deleting codes and revising code descriptors.)

HCPCS level II national codes do not carry the copyright of a private organization; they are in the public domain, which allows many publishers to print annual coding manuals. Each publisher may elect to color-code the print or pages, include supplemental explanatory material, or provide reimbursement information from the *Medicare Carriers Manual* (*MCM*) for Part B or the *Medicare National Coverage Determinations Manual*. The **Medicare Carriers Manual (MCM)** provides direction about services and procedures to be reimbursed by the MAC. The **Medicare National Coverage Determinations Manual** indicates whether a service is covered or excluded under the Medicare program.

Some publishers include the following HCPCS level II references in their version of the coding manual:

- General instructions or guidelines for each section

- Appendix that summarizes additions, deletions, and terminology revisions in level II codes

- Separate tables of drugs or deleted codes

- Symbols to identify codes excluded from Medicare coverage

- Codes for which payment is left to the discretion of the responsible MAC

- Codes with special coverage instructions

- Current HCPCS level II national modifiers

CMS has stated that it is not responsible for any errors that might occur in or from the use of these private printings of HCPCS level II national codes.

Types of HCPCS Level II Codes

HCPCS level II codes are organized according to type depending on the purpose of the codes and the entity responsible for establishing and maintaining them. The four types are as follows:

- Permanent national codes
- Miscellaneous codes
- Temporary codes
- HCPCS level II modifiers

Permanent National Codes

HCPCS level II permanent national codes are maintained by the HCPCS National Panel, which unanimously makes decisions about additions, revisions, and deletions. Because HCPCS level II is a national coding system, none of the parties, including CMS, can make unilateral decisions regarding permanent level II national codes, which are intended for use by all private and public health insurers.

Miscellaneous Codes

HCPCS level II miscellaneous codes include *miscellaneous/not otherwise classified* codes that are reported when a DMEPOS dealer submits a claim for a product or service for which there is no existing HCPCS level II code. Miscellaneous codes allow DMEPOS dealers to submit a claim for a product or service as soon as it is approved by the Food and Drug Administration (FDA) even though there is no code that describes the product or service. The use of miscellaneous codes also helps avoid the inefficiency of assigning codes for items or services that are rarely furnished or for which carriers expect to receive few claims.

Claims that contain miscellaneous codes are manually reviewed by the payer, and the following must be provided for use in the review process:

- Complete description of product or service
- Pricing information for product or service
- Documentation to explain why the item or service is needed by the beneficiary

Before reporting a miscellaneous code on a claim, a DMEPOS dealer should check with the payer to determine if a specific code has been identified for use (instead of a miscellaneous code).

Temporary Codes

HCPCS level II temporary codes (Table 7-1) are maintained by the CMS and other members of the HCPCS National Panel, independent of permanent level II codes. Permanent national codes are updated once a year on

Note:

- Decisions regarding temporary codes are made by an internal CMS HCPCS workgroup, and other payers may also use these codes.
- Whenever a permanent code is established by the HCPCS National Panel to replace a temporary code, the temporary code is deleted and cross-referenced to the new permanent code.

Table 7-1 Categories of HCPCS Level II Temporary Codes

Category	Descriptions
C codes	• Reported to Medicare administrative contractors (MACs) for hospital outpatient department procedures and services provided exclusively for Outpatient Prospective Payment System (OPPS) purposes.
G codes	• Identify professional health care procedures and services that do not have codes identified in CPT. • G codes can be reported to all payers.
H codes	• Reported to state Medicaid agencies that are mandated by state law to establish separate codes for identifying mental health services (e.g., alcohol and drug treatment services).
K codes	• Reported to MACs when existing permanent national codes do not include codes needed to implement a medical review coverage policy.
Q codes	• Identify services that would not ordinarily be assigned a CPT code (e.g., drugs, biologicals, and other types of medical equipment or services). • Q codes can be reported to all payers.
S codes	• Developed by the Blue Cross/Blue Shield Association (BCBSA) and the Health Insurance Association of American (HIAA) when no HCPCS level II national codes exist to report drugs, services, and supplies, but codes are needed to implement private payer policies and programs for claims processing. • S codes are reported to BCBS and private third-party payers.
T codes	• Reported to state Medicaid agencies when no HCPCS level II permanent codes exist, but codes are needed to administer the Medicaid program. • T codes are not reported to Medicare, but they can be reported to private third-party payers.

HCPCS Level II Modifiers	
AA	Anesthesia services performed personally by anesthesiologist
AD	Medical supervision by a physician: more than 4 concurrent anesthesia procedures
AE	Registered dietician
AF	Specialty physician
AG	Primary physician
AH	Clinical psychologist

Permission to reprint granted by Optuminsight, Inc.

Figure 7-1 Sample listing of HCPCS level II modifiers

January 1, but temporary codes allow payers the flexibility to establish codes that are needed before the next January 1 annual update. Approximately 35 percent of the HCPCS level II codes are temporary codes. Certain sections of the HCPCS level II codes were set aside to allow HCPCS National Panel members to develop temporary codes, and decisions regarding the number and type of temporary codes and the way they are used are made independently by each HCPCS National Panel member. Temporary codes serve the purpose of meeting short time frame operational needs of a particular payer.

Although the HCPCS National Panel may decide to replace temporary codes with permanent codes, if permanent codes are not established, the temporary codes remain "temporary" indefinitely.

HCPCS Level II Modifiers

HCPCS level II modifiers are attached to any HCPCS level I (CPT) or II (national) code to provide additional information regarding the product or service reported. Modifiers supplement the information provided by a HCPCS code descriptor to identify specific circumstances that may apply to an item or a service. HCPCS level II modifiers contain alpha or alphanumeric characters (Figure 7-1) (unlike CPT modifiers, which contain numeric characters only, as covered in Chapter 8).

 Note:

Because modifiers are attached to HCPCS level II codes, chapter content about modifiers precedes content about the assignment of HCPCS level II codes.

Coding Tip:

- HCPCS level II alpha and alphanumeric modifiers may also be added to CPT codes to further define the procedure or service reported (e.g., 69436-RT, tympanostomy, right ear).
- Refer to the inside cover (or an appendix) of the HCPCS Level II and CPT coding manuals for a comprehensive list of modifiers.
- Encoder software often contains guidance regarding selection of modifiers. For example, www.EncoderPro.com contains a clickable M icon that displays a list of applicable modifiers for a code.

EXAMPLE: A clinical psychologist provides 45 minutes of group psychotherapy in a partial hospitalization setting. Report G0410-AH.

A Medicare patient undergoes tendon surgery on the right palm (CPT code 26170) and left middle finger (CPT code 26180). Report 26170-RT and 26180-59-F2.

General Guidelines for Modifier Use

Not all HCPCS level I and II codes require modifiers. The CMS has clarified the use of modifiers when codes are reported for outpatient hospital services. (These rules also apply to the use of modifiers when reporting codes for physician services. Modifiers for physician services that differ from those used to report outpatient hospital services are clarified here.)

- Do not add a modifier to a code when its description indicates multiple occurrences, such as:

  - Two or more lesions

  - Multiple extremities

  - Different body parts

  EXAMPLE: 11600 Excision malignant lesion, trunks, arms, or legs; excised diameter 0.5 cm or less.

- Modifiers -GN, -GO, and -GP are added to codes reported for an outpatient plan of care:

  - Speech language therapy (-GN).

  - Occupational therapy (-GO).

  - Physical therapy (-GP).

- The following modifiers are added to codes reported for hospital outpatient surgical procedures *from the CPT Surgery section and certain codes from the CPT Medicine section (e.g., cardiac catheterization) only*:

  - Modifier -50 (Bilateral Procedure)

  - Modifier -73 (Discontinued Outpatient Hospital/Ambulatory Surgery Center (ASC) Procedure Prior to the Administration of Anesthesia)

  - Modifier -74 (Discontinued Outpatient Hospital/Ambulatory Surgery Center (ASC) Procedure After Administration of Anesthesia)

Coding Tip:

- For physician services, the following modifiers are added to codes reported for Surgery and Medicine procedures:

  - -50 (Bilateral Procedure)

  - -52 (Reduced Services)

  - -53 (Discontinued Procedure)

- Modifiers are added to codes reported for procedures and services when they:

  - Add more information regarding the anatomic site of the procedure.

  EXAMPLE: Cataract surgery on the right or left eye. Add modifier -RT or -LT to the CPT code reported for cataract surgery.

  - Help to eliminate the appearance of duplicate billing.

  EXAMPLE: Add modifier -76 to the reported code when the same procedure is performed more than once by the same physician.

  - Help to eliminate the appearance of unbundling.

  EXAMPLE: When codes Q0081 (Infusion therapy, using other than chemotherapeutic drugs, per visit) and 36000 (Introduction of needle or intracatheter, vein) are reported on the same claim, the payer will deny payment for one of the codes because they are duplicate services. Adding modifier -59 to code 36000, *if that procedure was performed for a reason other than as part of the IV infusion*, ensures appropriate processing of the claim and reimbursement for both procedures.

- Report modifiers on the hard copy UB-04 (CMS-1450) in Form Locator 44 (next to Form Locators where HCPCS codes are entered). (There is space for two modifiers on each hard copy UB-04.) For electronic claims, the UB-04 flat file allows entry of modifiers as record type 61, field numbers 6 and 7. (There is space for two modifiers, one in field 6 and one in field 7.)

- Report modifier(s) in Block 24D of the CMS-1500 claim, spacing once after the CPT or HCPCS level II code. (Space once between modifiers when multiple modifiers are added to the same code.)

- Do not report the dash that precedes a modifier.

  EXAMPLE: Modifier -AH is reported as AH in Block 24D of the CMS-1500.

24.	A DATE(S) OF SERVICE				B Place of Service	C Type of Service	D PROCEDURES, SERVICES, OR SUPPLIES (Explain Unusual Circumstances) CPT/HCPCS MODIFIER	E DIAGNOSIS CODE	F $ CHARGES	G DAYS OR UNITS	H EPSDT Family Plan	I EMG	J COB	K RESERVED FOR LOCAL USE
	From MM DD YY		To MM DD YY											
1							G0410	AH							

  Permission to reuse in accordance with http://www.cms.hhs.gov Content Reuse and Linking policy.

- When multiple modifiers are added to a code, the most specific modifier is listed first. For example, the following HCPCS level II modifiers are added (instead of modifier -LT or -RT):

  - -E1 through -E4
  - -FA and -F1 through -F9
  - -LC
  - -LD
  - -RC
  - -TA and -T1 through -T9

Modifiers Added to Surgical Procedures

Add modifier -50 (Bilateral Procedure) to codes for procedures that are performed on both sides during the same operative session.

  EXAMPLE: Patient underwent correction of hallus valgus (bunion) with simple exostectomy, right and left feet. Since this procedure was performed bilaterally, report 28290-50. (*Do not report 28290-RT and 28290-LT.*)

  The following rules clarify the use of modifier -50:

- Do not add modifiers -RT and -LT to a code when modifier -50 is added to that code.

- Add modifier -50 to surgical procedures only (CPT Surgery section codes, 10040–69990).

- Modifier -50 is *not* added to surgical procedure codes when the code description contains the following terminology:

  - Bilateral
  - Unilateral or bilateral

- Modifier -LT or -RT is added to the code that identifies a procedure performed on just one of two paired organs (e.g., ears, eyes, nostrils, kidneys, lungs, or ovaries).

  EXAMPLE: Code 69100 is eligible for modifier -50 if the procedure is performed on both ears. However, if a procedure (e.g., biopsy) is performed on the right or left ear, report code 69100-RT or 69100-LT.

Coding Tip:

- Do not add modifier -50 to codes reported for Evaluation and Management, Anesthesia, Radiology, Pathology and Laboratory, or Medicine procedures and services. Do not add modifier -50 to HCPCS level II codes.

- Modifier -LT or -RT is added to the code for a procedure that is performed on just one side.

- Modifiers for discontinued procedures for Outpatient Hospital/Ambulatory Surgery Center (ASC) (-73 and -74) are added to diagnostic and surgical procedure codes so hospitals can be reimbursed for expenses incurred during the preparation of a patient for surgery, which includes scheduling a room for performing the procedure.

  - Add modifier -73 when an Outpatient Hospital/Ambulatory Surgery Center (ASC) diagnostic or surgical procedure is terminated after a patient has been prepared for surgery (including sedation when provided) and taken to the room where the procedure is to be performed, but before the induction of anesthesia (e.g., local, regional block, or general anesthesia).

  - Add modifier -74 when an Outpatient Hospital/Ambulatory Surgery Center (ASC) procedure is terminated after the induction of anesthesia (e.g., local, regional block, or general anesthesia) or after the procedure was started (incision made, intubation started, or scope inserted).

  - Do *not* add modifier -73 or -74 to a code for the *elective* cancellation of a procedure.

Coding Tip:

- Add modifiers -73 and -74 to codes reported from the CPT Surgery section and to certain codes reported from the Medicine (e.g., cardiac catheterization) section. Do not add modifiers -73 and -74 to codes reported for Evaluation and Management, Anesthesia, Radiology, or Pathology and Laboratory procedures and services.

- When services are discontinued in the physician's office, report modifier -52 or -53 (instead of modifier -73 or -74).

- Add modifier -76 to the code for a procedure or service that was repeated during a separate operative session on the same day by the same physician. Add modifier -77 to the code for a procedure or service that was repeated during a separate operative session on the same day by another physician. The following rules apply to adding modifier -76 or -77:

  - Adding modifier -76 or -77 is based on whether the physician performing the procedure is the same or different.

  - The repeated procedure must be the same as the originally performed procedure. (On the claim, the code for the original procedure is entered once. Then it is entered again with the appropriate modifier.)

Modifiers Added to Radiology Services

The following modifiers are added to codes for CPT Radiology services:

- -52 (Reduced Services)

- -59 (Distinct Procedural Service)

- -76 (Repeat Procedure by Same Physician or Other Qualified Health Care Professional)

- -77 (Repeat Procedure by Another Physician or Other Qualified Health Care Professional)

- HCPCS level II modifiers

Coding Tip:

Do not add modifiers -53, -73, and -74 to Radiology codes.

When a radiology procedure is canceled, report a code to describe the extent of the procedure performed. If no code exists for what was done, report the intended code and add modifier -52.

EXAMPLE: The physician orders a chest X-ray, two views, frontal and lateral (code 71020). Just the frontal view is performed because the patient started feeling faint and needed to lie down. Report code 71010 (Radiologic examination, chest: single view, frontal). (Do *not* report code 71020-52.)

Reporting HCPCS Level II Modifiers

HCPCS level II modifiers are added to HCPCS level I (CPT) and level II (national) codes. When more than one level II modifier applies, report the code on more than one line of the UB-04 claim, with the appropriate HCPCS level II modifier:

EXAMPLE: Patient underwent simple drainage of a finger abscess, left-hand thumb and second finger (code 26010). On the UB-04, report the code on two lines as follows:

- 26010 FA
- 26010 F1

Note:

On the CMS-1500, report the code and multiple modifiers on just one line of Block 24D, such as 26010 FA F1.

Do not add modifiers -LT or -RT to:

- Allergy and clinical immunology codes
- Ambulance codes
- Codes that do not specify a limb or paired organ
- Drug administration codes (J and Q codes)
- DME (HCPCS level II E codes) that do not specify a limb
- Evaluation and management codes
- Immunization and vaccines/toxoid codes
- Medicine codes that contain *right* or *left* in the code description
- Orthotics/prosthetics codes that do not specify a limb
- Osteopathic and chiropractic manipulation codes
- Pathology and laboratory codes
- Physical medicine and rehabilitation codes
- Supply codes
- Temporary procedure and service codes (G codes) that do not specify a limb

Exercise 7.2 – HCPCS Level II National Codes

Instructions: Complete each statement.

1. HCPCS level II codes are developed and maintained by the _____.
2. Services and procedures that are reimbursed by a MAC can be found in the _____.
3. Whether a service is covered or excluded under the Medicare program can be found in the _____.
4. HCPCS level II permanent codes are maintained by the _____.
5. Dental codes (D0000–D9999) are copyrighted and published by the _____.
6. HCPCS level II miscellaneous codes are reported when a(n) _____ submits a claim for a product or service for which there is no existing HCPCS level II national code.
7. HCPCS level II temporary codes allow payers the flexibility to establish codes that are needed before the next _____ update.
8. Refer to Figure 7-1, and identify the modifier that is added to a code when a procedure is performed by a registered dietician: _____.
9. Modifier _____ is added to codes for procedures that are performed on both sides during the same operative session.
10. HCPCS level II _____ are added to HCPCS level I (CPT) and level II (national) codes.

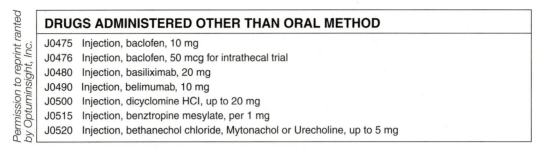

DRUGS ADMINISTERED OTHER THAN ORAL METHOD	
J0475	Injection, baclofen, 10 mg
J0476	Injection, baclofen, 50 mcg for intrathecal trial
J0480	Injection, basiliximab, 20 mg
J0490	Injection, belimumab, 10 mg
J0500	Injection, dicyclomine HCl, up to 20 mg
J0515	Injection, benztropine mesylate, per 1 mg
J0520	Injection, bethanechol chloride, Mytonachol or Urecholine, up to 5 mg

Figure 7-2 Sample listing of HCPCS level II J codes

Assigning HCPCS Level II Codes

Some services must be reported by assigning both a CPT and an HCPCS level II national code. The most common scenario uses the CPT code for the administration of an injection and the HCPCS code to identify the medication. Most drugs have qualifying terms such as *dosage limits* that could alter the quantity reported (Figure 7-2):

- If a drug is administered in a 70-mg dose and the HCPCS level II code description states "per 50 mg," the quantity billed is 2.

- If just 15 mg of a drug were administered and the HCPCS level II code description stated "up to 20 mg," the quantity billed is 1.

Imagine how much money providers lose by reporting only the CPT code for injections. Unless the payer or insurance plan advises the provider that it does not pay separately for the medication injected, always report this combination of codes. It is possible that a particular service would be assigned a CPT code and a level II HCPCS code. Which one should you report? The answer is found in the instructions from the payer. Most commercial payers require the CPT code. Medicare gives HCPCS level II codes the highest priority if the CPT code is general and the HCPCS national (level II) code is more specific.

Most supplies are included in the charge for the office visit or the procedure. CPT provides code 99070 for all supplies and materials exceeding those usually included in the primary service or procedure performed. However, this CPT code may be too general to ensure correct payment. If the office provides additional supplies when performing a service, the HCPCS level II codes may identify the supplies in sufficient detail to secure proper reimbursement.

Although CMS developed this system, some HCPCS level I and II services are not payable by Medicare. Medicare may also place qualifications or conditions on payment for some services. As an example, an electrocardiogram (ECG) is a covered service for a cardiac problem but is not covered when performed as part of a routine examination. Also, the payment for some services may be left to the discretion of the MAC. Two CMS publications assist MACs in correctly processing claims: the *Medicare National Coverage Determinations Manual* advises the MAC as to whether a service is covered or excluded under Medicare regulations, and the MCM directs the MAC to pay or reject a service, using a specific "remark" or explanation code.

There are more than 4,000 HCPCS level II codes, but you may find that no code exists for the procedure or service you need to report. Unlike CPT, HCPCS level II does not have a consistent method of establishing codes for reporting "unlisted procedure" services. If the MAC does not provide special instructions for reporting these services in HCPCS, report them with the proper "unlisted procedure" code from CPT. Remember to submit documentation explaining the procedure or service when using the "unlisted procedure" codes.

> **Note:**
>
> CMS developed HCPCS level II codes for Medicare, but commercial payers also adopted them.

Index	
Abatacept, J0129	
Abciximab, J0130	
Abdomen/abdominal	
dressing holder/binder, A4461, A4463	
pad, low profile, L1270	
Abduction	
control, each, L2624	
pillow, E1399	
rotation bar, foot, L3140-L3170	
Abortion, S0199, S2260-S2267	
Absorption dressing, A6251-A6256	

Permission to reprint granted by Optuminsight, Inc.

Figure 7-3 Sample listing of HCPCS level II index entries

Drug Name	Unit Per	Route	Code
10% LMD	500 mL	IV	**J7100**
5% Dextrose and .45% Normal Saline	1000 mL	IV	**S5010**
5% Dextrose in Lactated Ringers	1000 mL	IV	**S5011**
5% Dextrose with Potassium Chloride	1000 mL	IV	**S5012**

Permission to reprint granted by Optuminsight, Inc.

Figure 7-4 Sample listing of HCPCS level II table of drugs

HCPCS Level II Index

Because of the wide variety of services and procedures described in HCPCS level II, the alphabetical index (Figure 7-3) is very helpful in finding the correct code. The various publishers of the reference may include an expanded index that lists "alcohol wipes" and "wipes," as well as "Ancef" and "cefazolin sodium," making the search for codes easier and faster. Some references also include a table of drugs (Figure 7-4) that lists J codes assigned to medications. Some publishers print brand names beneath each generic description, and others provide a special expanded index of the drug codes. It is important never to code directly from the index and always to verify the code in the appropriate code section of the coding manual. You may want to review the HCPCS references from several publishers and select the one that best meets your needs and is easiest for you to use. If you have difficulty locating the service or procedure in the HCPCS level II index, review the table of contents (if available in your coding manual) to locate the code section (Figure 7-5). Or, page through the tabular list to familiarize yourself with the procedures and services classified in the coding manual. Read the code descriptions very carefully before selecting a code.

HCPCS Level II Code Sections

HCPCS level II code sections are identified by an alphabetical first character (e.g., *B* for *enteral and parenteral therapy* and *C* for *outpatient PPS*). Some code sections are logical, such as *R* for *radiology*, whereas others, such as *J* for *drugs*, appear to be arbitrarily assigned.

Transportation Services Including Ambulance (A0000–A0999)

The Transportation Services Including Ambulance section of HCPCS level II includes codes for ancillary transportation-related fees, ground and air ambulance, and nonemergency transportation (e.g., automobile, bus, taxi, and wheelchair van).

EXAMPLE: A Medicaid patient received emergency transport from her home to the hospital emergency department in an ambulance that contained basic life support (BLS). Report code A0429-RH. (The origin was the patient's residence, and the destination was the hospital; therefore, modifier -RH is added to code A0429.)

Permission to reuse in accordance with http://www.cms.hhs.gov Web site Content Reuse Policy.

Contents

Figure 7-5 Sample HCPCS level II coding manual table of contents

Medical and Surgical Supplies (A4206–A9999)

The Medical and Surgical Supplies section of HCPCS level II includes codes for DME-related supplies, accessories, maintenance, and repair (to ensure proper functioning of DME); medical supplies and accessories; and surgical supplies and accessories.

> **EXAMPLE:** A 68-year-old patient who is undergoing treatment for unresected liver cancer was supplied with a refill kit for an implantable infusion pump. Report code A4220.

Administrative, Miscellaneous, and Investigational (A9000–A9999)

The Administrative, Miscellaneous, and Investigational section of HCPCS level II includes codes for exercise equipment, noncovered items and services, nonprescription drugs, and radiopharmaceutical diagnostic imaging agents.

> **EXAMPLE:** A 99-year-old patient was administered a single multivitamin by mouth. Report code A9152.

Enteral and Parenteral Therapy (B4000–B9999)

The Enteral and Parenteral Therapy section of HCPCS level II includes codes for enteral and parenteral infusion pumps, enteral and parenteral supplies, enteral formulae, and parenteral nutritional solutions.

> **EXAMPLE:** The patient was supplied with a fiber additive for enteral formula. Report code B4104.

Outpatient PPS (C1300–C9899)

The Outpatient PPS section of HCPCS level II includes codes for biologicals, devices, and drugs eligible for transitional pass-through payments for hospitals, as well as items included in the new technology APCs under the OPPS. **Transitional pass-through payments** are temporary additional payments (over and above the OPPS payment) made for certain innovative medical devices, drugs, and biologicals provided to Medicare beneficiaries.

> **EXAMPLE:** Patient underwent insertion of a directional transluminal atherectomy catheter. Report code C1714.

Coding Tip:

> Some supplies are included during the administration of an evaluation and management (E/M) service, and separate HCPCS level II codes are not assigned (e.g., sterile gauze). E/M services are assigned separate CPT codes, which is discussed in Chapter 9.

Coding Tip:

> The OPPS requires hospitals and ambulatory surgery centers to report product-specific HCPCS level II "C codes" to obtain reimbursement for biologicals, devices, drugs, and other items associated with implantable device technologies. Reporting C codes in conjunction with CPT procedure codes greatly improves the quality of claims data Medicare uses to establish future APC payments. Outpatient coding edits (updated on a quarterly basis) identify C codes that should be billed with CPT procedure codes.
>
> Applications are also submitted to CMS for "new" biologicals, devices, and drugs for consideration of "transitional pass-through payment status" and items for consideration of "new-technology APC designation." If certain criteria are met and CMS approves the "new" biologicals, devices, drugs, and items, C codes are assigned and published in program memorandums.

Durable Medical Equipment (E0100–E9999)

The Durable Medical Equipment section of HCPCS level II includes codes for equipment (e.g., artificial kidney machines, oxygen and related respiratory equipment, and pacemakers) and supplies (e.g., bath and toilet aids, commodes, cranes, crutches, hospital beds, and walkers).

> **EXAMPLE:** The patient was supplied with a pair of aluminum underarm crutches. Report code E0114.

Procedures/Professional Services (Temporary) (G0000–G9999)

The Procedures/Professional Services (Temporary) section of HCPCS level II includes codes for professional health care procedures and services that do not have codes identified in the CPT.

EXAMPLE: A patient became a Medicare beneficiary on March 1 and underwent an initial preventive physical examination (IPPE) and in-office electrocardiogram (ECG) on May 30. Report codes G0402 and G0403. (Make sure you report the appropriate ICD-9-CM V or ICD-10-CM Z code as the first-listed diagnosis.)

Alcohol and Drug Abuse Treatment Services (H0001–H2037)

The Alcohol and Drug Abuse Treatment Services section of HCPCS level II includes codes used by state Medicaid agencies mandated by state law to establish separate codes for identifying mental health services that include alcohol and drug treatment services.

EXAMPLE: A patient underwent alcohol assessment prior to participating in psychotherapy. Report code H0001.

Drugs Administered Other Than Oral Method (J0000–J9999)

The Drugs Administered Other Than Oral Method section of HCPCS level II includes codes for drugs that ordinarily cannot be self-administered, chemotherapy drugs, immunosuppressive drugs, inhalation solutions, and other miscellaneous drugs and solutions.

EXAMPLE: A female home health patient received an injection of 10 mcg of teriparatide (brand name Forteo) for treatment of osteoporosis. Report code J3110.

Temporary Codes (K0000–K9999)

The Temporary Codes section of HCPCS level II includes codes for DME, as established by DME MACs (formerly DMERCs), when permanent national codes do not include codes needed to implement a DME MAC medical review policy.

EXAMPLE: The patient was supplied with a standard wheelchair. Report code K0001.

Orthotic Procedures and Devices (L0000–L4999)

The Orthotic Procedures section of HCPCS level II includes codes for orthopedic shoes, orthotic devices and procedures, and scoliosis equipment. **Orthotics** is the branch of medicine that deals with the design and fitting of orthopedic (relating to bone disorders) devices (e.g., braces). Several orthotic procedures subsections include "addition" codes, which means they are reported in addition to base codes from the same subsection or a previous subsection.

EXAMPLE: Patient underwent a halo procedure during which the cervical halo was incorporated into a jacket vest. Patient also received a magnetic resonance image compatible system during the same encounter. Report codes L0810 and L0859.

Because the description for code L0859 states "Addition to halo procedure, magnetic resonance image compatible system," it must be reported in addition to another HCPCS code, such as L0810.

Prosthetic Procedures (L5000–L9999)

The Prosthetic Procedures section of HCPCS level II includes codes for prosthetic devices, implants, and procedures. **Prosthetics** is the branch of medicine that deals with the design, production, and use of artificial body parts (e.g., artificial limbs). Several prosthetic procedures subsections include "addition" codes, meaning that they are reported in addition to base codes from the same subsection or from a previous subsection.

EXAMPLE: The patient received a below-knee PTB type socket, non-alignable system, pylon, no cover, SACH foot, plaster socket, direct-formed. The patient also received a test socket, below knee, during the same encounter. Report codes L5500 and L5620.

Because the description for code L5620 states "Addition to lower extremity, test socket, below knee," it must be reported in addition to another HCPCS code, such as L5500.

Medical Services (M0000–M0301) 🟢

The Medical Services section of HCPCS level II includes codes for office visits for the sole purpose of monitoring or changing drug prescriptions used in the treatment of mental psychoneurotic and personality disorders, in addition to cellular therapy, fabric wrapping of an abdominal aneurysm, intragastric hypothermia, intravenous (IV) chelation therapy, and prolotherapy.

- *Cellular therapy* involves injecting processed tissue from animal embryos, fetuses, or organs for the purpose of rejuvenating diseased tissue; its therapeutic effect has not been established.

- *Fabric wrapping of an abdominal aneurysm* is performed to reinforce an aneurysm with a fabric-wrapped stent (a small, flexible mesh tube used to "patch" the blood vessel). This procedure has largely been replaced with other more effective treatment methods.

- *Intragastric hypothermia* is a form of gastric freezing for the treatment of chronic peptic ulcer disease; CMS considers this procedure obsolete.

- *IV chelation therapy* is also called chemical endarterectomy, and it is performed to treat arteriosclerosis; it is considered experimental in the United States.

- *Prolotherapy* is a form of nonsurgical ligament reconstruction as a treatment for chronic pain; its therapeutic effect has not yet been established.

🟢 **Coding Tip:**

The National Correct Coding Policy Manual states that "HCPCS code M0064 is not reported with CPT codes 90801–90857 (psychiatric services)" because code M0064 "describes a brief office visit for the sole purpose of monitoring or changing drug prescriptions used in the treatment of mental psychoneurotic and personality disorders." If the patient is seen for the sole purpose of monitoring or changing drug prescriptions, report code M0064 only.

EXAMPLE: A psychoneurotic patient was seen by his provider for the purpose of changing one of his prescription medications from Prozac to Paxil. Report code M0064.

Pathology and Laboratory Services (P0000–P9999)

The Pathology and Laboratory Services section of HCPCS level II includes codes for chemistry, microbiology, and toxicology tests; screening Papanicolaou smears; and miscellaneous blood tests.

EXAMPLE: The patient underwent screen cervical Papanicolaou smear, which was interpreted by the physician. Report code P3001.

Q Codes (Temporary) (Q0035–Q9968)

The Q Codes (Temporary) section of HCPCS level II includes temporary codes for drugs, services, supplies, and tests until permanent codes are available. Effective 2001, casting supplies were removed from the practice expenses for all HCPCS codes, including CPT codes for fracture management, casts, and splints. This means that when CPT codes are reported for services that include the provision of a cast or splint, codes Q4001–Q4051 are also reported to provide reimbursement to providers for the supplies used in creating casts.

EXAMPLE: A Medicare patient received brachytherapy services, which included the administration of radioisotopes. Report code Q3001.

🟢 **Coding Tip:**

The National Correct Coding Initiative (NCCI) Policy Manual states that HCPCS code Q0091 (screening Pap smears) includes "services necessary to procure and transport the specimen to the laboratory." This means that if an evaluation and management (E/M) service is performed during the same visit solely for the purpose of performing a screening Pap smear, do not report a separate CPT E/M code. However, if a significant, separately identifiable E/M service is performed to evaluate other medical problems, report both Q0091 (screening Pap smear) and the appropriate CPT E/M code and add modifier -25 to the E/M code to indicate that the provider performed a significant, separately identifiable service.

CPT code 79900 was deleted in 2005, and HCPCS level II code Q3001 was created to report the administration of radioisotopes during brachytherapy. Report as the first-listed procedure the appropriate CPT brachytherapy code from 77326–77328 and/or 77750–77799.

Diagnostic Radiology Services (R0000–R5999)

The Diagnostic Radiology Service section of HCPCS level II includes codes that are reported for the transportation of portable X-ray and/or EKG equipment, including testing.

> **EXAMPLE:** The provider transported portable EKG equipment to the nursing facility for the purpose of testing his patients. Report code R0076.
>
> When more than one patient undergoes EKG testing, report code R0076, but prorate the single allowed transportation cost among all patients. For example, if the single allowed transportation cost is $50 and five patients underwent EKG testing, the prorated cost for each patient is $10.

Temporary National Codes (Non-Medicare) (S0000–S9999)

The Temporary National Codes (Non-Medicare) section of HCPCS level II includes codes reported to non-Medicare third-party payers (e.g., Blue Cross/Blue Shield, commercial payers, and Medicaid) for drugs, services, and supplies that are not classified in CPT or another section of HCPCS level II.

> **EXAMPLE:** The patient was administered butorphanol tartrate (trade name Stadol NS), nasal spray, 25 mg. Report code S0012.

National T Codes Established for State Medicaid Agencies (T1000–T9999)

The National T Codes Established for State Medicaid Agencies section of HCPCS level II includes codes that are reported to Medicaid state agencies for behavioral health, home health, hospice, long-term care, nursing, and other services; substance abuse treatment; supplies; and certain training-related procedures that are not classified in CPT or another section of HCPCS level II.

> **EXAMPLE:** The Medicaid patient required sign language services for 30 minutes. Report codes T1013 and T1013 (because the description of code T1013 states "per 15 minutes").

Vision Services (V0000–V2999)

The Vision Services section of HCPCS level II includes codes for vision-related supplies (e.g., contact lenses, intraocular lenses, lenses, and spectacles).

> **EXAMPLE:** The patient was supplied with a custom plastic prosthetic eye. Report code V2623.

Hearing Services (V5000–V5999)

The Hearing Services section of HCPCS level II includes codes that describe hearing tests and related supplies and equipment, speech-language pathology screenings, and repair of augmentative communicative systems.

> **EXAMPLE:** The audiologist dispenses a monaural, in-the-ear (ITE) hearing aid for a patient -diagnosed with sensorineural hearing loss, combined types. Report codes V5050 and V5241.

Exercise 7.3 – Assigning HCPCS Level II Codes

Instructions: Complete each statement.

1. Some services must be reported by assigning both a CPT and a HCPCS code; the most common scenario uses a CPT code for administration of a(n)_____ and the HCPCS code to identify the _____.

2. If a drug is administered in a 100 mg dose and the HCPCS level II code description states "per 50 mg," the quantity billed is _____.

3. If just 10 mg of a drug were administered and the HCPCS level II code description stated "up to 15 mg," the quantity billed is _____.

4. The charge for office visit or procedure usually includes _____ used to perform the procedure or service.

5. Although CMS developed this system, some HCPCS Levels I and II services are not payable by _____.

6. Some HCPCS level II coding manuals include a table of drugs that lists J codes assigned to _____.

7. If you have difficulty locating the service or procedure in the HCPCS level II index, review the _____ to locate the code section and read the code descriptions very carefully before selecting a code.

8. Codes sections in HCPCS level II are identified by a(n) _____.

9. CMS developed the level II codes for Medicare, but _____ also adopted them.

10. If no code exists for a procedure or service, report the proper "unlisted procedure" code from _____ and submit documentation explaining the procedure or service.

Determining Payer Responsibility

The specific HCPCS level II code determines whether the claim is sent to the primary MAC that processes provider claims or the DME MAC that processes DMEPOS dealer claims. Providers and DMEPOS dealers obtain annual lists of valid level II national codes, which include billing instructions for services.

Sample HCPCS Level II Codes	Jurisdiction
A0021–A0999	Primary MAC
A4206–A4209	Primary MAC (if incidental to a physician's service) *or* DME MAC
A4252–A4259	DME MAC

© Cengage Learning 2014

Note:

At one time, LMCs (now called MACs) processed all claims for DME. The emphasis on keeping seniors in their own homes led to a rapid expansion in DME services and dealers. Also, many of the larger companies operated in several states and sent their claims to multiple Medicare carriers. Unfortunately, a few dealers formed for the sole purpose of collecting as much money as possible from the Medicare program and then closed down. When CMS began to investigate and pursue fraudulent claims, it became apparent that DME billings were out of control. CMS decided to have all DME claims processed by only four DME regional carriers (DMERCs) (now called DME MACs). This allowed the LMC (now called primary MAC) to concentrate on the familiar, traditional claims of providers billing for services, not equipment.

When the doctor treats a Medicare patient for a broken ankle and supplies the patient with crutches, two claims are generated. The claim for the fracture care, or professional service, is sent to the primary MAC; the claim for the crutches is sent to the DME MAC. The physician must register with both, review billing rules, comply with claims instructions, and forward claims correctly to secure payment for both services. If the physician is not registered with the DME MAC to provide medical equipment and supplies, the patient is given a prescription for crutches to take to a local DMEPOS dealer.

Some services, such as cosmetic procedures, are excluded as Medicare benefits by law and will not be covered by either MAC. Splints and casts for traumatic injuries have CPT numbers that are used to report these supplies or services to the primary MAC. Because the review procedure for adding new codes to level II is a much shorter process, new medical and surgical services may first be assigned a level II code and then incorporated into CPT at a later date.

Patient Record Documentation

The patient record includes documentation that justifies the medical necessity of procedures, services, and supplies coded and reported on an insurance claim. This means that the diagnoses reported on the claim must justify diagnostic and/or therapeutic procedures or services provided. The patient's record should include documentation of the following:

- Patient history, including review of systems
- Physical examination, including impression
- Diagnostic test results, including analysis of findings
- Diagnoses, including duration (e.g., acute or chronic) and comorbidities that impact care
- Patient's prognosis, including potential for rehabilitation

When DMEPOS items are reported on a claim, the DMEPOS dealer must keep the following documents on file:

- Provider order for DMEPOS item, signed and dated
- Signed advance beneficiary notice if medical necessity for an item cannot be established

> **Note:**
>
> An **advance beneficiary notice (ABN)** is a waiver signed by the patient acknowledging that because medical necessity for a procedure, service, or supply cannot be established (e.g., due to nature of patient's condition, injury, or illness), the patient accepts responsibility for reimbursing the provider or DMEPOS dealer for costs associated with the procedure, service, or supply.

When the provider reports DMEPOS items on a claim, the provider must keep the following documents on file:

- Diagnosis establishing medical necessity for the item
- Clinical notes that justify the DMEPOS item ordered
- Provider order for DMEPOS item, signed and dated
- Signed advance beneficiary notice if medical necessity for an item cannot be established

DMEPOS Claims

For certain items or services reported on a claim submitted to the DME MAC, the DMEPOS dealer must receive a signed certificate of medical necessity (CMN) (Figure 7-6) from the treating physician before submitting a claim to Medicare. A copied, electronic, faxed, or original certificate of medical necessity (CMN) must be maintained by the DMEPOS dealer and must be available to the DME MAC on request. The **certificate of medical necessity (CMN)** is a prescription for DME, services, and supplies.

DME MAC medical review policies include **local coverage determinations (LCDs)** (formerly called local medical review policies, or LMRPs) and **national coverage determinations (NCDs)**, both of which define coverage criteria, payment rules, and documentation required as applied to DMEPOS claims processed by DME MACs for frequently ordered DMEPOS equipment, services, and supplies. (National policies are included in the *Medicare Benefit Policy Manual, Medicare Program Integrity Manual,* and *Medicare National Coverage Determinations Manual.*) If DMEPOS equipment, services, or supplies do not have medical review policies established for coverage, the general coverage criteria applies. The DMEPOS equipment, services, or supplies must:

- Fall within a benefit category.
- Not be excluded by statute or by national CMS policy.
- Be reasonable and necessary to diagnose and/or treat an illness or injury or to improve the functioning of a malformed body.

The DME MACs are required to follow national policy when it exists; when there is no national policy on a subject, DME MACs have the authority and responsibility to establish local policies. Because many DMEPOS dealers operate nationally, the CMS requires that the medical review policies published by the DME MACs be identical in all four regions.

Exercise 7.4 – Determining Payer Responsibility

Instructions: Match the Medicare administrative contractor (MAC) responsible for processing a claim submitted with each code. Answers may be assigned more than once.

_____ **1.** A4208

_____ **2.** A4255

_____ **3.** A0988

_____ **4.** E0153

_____ **5.** A4209

a. Primary MAC

b. DME MAC

c. Primary MAC or DME MAC

U.S. DEPARTMENT OF HEALTH & HUMAN SERVICES
CENTERS FOR MEDICARE & MEDICAID SERVICES

FORM APPROVED
OMB NO. 0938-0679

CERTIFICATE OF MEDICAL NECESSITY

DMERC 01.02A

HOSPITAL BEDS

SECTION A   Certification Type/Date: INITIAL __/__/__   REVISED __/__/__

PATIENT NAME, ADDRESS, TELEPHONE and HIC NUMBER	SUPPLIER NAME, ADDRESS, TELEPHONE and NSC NUMBER
(___) ___-____ HICN _____	(___) ___-____ NSC # _____

PLACE OF SERVICE _____	HCPCS CODE	PT DOB __/__/__ ; Sex ___ (M/F) ; HT.____(in.) ; WT.____(lbs.)
NAME and ADDRESS of FACILITY if applicable (See reverse	_____ _____ _____	PHYSICIAN NAME, ADDRESS (Printed or Typed) PHYSICIAN'S UPIN: _____ PHYSICIAN'S TELEPHONE #: (___) ___-____

SECTION B   Information in this Section May Not Be Completed by the Supplier of the Items/Supplies.

EST. LENGTH OF NEED (# OF MONTHS): _____ 1-99 (99=LIFETIME)   DIAGNOSIS CODES (ICD-9): _____ _____ _____ _____

ANSWERS	ANSWER QUESTIONS 1, AND 3-7 FOR HOSPITAL BEDS
	(Circle **Y** for Yes, **N** for No, or **D** for Does Not Apply)
	QUESTION 2 RESERVED FOR OTHER OR FUTURE USE.
Y N D	1. Does the patient require positioning of the body in ways not feasible with an ordinary bed due to a medical condition which is expected to last at least one month?
Y N D	3. Does the patient require, for the alleviation of pain, positioning of the body in ways not feasible with an ordinary bed?
Y N D	4. Does the patient require the head of the bed to be elevated more than 30 degrees most of the time due to congestive heart failure, chronic pulmonary disease, or aspiration?
Y N D	5. Does the patient require traction which can only be attached to a hospital bed?
Y N D	6. Does the patient require a bed height different than a fixed height hospital bed to permit transfers to chair, wheelchair, or standing position?
Y N D	7. Does the patient require frequent changes in body position and/or have an immediate need for a change in body position?

NAME OF PERSON ANSWERING SECTION B QUESTIONS, IF OTHER THAN PHYSICIAN (Please Print):
NAME: _____   TITLE: _____   EMPLOYER: _____

SECTION C   **Narrative Description Of Equipment And Cost**

(1) <u>Narrative</u> description of all items, accessories and options ordered; (2) Supplier's charge; and (3) Medicare Fee Schedule Allowance for <u>each</u> item, accessory, and option. *(See Instructions On Back)*

SECTION D   **Physician Attestation and Signature/Date**

I certify that I am the physician identified in Section A of this form. I have received Sections A, B and C of the Certificate of Medical Necessity (including charges for items ordered). Any statement on my letterhead attached hereto, has been reviewed and signed by me. I certify that the medical necessity information in Section B is true, accurate and complete, to the best of my knowledge, and I understand that any falsification, omission, or concealment of material fact in that section may subject me to civil or criminal liability.

PHYSICIAN'S SIGNATURE _____   DATE __/__/__   (SIGNATURE AND DATE STAMPS ARE NOT ACCEPTABLE)

CMS-841 (04/96)

Permission to reuse in accordance with http://www.cms.hhs.gov Web site Content Reuse Policy.

Figure 7-6 Sample certificate of medical necessity required of DMEPOS dealer

Summary

Three levels of codes are associated with HCPCS, commonly referred to as HCPCS level I, II, and III codes. HCPCS level I includes the five-digit Current Procedural Terminology (CPT) codes developed and published by the American Medical Association (AMA). HCPCS level II (or HCPCS national codes) were created in the 1980s to describe common medical services and supplies not classified in CPT. (Effective December 31, 2003, HCPCS level III local codes were no longer required; however, some third-party payers continue to use them.)

The HCPCS level II national coding system classifies similar medical products and services for the purpose of efficient claims processing. Each code contains a description, and the codes are used primarily for billing purposes. The codes describe DME devices, accessories, supplies, and repairs; -prosthetics; orthotics; medical and surgical supplies; medications; provider services; temporary Medicare codes (e.g., Q codes); and other items and services (e.g., ambulance services). Some services must be reported by assigning both a CPT and an HCPCS level II national code. The most common scenario uses the CPT code for the administration of an injection and the HCPCS code to identify the medication.

The specific HCPCS level II code determines whether the claim is sent to the primary Medicare administrative contractor (MAC) that processes provider claims or the DME MAC that processes DMEPOS dealer claims. Providers and DMEPOS dealers obtain annual lists of valid level II national codes, which include billing instructions for services.

Internet Links

CMS Online Manual System: Go to *www.cms.gov* and click on the Regulations & Guidance link, then click on the Manuals link.

HCPCS at eICD.com (free registration required): Go to *www.eicd.com* and click on the eHCPCS Online link.

HCPCS coding system: Go to *www.cms.gov* and click on the Medicare link, then scroll down to the Coding heading and click on the HCPCS—General Information link.

Online drug reimbursement coding and pricing database: *www.reimbursementcodes.com*

Noridian Medicare Durable Medical Equipment: Go to *www.noridianmedicare.com* and select Home from the Durable Medical Equipment drop-down menu.

Study Checklist

- ❑ Read this chapter and highlight key concepts.
- ❑ Create an index card for each key term.
- ❑ Access the chapter Internet links to learn more about concepts.
- ❑ Complete the chapter review, verifying answers with your instructor.
- ❑ Complete WebTutor assignments and take online quizzes.
- ❑ Complete Workbook chapter, verifying answers with your instructor.
- ❑ Go to *www.cengagebrain.com* to access StudyWARE™ and the Premium Website. Login instructions are located in the Preface and on the Printed Access Card.
- ❑ Form a study group with classmates to discuss chapter concepts in preparation for an exam.

Review

Multiple Choice

Instructions: Circle the most appropriate response.

1. Which would be assigned to report DMEPOS on insurance claims?
   - a. CPT codes
   - b. HCPCS level I codes
   - c. HCPCS level II codes
   - d. HCPCS level III codes

2. Which provides suppliers and manufacturers with assistance in determining HCPCS codes to be reported?
   - a. CMS
   - b. DME MAC
   - c. DMEPOS dealers
   - d. PDAC

3. Which temporary codes are reported to all payers?
   - a. G codes
   - b. G codes and Q codes
   - c. H codes and K codes
   - d. H codes, S codes, and T codes

4. When both a CPT code and a HCPCS level II code are available for a procedure, service, or supply, the coder should assign the:
   - a. code according to payer instructions.
   - b. CPT code.
   - c. HCPCS level II code.
   - d. more specific code.

5. Which are reported to generate transitional pass-through payments under the Outpatient Prospective Payment System?
   - a. C codes
   - b. G codes
   - c. Q codes
   - d. S codes

6. HCPCS level II "addition" codes are included in subsections of _____ codes.
   - a. alcohol and drug abuse treatment services
   - b. cellular therapy and chelation therapy
   - c. enteral and parenteral therapy
   - d. orthotics and prosthetics procedures

7. HCPCS level II modifiers:
   - a. contain alphanumeric characters only.
   - b. contain numeric characters only.
   - c. may also be added to CPT codes.
   - d. may be attached to HCPCS level II codes only.

8. Which processes claims for providers?
   - a. DME MAC
   - b. DMEPOS dealer
   - c. DMERC
   - d. primary MAC

9. Which processes claims for DMEPOS dealers?
   - a. DME MAC
   - b. LMC
   - c. primary MAC
   - d. SADMERC

10. Which is an example of a certificate of medical necessity?
    - a. advance beneficiary notice signed by the patient
    - b. local medical review policy
    - c. national coverage determination
    - d. prescription for DMEPOS from treating physician

11. A patient was supplied with an air pressure mattress. Report code _____.
    - a. E0181
    - b. E0184
    - c. E0185
    - d. E0186

12. Magnetic resonance imaging without contrast followed by with contrast, left breast. Report code _____.
    - a. C8903-LT
    - b. C8904-LT
    - c. C8905-LT
    - d. C8908-LT

13. A patient received an injection of hydrocortisone acetate, 15 mg, for contact dermatitis. Report code(s) _____.
    - a. J1700
    - b. J1700, J1700
    - c. J1720
    - d. J1720, J1720

14. A patient received a gradient compression stocking, full length/chap style 30-40 mmHg. Report code _____.
     a. A6531   b. A6534   c. A6537   d. A6539

15. A patient required catheterization for the collection of a specimen. Report code _____.
     a. A4300   b. A4305   c. P9612   d. P9615

16. A patient received 2 mg leuprolide acetate for treatment of prostate cancer. Report code(s) _____.
     a. J1950   b. J9217   c. J9218, J9218   d. J9219

17. A patient in a drug and alcohol rehabilitation hospital received an injection of methadone by the treating physician. Report code _____.
     a. H0020   b. H0029   c. H0033   d. J1230

18. An 8-year-old boy is fitted with a long-arm plaster cast. Service is performed in part by a resident under the direction of a teaching physician. Report code _____.
     a. Q4007   b. Q4007-GC   c. Q4008-GC   d. Q4010

19. The patient's family received 30 minutes of family training and counseling, which was provided for the purpose of child development. Report code(s) _____.
     a. T1025   b. T1026   c. T1027   d. T1027, T1027

20. A patient received a hand-held low vision aid. Report code _____.
     a. V2020   b. V2510   c. V2600   d. V2610

🔵 Note:

The main term *Ambulance* requires review of codes A0021–A0999 to locate the appropriate five-character HCPCS level II code and two-character modifier.

Coding Practice I

Instructions: Assign HCPCS level II code(s) to each statement.

Transportation Services Including Ambulance (A0000–A0999)

_____ 21. Ambulance transport of patient from physician's office to hospital emergency department, including advanced life support, level 2.

_____ 22. Ambulance transport of newborn from rural hospital to a children's specialty hospital.

_____ 23. Patient received basic life support (BLS) during emergency transport from his home to the hospital via ambulance.

_____ 24. Patient received life-sustaining oxygen in an ambulance during transport to the hospital from a skilled nursing facility.

_____ 25. Patient transported in wheelchair van from residential assisted living facility to physician's doctor's office.

Medical and Surgical Supplies (A4000–A8999)

_____ 26. Patient's primary care physician administered injection using a sterile 3 cc syringe with needle.

_____ 27. RN swabbed the patient's upper torso with one pint of pHisoHex solution in preparation for an office procedure.

_____ 28. Physician inserted a cervical cap for contraceptive use.

_____ 29. Patient purchased a brand-new replacement adapter for her breast pump from a local DMEPOS dealer.

_____ 30. Patient was supplied with a sterile eye pad.

Administrative, Miscellaneous and Investigational (A9000–A9999)

_____ 31. Patient underwent diagnostic radiology procedure, which required injection of one 30-mcg dose of ammonia N-13 as the radiopharmaceutical diagnostic imaging agent.

_____ 32. Patient rented prescribed exercise equipment from a local DMEPOS dealer.

_____ 33. Patient was administered a 2-millicurie I-131 sodium iodide capsule as the radiopharmaceutical diagnostic agent prior to a diagnostic radiology procedure.

_____ 34. Patient was injected with contrast material prior to echocardiography.

_____ 35. Patient was administered one dose of an oral multivitamin.

Enteral and Parenteral Therapy (B4000–B9999)

_____ 36. Patient was provided with parenteral nutrition administration kits for two days of care.

_____ 37. Patient received one unit of nutritionally incomplete/modular nutrients enteral formula via enteral feeding tube.

_____ 38. A new enteral infusion pump with alarm was attached to the patient's enteral feeding tube system.

_____ 39. Patient was provided with a new gravity fed enteral feeding supply kit, one day.

_____ 40. A Levine type stomach tube was used during the procedure.

Outpatient PPS (C1300–C9899)

_____ 41. One brachytherapy source of high-dose-rate iridium-192 was inserted into the patient by the radiation oncologist.

_____ 42. A cardiac event recorder was implanted in the patient as a medically necessary service/supply.

_____ 43. Implantable breast prosthesis was provided during surgery.

_____ 44. Patient underwent left breast MRI without contrast, followed by left breast MRI with contrast.

_____ 45. A short-term hemodialysis catheter was inserted in the patient's right forearm (patient is left-handed).

Durable Medical Equipment (E0100–E9999)

_____ 46. "Patient helper" trapeze bars and a grab bar were attached to the patient's bed.

_____ 47. An adult oxygen tent was supplied to the patient.

_____ 48. A bilirubin light with photometer was used to treat the patient.

_____ 49. Provider reported a dispensing fee for use of a DME nebulizer with compressor (covered drug).

_____ 50. Patient purchased a new folding walker, which has adjustable and fixed height features.

Procedures/Professional Services (Temporary) (G0000–G9999)

_____ 51. A complete CBC, automated, was performed.

_____ 52. Trimming of 5 dystrophic nails.

_____ 53. Patient received 20 minutes of individual smoking cessation counseling as part of a demonstration project.

_____ 54. Patient underwent colorectal cancer screening via flexible sigmoidoscopy.

_____ 55. Patient underwent full positron emission tomography (PET) imaging for initial diagnosis of breast cancer.

Alcohol and/or Drug Abuse Treatment Services (H0001–H2037)

_____ 56. Patient received 30 minutes of behavioral health counseling and therapy as provided through his employee assistance program.

_____ 57. Patient received 18 hours of partial hospitalization care for mental health crisis.

_____ 58. One day of psychiatric health care facility services was provided to the patient.

_____ 59. Three days of respite care services were provided to the patient in the hospice unit of the hospital.

_____ 60. Patient received 30 minutes of activity therapy delivered as part of outpatient physical therapy plan of care.

Drugs Administered Other than Oral Method (J0000–J9999)

_____ 61. Injection, caffeine citrate, 5 mg.

_____ 62. Injection, gamma globulin, intramuscular, 10 cc.

_____ 63. Injection, paricalcitol, 1 mcg.

_____ 64. Injection, torsemide, 10 mg/mL.

_____ 65. Infusion, doxorubicin HCl, 10 mg.

Temporary Codes (K0000–K9999)

_____ 66. Repair service of 10-year-old DMEPOS device required supply of complete front caster assembly for wheelchair with two semi-pneumatic tires.

_____ 67. Patient was supplied with one IV hanger.

_____ 68. Patient was supplied with two leg straps for use with her wheelchair.

_____ 69. Patient rented a prescribed lightweight portable motorized wheelchair.

_____ 70. A replacement alkaline battery, 1.5 volt, was provided for the patient-owned external infusion pump.

Orthotic Procedures (L0000–L4999)

_____ 71. Patient was provided with a cervical wire frame, semi-rigid, for occipital/mandibular support.

_____ 72. Patient purchased a prescribed custom-fabricated thoracic rib belt.

_____ 73. Patient underwent halo procedure (cervical halo incorporated into Milwaukee orthosis).

_____ 74. Patient purchased a prescribed 2-inch neoprene heel and sole elevation lift.

_____ 75. In conjunction with a previously furnished orthotics prosthetic device, patient was supplied with a posterior solid ankle, plastic, custom-fabricated, ankle foot orthosis (AFO).

Prosthetic Procedures (L5000–L9999)

_____ 76. Patient was fitted with a below-knee disarticulation prosthesis that contained a molded socket, shin, and solid ankle cushion heel (SACH) foot.

_____ 77. Patient (adult) was fitted with an Otto Bock electric hand, myoelectrically controlled.

_____ 78. Patient was fitted with a partial foot prosthesis that contained a shoe insert with longitudinal arch, toe filler.

_____ 79. Patient was provided with a glove (for terminal device), right-hand prosthesis.

_____ 80. During breast reconstruction surgery, a silicone breast prosthesis was inserted.

Medical Services (M0000–M0301)

_____ 81. Brief office visit to change prescription medication to treat patient's personality disorder.

_____ 82. Cellular therapy.

_____ 83. Chemical endarterectomy via intravenous (IV) chelation therapy.

_____ 84. Fabric wrapping of abdominal aneurysm.

_____ 85. Prolotherapy.

Pathology and Laboratory Services (P0000–P9999)

_____ 86. Catheterization for collection of specimen was performed for one patient.

_____ 87. Screening Pap smear, cervical, by technician under physician supervision.

_____ 88. Infusion of 250 mL of 5% albumin (human).

_____ 89. Two units of platelets were infused.

_____ 90. Two units of whole blood were used during transfusion.

Q Codes: Temporary Codes (Q0035–Q9968)

_____ 91. Patient received chemotherapy administration, push technique.

_____ 92. Patient underwent a collagen skin test.

_____ 93. Patient injected with 1 mL of 50 mg of teniposide.

_____ 94. As part of fracture treatment, 10-year-old patient received short-arm plaster splint.

_____ 95. Potassium hydroxide (KOH) preparation included as part of patient's treatment.

Diagnostic Radiology Services (R0000–R5999)

_____ 96. Transportation of portable chest X-ray and X-ray technician to nursing home; 20 patients underwent X-ray.

_____ 97. Transportation of portable EKG equipment to nursing facility; five patients underwent EKG.

_____ 98. Transportation of portable X-ray equipment and X-ray technician to patient's home; husband and wife underwent X-ray.

Temporary National Codes (Non-Medicare) (S0000–S9999)

_____ 99. Allogenic cord blood-derived stem cell transplantation.

_____ 100. Echosclerotherapy.

_____ 101. Gastrointestinal fat absorption study.

_____ 102. Global fee for extracorporeal shock wave lithotripsy (ESWL) treatment of kidney stone.

_____ 103. Harvesting of multivisceral organs from cadaver donor with preparation and maintenance of allografts.

National T Codes Established for State Medicaid Agencies (T1000–T9999)

_____ 104. Patient underwent 15 minutes of family training and counseling for child development.

_____ 105. Human breast milk processing, storage, and distribution.

_____ 106. Intramuscular medication administration by home health licensed practical nurse (LPN).

_____ 107. Patient received 30 minutes of private-duty nursing from a registered nurse (RN).

_____ 108. Waiver of utility services to support medical equipment and assistive technology/devices.

Vision Services (V0000–V2999)

_____ 109. Bifocal lenses, bilateral, 5.25 sphere, 2.12 cylinder, two lenses.

_____ 110. Deluxe frame.

_____ 111. Photochromatic tinting of two lenses.

_____ 112. Processing, preserving, and transporting corneal tissue.

_____ 113. Reduction of ocular prosthesis.

Hearing Services (V5000–V5999)

_____ 114. Patient underwent assessment for hearing aid.

_____ 115. Provision of binaural, behind-the-ear hearing aid.

_____ 116. Provision of digitally programmable monaural hearing aid, analog, in the canal (ITC).

_____ 117. Dispensing fee, binaural contralateral routing of signals (BICROS).

_____ 118. Patient purchased prescribed telephone amplifier assistive living device.

Coding Practice II

Instructions: Assign appropriate HCPCS level II code(s) and modifier(s) to each case.

119. SUBJECTIVE: The patient is an 89-year-old white female resident of the county nursing facility. I was asked to see her today because the nursing staff had noticed the patient was having difficulty breathing and was coughing up purulent material. A chest X-ray was ordered, and the mobile X-ray service arrived and took the X-ray while I was seeing my other patients.

OBJECTIVE: The patient appears ill. Temperature is 100.7. CHEST: Scattered rhonchi throughout all lung fields, with severely diminished breath sounds in the left lower lung. Expiratory and inspiratory wheezes present. HEART: Within normal limits. ABDOMEN: No tenderness on palpation.

EXTREMITIES: Mild dependent edema is noted; otherwise within normal limits.

ASSESSMENT: The chest X-ray revealed a density consistent with left lower lobe pneumonia.

PLAN: The patient was administered an injection of Zithromax 500 mg. The cough does not seem to be bothersome to the patient right now, so the nursing staff will wait and watch. The nursing staff is to monitor her for any signs of increased fever, lethargy, or medication reaction. They are to encourage fluids and keep the patient up in a chair as much as possible when she is not sleeping. The staff is to contact me immediately if the patient's symptoms worsen.

---

120. SUBJECTIVE: This 45-year-old construction worker was seen in the office today on an emergency basis because he stepped on a sharp edge of steel and lacerated his right foot. He states that he cannot recall his last tetanus shot.

OBJECTIVE: Examination of the right foot reveals a laceration of approximately 3.5 cm at the lateral edge of the foot that extends medially across the heel. PROCEDURE: The right heel was cleansed with pHisoHex and prepped with Betadine. The wound edges were infiltrated with 1% Xylocaine. After adequate anesthesia was obtained, the laceration was repaired with 3-0 nylon sutures. The wound was dressed with gauze and secured with paper tape.

ASSESSMENT: Laceration of right heel, repaired in the office.

PLAN: The patient was given a tetanus shot today. He was given instructions on wound care and signs of infection and was also given reference sheets on the same. He is to be nonweightbearing for the next 3 days and was given a pair of wooden crutches. He will return to the office in three days for reevaluation. The patient was also reminded to call immediately if pain increases or if he shows any signs of fever.

PART IV

Current Procedural Terminology (CPT) Coding System

Introduction to CPT Coding

Chapter Outline

Chapter Objectives

At the conclusion of this chapter, the student should be able to:

- Define key terms.
- Explain the organization, format, and content of CPT.
- Interpret CPT section guidelines, coding notes, and modifiers.
- Assign CPT procedure and service codes for outpatient care.
- Add CPT and/or HCPCS level II modifiers to codes, as appropriate.

Key Terms

add-on code

Appendix A of CPT

Appendix B of CPT

Appendix C of CPT

Appendix D of CPT

Appendix E of CPT

Appendix F of CPT

Appendix G of CPT

Appendix H of CPT

Appendix I of CPT

Appendix J of CPT

Appendix K of CPT

Appendix L of CPT

Appendix M of CPT

Appendix N of CPT

bullet symbol (•)

bull's-eye symbol (⊙)

Category I code

Category II code

Category III code

column 1/column 2 edit

descriptive qualifiers

flash symbol (↗)

forbidden (or prohibitory)
symbol (⊘)

functional modifier

green reference symbol (⮌)

guidelines

hollow circle symbol (○)

horizontal triangle
symbols (▶◀)

inferred words

informational modifiers

mutually exclusive edit

National Correct Coding
Initiative (NCCI)

notes

Notice of Exclusions
from Medicare
Benefits (NEMB)

number symbol (#)

plus symbol (+)

pricing modifier

range of codes

red reference symbol (⛔)

semicolon (;)

single code

special report

triangle symbol (▲)

unlisted procedure

unlisted service

Introduction

This chapter introduces the Current Procedural Terminology (CPT) coding system (or HCPCS level I), a proprietary coding system published annually by the American Medical Association (AMA). Current Procedural Terminology (CPT) is a listing of descriptive terms and identifying codes for reporting medical services and procedures. It provides a uniform language that describes medical, surgical, and diagnostic services to facilitate communication among providers, patients, and third-party payers.

Note:

When reviewing examples and completing exercises and review questions in this chapters (and in Chapters 10 through 18), use your CPT coding manual to locate index entries and to verify them in the tabular list.

History of CPT

The AMA first published CPT in 1966, and subsequent editions expanded its descriptive terms and codes for diagnostic and therapeutic procedures. Five-digit codes were introduced in 1970, replacing the four-digit classification. In 1983, CPT was adopted as part of the Healthcare Common Procedure Coding System (HCPCS) (as HCPCS level I) and its use was mandated for reporting Medicare Part B physician services. In 1986, HCPCS was required for reporting to Medicaid agencies, and the Omnibus Budget Reconciliation Act (OBRA) of 1986 mandated that CPT codes be reported for outpatient hospital surgical procedures.

The Health Insurance, Portability, and Accountability Act of 1996 (HIPAA) named CPT and HCPCS level II as the procedure code sets for physician services, physical and occupational therapy services, radiological procedures, clinical laboratory tests, other medical diagnostic procedures, hearing and vision services, and transportation services including ambulance. (HIPAA also named ICD-9-CM as the code set for diagnosis codes and inpatient hospital services, CDT for dental services, and NDC for drugs. It eliminated HCPCS Level III local codes effective December 2003.)

CMS enforced regulations resulting from the Medicare Prescription Drug, Improvement, and Modernization Act (MMA) in October 2004, which required that new, revised, and deleted CPT codes be implemented each January 1. In the past, a 90-day grace period (from January 1 through March 31) had been allowed so providers and health care facilities had time to update billing systems and coders had an opportunity to undergo training regarding new, revised, and deleted codes. It is important to purchase updated coding manuals to avoid billing delays and claims rejections. If outdated codes are submitted on claims, providers and health care facilities will incur administrative costs associated with resubmitting corrected claims and delayed reimbursement for services provided.

Note:

The AMA's CPT Editorial Board publishes an "early release" of new and revised codes (e.g., vaccination codes) each July and January (for implementation six months later). Early release codes are further discussed later in this chapter.

Exercise 8.1 – History of CPT

Instructions: Match the year with the event.

_____ **1.** Introduction of five-digit CPT codes.   **a.** 1966

_____ **2.** 90-day grace period for new/revised/deleted CPT codes.   **b.** 1970

_____ **3.** AMA first published CPT.   **c.** 1983

_____ **4.** Required reporting CPT codes for outpatient surgical procedures.   **d.** 1986

_____ **5.** Mandated reporting CPT codes for Medicare services.   **e.** 2004

Overview of CPT

CPT codes are used to report services and procedures performed on patients by the following types of providers:

- Home health care and hospice agencies
- Outpatient hospital departments (e.g., ambulatory surgery, emergency department, and outpatient laboratory or radiographic procedures)
- Physicians who are employees of a health care facility (e.g., Veterans Administration Medical Centers physicians)
- Physicians who see patients in their offices or clinics and in patients' homes

CPT codes and descriptions are based on consistency with contemporary medical practice as performed by clinical providers throughout the country. The assignment of CPT codes simplifies reporting and assists in the accurate identification of procedures and services for third-party payer consideration. As such, procedures and services reported on a claim must be linked to the ICD-9-CM code that justifies the need for the service or procedure. This demonstrates medical necessity for the service or procedure provided so the payer can judge whether the claim should be paid.

When reporting CPT codes, some services are considered integral to the standard of practice, which means that certain medical and surgical services are not assigned CPT codes. Such services include the following:

- Administering local, topical, or regional anesthetic (by physician performing procedure)
- Administering sedatives (by physician performing procedure)
- Applying, managing, and removing postoperative dressings and analgesic devices
- Cleansing, shaving, and prepping of skin
- Documenting preoperative, intraoperative, and postoperative procedures provided
- Draping and positioning of patient
- Inserting and removing drains, suction devices, dressings, and pumps into same site
- Inserting intravenous access for medication
- Irrigating a wound
- Providing surgical approach, closure, cultures, and supplies (unless CMS policy states otherwise)

Changes to CPT

CPT now supports EDI, the computer-based patient record (CPR) (or electronic medical record [EMR]), and reference/research databases. CPT can also be used to track new technology and performance measures. Code descriptors were improved to eliminate ambiguous terms; and guidelines and notes underwent revision to make them more comprehensive, easier to interpret, and more specific. A CPT glossary was created to standardize definitions and differentiate the use of synonymous terms. A searchable electronic CPT index is under development along with a computerized database to delineate relationships among CPT code descriptions.

 Note:

According to the AMA, Category II codes minimize administrative burdens because they facilitate data collection about quality of care. Services and/or tests results are assigned codes that support performance measures and that contribute to good patient care. Category II codes also relate to compliance with state or federal law.

Improvements to CPT are under way to address the needs of hospitals, managed care organizations, and long-term care facilities. In 2000, the AMA completed the CPT-5 Project (with changes phased in starting with CPT 2000 and concluding with CPT 2003), resulting in the establishment of three categories of CPT codes:

- **Category I codes** (e.g., 99201): Procedures/services identified by a five-digit CPT code and descriptor nomenclature; these are codes traditionally associated with CPT and organized into six sections.

- **Category II codes** (e.g., 0001F): Optional "performance measurements" tracking codes that are assigned an alphanumeric identifier with a letter in the last field (e.g., 1000F); these codes will be located after the Medicine section.

  EXAMPLE: A physician counsels a patient who smokes during an evaluation and management (E/M) service. Report code 4000F (tobacco use cessation intervention, counseling). If the physician also prescribes a smoking cessation medication, report code 4001F (tobacco use cessation intervention, pharmacologic therapy). (CPT Category II codes are reported in addition to the E/M service code.)

- **Category III codes** (e.g., 0058T): Contain "emerging technology" temporary codes assigned for data collection purposes that are assigned an alphanumeric identifier with a letter in the last field (e.g., 0003T); these codes are located after the Medicine section, and they will be archived after five years if they are not accepted for placement within Category I sections of CPT.

  EXAMPLE: Prior to 2005, Category III code 0012T was reported for a surgical arthroscopy of the knee with osteochondral autograft(s). In 2005, code 0012T was deleted and a Category I code 29866 was created with a code description of "arthroscopy, knee, surgical; osteochondral autograft(s) (eg, mosaicplasty) (including harvesting of the autograft[s])."

Note:

According to the AMA, Category III codes allow for data collection of "emerging technology" services and procedures, which are conducted as part of ongoing or planned research. Effective 2006, modifiers are reported with Category III codes.

The CPT Editorial Panel also approved the "early release" of new CPT codes. All changes provided as an "early release" are not intended to take effect until the implementation date, which is six months after the "early release" of the codes. This means that codes included in an "early release" in January are implemented for use in July (and codes included in an "early release" in July are implemented the following January). To assist users in reporting the most recently approved codes, the AMA's CPT website will feature updates of the CPT Editorial Panel's actions and early release of the codes in July and January during a given CPT cycle. These dates for early release correspond with the quarterly CPT Editorial Panel's meetings for each CPT cycle (May, August, November, and February).

Exercise 8.2 – Overview of CPT

Instructions: Complete each statement.

1. CPT codes and descriptions are based on consistency with contemporary medical practice as performed by _____ throughout the United States.

2. The assignment of CPT codes simplifies reporting and assists in the accurate identification of procedures and services for _____ consideration.

3. CPT codes for procedures and services that are reported on a claim must be linked to the ICD-9-CM code that justifies the need for the service or procedure, which demonstrates _____ for the service or procedure provided.

(continues)

Exercise 8.2 (continued)

4. Category _____ codes contain optional "performance measurements" tracking codes that are assigned an alphanumeric identifier with a letter in the last field.

5. Category _____ codes contain "emerging technology" temporary codes, which are assigned for data collection purposes and contain an alphanumeric identifier with a letter in the last field.

Organization of CPT

To assign CPT codes, it is necessary to become familiar with CPT's organizational characteristics:

- CPT sections
- CPT code number format
- Boldfaced type
- Italicized type
- Cross-reference term
- Single codes and code ranges
- Inferred words
- Guidelines
- Unlisted procedures and services
- Notes
- Descriptive qualifiers

CPT Sections

CPT organizes Category I procedures and services into six sections:

- Evaluation and Management (E/M) (99201–99499)
- Anesthesia (00100–01999, 99100–99140)
- Surgery (10021–69990)
- Radiology (including Nuclear Medicine and Diagnostic Ultrasound) (70010–79999)
- Pathology and Laboratory (80047–89398)
- Medicine (90281–99199, 99500–99607)

> **Note:**
>
> The E/M section is located at the beginning of CPT because these codes are reported by all specialties.

> **Note:**
>
> Medicine section codes 99100–99140, which classify Qualifying Circumstances for Anesthesia, are explained in the Anesthesia section guidelines. They are reported with Anesthesia section codes.

CPT Code Number Format

A five-digit code number and a narrative description identify each procedure and service listed in CPT. Most procedures and services contain stand-alone descriptions. To save space, some descriptions are not printed in their entirety next to a code number. Instead, the entry is indented and the coder must refer back to the common portion of the code description that is located before the semicolon.

EXAMPLE 1: STAND-ALONE CODE DESCRIPTION:

```
27870   Arthrodesis, ankle, open
```

EXAMPLE 2: INDENTED CODE DESCRIPTION:

```
27780   Closed treatment of proximal fibula or shaft fracture; without
        manipulation
27781      with manipulation
```

The code description for 27781 is *closed treatment of proximal fibula or shaft fracture <u>with manipulation</u>*.

Exercise 8.3 – Organization of CPT

Instructions: Complete each statement.

1. CPT organizes Category I procedures and services into _____ sections.

2. The Evaluation and Management section of CPT is located at the beginning of CPT because _____.

3. Medicine section codes 99100–99140, which classify *Qualifying Circumstances for Anesthesia*, are explained in the _____ section guidelines.

4. Refer to CPT code 55605. Its code description is _____.

5. Refer to CPT code 47560 and review all code descriptions through code 47570. How does code 47560 differ from code 47562? _____ _____

CPT Index

The CPT index (Figure 8-1) is organized by alphabetical main terms printed in boldface. The main terms represent procedures or services, organs, anatomic sites, conditions, eponyms, or abbreviations. The main term may be followed by indented terms that modify the main term; these are called *subterms*.

The CPT index organizes procedures and services according to:

- Procedure or service (e.g., arthroscopy)

- Organ or other anatomic site (e.g., ankle)

- Condition (e.g., wound)

- Synonyms (e.g., finger joint or intercarpal joint)

- Eponyms (e.g., Billroth I or II)

- Abbreviations (e.g., EKG)

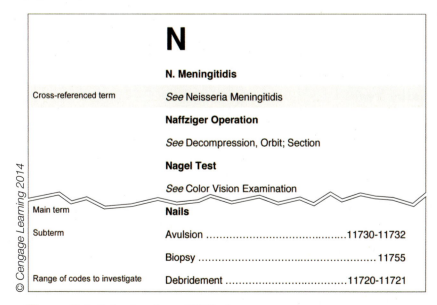

Figure 8-1 Selection from CPT index

To locate a CPT code, review patient record documentation to locate the service and/or procedure performed and locate the main term in the index (located in the back of the coding manual).

EXAMPLE: For the procedure "surgical temporomandibular joint (TMJ) arthroscopy," refer to the index and locate main term *Temporomandibular Joint*, subterm *arthroscopy*, and qualifier *surgical*. 29804 is the listed code. Next, verify code 29804 in the tabular portion of the coding manual before reporting it on a claim for submission to a third-party payer. (A diagnosis code must be reported on the claim to justify medical necessity of the procedure. The diagnosis code for articular disc disorder of temporomandibular joint, would justify medical necessity.)

Boldfaced Type

Main terms in the CPT index are printed in boldfaced type. CPT category and subcategory titles and code numbers are also printed in boldfaced type.

Italicized Type

Italicized type is used for the cross-reference term *See* in the CPT Index.

Coding Tip:

The descriptions of all codes listed in the index for a specific procedure must be carefully investigated before selecting a final code. CPT coding must never be performed solely from the index.

Cross-Reference Term

See is a cross-reference that directs coders to an index entry under which codes are listed. No codes are listed under the original entry.

EXAMPLE: The instructional term *See* directs the coder to index entry "Arteriovenous Shunt" because no codes are listed for the abbreviation *AV Shunt*.

```
AV Shunt
    See Arteriovenous Shunt
```

Single Codes and Code Ranges

Index code numbers for specific procedures may be represented as a **single code** number, a **range of codes** separated by a dash, a series of codes separated by commas, or a combination of single codes and ranges of codes. All codes should be investigated before assigning a code for the procedure or service.

EXAMPLE: The main term *Acid fast stain* contains just one code. Subterm *esophagus*, which is located below main term *Acid perfusion test,* contains two codes separated by commas. Main term *Acid phosphatase* contains a range of codes.

```
Acid Fast Stain ........................................................ 88312
Acid Perfusion Test
    Esophagus ................................... 0241T, 91013, 91030
Acid Phosphatase ............................................. 84060-84066
```

Inferred Words

To save space in the CPT Index when referencing subterms, **inferred words** are used.

EXAMPLE: The word *(of)* in parentheses is inferred and does not actually appear in the CPT index.

```
Abdomen
    Exploration (of) ....................................... 49000-49002
```

Exercise 8.4 – CPT Index

Instructions: Indicate whether each statement is true (T) or false (F).

_____ **1.** The cross-reference that directs coders to refer to a different index entry because no codes are found under the original entry is called *See.*

_____ **2.** Main terms appear in *italics* in the CPT index.

_____ **3.** Inferred words appear in the CPT index to assist coders in assigning appropriate codes.

_____ **4.** The main term may be followed by indented terms, known as subterms, which modify the main term.

_____ **5.** Cross-reference terms are printed in bold in the CPT index.

CPT Appendices

CPT contains appendices, located between the Medicine section and the index. Insurance specialists should carefully review these appendices to become familiar with coding changes that affect the practice annually:

- **Appendix A** (Modifiers) contains a list of CPT modifiers and detailed descriptions. Place a marker at the beginning of Appendix A because you will refer to it often.

- **Appendix B** (Summary of Additions, Deletions, and Revisions) contains annual CPT coding changes that include added, deleted, and revised CPT codes. Carefully review Appendix B of current CPT manual because it will serve as the basis for updating interoffice documents and billing tools.

- **Appendix C** (Clinical Examples) contains clinical examples for codes found in the E/M section.

- **Appendix D** (Summary of CPT Add-on Codes) contains a list of add-on codes that are identified throughout CPT with a + symbol. An **add-on code** is reported when another procedure is performed in addition to the primary procedure during the same operative session. Modifier -51 (multiple procedures) is *not* added to add-on codes.

- **Appendix E** (Summary of CPT Codes Exempt from Modifier 51) contains a list of codes that are exempt from modifier -51 reporting rules and that are identified throughout CPT with a forbidden (⊘) symbol.

- **Appendix F** (Summary of CPT Codes Exempt from Modifier 63) contains a list of codes that are exempt from modifier -63.

- **Appendix G** (Summary of CPT Codes That Include Moderate (Conscious) Sedation) contains a summary of CPT codes that include moderate (conscious) sedation and that are identified throughout CPT with a bull's-eye (⊙) symbol.

- **Appendix H** (Alphabetic Clinical Topics Listing) was removed from the CPT coding manual in 2010 and relocated to the AMA website. (Go to http://www.ama-assn.org, click on the *Physicians* link, and click on the *CPT – Current Procedural Terminology* link that is located below *Feature Resources*. Then, click on the Category II Codes link where you will find a link to the CPT Category II Codes Alphabetical Clinical Topics Listing PDF file.)

Coding Tip:

A complete list of code additions, deletions, and revisions is found in Appendix B of CPT. Revisions marked with horizontal triangles (►◄) are not included in Appendix B, and coders need to carefully review all CPT guidelines and notes in the new edition of CPT.

- **Appendix I** (Genetic Testing Code Modifiers) contains genetic testing code modifiers.

- **Appendix J** (Electrodiagnostic Medicine Listing of Sensory, Motor, and Mixed Nerves) contains an electrodiagnostic medicine listing of sensory, motor, and mixed nerves that are reported for motor and nerve studies codes 95900, 95903, and 95904, respectively. There is also a table that indicates the "type of study and maximum number of studies" generally performed for needle electromyogram (EMG), nerve conduction studies, and other EMG studies. The AMA's *CPT Changes 2006: An Insider's View* calls this table a ". . . tool to detect outliers."

- **Appendix K** (Product Pending FDA Approval) contains a list of products that are pending FDA approval but that have been assigned CPT codes. In the CPT manual, these codes are preceded by the flash symbol (𝄍).

- **Appendix L** (Vascular Families) contains a list of vascular families that is intended to assist in the selection of first-, second-, third-, and beyond third-order branch arteries.

- **Appendix M** (Deleted CPT Codes) contains a summary list of crosswalked current CPT codes with deleted/former codes, year codes were deleted, and citations referencing former codes that are applicable to current codes. (Renumbered codes for 2007–2009 are also included.)

- **Appendix N** (Summary of Resequenced CPT Codes) contains a list of CPT codes that do not appear in numeric order. CPT codes are resequenced (instead of deleted and renumbered) so that existing codes can be relocated to a more appropriate location. In the CPT manual, out-of-sequence codes are preceded by the number symbol (**#**).

Exercise 8.5 – CPT Appendices

Instructions: Match the appendix with its description. Answers may be assigned more than once.

_____ 1. Contains a list of add-on codes identified throughout CPT with a **+** symbol

_____ 2. Contains a list of CPT modifiers and detailed descriptions

_____ 3. Contains a list of codes that are exempt from modifier -63

_____ 4. Contains a list of vascular families to assist in the determination of first-, second-, third-, and beyond third-order branches of arteries

_____ 5. Contains a summary of CPT codes that include conscious sedation and that are identified in CPT with a ⊙ symbol

_____ 6. Contains added, deleted, and revised CPT codes

_____ 7. Contains annual CPT coding changes

_____ 8. Contains an alphabetic clinical topics listing at the AMA website

_____ 9. Contains an electrodiagnostic medicine listing of sensory, motor, and mixed nerves

_____ 10. Contains clinical examples for codes in the E/M section

_____ 11. Contains codes for vaccine products that are pending FDA approval

_____ 12. Contains codes that are exempt from modifier -51 reporting rules and that are identified in CPT with a ⊘ symbol

_____ 13. Contains genetic testing modifiers

_____ 14. Contains a crosswalk of resequenced codes that are identified with a **#** symbol

_____ 15. Contains a crosswalk of current and deleted/former CPT codes

a. Appendix A
b. Appendix B
c. Appendix C
d. Appendix D
e. Appendix E
f. Appendix F
g. Appendix G
h. Appendix H
i. Appendix I
j. Appendix J
k. Appendix K
l. Appendix L
m. Appendix M
n. Appendix N

CPT Symbols

Eight symbols (Figure 8-2 contains a partial selection) are located throughout the CPT coding manual:

- ● A **bullet symbol** located to the left of a code number identifies new procedures and services added to CPT.

- ▲ A **triangle symbol** located to the left of a code number identifies a code description that has been revised.

- ►◄ **Horizontal triangle symbols** surround revised guidelines and notes. These symbols are *not* used for revised code descriptions.

- ; To save space in CPT, some code descriptions are not printed in their entirety next to a code number. Instead, the entry is indented; and the coder must refer back to the common portion of the code description that is located before the **semicolon**. The common portion begins with a capital letter, and the abbreviated (or subordinate) descriptions are indented and begin with lowercase letters.

    EXAMPLE:

    ```
    20910   Cartilage graft; costochondral
      20912 nasal septum
    ```

    - For a patient who undergoes costochondral cartilage graft procedure, report code 20910.

    - For a patient who undergoes a nasal septum cartilage graft procedure, report code 20912.

    - For a patient who undergoes costochondral and nasal septum cartilage graft procedures during the same operative session, report codes 20910 and 20912-51. (Modifier -51 indicates that a multiple procedure was performed. The payer will discount reimbursement for the procedure assigned code 20912.)

- ＋ The **plus symbol** identifies add-on codes (Appendix D of CPT) for procedures that are commonly, but not always, performed at the same time and by the same surgeon as the primary procedure. Parenthetical notes, located below add-on codes, often identify the primary procedure to which add-on codes apply.

Note:

Review your CPT coding manual to locate codes preceded by the bullet, triangle, and horizontal triangle symbols.

Coding Tip:

CPT is printed using proportional spacing, and careful review of code descriptions to locate the semicolon may be necessary.

Symbol:	CPT Entry:	
Use of semicolon	**11000**	Debridement of extensive eczematous or infected skin; up to 10% of body surface
Use of plus symbol	＋ **11001**	each additional 10% of the body surface, or part thereof (List separately in addition to code to primary procedure)
Use of -51 modifier exemption symbol	⊘ **17004**	Destruction (eg, laser surgery, electrosurgery, cryosurgery, chemosurgery, surgical curettement), premalignant lesions (eg, actinic keratoses), 15 or more lesions
Use of bull's-eye symbol	⊙ **33010**	Pericardiocentesis; initial

© Cengage Learning 2014

Figure 8-2 Selection from CPT illustrating symbols

EXAMPLE: For a patient who undergoes posterior osteotomy of the spine, two cervical vertebral segments, report codes 22210 and 22216.

```
22210        Osteotomy of spine, posterior or posterolateral approach, one
             vertebral segment; cervical

22212          thoracic

22214          lumbar

+ 22216        each additional vertebral segment (List separately in addition
               to primary procedure)
```

(Use 22216 in conjunction with codes 22210, 22212, and 22214.)

Coding Tip:

- Do not report codes identified with **+** (add-on codes) as stand-alone codes; they must be reported with a primary code.
- Do not add modifier -51 to codes identified with **+** because payers discount reimbursement for such add-on codes; adding modifier -51 to codes that have the **+** symbol incorrectly reduces reimbursement even more.

⊘   This **forbidden** (or **prohibitory**) **symbol** identifies codes that are exempt from modifier -51. These codes are reported in addition to other codes, but they are not classified as add-on codes.

EXAMPLE: The patient underwent emergency endotracheal intubation.

```
⊘ 31500    intubation, endotracheal, emergency procedure
```

When code 31500 is reported with other procedures performed during the same encounter, do not add modifier -51.

⊙   The **bull's-eye symbol** indicates a procedure that includes moderate (conscious) sedation. (CPT Appendix G contains a list of CPT codes that includes moderate conscious sedation.)

CPT distinguishes between moderate (conscious) sedation performed by the physician doing the invasive procedure (e.g., thoracic surgeon) and anesthesia provided by a second clinician (e.g., anesthesiologist). CPT states, "The inclusion of a procedure on this list does not prevent separate reporting of an associated anesthesia procedure/service (CPT codes 00100–01999) when performed by a physician other than the operating physician or a qualified professional under the responsible supervision of a physician other than the operating physician." This means that an anesthesia service provided to the patient (in addition to conscious sedation) by an anesthesiologist or another qualified anesthesia provider is considered medically necessary and is payable.

EXAMPLE: Patient underwent insertion of permanent pacemaker with transvenous electrodes, atrial and ventricular. Report code 33208.

```
⊙ 33206    Insertion of new or replacement of permanent pacemaker with
           transvenous electrode(s); atrial

⊙ 33207    ventricular

⊙ 33208    atrial and ventricular
```

If a procedure (e.g., 33206) is performed under general anesthesia and the anesthesia is administered by a physician other than the surgeon (e.g., anesthesiologist), and that physician is present at all times during the procedure and personally supervises the delivery of anesthesia, also code the general anesthesia (CPT codes 00100–01999). If the surgeon administers general anesthesia, code only the procedure and do not assign a code from the CPT Anesthesia section.

If the patient undergoes a procedure for which the CPT code has a bull's-eye symbol and the patient does not receive moderate (conscious) sedation, report the CPT procedure code only (e.g., 33208). Do not assign modifier -52 (reduced services) to the procedure code.

✗ The **flash symbol** indicates codes that classify products pending FDA approval but that have been assigned a CPT code.

> **EXAMPLE:** Patient was administered an influenza virus vaccine, pandemic formulation
>
> ✗ `90663    Influenza virus vaccine, pandemic formulation`

○ The **hollow circle symbol** indicates a reinstated or recycled code in Category III of CPT. (It is unknown whether the *hollow circle symbol* will also appear in front of CPT's Category I and II codes in the future.)

> **EXAMPLE:** A performance measurement study was conducted on a patient, and it was determined that a new episode for his condition was documented in the patient record.
>
> ○ `1127F    New episode for condition (NMA-No Measure Associated)`

In CPT 2010, Category II code 1127F was deleted. In CPT 2012, the code was reinstated; thus, a *hollow circle symbol* appears before code 1127F.

\# The **number symbol** indicates out-of-numerical sequence codes. Resequencing allows existing codes to be relocated to a more appropriate location (rather than deleting and renumbering codes).

> **EXAMPLE:** Patient underwent excision of 4-cm subcutaneous soft tissue tumor of the neck.
>
> `  21555    Excision, tumor, soft tissue of neck or anterior thorax,`
> `           subcutaneous; less than 3 cm`
>
> `# 21552    3 cm or greater`

Note:

Prior to 2010, when a new code was added and there was no available code in a "code range," a new range of codes was added to accommodate the new code(s). This meant that all codes in a range were deleted (and added as new codes) for certain procedures even though the procedure text and meaning or applicability of the procedure had not changed.

The new policy facilitates historical data analysis, reduces the number of codes that providers must revise (e.g., Superbill), and eliminates the need for payers to modify related reimbursement policies. (Payers typically interpreted a new range of codes as "new codes" to CPT, resulting in payment denials.)

Resequenced codes will appear "out of sequence" in the print version of CPT, but that means the codes will be located with concepts to which they are related. CPT code description content will determine placement of out-of-sequence codes. (Codes in the electronic version of CPT will be in numerical order.)

⮌ The **green reference symbol** located below a code description in some CPT coding manuals indicates that the coder should refer to the *CPT Assistant* monthly newsletter and/or the *CPT Changes: An Insider's View* annual publication that contains all coding changes for the current year.

> **EXAMPLE:**
>
> `43882    Revision or removal of gastric neurostimulator electrodes, antrum, open`
>
> ⮌ `CPT Assistant Mar 07:4; CPT Changes: An Insider's View 2007`

⮌ The **red reference symbol** located below a code description in some CPT coding manuals indicates that the coder should refer to the *Clinical Examples in Radiology* quarterly newsletter.

EXAMPLE:

```
73500    Radiologic examination, hip, unilateral; 1 view
         ⊃ Clinical Examples in Radiology Spring 05:12
```

Exercise 8.6 – CPT Symbols

Instructions: Match the symbol with its description

_____	**1.** Identifies a procedure that includes conscious sedation	**a.** ⊙
_____	**2.** Identifies add-on codes	**b.** ▲
_____	**3.** Identifies codes that are exempt from modifier -51	**c.** •
_____	**4.** Identifies codes that classify products pending FDA approval	**d.** +
_____	**5.** Identifies new procedures and services added to CPT	**e.** ⊘
_____	**6.** Identifies revised code descriptions	**f.** ⁄
_____	**7.** Refers coders to *Clinical Examples in Radiology* newsletter	**g.** ○
_____	**8.** Indicates an out-of-numerical sequence code	**h.** #
_____	**9.** Refers coders to *CPT Assistant* newsletter and/or *CPT Changes: An Insider's View* annual publication of coding changes for current year	**i.** ⊃
_____	**10.** Indicates a reinstated or recycled code in Category III of CPT	**j.** ⊃

CPT Sections, Subsections, Categories, and Subcategories

CPT Category I codes are organized according to six sections that are subdivided into subsections, categories, and subcategories (Figure 8-3). Guidelines are located at the beginning of each CPT section; and the following are located in CPT subsections, headings or categories, subheadings or subcategories, and codes:

- Notes

- Descriptive qualifiers

Note:

CPT is inconsistent in its use of subsection, category, and subcategory terminology. For example, Table 1 in the CPT E/M section guidelines lists categories and subcategories (instead of the more logical subsections and categories). (Many years ago, the E/M section was a subsection of the Medicine section. When the codes were relocated to the beginning of the CPT coding manual for easy reference, the E/M section was created. The category and subcategory terminology associated with the E/M codes was retained.)

Remaining CPT section guidelines include lists of subsections except for the Radiology section, which includes some subcategories in the list of subsections. To make matters even more complicated, CPT refers to headings and subheadings in some section guidelines and categories and subcategories in other section guidelines. In addition, the Surgery guidelines include "Subsection Information," which refers to "subheadings or subsections." It would be more logical if the latter phrase had been written as "subheadings or subcategories."

Section	Surgery
Subsection	Integumentary System
Heading	Skin, Subcutaneous and Accessory Structures
Subheading	Incision and Drainage
Note	(For excision, see 11400, et seq)
Descriptive qualifier (underlined phrase)	10060 Incision and drainage of abscess (eg, carbuncle, suppurative hidradenitis, cutaneous or subcutaneous abscess, cyst, furuncle, or paronychia); simple or single

© Cengage Learning 2014

Figure 8-3 Selection from CPT illustrating sections, subsections, categories, subcategories, notes, and descriptive qualifiers

ICD-10 Alert!

HIPAA has designated CPT as a national code set for reporting outpatient (including physician's office) procedures and services. It further designated *CPT Assistant* as an official source of coding guidelines. CPT guidelines and notes and *CPT Assistant* coding guidelines take precedence over payer-specific rules for reporting codes. However, payers (e.g., CMS and commercial insurance companies) are selective about the guidelines and notes they implement for reimbursement purposes. Thus, payer-specific reimbursement rules often contradict CPT guidelines and notes and *CPT Assistant* coding guidelines. This means that coders must review and follow payer-specific reimbursement rules for reporting codes to obtain appropriate reimbursement.

EXAMPLE: Cautery was used to correct everted lacrimal puncta (small openings in the inner canthus of eyelids that channel tears), right and left eye. (There are two puncta in each eye, an upper and a lower punctum.) According to *CPT Assistant* (June 1995), code 68705 is reported four times. However, Medicare reimbursement rules require code 68705 to be reported twice with modifier -50 (Bilateral Procedure) added to each code.

PROCEDURES, SERVICES, OR SUPPLIES	
(Explain Unusual Circumstances)	
CPT/HCPCS	MODIFIER
68705	
68705	
68705	
68705	

PROCEDURES, SERVICES, OR SUPPLIES	
(Explain Unusual Circumstances)	
CPT/HCPCS	MODIFIER
68705	50
68705	50

© Cengage Learning 2014

This is just one of many cases where official CPT coding guidelines differ from payer reimbursement rules. To obtain appropriate reimbursement, make sure you determine payer reimbursement rules for submitting codes.

Guidelines

Guidelines located at the beginning of each CPT section should be carefully reviewed before assigning a code. **Guidelines** define terms and explain the assignment of codes for procedures and services located in a particular section (Figure 8-4). This means that guidelines in one section do not apply to another section in CPT.

Surgery Guidelines

Items used by all physicians in reporting their services are presented in the **Introduction**. Some of the commonalities are repeated here for the convenience of those physicians referring to this section on **Surgery**. Other definitions and items unique to Surgery are also listed.

Physicians' Services

Physicians' services rendered in the office, home, or hospital, consultations, and other medical services are listed in the section entitled **Evaluation and Management Services** (99201-99499) found in the front of the book, beginning on page 9. "Special Services and Reports" (99000 series) is presented in the **Medicine** section.

Follow-Up Care for Therapeutic Surgical Procedures

Follow-up care for therapeutic surgical procedures includes only that care which is usually a part of the surgical service. Complications, exacerbations, recurrence, or the presence of other diseases or injuries requiring additional services should be separately reported.

Materials Supplied by Physician

Supplies and materials provided by the physician (e g, sterile trays/drugs), over and above those usually included with the procedure(s) rendered are reported separately. List drugs, trays, supplies, and materials provided. Identify as 99070 or specific supply code.

© Cengage Learning 2014

Figure 8-4 Portion of CPT Surgery Guidelines

Unlisted Procedures and Services

An **unlisted procedure** or **unlisted service** code is assigned when the provider performs a procedure or service for which there is no CPT code. When an unlisted procedure or service code is reported, a **special report** (e.g., copy of the procedure report) must accompany the claim to describe the nature, extent, and need for the procedure or service.

Note:

Medicare and third-party payers often require providers to report HCPCS level II national codes instead of unlisted procedure or service CPT codes.

Notes

Instructional **notes** appear throughout CPT sections to clarify the assignment of codes. They are typeset in two patterns (Figure 8-5):

- A *blocked unindented note* is located below the title of a subsection, heading (or category), or subheading (or subcategory). It contains instructions that apply to all codes in the subsection, heading/category, or subheading/subcategory.

- An *indented parenthetical* note is located below the:

  ○ Title of a subsection, heading (or category), and subheading (or subcategory).

  ○ Code description (and the note applies to that code only unless the note indicates otherwise).

- A *parenthetical note* is located in the code description to provide an example. Such notes contain the abbreviation e.g., and terminology in the example is *not* required to appear in the procedural statement documented by the provider.

Coding Tip:

Within a code series, parenthetical notes provide information about deleted codes.

Descriptive Qualifiers

Descriptive qualifiers are terms that clarify the assignment of a CPT code. They can occur in the middle of a main clause or after the semicolon and may or may not be enclosed in parentheses. Make sure you read all code descriptions very carefully to properly assign CPT codes that require descriptive qualifiers.

EXAMPLE: The underlining in code descriptions for 17000 and 17003 identify descriptive qualifiers for each.

```
17000     Destruction (eg, laser surgery, electrosurgery, cryosurgery,
          chemosurgery, surgical curettement), premalignant lesions (eg,
          actinic keratoses); first lesion
```

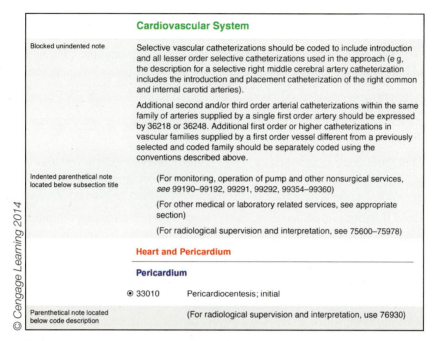

Figure 8-5 Selection from CPT illustrating different types of instructional notes

+ 17003   second through 14 lesions, each (List separately in addition to
            code for first lesion)

Coding Tip:

Coders working in a provider's office should highlight descriptive qualifiers in CPT that pertain to the office's specialty. This will help ensure that qualifiers are not overlooked when codes are assigned.

Exercise 8.7 – CPT Sections, Subsections, Categories, and Subcategories

Instructions: Indicate whether the statement is true (T) or false (F).

_____ **1.** The major sections of CPT are nuclear medicine, surgery, medicine, pathology, and radiology.

_____ **2.** When a parenthetical statement within a code description begins with e.g., one of the terms that follows must be included in the provider's description of the surgery for the code number to apply.

_____ **3.** The numeric format for a reported procedure should be expressed with a five-digit main number and a two-digit modifier.

_____ **4.** A blocked unindented note is located below a subsection title and contains instructions that apply to all codes in the category.

_____ **5.** All descriptive qualifiers for a particular code are found in an indented code description.

CPT Modifiers

CPT modifiers clarify services and procedures performed by providers. Although the CPT code and description remain unchanged, modifiers indicate that the description of the service or procedure performed has been altered.

- CPT modifiers are reported as two-digit numeric codes added to the five-digit CPT code (e.g., 99213-25).

- HCPCS level II national modifiers are reported as two-character alphabetic and alphanumeric codes added to the five-digit CPT code (e.g., 11760-TA and 11760-T1).

  EXAMPLE: A patient undergoes repair of nasal septal perforations (30630), which was unsuccessful. Three months later the patient undergoes repeat repair of nasal septal perforations by a different surgeon (30630-77). The same CPT code is assigned, and a modifier is added to indicate the repeat procedure.

CPT and HCPCS level II national modifiers have always been reported on claims submitted for provider office services and procedures. In April 2000, hospitals also began reporting CPT and HCPCS level II modifiers for outpatient services. When reporting codes with more than one modifier, enter the **functional modifier** (or **pricing modifier**), which assists in reimbursement decision-making (e.g., assistant surgeon). Next, enter **informational modifiers**, which clarify aspects of the procedure or service provided for the payer (e.g., procedure performed on right or left side only). (Medicare carriers originally created the terms functional modifier, pricing modifier, and information modifier, which means some payers do not use the terms.)

  EXAMPLE: A patient fractured his left femur. An assistant surgeon participated in the open treatment and internal fixation of the femoral fracture, proximal end, neck. Report code 27236-80-LT. (Modifier 80, Assistant Surgeon, is a functional modifier that impacts the reimbursement rate paid by the third-party payer. Modifier -LT is an informational modifier, which indicates that the surgery was performed on the patient's left side. It does not impact the reimbursement amount paid to the physician.)

When multiple modifiers are added to a CPT (or HCPCS level II) code and an informational modifier is listed first, third-party payers manually review the claim. Manual review slows claims processing and results in reimbursement delays to physicians.

Not all CPT modifiers apply to each section of CPT. Table 8-1 summarizes CPT modifiers in numerical order and identifies applicable CPT sections that are recommended for each. (Coders should contact third-party payers to obtain a list of modifiers and applicable CPT sections because each payer has different reporting requirements.)

Coding Tip:

As a general rule, list HCPCS level II modifiers after CPT modifiers (except for HCPCS level II modifier TC, which is listed before other HCPCS level II modifiers).

Note:

HCPCS Level II national modifiers were explained in Chapter 7.

Coding Tip:

Some CPT coding manuals include modifiers with brief descriptions inside the front cover, including CPT and HCPCS level II national modifiers approved for hospital outpatient reporting purposes. Appendix A of the CPT coding manual contains a comprehensive list of modifiers with descriptions.

The AMA and CMS develop new modifiers on a continuous basis, and next available numbers are assigned. This means that there is no relationship among groups of modifier numbers. Reviewing modifiers in strict numerical order does not allow for comparison of those that are related to one another in terms of content; therefore, Table 8-2 organizes modifiers according to reporting similarity.

Table 8-1 CPT Modifiers in a Quick View Format

Modifier	Title of Modifier	E/M	Anesthesia	Surgery	Radiololgy	Laboratory	Medicine	Approved for Hospital Outpateint Use
-22	Increased Procedural Services			X	X	X	X	
-23	Unusual Anesthesia		X					
-24	Unrelated Evaluation and Management Service by the Same Physician or Other Qualified Health Care Professional During a Postoperative Period	X						
-25	Significant, Separately Identifiable Evaluation and Management Service by the Same Physician or Other Qualified Health Care Professional on the Same Day of the Procedure or Other Service	X						X
-26	Professional Component				X			
-27	Multiple Outpatient Hospital E/M Encounters on the Same Date	X						X
-32	Mandated Services	X						
-33	Preventive Services	X						
-47	Anesthesia by Surgeon			X				
-50	Bilateral Procedure			X				X
-51	Multiple Procedures			X				
-52	Reduced Services			X	X	X	X	X
-53	Discontinued Procedure		X	X	X	X	X	
-54	Surgical Care Only			X				
-55	Postoperative Management Only			X				
-56	Preoperative Management Only	X		X				
-57	Decision for Surgery	X						
-58	Staged or Related Procedure or Service by the Same Physician or Other Qualified Health Care Professional During the Postoperative Period			X			X	X
-59	Distinct Procedural Service		X	X				X
-62	Two Surgeons			X				
-63	Procedure Performed on Infants less than 4 kg			X				
-66	Surgical Team			X				
-73	Discontinued Outpatient Hospital/Ambulatory Surgery Center (ASC) Procedure Prior to the Administration of Anesthesia			X				X
-74	Discontinued Outpatient Hospital/Ambulatory Surgery Center (ASC) Procedure After Administration of Anesthesia		X	X				X
-76	Repeat Procedure or Service by Same Physician or Other Qualified Health Care Professional			X				X
-77	Repeat Procedure by Another Physician or Other Qualified Health Care Professional			X				X
-78	Unplanned Return to the Operating/Procedure Room by the Same Physician or Other Qualified Health Care Professional Following Initial Procedure for a Related Procedure During the Postoperative Period			X				X
-79	Unrelated Procedure or Service by the Same Physician or Other Qualified Health Care Professional During the Postoperative Period			X				X
-80	Assistant Surgeon			X				
-81	Minimum Assistant Surgeon			X				
-82	Assistant Surgeon (when qualified resident surgeon not available)			X				

(continues)

Table 8-1 (*continued*)

Modifier	Title of Modifier	E/M	Anesthesia	Surgery	Radiolology	Laboratory	Medicine	Approved for Hospital Outpateint Use
-90	Reference (Outside) Laboratory					X		
-91	Repeat Clinical Diagnostic Laboratory Test					X		X
-92	Alternative Laboratory Platform Testing					X		
-99	Multiple Modifiers		X	X	X	X	X	

The following example illustrates how and why modifiers are used.

🔵 **EXAMPLE:** Mrs. T has a history of gallbladder disease. After several hours of acute pain, she was referred to Dr. S for an evaluation of her condition. Dr. S performed a complete history and physical examination and decided to admit the patient to the hospital for an immediate work-up for cholecystitis. When the results of laboratory tests and sonogram were received, the patient was scheduled for an emergency laparoscopic cholecystectomy.

Note:

In an attempt to simplify the explanation of modifiers, the wording does not correspond word for word with descriptions found in CPT.

The surgeon was Dr. S and the assistant surgeon was Dr. A. The surgery was successful, and the patient was discharged the next day and told to return to the office in seven days. Four days later Mrs. T returned to Dr. S's office complaining of chest pains. Dr. S performed another examination and ordered the necessary tests. After reviewing the test results and confirming with the patient's primary care physician, it was determined that the patient was suffering from mild angina.

Dr. S reports the following services (Figure 8-6):

- Initial hospital visit, comprehensive, with medical decision making of high complexity (99223-57) (Modifier -57 indicates that the decision to perform surgery was made during the hospital evaluation.)

- Laparoscopic cholecystectomy (47562)

- Office visit, established patient, expanded problem focused, with medical decision making of low complexity (99213-24) (Modifier -24 indicates that the reexamination of the patient revealed the problem to be unrelated to the normal postoperative care provided to a cholecystectomy patient. The diagnosis linked to this visit is angina.)

Dr. A reports (Figure 8-7) the following service:

- Laparoscopic cholecystectomy 47562-80 (Modifier -80 indicates that Dr. A is the assistant surgeon.)

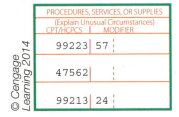

Figure 8-6 Completed Block 24D of CMS-1500 claim

Figure 8-7 Completed Block 24D on CMS-1500 claim

Table 8-2 Organization of CPT Modifiers According to Reporting Similarity

Special Evaluation and Management (E/M) Cases			
Modifier	Description	Interpretation	Coding Tips and Examples
-24	Unrelated Evaluation and Management Service by the Same Physician or Other Qualified Health Care Professional During a Postoperative Period	Assign to indicate that an E/M service was performed during the standard postoperative period for a condition unrelated to the surgery. The *service* to which the modifier is attached *must be* linked to a diagnosis that is *unrelated* to the surgical diagnosis previously submitted. Make sure you submit a copy of documentation with the claim to explain the circumstances.	**EXAMPLE:** One week after surgical treatment to release a frozen shoulder, patient received level 3 evaluation and management services for treatment of the flu. Report code 99213-24.
-25	Significant, Separately Identifiable Evaluation and Management Service by the Same Physician or Other Qualified Health Care Professional on the Same Day of the Procedure or Other Service	Assign when a documented E/M service was performed on the same day as another procedure because the patient's condition required the assignment of a significant, separately identifiable, additional E/M service that was provided "above and beyond the other service provided or beyond the usual preoperative and postoperative care associated with the procedure performed." The documented history, examination, and medical decision making must "stand on its own" to justify reporting modifier -25 with the E/M code. The E/M service provided must be "above and beyond" what is normally performed during a procedure.	**EXAMPLE:** During a routine annual examination, it was discovered that the 65-year-old established patient had an enlarged liver expanding the scope of level 4 evaluation and management services. Report codes 99397 and 99214-25. (Make sure you submit supporting documentation to the payer.)
-57	Decision for Surgery	Assign when the reported E/M service resulted in the *initial* decision to perform surgery on the day before *or* the day of surgery, to exempt it from the global surgery package.	**EXAMPLE:** The patient received level 4 evaluation and management services for chest pain in the emergency department, and a decision was made to insert a coronary artery stent. Report code 99284-57.
Greater, Reduced, or Discontinued Services			
-22	Increased Procedural Services	Assign when a procedure *requires greater than usual service(s).* Documentation that would support using this modifier includes difficult, complicated, extensive, unusual, or rare procedure(s).	**EXAMPLE:** The patient experienced blood loss of 600 cc, which required intraoperative transfusions. Report the CPT surgery code with modifier -22.
-52	Reduced Services	Report when a service has been partially reduced or eliminated at the provider's discretion and does not completely match the CPT code description. (Attach a copy of documentation to the claim.)	**EXAMPLE:** A surgeon removed a coccygeal pressure ulcer and performed a coccygectomy. However, the surgeon did not use a primary suture or perform a skin flap closure because the wound had to be cleansed for a continued period of time postoperatively. Report code 15920-52. (When the surgeon eventually performs the wound closure procedure, an appropriate code would be reported.)
-53	Discontinued Procedure	Report when a provider has elected to terminate a procedure because of extenuating circumstances that threaten the well-being of the patient. **NOTE:** This modifier applies only to provider office settings and is *not* reported for elective cancellation (e.g., by the patient) prior to anesthesia induction and/or surgical preparation in the operating suite.	**EXAMPLE:** The surgeon inserted the colonoscope and removed it right away because the patient had not been properly prepared for the procedure. Report code 45378-53. (The patient received instruction about properly preparing for the colonoscopy procedure, and the procedure was rescheduled.)

(continues)

Table 8-2 (*continued*)

Modifier	Description	Interpretation	Coding Tips and Examples
Greater, Reduced, or Discontinued Services			
-73	Discontinued Outpatient Hospital/Ambulatory Surgery Center (ASC) Procedure Prior to the Administration of Anesthesia	Report to describe discontinued procedures *prior to the administration of any anesthesia* because of extenuating circumstances threatening the well-being of the patient. (Also report an ICD code to document the reason the procedure was halted.) **NOTE:** This modifier applies only to ASC settings and is *not* reported for elective cancellation (e.g., by the patient) prior to anesthesia induction and/or surgical preparation in the operating suite.	**EXAMPLE:** Patient developed a heart arrhythmia prior to anesthesia administration, and the laparoscopic cholecystectomy procedure was canceled. Report code 47562-73.
-74	Discontinued Outpatient Hospital/Ambulatory Surgery Center (ASC) Procedure After the Administration of Anesthesia	Report to describe discontinued procedures *after the administration of anesthesia* due to extenuating circumstances. (Also report an ICD code to document the reason the procedure was halted.) **NOTE:** This modifier applies only to ASC settings.	**EXAMPLE:** The patient was prepped and draped, and general anesthesia was administered. The anesthesiologist noted a sudden increase in blood pressure, and the laparoscopic cholecystectomy procedure was terminated. Report code 47562-74.

Global Surgery

- These modifiers apply to the four areas related to the CPT *surgical package* (Figure 8-8), which includes local infiltration; metacarpal/digital block or topical anesthesia when used; the procedure; and normal, uncomplicated follow-up care.
- These modifiers do *not* apply to obstetrical coding, where the CPT description of specific codes clearly describes separate antepartum, postpartum, and delivery services for both vaginal and cesarean deliveries.

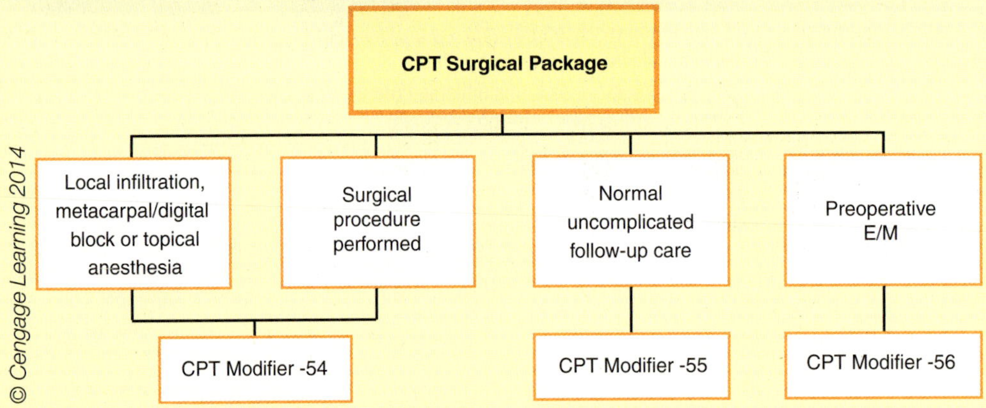

Figure 8-8 Modifiers that apply to components of the CPT surgical package

© Cengage Learning 2014

| -54 | Surgical Care Only | Report when a provider performed only the surgical portion of surgical package and personally administered required local anesthesia. Different provider(s) will have performed preoperative evaluation and/or provided postoperative care. | **EXAMPLE:** While on vacation, John Jones sustained a tibial shaft fracture and underwent closed treatment by Dr. Charles. Upon return to his hometown, John received follow-up care from Dr. Smith, a local orthopedist. Dr. Charles reports code 27750-54. |

(*continues*)

Global Surgery

Modifier	Description	Interpretation	Coding Tips and Examples
-55	Postoperative Management Only	Report when a provider other than the surgeon is responsible for postoperative management only of a surgery performed by another provider. Documentation in the patient's chart should detail the date of transfer of care to calculate the percentage of the fee to be billed for postoperative care. (The modifier is added to the surgical procedure code. Modifier -54 does *not* apply when a second provider occasionally covers for the surgeon and where no transfer of care occurs.)	**EXAMPLE:** While on vacation, John Jones sustained a tibial shaft fracture and underwent closed treatment by Dr. Charles. Upon return to his hometown, John received follow-up care from Dr. Smith, a local orthopedist. Dr. Smith reports code 27750-55.
-56	Preoperative Management Only	Report when a provider *other than* the operating surgeon performs preoperative care and evaluation of the patient for surgery (e.g., preoperative clearance).	**EXAMPLE:** Dr. Berger preoperatively cleared his patient during a level 4 E/M service for scheduled surgery by Dr. Charles. Dr. Berger reports code 99214-56.

Special Surgical and Procedural Events

Modifier	Description	Interpretation	Coding Tips and Examples
-58	Staged or Related Procedure or Service by the Same Physician or Other Qualified Health Care Professional During the Postoperative Period	Report to indicate that additional related surgery was required during the postoperative period of a previously completed surgery and was performed by the same provider. Documentation should include one of the following: • Original plan for surgery included additional stages to be performed within postoperative period of first stage of procedure. • Underlying disease required a second related, but unplanned, procedure to be performed. • Additional related therapy is required after the performance of a procedure.	**CODING TIP:** Do not report modifier -58 if the CPT code description describes multiple sessions of an event. **EXAMPLE:** A surgical wound is not healing properly because of the patient's underlying diabetes. Patient was told prior to the original surgery that if this happened, additional surgery would be required for subcutaneous tissue debridement of the wound. Report code 11042-58 for debridement surgery.
-59	Distinct Procedural Service	Report when same provider performs one or more *distinctly independent procedures* on the same day as other procedures or services, according to the following criteria: • Procedures are performed at different sessions or during different patient encounters. • Procedures are performed on different sites or organs and require a different surgical prep. • Procedures are performed for multiple or extensive injuries, using separate incisions/excisions; for separate lesions; or for procedures not ordinarily encountered/performed on the same day.	**EXAMPLE:** Patient has two basal cell carcinomas removed, one from the forehead with a simple closure (11640) and the other from the nose requiring adjacent tissue transfer (14060). Report codes 14060, 11640-51 (forehead), and 11640-59-51 (nose).
-63	Procedure Performed on Infants Less Than 4 kg	Report when infant weighs less than 4 kilograms (kg) because procedures performed may require increased complexity and provider work.	**EXAMPLE:** Baby Girl Markel's weight was 3.5 kg at the time she underwent diagnostic thoracoscopy. Report 32601-63.
-78	Unplanned Return to the Operating/Procedure Room by the same Physician or Other Qualified Health Care Professional Following Initial Procedure for a Related Procedure During the Postoperative Period	Report for unplanned circumstances that require return to operating room for complications of initial operation. (Also report an ICD code to document the surgical complication that necessitated a return to operating room.) **NOTE:** This modifier applies only to ASC settings.	**EXAMPLE:** Surgical sutures did not hold, and a 12-cm layer closure of axillary wound was performed. Report code 12034-78.

Table 8-2 (*continued*)

Special Surgical and Procedural Events			
Modifier	Description	Interpretation	Coding Tips and Examples
-79	Unrelated Procedure or Service by the Same Physician or Other Qualified Health Care Professional During the Postoperative Period	Report when a new procedure or service is performed by a provider during the normal postoperative period of a previously performed but unrelated surgery. **NOTE:** This modifier applies only to ASC settings.	**EXAMPLE:** Six weeks following cataract surgery performed on the left eye, the patient underwent diathermic repair of retinal detachment, right eye. Report code 67101-79.
Bilateral and Multiple Procedures			
-27	Multiple Outpatient Hospital E/M Encounters on the Same Date	Report for patients who receive multiple E/M services performed by *different providers* on the same day.	**EXAMPLE:** A patient was seen in the hospital's emergency department and received level 4 evaluation and management services due to a fractured ankle. The patient was seen later the same day in the urgent care center and provided with level 3 evaluation and management services due to a migraine that did not respond to prescribed medication taken at home. Report codes 99284-27 and 99213-27
-50	Bilateral Procedure	Report when a procedure was performed bilaterally *during the same session and when the code description does not specify that the procedure is bilateral.*	**EXAMPLE:** Patient underwent bilateral arthrodesis of the knees. Report code 27580-50 (*or* report HCPCS level II national modifiers as codes 27580-LT and 27580-RT).
-51	Multiple Procedures	Report when multiple procedures *other than E/M services* are performed during a single patient encounter by the same provider. The procedures performed are characterized as: • Multiple related surgical procedures performed at the same session. • Surgical procedures that are performed in combination, whether through the same or another incision, or that involve the same or different anatomy. • Combination medical and surgical procedures performed at the same session.	**EXAMPLE:** Patient underwent right tibial shaft fracture repair and arthrodesis of left knee. Report codes 27750 and 27580-51.
Repeat Services			
-76	Repeat Procedure or Service by Same Physician or Other Qualified Health Care Professional	Report when a procedure was repeated because of special circumstances involving the original service and the same physician performed the repeat procedure. **NOTE:** This modifier applies only to ASC settings.	**EXAMPLE:** A repeat EKG is performed due to changes in the patient's condition or the need to assess the effect of therapeutic procedures. Report code 93041-76.
-77	Repeat Procedure by Another Physician or Other Qualified Health Care Professional	Report when a physician *other than the original physician* performs a repeat procedure because of special circumstances involving the original study or procedure. **NOTE:** This modifier applies only to ASC settings.	**EXAMPLE:** Patient underwent sterilization procedure (e.g., tubal ligation), but became pregnant. After C-section delivery, she underwent a second sterilization procedure. Report codes 58611-77 for the second sterilization procedure.

(*continues*)

Multiple Surgeons

Modifier	Description	Interpretation	Coding Tips and Examples
-62	Two Surgeons	Report when two primary surgeons are required during an operative session, each performing distinct parts of a reportable procedure. Ideally, the surgeons represent different specialties.	**EXAMPLE:** A spinal surgeon and a general surgeon work together as primary surgeons to perform an anterior spinal fusion of L5-S1. The spinal surgeon also inserts an intervertebral synthetic cage and performs iliac bone grafting. Each surgeon reports code 22558-62. The spinal surgeon also reports codes 22851-51 and 20937-51.
-66	Surgical Team	Report when surgery performed is highly complex and requires the services of a skilled team of three or more surgeons. The procedure reported on the claim for each participating surgeon must include this modifier. The operative reports must document the complexity of the surgery and refer to the actions of each team member.	**EXAMPLE:** Reattachment of severed forearm. Each surgeon reports code 20805-66.
-80	Assistant Surgeon	Report when one physician assists another during an operative session. The assistant surgeon reports the same CPT code as the operating physician.	**EXAMPLE:** Dr. Landry assisted Dr. Bartron during single coronary artery bypass surgery. Dr. Landry reports code 33510-80. (Dr. Bartron reports code 33510 without the modifier.)
-81	Minimum Assistant Surgeon	Report when primary operating physician has planned to perform a surgical procedure alone, but circumstances arise that require the services of an assistant surgeon for a short time. The second surgeon reports the same CPT code as the operating physician.	**EXAMPLE:** Dr. Kelly begins an invasive cholecystectomy procedure and discovers that the gallbladder is the size of a hot dog bun, which necessitates calling Dr. Pietro to assist for a short time. Dr. Pietro reports code 47600-81. (A gallbladder is supposed to be the size of your little finger.)
-82	Assistant Surgeon (when qualified resident surgeon not available)	Report when a qualified resident surgeon is unavailable to assist with a procedure. In teaching hospitals, the physician acting as the assistant surgeon is usually a qualified resident surgeon. If circumstances arise (e.g., rotational changes) and a qualified resident surgeon is not available, another surgeon may assist with a procedure. The nonresident-assistant surgeon reports the same CPT code as the operating physician.	**EXAMPLE:** Resident surgeon Dr. Smith was to assist surgeon Dr. Manlin with a routine laparoscopic appendectomy. Dr. Smith was temporarily reassigned to the emergency department, and Dr. Manlin's partner assisted with the procedure. Code 44970-82 is reported.

Preventive Services

Modifier	Description	Interpretation	Coding Tips and Examples
-33	Preventive Service	Alerts third-party payers that the procedure or service was preventive under applicable laws and that patient cost sharing (e.g., coinsurance, copayment, deductible) does not apply when furnished by in-network providers.	**EXAMPLE:** The patient's primary care provider provided 20 minutes of smoking and tobacco use cessation counseling. Report code 99407-33.

Professional and Technical Components

Modifier	Description	Interpretation	Coding Tips and Examples
-26	Professional Component	Report when the provider either interprets test results or operates equipment for a procedure. *Do not report this modifier when a specific separately identifiable code describes the professional component of a procedure (e.g., 93010).*	**EXAMPLE:** Independent radiologist Dr. Minion interprets a stereo frontal chest X-ray that was performed by another provider. Dr. Minion reports code 71021-26.

(continues)

Table 8-2 (*continued*)

Mandated Services			
Modifier	**Description**	**Interpretation**	**Coding Tips and Examples**
-32	Mandated Services	Report when services (e.g., second or third opinion for a surgical procedure) provided were mandated by a third party (e.g., attorney or payer).	**EXAMPLE:** A patient's primary care provider respiratory therapy. The payer requires the patient to undergo a level 3 evaluation and management service by a respiratory specialist Code 99243-32 is reported.

Unusual Anesthesia			
-23	Unusual Anesthesia	Report when circumstances (e.g., extent of service or patient's physical condition) require anesthesia for procedures that usually require either no anesthesia or local anesthesia.	**EXAMPLE:** The 30-year-old patient is mentally retarded and extremely apprehensive and requires the administration of general anesthesia for ventral hernia repair (instead of regional anesthesia.) Code 00832-23 is reported.
-47	Anesthesia by Surgeon	Report when the surgeon provides regional or general anesthesia in addition to performing the surgical procedure.	**CODING TIP:** Modifier -47 is added to the CPT surgery code. It is not reported with Anesthesia codes 00100–01999.

EXAMPLE: The surgeon administers the regional anesthesia and performs the spigelian hernia repair. Code 49590-47 is reported. |

Laboratory Services			
-90	Reference (Outside) Laboratory	Report when a laboratory test is performed by an outside or reference laboratory	**EXAMPLE:** The provider orders a complete blood count (CBC). Because the office does not perform lab testing, arrangements are made with an outside laboratory to perform the CBC and bill the physician. The physician reports code 85025-90. (Code 36415 is also reported for routine venipuncture.)
-91	Repeat Clinical Diagnostic Laboratory Test	Report when a clinical diagnostic laboratory test is repeated on the same day to obtain subsequent (multiple) test results. *This modifier is not reported when lab tests are repeated to confirm initial results* (e.g., due to equipment problems).	**EXAMPLE:** The patient was in the emergency department for 18 hours for observation of chest pain. He underwent serial (repeated) lab tests for cardiac enzyme testing every six hours. Report codes 82657, 82657-91, and 82657-91.
-92	Alternative Laboratory Platform Testing	Report when laboratory testing is performed using a kit or transportable instrument that wholly or in part consists of a single-use, disposable analytical chamber. Such testing does not require permanent dedicated space because the testing materials can be carried or transported to the patient care area.	**EXAMPLE:** The hospital laboratory technician brought all of the HIV-1 testing materials to emergency department examination room #1 and performed an HIV-1 test on Mary Jones. Report code 86701-92.

Multiple Modifiers			
-99	Multiple Modifiers	Report to alert third-party payers that more than four modifiers are added to a procedure or service code.

The CMS-1500 claim allows up to four modifiers to be listed after a CPT or HCPCS level II code. If more than four modifiers are required to report a procedure or service, enter the first three modifiers and modifier 99 on line 1 of Block 24D. On line 2, report the same CPT or HCPCS level II code and enter the remaining modifiers (Figure 8-9). | **EXAMPLE:** An assistant surgeon (-80) reports an unusual service (-22), bilateral (-50), surgeon-provided general anesthesia services (-47) for lumbar hernia repair procedure (49540).

- On the CMS-1500 claim, report as 49540 22 47 50 99 and 49540 80.
- On the UB-04, report as 49540 22 47 99, 49540 and 49540 50 80. |

(*continues*)

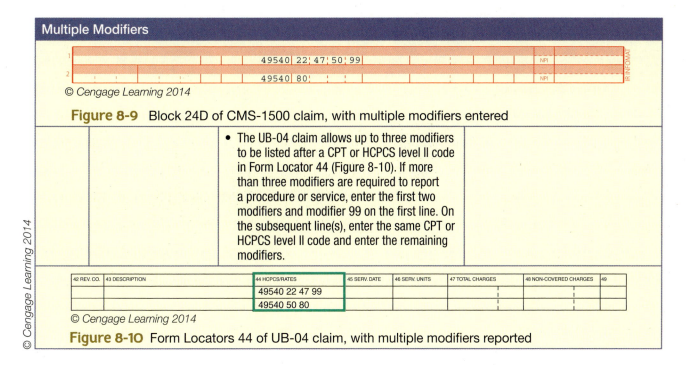

Multiple Modifiers

| 1 | | | | | 49540 | 22 | 47 | 50 | 99 | | | | NPI | | IR INFO/MAT |
| 2 | | | | | 49540 | 80 | | | | | | | NPI | | |

© Cengage Learning 2014

Figure 8-9 Block 24D of CMS-1500 claim, with multiple modifiers entered

• The UB-04 claim allows up to three modifiers to be listed after a CPT or HCPCS level II code in Form Locator 44 (Figure 8-10). If more than three modifiers are required to report a procedure or service, enter the first two modifiers and modifier 99 on the first line. On the subsequent line(s), enter the same CPT or HCPCS level II code and enter the remaining modifiers.

42 REV. CO.	43 DESCRIPTION	44 HCPCS/RATES	45 SERV. DATE	46 SERV. UNITS	47 TOTAL CHARGES	48 NON-COVERED CHARGES	49
		49540 22 47 99					
		49540 50 80					

© Cengage Learning 2014

Figure 8-10 Form Locators 44 of UB-04 claim, with multiple modifiers reported

Exercise 8.8 – CPT Modifiers

Instructions: Assign appropriate modifier(s) to each statement.

_____   **1.** Assistant surgeon reporting patient's cesarean section, delivery only

_____   **2.** Cholecystectomy reported during postoperative period for treatment of leg fracture

_____   **3.** Treatment for chronic conditions at same time preventive medicine is provided

_____   **4.** Inpatient visit performed by surgeon, with decision to perform surgery tomorrow

_____   **5.** Office consultation as preoperative clearance for surgery

_____   **6.** Postoperative management of vaginal hysterectomy

_____   **7.** Repeat gallbladder X-ray series, same physician

_____   **8.** Arthroscopy of right elbow and closed fracture reduction of left wrist

_____   **9.** Needle core biopsy of right and left breasts

_____   **10.** Consultation required by payer

National Correct Coding Initiative (NCCI)

To promote national correct coding methodologies and control the improper assignment of codes that results in inappropriate reimbursement of Medicare Part B claims, the Centers for Medicare & Medicaid Services (CMS) implemented the **National Correct Coding Initiative (NCCI)**. NCCI edits (Table 8-3) are used to process Medicare Part B claims for hospital outpatient and physiican services, and NCCI coding policies are based on the following:

• Analysis of standard medical and surgical practice

• Coding conventions included in CPT

Table 8-3 Partial Listing of National Correct Coding Initiative (NCCI) Edits

NCCI Edit	Description	Disposition of Claim
1	Invalid diagnosis code	Return to Provider
2	Diagnosis and age conflict	Return to Provider
3	Diagnosis and sex conflict	Return to Provider
4	Medicare secondary payer alert	Suspend
19	Mutually exclusive procedure that is not allowed by CCI even if appropriate modifier is present	Line Item Rejection
20	Component of a comprehensive procedure that is not allowed by CCI even if appropriate modifier is present	Line Item Rejection
39	Mutually exclusive procedure that would be allowed by CCI if appropriate modifier were present	Line Item Rejection
40	Component of a comprehensive procedure that would be allowed by CCI if appropriate modifier were present	Line Item Rejection

- Coding guidelines developed by national medical specialty societies (e.g., CPT advisory committee, which contains representatives of major medical societies)

- Local and national coverage determinations

- Review of current coding practices

 The NCCI was initially developed for use by Medicare administrative contractors (MACs) that process Medicare Part B claims for physician office services. NCCI edits were added to the Outpatient Code Editor (OCE) in August 2000, and they are used by MACs to process Medicare Part B claims for outpatient hospital services. (Some OCE edits that apply to outpatient hospital services claims differ from comparable edits in the NCCI used to process physician office services claims.)

Note:

Locate Medlearn articles that contain OCE updates by going to http://www.cms.hhs.gov and clicking on the Outreach & Education link, then clicking on the MLN Matters Articles link.

 Note:

In 2010, 23 Medicare Administrative Contractors (MACs) replaced the 23 fiscal intermediaries (FIs) that processed hospital inpatient and outpatient claims for Medicare Part A and Part B services and 17 Medicare carriers that processed physician claims for Medicare Part B services. MACs process both hospital inpatient/outpatient and physician Medicare Part A and Part B claims, and are abbreviated as A/B MACs. In addition MACs also process durable medical equipment claims and home health/hospice claims, abbreviated as DME MACs and HH&H MACs, respectively. (Although FIs and carriers continue to be referenced on government and private websites and newsletters, MACs replaced both entities in 2010.)

Carefully review parenthetical notes below CPT code descriptions to locate procedures that are separately reported (in addition to the major procedure performed). When reporting codes for outpatient hospital services and physician office services, make sure you use OCE software or NCCI software, respectively, to identify bundled codes for procedures and services considered necessary to accomplish the major procedure. Bundled procedure codes are *not* separately coded and reported with the major procedure code. Reporting bundled procedure codes in addition to the major procedure code is characterized as unbundling (fraud). The OCE edits are packaged with commercial software, such as Ingenix's Encoder Pro Expert. The NCCI edits are available at http://cms.hhs.gov. Click on the Medicare link, scroll down to the Coding heading, and click on the National Correct Coding Initiative Edits. (The OCE and NCCI edits are available for purchase from the National Technical Information Service (NTIS) at http://www.ntis.gov)

CMS POSTS CORRECT CODING INITIATIVE (CCI) EDITS ON INTERNET

The Centers for Medicare & Medicaid Services (CMS) has made it easier for physicians and other providers to bill properly and be paid promptly for their services to people with Medicare coverage. CMS has posted on its website (http://cms.hhs.gov/physicians/cciedits) the automated edits used to identify questionable claims and adjust payments to reflect what would have been paid if the claim had been filed correctly. The edits, known as the National Correct Coding Initiative (NCCI), identify pairs of services that normally should not be billed by the same physician for the same patient on the same day. The NCCI also promotes uniformity among the contractors that process Medicare claims in interpreting Medicare payment policies.

The posting of NCCI edits is the most recent in a series of steps CMS has taken to use the Internet creatively to reduce the regulatory burden on physicians and make it easier for them to work with Medicare to improve services to beneficiaries. CMS has also added a feature to its website (http://cms.hhs.gov/physicians) that makes it possible for physicians to determine in advance what they will be paid for a particular service or range of services. The Medicare Physician Fee Schedule Look-Up provides the unadjusted payment rates as well as the payment rates by geographic location.

While the NCCI is a cornerstone of efforts to ensure that Medicare and beneficiaries do not pay twice for the same service or for duplicative services, CMS believes physicians should have easy access to the edits used to identify incorrect claims. The NCCI includes two types of edits:

- **Column 1/column 2 edits:** Code pairs that should not be billed together because one service inherently includes the other; previously called comprehensive/component edits

- **Mutually exclusive edits:** Code pairs that, for clinical reasons, are unlikely to be performed on the same patient on the same day (e.g., two different types of testing that yield equivalent results)

CPT codes representing services denied based on NCCI edits may not be billed to Medicare beneficiaries. Since these denials are based on incorrect coding rather than medical necessity, the provider cannot submit an *Advanced Beneficiary Notice (ABN)* to seek payment from a Medicare beneficiary. An ABN is a form completed and signed by a Medicare beneficiary each time a provider believes a normally covered service will not be covered *and* the provider wants to bill the beneficiary directly for the service. In addition, because the denials are based on incorrect coding (rather than a legislated Medicare benefit exclusion), the provider *cannot* seek payment from the beneficiary even if a Notice of Exclusions from Medicare Benefits (NEMB) was obtained.

A **Notice of Exclusions from Medicare Benefits (NEMB)** is a form completed and signed by a Medicare beneficiary before items, procedures, and services excluded from Medicare benefits are provided; it alerts Medicare beneficiaries in advance that Medicare does not cover certain items and services because they do not meet the definition of a Medicare benefit or because they are specifically excluded by law. NEMB is completed when an ABN is not appropriate.

The NCCI edits, which are updated quarterly, were previously available to physicians and other providers on a paid subscription basis; but they are now available to anyone with a computer. The NCCI edits are posted as a spreadsheet that allows users to sort by procedural code and effective date. A *Find* feature allows users to look for a specific code. The NCCI edit files are also indexed by procedural code ranges to allow for easy navigation.

The new Web page also includes links to documents that explain the edits, including the following:

- Medicare Claims Processing Manual

- NCCI Edits Program Transmittals

- NCCI FAQs (frequently asked questions)

- NCCI Policy Manual for Part B MACs

(Permission to reuse in accordance with http://www.cms.hhs.gov Web site Content Reuse Policy.)

EXAMPLE: Code 67911 describes the "Correction of lid retraction." A parenthetical note below the code description advises that if autogenous graft materials are used during the same operative session, tissue graft codes 20920, 20922, or 20926 are reported in addition to code 67911.

According to the Medicare Code Editor (MCE), *other procedures necessary to accomplish* the "correction of lid retraction" are included in code 67911, such as full-thickness graft placement (15260). Other such procedures are not separately coded and reported when performed during the same operative session as the "correction of lid retraction."

Unbundling CPT Codes

Providers are responsible for reporting the CPT (and HCPCS level II) code that most comprehensively describes the services provided. NCCI edits determine the appropriateness of CPT code combinations for claims submitted to MACs. NCCI edits are designed to detect *unbundling*, which involves reporting multiple codes for a service when a single comprehensive code should be assigned. The practice of unbundling occurs because:

Note:

Additional content about the NCCI is located in Chapter 19.

- Provider's coding staff unintentionally reports multiple codes based on misinterpreted coding guidelines.

- The reporting of multiple codes is intentional and is done to maximize reimbursement.

Unbundling occurs when one service is divided into its component parts and a code for each component part is reported as if they were separate services.

EXAMPLE: A 64-year-old female patient undergoes total abdominal hysterectomy with bilateral salpingectomy and oophorectomy. Review CPT Surgery code descriptions for 58150, 58700, and 58720. Reporting codes 58700 and 58720 in addition to 58150 is considered unbundling. If all three codes were submitted on a claim, reimbursement for codes 58700 and 58720 would be disallowed (and the provider might be subject to allegations of fraud and abuse).

Unbundling occurs when a code for the separate surgical approach (e.g., laparotomy) is reported in addition to a code for the surgical procedure. Procedures performed to gain access to an area or organ system are not separately reported.

EXAMPLE: A 54-year-old female patient underwent excision of ileoanal reservoir with ileostomy, which required lysis of adhesions to gain access to the site of surgery. Review CPT Surgery code descriptions for 45136 and 44005. Report CPT code 45136 only because code 44005 is considered a component part of the total procedure (45136). Reporting both codes would be considered unbundling.

Exercise 8.9 – National Correct Coding Initiative

Instructions: Complete each statement.

1. To promote national correct coding methodologies and control the improper assignment of codes that result in inappropriate reimbursement of _____, CMS implemented the NCCI.

2. The NCCI was initially developed for use by Medicare administrative contractors (MACs) that process Medicare Part B claims for physician office services; and in August 2000, NCCI edits were added to the _____ for use by MACs to process Medicare Part B claims for outpatient hospital services.

3. The NCCI code pairs that should not be billed together because one service inherently includes the other are called _____ edits, while the NCCI code pairs that, for clinical reasons, are unlikely to be performed on the same patient on the same day are called _____ edits.

4. When a submitted claim for reimbursement is denied because of incorrect coding rather than medical necessity, the provider cannot submit a(n) _____ or a(n) _____ to seek payment from a Medicare beneficiary.

5. A 34-year-old male underwent upper gastrointestinal endoscopy, which included visualization of the esophagus, stomach, and duodenum. During endoscopy, brushings collected esophageal specimens and esophageal biopsy was performed. Upon review of CPT Surgery code descriptions for 43235 and 43239, the coder assigned 43239 only (because 43235 is considered a component of the total procedure, 43239). Reporting both codes would be considered _____.

Summary

CPT codes are reported for services and procedures provided by home health care and hospice agencies, outpatient hospital departments, physicians who are employees of a health care facility, and physicians who see patients in their offices or clinics and in patients' homes. To promote national correct coding methodologies and to control the improper assignment of codes that result in inappropriate reimbursement of Medicare Part B claims, the Centers for Medicare & Medicaid Services (CMS) implemented the National Correct Coding Initiative (NCCI).

CPT organizes Category I procedures and services into six sections: Evaluation and Management (E/M), Anesthesia, Surgery, Radiology (including Nuclear Medicine and Diagnostic Ultrasound), Pathology and Laboratory, and Medicine. The CPT index is organized by alphabetical main terms printed in boldface, and appendices are located between the Medicine section and the index.

Symbols are located throughout the CPT coding book. A bullet (•) located to the left of a code number identifies new procedures and services added to CPT. A triangle (▲) located to the left of a code number identifies a code description that has been revised. Horizontal triangles (►◄) surround revised guidelines and notes. This symbol is *not* used for revised code descriptions. A semicolon (;) is used in CPT to save space. The plus symbol (✚) identifies add-on codes. The forbidden symbol (⊘) symbol identifies codes that are exempt from modifier -51. The bull's-eye symbol (⊙) indicates a procedure that includes conscious sedation. The flash symbol (↗) indicates codes that classify products pending FDA approval but that have been assigned a CPT code. The hollow circle symbol (○) indicates reinstated or recycled code. The number symbol (#) indicates out-of-sequence codes.

CPT Category I codes are organized according to six sections that are subdivided into subsections, categories, and subcategories. Guidelines, notes, and descriptive qualifiers are also found in CPT sections, subsections, categories, and subcategories. Two-digit modifiers are added to five-digit CPT codes to clarify services and procedures performed by providers.

Internet Links

CodingPro-L Listserv: *www.decisionhealth.com/codingpro-l-enroll*

Current Procedural Terminology: Go to *www.ama-assn.org* and scroll your mouse over the Professional Resources link, then click on the CPT link.

JustCoding.com: Go to *www.justcoding.com* and sign up for the free e-newsletter.

Medicare PFS look-up: Go to *www.cms.gov* and click on the Resources & Tools link, then click on the Medicare Physician Fee Schedule Look-Up link.

MedlinePlus: *www.medlineplus.gov*

National Correct Coding Initiative (NCCI) Edits: Go to *www.cms.gov* and click on the Medicare link. Scroll down to the Coding heading and click on the National Correct Coding Initiative Edits link.

Order CPT coding books online: *www.cengage.com*

RiteCode.com: Go to *www.ritecode.com* and click on the "Free Coding Quizzes" link.

Study Checklist

❏ Read this chapter and highlight key concepts.

❏ Create an index card for each key term.

❏ Access the chapter Internet links to learn more about concepts.

❏ Complete the chapter review, verifying answers with your instructor.

❏ Complete WebTutor assignments and take online quizzes.

❏ Complete Workbook chapter, verifying answers with your instructor.

❏ Go to *www.cengagebrain.com* to access StudyWARE™ and the Premium Website. Login instructions are located in the Preface and on the Printed Access Card.

❏ Form a study group with classmates to discuss chapter concepts in preparation for an exam.

Review

Multiple Choice

Instructions: Circle the most appropriate response.

1. Which mandated that CPT codes be reported for outpatient hospital surgical procedures?
   a. Health Insurance, Portability, and Accountability Act of 1996 (HIPAA)
   b. Healthcare Common Procedure Coding System (HCPCS)
   c. Medicare Prescription Drug, Improvement, and Modernization Act (MMA)
   d. Omnibus Budget Reconciliation Act (OBRA) of 1986

2. New, revised, and deleted CPT codes that are provided as an "early release" in July by the CPT Editorial Panel are intended to take effect:
   a. after the FDA approves the product.
   b. immediately upon "early release."
   c. 6 months later.
   d. within a 90-day grace period.

3. The E/M section is located at the beginning of CPT because these codes are:
   a. reported by all specialties.
   b. sequenced first on all claims.
   c. the most frequently reported.
   d. used to establish medical necessity.

4. *Arthroscopy, ankle*, and *wound* are examples of _____ in the CPT index.
   a. cross-references   b. main terms   c. qualifiers   d. subterms

5. Which is the best example of a CPT index cross-reference term?
   a. also   b. and   c. see   d. see also

6. When a range *or* series of single codes is listed in the CPT index for a procedure or service:
   a. a cross-reference will direct the coder to another index entry.
   b. each code must be verified in the CPT manual before a code is assigned.
   c. the range of codes is separated by a comma.
   d. the series of single codes is separated by a dash.

7. Codes identified throughout CPT with a forbidden (⊘) symbol are summarized in Appendix _____.
   a. C   b. D   c. E   d. F

8. Horizontal triangles (►◄):
   a. identify a code description that has been revised.
   b. mark revisions that are included in Appendix B.
   c. surround new procedures and services that have been added to CPT.
   d. surround revised guidelines and notes.

9. Codes identified with a plus symbol (+):
   a. are exempt from modifier -51.
   b. are reported as stand-alone codes.
   c. contain parenthetical notes.
   d. identify add-on codes.

10. A code identified by a bull's-eye symbol (◉) indicates that:
    a. anesthesia is considered medically necessary and payable.
    b. conscious sedation was administered by the physician performing an invasive procedure.
    c. general anesthesia was administered by an anesthesiologist.
    d. no other anesthesia procedures or services may be reported.

11. Which are located at the beginning of each CPT section, define terms, and explain the assignment of codes for procedures and services located in a particular section?
    a. descriptive qualifiers   c. notes
    b. guidelines   d. unlisted procedures or services

12. Which are typeset as a blocked unindented or a blocked indented parenthetical pattern?
    a. descriptive qualifiers   c. notes
    b. guidelines   d. unlisted procedures or services

13. Which requires the submission of a special report that describes the nature, extent, and need for the procedure or service?
    a. descriptive qualifier   c. note
    b. guideline   d. unlisted procedure or service

14. Which code is assigned for "unattended sleep study, interpretation only?"
    a. 95805   b. 95805-90   c. 95806   d. 95806-26

15. A patient was seeking loss-of-wages benefits due to injuries sustained in a motor vehicle accident. The insurance company requested a second opinion regarding injuries and sent the patient for an Independent Medical Exam (IME), where a level 3 outpatient consultation service was provided. The IME physician reviewed medical records from the emergency department, the primary care physician, and pain management center. The IME report was sent to the insurance company. Which code is assigned?
    a. 99243-26   b. 99243-32   c. 99243-77   d. 99243-90

16. A patient presented to the physician's office for removal of ten skin tags on his torso. During the procedure, the patient became anxious and the procedure was discontinued. No skin tags were removed. Which code is reported?
    a. 11200-52   b. 11200-53   c. 11200-73   d. 11200-74

17. The patient underwent osteotomy of cervical spine, anterior approach, single segment, by two surgeons. Which code is reported?
    a. 22220-62   b. 22220-66   c. 22220-80   d. 22220-81

18. The patient underwent a T7 index (total thyroxine) lab test, which was sent to an outside laboratory. Which code is reported?
    a. 84436-90   b. 84436-91   c. 84439-90   d. 84437-91

19. If payment of a service or procedure is denied based on National Correct Coding Initiative (NCCI) edits, the provider:
    a. can seek payment from a Medicare beneficiary if an Advanced Beneficiary Notice (ABN) or a Notice of Exclusions from Medicare Benefits (NEMB) is obtained.
    b. can seek payment from the beneficiary if a Notice of Exclusions from Medicare Benefits (NEMB) is obtained.
    c. can submit an Advanced Beneficiary Notice (ABN) to seek payment from a Medicare beneficiary.
    d. cannot seek payment from a Medicare beneficiary even if an Advanced Beneficiary Notice (ABN) or a Notice of Exclusions from Medicare Benefits (NEMB) is obtained.

20. National Correct Coding Initiative (NCCI) edits were developed to promote national correct coding methodologies and control the improper assignment of codes that results in inappropriate reimbursement of Medicare Part _____ claims.
    a. A   b. B   c. C   d. D

Coding Practice I—CPT Index

Instructions: Refer to the CPT index to respond to each case.

21. Patient underwent debridement of infected subcutaneous tissue, lower left leg. Use the CPT index to identify the following:
    Main term _____
    Subterm _____
    2nd qualifier _____
    3rd qualifier _____
    Code range _____

22. Patient underwent arthrodesis of the elbow. Use the CPT index to identify the following:
    Main term _____
    Subterm _____
    Code range _____

23. Patient underwent Kocher Pylorectomy. Use the CPT index to locate the cross-reference for the procedure. Then identify the main term, subterm, and code range.
    Main term _____
    Cross-reference _____
    Main term _____
    Subterm _____
    Code range _____

24. Patient underwent abdominal hysterectomy with resection of both ovaries due to malignancy. Use the CPT index to locate the following:
    Main term _____
    Subterm _____
    2nd qualifier _____
    Code range _____

25. Patient underwent PET scan, brain. Use the CPT index to locate the cross-reference for the procedure. Then identify the main term, subterm, and code range.

   Main term _____

   Cross-reference _____

   Main term _____

   Subterm _____

   Code range _____

Coding Practice II—CPT Appendices

Instructions: Refer to the CPT appendices to respond to each case.

26. A rheumatology practice manager gathers data on patients with osteoarthritis of the knee by reviewing 135 patient records from the past 6 months. Of the 135 patients, she determines that 100 patients use over-the-counter anti-inflammatory or analgesic medications to relieve pain. Refer to CPT Appendix H (by going to the AMA website at http://www.ama-assn.org, and clicking on the *CPT–Current Procedural Terminology link*) and identify the performance measure the manager is assessing. Then verify the code and description in the Category II Codes section of CPT.

   _____

27. A 25-year-old female presents to the clinic and undergoes genetic testing for Jackson-Weiss syndrome. Her twin sister has a 2-year-old child who was recently diagnosed with this syndrome. Refer to CPT Appendix I and identify the genetic testing category and modifier for Jackson-Weiss syndrome.

   Category _____

   Modifier _____

28. A patient undergoes repeat evaluation of radiculopathy, which includes two nerve conduction studies: an amplitude study and an F-wave study. Code 95903 is reported. Refer to the table on the last page of CPT Appendix J and locate *Radiculopathy* in Column 1. Then locate the number below the heading "Motor NCS With and/or Without F Wave." What is the maximum number of "nerve conduction studies" the patient can undergo?

   _____

29. The right internal carotid artery is a third-order branch of the innominate artery. The left external carotid artery is a second-order branch of the left common carotid artery. Refer to CPT Appendix L and identify the first-order artery from which third-order gastroduodenal and proper hepatic arteries branch?

   _____

30. A 55-year-old patient undergoes an esophagoscopy at an ambulatory surgical center. The patient is administered a mixture of midazolam and fentanyl for moderate (conscious) sedation. Code 43228 is assigned. Refer to CPT Appendix G to locate code 43228. Does code 43228 include moderate (conscious) sedation, or should a code from range 99143–99145 be assigned as a secondary code.

   _____

Coding Practice III—CPT Symbols

Instructions: Interpret the use of CPT symbols to respond to each case.

31. A 60-year-old patient presents to the physician's office for a vaccination, and the coder notices the flash (/\) precedes the code to be assigned. Explain the meeting of the flash (/\) symbol that precedes the code.

   _____

32. A 37-year-old female presents to a local hospital for the birth of her second child. After a difficult labor, the patient undergoes a cesarean section. The patient also undergoes a subtotal hysterectomy due to endometriosis. Codes 59510 and 59525-51 are reported. Refer to code 59525 and explain the meaning of the plus (+) symbol that precedes the code.

   _____

33. A patient undergoes a screening colonoscopy; during the procedure, several biopsies are taken of the splenic flexure and the transverse colon. Code 45380 is reported. Refer to code 45380 and explain the meaning of the bull's-eye (◉) symbol that precedes the code.

   _____

34. A patient presents to the emergency department (ED) following an accident in his garage. The patient was working under his car when the jack failed, and the car fell on the patient's chest. The patient requires 65 minutes of critical care time during which he is evaluated and undergoes emergency endotracheal intubation. The patient is admitted as an inpatient and scheduled for an exploratory laparotomy with possible splenectomy. Codes 99291 and 31500 are reported for the ED visit. Refer to code 31500 and explain the meaning of the forbidden (⊘) symbol that precedes the code.

   _____

35. Patient underwent initial closed treatment of a temporomandibular dislocation. Code 21480 is reported. Refer to code 21480 and explain the meaning of the semicolon (;) symbol in the code description.

   _____

Coding Practice IV—CPT Modifiers

Instructions: Assign CPT modifiers to each case.

36. A patient undergoes simple repair of multiple skin lacerations, left foot and toes. The patient also undergoes intermediate repair of left heel laceration. The patient is discharged home after suturing, bandaging, and placing in a soft cast. Codes assigned include 12041 and 12002. Refer to CPT Appendix A and identify the modifier that should be added to code 12002.

   _____

37. An 80-year-old male patient undergoes bilateral posterior packing of the nasal cavity. Code 30905 is assigned. Refer to CPT Appendix A and identify the modifier that should be added to code 30905.

   _____

38. A patient undergoes magnetic resonance imaging (MRI), lower left leg. Dr. Miller interprets the MRI and documents a report. What modifier is added to the CPT code reported for the MRI?

   _____

39. Patient underwent incision and drainage (I&D) of a Bartholin's gland abscess done on April 5. The global period is 30 days. The abscess recurred; on April 28, the patient underwent repeat I&D by the same surgeon. Code 56420 was reported for the procedure performed on April 5. What modifier is added to code 56420 for the procedure performed on April 28?

_____

40. A male patient underwent biopsy of the prostate gland on October 11, performed by Dr. Smith. The global period is zero days. The pathology results were of uncertain behavior; per the pathologist's recommendations, the patient underwent repeat biopsy on November 15, by Dr. Jones, to obtain a larger sample. Code 55700 was reported for the procedure performed on October 11. What modifier is added to code 55700 for the procedure performed on November 15?

_____

CPT Evaluation and Management

Chapter Outline

Overview of Evaluation and Management Section

Evaluation and Management Section Guidelines

Levels of Evaluation and Management Services

Evaluation and Management Categories and Subcategories

Chapter Objectives

At the conclusion of this chapter, the student should be able to:

- Define key terms.
- Explain the organization, format, and content of the CPT Evaluation and Management section.
- Interpret CPT Evaluation and Management section guidelines, coding notes, and modifiers.
- Select CPT evaluation and management levels of service for documented patient care.
- Assign CPT evaluation and management service codes for patient care.
- Add CPT and/or HCPCS level II modifiers to codes as appropriate.

Key Terms

care plan oversight services

chief complaint (CC)

clinical examples

comprehensive examination

comprehensive history

concurrent care

consultation

contributory components

coordination of care

counseling

critical care

critical illness or injury

detailed examination

detailed history

Documentation Guidelines for Evaluation and Management Services

emergency department service

established patient

expanded problem focused examination

expanded problem focused history

extent of examination

extent of history

face-to-face time

family history

history

history of present illness (HPI)

home services

hospital discharge service

hospital inpatient service

infant

inpatient neonatal and pediatric critical care and intensive service

intensivist

interfacility transport

intraservice time

key components

low birth weight

medical decision making (MDM)

nature of the presenting problem

neonate

new patient

newborn care services

observation service

office or other outpatient services

partial hospitalization

past medical history

pediatric critical care patient transport

physical examination

physician case management

place of service (POS)

preoperative clearance

preventive medicine services

problem focused examination

problem focused history

professional services

prolonged services

referral

review of systems (ROS)

social history

special evaluation and management services

standby service

system review

type of service (TOS)

unit/floor time

very low birth weight

Introduction ●

The Evaluation and Management (E/M) section (codes 99201–99499) is located at the beginning of the CPT coding manual because these codes describe services most frequently provided by physicians. This makes it easier to locate these frequently reported codes. Accurate assignment of E/M codes is essential to the success of a physician's practice because most of the revenue generated by the office is based on provision of these services. Before assigning E/M codes, make sure you review the guidelines (located at the beginning of the E/M section) and apply any notes (located below category and subcategory titles).

Most E/M services are cognitive services. This means that the provider must acquire information from the patient, use reasoning skills to process the information, interact with the patient to provide feedback, and respond by creating an appropriate plan of care. E/M services do *not* include significant procedural services (e.g., diagnostic tests or surgical procedures), which are coded separately. However, some services that arise directly from the E/M service provided are included (e.g., cleansing traumatic lesions, closing lacerations with adhesive strips, applying dressings, and providing counseling and educational services).

● **Coding Tip:**

Notes located beneath categories and/or subcategories apply to all codes in the categories or subcategories. Parenthetical notes that are located below a specific code apply to that code only unless the note indicates otherwise.

Overview of Evaluation and Management Section

CPT 1992 introduced the E/M level of service codes, replacing the office visit codes that were included in the Medicine section of past editions of CPT. The E/M section is organized according to place of service (POS) (e.g., office, hospital, home, nursing facility [NF], emergency department [ED], or critical care), type of service (TOS) (e.g., new or initial encounter, follow-up or subsequent encounter, or consultation), and miscellaneous services (e.g., prolonged physician service or care plan oversight service). The E/M level of service reflects the amount of work involved in providing health care to a patient, and correct coding requires determining the extent of history and examination performed as well as the complexity of medical decision making.

Documentation in the patient's chart must support the E/M level of service reported. CMS often refers to E/M codes by level numbers, and the level often corresponds to the last digit of the CPT code (e.g., 99204 is a level 4 E/M service).

Accurate assignment of E/M codes depends on (1) identifying the place of service (POS) and/or type of service (TOS) provided to the patient, (2) determining whether the patient is new or established to the practice, (3) reviewing the patient's record for documentation of level of service components, and (4) applying CMS's Documentation Guidelines for Evaluation and Management Services.

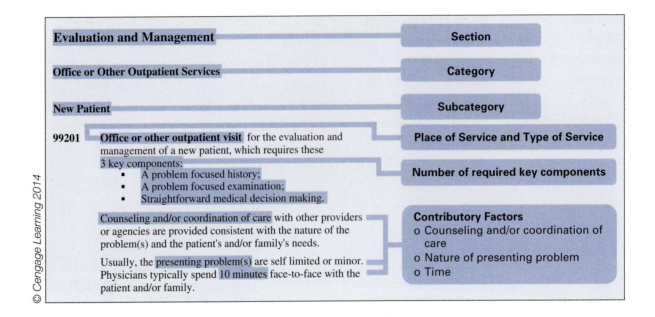

© Cengage Learning 2014

Place of Service (POS)

Place of service (POS) refers to the physical location where health care is provided to patients (e.g., office or other outpatient settings, hospitals, NFs, home health care, or EDs).

> **EXAMPLE 1:** The provider treated the patient in her office.
>
> *Place of Service:* Office
>
> *E/M Category:* Office or Other Outpatient Services

> **EXAMPLE 2:** The patient received care in the hospital's emergency department (ED).
>
> *Place of Service:* Hospital ED
>
> *E/M Category:* Emergency Department Services

 Note:

Refer to the Office or Outpatient Services category of E/M and notice that it contains two subcategories (New Patient and Established Patient). The New Patient subcategory contains five codes, and the Established Patient subcategory also contains five codes. Each code represents a level of E/M service ranked from lowest to highest level. CMS would consider E/M code 99201 a level 1 code.

Type of Service (TOS)

Type of service (TOS) refers to the kind of health care services provided to patients. It includes critical care, consultation, initial hospital care, subsequent hospital care, and confirmatory consultation.

> **EXAMPLE 1:** The patient underwent an annual physical examination in the provider's office.
>
> *Type of Service:* Preventive care
>
> *E/M Category:* Preventive Medicine Services

> **EXAMPLE 2:** The hospital inpatient was transferred to the regular medical-surgical unit where he was recovering from surgery. He suddenly stopped breathing and required respirator management by his physician.
>
> *Type of Service:* Critical care
>
> *E/M Category:* Critical Care Services

Sometimes *both the TOS and POS* must be identified before the proper code can be assigned.

EXAMPLE 1: Dr. Smith completed Josie Black's history and physical examination on the first day of her inpatient admission.

> *Place of Service:* Hospital
>
> *Type of Service:* Initial inpatient care
>
> *E/M Category:* Hospital Inpatient Services
>
> *E/M Subcategory:* Initial Hospital Care

EXAMPLE 2: Dr. Charles saw Josie Black (age 38) in her office to perform an annual physical examination.

> *Place of Service:* Office
>
> *Type of Service:* Preventive medicine
>
> *E/M Category:* Preventive Medicine Visits

Coding Tip:

The CPT Medicine section includes codes describing specialty services (e.g., ophthalmology, psychiatry) that require E/M. When codes for specialty services are reported, a separate E/M service from the CPT E/M section is *not* reported on the same date *unless a significant, separately identifiable E/M service was provided (and modifier -25 is attached).*

Exercise 9.1 – Overview of Evaluation and Management Section

Instructions: Use your CPT coding manual to complete each statement.

1. When a 49-year-old female patient is seen in the physician's office for an annual physical examination, the coder should refer to the E/M category entitled _____.

2. For a 24-year-old male patient who received immediate care in the hospital emergency room, the coder should refer to the E/M category entitled _____.

3. Codes for E/M levels of service reflect the amount of work involved in providing health care to a patient, and correct coding primarily involves determining the extent of _____ performed and the complexity of medical decision making.

4. CMS often refers to E/M codes by level numbers, and the level often corresponds to the last digit of the CPT code. Therefore, code 99215 is a level _____ service.

5. The physical location where health care is provided to patients is called the _____.

6. The kind of health care services provided to patients is called the _____.

7–10. Mary Smith was seen in her primary care provider's office two months ago when she underwent a routine physical examination. She returns today with complaints of severe abdominal pain and discomfort. Diagnostic testing revealed Crohn's disease, and a treatment plan was discussed. Identify each of the following for services provided to Mary Smith today.

> 7. Type of Service: _____
>
> 8. Place of Service: _____
>
> 9. E/M Category: _____
>
> 10. E/M Subcategory: _____

Evaluation and Management Section Guidelines

The E/M section guidelines are located at the beginning of the section and include the following contents:

- Classification of evaluation and management (E/M) services
- Definitions of commonly used terms
- Unlisted service
- Special report
- Clinical examples
- Instructions for selecting a level of E/M service

Classification of E/M Services

The E/M section of CPT is organized into categories, including office and other outpatient visits, hospital observation and inpatient services, consultations, and emergency department services. Many categories contain subcategories (e.g., new and established patients and team conferences and telephone calls). Each category of E/M contains five-digit numerical codes ranging from 99201 to 99499; most code descriptions include the place and/or type of service, content of service (e.g., detailed history and detailed examination), nature of presenting problem, and time typically required to provide the service. E/M codes classify provider services according to the extent of work (e.g., counseling, history, or physical) and the intensity of the medical encounter (e.g., complexity of medical decision making). This means that a provider who performs and documents extensive work in the diagnosis and treatment of a patient (e.g., comprehensive history and examination, and medical decision making of high complexity) can assign a higher-level E/M code than a provider who performs and documents less extensive work.

Assigning E/M codes can be difficult and confusing; although guidelines and notes include definitions and instructions for selecting codes, they were perceived as insufficient to guarantee consistent coding by providers and reliable medical review by payers. In response, CMS developed **Documentation Guidelines for Evaluation and Management Services**, which explain how E/M codes are assigned according to elements associated with comprehensive multisystem and single-system examinations. The first set of guidelines created by CMS in 1995 was criticized by providers as containing unclear criteria for single-system examinations. CMS then created an alternative set of guidelines in 1997, which was also criticized as being confusing and requiring extensive counting of services and other elements. CMS, therefore, instructed Medicare administrative contractors to use both sets of guidelines when reviewing records, and providers were instructed to use whichever set of guidelines was most advantageous to their practice reimbursement. (The American Medical Association (AMA) continues to work with CMS to develop an acceptable approach for classifying E/M services.)

Definitions of Commonly Used Terms

The E/M guidelines organize definitions of commonly used terms in alphabetical order (except for new and established patient terms). The following terms are discussed below:

- New and established patient
- Concurrent care

The following terms are discussed under the "Levels of Evaluation and Management Services" Section in this chapter:

- Key components
  - History
    - Chief complaint
    - History of present illness
    - Family history

- Past history
- Social history
- System review (review of systems)
  - Examination
  - Medical decision making
- Contributory components
  - Counseling
  - Coordination of care
  - Nature of presenting problem
  - Time

New and Established Patient

A **new patient** is one who has *not* received any professional services from the physician or from another physician of the exact same specialty and subspecialty who belongs to the same group practice, within the past three years.

An **established patient** is one who *has* received professional services from the physician or from another physician of the same exact specialty and subspecialty who belongs to the same group practice, within the past three years.

Coding Tip:

- **Professional services** are face-to-face services provided by a physician or by nonphysician practitioners (e.g., nurse practitioner, physician assistant) and reported by assigning an E/M code.
- Definitions of new and established patients include professional services rendered by other physicians of the same specialty in the same group practice.
- CPT Evaluation and Management section guidelines contain a decision tree that can be used to determine new versus established patients.

EXAMPLE 1: Sally Dunlop had a prescription renewed by Dr. Smith's office on January 1, 2009, but she did not see the physician. She has been Dr. Smith's patient since her initial office visit on March 15, 2006. On December 1, 2009, Dr. Smith treated Sally during an office visit.

New Patient: March 15, 2006

New Patient: December 1, 2009

Although the patient had the prescription renewed on January 1, 2009, because there was no face-to-face service provided Sally Dunlop is considered a new patient for the December 1, 2009, visit.

EXAMPLE 2: Dr. Charles and Dr. Black share a practice. Dr. Charles is a general surgeon who treated Mary Smith in the office on July 1, 2009. Mary was first seen by the practice on February 15, 2006, when Dr. Black provided preventive care services to her. Mary returned to the practice on November 1, 2009, for her annual physical examination conducted by Dr. Black.

New Patient: February 15, 2006, and July 1, 2009.

Established Patient: November 1, 2009

EXAMPLE 3: Dr. Corey left Alfred Medical Group to join Buffalo Physician Group as a family practitioner. At Buffalo Physician Group, when Dr. Corey provides professional services to patients, are those patients considered new or established?

Answer: Patients who have not received professional services from Dr. Corey or another physician of the same specialty at Buffalo Physician Group are considered new. Patients who have been treated by another family practitioner at Buffalo Physician Group within the past three years are considered established. If any of Dr. Corey's patients from the Alfred Medical Group choose to seek care from him at the Buffalo Physician Group, they will be considered established patients.

Concurrent Care

Concurrent care is the provision of similar services, such as hospital inpatient visits, to the same patient by more than one provider on the same day. CMS permits the provision of concurrent care by two or more providers on the same day even if the providers are of the same specialty. To avoid reimbursement denials by third-party payers and Medicare administrative contracts, the attending physician is to add modifier -A1 (Principal Physician of Record) to the E/M code reported. When possible, each provider should also report different ICD-9-CM diagnosis codes from those reported by other providers who provide E/M services to the patient on the same day.

> **EXAMPLE:** Laurie Birch was admitted to the hospital on October 5 for an acute myocardial infarction. On October 7, her attending physician (a cardiologist) wrote a physician's order requesting a psychiatrist to consult with the patient regarding her anxiety and depression. The cardiologist's insurance specialist should report the ICD code for "acute myocardial infarction" to justify inpatient E/M services provided to the patient (and add modifier -A1, Principal Physician of Record, to the CPT code reported). The psychiatrist's insurance specialist should report the ICD codes for "anxiety and depression" to justify inpatient consultation E/M services provided to the patient. If each provider reported the ICD code for "acute myocardial infarction," the provider who submitted the claim first would be reimbursed (and the other provider's claim would be denied).

Unlisted Service

An unlisted service code is assigned when the provider furnishes an E/M service for which there is no CPT code. When an unlisted procedure or service code is reported, a special report (e.g., copy of documented encounter note record) must accompany the claim to describe the nature of, extent of, and need for the procedure or service.

> **Coding Tip:**
>
> Medicare and third-party payers often require providers to report HCPCS level II national codes (if available) instead of unlisted procedure or service CPT codes.

Special Report

When an unlisted service code is reported, a special report must be submitted with the insurance claim to demonstrate medical appropriateness. The provider should document the following elements in the special report:

- Complexity of patient's symptoms
- Description of nature of, extent of, and need for service
- Diagnostic and therapeutic procedures performed
- Follow-up care
- Patient's final diagnosis and concurrent problems
- Pertinent physical findings
- Time, effort, and equipment required to provide the service

Clinical Examples

Appendix C of the CPT coding manual contains **clinical examples** of E/M service codes. Along with a careful review of the E/M code descriptions, they assist providers in selecting the appropriate code for documented E/M services. The AMA cautions providers that the clinical examples "do not encompass the entire scope of medical practice." They can be used in addition to documented key components (history, examination, and/or medical decision making) that are required to determine a particular level of service.

Exercise 9.2 – Evaluation and Management Section Guidelines

Instructions: Complete each statement.

1. Tim Turner was seen by Dr. Chambers on February 5 of this year for follow-up of his type 2 diabetes mellitus. Tim has been Dr. Chambers' patient since 1984, when he was seen for an initial visit. Tim returned to the office each year since 1984 for an annual physical examination until last year, when he was diagnosed with type 2 diabetes mellitus. Since then, Tim has returned for a recheck office visit with Dr. Chambers every three months. Tim is considered a(n) _____ (new or established) patient for Dr. Chambers' practice.

2. Kristin Broome was seen by Dr. Marlot on March 8 six years ago for treatment of influenza. She returned on January 5 one year later for her annual physical examination, which included a prescription for birth control pills. Kristin called the office on April 10 of that same year to request that the local pharmacy be called so she could receive a refill of her birth control pills. Dr. Marlot called in the prescription that afternoon. Kristin next returned to the office on April 15 of this year for an annual physical examination. Kristin is considered a(n) _____ (new or established) patient for Dr. Marlot's practice.

3. Dr. Peterson, Dr. Slatterly, and Dr. Vaughan are members of the Medex Pediatric Group Practice. Eric Webb is a 15-year-old boy who was initially seen by Dr. Vaughan on August 5 of last year for a sports physical. Eric returned to the office on September 10 of this year and was seen by Dr. Peterson for treatment of an ear infection. Eric is considered a(n) _____ (new or established) patient for Dr. Peterson's practice.

4-5. Sandy Tyler was admitted to the hospital on July 4 for treatment of a fractured pelvis, which he sustained while parasailing earlier in the day. On July 5, his attending physician (an orthopedic surgeon) wrote a physician's order requesting a neurologist to consult with the patient regarding numbness of his left foot.

4. Which diagnosis should the orthopedic surgeon report to justify inpatient E/M services?

_____

5. Which diagnosis should the neurologist report to justify inpatient E/M consultation services?

_____

Levels of Evaluation and Management Services

E/M categories and subcategories contain codes that are classified according to level of services for reporting to third-party payers. Although the last number of some E/M codes represents the level of service (e.g., code 99213 is a level 3 E/M service), the levels within categories and subcategories are not interchangeable. Levels of E/M services include conferences with or about patients, evaluations, examinations, preventive adult and pediatric health supervision, treatments, and other medical services (e.g., determining the need for and/or location of appropriate care, such as hospice care for a terminally ill patient).

Coding Tip:

- CPT code 99201 classifies a level 1 office or other outpatient service reported for new patients, and it includes a problem focused history and examination and straightforward medical decision making.

- CPT code 99211 classifies a level 1 office or other outpatient service reported for established patients, but it is reported when the physician's presence may not be required (e.g., office nurse takes patient's blood pressure and records it in the record).

- The CPT code that classifies a problem focused history and examination and straightforward medical decision making is 99212, a level 2 office or other outpatient service.

Typically, just one E/M code is reported each day by a provider who provides outpatient services. When a separately identifiable E/M service is provided in addition to a surgical procedure, the E/M code is reported with modifier -25.

Coding Tip:

- When more than one provider furnishes E/M services to the same patient on the same day, CPT classifies that as concurrent care.
- Medicare no longer processes claims that include Consultation subsection codes. Thus, when *inpatient* E/M services are performed by more than one provider on the same date of service, to ensure payment, the attending physician adds modifier -A1 (Principal Physician of Record) to the E/M code reported.

EXAMPLE 1: A physician sutured a patient's 2.5-cm scalp wound in the ED and performed a comprehensive neurological history and exam of the patient. The patient had sustained head trauma as the result of a car accident, and EMT personnel documented that he had been unconscious at the scene. Medical decision making was of high complexity. Report code 12001 for the simple repair of the scalp wound, and report code 99285-25 for the E/M service provided.

EXAMPLE 2: A physician sutured a 5-cm laceration of a patient's left hand and confirmed that the patient was up to date regarding tetanus toxoids immunization status. Report code 12002 for the simple repair of the skin laceration, hand. Do not report an E/M code because the patient was not evaluated other than for confirmation of her tetanus immunization status.

The levels of E/M services code descriptions include seven components, six of which determine the level of E/M service code to be assigned:

- History
- Examination
- Medical decision making
- Counseling
- Coordination of care
- Nature of presenting problem
- Time

The **key components** of history, examination, and medical decision making are required when selecting an E/M level of service code. **Contributory components** include counseling, coordination of care, nature of presenting problem, and time; and they are used to select the appropriate E/M service code when patient record documentation indicates that they were the focus of the visit.

Key Components

E/M code selection is based on three key components:

- Extent of history
- Extent of examination
- Complexity of medical decision making

All three key components must be considered when assigning codes for new patients. For established patients, two of the three key components must be considered. This means that documentation in the patient's chart must support the key components used to determine the E/M code selected.

The E/M code reported to a payer must be supported by documentation in the patient's record (e.g., SOAP or clinic note, diagnostic test results, or operative findings). Although providers are responsible for selecting the E/M code at the time patient care is rendered, insurance specialists audit records to make sure that the appropriate level of E/M code was reported to the third-party payer.

Extent of History

A **history** is an interview of the patient that includes the following elements: history of present illness (HPI) (including the patient's chief complaint, CC), a **review of systems (ROS)**, and a past-/family/social history (PFSH) (Table 9-1). The **extent of history** (Figure 9-1A) is categorized according to four types:

- **Problem focused history**: Chief complaint, brief history of present illness or problem.
- **Expanded problem focused history**: Chief complaint, brief history of present illness, problem pertinent system review.
- **Detailed history**: Chief complaint, extended history of present illness, problem pertinent system review extended to include a limited number of additional systems, pertinent past/family/social history directly related to patient's problem.
- **Comprehensive history**: Chief complaint, extended history of present illness, review of systems directly related to the problem(s) identified in the history of the present illness in addition to a review of all additional body systems, complete past/family/social history.

Table 9-1 History Elements, Definitions, and Examples

History Element	Definition	Example
Chief complaint (CC)	Patient's description of medical condition stated in the patient's own words.	**EXAMPLE:** Patient states, "My knee gives out, and it really hurts when I walk."
History of present illness (HPI)	Chronological description of patient's present condition from time of onset to present. HPI should include location, quality, severity, duration of the condition, and associated signs and symptoms.	**EXAMPLE:** Patient states that for the past several months, his left knee has caused discomfort, especially when walking. Previous evaluation resulted in a diagnosis of probable torn cartilage. Today the knee is very bruised, and the patient complains of severe pain that started one week ago and is constant. The knee is painful when the patient is either resting or walking. Nothing helps reduce the pain. The patient has taken prescription Motrin and has tried using a heating pad as well as an ice pack. He states that nothing helps. Patient denies current injury.
		Item / Documentation location — left knee quality — bruised, painful severity — extremely severe duration — one week timing — constant context — resting or walking modifying factors — nothing makes it better
Past medical history	Summary of past illnesses, operations, injuries, treatments, and known allergies.	**EXAMPLE:** Reveals a healthy individual who has been hospitalized in the past x3 for childbirth; the patient has no known allergies, has no history of diseases, and is not currently on any medications.
Family history	A review of the medical events in the patient's family, including diseases that may be hereditary or that may present a risk to the patient.	**EXAMPLE:** Patient states that father died at age 51 of heart disease and that mother is living and well.
Social history	An age-appropriate review of past and current activities such as daily routine, dietary habits, exercise routine, marital status, occupation, sleeping patterns, smoking, use of alcohol and other drugs, and sexual activities.	**EXAMPLE:** Patient has history of marijuana use as a teenager and currently drinks alcohol socially; previous history of smoking cigarettes (quit three years ago).

(continues)

Table 9-1 (*continued*)

History Element	Definition	Example
System review [ROS]	Inventory by systems to document subjective symptoms stated by the patient. Provides an opportunity to gather information that the patient may have forgotten to mention or that may have seemed unimportant. The ROS includes: • constitutional • cardiovascular • skin • gastrointestinal • head • genitourinary • eyes • musculoskeletal • ears • neurological • nose • endocrine • mouth • psychological • throat • hematologic/lymphatic • breasts • allergic/immunologic • respiratory	**EXAMPLE:** Respiratory: The patient denies shortness of breath. **NOTE:** Providers should not document *negative* or *normal* in response to ROS items. Instead, they should document a statement relative to the item. **NOTE:** The *constitutional* as performed during a system review includes nonspecific symptoms that indicate a person is unwell, such as general aches. During a physical examination, the *constitutional* includes the patient's vital signs (e.g., blood pressure, pulse, and respirations).

Extent of Examination

A **physical examination** (Table 9-2) is an assessment of the patient's organ (e.g., extremities) and body systems (e.g., cardiovascular). The **extent of examination** (Figure 9-1B) is categorized according to four types:

- **Problem focused examination**: A limited examination of the affected body area or organ system.

- **Expanded problem focused examination**: A limited examination of the affected body area or organ system and other symptomatic or related organ system(s).

- **Detailed examination**: An extended examination of the affected body area(s) and other symptomatic or related organ system(s).

- **Comprehensive examination**: A general multisystem examination or a complete examination of a single organ system.

Complexity of Medical Decision Making

Medical decision making (MDM) refers to the complexity of establishing a diagnosis and/or selecting a management option as measured by the:

- Number of diagnoses or management options.

- Amount and/or complexity of data to be reviewed.

- Risk of complications and/or morbidity or mortality.

Complexity of medical decision-making criteria (Figure 9-1C) reflects the provider's level of uncertainty, volume of data to review, and risk to the patient. Documentation in the patient's record includes:

- Laboratory, imaging, and other test results that are significant to the management of the patient care.

- List of known diagnoses as well as those that are suspected.

- Opinions of other physicians who have been consulted.

- Planned course of action for the patient's treatment (plan of treatment).

- Review of patient records obtained from other facilities.

The physician is responsible for determining the complexity of medical decision making, and that decision must be supported by documentation in the patient's chart. CPT includes a table in the E/M guidelines that can assist in

SELECTING EXTENT OF HISTORY: To select extent of history, review the following elements documented in the patient record. If an element is not documented, it cannot be considered when selecting the level of E/M service code.

■ History of Present Illness (HPI)
■ Review of Systems (ROS)
■ Past, Family, and Social History (PFSH)

HISTORY OF PRESENT ILLNESS (HPI): Review the patient's record, and for each documented HPI element listed below, enter an **x** in the box located in front of the element on this form.

☐ **Duration:** of pain/discomfort or illness; length of time condition has persisted (e.g., pain began 3 days ago)
☐ **Location:** of pain/discomfort (e.g., is pain diffuse/localized, unilateral/bilateral, does it radiate or refer?)
☐ **Quality:** a description of the quality of the symptom (e.g., is pain described as sharp, dull, throbbing, stabbing, constant, intermittent, acute or chronic, stable, improving or worsening)
☐ **Severity:** use of self-assessment scale to measure subjective levels (e.g., "on a scale of 1–10, how severe is the pain?"), or comparison of pain quantitatively with previously experienced pain
☐ **Timing:** establishing onset of pain and chronology of pain development (e.g., migraine in the a.m.)
☐ **Context:** where was the patient and what was he doing when pain begins (e.g., was patient at rest or involved in an activity; was pain aggravated or relieved, or does it recur, with a specific activity; did situational stress or some other factor precede or accompany the pain)
☐ **Modifying factors:** what has patient attempted to do to relieve pain (e.g., heat vs. cold; does it relieve or exacerbate pain; what makes the pain worse; have over-the-counter drugs been attempted - with what results)
☐ **Associated signs/symptoms:** clinician's impressions formulated during the interview may lead to questioning about additional sensations or feelings (e.g., diaphoresis associated with indigestion or chest pain, blurred vision accompanying a headache, etc.)
_____ **Total Score:** Enter the number of **x**'s entered above. Place an **x** in front of the HPI type below.
     ☐ BRIEF HPI (1–3 elements)
     ☐ EXTENDED HPI (4 or more elements)

REVIEW OF SYSTEMS (ROS): Review the clinic or SOAP note in the patient's record, and for each documented ROS element listed below, enter an **x** in the box located in front of the element on this form.

☐ Constitutional symptoms	☐ Eyes	☐ Musculoskeletal
☐ Allergic or immunologic	☐ Gastrointestinal	☐ Neurologic
☐ Cardiovascular	☐ Genitourinary	☐ Psychiatric
☐ Ears, nose, throat, mouth	☐ Hematologic/Lymphatic	☐ Respiratory
☐ Endocrine	☐ Integumentary	

_____ **Total Score:** Enter the number of **x**'s entered above. Place an **x** in front of the ROS type below.
     ☐ NONE
     ☐ PROBLEM PERTINENT ROS (1 body system documented)
     ☐ EXTENDED ROS (2–9 body systems documented)
     ☐ COMPLETE ROS (all body systems documented)

PAST, FAMILY AND/OR SOCIAL HISTORY (PFSH): Review the clinic or SOAP note in the patient's record, and for each documented PFSH element (below), enter an **x** in the box located in front of the element on this form.
☐ Past history (current medications, drug allergies, immunizations, and prior illnesses/ injuries, hospitalizations, surgeries)
☐ Family history (health status/cause of death of relatives, specific disease related to CC, HPI, ROS, hereditary diseases for which patient is at risk)
☐ Social history (alcohol use, current employment, illicit drug use, level of education, nutritional status, occupational history, sexual history, tobacco use)

_____ **Total Score:** Enter the number of **x**'s entered above. Place an **x** in front of the PFSH type below.
     ☐ NONE
     ☐ PERTINENT PFSH (1 history area documented)
     ☐ COMPLETE PFSH (2 or 3 history areas documented)

Circle the type of HPI, ROS and PFSH. Select the Extent of History. (Note: 3 of 3 elements must be met or exceeded.)

HPI	Brief	Brief	Extended	Extended
ROS	None	Problem Pertinent	Extended	Complete
PFSH	None	None	Pertinent	Complete
EXTENT OF HISTORY	PROBLEM FOCUSED	EXPANDED PROBLEM FOCUSED	DETAILED	COMPREHENSIVE

Figure 9-1A Extent of history

Table 9-2 Physical Examination Elements and Examples

Element	Example
General Survey	Reveals well-developed, somewhat obese, elderly, white male in severe distress with severe substernal discomfort and pain in upper arms. Conscious. Alert. Appears to be stated age. No deformity. Patient cannot sit or stand still because he is in such agony. Gait affected only by pain; otherwise it is normal. Carriage normal. Age 67. Sex male. Height 5'11". Weight 188 lbs. Temperature 98.0°F orally. Pulse 56 and regular. Blood pressure 150/104.
Skin	Reveals pale, cool, moist surface with no cyanosis or jaundice. No eruption. No tumors.
Head	Hair, scalp, skull within normal limits. Facies anxious.
Eyes	Pupils round, regular, equal. Pupils react normally to light and accommodation. Extraocular muscles intact. Corneae, sclerae, conjunctivae clear. Fields intact. Ophthalmoscopic examination reveals fundi discs to be well outlined.
Ears	Examination reveals grossly intact hearing. No lateralization. External canals and ears, and left membrana tympanica clear. No tumor.
Nose and Sinuses	Inspection reveals grossly intact sense of smell. No deformity. No tenderness. Septum benign. Only residual mucous in both nostrils. No tumor. Sinuses within normal limits.
Mouth	Mouth edentulous. Lips, gums, buccal mucosa, and tongue within normal limits.
Throat	Examination reveals posterior oropharynx and tonsils to be very red and inflamed. Palate and uvula benign. Larynx not visualized.
Neck	Reveals cervical structures to be supple with no masses, scars, or abnormal glands or pulsations.
Chest	Chest inspection reveals it to have normal expansion. Thorax observation reveals it to be somewhat obese but with normal shape and symmetry without swellings or tumors or significant lymphadenopathy. Respiratory motions normal. Palpable tactile fremitus physiologically normal.
Breasts	Felt to be symmetrical and without masses or tenderness. Nipples normal. No axillary lymphadenopathy.
Lungs	Investigation reveals lungs clear on inspection, palpation, percussion, and auscultation.
Heart	Examination reveals heart to be indicated as normal since the area of cardiac dullness is normal is size, shape, and location. Heart rate slow. Rhythm regular. No accentuation of A2 and P2.
Abdomen	Appearance is slightly obese with no striae. Has a well-healed herniorrhaphy scar on the right inguinal area. No tenderness, guarding, rigidity, or rebound phenomena. No abnormal abdominal masses palpable. No organomegaly. No distention. No herniae. Bowel sounds are normal.
Genitalia	Reveals male type and circumcised penis. Scrotum, testes, and epididymes appear to be normal in size, shape, and color without skin lesions or tumors.
Rectal	Inspection proves sphincter tone good. Lumen clear. Hemorrhoids, internal and external, found on examination.
Extremities	Examination reveals no loss of motor function of the extremities or back. Patient can sit, stand, squat, and walk although it causes excruciating pain and this is in the substernal chest area. Patient advised to avoid doing these things. No evidence of injury. No paralysis. Patient squirms and moves constantly in his agony. He cannot sit long nor can he stand in one position. Extremities exam reveals them to be intact. Shoulder girdle inspection reveals no tenderness, muscle spasms, or abnormality or motion. No crepitation. Examination of the back reveals a slight infected and tender pilonidal cyst over the sacrum. No deformity or limitation of motion of the back noted. No other tenderness. Arms, hands, legs, and feet investigation reveals no deformity, fracture, dislocations, injury, tremors, atrophic muscles, swelling, tenderness, muscle spasms, or abnormality of motion.
Lymphatics	System check reveals lymph glands to be normal throughout.
Blood Vessels	Investigation reveals veins to be normal. Arteries are arteriosclerotic and all peripheral pulses are palpable and undiminished.
Neurological	Examination reveals the patient generally conscious, cooperative, mentally alert, and reasonably intelligent, although he seems to be somewhat confused. Cranial nerves intact. Superficial and deep tendon reflexes intact and equal bilaterally. No pathological reflexes. No abnormality of the sensory perception or of the associated movements, or of the autonomic or endocrine systems felt to be due to neurological disorder. IMPRESSION: Acute myocardial infarction. Essentials hypertension. Arteriosclerosis. Pilonidal cyst with mild infection. Internal and external hemorrhoids. NOTE: Impression is documented at the end of a history and physical examination report. It is not an element of the physical examination

SELECTING EXTENT OF EXAMINATION: To select the level of examination, first determine whether a *single organ examination* (e.g., specialist exam, such as ophthalmologist) or a *general multisystem examination* (e.g., family practitioner) was completed.

SINGLE ORGAN SYSTEM EXAMINATION: Refer to single organ system examination requirements in CMS's *Documentation Guidelines for Evaluation and Management Services.* Place an **x** in front of the appropriate exam type below.

☐ PROBLEM FOCUSED EXAMINATION (1–5 elements identified by a bullet)

☐ EXPANDED PROBLEM FOCUSED EXAMINATION (at least 6 elements identified by a bullet)

☐ DETAILED EXAMINATION (at least 12 elements identified by a bullet)

☐ COMPREHENSIVE EXAMINATION (all elements identified by a bullet; document every element in each box with a shaded border and at least 1 element in each box with an unshaded border)

NOTE: for eye and psychiatric examinations, at least 9 elements in each box with a shaded border and at least 1 element in each box with a shaded or unshaded border is documented

GENERAL MULTISYSTEM EXAM: Refer to the general multisystem examination requirements in CMS's *Documentation Guidelines for Evaluation and Management Services.* Place an **x** in front of the organ system or body area for up to the total number of allowed elements (e.g., up to 2 marks can be made for the Neck exam).

☐ Constitutional (2)   ☐ Gastrointestinal (5)   ☐ Psychiatric (4)
☐ Cardiovascular (7)   ☐ Genitourinary (M–3; F–6)   ☐ Respiratory (4)
☐ Chest (Breasts) (2)   ☐ Musculoskeletal (6)   ☐ Skin (2)
☐ Eyes (3)   ☐ Neck (2)
☐ Ears, nose, mouth, throat (6)   ☐ Neurologic (3)

_____ **Total Score:** Enter the number of **x**'s entered above. Place an **x** in front of the Examination type below.

☐ PROBLEM FOCUSED EXAMINATION (1–5 elements identified by a bullet on CMS's *E/M Documentation Guidelines*)

☐ EXPANDED PROBLEM FOCUSED EXAMINATION (at least 6 elements identified by a bullet on CMS's *E/M Documentation Guidelines*)

☐ DETAILED EXAMINATION (at least 2 elements identified by a bullet from each of 6 organ systems or body areas or at least 12 elements identified by a bullet in 2 or more systems or areas, on CMS's *E/M Documentation Guidelines*)

☐ COMPREHENSIVE EXAMINATION (documentation of all elements identified by a bullet in at least 9 organ systems or body areas, and documentation of at least 2 elements identified by a bullet from each of 9 organ systems or body areas, on CMS's *E/M Documentation Guidelines*)

Figure 9-1B Extent of examination

determining complexity of medical decision making (Table 9-3). Once the key components for extent of history and examination are determined, the type of medical decision making can be selected, as follows:

- Straightforward
- Moderate complexity
- Low complexity
- High complexity

Assigning the E/M Code

Once the extent of history, extent of examination, and complexity of medical decision making are determined, select the appropriate E/M code (Figure 9-1D).

EXAMPLE: Use Figures 9-1A, 9-1B, 9-1C, and 9-1D and Table 9-3 to determine extent of history and examination and complexity of medical decision making for a patient who is seen by his general practitioner.

SUBJECTIVE: The patient is a 35-year-old established male patient seen today with a CC of severe snoring. He says that this has gone on for years and that he's finally ready to do something about it because he awakens during the night from it and his wife is also losing sleep from his snoring. He says that he wakes up in the morning feeling very tired and notices that he gets very tired during the day. ROS reveals allergies. He denies smoking or alcohol use. He is on no medications.

Criteria to Determine Minimal, Low, Moderate, and High Levels of Medical Decision Making

	Minimal	Low	Moderate	High
Number of Diagnoses	• One self-limited or minor problem (e.g., cold, insect bite)	• Two or more self-limited minor problems • One stable chronic illness (e.g., controlled hypertension) • Acute, uncomplicated illness or injury (e.g., allergic rhinitis, simple sprain)	• One or more chronic illnesses with mild exacerbation, progression, or side effects of treatment • Two or more stable chronic illnesses • Undiagnosed new problem with uncertain prognosis (e.g., breast lump) • Acute illness with systemic symptoms (e.g., pyelonephritis) • Acute complicated injury (e.g., head injury with unconsciousness)	• One or more chronic illnesses with severe exacerbation, progression, or side effects of treatment • Acute or chronic illnesses or injuries that pose a threat to life or bodily function (e.g., acute myocardial infarction) • An abrupt change in neurologic status (e.g., seizure)
Amount/ Complexity of Data to be Reviewed	• Lab tests requiring venipuncture • Chest X-ray • ECG/EEG • Urinalysis • Ultrasound • KOH prep	• Physiologic tests not under stress (e.g., pulmonary function tests) • Noncardiovascular imaging studies with contrast (e.g., barium enema) • Superficial needle biopsies • Clinical lab tests requiring arterial puncture • Skin biopsies	• Physiologic tests under stress (e.g., cardiac stress test) • Diagnostic endoscopies with no identified risk factors • Deep needle or incisional biopsies • Cardiovascular imaging studies with contrast and no identified risk factors • Obtain fluid from body cavity (e.g., thoracentesis)	• Cardiovascular imaging studies with contrast with identified risk factors • Cardiac electrophysiologic tests • Diagnostic endoscopies with identified risk factors • Discography
Management Options	• Rest • Gargles • Elastic bandages • Superficial dressings	• Over-the-counter drugs • Minor surgery with no identified risk factors • Physical therapy • Occupational therapy • IV fluids without additives	• Minor surgery with identified risk factors • Elective major surgery (open, percutaneous, or endoscopic) with no identified risk factors • Prescription drug management • Therapeutic nuclear medicine • IV fluids with additives • Closed treatment of fracture or dislocation without manipulation	• Elective major surgery (open, percutaneous, or endoscopic) with identified risk factors • Emergency major surgery (open, percutaneous, or endoscopic) • Parenteral controlled substances • Drug therapy requiring intensive monitoring for toxicity • Decision not to resuscitate or to de-escalate care because of poor prognosis

Figure 9-1C Complexity of medical decision making

EXAMPLE OF MEDICAL DECISION MAKING DOCUMENTATION

Review the progress note to identify:

- diagnoses documented.
- whether data were reviewed.
- management options available to treat the patient.
- any risk of complications, morbidity, or mortality.

PROGRESS NOTE

SUBJECTIVE: The patient states that she has had an upset stomach for the past five days, and that it just won't go away. The patient denies recent changes in dietary habits or activities. She states that she was recently notified by her son that he is getting a divorce, and she admits that she is very upset about this news.

OBJECTIVE: GI: Normal bowel sounds. No rigidity. Some pain upon deep organ palpation. No organomegaly. Upon review of the record, it was noted that the patient has not complained about this problem in the past.

ASSESSMENT: Dyspepsia due to anxiety.

PLAN: (1) Gaviscon Extra Strength Relief Formula Liquid, 2 to 4 teaspoonfuls 4 times a day after meals and at bedtime. Follow with half a glass or water or other liquid. (2) Referral to James Kaplan, PhD, Clinical Psychologist. (3) Follow-up appointment in one month.

Notice that documentation included a review of data and a diagnosis. However management options and risk of complications, morbidity or mortality were not documented.

OBJECTIVE: Blood pressure is 126/86. Pulse is 82. Weight is 185. EYES: Pupils equal, round, and reactive to light and accommodation; extraocular muscles intact. EARS & NOSE: Tympanic membranes normal; oropharynx benign. NECK: Supple without jugular venous distention, bruits, or thyromegaly. RESPIRATORY: Breath sounds are clear to percussion and auscultation. EXTREMITIES: Without edema; pulses intact.

ASSESSMENT: Possible sleep apnea.

PLAN: Patient to undergo sleep study in two weeks. Results to be evaluated by Dr. Jones, ENT specialist, to determine whether patient is candidate for laser-assisted uvuloplasty (LAUP) surgery.

Table 9-3 Complexity of Medical Decision Making

Two of Three Elements Must Be Met or Exceeded			
Number of Diagnoses or Management Options	Amount/Complexity of Data to be Reviewed	Risk of Complications and/or Morbidity/ Mortality	Medical Decision Making
Minimal	Minimal or none	Minimal	Straightforward
Limited	Limited	Low	Low complexity
Multiple	Moderate	Moderate	Moderate complexity
Extensive	Extensive	High	High complexity

Select the E/M code based on extent of history and examination and complexity of medical decision making:				
History	Problem focused	Expanded problem focused	Expanded problem focused	Detailed	Comprehensive
Examination	Problem focused	Expanded problem focused	Expanded problem focused	Detailed	Comprehensive
Medical Decision Making	Straightforward	Low complexity	Moderate complexity	Moderate complexity	High complexity

Go to the appropriate E/M category/subcategory, and select the code based upon the information above

Current Procedural Terminology © 2010 American Medical Association. All rights reserved.

Figure 9-1D E/M code selection based on extent of history, extent of examination, and complexity of medical decision making

To assign the E/M code, the following is determined:

- **NEW OR ESTABLISHED PATIENT:** This is an established patient.

- **EXTENT OF HISTORY:** HPI elements include quality, severity, timing, and context; extended HPI (four elements) is documented. ROS elements include allergic; problem pertinent ROS (one body system) is documented. PFSH elements include documentation of social history; pertinent PFSH (one history area) is documented for a score of 1. Because three out of three HPI/ROS/PFHS types must be selected to determine the higher-level extent of history, expanded problem focused history is assigned.

- **EXTENT OF EXAMINATION:** Constitutional (1), Eyes (1), ENT (2), Neck (1), Respiratory (1), Cardiovascular (1); expanded problem focused examination (six elements) is documented.

- **COMPLEXITY OF MEDICAL DECISION MAKING:** Undiagnosed new problem with uncertain prognosis is documented (possible sleep apnea). Although "physiologic test not under stress" (sleep study) is documented as being ordered, results are not reviewed by this provider. In addition, this provider will not follow through on management options because the patient is referred to an ENT specialist. Therefore, complexity of medical decision making is straightforward because two of three elements are required and just one element is documented.

- **E/M CODE ASSIGNED:** 99213 (Two of three key components are required.)

Contributory Components

The contributory components of counseling, coordination of care, nature of presenting illness, and time play an important role in selecting the E/M code when documentation in the patient record indicates that they were the focus of the visit. Counseling and/or coordination of care components drive CPT code selection only when they dominate the encounter (e.g., office visit), requiring that more than 50 percent of the provider's time be spent on such components. In such circumstances, the provider must be sure to carefully document these elements so as to support the higher-level code selected. (Some E/M code descriptions include notes about time and nature of the presenting problem to assist in determining the appropriate code number to report.)

Counseling

CPT defines **counseling** as it relates to E/M coding as a discussion with a patient and/or family concerning one or more of the following areas:

- Diagnostic results, impressions, and/or recommended diagnostic studies

- Prognosis

- Risks and benefits of management (treatment) options

- Instructions for management (treatment) and/or follow-up

- Importance of compliance with chosen management (treatment) options

- Risk factor reduction

- Patient and family education

Providers typically select the level of E/M code based on extent of history and examination and complexity of medical decision making. However, some patients require counseling services (e.g., nutrition instruction, smoking cessation, and weight management) during an E/M visit. If provided, such counseling should be properly documented and the appropriate level of E/M code selected.

Note:

The E/M CodeBuilder located in Appendix I will help you to select the correct E/M code.

Coding Tip:

Do not confuse E/M counseling with psychotherapy. Psychotherapy codes are located in the CPT Medicine section and are reported for behavioral health modification or the treatment of mental illness.

EXAMPLE: Sherry Salins is a 52-year-old established female patient who was diagnosed with type 2 diabetes mellitus five years ago. She has never been able to control her diabetes with diet and exercise alone and was prescribed oral insulin upon onset. During today's expanded problem focused history and examination E/M office visit, Sherry informed me that she is determined to reduce the amount of oral insulin she takes daily, and she requested nutrition instruction and weight counseling. I subsequently spent 45 minutes (of the 70-minute office visit) discussing the fundamentals of nutrition and weight as related to diabetes mellitus. Sherry is scheduled to return in one month for recheck, and she was provided with a referral to a nutritionist as well as a weight counselor.

The patient received 45 minutes of counseling services *in addition to the expanded problem focused E/M service (code 99213), which was 25 minutes in length*. The 45 minutes of additional time represents more than 50 percent of the time associated with the total 70-minute office visit. Thus, code 99215 is reported because its description states *40 minutes face-to-face time with patient*.

Coordination of Care

When the physician makes arrangements with other providers or agencies for services to be provided to a patient, this is called **coordination of care**.

EXAMPLE: Dr. Smith writes a discharge order for inpatient Carol Clark to be discharged home and to receive home health care. Dr. Smith spends 30 minutes contacting the home health agency to make the appropriate arrangements for the patient and instructing the hospital to send copies of the patient's record to the home health care agency.

Nature of the Presenting Problem

CPT defines **nature of the presenting problem** as "a disease, condition, illness, injury, symptom, sign, finding, complaint, or other reason for the encounter, with or without a diagnosis being established at the time of the encounter." The *nature of the presenting problem* is considered when determining the number of diagnoses or management options for medical decision making complexity (Table 9-3). Five types of presenting problems are recognized:

> **Note:**
>
> Time spent with the patient (and/or persons responsible for the patient) is the key factor to selecting a level of E/M services *when counseling and/or coordination of care consists of more than 50% of face-to-face time*. The extent of counseling and/or coordination of care must be documented in the patient record.

- *Minimal*: A problem may not require the presence of the physician, but service is provided under the physician's supervision (e.g., patient who comes to the office once a week to have blood pressure taken and recorded).

- *Self-limited or minor*: A problem that runs a definite and prescribed course, is transient in nature, and is not likely to permanently alter health status or that has a good prognosis with management/compliance (e.g., patient diagnosed with adult-onset diabetes mellitus controlled by diet and exercise).

- *Low severity*: A problem where the risk of morbidity without treatment is low; there is little to no risk of mortality without treatment; full recovery without functional impairment is expected (e.g., patient diagnosed with eczema that does not respond to over-the-counter medications).

- *Moderate severity*: A problem where the risk of morbidity without treatment is moderate; there is moderate risk of mortality without treatment; uncertain prognosis; increased probability of prolonged functional impairment (e.g., 35-year-old male patient diagnosed with chest pain on exertion).

- *High severity*: A problem where the risk of morbidity without treatment is high to extreme; there is a moderate to high risk of mortality without treatment; high probability of severe, prolonged functional impairment (e.g., infant hospitalized with a diagnosis of respiratory syncytial virus).

Time (Face-to-Face versus Unit/Floor)

Intraservice time is a variable that includes *face-to-face time and unit/floor time*. **Face-to-face time** is the amount of time the office or outpatient care provider spends with the patient and/or family. **Unit/floor time** is the amount of time the provider spends at the patient's bedside and managing the patient's care on the unit or floor (e.g., reviewing test results). Unit/floor time applies to inpatient hospital care, hospital observation care, initial and follow-up inpatient hospital consultations, and nursing facility services.

As mentioned above, although the key components of history, examination, and medical decision making usually determine the E/M code, visits consisting predominantly of counseling and/or coordination of care are the exception. When counseling and/or coordination of care dominates (more than 50 percent) the physician-patient and/or family encounter, it can be considered a key factor in selecting a particular E/M code. The extent of counseling must be documented in the patient's chart to support the E/M code selected.

EXAMPLE: Anne Sider is seen by Dr. Cyrix in the office for her three-month check-up. (She has chronic hypertension controlled by diet and exercise.) During the visit, Dr. Cyrix notes that the patient seems distracted and stressed, and he asks her about these symptoms. Anne starts to cry and spends 10 minutes telling Dr. Cyrix that her "life is falling apart" and that she wakes up in the middle of the night with a pounding heart, feeling as though she's going to die. Dr. Cyrix spends the next 45 minutes (of the 70-minute visit) counseling Anne about these symptoms. He determines that Anne is suffering from panic attacks, so he prescribes a medication and contacts ABC Counseling Associates to arrange an appointment for mental health counseling.

In this example, a routine three-month check-up (for which code 99212 or 99213 would be selected) evolves into a higher-level service (for which code 99215 can be reported). The provider must carefully document all aspects of this visit, which includes the recheck for hypertension, provision of counseling, coordination of care provided, and length of time spent face-to-face with the patient. (The coder should report an ICD-9-CM disease code from subcategory V65.4, in addition to the hypertension disease code, when counseling and/or coordination of care dominates the patient encounter *and is documented by the provider*.)

To properly bill an E/M level of service for an encounter based on time, the provider must provide counseling and/or coordination of care *in the presence of the patient* and document the following:

- Total length of time for the encounter
- Length of time spent coordinating care and/or counseling patient
- Issues discussed
- Relevant history, exam, and medical decision making (if performed)

EXAMPLE: Lucy Moreno is a 45-year-old established female patient who was seen in the office on April 22 for problem focused history and examination as follow-up for her diagnosis of lower back pain. Patient states that she is having great difficulty managing her pain, and she says that she realizes part of the problem is that she needs to lose 50 pounds. I discussed a variety of weight loss management options with the patient, including an appropriate exercise program; and she is scheduled to return in one month for recheck. Today's visit was 30 minutes in length, more than half of which was spent discussing weight loss management. Report code 99214.

Exercise 9.3 – Levels of Evaluation and Management Services

Instructions: Complete each of the following.

1. Refer to the Evaluation and Management section of CPT and identify a code for each level of service listed below.

    a. Office or other outpatient visit, new patient, level 4 _____

    b. Office or other outpatient visit, established patient, level 1 _____

    c. Hospital inpatient services, initial hospital care, level 2 _____

d. Home visit, new patient, level 5 _____

e. Emergency department services, level 3 _____

2. An 89-year-old diabetic female presented to the hospital emergency room for evaluation of a very painful lower left arm. An X-ray revealed a left ulnar fracture. After taking a detailed history and performing a detailed exam, the physician reduced the fracture and applied a short-arm cast. Medical decision making was of moderate complexity.

a. Should an E/M code be reported for this case? _____

b. If so, which code? _____

3. A 14-year-old male presented to his primary care provider's office for treatment of 3-cm laceration, which the physician sutured. The physician also administered a tetanus toxoid after confirming that the patient's tetanus immunization status was not up-to-date.

a. Should an E/M code be reported for this case? _____

b. If so, which code? _____

4. Name the three key components that determine an E/M code. _____

5. When assigning an E/M code for a new patient, the number of key components that must be considered is _____.

6. When an E/M code is assigned for an established patient, the number of key components that must be considered is _____.

7. Name the contributory components that are considered when determining an E/M code; they are not considered key components. _____

8. Dr. Kuhl performed a level 3 E/M service to treat an 18-year-old established female patient in the office for a urinary tract infection. Urine culture revealed *Escherichia coli* bacteria. The patient was prescribed antibiotics and instructed to return for recheck in 10 days.

a. Identify the CPT E/M category and subcategory. _____

b. Identify the appropriate CPT code. _____

9. Review the case below and answer the questions to assign the E/M office or other outpatient code. (You will have to identify the elements documented in the case to determine the level of history, level of examination, and complexity of medical decision making.)

SUBJECTIVE: A 54-year-old female patient is seen in the office for routine three-month follow-up for evaluation and management of type 2 diabetes mellitus and hypertension. The patient has no new complaints today; she denies chest pain, headache, numbness of the extremities, shortness of breath, or visual changes. The patient states that she has remained on the diet recommended during the last E/M visit and that she is regularly exercising. Home monitoring of blood pressure and glucose levels are within normal limits.

OBJECTIVE: Blood pressure 130/78. Weight 145. Pulse 78, regular. HEAD, EYES, EARS, NOSE, THROAT: Pupils equal, round, and reactive to light and accommodation. External auditory canals and tympanic membranes negative. Oropharynx benign. NECK: Supple. No bruits, jugular venous distention, or thyromegaly. CHEST: Breath sounds clear to auscultation and percussion. No rubs, rales, rhonchi, or wheezing. HEART: No click, gallop, irregularity, murmur, or rub. EXTREMITIES: Distal pulses intact. No cyanosis, clubbing, or edema. NEUROGICAL: Deep tendon reflexes within normal limits and symmetrical. No decreased lower extremity sensation noted. LAB RESULTS: Fasting blood sugar 132. Urinalysis within normal limits.

ASSESSMENT: Type 2 diabetes mellitus, controlled. Benign hypertension.

PLAN: Glucotrol 5 milligrams daily, every morning. Procardia XL 30 milligrams daily. Relafen 1000 milligrams daily. Continue home glucose monitoring. SMA-7 and glycosylated hemoglobin today. Return for routine follow-up in three months.

(continues)

Exercise 9.3 (continued)

    a. Is this patient new or established? _____

    b. What is the extent of history? _____

    c. What is the extent of examination? _____

    d. What is the complexity of medical decision making? _____

    e. Which E/M code is assigned? _____

10. A home care physician provided E/M home care services to a 54-year-old male who complained of dyspnea due to cirrhosis of the liver and ascites. The home care physician spent 60 minutes reviewing the patient's record, taking a comprehensive history, and performing a comprehensive examination. Medical decision making was of moderate complexity. The home care physician then spent an additional 20 minutes documenting the home visit report and coordinating care with the patient's primary care physician. Identify the appropriate CPT code.

Evaluation and Management Categories and Subcategories

The E/M section (99201–99499) contains notes unique to each category and subcategory. *Remember to review notes before assigning an E/M code.* (As discussed in Chapter 8, CPT refers to E/M subsections and categories as categories and subcategories, respectively.)

CMS NO LONGER RECOGNIZES CPT CONSULTATION CODES FOR MEDICARE PART B PAYMENT

According to CMS, effective January 1, 2010, CPT's consultation codes were no longer recognized for Medicare Part B payment. Instead, providers who perform initial evaluation services for Medicare patients assign CPT's evaluation and management (E/M):

- Outpatient or Other Visits (99201–99215) codes for physician office/outpatient consultations.
- Inpatient Hospital Visits: Initial and Subsequent (99221–99223) for hospital inpatient consultations.
- Nursing Facility Visits (99304–99306) for nursing facility inpatient consultations.

This new rule means that when codes from the Consultations subsection of CPT (99241–99255) are reported on a CMS-1500 claim (or on a UB-04 claim or via electronic data interchange) payment will be denied. All of the codes in the CPT Consultations subsection do not map exactly to codes in the Outpatient or Other Visits, Inpatient Hospital Visits: Initial and Subsequent, or Nursing Facility Visits subsections. (CMS has stated that they will not create a crosswalk of Consultation codes to the CPT codes that are to be reported for each type of service. The mapping tables below are provided for illustrative purposes only.)

Outpatient Consultations: Instead of using criteria for CPT's Consultation subsection codes 99241–99245, providers will use coding guidelines for CPT's Office or Other Outpatient Visit *new patient* codes 99201–99205 and *established patient* codes 99211-99215 to determine (1) whether the patient is new or established and (2) level of history, examination and medical decision making provided.

CPT's outpatient consultation codes 99241–99245 actually do map to the outpatient or other visit codes (after it is determined whether the service was provided to a new or established patient).

Inpatient Hospital Visits: Instead of using criteria for CPT's Consultation subsection codes 99241–99255, when providers perform an initial consultation on a hospital inpatient, they will use coding guidelines for CPT's Inpatient Hospital Visits *initial* hospital care codes 99221–99223.

Nursing Facility Services: Instead of using criteria for CPT's Consultation subsection codes 99241–99255, when providers perform an initial consultation on a nursing facility patient, they will use coding guidelines for CPT's Nursing Facility Visits initial nursing facility care codes 99304–99306.

Note:

Multiple reporting of initial hospital care and nursing facility care codes can occur for a single date of service.

- The principal physician of record will add modifier -AI (Principal Physician of Record) to reported initial hospital care codes 99221–99223 and initial nursing facility care codes 99304–99306.

- Any other provider who provides initial hospital care or initial nursing facility care for the same patient will report the appropriate E&M code without modifier -AI.

- Follow-up inpatient visits will be billed as subsequent hospital care visits or subsequent nursing facility care visits without modifier -AI.

CPT's inpatient consultation codes do not map exactly to initial inpatient hospital visits or initial nursing facility visits. Thus, providers should report the appropriate E/M code (other than a CPT consultation code) that describes the service provided. The general guideline is that the provider reports the most appropriate available code to bill Medicare for services that were previously billed using the CPT consultation codes. For services that can be described by previously used inpatient consultation CPT codes, CMS has stated that providers may bill the corresponding initial hospital care service codes or initial nursing facility care codes (where those codes appropriately describe the level of service provided). When the previously used inpatient consultation codes do not apply, providers should report the E/M code that most closely describes the service provided.

Note:

Low level inpatient consultation codes 99251–99252 do not match any of the initial hospital care codes 99221–99223. For example, inpatient consultation codes 99251 and 99252 require "a problem focused history" and "an expanded problem focused history," respectively. In contrast, initial hospital care code 99221 requires "a detailed or comprehensive history."

CMS has stated that providers can report code 99221 for an E/M service if the requirements for billing that code, which are greater than CPT consultation codes 99251 and 99252, are met by the service furnished to the patient. CMS has also stated that because subsequent hospital care codes 99231 and 99232, respectively, require a problem focused interval history" and "an expanded problem focused interval history," they could potentially meet the component work and medical necessity requirements to be reported for an E/M service that could be described by CPT consultation code 99251 or 99252. However, nothing official has been released by CMS that states reporting codes 99231 and 99232 is permitted.

Note:

To review CMS's Q&A regarding the changes in reporting consultation codes, go to http://www.cms.gov, click on the Outreach & Education link, click on the MLN Matters Articles link, click on the 2010 MLN Matters Articles link, enter SE1010 in the "Show only items containing the following word" box, click the box to populate it with a checkmark, click Show Items, click on the SE1010 link, and scroll down and click on the SE1010.pdf file.

Office or Other Outpatient Services

The Office or Other Outpatient Services category of E/M includes the following subcategories:

- New Patient

- Established Patient

Office or other outpatient services are provided in a physician's office, a hospital outpatient department, or another ambulatory care facility (e.g., stand-alone ambulatory care center). Before assigning an E/M level of service code from this category, make sure you apply the definition of *new* and *established patient* and consider the following:

Note:

Medicare does not allow physicians to report codes from the Consultations category. Thus, physicians (e.g., specialists) who provide office consultation services to new and established Medicare patients are to report codes from the Office or Other Outpatient Services category. (It is unknown whether other third-party payers will adopt Medicare's ruling.)

- When a physician provides two E/M services for the same patient on the same day and the patient's problem is the same for each encounter, report just one E/M service. (Physicians in the same group practice who are in the same specialty submit claims as though they are a single physician.) This means that when a physician provides E/M office or other outpatient services to the same patient multiple times on the same day for the same problem, the highest-level E/M service is reported. (*An exception to this rule is reporting of critical service codes with an E/M service code.*)

- When a physician provides multiple E/M office or other outpatient services to the same patient on the same day and the patient's problems are different for each E/M service, report multiple E/M codes. To justify medical necessity, make sure you link the appropriate diagnosis or condition code to its respective E/M code. Add modifier -25 to the second and subsequent E/M codes.

- When the patient receives office or other outpatient E/M services *and is admitted to the hospital as an inpatient by the same physician*, report an E/M code for the initial hospital care only. Do not report an office or other outpatient E/M service code.

- When the provider performs a comprehensive exam in the office and the patient is later admitted to the hospital *on another day as a planned admission*, report a lower-level-of-service initial hospital care E/M code for the hospital admission (because the provider already performed and reported the predominant portion of the E/M during the office encounter). (When the patient is admitted on another day but the admission is unplanned, report the appropriate E/M code for the office visit and an appropriate-level-of-service E/M code for the initial hospital care.)

 ## Coding Tip:

The provider does not have to redocument the history, review of symptoms, and past/family/social history documented during a previous encounter if the provider documents that the previous information was reviewed and then updates the information. The period of time since the previous encounter should generally be no more than one or two years. In addition, the provider should indicate in the current note where the previous documentation can be found (e.g., Refer to office records dated April 14, YYYY.).

EXAMPLE 1: Dr. Smith provides a level 3 E/M service to a new patient in the office for treatment of anxiety. The patient is prescribed medication and referred to a psychologist for therapy. The same patient returns four hours later because she is having difficulty dealing with her anxiety, and Dr. Smith provides a level 2 E/M service and 30 minutes of counseling. The insurance specialist should report code 99203 on the insurance claim. (An E/M code for the return visit four hours later is not reported because the patient's problem was the same as for the first visit.)

EXAMPLE 2: An 89-year-old established patient receives level 3 E/M services from Dr. James to evaluate her blood pressure medication. The same patient returns five hours later and receives level 4 E/M services from Dr. James to evaluate hip pain due to falling at home. The insurance specialist should report 99213 and 99214-25 because this patient received E/M services for two different problems. (The payer may request copies of the patient record to verify the claim.)

EXAMPLE 3: An established patient receives level 4 E/M services in the office from Dr. Peterson and is later admitted to the hospital, where Dr. Peterson provides level 3 initial hospital care E/M services. The insurance specialist should report code 99223 on the insurance claim. (An office or other outpatient services E/M code is not reported.)

Teaching Physicians and Resident Physicians

A teaching physician is a physician (other than another resident) who involves and supervises resident physicians in the care of his or her patients. A resident physician (or resident) is an individual who participates in an approved graduate medical education (GME) program.

Teaching physicians are no longer required to rewrite in its entirety the key elements of a resident physician's E/M documentation. However, a teaching physician cannot bill for a resident physician's history or physical exam *unless present for a significant portion of the exam*. The teaching physician can select an E/M level of service based on time spent later reviewing the resident's documented history and exam (as part of the medical decision-making process), adding it to the history and examination performed by the provider. (These conditions also apply when *any* provider reviews a history and examination performed, for example, six months previously.)

Teaching physicians are also required to substantiate any services reported on a claim by documenting a summary note of services provided personally or directly observed. The summary note can confirm or revise the HPI, physical examination, and medical decision-making activities. (For services such as a single surgical procedure and/or diagnostic test, the teaching physician can indicate his or her physical presence during the key portion of the procedure or test.)

EXAMPLE 1: When all required elements are obtained personally by a teaching physician without a resident present, the teaching physician documents the E/M service as if in a nonteaching setting. The teaching physician's documentation should also include a statement such as "I performed a history and physical examination of the patient and discussed his management with the resident. I reviewed the resident's note and agree with the documented findings and plan of care."

EXAMPLE 2: When all required elements are obtained by the resident in the presence of or jointly with the teaching physician and documented by the resident, the teaching physician documents that he or she was present during performance of critical or key portion(s) of the service and that he or she was directly involved in the management of the patient's care. The teaching physician's note should also reference the resident's note. The combination of entries must be adequate to substantiate the level of service billed and the medical necessity of the service. The teaching physician's documentation should also include a statement such as, "I was present with resident during the history and exam. I discussed the case with the resident and agree with the findings and plan as documented in the resident's note."

EXAMPLE 3: When selected required elements of the service (e.g., history and physical examination) are obtained by the resident *in the absence of the teaching physician*, the resident documents the services provided. The teaching physician must independently perform the critical or key portion(s) of the service with or without the resident present and discuss the case with the resident. In this situation, the teaching physician must document that he or she personally saw the patient, personally performed critical or key portions of the service, and participated in the management of the patient. The teaching physician's note should also reference the resident's note. For payment consideration by the third-party payer, the combined entries of the teaching physician and resident must be adequate to substantiate the level of service billed and the medical necessity of the service. The teaching physician's documentation should also include a statement such as "I saw and evaluated the patient. Discussed with resident and agree with resident's findings and plan as documented in the resident's note."

Code 99211

Code 99211 is commonly thought of as a "nurse visit" because it is typically reported when ancillary personnel provide E/M services. However, the code can be reported when the E/M service is rendered by any other provider (e.g., nurse practitioner, physician assistant, or physician). CMS "incident to" guidelines apply when the 99211 E/M level of service is provided by ancillary personnel in the office. The guidelines state that the physician must be physically present in the suite of offices when the service is provided. Documentation of a 99211 level of service includes a CC and a description of the service provided. Because the presenting problem is considered of minimal severity, documentation of a history and examination is not required.

> **EXAMPLE 1:** The office nurse administers a patient's monthly injection of vitamin B12 cyanocobalamin (1000 µg) based on standing orders. Before administering the injection, the nurse takes and documents the patient's vital signs (blood pressure, height, weight, and body temperature). Report CPT code 99211 and HCPCS level II national code J3420.

> **EXAMPLE 2:** The patient comes to the physician's office, and the office nurse administers the monthly injection of testosterone enanthate (100 mg). The patient had received E/M level 3 services from the physician last week. Report HCPCS level II national code J3120 only. Do not report CPT code 99211 because the only service provided was the injection and the patient did not require or receive other E/M services (e.g., taking vital signs).

Hospital Observation Services

The Hospital Observation Services category includes the following subcategories:

- Observation Care Discharge Services
- Initial Observation Care
- Subsequent Observation Care

Observation services are provided in a hospital 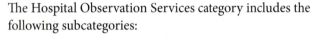 outpatient setting, and the patient is considered an outpatient. Observation status is "an outpatient in a bed" because services include use of a bed (including overnight use of a bed) and hourly monitoring by a hospital's nursing or other staff that is reasonable and necessary to evaluate an outpatient's condition or determine the need for possible admission to the hospital as an inpatient. An observation patient may improve and be released *or* be admitted as an inpatient, which requires documentation of a proper admission order that serves as a rationale for an inpatient stay; the word "Admit" as an admission order for inpatient hospitalization is insufficient. Observation services are reimbursed only when ordered by a physician (or another individual authorized by state licensure law and hospital staff bylaws to admit patients to the hospital or to order outpatient tests). Medicare says that "the decision whether to discharge a patient from the hospital following resolution of the reason for the observation care or to admit the patient as an inpatient can be made in less than 48 hours, usually less than 24 hours," after which the physician must order an inpatient admission.

> **Note:**
>
> Observation care is a service that is provided to a patient (e.g., initial observation care). It is *not* a patient status (e.g., inpatient, outpatient). For example, both outpatients and emergency department patients receive observation services.

 Coding Tip:

> When observation care is initiated during an encounter for another service (e.g., outpatient surgery), evaluation and management services provided by the physician initiating observation care are considered part of the initial observation care *when performed on the same date*. For example, a patient is treated in the emergency department (ED) and then placed under observation in the hospital. The observation service code only is reported to the payer because the ED service is included in the observation service. This rule applies to the supervising physician (who places the patient under observation); other physicians who provide services to patients under observation will report such services separately. For example, a thoracic surgeon who provides consultative services to a patient under observation reports codes for those services to the payer.

EXAMPLE: A patient underwent open reduction internal fixation (ORIF) in the hospital's outpatient surgery department. The surgeon ordered observation care due to unusual postoperative pain, and the patient is discharged home the next day. CPT codes reported for this encounter include the ORIF procedure, initial observation care, and observation care discharge services. (ICD codes reported include the reason for surgery and the reason for observation care, which was postoperative pain.)

Coding Tip:

A patient who is referred by a physician for hospital observation services, bypassing the outpatient or emergency department, is considered a "direct admission to observation." This can occur when the patient receives E/M services in the physician's office and the physician determines that the patient's status requires observation services. Instead of reporting an office or other outpatient service E/M code, the physician reports an observation service code.

The following services are *not* reported as observation services, and claims submitted for such services will be denied as not reasonable or necessary.

- Services *not* reasonable or necessary for the diagnosis or treatment of the patient but provided for the convenience of the patient, patient's family, or physician (e.g., patient is waiting for transfer to NF or physician is busy when patient is physically ready for discharge).

- Services covered by Medicare Part A (e.g., medically appropriate inpatient admission).

- Services that are bundled with another Medicare Part B service (e.g., postoperative monitoring during standard recovery period of four to six hours). (Such services are billed as recovery room services.)

- Services provided to patients who undergo diagnostic testing in a hospital outpatient department (e.g., routine preparation services furnished prior to the testing and recovery afterward).

- Therapeutic services associated with other treatments (e.g., chemotherapy).

- Standing orders for observation following outpatient surgery. (Such services are provided as part of outpatient surgery services.)

Coding Tip:

No differentiation is made as to patient status (new versus established) when assigning hospital observation services codes.

Observation Care Discharge Services

Observation care discharge services include documentation of the following:

- Final examination of the patient

- Discussion of the hospital stay

- Instructions for continuing care

Services also include preparation of discharge records.

Initial Observation Care

Initial observation care codes are reported for patients who are admitted for observation services on one date and discharged from observation status on a different date. Reference times are included in descriptions of initial observation care codes, which means the service can be based on time (instead of key components of history, examination, and medical decision making) *when counseling and/or coordination of care dominates (more than 50 percent) of the physician/ patient encounter.* This means that the insurance specialist assigns a code from range 99218–99220 along with code 99217.

Coding Tip:

For patients who are admitted and discharged from observation care on the same date, report codes from the Observation or Inpatient Care Services (including Admission and Discharge Services) subcategory of the Hospital Inpatient Services category.

Subsequent Observation Care

Subsequent observation care codes 99224–99226 are reported when a patient receives observation services for a second calendar day and is *not* admitted as a hospital inpatient or discharged from observation services.

> **EXAMPLE:** A patient was treated in the hospital's ED for acute asthmatic bronchitis at 9:30 PM on May 14. The ED physician determined that the patient needed to be observed for a period of six to eight hours after provision of emergency treatment. The patient received a detailed level of observation services and was discharged from observation services at 5 AM on May 15. Report codes 99218 and 99217.

Quick Guide to Coding Observation Care Services		
For Patients Admission/Discharged on the:	Whose Length of Observation Time Is:	Report Codes:
Same date	<8 hours	99218-99220
Same date	>8 hours	99234-99236
Different dates	Any length of time	99218-99220 and 99224-99226 and 99217

© Cengage Learning 2014

Hospital Inpatient Services

The Hospital Inpatient Services category of E/M includes the following subcategories:

- Initial Hospital Care
- Subsequent Hospital Care

Note:

Medicare does not allow physicians to report codes from the Consultations category. Thus, physicians (e.g., specialists) who provide inpatient consultation services to Medicare patients are to report codes from the Initial Hospital Care subcategory. (It is unknown whether other third-party payers will adopt Medicare's ruling.)

When more than one physician (e.g., attending physician and a consultant) provides inpatient services on the same date of service, the attending physician adds modifier -A1 (Principal Physician of Record) to the reported E/M code.

The Subsequent Hospital Care subcategory includes the following headings:

- Observation or Inpatient Care Services (Including Admissions and Discharge Services)
- Hospital Discharge Services

Hospital inpatient services are provided to hospital inpatients, including partial hospitalization services; they are indicated when the patient's condition requires services and/or procedures that cannot be performed in any other POS without putting the patient at risk. **Partial hospitalization** is a short-term, intensive treatment program where individuals who are experiencing an acute episode of an illness (e.g., geriatric, psychiatric, or rehabilitative) can receive medically supervised treatment during a significant number of daytime or nighttime hours. This type of program is an alternative to 24-hour inpatient hospitalization and allows the patients to maintain their everyday life without the disruption associated with an inpatient hospital stay.

Note:

Hospitals include acute care hospitals, inpatient psychiatric facilities, and comprehensive inpatient rehabilitation facilities.

Coding Tip:

No differentiation is made as to patient status (new versus established) when assigning hospital inpatient services codes.

REPORTING CODES FOR HOSPITALIST SERVICES

The Society of Hospital Medicine defines hospitalists as physicians whose primary focus is the general medical care of hospitalized patients; their activities include patient care, teaching research, and leadership related to hospital medicine. Hospitalists may be employed directly by the hospital, serve as independent contractors, or be part of a group practice of hospitalists.

EXAMPLE: An orthopedic surgeon admits a 40-year-old patient from the emergency department on May 1 and schedules surgery on May 2 to repair a hip fracture. She requests that Dr. Jones, an internal medicine hospitalist, evaluate the patient on May 1 for chronic bronchitis and to provide preoperative clearance.

The orthopedic surgeon reports a code for the initial hospital care (99221–99223), and the hospitalist reports a code for the inpatient consultation (99251–99255). [If Dr. Jones saw a Medicare patient, he would report a code from the Initial Hospital Care (99221–99239) subcategory instead of the Inpatient Consultations subcategory.]

Initial Hospital Care

Initial hospital care services cover the first inpatient encounter the attending physician has with the patient for each admission. An initial hospital care code is reported once per hospitalization by the admitting or attending physician or another qualified nonphysician practitioner (e.g., nurse practitioner, physician assistant, or clinical nurse specialist). In addition, providers may not bill for both an admission visit and a discharge visit on the same day; for a patient who is admitted and discharged on the same date, report a code from the Observation or Inpatient Care Services (including Admission and Discharge Services) subcategory (99234–99236). When a patient placed under observation is admitted as an inpatient by the same physician on the same day he or she is placed under observation, report an initial hospital care code (99221–99223) only for that day.

A hospital inpatient is someone who is admitted and discharged and has a length of stay (LOS) of one or more days. These codes cover all E/M services performed by that physician as related to the admission, regardless of where other E/M services were performed (e.g., preoperative history and examination performed in the office just days prior to an elective admission). Physicians involved in care of the patient but not designated as the attending physician report services from a different category of E/M depending on where services were rendered (e.g., ED services or consultations).

EXAMPLE: On the day of inpatient admission, Dr. Thompson provided initial hospital care E/M level 3 services to a 42-year-old male patient who was admitted for antibiotic therapy to treat pneumonia due to *Klebsiella pneumoniae* bacteria. Report code 99223.

If Dr. Thompson had provided level 4 or 5 E/M services to the patient in the office, which resulted in admission the next day, the report code would be 99214 or 99215 for the office or other outpatient services encounter and code 99221 for the initial hospital care service.

Subsequent Hospital Care

Subsequent hospital care includes the review of the patient's record for changes in the patient's condition, the results of diagnostic studies, and/or the reassessment of the patient's condition since the last assessment performed by the physician.

- Code 99231 is reported for a stable, recovering, or improving patient.

- Code 99232 is reported for a patient who did not readily respond to inpatient therapy or who developed a minor complication during the inpatient stay.

- Code 99233 is reported for a patient who is considered unstable because he or she developed a significant complication or a new problem. (Such patients are transferred to NFs or discharged home to receive home health care services.)

EXAMPLE: Dr. Thompson provided subsequent hospital care level 2 services to the 42-year-old male patient who was admitted for antibiotic therapy to treat pneumonia due to *Klebsiella pneumoniae* bacteria. Report code 99232.

If the physician had identified an additional condition (e.g., neurologic disorder) that required the participation of another physician in this patient's care, both physicians would report an E/M level of service code and link the appropriate ICD condition code to the E/M code. The other physician would provide consultation services initially; if that physician continued to participate in the patient's inpatient care, report E/M codes from the Subsequent Hospital Care subcategory.

Observation or Inpatient Care Services (Including Admission and Discharge Services)

When observation *or* inpatient care services are provided to patients who are admitted and discharged on the same date, report a code from 99234–99236.

- When a patient is admitted as a hospital inpatient after receiving observation services on the same date, report only an initial hospital care code. (That code should reflect the services provided by the physician during the patient's observation status.)

- When a patient receives observation services on the same date as the result of services provided at another site of service (e.g., physician's office, hospital ED, or NF), report only an observation or an inpatient care services code. (That code should reflect the services provided by the physician at the other site.)

EXAMPLE 1: A patient receives treatment in the hospital ED for an acute asthma attack. The ED physician orders a blood gas analysis laboratory test and an injection of medication to help the patient breathe more easily. The ED physician then orders the patient to be placed in the hospital outpatient observation unit to monitor the patient's breathing and to ensure that the treatment resolves the patient's problem. Five hours later the ED physician examines the patient, who has normal vital signs and has resumed normal breathing. The patient is discharged to follow up with his primary care provider (PCP). The patient's record reveals documentation of a comprehensive history, comprehensive examination, and medical decision making that is of moderate complexity. Report code 99235 only. (*Do not report ED services code 99283 for this encounter.*)

EXAMPLE 2: A 38-year-old female patient undergoes a scheduled hospital ambulatory surgical procedure and is taken to the recovery room, where she has difficulty awakening from anesthesia and an elevated blood pressure. Both conditions persist during the usual recovery period, and the surgeon orders the ED physician to evaluate the patient. The patient is placed in the hospital's outpatient observation unit, and the ED physician orders the nursing staff to monitor the patient's condition and note any continued abnormalities that could indicate a drug reaction or other postsurgical complications. After four hours in the observation unit, the patient is no longer lethargic, has a normal blood pressure, and shows no signs of postsurgical complications. The ED physician discharges the patient from the observation unit to home. The patient record documents a comprehensive history, comprehensive examination, and medical decision making of high complexity. Report code 99236. (The coverage of outpatient observation services began when the patient was placed in the observation unit. Services provided to the patient in the hospital's outpatient surgical suite and recovery room are not considered observation status services.)

EXAMPLE 3: A patient is scheduled to undergo outpatient cataract extraction surgery. The patient expresses a preference for spending the night following the procedure at the hospital despite the fact that the procedure does not require an overnight stay. The hospital registered and treated the patient on an outpatient basis to perform the surgery and then permitted the patient to remain at the hospital overnight. Do not report a code for the overnight stay because it is not covered as medically necessary observation status services. (When a patient is accommodated in this manner, make sure that you notify the patient in advance that the overnight stay is not medically necessary and that the patient will be charged for the additional services. If the patient experiences complications postsurgically that necessitate an inpatient admission, the patient is admitted and a Medicare Part A claim is submitted.)

Hospital Discharge Services

Hospital discharge services include the final examination of the patient; discussion of the hospital stay with the patient and/or caregiver; instructions for continuing care provided to the patient and/or caregiver; and preparation of discharge records, prescriptions, and referral forms. Hospital discharge day management codes are reported for services provided by the physician as part of the final hospital discharge of a patient.

EXAMPLE 1: Dr. Taylor provided 30 minutes of hospital discharge day management services to a 44-year-old female patient who was admitted for management of newly diagnosed type 2 diabetes mellitus. The patient responded well to inpatient insulin treatment and, upon examination, is discharged in improved condition. The patient was provided with discharge instructions for diabetes care, including the administration of insulin injections at home. Follow-up appointment in 10 days was scheduled. Report code 99238.

EXAMPLE 2: Dr. Collins provided 70 minutes of hospital discharge day management services to a 94-year-old female patient who was admitted for surgical treatment of a fractured pelvis. During inpatient hospitalization, the patient developed pneumonia, which was successfully treated. Arrangements were made to transfer the patient to a nursing facility (NF) for follow-up care. Orders for pain management were provided to the NF. The patient was informed that Dr. Collins would visit her tomorrow to perform a comprehensive nursing facility assessment. Report code 99239.

Consultations

The Consultations category of E/M includes the following subcategories:

- Office or Other Outpatient Consultations
- Inpatient Consultations

 Note:

CMS no longer allows physicians or other providers to report codes from the Consultations category of CPT. Physicians (e.g., specialists) who provide consultation services to Medicare patients in a(n):

- Office or hospital outpatient setting are to report codes from the Office or Other Outpatient Services category.
- Inpatient setting are to report codes from the Hospital Inpatient Services category.
- Nursing facility setting are to report codes from the Nursing Facility Services category.
  - The attending physician reports modifier -A1 (Principal Physician of Record) with the initial hospital care code or initial nursing facility care code to distinguish the admitting or attending physician's service from those who provide consultation services.

The OIG reported that most consultation services reported to Medicare in 2001 were inappropriate, and subsequent education efforts to improve reporting failed to produce desired results. Other third-party payers will likely adopt the elimination of CPT's consultation codes. It is unknown whether the AMA will eliminate the "Consultations" category from a future revision of CPT.

EXAMPLE: On May 1, Mary Smith is seen in the hospital's emergency department (ED) and received level 4 evaluation and management services from Dr. Axel (ED physician). The patient complained of severe shortness of breath, chest pain radiating down the left arm, back pain, and extreme anxiety. The patient was admitted to the hospital on May 1, and Dr. Rodney (attending physician) provided level 3 initial hospital care. Dr. Axel reported code 99284, and Dr. Rodney reported code 92222-A1.

A **consultation** is an examination of a patient by a health care provider, usually a specialist, for the purpose of advising the referring or attending physician in the evaluation and/or management of a specific problem with a known diagnosis. Consultants may initiate diagnostic and/or therapeutic services as necessary during the consultative encounter. The following criteria are used to define a consultation:

- The consultation is requested by another physician or source such as a third-party payer. (If the consultation is mandated by a payer or other source, attach modifier 32 to the consultation code.)

- The consultant renders an opinion or advice.

- The consultant initiates diagnostic or therapeutic services.

- The requesting physician has documented in the patient's record the request and the need for the consultation.

- The consultant's opinion, advice, and any services rendered are documented in the patient's record and communicated to the requesting physician or source, generally in the form of a written report.

Coding Tip:

- Do not confuse a consultation with a referral. A **referral** is a recommendation to transfer a patient's care from one provider to another. A referring physician does not schedule the appointment or document a request for referral. A referral is not a consultation. To ensure proper coding of the encounter, call the referring provider to inquire whether a consultation was intended instead of a referral.

- No differentiation is made as to patient status (new versus established) when assigning consultation codes.

- When a confirmatory consultation is required by a third-party payer or another party, add modifier -32 to the appropriate code from the Consultations category (non-Medicare patient), Office or Other Outpatient Services category (Medicare office or hospital outpatient), Inpatient Hospital Care subcategory (Medicare inpatient), or Initial Nursing Facility Care subcategory (Medicare nursing facility patient).

Office or Other Outpatient Consultations

The Office or Other Outpatient Consultation category includes services provided in the following health care settings:

- Physician's office

- Outpatient or other ambulatory care facility

- Hospital observation services

- Home services

- Domiciliary, rest home, or custodial care

- Emergency department

Coding Tip:

When a consultant provides follow-up office or other outpatient consultation services, report codes from Office or Other Outpatient Services, Established Patient (99211–99215).

Coding Tip:

- When office or other outpatient consultation services are provided to Medicare patients, report codes from the Office or Other Outpatient Services category.

- Guidelines about consultation requests and documentation also apply to consulting physicians who report codes from the Office or Other Outpatient Services category.

For a code from the Office or Other Outpatient Consultations category to be reported, the consultation request must be initiated by the attending physician or another health care provider and the attending physician must document all consultation requests in the patient's record. The consultant must document a written report that includes the name of the person requesting the consultation, the reason for the consultation, and the way the findings were communicated to the referring health care provider. Any specifically identifiable diagnostic or therapeutic service performed on the same day as the examination may be billed separately. These separate services must be linked to the appropriate diagnosis to ensure that medical necessity criteria are met. (Some Medicare administrative contractors and third-party payers may disallow payment when surgical procedures and E/M services are performed during the encounter.)

Coding Tip:

- When a consultant provides consultation services in the hospital's emergency department (ED) (at the request of the ED physician), report a code from the Office or Other Outpatient Consultations category of the Consultations subsection.
- When a consultant assumes responsibility for a portion or all management of the case, subsequent care provided by the consultant is reported with the appropriate office or other outpatient services or subsequent hospital care code.
- A **preoperative clearance** occurs when a surgeon requests that a specialist or another physician (e.g., general practitioner) examine a patient and indicate whether the patient can withstand the expected risks of a specific surgery. This is considered a consultation even if the physician performing the preoperative clearance is the patient's primary care physician. (A written request must be documented in the patient's record.)

Note:

A history and physical examination is performed by the patient's surgeon (in the office or at the hospital).

EXAMPLE: On March 15, a 42-year-old female patient was seen by Dr. Verde, her general practitioner, due to symptoms of chest pain and heart palpitations. Dr. Verde determined that the patient needed to be evaluated by a specialist and arranged for the patient to be seen in consultation by Dr. Falco, a cardiologist. Dr. Falco provided a level 4 office or other outpatient consultation service, to the patient on March 20 and ordered diagnostic testing to establish a definitive diagnosis. Code 99244 is reported for the visit to Dr. Falco's office. (If, upon review of diagnostic testing results, Dr. Falco establishes a definitive diagnosis that requires the provision of further E/M services to the patient, report codes from the Office or Other Outpatient Services category of E/M.)

Inpatient Consultations

Inpatient consultation codes are reported when consultation services are provided to non-Medicare inpatients, nursing facility residents, or partial hospitalization patients. Just one inpatient consultation code is reported by a consulting physician per non-Medicare admission. When consulting physicians participate in the patient's inpatient care, report codes from the Subsequent Hospital Care or Subsequent Nursing Facility subcategory of E/M, depending on health care setting. When follow-up care is provided in the consultant's office, report a code from the Office or Other Outpatient Services category of E/M.

Coding Tip:

- When an inpatient consultation is provided to Medicare patients, consultants report a code from the Initial Hospital Care category or the Initial Nursing Facility Care category.
- Guidelines about consultation requests and documentation also apply to consulting physicians who report codes from the Initial Hospital Care or Initial Nursing Facility Care category.

EXAMPLE: A 52-year-old female patient was admitted to the hospital by her PCP to control her type 2 diabetes mellitus and to evaluate possible gangrene of her left foot. The provider ordered inpatient consultation services from an orthopedic surgeon, who provided level 4 E/M initial inpatient consultation services during evaluation of the patient. The orthopedic surgeon told the patient and her PCP that immediate surgical debridement was necessary. (Surgical debridement was performed.) Report code 99254-57 for the consultation services, along with a code from the CPT Surgery section for surgical debridement. (Modifier -57 is attached to code 99254 because the E/M services resulted in a decision to perform surgery. When the orthopedic surgeon provides inpatient and office E/M services to the patient postoperatively, do not report E/M codes. Such follow-up care is part of the global period of surgery; the orthopedic surgeon is paid a fee for having performed the surgery and providing routine follow-up care.)

Coding Tip:

- When a physician provides consultation services to a nursing facility resident, just one non-Medicare inpatient consultation code (or Medicare patient Initial Nursing Facility Care code) may be reported per nursing facility admission, regardless of the length of time the resident remains in the facility (e.g., years). For additional consultation services, report subsequent nursing care visit codes (even when months or years have passed since the initial consultation service).

- For follow-up inpatient consultation services, report codes from the Subsequent Hospital Care subcategory of E/M.

Emergency Department Services

Emergency department services are provided in a hospital, which is open 24 hours for the purpose of providing unscheduled episodic services to patients who require immediate medical attention. A medical emergency is the sudden and unexpected onset of a medical condition or the acute exacerbation of a chronic condition that is threatening to life, limb, or sight and that requires immediate medical treatment or that manifests painful symptomatology requiring immediate palliative effort to relieve suffering. A maternity emergency is a sudden unexpected medical complication that puts the mother or fetus at risk. A psychiatric inpatient admission is an emergency when, based on a psychiatric evaluation performed by a physician (or another qualified mental health care professional with hospital admission authority), the patient is at immediate risk of serious harm to self or others as a result of a mental disorder, and requires immediate continuous skilled observation at the acute level of care.

While ED physicians employed by the facility usually provide ED services, any physician who provides services to a patient registered in the ED may report the ED services codes. The physician does not have to be assigned to the hospital's ED. When services provided in the ED are determined not to be an actual emergency, ED services codes (99281–99288) are still reportable if ED services were provided. Typically, the hospital reports a lower-level ED services code for nonemergency conditions.

If a physician provides emergency services to a patient in the office, it is not appropriate to assign codes from the Emergency Department Services category of E/M. If the patient's PCP asks the patient to meet him in the hospital's ED as an alternative to the physician's office and the patient is not registered as a patient in the ED, the physician should report a code from the Office or Other Outpatient Services category of E/M. ED services codes are reported only if the patient receives services in the hospital's ED.

When the same physician provides ED services on the same day as a comprehensive nursing facility assessment, do not report an ED services code. Any E/M services provided at a site other than the NF are included in reimbursement for initial nursing facility care when performed on the same date as the nursing facility admission. (When a different physician provides ED services in addition to services provided by a physician at the NF, each physician reports an appropriate E/M code.)

When a patient's PCP directs the patient to go to the hospital's ED to receive care and that physician is subsequently asked by the ED physician to evaluate the patient and advise the ED physician as to whether the patient should be admitted to the hospital or be sent home, assign codes as follows:

- If the patient is admitted to the hospital by the patient's PCP, the PCP should report a code for the appropriate level of the initial hospital care (99221–99223) only. All E/M services provided by the PCP in conjunction with an inpatient admission are considered part of initial hospital care when performed on the same date as the admission. The ED physician who treated the patient in the ED should report the appropriate ED services code.

- If the ED physician, based on the advice of the patient's PCP who came to the ED to evaluate the patient, sends the patient home, the ED physician should report the appropriate ED services code. The patient's

PCP should also report an ED services code that describes the services provided in the ED. The PCP should not report a consultation services code because no information was provided to the ED physician for use in the patient's treatment. If the PCP does not come to the hospital to evaluate the patient but provides advice to the ED physician via telephone, the PCP should not report any E/M code.

When an ED physician requests that another physician evaluate an emergency patient, the other physician should report a consultation services code if criteria for providing a consultation have been met. If those criteria are not met and the patient is discharged from the ED or admitted to the hospital by another physician, the physician contacted by the ED physician should report an ED services code. If the consulted physician admits the patient to the hospital and the criteria for a consultation have not been met, the physician should report an initial hospital care code.

EXAMPLE: A 54-year-old female patient presented to the hospital ED with the symptoms of abdominal discomfort, severe shortness of breath, and numbness in both hands. The ED physician provided level 5 E/M services, which included diagnostic work-up. Report code 99285.

Other Emergency Services

Code 99288 is reported when the physician is in two-way communication contact with ambulance or rescue crew personnel located outside the hospital. The physician directs performance of the following procedures:

- Administration of intramuscular, intratracheal, or subcutaneous drugs

- Administration of intravenous fluids

- Cardiac and/or pulmonary resuscitation

- Electrical conversion of arrhythmia

- Endotracheal or esophageal obturator airway intubation

- Telemetry of cardiac rhythm

Coding Tip:

- No differentiation is made as to patient status (new versus established) when assigning ED services codes.

- Usually Medicare administrative contractors and third-party payers do not provide a separate payment for services reported as code 99288 because they are considered included in the payment for services (e.g., emergency department services reported with CPT codes or ambulance services reported with HCPCS level II codes).

Critical Care Services

Critical care is the direct delivery of medical care by a physician to a patient who is critically ill or injured and who requires the full, exclusive attention of the physician. A **critical illness or injury** is one that acutely impairs one or more vital organ systems, jeopardizing the patient's survival. Critical care involves high-complexity medical decision making to assess and manage life-threatening conditions (e.g., central nervous system failure, circulatory failure, shock, renal failure, hepatic failure, metabolic failure, respiratory failure, postoperative complications, overwhelming infection, and other vital system functions), to treat single or multiple vital organ system failure, or to prevent further deterioration of vital functions. Critical care is usually, but not always, provided in a critical care area (e.g., coronary care unit, intensive care unit (ICU), pediatric intensive care unit (PICU), respiratory care unit, or emergency care facility). Payers will reimburse critical care services provided in any location as long as the care provided meets the definition of critical care and supporting documentation is in the patient's record.

Critical care services are reported when a physician directly delivers medical care for a critically ill or critically injured patient. Critical care services can be provided on multiple days even if no changes are made to the treatment rendered to the patient, as long as the patient's condition requires the direct delivery of critical care services by the provider. Time spent away from the patient's bedside that is documented in the patient's record qualifies as critical care services (e.g., time spent with family members or surrogate decision makers to obtain the patient's history

Note:

Critical care services require personal management by the physician. They are life- and organ-supporting interventions that require personal assessment and manipulation by the physician. Withdrawal of or failure to initiate these interventions on an urgent basis would likely result in sudden and clinically significant or life-threatening deterioration in the patient's condition. The service is of such intensity that the physician must devote his or her full attention to the patient and, therefore, cannot render services to any other patient during that same period of time.

or to discuss treatment options). The documented progress note must include any family discussion to a specific treatment issue and *explain why the discussion was necessary on that day*.

Critical care time may be continuous or interrupted; and the time spent engaged in critical care services is directly related to the patient's care, whether that time was spent at the immediate bedside or elsewhere on the floor or unit. The following services performed elsewhere by the physician represent critical care:

- Spending time at the nursing station reviewing test results

- Discussing the patient's care with other medical staff

- Documenting critical care services in the patient's record

- Obtaining the patient's medical history and discussing treatment options with family members if the discussion is absolutely necessary for treatment decision under consideration that day

Critical care services include the following procedures, which are not coded or reported separately:

- Blood gases

- Chest X-rays

- Gastric intubation

- Information data stored in computers (e.g., EKGs, blood pressures, and hematologic data)

- Interpretation of cardiac output measurements

- Pulse oximetry

- Temporary transcutaneous pacing

- Vascular access procedures

- Ventilatory management

Coding Tip:

- Just because a patient is located in a critical care unit does not mean that he or she is receiving critical care; if the patient is stable, report the appropriate subsequent hospital care service code.

- Report services, such as Swan-Ganz catheterization (93503) and intubation (31500), when provided in addition to critical care services codes.

When a patient receives critical care services while located in a critical care unit, on a medical or surgical unit, or in the hospital ED, the critical care services codes are reported *in addition to initial hospital care, subsequent hospital care, and/or initial inpatient consultations service codes*. (Add modifier -25 to the E/M level of service code to report it as a separately identified service provided to the patient.) Comprehensive documentation of critical care services provided is crucial, including the length of time the physician spent providing services. Critical care services codes are selected according to the total duration of time the provider spent delivering services to the patient, even if the time spent was not continuous (Table 9-4). To calculate duration of time, the provider must devote his or her full attention to the patient, and cannot provide services to any other patient during that same period of time.

Table 9-4 Critical Care Services: Total Duration of Critical Care and Codes

Total Duration of Critical Care	Codes
Less than 30 minutes	Assign appropriate E/M code(s)
30–74 minutes	99291
75–104 minutes	99291, 99292
105–134 minutes	99291, 99292, 99292
135–164 minutes	99291, 99292, 99292, 99292
165–194 minutes	99291, 99292, 99292, 99292, 99292
194 minutes or longer	99291 and 99292 as appropriate based on total duration of time

Coding Tip:

- Critical care code 99292 is reported for up to 30 minutes each beyond the first 74 minutes. Throughout CPT, interpret length of time, burn percentage, number of lesions, and so on, as "up to" the number in the code description.

- If critical care services are provided on the same date as a surgical procedure that has a global period and the services are related to the reason for surgery, critical care services are bundled (included) in the reimbursement for the surgical procedure. In this situation, do not report codes for critical care services.

- If critical care services provided are unrelated to the reason for surgery, report codes for services provided (in addition to the surgery code). Attach modifier -24 or -25 to the critical care services code(s). (The surgeon must document that the critical care was unrelated to the surgical procedure performed or was beyond the typical work of pre- or postoperative care associated with the procedure.)

- If the surgeon is also an intensivist, the surgeon should not report codes for critical care services provided to his or her patient during the pre- or postoperative period. Such critical care services are included in the global surgical fee.

- If a surgeon requires the assistance of another intensivist, the intensivist should report codes for critical care services provided. An **intensivist** is a physician who has received extensive training and experience in critical care and who specializes in the care of critically ill patients, usually in an intensive care unit (ICU). Usually an intensivist has completed a fellowship in critical care following completion of a residency in internal medicine, pulmonary medicine, anesthesia, or surgery. Most intensivists are board-certified or board-eligible in critical care medicine.

- Critical care services (99291–99292) are reported for services provided to patients whose age is over 24 months.

- To report critical care services for patients 24 months and younger, refer to codes 99289–99290 for pediatric critical care patient transport or codes 99471–99746 for inpatient neonatal and pediatric critical care services.

EXAMPLE 1: Mary Jones is seen in the hospital ED for trauma as the result of an automobile accident. The ED physician also provides 60 continuous minutes of critical care services. Report the appropriate ED level of service code along with code 99291. (Attach modifier -25 to the ED level of service code.)

EXAMPLE 2: Dr. Smith delivers critical care services to his patient on June 15 from 8–9 AM, 10:30–10:45 AM, and 3:00–3:45 PM To assign a critical care services code to this case, total the minutes of critical care services directly delivered by the provider. Codes 99291, 99292, and 99292 are reported.

Nursing Facility Services

Nursing facility services are provided at a nursing facility (NF), skilled nursing facility (SNF), intermediate care facility/mentally retarded (ICF), long-term care facility (LTCF), or psychiatric residential treatment facility. NFs provide convalescent, rehabilitative, or long-term care for patients, and a comprehensive assessment must be completed on each patient that meets the resident's medical, nursing, mental, and psychological needs. The patient's functional capacity, identification of potential problems, and nursing plan to enhance (or at least maintain) the patient's physical and psychosocial functions are assessed and documented. The assessments are written when the patient is admitted or readmitted to the facility or when a reassessment is necessary because of a substantial change in the patient's status.

Note:

Medicare does not allow physicians to report codes from the Consultations category. Thus, physicians (e.g., specialists) who provide inpatient consultation services to Medicare residents are to report codes from the Initial Nursing Facility Care subcategories. (It is unknown whether other third-party payers will adopt Medicare's ruling.)

When more than one physician (e.g., attending physician and a consultant) provides inpatient services on the same date of service, the attending physician adds modifier -A1 (Principal Physician of Record) to the reported E/M code.

EXAMPLE: The nursing facility assessment code (99318) is reported when the nursing facility patient's attending physician conducts an annual assessment. The attending physician is responsible for reviewing and affirming the patient's plan of care.

 Coding Tip:

No differentiation is made as to patient status (new versus established) when assigning nursing facility services codes.

Third-party payers usually reimburse E/M services provided in a nursing facility when the purpose of the visit is to fulfill the minimum federal requirement of at least one physician visit every 30 days for the first three months and at least once every 60 days thereafter and/or the service is reasonable and necessary for the diagnosis or treatment of illness or injury or to improve the functioning of a malformed body member and all of the following conditions are fulfilled:

- The service requires the skill of a physician.

- The service is sufficiently well-documented to satisfy the criteria of the 1995 or 1997 Evaluation and Management Documentation Guidelines for the level of service and code reported.

- The service is performed by the attending physician, a consulting physician requested by the attending physician, or a named physician requested by the patient or the patient's interested family member or legal guardian.

For an E/M service in an NF to be considered reasonable and necessary, it must be furnished in accordance with accepted standards of medical practice for the diagnosis or treatment of the patient's condition or with the goal of improving the function of a malformed body member; be ordered and furnished by qualified personnel; and meet, but not exceed, the patient's medical need.

EXAMPLE: On October 14, a 97-year-old female patient was transferred from the hospital to the NF in stable condition. The patient's attending physician provided hospital discharge day management services and provided a level 2 initial nursing facility care service. On November 14, the physician provided level 1 subsequent nursing facility care. The patient expired on November 30, and the physician was not in attendance. Report codes 99305 (10/14) and 99307 (11/14). (A discharge service code is not reported.)

Domiciliary, Rest Home (e.g., Boarding Home), or Custodial Care Services

Domiciliary, rest home (e.g., boarding home), or custodial care services are provided to residents of a facility that provides room, board, and other personal assistance services, usually on a long-term basis. Medical services (e.g., 24-hour nursing care) are *not* provided to residents.

Coding Tip:

- Report a code for hospital discharge services (99238–99239), observation care discharge (99217), or observation or inpatient hospital care (same day admission/discharge) (99234–99236) and initial nursing facility care (99304–99306) *if a patient is discharged and admitted to an NF, an SNF, an ICF, or an LTCF on the same date.*

- Do not report codes for ED or office or other outpatient services with initial nursing facility care when provided on the same day for the same patient by the same physician. E/M services provided at sites other than the NF are bundled into initial nursing facility care when performed on the same date as the nursing facility admission by the same physician.

- Do not report codes for initial or subsequent nursing facility care and initial hospital care on the same date for the same patient by the same physician. Payment for initial hospital care services includes all work performed by the physician in all sites of service on that date.

- Report a code for subsequent nursing facility care when the evaluation of the patient's assessment plan is not required and/or when the patient has not had a major or permanent change of health status.

- For discharge from a nursing facility, report code 99315 or 99316. If the patient has expired, report code 99315 or 99316 if the primary service provided by the physician is pronouncement of death, completion of the death summary, and discussion with the deceased patient's family. The provider must personally visit the patient and document pronouncement of death before midnight on the date the patient expired.

Domiciliary, rest home (e.g., boarding home), or custodial care services are also provided to residents of adult living facilities, assisted living facilities, custodial care facilities, group homes, and residential substance abuse treatment facilities. *Assisted living facilities* offer nonmedical senior housing that assists residents with tasks such as cooking and laundry and provides reminders to take medications. *Assisted living* is a general term for living arrangements in which some services are available to residents who still live independently within the assisted living complex. In most cases, assisted living residents pay a regular monthly rent and then pay additional fees for the services they require. *Board and care homes* (or *boarding homes*) are group living arrangements designed to meet the needs of people who cannot live independently but who do not require nursing facility services. These homes offer a wider range of services than assisted living facilities, and most provide help with activities of daily living (e.g., eating, walking, bathing, and toileting). In some cases, private long-term care insurance and medical assistance programs help pay for board and care home services.

Coding Tip:

Make sure you differentiate as to patient status (new versus established) when assigning domiciliary, rest home (e.g., boarding home), or custodial care services codes.

EXAMPLE: A 92-year-old established female patient who resides in an assisted living facility received E/M level 1 services from her primary care physician on December 4. Report code 99334 for the December 4 E/M service.

Domiciliary, Rest Home (eg., Assisted Living Facility), or Home Care Plan Oversight Services

Codes 99339–99340 are reported for care plan oversight services provided for patients who reside at home or in a domiciliary, facility, or rest home. These codes are not reported for home health or hospice patients or for nursing facility residents.

Home Services ●

Home services are provided to individuals and individuals and families in their place of residence to promote, maintain, or restore health and/or to minimize the effects of disability and illness, including terminal illness. Services are provided by nurses, doctors, social workers, therapists, and home health aides. Services are ordered by a physician (instead of treatment in a hospital or SNF) and may result in a shorter acute care hospital or SNF LOS. Home health care programs must be organized, administered, and supervised by a hospital or qualified licensed personnel under the medical direction of a physician. Home services allow patients to recuperate while remaining the home. Since most home health care is temporary and part-time, in addition to providing direct care, the home health staff teaches patients (and their families or others) how to continue needed care (e.g., medication administration, wound care, and therapy).

The home health care physician is responsible for documenting a plan of care and reviewing data. If the written plan of care was not initially prepared by the physician (e.g., prepared by the home health agency), the patient record must include documentation of the physician's contribution to the development of the plan and/or a review of the specific items entered into the plan. It is not sufficient for a home health agency to maintain documentation in its records for the physician. The physician must maintain his or her own records, including periodic summary reports provided by the home health agency. Documentation of all face-to-face E/M home services visits and any telephone communications with the patient or caretakers must be documented in the patient's record. This documentation must indicate an ongoing knowledge of any changes in the patient's condition, drugs, or other needs and the way they are being addressed.

Coding Tip:

When home services codes are reported (99341–99350), make sure you differentiate as to patient status (new versus established).

EXAMPLE: A primary care physician provides level 2 home services to a 72-year-old established patient to evaluate the status of the patient's wound healing. The patient has been receiving daily skilled wound care. The physician determines that an additional 10 days of daily skilled wound care is needed, and he documents that order for the home health agency. Report code 99348.

HOME HEALTH AGENCY FACE-TO-FACE ENCOUNTERS FOR MEDICARE BENEFICIARIES

For Medicare purposes, certifying physicians are responsible for documenting all face-to-face encounters with patients in the patient record, and the encounter must occur no more than 90 days prior to the home health start of care date or within 30 days after the start of care. Such face-to-face encounters can be performed using telehealth services at an approved originating site, which is the location of an eligible Medicare beneficiary at the time such services occur. Originating sites must be located in Rural Health Professional Shortage Areas or in counties outside of metropolitan statistical areas, and they can include physician/practitioner offices, hospitals, critical access hospitals (CAHs), rural health clinics (RHCs), federally qualified health centers (FQHCs), hospital-based or CAH-based renal dialysis centers, skilled nursing facilities (SNFs), and community mental health centers (CMHCs). Nonphysician providers (e.g., certified nurse-midwife, nurse practitioners, physician assistants) can also provide face-to-face E/M home services, but they must inform the certifying physician of any clinical findings exhibited by the patient during the encounter. Then, the physician must document the encounter and countersign the certification. Documentation requirements include:

- Date of face-to-face encounter between the physician or nonphysician provider and the patient.
- Brief narrative describing how the patient's observed clinical condition supports the patient's homebound status and need for skilled services.
- Documentation of the encounter (e.g., handwritten, keyboarded, or EHR format) by the certifying physician on the signed/dated certification form or as a signed/dated addendum to the certification.

Certifying physicians or nonphysician providers are permitted to verbally communicate the brief narrative describing how the patient's observed clinical condition supports the patient's homebound status and need for skilled services to the home health agency (HHA). The HHA provider documents the encounter on the certification form, and the certifying physician must sign the form.

Prolonged Services

Physicians' services involving patient contact that are considered beyond the usual service in either an inpatient or outpatient setting may be reported as **prolonged services**. Codes for prolonged services are reported *in addition to* other physician services (e.g., office or other outpatient services and hospital inpatient services). Prolonged physician services are reported only when the time involved *exceeds* the typical time associated with an E/M service by at least 30 minutes. Prolonged services of less than 30 minutes' total duration on a given date are not separately reported because the work involved is included in the total work for the E/M service code. In addition, prolonged services of less than 15 minutes beyond the first hour and less than 15 minutes beyond the final 30 minutes are not reported separately.

Prolonged Service with Direct Patient Contact

Codes 99354–99357 are add-on codes reported for the total duration of time during which the physician or other qualified health care professional (e.g., nurse practitioner, physician assistant) provided services involving direct face-to-face patient contact that is beyond the usual service provided in an inpatient or outpatient setting. Direct patient contact includes additional non-face-to-face services (e.g., discussing medical management of patient with consulting physician) on the patient's floor or unit in the hospital or nursing facility during the same session. Because the time spent by the physician does not have to be continuous, report code(s) for cumulative time. Codes 99354–99355 are reported when prolonged services are provided in the physician's office or in another outpatient location, and codes 99356–99357 are reported when prolonged services are provided to inpatients.

> **EXAMPLE 1:** A phy†sician provided level 3 office or other outpatient services to an acutely ill established patient who was treated for an asthma attack with intermittent bronchial dilation and subcutaneous epinephrine. The physician provided intermittent direct services over a period of 65 minutes. Report codes 99213 and 99354.

> **EXAMPLE 2:** A physician provided level 3 initial hospital care services to an acutely ill 4-year-old patient who was admitted with respiratory distress, requiring direct contact by the physician. Total duration of time was 115 minutes. Report codes 99223, 99356, and 99357.

Prolonged Service Without Direct Patient Contact

Codes 99358-99359 are add-on codes reported for the total duration of time during which the physician or other qualified health care professional provided services *without direct patient contact* (e.g., extensive record review) on an outpatient or inpatient basis occurring before and/or after direct patient care.

> **EXAMPLE:** A physician provided level 4 office or other outpatient services to an established elderly male patient who was seen for senile dementia, hypertension, diabetes mellitus, and arrhythmia. It becomes clear during the encounter that the patient needs to be placed in an SNF immediately. The patient's wife becomes upset when the physician discusses this recommendation with her, and the physician spends 45 minutes talking with her about what she and the patient can expect regarding SNF care. The physician also calls the local SNF to arrange for patient admission and to coordinate the patient's plan of care; 15 minutes are spent during this phone call. The total duration of time providing non-face-to-face contact was 65 minutes. Report codes 99214 and 99358.

Standby Services

Standby services involve a physician or other qualified health care professional spending a prolonged period of time *without patient contact* waiting for an event to occur that will require the physician's services. Such services must be requested by another physician (e.g., attending physician) and are reported only if the standby time is

30 minutes or longer. However, if a physician who provides standby services performs surgery, the standby services are included in the surgical procedure's global period. Standby services include the following:

- Operative standby: Surgeon is requested to stand by in the event surgery is required, such as for a trauma case.

- Pathology standby: Pathologist is requested to stand by to evaluate a frozen section while the patient is in the operating room.

- Diagnostics standby: Cardiologist is requested to stand by to monitor diagnostics, such as telemetry.

- Obstetrics standby: Surgeon is requested to stand by in the event that a cesarean section is required.

- Pediatrics standby: Pediatrician is requested to stand by in the event that services are needed after the delivery of a high-risk newborn.

Code 99360 is reported in addition to codes 99460 (history and examination of normal newborn) and 99465 (newborn resuscitation), *but not* 99464 (attendance at delivery and initial stabilization of newborn).

> **EXAMPLE:** An obstetric surgeon was called in for consultation by the patient's attending physician (a family practitioner) and provided 30 minutes of standby services due to fetal distress, as noted on the fetal monitor. During standby, the fetal distress resolved, the patient went into active labor, and the patient's attending physician (not the obstetric surgeon) delivered the baby vaginally. The insurance specialist should report 99360 for the obstetric surgeon (because no cesarean section was required).

Coding Tip:

The patient's record must include documentation that supports the E/M level of service code reported, as well as the duration and content of prolonged services that the physician furnished.

- Time the office staff spends with the patient or time the patient remains unaccompanied in the office is not reported using prolonged services codes.

- Time spent waiting for inpatient test results, changes in the patient's condition, end of therapy, or use of facilities is not reported using prolonged services codes.

Case Management Services

According to CPT, "**physician case management** is a process in which a physician or another qualified health care professional is responsible for direct care of a patient, and for coordinating and managing access to, initiating, and/or supervising other health care services needed by the patient." Case management services include anticoagulant management and medical team conferences.

> **EXAMPLE:** The physician participated in a 30-minute interdisciplinary medical team conference of mental health professionals to discuss a 49-year-old patient's plan of care. Report code 99367.

Care Plan Oversight Services

Care plan oversight services cover the physician's time supervising a complex and multidisciplinary care treatment program for a specific patient who is under the care of a home health agency, hospice, or nursing facility. These codes are classified separately from other E/M codes when the physician is involved in direct patient examinations. The billing covers a 30-day period, and only one physician in a group practice may bill for this service in any given 30-day period.

> **EXAMPLE:** The physician reviewed and revised the hospice agency care plan for a 64-year-old female patient with terminal breast cancer. Care plan oversight services required 25 minutes of the physician's time. Report code 99377.

Preventive Medicine Services

Preventive medicine services include routine examinations or risk management counseling for children and adults who exhibit no overt signs or symptoms of a disorder while presenting to the medical office for a preventive medical physical. Such services are also called wellness visits. Discussion of risk factors such as diet and exercise counseling, family problems, substance abuse counseling, and injury prevention are an integral part of preventive medicine. Care must be taken to select the proper code according to the age of the patient and the patient's status (new versus established).

Coding Tip:

- Make sure you determine the patient's status (new versus established) when assigning preventive medicine services codes.
- Preventive medicine services are not reported when a patient who is receiving treatment for a specific disorder returns to the office for a "recheck of a known problem."

When a significant abnormality or preexisting condition is treated during the same encounter as a preventive medicine service (e.g., annual physical exam), it is appropriate to report an office or other outpatient services code (99201–99215) in addition to the preventive medicine services code. To report both codes, the preventive medicine services portion of the visit must be complete and comprehensive and the work-up for the significant problem must meet the required key components for assignment of codes 99201–99215. Attach modifier -25 to the code reported from 99201–99215 and make sure you link the appropriate diagnosis code to justify medical necessity.

EXAMPLE 1: A 24-year-old new patient receives preventive medicine services from a family practitioner. Report code 99385.

EXAMPLE 2: A 45-year-old established patient receives preventive medicine services as part of an annual physical exam; during examination, the physician notices a breast lump. The physician provides level 3 E/M office or other outpatient services to evaluate the breast lump, which includes additional examination and discussion of diagnostic testing plans with the patient. Report codes 99396 and 99213-25.

Counseling Risk Factor Reduction and Behavior Change Intervention

Counseling risk factor reduction and behavior change intervention are reported by physicians or other qualified health care professionals who provide face-to-face services to promote patients' health and prevent illness or injury.

- Risk factor reduction services include preventive medicine counseling to patients who do not have a specific illness, but for whom such counseling might otherwise be used as part of treatment. Patient issues include family problems, substance use, sexual practices, and so on.

- Behavior change interventions are provided to patients who exhibit a behavior, which is often considered an illness (e.g., obesity, substance abuse or misuse, tobacco use or addiction).

EXAMPLE 1: A patient who has been identified as being the adult child of an alcoholic receives preventive medicine individual counseling lasting 60 minutes. Report code 99404.

EXAMPLE 2: A patient who has a two-pack per day history of smoking cigarettes receives individual behavior change intervention counseling as part of his level 3 E/M service for treatment of type 2 diabetes mellitus. Report codes 99213 and 99406-25.

Non-Face-to-Face Physician Services

Non-face-to-face physician services include telephone services and online medical evaluations. Telephone services are provided by a physician to an established patient using the telephone. Online medical evaluations are provided by a physician to an established patient using Internet resources to respond to a patient's online inquiry.

- If the telephone service results in a scheduled appointment within 24 hours or for the next urgent visit, the telephone services code is not reported.

- If the telephone service or online medical evaluation refers to an E/M service provided during the previous seven days or within the postoperative period of a previously performed surgical procedure, the telephone service or online medical evaluation is not reported.

- Online medical evaluation services are reported just once within a 7-day period, although multiple physicians can report codes for such services for the same patient.

  EXAMPLE 1: A physician called an established patient to discuss the results of laboratory testing and to revise the instructions for taking a prescribed medication. The call was 12 minutes in duration. The patient had previously been seen in the office 10 days ago, and is scheduled to return to the office for follow-up in two months. Report code 99442.

  EXAMPLE 2: A patient e-mailed her physician to ask whether her prescribed Effexor could be increased from 75 to 150 mg per day, per the recommendation of her marriage counselor. The counselor suggested that 75 mg per day was not a therapeutic dosage for the patient, and her physician agreed and instructed the patient to take two 75-mg capsules daily. The patient had previously been seen by the physician in the office 30 days ago, and she is scheduled to receive office E/M services in 60 days as part of her routine care. Report code 99444.

Special Evaluation and Management Services

According to CPT, **special evaluation and management services** are provided for establishment of baseline information prior to life or disability insurance certificates being issued and for examination of a patient with a work-related or medical disability problem. During special evaluation and management services, the examining provider does *not* assume active management of the patient's health problems.

  EXAMPLE 1: A life insurance company's representative examines a 27-year-old male patient in his home to determine whether a base life insurance policy will be issued. Report code 99450.

  EXAMPLE 2: A 42-year-old male who had sustained an on-the-job injury about 10 years ago is evaluated by a court-appointed workers' compensation physician to determine whether the patient's current condition is considered work-related. Report code 99456.

Newborn Care Services

Newborn care services are provided to newborns in a variety of health care settings (e.g., hospital, birthing center, and home birth).

  EXAMPLE 1: A 34-year-old female patient was admitted to the hospital on May 19 for vaginal delivery, which resulted in a healthy 10-pound newborn boy. The pediatrician provided newborn care services on May 19 to complete a history and examination of the infant; and on the morning of May 20, the patient and her infant boy were discharged home. Report codes 99460 and 99462 for the newborn case.

  EXAMPLE 2: A 34-year-old female patient delivered a healthy 8-pound newborn girl at home, and the physician in attendance performed a physical examination of the neonate and provided instruction to the parents about initial care. The patient and her daughter are scheduled to follow up in the office in three days. Report code 99461 for the newborn case.

  EXAMPLE 3: A 42-year-old female patient was admitted to the hospital on the morning of September 4 and delivered a healthy 9-pound infant boy. At 9 PM, the patient requested discharge because she had been informed that her 5-year-old son had been injured and was in another hospital for treatment of a broken leg. The physician examined the patient and her infant son and discharged both to home for follow-up in the office the next day. Report code 99463.

Inpatient Neonatal Intensive Care Services and Pediatric and Neonatal Critical Care Services

Inpatient neonatal and pediatric critical care and intensive services are provided to critically ill neonates and infants by a physician. A **neonate** is a newborn, up to 28 days old. An **infant** is a very young child, up to one year old. The definitions for critical care services codes provided to neonates are the same as those provided to adults. (Refer to the previous section of this chapter for discussion of critical care services definitions and coding guidelines.) Inpatient neonatal and pediatric critical care and intensive services begin on the date of admission, and codes are reported once per day per patient. These codes are reported for each 24-hour period, not according to total duration of critical care; and the appropriate code is reported once per day per patient.

Coding Tip:

- When a neonate or an infant is no longer considered critically ill (e.g., attains a body weight that exceeds 5000 grams), report subsequent hospital care codes (99231–99233) for inpatient services provided.
- For infants with less than 5000 grams body weight, who are no longer considered critically ill, report continuing intensive care services codes (99478–99480).

Pediatric Critical Care Patient Transport

Pediatric critical care patient transport (99466, 99467) includes the physical attendance and direct face-to-face care provided by a physician during the interfacility transport of a critically ill or critically injured patient, aged 24 months or younger. **Interfacility transport** is the transfer of a patient from one health care facility to another (e.g., community hospital to children's hospital), and it usually involves use of an ambulance or a helicopter.

EXAMPLE 1: A 4-month-old infant requires pediatric critical care patient transport services due to respiratory failure. The infant's pediatrician provided critical care services during a 95-minute interfacility transfer from a rural community hospital, where the patient was initially treated to stabilize him, to a specialty children's hospital in a city located 70 miles away. Report codes 99466 and 99467.

EXAMPLE 2: A 14-day-old infant received critical care services on August 5, August 6, and August 7, at which time the patient was transferred out of the neonatal ICU to the pediatric nursing unit. Report codes 99468, 99469, and 99469.

Inpatient Neonatal and Pediatric Critical Care

Inpatient neonatal critical care services provided to patients 28 days of age or less are reported with codes 99468 and 99469. Inpatient pediatric critical care services provided to patients 29 days of age through 24 months are reported with codes 99471–99476.

Initial and Continuing Intensive Care Services

Continuing intensive care services codes are reported for services provided subsequent to the day of admission to **very low birth weight** (less than 1500 grams) or **low birth weight** (1500–2500 grams) infants who are no longer considered critically ill. These codes are reported for each 24-hour period, not according to total duration of critical care, and the appropriate code is reported once per day per patient.

EXAMPLE: A 25-day-old infant weighing 1400 grams received subsequent intensive care services from her pediatrician on days two and three of her inpatient admission. Report 99478, 99478.

Complex Chronic Care Coordination Services

Complex chronic care coordination services are provided by physicians, other qualified health care professionals, and clinical staff. Services include patient-centered management and support services that are provided to patients who reside at home or in a domiciliary, rest home, or assisted living facility.

Transitional Care Management Services

Transitional care management services are provided to established patients in their community setting, which can include their home, domiciliary, rest home, or assisted living facility. Services are provided for medical and/or psychosocial problems that require moderate or high complexity medical decision making during transitions in care from an inpatient hospital setting (e.g., acute care hospital, rehabilitation hospital, long-term acute care hospital), partial hospital, observation status in a hospital, or skilled nursing facility.

Other Evaluation and Management Services

Code 99499 is assigned when the E/M service provided is not described in any other listed E/M codes. The use of modifiers with this code is not appropriate. In addition, a special report must be submitted with the CMS-1500 claim.

Exercise 9.4 – Evaluation and Management Categories and Subcategories

Instructions: Indicate whether each statement is true (T) or false (F).

_____   **1.** When a physician provides more than one evaluation and management service for the same patient on the same day and the patient's problem is the same for each encounter, report an E/M service code for each encounter.

_____   **2.** When a physician provides two E/M office or other outpatient services to the same patient on the same day and the patient's problems are different for each E/M service, report multiple E/M codes and attach modifier -51 to the second code.

_____   **3.** When the patient receives office or other outpatient E/M services *and is admitted to the hospital as an inpatient by the same physician*, report an E/M code for the initial hospital care only.

_____   **4.** When the provider performs a comprehensive exam in the office and the patient is later admitted to the hospital *on another day*, void the previously submitted claim on which the office E/M code was reported and report a higher level of service initial hospital care E/M code for the hospital admission.

_____   **5.** The provider does not have to redocument the history, review of symptoms, and past/family/social history documented during a previous encounter *if the provider documents that the previous information was reviewed and then updates the information.*

_____   **6.** Teaching physicians are required to rewrite in entirety the key elements of a resident physician's E/M documentation.

_____   **7.** Code 99211 is commonly thought of as a "nurse visit" because it can be reported only when a nurse provides office E/M services for an established patient.

_____   **8.** Observation services are provided in a hospital outpatient setting, and the patient is considered an outpatient.

_____   **9.** A patient who is referred by a physician for hospital observation services, bypassing the outpatient or emergency department, is considered a "direct admission to observation."

_____   **10.** Initial observation care codes are reported for patients who are admitted and discharged from observation services on the same date.

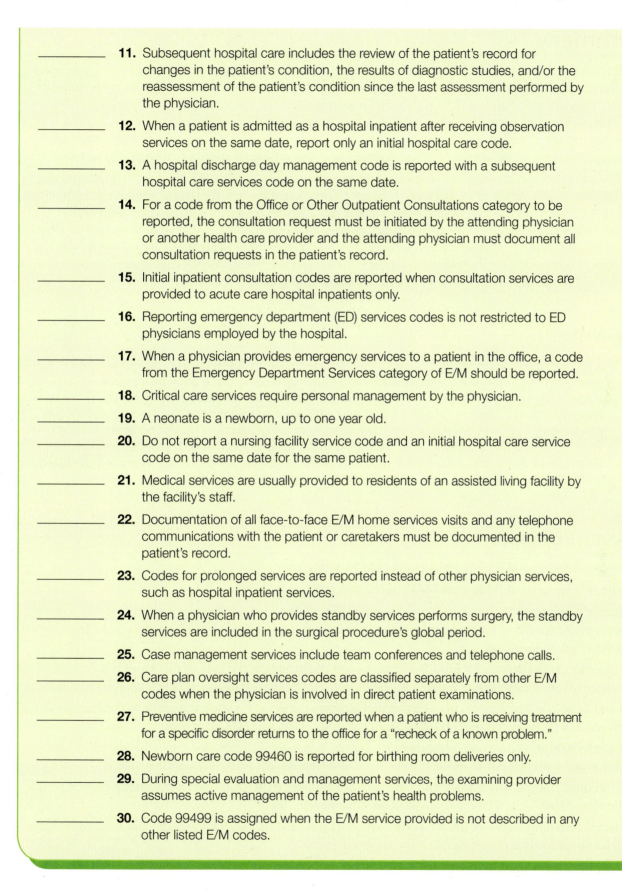

11. Subsequent hospital care includes the review of the patient's record for changes in the patient's condition, the results of diagnostic studies, and/or the reassessment of the patient's condition since the last assessment performed by the physician.

12. When a patient is admitted as a hospital inpatient after receiving observation services on the same date, report only an initial hospital care code.

13. A hospital discharge day management code is reported with a subsequent hospital care services code on the same date.

14. For a code from the Office or Other Outpatient Consultations category to be reported, the consultation request must be initiated by the attending physician or another health care provider and the attending physician must document all consultation requests in the patient's record.

15. Initial inpatient consultation codes are reported when consultation services are provided to acute care hospital inpatients only.

16. Reporting emergency department (ED) services codes is not restricted to ED physicians employed by the hospital.

17. When a physician provides emergency services to a patient in the office, a code from the Emergency Department Services category of E/M should be reported.

18. Critical care services require personal management by the physician.

19. A neonate is a newborn, up to one year old.

20. Do not report a nursing facility service code and an initial hospital care service code on the same date for the same patient.

21. Medical services are usually provided to residents of an assisted living facility by the facility's staff.

22. Documentation of all face-to-face E/M home services visits and any telephone communications with the patient or caretakers must be documented in the patient's record.

23. Codes for prolonged services are reported instead of other physician services, such as hospital inpatient services.

24. When a physician who provides standby services performs surgery, the standby services are included in the surgical procedure's global period.

25. Case management services include team conferences and telephone calls.

26. Care plan oversight services codes are classified separately from other E/M codes when the physician is involved in direct patient examinations.

27. Preventive medicine services are reported when a patient who is receiving treatment for a specific disorder returns to the office for a "recheck of a known problem."

28. Newborn care code 99460 is reported for birthing room deliveries only.

29. During special evaluation and management services, the examining provider assumes active management of the patient's health problems.

30. Code 99499 is assigned when the E/M service provided is not described in any other listed E/M codes.

Summary

The E/M section is organized according to place of service (e.g., office, hospital, home, nursing facility, emergency department, or critical care), type of service (e.g., new or initial encounter, follow-up or subsequent encounter, or consultation), and miscellaneous services (e.g., prolonged physician service or care plan oversight service). The evaluation and management (E/M) section guidelines are located at the beginning of the section and include the following contents: classification of evaluation and management (E/M) services, definitions of commonly used terms, unlisted service, special report, clinical examples, and instructions for selecting a level of E/M service.

E/M categories and subcategories contain codes that are classified according to level of services for reporting to third-party payers. Although the last number of some E/M codes represents the level of service (e.g., code 99213 is a level 3 E/M service), the levels within categories and subcategories are not interchangeable. Levels of E/M services include conferences with or about patients, evaluations, examinations, preventive adult and pediatric health supervision, treatments, and other medical services (e.g., determining the need for and/or location of appropriate care, such as hospice care for a terminally ill patient). The E/M section (99201–99499) contains notes unique to each category and subcategory. *Remember to review notes before assigning an E/M code.*

 Note:

Medicare no longer allows physicians to report codes from the Consultations category. Thus, physicians (e.g., specialists) who provide consultation services to office patients, hospital outpatients, hospital inpatients, or nursing facility residents are to report codes from the Office or Other Outpatient Services category, Initial Hospital Care subcategory, or Initial Nursing Facility Care subcategory of CPT. (It is unknown whether other third-party payers will adopt Medicare's ruling.) When more than one physician (e.g., attending physician and a consultant) provides services to a Medicare inpatient or nursing facility resident on the same date of service, the attending physician adds modifier -A1 (Principal Physician of Record) to the reported E/M code.

Internet Links

American Academy of Family Physicians (AAFP): *www.aafp.org*

American Academy of Pediatrics (AAP): *www.aap.org*

American College of Emergency Physicians (ACEP) coding and reimbursement articles: Go to *www.acep.org*, and scroll over the Practice Resources link, then click on the Issues by Category link and select a topic from the Reimbursement list.

Documentation Guidelines for E&M Services: Go to *www.cms.gov*, and click on the Outreach & Education link, click on the MLN Educational Web Guides link, and click on the Documentation Guidelines for E&M Services link.

E/M and Specialty Scoresheets from Highmark Medicare Services: Go to *www.highmarkmedicareservices.com*, and click on the Physicians/Providers [Part B] link, and click on the E/M Center Link.

E/M CodeBuilder: Go to *www.cengage.com*, and use the login instructions located in the Preface and on the Printed Access Card to locate an online version of the E/M CodeBuilder on the Premium Website.

International Trauma Anesthesia and Critical Care Society (ITACCS): Go to *www.itaccs.com*, and click on the More About Trauma link to access additional trauma websites.

Medicare Learning Network (MLN): Go to *www.cms.gov*, and click on "Outreach & Education," then click on a link below the Medicare Learning (MLN) heading.

Society of Critical Care Medicine (SCCM) coding and billing articles: Go to *www.sccm.org*, and scroll over the Public Health and Policy heading, then scroll over the Regulatory Matters heading, and click on the Coding and Billing link.

Study Checklist

- ❏ Read this chapter and highlight key concepts.
- ❏ Create an index card for each key term.
- ❏ Access the chapter Internet links to learn more about concepts.
- ❏ Complete the chapter review, verify answers with your instructor.
- ❏ Complete WebTutor assignments and take online quizzes.
- ❏ Complete Workbook chapter, verifying answers with your instructor.
- ❏ Go to *www.cengagebrain.com* to access StudyWARE™ and the Premium Website. Login instructions are located in the Preface and on the Printed Access Card.
- ❏ Form a study group with classmates to discuss chapter concepts in preparation for an exam.

Review

Multiple Choice

Instructions: Circle the most appropriate response.

1. The E/M level of service reflects the:
   a. amount of work involved in providing health care to a patient.
   b. kind of health care services provided to a patient.
   c. physical location where health care is provided to a patient.
   d. type of condition for which the patient is being treated.

2. Concurrent care is the provision of similar services to:
   a. different patients by the same provider on the same day.
   b. the same patient by more than one provider on the same day.
   c. the same patient by the same provider on different days.
   d. the same patient by the same provider on the same day.

3. Dr. Benjamin practiced at Hopewell Medical Center until 2002, when he began to practice with Dr. Evans at the Lakewood Clinic. Which would be considered a new patient at Lakewood Clinic?
   a. Debra injured her back two years ago and has been under continuous treatment at another facility. She had her records transferred to Lakewood Clinic and is going to be seen by Dr. Evans for continuing treatment of her chronic condition.
   b. Henrique, who had last seen Dr. Benjamin at Hopewell Medical Center in April 2001, is treated by Dr. Benjamin at the Lakewood Clinic in March 2004.
   c. Martha had a physical performed on June 1, 2003, by Dr. Benjamin and is seen by Dr. Evans on September 30, 2005, for a sinus condition.
   d. Sheryl was treated last month by Dr. Evans. This week she needs to be seen again, but Lakewood Clinic is closed for the holiday. She is seen by an on-call physician who is covering for Dr. Evans.

4. *Problem focused*, *expanded problem focused*, *detailed*, and *comprehensive* are terms used to describe which components of an E/M level of service code?
   a. extent of exam
   b. extent of history
   c. extent of history and extent of exam
   d. review of systems

5. Which contributory component would be considered when determining the number of diagnoses or management options for medical decision making complexity?
   - a. coordination of care
   - b. counseling
   - c. nature of the presenting problem
   - d. time

6. There are seven components to a level of E/M service code descriptions. Which are considered key components when selecting the E/M code?
   - a. counseling, coordination of care, and nature of presenting problem
   - b. history, exam, and medical decision making
   - c. history, exam, and time
   - d. medical decision making, time, and nature of presenting problem

7. Time is a contributing factor in E/M code selection for which scenario?
   - a. A patient had an encounter solely for the purpose of discussing treatment options for a recently diagnosed condition.
   - b. After Dr. Harris diagnosed Ellen with an ear infection, he explained the prognosis and wrote a prescription for an antibiotic.
   - c. Dr. Bender showed frightened little Jimmy the X-ray of his broken arm and explained why a cast would help him get better.
   - d. Dr. Knolles spent 10 minutes reviewing information on drugs to find one that the patient could tolerate.

8. Documentation of the review of systems is used to establish:
   - a. complexity of medical decision making.
   - b. extent of examination performed.
   - c. extent of history obtained.
   - d. presence of contributing factors.

9. A physician discussed the results of diagnostic testing with his patient. This portion of the encounter is considered:
   - a. coordination of care.
   - b. counseling.
   - c. examination.
   - d. history of present illness.

10. Which is reported using a non-face-to-face physician service code?
    - a. A patient came into the emergency department with severe pain in the lower back. She told the physician that she had recently had an MRI at that facility but hadn't received the results yet. The physician looked up the test results and verified that a displaced disc was causing the pain.
    - b. A patient involved in a motor vehicle accident came to the emergency department with complaints of a sore neck and blurry vision. The patient was diagnosed with whiplash. The attending physician requested an ophthalmology consultation during the encounter, but no physicians were available so he scheduled the consultation for the following day. He instructed the patient to follow up with her primary care physician if symptoms persisted.
    - c. A physician called the patient at home to discuss the results of her lab tests. After reviewing the reports, he believed that further testing was necessary and advised her to make an appointment as soon as possible.
    - d. During an encounter, a physician recommended physical therapy to a patient with rheumatoid arthritis. She expressed concern over which facility she should contact and how she would get there. Before she left, the physician provided her with names and numbers of facilities she could contact for treatment, as well as agencies that would assist in her transportation needs.

11. A patient is admitted with head injury. On the initial visit, the physician observes that the patient is unconscious and is bleeding from the right ear. The physician spends 70 minutes treating the patient and coordinating care, during which time a comprehensive history and exam are obtained. Which E/M code is reported?
    - a. 99221
    - b. 99222
    - c. 99223
    - d. 99285

12. A 6-year-old child is seen by her family physician for her annual check-up and immunizations. Her last encounter was one year ago. Which E/M code is reported?
    a. 99211   b. 99251   c. 99383   d. 99393

13. A patient with severe chest pain is admitted for observation. A comprehensive history and examination are performed. Medical decision making is moderate. The patient is released the same day. Which E/M code is reported?
    a. 99202   b. 99219   c. 99222   d. 99235

14. A 38-year-old patient with neck stiffness and pain radiating down the right arm presents to the neurosurgeon for an office consultation. A detailed history and exam are obtained during the 40-minute encounter. Which E/M code is reported?
    a. 99204   b. 99221   c. 99243   d. 99244

15. A patient was seen in the emergency department after she burned her hand with scalding water. An expanded problem focused history and exam were performed. Medical decision making was of low complexity. Which E/M code is reported?
    a. 99213   b. 99232   c. 99282   d. 99283

16. A physician performs a scheduled follow-up visit to a 65-year-old patient in a nursing facility who is recovering from pneumonia. The patient has responded well to the treatment, and no complications are noted. Which E/M code is reported?
    a. 99307   b. 99308   c. 99324   d. 99341

17. A new patient presents to the physician's office with complaints of severe earache, jaw pain, and facial swelling. The physician obtains a detailed history of the chief complaint, an extended review of systems, and a problem pertinent past/family/social history. Medical decision making is of low complexity. Which E/M code is reported?
    a. 99203   b. 99204   c. 99205   d. 99214

18. An established patient has a four-month office check-up for medical management of high triglyceride levels. A brief history of present illness and a problem pertinent review of systems are obtained. The physician counsels the patient on diet and exercise and advises the patient to return again in four months. Which E/M code is reported?
    a. 99202   b. 99213   c. 99214   d. 99232

19. A subsequent hospital visit is required for a 58-year-old patient admitted with an esophageal neoplasm who has begun to spit up blood. Metastasis is suspected. Which E/M code is reported?
    a. 99233   b. 99236   c. 99255   d. 99285

20. An inpatient follow-up consultation is performed for a 40-year-old patient who is experiencing foot drop after leg surgery. The foot has regained normal positioning. Which E/M code is reported?
    a. 99221   b. 99231   c. 99241   d. 99251

Coding Practice

Instructions: Review each case and assign CPT code(s) and appropriate modifier(s).

Office or Other Outpatient Services

21. A 4-year-old female established patient received evaluation and management services, which included a problem focused history, an expanded problem focused exam, and medical decision making (MDM) of a low level. The patient is diagnosed with influenza.

_____

22. A 16-year-old outpatient who is a new patient to the office complains of severe facial acne. The history and physical examination are expanded problem focused. The physician must consider related organ systems in addition to the integumentary system in order to treat the condition. With minimal number of diagnoses to consider and the minimal amount of data to review, the physician's decision making is straightforward with regard to the treatment of this patient.

Hospital Observation Services

23. A patient was in an automobile accident and is complaining of a minor headache and no other apparent injuries. History gathered from bystanders states that the patient was not wearing a seat belt and hit his head on the windshield. A 15-minute loss of consciousness was noted. The patient was then admitted for 24-hour observation to rule out head injury. A comprehensive history and exam are performed by the physician. The MDM is of moderate complexity.

24. A 55-year-old female came in with the complaint of severe abdominal pain. The patient was admitted on 05/07 to observation due to the severity and location of her pain. The admitting physician performed a comprehensive history and a detailed examination and documented medical decision making of a moderate complexity given the amount of possible diagnoses, including appendicitis, gastric ulcer, cholelithiasis, and pyelonephritis. Various diagnostic tests were ordered and done, including barium enema, upper gastrointestinal endoscopy, and KUB (kidneys, ureters, bladder) X-ray. No disease or disorder was found, and the patient was discharged from observation on 05/08. The patient reported a decrease in her pain after 30 hours of IV analgesics and antispasmodics. The physician documented that the patient should follow up with her primary care physician in two days or return to the hospital if the pain worsens. The physician also documented a final detailed examination of the patient and dictated a discharge summary report.

Hospital Inpatient Services

25. A 50-year-old female patient was admitted to the hospital on 10/10 with a diagnosis of pneumonia due to *Staphylococcus aureus*, at which time she received level 2 E/M services from her attending physician. On 10/11 and 10/12, the patient received level 2 E/M services. On 10/13, the patient was discharged from the hospital in improved condition to follow up with the physician at home; the physician spent 30 minutes performing discharge day management functions.

26. An established patient is seen in the hospital on day two of his hospital stay. The patient had been admitted through the emergency department with status asthmaticus and had been undergoing extensive respiratory therapy over the past 24 to 30 hours. The physician performs a detailed interval history and a detailed physical exam. The possibility of pneumonia complicating the asthma must be considered. The patient's respiratory condition is still unstable. The MDM complexity was high.

Consultations

27. A 52-year-old patient was sent to a surgeon for an office consultation concerning hemorrhoids. An expanded problem focused history and examination were performed. The consultant recommended treating with medication after a straightforward MDM.

28. A 13-year-old male was admitted yesterday for a tympanotomy. Postsurgically, the child developed fever and seizures of unknown origin. A pediatric consultation was requested. This was done on the second hospital admission day and 24 hours after surgery. The history of present illness (HPI) was extended with a complete review of systems (ROS). A complete past/family/social history (PFSH) was elicited from the mother as part of a comprehensive history. A comprehensive examination was conducted on all body areas and organ systems. The MDM complexity was high.

Emergency Department Services

29. A patient in the emergency department (ED) has a temperature of 103°F and is in acute respiratory distress. Symptoms include shortness of breath, chest pain, and gasping. The physician is unable to obtain a history or perform a comprehensive physical examination because the patient's condition is critical. The MDM complexity is high.

30. With two-way communication, the physician directs the emergency medical technicians (EMTs) in an ambulance en route to the emergency department with a patient in apparent cardiac arrest.

Critical Care Services

31. A patient presents with the complaint of hematemesis. The patient also has a rapid pulse rate and low blood pressure. In the ED, critical care is provided by the ED attending to raise the patient's blood pressure and decrease blood loss. This is done for 70 minutes before the patient is transferred to the surgical suite for an endoscopic procedure to evaluate his esophagus. The physician documents a detailed examination and MDM of high complexity. Due to the patient's medical condition, he is unable to provide any history; and no family is present to provide information.

32. A physician is called to the intensive care unit to provide care for a patient who received second- and third-degree burns over 50 percent of his body due to a chemical fire. The patient is in respiratory distress and is suffering from severe dehydration. The physician provides support for two hours. Later that day the physician returns and provides an additional hour of critical care support to the patient.

Nursing Facility Services

33. A 72-year-old patient suffered a cerebral vascular accident (CVA). Today the patient is admitted to a skilled nursing facility (SNF) for rehab and medical care. The patient was just discharged from an acute care facility. The SNF medical director documents a comprehensive history, including the patient's chief complaint of paralysis and weakness, an extended HPI, and a complete ROS. A detailed exam of the patient's cardiovascular, respiratory, musculoskeletal, neurological, and genitourinary systems is documented. The physician orders a multidisciplinary rehabilitation care plan for the patient and the continued treatment of the patient's other medical conditions, including hypertension and diabetes. The MDM complexity is high.

34. Subsequent follow-up care is provided for a comatose patient transferred to a long-term care center from the hospital two days ago. The resident shows no signs of consciousness on examination but appears to have developed a minor upper respiratory tract infection with a fever and rales heard on auscultation. The physician performs an expanded problem focused interval examination with respiratory status and status of related organ systems such as cardiovascular. The physician is concerned that the respiratory infection could progress to pneumonia and orders the appropriate treatment. The MDM complexity is moderate.

Domiciliary, Rest Home, or Custodial Care Services

35. A new patient diagnosed with mild intellectual disabilities (specifically, mild mental retardation) and self-abuse is sent to a custodial care facility for admission. The patient's family is no longer able to care for the patient at home. The care facility physician documents a problem focused history with a problem focused exam. The medical decision making documented was straightforward.

36. A 21-year-old patient with a recent history of drug abuse is admitted to a rehab center for treatment. In the patient's second week of treatment, she complains of back pain and is seen by the same physician who evaluated her medically upon admission. At this time, the physician documents a problem focused interval history, an expanded problem focused examination, and MDM of moderate complexity.

Home Services

37. A 64-year-old female patient has diabetes and has been having problems adjusting her insulin doses. She has had an onset of dizziness and sensitivity to light. Her primary care physician, who has treated her for this condition during the past four years, makes a home visit today. At this visit, the physician gathers a brief HPI and a problem pertinent ROS during the problem focused history. The physical exam focuses on the body systems currently affected by the diabetes. The patient's condition is moderately severe and the MDM complexity is of a moderate level.

38. A 15-year-old new patient has cystic fibrosis and is having problems with her Pulmozyme dosage. This medication is used to thin the mucus that clogs her lungs. The patient is having moderate throat pain and slight tightness in her chest. The physician makes a home visit to gather HPI and ROS and pertinent past personal medical information for a detailed history. The detailed exam focuses on the body systems currently affected by the cystic fibrosis and related organ systems: ears, nose, throat, mouth, respiratory, gastrointestinal, and cardiovascular. The MDM complexity is of a moderate level.

Prolonged Physician Service

39. An established patient with a history of asthma presents in an office visit with acute bronchospasm and moderate respiratory distress. The physician conducts a problem focused history followed by a detailed examination, which shows a respiratory rate of 30. Office treatment is initiated: intermittent bronchial dilation and subcutaneous epinephrine. This service requires the physician to have intermittent direct contact with the patient over a two-hour period. The MDM complexity is moderate.

Physician Standby Services

40. A patient was in the delivery room ready to give birth. When the physician had the patient start pushing, possible complications for the infant were noted and the hospital pediatric neonatal specialist was notified of a possible need for her evaluation of this newborn. The pediatric specialist was notified at 9:20 AM At 10 AM, she was informed via phone call from the OB/GYN that the infant had normal APGAR scores of 9 and 9.

_____

Case Management Services

41. A 72-year-old patient with a history of breast cancer has a suspicious mass in her uterus. A biopsy was done. The determination was that the patient had a carcinoma _in situ._ of the uterus. The physician who conducted the surgery called a face-to-face meeting with his fellow surgeons and discussed the case and the patient's outcome for 30 minutes.

_____

42. A 14-year-old boy twisted his ankle while playing soccer. He received level 3 E/M services from his physician the next morning. The physician ordered an X-ray of the ankle, and the the child left the office after the X-ray but did not see the physician. Later that afternoon the physician called and spoke to the patient's mother about the X-ray results and treatment of the patient's sprain. Medical discussion was 10 minutes in duration.

_____

Care Plan Oversight Services

43. A 75-year-old patient was just diagnosed with type 1 diabetes. This means that the patient will have to give himself insulin shots. The physician supervised the coordination of home health care, which required 30 minutes of his time.

_____

44. A 50-year-old female has brain cancer, and the physician supervised the coordination of hospice services, which required 45 minutes of his time.

_____

Preventive Medicine

45. A 13-year-old new patient presents for a well-check examination. The patient does not report any medical complaints.

_____

46. 75-year-old established patient presents for his annual physical examination. The patient's chronic conditions are well controlled wtih diet and exercise.

_____

Non-Face–to–Face Physician Services

47. A physician called an established patient to inform her that the results of a chest X-ray were negative. The call was 5 minutes in duration. The patient had previously been seen in the office 10 days ago.

_____

48. A patient e-mailed his physician to ask whether taking 500 mg of cinnamon tablets daily would be acceptable, given the prescribed medications he takes. The physician replied, approving his taking 500 mg of cinnamon tablets daily. The patient had previously been seen by the physician in the office 15 days ago, and he is scheduled to receive office E/M services in 60 days as part of his routine care.

Special Evaluation and Management Services

49. A 58-year-old man was seen by his private physician for an examination as part of his claim for long-term medical disability. The patient has chronic obstructive lung disease with severe emphysema and has been unable to work during the past year. The physician documents a comprehensive medical history and a detailed examination. The physician reviews the patient's current medical treatment plan and recommends that it continue. All of the necessary documentation required by the insurance company is completed, including the physician's opinion that the patient would be unable to work in the future, as his pulmonary function is markedly impaired in spite of continual respiratory and pharmacologic therapy.

Newborn Care

50. A full-term baby girl received initial and subsequent care services on July 7 and July 8, respectively.

CPT Anesthesia

Chapter Outline

Anesthesia Terminology

Overview of Anesthesia Section

Anesthesia Section Guidelines

Anesthesia Subsections

Chapter Objectives

At the conclusion of this chapter, the student should be able to:

- Define key terms.
- Explain the organization, format, and content of the CPT Anesthesia section.
- Interpret CPT Anesthesia section guidelines, coding notes, and modifiers.
- Assign CPT evaluation and management service codes.
- Add CPT and/or HCPCS level II modifiers to codes, as appropriate.
- Calculate anesthesia fees.

Key Terms

airway management

A-line

analgesia

analgesic

anesthesia

anesthesia conversion factor

anesthesia time unit

anesthesiologist

anesthetic

arteriography

base unit value

Bier block

cannula

capnography

caudal anesthesia

central nervous system (CNS)

central venous access device (CVAD)

central venous pressure catheter

central venous pressure (CVP) line

certified registered nurse anesthetist (CRNA)

cleft lip

concurrent medically directed anesthesia procedure

contrast medium

dura mater

electroconvulsive therapy (ECT)

electromyogram (EMG)

emergency condition

endotracheal tube (ET)

epidural anesthesia

external catheter

extracorporeal shock wave lithotripsy (ESWL)

extradural procedure

field block

fluid management

general anesthesia

heparin

hypovolemia

implanted port

infiltration anesthesia

internal catheter

interventional therapeutic radiological procedure

intra-arterial cannula

intra-arterial catheter

intra-arterial line

intracranial

intravenous regional anesthesia

lesion

lithotripter

local anesthesia

lumbar puncture (LP)

lumen

mass spectrometry

modifying unit

monitored anesthesia
care (MAC)

nerve plexus

nontunneled catheter

one-lung ventilation
(OLV)

organ harvest

panniculectomy

panniculus adiposus

pannus

peripheral nerve block

physical status modifier

plexus anesthesia

post-anesthesia
evaluation

postoperative pain
management

pre-anesthesia
evaluation

pulmonary wedge
pressure

pulse oximetry

pump oxygenator

qualifying circumstance

radiopaque

regional anesthesia

saddle block anesthesia

sedation

shock therapy

spinal anesthesia

spinal tap

surface anesthesia

Swan-Ganz catheter

tunneled catheter

urethrocystoscopy

Introduction

The Anesthesia section is located after the Evaluation and Management section in the CPT coding manual, and the codes range from 00100 to 01999. Anesthesia codes are reported for services related to the administration of anesthesia (including general and regional), the supplementation of local anesthesia, and other supportive anesthesia services. Anesthesia subsections are organized according to anatomic site, except the last four subsections, which are listed as types of procedure. Any qualified health care provider who administers analgesic or anesthetic agents is permitted to report codes from the Anesthesia section of CPT. Providers include anesthesiologists, certified registered nurse anesthetists (CRNAs), surgeons, and other physicians. However, when the same physician (e.g., surgeon) performs the procedure and administers anesthesia, add modifier -47 to the CPT Surgery Section code (and do not report a separate code from the Anesthesia Section).

An **anesthesiologist** is a physician who, after medical school, completes a one-year internship and three-year residency in anesthesia. A **certified registered nurse anesthetist (CRNA)** is a licensed registered nurse (RN) who has earned a bachelor's degree in science or nursing, has at least one year of acute care nursing experience (e.g., intensive care, coronary care, or emergency/trauma), has completed a 24- to 36-month nurse anesthesia program leading to a master's degree, and has passed the national certification exam. (Doctorate programs are also available.)

Anesthesia Terminology

Patients who undergo surgical or other invasive procedures (e.g., radiological procedure) require anesthesia services so the procedure can be performed. **Anesthesia** is the process of inducing a loss of sensitivity to pain in all or part of the body, resulting from the administration of an **anesthetic** (drug or agent that causes a loss of feeling, awareness, and/or consciousness). An **analgesic** is a drug that reduces pain, such as aspirin, acetaminophen, and ibuprofen; for surgery, other substances (e.g., morphine) are used to cause **analgesia** (loss of pain sensation without loss of consciousness).

Types of Anesthesia

The following types of anesthesia are used in surgical practice:

- General anesthesia
- Local anesthesia
- Regional anesthesia

General anesthesia is used for extensive surgeries and involves the administration of anesthetic agents that are inhaled (e.g., sevoflurane combined with nitrous oxide) or administered intravenously (e.g., propofol). They act as hypnotics, muscle relaxants, and painkillers and serve to block any memory of the surgery. General anesthesia renders a patient unconscious, which means the brain doesn't perceive pain signals. To determine the general anesthetic agents to administer, the patient's age and health must be considered, along with the type of surgery to be performed.

Local anesthesia is appropriate for minor surgeries (e.g., dental work, skin biopsy, and suture of a laceration) and involves applying a topical agent (e.g., lidocaine) on the body's surface or injecting a local anesthetic agent (e.g., procaine) for the purpose of numbing a small part of the body. As a result, pain signals are blocked and the patient remains alert. Local anesthesia administration techniques include:

- **Surface anesthesia**: Topical application of local anesthetic cream, solution, or spray to skin or mucous membranes.

- **Infiltration anesthesia**: Topical injection of local anesthetic into tissue.

- **Field block**: Subcutaneous injection of local anesthetic in area bordering the field to be anesthetized.

- **Peripheral nerve blocks**: Injection of local anesthetic in the vicinity of a peripheral nerve to anesthetize that nerve's area of innervation.

- **Plexus anesthesia**: Injection of local anesthetic in the vicinity of a **nerve plexus**, which is a network of intersecting nerves (Figure 10-1).

Regional anesthesia is appropriate when there is a need to block pain from a large part of the body (e.g., lower extremity and pelvic surgeries). Regional anesthetic agents are injected into or near the spinal fluid and around a nerve or network of nerves to block the nerve supply to a specific part of the body (Figure 10-2). The patient cannot feel pain in that area when a procedure is performed, and the patient remains awake (or sedated). Intravenous (IV) sedation may be administered prior to regional anesthesia to relax the patient and make him or her drowsy, but the patient remains conscious. Regional anesthesia includes the following:

- **Caudal anesthesia,** or **saddle block anesthesia**: Local anesthetic is injected into the caudal canal, which is the sacral portion of the spinal canal; anesthetized area is the umbilicus, below the navel.

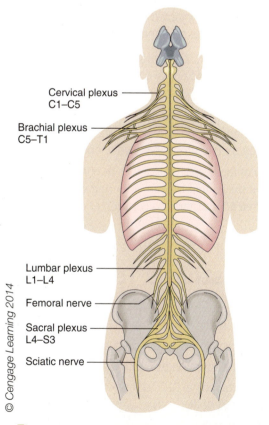

© Cengage Learning 2014

Figure 10-1 Spinal cord and nerves. (Most spinal nerves are named for the corresponding vertebrae)

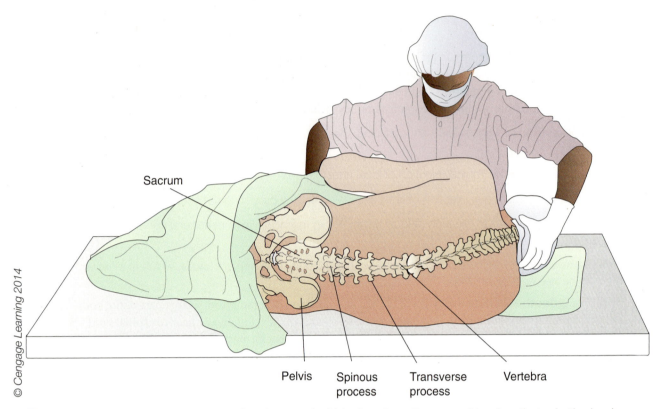

Figure 10-2 Correct position for performing a spinal block or inserting an epidural-catheter in the lumbar region.

- **Epidural anesthesia**: Local anesthetic is injected into the epidural space where it acts primarily on spinal nerve roots; anesthetized area includes the abdomen, chest, and large regions of the body.

- **Spinal anesthesia**: Local anesthetic is injected into cerebrospinal fluid (CSF) at the lumbar spine, where it acts on spinal nerve roots and part of the spinal cord; anesthetized area extends from the legs to the abdomen or chest.

- **Intravenous regional anesthesia**, or **Bier block**: An IV cannula is inserted into the extremity on which the procedure is to be performed and a tourniquet is applied to interrupt blood circulation; then a large volume of local anesthetic is injected into a peripheral vein, anesthetizing the extremity.

Sedation is the administration of medication into a vein to relieve pain and anxiety; it makes the patient feel calm. Such medications may result in the patient not remembering surgical events (even though the patient remains awake). Sedation medications are often administered in addition to other forms of anesthesia.

Exercise 10.1 – Anesthesia Terminology

Instructions: Match the term with its definition.

_____ **1.** Administration of anesthetic agents that are inhaled

_____ **2.** Administration of medication to relieve pain/anxiety

_____ **3.** Application of a topical agent on the body's surface

_____ **4.** Injected into or near the spinal fluid to block the nerve supply to a specific part of the body

_____ **5.** Intravenous regional anesthesia

a. Bier block

b. General anesthesia

c. Local anesthesia

d. Regional anesthesia

e. Sedation

Instructions: Match the term with its definition.

_____ **6.** Injection of local anesthetic in the vicinity of a network of intersecting nerves

_____ **7.** Injection of local anesthetic in the vicinity of a peripheral nerve to anesthetize area of innervation

_____ **8.** Subcutaneous injection of local anesthetic in area bordering the field to be anesthetized

_____ **9.** Topical application of local anesthetic cream to skin

_____ **10.** Topical injection of local anesthetic into tissue

a. Field block

b. Infiltration anesthesia

c. Peripheral nerve block

d. Plexus anesthesia

e. Surface anesthesia

Overview of Anesthesia Section

The Anesthesia section includes 15 anatomic sites, followed by four additional subsections for radiological procedures, burn excisions or debridement, obstetrics, and other procedures. Codes are organized according to type of procedure (open, closed, endoscopics, and so on), and each anesthesia code relates to corresponding surgical procedures. Because a one-to-one correspondence for anesthesia to surgery codes does not exist, one anesthesia code is often reported for many different surgical procedures that share similar anesthesia requirements. The Anesthesia section guidelines also include four codes (99100–99140) that are located in the Medicine section, which are used to report qualifying circumstances for anesthesia.

 Coding Tip:

Notes located beneath headings and/or subheadings apply to all codes in the headings or subheadings. Parenthetical notes that are located below a specific code apply to that code only unless the note indicates otherwise.

Anesthesia services include the preparation and monitoring of the patient, and the services included (bundled) in the anesthesia code reported include the following:

- Draping, positioning, prepping, and transporting the patient
- Inserting nasogastric or orogastric tubes
- Inserting peripheral IV lines for fluid and medication administration
- Interpreting laboratory results (e.g., arterial blood gases, hematology, and blood chemistries)
- Interpreting monitored functions (e.g., blood pressure, brain stem evoked response (BSER), capnography, central nervous system (CNS) pressure, Doppler flow, electroencephalogram, heart rate, oximetry, respirations, and temperature)
- Placing airway tubes (e.g., endotracheal tube (ET) and orotracheal tube), including laryngoscopy (direct or endoscopic) for airway management
- Positioning external devices for capnography, cardiac monitoring, CNS evoked responses, Doppler flow, pulse oximetry, and temperature
- Stimulating nerves to determine level of paralysis or localization of nerve(s)

When the above services are provided to surgical patients, they are included as part of the anesthesia service. They are not coded and reported or reimbursed in addition to the anesthesia code. The above services are typically provided on the same date as the surgery performed.

EXAMPLE: A patient with sepsis underwent a sternal debridement surgical procedure for which the CRNA provided general anesthesia services. The procedure ended at 2 P.M., and by noon the next day, anesthesia services were concluded. Later that night at 10 P.M., the CRNA inserted an ET to establish an airway for the patient. Report codes 00550-P3 and 31500.

- Go to the CPT index and locate main term *Anesthesia* and subterm *Sternum* to locate code 00550. Refer to the Anesthesia section guidelines to assign physical status modifier -P3. (Sepsis is considered a severe systemic disease.)

- Go to the CPT index and locate main term *Endotracheal Tube* and subterm *Intubation* to locate code 31500.

>
> ## Note:
> Modifier -59 is added to code 31500 if allowed as a bundled service under the NCCI. This alerts the third-party payer that insertion of the ET was a distinct procedural service.

Coding Tip:

When an electromyogram (EMG) is performed to assess level of paralysis or localization of nerve(s), and results are documented in the patient's record, report the EMG code separately. An **electromyogram (EMG)** is a graphic tracing of a muscle's electrical activity at rest or during contraction, and it is used to diagnose nerve dysfunction and muscle disorders.

Monitored Anesthesia Care (MAC)

Monitored anesthesia care (MAC) is the administration of varying amounts of local, regional, and certain mind-altering drugs by an anesthesiologist or a CRNA during a patient's diagnostic or therapeutic procedure. CMS defines MAC as "the intraoperative monitoring of the surgical patient's vital physiological signs, in anticipation of the patient's need for general anesthesia or development of adverse physiological patient reaction to the surgery."

During MAC, the anesthesiologist or CRNA administers anesthetic medication through an IV line, monitors the patient's comfort level, and increases or decreases medication as needed (hence the name *monitored anesthesia care*). MAC includes a preoperative visit, intraoperative care, and postoperative anesthesia management. The anesthesiologist or CRNA provides the following services:

- Monitors vital signs and maintains patient's airway and continual evaluation of vital functions

- Diagnoses and treats clinical problems that occur during the procedure

- Administers analgesics, anesthetic agents, hypnotics, sedatives, or other medications as necessary to ensure patient safety and comfort

- Provides other medical services as needed for the safe completion of the procedure

Coding Tip:

Because monitored anesthesia care is a physician service provided to an individual patient and is based on medical necessity, reimbursement may be the same amount as for full general anesthesia services if all required services are properly documented. Report the appropriate anesthesia code and add an appropriate physical status modifier along with modifier -QS (monitored anesthesia care). In addition, report a qualifying circumstances code (from the Medicine section) when indicated. When appropriate, add one or more of the HCPCS level II anesthesia modifiers (discussed in the next section of this chapter) to the anesthesia code. Make sure you report the appropriate ICD code(s) that support(s) medical necessity for MAC and identifies the reason for the surgical procedure.

Note:

Monitored anesthesia care is not the same as moderate (conscious) sedation, which is reported with codes from the CPT Medicine section. Refer to Chapters 11 and 18 for information about moderate (conscious) sedation.

Exercise 10.2 – Overview of Anesthesia Section

Instructions: Enter a response for each item.

1. Anesthesia services include the preparation and monitoring of the patient, along with other services. Name five other services that are bundled with Anesthesia services.

_____

_____

_____

_____

_____

2. When services are provided to surgical patients that are not included as part of the anesthesia service code, they are reported separately. Modifier _____ is added to each code to indicate that the service provided was independent of the anesthesia service.

3. When an electromyogram (EMG) is performed to determine nerve dysfunction and report results are documented in the patient's record, the service is included in the reported anesthesia code. True or False?

4. With monitored anesthesia care (MAC), an anesthesiologist participates in care provided to a patient during a diagnostic or therapeutic procedure. List three services provided by the anesthesiologist as part of MAC.

_____

_____

_____

5. When reporting an anesthesia services code for which monitored anesthesia care was provided, add modifier to the code along with appropriate HCPCS level II anesthesia modifiers.

_____

Anesthesia Section Guidelines

Anesthesia services are reported by assigning a five-digit procedure code and adding appropriate modifiers. A physician (e.g., anesthesiologist) is responsible for supervising anesthesia services (which include general and regional), supplementation of local anesthesia, and other supportive services so the patient receives appropriate and optimal anesthesia care. The administration of local infiltration, metacarpal/metatarsal/ digital block, or topical anesthesia by the operating surgeon or obstetrician is included (bundled) in the surgery code; separate codes are not reported. Such anesthesia is not coded or reported separately because it is included in the surgery code (e.g., surgical procedure fee in physician's office, facility charge at an ambulatory surgical center or hospital outpatient department, and accommodation revenue code for a hospital inpatient).

An anesthesiologist's responsibilities include the following services, which are included (bundled) in the anesthesia code:

- Providing **airway management**: Ensuring an open airway to the patient's lungs.
- Administering analgesics and general anesthetic drugs and agents.
- Providing **fluid management**: Administering IV fluids to avoid dehydration, maintain an effective circulating volume, and prevent inadequate tissue perfusion.

Addressograph

PRE- AND POST-ANESTHESIA EVALUATION RECORD

PRE-ANESTHESIA EVALUATION

HISTORY TAKEN FROM:	❑ Patient	❑ Parent/ Guardian	❑ Significant Other	❑ Chart	❑ Poor Historian	❑ Language Barrier

PROPOSED PROCEDURE:

AGE	GENDER ❑ Male ❑ Female	HEIGHT	WEIGHT	BLOOD PRESSURE	PULSE	RESPIRATIONS	TEMPERATURE	O2 SAT%

PREVIOUS ANESTHESIA:	❑ None
PREVIOUS SURGERY:	❑ None
CURRENT MEDICATIONS:	❑ None
FAMILY HX – ANES. PROBLEMS:	❑ None
ALLERGIES	❑ None

AIRWAY	❑ MP1	❑ MP2	❑ MP3	❑ MP4	❑ Unrestricted neck ROM	❑ T-M distance = ________
(Enter X in appropriate boxes)	❑ Obesity		❑ ↓ neck ROM		❑ History of difficult airway	❑ Short muscular neck
	❑ Teeth poor repair		❑ Teeth chipped/loose		❑ Edentulous	❑ Facial hair

BODY SYSTEM	COMMENTS
RESPIRATORY	❑ WNL Tobacco Use: ❑ Yes ❑ No ❑ Quit ________ Packs/Day for ____ Years
CARDIOVASCULAR	❑ WNL Pre-procedure Cardiac Assessment:
GASTROINTESTINAL	❑ WNL Ethanol Use: ❑ Yes ❑ No ❑ Quit Frequency ____________ ❑ History of Ethanol abuse
MUSCULOSKELETAL	❑ WNL
GENITOURINARY	❑ WNL
OTHER	❑ WNL
PREGNANCY	❑ WNL ❑ AROM ❑ SROM ❑ Pitocin Drip ❑ Induction ❑ MgDrip Weeks Gestation: ____ G: ____ P: ____ EDC: ______

DIAGNOSTIC STUDIES
ECG
CHEST X-RAY
PULMONARY STUDIES

LABORATORY STUDIES
PT/PTT/INR:
T&S / T&C:
HCG:
LMP:
UA:

OTHER DIAGNOSTIC TESTS

PLANNED ANESTHESIA/MONITORS

PRE-ANESTHESIA MEDICATION

SIGNATURE OF ANESTHESIOLOGIST OR C.R.N.A.

POST-ANESTHESIA EVALUATION

Location	Time	B/P	O_2Sat	Pulse	Respirations	Temperature

❑ Awake ❑ Mask O_2 ❑ Somnolent ❑ Unarousable ❑ Oral/nasal airway
❑ Stable ❑ NC O_2 ❑ Unstable ❑ T-Piece ❑ Intubated ❑ Ventilator
❑ Regional – dermatome level: ❑ Continuous epidural analgesia
❑ Direct admit to hospital room ❑ No anesthesia related complications noted
❑ See notes for anesthesia related concerns ❑ Satisfactory postanesthesia/analgesia recovery

CONTROLLED MEDICATIONS

Medication	Used	Destroyed	Returned

SIGNATURE OF ANESTHESIOLOGIST OR C.R.N.A.

ALFRED STATE MEDICAL CENTER ■ 100 MAIN ST, ALFRED NY 14802 ■ (607) 555-1234

Permission to reprint granted by Alfred State College.

Figure 10-3 Sample pre- and post-anesthesia evaluation record

- Performing and documenting pre-anesthesia and post-anesthesia evaluations (Figure 10-3) and an anesthesia record (Figure 10-4).
- Monitoring the patient's cardiorespiratory status during surgery to include:
  - Blood pressure and temperature
  - **Capnography** (monitoring carbon dioxide levels)
  - Continuous electrocardiogram
  - Continuous **pulse oximetry** (arterial oxyhemoglobin saturation)
  - Low oxygen and circuit disconnect alarms
  - **Mass spectrometry** (monitors proper levels of the anesthetic)

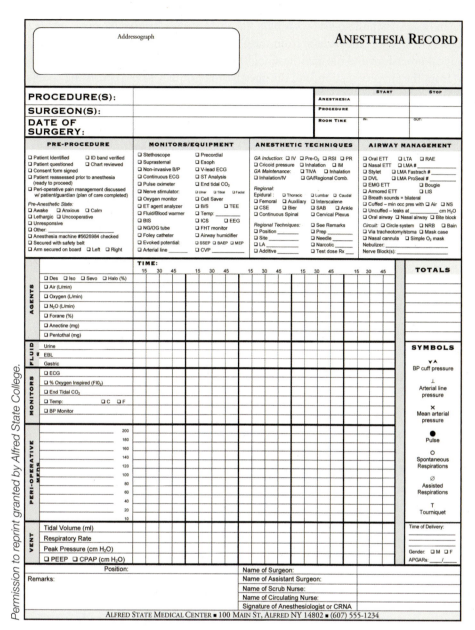

Figure 10-4 Sample anesthesia record

The anesthesiologist or CRNA is responsible for conducting a **pre-anesthesia evaluation** of the patient prior to surgery, which includes assessing information from the patient's record, interviewing the patient (e.g., history), conducting a physical examination, evaluating preoperative test results, and ensuring that informed anesthetic consent has been obtained. The pre-anesthesia evaluation is included (bundled) in the anesthesia services code. If the surgery for which a pre-anesthesia evaluation was performed is canceled, the anesthesiologist should report an evaluation and management service code (e.g., office or other outpatient consultation or inpatient consultation).

A **post-anesthesia evaluation** is also included (bundled) in the anesthesia services code and includes an evaluation of the patient during recovery from anesthesia, as well as evaluation, treatment, and follow-up of possible anesthesia-related complications. When an anesthesiologist or a CRNA provides significant, separately identifiable services (e.g., critical care services, postoperative pain management services, or unrelated ventilator management), the appropriate code(s) are reported for each service.

When a physician (e.g., anesthesiologist) *other than the physician performing the procedure* (e.g., surgeon) provides anesthesia services, report the code(s) from the CPT Anesthesia section. (This means that a surgeon is performing the surgical procedure and the anesthesiologist or CRNA is providing anesthesia services. The surgeon reports the code(s) from the Surgery section, and the anesthesiologist or CRNA reports the code(s) from the Anesthesia section.)

EXAMPLE: An anesthesiologist provides general anesthesia services for a patient who undergoes carpal tunnel surgery. Report code 01810 (with appropriate modifiers, discussed later in this chapter). (In the CPT index, locate main term *Anesthesia* and subterm *Wrist* to locate code 01810.)

When the surgeon (or another physician) provides general or regional anesthesia *in addition to performing the procedure for which anesthesia is administered*, report the code(s) from the CPT Surgery section and attach modifier -47 to each code. *Do not attach modifier -47 to an anesthesia code.* (This means that the surgeon is performing the surgical procedure and providing general or regional anesthesia services to the same patient during the same operative session. No anesthesiologist or CRNA is in the operating room providing anesthesia services.)

EXAMPLE: The surgeon provides regional anesthesia services for a 38-year-old female patient who undergoes a needle biopsy of the thyroid. Report code 60100-47.

• In the CPT index, locate main term *Thyroid Gland* and subterm *Needle Biopsy* to locate code 60100.

• Add modifier -47 to code 60100 to indicate that the physician who performed the surgical procedure also provided anesthesia services.

• Do *not* report code 00322 from the Anesthesia section of CPT.

Reporting Codes for Monitoring or Providing Other Services

When an anesthesiologist or a CRNA (or the surgeon if he or she is providing anesthesia services) performs unusual forms of monitoring or other services, report codes for each procedure or service separately. Add modifier -59 to each code reported in addition to the anesthesia code. Modifier -59 is added to codes that describe distinct procedural services performed during the same encounter, operative session, or patient's stay as the provision of anesthesia services (e.g., endotracheal intubation by anesthesiologist or CRNA after completion of anesthesia services).

 Note:

Peripheral venous access is the IV line that is inserted in a small peripheral vein in the hand or forearm. It is temporary and has to be routinely changed. A midline peripheral catheter (e.g., Landmark) is inserted in the patient's arm near the inside of the elbow and threaded up inside the arm about 6 inches. The catheter can remain inserted for about six weeks (e.g., short-term course of antibiotics) but is not practical for long-term IV therapy. Peripheral venous access and midline peripheral catheters are fl ushed with saline (to clean the catheter) and heparin (to prevent blood from clotting in the catheter). Neither type can be used to draw blood lab tests. (A peripheral venous access IV line uses a shorter catheter than that used for central venous pressure lines, described later in the chapter.)

EXAMPLE: An anesthesiologist inserts a percutaneous arterial line (catheter) to monitor the patient while providing the anesthesia services during an intracranial surgical procedure. Following surgery, the anesthesiologist inserts a Swan-Ganz (flow-directed) cardiac catheter. The anesthesiologist reports codes 00210, 36620-59, and 93503-59.

• In the CPT index, locate main term *Anesthesia* and subterm *Intracranial* to locate code 00210.

• In the CPT index, locate main term *Catheterization*, subterm *Arterial*, and 2nd qualifier *Percutaneous* to locate code 36620.

• In the CPT index, locate main term *Insertion*, subterm *Catheter*, 2nd qualifier *Cardiac*, and 3rd qualifier *Flow Directed* to locate code 93503.

- Modifier -59 indicates that the anesthesiologist provided distinct procedures in addition to anesthesia services on the same date.

Emergency Endotracheal Tube Intubation

An **endotracheal tube (ET)** is an artificial airway used for short-term airway management or mechanical ventilation due to potential or actual respiratory system insufficiency. The indications for endotracheal intubation include administration of medications during cardiopulmonary arrest, airway maintenance, oxygenation and ventilation, and secretion control.

Central Venous Access Devices (CVADs)

A **central venous access device (CVAD)** is a thin plastic tube (or catheter) that is inserted (or placed) into a vein and connected to a monitor. After insertion, a chest X-ray is done to verify that the catheter's tip is in the proper location above the heart. It measures a patient's central venous pressure (CVP) as an indicator of circulating blood volume, the heart's effectiveness as a pump, and the patient's vascular tone and response to treatment. CVADs are inserted due to the absence of a suitable peripheral access for fluid administration (e.g., rapid infusion of a high volume of fluid in a patient with **hypovolemia**, which is abnormally decreased blood volume). CVADs are also used for the administration of medications (e.g., potassium chloride and dopamine) that may be harmful to smaller **lumen** (opening) peripheral veins and/or for the insertion of a pacing wire.

 A **central venous pressure (CVP) line** (or **central venous pressure catheter**) is inserted through a vein in the neck (e.g., external or internal jugular vein) or a vein in the upper chest under the collarbone (e.g., subclavian vein) and then into a large central vein in the chest (e.g., superior vena cava). A CVP line can also be inserted through a vein in the leg (e.g., femoral) and then into a large central vein below the chest (e.g., inferior vena cava).

> **Note:**
>
> A CVP line (or CVP catheter) is also called a central venous catheter (CVC) or central venous line (CVL).

CVP lines are inserted as internal or external catheters depending on the patient's condition as well as the frequency and duration of infusions. An **external catheter** or **nontunneled catheter** is not implanted under the patient's skin, and it does not require a needle to be inserted into the skin to deliver medications. It is used when the patient requires frequent infusions that last several hours, and it requires a sterile dressing that must be changed once or twice daily. In addition, external catheters may require period injections of **heparin** (anticoagulant that prevents blood clots from developing in the catheter). The Cook (cystotomy catheter) is an example of an external catheter. Some nontunneled catheters require just a saline flush, and others require both a saline and a heparin flush. Blood can be drawn from a nontunneled catheter.

An **internal catheter** (or **tunneled catheter**) is implanted completely under the skin. (The catheter's tip is inserted in the superior vena cava, and the other end is "tunneled" about 6 inches away under the chest's skin and sealed with a Dacron cuff to prevent infection.) An internal catheter requires no special care when it is not being used since it is located completely under the skin. The AshSplit Cath (hemodialysis catheter), Groshong, and Hickman are examples of internal catheters. Some tunneled catheters require just a saline flush, and others require both a saline and heparin flush. Blood can be drawn from a tunneled catheter.

An **implanted port** is a small reservoir that has a rubber plug attached to the catheter that enters the patient's vein below the collarbone and is threaded into the superior vena cava. The port is implanted underneath the skin (local anesthesia and IV sedation). To access the catheter, the site must be located and cleaned and a special needle is inserted through the skin and into the rubber plug. Blood can be drawn from an implanted port.

Intra-Arterial Lines

An **intra-arterial line** (also called **intra-arterial cannula**, or **intra-arterial catheter**, or **A-line**) is a thin plastic tube, cannula, or catheter that is inserted into an artery and connected to a monitor. Its purpose is to measure immediate changes in intra-arterial blood pressure and concentrations of oxygen and carbon dioxide; it also is used to collect frequent blood samples for lab tests. An A-line is inserted when cardiopulmonary status is unstable or when serial (repeat) blood sampling is necessary.

Swan-Ganz Catheterization

A **Swan-Ganz catheter** is a thin, flexible, flow-directed multilumen plastic tube (or catheter) that is advanced from a peripheral vein into the right atrium and then positioned in a branch of the pulmonary artery. The catheter's balloon tip travels through the pulmonary artery, and pulmonary wedge pressure is measured in front of the temporarily inflated and wedged balloon. **Pulmonary wedge pressure** is the indirect measurement of left atrial pressure that is useful in the diagnosis of left ventricular failure and mitral valve disease. The Swan-Ganz catheter serves to obtain diagnostic information about the heart and to provide continuous monitoring of heart function in critically ill patients. The result is that the physician can evaluate circulatory volume due to acute valvular regurgitation, burns, congenital heart disease, heart failure, kidney disease, or shock. It is also used to monitor complications of myocardial infarction and the effects of certain heart medications.

Postoperative Pain Management

Postoperative pain management includes the administration of epidural or subarachnoid medications on the date(s) of service after the date of surgery. It is provided by the surgeon as part of the surgical procedure's global package, which means reimbursement is included in the CPT surgery code reported. When postoperative pain management is performed by the anesthesiologist, the surgeon must document the reason such care was transferred to the anesthesiologist. The anesthesiologist reports code 01996 just once each day that services are provided. Add modifier -59 to code 01996 on the day of *surgery* to indicate that a distinct procedural service was provided (in addition to administration of anesthesia during surgery that day). On subsequent postoperative days, if services are provided, do not add modifier -59 to code 01996.

Drug Administration Codes

Anesthesiologists and CRNAs do not report drug administration CPT codes from the Medicine section or HCPCS level II codes for anesthetic agents or other drugs administered from the time of the patient's arrival in the operating room through discharge from post-anesthesia care.

Anesthesia Modifiers

All anesthesia services require the following types of modifiers to be reviewed for assignment with reported anesthesia codes:

- HCPCS level II modifiers

- Physical status modifiers

- CPT modifiers

HCPCS Level II Anesthesia Modifiers

When applicable, the following HCPCS level II modifiers are added to reported anesthesia codes:

- -AA: Anesthesia services performed personally by anesthesiologist

- -AD: Medically supervised by a physician for more than four concurrent procedures

- -G8: Monitored anesthesia care for a deep, complex, complicated, or markedly invasive surgical procedure

Note:

Report modifier -G8 with CPT codes 00100, 00400, 00160, 00300, 00532, and 00920 only. Do not report modifier -G8 modifier with modifier -QS.

- -G9: Monitored anesthesia care for patient who has history of severe cardiopulmonary condition

- -QK: Medical direction of two, three, or four concurrent procedures involving qualified individuals

- -QS: Monitored anesthesia care

Note:

Add -QS to the anesthesia code if monitored anesthesia care (MAC) is provided. MAC involves the intraoperative monitoring of the patient's vital physiologic signs in anticipation of the need for administration of general anesthesia or of the development of adverse physiologic patient reaction to the surgical procedures.

- -QX: CRNA service with medical direction by physician

Note:

Assign modifier -QX when the CRNA alone provides anesthesia service to the patient and the anesthesiologist is not in the operating room with the CRNA but provides medical direction for the CRNA (e.g., from another operating room).

- -QY: Medical direction of one CRNA by an anesthesiologist

Note:

Assign modifier -QY when the CRNA and the anesthesiologist both provide anesthesia services to the same patient in the same operating room and the anesthesiologist provides medical direction for the CRNA.

- -QZ: CRNA service without medical direction by physician

  EXAMPLE: A CRNA provided general anesthesia services to an otherwise healthy patient who underwent a vaginal hysterectomy due to uterine fibroids. The CRNA received medical direction from an anesthesiologist. Report code 00944-P1-QX. (Modifier -P1 is a physical status modifier added to the anesthesia code, indicating a "normal healthy patient." Physical status modifiers are discussed in the next section of this chapter.)

Physical Status Modifiers

A **physical status modifier** is added to each reported anesthesia code to indicate the patient's condition at the time anesthesia was administered. The modifier also serves to identify the complexity of services provided. (The physical status modifier is determined by the anesthesiologist or CRNA and is documented as such in the patient record.) Physical status modifiers are represented by the letter *P* followed by a single digit from 1 to 6 as follows:

- -P1: Normal healthy patient (e.g., no biochemical, organic, physiologic, or psychiatric disturbance)

- -P2: Patient with mild systemic disease (e.g., anemia, chronic asthma, chronic bronchitis, diabetes mellitus, essential hypertension, heart disease that only slightly limits physical activity, or obesity)

- -P3: Patient with severe systemic disease (e.g., angina pectoris; chronic pulmonary disease that limits activity; history of prior myocardial infarction; heart disease that limits activity; poorly controlled essential hypertension; morbid obesity; or diabetes mellitus, type 1)

- -P4: Patient with severe systemic disease that is a constant threat to life (e.g., advanced pulmonary/renal/hepatic dysfunction, congestive heart failure, persistent angina pectoris, or unstable/rest angina)

- -P5: Moribund patient who is not expected to survive without the operation (e.g., abdominal aortic aneurysm)

- -P6: Patient declared brain dead whose organs are being removed for donor purposes

  EXAMPLE: An anesthesiologist provided general anesthesia services to a 65-year-old male with mild systemic disease who underwent total knee replacement. Report code 01402-P2.

CPT Modifiers

The following CPT modifiers should be reviewed to determine whether they need to be added to the reported anesthesia codes:

- -23: Unusual anesthesia

Coding Tip:

- When a patient's circumstances warrant the administration of general or regional anesthesia (instead of the usual local anesthesia), add modifier -23 to the anesthesia code. The following may require general or regional anesthesia services (when local anesthesia services are usually provided):
  - Extremely apprehensive patients
  - Mentally retarded individuals
  - Patients who have a physical condition (e.g., spasticity or tremors)

EXAMPLE: An anesthesiologist provided general anesthesia services to a 49-year-old male patient with chronic obstructive pulmonary disease who underwent extracorporeal shock wave lithotripsy with water bath. The patient was extremely anxious about the procedure, which normally does not require general anesthesia. Report code 00872-P3-23-AA.

- -59: Distinct procedural service

Coding Tip:

- An anesthesiologist or a CRNA reports the anesthesia code with the highest base unit value first. Modifier -59 is added to each separately reported anesthesia code.

- -74: Discontinued outpatient hospital/ambulatory surgery center procedure after anesthesia administration
- -99: Multiple modifiers

Time Reporting

Anesthesia services are reported based on time, which begins when the anesthesiologist or CRNA starts preparing the patient to receive anesthesia and ends when the anesthesiologist or CRNA is no longer in personal attendance. Anesthesia time units are reported for the amount of time the anesthesiologist or CRNA spends administering anesthesia, and reimbursement for anesthesia services varies according to increments of time. (Nonmonitored time is *not* considered when calculating time units.)

Note:

Teaching anesthesiologists must be present with the resident physician during all critical or key portions of the anesthesia service, and they must be immediately available to furnish anesthesia services during the entire procedure. Teaching CRNAs who are involved with two concurrent cases must be present with the student nurse anesthetist during pre- and post-anesthesia care for each case. They are prohibited from being involved in any other activities (e.g., pre-anesthesia evaluation of the patient for a third case) when two concurrent cases are ongoing.

EXAMPLE: A patient undergoes a cataract extraction and requires 90 minutes of MAC by the anesthesiologist, which includes the administration of a sedative along with a retrobulbar injection for regional block anesthesia. Subsequently, an interval of 30 minutes transpires, during which time the patient does not require monitoring by the anesthesiologist. After this period, monitoring commences for

Table 10-1 Sample Portion of Anesthesia Base Unit Values

© Cengage Learning 2014

CPT Code	Description Base Unit Value
00100	5
00102	6
00103	5
00104	4
00120	5

30 additional minutes until the patient is released to the recovery room. The anesthesiologist reports 120 minutes of time on the claim.

Payment for anesthesia services is based on the sum of an anesthesia code-specific base unit value plus anesthesia time units and modifying units multiplied by the locality-specific anesthesia conversion factor. The formula for calculating the anesthesia fee is as follows: [code-specific base unit value + anesthesia time unit(s) + modifying unit(s)] × locality-specific anesthesia conversion factor (e.g., [5 + 3 + 0] × $17.04 = anesthesia fee).

- The code-specific **base unit value** for anesthesia codes (00100–01999) represents the degree of difficulty associated with providing anesthesia for a surgical procedure (Table 10-1).

- **Anesthesia time units** are based on the total anesthesia time, and they are reported as one unit for each 15 minutes (or fraction thereof) of anesthesia time. (Anesthesia time begins when the anesthesiologist or CRNA begins to prepare the patient for anesthesia care and ends when the anesthesiologist is no longer in personal attendance.)

- **Modifying units** recognize added complexities associated with the administration of anesthesia, including physical factors and difficult circumstances. Physical factors indicating the patient's condition at the time anesthesia was administered are reported by adding the appropriate physical status modifier (P1–P6) to the anesthesia code. Difficult circumstances are reported with qualifying circumstances codes, located in the CPT Medicine section. The relative values for physical status modifiers and qualifying circumstances codes are located in the current year's American Society of Anesthesiologists (ASA) *Relative Value Guide* publication (Table 10-2).

- The locality-specific **anesthesia conversion factor** is the dollar amount assigned to a geographic location (Table 10-3).

 When the patient undergoes more than one procedure during the same operative episode and the anesthesiologist or CRNA provides multiple anesthesia services for the same patient during the same operative session, the anesthesia fee is based on the *highest* code base unit value when multiple stand-alone anesthesia codes are reported (which is added to the total anesthesia time for all services provided). (The anesthesia code with the highest code base unit is reported. The exception is when an anesthesia code has add-on codes, which are also reported, and reimbursement for multiple anesthesia services is based on the sum of the base unit values.)

Note:

Anesthesia time reported includes monitoring during administration of regional block anesthesia and during the procedure. Interval and recovery room times are not included when calculating time, although the anesthesiologist or CRNA is required to document the patient's condition on the recovery room record (Figure 10-5).

Note:

Base unit values and modifying unit relative values are available as downloadable files at http://www.cms.hhs.gov. Click on the All Fee-for-Service Providers link (located toward the bottom of the page), and click on the Anesthesiologists Center link to locate the Anesthesia Base Units file.

Table 10-2 Sample Portion of Modifying Units and Relative Values

CPT Physical Status Modifier	Relative Value
-P1	0
-P2	0
-P3	1
-P4	2
-P5	3
-P6	0
CPT Qualifying Circumstances Code	**Relative Value**
99100	1
99116	5
99135	5
99140	2

© Cengage Learning 2014

Table 10-3 Sample Portion of Locality-Specific Anesthesia Conversion Factors

Payer Number	Locality Number	Locality Name	Conversion Factor
00500	00	Alabama	$17.04
00830	01	Alaska	$29.66
00832	00	Arizona	$17.83
00520	13	Arkansas	$16.52

Permission to reuse in accordance with Centers for Medicare & Medicaid Services http://www.cms.hhs.gov Digital Rights, Copyrights, Trademarks & Patents Policy Web site.

EXAMPLE 1: A 22-year-old female patient who has chronic asthma underwent a planned vaginal delivery on May 14, during which neuraxial labor anesthesia was administered by an anesthesiologist. Report code 01967-P2. (Anesthesia code 01967 has a base unit value of 5, and physical status modifier -P2 has a relative value of 0.) A review of the patient record indicates 45 minutes of anesthesia time, which is calculated as 3 anesthesia time units (45 ÷ 15 = 3). If a conversion factor of $17.45 is assigned to New York State, payment for anesthesia services is calculated as $139.60. The formula for calculating anesthesia services reimbursement is as follows:

    STEP 1: (5 + 3 + 0) × $17.45

    STEP 2: 8 × $17.45

    AMOUNT: $139.60

EXAMPLE 2: A 22-year-old female patient who has chronic asthma was prepared for a planned vaginal delivery on May 14, during which neuraxial labor anesthesia was administered by an anesthesiologist. Complications required that an emergency cesarean delivery be performed instead of the planned vaginal delivery. Report codes 01968-P2 and 99140 *in addition to* code 01967-P2. (Reimbursement for multiple anesthesia services is based on the sum of each base unit value because code 01968 is an add-on code.) Anesthesia code 01967 has a base unit value of 5, and code 01968 has a base unit value of 2. The total length of anesthesia time for both procedures was 75 minutes, which is calculated as 5 anesthesia time units (75 ÷ 15 = 5). The patient is assigned physical status modifier -P2, which has a relative value of 0, and code 99140 has a relative value of 2. If the conversion factor is $17.45, payment

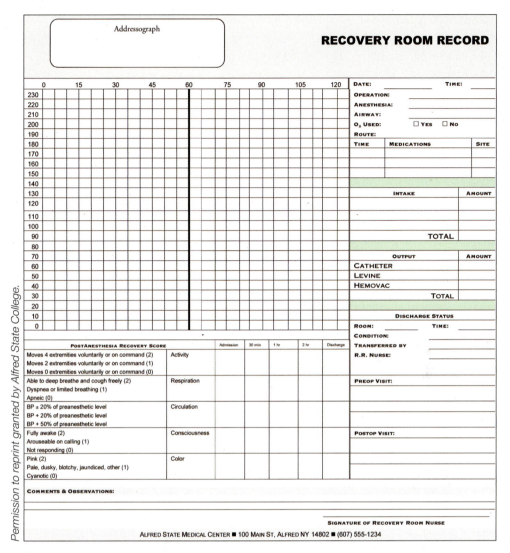

Figure 10-5 Sample recovery room record

for anesthesia services is calculated as $244.30. The formula for calculating anesthesia services reimbursement is as follows:

STEP 1: $(5 + 2 + 5 + 2) \times \$17.45$

STEP 2: $14 \times \$17.45$

AMOUNT: $\$244.30$

EXAMPLE 3: A 39-year-old male patient who has otherwise been healthy sustained multiple trauma and was administered general anesthesia by an anesthesiologist during cranial surgery and upper abdominal surgery. Both surgical procedures were performed during the same operative session. (Reimbursement for multiple anesthesia services is based on the highest ASA base unit value when anesthesia for two separate procedures is provided.) Assign codes 00210-P5, and 99140. (Do not report code 00790 for the administration of anesthesia for the upper abdominal surgery because it was provided during the same operative episode as anesthesia administered for the cranial surgery.) If anesthesia code 00210 has a base unit value of 11 and code 00790 has a base unit value of 7, use value 11 when determining anesthesia reimbursement (because code 00790 is not reported). The total length of anesthesia time for both procedures was 120 minutes, which is calculated as 8 anesthesia time units ($120 \div 15 = 8$). Physical status modifier -P5 is assigned a relative value of 3, and code 99140 is assigned a relative value of 2. If the conversion factor is $17.45, payment for anesthesia services is calculated as $418.80. The formula for calculating anesthesia services reimbursement is as follows:

STEP 1: (11 + 8 + [3 + 2]) × $17.45

STEP 2: (19 + 5) × $17.45

STEP 3: 24 × $17.45

AMOUNT: $418.80

Medicare defines **concurrent medically directed anesthesia procedures** as "the maximum number of procedures an anesthesiologist or CRNA medically directs within the context of a single procedure and when the procedures overlap each other." The ASA base unit value is reduced for subsequent anesthesia services when the definition of *concurrent medically directed anesthesia procedures* applies to the submission of multiple anesthesia codes. (Base unit value reduction of services is determined by the third-party payer.)

EXAMPLE: Procedures A through E are concurrent medically directed anesthesia procedures provided by an anesthesiologist on May 20. The start and end times for each procedure represent the periods during which anesthesia time is counted.

Procedure	Start Time	End Time	Number of Concurrent Procedures	Base Unit Value Reduction
A	8:00 A.M.	8:20 A.M.	2	10%
B	8:10 A.M.	8:45 A.M.	2	10%
C	8:30 A.M.	9:15 A.M.	2	10%

© Cengage Learning 2014

- During procedure A, the anesthesiologist medically directed two concurrent procedures A and B (from 8:10 A.M. to 8:20 A.M.).

- During procedure B, the anesthesiologist medically directed two concurrent procedures A and B from 8:10 A.M. to 8:20 A.M. and then procedures B and C from 8:30 A.M. to 8:45 A.M.

- Thus, during each procedure A and B, the anesthesiologist medically directed, at most, two concurrent procedures.

Anesthesia Services

Assign the appropriate CPT evaluation and management (E/M) code when anesthesia services are provided in an office, home, or hospital, which includes consultation services and other medical services. (When an anesthesiologist or a CRNA administers anesthesia during a surgical procedure and provides pre-anesthesia and post-anesthesia care, do *not* assign a CPT E/M consultation code.) When an anesthesiologist or a CRNA performs a pre-anesthesia evaluation and determines that anesthesia cannot be administered, report an E/M consultation code.

Supplied Physician

When an anesthesiologist or a CRNA provides materials and supplies (e.g., sterile trays and drugs) over and above those usually included with the office visit or other services rendered, report the materials and supplies separately with CPT code 99070.

Separate or Multiple Procedures

When multiple surgical procedures are performed during the provision of anesthesia services, report the anesthesia code that represents the most complex procedure performed. However, if the additional anesthesia code for multiple surgical procedures performed is an add-on code, report all codes. The time reported for the provision of anesthesia services is the combined total for all procedures performed.

Separate Report

When an unlisted service code is reported, a special report must be submitted with the insurance claim to demonstrate medical appropriateness. The provider should document the following elements in the special report:

- Complexity of patient's symptoms

- Description of nature, extent, and need for service

- Diagnostic and therapeutic procedures performed

- Follow-up care

- Patient's final diagnosis and concurrent problems

- Pertinent physical findings

- Time, effort, and equipment required to provide the service

 Note:

For hernia repair procedures performed on infants younger than 1 year of age at the time of surgery, assign code 00834 or 00836, depending on the infant's age.

Qualifying Circumstances

When anesthesia services are provided during situations or circumstances that make anesthesia administration more difficult, report a **qualifying circumstances** code from the CPT Medicine section (in addition to the anesthesia code). Difficult circumstances depend on factors such as extraordinary condition of patient, notable operative conditions, or unusual risk factors. These codes are reported in addition to the anesthesia codes. Qualifying circumstances codes include the following:

Note:

An **emergency condition** results when a delay in treatment of the patient would lead to a significant increase in threat to life or body part.

- 99100: Anesthesia for patient of extreme age, under 1 year and over 70

- 99116: Anesthesia complicated by utilization of total body hypothermia

- 99135: Anesthesia complicated by utilization of controlled hypotension

- 99140: Anesthesia complicated by emergency conditions (specify)

  EXAMPLE: A 92-year-old female patient received general anesthesia services from a CRNA and was monitored by an anesthesiologist during total left hip arthroplasty. Report codes 01214-P2-QX and 99100.

Exercise 10.3 – Anesthesia Section Guidelines

Instructions: Match the term with its definition.

_____ **1.** Administering intravenous fluids to avoid dehydration   **a.** Airway management

_____ **2.** Arterial oxyhemoglobin saturation   **b.** Capnography

_____ **3.** Ensuring an open airway to the patient's lungs   **c.** Fluid management

_____ **4.** Monitoring proper levels of the anesthetic   **d.** Mass spectrometry

_____ **5.** Monitoring carbon dioxide levels   **e.** Pulse oximetry

(continues)

Exercise 10.3 (continued)

Instructions: Match the type of evaluation with its description. Answers may be assigned more than once.

_____ 6. Conducting a physical examination

_____ 7. Evaluating the patient during anesthesia recovery

_____ 8. Interviewing the patient

_____ 9. Obtaining informed anesthetic consent

_____ 10. Treatment of anesthesia-related complications

a. Pre-anesthesia evaluation

b. Post-anesthesia evaluation

Instructions: Indicate whether each statement is true (T) or false (F).

_____ 11. When an anesthesiologist or a CRNA performs unusual forms of monitoring or other services, the codes are reported separately and modifier -59 is added to each code.

_____ 12. When local infiltration, metacarpal/metatarsal/digital block, or topical anesthesia is administered by the operating surgeon or obstetrician, it is included in the surgery code.

_____ 13. When a physician (e.g., anesthesiologist) other than the physician performing the procedure provides anesthesia services, report the code(s) from the CPT Anesthesia section.

_____ 14. When the surgeon (or other physician) provides general or regional anesthesia in addition to performing the procedure for which anesthesia is administered, report the anesthesia code for the procedure performed and attach modifier -47 to that code.

_____ 15. Anesthesia services are reported based on time, which begins when the anesthesiologist or CRNA starts preparing the patient to receive anesthesia and ends when the patient is discharged from the recovery room.

_____ 16. Anesthesia time units are reported for the amount of time the anesthesiologist or CRNA spends administering anesthesia, and reimbursement for anesthesia services varies according to increments of time.

_____ 17. When calculating anesthesia time units, do not include nonmonitored time.

_____ 18. A patient undergoes a surgical procedure that requires 30 minutes of monitored anesthesia care by the anesthesiologist. Then 15 minutes transpires when the patient does not require monitoring by the anesthesiologist. After this interval, the anesthesiologist commences monitoring for 15 additional minutes until the patient is released to the recovery room. The number of anesthesia time units is 3.

_____ 19. Payment for anesthesia services is based on the following formula: [code-specific base unit value + anesthesia time unit(s) + modifying unit(s)] × locality-specific anesthesia conversion factor = anesthesia fee.

_____ 20. A 38-year-old female patient who has diabetes mellitus underwent a planned vaginal delivery on November 14, during which neuraxial labor anesthesia was administered by an anesthesiologist. Code 01967-P2 is reported (base unit value of 5 and relative value of 0). A review of the patient record indicates 60 minutes of anesthesia time. The conversion factor is $17.45. The payment for anesthesia services is calculated as $139.60.

Instructions: Match the physical status modifier with the example.

_____ 21. A patient who is on medication for petit mal seizures undergoes emergency appendectomy.

_____ 22. A patient with late-stage adenocarcinoma of the left breast undergoes left mastectomy.

_____ 23. A healthy patient undergoes colonoscopy.

_____ 24. A patient with end-stage renal disease undergoes laparoscopic cholecystectomy.

_____ 25. A patient with cardiomyopathy undergoes heart transplant.

a. P1 (normal healthy patient)

b. P2 (patient with mild systemic disease)

c. P3 (patient with severe systemic disease)

d. P4 (patient with severe systemic disease that is a constant threat to life)

e. P5 (moribund patient who is not expected to survive without the operation)

f. P6 (patient declared brain dead whose organs are being removed for donor purposes)

Anesthesia Subsections

The Anesthesia section is organized according to general anatomic areas or services that relate to a number of surgical procedures. For Medicare purposes, just one anesthesia code is usually reported unless the second and subsequent anesthesia codes are add-on codes. When unusual procedures and services are provided by the anesthesiologist, report separate anesthesia codes. The code that describes the anesthesia service for the procedure that has the *highest* base unit value is reported first.

The Anesthesia section includes add-on codes for anesthesia services provided to patients undergoing burn excisions or debridement and obstetrics procedures. The add-on code is reported in addition to the code for the primary anesthesia service.

Head

Anesthesia services for the Head subsection include procedures on the following anatomic sites: accessory sinuses, ears, eyelids, eyes, facial bones, lips, nose, salivary glands, and skull. Codes for anesthesia services provided for electroconvulsive therapy (ECT) and intraoral and intracranial procedures are also included. Refer to Table 10-4 for coding rules associated with Head subsection anesthesia codes.

Coding Tip:

- When an anesthesiologist or a CRNA provides distinct procedural services (e.g., insertion of the Swan-Ganz catheter) in addition to anesthesia services, codes are reported separately and modifier -59 is added to each code.
- Surgical endoscopy/arthroscopy always includes diagnostic endoscopy/arthroscopy. This means that if an anesthesiologist or a CRNA provides anesthesia services for a diagnostic and a surgical endoscopy/arthroscopy that are performed during the same operative session, report just one anesthesia services code with appropriate modifiers. This coding tip applies to the following subsections: knee and popliteal area, lower leg (below knee, includes ankle and foot), shoulder and axilla, and upper arm and elbow.

Table 10-4 Coding Rules Associated with Neck Subsection Anesthesia Codes

Code(s)	Coding Rule
00102	Code 00102 is reported when anesthesia services are provided for plastic repair of a cleft lip, and code 00172 is reported when a cleft lip repair is performed. To report non-cleft lip repairs, assign code 00300. A **cleft lip** is a congenital deformity of the upper lip that failed to close during development; types include unilateral, bilateral, and median (harelip) and may be accompanied by defects of the maxilla and hard palate. NOTE: Bilateral cleft lip describes the type of defect, not the surgery performed.
00104	When a procedure code for electroconvulsive therapy is reported on a claim that is submitted to a Medicare administrative contractor, it is denied as a noncovered service. This means that code 00104, anesthesia for electroconvulsive therapy, will also be denied by Medicare. **Electroconvulsive therapy (ECT)** (or **shock therapy**) involves briefly applying an electric current to the brain to produce a seizure; its purpose is to relieve depression, schizophrenia, and severe affective disorders.
00170	To justify medical necessity for code 00170, make sure you report an appropriate ICD diagnosis code. Medicare does not cover anesthesia services for the care, filling, removal, replacement, or treatment of teeth or structures directly supporting the teeth.
00190	Code 00190 is reported when anesthesia services are provided during extradural procedures on bone(s) of the skull. An **extradural procedure** is performed on the outer side of the **dura mater**, which is the membrane that forms the outer covering of the **central nervous system (CNS)** (brain and spinal cord).
00218	Code 00218 is reported for anesthesia services provided during any **intracranial** (introduced into or within the skull) procedure performed while the patient is in a seated position.

Table 10-5 Coding Rules Associated with Head Subsection Anesthesia Codes

Code(s)	Coding Rule
00300	When a patient who undergoes removal of a **lesion** (abnormal tissue resulting from autoimmune or metabolic disorders, infection, neoplasm, or trauma) that requires an anesthesiologist or a CRNA to provide anesthesia services, report code 00300. When such services are provided, make sure you report an appropriate ICD diagnosis code to justify medical necessity (e.g., mentally retarded patient who exhibits severe anxiety about undergoing the procedure). (And make sure you are prepared to send the payer a copy of the patient record.) The surgeon who removes a lesion usually provides anesthesia services, which involve administration of local anesthesia. If general or regional anesthesia is administered by the surgeon, add modifier -47 to the surgery code. NOTE: Modifier -47 is never added to an anesthesia code.
00326	When procedures on the larynx and trachea are performed on a patient who is younger than 1 year of age, report 00326. *Do not report code 99100 on the same claim as code 00326.*
00350–00352	Codes 00350–00352 are not reported when anesthesia services are provided during arteriography. Instead, report code 01916.

© Cengage Learning 2014

EXAMPLE: A healthy patient underwent soft tissue biopsy of the accessory sinuses, for which a CRNA provided anesthesia services. The CRNA was supervised by an anesthesiologist. Report code 00164-P1-QX.

Neck

Anesthesia services for the Neck subsection include procedures on the following anatomic sites: integumentary system; muscles and nerves of the head, neck, and posterior trunk; esophagus, thyroid, larynx, trachea, and lymphatic system of the neck; and major vessels of the neck. Refer to Table 10-5 for coding rules associated with Neck subsection anesthesia codes.

EXAMPLE: An anesthesiologist provided anesthesia services to a terminally ill 1-year-old patient who underwent laryngoscopy. Report code 00320-P4-AA.

Thorax (Chest Wall and Shoulder Girdle)

Anesthesia services for the Thorax (Chest Wall and Shoulder Girdle) subsection include procedures on the following anatomic sites: integumentary system on the extremities, anterior trunk and perineum; breast; clavicle; scapula; and ribs. Anesthesia services for an electrical conversion of arrhythmias procedure are also included. Refer to Table 10-6 for coding rules associated with Thorax (Chest Wall and Shoulder Girdle) subsection anesthesia codes.

EXAMPLE: A 79-year-old female patient underwent bilateral radical mastectomy with internal mammary node dissection (12 lymph nodes). She was recently diagnosed with metastatic adenocarcinoma of the breast to the lung. The anesthesiologist provided general anesthesia services. Report codes 00406-P5-AA and 99100.

The surgeon who removes a skin lesion usually provides local anesthesia or MAC. If general or regional anesthesia services are provided by the surgeon, add modifier -47 to the surgery code. (*Do not add modifier -47 to an anesthesia code.*) If general anesthesia, regional anesthesia, or MAC is provided by an anesthesiologist or a CRNA, report the appropriate code, physical status modifier, and qualifying circumstances codes. (Add modifier -QS to the anesthesia code if MAC is provided.) Make sure you report an appropriate ICD diagnosis code to justify medical necessity (e.g., mentally retarded patient who exhibits severe anxiety about undergoing the procedure).

EXAMPLE: An anesthesiologist provided MAC for a 5-year-old patient who underwent a biopsy of the perineum. Report 00400-P1-QS-AA.

Table 10-6 Coding Rules Associated with Thorax (Chest Wall and Shoulder Girdle) Subsection Anesthesia Codes

Code	Coding Rule
00400	Surgical procedures of the skin are often performed under local anesthesia. When monitored anesthesia care (MAC) is provided by an anesthesiologist or a CRNA due to the patient's age, mental status, or size of the skin lesion, report the appropriate anesthesia code, physical status modifier, and HCPCS level II modifier -QS. Also report a qualifying circumstances code if indicated.
00402	Reconstructive breast procedures are reported with code 00402.
00404	Radical or modified radical breast procedures that do not include internal mammary node dissection are reported with code 00404.
00406	When an internal mammary node dissection is performed *in addition to a radical or modified radical breast procedure,* report code 00406. (If internal mammary node dissection is *not* performed, report code 00404.)

- If the surgeon had provided MAC, you would have reported code 56605. (*Do not report modifier -QS or modifier -47.*)
- If the surgeon had provided general or regional anesthesia services, you would have reported code 56605-47.

Intrathoracic

Anesthesia services for the Intrathoracic subsection include procedures on the following anatomic sites: bronchus, coronary arteries, diaphragm, esophagus, great vessels of chest, heart, lungs, mediastinum, pericardial sac, pleura, sternum, and thorax. Refer to Table 10-7 for coding rules associated with Intrathoracic subsection anesthesia codes.

EXAMPLE: A 39-year-old female patient with severe systemic disease underwent sternal debridement for which the anesthesiologist provided general anesthesia services. Report code 00550-P3-AA.

Spine and Spinal Cord

Anesthesia services for the Spine and Spinal Cord subsection include procedures on the following anatomic sites: cervical, thoracic, and lumbar spine and spinal cord. Refer to Table 10-8 for coding rules associated with Spine and Spinal Cord subsection anesthesia codes.

EXAMPLE: General anesthesia services were provided by an anesthesiologist during an otherwise healthy patient's thoracic spine surgery. Report code 00620-P1-AA.

Note:

When a physician performs spinal manipulation under anesthesia, report code 22505. Other manipulation under anesthesia codes include 23700, 24300, 25259, 26340, 27275, 27570, and 27860. For these codes, *manipulation* refers to "reduction" of a fracture, which is typically reimbursed by payers. When spinal manipulation is performed without anesthesia, report code 97140, which is located in the Physical Medicine and Rehabilitation subsection of the CPT Medicine section.

Upper Abdomen

Anesthesia services for the Upper Abdomen subsection include procedures on the following anatomic sites: upper abdominal wall, liver, major abdominal blood vessels, pancreas, and stomach. This subsection also includes

Table 10-7 Coding Rules Associated with Intrathoracic Subsection Anesthesia Codes

Code(s)	Coding Rule
00500	The "procedures on esophagus" described in code 00500 require (intrathoracic) chest incision. For "procedures on esophagus" that do *not* require (intrathoracic) chest incision, report 00320.
00528, 00529	Anesthesia services for endoscopic procedures (e.g., esophagoscopy, bronchoscopy, mediastinoscopy, and thoracoscopy) are usually provided by the surgeon who performs the procedure. If an anesthesiologist or a CRNA provides general or regional anesthesia services, report 00528 or 00529 and the appropriate physical status and HCPCS level II modifiers. (When MAC is provided by the anesthesiologist or CRNA, also add HCPCS level II modifier -QS.)
00530-00534	General anesthesia or monitored anesthesia care may be reimbursed by Medicare if they are determined to be reasonable and necessary. Adequate documentation of medical necessity is reviewed on a case-by-case basis. When pacemaker surgery involves the use of the transthoracic method of implantation (code 00560), which requires open surgery, it is accepted practice that general anesthesia services will be provided. Medicare will reimburse such services, and it is unnecessary to submit special medical documentation to Medicare for consideration. According to Ingenix's *Coding and Payment Guide for Anesthesia Services*, Medicare will reimburse general anesthesia or MAC when the patient's record documents: • Diagnoses of other hyperalimentation (278.8), intermediate coronary syndrome (411.1), pulmonary valve disorders (424.3), and/or congestive heart failures (category 428). • The fact that the patient is uncontrollable under local anesthesia (e.g., small child) is disoriented, or has mental confusion.
00528–00529 00540–00541	**One lung ventilation (OLV)** is the isolation of the right or left lung so that one lung is ventilated and the other is allowed to collapse. OLV is performed to (1) improve surgical access so the surgeon can perform lung surgery, (2) prevent the other lung from being contaminated by blood or pus from the diseased lung during surgery (because an anesthetized patient loses the ability to cough and, thus, the ability to prevent infected material or blood from entering the normal lung), or (3) provide intensive care ventilation to prevent the normal lung from being subjected to the high pressure required to ventilate an abnormal lung (e.g., after a single lung transplant). When OLV is provided, assign code 00529 or 00541. When OLV is not provided (because bilateral lung ventilation is provided), assign code 00528 or 00540.
00561	Do not report qualifying circumstances codes 99100 with code 00561, which includes in its description "under one year of age." Also do not report qualifying circumstances code 99116 or 99135 with code 00561 because "total body hypothermia" and "controlled hypotension" are included in general anesthesia services for procedures on the heart, pericardial sac, and great vessels of the chest.
00560–00566	A **pump oxygenator** is a device that substitutes for the heart (pump) and lungs (oxygenator) during open heart surgery. A pump oxygenator is not typically used for coronary artery bypass grafting (CABG) or laser myocardial revascularization surgery, and the patient's beating heart provides circulatory support.

anesthesia codes for upper gastrointestinal (GI) endoscopic procedures and hernia repairs and laparoscopy. Refer to Table 10-9 for coding rules associated with Upper Abdomen subsection anesthesia codes.

EXAMPLE: An anesthesiologist provides general anesthesia services for a patient who undergoes a liver transplant. Report 00796-P5-AA.

Lower Abdomen

Anesthesia services for the Lower Abdomen subsection include procedures on the following anatomic sites: lower abdominal wall, **panniculus adiposus**, or **pannus**, (layer of subcutaneous adipose tissue, or fat, below the dermis that contains fat deposits, blood vessels, and nerves). The following anatomic sites are accessed via transabdominal incision: uterus; fallopian tubes; and urinary tract, including kidneys, and urinary bladder; prostate

Table 10-8 Coding Rules Associated with Spine and Spinal Cord Subsection Anesthesia Codes

Code	Coding Rule
00600	When anesthesia services for diagnostic and therapeutic percutaneous image-guided spine and spinal cord procedures are provided, report codes 01935–01936 instead of 00600.
00604	When anesthesia services are provided for a patient who undergoes cervical spine and cord surgery in a sitting position, report code 00604.
00635	A **lumbar puncture (LP)** or **spinal tap**, involves inserting a **cannula** (hollow needle) at the L3-4 or L4-5 (lumbar vertebrae) to remove cerebrospinal fluid (CSF) for diagnostic or therapeutic purposes (e.g., measure CSF pressure or analyze CSF fluid).
00640	Report code 00640 when anesthesia is provided for closed procedures on the cervical, lumbar, or thoracic spine. Third-party payers do not usually reimburse 00640 when reported for spinal manipulation under anesthesia (SMUA) to treat low back pain or other neuromusculoskeletal disorders by improving range of motion and reducing spinal pain.

© Cengage Learning 2014

Table 10-9 Coding Rules Associated with Upper Abdomen Subsection Anesthesia Codes

Code	Coding Rule
00740	Anesthesia services (e.g., sedation) for endoscopic procedures (e.g., upper GI endoscopy) are usually provided by the surgeon who performs the procedure. If an anesthesiologist or a CRNA provides general or regional anesthesia services, report 00740 and the appropriate physical status and HCPCS level II modifiers. (When MAC is provided by the anesthesiologist or CRNA, also add HCPCS level II modifier -QS.)
00796	Code 00796 is reported for anesthesia services provided to the recipient of a liver transplant. Assign code 01990 for anesthesia services provided to a brain-dead patient who undergoes liver **organ harvest** (removal of an organ for transplantation).

© Cengage Learning 2014

gland; adrenal glands; lower abdominal vessels; and inferior vena cava. This subsection also includes anesthesia codes for lower intestinal endoscopic procedures and hernia repairs and lower abdomen intraperitoneal procedures including laparoscopy. Refer to Table 10-10 for coding rules associated with Lower Abdomen subsection anesthesia codes.

EXAMPLE: An anesthesiologist provided regional anesthesia services to a diabetic patient who underwent total cystectomy. Report code 00864-P2-AA.

Perineum

Anesthesia services for the Perineum subsection include procedures on the following anatomic sites: anus, rectum, perineum, vulva, vas deferens, seminal vesicles, testes, penis, vagina, labia, cervix, endometrium, uterus, prostate, urethra, urinary bladder, and ureters. Refer to Table 10-11 for coding rules associated with Perineum subsection anesthesia codes.

EXAMPLE: An anesthesiologist provided general anesthesia services to a hypertensive patient who underwent vulvectomy. Report code 00906-P2-AA.

For anesthesia services provided during perineal muscle and nerve procedures, report code 00300. For anesthesia services provided during perineal skin procedures, report code 00400.

EXAMPLE 1: An anesthesiologist provided general anesthesia services to 4-year-old female healthy patient who underwent perineal skin biopsy. Report code 00400-P1-AA.

EXAMPLE 2: An anesthesiologist provided regional anesthesia services to an anxious diabetic patient who underwent left gluteus maximus muscle biopsy. Report code 00300-P2-AA.

Table 10-10 Coding Rules Associated with Lower Abdomen Subsection Anesthesia Codes

Code(s)	Coding Rule
00802	**Panniculectomy** is the surgical removal of excess abdominal panniculus (or pannus), which is a redundant layer of fat tissue (or apron) located at the lowest portion of the abdominal wall. (Patients who have lost significant weight after undergoing a previous gastric restrictive procedure for morbid obesity often develop excess pannus.)
00810, 00840	Anesthesia services (e.g., sedation) for endoscopic procedures (e.g., lower intestinal endoscopy and laparoscopy) are usually provided by the surgeon who performs the procedure. If an anesthesiologist or a CRNA provides general or regional anesthesia services, report 00810 or 00840 and the appropriate physical status and HCPCS level II modifiers. (When MAC is provided by the anesthesiologist or CRNA, also add HCPCS level II modifier -QS.)
00834–00836	When a hernia repair is performed on an infant less than 1 year of age, report code 00834 or 00836 (depending on age). *Do not report qualifying circumstances code 99100 with code 00834 or 00836.* For patients 1 year of age or older who undergo hernia repair surgery, report code 00830 or 00832 (depending on type of hernia).
00868	Code 00868 is reported for anesthesia services provided to the recipient of a kidney transplant. Assign code 00862 for anesthesia services provided to a living kidney donor. Assign code 01990 for anesthesia service provided to a brain-dead patient who undergoes a kidney organ harvest.
00872	**Extracorporeal shock wave lithotripsy (ESWL)** uses ultrasound shock waves to crush calculi (stones) located in the bladder, renal pelvis, or ureter. A **lithotripter** is the device that administers a high-voltage electrical discharge through a spark gap under water, which produces a compressive force and breaks apart the stones so they can pass in urine. Typically, the surgeon provides monitored anesthesia case (MAC) to the patient. However, if an anesthesiologist or a CRNA provides general or regional anesthesia services, report 00872 and the appropriate physical status and HCPCS level II modifiers. If MAC is provided by the anesthesiologist, add HCPCS level II modifier -QS.

Table 10-11 Coding Rules Associated with Perineum Subsection Anesthesia Codes

Code(s)	Coding Rule
00902	For anesthesia services provided during lower intestinal endoscopic procedures, report code 00810.
00910–00918	When anesthesia services are provided for **urethrocystoscopy** (visualization of urethra and urinary bladder) and the surgeon completes other procedures through the urethrocystocope (e.g., biopsy of urinary bladder), report the appropriate code from range 00910–00918.
00920–00938	When anesthesia services are provided for procedures performed on male genitalia and an open urethral procedure (incision into urethra) is done to access anatomic sites, report the appropriate code from range 00920–00938.

Pelvis (Except Hip)

Anesthesia services for the Pelvis (Except Hip) subsection include procedures on the following anatomic sites: anterior or posterior iliac crest, bony pelvis, interpelviabdominal (hindquarter), pelvis, symphysis pubis, sacroiliac joint, acetabulum, and extrapelvic and intrapelvic obturator nerves. (There are no coding rules for the Pelvis [Except Hip] subsection.)

EXAMPLE: An anesthesiologist provided general anesthesia services to a chronic asthmatic patient who underwent an open procedure involving the sacroiliac joint. Report code 01170-P2-AA.

Upper Leg (Except Knee)

Anesthesia services for the Upper Leg (Except Knee) subsection include procedures on the following anatomic sites: hip joint; upper two-thirds of femur; and arteries, veins, nerves, muscles, tendons, fascia, and bursae of upper leg. (There are no coding rules for the Upper Leg [Except Knee] subsection.)

> **EXAMPLE:** An anesthesiologist provided general anesthesia services to a mentally retarded patient with mild systemic disease who underwent nerve biopsy of the upper leg. Report code 01250-P2-AA.

Knee and Popliteal Area

Anesthesia services for the Knee and Popliteal Area subsection include procedures on the following anatomic sites: arteries, veins, nerves, muscles, tendons, fascia, and bursae of knee and/or popliteal area; lower one-third of femur; knee joint; upper ends of the tibia and fibula; and patella. (There are no coding rules for the Knee and Popliteal Area subsection.)

> **EXAMPLE:** An anesthesiologist provided general anesthesia services to a normal healthy patient with mild systemic disease who underwent diagnostic arthroscopy, left knee. Report code 01382-P1-AA.

Lower Leg (Below Knee, Includes Ankle and Foot)

Anesthesia services for the Lower Leg (Below Knee, Includes Ankle and Foot) subsection include procedures on the following anatomic sites: lower leg; ankle; foot; and arteries, veins, bones, nerves, muscles, tendons, and fascia of leg, ankle, and foot. (There are no coding rules for the Lower Leg [Below Knee, Includes Ankle and Foot] subsection.)

> **EXAMPLE:** An anesthesiologist provided general anesthesia services to a normal healthy patient who underwent arthroscopic procedure, right ankle. Report code 01464-P1-AA.

Shoulder and Axilla

Anesthesia services for the Shoulder and Axilla subsection include procedures on the following anatomic sites: arteries, veins, nerves, muscles, tendons, fascia, and bursae of shoulder and axillae; humeral head and neck; sternoclavicular joint; acromioclavicular joint; and shoulder joint. (There are no coding rules for the Shoulder and Axilla subsection.)

> **EXAMPLE:** An anesthesiologist provided general anesthesia services to a normal healthy patient who underwent muscle biopsy, left shoulder. Report code 01610-P1-AA.

Upper Arm and Elbow

Anesthesia services for the Upper Arm and Elbow subsection include procedures on the following anatomic sites: arteries, veins, nerves, muscle, tendons, fascia, and bursae of upper arm and elbow; humerus; and elbow. (There are no coding rules for the Upper Arm and Elbow subsection.)

> **EXAMPLE:** An anesthesiologist provided general anesthesia services to a patient with mild systemic disease who underwent excision of tumor of the right humerus. Report code 01758-P2-AA.

Forearm, Wrist, and Hand

Anesthesia services for the Forearm, Wrist, and Hand subsection include procedures on the following anatomic sites: arteries, veins, nerves, muscles, tendons, fascia, and bursae of forearm, wrist, and hand; radius; ulna; wrist; hand bones; distal radius; distal ulna; and hand joints. (There are no coding rules for the Forearm, Wrist, and Hand subsection.)

> **EXAMPLE:** An anesthesiologist provided general anesthesia services to a normal healthy but very anxious patient who underwent diagnostic and surgical arthroscopy with bone biopsy, right wrist. Report code 01830-P1-AA-23. (Modifier -23 indicates general anesthesia services were provided for a procedure that usually is performed under local anesthesia.)

Radiological Procedures

Anesthesia services for radiological procedures include the following: myelography, diskography, and vertebroplasty; diagnostic arteriography/venography; cardiac catheterization, including coronary angiography and ventriculography; noninvasive imaging or radiation therapy; and therapeutic interventional radiology involving the arterial/venous/lymphatic systems. (Refer to Table 10-12 for Radiological Procedures subsection coding rules.)

EXAMPLE: An anesthesiologist provided MAC to a patient with severe systemic disease who underwent cardiac catheterization, including coronary angiography and ventriculography. Report code 01920-P3-AA-QS.

Note:

Refer to Chapter 16, CPT Radiology, for coding rules about radiological procedures and services.

Coding Tip:

- Medicare anesthesia billing guidelines require that just one code be reported for anesthesia services provided in conjunction with radiological procedures.

- Radiological supervision and interpretation codes applicable to radiological procedures being performed are reported by the appropriate provider (e.g., radiologist, cardiologist, neurosurgeon, or radiation oncologist). Such codes are not included (bundled) in anesthesia services codes for radiological procedures, and the appropriate provider must report the radiology procedure or service code.

Table 10-12 Coding Rules Associated with Radiological Procedures Subsection Anesthesia Codes

Code (s)	Coding Rule
01916	An **arteriography** is the visualization of an artery via X-ray after injection of a **radiopaque** (cannot be penetrated by electromagnetic radiation). A **contrast medium** is a radiopaque substance (e.g., Renografin dye used for intravenous pyelogram) that obstructs the passage of X-rays so structures containing it appear white on radiographic film. This allows the radiologist to visualize abnormalities and define body structure contours.
01920	CPT code 01920 (Anesthesia for cardiac catheterization including coronary angiography and ventriculography (not to include Swan-Ganz catheter)) is reported for monitored anesthesia care (MAC) in patients who are critically ill or critically unstable. If the physician performing the radiological service inserts a catheter (other than a Swan-Ganz catheter) as part of the anesthesia services provided and a catheter is left in place and used for monitoring purposes, do not report a code for placement of the monitoring catheter (e.g., CPT codes 36500, 36555–36556, 36568–36569, 36580, 36584, and 36597).
01922	When anesthesia is required for a CT scan or MRI due to medical necessity (e.g., mentally retarded patient), report code 01922 (Anesthesia for noninvasive imaging or radiation therapy) with appropriate modifiers.
01924–01933	**Interventional therapeutic radiological procedures** are the therapeutic application of radiation that includes the following aspects: • Analysis and interpretation of radiation equipment performance measurements • Calibration of equipment associated with production and use of radiation • Analysis and interpretation of measurements associated with patient dosages • Radiation safety aspects associated with production and use of radiation
01935–01936	Percutaneous image guided procedures on the spine and spinal cord involve inserting a peripheral intravenous catheter, administering an anxiolytic (anti-anxiety) medication, and accompanying the patient to the radiology suite. Once in the radiology suite, sedation and analgesic agents (e.g., diagnostic procedures) or general anesthesia (e.g., therapeutic procedures) are administered.

Burn Excisions or Debridement

Anesthesia services for burn excisions or debridement procedures include the following: second- and third-degree burn excision or debridement with or without skin grafting according to total body surface area. (Refer to Chapter 11, CPT Surgery I, for discussion of total body surface area calculations.) (Refer to Table 10-13 for Burn Excisions or Debridement subsection coding rules.)

> **EXAMPLE:** An anesthesiologist provided general anesthesia services to a 2-year-old type 1 diabetic patient who underwent second-degree burn debridement of the chest, 5 percent of total body surface area. Report code 01952-P2-AA.

Obstetric

Anesthesia services for obstetric procedures include the following: external cephalic version procedure, vaginal delivery, cesarean delivery, urgent hysterectomy following delivery, cesarean hysterectomy without labor analgesia/anesthesia care, abortion procedures, neuraxial labor analgesia/anesthesia for planned vaginal delivery, neuraxial labor analgesia/anesthesia for cesarean delivery following planned vaginal delivery, and cesarean hysterectomy following neuroaxial labor analgesia/anesthesia. (Refer to Chapter 15, CPT Surgery V, for detailed discussion of obstetric procedures and services.) (Refer to Table 10-14 for Obstetric subsection coding rules.)

> **EXAMPLE:** An anesthesiologist provided general anesthesia services to a normal healthy patient who suffered a miscarriage and underwent surgery to remove the remaining products of conception. Report code 01965-P1-AA.

Table 10-13 Coding Rules Associated with Burn Excisions or Debridement Subsection Anesthesia Codes

Code(s)	Coding Rule
01952–01953	Code 01953 is reported with code 01952 when the percent of total body surface area or part thereof treated is greater than 9 percent. Do not add modifier -51 (Multiple Procedures) to code 01953 because the word "each" is included in its code description. Be sure to interpret percent of total body surface in code 01952 as up to 4 percent and in code 01953 as up to 9 percent.

© Cengage Learning 2014

Table 10-14 Coding Rules Associated with Obstetric Subsection Anesthesia Codes

Code(s)	Coding Rule
01967–01969	If documentation supports procedures or services provided, code 01968 is reported with 01967, or code 01969 is reported with 01967 and 01968.

© Cengage Learning 2014

Other Procedures

Anesthesia services for other procedures include the following: physiologic support for harvesting organ(s) from brain-dead patients, anesthesia for diagnostic/therapeutic nerve blocks and injections, daily hospital management of epidural or subarachnoid continuous drug administration, and unlisted anesthesia procedure(s). (Refer to Table 10-15 for Other Procedures subsection coding rules.)

Table 10-15 Coding Rules Associated with Other Procedures Subsection Anesthesia Codes

Code(s)	Coding Rule
01996	Report code 01996 when the anesthesiologist or CRNA provides daily hospital management of continuous epidural or subarachnoid drug administration. This management is provided because the anesthesiologist or CRNA inserted an epidural or subarachnoid catheter during a surgical procedure as part of anesthesia services provided.
01999	When reporting code 01999, make sure you submit a copy of the operative report and other pertinent documents to the third-party payer for review.

© Cengage Learning 2014

Note:

- To report regional intravenous administration of local anesthetic agents or other medication in the upper or lower extremity, assign an Anesthesia code from the appropriate Anesthesia subsection.

- To report a Bier block for pain management, assign code 64999. A *Bier Block* is an intravenous regional block, which involves using a tourniquet to restrict the effects of anesthesia to a region of the body (e.g., leg).

- To report intra-arterial or intravenous injections, including that for pain management, assign a code from 96373-96379.

EXAMPLE: An anesthesiologist managed the continuous drug administration of an epidural for a 50-year-old patient who has COPD. Report code 01996-P2-AA.

Exercise 10.4 – Anesthesia Subsections

Instructions: Complete each statement below.

1. For Medicare purposes, just one anesthesia code is usually reported unless the second and subsequent anesthesia codes are _____ codes.

2. When an anesthesiologist or a CRNA provides distinct procedural services such as the insertion of a Swan-Ganz catheter in addition to anesthesia services, codes are reported separately and modifier _____ is added to the anesthesia code.

3. When procedures on the larynx and trachea are performed on a patient who is younger than 1 year of age, report qualifying circumstances code 99100 in addition to 00326. True or False?

4. When an internal mammary node dissection is performed *in addition to a radical or modified radical breast procedure*, report code _____.

5. Anesthesia services for endoscopic procedures are usually provided by the surgeon who performs the procedure. When monitored anesthesia care (MAC) is provided by the anesthesiologist or CRNA, add HCPCS level II modifier _____ for MAC.

6. When anesthesia services for therapeutic percutaneous image-guided procedure on the spine and spinal cord are provided, report a code from range _____.

7. When anesthesia services are provided to the recipient of a liver transplant, report code _____.

8. When anesthesia services are provided to a brain-dead patient who undergoes a kidney organ harvest, report code _____.

9. When anesthesia is required for a CT scan or MRI due to medical necessity (e.g., mentally retarded patient), report code _____.

10. When the percentage of total body surface area or part thereof treated is greater than 9 percent, report code _____ in addition to 01952.

Summary

The Anesthesia section is located after the Evaluation and Management section in the CPT coding manual, and codes (00100 to 01999) with appropriate modifiers are reported for services related to the administration of anesthesia (including general and regional), supplementation of local anesthesia, and other supportive anesthesia services. The Anesthesia section is organized according to general anatomic areas or services that relate to a number of surgical procedures. For Medicare purposes, just one anesthesia code is reported unless the second and subsequent anesthesia codes are add-on codes. When separate anesthesia codes are reported, the code that describes the anesthesia service for the procedure that has the *highest* base unit value is reported first.

A physician (e.g., anesthesiologist) is responsible for supervising anesthesia services (which include general and regional), supplementation of local anesthesia, and other supportive services so the patient receives appropriate optimal anesthesia care. The administration of local infiltration, metacarpal/metatarsal/digital block, or topical anesthesia by the operating surgeon or obstetrician is included (bundled) in the surgery code; separate codes are not reported. Anesthesia services include the preparation and monitoring of the patient, as well as the following services: draping, positioning, prepping, and transporting the patient; inserting nasogastric or orogastric tubes; inserting peripheral IV lines for fluid and medication administration; interpreting laboratory results; interpreting monitored functions; placing airway tubes, including laryngoscopy for airway management; positioning external devices for capnography, cardiac monitoring, CNS evoked responses, Doppler flow, pulse oximetry, and temperature; and stimulating nerves to determine level of paralysis or localization of nerve(s).

Internet Links

American Society of Anesthesiologists (ASA): Go to *www.asahq.org*, and click on the Practice Management link to access reimbursement information.

Anesthesia Nursing & Medicine: *www.anesthesia-nursing.com*

Medicare Information for Anesthesiologists: Go to *www.cms.gov*, and click on the Medicare link, then click on the Anesthesiologists Center link, located toward the bottom of the page.

Vascular Access Doc: Go to *www.vascularaccessdoc.com*, and click on the Photos/Videos link to view vascular access catheters images and videos.

Virtual Anaesthesia Textbook: *www.virtual-anaesthesia-textbook.com*

Study Checklist

- ❏ Read this chapter and highlight key concepts.
- ❏ Create an index card for each key term.
- ❏ Access the chapter Internet links to learn more about concepts.
- ❏ Complete the chapter review, verifying answers with your instructor.
- ❏ Complete WebTutor assignments and take online quizzes.
- ❏ Complete Workbook chapter, verifying answers with your instructor.
- ❏ Go to *www.cengagebrain.com* to access StudyWARE™ and the Premium Website. Login instructions are located in the Preface and on the Printed Access Card.
- ❏ Form a study group with classmates to discuss chapter concepts in preparation for an exam.

Review

Multiple Choice

Instructions: Circle the most appropriate response.

1. Local anesthesia administration techniques include:
   a. caudal anesthesia, saddle block anesthesia, and epidural anesthesia.
   b. general anesthesia, local anesthesia, and regional anesthesia.
   c. spinal anesthesia, intravenous regional anesthesia, and Bier block.
   d. surface anesthesia, infiltration anesthesia, field block, peripheral nerve block, and plexus anesthesia.

2. The Anesthesia of the CPT section includes:
   a. subsections for anatomic sites followed by subsections for procedures.
   b. subsections for procedures followed by subsections for anatomic sites.
   c. subsections for anatomic sites only.
   d. subsections for procedures only.

3. Prior to surgery, a professional assesses information from the patient's record, performs a physical examination, evaluates preoperative test results, and ensures that informed anesthetic consent has been obtained. This service is called:
   a. monitored anesthesia care.
   b. post-anesthesia evaluation.
   c. postoperative pain management.
   d. pre-anesthesia evaluation.

4. The professional who assesses information from the patient's record, performs a physical examination, evaluates preoperative test results, and ensures that informed anesthetic consent has been obtained is called a(n):
   a. anesthesiologist or CRNA.
   b. primary care physician.
   c. registration technician.
   d. surgeon.

5. The information assessed from the patient's record, physical examination performed on the patient, evaluation of preoperative test results, and verification that informed anesthetic consent has been obtained is:
   a. documented in the operative report.
   b. included in the anesthesia code.
   c. part of post-anesthesia services.
   d. reported as a separate service.

6. If the surgery for which pre-anesthesia services are performed is canceled, the anesthesiologist should:
   a. not report any codes.
   b. report an evaluation and management service code instead of an anesthesia code.
   c. report the anesthesia code for the procedure that was canceled.
   d. report the anesthesia code for the procedure that was canceled and add modifier -53 for discontinued procedure.

7. When an anesthesiologist provides anesthesia services for a 5-month-old healthy patient who undergoes a procedure on the larynx and trachea, report code(s):
   a. 00326-P1-AA.
   b. 00326-P1-AA and 99100.
   c. 99100.
   d. 99100 and 00326-P1-AA.

8. Code 00218 is reported for anesthesia services provided during an _____ procedure, which is performed on the skull while the patient is in a seated position.
   a. endocranial   b. innercranial   c. intercranial   d. intracranial

9. Which is considered a diagnostic radiological procedure?
   a. analysis and interpretation of measurements associated with patient dosages
   b. analysis and interpretation of radiation equipment performance measurements
   c. calibration of equipment associated with production and use of radiation
   d. visualization of abnormalities and definition of body structure contours

10. Code 00802 is reported for anesthesia services administered during a procedure in which a redundant layer of fat tissue located at the lowest portion of the abdominal wall is surgically removed. This procedure is called a:
    a. panniculectomy.   b. panniculotomy.   c. panniculus.   d. pannus.

11. An anesthesiologist provided anesthesia services on an otherwise healthy patient who underwent left corneal transplant. Which CPT code is assigned?
    a. 00144-P1-AA   b. 0580-P1-AA   c. 65410-P1-AA   d. 65710-P1-AA

12. An anesthesiologist provided anesthesia services on a 30-year-old otherwise healthy male patient who underwent thyroidectomy. Which CPT code is assigned?
    a. 00320-P1-AA   b. 00322-P1-AA   c. 01442-P1-AA   d. 60210-P1-AA

13. An anesthesiologist provided monitored anesthesia care to a patient with history of severe cardiopulmonary condition who underwent a procedure to access central venous circulation. Which CPT code is assigned?
    a. 0050-P3-AA-G9   c. 00560-P4-AA-G9
    b. 00532-P4-AA-G9   d. 01916-P4-AA-G9

14. An anesthesiologist provided anesthesia services on a patient with mild systemic disease who underwent upper abdomen vascular surgery. Which CPT code is assigned?
    a. 00700-P2-AA   b. 00770-P2-AA   c. 00880-P2-AA   d. 00882-P2-AA

15. An anesthesiologist provided anesthesia services on an otherwise healthy patient who underwent intra-pelvic obturator neurectomy. Which CPT code is assigned?
    a. 01140-P1-AA   b. 01180-P1-AA   c. 01190-P1-AA   d. 27326-P1-AA

16. An anesthesiologist provided anesthesia services on a patient with mild systemic disease who underwent popliteal thromboendarterectomy. Which CPT code is assigned?
    a. 01440-P2-AA   b. 01442-P2-AA   c. 01400-P2-AA   d. 35303-P2-AA

17. An anesthesiologist provided anesthesia services on an otherwise healthy patient who underwent repair of the Achilles tendon. Which CPT code is assigned?
    a. 01462-P1-AA   b. 01472-P1-AA   c. 27650-P1-AA   d. 28200-P1-AA

18. An anesthesiologist provided anesthesia services on a patient with severe systemic disease who underwent an interthoracoscapular amputation. Which CPT code is assigned?
    a. 01630-P3-AA   b. 01636-P3-AA   c. 01710-P3-AA   d. 23900-P3-AA

19. An anesthesiologist provided anesthesia services to a 5-year-old otherwise healthy patient who underwent bilateral orchiopexy. Which CPT code is assigned?
    a. 00926-P1-AA   b. 00928-P1-AA   c. 00930-P1-AA   d. 54650-P1-AA

20. An anesthesiologist provided anesthesia services on an otherwise healthy patient who underwent phleborraphy, right wrist. Which CPT code is assigned?
    a. 01782-P1-AA   b. 01852-P1-AA   c. 15850-P1-AA   d. 37650-P1-AA

Coding Practice I—Modifiers

Instructions: Review each case and assign CPT anesthesia code(s) and appropriate modifier(s). Some cases require assignment of CPT surgery codes and appropriate modifier(s), per chapter content about anesthesia coding guidelines.

21. While providing regional anesthesia services for a healthy patient who underwent an emergency cesarean section, the anesthesiologist inserted a catheter to provide continuous epidural analgesia pain management (morphine bolus).

_____

22. A CRNA (with medical direction by the surgeon) provided general anesthesia services for a controlled diabetic patient who underwent total wrist replacement. At the conclusion of the surgical procedure, the CRNA inserted an epidural catheter to provide continuous postoperative analgesia for pain management. The CRNA monitored the patient's pain management on the day after surgery.

_____

23. A healthy patient underwent total knee replacement surgery; regional anesthesia services were provided by an anesthesiologist.

_____

24. An anesthesiologist provided regional pain block for an arthroscopic anterior cruciate ligament repair of the left knee of a healthy 40-year-old male patient. The anesthesiologist also performed a femoral nerve block for postoperative pain management.

_____

25. A patient with chronic asthma underwent a thoracotomy. The CRNA (without medical direction by a physician) provided general anesthesia services and, at the conclusion of the procedure, inserted an epidural catheter and infused morphine for postoperative pain control.

_____

Coding Practice II—Anesthesia

Instructions: Review each case and assign the appropriate anesthesia code(s) and physical status modifier(s). Make sure you assign qualifying circumstance code(s) where appropriate. All anesthesia services were provided by the anesthesiologist, which means that modifier -AA is added to each anesthesia code. Some cases require assignment of CPT surgery codes and appropriate modifier(s), per chapter content about anesthesia coding guidelines.

Head

26. A 77-year-old healthy male patient with controlled diabetes mellitus underwent intraocular lens transplant surgery for which general anesthesia was administered.

_____

27. A 5-year-old healthy boy was admitted to the pediatrics floor of an acute care hospital and underwent tympanostomy for which general anesthesia was administered.

_____

Neck

28. A 9-month-old female patient underwent tracheostomy under general anesthesia after having sustained injuries in a motor vehicle accident. The child lost consciousness for 60 minutes after the accident and required cardiopulmonary resuscitation.

_____

29. A 47-year-old male patient with a history of hypertension underwent a partial thyroid lobectomy due to a thyroid tumor. General anesthesia was administered.

_____

Thorax (Chest Wall and Shoulder Girdle)

30. A 33-year-old healthy male construction worker fell from a ladder onto a wooden platform. He was brought into the emergency room and diagnosed with a concussion; there was no loss of consciousness. The patient went to the operating room for the complicated removal of wood from his shoulder. He received general anesthesia.

_____

31. A 14-year-old male is admitted to the pediatrics ward with chest pain, shortness of breath, and possible lordosis. After examination, the diagnosis of pectus excavatum was made. The boy had the condition corrected with an open procedure under general anesthesia.

_____

Intrathoracic

32. A 78-year-old female smoker was admitted for shortness of breath, hypertension, and bloody sputum. She was diagnosed with pneumonia and underwent pneumocentesis performed under general anesthesia.

_____

33. A 45-year-old male with a history of coronary disease and mild hypertension underwent insertion of a permanent pacemaker with epicardial electrodes by thoracotomy. General anesthesia was administered.

_____

Spine and Spinal Cord

34. A 57-year-old female with a history of osteoporosis underwent posterior arthrodesis in the craniocervical (occipital C2) region. General anesthesia was administered.

_____

35. A 25-year-old male heroin addict complaining of severe headaches was admitted to the psychiatric floor of an acute care hospital. After detoxification, the patient still had headaches; increased spinal fluid pressure was noted. He underwent diagnostic lumbar spinal puncture performed under regional anesthesia.

_____

Upper Abdomen

36. An obese 56-year-old male with benign hypertension complained of recurring heartburn. After examination, he was admitted for surgery and underwent a transabdominal repair of a diaphragmatic hernia. General anesthesia was administered.

_____

37. An otherwise healthy 5-year-old female underwent percutaneous liver biopsy under general anesthesia.

_____

Lower Abdomen

38. A 54-year-old female who lost 100 pounds two years go underwent panniculectomy under general anesthesia. The patient has no significant medical history or chronic conditions.

_____

39. A healthy 36-year-old female underwent tubal ligation under general anesthesia for voluntary sterilization.

_____

Perineum

40. A 45-year-old female presented with moderate vaginal bleeding. After being admitted and tested, she underwent hysteroscopy with endometrium biopsy under general anesthesia.

_____

41. A healthy 38-year-old male requested voluntary sterilization and underwent vasectomy. Regional anesthesia was administered.

_____

Pelvis

42. A volunteer offered bone marrow to a needy recipient. He underwent bone marrow aspiration of the posterior iliac crest with general anesthesia to provide a sample to test for a match. The donor has no chronic or current medical conditions.

_____

43. A healthy 14-year-old-male fell while skateboarding and landed on his back. After radiological exam, he was diagnosed with fractured sacroiliac joint. Open treatment of the anterior ring fracture was performed under general anesthesia.

_____

Upper Leg

44. A 46-year-old female fell while in-line skating and fractured her femur at the proximal end. She underwent open treatment of the femoral fracture with internal fixation under general anesthesia. The patient has type 2 diabetes mellitus, controlled.

_____

45. A 76-year-old female with Parkinson's disease fell while getting out of bed. She was unable to walk and was found two days later by her son. She was dehydrated and disoriented. She was seen and evaluated in the emergency department. She was admitted with the diagnosis of a hip fracture. The patient's hip was repaired with total hip arthroplasty under general anesthesia on the day of admission.

_____

Knee and Popliteal Area

46. A 17-year-old male high school football player's knee was injured during a game. Examination revealed fractured patella. He underwent open treatment of the fractured patella under general anesthesia.

_____

47. A 15-year-old female high school gymnast's knee was injured during a meet. Radiological examination revealed torn meniscus. She underwent a surgical arthroscopic procedure of her knee to repair the meniscus, with general anesthesia.

_____

Lower Leg

48. A 14-year-old Down syndrome male was stepped on by a horse. Upon radiological exam, it was noted that the boy had a trimalleolar fracture. He underwent closed treatment of the fracture without manipulation under general anesthesia.

_____

49. A 23-year-old female smoker was seen in the emergency room with pain, swelling, and disfigurement in her right lower leg. Radiological exam revealed a fractured tibia. She underwent closed reduction and casting under general anesthesia.

_____

Shoulder and Axilla

50. A 27-year-old male fell while riding his motorcycle. He complained of right shoulder pain and swelling. Upon radiological exam, it was noted that he had a fractured humerus. He underwent closed treatment of the humeral head under general anesthesia.

_____

51. A healthy 37-year-old female iron worker had an I beam fall on her shoulder. The joint was crushed. She went to the emergency room and was brought to the operating room for interthoracoscapular amputation under general anesthesia.

_____

Upper Arm and Elbow

52. A healthy 21-year-old female college tennis player complained about pain in her left elbow. The joint was swollen and tender. After orthopedic and radiological exam, reconstruction of the lateral collateral ligament was performed under general anesthesia.

_____

53. A 50-year-old bodybuilder heard a pop and felt severe pain in his right upper arm while lifting heavy weights. Radiological exam revealed a ruptured bicep tendon. He underwent reinsertion of the ruptured tendon under general anesthesia.

_____

Forearm, Wrist, and Hand

54. A 68-year-old male noticed a lump on his left forearm. Examination determined that he was in need of incision and drainage of a bursa. The procedure was performed under general anesthesia.

_____

55. A 47-year-old healthy male factory worker caught his lower left arm in a commercial washing machine. The patient sustained a fracture and dislocated distal radius. The patient underwent open reduction of the fracture and dislocation under general anesthesia.

_____

Radiological Procedures

56. A 57-year-old obese female with hypertension showed coronary problems during a stress test. A cardiac catherization under general anesthesia was performed.

_____

57. A 63-year-old male was diagnosed with a glioblastoma multiforme. He underwent radiation therapy under regional anesthesia.

_____

Burn Excisions or Debridement

58. A firefighter sustained second-degree burns over 35 percent of his body while on duty. He received general anesthesia during the burn debridement.

_____

59. A 59-year-old female chemical factory worker sustained second-degree burns due to a caustic chemical spill to her left arm. Nine percent of her body was burned. She received general anesthesia during burn excision.

_____

Obstetric

60. A healthy 24-year-old female had a normal vaginal delivery under regional anesthesia.

_____

61. A controlled noninsulin diabetic 29-year-old female underwent cesarean delivery with general anesthesia.

_____

Other Procedures

62. A 37-year-old male has recurring back pain. He underwent spinal disc surgery and continued to need daily epidural continuous drug anesthesia while in the hospital.

_____

63. An anesthesiologist provided physiologic support for harvesting organs from a brain-dead patient.

_____

64. A healthy 30-year-old patient presented to the emergency department with a lump on the palm of his hand. After examination, the patient was diagnosed with a cyst. The patient consented to removal of the cyst in the emergency department. However, the patient does not want conscious sedation or a regional nerve block. After consulting with the anesthesiologist, the patient received local anesthesia administered via IV for 15 minutes.

_____

65. General anesthesia was administered to a 6-month-old male child who underwent repair of his cleft palate. The patient was observed in recovery by the nursing staff and evaluated by the anesthesiologist before being transferred to the pediatric unit of the hospital. The nursing staff placed an IV line for saline and postoperative pain medication.

_____

CPT Surgery I

Chapter Outline

Overview of Surgery Section
Surgery Guidelines

General Subsection
Integumentary System Subsection

Chapter Objectives

At the conclusion of this chapter, the student should be able to:

- Define key terms.
- Explain the organization, format, and content of the CPT Surgery section.
- Interpret CPT Surgery section guidelines.
- Interpret CPT Surgery coding notes for the General and Integumentary System subsections.
- Assign CPT Surgery codes from the General and Integumentary System subsections.
- Add CPT and/or HCPCS level II modifiers to codes, as appropriate.

Key Terms

ablation
acellular dermal
  replacement
actinic keratosis (AK)
adjacent tissue transfer/
  rearrangement
advancement flap
allograft
autograft
bedsore
biopsy
blepharoplasty
chemical peel
chemosurgery
cryosurgery

decubitus ulcer
defect
dermabrasion
destruction
diagnostic procedure
donor site
double pedicle flap
electrosurgery
endoscopy
excision
excisional biopsy
extensive cellulitis
fine-needle aspiration
  (FNA)
flap

free flap
free skin graft
full-thickness
  skin graft
glabellar frown lines
global period
global surgical package
graft
incision
incision and drainage
  (I&D)
incisional biopsy
introduction
island flap
island pedicle flap

LASER (light
  amplification by
  stimulated emission
  of radiation)
Limberg flap
lumpectomy
microdermabrasion
moderate (conscious)
  sedation
modified radical
  mastectomy
Mohs microsurgery
mycocutaneous flap
needle core biopsy
open biopsy
paring and curettement

partial mastectomy	repair	simple repair	tissue-cultured autograft
pedicle skin graft	revision	split-thickness skin graft	tissue rearrangement
pilonidal cyst	rhomboid flap	stereotactic localization	total mastectomy
pressure ulcer	rhytidectomy	stroma	undermining
primary defect	rotation flap	surgical curettement	V-Y plasty
radical mastectomy	rule of nines	surgical package	W-plasty
random pattern flap	secondary defect	suture	xenograft
recipient site	separate procedure	therapeutic surgical procedure	Z-plasty
reconstruction	shaving	tissue approximation	
removal	simple closure		

Introduction

The Surgery section of CPT is the largest, and it contains codes and code descriptions for surgical procedures performed by physicians. Because procedures can be performed using a variety of methods and different combinations, the Surgery section contains multiple codes that describe similar procedures. The intention is to allow for coding specificity and to accurately reflect the actual procedure performed. The patient's diagnosis and physical status (e.g., normal, healthy patient versus patient with severe systemic disease) guides the physician, who determines whether just one procedure or multiple procedures will be performed during an encounter (e.g., office visit) or operative session (e.g., ambulatory surgery). The documented operative report and other patient record documentation guide the selection of appropriate codes for reporting to third-party payers.

Overview of Surgery Section

The Surgery section is the largest in CPT, and its subsections are organized anatomically (e.g., body area or organ system). Categories and subcategories are organized within subsections according to type of procedure. Selecting the appropriate surgery code requires a careful review of the patient record to determine the procedures and services provided. Before referring to the CPT index to begin the process of locating a surgery code, review the documented operative report (Figure 11-1) to determine the following:

- Body system (e.g., digestive)

- Anatomic site (e.g., stomach)

- Surgical approach (e.g., laparotomy)

- Type of procedure performed (e.g., removal, as for partial gastrectomy)

- Fact that multiple procedures were performed during the same operative session (e.g., gastroscopy followed by exploratory laparotomy and removal of a portion of the stomach)

EXAMPLE 1: When reporting the CPT code for "excision of cervical stump," if an abdominal approach was documented in the operative report, assign code 57540. If a vaginal approach was documented, assign code 57550.

```
57540   Excision of cervical stump, abdominal approach;
57545     with pelvic floor repair
57550   Excision of cervical stump, vaginal approach;
```

EXAMPLE 2: When reporting the CPT code for "removal of a 0.5-cm malignant lesion of the arm," if a surgical excision was documented in the operative report, assign code 11600. If a destruction procedure (e.g., laser ablation) was documented, assign code 17260.

```
11600   Excision, malignant lesion including margins, trunk, arms, or legs;
          excised diameter 0.5 cm or less
```

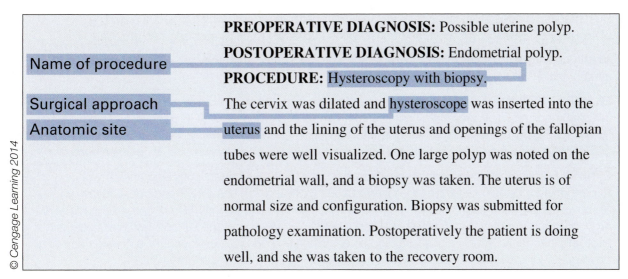

PREOPERATIVE DIAGNOSIS: Possible uterine polyp.

POSTOPERATIVE DIAGNOSIS: Endometrial polyp.

Name of procedure

PROCEDURE: Hysteroscopy with biopsy.

Surgical approach

The cervix was dilated and hysteroscope was inserted into the

Anatomic site

uterus and the lining of the uterus and openings of the fallopian tubes were well visualized. One large polyp was noted on the endometrial wall, and a biopsy was taken. The uterus is of normal size and configuration. Biopsy was submitted for pathology examination. Postoperatively the patient is doing well, and she was taken to the recovery room.

Figure 11-1 Sample operative report with name of procedure, surgical approach, and anatomic site highlighted to illustrate how to locate information needed to assign CPT code.

```
17260    Destruction, malignant lesion (eg, laser surgery, electrosurgery,
         cryosurgery, chemosurgery, surgical curettement), trunk, arms or
         legs; lesion diameter 0.5 cm or less
```

CPT coding descriptions include the procedure performed, but they do not include the numerous activities integral to the procedure. It would be impractical to list every event common to all procedures of a similar nature in the code's narrative description. Many common activities reflect the principles of medical and surgical care; and while considered acceptable medical/surgical practice, they are not coded separately. In addition, although many activities are common to all procedures, some are integral only to certain groups of procedures.

The services integral to the standard practice of medical/surgical services, for which no separate code is assigned, include:

- Cleansing, shaving, and prepping the patient's skin

- Draping and positioning the patient

- Inserting intravenous access for medication

- Administering sedatives (by physician performing procedure)

- Administering local, topical, and/or regional anesthetic (by physician performing procedure)

- Establishing the surgical approach (identifying anatomic landmarks, making the incision, evaluating the surgical field, and performing simple debridement of traumatized tissue)

- Performing lysis of simple adhesions

- Isolating neurovascular, muscular (including stimulation for identification), bony, or other structures that limits access to surgical field

- Taking surgical cultures

- Irrigating wounds

- Inserting and removing drains, suction devices, dressings, and pumps into same site

- Closing the surgical incision

- Applying, managing, and removing postoperative dressings, including analgesic devices (e.g., peri-incisional TENS unit, institution of patient-controlled analgesia)

© Cengage Learning 2014

- Documenting preoperative, intraoperative, and postoperative reports, which includes providing photographs, drawings, dictation, and transcription necessary to document services provided

- Identifying surgical supplies (unless third-party payer policy states that they are separately coded and reimbursable)

  EXAMPLE 1: The physician removed cerumen (ear wax) impaction prior to performing a myringotomy. The cerumen impaction prevented access to the tympanic membrane, and its removal was necessary for the successful completion of the myringotomy. Report code 69420 (Myringotomy including aspiration and/or eustachian tube inflation) only. *Do not report a separate code for removal of cerumen impaction.*

  EXAMPLE 2: The physician performed a bronchoscopy to assess the patient's lung anatomy prior to performing a lobectomy (single lobe). Report code 32480, which has a CPT code description of "removal of lung, other than total pneumonectomy; single lobe (lobectomy)." *Do not report a code for the bronchoscopy,* which was performed as a scout endoscopy to assess the surgical field and to establish anatomic landmarks, extent of disease, and so on. When an endoscopic procedure is done as part of an open procedure, such as a lobectomy, it is not separately coded and reported.

  If an endoscopy is performed initially to diagnose the patient on the same day as the open procedure, the endoscopy is separately coded and reported. Modifier 58 is added to the endoscopy code to indicate that the procedures are staged or planned services. Also, if endoscopic procedures are performed on distinct, separate areas during the same operative session, separately code and report each procedure (e.g., thoracoscopy and mediastinoscopy). However, if a cursory (brief) evaluation of the upper airway is done as part of a bronchoscopy, do not separately code and report procedures (e.g., laryngoscopy or sinus endoscopy).

Organization of Surgery Section

The guidelines located at the beginning of the Surgery section apply to all codes in the section. Notes located throughout the Surgery section apply to a specific subsection, heading, or subheading. The basic organization of the Surgery section is by major body system, with headings and subheadings based on anatomic site and/or type of procedure (Table 11-1). The Surgery section contains the following subsections, which represent organ systems, anatomic sites, or other designations:

- General (10021–10022)

- Integumentary System (10040–19499)

- Musculoskeletal System (20005–29999)

- Respiratory System (30000–32999)

- Cardiovascular System (33010–37799)

- Hemic and Lymphatic Systems (38100–38999)

- Mediastinum and Diaphragm (39000–39599)

- Digestive System (40490–49999)

- Urinary System (50010–53899)

- Male Genital System (54000–55899)

- Reproductive System Procedures (55920)

- Intersex Surgery (55970–55980)

- Female Genital System (56405–58999)

- Maternity Care and Delivery (59000–59899)

- Endocrine System (60000–60699)

Table 11-1 Subheadings Typically Organized Below CPT Surgery Subsections

Subheading	Description
Incision	Cut made into body tissue during surgery using a knife, electrosurgical unit, or laser (e.g., 66500)
Incision and Drainage (I&D)	Cutting open a lesion (e.g., abscess) and draining its contents (e.g., 10120)
Excision	Removing a portion or all of an organ or another tissue (e.g., skin), using a scalpel or another surgical instrument (e.g., 11402)
Introduction	Injecting, inserting, or puncturing body tissue (e.g., 11900) or scoping an organ (e.g., 47500)
Removal	Eliminating tissue (e.g., amputating a body part) or taking something out (e.g., removing implants, such as buried wire, pins, or screws) (e.g., 20694)
Endoscopy	Visualizing a body cavity using an instrument that can be inserted into the body through a small incision or a natural opening (e.g., nose) (e.g., 31231) **NOTE:** An endoscope is also used as a surgical approach for performing other procedures (e.g., laparoscopic cholecystectomy, sigmoidoscopy with removal of polyps)
Repair	Improving improperly functioning body parts (e.g., 49520); types of repair include: • **Grafts:** Moving healthy tissue from one site to another to replace diseased or defective tissue. • **Suture:** Closing a wound using catgut, glue, silk thread, wire, or other materials. (Figure 11-2)
Revision	Modifying a previous procedure (e.g., gastric restrictive procedure) or a device (e.g., shunt) (e.g., 49426)
Reconstruction	Rebuilding a body part, such as the breast (e.g., 19357)
Destruction	**Ablation** (or removal) of benign, premalignant, or malignant tissue (e.g., 17000); types of destruction include: • **Chemosurgery:** Using chemicals to destroy diseased tissue, such as for skin cancer. • **Cryosurgery:** Applying extreme cold, such as liquid nitrogen, to destroy abnormal tissue cells, such as warts or small skin lesions. • **Electrosurgery:** Using an electrical device, such as electrocautery, to destroy abnormal tissue. • **LASER (light amplification by stimulated emission of radiation):** Using a device that is filled with a gas, liquid, or solid substance that is stimulated to emit light to a specific wavelength to burn, cut, or dissolve tissue. • **Surgical curettment:** Scraping abnormal tissue.
Other Procedures	Unrelated procedures, which include arthrodesis, Mohs micrographic surgery, manipulation (of fractures/dislocations), splinting, or casting.

© Cengage Learning 2014

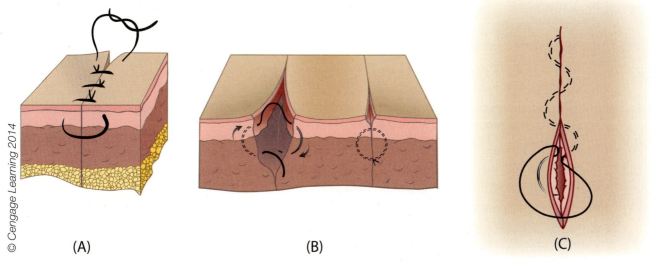

© Cengage Learning 2014

(A)   (B)   (C)

Figure 11-2 (A) Simple interrupted sutures (B) Buried sutures (C) Running subcuticular sutures

- Nervous System (61000–64999)

- Eye and Ocular Adnexa (65091–68899)

- Auditory System (69000–69979)

- Operating Microscope (69990)

In the Surgery section, procedures are categorized as diagnostic procedures or therapeutic surgical procedures. **Diagnostic procedures** (e.g., arthroscopy, biopsy, and endoscopy) are performed to evaluate the patient's complaints or symptoms and to establish the diagnosis. **Therapeutic surgical procedures** (e.g., removal and repair) are performed to treat specific conditions or injuries; they include the procedure itself and normal, uncomplicated follow-up care.

Surgery section procedures are typically organized according to the following subheadings (below the heading of a subsection). (Some subheadings are not located below each heading, while some headings include additional subheadings, such as fracture and/or dislocation in the Musculoskeletal System subsection.)

- Incision or Incision and drainage

- Excision

- Introduction or removal

- Endoscopy

- Repair, revision, and/or reconstruction

- Destruction

- Other procedures

Exercise 11.1 – Overview of Surgery Section

Instructions: Complete each statement.

1. The organization of the CPT Surgery section is according to _____.

2. Endoscopy, arthroscopy, and biopsy are considered _____ services.

3. Gastric resection and knee replacement procedures are considered _____ services.

4. The patient underwent cystourethroscopy with biopsy of urinary bladder wall. Identify the following:

   a. Body system: _____

   b. Anatomic site: _____

   c. Surgical approach: _____

   d. Type of procedure performed: _____

   e. Name of the procedure: _____

   f. Code number assigned: _____

5. The physician performed lysis of adhesions, exploratory laparotomy, and partial colon resection with end-to-end anastomosis. Identify the following:

   a. Body system: _____

   b. Anatomic site: _____

   c. Surgical approach: _____

   d. Type of procedure performed: _____

   e. Name of the procedure: _____

   f. Code number assigned: _____

Surgery Guidelines

Guidelines located at the beginning of the CPT Surgery section clarify the assignment of codes and explain terms. Surgery guidelines include the following:

- Services
- CPT surgical package definition
- Follow-up care for diagnostic procedures
- Follow-up care for therapeutic surgical procedures
- Supplied material

- Reporting more than one procedure/service
- Separate procedure
- Subsection information
- Unlisted service or procedure
- Special report
- Surgical destruction

Services

Codes for physician services that are provided in the office, patient's home, hospital, and other health care facilities are located in the Evaluation and Management (E/M) section of the CPT. This section also includes codes for consultations and other medical services. Codes for special services and reports are located in the CPT Medicine section.

CPT Surgical Package Definition

Many services performed are integral to the standard of medical/surgical services, such as the cleansing, shaving, and prepping of skin and the insertion of intravenous access for medication. The CPT **surgical package** includes the following services, in addition to the surgical procedure:

- Local infiltration, metacarpal/metatarsal/digital block, or topical anesthesia
- One related E/M service following the decision for surgery, which includes the history and physical, on the date of procedure or immediately prior to performance of the procedure
- Immediate postoperative care, which includes dictating the operative report and talking with the family and other physicians or qualified health care professionals
- Documentation of postoperative physician orders
- Evaluation of the patient in the postanesthesia recovery area
- Typical postoperative follow-up care (e.g., removal of sutures)

Note:

When reporting a CPT surgery code, surgical package services are included in that code. They are not separately coded and reported.

In 1992, The Centers for Medicare & Medicaid Services (CMS) established a national definition for a **global surgical package** (that differs from the definition of the CPT *surgical package*) to ensure that payments are made consistently for the same services across all Medicare administrative contractor jurisdictions. The *global surgical package* definition prevents Medicare payments for services that are more or less comprehensive than intended. The CMS global surgical package includes the surgical procedure and a standard package of preoperative, intraoperative, and postoperative services. In addition, CMS categorizes surgeries as major or minor, and it establishes a postoperative **global period** (0, 10, or 90 days) (Figure 11-3) for each surgical procedure, which includes the following policies:

- The global period for major surgery is 90 days
- The global period begins the day following surgery
- The global period includes a one-day preoperative period

CPT Code	Brief Description	Global Period
59050	Fetal monitoring with report	XXX
59160	Dilatation and curettage after delivery	010
59200	Insertion of cervical dilator	000
59400	Obstetrical care	MMM
59525	Removal of uterus after cesarean section	ZZZ
59812	Treatment of miscarriage	090
59899	Maternity care procedure	YYY

© Cengage Learning 2014

Figure 11-3 Sample of CMS global periods

EXAMPLE: To determine the global period for major surgeries, count the day before the day of surgery, the day of surgery, and the 90 days immediately following the day of surgery. For a date of surgery on January 1, the:

- Preoperative day is December 31

- Last day of the 90-day postoperative period is April 1

To arrive at April 1, count January 2–31 as 30 days, February 1–28 as 28 days, March 1–31 as 31 days, and April 1 as 1 day, for a total of 90 days *after the day of surgery*.

- The global period for minor surgery (e.g., endoscopies) is zero or 10 days, and physician visits on the day of a minor surgical procedure or endoscopy are included in reimbursement for the procedure.

- The zero-day global period includes the day of surgery only.

  EXAMPLE: To determine the zero-day global period for a minor surgical procedure, count the day of surgery only. For a date of surgery on March 5, the last day of the postoperative period is also March 5.

- The 10-day global period includes the day of surgery and the 10 days that immediately follow the day of surgery.

  EXAMPLE: To determine the 10-day global period for a minor surgical procedure, count the day of surgery and the appropriate number of days immediately following the date of surgery. For a date of surgery on March 5, the last day of the postoperative period is March 15.

CMS publishes a list of the global periods (Figure 11-3) for each CPT code in the *Federal Register*. That list also includes the following alphabetic codes in the global period column:

- MMM: Global period policy does not apply; describes services furnished in uncomplicated maternity cases, including antepartum care, delivery, and postpartum care

- XXX: Global period policy does not apply

- YYY: Global period is established by each Medicare administrative contract (e.g., unlisted surgery codes)

- ZZZ: CPT code is related to another service provided, which is always included in the global period of the other service

Instructions for the CMS's global surgical package describe the components of a global surgical package and payment rules for minor surgeries, endoscopies, and global surgical packages that are split between physicians. In addition to the global surgical package policy, other payment policies and claims processing requirements were established for other surgical issues, including bilateral and multiple surgeries. The CMS global surgical package includes the following:

- Preoperative services (visits after the decision is made to operate)

- The day before the day of surgery for major procedures

- The day of surgery for minor procedures

- Intraoperative services (includes the operation and all usual and necessary parts of a surgical procedure, such as wound irrigation, insertion and removal of drains, surgical closure, and application and/or removal of postoperative dressings)

- Treatment of complications following surgery (additional services provided by the surgeon during the postoperative period because of the development of complications that do not require additional trips to the operating room)

- Postoperative visits (follow-up visits during the postoperative period that are related to recovery from surgery)

- Postsurgical pain management (provided by the surgeon)

- Miscellaneous services (e.g., dressing changes; local incisional care; removal of operative packing; removal of sutures and staples, tubes, drains, and casts; insertion or removal of urinary catheters and/or nasogastric tubes)

Note:

When a patient receives treatment for an unrelated condition during the global period, add modifier 24 to the CPT code for an E/M service or add modifier 79 to the CPT code for a surgical procedure/service.

The CMS global surgical package does *not* include the following:

- Initial consultation or evaluation services by the surgeon to determine need for major surgery

- Visits unrelated to the diagnosis for which a surgical procedure is performed

- Services provided by other physicians, except when the physicians agree on transfer of care

- Diagnostic tests and procedures, including diagnostic radiological procedures

Note:

The initial consultation or evaluation services by the surgeon is included to determine the need for minor surgery.

- Clearly distinct surgical procedures during the postoperative period that are *not* for treatment of complications or procedures done in "stages" (e.g., two or more parts of a procedure planned at the time of the first procedure to occur at a time after the initial surgery, such as a mastectomy, and insertion of a prosthesis during the postoperative global period)

- Treatment for postoperative complications that require a return trip to the operating room

- A required, more extensive procedure when a less extensive procedure fails; in this case, the second procedure is payable separately

It is important to understand that the procedure being performed determines the global follow-up care; the condition being treated does not. The global surgical packages deal with the procedure(s) performed during the global period by the operating surgeon; only the operating surgeon is associated with that particular global period of follow-up care.

EXAMPLE: A patient underwent ventral hernia repair performed by a general surgeon and one week later fractured her ankle. An orthopedic surgeon inserted a pin to repair the fractured ankle. A global follow-up period for the specific surgery performed is associated with the CPT code assigned by each physician. Thus, each physician receives appropriate reimbursement for services provided.

When the patient is seen by the general surgeon for follow-up care related to the ventral hernia repair and such care is provided within the global period, an E/M code for services provided is *not* reported.

Payment for such follow-up care is bundled in the CPT code reported for the ventral hernia repair surgery. Likewise, when the patient is seen by the orthopedic surgeon for follow-up care related to the ankle surgery, E/M services are bundled in the CPT code reported for that surgery.

If the patient develops complications subsequent to surgery and receives E/M services within the global period, the respective surgeon should report a CPT code for services provided to receive reimbursement from the third-party payer.

E/M services provided as follow-up to a surgical procedure are included in the reimbursement amount for the surgery, and codes for follow-up E/M services are not reported separately. However, when the patient receives E/M services for an unrelated condition, make sure you report an E/M code to receive reimbursement for services provided.

EXAMPLE: An excision of a malignant lesion on the left arm is performed in the office on May 10. The postoperative global period for code 11606 is 10 days. The patient returns to the office on May 15 and is treated for conjunctivitis. The physician should report an appropriate E/M code and add modifier 24 (Unrelated Evaluation and Management Service by the Same Physician During a Postoperative Period) (e.g., 99213-24).

When an E/M service provided is for the purpose of deciding to perform a major surgical procedure, the E/M service is considered a significant, separately identifiable service. Report an appropriate E/M code and add modifier 57 (decision for surgery) (e.g., 99214-57).

EXAMPLE: A surgeon provided level 5 consultation services to a patient in the office to determine whether surgery was necessary due to complaints of severe abdominal pain. After evaluation, the ambulance is called and the patient is transported to the hospital, where the surgeon performs an emergency gastrotomy with suture repair of a bleeding ulcer. Report code 43501 (Gastrotomy; with suture repair of bleeding ulcer) and 99245-57 (Office consultation for new or established patient, level 5).

Note:

Medicare administrative contractors use software that contains prepayment edits to detect the separate billing of services included in the global package. When E/M codes are reported for services provided during a global period and a modifier is not added to the code to indicate special circumstances, the claims are denied.

Local Infiltration, Metacarpal/Metatarsal/Digital Block, or Topical Anesthesia

Local infiltration, metacarpal/metatarsal/digital block, or topical anesthesia, when provided by the physician performing the procedure, is considered part of the procedure. When the surgeon provides general anesthesia, regional anesthesia, or monitored anesthesia care, add modifier -47 to the surgery code.

Note:

When a physician other than the surgeon (e.g., anesthesiologist) provides general anesthesia, regional anesthesia, or monitored anesthesia care, the other physician reports an anesthesia code for services provided. (Refer to Chapter 10 for anesthesia coding rules.)

EXAMPLE: A surgeon injected a local anesthetic in preparation for performing an inguinal hernia repair on a 42-year-old patient. The local anesthetic procedure performed by the surgeon is included in the surgical procedure and is not separately coded and reported.

Moderate (conscious) sedation is moderate sedation or analgesia that results in a drug-induced depression of consciousness. CPT established a package concept for conscious sedation, and a ⊙ (bull's-eye) symbol located next to the code number identifies conscious sedation as an inherent part of providing specific procedures. (Moderate [conscious] sedation codes are listed in Appendix G of the CPT coding manual.) Because these codes include conscious sedation, it is inappropriate for a physician to report a surgery code and a conscious sedation code (99143–99150).

> **EXAMPLE:** A surgeon performed a procedure to place radiotherapy afterloading brachytherapy catheters into the breast for interstitial radioelement following a partial mastectomy. The patient required the administration of moderate (conscious) sedation during the procedure. Locate code 19298 in the CPT coding manual and note that the bull's-eye symbol (⊙) appears next to the code. This means that a conscious sedation code (99143–99150) is *not* reported in addition to code 19298.

The management of postoperative pain by the surgeon, including epidural drug administration, is included in the global package with the operative procedure.

Follow-up Care for Diagnostic Procedures

Diagnostic procedures are performed to evaluate a patient's condition, to determine the nature of a condition, and to distinguish between one disease and another. According to CPT, follow-up care for diagnostic procedures includes only that care related to recovery from the diagnostic procedure itself. Codes for services provided should be reported when a physician treats:

- The patient's condition for which the diagnostic procedure was performed.

- Other conditions that are not related to the reason for performing the diagnostic procedure.

When a patient receives services from the physician who performed the diagnostic procedure and those services are in follow-up to the procedure performed (e.g., suture removal or dressing change), do not report a code for services provided.

Follow-up Care for Therapeutic Surgical Procedures

Therapeutic surgical procedures are performed for the definitive treatment of a disease or condition rather than for diagnostic or investigative purposes. Follow-up care for therapeutic surgical procedures includes only the care that is typically considered part of the surgical service. The physician generally sees the patient several times as part of normal, uncomplicated follow-up care (e.g., remove sutures, evaluate the results of the surgery, or check for complications). These postoperative visits are included as part of surgery's global period because normal follow-up care services are a necessary component of the surgical process.

Codes for services provided should be reported when a physician treats the following during the postoperative global period:

- Complications (e.g., postoperative wound infection)

- Exacerbations (e.g., macular degeneration that was treated, but worsens, requiring another treatment)

- Recurrence (e.g., return of cancer)

- Presence of other diseases (e.g., appendicitis during global period for gastric resection)

- Injuries (e.g., fracture resulting from car accident)

Supplied Materials

Supplies commonly included in surgical packages (e.g., dressings, tubing, and steri-strips) are not coded separately. *Only those supplies and materials provided by the physician over and above the supplies usually included with the procedure rendered are reported separately.* Assign code 99070 to report these supplies or assign specific HCPCS level II national codes for such supplies or drugs.

The CPT Surgery section guidelines do not identify procedures codes for which it is appropriate to report supply items (e.g., surgical trays) separately. Reimbursement of supplies and materials required to perform the procedure is a specific reimbursement issue, which varies from one third-party payer to another. CMS created specific instructions regarding the separate reporting of "supply" items. With the full implementation of the practice expense component of the Medicare Fee Schedule, all supplies, such as surgical trays, are now included (e.g., bundled) in the payment for the procedure; Medicare will no longer reimburse the physician for this code. Some non-Medicare payers may still use it; others may alternatively allow CPT code 99070, Supplies and materials (except spectacles), provided by the physician over and above those usually included with the office visit or other services rendered (list drugs, trays, supplies, or materials provided) instead.

> **EXAMPLE:** A patient underwent a repair of recurrent strangulated abdominal incisional hernia with implantation of mesh. Report code 49566 (Repair recurrent incisional or ventral hernia; incarcerated or strangulated) and HCPCS level II code C1781 (mesh) *or* CPT code 49568 (Implantation of mesh or other prosthesis for incisional or ventral hernia repair). (Do not add modifier -51 to code C1781 or 49568 because they are exempt from that modifier.)

Reporting More than One Procedure/Service

When a physician performs more than one procedure or service on the same date, during the same operative session, or during a postoperative period and the surgical package concept applies, report one or more CPT modifiers to receive reimbursement consideration from third-party payers.

> **Note:**
> Refer to Table 8-2 in Chapter 8 for a comprehensive list of modifiers, descriptions, and examples (including modifiers used for reporting more than one procedure/service).

Add-on Codes

CPT includes a ✚ (plus) symbol next to add-on codes that describe a service that can be reported only in addition to a primary procedure. Add-on codes can also be identified by specific language in the code descriptor, such as *each additional* or *(List separately in addition to primary procedure)*. Add-on codes are never reported as stand-alone codes because they are considered an integral part of another procedure. They are never reported alone because the procedures they describe would not be performed unless another primary procedure was performed.

Add-on codes allow physicians to separately report procedures and services performed in addition to the primary procedure. The key to identifying add-on codes is determining whether the code always has to be reported with another code. If that is the case, the code is considered an add-on code. Also, add-on codes are exempt from the multiple procedure concept, which means -51 is not added.

> **EXAMPLE:** A patient underwent open treatment of three lumbar vertebral fractures. Report codes 22325, 22328, and 22328.
>
> The description for code 22325 includes "one fractured vertebra," and the description for code 22328 states "each additional fractured vertebrae . . . (List separately in addition to code for primary procedure)." This patient underwent treatment for three vertebral fractures, which requires the reporting of three codes. (Do not add modifier -51 to the 22328 codes because they are exempt from that modifier.)

Separate Procedure

CPT code descriptions that contain the term **separate procedure** in parentheses are commonly performed as an integral component of a total service or procedure. When the total procedure or service is performed, do not report as an additional procedure the code that contains the term *(separate procedure)* in its code description. When a separate procedure (e.g., 53020, Meatotomy) is performed during the same operative session as a more comprehensive procedure (e.g., 52285, Cystourethroscopy for treatment of the female urethral syndrome), do *not* code the separate procedure in addition to the more comprehensive procedure.

> **EXAMPLE:** The patient underwent sesamoidectomy and excision of a bone cyst of the middle phalanx of the right hand. Report code 26210.

Do not mistakenly report code 26185 in addition to code 26210. Code 26185 contains the term *(separate procedure)* in its code description. The procedure described in code 26185 is a component part of the more comprehensive "excision of bone cyst" procedure.

When a procedure or service that contains *(separate procedure)* in its code description *is performed independently of or is considered unrelated to or distinct from other procedures performed during the same operative session, report the separate procedure code in addition to codes for other procedures (or services).*

Reporting separate procedure codes may be necessary to classify the following:

- Procedure performed during a different session or patient encounter, procedure or surgery, site, or organ system

- Procedure performed through a separate incision or excision

- Separate lesion excised during the same operative session as removal of another lesion

- Treatment of a separate injury (or area of injury for extensive injuries)

Add modifier -59 to the separate procedure code to indicate that the procedure is not considered a component of another procedure, but is a distinct, independent procedure.

EXAMPLE: A patient underwent a complete salpingo-oophorectomy, bilateral, during the same operative session as a total abdominal hysterectomy. Report code 58150, Total abdominal hysterectomy (corpus and cervix), with or without removal of tube(s), with or without removal of ovary(s). Do not report code 58720, Salpingo-oophorectomy, complete or partial, unilateral or bilateral (separate procedure), because it is considered an integral component of the procedures described for code 58150.

Subsection Information

Many of the Surgery subsections contain unique instructions called *notes,* which are located just below the title of the subsection (Figure 11-4), heading, or subheading. Parenthetical notes are located below codes, and they apply to just that code.

EXAMPLE: The note located above code 11200 in the CPT coding manual provides instruction that removal includes scissoring or any sharp method. . . . It applies to all codes under the heading "Removal of Skin Tags."

The parenthetical note located below code 11201 in the coding manual indicates that code 11201 is reported with 11200, which means that it is never reported as a stand-alone code. This note applies to code 11201 only.

Unlisted Service or Procedure

CPT unlisted procedure codes are assigned when no specific code accurately describes the procedure performed. When reporting an unlisted procedure code on an insurance claim, make sure you include a written report (e.g., copy of operative report) that describes the procedure(s) performed. (During the first year that laparoscopic appendectomies and cholecystectomies were performed, no procedure codes were included in CPT. Unlisted procedure codes were reported.)

EXAMPLE: A physician performs a pressure ulcer excision, using a technique that is not described by any existing pressure ulcer codes. Report code 15999 and include a copy of the operative report with the claim.

Special Report

When an unlisted procedure code is reported to a third-party payer, attach a special report that describes the procedure performed. Special reports may also be required for procedures and services that are rarely provided, unusual, or new to establish medical necessity. As a minimum, to document a special report, include the following:

- Adequate description of the nature, extent, and need for the procedure

- Time, effort, and equipment necessary to provide the procedure or service

Removal of Skin Tags

Removal by scissoring or any sharp method, ligature, strangulation, electrosurgical destruction or combination of treatment modalities including chemical destruction or electrocauterization of wound, with or without local anesthesia.

11200	Removal of skin tags, multiple fibrocutaneous tags, any area; up to and including 15 lesions
+ 11201	each additional 10 lesions, or part thereof (List separately in addition to code for primary procedure)
	(Use 11201 in conjunction with 11200)

Figure 11-4 Sample note in CPT

The following additional items may also be documented in a special report:

- Complexity of symptoms
- Concurrent problems
- Diagnostic and therapeutic procedures
- Final diagnosis
- Follow-up care
- Pertinent physical findings (e.g., location, number, and size of lesions)

EXAMPLE: An ear, nose, and throat specialist performed an experimental procedure on the pharynx of a 14-year-old prodigy opera singer to treat persistent pharyngitis that has not resolved with traditional medical treatment. Conventional procedures to treat the unusual condition are not an option for this patient because they pose too great a risk of damage to the patient's vocal cords. The procedure was approved by the patient's parents, the health care facility at which it was performed, and the third-party payer that will reimburse its costs. Because the procedure is experimental, no CPT code is available. Report 42999 and attach a copy of the transcribed operative report to the claim. The operative report is the "special report" required by the payer to process the claim for reimbursement.

Surgical Destruction

Surgical destruction is considered part of a surgical procedure, and different methods of destruction are not reported separately unless the technique substantially differs from the standard management of a problem or condition. (CPT codes are available for exceptions due to special circumstances.) Surgical destruction includes the ablation (or removal) of tissues by any method, including chemical treatment, cryosurgery, electrosurgery, or laser.

EXAMPLE: A physician performed argon laser treatments on a patient with a congenital port wine stain. Report code 17106.

Exercise 11.2 – Surgery Guidelines

Instructions: Indicate whether each statement is true (T) or false (F).

_____ **1.** When services performed are integral to the standard of medical/surgical services, they are coded and reported separately.

_____ **2.** The CPT surgical package includes typical postoperative follow-up care in addition to the surgical procedure.

_____ **3.** CMS categorizes surgeries as major or minor, and it establishes a postoperative global period of 0, 10, or 90 days.

4. The CMS global surgical package includes preoperative visits before the decision is made to operate.

5. Visits unrelated to postoperative follow-up for a surgical procedure are included in CMS's global surgical package.

6. It is inappropriate for a physician to report a code for conscious sedation with the surgical service-described CPT code 19298.

7. A diagnostic esophagogastroduodenoscopy was performed to rule out gastric ulcer disease. The findings confirmed the diagnosis, and the physician prescribed medication. The patient was seen in the physician's office one week later for a follow-up visit to determine whether the patient's symptoms had been alleviated by medication. The patient was still experiencing acute pain, and the physician increased the medication dosage. The patient was scheduled for a two-week follow-up visit. The evaluation and management code for the follow-up visit during which the physician increased the dosage of the patient's medication is reported separately.

8. Health care services that are provided above and beyond the original surgical procedure are included in follow-up care for therapeutic procedures.

9. A physician applied sterile dressing after repairing a laceration. The sterile dressings are not separately coded and reported.

10. The patient underwent esophageal dilation for esophageal stricture (43450); during the same operative session, the patient also underwent esophagoscopy (43200) to investigate the cause of the esophageal stricture. Upon review of both codes, the physician should report 43450 and 43200-59.

Instructions: Complete each statement.

11. The global period for a major surgical procedure performed on May 1 is 90 days. The last day of the postoperative period is _____.

12. The global period for a minor surgical procedure performed on March 15 is zero days. The last day of the postoperative period is _____.

13. The global period for a minor surgical procedure performed on October 4 is 10 days. The last day of the postoperative period is _____.

14. A surgeon performed an incision and drainage of an abscess in the office. The patient developed an infection of the surgical site that required a return visit within 3 days to the physician's office. Which CPT modifier is reported with the E/M visit? _____

15. Code 29870 is reported for diagnostic knee arthroscopy (separate procedure), which was performed to determine the extent of a knee injury. The next day the same physician performs an arthroscopic major synovectomy and reports code 29876 because _____.

16. A physician repairs bilateral inguinal hernias on a 2-year-old. The physician reports the code for the inguinal hernia repair and adds modifier _____.

17. The same physician performed the following procedures during the same operative session:

- Biopsy of vulva or perineum (separate procedure); one lesion (56605)
- Repair of initial inguinal hernia, age 5 years or over; reducible (49505)

It is acceptable to report 49505 and 56605-59 because _____.

18. A physician performs an experimental arthroscopic shoulder procedure and uses heat to shrink the capsule in the shoulder. Report unlisted arthroscopic code _____ and submit a special report.

19. CPT defines *destruction* as the _____.

20. A physician performed surgery on a patient to destroy 25 lesions. Review the description for code 17004. How many times should code 17004 be reported? _____ Why? _____

General Subsection

The General subsection contains just two codes:

- 10021 (fine-needle aspiration; without imaging guidance)

- 10022 (fine-needle aspiration; with imaging guidance)

Fine-needle aspiration (FNA) involves the removal of fluid from a cyst or cells from a solid mass. Then the cells are examined cytologically. FNA is a percutaneous procedure; if the cyst or mass is *not* palpable on physical exam, the procedure is typically performed under image guidance using fluoroscopy, ultrasound, or computed tomography (CT). Report code 10021 if FNA is performed without imaging guidance. Report code 10022 if imaging guidance is used to assist in locating the lump.

EXAMPLE 1: A physician aspirates a cyst, using FNA technique. Report code 10021.

EXAMPLE 2: A patient presents with a thyroid nodule. Using CT guidance, a FNA is performed on the thyroid nodule; the material is sent for cytologic review. In addition to code 10022, report 77012 (Computed tomography guidance for needle placement [e.g., biopsy, aspiration, injection, localization device], radiological supervision and interpretation). (Directional modifiers, such as -LT and -RT, are not added to codes in CPT's General Subsection.)

The parenthetical notes located below the General subsection applies to both codes (10021–10022). The first note specifies that when percutaneous needle aspiration requires imaging guidance, the appropriate radiological supervision and interpretation code is also reported (e.g., 77002, Fluoroscopic guidance for needle placement). The second and third notes specify that codes 10021–10022 are *not* reported for:

- Percutaneous needle biopsy other than FNA, which is reported with appropriate codes from the Surgery section (e.g., 20206, percutaneous needle biopsy of muscle).

- Evaluation of fine-needle aspirate, which is reported with code(s) from the Pathology and Laboratory section (e.g., 88172, Cytopathology, evaluation of fine-needle aspirate; immediate cytohistologic study to determine adequacy of specimen[s]).

Exercise 11.3 – General Subsection

Instructions: Assign the CPT code(s) and appropriate modifier(s) to each statement.

1. A patient presents with a palpable left breast mass for which fine-needle aspiration biopsy is performed.

2. A patient has a nonpalpable right breast mass that was identified on a previous screening mammogram. Ultrasound exam at that time revealed that the mass is not a simple cyst. Fine-needle aspiration biopsy of the right breast mass is performed under ultrasonic guidance during today's encounter.

Integumentary System Subsection

The Integumentary System subsection includes dermatological procedures, plastic surgery, and components of multiple surgical procedures (e.g., closure, flaps, grafts, and tissue transfer). Integumentary procedures (Table 11-2) are often performed as staged procedures (e.g., flaps and grafts) due to the complexity of services rendered. Integumentary procedures include incision, biopsy, removal, paring/curettement, shaving, destruction, excision, repair, adjacent tissue rearrangement, grafts, flaps, and specialized services (e.g., burn management,

Table 11-2 Integumentary Procedures and Definitions

Integumentary Procedure	Definition
Adjacent tissue transfer/rearrangement	Closure of defects by relocating a flap of adjacent normal, healthy tissue from a donor site to an nearby (adjacent) defect, such as a traumatic skin wound or the site of excised lesion; a portion of the flap remains intact to provide a blood supply to the grafted site
Biopsy	Removal and examination of tissue to establish a diagnosis, confirm a diagnosis, or determine the extent of a disease
Flap	Relocation of a mass of tissue (usually skin) that has been partially removed from one part of the body so that it retains its own blood supply
Graft	Any tissue or organ used for implantation or transplant
Mohs microsurgery	Technique of excising skin tumors by removing tumor tissue layer by layer, examining the removed portion microscopically for malignant cells, and repeating the procedure until the entire tumor is removed
Paring and curettement	Removal of growths or other material from the wall of a cavity or another surface, as with a curette; paring of lesions (e.g., corns and calluses) seldom, if ever, require local anesthesia
Shaving	Horizontal slicing to remove epidermal and dermal lesions (e.g., without a full-thickness dermal excision); removal includes scissoring or any sharp method

© Cengage Learning 2014

Mohs micrographic surgery). (Refer to the definitions of surgical terms earlier in this chapter. Additional terms are defined below.)

The CPT Surgery Integumentary subsection contains the following headings:

- Skin, Subcutaneous and Accessory Structures
- Nails
- Pilonidal Cyst
- Introduction
- Repair (Closure)
- Destruction
- Breast

Coding Tip:

- Do not add HCPCS level II modifiers LT and RT to codes in the Skin, Subcutaneous and Accessory Structures; Nails; Pilonidal Cyst; Introduction; Repair (Closure); or Destruction headings—the skin is not a paired organ.
- Add modifiers LT and RT to codes in the Breast heading.
- Add HCPCS level II modifiers FA through F9 or TA through T9 to codes for procedures performed on the fingernails and toenails.

Skin, Subcutaneous and Accessory Structures

The Skin, Subcutaneous and Accessory Structures heading includes the following subheadings: Incision and Drainage (I&D), Excision-Debridement, Paring or Cutting, Biopsy, Removal of Skin Tags, Shaving of Epidermal or Dermal Lesions, Excision—Benign Lesions, and Excision—Malignant Lesions.

Incision and Drainage (I&D)

The I&D subheading contains procedures that establish a drainage pathway for fluid that forms at sites of infection. CPT I&D procedures include cutaneous and subcutaneous drainage of cysts, fluid collections, infections, hematomas (Figure 11-5), pustules, and seromas. When a procedure to excise a lesion results in drainage of an area, either as a part of the procedure or as a way to gain access to the lesion, do not report a code for I&D if the excision or another

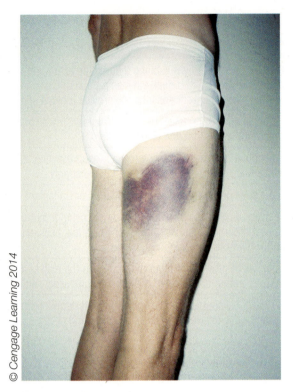

Figure 11-5 Hematoma

procedure is performed during the same operative session. It is also inappropriate to report a separate code for an I&D of a hematoma (10140) if it is performed during the same operative session as excision, repair, destruction, removal, and so on.

> **EXAMPLE:** A patient undergoes a scheduled procedure to treat a **pilonidal cyst** (entrapped epithelial tissue and hair located in the sacral area at the top of the crease between the buttocks, which can become infected). Treatment options include simple I&D (10080–10081), excision (11770–11772), or a combination of both *if extensive cellulitis is present.*

> ### Note:
> CPT does not define type of excision terms: simple, extensive or complicated. The provider is responsible for establishing the type of excision.

- When a patient undergoes simple I&D of a pilonidal cyst and there is no mention of infection, report CPT code 10080. During a simple I&D of a pilonidal cyst, if the provider also performs an excision of the pilonidal cyst, report just code 11770 (for simple excision).

- Report 11771 instead of 11770 when a cyst measures 2 cm or larger in size, is recurrent, or requires layered closure.

- If plastic repair (e.g., local flap) will be required in the future, report 11772 instead of 11770 or 11771.

- During simple I&D of a pilonidal cyst, if the provider encounters **extensive cellulitis** (acute inflammation of skin's connective tissue that is caused by infection with bacteria) and the excision of the pilonidal cyst cannot be performed, the provider will prescribe an antibiotic. Report CPT code 10081 for complicated I&D of the pilonidal cyst (due to presence of an infection). If after one week of antibiotic therapy, the patient returns and the provider performs an excision of the pilonidal cyst, report code 11770-78 (or 11771-78 or 11772-78 depending on complexity).

CPT codes describe procedures necessary to address complications, such as code 10180 (Incision and drainage, complex, postoperative wound infection). Such codes are *not* reported with codes for the original surgery that resulted in the complication. If the original surgery code is reported with the procedure to treat the complication, National Correct Coding Initiative (NCCI) edits will deny reimbursement for the procedure performed to treat the complication.

EXAMPLE: A patient who underwent a thoracotomy developed a surgical wound infection, which required I&D. Report code 10180-78 for I&D of the (skin) wound infection.

Exercise 11.4 – Incision and Drainage

Instructions: Assign the CPT code(s) and any appropriate modifier(s) to each statement.

1. Complex incision and drainage, postoperative wound infection.

_____

2. Incision and drainage of hematoma, skin.

_____

3. Incision and removal of foreign body, subcutaneous tissue.

_____

4. Marsupialization acne surgery.

_____

5. Simple incision and drainage of five infected cysts.

_____

Lesion Removal

Lesion removal is coded in CPT by referencing the following subheadings:

- Excision—Debridement
- Paring or Cutting
- Biopsy
- Removal of Skin Tags
- Shaving of Epidermal or Dermal Lesions
- Excision—Benign Lesions
- Excision—Malignant Lesions

A skin lesion (Figure 11-6) is a pathologic change in tissue (e.g., benign or malignant). To accurately code the removal of lesions, review the patient record to locate the following information:

- Method of removing the lesion (e.g., paring, shaving, or debridement)
- Malignant or benign status of lesion if excision method is performed
- Site or body part where lesion is located
- Size of the lesion in centimeters (Figure 11-7)
- Type of wound closure/repair (e.g., simple, intermediate, or complex)

Note:

- To calculate the size of a lesion, refer to "excised diameter" notes located in CPT Surgery (above the Excision-Benign Lesions heading in the Integumentary System subsection). The "excised diameter" includes the size of the lesion plus its margins.

- Documentation of the "excised diameter" should include dimensions for the greatest size (diameter) of the lesion as well as for the margin around the lesion. *When multiple lesions are removed, do not add together the greatest size (or diameter) of each separate lesions even when excised in one ellipse.*

- The margin is the amount of surrounding tissue that must be removed to adequately excise the lesion, and it is calculated as the shortest distance from the lesion to the edge of the skin ellipse.

  - An ellipse is a shape resembling an oval.

  - The narrowest amount of tissue removed from each end of the ellipse is measured and used to calculate the "excised diameter" of the lesion.

  - When multiple lesions are excised using one ellipse, the narrowest margin between lesions is measured and used *in addition to measurements of each end of the ellipse* to calculate the "excised diameter" of the lesion.

  EXAMPLE 1: A 2 × 1 cm benign lesion of the cheek was excised in an elliptical fashion with 2-mm margins in all directions. Simple closure was performed. The "excised diameter" is calculated as 2.4 cm because:

  - The greatest size (or diameter) of the lesion is 2 cm.

  - The narrowest margin of each end of the ellipse is 2 mm (or 0.2 cm), calculated as 0.2 cm × 2 = 0.4 cm.

  - 2 cm + 0.4 cm = 2.4-cm "excised diameter."

  - Report CPT code 11443. (Do not report a separate code for the simple closure procedure.)

  EXAMPLE 2: One elliptical excision was made to remove two nevi from the patient's left arm. Lesion A was 3 cm in diameter, and lesion B was 2 cm in diameter. Skin margins were 4 mm at each end of the ellipse, and 2 mm between the two lesions. Simple closure was performed. The "excised diameter" of lesion A is 3.5 cm and lesion B is 2.5 cm because:

  - The greatest size (or diameter) of each lesion is 3 cm and 2 cm, respectively. Do not add together the greatest size (or diameter) of separate lesions even when excised in one ellipse.

  - The narrowest margin of each end of the ellipse is 4 mm (or 0.4 cm). Thus, associate 0.4 cm with each lesion.

  - The narrowest margin between the lesions is 2 mm (or 0.2 cm). Thus, associate 0.1 cm (half of 0.2 cm) with each lesion.

  - 3 cm + 0.4 cm + 0.1 cm = 3.5-cm "excised diameter" of lesion A.

  - 2 cm + 0.4 cm + 0.1 cm = 2.5-cm "excised diameter" of lesion B.

  - Report CPT code 11404 for lesion A and 11403-51 for lesion B. (Do not report a separate code for the simple closure procedure.)

From a coding perspective, benign lesions include neoplasms, fibrous cysts, or other inflammatory cystic lesions. Malignant lesions are typically described as melanoma, basal cell carcinoma, or squamous cell carcinoma. When surgery is performed on a lesion, select the appropriate code according to the lesion's "excised diameter," which includes the lesion plus its margins. (Do not refer to the pathology report for the diameter because placing a lesion in formalin, the formaldehyde solution used to preserve organic specimens, can result in shrinkage.)

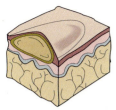

Bulla: (Large blister)
    Same as a vesicle only
    greater than 10 mm
Example:
    Contact dermatitis, large
    second-degree burns,
    bulbous impetigo, pemphigus

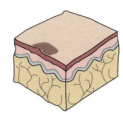

Macule:
    Localized changes in skin
    color of less than 1 cm
    in diameter
Example:
    Freckle

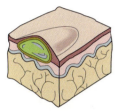

Nodule:
    Solid and elevated; however,
    they extend deeper than
    papules into the dermis or
    subcutaneous tissues, greater
    than 10 mm
Example:
    Lipoma, erythema, cyst, wart

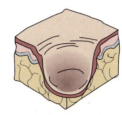

Papule:
    Solid, elevated lesion less
    than 1 cm in diameter
Example:
    Elevated nevi

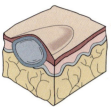

Pustule:
    Vesicles or bullae that
    become filled with pus,
    usually described as less
    than 0.5 cm in diameter
Example:
    Acne, impetigo, furuncles,
    carbuncles

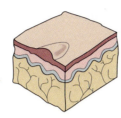

Ulcer:
    A depressed lesion of
    the epidermis and upper
    papillary layer of the dermis
Example:
    Stage 2 pressure ulcer

Tumor:
    The same as a nodule only
    greater than 2 cm

Example:
    Benign epidermal tumor
    basal cell carcinoma

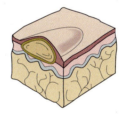

Vesicle: (Small blister)
    Accumulation of fluid between
    the upper layers of the skin;
    elevated mass containing
    serous fluid; less than 10 mm
Example:
    Herpes simplex, herpes
    zoster, chickenpox

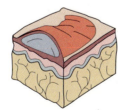

Urticaria, Hives:
    Localized edema in the
    epidermis causing irregular
    elevation that may be red
    or pale, may be itchy
Example:
    Insect bite, wheal

Figure 11-6 Skin lesions

© Cengage Learning 2014

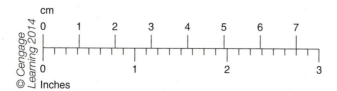

© Cengage Learning 2014

Figure 11-7 Lesions are measured in centimeters.
(Note: 2.5 centimeters equals 1 inch.)

EXAMPLE: A malignant lesion of the nose measuring 1.0 cm in diameter is excised, and the operative report states that skin margins are 1.1 cm. The "excised diameter" of the lesion is 2.1 cm (1.0 + 1.1 = 2.1). Therefore, report code 11643 (Excision, malignant lesion including margins, face, ears, eyelids, nose, lips; excised diameter 2.1 to 3.0 cm).

 Note:

If an operative report describes the diameter of a lesion as having multiple sides, select the largest size as the diameter (e.g., a lesion described as 2 cm × 3 cm × 5 cm is 5 cm in diameter).

Just one type of removal is reported for each lesion, whether it is destruction (e.g., laser or freezing), debridement, paring, curettement, shaving, or excision. CPT notes describe the nature of each of these forms of removal.

When multiple methods are used to remove one lesion, report a code for just one destruction method. When multiple distinct lesions are removed using different methods, report a code for each lesion removal and attach modifier 59 to each code. (Modifier 59 indicates different site, different method, or different lesion.) Make sure the provider has documented the distinct locations of each lesion in the patient's record.

The biopsy of a lesion involves the partial removal of a lesion, and it is frequently performed at the same time as the removal of the entire lesion to obtain a pathologic specimen. The lesion biopsy is performed first, the tissue is submitted to pathology for evaluation and pathologic diagnosis, and then the lesion is completely removed. When a lesion biopsy is performed as part of a lesion removal, it is considered part of the total procedure and is not assigned a separate code. Report only the CPT code for removal of the lesion.

Lesion removal by any method may require simple, intermediate, or complex closure; it is also possible that a tissue transfer procedure will have to be performed. When the lesion removal requires bandaging, strip closure, or simple closure, the closure is included in the lesion excision and is not coded and reported separately. A **simple repair**, or **simple closure**, (also called one-layer closure, nonlayered closure, and single-layer closure) involves the use of staples, sutures, and/or tissue adhesives to repair superficial wounds involving epidermis, dermis, and/or subcutaneous tissues.

Simple repair procedures are considered integral to lesion removal. Intermediate and complex repair (closure), when medically necessary, is coded separately. (For Mohs micrographic surgery, all necessary repairs are coded and reported separately.)

 Coding Tip:

- When a benign or malignant lesion is excised and complex closure is performed during the same operative session, two codes are reported:
  - Excision of benign or malignant lesion (11400–11446 or 11600–11646)
  - Complex closure (13100–13153)
- However, when a scar is excised followed by complex closure, report the complex repair code only.
- When multiple lesions are excised during the same operative session, report a code for the excision of each lesion.
- When a malignant lesion is excised and the patient returns for further excision to ensure that the malignancy has been completely resected, report a code for excision of a malignant lesion (even if the pathology report documents no residual malignancy).

Refer to the following table when assigning codes for excision of benign or malignant lesions that require wound repair (closure). When using the table to assign codes, it is important to note that:

- When multiple lesions are excised during the same operative session, the number of excision codes must be increased accordingly.

- When intermediate or complex repair (closure) is performed to repair defects resulting from excision of multiple lesions, codes are grouped according to the same anatomic sites.

Type of Procedure	# of Codes	Types of Codes
Simple repair	1	Excision (11400–11471 or 11600–11646)
Intermediate repair	2	Excision (11400–11471 or 11600–11646)
		Intermediate repair (12031–12057)
Complex repair	2	Excision (11400–11471 or 11600–11646)
		Complex repair (13100–13160)

Exercise 11.5 – Lesion Removal

Instructions: Assign the CPT code(s) and any appropriate modifier(s) to each statement.

1. A physician excises a 1-cm lesion of the left forearm, and the defect is closed with a simple repair.

   _____

2. Punch biopsy of a skin lesion on the back and another one on the arm.

   _____

3. Excision of a 2.1-cm malignant lesion of the nose and two malignant lesions, including margins, of the chest, each 1.5-cm in diameter, including margins.

   _____

4. Four warts were removed by paring.

   _____

5. A physician excised a 2-cm benign lesion from the face.

   _____

Nails

The Nails heading classifies procedures that are performed to treat a variety of nail conditions, such as infections, trauma, nail dystrophy, and neoplasms. Most nail surgery is performed using local or digital block anesthetic. These procedures are typically performed on toenails but can be done on fingernails as well.

Nondystrophic nails are normal nails with no abnormal development or changes due to aging, injury, or disease. Nail debridement is generally done to treat hypertrophic dystrophic nails and mycotic (fungal) infections. It is performed mechanically by using instruments such as a nail splitter, a nail elevator, and an electrical burr (sander). For lacerations to the nailbed, where the wound extends under the proximal nail fold, a portion or all of the nail plate must be removed in order to visualize the laceration.

Coding Tip:

Report HCPCS level II modifiers (-FA through -F9 and -TA through -T9) with codes for procedures performed on a patient's fingernails and toenails.

Pilonidal Cyst

The Pilonidal Cyst heading contains codes for procedures to report excision. A pilonidal cyst contains a tuft of hair that developed as the result of repeated friction, which caused hairs to penetrate the skin; it occurs primarily in the sacrococcygeal area. (For incision of a pilonidal cyst, report the appropriate code from the Incision and Drainage heading.)

Exercise 11.6 – Nails

Instructions: Assign the CPT code(s) and any appropriate modifier(s) to each statement.

1. A diabetic patient was seen by a podiatrist for trimming of nondystrophic nails, which are unaffected by abnormal development or changes in structure or appearance. Following cleansing and drying of all toenails of both feet, clippers are used to cut each nail straight across so that it is in line with the edge of the end of the toe.

   _____

2. Reconstruction of nailbed, second toe on left foot, with graft.

   _____

3. Avulsion of nail plate, simple, 5 nails, right foot.

   _____

4. The physician evacuated blood from a hematoma located beneath a patient's fingernail, second digit, left hand. The physician used an electrocautery needle to pierce the nail plate so the hematoma can drain. Pressure was applied to the nailbed to force the blood from beneath the nail plate. A loose dressing was applied so the area can continue to drain.

   _____

5. Wedge excision of skin of nail fold for ingrown toenail, third digit, right foot.

   _____

Exercise 11.7 – Pilonidal Cyst

Instructions: Assign the CPT code(s) and any appropriate modifier(s) to each statement.

1. Excision of complicated pilonidal cyst.

   _____

2. Pilonidal sinus excision, simple.

   _____

3. Excision of extensive pilonidal cyst.

   _____

4. The physician shaved hair adjacent to a pilonidal cyst and made an incision to allow drainage of cystic fluid.

   _____

5. The patient presented with an infected pilonidal cyst (complicated). The cyst was incised and drained.

   _____

Introduction

Codes located in the Introduction heading include the following procedures: injection of lesion(s); tattooing; subcutaneous infection of filling material (e.g., collagen); insertion, removal, and replacement of tissue expanders; insertion and removal of implantable contraceptive capsules; subcutaneous hormone pellet implantation; and insertion, removal, and removal with insertion of nonbiodegradable drug delivery implants.

CPT codes 11900–11901 describe intralesional injection(s) into one or more lesions, and they are reported for the treatment of lesions such as keloids, psoriasis, and acne (cystic or nodular). Drugs are injected directly into the lesion, and it is appropriate to report HCPCS level II national code(s) for medication(s) administered. CPT codes (11900–11901) reported are determined by the number of lesions treated (not by the number of injections).

Coding Tip:

- Codes 11900–11901 are not reported for local anesthetic injection in anticipation of chemotherapy or any other definitive service performed on a lesion or group of lesions (e.g., lesion destruction or removal).
- The administration (injection) of local anesthesia is included in the surgical procedure performed, and it is not coded separately.

Note:

CPT Medicine Section codes that describe intralesional chemotherapy involve the injection of chemotherapeutic agents into one or multiple lesions. Do not report lesion injection codes (11900–11901) with intralesional chemotherapy codes (96405–96406) unless separate lesions are injected with different agents. Make sure you attach modifier -59 to the intralesional injection code(s) if the procedure is performed during the same encounter as lesion injection(s).

EXAMPLE: A physician performed intralesional injection of eight lesions. Report code 11901. (Code 11901 is a stand-alone code; it does not contain the plus symbol next to the code, which would indicate an add-on code. Do not report 11900 with 11901. Report either 11900 or 11901 based on the number of lesions injected.)

Exercise 11.8 – Introduction

Instructions: Assign the CPT code(s) and any appropriate modifier(s) to each statement.

1. Patient presented for subcutaneous implantation of estradiol and testosterone compressed crystalline pellets.

_____

2. A patient presented with acne (cystic), and the physician injected drugs directly into six lesions.

_____

3. Subcutaneous injection of 15.0 cc of collagen was performed.

_____

4. Five implantable contraceptive capsules were removed.

_____

5. Intralesional injection, 12 lesions.

_____

Table 11-3 Medical Terms for Adjacent Tissue Transfer/Rearrangement, Flap, and Graft Procedures

Defect	Wound that is the result of surgical intervention or trauma
Donor site	Anatomic site from which healthy skin is removed
Primary defect	Wound resulting from initial surgical intervention (e.g., excision of lesion) or trauma (e.g., deep abrasions)
Recipient site	Anatomic site to which healthy skin is attached
Secondary defect	Wound resulting from removal of tissue to create flap(s) or graft(s)
Stroma	Supporting tissue (matrix) of an organ
Tissue approximation	Method of replacing sutures with material or substance (e.g., surgical glue), which facilitates enhanced cosmetic results and faster healing of defects
Undermining	Process of using a surgical instrument to separate skin and mucosa from its underlying stroma so that the tissue can be stretched and moved to overlay a defect

Repair (Closure)

The Repair (Closure) heading includes the following subheadings, which require knowledge of additional medical terms associated with repair (closure) procedures (Table 11-3):

- Repair—Simple
- Repair—Intermediate
- Repair—Complex
- Adjacent Tissue Transfer or Rearrangement
- Skin Replacement Surgery and Skin Substitutes
- Flaps (Skin and/or Deep Tissues)
- Other Flaps and Grafts
- Other Procedures
- Pressure Ulcers (Decubitus Ulcers)
- Burns, Local Treatment

Simple, Intermediate, Complex Repairs

Coding wound repairs is sometimes confusing because codes for repairs can be stand-alone procedures, separately reportable services when performed with certain other procedures (e.g., excisions requiring complex repair), or they can be an integral part of a more complex procedure and not separately reportable (e.g., surgical wound closure).

To add to the confusion, repairs are also divided into three categories:

- Simple: Superficial, only simple, one layer, primary suturing is required
- Intermediate: One of the deeper layers of subcutaneous tissue and fascia are involved
- Complex: Requiring more than layered closure; e.g., revision, debridement, creation of a defect, or preparation of the site

Note:

- Single-layer closure is coded as an intermediate repair if the wound is heavily contaminated and requires extensive cleaning.
- When a physician documents layered closure, do not assume an intermediate repair code is to be reported. Locate documentation of:
  - Closure of subcutaneous tissue or more than one layer of tissue beneath the dermis. Such closure of tissue layers under the skin uses dissolvable sutures before suturing the dermis and epidermis.

    or
  - Extensive cleaning or removal of foreign matter from a heavily contaminated wound that is closed with a single layer.

Assign codes in this section to report wound closures utilizing sutures, staples, or tissue adhesives (e.g., 2-cyanoacrylate tissue glue) either alone or in combination with one another or with adhesive strips.

To report wound repairs, review the patient record to locate the length of the repaired wound(s) in centimeters. Then group the wounds by type of repair (e.g., simple, intermediate, or complex) and anatomic site. Finally, add the lengths of multiple wounds in the same category and report the repair code for the total. Make sure you separately code and report wound repairs that are located in more than one anatomic site; report the most complicated service as the first-listed procedure.

Coding Tip:

Wound closure utilizing adhesive strips as the only repair material are reported with an appropriate E/M code.

EXAMPLE 1: A complex repair of two scalp lacerations measuring a total of 4-cm is located in the same anatomic site and is the same type of repair. Report code 13121.

EXAMPLE 2: A complex repair of a 6-cm forehead laceration, 3-cm cheek laceration, and 3-cm chin laceration and an intermediate repair of 3.5-cm lacerations to both hands represent two different sites and types of repair. Report codes 13132, 13133, and 12042-51. (Report codes 13132 and 13133 for complex repair of the total 12-cm laceration (forehead, cheek, and chin). Report code 12042-51 for the intermediate repair of the 3.5-cm lacerations of both hands.)

Note:

Modifier -51 is not reported with code 13133 because the plus symbol indicates that the code has "modifier -51 exempt" status. However, modifier -51 is reported with code 12042 because notes below the Repair (Closure) heading state, "When more than one classification of wounds is repaired, list the more complicated as the primary procedure and the less complicated as the secondary procedure, using modifier 51."

Coding Tip:

HCPCS level II national code G0168, Wound closure utilizing tissue adhesive(s) only (e.g., Dermabond), is considered a supply code. Therefore, code G0168 is reported in addition to the appropriate wound repair CPT code.

EXAMPLE: Patient sustained a 2.5-centimeter superficial laceration, right leg, which was repaired using Dermabond tissue adhesive. Report codes 12001 and G0168.

Coding Wound Repair (Closure) Procedures

When reporting wound repair (closure) codes, make sure that you do the following:

- Calculate the size of the wound in centimeters, whether angular, curved, or star-shaped.

- Add together the lengths of all wounds for the multiple repair of wounds in the same anatomic site (e.g., 12001–12007) and report just one code.

- Report the code for the most complicated repair first, followed by less complicated repair codes (with modifier -59).

- Report codes 11042–11047 for skin debridement when:

  ○ Gross contamination requires prolonged cleansing.

- ○ Large amounts of devitalized or contaminated tissue are removed.

- ○ Debridement is performed without immediate primary wound closure.

- Report codes 11010–11012 when extensive debridement of subcutaneous tissue, muscle fascia, muscle, and/or bone (including removal of foreign material) at the site of open fracture(s) and/or dislocation(s). To report these codes, debridement must include removal of foreign material *and* be performed to the level of skin and/or subcutaneous tissue (11010), but may extend to muscle (11011) or bone (11012), and documentation must specify precisely the depth of debridement.

- For debridement of skin only (or for active wound care management), without removal of foreign material, report codes 97597 or 97598 from the CPT Medicine section.

- Report codes for the repair of nerves, blood vessels, and tendons (from the specific body system involved, such as nervous, cardiovascular, or musculoskeletal). (However, codes for simple exploration of nerves, blood vessels, and tendons exposed in an open wound are not reported separately.)

- When physician locates a foreign body and removes it, report a code for its removal only.

  EXAMPLE 1: A diabetic male is diagnosed with with a 2.0 cm × 2.0 cm posterior left heel ulceration that involves skin, subcutaneous tissues, and the soleus muscle. Debridement at all levels was performed. Report code 11043 for the 4.0 cm treatment area. (2.0 cm × 2.0 cm = 4.0 sq cm)

  EXAMPLE 2: A motorcyclist lost control on 2-lane country road that was covered with loose stone. She suffered an open fracture of her right tibia and extensive abrasions directly over the fracture site, which required debridement down to muscle. The debridement procedure is reported with code 11011. (The open fracture repair is reported separately, according to documentation in the patient record.)

In addition, it is important to remember that:

- The simple ligation of vessels in an open wound is included in the wound repair code.

- The simple exploration of nerves, blood vessels, or tendons exposed in an open wound is included in the wound repair code.

- The reported wound repair codes are based on length of the wound (in centimeters), wound site, and complexity of repair.

- Code 13160 describes a secondary or complicated closure of a surgical wound because the initial closure reopened or failed.

- Wound repairs usually require local anesthesia, and the physician usually performs a neurovascular exam prior to administering the anesthetic. The administration of the local anesthesia is included in the wound repair code.

When the closure of a lesion excision cannot be accomplished by simple, intermediate, or complex closure, the following methods are used:

- Adjacent tissue transfer or rearrangement (Table 11-4)

- Skin replacement surgery and skin substitutes

Adjacent Tissue Transfer or Rearrangement

Adjacent tissue transfer or rearrangement codes include skin excision and are assigned according to anatomic site. To determine the correct code, calculate the combined area (as square centimeters) of the defect to be repaired *and the defect created by the tissue transfer*. Do not report a separate code for excision of a lesion or another defect when an adjacent tissue transfer or a rearrangement procedure is performed.

When a procedure is performed to repair a secondary defect (e.g., site of donor advancement flap), report an additional procedure code for the repair (e.g., full-thickness skin graft).

EXAMPLE 1: Patient previously underwent excision of lesion, chest. Today, the patient undergoes adjacent tissue transfer repair of resulting 1 sq cm skin defect via advancement flap, created from

Table 11-4 Adjacent Tissue Transfer or Tissue Rearrangement Methods and Definitions

Adjacent Tissue Transfer Method	Definition
Advancement flap	Movement of tissue in a straight line from donor to defect site using a sliding process; once movement is achieved, the flap is sutured in place; advancement flaps are not rotated or moved sideways
Double pedicle flap	Maintains blood supply from both ends of the flap incision made to create a curvilinear flap contiguous with the defect; flap is pivoted and sutured in place over the defect
Free flap	Island flap that is detached from donor site and reattached at recipient site via microvascular anastomosis
Island flap	Flap consisting of skin and subcutaneous tissue with a pedicle comprised only of nutrient vessels; also called island pedicle flap
Mycocutaneous flap	Autologous graft consisting of both skin and muscle tissue from the donor site
Random pattern flap	Mycocutaneous flap with a random pattern of arteries
Rhomboid flap	Random pattern flap that can be raised on any or all corners of a parallelogram configuration, typically 120 and 60 degrees; also called Limberg flap
Rotation flap	Incision made to create a curvilinear flap contiguous with the defect; flap is dissected, freed, pivoted, and sutured in place over the defect
Tissue rearrangement	Defined by anatomic site and size of defect; includes excision of the defect or lesion; terms used to describe transfer or rearrangement include *Z-plasty, W-plasty, V-Y-plasty, rotation flap, advancement flap,* and *double pedicle flap*
V-Y-plasty	After creation of a V-shaped incision, the edges of the incision are drawn together and sutured, converting the incision to a *Y* shape
W-plasty	Both edges of the wound or defect are trimmed into the shape of a *W* or multiple *W*s
Z-plasty	Involves making an incision along with two additional incisions, one above and another below, creating a *Z* formation

© Cengage Learning 2014

2 sq cm of adjacent chest tissue. Dressings were applied to both wounds. Report code 14000 (because 1 sq cm + 2 sq cm = 4 sq cm, and the chest is part of the body's trunk).

EXAMPLE 2: Patient previously underwent excision of nasal scar, which resulted in a skin defect. Today, the patient undergoes adjacent tissue transfer repair of the 2 sq cm nasal skin defect using an advancement flap (using 4 sq cm of skin from the left cheek). A full-thickness skin graft (using 6 sq cm of skin from right inner thigh) was required to close the 4 sq cm flap left cheek donor site defect. The right inner thigh was repaired using direct closure. Report codes 14060 (because 2 sq cm + 4 sq cm = 6 sq cm) and 15240-51 (which includes direct closure to repair the right inner thigh).

Skin Replacement Surgery and Skin Substitutes, Flaps (Skin and/or Deep Tissues), and Other Flaps and Grafts

CPT graft codes are organized as follows:

- Autograft/tissue cultured autograft
- Acellular dermal replacement
- Allograft/tissue cultured allogeneic skin substitute
- Allograft, skin
- Xenograft, skin

An **autograft** is the transplantation of tissue from the same individual (e.g., harvesting skin from the patient's thigh to graft a defect of the upper arm). **Tissue-cultured autografts** are supplied by laboratories. (Modifier -58 is added to tissue-cultured autograft codes because labs can grow a limited amount of tissue and such grafts are often performed as staged procedures.)

Acellular dermal replacement is a bioengineered artificial skin (e.g., Alloderm). An **allograft** is the transplantation of tissue from someone of the same species (e.g., harvesting skin from another person's thigh to graft a defect on the patient's upper arm). A **xenograft** is the transplantation of tissue from a different species (e.g., harvesting skin from a baboon or a pig to graft a defect on the patient's upper arm).

Types of skin grafts include the following:

- Free skin graft
  - Full-thickness skin graft
  - Split-thickness skin graft
- Pedicle skin graft

Free skin grafts are completely separated from the donor site before being transferred to the recipient site. They are classified as **full-thickness skin grafts** (graft of epidermis and dermis) or **split–thickness skin grafts** (graft of entire epidermis and a portion of the dermis). Full-thickness skin grafts are often harvested from the inguinal folds, supraclavicular region, abdomen, thigh, and postauricular skin (because of the availability of excess skin, which eases primary closure of the donor site). Split–thickness grafts are typically used to repair edematous, infected, or large wounds (e.g., result of burns).

Coding Tip:

- Before reporting codes 15002–15278 for free skin grafts, determine whether the graft is full-thickness or split-thickness, what the size of the recipient area is, and where the location of the recipient area is.
- When reporting codes 15100–15278, the area over which a skin graft is placed must be free of infection or other disease; if it is necessary to cleanse the recipient site of a skin graft, also report a code from 15002–15005 for the surgical preparation.
- Although codes 15002–15278 include simple debridement of the recipient area, they do not include repair of the donor site with skin grafts or local flaps. Report additional code(s) when the donor site is repaired in this manner.

Pedicle skin grafts are not immediately completely separated from their donor site. A portion of the graft is transferred to the recipient area, and a remaining portion (the base) is attached to the donor site so that there is a vasculature and nerve supply for the recipient area. Once blood flow to the recipient site is sufficient, the base is grafted to the recipient site.

Coding Tip:

Codes 15600–15630 are reported when the "delay technique" is used to improve the blood supply to the base of a flap. This is accomplished by temporarily obstructing the blood supply to the flap to allow a relatively long flap to be transferred onto a narrow pedicle.

When assigning codes for skin grafts, identify the following:

- Type of graft
  - Permanent or temporary
  - Natural or manufactured graft material
  - Use of skin components (e.g., epidermal, dermal, split-thickness, or full-thickness grafts) (Refer to Figure 11-8 to view full-thickness and split-thickness skin grafts.)

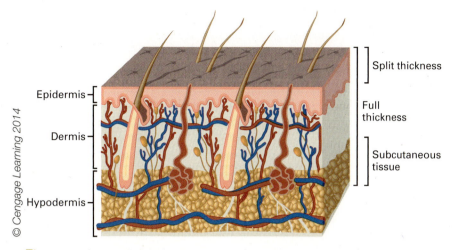

Figure 11-8 Depth of full-thickness and split-thickness skin cross-sections

- Recipient site (anatomic location)

- Surface area of the recipient site calculated as square centimeters

Just one type of skin graft is usually applied to an anatomic location. Thus, primary free skin graft codes are mutually exclusive of one another. When multiple anatomic locations require different grafts, add modifier -59 to the reported code(s) to indicate that different sites underwent grafting.

When a benign or malignant lesion is excised and surgical preparation and free skin grafting are performed, two codes are reported:

- Excision lesion code (11400–11446 or 11600–11646)

- Skin graft code

However, when a benign or malignant lesion is excised with flap closure, just the flap closure code is reported.

Generally, debridement of nonintact skin in anticipation of a skin graft is necessary prior to application of the skin graft and is included in the skin graft. When skin is intact, however, and the graft is being performed after excisional preparation of intact skin, codes 15002–15005 (Excisional preparation) are separately reported. CPT codes 15002–15005 do not describe debridement of nonintact, necrotic, or infected skin, nor is their use indicated with other lesion removal codes.

EXAMPLE: A patient with full-thickness burns of the left arm underwent surgical preparation of the burned tissue. After excision and hemostasis, 100 sq cm full thickness free graft with direct closure was performed. Report codes 15002, 15220, 15221, 15221, 15221 and 15221.

Refer to Table 11-5 when assigning codes for tissue rearrangement, free skin grafts, flaps (skin and/or deep tissues), and/or other flaps and grafts. When multiple tissue rearrangement and free skin grafts procedures are required during the same operative session, make sure you report each separately. (The total square centimeters for repair of different defects are not added together.)

Other Procedures

"Other procedures" codes classify the following integumentary system procedures:

- Dermabrasion

- Abrasion

- Chemical peel

- Cervicoplasty

- Blepharoplasty

- Rhytidectomy

- Excision, excessive skin and subcutaneous tissue (including lipectomy)

Table 11-5 Types of Codes for Tissue Rearrangement, Free Skin Grafts, and Flaps

Type of Procedure	# of Codes	Types of Codes
Adjacent tissue transfer or rearrangement	1	• Adjacent tissue transfer or rearrangement (14000–14350)
Free skin graft	2 or more	• Free skin graft (15050–15278) • Surgical preparation or creation of recipient site *(15002–15005) for burn and wound preparation and management procedures only* • Repair of donor site if local flap or skin graft is required (14000–14350)
Flap (skin and/or deep tissue)	1 or more	• Flap (skin and/or deep tissue) (15570–15738) • Repair of donor site if local flap or skin graft is required (14000–14350 or 15050)
Other flap and graft	1 or more	• Flap or graft (15740–15738) • Repair of donor site if local flap or skin graft is required (14000–14350)

- Graft for facial nerve paralysis
- Removal of sutures under anesthesia
- Dress change under anesthesia
- Intravenous injection of agent
- Suction-assisted lipectomy

Dermabrasion (Figure 11-9) is performed for conditions such as acne scarring and wrinkles (facial) and rhytids and general keratosis (facial and other than face). The physician uses a rotary device to sand down raised lesions or thickened tissue, regenerating smoother skin.

EXAMPLE: Patient underwent total face dermabrasion by use of a rotary instrument that penetrates into the dermis layer of skin. Report code 15780.

Coding Tip:

- The code description for code 15783 includes "tattoo removal" as an example. However, dermabrasion to remove a tattoo usually involves the dermis. According to the AMA's CPT Assistant, because code 15783 is reported for superficial abrasion, it should not be reported for tattoo removal. Report a code from 15780–15782 for tattoo removal.

- Microdermabrasion is not classified in CPT, which means that unlisted code 17999 is assigned. **Microdermabrasion** is a skin-freshening technique used to repair facial skin that is damaged by the sun and the effects of aging. A sandblaster device is used to spray tiny crystals across the face, mixing gentle abrasion with suction to remove the outer layer of skin.

A chemical peel involves the use of chemical agents (e.g., glycolic acid or phenol) to remove wrinkles and abnormal pigmentation. Be sure to determine if treatment is localized to surface layers of the facial skin or the deeper dermal layer.

Note:

Actinic keratosis (AK) is a common sun-induced skin lesion of the epidermis that has the potential to become skin cancer. The most commonly performed treatments for AK includes cryosurgery with liquid nitrogen, topical drug therapy, and curettage. However, AK treatments also include dermabrasion, excision, chemical peels, laser therapy, and photodynamic therapy (PDT).

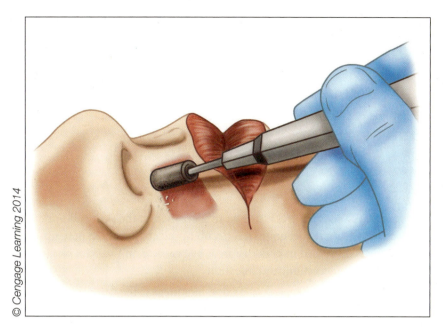

Figure 11-9 Dermabrasion

A **blepharoplasty** is any surgical repair of an eyelid. From a coding perspective, blepharoplasty describes the removal of the orbicularis muscle, orbital fat, and excess eyelid skin around the orbit. Make sure you review the operative report to identify the procedure performed and assign appropriate codes. A blepharoptosis repair is performed on the levator muscle of the eyelid. The code selected is based on the surgical approach used to performed blepharoptosis repair.

EXAMPLE: Patient underwent blepharoplasty of the left lower eyelid, which required the physician to dissect lower eyelid skin to the subcutaneous and muscle fascial layers and excise excess skin. Report code 15820-E2. (HCPCS level II modifier E2 is reported to indicate that the procedure was performed on the "lower left, eyelid.")

Note:

Medicare reimburses services that are reasonable and necessary to diagnose and treat or to improve the functioning of a malformed body member. When blepharoplasty procedures (15822–15823) are performed for cosmetic purposes, they are not covered by Medicare. When the function of the eye is impaired by overlying skin or fatty tissue, the repair is deemed medically necessary and is covered by Medicare.

A **rhytidectomy** involves excising a section of skin to eliminate wrinkles and can be done to reduce **glabellar frown lines**, which are vertical furrows in the forehead area between the eyebrows.

Graft procedures for facial nerve paralysis involve the removal of connective tissue (e.g., fascia) from the body. The graft is transplanted to the face to reanimate previously paralyzed areas.

The removal of sutures by the surgeon is included in the global period associated with that procedure. (The removal of sutures by a physician other than the surgeon who initially placed the sutures is usually reported with an E/M code.)

Abdominal panniculectomy (abdominoplasty) is performed to remove fatty tissue and excess skin from the lower to middle portions of the abdomen. This procedure is typically performed on individuals who have lost considerable weight, resulting in loose-hanging folds of skin in the abdominal area. A lipectomy is the removal of localized subcutaneous fat deposits by suction curettage or blunt cannulization to cosmetically correct obesity and other contour defects.

EXAMPLE: Report 15832 for removal of excess skin and subcutaneous tissue on the thigh, 15833 for the leg, 15834 for the hip, 15835 for the buttock, 15836 for the arm, 15837 for the forearm or hand, 15838 for the submental fat pad, and 15839 for any other area.

When a physician performs a suction-assisted lipectomy, a liposuction cannula is inserted through the fat deposits, removing excess deposits. From a CPT coding perspective, it would be appropriate to report code 15877 for *each* area of liposuction on the trunk.

EXAMPLE: Report 15877 for a lipectomy of the trunk, 15878 if liposuction is done on an upper extremity, and 15879 for a lower extremity. Modifier 59 should be appended to the subsequent procedures performed.

Pressure Ulcers (Decubitus Ulcers)

A **pressure ulcer**, or **decubitus ulcer**, or **bedsore**, is an ulceration of the skin and underlying tissue that occurs over a bony prominence (e.g., sacral decubitus). A decubitus ulcer appears in patients confined to bed or immobilized when blood supply is decreased in pressure areas by pressure on the skin, resulting in inflammation and swelling and ultimately necrosis, ulceration, and infection.

The primary excisional procedure of a staged process does not include the flap/graft procedures, which are reported separately. CPT includes notes that provide instruction to report appropriate repair and skin graft codes.

EXAMPLE: Patient underwent excision of ischial pressure ulcer with ostectomy. Report code 15946.

When a muscle or myocutaneous flap is planned for a subsequent session prospectively (e.g., at the time of the original procedure), report the appropriate flap code and add modifier 58 (Staged Procedure).

Burns, Local Treatment

The introduction to the Burns, Local Treatment heading states that the application of materials (e.g., Biobrane) is included. To assign appropriate codes for the treatment of burns, review the medical record to identify the following:

- Percentage of body surface
- Severity (depth) of the burn
  - Partial-thickness burns (e.g., first-degree or second-degree)
  - Full-thickness burns (e.g., third-degree)

To determine the extent of body surface involved, use the **rule of nines**, which divides total body surface area (BSA) into nine segments by percentage (Figure 11-10). When estimating the percentage of the body affected by burns, review the medical record to locate the patient's age. (The surface area for children is estimated differently than that for adults.)

EXAMPLE: The physician surgically debrided blisters and devitalized tissue that involved less than 5 percent of the total BSA. Report code 16020.

Exercise 11.9 – Repair (Closure)

Instructions: Assign the CPT code(s) and any appropriate modifier(s) to each statement.

1. Repair of 3.0-cm scalp laceration.

_____

2. A physician performed a 4-cm wound closure using adhesive strips.

_____

3. Debridement of partial-thickness burn of the right hand involving 1 percent of total body surface.

_____

4. Full-thickness skin graft, free, including direct closure of donor site, trunk (20 sq cm). Surgical preparation of recipient site (20 sq cm) was also performed during the same operative session.

_____

5. Dermabrasion, total face.

_____

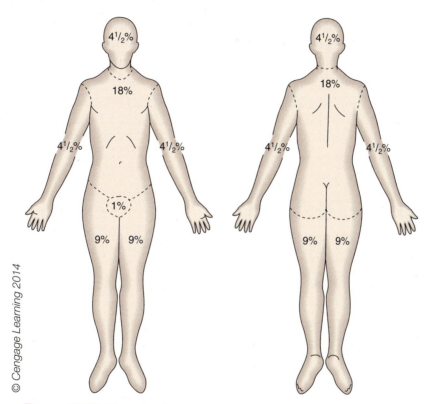

© Cengage Learning 2014

Figure 11-10 The rule of nines

Destruction

Destruction is the ablation of tissue by any method (e.g., electrosurgery, cryosurgery, or laser or chemical treatments). During destruction, excision, incision, removal, repair, or closure procedures, the debridement of nonviable tissue that surrounds a lesion, an injury, or an incision may be necessary to perform the intended procedure. Do not report the debridement codes when the intended procedure (e.g., destruction of lesion) is performed during the same operative session as the debridement procedure; the debridement procedure is considered a necessary part of the total procedure.

Destruction of Benign or Premalignant Lesions and Destruction of Malignant Lesions, Any Method

Each lesion treated is reported as a separate code for the destruction of benign, premalignant, and malignant lesions.

EXAMPLE: The physician uses a small applicator to apply liquid nitrogen directly to the patient's skin to remove a hypertrophic AK lesion. Report code 17000.

During destruction, excision, incision, removal, repair, or closure procedures, the debridement of nonviable tissue that surrounds a lesion, an injury, or an incision may be necessary to perform the intended procedure. Do *not* report a debridement code when the intended procedure (e.g., destruction of lesion) is performed during the same operative session as the debridement procedure. The debridement procedure is considered a necessary part of the total procedure.

EXAMPLE: A physician performed laser surgery to destroy a 0.5-cm malignant facial skin lesion. He also destroyed a premalignant lesion on the skin of the left shoulder. Report codes 17280 and 17000-51.

Mohs Micrographic Surgery

Mohs micrographic surgery is an advanced treatment procedure used to treat basal cell carcinoma and squamous cell carcinoma skin cancers. Dermatologists trained in this technique serve as surgeon, pathologist, and reconstructive surgeon. They use a microscope to trace and ensure the removal of skin cancer to its roots. Mohs micrographic surgery codes (17311–17315) are reported instead of excision codes and surgical pathology codes. Reporting Mohs micrographic surgery and surgical pathology codes on the same claim is inappropriate. A Mohs surgeon who obtains a diagnostic biopsy to make the decision to perform surgery reports the diagnostic biopsy code separately. Modifier -58 (staged or related procedure or service by same physician during postoperative period) is attached to the diagnostic biopsy and Mohs micrographic surgery codes to indicate staged or planned procedures.

EXAMPLE: A patient undergoes Mohs micrographic surgery for basal cell carcinoma of the head (behind the left ear). In Stage I, a layer of tissue is removed and the specimen is subdivided into two smaller specimens for pathologic review. In Stage II, the second layer is excised and subdivided into three smaller specimens for pathologic processing. Report codes 17311 and 17312.

Exercise 11.10 – Destruction

Instructions: Assign the CPT code(s) and any appropriate modifier(s) to each statement.

1. Destruction of three benign facial lesions.

2. Destruction of 17 skin tags.

3. Patient underwent removal of five flat warts, using photothermolysis laser.

4. Laser surgery destruction of two actinic keratoses lesions, chest.

5. Electrosurgical destruction of 10 skin tags.

6. Chemosurgery, 3.8-cm malignant lesion, scalp.

7. Surgical curettement of 1.5-cm malignant lesion, trunk.

8. Cryosurgery, 10.0-cm malignant lesion, neck.

9. Electrosurgery, 0.5-cm malignant lesion, nose.

10. Laser surgery, 2.3-cm malignant lesion, left shoulder.

Breast

Diagnostic testing used to detect breast cancer may include a mammogram, ultrasonography, magnetic resonance imaging (MRI), FNA, core biopsy, or surgical biopsy. Treatment plans can include a local therapy approach such as breast-conserving surgery or mastectomy, radiation therapy (e.g., internal or implant radiation or external radiation), and breast reconstruction (e.g., implant or tissue transfer).

Because of the unique nature of procedures developed to address breast disease, codes in CPT are established for services (e.g., incision, excision, introduction, repair, and reconstruction). FNA biopsies, core biopsies, open incisional or excisional biopsies, and related procedures performed to procure tissue from a lesion for which an established diagnosis exists are not to be reported separately at the time of a lesion excision unless performed on a different lesion or on the contralateral breast. However, if a diagnosis is not established *and the decision to perform the excision or mastectomy is dependent on the results of the biopsy*, the biopsy is separately reported. Modifier -58 is used to indicate that the biopsy and the excision or mastectomy are staged or planned procedures.

Breast Biopsies

Breast biopsies are performed according to the following methods:

- Fine-needle aspiration (FNA) (Figure 11-11A)
- Needle core biopsy
  - Hand-operated needle
  - Stereotactic localization
- Open biopsy
  - Excisional biopsy
  - Incisional biopsy (Figure 11-11B)

Fine-Needle Aspiration (FNA)

FNA of the breast is reported, depending on whether imaging guidance was used during the procedure. A FNA uses a thin needle (e.g., 20- or 22-gauge needle), which is inserted through the mass several times. Suction is applied as the needle is withdrawn to obtain strands of single cells for cytologic diagnosis.

Coding Tip:

- Do not report code 19100 (needle core breast biopsy) for fine-needle aspiration (FNA) of breast tissue. FNA procedures are reported with codes 10021–10022, which includes single and multiple lesions.
- Code 77031 is assigned as an additional code (for each lesion) if FNA (10022) is performed using imaging guidance and stereotactic localization.

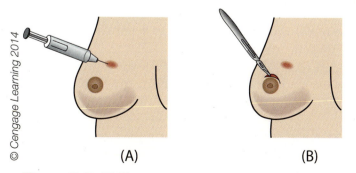

© Cengage Learning 2014

(A)   (B)

Figure 11-11 (A) Fine-needle aspiration. (B) Incisional biopsy

Needle Core Biopsy

A **needle core biopsy** is obtained using a hand-operated needle (e.g., Trucut or Vim-Silverman) or stereotactic localization. Once the tissue is obtained, it is fixed for routine pathologic section. **Stereotactic localization** is indicated for nonpalpable lesions because it uses specialized three-dimensional imaging to target the lesion. The breast is placed in a fixed position, and a biopsy gun (e.g., 14- or 18-gauge needle) is used to obtain needle core biopsies from the lesion.

Coding Tip:

- In addition to code 19100 for needle core biopsy, report code 77031 for stereotactic localization or code 77032 for mammographic guidance.
- A biopsy code (19100–19103) is assigned for each biopsied site (e.g., three-needle core biopsy sites are reported as codes 19100, 19100, and 19100).
- Differentiating a puncture aspiration of a breast cyst, a needle core biopsy of the breast, and fine-needle aspiration of breast tissue can be confusing:
  - Codes 10021–10022 are assigned for fine-needle aspirations of the breast, depending on whether imaging guidance was used during the procedure.
  - Codes 19000–19001 are assigned for puncture aspirations of breast cysts.
  - Codes 19100–19103 are assigned for needle core breast biopsies. (Code 19101 describes a breast biopsy obtained through an incision.)

However, if the entire lesion is subsequently removed during the same operative session as an excisional biopsy, code 19120 is reported instead of 19101.

Open Biopsy

An **open biopsy** can be incisional or excisional, depending on the amount of lesion removed. An **excisional biopsy** removes the lump or suspicious area in its entirety. An **incisional biopsy** removes a portion of the lesion by slicing into it or incising it; it is usually performed on large tumors (and the patient undergoes mastectomy later).

Excisional breast surgery includes certain biopsy procedures, the removal of cysts or other benign or malignant tumors or lesions, and the surgical treatment of breast and chest wall malignancies. Biopsy procedures may be percutaneous or open. Open excision of breast lesions without attention to surgical margins, with or without the preoperative placement of radiological markers, is reported with codes 19120–19126.

> ## Note:
>
> An excisional biopsy (19120) is not a **lumpectomy**, which is a partial mastectomy (19301–19302).

Coding Tip:

- Review the entire operative report and pathology report to determine whether the biopsy was excisional or incisional.
- For an excisional biopsy, report code 19120. (However, if the lesion was identified with preoperative placement of a radiological marker, report codes 19125–19126 and 19290–19291, depending on the number of localized lesions. Also report codes 77031–77032 for radiological supervision and interpretation.)
- For an open incisional biopsy, report code 19101. (However, if the operative report indicates that the biopsy was "incisional" and the pathology report indicates that the entire lesion was removed, report code 19120 for an excisional biopsy.)

EXAMPLE: The patient was registered for outpatient surgery on August 1. The patient received an explanation from the surgeon that she would undergo excisional left breast biopsy in the morning and that if pathology results were positive for cancer, the patient would undergo left breast lumpectomy during the late afternoon. The excisional left breast biopsy was performed at 9 a.m., and tissue was positive for adenocarcinoma. The patient returned to the operating room at 2 p.m. and underwent left breast lumpectomy. Report codes 19120-LT (Excisional breast biopsy) and 19301-58-LT (Breast lumpectomy, staged or related procedure performed by the same physician during the postoperative period). (Modifier -58 is added to just one CPT code. The pathologist reports an appropriate code from the Pathology and Laboratory section of CPT.)

Coding Tip:

Do not report code 19120 for a breast lumpectomy. Code 19120 (excisional biopsy) is reported when the physician makes an incision in the skin of the breast overlying the site of the mass and dissects skin and tissue (from the site of the aberrant tissue, areola, cyst, fibroadenoma, lesion of the duct, nipple, or tumor). This procedure involves excising the lesion and a rim of surrounding normal tissue. When the excision of more than one lesion is performed in different areas of the breast (through separate incision sites), report code 19120 for each excision site.

A breast lumpectomy is a type of partial mastectomy, and it is reported with code 19301. When more than one lumpectomy is performed in different areas of the breast (through separate incision sites), report code 19301 for each excision site. (Modifier -51 is added to the second and subsequent reporting of code 19301 when multiple lumpectomies are performed during the same operative episode.)

EXAMPLE: A breast mass biopsy was sent to the pathologist during the operative procedure for immediate diagnosis. The pathologist examined the specimen and diagnosed a malignancy. Immediate full-thickness (through the dermis) removal of the lesion, including margins, was performed. The procedure included simple (nonlayered) closure of the mass. Report code 19120. (The pathologist reports an appropriate code from the Pathology and Laboratory section of CPT.)

Mastectomy

Mastectomy (Figure 11-12) procedures are classified in CPT as follows:

- Partial mastectomy (including lumpectomy)
- Radical mastectomy
- Simple or total mastectomy
- Modified radical mastectomy

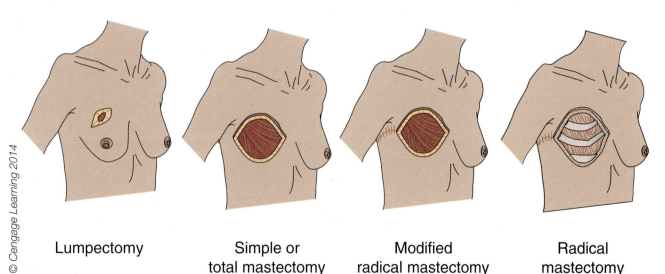

© Cengage Learning 2014

Lumpectomy   Simple or   Modified   Radical
                      total mastectomy   radical mastectomy   mastectomy

Figure 11-12 Types of mastectomy

Partial mastectomy procedures describe open excisions of breast tissue with specific attention to adequate surgical margins. A **partial mastectomy** involves making an incision through skin and fascia over the breast tumor and clamping lymphatic and blood vessels; the physician then excises the tumor mass along with a section of breast tissue. A partial mastectomy is also called a lumpectomy, quadrant-ectomy, segmental mastectomy, and tylectomy.

> **EXAMPLE:** A sentinel node biopsy is performed as part of an axillary lymphadenectomy during a partial mastectomy procedure. Report code 19302, which includes removal of the sentinel node and other axillary lymph nodes.

Total mastectomy procedures include complete mastectomy, modified radical mastectomy, simple mastectomy, and subcutaneous mastectomy. A **total mastectomy** is the surgical removal of the entire breast, including the pectoral fascia and a sampling of axillary lymph nodes. Radical mastectomy procedures include the removal of pectoral muscles, axillary lymph nodes, and/or internal mammary lymph nodes. A **radical mastectomy** is a total mastectomy that includes removal of the breast and nipple, pectoralis muscles (major and/or minor), axillary lymph nodes, and internal mammary lymph nodes. A **modified radical mastectomy** is a total mastectomy that includes removal of the breast and nipple, axillary lymph nodes, and pectoralis minor muscle.

Breast Repair and Reconstruction

CPT breast reconstruction codes include the following elements:

- Elevation and transfer of the flap
- Closure of the donor site
- Breast contouring
- Insertion of breast implant or prosthesis, when performed

Breast reconstruction with transverse rectus abdominis myocutaneous flap (TRAM), single pedicle includes closure of donor site. In addition, TRAM flap codes include the following:

- Creation of the breast pocket
- Elevation of the abdominal flap
- Muscle dissection
- Flap transfer
- Fascial closure (donor site) with or without mesh
- Abdominal closure including umbilicoplasty
- Breast contouring

> **Coding Tip:**
>
> Codes 19260–19272 are not restricted to reporting just the removal of breast tumors. They are used to report resections of chest wall tumors originating from any chest wall component. (Patients diagnosed with breast cancer who undergo mastectomy may be diagnosed with chest wall cancer at a later date, requiring surgical excision.)

Because excision of lesions is often done during the same operative session as a mastectomy, breast excisions are not separately reported in addition to the mastectomy code *unless performed to establish the malignant diagnosis before proceeding to the mastectomy.* Thus, CPT breast excision codes are not reported in addition to CPT mastectomy codes when performed on the same side. If the breast excision is performed to obtain tissue to determine pathologic diagnosis of malignancy prior to proceeding to a mastectomy, the excision is separately coded and reported with the mastectomy code and modifier -58 is added to the codes.

Use of other integumentary codes for incision and closure are included in the codes that describe various breast excision or mastectomy codes. Because of the frequent need to biopsy lymph nodes or remove muscle tissue in conjunction with mastectomies, these procedures are included in CPT coding for mastectomy. It is inappropriate to separately report ipsilateral lymph node dissection with mastectomy codes. When a breast lesion is identified and treated and medical necessity indicates that biopsy of contralateral nodes should be done, report the biopsy or lymph node dissection codes (and add an appropriate anatomic modifier, such as -LT or -RT for left or right). Breast reconstruction codes also include the insertion of a prosthetic implant, and they are not reported with CPT codes that describe the insertion of breast prosthesis only.

CPT coding for breast procedures generally refers to unilateral procedures; when performed bilaterally, add modifier -50 to the code. (The Repair and/or Reconstruction subheading includes a parenthetical note as a reminder to report modifier -50 when appropriate.) When breast reconstruction is performed unilaterally, add the applicable HCPCS Level II modifier -LT (left) or RT (right) to the procedure code.

Exercise 11.11 – Breast

Instructions: Assign the CPT code(s) and any appropriate modifier(s) to each statement.

1. Excision of two lesions, right breast, identified by the placement of radiological markers for each.

_____

2. A transverse rectus abdominis myocutaneous flap procedure for right breast reconstruction is performed using a single rectus abdominis muscle to transfer the necessary tissue to form a breast mound.

_____

3. Lumpectomy, left breast.

_____

4. Physician performed a partial mastectomy of the right breast with right axillary lymphadenectomy and biopsy of the right sentinel node.

_____

5. Patient's left breast lesion was localized for needle biopsy. Mammographic images were obtained to verify needle placement with regard to the lesion. After verifying the position, the biopsy was obtained and postbiopsy targeted mammographic imaging was performed. A metallic clip marker was placed through the same instrument at the site of tissue removal, using the same guidance. A mammogram after the procedure confirms the location of the clip in the breast for future reference.

_____

Summary

The Surgery section is the largest in CPT, and its subsections are organized anatomically (e.g., body area or organ system). Guidelines located at the beginning of the CPT Surgery section clarify the assignment of codes and explain terms. The General subsection contains just two codes. The Integumentary System subsection includes dermatological procedures, plastic surgery, and components of multiple surgical procedures (e.g., closure, flaps, grafts, and tissue transfer). Integumentary procedures are often performed as staged procedures (e.g., flaps and grafts) due to the complexity of services rendered.

Internet Links

American Academy of Dermatology (AAD): *www.aad.org*

Medicare Learning Network (MLN): Go to *www.cms.gov*, and click on "Outreach & Education," then click on a link below the Medicare Learning Network (MLN) heading.

Medscape: Go to *www.medscape.com*, and register for free access to Medscape's medical resource databases.

National Correct Coding Initiative (NCCI) Edits: Go to *www.cms.gov*, and click on the Medicare link, then click on the National Correct Coding Initiative Edits link.

National Institutes of Health Videos of Surgical Procedures: Go to *www.nlm.nih.gov*, and click on the MedlinePlus link, then click on the Surgery Videos link.

ORlive (TM) Broadcasts: Go to *www.or-live.com*, and click on Email Notifications link to sign up for event announcements about live Webcasts in selected health specialties.

Study Checklist

- ❏ Read this chapter and highlight key concepts.
- ❏ Create an index card for each key term.
- ❏ Access the chapter Internet links to learn more about concepts.
- ❏ Complete the chapter review, verifying answers with your instructor.
- ❏ Complete WebTutor assignments and take online quizzes.
- ❏ Complete Workbook chapter, verifying answers with your instructor.
- ❏ Go to *www.cengagebrain.com* to access StudyWARE™ and the Premium Website. Login instructions are located in the Preface and on the Printed Access Card.
- ❏ Form a study group with classmates to discuss chapter concepts in preparation for an exam.

Review

Multiple Choice

Instructions: Circle the most appropriate response.

1. Which is a therapeutic surgical procedure?
   - a. arthroscopy
   - b. biopsy
   - c. endoscopy
   - d. repair

2. A patient undergoing a surgical procedure was draped and positioned. The surgical area was cleansed and shaved, an IV was started, and a sedative was administered. The surgical approach was identified, and an incision was made. The wound was irrigated, and cultures were taken. The incision was closed, and dressings were applied. The procedure was then dictated and transcribed. Which service is assigned a separate code?
   - a. administration of a sedative
   - b. none of the services are reported separately.
   - c. taking cultures
   - d. transcription of the dictated report

3. Which modifier indicates a staged procedure or service?
   - a. -58
   - b. -59
   - c. -66
   - d. -76

4. When a patient receives treatment for an unrelated condition during the global period, which modifier is added to the CPT code?
   - a. -51
   - b. -57
   - c. -59
   - d. -79

5. The CMS global surgical package includes:
   - a. diagnostic tests and procedures, including diagnostic radiological procedures.
   - b. initial consultation or evaluation of the problem by the surgeon to determine the need for surgery.
   - c. the day before the day of surgery for major procedures.
   - d. treatment for postoperative complications that require a return trip to the operating room.

6. When an evaluation and management (E/M) service provided is for the purpose of deciding to perform a major surgical procedure, which is reported?
   - a. E/M code
   - b. E/M code with modifier -57
   - c. E/M code with modifier -59
   - d. No E/M code is reported because the service is bundled in the surgery code.

7. The code reported for fine-needle aspiration is determined based on whether:
   - a. fluid is aspirated from a cyst or cells are aspirated from a solid mass.
   - b. imaging guidance is used during the procedure.
   - c. the cyst or mass is visible.
   - d. the procedure is performed percutaneously.

8. If the operative report describes a lesion as 3.5 cm × 4 cm × 5 cm, which is reported as the diameter?
   - a. 3.5 cm
   - b. 4 cm
   - c. 5 cm
   - d. 17.5 cm

9. When Mohs micrographic surgery is performed, Mohs micrographic surgery codes are reported instead of:
   - a. a diagnostic biopsy code.
   - b. excision codes and a diagnostic biopsy code.
   - c. excision codes and surgical pathology codes.
   - d. surgical pathology codes.

10. Wound repair is coded with an appropriate evaluation and management code when the sole repair material used is:
    - a. adhesive strips.
    - b. staples.
    - c. sutures.
    - d. tissue adhesives.

11. Evacuation of subungual hematoma. Which CPT code is assigned?
    - a. 10140
    - b. 10160
    - c. 11740
    - d. 11750

12. Collagen injection, face, 5.1 cc. Which CPT code is assigned?
    - a. 11950
    - b. 11951
    - c. 11952
    - d. 11954

13. Puncture aspiration of abscess on lower left eyelid. Which CPT code is assigned?
    - a. 10120-E2
    - b. 10140-E2
    - c. 10160-E2
    - d. 10180-E2

14. Open excision of fibroadenomas, right breast. Which CPT code is assigned?
    - a. 19100-RT
    - b. 19120-RT
    - c. 19301-RT
    - d. 19260-RT

15. Suction-assisted abdominal lipectomy. Which CPT code is assigned?
    - a. 15876
    - b. 15877
    - c. 15878
    - d. 15879

16. Adjacent tissue transfer of 12 sq cm defect of forehead. Which CPT code is assigned?
    - a. 14020
    - b. 14021
    - c. 14040
    - d. 14041

17. Mohs micrographic surgery of upper left arm (first stage) with excision of five specimens. Diagnostic skin biopsy performed the same day. Which CPT code(s) are assigned?
    a. 11100, 17313-51
    b. 17313, 11100-59
    c. 17313
    d. 17313, 11406

18. Modified radical mastectomy, including axillary lymph nodes, excluding pectoral muscles. Which CPT code is assigned?
    a. 19301
    b. 19305
    c. 19306
    d. 19307

19. Epidermal facial chemical peel. Which CPT code is assigned?
    a. 15788
    b. 15789
    c. 15792
    d. 15793

20. Cryosurgery of two plantar warts. Which CPT code(s) are assigned?
    a. 17000, 17000
    b. 17000, 17003
    c. 17000, 17003-51
    d. 17110

Coding Practice

Instructions: Assign the CPT code(s) and appropriate modifier(s) to each case.

General

21. Patient underwent fine-needle aspiration to remove fluid sample from a cyst, anterior neck. Physician palpated the cyst, cleansed the site with Betadine solution, and inserted a 25-gauge needle into the cyst. Approximately 2 cc of fluid were removed. The needle was withdrawn, and a small bandage was placed over the insertion area.

_____

22. Patient underwent fine-needle aspiration to remove a cluster of cells from a solid mass, subcutaneous layer of the left upper quadrant, abdomen. Computed tomography imaging guidance for needle placement was performed. Physician palpated the mass, cleansed the area with Betadine solution, and inserted a 22-gauge needle into the solid mass. Approximately 1 cc of tissue was removed. The needle was withdrawn, and a small bandage was placed over the insertion area.

_____

Integumentary System

23. A large mass, soft and movable, located on the patient's back between the lower scapular area and midline on the left, was palpated. An elliptical incision was made, a section of the tissue was removed, and the 4.0 cyst was resected completely. Bleeding vessels were clamped and coagulated. Penrose drain was left in the wound; and skin edges were closed along with subcutaneous tissue, using interrupted silk sutures.

_____

24. Patient was prepped and draped; after adequate general endotracheal anesthesia, the body was somewhat flexed at the waist to provide adequate exposure after taping in preparation to separate the buttocks at the sacral crease. A probe was inserted into the inferior sinus, and only 3 to 4 cm of fluid were obtained. The area was prepped for excision, and an oval-shaped piece of skin was excised in total, including the 5.0-cm subcutaneous pilonidal cyst sinus end. Bleeding was controlled with electrocautery, the area was copiously irrigated with Betadine saline solution and suctioned and sponged off, and vertical mattress sutures of Prolene were placed in layers to obliterate the dead space.

_____

25. Local anesthesia was injected using 1 percent lidocaine with epinephrine 1.5 cc. Incision was made along the postauricular sulcus through the drainage point with retraction applied. A 3.0 cm sebaceous cyst was evident, and it was drained. A small bandage was placed over the incision and drainage site.

26. Split-thickness skin graft of about 7 sq cm was removed from the left thigh, and sterile dressings were applied. A 6-cm malignant lesion was removed from the left calf by a wide excision, including at least 1 cm of normal skin all around, taking it all the way down to include fascia and overlying muscle. Bleeding points were carefully ligated, wound was treated with Hibiclens, and skin graft was applied and sutured in place with 4-0 Mersilene sutures.

27. Patient was using a chain saw, which slipped, and the patient sustained a 5.0-cm laceration to the dorsum of the proximal portion of the left index finger, extending through the extensor tendon and capsule. Debridement of tissue was done to facilitate a better repair of this deep laceration. Tendon and capsule were sutured with five 6-0 silk sutures. Bleeders were ligated with plain catgut. Skin was debrided extensively and approximated with seven sutures of 4-0 Dermal.

28. Patient sustained second-degree burn of the right thigh that was less than 5 percent of the total body surface. The skin was completely necrotic. The right thigh was prepared with pHisoHex, and the wound was debrided using a dermatome. Partial thickness, superficial layer of dead skin tissue was removed. Wound was treated with pHisoHex and cleaned, and a sterile outside dressing was applied.

29. Digital nerve block was applied to numb the top of the right great toe and the left great toe. Blunt dissection of the nail plate from the nailbed, right great toe, was performed. Bleeding was cauterized. Right great toe was bandaged. Next, the left great toenail plate was removed from the nailbed, bleeding was cauterized, and left great toe was bandaged.

30. Patient sustained a 3.0-cm scalp laceration and a 2.0-cm neck laceration after being cut with a knife during a bar fight. Local anesthetic was injected around the scalp and neck laceration sites. Wounds were thoroughly cleansed, explored, and irrigated with a saline solution. One-layer suture repair of scalp and neck wounds was performed.

31. An island pedicle flap was formed on the left thigh, and the defect was covered by elevating a flap of skin and subcutaneous tissue. The flap was then rotated into the defect, with transfer being accomplished through a tunnel underneath the skin. The flap was sutured into its new position, and the donor site was closed.

32. Bell's palsy patient underwent harvesting of a graft for residual facial nerve paralysis. Connective tissue fascia was removed from the fascia lata, right leg. Fascia graft was transplanted to the face and sutured into place underneath skin to reanimate paralyzed area of the face.

33. Using surgical curettement, 3.0 malignant lesion of the neck was removed.

34. Procedure: Lumpectomy, left breast. Incision was made through skin and fascia over a left breast mass, and lymphatic and blood vessels were clamped. Tumor mass was excised in its entirety along with normal breast tissue. Drainage tube was placed through a separate stab incision. Layered closure was performed, and a sterile dressing was applied.

_____

35. Right breast cyst was palpated, and needle was inserted into skin of the breast overlying the cyst. Needle was inserted into the cyst, and fluid was evacuated into the syringe. Needle was withdrawn, and pressure was applied to the puncture wound.

_____

CPT Surgery II

CHAPTER 12

Chapter Outline

Musculoskeletal System Subsection
Respiratory System Subsection

Chapter Objectives

At the conclusion of this chapter, the student should be able to:

- Define key terms.
- Explain the organization, format, and content of the CPT Surgery Musculoskeletal System and Respiratory System subsections.
- Interpret CPT surgery coding notes for the Musculoskeletal System and Respiratory System subsections.
- Assign CPT surgery codes from the Musculoskeletal System and Respiratory System subsections.
- Add CPT and/or HCPCS level II modifiers to codes, as appropriate.

Key Terms

allogenous
arthrocentesis
arthrodesis
arthroscopy
artificial ankylosis
arytenoidectomy
arytenoidopexy
augmentation
autogenous
backbench work
bronchoscopy
brushing
bunion

cadaver donor
  pneumonectomy
cell washing
closed fracture
  treatment
concha
direct laryngoscopy
dislocation
extensor tendons
external fixation device
femur
flail chest
flexor tendons

harvesting
immobilize
indirect laryngoscopy
internal fixation device
knee
laryngoscopy
larynx
LeFort I
LeFort II
LeFort III
ligament
lobectomy
luxation

manipulation
nasal vestibule
obturator
open fracture treatment
osteogenesis
osteotomy
percutaneous needle
  biopsy
percutaneous skeletal
  fixation
percutaneous
  vertebroplasty
pleura

pleural effusion	replantation	subluxation	trachea
pneumocentesis	rhytides	thoracentesis	tracheobronchoscopy
pyramidal fracture	segmentectomy	thoracoscopy	turbinates
recipient lung allotransplantation	skeletal traction	tibia	wedge resection
reduction	stabilize	tibial plateau	
	subglottic stenosis	total pneumonectomy	

Introduction

The Musculoskeletal System subsection classifies procedures performed on bones, cartilage, joints, ligaments, muscles, and tendons (including casting and strapping). The Respiratory System subsection classifies procedures performed on the nose, accessory sinuses, larynx, trachea and bronchi, and lungs and pleura. CPT guidelines that apply to the subsections are located at the beginning of the Surgery section. Unique coding instructions for Musculoskeletal or Respiratory System subsections are located in notes below headings or codes.

Note:

The content in Chapter 12 (and Chapters 13 through 15) is organized exactly as it appears in the CPT Surgery section. This organization facilitates learning by allowing students to move from one CPT Surgery subsection to the next, in order.

 Coding Tip:

Notes located beneath headings and/or subheadings apply to all codes under the heading or subheading. Parenthetical notes located below a specific code apply to that code only, unless the note indicates otherwise.

Musculoskeletal System Subsection

The CPT Musculoskeletal System subsection is arranged from head to toe according to body area and includes the following headings:

- General
- Head
- Neck (Soft Tissues) and Thorax
- Back and Flank
- Spine (Vertebral Column)
- Abdomen
- Shoulder
- Humerus (Upper Arm) and Elbow
- Forearm and Wrist
- Hand and Fingers
- Pelvis and Hip Joint
- Femur (Thigh Region) and Knee Joint

- Leg (Tibia And Fibula) and Ankle Joint
- Foot and Toes
- Application of Casts and Strapping
- Endoscopy/Arthroscopy

Each heading includes one or more of the following subheadings:

- Incision
- Excision
- Introduction or Removal
- Repair, Revision, and/or Reconstruction
- Fracture and/or Dislocation (Table 12-1)
- Manipulation
- Arthrodesis
- Amputation
- Other Procedures

Musculoskeletal System Notes

Musculoskeletal System subsection notes include definitions of fractures (e.g., closed and open) and clarify that the type of fracture does not necessarily correspond to the type of treatment (e.g., closed, open, or percutaneous) provided. In addition, types of injury codes include open or closed fractures and joint injuries.

Coding Tip:

Open and closed fractures may not receive the same type of treatment. Closed fractures can receive open treatment, and open fractures can receive closed treatment. Either type of fracture can receive **percutaneous skeletal fixation** treatment.

Coding Tip:

Fracture management codes are found throughout the Musculoskeletal System subsection. The codes include the following:

- Pinning
- Open or closed treatment of the fracture
- Application and removal of the initial cast or splint
- Normal, uncomplicated follow-up care

  Do not report separate codes for the above services when they are provided, because they are included in the fracture treatment code. Codes for treatment of fractures and joint injuries (dislocations) are classified according to type of manipulation (reduction) and stabilization (fixation or immobilization).

Table 12-1 Types of Fractures, Joint Injuries, and Fracture Treatment

Term	Definition
Types of Fractures	
Closed fracture (or simple fracture) (Figure 12-1)	• Broken bone(s) do not protrude through skin. • No open wounds • Described clinically as "closed" • May include burns, deep abrasions, involvement of subcutaneous requiring debridement, and skin contusions
Dislocation, or **luxation** (Figure 12-1)	• Total displacement of bone from its joint • **Subluxation** is the partial displacement of a bone from its joint.
Open fracture (or compound fracture) (Figure 12-1)	• Broken bone(s) that can be seen through an open wound or that protrudes through skin • Clinically requires an injury with sufficient force to penetrate skin, subcutaneous tissue, muscle fascia/muscle, and/or bone or joint
Types of Fracture Treatment	
Closed fracture treatment	• Fracture site is not surgically opened or exposed. • Three methods of treatment: ○ With **manipulation**, or **reduction** (Figure 12-2), which means that the bones are realigned ○ Without manipulation, which means that the bones are not realigned and a cast or strapping device is placed around the limb to **stabilize**, or **immobilize**, it, which secures the bone(s) in fixed position ○ With or without **skeletal traction** (Figure 12-3), which exerts a pulling force on the affected limb to realign bone or joint
Open fracture treatment	• Fracture site is surgically opened or exposed.
Percutaneous Skeletal Fixation	
External fixation device (Figure 12-4)	• Hardware is inserted through bone and skin and held rigid with cross braces outside of the body • Always removed after the fracture has healed • Removal procedure is included in the global service, which means it is *not* separately coded and reported
Internal fixation device (Figure 12-5)	• Pins, screws, and/or plates are inserted through or within the fracture area to stabilize and immobilize the injury • Often called open reduction with internal fixation, or ORIF

Exercise 12.1 – Musculoskeletal System Notes

Instructions: Complete each statement.

1. The Musculoskeletal subsection is arranged from head to toe according to _____.

2. Types of injury codes include _____.

3. Open and closed fractures may not receive the same type of _____.

4. Fracture management codes include pinning, open or closed treatment of the fracture, application and removal of the initial cast or splint, and _____.

5. Codes for treatment of fractures and joint injuries are classified according to type of _____ and stabilization.

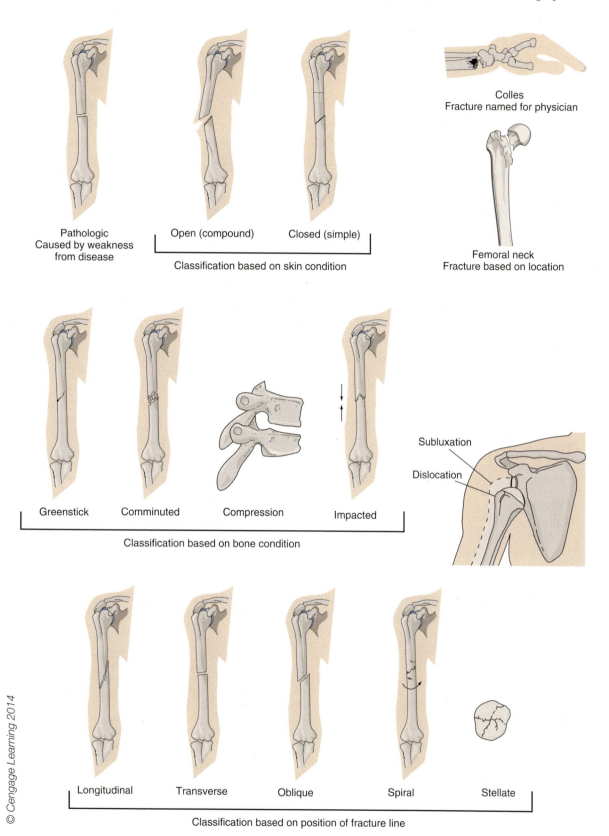

Pathologic
Caused by weakness
from disease

Open (compound)   Closed (simple)

Classification based on skin condition

Colles
Fracture named for physician

Femoral neck
Fracture based on location

Greenstick   Comminuted   Compression   Impacted

Classification based on bone condition

Subluxation

Dislocation

Longitudinal   Transverse   Oblique   Spiral   Stellate

Classification based on position of fracture line

Figure 12-1 Fractures and dislocations

© Cengage Learning 2014

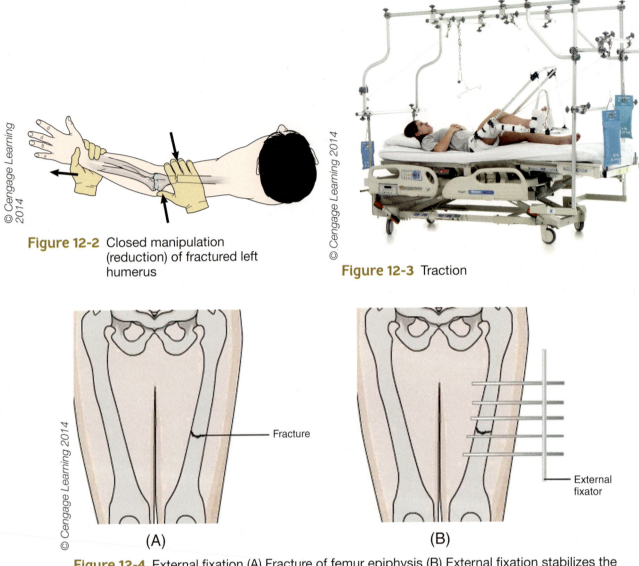

© Cengage Learning 2014

Figure 12-2 Closed manipulation (reduction) of fractured left humerus

© Cengage Learning 2014

Figure 12-3 Traction

Fracture

(A)   (B)

External fixator

© Cengage Learning 2014

Figure 12-4 External fixation (A) Fracture of femur epiphysis (B) External fixation stabilizes the bone and is removed after the bone has healed

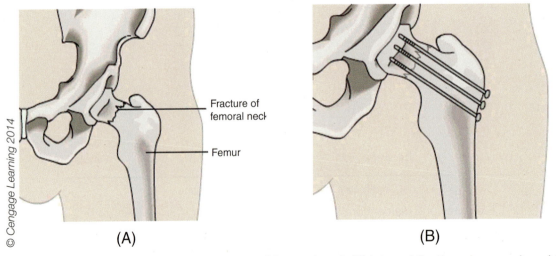

© Cengage Learning 2014

Fracture of femoral neck

Femur

(A)   (B)

Figure 12-5 Internal fixation (A) Fracture of femoral neck (B) Internal fixation pins are placed to stabilize the bone; these are not removed

General

The General heading contains the following subheadings, several of which are unique to the heading:

- Incision
- Wound Exploration—Trauma (e.g., Penetrating Gunshot, Stab Wound)
- Excision
- Introduction or Removal
- Replantation
- Grafts (or Implants)
- Other Procedures

Incision

When an incision of a soft tissue abscess is performed and it is located in deeper tissues than those associated with the integumentary system, report code 20005. Code 20005 is reported for the incision and drainage of a soft tissue abscess, subfascia, which involves the soft tissue below the deep fascia; the physician thoroughly debrides and irrigates the affected area, examines underlying tissue and bone for signs of infection, removes dead bone or tissue, and closes the site.

Wound Exploration—Trauma

CPT codes 20100–20103 are reported for the treatment of wound(s) resulting from penetrating trauma (e.g., gunshot or stab wound), and they include the following:

- Surgical exploration and enlargement of the wound
- Extension of dissection (to determine penetration)
- Debridement
- Removal of foreign body(s)
- Ligation or coagulation of minor subcutaneous and/or muscular blood vessel(s) of the subcutaneous tissue, muscle fascia, and/or muscle, not requiring thoracotomy or laparotomy

When major structures or major blood vessels require repair via thoracotomy or laparotomy, do not report the -otomy code. Report the repair code. When a simple, intermediate, or complex repair of wound(s) is performed *only* (without enlargement of wound area, extension of dissection to determine penetration, debridement, removal of foreign body, ligation/coagulation of minor blood subcutaneous/muscular blood vessels), report the appropriate repair code(s) from the Integumentary System section.

EXAMPLE: A patient was treated for a 2.5-cm stab wound located above the base of the neck. The physician extended the wound to explore and assess damage; it was determined that the injury extended to the muscle. Muscle fascia and subcutaneous tissue were closed in layers, and the skin was closed. Report code 20100.

Excision

Report excision codes for epiphyseal bar procedures (performed on bone) and biopsies performed on muscle or bone.

EXAMPLE: Patient underwent open bone biopsy of the right femur. Report code 20245-RT.

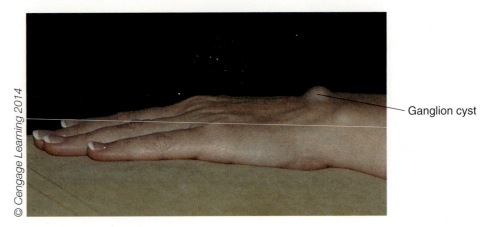

© Cengage Learning 2014

Ganglion cyst

Figure 12-6 Ganglion cyst

Introduction or Removal

Introduction and removal procedure codes are reported for injection procedures, removal of a foreign body, insertion and application of surgical hardware, arthrocentesis, and aspirations. Surgical injections are performed by inserting a needle directly into a joint or tendon sheath, trigger point, or ganglion cyst (Figure 12-6) to aspirate fluid or inject medications. Codes for injections are based on anatomic site. **Arthrocentesis** is a procedure done to puncture a joint for fluid removal or medication injection.

EXAMPLE 1: A patient underwent aspiration of ganglion cyst, left wrist. Report code 20612-LT.

EXAMPLE 2: Using ultrasound guidance for needle placement, the physician injected patient's left knee joint with 30 mg of Kenalog for therapeutic relief of knee pain. Report code 20610-LT, 76942 and HCPCS level II codes J3301, J3301, and J3301.

Code 20692 is reported in addition to the code for treatment of the fracture or joint injury (unless application of an external fixation system is included in the fracture or joint injury code description).

EXAMPLE: A patient underwent closed treatment of a femoral shaft fracture with manipulation and application of an external fixation system. Report codes 27502 and 20692-51. Code 27502 does not specify the use of an external fixation device in its code description; therefore, also report code 20692 with modifier -51.

When a traumatic injury with an open wound requires surgical debridement but the type of fracture requires manipulation and casting (instead of an external or internal fixation device), report the appropriate code for closed fracture treatment *in addition to the appropriate debridement code.*

EXAMPLE: A patient underwent closed treatment of tibial fracture with manipulation, application of a cast, and open wound debridement of 15 sq cm of skin using a scalpel around the fracture site. Report codes 27752 and 97597. There is mention of manipulation; therefore, report code 27752. Report code 97597 for the debridement procedure.

Replantation

Replantation is the surgical reattachment of a finger, a hand, a toe, a foot, a leg, or an arm that has been completely severed from a person's body. (A severed body part is also called an amputation.) Replantation codes include arthrodesis, cleansing, debridement, internal fixation, and repair of tendons (as well as the surgical reattachment procedure).

EXAMPLE 1: A patient who severed his left arm at the humeral diaphysis in a machine accident underwent replantation of the arm. Wound debridement and shortening were performed on the stump and the amputated part of the arm, along with primary repair of muscles and microsurgical repair of arteries, veins, and nerves and internal fixation. A splint was also applied. Report code 20802-LT.

EXAMPLE 2: A patient who suffered a partially severed right leg in an automobile accident underwent repair of the cruciate and collateral ligaments of the right knee; suture of tendon, right knee; repair of one arterial blood vessel, right knee; and 7.5-cm complex closure of wound. Report codes 27409-RT, 35226-51-RT, 27380-51-RT, and 13121-51-RT. (Modifier -51 is reported to indicate that multiple procedures were performed *in addition* to the first-listed procedure.)

Grafts (or Implants)

Codes 20900–20938 are reported when **autogenous** (originating in the patient's body) tissue is obtained through separate skin or fascial incisions, *except when the graft procedure code includes* **harvesting** (removing tissue for transplantation) *the graft (or implant) for which a combination code is reported.* Codes with the ✚ (add-on code) symbol mean that modifier -51 is not added. (**Allogenous** grafts involve tissue organ transplanted from one person to another; for example, bone tissue can be obtained from a bone bank. Xenografts are obtained from another species, such as pigs.)

Codes 20900–20926 are reported when graft material is harvested (obtained) from bone, cartilage, fascia, or tendon. Harvested bone tissue is transplanted to another site to promote **osteogenesis** (bone growth) or to provide structural stability (e.g., spinal fusion). Harvested cartilage tissue is often used for reconstruction purposes (e.g., facial reconstruction to relieve temporomandibular joint (TMJ) pain). Fascia lata tissue is harvested from gastrocnemius fascia (from the calf) or tensor fascia lata (from the thigh) for soft tissue augmentation (e.g., repair skin defects, such as multiple depressed acne scars or **rhytides**, or wrinkles). (**Augmentation** is the process of enlarging or increasing.) Tendon tissue is harvested for the purpose of repairing another tendon (e.g., reconstruct anterior cruciate ligament).

EXAMPLE: Costochondral cartilage graft was harvested from the left rib of a 4-year-old child for laryngotracheal reconstruction to treat **subglottic stenosis** (narrowing of the airway below the vocal cords, adjacent to the cricoid cartilage). Report codes 31582 and 20910-51.

Codes 20930–20938 are reported for bone grafts obtained for spine surgery. Just one bone graft code is reported for each operative session (in addition to codes for the definitive procedure, such as spinal fusion) even if graft material is obtained from more than one spinal level (e.g., C1 and C2).

EXAMPLE: A patient diagnosed with spinal stenosis undergoes laminectomy with cervical spine fusion, which requires harvesting a large structural bone graft from the iliac crest (through a separate incision). Report codes 22800, 20902-51, and 20931 in addition to the spinal fusion procedure code. (Do not add modifier -51 to code 20931 because it is an add-on code.)

> **Note:**
>
> When a bone marrow biopsy is performed using a needle or trocar, report code 38221 (Bone marrow; biopsy, needle or trocar), which describes the procedure for obtaining the bone marrow tissue for biopsy.

Other Procedures

Report "other procedures" codes when procedures are performed (e.g., bone grafts with microvascular anastomosis) that are not reportable with codes from the grafts (or implants) codes.

EXAMPLE: The patient undergoes bone graft of the left fibula, with microvascular anastomosis. This means that the bone tissue is harvested along with its blood supply (but without overlying skin). (The grafted tissue will be used to reconstruct the patient's right tibial bone, which has a filling defect as the result of trauma; and surgery will involve microsurgical anastomosis of blood vessels.) Report code 20955-LT for the "bone graft of left fibula, with microvascular anastomosis."

Exercise 12.2 – General

Instructions: Assign the CPT code(s) and appropriate modifier(s) to each statement.

1. The physician treated a soft tissue abscess that was due to osteomyelitis by making an incision and examining, debriding, and draining the subfascia; the physician also irrigated the affected area, examined underlying tissue and bone for signs of infection, and closed the site.

   _____

2. Patient underwent exploration of a penetrating wound of the chest, which involved surgical exploration and enlargement of the wound, debridement, removal of a foreign body, and ligation of subcutaneous tissue.

   _____

3. Open bone biopsy, superficial, left femur.

   _____

4. Patient underwent aspiration of ganglion cyst, right wrist.

   _____

5. Patient received a cortisone injection to a single trigger point, which consisted of the trapezius, deltoid, and latissimus dorsi muscles.

   _____

6. A patient diagnosed with joint contracture of the right ankle underwent application of a multiplane external fixation device.

   _____

7. A patient severed his right index finger while using a chain saw. He underwent successful replantation of the index finger, which included metacarpophalangeal (MCP) joint to insertion of flexor sublimis tendon.

   _____

8. Fascia lata graft was harvested using a stripper.

   _____

9. Patient underwent structural allograft as part of an arthrodesis, posterior technique, craniocervical (occiput-C2)

   _____

10. Electrical stimulation procedure was performed to aid bone healing, invasive type.

   _____

Head

CPT codes located in the Head category include procedures performed on the skull, facial bones, and temporomandibular joint (TMJ).

Incision

The Incision subheading contains just one code for Arthrotomy, temporomandibular joint. When performed on both sides of the joint, add modifier -50 to the code.

> **EXAMPLE:** A patient underwent TMJ arthrotomy, left, to release scar tissue. Report code 21010-LT.

Excision

Report excision codes for surgery performed on bone and soft tissue of the face and/or scalp.

> **EXAMPLE:** Patient underwent TMJ condylectomy, left. Report code 21050-LT.

Manipulation

The Manipulation subheading contains a code for reporting TMJ manipulation, which requires anesthesia services.

> **EXAMPLE:** Patient underwent therapeutic TMJ manipulation for which general anesthesia was administered. Report code 21073. (Do not report modifier -50, -LT, or -RT with code 21073.)

Coding Tip:

When an outside laboratory prepares the prosthetic device, do not report codes 21076–21089 for physician professional services. (The physician who fits a device made by an outside laboratory should report an appropriate evaluation and management code.)

Head Prosthesis

Head prosthesis codes describe professional services that involve designing and preparing a prosthesis for a patient. Prostheses are created for rehabilitation patients who have facial, oral, or other anatomic deficiencies that require an artificial ear, eye, or nose or an intraoral **obturator**, which is used to close a gap (e.g., cleft).

> **EXAMPLE:** A patient was fitted for a mandibular resection prosthesis, which was custom prepared by the physician. Report code 21081.

Introduction or Removal

Codes 21100–21116 are reported for other introduction or removal procedures, such as application of halo-type appliance for maxillofacial fixation (including removal), interdental fixation device (e.g., arch bar) for conditions other than fracture or dislocation (including removal), or injection procedure for TMJ arthrography.

> **EXAMPLE:** A physician applied a halo-type appliance for maxillofacial fixation, and he removed it 30 days later. Report 21100. (Do not report a separate code for removal of the halo-type appliance because that procedure is included in the global period for code 21100.)

Repair, Revision, and/or Reconstruction

Codes 21141–21160 that describe reconstruction of the face are called LeFort I, II, or III procedures. **LeFort I** brings the lower midface forward (from the level of the upper teeth) to just above the nostrils. **LeFort II**, or **pyramidal fracture**, is a surgical fracture of the midfacial skeleton at an apex near the superior aspect of the nasal bones. **LeFort III** brings the entire midface forward, from the upper teeth to just above the cheekbones.

> **EXAMPLE:** A patient underwent a LeFort I reconstruction procedure of the midface, which required reconstruction of two pieces without bone graft. Report code 21142.

 Note:

- Colpocleisis, also known as a LeFort procedure, involves the surgical repair of a uterine prolapse or a vaginal vault prolapse.
- LeFort I, II, and III fractures are complex bilateral fractures of facial bones that contain large, unstable fragments.
- A Wagstaff-LeFort fracture is an avulsion of the fibula.

Other repair, revision, and/or reconstruction codes are reported for genioplasty, augmentation, and reduction procedures performed on the face, mandible, or forehead. Procedures include reconstruction, osteotomy, arthroplasty, repositioning, augmentation, revision, canthopexy, and reduction.

EXAMPLE: Patient underwent TMJ arthroplasty with allograft. Report code 21242.

Fracture and/or Dislocation

Codes 21310–21497 are reported for treatment of fractures and/or dislocations of the skull, facial bones, and TMJ.

EXAMPLE: A physician performs an open reduction and internal fixation of a left mandibular fracture. Report code 21470-LT.

Code 21497 describes interdental wiring for a condition other than fracture, which is a stabilization procedure that involves the insertion of wire between teeth. Compare this code description to code 21110 (Application of interdental fixation device for conditions other than fracture or dislocation, includes removal); an interdental fixation device is less permanent than wire.

Other Procedures

Just one unlisted code is included in the Other Procedures subheading.

Exercise 12.3 – Head

Instructions: Assign CPT code(s) and appropriate modifier(s) to each statement.

1. Arthrotomy of temporomandibular joint, right and left sides.

   _____

2. Excision of two facial bones (due to bone abscesses).

   _____

3. Impression and custom preparation of speech aid prosthesis.

   _____

4. Sliding osteotomy genioplasty, single piece.

   _____

5. Reconstruction midface, Lefort II with anterior intrusion.

   _____

6. Osteotomy of mandible, segmental.

   _____

7. Malar augmentation with prosthetic material.

   _____

8. Closed treatment of orbit fracture, with manipulation.

   _____

9. Closed treatment of maxillary alveolar ridge fracture.

   _____

10. Open treatment of mandibular condylar fracture.

    _____

Neck (Soft Tissues) and Thorax

The Neck (Soft Tissues) and Thorax heading includes codes for procedures performed on the soft tissues of the neck and thorax (e.g., incision and drainage, excisional biopsies, repairs, revisions, and reconstruction).

Incision

Report a code from 21501–21502 for incision and drainage of abscesses or hematomas, and report code 21510 for deep incision with opening of bone cortex of the thorax.

> **EXAMPLE:** Patient underwent incision and drainage of deep abscess, soft tissues of thorax, with partial rib ostectomy. Report code 21502.

Excision

Codes 21550–21632 are reported for excision of soft tissue of the neck or thorax (e.g., biopsy or excision of tumor), radical resection of a tumor, partial and total excision of ribs, costotransversectomy, ostectomy of sternum, sternal debridement, and radical resection of sternum. Note that code 21555 describes the type of lesion removed (e.g., tumor) and the anatomic location (e.g., soft tissue of neck or thorax), but it does not indicate the size of the tumor. Therefore, regardless of tumor size, report 21555 if that procedure is performed.

> **EXAMPLE:** Patient underwent costotransversectomy for decompression of paravertebral mass. Report code 21610.

Repair, Revision, and/or Reconstruction

Codes 21685–21750 describe the repair, revision, and/or reconstruction of soft tissues of the neck (e.g., muscle) and thoracic soft tissues and bones. When procedures are performed to repair superficial wounds, refer to the Integumentary System subsection to assign an appropriate code.

> **EXAMPLE:** Patient underwent open reconstructive repair of pectus excavatum. Report code 21740.

Fracture and/or Dislocation

Codes 21800–21825 are reported for procedures performed to treat rib and sternum fractures or dislocations.

> **EXAMPLE:** Patient underwent bilateral rib fracture treatment with external fixation device for **flail chest**, a condition in which a segment of the thoracic wall becomes detached from the remainder of the chest wall. Report code 21810-50.

Other Procedures

Just one unlisted code is included in the Other Procedures subheading.

Back and Flank

The Back and Flank heading contains just one subheading.

Excision

Back and Flank codes are reported for biopsy, tumor excision, and radical resection of tumor procedures performed on the back and flank. When a drain is inserted and/or the incision is repaired with multiple layers of sutures, staples, or steri-strips, do not separately report codes for those procedures; they are bundled in back and flank codes.

> **EXAMPLE:** Patient underwent soft tissue biopsy of the back, deep. Report code 21925.

Exercise 12.4 – Neck (Soft Tissues) and Thorax and Back and Flank

Instructions: Assign the CPT code(s) and appropriate modifier(s) to each statement.

1. Deep incision with opening of bone cortex, thorax.

_____

(continues)

Exercise 12.4 (continued)

2. Hyoid myotomy and suspension.

_____

3. Closed treatment of sternum fracture.

_____

4. Partial excision of rib.

_____

5. Sternal debridement.

_____

6. Needle biopsy, soft tissue, thorax.

_____

7. Excision of tumor, soft tissue of back, 2.5 cm.

_____

8. The physician removed a 4 cm malignant soft tissue tumor from the patient's flank, and radical resection was performed to remove the tumor and adjacent tissue. The surgical wound was repaired with complex closure.

_____

9. Patient underwent biopsy of superficial soft tissues of the back.

_____

10. Biopsy, soft tissue of flank, deep.

_____

Spine (Vertebral Column)

Spine (vertebral column) codes classify procedures performed on the cervical, thoracic, and lumbar spine. Vertebral procedures are sometimes followed by arthrodesis, and they may also include bone grafts and instrumentation. When reporting codes for spinal procedures, make sure you differentiate spinal segments (e.g., T1) and interspaces (e.g., T1-T2 interspace).

- T1-T2 represents two spinal segments of the thoracic vertebra, at levels 1 and 2.
- L1-L4 represents four spinal segments of the lumbar vertebra, at levels 1, 2, 3, and 4.
- T1-T2 represents one interspace of the thoracic vertebra, between levels T1 and T2.
- C1-C2 and C2-C3 represent two interspaces of the cervical vertebra, between levels C1 and C2 as well as between C2 and C3.

Coding Tip:

- Procedures performed on the bones, connective tissue, and muscles of the spinal column are classified in the Musculoskeletal subsection of CPT.

- Procedures performed on the spinal cord and spinal nerves are classified in the Nervous System subsection of CPT.

The notes located just below the Spine (Vertebral Column) heading should be reviewed before assigning codes.

- Bone graft procedure codes (20930–20938) are reported separately, in addition to arthrodesis procedure codes.

- Instrumentation procedure codes (22840–22848, 22851) are reported separately, in addition to arthrodesis procedure codes.

- When an arthrodesis procedure is performed in addition to another procedure, report the arthrodesis procedure code in addition to codes for other procedures performed. Make sure you add modifier -51 to the arthrodesis procedure code(s).

- When two surgeons collaborate to perform a spinal procedure during the same operative session on the same patient and each performs a distinct part of the procedure, add modifier -62 to the procedure code reported by each surgeon. (Additional procedure codes reported by each surgeon are also reported with modifier -62 if the surgeons continue to work as primary surgeons.)

EXAMPLE 1: Patient underwent arthrodesis of T1-T3 using local autograft from the ribs. Dual rods were inserted with multiple hooks and sublaminar wires. Report codes 22610, 22614, 22614, 22842, and 20936.

Three thoracic segments were fused; therefore, report codes 22610, 22614, and 22614. (Code 22614 is an add-on code; therefore, do not add modifier -51.) Report code 22842 for insertion of dual rods with multiple hooks and sublaminar wires; it is also exempt from the addition of modifier -51. Code 20936 describes the local autograft from the ribs.

EXAMPLE 2: Surgeon A performed a posterior exposure procedure on Mary Jones by making an incision overlying the lumbar vertebrae, separating the fascia and supraspinous ligaments in line with the incision. He then lifted ligaments and muscles out of the way. Next, Surgeon B performed a posterior discectomy and fusion at L2, and he performed a partial excision of the vertebral body at L3.

- Surgeon A reports code 22612-62.
- Surgeon B reports codes 22612-62 and 22114.

Although Surgeon A performed just the posterior exposure part of the procedure, because it is significant to the entire procedure, Surgeon A reports code 22612 with modifier -62.

Incision

Codes 22010 and 22015 are reported for the open incision and drainage of deep abscesses (subfascial) of the following sites:

- Cervical
- Thoracic
- Cervicothoracic
- Lumbar
- Sacral
- Lumbosacral

EXAMPLE: A patient underwent open incision and drainage of a deep subfascial abscess, sacral region. Report code 22015.

Excision

The Excision subheading contains a note stating that when two surgeons work together to perform a spinal procedure during the same operative session on the same patient, when each performs a distinct part of the procedure, modifier -62 is added to the procedure code reported by each surgeon. (Additional procedure codes are also reported with modifier -62 if the surgeons continue to work as primary surgeons.)

EXAMPLE: A patient underwent surgical repair of L1-L2 and L3-L4. Dr. Berry performed a posterior exposure of the spine with mobilization of great vessels. Dr. Thomas performed posterior discectomy and spinal fusion at L2-L3 and L4, using anterior interbody technique.

Dr. Berry reports codes 22612-62 and 22614-62. Dr. Thomas reports 22612-62 and 22614-62. (Do not add modifier -51 to code 22614.)

Osteotomy

An **osteotomy** is an incision into bone. Spinal osteotomy involves making incisions in vertebral bone to remove pieces or wedges of bone to correct a deformity such as kyphosis, lordosis, or scoliosis (Figure 12-7). Because the osteotomy codes include corpectomy, discectomy, and laminectomy, separate codes are not reported for

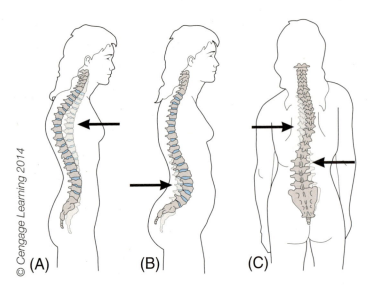

© Cengage Learning 2014

Figure 12-7 Spinal deformities (A) Kyphosis (B) Lordosis (C) Scoliosis

these procedures when they are documented in the operative report. Osteotomy codes differentiate anterior and posterior approach.

When an osteotomy is performed during the same operative session as a(n):

- Arthrodesis, report the appropriate code(s) from 22590–22634.

- Spinal instrumentation procedure, report the appropriate code(s) from 22840–22848 and 22851–22855; do not add modifier -51 to instrumentation procedure codes. (Do not add modifier -62 to 22840–22848 and 22850–22855.) (When two surgeons perform a procedure that also includes spinal instrumentation, just one of the surgeons performs the spinal instrumentation procedure. Therefore, do not add modifier -62 to the spinal instrumentation code.)

- Bone graft procedure, report an appropriate code from 20930–20938 (and do not add modifier -51 or -62 to the bone graft code). (When two surgeons perform a procedure that also includes bone grafting, just one of the surgeons performs the bone graft procedure. Therefore, do not add modifier -62 to the bone graft code.)

The Osteotomy subheading also includes a note indicating that when two surgeons work together to perform an anterior spine osteotomy procedure during the same operative session on the same patient and each performs a distinct part of the procedure, modifier -62 is added to the appropriate procedure codes (reported by each surgeon).

EXAMPLE 1: Patient underwent spinal osteotomy of spine, posterolateral approach, C1. Report code 22210.

EXAMPLE 2: Patient underwent anterior osteotomy of the spine with discectomy, T1. Report code 22222. (Do not report a separate code for the discectomy procedure.)

EXAMPLE 3: Patient underwent anterior spinal osteotomy, L1-L2. Dr. James performed anterior exposure of the spine with mobilization of great vessels. Dr. Smith performed anterior spinal osteotomy of L1-L2 with discectomy. Then Dr. James performed closure procedures. Dr. James reports 22224-62 and 22226-62. Dr. Smith also reports 22224-62 and 22226-62. (Do not add modifier -51 to code 22226 because it is an add-on code.)

Fracture and/or Dislocation

When treatment of fractures and/or dislocations is performed during the same operative session as a(n):

- Bone graft procedure, report an appropriate code from 20930–20938 (and do not add modifier -51 or -62 to the bone graft code).

- Arthrodesis, report the appropriate code(s) from 22590–22634.

- Spinal instrumentation procedure, report the appropriate code(s) from 22840–22848. (Do not add modifier -62 to 22840–22848).

The Fracture and/or Dislocation subheading also includes a note indicating that when two surgeons work together to treat distinct parts of *open fracture and/or dislocation* procedures during the same operative session and each performs a distinct part of the procedure, modifier -62 is added to procedure codes 22318–22328. Both surgeons must work together as primary surgeons.

> **EXAMPLE 1:** Patient underwent closed treatment of vertebral process fracture, L1. Report code 22305.

> **EXAMPLE 2:** Patient underwent open treatment and reduction of T3-T4 vertebral fracture with grafting. Dr. Lawson performed anterior exposure of the spine with mobilization of great vessels. Dr. Timber performed open treatment and reduction of T3-T4 vertebral fracture with spinal allograft. Then Dr. Lawson performed closure procedures. Dr. Lawson reports 22327-62 and 22328-62. Dr. Timber also reports 22327-62, 22328-62, and 20931. (Do not add modifier -51 to code 22328.)

Manipulation

"Manipulation of spine" under anesthesia is performed to treat back pain and other disorders. The idea is that the patient is more relaxed while under anesthesia, and better spinal manipulation results. Report code 22505 once for manipulation of any region of the spine, including multiple regions during the same operative session. (For "manipulation of the spine *without* anesthesia," report code 97140 from the Medicine section.)

> **EXAMPLE:** Patient underwent lumbar spinal manipulation under anesthesia. Report code 22505.

Vertebral Body, Embolization or Injection

Percutaneous vertebroplasty, reported with code(s) under the Vertebral Body, Embolization or Injection heading, is typically performed to relieve pain due to (1) vertebral compression fractures (e.g., pathologic fractures due to osteoporosis) and (2) benign and malignant infiltrating vertebral lesions (e.g., aneurysmal bone cysts, giant cell tumor, hemangioma, metastatic cancer, or myeloma). Patients who are candidates for percutaneous vertebroplasty have experienced functional disability and severe pain, which is unrelieved by pain medication and application of a brace (for support).

Percutaneous vertebroplasty is usually performed with the patient under conscious sedation; a bone cement (that hardens in about 10 minutes) is injected under pressure directly into a fractured vertebra. The cement causes fragments of fractured vertebra to congeal, providing stability. Bone cement is also injected to fill minor spaces in cancellous bone. Because percutaneous vertebroplasty is performed under fluoroscopic or computed tomography guidance, also report an appropriate code from the Radiology section for the radiological supervision and interpretation.

> **EXAMPLE:** Patient underwent percutaneous vertebroplasty under fluoroscopic guidance, L1 and L2, to stabilize pathologic fractures due to osteoporosis. Report codes 22521 and 22522. (Do not add modifier -51 to code 22522.) In addition, report code 72291.

Arthrodesis

Arthrodesis, or **artificial ankylosis**, is the surgical fixation (e.g., fusion) of a joint. Arthrodesis may be performed independently of other procedures; when arthrodesis is performed with another procedure, report the arthrodesis code in addition to the definitive procedure and add modifier -51 to the arthrodesis code if applicable. (Some arthrodesis codes are exempt from modifier -51.)

Arthrodesis performed for reasons other than to correct a spinal deformity is classified according to anatomic approach (22548–22634), such as anterior or anterolateral approach, posterior or posterolateral approach, or anterior or posterior interbody technique. Arthrodesis for spinal deformities (e.g., scoliosis and kyphosis) is reported with codes 22800–22812.

- Spinal instrumentation procedures are reported in addition to the arthrodesis code(s), and modifier -51 is added to the instrumentation code(s).

- Bone graft procedures are reported in addition to the arthrodesis code(s).

    EXAMPLE: A physician performed posterior arthrodesis of L5-S1 using autogenous iliac bone graft harvested through a separate incision. Report codes 22612 and 20937. (Do not add modifier -51 to code 20937.)

Exploration

Just one code is reported for exploration of spinal fusion.

- When spinal instrumentation is performed during the same operative session as the exploration of spinal fusion, report the appropriate instrumentation code from 22840–22855.

- When exploration of spinal fusion is performed in addition to other definitive procedures (e.g., arthrodesis), add modifier -51 to the "exploration of spinal fusion" code.

Spinal Instrumentation

Report codes 22840–22855 when spinal instrumentation is performed during a surgical procedure. Make sure you add modifier -51 to codes 22849–22850 and 22852–22855 only when spinal instrumentation is performed during the same operative session as other definitive procedure(s).

    EXAMPLE: Patient underwent anterior interbody technique arthrodesis of C1-C2. Autogenous iliac bone graft was used, and it was harvested through a separate incision. Anterior instrumentation of the two vertebral segments was also performed. Report codes 22554, 22845, and 20937. (Do not add modifier -51 to code 20937.)

Exercise 12.5 – Spine (Vertebral Column)

Instructions: Assign the CPT code(s) and appropriate modifier(s) to each statement.

1. Patient underwent arthrodesis at L4-L5 interspace. Posterior interbody technique laminectomy was performed. Discectomy was also performed to prepare the vertebral interspace for fusion.

    _____

2. Physician performed "spinal manipulation under anesthesia," cervical, thoracic, and lumbar spine.

    _____

3. Patient underwent osteotomy and discectomy of a single cervical spine vertebral segment. Anterior approach was used.

    _____

4. Physician performed arthrodesis using posterior technique of atlas-axis (C1-C2) with internal spinal fixation by wiring the spinous processes.

    _____

5. Patient underwent posterior arthrodesis of L2-L3 for spinal deformity, with casting. Autogenous iliac bone graft was harvested through a separate incision.

    _____

Abdomen

The Abdomen subheading contains just two headings:

- Excision

- Other Procedures

The excision procedure code is reported for excision of abdominal wall tumor. The "other procedures" code is reported for unlisted procedures.

> **EXAMPLE:** Patient underwent excision of subfascial abdominal wall tumor. Report code 22900.

Shoulder

The Shoulder heading contains codes for procedures performed on the clavicle, scapula, humerus head and neck, sternoclavicular joint, acromioclavicular joint, and shoulder joint.

> **EXAMPLE:** Physician performed removal of a "total shoulder" implant with replacement of a new implant. Report codes 23332 for removal of the implant and 23472-51 for arthroplasty and insertion of a new total shoulder implant.

Note:

To report magnetic resonance imaging (MRI) of the shoulder with intra-articular contrast, report code 23350 (Injection procedure for shoulder arthrography or enhanced CT/MRI shoulder arthrography) in addition to the MRI code (from the Radiology section).

Humerus (Upper Arm) and Elbow

The Humerus (Upper Arm) and Elbow heading includes codes for procedures performed on the humerus, elbow, and head and neck of the radius and olecranon process.

> **EXAMPLE:** Patient underwent closed treatment with manipulation, medial humeral epicondylar fracture. Report code 24565.

Forearm and Wrist

The Forearm and Wrist heading includes codes for procedures performed on the radius, ulna, carpal bones, and joints.

> **EXAMPLE:** A patient was diagnosed with subluxation of extensor carpi ulnaris (ECU) tendon at the wrist. The physician reconstructed the ECU tendon sheath with a retinacular graft harvest from the fourth dorsal compartment. Report code 25275, which includes the procedure for obtaining the graft.

Coding Tip:

- Open carpal tunnel decompression surgery (for carpal tunnel syndrome) is classified in the Nervous System subsection of surgery.
- Surgical endoscopy to release the transverse carpal ligament to treat carpal tunnel syndrome surgery is assigned code 29848, which is located under the Endoscopy/Arthroscopy heading of the Musculoskeletal System subsection.

Hand and Fingers

The Hand and Fingers heading includes codes for procedures performed on the hands and fingers, which include repairs to tendons, nerves, and blood vessels to provide treatment for injuries or to correct deformities. Tendons include two types:

- **Flexor tendons**: Bend the fingers
- **Extensor tendons**: Straighten the fingers

The following procedures are bundled in the tendon repair codes:

- Application of immobilization
- Extension of the excision
- Repair and closure of tendon sheath

Codes for harvesting and inserting tendon grafts from another site, repairing nerves or arteries, and treating fractures are reported in addition to the tendon repair.

Exercise 12.6 – Abdomen, Shoulder, Humerus (Upper Arm) and Elbow, Forearm and Wrist, and Hand and Fingers

Instructions: Assign the CPT code(s) and appropriate modifier(s) to each statement.

1. The physician performed an excision of a 4 cm subfascial abdominal wall tumor and the surrounding tissue. Incision was repaired in multiple layers with sutures.

2. The physician removed subdeltoid calcareous deposits, left shoulder joint, by incising the raised area over the calcium deposits and removing the calcareous deposits.

3. The physician performed a forequarter interthoracoscapular amputation, right shoulder.

4. The physician performed removal of a deep foreign body, left shoulder.

5. Excision of malignant tumor from subcutaneous tissue around right elbow.

6. Percutaneous medial tenotomy for treatment of tennis elbow, right.

7. Patient who sustained left elbow trauma developed an elbow contracture that required manipulation under anesthesia.

8. Percutaneous skeletal fixation of left Colles fracture with manipulation.

9. Injection procedure performed to prep patient for right wrist arthrography.

10. Left palmar fasciectomy with Z-plasty.

Pelvis and Hip Joint

The Pelvis and Hip Joint heading includes codes for procedures performed on the head and neck of the femur (hip joint). (Codes for procedures performed on the femur and its tibial plateau are located under the Femur [Thigh Region] and Knee Joint heading.)

EXAMPLE: Patient underwent partial hemiarthroplasty of the left hip with insertion of femoral stem prosthesis. Report code 27125-LT. (Insertion of the femoral stem prosthesis is included in code 27125.)

Femur (Thigh Region) and Knee Joint

The Femur (Thigh Region) and Knee Joint heading includes codes for procedures performed on the femur and its tibial plateau and the knee joint. (Codes for procedures performed on the head and neck of the femur are located under the Pelvis and Hip Joint heading.)

The **femur** (Figure 12-8) is the long bone of the thigh, and it articulates with the hip bone, tibia, and patella. The **tibial plateau** is the lower portion of the femur that articulates with the **tibia** (larger of the two lower leg bones). The **knee** is a "hinge" joint comprised of bones, cartilage, ligaments, and tendons. **Ligaments** (e.g., medical collateral ligament) are connective tissue that connects bone to bone (e.g., patella to femur), and they control stability of the knee. Trauma to knee joints can result in ligament tears, which require surgical repair (Figure 12-9).

EXAMPLE: Patient was diagnosed with an anterior medial left thigh mass, which was 2 × 2 × 1.5 cm in size. With the patient under local anesthesia, biopsy of the mass above the superficial fascia was performed. Report code 27323-LT (because the mass was removed from "above the superficial fascia.")

> **Note:**
>
> Arthroscopic knee surgery is a commonly performed procedure, and codes are located under the Endoscopy/Arthroscopy heading of the Musculoskeletal System subsection.

Leg (Tibia and Fibula) and Ankle Joint

The Leg (Tibia and Fibula) and Ankle Joint heading includes codes for procedures performed on the tibia, fibula, and ankle joint.

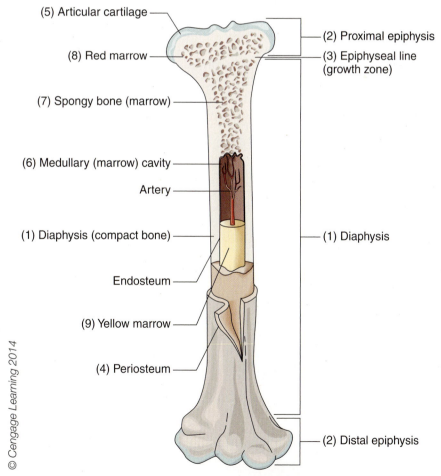

(5) Articular cartilage
(8) Red marrow
(7) Spongy bone (marrow)
(6) Medullary (marrow) cavity
Artery
(1) Diaphysis (compact bone)
Endosteum
(9) Yellow marrow
(4) Periosteum

(2) Proximal epiphysis
(3) Epiphyseal line (growth zone)
(1) Diaphysis
(2) Distal epiphysis

© Cengage Learning 2014

Figure 12-8 Structure of (femur long bone), including proximal (near) and distal (far) references to the bone's shaft

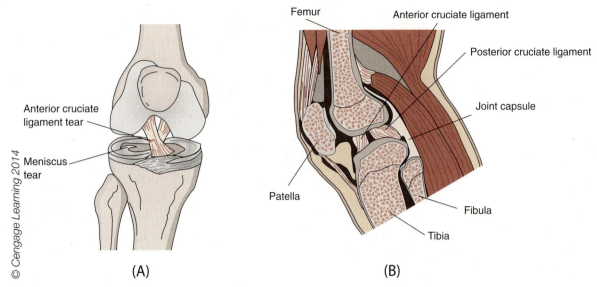

Figure 12-9   (A) Meniscus and anterior cruciate ligament tears. (B) Knee joint

EXAMPLE: Patient underwent flexor tenolysis of the right ankle, single tendon. Report code 27680-RT. (When the procedure is performed on multiple tendons that are accessed through separate incisions, report code 27681. When multiple tendons are accessed through the same incision, report code 27680 for each tendon.)

Foot and Toes

The Foot and Toes heading includes codes for procedures performed on the feet and toes. Hallux valgus repair codes (28290–28299) are reported to correct **bunions** (Figure 12-10), which are caused by bone inflammation and swelling and result in medial deviation and axial rotation of the first metatarsophalangeal (MTP) joint. Bunion deformities develop differently, and repair requires different levels of complexity and different techniques, as follows:

- Keller procedure: Simple resection of the base of the proximal phalanx with removal of the medial eminence

- McBride procedure: Distal soft tissue release that corrects soft tissue deformity at the MTP joint

- Mitchell procedure: Complex, double cut osteotomy through the neck of the first metatarsal

  EXAMPLE: Patient underwent bilateral hallux valgus correction with sesamoidectomy and simple exostectomy. Report code 28290-50.

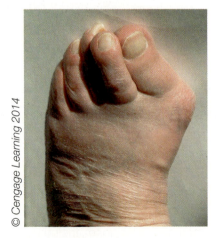

Figure 12-10 Bunion

Exercise 12.7 – Pelvis and Hip Joint, Femur (Thigh Region) and Knee Joint, Leg (Tibia and Fibula) and Ankle Joint, and Foot and Toes

Instructions: Assign the CPT code(s) and appropriate modifier(s) to each statement.

1. Proximal hamstring release.

2. Partial hip replacement with bipolar arthroplasty to treat right hip fracture.

3. Removal of a foreign body deep in the left thigh.

4. Complete 1 × 1 × 0.5 cm excision of superficial mass, posterior left thigh.

5. Excision of 2 cm bone cyst with autograft of harvested femur graft, left, which was performed during the same operative session.

6. Decompression fasciotomy of the lateral and posterior compartments, right knee.

7. Percutaneous repair of ruptured Achilles tendon, right.

8. Incision and drainage of infected bursa, left ankle.

9. Distal Chevron osteotomy, right.

10. Partial ostectomy to surgically correct bunionette involving the right fifth metatarsal head.

Application of Casts and Strapping

The Application of Casts and Strapping heading includes codes that are reported when the cast (or splint) application or strapping is a(n):

- Replacement procedure performed during or after the period of follow-up care.

- Initial service performed *without restorative treatment or procedure* to stabilize or protect a fracture, a dislocation, or another injury and/or to provide comfort to a patient.

   EXAMPLE 1: A 5-year-old patient was seen in the office to have his left short-arm cast replaced. He was playing a game he invented called "bop it," which involved knocking his cast on top of one of his bedposts. The cast cracked and had to be replaced. The patient was instructed to stop playing "bop it." Report code 29075-LT.

   EXAMPLE 2: A 7-year-old patient injured his left arm while roller-skating. A two-view left forearm X-ray performed at Sylvania Community Hospital's emergency department, revealed fractures of the radial and ulnar shafts. A level III emergency department evaluation and management service was provided. The patient's arm was placed in a splint to stabilize the fracture, and the mother was informed that treatment would have to be performed the next day because no orthopedic physician was available in the facility or on call. Report codes 99283, 29125-LT, and 73090-LT. (Do not add modifier -57 to the E/M code or modifier -51 to the surgery and radiology codes.)

Upon being informed that treatment would not be performed that day, the mother called the facility from which the family normally receives treatment and asked to speak with the orthopedic surgeon on call. That physician called her back within 15 minutes; and when the mother explained the circumstances, she was told to bring the X-rays and her child to St. Francis Hospital to meet the surgeon there so he could assess her son and perform treatment. Upon outpatient evaluation and management (level III) of this new patient by the orthopedic surgeon, the mother was informed that same-day treatment was preferred because waiting until the next day would result in swelling, inflammation, and pain, making it more difficult to treat the fractures. Later that day the patient underwent closed manipulation of radial and ulnar shaft fractures under general anesthesia, and a short-arm cast was applied. The patient remained in the hospital until 10 p.m., at which time he was released to return home with his parents. Report codes 25565 and 99203-57.

When one physician applies a cast, splint, or strapping device as initial treatment of a fracture or dislocation and a different physician later performs a restorative treatment or procedure, report "treatment of fracture and/or dislocation" code(s) from the appropriate heading in the Musculoskeletal System subsection.

When a physician performs an initial restorative treatment or procedure and an initial cast, splint, or strap is also applied, the physician is responsible for providing all subsequent fracture, dislocation, and/or injury care. Do not report a code for the application of a cast, splint, or strapping device with the initial restorative treatment or procedure; the first cast, splint, or strapping device application is included in the "treatment of fracture and/or dislocation" code.

Coding Tip:

Do not report modifier -58 (Staged or related procedure or service by the same physician during the postoperative period) when a temporary cast, splint, or strapping device is applied and the patient later undergoes a restorative treatment or procedure. In addition, do not report evaluation and management service codes unless significant identifiable further services are provided at the time of the cast application or strapping. (Report only the "treatment of fracture and/or dislocation" code.)

Endoscopy/Arthroscopy

The Endoscopy/Arthroscopy heading includes codes for procedures performed using an endoscope or arthroscope. Endoscopy is the visual examination of the interior of a body cavity or an organ. **Arthroscopy** (Figure 12-11) is the visual examination of the inside of a joint.

Endoscopic and arthroscopic procedures are diagnostic or surgical, and CPT notes indicate that surgical endoscopy/arthroscopy always includes diagnostic endoscopy/arthroscopy. An endoscopy/arthroscopy is considered diagnostic when it is performed to visualize an abnormality or to determine the extent of disease. When anything in addition to visualization is performed, the procedure is considered surgical.

Coding Tip:

- A surgical endoscopy/arthroscopy always includes a diagnostic endoscopy/arthroscopy. This means that a code for diagnostic endoscopy/arthroscopy is not reported with a code for surgical endoscopy/arthroscopy. A diagnostic endoscopy/arthroscopy code is reported when it is the only endoscopic/arthroscopic procedure performed. (Codes for other procedure codes, other than surgical endoscopy/arthroscopy, can be reported with diagnostic endoscopy/arthroscopy codes.)

- Diagnostic knee arthroscopy is probably the most common type of procedure performed. It is done to examine and diagnose knee joint abnormalities. Diagnostic knee arthroscopy involves inserting an arthroscopy through small incisions and using a camera to transmit images onto a monitor so the knee joint's interior can be visualized. During arthroscopic knee surgery, the knee is subdivided into three compartments: medial, lateral, and patellofemoral.

- Surgical knee arthroscopy is often performed to treat diseased or damaged structures of the knee joint (e.g., torn meniscus, meniscal lesions, damaged patella or ligaments, and inflamed or damaged synovium).

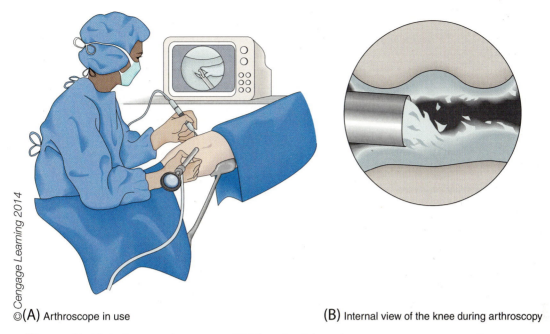

(A) Arthroscope in use

(B) Internal view of the knee during arthroscopy

Figure 12-11 Arthroscopic surgery (A) The physician views progress on a monitor. (B) Internal view as diseased tissue is removed during surgery.

Exercise 12.8 – Application of Casts and Strapping and Endoscopy/Arthroscopy

Instructions: Assign the CPT code(s) and appropriate modifier(s) to each statement.

1. Diagnostic arthroscopy, left elbow, with synovial biopsy.

   _____

2. Patient's left long-arm cast was removed after getting wet, the site was evaluated, and another long-arm fiberglass cast was reapplied. The same physician who applied the first cast removed the wet cast and applied the new cast.

   _____

3. Physician treated flexion contracture of right small finger proximal interphalangeal joint by applying a cast to stabilize the joint.

   _____

4. Patient with diabetic neuropathic ulcers had rigid total contact leg cast applied, left.

   _____

5. Patient sustained nondisplaced fracture of distal left ulna, and emergency department physician applied a molded splint for immobilization and protection of the fracture. Patient was referred to orthopedic specialist.

   _____

6. Patient underwent arthroscopic repair of large osteochondritis dissecans lesion and talar dome fracture with internal fixation, right.

   _____

7. Surgical arthroscopy of the metacarpophalangeal joint on the right with debridement.

   _____

(continues)

Exercise 12.8 (continued)

8. Patient underwent Mumford procedure of distal 1 cm of left clavicle.

_____

9. Arthroscopic superior labrum anterior/posterior (SLAP) lesion tear repair, right shoulder.

_____

10. Left knee diagnostic and surgical arthroscopy with partial medial meniscectomy.

_____

Respiratory System Subsection

The CPT Respiratory System (Figure 12-12) subsection is arranged according to body area from nose to lungs. It includes the following headings:

- Nose
- Accessory Sinuses
- Larynx
- Trachea and Bronchi
- Lungs and Pleura

Respiratory system headings include one or more of the following subheadings:

- Incision
- Excision
- Introduction (and Removal)
- Removal of Foreign Body
- Repair
- Destruction
- Endoscopy
- Other Procedures

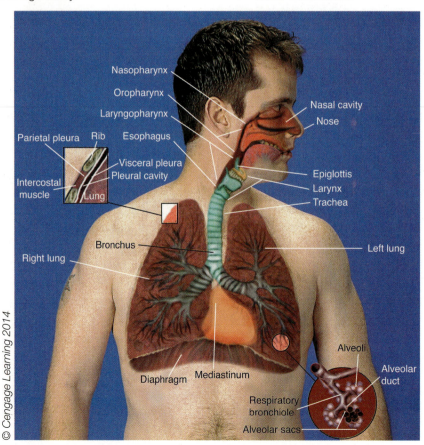

© Cengage Learning 2014

Figure 12-12 Respiratory system

The Respiratory System subsection's Lungs and Pleura heading also contains the following subheadings:

- Lung Transplantation
- Surgical Collapse Therapy; Thoracoplasty

Respiratory section guidelines define procedures and provide instruction for the selection of appropriate codes, as follows:

- Approach used for lung procedures
- Amount and type of tissue removed
- Difference between diagnostic and therapeutic procedures
- Ways various removal procedures may be performed

Nose

The Nose heading contains codes for procedures that are performed on the nose, nasal septum, intranasal tissue, nasal turbinates, and skin of the nose. (Refer to Figure 12-13 for structure of the upper respiratory system, including nasal anatomy.) Codes for procedures range from simple control of a nosebleed (30901) to complex surgery (e.g., rhinoplasty, coded as 30400).

Coding Tip:

When the control of bleeding is performed during a procedure, it is considered an integral part of that procedure and is not separately coded and reported. This means that codes that classify "control of nasal hemorrhage" (30901–30906) are not reported with other procedure codes.

Excision

Turbinates, or **conchae**, are bony plates covered by spongy mucosa with curved margins. There are three turbinates on each side of the **nasal vestibule** (nose's entrance): inferior, middle, and superior. When surgery is performed on turbinates, it is important to identify the type of turbinate procedure and technique used. Turbinates can be removed by

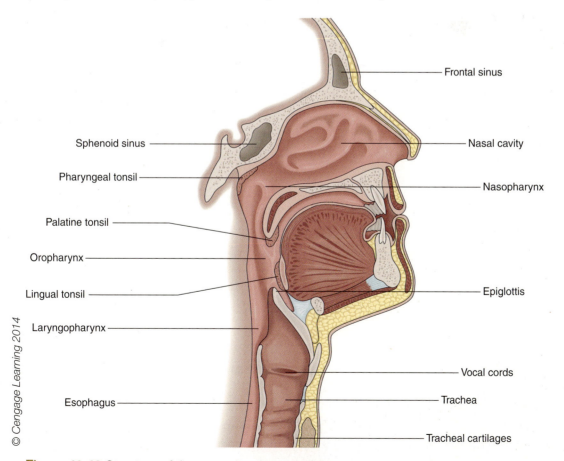

© Cengage Learning 2014

Figure 12-13 Structure of the upper respiratory system

resection or excision with or without endoscopy, cauterization, debridement, laser, cryotherapy, radiofrequency reduction, or ablation. Turbinate excision and submucous resection codes (30130–30140) are typically reported for inferior turbinate surgery. These codes can also be reported separately with other surgical procedures performed on the nose (e.g., sphenoid, maxillary, or frontal sinus procedures; septoplasty). Codes 30130–30140 describe unilateral procedures, which means that if the surgery is performed on both sides, modifier -50 (bilateral procedure) is added to the reported code.

> **EXAMPLE:** Patient underwent anterior intranasal ethmoidectomy for chronic sinusitis. A partial inferior turbinate excision was performed to gain access to the ethmoid bone. Report code 31200. (Code 30130 is not reported for the partial inferior turbinate excision because it was performed only to gain access to the ethmoid bone.)

Coding Tip:

When a turbinate procedure is performed to gain access to the ethmoid bone, do not report codes 30130–30140. However, if a separate diagnosis justifies medical necessity for excision of turbinate (30130) or submucous resection of turbinate (30140), report the appropriate code and add modifier -59. (NOTE: Even if medical necessity justifies reporting codes 30130–30140, some third-party payers will not reimburse the turbinate excision or submucous resection because the code descriptions do not specify middle or superior turbinates.)

> **EXAMPLE:** Patient underwent a total intranasal ethmoidectomy for chronic sinusitis and a complete excision of the inferior turbinate for sleep apnea. Report codes 31201 and 30130-59.

Repair

When a physician performs surgical nasal/sinus endoscopy with partial ethmoidectomy (anterior) and septoplasty or submucous resection, report codes 31254 *and* 30520 because each is a separate and distinct service.

> **EXAMPLE:** Patient underwent bilateral surgical endoscopic nasal septoplasty with cartilage scoring. Report codes 30520-50 and 31254-50-51.

Exercise 12.9 – Nose

Instructions: Assign the CPT code(s) and appropriate modifier(s) to each statement.

1. Physician made therapeutic injections into the right and left turbinates.

2. Excision of polyp from inside of nose, left side, via scalpel. Single-layer closure was also performed.

3. Removal of nasal mucosa from inside left side of nose for biopsy. Some normal tissue adjacent to diseased mucosa is also removed during biopsy.

4. Lateral rhinotomy, left.

5. Rhinoplasty for nasal deformity secondary to congenital cleft lip and palate, including columellar lengthening of the tip and septum, with osteotomies.

Accessory Sinuses

The Accessory Sinuses heading contains codes for procedures performed on the maxillary, frontal, ethmoid, and sphenoid sinuses. The Accessory Sinuses heading contains unique coding guidelines for endoscopy procedures. (Refer to Figure 12-13 for location of accessory sinuses.)

Endoscopy

Endoscopy codes classify unilateral procedures unless the code description indicates otherwise. This means that HCPCS level II modifier -LT or -RT is added to the endoscopy code unless the procedure is performed bilaterally and modifier -50 is added to the code.

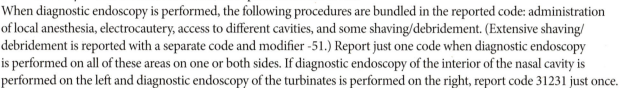

Note:

Modifier -50 is not added to code 31231 because "bilateral" is included in its description. However, modifier -LT or -RT can be added to code 31231 if the procedure is performed unilaterally.

Diagnostic endoscopy codes include inspection of the interior of the nasal cavity and its meatus, turbinates, and sphenoethmoid recess. When diagnostic endoscopy is performed, the following procedures are bundled in the reported code: administration of local anesthesia, electrocautery, access to different cavities, and some shaving/debridement. (Extensive shaving/debridement is reported with a separate code and modifier -51.) Report just one code when diagnostic endoscopy is performed on all of these areas on one or both sides. If diagnostic endoscopy of the interior of the nasal cavity is performed on the left and diagnostic endoscopy of the turbinates is performed on the right, report code 31231 just once.

Surgical sinus endoscopy is performed through the nose, using a fiberoptic endoscopy; and it includes sinusotomy (when performed) and diagnostic endoscopy. When a physician performs surgical endoscopy of accessory sinuses, evaluation of nasal access regions (diagnostic endoscopy) is also performed as part of the medically necessary service. Do not report a code for diagnostic endoscopy in addition to the surgical endoscopic procedure. This means that when surgical and diagnostic endoscopies are performed during the same operative session, just one code from 31233–31297 is reported to classify both procedures.

EXAMPLE: Patient undergoes surgical endoscopy with anterior ethmoidectomy, left; and the physician uses the endoscope to evaluate other regions of the nasal cavity. Report code 31254-LT. (Do not report code 31231 for the diagnostic nasal endoscopy.)

Note:

Recognize the difference between endoscopic and open surgical approaches. An endoscopic nasal surgical approach utilizes a fiberoptic endoscope instrument, which is inserted through the nostril(s). An open nasal surgical approach is performed by making an incision into skin or tissues inside the nasal cavity.

Anatomically, the middle turbinate is part of the ethmoid bone. Therefore, if the middle turbinate is removed during endoscopic polypectomy or endoscopic ethmoidectomy, a code for removal of the middle turbinate is *not* reported.

Code 30930, Fracture nasal turbinate(s), therapeutic, usually applies to inferior turbinate surgery. It is considered a distinct and separate procedure from that described in codes 31255 (Nasal/sinus endoscopy, surgical; with ethmoidectomy, total (anterior and posterior)) and 30520 (Septoplasty or submucous resection, with or without cartilage scoring, contouring or replacement with graft). Therefore, when one or more of the above procedures is performed during the same operative session, report each code (and add the appropriate HCPCS level II or CPT modifiers). When the surgeon fractures the middle turbinates to facilitate a sinus procedure, that is considered part of the sinus procedure and a separate "fracture nasal turbinate(s)" code is *not* reported.

EXAMPLE: Patient underwent bilateral nasal/sinus surgical endoscopy with total ethmoidectomy and bilateral nasal septoplasty. Report codes 31255-50 and 30520-50-51.

When biopsy of a lesion from the accessory sinuses is obtained as part of an excision, destruction, or other type of removal during the same operative session, do not report a biopsy code in addition to the excision/destruction/removal code. Also, biopsy codes are not separately reported for multiple similar or identical lesions even if the lesions are taken from a different area of the respiratory system.

EXAMPLE: A patient presents with multiple nasal polyps. Patient undergoes surgical endoscopy with polypectomy and total ethmoidectomy. Report code 31255. (Do not report code 31237 for the surgical endoscopy with polypectomy because that procedure is bundled with code 31255.) Even though polypectomy may have been performed prior to total ethmoidectomy, the polypectomy procedure is included in the more invasive ethmoidectomy procedure.

Coding Tip:

When a sinusotomy (31000–31090) is performed in conjunction with a sinus endoscopy, just one code is reported for both services. If the endoscopy was performed to evaluate the sinus cavity prior to sinusotomy, report just the sinusotomy procedure code. CPT instructions state that a surgical sinus endoscopy always includes sinusotomy and diagnostic endoscopy.

Exercise 12.10 – Accessory Sinuses

Instructions: Assign the CPT code(s) and appropriate modifier(s) to each statement.

1. Anterior ethmoidectomy via intranasal approach.

   _____

2. Endoscopic treatment of a nosebleed.

   _____

3. Endoscopic anterior and posterior (total) ethmoidectomy, left, with left maxillary antrostomy.

   _____

4. Nasal endoscopy with biopsy.

   _____

5. Endoscopic frontal nasal exploration with removal of tissue from left frontal sinus and diagnostic endoscopy of left turbinates.

   _____

Larynx

The Larynx (Figure 12-14) heading contains codes for procedures performed on the epiglottis and larynx and inside the trachea.

Excision

When a total laryngectomy with bilateral radical neck dissection (31365) is performed, do not add modifier -50 to the code. Because the larynx is a single midline organ, it is not appropriate to add modifier -50 to code 31365. (A laryngectomy cannot be performed bilaterally.) Instead, report code 31365 for the total laryngectomy and radical neck dissection on one side. Report code 38720-59 for the radical neck dissection on the other side. (The description of code 38720 is "Cervical lymphadenectomy (complete).") (Modifier -59 is added to indicate a distinct procedural service.)

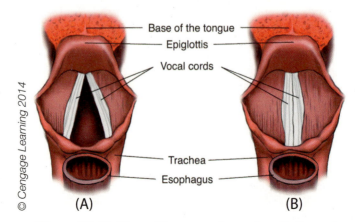

© Cengage Learning 2014

Figure 12-14 View of larynx and vocal cords from above
(A) Vocal cords are open during breathing.
(B) Vocal cords vibrate together during speech.

When an arytenoidectomy or arytenoidopexy is performed as an open procedure, report code 31400. When an arytenoidectomy is performed endoscopically, report code 31560. An **arytenoidectomy** is the excision of arytenoid cartilage, which is located in the bilateral vocal fold. An **arytenoidopexy** is the surgical fixation of arytenoidal cartilage and/or surrounding muscles. Both procedures are done to improve patient breathing.

EXAMPLE: Patient underwent endoscopic arytenoidectomy. Report code 31560. (Do *not* report code 31400.)

Endoscopy

Endoscopy codes (31505–31579) include the following types of laryngoscopy, and the documented operative report will indicate the instrumentation used:

- Direct
- Indirect
- Use of operating microscope (for magnification)
- Use of fiberoptic scope (that transmits light)

Laryngoscopy is the visualization of the back of the throat, including the **larynx** (voice box) and vocal cords. **Direct laryngoscopy** is the insertion of a flexible or rigid fiberoptic scope or a rigid laryngoscope to visualize throat structures. **Indirect laryngoscopy** is the insertion of a small hand mirror in the patient's mouth at the back of the throat while the physician wears headgear that contains a mirror and light source; the mirror worn by the physician reflects light into the patient's mouth, allowing the physician to visualize the patient's throat.

EXAMPLE: Patient underwent indirect diagnostic laryngoscopy. Report code 31505.

When a laryngoscopy procedure is required for placement of an endotracheal tube to provide air passage in an emergency situation, *do not separately code and report the laryngoscopy*. Report code 31500 (Intubation, endotracheal, emergency procedure) only.

When a laryngoscopy procedure is used to place an endotracheal tube for nonemergent reasons (e.g., general anesthesia or bronchoscopy), *do not separately code and report the laryngoscopy*. (Code 31500, Intubation, endotracheal emergency procedure) is not reported when an elective intubation is performed.) When a laryngoscopy procedure is required for placement of a tracheostomy, report just the tracheostomy code (31603–31614). Do not report a code for the laryngoscopy. When tracheostomy is performed as an essential part of laryngeal surgery (e.g., laryngectomy, laryngoplasty, or laryngotomy), do not separately report code 31600, Tracheostomy, planned (separate procedure).

Coding Tip:

Report code 31500 when emergency endotracheal intubation is performed during the provision of critical care services (99291–99292).

Exercise 12.11 – Larynx

Instructions: Assign the CPT code(s) and appropriate modifier(s) to each statement.

1. Emergency department physician places endotracheal tube for a patient in respiratory distress.

   _____

2. Total laryngectomy with radical neck dissection.

   _____

3. Patient with cricoid split (break in the circular cartilage of the larynx) undergoes laryngoplasty.

   _____

4. Complicated tracheotomy tube change (prior to establishment of fistula tract).

   _____

5. Total laryngectomy with bilateral radical neck dissection.

   _____

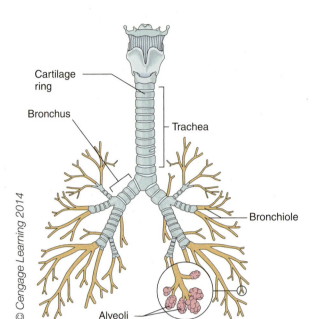

© Cengage Learning 2014

Figure 12-15 Trachea, bronchi, bronchial tree, and alveoli (air sacs)

Trachea and Bronchi

The Trachea and Bronchi (Figure 12-15) heading contains codes for procedures performed through the trachea and on tracheal cartilage (carinii) and the bronchi.

Endoscopy

A **bronchoscopy** (Figure 12-16) is the visual examination of the interior of the bronchus. A tracheoscopy is the visual examination of the interior of the **trachea** (windpipe). A **tracheobronchoscopy** is the visual examination of the interior of the trachea and bronchus. Endoscopy of the trachea and bronchus is performed with either a flexible fiberoptic scope or a rigid scope, with or without cell washings or brushing. A **brushing** involves combing the mucous lining of the trachea or bronchus with a bronchial brush to collect cells. **Cell washing** involves flushing fluid into an area and removing the fluid, using aspiration technique to collect cells.

Codes 31622–31656 describe procedures that involve use of a bronchoscope, with or without fluoroscopic guidance, to visualize all major lobar and segmental bronchi. These procedures may also include obtaining diagnostic specimens as part of the examination. Fiberoptic bronchoscopy services routinely include inspection of the nasal cavity, pharynx, and larynx. When nasal endoscopy, laryngoscopy is performed, in addition to bronchoscopy, report a code for the bronchoscopy procedure only.

 Coding Tip:

Procedures described in codes 31622–31629 are distinct surgical procedures, and they are not considered integral components of one another. Therefore, when multiple procedures are performed via bronchoscopy that can be reported with codes 31622–31629, report each code separately and do not add modifier -51 to any of the codes.

Diagnostic endoscopy of the trachea and bronchi performed during the same operative session as a surgical endoscopy is included in the surgical endoscopy. Do not report a code for diagnostic endoscopy when it is performed with surgical endoscopy.

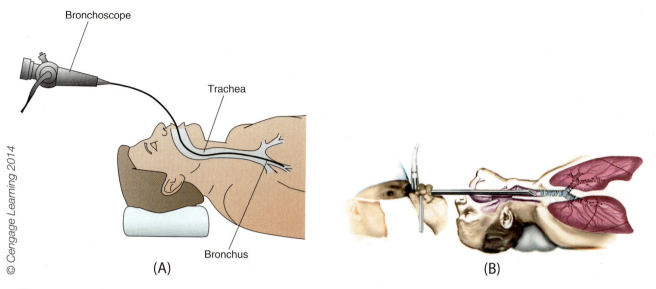

Figure 12-16 (A). Flexible bronchoscopy (B). Rigid bronchoscopy

Diagnostic endoscopy is often performed during an open surgical procedure to evaluate (or scout or investigate) the surgical field. Do not report a code for diagnostic endoscopy when it is performed with an open surgical procedure.

When a surgical endoscopic procedure fails and is converted to an open procedure, do not report a code for the surgical endoscopic procedure. Report only a code for the open procedure.

EXAMPLE: A patient presents with aspiration of a foreign body. A diagnostic bronchoscopy is performed to locate the foreign body, and a surgical bronchoscopy is performed to remove the foreign body. Report code 31635. (Do not report a code for the diagnostic bronchoscopy.)

Exercise 12.12 – Trachea and Bronchi

Instructions: Assign the CPT code(s) and appropriate modifier(s) to each statement.

1. Emergency transtracheal tracheostomy of 18-month-old child.

   _____

2. Bronchial brush biopsy via transglottic catheterization.

   _____

3. Flexible bronchoscopy to remove a piece of food inhaled into the left bronchus.

   _____

4. Bronchoscopy with bronchial alveolar lavage.

   _____

5. Bronchoscopy with brushings, biopsy, and removal of foreign body.

   _____

Lungs and Pleura

The Lungs and Pleura (Figure 12-17) heading contains codes for procedures performed on the lungs and **pleura** (membrane that envelops the lungs and lines the walls of the pleural cavity).

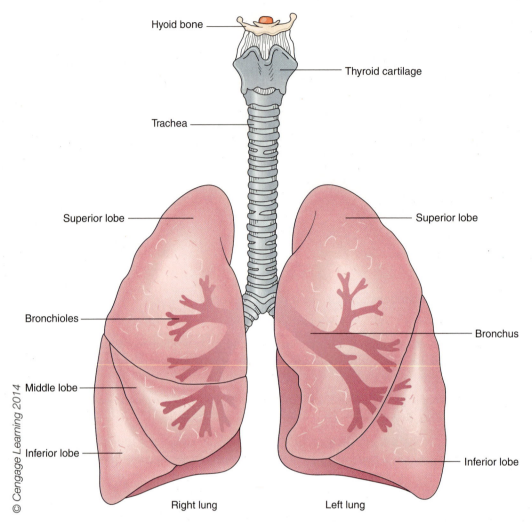

Figure 12-17 External view of lungs. Note three lobes in the right lung and two lobes in the left lung.

Excision

For **percutaneous needle biopsy**, a long needle is inserted through the skin and into other tissue (e.g., chest wall, lung, or mediastinum) to obtain tissue for diagnostic evaluation. Code 32400 is reported for "biopsy, pleura; percutaneous needle." When fine-needle aspiration is documented, report an appropriate code from the General subsection.

Removal

Thoracentesis (Figure 12-18A) is the surgical puncture of the chest wall with a needle to obtain fluid from the pleural cavity. It is performed to make a diagnostic evaluation or to drain excess fluid from a patient with severe **pleural effusion** (Figure 12-18B) (fluid in the pleural cavity prevents the lung from fully expanding, making it difficult for the patient to breathe).

Make sure you appropriately report codes for the following procedures, which may appear similar but are very different procedures:

- Percutaneous pleural biopsy involves inserting a long needle through skin into the chest wall to obtain pleural tissue (without direct visualization of the pleura).

- **Pneumocentesis** is the puncture of the pleural space with a transthoracic needle to drain *fluid* or to obtain material for diagnostic study.

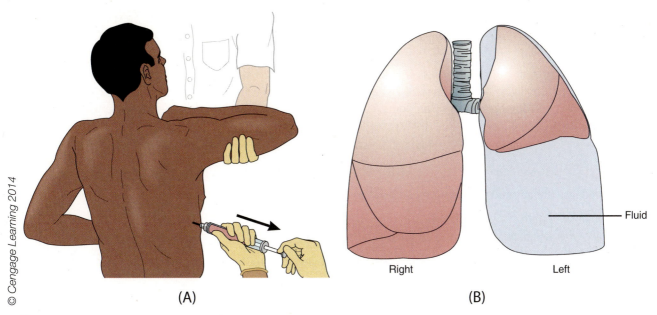

© Cengage Learning 2014

Figure 12-18 (A) Thoracentesis. (B) Lung with pleural effusion

A **total pneumonectomy** is removal of the entire lung, and a **lobectomy** is the removal of a single lobe of the lung. Each lobe contains multiple segments, and a **segmentectomy** is the removal of one segment of a lobe. A **wedge resection** is the removal of a portion of lung that is less than a segment. A wedge resection may be performed on any portion of a diseased lung (e.g., a limited resection involves excising a lesion and the margin of surrounding normal lung tissue).

According to CPT, a therapeutic wedge resection requires attention to margins and complete resection [of diseased tissue] even when a more extensive resection is performed during a later operative episode. During a wedge resection, when an intraoperative pathology consultation determines that a more extensive resection is required in the same anatomic location, the original wedge resection is coded as a diagnostic wedge resection. If intraoperative pathology consultation determines that a more extensive resection is *not* required, the original procedure is coded as a therapeutic wedge resection.

EXAMPLE: Code 32480 describes the removal of one of the three lobes in the right lung (right upper lobe, right middle lobe, or right lower lobe) or one of the two lobes in the left lung (left upper lobe or left lower lobe).

Endoscopy

A **thoracoscopy** is the visual examination of the pleural cavity and it provides an alternative to open lung or thoracotomy procedures to treat pleural disorders surgically. When an open lung procedure, a thoracotomy, or another open chest procedure immediately follows diagnostic thoracoscopy, report codes for both procedures (and sequence the open procedure first). When a surgical thoracoscopy is converted to an open procedure, report code(s) for the open lung procedure(s) only. Do not report a code for the surgical thoracoscopy procedure.

EXAMPLE: Patient presents with lower lateral chest wall pain and shortness of breath. Thoracoscopy is performed, and biopsy of lobulated mass reveals mesothelioma. Report code 32608.

Lung Transplantation

Lung transplants include the following distinct components, and a code is assigned to each by the physician who performs the component procedure:

- **Cadaver donor pneumonectomy**, which involves harvesting the allograft (graft such as lung tissue that is transplanted between genetically nonidentical individuals of the same species) and preserving the allograft with cold preservation solution and cold maintenance

- **Recipient lung allotransplantation**, which includes transplantation of a single or double lung allograft and care of the recipient

- **Backbench work** for lung transplantation, which involves preparing the cadaver donor lung allograft prior to lung transplantation and dissecting allograft from surrounding soft tissues to prepare the pulmonary venous/atrial cuff, pulmonary artery, and bronchus

  EXAMPLE: Patient with severe respiratory system complications due to cystic fibrosis underwent lung transplant procedure to remove diseased lungs and replace them with healthy lungs from a recently deceased donor. Transplant physician performed donor pneumonectomy including cold preservation from cadaver donor, backbench standard preparation of cadaver donor lung allografts, and double lung transplant with cardiopulmonary bypass. Report codes 32854, 32850-51, and 32856-51.

Surgical Collapse Therapy; Thoracoplasty

Surgical collapse therapy and thoracoplasty codes classify procedures performed to therapeutically collapse a patient's lung(s):

- *Extrapleural resection of ribs* is the removal of rib(s).

- *Thoracoplasty* is the resection of ribs to allow the chest wall to retract, reducing the size of the pleural space.

- *Pneumonolysis* is the division of tissues that attach the lung to the wall of the chest cavity.

- *Therapeutic pneumothorax* is the injection of air into the pleural space.

  EXAMPLE: A patient underwent extraperiosteal pneumonolysis. Report code 32940.

Other Procedures

When a total lung lavage is performed bilaterally, add modifier -50 to code 32997 (because the code description specifies "unilateral"). When bronchoscopic bronchial alveolar lavage is performed, report code 31624 under the Trachea and Bronchi heading.

  EXAMPLE: Patient underwent total lung lavage, left. Report code 32997-LT.

Exercise 12.13 – Lungs and Pleura

Instructions: Assign the CPT code(s) and appropriate modifier(s) to each statement.

1. Emergency department physician performed a tube thoracostomy for hemothorax, inserting a tube for drainage.

2. Total unilateral lung lavage.

3. Percutaneous needle biopsy of lung and fine-needle aspiration of lung.

4. Diagnostic thoracoscopy with lung biopsy (left side) and surgical thoracoscopy with segmental lobectomy (left side) (both procedures performed during same operative session).

5. Patient with severe respiratory system complications due to chronic obstructive pulmonary disease underwent unilateral lung transplant procedure to remove one diseased lung, on the right, and replace it with a healthy lung from a recently deceased donor. Donor lung also required repair of intrathoracic blood vessel. Transplant physician performed donor pneumonectomy including cold preservation from cadaver donor, backbench standard preparation of cadaver donor lung allografts, and single lung transplant without cardiopulmonary bypass.

Summary

CPT codes in the Musculoskeletal System subsection are reported for procedures on bones, cartilage, joints, ligaments, muscles, and tendons. The subsection is arranged from head to toe according to body area. The Musculoskeletal System subsection also classifies fracture management, casting and strapping, and endoscopy/arthroscopy. The CPT Respiratory System subsection is arranged from nose to lungs according to body area.

Internet Links

American Academy of Otolaryngology—Head and Neck Surgery (AAO-HNS): Go to *www.entnet.org*, and click on the Health Information link (located at the top of the website) for information about ENT diseases, disorders, and anatomic structures.

American Lung Association: *www.lungusa.org*

Musculoskeletal Radiology of Fractures: Go to *www.gentili.net*, and scroll down, then click on the Fracture Atlas link below "General".

National Institute of Arthritis and Musculoskeletal and Skin Diseases (NIAMS): *www.niams.nih.gov*

Physiology Education Research Consortium (PERC): Go to *www.physiologyeducation.org*, and click on "Educational Materials." Scroll down to the Software heading and select "Simulations in Physiology—The Respiratory System" (to complete a computer simulation).

YourLungHealth.org: *www.yourlunghealth.org*

Study Checklist

- ❏ Read this chapter and highlight key concepts.
- ❏ Create an index card for each key term.
- ❏ Access the chapter Internet links to learn more about concepts.
- ❏ Complete the chapter review, verifying answers with your instructor.
- ❏ Complete WebTutor assignments and take online quizzes.
- ❏ Complete Workbook chapter, verifying answers with your instructor.
- ❏ Go to *www.cengagebrain.com* to access StudyWARE™ and the Premium Website. Login instructions are located in the Preface and on the Printed Access Card.
- ❏ Form a study group with classmates to discuss chapter concepts in preparation for an exam.

Review

Multiple Choice

Instructions: Circle the most appropriate response.

1. Which is a type of open fracture treatment?
   - a. closed reduction
   - b. internal fixation
   - c. stabilization
   - d. traction

2. Which is performed to puncture a joint for fluid removal or medication injection?
   - a. arthrocentesis
   - b. arthrodesis
   - c. arthroscopy
   - d. artificial ankylosis

3. Which are included with osteotomy codes (22210–22226), which means that separate codes are not reported when these procedures are performed during the same operative session as the osteotomy?
   a. arthrocentesis, arthroscopy, artificial ankylosis
   b. corpectomy, discectomy, laminectomy
   c. grafting, reduction, stabilization
   d. skeletal fixation, stabilization, traction

4. Open carpal tunnel decompression surgery (for carpal tunnel syndrome) is classified in which CPT Surgery subsection and/or under which heading?
   a. Integumentary System
   b. Musculoskeletal System
   c. Nervous System
   d. Operating Microscope Section

5. The application of casts and strapping are reported when the cast (or splint) or strapping is an initial service performed _____ to stabilize or protect a fracture, a dislocation, or another injury and/or to provide comfort to a patient.
   a. during restorative treatment/procedure
   b. instead of placing a cast (or splint) or strap
   c. when a reduction or manipulation is completed
   d. without restorative treatment/procedure

6. Calcaneous ostectomy for removal of spurs, left foot. Which CPT code is assigned?
   a. 28111-LT
   b. 28116-LT
   c. 28118-LT
   d. 28119-LT

7. Unlisted maxillofacial prosthetic procedure. Which CPT code is assigned?
   a. 21089
   b. 21299
   c. 22899
   d. 23929

8. C3-C4 anterior discectomy performed by two primary surgeons. Which CPT codes are reported by Surgeon A?
   a. 22554, 22585-51
   b. 22554-62, 22585-51
   c. 22554-62
   d. 22554-62, 22585-62

9. Reconstruction of complete shoulder (rotator) cuff avulsion, chronic, right side. Which CPT code(s) are assigned?
   a. 23130-RT, 23420-RT
   b. 23130-RT, 23420-51-RT
   c. 23410-RT
   d. 23420-RT

10. Incision and drainage of deep abscess, right forearm. Which CPT code is assigned?
    a. 10060
    b. 24310-RT
    c. 25028-RT
    d. 25031-RT

11. When a physician performs surgical nasal/sinus endoscopy with partial ethmoidectomy (anterior) and septoplasty or submucous resection, report the:
    a. septoplasy code (30520).
    b. endoscopy code (31254).
    c. endoscopy code (31254) and the septoplasty code (30520).
    d. endoscopy code (31254) or the septoplasty code (30520).

12. Which is considered part of the ethmoid bone and, if removed during endoscopic polypectomy or endoscopic ethmoidectomy, is not coded and reported separately?
    a. frontal sinus
    b. maxillary sinus
    c. middle turbinate
    d. nasal vestibule

13. Which is the surgical fixation of arytenoidal cartilage and/or surrounding muscles?
    a. arytenoidectomy
    b. arytenoidopexy
    c. arytenoidostomy
    d. arytenoidotomy

14. Which procedure is performed to comb the mucous lining of the trachea or bronchus and uses a bronchial brush to collect cells?
    a. brushing
    b. cell washing
    c. tracheotomy
    d. bronchoscopy

15. Which component(s) of a lung transplant are reported as distinct code(s) by the physician who performs the component procedure(s)?
    a. cadaver donor pneumonectomy
    b. backbench work for lung transplantation
    c. recipient lung allotransplantation
    d. each of the above

16. Initial cautery to control posterior nasal hemorrhage. Which CPT code is assigned?
    a. 30901
    b. 30903
    c. 30905
    d. 30906

17. Surgical nasal endoscopy with repair of cerebrospinal fluid leak, sphenoid region, right side. Which CPT code is assigned?
    a. 31287-RT
    b. 31290-RT
    c. 31291-RT
    d. 31292-RT

18. A 3-year-old child undergoes direct laryngoscopy for aspiration of fluid. Which CPT code is assigned?
    a. 31515
    b. 31520
    c. 31520-63
    d. 31525

19. Catheterization with bronchial brush biopsy. Which CPT code is assigned?
    a. 31715
    b. 31717
    c. 31720
    d. 31725

20. Surgical thoracoscopy with excision of a pericardial cyst. Which CPT code is assigned?
    a. 32604
    b. 32658
    c. 32659
    d. 32661

Coding Cases

Instructions: Assign the CPT code(s) and appropriate modifier(s) to each case.

Musculoskeletal System

21. Patient sustained a stab wound to the neck during a domestic dispute and underwent wound exploration. The stab wound was extended; and examination of surrounding bones, connective tissue, muscles, and nerves revealed normal findings. No foreign bodies were found. The area was debrided and irrigated. Coagulation of minor subcutaneous and muscular blood vessels was achieved with electrocautery. The wound was cleaned and closed with 3-0 Vicryl.

_____

22. Patient underwent reconstruction of the entire forehead and supraorbital rims, requiring grafts, to correct a congenital skeletal deformity. After administration of general anesthesia, scalp and upper eyelid incisions were made to access the surgical site. The forehead bones were reshaped and repositioned, and bone allografts were inserted to augment the forehead and supraorbital rims. Incisions were closed after wires were inserted as fixation devices to maintain the proper shape of the facial bones.

_____

23. A 13-year-old male sustained a fractured right femur during a soccer game and underwent open treatment with insertion of two screws and two pins. After administration of general anesthesia, an incision was made over the fracture site and a metal rod was inserted through the bone's shaft to stabilize it. The rod was secured with screws, and the leg was placed in a cast.

_____

24. Patient underwent incision and drainage of bursa, right knee. Needle was inserted into bursa; and fluid was drained from the sac, which was located deep within the knee's soft tissue.

_____

25. Patient underwent knee replacement surgery one month ago. Today "manipulation of the left knee under general anesthesia" was performed to flex the knee joint and increase its range of motion.

_____

26. 2-year-old patient underwent reapplication of a long-leg cast to the left femur, which extended from the thigh to the toes. The patient sustained femur fracture four weeks ago when initial reduction was performed and application of long-leg cast was applied. Today that cast was removed and replaced with a long-leg cast due to the patient's age, to ensure optimal bone healing.

_____

27. Patient underwent open reduction of left tibia fracture four weeks ago. Today the orthopedic surgeon cut a hole in the patient's short-leg cast to check for incisional infection. No infection was noted.

_____

28. Patient underwent diagnostic arthroscopy of the left elbow due to unexplained pain. Surgeon inserted arthroscope into the left elbow joint to determine presence of disease or injury.

_____

29. Patient underwent removal of a metal sliver from the index finger, right hand. The surgeon made an incision between the first and second bones of the right index finger. Joint exploration revealed the presence of a metal sliver, which was removed.

_____

30. Patient underwent closed treatment of fractured tip of the right radius at distal end, which included application of a short-arm cast.

_____

Respiratory System

31. Patient underwent bilateral diagnostic nasal endoscopy. The physician inserted an endoscope into the left nostril to evaluate nasal structures. The right nostril was also examined.

_____

32. Patient underwent indirect endoscopy of the larynx with biopsy. The physician used a small, round mirror to examine the vocal cords, tongue, and top of the throat for signs of disease or injury. Biopsy of larynx was performed for evaluation and diagnosis.

_____

33. Patient presents with a six-month history of hoarseness. The physician performs a laryngoscopy. The patient is prepped in the usual fashion. A fiberoptic laryngoscope is passed; the vocal cords are examined under direct visualization. Slight swelling is noted. A biopsy sample is taken to be sent to pathology.

_____

34. Patient with a history of recurrent spontaneous left pneumothorax was prepped for a thoracoscopy and underwent parietal pleurectomy. An incision was made at the eighth intercostal space, and a thoracoscope was inserted to view patient's lungs. No evidence of disease was found in the lobes. Trocars were then placed, and the pleura was stripped away from the chest wall. A nice surface was accomplished. A chest tube was placed for drainage. The remaining incision was closed with mattress sutures of 4-0 nylon.

_____

35. A 45-year-old female nonsmoker has had a cough for the last 6 months. With the patient placed under intravenous sedation, a bronchoscope was passed in the patient's oral cavity. Primary structures of upper area visualized and found to be normal. The transbronchial area was examined. A biopsy sample was taken of the lobe. The patient had minimal blood loss. The bronchoscope was then removed, and the patient returned to the outpatient area in satisfactory condition.

_____

36. A patient with bilateral vocal cord paralysis presents for removal of arytenoid cartilage. This is being done to improve the patient's breathing. With the patient placed under general anesthesia, the laryngoscope with operating microscope is inserted into the oral cavity. The pharynx and larynx are examined under the microscope. After adequate visualization is established, the arytenoids cartilage is exposed by excision of the mucosa overlying it.

_____

37. A 50-year-old patient has difficulty breathing through left nostril. The patient has a deformity of the septum and presents for a submucous resection of the septum (SMR). After making an incision, the lining of the septum is detached. The patient's deviated portion of his septum is removed, and the cartilage portion above is scored. Nasal packing is placed.

_____

38. Patient suffers from anosmia. The patient consents to a diagnostic biopsy of intranasal cavity. This procedure is done under local anesthesia delivered to nasal tissue. A small amount of tissue is removed under direct visualization. Minimal bleeding is noted.

_____

39. A 2-year-old patient presents to the office with a marble in his nose, per the mother. Using nasal forceps, the marble is removed.

_____

40. A 5-year-old patient had a cleft lip repair done at 3 months of age. Now the patient has a nasal deformity that requires repair. The physician makes intranasal incisions and pulls back skin from nasal bone tip. The bone is shaved and lengthened at the tip. The area is irrigated, and nasal packing is placed. The patient has little blood loss.

_____

CPT Surgery III

Chapter Outline

Cardiovascular System Subsection

Hemic and Lymphatic Systems Subsection

Chapter Objectives

At the conclusion of this chapter, the student should be able to:

- Define key terms.
- Explain the organization, format, and content of the CPT Surgery Cardiovascular System and Hemic and Lymphatic Systems subsections.
- Interpret CPT surgery coding notes for the Cardiovascular System and Hemic and Lymphatic Systems subsections.
- Assign CPT surgery codes from the Cardiovascular System and Hemic and Lymphatic Systems subsections.
- Add CPT and/or HCPCS level II modifiers to codes, as appropriate.

Key Terms

adenoids

adjuvant techniques

aneurysm

angiogenesis

angioscopy

aortic anomaly

aortic sinus

arteriovenous fistula

blood

bone marrow

bone marrow aspiration

bone marrow biopsy

cadaver donor cardiectomy with or without pneumonectomy

cancer staging

cardiac ablation

cardiac tumor

cardiac valve

cardiopulmonary bypass

chyle

commissurotomy

composite graft

coronary artery bypass graft (CABG)

coronary endarterectomy

cross-over vein graft

cutdown

dual chamber

electrophysiology

embolectomy

embolus

en bloc

endocardium

first-order vessels

heart murmur

hemic system

lymph

lymph nodes

lymphatic system

Maze procedure

modified Maze procedure

myocardium

nonselective vascular catheterization

open transluminal angioplasty

open transluminal atherectomy

pacemaker

pacing cardioverter-defibrillator (PCD)

patency

percutaneous myocardial revascularization (PMR)

percutaneous transluminal angioplasty (PTA)

percutaneous transluminal atherectomy

percutaneous transmyocardial laser revascularization (PTMR)

pericardial sac

pericardiectomy

pericardiocentesis

pericardiotomy

pericardium

peripherally

recipient heart with or without lung allotransplantation

reconstruction of the vena cava

saphenopopliteal vein anastomosis

second-order vessels

selective vascular catheterization

septal defects

septum

shunting procedure

single chamber

sinus of Valsalva

spleen

splenoportography

stab phlebectomy

stem cells

stented valve

stentless valve

sympathectomy

tetralogy of Fallot

therapeutic apheresis

third-order vessels

thrombectomy

thromboendarterectomy

thymus

tonsils

transluminal angioplasty

transluminal atherectomy

transmyocardial revascularization (TMR)

transposition of great vessels

truncus arteriosus

tube pericardiostomy

tunneled

valvular atresia

valvular heart disease

valvular prolapse

valvular regurgitation

valvular stenosis

valvuloplasty

valvulotomy

vascular family

venous anomaly

venous valve transposition

ventricular assist device (VAD)

visceral arteries

Introduction

The Cardiovascular System subsection classifies procedures performed on the heart and pericardium, valves (e.g., mitral and semilunar), and peripheral vascular vessels (e.g., arteries, veins, and capillaries). The Hemic and Lymphatic Systems subsection classifies procedures performed on the spleen, lymph nodes, and lymphatic channels. CPT guidelines that apply to the subsections are located at the beginning of the Surgery section. Unique coding instructions for the cardiovascular system and hemic and lymphatic system are located in notes below headings or codes.

Coding Tip:

Notes located beneath headings and/or subheadings apply to all codes in the heading or subheading. Parenthetical notes that are located below a specific code apply to that code only unless the note indicates otherwise.

Cardiovascular System Subsection

Cardiovascular System subsection codes are arranged anatomically and then according to procedure performed. The Cardiovascular System subsection includes the following headings:

- Heart and Pericardium

- Arteries and Veins

Cardiovascular System Notes

Notes located at the beginning of the Cardiovascular System subsection provide instruction about assigning codes for *selective vascular catheterization*. When performed as part of cardiovascular (and radiology) procedures, codes for *selective vascular catheterization* (e.g., 36011) are reported separately.

In addition, parenthetical notes are located just above the Heart and Pericardium heading. They serve as reminders to review the Radiology and/or Medicine sections of CPT to locate additional codes associated with

Table 13-1 CPT Surgery Cardiovascular System Subsection Headings with Notes to Report Radiology and/or Medicine Codes

Surgery Subsection and Heading	Radiology	Medicine
Heart and Pericardium		
Patient-Activated Event Recorder		X
Cardiac Valves		X
Shunting Procedures		X
Arteries and Veins		
Endovascular Repair of Abdominal Aortic Aneurysm	X	
Endovascular Repair of Iliac Aneurysm	X	
Transluminal Angioplasty	X	
Vascular Injection Procedures	X	X
Portal Decompression Procedures	X	
Transcatheter Procedures	X	
Endovascular Revascularization	X	
Intravascular Ultrasound Services	X	

© Cengage Learning 2014

certain cardiovascular system procedures (Table 13-1). (Notes are also located throughout the Cardiovascular System subsection as a reminder to report additional surgery codes with some procedures.)

Coding Tip:

During cardiovascular procedures, **cardiopulmonary bypass** is often required to divert blood from the heart to the aorta, using a pump oxygenator. Because some procedures can be performed without cardiopulmonary bypass, make sure you review the operative report to determine whether to assign the cardiopulmonary bypass code for the procedure performed.

EXAMPLE: Patient underwent repair of cardiac wound with cardiopulmonary bypass. Report code 33305.

Selective Vascular Catheterization

When reporting codes for selective vascular catheterization, knowledge of the flow of blood (Figure 13-1) throughout the body's circulatory system is crucial. (In fact, it's a good idea to reference an anatomy and physiology textbook such as Delmar's *Body Structures & Functions* when assigning codes to procedures classified in the Cardiovascular System subsection.) Selective vascular catheterization procedures are classified as "vascular injection procedures" (36000–36680), and require separate coding of the following:

- Diagnostic procedure (e.g., carotid angiogram) and/or therapeutic procedure (e.g., balloon dilation via catheter)

- Vascular access (e.g., selective vascular catheterization)

Separate codes are not reported for the administration of local anesthesia, introduction of the needle or catheter, or *injection* of contrast material. (The supply of contrast media *is* assigned a HCPCS level II code.) In addition, CPT codes are assigned to the point of catheter placement (not guidewire insertion); catheters

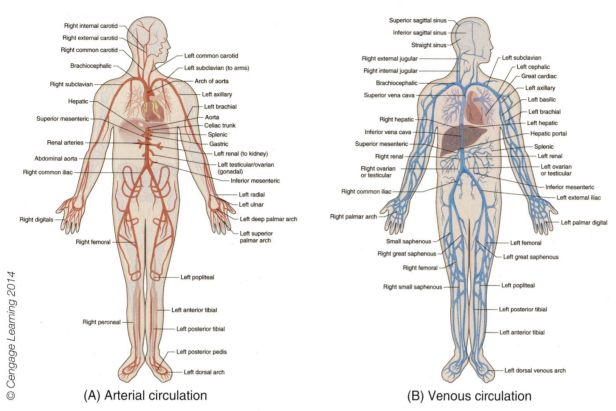

Figure 13-1 Circulatory system (A) Arterial circulation (B) Venous circulation

© Cengage Learning 2014

(or sheats) are conduits through which images are recorded and vascular procedures performed. A guidewire might be inserted beyond placement of the catheter, and no images are taken or procedures are performed at the insertion point of the guidewire; thus, code to the point of catheter placement (not guidewire insertion) (Figure 13-2).

Selective vascular catheterization is the insertion and manipulation or guidance of a catheter (that is attached to a guidewire) into the branches of the arterial system (other than the aorta or the vessel punctured) for the purpose of performing diagnostic or therapeutic procedures. Selective vascular catheterization is usually performed under fluoroscopic (moving X-ray) guidance. The code reported for selective vascular catheterization includes introduction of the catheter into the punctured vessel and guidance through all lesser- (or first-) order vessels (to get to the intended vessel that undergoes the diagnostic or therapeutic procedure). This means that codes are *not* reported for **nonselective vascular catheterization**, which involves introducing the catheter directly into a vessel without further advancement past the punctured vessel or introduction of a catheter into any portion of the aorta or vena cava from any approach (e.g., axillary, brachial, femoral, jugular).

Once the catheter reaches its intended vessel, assign an appropriate code for such selective vascular catheterization. When additional vessels are catheterized for the purpose of performing diagnostic and/or therapeutic procedures, assign appropriate codes for selective vascular catheterization of such second- and third- (and beyond) order vessels. First-, second-, and third- (and beyond) order vessel catheterization is discussed next.

> **Coding Tip:**
>
> When fluoroscopic guidance is provided during selective vascular catheterization, make sure you assign the appropriate supervision and interpretation code from the Radiology section (codes 75600–75978).

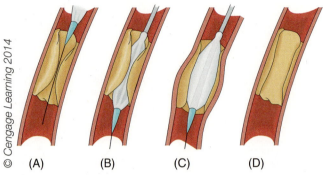

Figure 13-2 (A) Insertion of guidewire into and beyond plaque formation in artery (B) Insertion of catheter with attached balloon through plaque formation in artery (C) Expansion of balloon to compress plaque against arterial walls and open the arterial lumen (D) Compressed plaque, creating wider lumen in artery

A **vascular family** (Figure 13-3) (CPT Appendix L) is a group of vessels that is accessed by the same first order vessel, and it is supplied by the same primary branch from the aorta. A vascular family can be compared to a tree with branches. The trunk is the aorta, which contains large and small branches. (Think of the aorta as a zero-order vessel because it is a common starting point for catheterization. The femoral artery, as a starting point for catheterization, is an example of another zero-order vessel.) From the starting point, vessels branch outward (similar to a network of streets from a highway) into the following:

- First-order vessels

- Second-order vessels

- Third-order vessels

First-order vessels extend as primary arterial branches from the aorta (e.g., left common carotid artery in the neck and inferior mesenteric artery or common iliac artery in the abdomen). When an *initial* second- or third-order arterial catheterization is performed within a vascular family, report just one code from 36216–36217 or 36246–36247. **Second-order vessels** branch from first-order vessels, and **third-order vessels** branch from second-order vessels. (Refer to Figure 13-3 for an illustration of first-, second-, and third-order vessels of a vascular family.)

EXAMPLE: SELECTIVE VASCULAR CATHETERIZATION INTO FIRST-ORDER VESSELS: After being assaulted, a patient presented to the emergency department, complaining of severe upper left flank pain. Patient underwent left renal angiogram. This required insertion of a catheter into the right femoral artery. The catheter was advanced to the right external iliac and common iliac arteries and aorta and into left renal artery. Contrast media was injected for visualization of the left renal artery upon X-ray. Report code 36251. The right femoral, right external iliac, and right common iliac arteries underwent nonselective catheterization because they were used to access the left renal artery; and no diagnostic or therapeutic procedure was performed on them. (Thus, do not assign catheter placement codes for accessing the right femoral, right external iliac, or right common iliac arteries.)

Selective vascular catheterization was achieved by making a small incision in the skin and performing an arterial puncture into the left femoral artery (groin region). A needle containing a stylet (inner wire) was inserted through the skin into the left femoral artery. The stylet was removed and replaced with a guidewire. Under fluoroscopy, the guidewire was advanced through the external iliac artery and common iliac artery and then into the aorta. From the abdominal aorta, the guidewire was advanced into the left renal artery. The needle was removed, and a catheter was inserted over the length of the guidewire

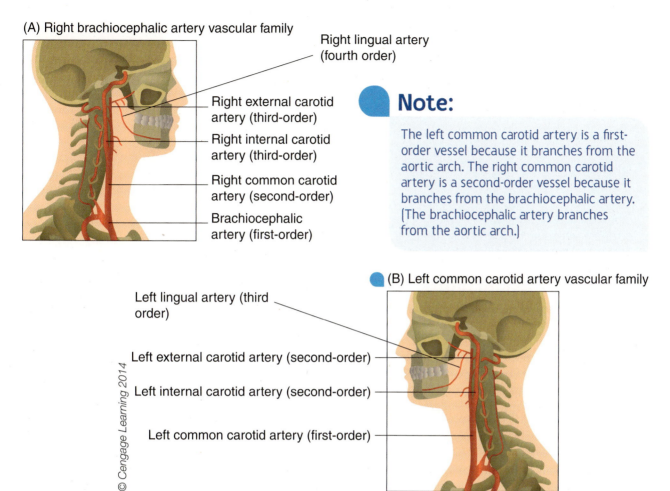

(A) Right brachiocephalic artery vascular family

Right lingual artery
(fourth order)

Right external carotid
artery (third-order)

Right internal carotid
artery (third-order)

Right common carotid
artery (second-order)

Brachiocephalic
artery (first-order)

Note:

The left common carotid artery is a first-order vessel because it branches from the aortic arch. The right common carotid artery is a second-order vessel because it branches from the brachiocephalic artery. (The brachiocephalic artery branches from the aortic arch.)

(B) Left common carotid artery vascular family

Left lingual artery (third order)

Left external carotid artery (second-order)

Left internal carotid artery (second-order)

Left common carotid artery (first-order)

© Cengage Learning 2014

Figure 13-3 Artery vascular families (A) First-, second-, third-, and fourth-order vessels in the right brachiocephalic artery vascular family (B) First-, second-, and third-order vessels in the left common carotid artery vascular family

until it reached the renal artery. The guidewire was removed, and the catheter was left in place. Under fluoroscopic guidance, contrast media was injected manually with a syringe or with an automatic injector connected to the catheter. (An automatic injector propels a large volume of dye quickly to the angiogram site.) X-rays were taken, and the catheter was slowly and carefully removed. Pressure was applied to the insertion site (to facilitate clotting and to allow the arterial puncture to reseal), and a pressure bandage was applied.

Review the operative report to determine which artery (or arteries) underwent diagnostic or therapeutic procedures after having a catheter inserted. Although multiple arteries might be involved in a catheter being threaded from the insertion point to the intended artery, only one code is reported if just one artery undergoes diagnostic or therapeutic procedures.

EXAMPLE: A catheter was introduced into the brachiocephalic artery (first-order) and then inserted into the right common carotid artery (second-order) and the right internal carotid artery (third-order) to the cerebral artery (fourth-order), where contrast media was injected to perform a cerebral angiography. In addition to the cerebral angiography code, report just one selective vascular catheterization code for the cerebral artery. The brachiocephalic, right common carotid, and right internal carotid arteries were used to access the (fourth-order) cerebral artery. No diagnostic or therapeutic procedures were performed on them. Therefore, do not assign selective vascular catheterization codes for catheterization of the brachiocephalic, right common carotid, or right internal carotid arteries.

The note at the beginning of the Cardiovascular System subsection also provides instruction to report add-on code 36218 or 36248 (in addition to the primary code 36215–36217 or 36245–36247) when *additional*:

- Selective arterial catheterization of second- and/or third-order vessels is achieved using a single first-order artery.

- First-, second-, or third-order vessels are accessed during selective arterial catheterization, and the vascular families supplied by a first-order vessel are from a *different* family of arteries.

  EXAMPLE: A catheter was introduced into the left common carotid artery (first-order) and inserted into the left internal carotid artery (second-order). Contrast media was injected and carotid arteriogram performed. The catheter was further advanced into the left cerebral artery (third-order), additional contrast media was injected, and cerebral angiogram was performed. In addition to radiology codes for the carotid arteriogram and cerebral angiogram, report a selective vascular catheterization code for the (second-order) left internal carotid artery and add-on code 36218 for the selective vascular catheterization of the (third-order) cerebral artery. The left common carotid artery was used to access the other two arteries; therefore, a selective vascular catheterization code is *not* assigned.

Heart and Pericardium

Codes 33010–33999 are reported for procedures performed on the heart and pericardium.

Pericardium

The **pericardium**, or **pericardial sac**, is the membrane that surrounds the heart. CPT codes 33010 and 33011 are reported for **pericardiocentesis**, which is the insertion of a needle to withdraw fluid from the pericardium. Radiologic guidance is often performed with pericardiocentesis, so make sure you report code 76930 as an additional service.

A **tube pericardiostomy** (code 33015) is the insertion of a tube for drainage or specimen collection. A **pericardiotomy** (code 33020) requires thoracotomy as incision for pericardial drainage, fluid collection, or foreign body removal.

Pericardiectomy is the removal of part of the pericardium (to treat chronic pericarditis). Report code 33031 when cardiopulmonary bypass is documented in the operative report.

  EXAMPLE: Patient underwent pericardiotomy for removal of blood clot. Report code 33020.

Coding Tip:

Do not report modifier -50 with selective arterial catheterization codes (36215–36248). When multiple selective arterial catheterization procedures of separate and distinct vascular families are performed during the same operative session, report modifier -59 and/or enter the appropriate number of units in Block 24F of the CMS-1500 claim or Form Locator 46 of the UB-04.

  EXAMPLE: Selective arterial catheterization of the thoracic artery and the brachiocephalic artery: Report codes 36215 and 36215-59 or code 36215 and the number of units on the CMS-1500 or UB-04 insurance claim (Figure 13-4).

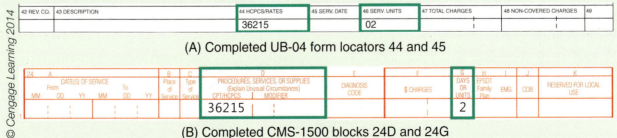

Figure 13-4 Reporting selective arterial catheterization codes on CMS-1500 and UB-04 claims (A) Completed form locators 44 and 45 on the UB-04 claim (B) Completed blocks 24D and 24G of the CMS-1500 claim

Coding Tip:

Report a code from 32658–32661 (instead of a code from the cardiovascular subsection) when surgical thoracoscopy is performed to:

- Remove a clot or foreign body from the pericardial sac.
- Create a pericardial window or partial resection of pericardial sac for drainage.
- Carry out a total pericardiectomy.
- Excise a pericardial cyst, tumor, or mass.

Cardiac Tumor

A **cardiac tumor** is a growth that develops in the heart's **endocardium** (inner lining), **myocardium** (muscle layer), or pericardium. The majority of cardiac tumors are benign, although a percentage are malignant. Methods for diagnosing cardiac tumors include complete history and physical examination and diagnostic procedures such as echocardiogram, electrocardiogram, computed tomography (CT scan), magnetic resonance imaging (MRI), chest X-ray, and coronary arteriogram or angiogram.

Benign cardiac tumors include myxoma, rhabdomyoma, and other rare tumors (e.g., fibroma, hemangioma, lipoma, lymphangioma, neurofibroma, and papillary fibroelastoma). Malignant cardiac tumors include cardiac sarcoma, fibrosarcoma, liposarcoma, and rhabdomyosarcoma. Surgical removal of a cardiac tumor is indicated if it causes an arrhythmia or obstructs blood flow through the heart. When a cardiac tumor cannot be removed, a heart transplant may be required.

EXAMPLE: Patient underwent complete resection of cardiac liposarcoma with cardiopulmonary bypass. Report code 33120.

Coding Tip:

When the scheduled resection of an external cardiac tumor requires cardiopulmonary bypass because a significant portion of the heart or a significant number of major vessels must be removed to ensure adequate tumor margins, the procedure becomes an excision of an intracardiac tumor and code 33120 is reported.

Transmyocardial Revascularization (TMR)

Transmyocardial revascularization (TMR) uses a high-powered laser to create small channels in the heart muscle to increase blood supply to the myocardium. The procedure also promotes **angiogenesis** (growth of new capillaries) as a blood supply to the heart muscle. TMR is performed to treat severe angina (in patients who are not candidates for coronary artery bypass graft (CABG) or angioplasty surgery), and the procedure may be performed with or without cardiopulmonary bypass. (TMR is usually performed with cardiopulmonary bypass.)

EXAMPLE: Patient underwent TMR, by thoracotomy. Report code 33140.

Coding Tip:

A variation of the TMR procedure is called **percutaneous myocardial revascularization (PMR)**, or **percutaneous transmyocardial laser revascularization (PTMR)**, during which a catheter with the laser inside is inserted through an artery (e.g., from femoral artery to external iliac artery to common iliac artery to aorta) into the left ventricle of the heart. The laser is used to create channels, which do not penetrate the entire heart muscle, as with the TMR. Because there is no specific CPT code, report unlisted code 33999 (and submit a copy of the operative report to the third-party payer).

Internal
jugular vein

Subclavian vein

Artificial pacemaker

External
jugular vein

Incision made through
skin layers to create
pocket into which
artificial pacemaker
is inserted

© Cengage Learning 2014

Figure 13-5 An artificial pacemaker is implanted under the skin

Pacemaker or Pacing Cardioverter-Defibrillator

A **pacemaker** (Figure 13-5) regulates the patient's heartbeat to prevent arrhythmias (e.g., atrial fibrillation and bradycardia) and includes a pulse generator (battery and electronic device) and electrodes (leads). A **pacing cardioverter-defibrillator (PCD)** (Figure 13-6) is similar to a pacemaker in that it includes a pulse generator and electrodes, but it uses a combination of antitachycardia pacing and low-energy cardioversion or defibrillating shocks to regulate the patient's heartbeat and prevent arrhythmias (e.g., ventricular fibrillation and ventricular tachycardia).

Pulse generators for pacemakers and PCDs are implanted internally under the skin (permanent), or they are attached externally (temporary). The PCD pulse generator is often inserted in a "pocket" below the skin in the infraclavicular region or abdomen. Electrodes are inserted through a vein or placed on the surface of the heart. The two types of pacemakers and PCDs are:

> **Coding Tip:**
>
> When an additional electrode is inserted into the left ventricle during a single-or dual-chamber procedure, report code 33224–33225 (in addition to the pacemaker or pacing cardioverter-defibrillator code). Add modifier -51 to code 33224. Do not add modifier -51 to add-on code 33225.

- **Single chamber**: Contains a single electrode that is positioned in the heart's right atrium *or* right ventricle.

- **Dual chamber**: Contain two electrodes; one is placed in the right atrium, and the other is placed in the right ventricle.

Before assigning the CPT code(s) for pacemaker or PCD insertions, determine the following:

- What type of pacemaker device or system is used (e.g., single or dual chamber)

- What surgical approach is used for electrode placement

  - *Epicardial approach:* Sternotomy or thoracotomy is performed or subcostal or xiphoid incision is made and pulse generator is inserted in a "pocket" created under the skin in the upper chest; electrodes are inserted through the incision into a vein and threaded to the heart under fluoroscopic guidance; one end of the electrode is attached to the heart muscle and the other end is attached to the pulse generator.

  - *Endocardial approach (or transvenous approach):* Cephalic vein cutdown or percutaneous subclavian vein puncture is performed to access the venous system, through which one end of the electrode is attached to the heart muscle; the other end is attached to the pulse generator, which is placed in a "pocket" created under skin in the abdomen.

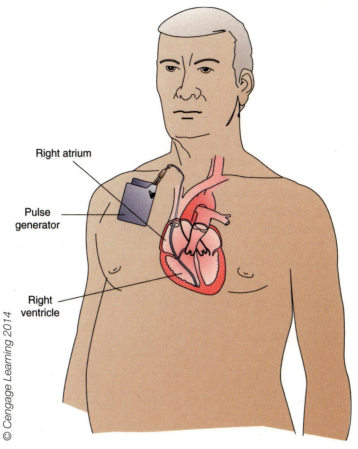

Figure 13-6 Implantable pacing cardioverter-defibrillator (PCD)

© Cengage Learning 2014

- Whether insertion is an initial, repair, replacement, or upgrade procedure

- Whether the procedure involves the entire pacemaker system or just a component (e.g., electrode)

- Whether fluoroscopic guidance was used

Coding Tip:

- A table of transvenous procedures contains codes that are reported for pacemakers and implantable cardioverter-defibrillator systems, which helps clarify code assignment.

- When PCD electrodes are removed, a transvenous extraction (code 33244) may be attempted; however, if unsuccessful, a thoracotomy may be required to remove the electrodes (code 33243).

- When a pacemaker or PCD "battery" is changed, it is actually the pulse generator that is changed. Replacement of a pulse generator is reported with two codes: a code for removal of the pulse generator and a code for insertion of a new pulse generator.

- When pacemaker or PCD electrodes are replaced, report appropriate code(s) from 33206–33208, 33210–33213, 33221, or 33224. Do not report a separate pacemaker removal code in addition to a replacement code, which would be considered overcoding.

EXAMPLE 1: Patient underwent subcutaneous insertion of permanent dual chamber pacemaker pulse generator with transvenous placement of existing electrodes in the right atrium and right ventricle. Procedure included fluoroscopic guidance. Report code 33213.

EXAMPLE 2: Patient underwent replacement of a single-chamber pacemaker pulse generator. The existing pocket was reopened, and the pulse generator was disconnected from its single lead and removed. The new pulse generator was inserted into the existing pocket and connected to the single existing lead. The incision was closed with sutures. Report code 33227.

EXAMPLE 3: Single-chamber pacemaker system was replaced with dual-chamber system, including insertion of new pulse generator and new electrodes. Report code 33214. (Do not report a code for removal of the existing pacemaker system, because it is included in code 33214.)

 EXAMPLE 4: Thirty days after initial insertion of transvenous pacemaker, pacemaker electrode was repositioned. Incision is made into the existing pocket; pulse generator and electrode are removed and tested to ensure that they are not defective. Because the electrode is not defective, the generator is replaced in the pocket. The electrode is reattached to the generator, placed in a new position (repositioned) in the right atrium, and retested. The incision is closed with sutures. Report code 33215.

EXAMPLE 5: Single transvenous electrode was repaired for a single-chamber pacemaker. Incision is made into the existing pocket, and the electrode is disconnected from the pulse generator. After repair, the electrode is reattached to the generator and the incision is closed with sutures. Report code 33218.

EXAMPLE 6: Previously implanted pacing cardioverter-defibrillator was repositioned. Report code 33215.

Electrophysiologic Operative Procedures

Electrophysiology is the study of heart arrhythmias and Electrophysiologic (EP) procedures analyze heart rhythm abnormalities and include operative ablation or operative incisions and reconstruction of the atria to correct abnormal pathways. The electrophysiology procedure is invasive, similar to a cardiac catheterization, in that electrode catheters are introduced into the right side of the heart from the femoral, brachial, or jugular vein. The catheters positioned in the heart are used to measure and record cardiac rhythm.

> **Note:**
>
> When electronic analysis of an internal pacemaker system is performed, report a code from 93279–93299 in the Medicine section. The code is reported for an encounter after the insertion procedure to determine whether the pacemaker or pacing cardioverter-defibrillator is functioning properly and/or has to be reprogrammed.

> **Note:**
>
> When the physician performs an "operative" cardiac ablation (also called a Maze procedure), a code is assigned from the CPT Surgery section of CPT (e.g., 33254). Cardiac ablation is sometimes called "cardiac catheter ablation;" however, that procedure is assigned a code from the CPT Medicine section (93650–93652).

- Operative **cardiac ablation** (**modified Maze procedure**) stops atrial or ventricular fibrillation by using radiofrequency waves (modified electrical energy) to create small scars on the heart's surface. Impulses are redirected and follow a normal electrical pathway through the heart.

- The **Maze procedure** stops atrial fibrillation or atrial flutter by using incisions in heart tissue to stop abnormal heart rhythm.

Both types of EP procedures require thoracotomy to access the heart, and cardiopulmonary bypass may or may not be used.

EXAMPLE: Patient underwent operative ablation of ventricular arrhythmogenic focus with cardiopulmonary bypass. Thoracotomy was used to access the heart. Report code 33261.

Patient-Activated Event Recorder

Cardiac event recorders document the heart's rhythms during transient (infrequent or recurrent) cardiac symptoms (e.g., recurrent syncope). The procedure for inserting and removing an event recorder is similar to that for implanting or removing a pacemaker pulse generator.

Coding Tip:

- Initial implantation of patient-activated event recorders includes programming. When subsequent electronic analysis and/or reprogramming are required, report codes 93279–93299 from the Medicine section.
- Holter monitor and external event recording are reported with codes 93268–93272 from the Medicine section.

EXAMPLE: Patient underwent thoracotomy and implantation of patient-activated cardiac event recorder with programming. Report code 33282.

Heart (Including Valves) and Great Vessels

CPT codes 33300–33335 describe repairs to injuries of the heart and/or great vessels (e.g., stab wounds and gunshot wounds). Cardiopulmonary bypass may or may not be required during the repair procedure; make sure you report the appropriate code.

EXAMPLE: Patient underwent repair of cardiac stab wound, with cardiopulmonary bypass. Separate incision was made to remove atrial thrombus. Report codes 33305 and 33315-59.

Cardiac Valves and Other Valvular Procedures

Cardiac valves are flaps of tissue that keep blood flowing in one direction to allow for the efficient one-way flow of blood through the heart's chambers. **Valvular heart disease** is the abnormality or dysfunction of one or more of the heart's four valves (aortic, mitral, pulmonary, and tricuspid):

- **Valvular atresia**: Valve fails to develop properly and is completely closed at birth.
- **Valvular prolapse**: Two valvular flaps do not close properly.
- **Valvular regurgitation**: Backflow of blood due to valvular prolapse.
- **Valvular stenosis**: Narrowing of one or more cardiac valves.

When coding procedures performed on cardiac valves, first determine the valve involved:

- Aortic
- Mitral
- Tricuspid
- Pulmonary

Then determine the type of procedure performed:

- **Valvuloplasty**: Open-heart surgery during which the surgeon removes the damaged valve and replaces it with a prosthetic, homograft or allograft, stented, or stentless valve. (Figure 13-7)

Coding Tip:

To report removal of a thrombus (33310–33315) in addition to codes for other cardiac procedures performed during the same operative session, a separate incision into the heart is required (to remove the atrial or ventricular thrombus). Add modifier -59 to code 33315 when it is reported for "removal of a thrombus with coronary bypass" in addition to codes for other cardiac procedures.

Coding Tip:

When nonsurgical, catheter-based, percutaneous balloon valvuloplasty is performed, report code(s) 92986–92990.

- **Valvulotomy**: Open-heart surgery in which an incision is made into a valve to repair valvular damage; includes **commissurotomy**, in which narrowed valve leaflets are widened by carefully opening the fused leaflets with a scalpel.

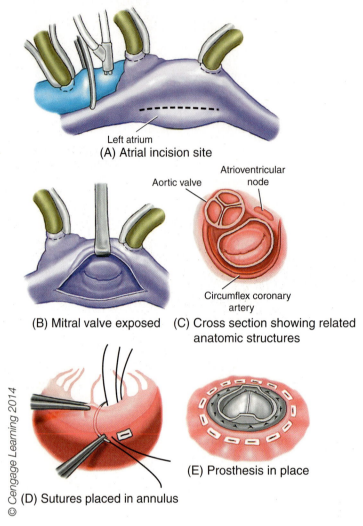

Left atrium
(A) Atrial incision site

Aortic valve

Atrioventricular node

(B) Mitral valve exposed

Circumflex coronary artery

(C) Cross section showing related anatomic structures

© Cengage Learning 2014

(D) Sutures placed in annulus

(E) Prosthesis in place

Figure 13-7 Mitral valve replacement: (A) Atrial incision site; (B) Mitral valve exposed; (C) Cross section showing related anatomical structures; (D) Sutures placed in annulus; (E) Prosthesis in place.

Coding Tip:

- When multiple valve procedures are performed during the same operative session, add modifier -51 to the second (and subsequent) valve procedure code(s).
- Do not add modifier -63 to codes 33401–33403.
- Codes 33401–33403 include aortic valve valvotomy or commissurotomy.
- When a valve requires insertion of a prosthetic ring, report codes 33426–33427.

Code 33405 describes replacement of the aortic valve with a prosthetic valve, with cardiopulmonary bypass. It is reported for procedures performed on valves *other than* homograft (human donor) or stentless (does not contain any framework) valves. (Code 33410 is reported when a stentless tissue valve is used to replace an aortic valve.) When an allograft (or a homograft) is used in aortic valve replacement, report code 33406.

Note:

A **stented valve** includes framework on which the replacement valve is mounted to provide support for the valve's leaflets. A **stentless valve** is often an actual heart valve obtained from either a human donor (homograft) or a pig, and it does not contain framework. Stentless valves are preferred because they are less obstructive and have improved long-term performance.

EXAMPLE 1: Patient underwent aortic valvuloplasty with cardiopulmonary bypass. Report code 33400.

EXAMPLE 2: Patient underwent right ventricular resection for infundibular stenosis, with commissurotomy. Report code 33476.

Coronary Artery Anomalies

An **arteriovenous fistula** is an abnormal passageway between an artery and a vein that allows blood to flow directly into a vein. It can occur as a congenital defect or as the result of trauma. (A fistula can also be surgically created to provide a site for vascular access.) An arteriovenous fistula can occur anywhere in the body, but it most often occurs in the legs or arms. The fistula might eventually develop into an **aneurysm** (bulge in an artery that can weaken the arterial wall and eventually burst, resulting in hemorrhage). For example, a coronary arteriovenous fistula (or coronary artery fistula) is a congenital fistula that is often located between the right coronary artery and the right heart.

> **EXAMPLE:** Patient underwent a Takeuchi procedure, which involved constructing an intrapulmonary artery tunnel. Report code 33505.

Endoscopy

CPT code 33508 is an add-on code that is reported when an endoscopic approach is used to harvest veins for coronary artery bypass procedures. Report code 33508 in addition to codes 33510–33523.

> **EXAMPLE:** Patient underwent coronary artery bypass graft (CABG) procedure, single coronary venous graft, with endoscopic harvesting of saphenous vein. Report codes 33510 and 33508.

Coronary Artery Bypass Graft (CABG) Procedures

Codes 33510–33545 describe coronary artery bypass graft (CABG) procedures, which are coded according to type of graft:

- Venous grafting (33510–33516)
- Combined arterial-venous grafting (33517–33530) (add-on codes)
- Arterial grafting (33533–33545)

Coronary artery bypass graft (CABG) (pronounced "cabbage") (Figure 13-8) is a procedure performed to improve the flow of blood to the heart. A blood vessel (called a graft) is removed from the arm, leg, or chest and anastomosed to bypass (detour) the blood flow around a narrowed or blocked coronary artery. (The surgery relieves angina symptoms, improves the patient's ability to exercise, and reduces the patient's risk of a heart attack.) Correctly reporting CABG requires careful review of the operative report to determine the number and type of grafts performed.

Coding Tip:

- Codes 33500–33507 include endarterectomy or angioplasty when performed during the same operative session.
- Do not add modifier -63 to codes 33502–33503 or 33505–33506.

Coding Tip:

When an open approach is used to harvest an upper extremity vein, report code 35500 (instead of code 33508).

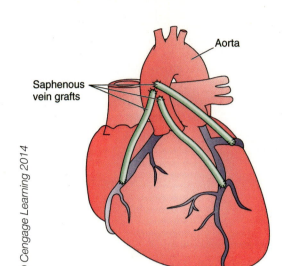

Figure 13-8 Coronary artery bypass graft (CABG) using saphenous vein grafts

Codes 33510–33516 are used to report CABG procedures using venous grafts only, and they are *not* reported when CABG procedures use a combination of arterial and venous grafts during the same procedure. Codes 33517–33530 are reported for combined arterial-venous grafts, and they are always reported in addition to an arterial graft codes (33533–33536).

EXAMPLE: Patient underwent CABG procedure for arteriosclerotic heart disease. A single arterial graft was performed. The sternum was opened, the heart was stopped and cooled, and the patient was connected to cardiopulmonary bypass. A long piece of the mammary artery was harvested, and one end was attached to the ascending aorta. The other end of the graft was attached to the circumflex coronary artery, just below the blocked area. Report code 33533-LC.

Coding Tip:

- CPT code 33530 is reported for repeat CABG or valve procedures that are performed more than one month after the original surgical procedure. Code 33530 is reported in addition to the appropriate code(s) for the CABG or valve procedure.

- Harvesting the vein or artery is included in codes 33510–33536 except when an upper extremity vein (e.g., axillary, brachial, radial, or ulnar vein) (code 35500), upper extremity artery (e.g., axillary, brachial, radial, or ulnar artery) (code 35600), or femoropopliteal vein segment (code 35572) is harvested. When harvesting of the vein or artery is documented in the operative report, assign codes 35500, 35600, and/or 35572 in addition to the CABG procedure code.

- HCPCS Level II modifiers identify placement of the bypass grafts and are added to the CABG code:

  - -LC (left circumflex coronary artery)

  - -LD (left anterior descending coronary artery)

  - -RC (right coronary artery)

Coronary Endarterectomy

Coronary endarterectomy is performed to remove the inner layer of coronary arteries that contain cholesterol plaques. When a patient's coronary arteries contain extensive cholesterol plaque, a CABG procedure cannot be performed until the plaque is removed via coronary endarterectomy.

EXAMPLE: Patient underwent coronary endarterectomy of the left anterior descending and left circumflex coronary arteries. During the same operative session, the patient also underwent double CABG. The graft sections were obtained from the internal mammary arteries. Report codes 33534-LC-LD, 33572, and 33572.

Single Ventricle and Other Complex Cardiac Anomalies

Codes 33600–33622 are reported for procedures performed to correct single ventricle and other complex cardiac anomalies. For example, the Norwood procedure is reported with code 33619 (to repair a single ventricle that has an aortic outflow obstruction and aortic arch hypoplasia). During the procedure, the pulmonary artery is connected to the right ventricle, using a shunt, and the underdeveloped aorta is enlarged and reconstructed.

EXAMPLE: Patient diagnosed with tricuspid atresia undergoes repair that involves closure of the atrial septal defect and anastomosis of the aorta to the pulmonary artery. Report code 33615.

Congenital Heart Defects

Congenital heart defects include the following:

- Septal defects
- Sinus of Valsalva defects
- Venous anomalies
- Shunting procedures
- Transposition of great vessels
- Truncus arteriosus
- Aortic anomalies

Septal Defects

The **septum** is tissue that separates the heart's left and right sides. **Septal defects** occur when the tissue doesn't completely close between the heart's chambers (atria or ventricles). This allows oxygen-rich blood from one side of the heart (e.g., left atrium) to mix with oxygen-poor blood on the other side (e.g., right atrium). The extra blood flows through the hole, causing a swishing sound, which is called a **heart murmur** (an extra heart sound).

EXAMPLE: Patient underwent repair of atrial septal defect, secundum, with cardiopulmonary bypass, without patch. The right atrium was opened, and the size and location of the atrial septal defect was assessed. Due to the small size of the atrial septal tissue, it was closed with a suture. Report code 33641.

Codes 33692–33697 describe repair procedures for **tetralogy of Fallot**, which is a congenital heart condition that includes ventral septal defect, stenosis of the infundibulum, hypertrophy of the right ventricle, and an abnormally positioned aorta.

EXAMPLE: Patient underwent complete repair of tetralogy of Fallot without pulmonary atresia using transannular patch. Report code 33694.

Sinus of Valsalva Defects

The **sinus of Valsalva** (or **aortic sinus**) is an anatomic dilation of the ascending aorta that occurs just above the aortic valve (e.g., left anterior aortic sinus that gives rise to the left coronary artery). Defects include aneurysms and fistulas for which repair and closure procedures are performed.

EXAMPLE: Patient underwent surgical repair of a sinus of Valsalva aneurysm. Report code 33720.

Venous Anomalies

Venous anomalies are associated with systemic veins and pulmonary veins and include conditions such as:

- *Cor triatriatum* (congenital anomaly in which left atrium or right atrium is divided into two parts by a fold of tissue, membrane, or fibromuscular band; referred to as a heart with three atria).
- *Pulmonary vein stenosis* (abnormal thickening and narrowing of walls of pulmonary veins).
- *Scimitar syndrome* (congenital condition in which aberrant vessel connects pulmonary vein in right lung to inferior vena cava).
- *Supravalvar mitral ring* (rare congenital defect characterized by an abnormal ridge of connective tissue on the atrial side of the mitral valve).
- *Total anomalous pulmonary venous return (TAPVR)* (rare congenital defect in which all four pulmonary veins do not connect normally to left atrium but instead drain to the right atrium by way of an abnormal connection).

EXAMPLE: Patient underwent surgical repair of supravalvular mitral ring via resection of left atrial membrane. Report code 33732.

Shunting Procedures

Shunting procedures are performed to move blood from one area to another, and they are performed for conditions such as:

- *Atrial septal defect (ASD)* (opening in atrial septum fails to close after birth).

- *Coarctation of the aorta* (part of the aorta has a very narrow section, similar in appearance to an hourglass timer, reducing blood flow).

- *Patent ductus arteriosus (PDA)* (opening between aorta and pulmonary artery fails to close after birth).

- *Tricuspid atresia* (tricuspid valve is deformed, narrow, or missing).

- *Ventricular septal defect (VSD)* (opening in ventricular septum fails to close after birth).

   EXAMPLE: Patient underwent a shunt procedure of the descending aorta to the pulmonary artery to correct patent ductus arteriosus. Report code 33762.

Transposition of Great Vessels

The **transposition of great vessels** is the congenital reversal of the aorta and pulmonary artery. The pulmonary arteries are supplied by the left ventricle, and the aorta is supplied by the right ventricle—the opposite of the normal arrangement. Surgery to correct the transposition of great vessels is reported with codes 33770–33783.

   EXAMPLE: Patient underwent repair of transposition of the great arteries with aortic and pulmonary artery reconstruction. Report code 33778.

Truncus Arteriosus

Truncus arteriosus is a congenital malformation in which just one artery arises from the heart to form the aorta and pulmonary artery. Surgery to correct truncus arteriosus is reported with codes 33786–33788.

   EXAMPLE: Patient underwent total repair of truncus arteriosus. Report code 33786.

   The repair of aortic anomalies is reported with codes 33800–33853. For example, code 33852 describes the repair of a hypoplastic or interrupted aortic arch using autogenous or prosthetic material, without cardiopulmonary bypass.

Aortic Anomalies

Aortic anomalies result from unusual patterns of aortic development and include conditions such as:

- *Tracheal decompression (or tracheomalacia)* (softness of cartridge that supports tracheal walls, which can be due to *vascular ring formation* and results in tracheal collapse and decreased airflow).

- *Aberrant vessels* (or *vascular ring formation*) (abnormal growth of vessels, which encircle trachea and esophagus and result in upper airway obstruction).

- *Aortopulmonary septal defect (APSD)* (deficiency in septum between aorta and pulmonary artery, resulting in abnormal communication between them).

- *Patent ductus arteriosus* (opening between aorta and pulmonary artery fails to close after birth).

- *Coarctation of aorta* (part of the aorta has a very narrow section, similar in appearance to an hourglass timer, reducing blood flow)

- *Hypoplastic aortic arch* (or *interrupted aortic arch*) (absence of a portion of the aortic arch, creating a gap between the ascending and descending aorta)

   EXAMPLE: Patient underwent surgical division of aberrant vessels with aortopexy to correct tracheomalacia. Report codes 33802 and 33800-51.

Thoracic Aortic Aneurysm

An aneurysm (Figure 13-9) is a bulge in an artery than can weaken the arterial wall and eventually burst, resulting in hemorrhage. Procedures to repair thoracic aortic aneurysms are reported with codes 33860–33877.

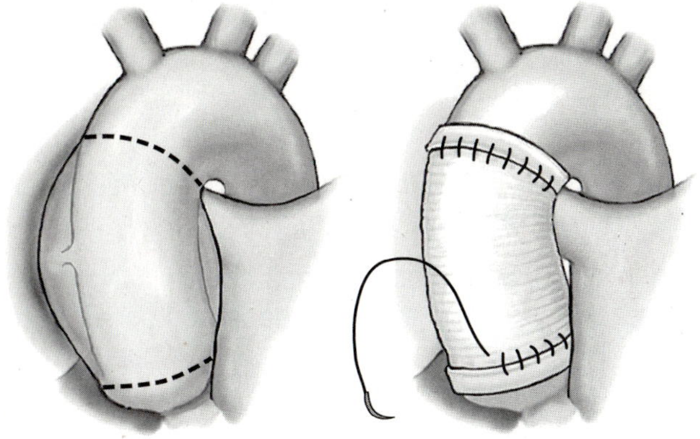

Figure 13-9 Aortic aneurysm repair

EXAMPLE: Patient underwent transverse arch graft to repair thoracic aortic aneurysm. Cardiopulmonary bypass was provided. Report code 33870.

Endovascular Repair of Descending Thoracic Aorta

Endovascular repair of descending thoracic aorta procedures involve the placement of grafts to repair defects of the thoracic aorta (e.g., aneurysm, intramural hematoma, penetrating ulcer, traumatic disruption). When fluoroscopic guidance is used during endovascular repair procedures, report a code from 75956–75959.

Note:

Interventional procedures performed with endovascular repair of the descending thoracic aorta are reported separately (e.g., innominate, carotid, subclavian, visceral, or iliac artery transluminal angioplasty or stenting; arterial embolization; and intravascular ultrasound).

EXAMPLE: Patient underwent placement of proximal extension prosthesis for endovascular repair of descending thoracic aorta dissecting aneurysm, initial extension only. Fluoroscopic guidance confirmed appropriate placement. Report codes 33883 and 79598.

Pulmonary Artery

Codes 33910–33926 describe procedures performed on the pulmonary artery section. For example, code 33917 describes repair of pulmonary artery stenosis by reconstruction with patch or graft.

EXAMPLE: Patient underwent repair of pulmonary atresia with ventricular septal defect, by construction or replacement of conduit from right or left ventricle to pulmonary artery. Report code 33920.

Heart/Lung Transplantation

Guidelines for heart/lung transplantation include three components:

- **Cadaver donor cardiectomy with or without pneumonectomy**, which involves harvesting the allograft (graft such as lung tissue that is transplanted between genetically nonidentical individuals of the same species) and preserving the allograft with cold preservation solution and cold maintenance (codes 33930 and 33940)

Note:

Cold preservation is a component of the donor organ harvesting procedure, not the backbench preparation. For example, cold preservation of a donor heart allograft is included in code 33940, Donor cardiectomy (including cold preservation).

- Backbench work, which involves preparing the cadaver donor heart and/or lung allograft prior to lung transplantation and dissecting allograft from surrounding soft tissues to prepare the aorta, superior vena cava, inferior vena cava, pulmonary artery, left atrium, and/or trachea for implantation (codes 33933 and 33944)

- **Recipient heart with or without lung allotransplantation**, which includes transplantation of the allograft and care of the recipient (codes 33935 and 33945)

   EXAMPLE: Patient with severe cardiomyopathy underwent heart transplant procedure to remove diseased heart and replace with healthy heart from a recently deceased donor. Transplant physician performed donor cardiectomy including cold preservation from cadaver donor, backbench standard preparation of cadaver donor heart allograft, and heart transplant with cardiopulmonary bypass. Report codes 33940, 33944, and 33945. (The 33940 procedure is performed on the donor, not the recipient. The 33944 and 33945 procedures are performed on the recipient, and modifier -51 is not added.)

   When donor cardiectomy and backbench preparation are performed at a facility other than the transplant facility (and the removed organ is transported to the transplant facility), codes 33940 and 33944 are reported by the first facility. Code 33945 is reported by the transplant facility.

Cardiac Assist

Cardiac assist procedures include the insertion, implantation, and removal of various devices. A **ventricular assist device (VAD)** provides temporary support for the heart by substituting for left or right heart function (e.g., after myocardial infarction).

   EXAMPLE: Patient underwent insertion of intra-aortic balloon assist device into the common femoral artery. Device was to the distal aortic arch. Report code 33967.

Exercise 13.1 – Heart and Pericardium

Instructions: Assign the CPT code(s) and appropriate modifier(s) to each statement.

1. Patient undergoes aortic valve replacement with stentless tissue valve by division. Cardiopulmonary bypass is provided.

2. 18-year-old patient underwent repair of ductus arteriosus. Posteriolateral thoracotomy was performed to access the heart.

3. Patient underwent coronary artery bypass, during which a single arterial and single vein graft was performed.

4. 7-year-old child underwent repair of pulmonary atresia, and a prosthetic conduit was used.

5. Patient underwent insertion of permanent pacemaker with transvenous electrode(s), ventricular. An additional electrode was inserted in the left ventricle to provide a biventricular pacing system and attached to the inserted pacemaker.

6. Patient underwent subtotal pericardiectomy with cardiopulmonary bypass.

7. Patient-activated cardiac event recorder was implanted in a 54-year-old male patient on May 1. Two weeks later the patient underwent electronic analysis and reprogramming of the recorder on May 16.

8. Patient underwent sinus of Valsalva fistula repair, with cardiopulmonary bypass.

9. Operative ablation of ventricular arrhythmogenic focus was performed on a 62-year-old female patient, with cardiopulmonary bypass.

10. Patient underwent transection of pulmonary artery with cardiopulmonary bypass.

11. The physician drained fluid from the pericardial space under fluoroscopic guidance.

12. The physician repositions a previously placed transvenous right ventricular electrode.

13. The physician performed an operative ablation of a supraventricular arrhythmia without cardiopulmonary bypass.

14. The physician performed a surgical vascular endoscopy with video-assisted harvesting of a vein for coronary artery bypass surgery (vein only, single coronary venous graft).

15. Patient underwent banding of pulmonary artery.

16. The physician initiated cardiopulmonary bypass, the right atrium was opened, and a stiff ring was inserted for valvuloplasty of the tricuspid valve.

17. Using cardiopulmonary bypass, the physician repaired an artificial prosthetic valve that was malfunctioning due to leakage.

18. The patient was brought to the operating room, and a triple coronary bypass was performed using only venous conduits.

19. The physician performed a coronary endarterectomy during the same operative session as a coronary artery bypass graft procedure (using an arterial graft).

20. The physician performed a Damus-Kaye-Stansel procedure.

21. Using cardiopulmonary bypass, the right atrium was opened and a patch of Dacron was sutured to the edge of the atrial septal defect to close it.

22. The physician repaired a hypoplastic aortic arch using prosthetic material, without cardiopulmonary bypass.

23. The surgeon repaired transposition of the great arteries via Jatene-type aortic pulmonary artery reconstruction, including closure of ventricular septal defect.

24. The physician repaired an atrial septal defect with cardiopulmonary bypass and patch.

25. Using hypothermic circulatory arrest methodology, the physician repaired a dissection of the ascending aorta with moderate aortic insufficiency; the ascending aorta was replaced with a prosthetic graft, and the aortic valve was resuspended.

Arteries and Veins

The Arteries and Veins subsection also requires an excellent understanding of the anatomy of vascular structures because it is organized according to artery or vein (and approach). Notes at the beginning of the arteries and veins subsection indicate the following:

- Codes for procedures performed on arteries and veins include the establishment of both inflow and outflow by whatever procedures are necessary. This means that separate codes for establishing inflow and outflow are not reported.

- The portion of the operative arteriogram that is performed by the surgeon is included in codes for procedures performed on arteries and veins. (When the radiologist participates by supervising and interpreting an arteriogram, a separate code is reported.)

- When a **sympathectomy** (excision of a segment of the sympathetic nerve) procedure is performed, it is included in the codes for aortic procedures. For example, a lumbar sympathectomy might be performed to improve collateral blood supply to the foot when reconstructive surgery is not possible.

- Unlisted vascular procedures are reported with code 37799.

Embolectomy/Thrombectomy

An **embolectomy** is the surgical removal of an **embolus** (blood clot that circulates throughout the bloodstream), and a **thrombectomy** (fixed blood clot) is the surgical removal of a thrombus. Before reporting a code, make sure you identify the type of blood vessel (artery or vein) and the approach used to remove the embolus or thrombus (e.g., catheter and/or incision).

> **EXAMPLE 1:** Patient underwent carotid embolectomy with catheter, by neck incision. Report code 34001.

> **EXAMPLE 2:** Patient underwent direct subclavian vein thrombectomy, by neck incision. Report code 34471.

Venous Reconstruction

Venous reconstruction procedures are performed to repair venous valves, the vena cava, and venous transposition. Leg veins contain valves, which contain two leaflets to allow blood to flow in one direction toward the heart. When venous valves become damaged and fail to function properly, the backflow of blood occurs, resulting in varicose veins, pain, leg swelling, hyperpigmentation (skin discoloration), and skin ulcers (breakdown of the skin). Valvuloplasty is performed to repair incompetent valves by opening the vein; exposing the leaflets after dissecting the vein from surrounding tissues; and placing very fine sutures to attach the valve edges to the vein wall, which tightens the valve flaps when the vein is closed.

Reconstruction of the vena cava is performed to correct a congenital defect or to repair the vena cava when the patient sustains trauma or the vena cava is damaged due to long-term drug therapy (e.g., chemotherapy). For example, the obstructed or damaged portion of the vena cava is resected and repaired with an autologous (graft from patient's own body) pericardial patch.

Venous valve transposition is performed to treat chronic deep venous insufficiency. An incision is made to expose the venous valve, and the section of the vein that contains the malfunctioning valve is excised. Then a harvested vein that contains functional valves is anastomosed end to end to the remaining vein.

A **cross-over vein graft** procedure involves making an incision to expose the vein's incompetent valve, dividing that section of the vein, and connecting it to a nearby vein that has functioning valves.

A **saphenopopliteal vein anastomosis** involves making an incision to expose the saphenous vein and connecting it to the popliteal vein using end-to-end anastomosis.

> **EXAMPLE:** Patient developed chronic benign superior vena cava syndrome due to long-term use of central venous catheters (CVCs) for administration of chemotherapy. Reconstruction of vena cava was performed by resecting the obstructed segment and placing an autologous pericardial patch. Report code 34502.

Coding Tip:

The list of procedures included and excluded from endovascular repair of an abdominal aortic aneurysm varies slightly from those associated with endovascular repair of an iliac aneurysm. For example, open femoral or iliac artery exposure is included with endovascular repair of an abdominal aortic aneurysm, but it is reported separately when performed with endovascular repair of an iliac aneurysm.

Repair of Aneurysms

An aneurysm is an abnormal "bulging" of a portion of a vessel, usually due to a weakness or thinning of the vessel wall at that location (Figure 13-10). It can be caused by congenital or acquired weakness of the vessel wall. Minimally invasive procedures are performed to implant endovascular devices (e.g., endovascular graft) for treatment of aortic aneurysms (codes 34800–34834) and iliac aneurysms (code 34900). Direct (open) repair includes partial or total excision of the arterial segment that contains the aneurysm and insertion of a graft, using end-to-end anastomosis (codes 35001–35152) (Figure 13-11).

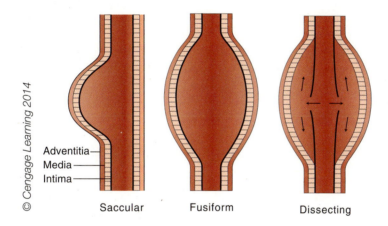

Figure 13-10 Three types of aneurysms

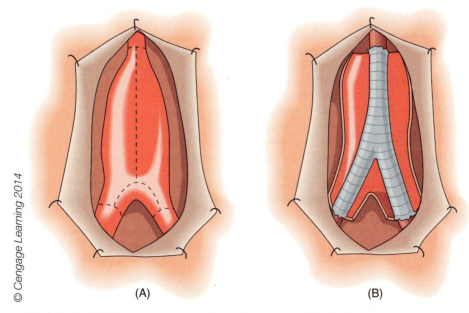

Figure 13-11 (A) Surgical resection of aneurysm (B) Grafting of aneurysm

Because a number of different methods are used to repair abdominal aortic aneurysms, the coder must review the operative report to identify:

- Whether an endovascular or direct (open) repair of the abdominal aortic aneurysm was performed.
- What the artery and type of exposure were (e.g., open femoral artery exposure for delivery of endovascular prosthesis, by groin incision, unilateral).
- What type of device was used for repair (e.g., modular bifurcated prosthesis).
- What other separately reported procedures or services were provided (e.g., fluoroscopy).

Coding Tip:

- Codes for endovascular repair of aneurysms include balloon angioplasty with target treatment zone either before or after graft deployment, deployment, distal extensions, manipulation, and positioning.
- When assigning codes for aneurysm repair, review the patient record to determine if the type of repair is direct (open) or endovascular. Direct (open) repairs include procedures performed on the thoracic aorta and all other arteries. Endovascualr repairs include procedures performed on the thoracic aorta, abdominal aorta, and the iliac artery.

EXAMPLE 1: Patient underwent open iliac artery exposure and placement of endovascular prosthesis during endovascular therapy to treat an abdominal aortic aneurysm. Report code 34820.

EXAMPLE 2: Abdominal incision was made to expose the right iliac artery, and endovascular graft was placed under fluoroscopic guidance to repair right iliac aneurysm. Report codes 34900-RT, 34820-RT, and 75954-RT.

EXAMPLE 3: Patient underwent direct repair with partial excision of aneurysm and graft insertion to treat a left carotid aneurysm. Report code 35001-LT.

Repair of Fistulas

An *arteriovenous fistula* is an abnormal connection or passageway between an artery and a vein, which means blood flows directly from an artery into a vein, bypassing the capillaries. A person may be born with an arteriovenous fistula (congenital fistula), or a fistula may develop after birth (acquired fistula due to trauma or other pathology).

EXAMPLE 1: Patient underwent repair of a congenital arteriovenous fistula, neck. Report code 35180.

EXAMPLE 2: Patient sustained a knife wound to the abdomen, and a traumatic arteriovenous fistula developed. Surgical repair of the abdominal arteriovenous fistula was performed. Report code 35189.

Repair of Blood Vessels Other Than for Fistula, With or Without Patch Angioplasty

Generally, the *repair of blood vessels (other than for fistula)* is due to an injured artery or vein, such as a lacerated or torn blood vessel. Repairs include the following types:

- Direct (e.g., a partly divided vessel or one that has been lacerated longitudinally can be sutured, with the cut ends anastomosed)
- Vein graft (e.g., a piece of saphenous vein is harvested from the patient and sutured over lacerated blood vessel to bypass the abnormal section of the vessel)
- Graft other than vein (e.g., synthetic graft material is sutured end-to-end to the vessel, replacing the excised portion)

EXAMPLE 1: Patient underwent direct repair of superficial basilica vein, left hand. Report code 35207-LT.

EXAMPLE 2: Patient underwent repair of peroneal artery with synthetic graft, right lower leg. Report code 35286-RT.

Thromboendarterectomy

A **thromboendarterectomy** is the surgical excision of a thrombus and atherosclerotic inner lining from an obstructed artery. It is typically performed to treat calcified plaque or clot formations that don't respond to balloon angioplasty procedures. Coders must carefully review documentation to distinguish between a thrombectomy (e.g., procedure to remove a thrombus or blood clot) and a thromboendarterectomy (e.g., procedure to remove a thrombus and the lining of the artery, including possible placement of a patch graft).

Coding Tip:

When a carotid thromboendarterectomy procedure is repeated more than one month after the original procedure, report code 35390 in addition to code 35301.

EXAMPLE: Patient underwent abdominal aortic thromboendarterectomy with patch graft. Report code 35331.

Angioscopy

Angioscopy is the microscopic visualization of substances (e.g., contrast media and radiopaque agents) as they pass through capillaries. The intravenous injection of the substance is performed as part of the procedure.

EXAMPLE: Patient underwent endovascular repair of infrarenal abdominal aortic aneurysm using aorto-aortic tube prosthesis. Prior to performing the therapeutic portion of the procedure, angioscopy was performed to visualize the interior of the aortic arch. Subsequently, under abdomional aortographic guidance, initial third-order vascular catheterization of left infrarenal artery was performed and atherectomy catheter device was advanced to the aorta. In addition to codes for the endovascular repair (34800, 36247-LT, 75625), report code 35400. (Do not add modifier -51 to code 35400.)

Coding Tip:

Code 35400 (Angioscopy) is reported in addition to the code for the primary procedure performed (e.g., percutaneous transluminal angioplasty, PTA).

Transluminal Angioplasty

Transluminal angioplasty is the surgical repair of a blood vessel through its lumen (opening). Angioplasty procedures may be open (inside of blood vessel is exposed) or percutaneous (through the skin), and codes for procedures are selected according to the artery or vein treated.

- An **open transluminal angioplasty** involves making an incision in the skin overlying the artery and carrying it down to free the artery from surrounding structures. Clamps are applied, and a small incision is made to create an opening in the artery. The balloon catheter is inserted and threaded up to the narrow portion of the artery, where the balloon is inflated to increase the artery's diameter. The incision in the artery is closed, and the skin incision is closed in layers.

  EXAMPLE: Patient underwent open angioplasty of the aorta; insertion of balloon catheter into the aorta; and thoracic aortographic radiological supervision and interpretation. Report codes 35452, 36200, and 75600. (Refer to notes in the "Vascular Injection Procedure" category of the Cardiovascular System subsection of CPT Surgery.)

- A **percutaneous transluminal angioplasty (PTA)** involves puncturing the artery and inserting a sheath, guidewire, and guiding catheter (after removing the guidewire). The guiding catheter is advanced to the narrow portion of the artery, and a balloon catheter is inserted through the guiding catheter. The balloon is inflated to increase the artery's diameter. A single suture may be used to repair the puncture.

Note:

Codes for placement of the catheter and radiological supervision and interpretation services are reported separately, in addition to the codes for the percutaneous transluminal angioplasty.

EXAMPLE: Patient underwent percutaneous transluminal balloon angioplasty of the left renal artery. Skin puncture was made; and under fluoroscopic guidance, catheter was inserted into the left femoral and threaded through to the left common iliac artery. The narrowed portion of the left common iliac artery was located, and the balloon was inflated three times to widen its diameter. Report codes 35471-LT, 36246-51-LT (external iliac and internal iliac arteries, second-order), and 75966.

Note:

Percutaneous transluminal coronary angioplasty (PTCA) (Figure 13-12) is performed on the coronary arteries, and codes are located in the Medicine section (92982–92984). Coronary angioplasty is accomplished by inserting a balloontipped catheter through an artery in the groin or arm and threading it to the coronary artery, where the balloon is inflated (once or several times) to enlarge a narrowing in the coronary artery.

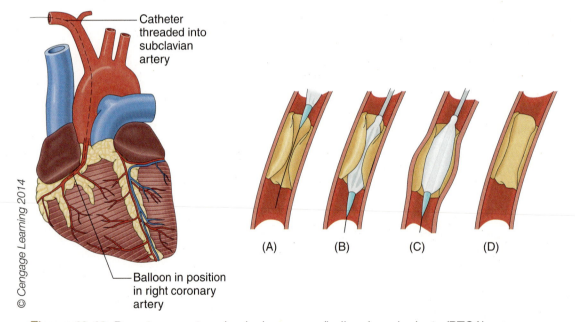

Catheter threaded into subclavian artery

Balloon in position in right coronary artery

© Cengage Learning 2014

(A)   (B)   (C)   (D)

Figure 13-12 Percutaneous transluminal coronary (balloon) angioplasty (PTCA)

Transluminal Atherectomy (for Endovascular Revascularization)

Transluminal atherectomy (Figure 13-13) is the excision of plaque from inside a blood vessel. Atherectomy procedures may be open (inside of blood vessel is exposed) or percutaneous (through the skin), and codes for procedures are selected according to the artery or vein treated. The following atherectomy devices are inserted into the vessel to remove plaque:

- Catheter with a rotating blade, which shaves and dislodges plaque
- Laser catheter, which vaporizes plaque
- Dissectional catheter, which shaves off plaque

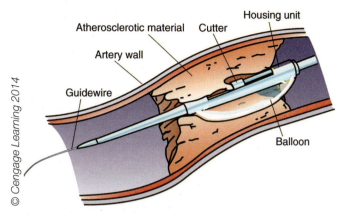

Figure 13-13 Atherectomy catheter with a rotating blade that shaves and dislodges plaque.

For an **open transluminal atherectomy**, an incision is made in the skin overlying the artery and the artery is punctured with a large needle. A guidewire is inserted, and the needle is removed. An introducer sheath is inserted over the guidewire into the artery's lumen. The atherectomy device is positioned under fluoroscopic guidance, and plaque is removed. The opening into the artery is closed, and the skin incision is closed in layers.

A **percutaneous transluminal atherectomy** involves puncturing the artery with a large needle and inserting a guidewire into the artery. An introducer sheath is inserted over the guidewire into the artery's lumen. The atherectomy device is positioned under fluoroscopic guidance, and plaque is removed. The artery is compressed to achieve hemostasis. (CPT's category III codes are reported for some PTA procedures.)

EXAMPLE 1: Patient underwent endovascular revascularization via open transluminal atherectomy of the right femoral-popliteal artery. Under fluoroscopic guidance, laser catheter was inserted into the right common iliac artery, advanced into the right common femoral artery, advanced into the right superficial femoral artery, and advanced into the right popliteal artery. Plaque was vaporized from inside the right popliteal artery. Report codes 37225-RT, and 36247-51-RT. (Fluoroscopic guidance and atherectomy are included in code 37225.)

EXAMPLE 2: Patient underwent percutaneous transluminal atherectomy of the right brachio-cephalic artery. Skin puncture was made; and under fluoroscopic guidance, selective catheterization into the right brachiocephalic artery was performed. The narrowed portion of the artery was located, the laser atherectomy device was inserted, and plaque was vaporized. Right brachiocephalic artery was compressed to achieve hemostasis. Report codes 0237T-RT, and 36215-51-RT. (Fluoroscopic guidance and atherectomy are included in code 0237T.)

Coding Tip:

- CPT's revascularization codes allow a single code to be reported for open or percutaneous transluminal atherectomy, fluoroscopic guidance, and angioplasty within the same vessel if performed.
- Codes for placement of the catheter are reported separately in addition to codes for revascularization.

Bypass Graft

The Bypass Graft heading includes codes that describe procedures performed on veins and *in situ* veins. Codes also classify the use of "other than vein" material (e.g., synthetic graft) as bypass grafts for arteries. Each code describes the bypass graft anastomosis location. For example, code 35506 describes *carotid-subclavian*, which means that the bypass graft is anastomosed from the carotid artery to the subclavian artery.

EXAMPLE 1: Patient underwent bypass graft, with vein, of the left femoral-popliteal artery. Report code 35556-LT.

EXAMPLE 2: Patient underwent *in situ* vein bypass of the right femoral-popliteal artery. Report code 35583-RT.

EXAMPLE 3: Patient underwent synthetic bypass graft of the right carotid artery. Report code 35601-RT.

Composite Grafts

Add-on codes 35681–35683 describe composite bypass graft harvesting and anastomosis of multiple vein segments as arterial bypass graft conduits. A **composite graft** is comprised of vein and synthetic graft material (code 35681) *or* segments of veins from two or more locations, such as saphenous vein and femoral vein (codes 35682–35683).

EXAMPLE 1: Patient underwent bypass graft procedure of right femoral-popliteal artery with Gore-Tex synthetic graft and a portion of the right saphenous vein. Report 35556-RT and 35681. (Do not add modifier -51 to code 35681.)

EXAMPLE 2: Patient underwent bypass graft procedure of right femoral-popliteal artery. Vein grafts were obtained from the left brachial and left basilic veins. Report codes 35556-RT and 35682-LT. (Do not add modifier -51 to code 35682.)

Note:

The most common material used for "other than vein" includes synthetic materials such as Gore-Tex.

Coding Tip:

Report code 35682 or 35683 when more than one vein segment is documented as harvested.

Adjuvant Techniques

Add-on codes 35685–35686 describe **adjuvant techniques**, which are additional procedures or techniques that may be required during a *lower extremity* bypass graft procedure. They are performed to improve the **patency** (open and unblocked status of a blood vessel or another tube in the body) of *lower extremity* synthetic or autogenous arterial bypass grafts.

- Add-on code 35685 is reported when a venous patch or cuff is anastomosed between the synthetic bypass and the involved artery.

- Add-on code 35686 is reported when an autogenous vein is used to create a fistula (passageway) during lower extremity bypass graft surgery.

EXAMPLE 1: Patient underwent right popliteal-tibial bypass grafting with Gore-Tex synthetic graft material. Adjuvant distal vein cuff (DVC) of the popliteal-tibial bypass graft was performed during the same operative session. Report codes 35671-RT and 35685-RT. (Do not report modifier -51 with code 35685.)

EXAMPLE 2: Patient underwent left femoral-popliteal bypass grafting with polytetrafluoroethylene synthetic material. Adjuvant distal arteriovenous fistula (DAVF) of the femoral-popliteal graft was performed during the same operative session. Report codes 35656-LT and 35686-LT. (Do not report modifier -51 with code 35686.)

Arterial Transposition

Arterial transposition and/or reimplantation procedures are performed to improve arterial blood flow. Codes 35691–35697 describe the pairs of arteries that are anastomosed to each other. For example, code 35691 is reported when the vertebral artery is anastomosed to the carotid artery (to improve arterial blood flow).

EXAMPLE 1: Patient underwent transposition surgery to anastomose the right vertebral artery to the right subclavian artery. Report code 35693.

Coding Tip:

Add-on code 35697 is reported in addition to a code for the primary procedure. **Visceral arteries** supply blood to the intestines, liver, and spleen.

EXAMPLE 2: Patient underwent bypass graft surgery of splenorenal artery, during which synthetic graft material was used. Replantation of splenic artery to infrarenal aortic prosthesis was performed during the same operative session to ensure adequate blood supply to the spleen. Report codes 35636 and 35697. (Do not add modifier -51 to code 35697.)

Excision, Exploration, Repair, Revision

When assigning CPT codes to excision, exploration, repair, and revision procedures:

- Code 35700 is reported when a patient returns to the operating room more than one month after an original procedure on the femoral-popliteal or femoral (popliteal)-anterior tibial, posterior tibial, or peroneal artery or other distal vessels.

- Codes 35701–35761 are reported when a patient undergoes exploration (*not followed by surgical repair*) of the carotid, femoral, or popliteal arteries or other vessels.

- Codes 35800–35860 are reported when a patient returns to the operating room for exploration and control of postoperative hemorrhage and/or treatment of thrombosis or infection.

- Code 35870 is reported for repair of graft-enteric fistula. An aortic graft-enteric fistula is a complication of aortic reconstruction surgery; repair includes graft excision with extra-anatomic bypass.

- Codes 35875–35876 are reported when a patient undergoes thrombectomy of arterial or venous graft and/or revision of arterial or venous graft.

- Codes 35879–35884 are reported for revision of bypass grafts.

- Codes 35901–35907 are reported for excision of infected grafts.

    EXAMPLE: Patient underwent exploration for suspected postoperative hemorrhage, chest. Five days ago patient underwent CABG surgery. Report 35820-78.

Coding Tip:

- Codes 35800–35860 are not reported when bleeding occurs during the initial operation.

- Add modifier -78 to codes 35800–35860 when the service provided represents a return to the operating room for a related procedure during the postoperative period.

Vascular Injection Procedures

Vascular injection procedure codes describe common procedures performed to gain venous access for phlebotomy, prophylactic intravenous access, infusion therapy, chemotherapy, and drug administration. They are reported for:

- Diagnostic catheterization (e.g., injecting contrast media into vasculature for radiologic imaging).

- Therapeutic (interventional) catheterization (e.g., balloon dilation or stent placement to open narrowed valves and vessels).

 Note:

When you look up "Vascular Injections" in the CPT index, you'll notice that code 36299 for "Unlisted Services and Procedures" is the only entry. There is also no index entry for "Injection, Vascular" in the CPT index. (Some codes are listed for the "Catheter" entry in the CPT index.) Thus, coders must become familiar with codes and descriptions in the Vascular Injection Procedures heading (and subheadings) of CPT.

CPT also classifies cardiovascular procedures in multiple locations. For example, vascular ultrasound procedures for noncoronary vessels are classified in the Cardiovascular Surgery section, but vascular ultrasound procedures for coronary vessels and cardiac catheterizations are located in the Medicine section.

Vascular injection procedures include the following services, which are not coded and reported separately:

- Injection of contrast media, with or without automatic power injection

 Note:

Although the injection procedure is not reported separately, an HCPCS level II code for provision of contrast media is reported separately.

- Introduction of needles or catheters

 Note:

Although the introduction of a needle or catheter is not reported separately, a CPT code for selective vascular catheterization is reported separately.

- Necessary local anesthesia

- Necessary pre- and postinjection care specifically related to the injection procedure

The following supplies are reported with HCPCS level II codes if provided during a vascular injection procedure:

- Catheters

- Drugs

- Contrast media

Notes below the Vascular Injection Procedures subheading provide instruction about coding selective vascular catheterization. (Be sure to review previous content about selective vascular catheterization.)

Codes for vascular injection procedures include the following routes:

- Intravenous (36000–36015)

- Intra-arterial–intra-aortic (36100–36299) (including placement of shunts for dialysis)

- Venous (36400–36598)

- Arterial (36600–36660)

- Intraosseous (36680)

Vascular injection procedures include the introduction of the catheter or needle into a blood vessel and insertion into lesser- (first-) order vessels. Then when the catheter is inserted as follows for the purpose of performing diagnostic and/or therapeutic procedures, the code(s) for selective vascular catheterization is reported:

- Second-, third- (and beyond) order vessels (e.g., popliteal angiogram)

- Aorta and first-, second-, third- (and beyond) vessels (e.g., carotid angiogram)

Coding Tip:

- When two separate access procedures (e.g., punctures of two different vessels) are performed, report a separate code for each.

- When a nonselective vascular catheterization is converted to a selective vascular catheterization, report a code for the selective vascular catheterization only.

Coding Tip:

Codes for cardiac catheterization are assigned from the Medicine section of CPT.

Intravenous vascular injection procedures (36000–36015) do not include codes for catheterization of third- (or beyond) order vessels. When higher-order vessels undergo venous catheterization procedures, report code 36012 for *each* second-order and third- (and beyond) order vessel.

> **EXAMPLE:** Patient underwent left arm venogram. Catheter was introduced into the superior vena cava and inserted into the brachiocephalic vein and left subclavian vein. Catheter was manipulated into the left axillary vein, and contrast media was injected. Catheter was further advanced into the left brachial and left basilic veins, and contrast media was injected. Good visualization of the left axillary, brachial, and basilica veins was obtained. No deformities were noted. Report code 75820-LT for the left arm venogram. Report code 36011-LT for selective vascular catheterization of the left axillary vein. Report 36012-LT and 36012-LT for selective vascular catheterization of the left brachial and basilica veins, respectively.

Coding Tip:

When a catheter is removed from a vessel, do not report a separate code for that procedure. However, when implantable venous access devices and/or subcutaneous reservoirs are removed, report an appropriate code (e.g., code 36589).

CPT code 36200 is reported just once for "introduction of catheter, aorta" regardless of the number of times the catheter is repositioned in the aorta. When multiple vessels are accessed during catheterization, in different vascular families, report the code for the highest level of selectivity in each vascular family (36215–36217 and 36245–36248).

Venous procedures are coded according to the type of procedure, patient's age, and the puncture site (e.g., 2-year-old patient underwent scalp vein venipuncture, 36405). Make sure you carefully review the patient record and code descriptions to determine whether the procedure was a direct puncture or a cutdown and whether a physician's skill was required.

Therapeutic apheresis is the removal of blood components, cells, or plasma solute and the retransfusion of the remaining components into the patient. Procedure codes are based on blood components:

- White blood cells
- Red blood cells
- Platelets
- Plasmapheresis
- Extracorporeal immunoadsorption and plasma reinfusion
- Extracorporeal selective adsorption or selective filtration and plasma reinfusion

Central Venous Access Procedures

Central venous access procedures include insertion, repair, partial replacement, complete replacement, and/or removal of the catheter or device. A venous access device is inserted:

- Centrally (e.g., femoral, jugular, or subclavian vein or inferior vena cava)
- Peripherally (e.g., basilic or cephalic vein)

A CVC or a central venous access device (CVAD) is used to deliver intravenous fluids and medications and to obtain blood samples. These infusions may be administered for short or prolonged periods, using a single-lumen (allows for infusion of one solution) or multiple-lumen catheter (allows for infusion of several solutions simultaneously).

To be considered a central venous access catheter or device, the tip of the CVC or CVAD must terminate in the subclavian, brachiocephalic, or iliac veins; the superior or inferior vena cava; or the right atrium. (Otherwise, the catheter is considered a midline catheter, MLC.) The device is accessed for use (e.g., administration of medications or hyperalimentation) through a(n):

- Exposed catheter (external to the skin).

- Subcutaneous port.

- Subcutaneous pump.

CVAD codes are reported according to the patient's age and whether the device is nontunneled (not implanted) or tunneled (implanted).

Peripherally inserted CVADs include peripherally inserted central (venous) catheters (PICCs) and MLCs. The type of catheter inserted depends on the technique used, solutions infused, and duration of the intravenous therapy. Any catheter placed with the tip between the antecubital area and the head of the clavicle is called an MLC. Such placement is typically done for infusion therapy, which is expected to last from 1 to 8 weeks (when the catheter tip doesn't need to terminate in the superior vena cava). The PICC can also be shortened if it is needed for midline placement. It is usually inserted below the antecubital fossa and does not require use of a guidewire.

When reporting codes for central venous access procedures (Table 13-2), make sure you determine the following:

- Patient's age

- Whether the catheter was **tunneled** (implanted) or nontunneled

- Whether the procedure was done via:

  - **Cutdown**: Catheter is inserted directly into a vein through an incision.

  - **Peripherally**: Catheter is inserted into peripheral vein using a needle or trocar.

Note:

Tunneled (implantable) venous access ports are typically used for long-term intravenous therapy, and they contain two parts: catheter and port.

Coding Tip:

When blood is collected from a partially or completely implantable venous access device, report code 36591.

Codes 36575–36590 are reported for procedures performed to repair, replace, and/or remove CVADs and CVCs. These codes do not require selection based on the patient's age or central/peripheral insertion site. However, they do distinguish between nontunneled (with exposed access) and tunneled catheters (require subcutaneous port/pump pocket and connection). They also require knowledge of whether a subcutaneous port or pump was inserted. (Refer to Table 13-2 for a list of centrally inserted and peripherally inserted CVC and CVAD devices.)

Codes 36595–36596 are reported for the mechanical removal of obstructive material (e.g., blood clot) from a central venous device. Code 36597 requires fluoroscopic guidance to reposition a previously placed CVC. (Report code 76000 for fluoroscopic guidance.)

Arterial

Arterial blood gases (e.g., arterial blood oxygen, carbon dioxide, and bicarbonate levels) are commonly performed to diagnose the patient's effectiveness of respiration. To report an arterial puncture for the purpose of obtaining a sample for arterial blood gas analysis, report code 36600. During an arterial puncture, a needle is inserted into the artery to obtain a sample of blood; a catheter is *not* inserted into the artery.

Table 13-2 Coding Central Venous Access Catheters and Devices

Code	Age	Nontunneled	Tunneled (Implanted)	Types of Venous Access Catheters and Devices	Venous Insertion Sites
36555 36556	< 5 ≥ 5	X X		Centrally inserted central venous catheter (CVC), such as: • Cook • Leonard • Quinton • Shiley • Triple lumen	• Femoral vein • Inferior vena cava • Jugular vein • Subclavian vein
36557 36558	< 5 ≥ 5		X X	Centrally inserted CVC, without subcutaneous port or pump, such as: • Ash Split • Broviac • Double lumen • Groshorg • Hickman • PermCath	• Femoral vein • Inferior vena cava • Jugular vein • Subclavian vein
36560 36561	< 5 ≥ 5		X X	Centrally inserted central venous access device (CVAD), with subcutaneous port, such as: • Bard port • Infuse-a-Port • MediPort • Port-a-Cath • Q-Port	• Femoral vein • Inferior vena cava • Jugular vein • Subclavian vein
36563			X	Centrally inserted CVAD, with subcutaneous pump, such as: • Chemotherapy pump • Infusion pump • Intravenous pump	• Femoral vein • Inferior vena cava • Jugular vein • Subclavian vein
36565			X	Centrally inserted CVAD requiring two catheters via two separate venous access sites, without subcutaneous port or pump, such as Tesio type catheter	• Femoral vein • Inferior vena cava • Jugular vein • Subclavian vein
36566			X	Centrally inserted CVAD requiring two catheters via two separate venous access sites, with subcutaneous port(s), such as Tesio type catheter, with port	• Femoral vein • Inferior vena cava • Jugular vein • Subclavian vein
36568 36569	< 5 ≥ 5			Peripherally inserted central venous catheter (PICC), without subcutaneous port or pump, such as: • Abbott • Angiocath • Jelco • Triple lumen	Superficial veins in the arms, legs, feet, or head, such as: • Basilic vein • Cephalic vein • Saphenous vein
36570 36571	< 5 ≥ 5			Peripherally inserted CVAD, with subcutaneous port, such as: • Bard port • Infuse-a-Port • Medi-Port • Port-a-Cath • Q-Port	Superficial veins in the arms, legs, feet, or head, such as: • Basilic vein • Cephalic vein • Saphenous vein

Coding Tip:

- When mechanical removal of obstructive material code 36595 or 36596 is reported, report code 75901 or 75902 for radiological supervision and interpretation, respectively. A venous catheterization code (36010–36012) is also reported when performed.

- When a CVC is repositioned, report code 36597 with the appropriate Radiology code.

Code 36620 is reported when a catheter or cannula is inserted into the artery *percutaneously* for blood sampling, monitoring, infusion, or transfusion. Once the procedure is complete, the catheter or cannula is removed. Code 36625 is reported when the physician performs a *cutdown* procedure to access the artery, inserts a catheter or cannula, sutures the artery, and closes the incision in layers.

Intraosseous

Code 36680 is reported when the physician inserts a special needle to puncture the bone marrow cavity (e.g., tibia or femur) to infuse fluids into bone marrow blood vessels.

Hemodialysis Access, Intervascular Cannulation for Extracorporeal Circulation, or Shunt Insertion

Codes 36800–36870 describe the following procedures:

- Arteriovenous anastomosis, direct

- Insertion of cannulas for prolonged extracorporeal circulation of membrane oxygenation (ECMO)

- Arteriovenous fistula

    Arteriovenous hemodialysis access is created by using autogenous venous tissue or inserting a prosthetic graft.

    EXAMPLE 1: Patient underwent forearm vein transposition between the elbow and the wrist. Report code 36820.

    EXAMPLE 2: Patient underwent open arteriovenous anastomosis of the right cephalic vein. (The cephalic vein is located in the upper arm.) Report code 36818-RT.

    EXAMPLE 3: Patient underwent open arteriovenous anastomosis via left basilic vein transposition. (The basilic vein is in the upper arm.) Report code 36819-LT.

Portal Decompression Procedures

Codes 37140–37183 are reported for the insertion and revision of transvenous intrahepatic portosystemic shunt (TIPS) procedures. A TIPS is inserted to reduce portal pressure associated with portal hypertension. Portal blood flow is diverted into the hepatic vein, which reduces pressure between the portal and systemic circulations.

> **EXAMPLE:** Patient underwent insertion of TIPS. Report code 37182.

Transcatheter Procedures

The Transcather Procedures subheading contains notes that provide instruction to report codes separately for catheter placement and

Note:

A heparin flush is performed to maintain patency of the catheter/port and to reduce the risk of blood clotting in the catheter. When a heparin flush is performed as a part of an injection or infusion procedure, it is not separately coded.

Coding Tip:

Codes 37182 and 37183 include radiological supervision and interpretation (e.g., portography and all associated imaging guidance and documentation). Therefore, do not report codes 75885 and 75887 with codes 37182 and 37183.

radiological supervision and interpretation. When transcatheter therapy services are provided, the introduction of the needle and catheter are included in the code for the primary service.

EXAMPLE 1: Patient underwent open transcatheter placement of an intravascular stent under fluoroscopic guidance. The catheter was introduced into the right femoral artery (second-order artery), and contrast medium was injected. Femoral angiogram was performed and revealed blockage of the femoral artery. Under fluoroscopic guidance, an intravascular stent was placed in the femoral artery. Repeat femoral angiogram (Figure 13-14), after stent placement, revealed good arterial circulation in the femoral artery. Report codes 37207-RT, 36246-RT, and 75960-RT.

EXAMPLE 2: Patient underwent cerebral thrombolysis as therapy for acute ischemic stroke. Report code 37195.

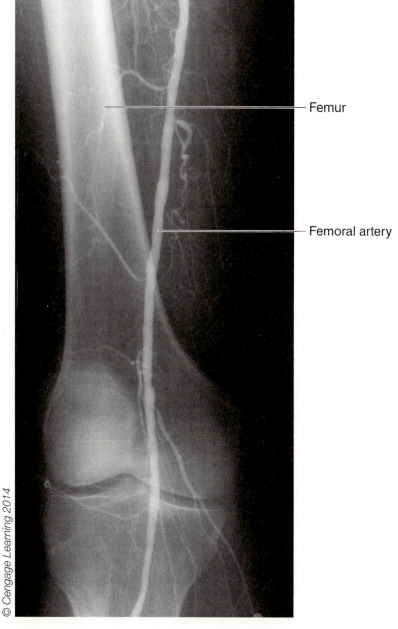

Femur

Femoral artery

© Cengage Learning 2014

Figure 13-14 Femoral angiogram. The use of contrast medium makes arteries visible.

Endovascular Revascularization

Endovascular revascularization procedures are performed for lower extremity occlusive disease, and include open, percutaneous, and transcatheter methods. The CPT codes are inclusive of all services provided for the vessel treated, and codes from one vascular family are reported for the purpose of revascularization:

- *Iliac Vascular Territory*, which is subdivided into the common iliac, internal iliac and external iliac arteries.

- *Femoral/Popliteal Vascular Territory*, which includes the femoral and popliteal arteries in one extremity.

- *Tibial/Peroneal Vascular Territory*, which includes the anterior tibial, posterior tibial, and peroneal arteries.

  EXAMPLE: Patient underwent percutaneous transluminal angioplasty for endovascular revascularization of the right common iliac, right internal iliac and right external iliac arteries. Report codes 37220, 37222, 37222. (Code 37220 is the primary endovascular revascularization code, and code 37222 is reported twice for endovascular revascularization of the two additional arteries. Code 37222 is an add-on code and, thus, exempt from modifier -51.)

Intravascular Ultrasound Services

Intravascular ultrasound services to of noncoronary vessels are performed during diagnostic evaluation and/or therapeutic intervention. Notes provide instruction to report codes 75945 and 75946 for the radiological supervision and interpretation of the intravascular ultrasound procedure.

Endoscopy

CPT codes 37500–37501 describe vascular endoscopy procedures, and surgical vascular endoscopy always include diagnostic endoscopy.

  EXAMPLE: Patient underwent surgical vascular endoscopy with ligation of subfascial perforator veins. Report code 37500.

Ligation

Ligation of arteries and veins is performed to control bleeding of a ruptured or dissected (torn) artery/vein.

CPT codes 37700–37735 describe ligation, division, and stripping of the saphenous veins. These procedures are different from the stab phlebectomy procedure described in codes 37765 and 37766. For a **stab phlebectomy**, multiple tiny incisions are made over varicose vein sites. At each stab site, the varicosity is extracted and then the varicose segment is removed. (The stab phlebectomy procedure is not typically performed on saphenous veins.)

Code 37760 describes the subfascial ligation of incompetent perforator veins (e.g., connecting superficial veins located below the skin's surface to deep veins in the leg muscle). Perforator vein ligation may also be performed endoscopically, which is reported with code 37500.

Code 37780 describes the ligation and division of short saphenous vein at the saphenopopliteal junction. An incision is made in the skin overlying the short saphenous vein at its junction with the saphenopopliteal vein at the knee. Vessels are dissected and ties are placed around the short saphenous vein, which is divided between the ties.

Code 37785 describes the ligation, division, and/or excision of varicose vein "clusters." These are large varicose veins that cannot be effectively treated using the stab phlebectomy technique because they require a larger incision. An open surgical dissection of the vein cluster is made using long incisions rather than short stab incisions.

Exercise 13.2 – Arteries and Veins

Instructions: Assign the CPT code(s) and appropriate modifier(s) to each statement.

1. During a cardiac catheterization procedure, the physician performed infusion of nitroglycerin as transcatheter therapy.

   _____

2. A physician performs a right upper extremity arteriogram. Catheter is inserted into the right brachial artery.

   _____

3. Physician uses a transfemoral approach to advance the catheter to the ascending aorta, where contrast media is injected and the descending thoracic aorta and abdominal aorta are imaged.

   _____

4. Physician punctures the subclavian vein of a 4-year-old, passes a guidewire centrally, and inserts a central venous catheter.

   _____

5. Patient underwent left renal venogram, which required introduction of a catheter into the inferior vena cava, insertion into the left renal vein, and manipulation into the left suprarenal vein. Contrast media was injected into both veins, and the structures were well visualized. No obstruction or other deformity was noted.

   _____

Hemic and Lymphatic Systems Subsection

The Hemic and Lymphatic Systems subsection headings include the following:

- Spleen

- General

- Lymph Nodes and Lymphatic Channels

The Hemic and Lymphatic Systems subsection contains codes that describe procedures on the spleen, bone marrow transplantation services, the lymph nodes and lymph channels, the mediastinum, and the diaphragm. The **hemic system** is a blood-producing system. **Blood** is tissue that consists of plasma, red blood cells, white blood cells, and platelets (or thrombocytes). The **lymphatic system** (Figure 13-15) consists of the spleen, thymus, tonsils, adenoids, vessels that carry lymph, and lymph nodes. The **spleen** (Figure 13-16) produces mature lymphocytes, destroys worn out red blood cells, and serves as a reservoir for blood. The **thymus** produces T lymphocytes, which are important to the body's immune function. The **tonsils** are located at the back of the throat, and they contain lymphoid tissue that helps fight infections. The **adenoids** are located at the rear of the nose, and they contain lymphoid tissue that helps fight infections. **Lymph** is a clear fluid that contains **chyle** (digestive fluid that contains proteins and fats), some red blood cells, and lymphocytes, which help fight infection and disease. **Lymph nodes** are clusters of bean-shaped nodules that act as the body's filtration system, removing cell waste and excess fluid and helping to fight infection. They are located in the:

- Back of the head, just above the hairline (occipital region)

- Neck (cervical region)

- Armpits (axillary region)

- Elbow (cubital region)

- Chest (supraclavicular region)

- Abdomen (retroperitoneal region)

- Groin (inguinal region)

- Knee (popliteal region)

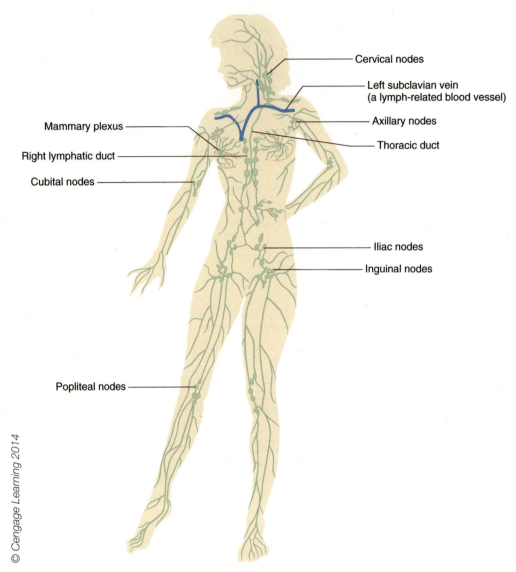

Figure 13-15 Lymphatic circulation and major lymph node locations

Spleen

Codes 38100–38115 are reported for the excision or repair of the spleen. (In code 38102, **_en bloc_** means "as a whole.") Codes 38120–38129 are reported for laparoscopic procedures performed on the spleen. A note below the Laparoscopy subheading provides instruction that "surgical laparoscopy always includes diagnostic laparoscopy." This means that when the physician performs diagnostic and surgical laparoscopies during the same operative session, just the code for surgical laparoscopy is reported. When the physician performs a diagnostic laparoscopy as a separate procedure, report 49320 as an additional code.

> **EXAMPLE:** Patient underwent diagnostic laparoscopy followed by open repair of ruptured spleen with partial splenectomy. Report codes 38115 and 49320.

 Code 38200 is reported when a needle is inserted percutaneously and contrast media is injected into the spleen for direct **splenoportography**, which is the radiographic visualization of the splenic and portal veins.

> **Coding Tip:**
>
> When reporting code 38200, make sure you report the code for radiological supervision and interpretation (75810).

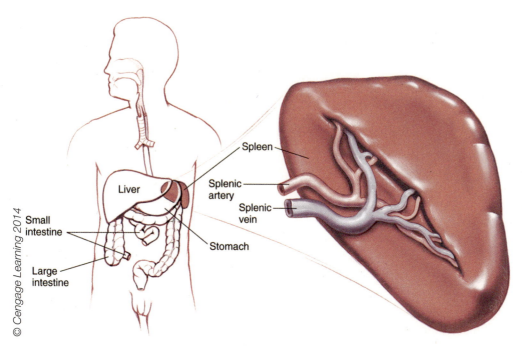

Figure 13-16 The spleen performs many important functions related to the immune system.

EXAMPLE: Patient underwent splenoportography, with percutaneous injection of contrast medium into the spleen. Report codes 75810 and 38200.

General

The General heading includes the Bone Marrow or Stem Cell Services/Procedures subheading. **Bone marrow** is spongy material that fills large bones' cavities and consists of two types:

- Red marrow: Produces red blood cells, white blood cells, and platelets.

- Yellow marrow: Replaces red marrow with fatty tissue that does not produce blood cells.

  Bone marrow contains two types of **stem cells**:

- Hemopoietic: Produce red blood cells, white blood cells, and platelets.

- Stromal: Produce fat, cartilage, and bone and have the ability to differentiate into many kinds of tissue, such as nervous tissue.

Codes are reported for the harvesting, aspiration, biopsy, and transplantation of bone marrow and/or stem cells. Codes are also reported for the steps involved in the preservation, preparation, and purification of bone marrow and stem cells prior to transplantation or reinfusion.

Codes 38205–38206 are reported when stem cells are harvested from a suitable donor (allogenic) or the patient's bone marrow (autologous). Codes 38240–38241 are reported when bone marrow or stem cells are transplanted for the purpose of restoring bone marrow stem cells using the donor's or the patient's marrow. Code 38242 is reported when allogenic donor lymphocyte infusions are performed as a bone marrow or blood-derived peripheral stem cell transplantation, which is often used to treat chronic myelogenous leukemia.

A **bone marrow aspiration** uses a needle to remove a sample of the liquid bone marrow for examination under a microscope. A **bone marrow biopsy** involves boring a small hole into a long bone (e.g., hip) and using a large, hollow needle to remove bone marrow for examination under a microscope. When bone marrow aspiration and bone marrow biopsy procedures are performed at the same site through the same skin incision (during the

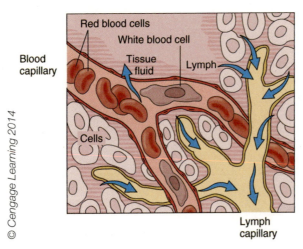

Figure 13-17 Lymph circulation showing interaction with blood vessels and cells.

same operative session), report just bone marrow biopsy code 38221. When the procedures are performed at separate sites (e.g., different bones or separate skins incisions in the same bone), report codes 38220 and 38221-59.

Lymph Nodes and Lymphatic Channels

Capillaries surround cells but are not actually connected to cells, which results in the leakage of watery blood plasma (containing oxygen, proteins, glucose, and white blood cells) or lymph (Figure 13-17). This lymph (fluid) is recirculated away from the body's cells in the lymphatic circulatory system, which contains lymphatic channels, called capillaries and lymphatic vessels. The lymph eventually reaches one of about one hundred lymph nodes located throughout the body, which filter the fluid. (Lymph nodes contain white blood cells that filter debris and foreign cells from lymph.) When a patient becomes infected (e.g., bacteria or virus), the number of white blood cells in lymph nodes increases to billions. The lymph nodes work to fight the infection and release the filtered lymph (fluid) back into the bloodstream. Sometimes lymph nodes become infected or abscessed and require surgical treatment.

> **EXAMPLE:** A patient is diagnosed with cervical lymphadenitis and undergoes incision and drainage. The surgeon makes a skin incision overlying the abscessed cervical lymph node, a needle with a syringe attached is inserted into the lymph node, and the abscess is drained. The wound is closed with steri-strips. Report code 38300.

Codes 38562–38564 describe the limited excision of lymph nodes for **cancer staging**, which is the determination that cancer has or has not spread anatomically from its point of origin. Codes 38700–38780 describe the complete removal of the lymph nodes, and surgical wound closure is often performed in layers.

Exercise 13.3 – Hemic and Lymphatic Systems Subsection

Instructions: Assign the CPT code(s) and appropriate modifier(s) to each statement.

1. Patient underwent bilateral total pelvic lymphadenectomy via laparoscope with multiple periaortic lymph node samplings.

   _____

2. Physician conducted a donor search to locate a suitable match for a transplant patient and arranged acquisition of cells.

   _____

3. Physician infused a patient with allogenic lymphocytes.

4. Previously frozen stem cells were thawed, without washing.

5. Bone marrow biopsy, sternum, using trocar.

6. Progenitor cells (allogeneic) were harvested from umbilical and placental blood, cryopreserved, and maintained for transplantation.

7. Physician made a subcostal incision, dissected tissue surrounding the spleen, doubly ligated the vessels, and removed the spleen.

8. Physician sutured lacerations in a ruptured spleen and then resected and removed a damaged segment of the spleen.

9. Physician inserted a catheter into the spleen and injected 20 cubic centimeters of radiopaque dye for splenoportography.

10. Physician performed a total splenectomy.

11. A patient with idiopathic thrombocytopenic purpura underwent a laparoscopic splenectomy.

12. Patient underwent suprahyoid lymphandenectomy.

13. Patient underwent glossectomy with a composite resection on the left side of the neck with mandibular resection and radical neck dissection (Commando), and a modified radical neck dissection on the right side.

14. Patient underwent total laryngectomy with bilateral radical neck dissection.

15. Patient underwent injection of dye to visualize the sentinel node on lymphangiography.

Summary

The Cardiovascular System subsection classifies procedures performed on the heart and pericardium, valves (e.g., mitral and semilunar), and peripheral vascular vessels (e.g., arteries, veins, and capillaries). Cardiovascular System subsection codes are arranged anatomically and then according to procedure performed.

The Hemic and Lymphatic Systems subsection classifies procedures performed on the spleen, lymph nodes, and lymphatic channels.

Internet Links

CardioDynamics (impedance cardiography technology): *www.cardiodynamics.com*

CTSNet (Cardiothoracic Surgery Network): *www.ctsnet.org*

Medcomp (dialysis and vascular access catheters): *www.medcompnet.com*

Peripheral Vascular Surgery Society: Go to *www.pvss.org* and scroll over "Patients" and click on the Info for Patients link.

The Gross Physiology of the Cardiovascular System: *www.cardiac-output.info*

Study Checklist

☐ Read this chapter and highlight key concepts.

☐ Create an index card for each key term.

☐ Access the chapter Internet links to learn more about concepts.

☐ Complete the chapter review, verifying answers with your instructor.

☐ Complete WebTutor assignments and take online quizzes.

☐ Complete Workbook chapter, verifying answers with your instructor.

☐ Go to *www.cengagebrain.com* to access StudyWARE™ and the Premium Website. Login instructions are located in the Preface and on the Printed Access Card.

☐ Form a study group with classmates to discuss chapter concepts in preparation for an exam.

Review

Multiple Choice

Instructions: Circle the most appropriate response.

1. When coding cardiovascular system procedures, from which section(s) of CPT are additional codes often reported?

    a. E/M   b. Medicine   c. Pathology/Laboratory   d. Radiology, Medicine

2. When reporting codes 33880 and 33881 for endovascular repair of the descending thoracic aorta, which is included?
    a. placement of all extensions in the distal thoracic aorta
    b. placement of proximal extensions
    c. subclavian artery-to-carotid bypass
    d. subclavian carotid-to-carotid bypass

3. Codes 33500–33507, Coronary Artery Anomalies, include _____ when performed during the same operative session?
    a. arterial embolization   c. endarterectomy or angioplasty
    b. coronary artery bypass grafting   d. intravascular ultrasound

4. Review code 33282 (Implantation of a patient-activated cardiac event recorder). The parenthetical note below code 33282 provides instruction to assign codes 93285, 93291, or 93298 for:
    a. Holter monitor and external event recording.
    b. initial implantation, including programming.
    c. removal and reinsertion of a pacing cardioverter.
    d. subsequent electronic analysis and/or reprogramming.

5. When the "battery" of a pacemaker or pacing cardioverter-defibrillator (PCD) is changed, it is actually the _____ that is changed.

    a. catheter   b. electrode   c. pacemaker   d. pulse generator

6. An angioscopy (35400) is performed in addition to a transluminal balloon angioplasty of the renal artery during the same operative session. Which code(s) are reported?
   a. transluminal balloon angioplasty of renal artery only
   b. transluminal balloon angioplasty of renal artery and angioscopy
   c. transluminal balloon angioplasty of renal artery, angioscopy, and injection of contrast medium
   d. transluminal balloon angioplasty of renal artery, angioscopy, injection of contrast medium, and angiography

7. A coder reviews the patient record to determine the patient's age, whether the inserted catheter was tunneled or nontunneled, and whether the procedure was performed peripherally or via cutdown. Which procedure is being coded?
   a. arteriovenous anastomosis
   b. central venous access
   c. portal decompression
   d. therapeutic aspheresis

8. Which is the removal of a fixed blood clot?
   a. atherectomy
   b. embolectomy
   c. sympathectomy
   d. thrombectomy

9. The two types of aneurysm repair are:
   a. arteriovenous and open.
   b. endocardial and endovascular.
   c. endovascular and direct.
   d. transluminal and direct.

10. *En bloc* means:
   a. closed and blocked status of incision.
   b. implanted.
   c. insertion directly into a vein through a blood vessel.
   d. surgical removal as a whole.

11. Excision of mediastinal cyst. Which CPT code is assigned?
   a. 39000   b. 39010   c. 39200   d. 39220

12. Pericardiectomy with cardiopulmonary bypass. Which CPT code(s) are assigned?
   a. 33030, 33935
   b. 33030, 33935-51
   c. 33030, 33935-59
   d. 33031

13. Suture repair of aorta without shunt or cardiopulmonary bypass. Which CPT code is assigned?
   a. 33300   b. 33320   c. 33322   d. 33330

14. 15-year-old patient admitted for repair of patent ductus arteriosus by division. Which CPT code(s) are assigned?
   a. 33820   b. 33822   c. 33824   d. 33840

15. Patient with cardiopulmonary insufficiency receives 72 hours of extracorporeal circulation. Which CPT code(s) are assigned?
   a. 33960
   b. 33960, 33961
   c. 33960, 33961, 33961
   d. 33961, 33961

16. Open biopsy of deep cervical nodes. Which CPT code is assigned?
   a. 38500   b. 38510   c. 38520   d. 38525

17. Patient underwent percutaneous thrombectomy of the arteriovenous fistula with autogenous graft. Which CPT code is assigned?
   a. 36825   b. 36831   c. 36832   d. 36870

18. Percutaneous venous transluminal balloon angioplasty performed as a distinct procedural service. Which CPT code is assigned?
   a. 35460-59   b. 35460-79   c. 35476   d. 35476-59

19. Percutaneous transcatheter retrieval of intravascular foreign body. Which CPT code is assigned?
    a. 37201   b. 37202   c. 37203   d. 37204

20. Direct repair of a ruptured aneurysm of the abdominal aorta. Which CPT code is assigned?
    a. 33877   b. 34800   c. 35082   d. 35092

Coding Practice

Instructions: Assign the CPT code(s) and appropriate modifier(s) to each case.

Cardiovascular System

21. A patient presents to the ambulatory surgery center for stripping of the long saphenous veins in the right leg and the long and short saphenous veins in the left leg. The long saphenous veins were stripped from the saphenofemoral junction to the knee.

_____

22. A patient has a 3-year history of mitral regurgitation. The patient presents for mitral valve replacement. The procedure begins with placing the patient on heart-lung bypass machine. After gaining access to the thoracic cavity, the left atrium is identified. The damaged mitral valve is identified and removed. This is replaced with a biprosthetic valve and sewn in. Total time on bypass machine was 2.5 hours.

_____

23. A patient presents for pacemaker insertion due to diagnosis of bradycardia. After intravenous sedation was obtained, the entire left chest and neck were prepped. A standard incision was made in the left deltopectoral groove. A small venotomy was made, and the ventricular and then the atrial leads were placed into position. These were tested and found to be functioning properly. The leads were anchored at exit sites from the vein attached to the pacemaker. The pacemaker was tested, was functioning, and was placed in the subcutaneous pocket. All connections are checked. The patient will have another check before discharge from the hospital tomorrow.

_____

24. A 20-year-old male patient presents for surgical treatment of his patent ductus arteriosus (PDA). Under general anesthesia, a thoracotomy is done for access to the PDA. After the pericardium is opened to get to the mediastinum, the ductus is identified and closed via ligation.

_____

25. A 2-year-old patient presents to the ED after having fallen in a lake, with a near drowning. The patient is in shock. Regular venous access methods have failed, and the emergency department attending physician decides to do a venous cutdown. After a transverse incision over the vein of the patient's ankle is made, a small stab incision is done distal to the first incision. Two sutures are placed around the vein. A cannula is passed though the incision of the vein. The skin is closed in layers with.sutures.

_____

26. A 45-year-old patient diagnosed with chronic renal failure underwent surgery to facilitate dialysis access. The surgeon created an arteriovenous fistula by other than direct arteriovenous anastomosis with placement of nonautogenous graft access. The patient was prepped and draped in the usual fashion. Dissection was carried down the brachial artery and basilica vein. Prolene sutures were used to expose the vein. A thermoplastic graft was tunneled subcutaneously. The vein graft was sewn end to side. The graft was flushed with saline and then clamped below the anastomosis. The proximal graft at the 4 mm end was beveled and sewn to the small caliber brachial artery. Anastomosis was secured, and the native artery was flushed up through the graft first. All wounds were closed with Vicryl and nylon sutures.

_____

27. A 57-year-old patient was found to have carotid stenosis after duplex scan and angiogram. The patient presents today for a left carotid thromboendarterectomy with patch angioplasty. The neck area of the patient was prepped. An oblique incision along the sternomastoid muscle was made. Dissection was done through the platysma to the carotid sheath. The hypoglossal and vagus nerves were identified during dissection and preserved with care. The sheath dissection was performed along the anterior border of the left internal jugular vein. The common, external, and internal carotid arteries were dissected. The patient was given heparin, and clamping of the internal carotid did not reveal any changes on EEG monitor. The common and external carotids were clamped. A longitudinal arteriotomy was made. Standard thromboendarterectomy was performed, transecting the proximal end and working distally. The arteriotomy was closed with a patch cut to an ellipse and parachuted into the distal apex. The external and common carotids were opened. There was a good signal in the arteries. No changes were noted on the EEG. The wound was irrigated and closed.

28. The patient had an implantable cardioverter defibrillator (ICD) placed 6 months ago. The patient now has a malfunction of this device. After adequate anesthesia, an incision was made and the electrodes were removed from the generator. There was a screw problem with the generator that was producing a noise. The leads were tested and found to be working satisfactorily. The original pacing cardioverter-defibrillator pulse generator was removed and then replaced with a pacing cardioverter-defibrillator pulse generator. Both generators were a dual lead system. The ICD was placed back in the pocket, and the wound was closed after irrigation with 3-0 and 4-0 Vicryl.

29. A 35-year-old female patient has been found to have a pericardial cyst via echocardiogram. After adequate anesthesia, a lateral thoracotomy is performed to gain access to the pericardium. The patient's heart is stopped via cardioplegia infused through a heart-lung bypass machine. The pericardial cyst is seen lying next to the diaphragm. It is removed in total. Drainage tubes are placed. The cardioplegia is reversed. The cyst will be sent to pathology for analysis. The wound is closed in layers with Prolene and Vicryl.

30. A patient presents with a history of atherosclerosis. The patient is having surgery to bypass his blocked heart arteries. After anesthesia is administered and the patient is placed on a heart bypass machine, the surgeon makes a thoracic incision. The blockage of the heart is identified. The physician harvests a vein from the patient's leg to use in the bypass. An opening is made in the aorta. The grafted vein is sutured to the opening in the aorta at one end and below the blockage at the other end.

Hemic and Lymphatic Systems

31. A patient with a history of pancytopenia presents for a bone marrow biopsy. The physician numbs the skin and inserts a needle into the iliac bone. The core of the needle is discharged, and the sample is placed. The needle is withdrawn. The sample is sent for analysis.

32. A 14-year-old patient was in a motor vehicle crash and suffered blunt abdominal trauma. Due to internal bleeding and a ruptured spleen, the patient requires a splenectomy. After making the initial abdominal incision, the physician identifies the spleen. Splenic blood vessels are tied off. The spleen is removed in total. The remainder of the abdominal cavity is examined for any injuries or bleeding. No injury or additional bleeding is found. The wound is closed in layers.

33. A 3-year-old patient with a cystic hygroma of the neck presents for dissection. An incision is made in the neck. The tissue surrounding the hygroma is removed via excision. The hygroma is deep in the neurovascular section of the neck. Extensive and deep dissection is required for complete removal. The cyst is accessed and removed. The skin is closed in multiple layers.

_____

34. A patient underwent pelvic lymphadenectomy, which included removal of the external iliac, hypogastric, and obturator nodes. The patient has a history of ureteral cancer and now has pelvic pain and swelling. The patient is placed in the supine position. An incision is made over the iliac crest. Blood vessels are identified, and bleeders are cauterized. Enlarged pelvic lymph nodes are identified and removed in total. These are sent to pathology. The wound is closed with sutures.

_____

35. A patient presents for a cervical node removal. The patient's left neck area is prepped and draped in the usual fashion. An incision is made to access the cervical node. A scalene fat pad is identified and removed to access the deeper node. Both the cervical node and the pad are sent to pathology for analysis. The wound is closed in layers.

_____

36. A patient suffered a fall from 20 feet. The patient has internal bleeding and has consented for a laparoscopic procedure to identify internal structures that may be causing hemorrhage. The patient is placed in the normal lateral decubitus position. A trocar is placed above the umbilical region through an incision. Gas is introduced into the abdominal cavity. Laparoscopic examination identifies damage to the patient's spleen. An additional two incisions are made to insert trocars for the procedure. The spleen is dissected with hemostasis achieved. The spleen is removed via pouch method through the trocar. The three incision sites are closed with sutures.

_____

37. The patient presents for lymphangiography of the right pelvic lymph nodes. The radiologist accesses the patient's vein and puts dye in to highlight subcutaneous tissues. A lymph vessel is identified. A small incision is made to allow for the introduction of a needle and catheter. More dye is injected into this vessel. The needle and catheter are secured with a suture. The first set of films is done. The second set of films is done on the next day. After the second set of films, the radiologist removes the catheter and sutures the incision site closed.

_____

38. A patient with a history of chyle in the pleural cavity presents for suturing of his thoracic duct. Via an abdominal incision, the duct is identified and tied off. The incision is closed in layers with sutures.

_____

39. A patient with leukemia requires a bone marrow donor. The physician contacts the national bone marrow donor and provides medical information on the patient. The physician receives two potential matches.

_____

40. A patient has an enlarged lymph node of the axillary region. The physician makes an incision over the lymph node area after adequate local anesthesia. The node is identified and found to be inflamed; drainage of the node yields a pustulant material. The area is thoroughly irrigated, and the incision wound is closed with 4-0 Prolene sutures.

_____

CPT Surgery IV

Chapter Outline

Mediastinum and Diaphragm Subsection
Digestive System Subsection
Urinary System Subsection

Chapter Objectives

At the conclusion of this chapter, the student should be able to:

- Define key terms.
- Explain the organization, format, and content of the CPT Mediastinum and Diaphragm, Digestive System, and Urinary System subsections.
- Interpret CPT surgery coding notes for the Mediastinum and Diaphragm, Digestive System, and the Urinary System subsections.
- Assign CPT surgery codes from the Mediastinum and Diaphragm, Digestive System, and Urinary System subsections.
- Add CPT and/or HCPCS level II modifiers to codes, as appropriate.

Key Terms

anoscopy
biliary system
bipolar cautery
cheiloplasty
cholecystectomy
closed laparoscopy
cold biopsy forceps
colectomy
colonoscopy
colostomy
complex fistulectomy

continent ileostomy
cystometrogram
cystoscopy
cystourethroscopy
diagnostic endoscopy
diaphragm
digestive system
diverticula
diverticulosis
electrocautery snare
endorectal pull-through

endoscopic retrograde
   cholangiopancrea-
   tography (ERCP)
enterectomy
enterolysis
esophageal varices
esophagogastroduo-
   denoscopy (EGD)
esophagogastroscopy
esophagoscopy
gastrectomy
hepatotomy

hernia
hot biopsy forceps
hypopharynx
ileoanal anastomosis
ileostomy
J-pouch
kidney
Kock pouch
laparoscopy
laser technique
laser-assisted
   uvulopalatoplasty

lithotripsy	percutaneous lithotomy	sigmoidoscopy	upper GI endoscopy
Meckel's diverticulum	peristalsis	stoma	ureter
mediastinum	peritoneoscopy	subcutaneous fistulectomy	ureterolithotomy
mucocutaneous margin	proctectomy	submuscular fistulectomy	urethra
nasopharynx	proctosigmoidoscopy	submuscular fistulectomy	urethroplasty
nephrectomy	pull-through	surgical endoscopy	urinary bladder
Nissen fundoplasty	rhinoplasty	transurethral resection of the prostate (TURP)	urinary system
open laparoscopy	second-stage fistulectomy/ fistulotomy	transurethral resection of the prostate (TURP)	uroflowmetry
oropharynx	second-stage fistulectomy/ fistulotomy	transurethral ureteroscopic lithotripsy	volvulus
ostomy	seton	transurethral ureteroscopic lithotripsy	Whipple procedure
palatopharyngoplasty			

Introduction

The Mediastinum and Diaphragm subsection classifies procedures performed on the mediastinum and diaphragm. The Digestive System subsection classifies procedures performed on gastrointestinal (GI) tract organs as well as the teeth, palate and uvula, adenoids and tonsils, Meckel diverticulum and mesentery, appendix, biliary tract, pancreas, abdomen, peritoneum, and omentum. The Urinary System subsection classifies procedures performed on the kidneys, ureters, bladder, and urethra.

CPT guidelines that apply to the subsections are located at the beginning of the Surgery section. Unique coding instructions for the mediastinum and diaphragm, digestive system, and urinary system subsections are located in notes below headings or codes.

Coding Tip:

Notes located beneath headings and/or subheadings apply to all codes in the heading or subheading. Parenthetical notes that are located below a specific code apply to that code only, unless the note indicates otherwise.

Mediastinum and Diaphragm Subsection

Mediastinum and diaphragm subsection headings include the following:

- Mediastinum

- Diaphragm

The **mediastinum** is the space in the thoracic cavity between the lungs that contains the aorta, the esophagus, the heart, and other structures. Codes 39000–39499 are reported for procedures performed on the mediastinum.

The **diaphragm** is the thin muscle below the heart and lungs that separates the chest from the abdomen. It functions in respiration by contracting during inspiration, which means that the size of the chest cavity expands when a person is breathing in. Codes 39501–39599 are reported for procedures performed on the diaphragm (e.g., laceration).

The repair of two types of hernias is coded from the Mediastinum and Diaphragm heading:

- Hiatus hernia (Figure 14-1)

- Diaphragmatic hernia

    EXAMPLE 1: Patient underwent resection of mediastinal cyst. Report code 39200.

    EXAMPLE 2: Patient underwent resection of the diaphragm, with simple repair. Report code 39560.

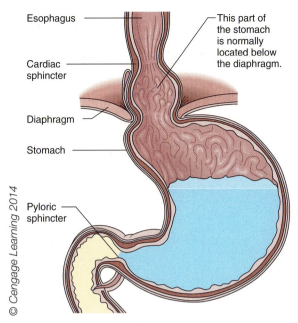

© Cengage Learning 2014

Esophagus

This part of the stomach is normally located below the diaphragm.

Cardiac sphincter

Diaphragm

Stomach

Pyloric sphincter

Figure 14-1 In a hiatus hernia (or hiatal hernia), part of the stomach protrudes through the esophageal opening in the diaphragm.

Exercise 14.1 – Mediastinum and Diaphragm Subsection

Instructions: Assign the CPT code(s) and appropriate modifier(s) to each statement.

1. The physician performed a complex repair during resection of the diaphragm and closed the residual defect with synthetic graft material.

   _____

2. Patient underwent median sternotomy to remove a foreign body.

   _____

3. Patient underwent repair, laceration of diaphragm.

   _____

4. Physician inserted a medastinoscope through an incision in the sternal notch and performed a mediastinal lymph node biopsy.

   _____

5. Physician repaired an acute traumatic diaphragmatic hernia.

   _____

Digestive System Subsection

The **digestive system** (Figure 14-2) begins at the mouth and extends to the anus. The upper digestive tract consists of the mouth, pharynx, esophagus, and stomach. The esophagus passes through the diaphragm and enters the stomach between its body and fundus. The stomach lies below the diaphragm and is composed of the fundus (upper portion under the diaphragm), body (middle), and antrum (lower).

The liver, the gallbladder, and the pancreas are digestive accessory organs that produce enzymes and substances that assist with digestion in the small intestine. The absorption of nutrients into the bloodstream occurs in the

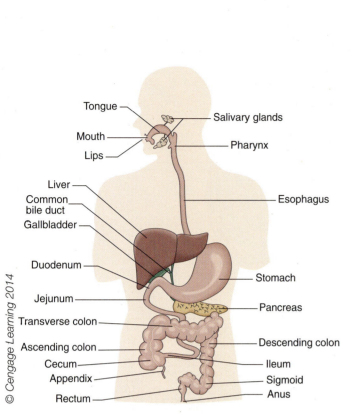

Figure 14-2 Digestive system organs

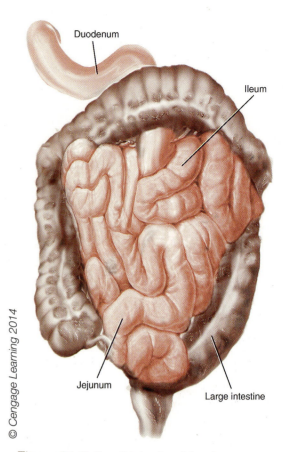

Figure 14-3 Small intestine (duodenum, jejunum, ileum)

small intestine (Figure 14-3). The pyloric sphincter controls the passage of digested food from the stomach into the duodenum (first part of the small intestine). The small intestine also contains the jejunum and the ileum, where the ileocecal valve allows for the controlled passage of digested material into the large intestine. The last section of the digestive tract is called the large intestine (Figure 14-4). It includes the cecum, colon, rectum, and anus. The appendix, located off the large intestine, has no known function.

Note:

When a lesion of the **mucocutaneous margin** (mucous membrane and skin) borders the digestive tract, it may appear that treatment (e.g., biopsy, destruction, or excision) requires the reporting of codes from multiple subsections of CPT to classify procedures performed. In fact, codes from just one of the following CPT subsections are reported:

- Integumentary system (10040–19499), *or*
- Digestive system (40490–49999).

The Digestive System subsection includes procedures to diagnose and treat disorders of the digestive system (e.g., GI endoscopy, laparoscopy, and gastric analysis). Similar to other Surgery subsections, procedures are classified first by anatomic area and then by type.

EXAMPLE: Patient underwent upper GI endoscopy of the esophagus, stomach, and duodenum, with specimen collection via brushing technique. Report code 43235.

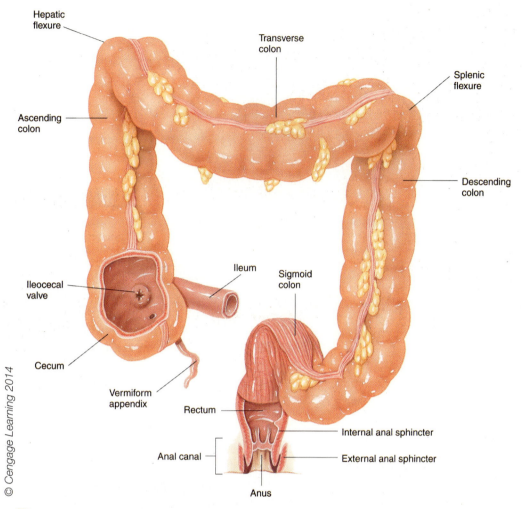

Figure 14-4 Large intestine

Digestive System subsection codes are reported for open, endoscopic, and laparoscopic procedures. The operative report must be carefully reviewed to correctly identify the surgical approach.

The following codes are reported for gastrostomy procedures (Figure 14-5). Their code descriptions differ based on the surgical approach (underlined in each code description below) used to perform the gastrostomy.

- 43246   Upper gastrointestinal <u>endoscopy</u> including esophagus, stomach, and either the duodenum and/or jejunum as appropriate; with directed placement of percutaneous gastrostomy tube

- 43653   Laparoscopy, <u>surgical</u>; gastrostomy, without construction of gastric tube (eg, Stamm procedure) (separate procedure)

- 43830   Gastrostomy, <u>open</u>; without construction of gastric tube (eg, Stamm procedure) (separate procedure)

- 49440   Insertion of gastrostomy tube, <u>percutaneous</u>, under fluoroscopic guidance...

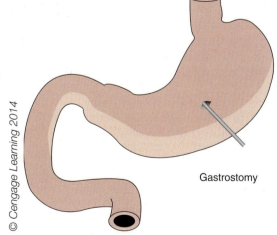

Figure 14-5 A gastrostomy is the surgical creation of an artificial opening into the stomach.

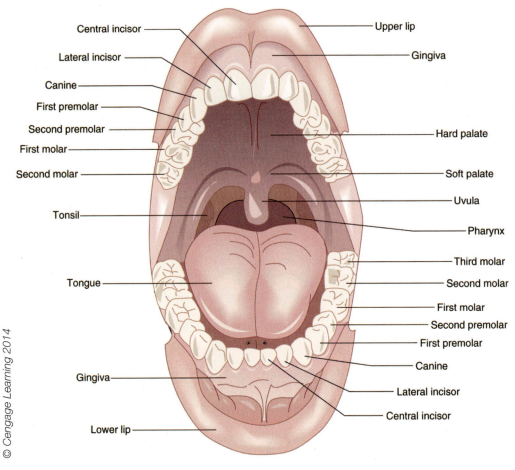

Figure 14-6 Oral cavity

© Cengage Learning 2014

Note:

The CPT Medicine section also contains codes for digestive system procedures. They are located under the Gastroenterology heading (91010–91299), which classifies diagnostic tests such as electrogastrography. Such tests are generally included in endoscopic procedures, which means that they are not separately coded and reported.

The following headings contain codes that classify procedures performed on the oral cavity (Figure 14-6):

- Lips
- Palate and Uvula
- Vestibule of Mouth
- Salivary Gland and Ducts
- Tongue and Floor of Mouth
- Pharynx, Adenoids, and Tonsils
- Dentoalveolar Structures

Lips

CPT codes 40490–40799 are reported for procedures performed on the lips (e.g., biopsy of lip). Codes 40490–40530 are reported for excision procedures performed on the lip. When a procedure is performed on the *skin* of the lip, report an appropriate code from the Integumentary System subsection. Do *not* report codes from both subsections for the same procedure.

Cheiloplasty is the plastic surgery of the lips. To properly assign codes 40650–40654, review the operative report to determine the vertical height associated with the repair (e.g., up to one-half vertical height or over one-half vertical height).

EXAMPLE 1: Patient underwent a lip biopsy. Report code 40490.

EXAMPLE 2: Patient underwent biopsy of the skin of the lip. The surgeon removed a skin lesion from the lateral side of the bottom lip. Report code 11100 (from the Integumentary System subsection).

The *full-thickness* repair of a lip laceration is reported with a code from the Repair (Cheiloplasty) heading. Do *not* report a code from the Integumentary System subsection instead of *or* in addition to full-thickness repairs of lip lacerations. (Simple and intermediate repairs of *skin* on the lip are reported with codes from the Integumentary System subsection.)

For procedures performed to repair cleft lip and nasal deformities, review the operative report to identify whether the procedure is:

- Primary or secondary.

- One-stage or two-stage.

A primary procedure repairs the cleft lip/nasal deformity without re-creating the defect. A secondary procedure re-creates the defect and includes reclosure to repair the cleft lip/nasal deformity.

Codes 40700, 40720, and 40761 are performed unilaterally. For a bilateral procedure, add modifier -50 to the reported code. For a **rhinoplasty** (repair of skin defect of the nose using harvested tissue or plastic surgery to change the nose's shape or size), report a code from the Respiratory subsection (30460–30462). For repair of a cleft lip using a cross-lip pedicle flap (Abbe-Estlander type), report code 40527. For more complicated plastic repair of a cleft lip or nasal deformity using a cross-lip pedicle flap (Abbe-Estlander type) with sectioning/inserting of pedicle (flap), report code 40761.

EXAMPLE 1: Patient underwent full-thickness repair of the vermilion border of the upper lip. Patient sustained a laceration while replacing spark plugs in his classic 1967 Pontiac Bonneville. Report code 40650.

EXAMPLE 2: Patient underwent up to half vertical height full-thickness repair of the lower lip due to laceration acquired during a bar fight. The wound extended through the full thickness of the lip, including the vermilion border. Wound size was up to one-half the vertical height of the lip. Report code 40652.

Vestibule of Mouth

Codes 40800–40899 are reported for the following procedures performed on the vestibule of the mouth, which includes mucosal and submucosal tissue (inner lining) of the lips and cheeks:

- Incision

- Excision, destruction

- Repair

- Other procedures (unlisted procedure)

EXAMPLE: The patient has a habit of sucking on toothpicks; and during a recent automobile accident, a toothpick became embedded in submucosal tissue in his mouth. Patient underwent simple removal of embedded foreign body (toothpick). Report code 40804.

Tongue and Floor of Mouth

Codes 41000–41599 are reported for procedures performed on the tongue and floor of the mouth include the following:

- Incision

- Excision

- Repair

- Other procedures

When reporting codes for excision of a tongue lesion, review the operative report to identify the:

- Location of the lesion (e.g., posterior one-third or anterior two-thirds of the tongue).

- Type of excision (partial or complete/total).

Note:

When a partial glossectomy with bilateral radical neck dissection is performed, report code 41135 for the glossectomy and radical neck dissection on one side. (There is just one tongue, which means modifier -50 cannot be added to code 41135.) Report code 38720-59 for the radical neck dissection on the other side. (Modifier -59 is added to indicate a distinct procedural service.)

EXAMPLE: Patient underwent partial glossectomy with unilateral radical neck dissection. Report code 41135.

Dentoalveolar Structures

Codes 41800–41899 are reported for procedures performed on dentoalveolar structures (e.g., teeth or gums). These codes are classified in the Digestive System subsection of CPT because most commonly performed dental procedures are not actually found in CPT. Such procedures are classified in the *Current Dental Terminology* (CDT).

EXAMPLE: Patient underwent drainage of gum abscess. Report code 41800.

Palate and Uvula

CPT codes 42000–42299 describe procedures performed on the hard and soft palates and the uvula. A **palatopharyngoplasty** (code 42145) is performed to treat oropharyngeal obstructions; it involves surgically resecting excess tissue from the uvula, soft palate, and pharynx to open the airway (e.g., cure extreme cases of snoring with or without sleep apnea).

Note:

Do not report code 42145 (Palatopharyngoplasty) for a **laser-assisted uvulopalatoplasty** procedure, which uses a laser technique to remove tissue from the uvula, soft palate, and pharynx. CPT does not list a specific code for laser-assisted uvulopalatoplasty. Therefore, either report unlisted code 42299 and submit a copy of the operative report with the claim or report HCPCS level II code S2080. Because more than one treatment session may be required to achieve optimal results, subsequent visits to repeat the laser-assisted uvulopalatoplasty are included in the global period for the code reported. Therefore, a code for each repeat session is *not* reported separately.

Codes 42200–42235 describe cleft palate repairs (Figure 14-7). The size and location of the cleft determine the type of repair performed (and reported code).

Coding Tip:

Cleft lip/nasal deformity repairs are reported with codes 40700–40761. When a cleft palate repair is performed during the same operative session as a cleft lip/nasal deformity repair, report a code from 42200–42235 and 40700–40761.

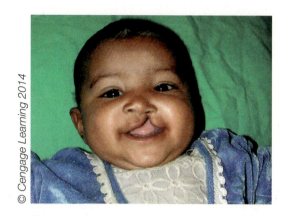

© Cengage Learning 2014

© Cengage Learning 2014

Figure 14-7 A child with a cleft palate before and after treatment.

EXAMPLE: The patient underwent primary plastic repair of cleft lip/nasal deformity, complete, unilateral. During the same operative session, the patient also underwent palatoplasty for cleft palate, with closure of alveolar ridge, soft tissue only. Report codes 40700 and 42205-51.

Salivary Gland and Ducts

Codes 42300–42699 are reported for procedures performed to treat conditions involving the salivary gland and salivary ducts (e.g., abscess, cyst, and tumor). The selection of a code for the excision of a parotid tumor or the parotid gland (42410–42426) is based on the following:

- What amount of tissue was excised

- Where the location was (e.g., lateral lobe)

- Whether the procedure included nerve dissection

- Whether the procedure included radical neck dissection

Note:

When the excision of a parotid tumor or the parotid gland is performed with bilateral radical neck dissection, report code 42426 for the excision and radical neck dissection on one side. (There is just one parotid gland, which means that modifier -50 *cannot* be added to code 42426.) Report code 38720-59 for the radical neck dissection on the other side. (Modifier -59 is added to indicate that a distinct procedural service was provided.)

Pharynx, Adenoids, and Tonsils

Codes 42700–42999 are reported for procedures performed on the pharynx, adenoids, and tonsils. The pharynx contains three segments:

- **Nasopharynx**: Located above the soft palate.

- **Oropharynx**: Area between the soft palate and the upper portion of the epiglottis, including the tonsils.

- **Hypopharynx**: Extends from the upper edge of the epiglottis to the larynx/esophagus juncture.

A variety of techniques and approaches are used when treating conditions of the pharynx (e.g., oral, cervical, thoracic, and horizontal or lateral neck incisions).

EXAMPLE: Patient underwent removal of a lesion of the pharynx via oral approach using curettage. Report code 42808.

Tonsillectomy and Adenoidectomy

Tonsillectomy and adenoidectomy are the most frequently performed procedures coded from this heading. Codes 42820–42836 are reported for the removal of diseased tonsils or adenoids, using any of the following techniques:

- Cryogenic

- Electrocautery

- Laser

   The selection of a tonsillectomy or adenoidectomy code is based on the following:

- Type of procedure performed (e.g., primary or secondary)

- Age of the patient

   A primary procedure code is reported the first time the tonsils or adenoids are removed. A secondary procedure code is reported when there is tissue regrowth requiring subsequent removal. The age of the patient is a factor because age increases the complexity (level of difficulty) of the procedure and lengthens the recovery time.

   Separate codes are included to report hemorrhage control following tonsillectomy and adenoidectomy procedures. Make sure you report these procedure codes with modifier -78 to indicate the return to the operating room for a related procedure performed during the postoperative (global) period.

   Codes 42842–42845 are reported for the radical resection of tonsils, which involves the removal of the tonsils, tonsillar pillars, retromolar trigone, and any infected portions of the maxilla and mandible. Radical resection may also include a hemi- or total glossectomy and/or a full neck dissection.

   A limited pharyngectomy (42890) is performed to remove a small portion of the pharyngeal wall (e.g., pyriform sinus).

Coding Tip:

Tonsillectomy and adenoidectomy are routinely performed bilaterally, and modifier -50 is not added to the codes.

Exercise 14.2 – Oral Cavity

Instructions: Assign the CPT code(s) and appropriate modifier(s) to each statement.

1. Patient underwent alveoloplasty to remove sharp areas or undercuts of alveolar bone, one quadrant.

   _____

2. Surgeon used a scalpel to slice off a cancerous portion of the vermilion border of the patient's lip; mucosal advancement was performed after excision.

   _____

3. Surgeon made an incision through submucosal tissue and removed a lesion in the vestibule of the mouth. Wound repair was not required.

   _____

4. Patient underwent simple incision of the lingual frenum to free the tongue.

   _____

5. Patient underwent incision in the parotid gland to remove a calcified stone.

   _____

6. Surgeon repaired a tear at the pharyngeal esophageal junction.

   _____

7. Physician drained an abscess near the tonsil.

_____

8. Surgeon removed an 8-year-old patient's tonsils and adenoids.

_____

9. Physician controlled secondary oropharyngeal hemorrhaging, status post-tonsillectomy, by using cellulose sponges that expanded when placed in the tonsillar cavity.

_____

10. Physician performed a tonsillectomy on a 12-year-old male patient.

_____

Esophagus

Codes 43020–43499 are reported for procedures performed on the esophagus. When assigning codes to procedures performed on the esophagus, review documentation carefully to identify the approach (e.g., incision or endoscopy).

EXAMPLE 1: Patient underwent esophagotomy via cervical approach, with removal of foreign body. Report code 43020.

EXAMPLE 2: Patient underwent cricopharyngeal myotomy via esophagotomy, thoracic approach, with removal of foreign body. Report code 43045.

Endoscopy

Endoscopic procedures performed to visualize digestive system organs generally use a flexible fiber-optic tube. (Rigid instruments are also used to perform endoscopy.) GI endoscopy is performed to diagnose and treat disorders of the GI tract. Codes are assigned according to the type of instrument used and the anatomic area visualized. The codes are classified in CPT as the following series:

- **Esophagoscopy** (43200–43232) is the direct visualization of the esophagus, using an endoscope.

- **Upper GI endoscopy (esophagogastroscopy)** (43234) is the direct visualization of the esophagus and the stomach.

- **Esophagogastroduodenoscopy (EGD)** (43235–43259) (Figure 14-8) uses a fiber-optic endoscope to visualize the esophagus, stomach, and proximal duodenum.

- **Endoscopic retrograde cholangiopancreatography (ERCP)** (43260–43272) involves passing an endoscope through the esophagus, stomach, and duodenum to the ducts of the biliary tree and pancreas. A small plastic tube is passed through the endoscope, through which dye is injected (to allow for visualization of the ducts on X-rays). A radiologist then takes X-rays to diagnose liver, gallbladder, bile duct, and pancreas problems.

Coding Tip:

Code 43200 is the parent code in the GI endoscopy series of codes (43200–43232). This means that descriptions for codes 43201–43232 are indented below code 43200. Review the partial listing of rigid or flexible esophagoscopy codes and descriptions below. Note that code 43202 is reported for a patient who undergoes flexible or rigid esophagoscopy with single or multiple biopsies.

- 43200 Esophagoscopy, rigid or flexible; diagnostic, with or without collection of specimen(s) by brushing or washing (separate procedure)

- 43201 with directed submucosal injections(s), any substance

- 43202 with biopsy, single or multiple

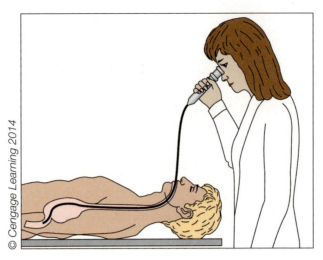

Figure 14-8 Esophagogastroduodenoscopy (EGD)

Endoscopic procedures are considered diagnostic or surgical, and surgical endoscopy always includes diagnostic endoscopy. This means that when both procedures are performed during the same operative session, report the code for surgical endoscopy only.

- **Diagnostic endoscopy** is performed to visualize an abnormality or determine the extent of disease.

- **Surgical endoscopy** is performed when anything in addition to visualization is performed (e.g., removal of foreign body).

  EXAMPLE: Patient underwent diagnostic flexible sigmoidoscopy and biopsy of a lesion during the same operative session. The code for the diagnostic endoscopy (45330) is not reported. Only the code for the surgical procedure (45331) is reported.

Code 43202 (Esophagoscopy, rigid or flexible; with biopsy, single or multiple) is reported just once regardless of the number of biopsies performed. Likewise, codes 43216 and 43217 are reported just once regardless of the number of lesions treated.

  EXAMPLE 1: Patient underwent flexible esophagoscopy with multiple biopsies. Report code 43202.

  EXAMPLE 2: Patient underwent flexible esophagoscopy with removal of five polyps by bipolar cautery. Report code 43216 (just once even though five polyps were removed).

  EXAMPLE 3: Patient underwent flexible esophagoscopy with removal of three lesions by snare technique. Report code 43217 (just once even though three lesions were removed).

The endoscopic treatment of **esophageal varices** (uneven, enlarged, tortuous veins) (Figure 14-9) includes the following:

- Ligation (similar to the technique used to band hemorrhoids)

- Endoscopic injection of a sclerosing agent (e.g., concentrated saltwater)

Code 43204 is reported for an esophagoscopy that includes injection sclerosis of esophageal varices. During injection sclerosis, the physician passes a sclerotherapy needle through the scope and injects the sclerosing agent into the varices.

Code 43243 is reported when the physician performs an esophagogastroduodenoscopy (EGD), passes a sclerotherapy needle through the endoscope, and injects varices with an agent to obliterate them. Code 43244 is reported when the physician performs an EGD, passes a suction tip through the endoscope to lift the varix, and places a rubber band around the base of the varix to ligate it.

  EXAMPLE 1: Patient underwent flexible esophagoscopy with band ligation of esophageal varices. Report code 43205.

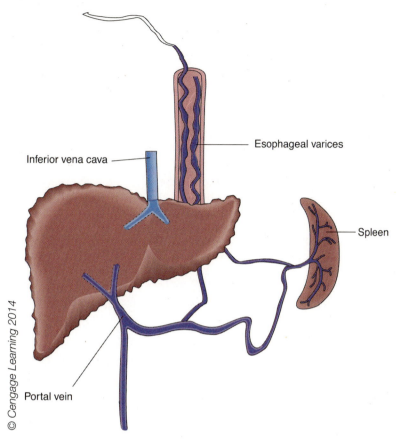

Figure 14-9 Esophageal varices

EXAMPLE 2: Patient underwent direct ligation of esophageal varices. Physician accessed the esophagus through a thoracic incision and ligated the varices with sutures. Report code 43400.

EXAMPLE 3: Patient underwent esophageal transection with repair of esophageal varices. The physician used a stapler that was inserted through an incision in the anterior wall of the stomach to transect and repair the esophagus to remove esophageal varices. Report code 43401.

EXAMPLE 4: Patient underwent ligation at the gastroesophageal junction for preexisting esophageal perforation. The physician ligated the junction of the stomach and esophagus, and a gastrostomy was created for feeding. Report code 43405.

Procedures performed to treat gastroesophageal reflux disease (GERD) (43257) typically use conscious sedation as well as radiofrequency energy delivered via endoscopy. The physician performs an EGD with ultrasound examination, and radiofrequency energy is subsequently applied through the endoscope to the muscle of the lower esophageal sphincter and/or the gastric cardia to treat GERD.

Note:

Do not add code 43653 for the gastrostomy because its (separate procedure) note means that part of the procedure is included in code 43404. However, if the gastrostomy was performed through a (documented) separate incision, reporting 43404 with modifier -59 (Distinct Procedural Service) is permitted.

EXAMPLE: Patient underwent upper GI endoscopy of the esophagus, stomach, and duodenum with delivery of thermal energy to the lower esophageal sphincter muscle for treatment of GERD. Report code 43257.

Codes 43260–43272 are reported for ERCP. For example, if gallstones are present in the gallbladder (or bile duct), the doctor can remove them through the endoscope. Biopsies may also be taken for evaluation by the pathologist.

EXAMPLE: Patient underwent diagnostic ERCP with single biopsy. Report code 43261.

When a sphincterotomy of the bile duct or pancreatic duct is performed, it includes a diagnostic ERCP. A guidewire is advanced into the biliary tree, and an electrocautery current is applied to make the incision (code 43262). When the patient undergoes gallstone and pancreatic duct stone removal (43264–43265) and a sphincterotomy is performed during the same operative session, code 43262 is also reported.

EXAMPLE: A patient undergoes ERCP basket removal of gallstones following a sphincterotomy. Report codes 43262 and 43264–51.

Laparoscopy

A **laparoscopy**, or **peritoneoscopy**, is the examination of the peritoneal contents using a laparoscope that is inserted through the abdominal wall.

> **Note:**
>
> Surgical laparoscopy always includes diagnostic laparoscopy.

- **Closed laparoscopy** is the insufflation of the abdominal cavity and is performed using a percutaneously placed needle.

- **Open laparoscopy** is the insufflation of the abdomen and is performed using a trocar, which is placed under direct vision after making a small celiotomy incision.

  EXAMPLE: Patient underwent surgical laparoscopy with Nissen esophagogastric fundoplasty. Report code 43280. (**Nissen fundoplasty** involves mobilizing the lower end of the esophagus by suturing the fundus of the stomach around the circumference of the lower esophagus at the esophagogastric junction.)

Manipulation

When endoscopic esophageal procedures are performed, the advancement of the endoscope through the esophagus expands any stricture. The dilation is considered an integral part of the esophagoscopy procedure. This means that a code from 43450–43458 (Dilation of the esophagus without the use of an endoscope) is not reported with a code for endoscopy of the esophagus (even if the operative report documents esophageal dilation during endoscopy). When esophagogastric tamponade is performed with a balloon (Sengstaaken type), report code 43460.

 Note:

> Esophageal dilation (without endoscopy) is usually performed under fluoroscopic guidance. Make sure you report the appropriate fluoroscopic guidance (X-ray) code in addition to the manipulation code, when performed.

 EXAMPLE: The physician uses fluoroscopy to insert a guidewire and to dilate the esophagus by passing dilators over the guidewire. Report 43453. (Code 74360 is reported for fluoroscopy, which is radiological guidance of "intraluminal dilation of strictures and/or obstructions, such as the esophagus.")

> **Coding Tip:**
>
> When a procedure is performed for the purpose of endoscopic dilation, report the appropriate code (43226, 43248, or 43249).

Other Procedures

The free transfer of a short segment of jejunum (43496) is usually performed after portions of the pharynx or esophagus have been resected (e.g., cervical esophageal and hypopharyngeal carcinoma).

Stomach

Codes 43500–43999 are reported for procedures performed on the stomach.

- **Gastrectomy** (removal of all or a portion of the stomach) is typically performed to treat ulcers (Figure 14-10) or malignancy and includes codes 43620–43635.

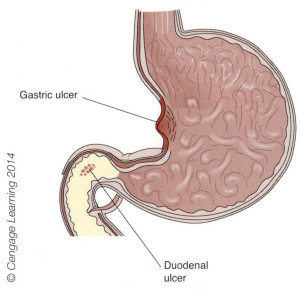

Figure 14-10 Gastric and duodenal ulcers

- The Roux-en-Y gastric bypass and small bowel reconstruction procedures (43644–43645) use a Y-shaped anastomosis that includes the intestines.

- Surgical laparoscopic procedures performed on the stomach are reported with codes 43651–43659. Codes reported for procedures involving the field of bariatric surgery use laparoscopic techniques to perform gastric restrictive procedures for morbid obesity.

- Naso- or orogastric tube placement (43752) that requires a physician's skill and fluoroscopic guidance is reported when the nursing staff is unable to successfully insert the tube. Code 43752 is not reported when nursing staff inserts the tube.

- Gastric restrictive procedures involve placement of an adjustable gastric band (43770–43774).

- Code 43845 is reported for a gastric restrictive procedure that includes two reconstructive anastomosis (biliopancreatic diversion with duodenal switch).

- Code 43846 is reported for a gastric bypass procedure that includes Roux-en-Y gastroesterostomy.

  EXAMPLE: Patient underwent surgical laparoscopic gastric restrictive procedure, which included gastric bypass and Roux-en-Y gastroenterostomy (roux limb 150 cm or less). Report code 43644.

Intestines (Except Rectum)

Codes 44005–44799 are reported for procedures performed on the intestines (except rectum). (Codes 45000–45999 are reported for procedures performed on the rectum.) Because codes 44005–44799 describe similar-sounding procedures (e.g., enterolysis, enterectomy, and enteroenterostomy), coders must carefully review operative report documentation to ensure correct code assignment.

Incision

The **enterolysis** (freeing of intestinal adhesions) (44005) is classified as a separate procedure code, and it is considered an integral component of hernia repair codes. Therefore, do not report code 44005 when other surgical procedures include the lysis of intestinal adhesions. However, if documentation indicates that enterolysis was extensive and added significantly to the procedure, add modifier -22 (Increased Procedural Services) to code 44005. There are, however, some instances when it is appropriate to report code 44005 with other intestine procedure codes.

Exercise 14.3 – Esophagus and Stomach

Instructions: Assign the CPT code(s) and appropriate modifier(s) to each statement.

1. Physician inserted a flexible esophagoscope into the esophagus and destroyed a lesion, using snare technique.

   _____

2. Surgeon made an incision in the left posterior chest wall into the esophagus to remove a foreign body from the esophagus.

   _____

3. Physician inserted a balloon endoscopically for tamponade of bleeding esophageal varices.

   _____

4. Dr. Smith performed a cervical esophagectomy while Dr. Jones performed a jejunum transfer with microvascular anastomosis.

   _____

5. The physician passed an endoscope through the patient's mouth and visualized the entire esophagus, stomach, duodenum, and jejunum. One lesion was removed using biopsy forceps. Another lesion was removed using a snare.

   _____

6. Patient underwent incision of the pyloric muscle.

   _____

7. The physician performed an open revision of a previously performed gastric restrictive procedure and reversed the previously partitioned stomach to restore normal gastrointestinal continuity.

   _____

8. Using fluoroscopic guidance, the physician repositioned a gastric feeding tube through the duodenum.

   _____

9. The physician performed a laparoscopic surgical gastric restrictive procedure with gastric bypass and Roux-en-Y gastroenterostomy.

   _____

10. The physician percutaneously placed a gastrostomy tube into the stomach.

    _____

Codes 44050–44055 describe the surgical treatment of a **volvulus** (twisting or displacement of the intestines, causing obstruction). (Figure 14-11)

EXAMPLE: Patient underwent reduction of volvulus (Figure 14-11) via laparotomy. Report code 44050.

Excision

Enterectomy (resection of small bowel segments) procedure codes (44120–44128) describe resection of a segment of the intestine and they require the coder to determine the:

- Amount of tissue removed.

- Type of repair performed.

  (When the procedure is performed for congenital atresia, refer to codes 44126–44128.) An enteroenterostomy (44130) is the creation of an artificial external opening or fistula in the intestines.

EXAMPLE: Patient underwent enterectomy, which involved resection of two segments of the small intestine with anastomosis. Report codes 44120 and 44121.

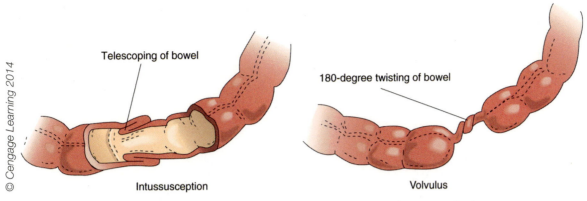

© Cengage Learning 2014

Figure 14-11 Bowel obstructions can be caused by an intussusception or a volvulus.

Colectomy is the removal of part or all of the large intestine (e.g., colon); however, a partial colectomy is more common. Four types of partial colectomies include removal of:

- All/part of the right colon (e.g., right colectomy).
- All/part of the left colon (e.g., left colectomy).
- All/part of the rectosigmoid colon (e.g., anterior resection).
- The lower rectosigmoid colon, rectum, and anus (e.g., abdominal perineal resection).

    EXAMPLE: Patient underwent total colectomy with proctectomy and ileostomy. Report code 44155.

Laparoscopy

Surgical laparoscopy includes diagnostic laparoscopy, which means if both procedures are documented a code for the surgical laparoscopy only is reported. If a diagnostic laparoscopy (peritoneoscopy) only is performed, report code 49320.

    EXAMPLE: Patient underwent laparoscopic jejunostomy for feeding. Report code 44186.

Enterostomy — External Fistulization of Intestines

An **ostomy** refers to surgically creating an opening in the body for the discharge of body wastes. (A **stoma** is a surgically created opening between to the ureter, small intestine, or large intestine through the abdominal wall.) Ostomy procedures are classified according to the portion of the digestive tract that is brought to the surface. (They may be permanent or temporary.) Types of ostomies are the following:

- **Colostomy**: A portion of the colon or rectum is removed, and the remaining colon is brought to the abdominal wall (Figure 14-12).
- **Ileostomy**: The colon and rectum are removed, and the small intestine is brought to the abdominal wall.

    A **continent ileostomy**, or **Kock pouch**, is a surgical variation of an ileostomy. A reservoir pouch is created inside the abdomen using a portion of the terminal ileum, a valve is constructed in the pouch, and a stoma is brought through the abdominal wall. A catheter is inserted into the pouch several times each day to empty feces from the reservoir.

    EXAMPLE: Patient underwent continent ileostomy. Report code 44316.

Endoscopy, Small Intestine and Stomal

Jejunal feedings (44373) are performed via small intestinal endoscopy. This type of endoscopy is an enteroscopy that is performed beyond the second portion of duodenum (not including the ileum), and the procedure (44373) includes conversion of a percutaneous gastrostomy tube to a percutaneous jejunostomy tube. During this procedure, a thin tube is passed through the gastrostomy tube into the stomach and advanced; a direct puncture is *not* made into the jejunum. (Code 44372 classifies an infrequently performed procedure, the endoscopic placement of a percutaneous jejunostomy tube using a percutaneous puncture and endoscopic guidance.)

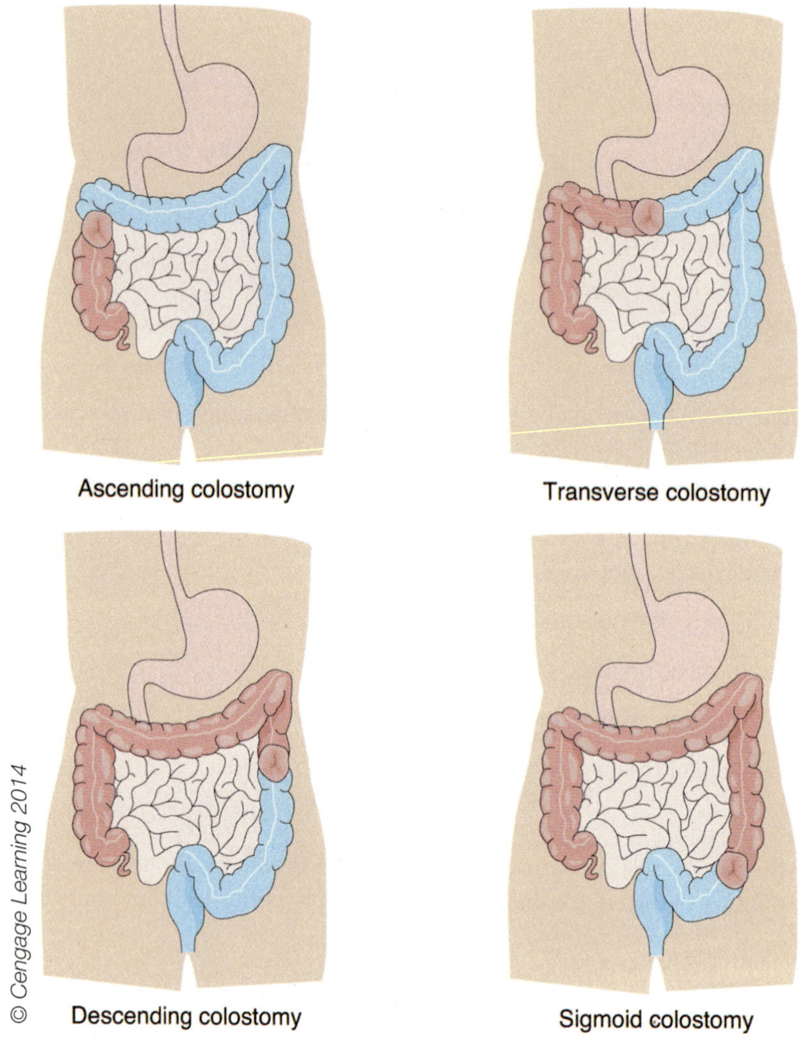

Ascending colostomy

Transverse colostomy

© Cengage Learning 2014

Descending colostomy

Sigmoid colostomy

Figure 14-12 Colostomy locations (Blue section may be surgically removed if colostomy is permanent.)

Codes 44376–44379 are reported for small intestinal endoscopy, enteroscopy beyond second portion of duodenum, procedures. Codes 44380–44383 are reported for ileoscopy, through stoma. Codes 44385–44386 are reported for the endoscopic evaluation of a small intestinal pouch. Codes 44388–44397 are reported for colonoscopy through stoma procedures.

EXAMPLE: Patient underwent small intestinal endoscopy with enteroscopy beyond the second portion of the duodenum and single biopsy. Report code 44361.

Introduction

The introduction of a long gastrointestinal (GI) tube with an inflatable balloon at the end (e.g., Miller-Abbott) (44500) is performed to clear GI strictures.

EXAMPLE: Patient underwent introduction of a Miller-Abbott GI tube to clear GI strictures. Report code 44500.

Repair

Codes 44602–44680 are reported for procedures performed to repair the small intestine.

EXAMPLE: Code 44602 is reported for the suturing of a single perforation of the small intestine, while code 44603 is reported for the suturing of multiple perforations.

Other Procedures

Code 44700 describes a procedure performed to exclude the small intestine from the pelvis by implanting mesh or other prosthesis or by using native tissue. When the small intestine is elevated to prevent damage from radiation therapy, mesh, other prosthesis, or native tissue is used (44700). An instructional note below code 44700 provides instruction to report codes from the Radiology Oncology heading for therapeutic radiation treatment.

> **EXAMPLE:** Patient underwent exclusion of the small intestine from the pelvis with placement of mesh. Report code 44700.

Meckel's Diverticulum and the Mesentery

Diverticula (Figure 14-13) are small pouches (herniations) in the colon that bulge outward through weak spots. **Diverticulosis** is the presence of diverticula in the mucosa and submucosal, through or between fibers of the colon's major muscle layer. Codes 44800–44899 are reported for procedures performed to treat diverticular and mesenteric diseases.

Meckel's diverticulum is a common congenital abnormality of the GI tract that results in a pouch in the wall of the small bowel that contains remnants of fetal GI tissue. The diverticulum may contain gastric, stomach, ectopic, or pancreatic tissue. Treatment includes excision of Meckel's diverticulum.

> **EXAMPLE:** Patient underwent excision of Meckel's diverticulum. Report code 44800.

Appendix

Appendectomies (44950–44970) are performed laparoscopically or through an open abdominal incision. An instructional note below code 44950 states that when an appendectomy is performed during intra-abdominal surgery, it is considered incidental; it is not coded and reported separately. When an appendectomy is performed for an indicated purpose during the same operative session as another major procedure, report code 44955.

> **EXAMPLE 1:** Patient underwent laparoscopic appendectomy for acute appendicitis. Report code 44970.

> **EXAMPLE 2:** Patient underwent excision of Meckel's diverticulum. During surgery, the physician noted that the appendix was inflamed and enlarged; an appendectomy was also performed. Report codes 44800 and 44955 (According to Ingenix's Encoder Pro Expert, modifier -51 is not reported with add-on code 44955. Also, modifier -59 is not added to code 44955 because a separate incision was *not* made to perform the appendectomy).

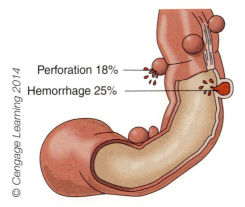

© Cengage Learning 2014

Perforation 18%
Hemorrhage 25%

Figure 14-13 Diverticula in the sigmoid colon. Diverticulosis is almost always located in the descending or sigmoid colon.

Rectum

Codes 45000–45999 are reported for procedures performed on the rectum. Endoscopic procedure codes specify the type of instrument used, the purpose of the endoscopy, and the site involved. When reporting codes for colonoscopies (e.g., colostomy or rectum), the coder must also determine the approach. GI endoscopic procedures involve the small bowel, colon, and rectum and include the following:

- **Proctosigmoidoscopy**: Visual examination of the rectum and sigmoid colon.

- **Sigmoidoscopy**: Visual examination of the entire rectum and sigmoid colon and may include a portion of the descending colon (Figure 14-14).

- **Colonoscopy**: Visual examination of the entire colon, from the rectum to the cecum, and may include the terminal ileum (Figure 14-15).

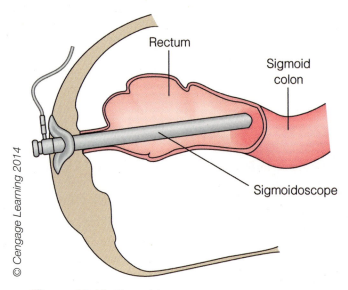

Figure 14-14 Sigmoidoscopy

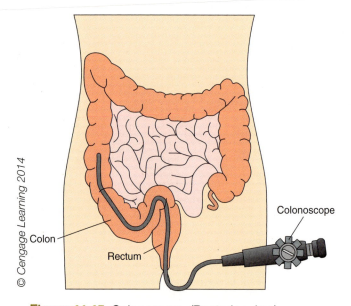

Figure 14-15 Colonoscopy (Posterior view)

Coding Tip:

- When an incomplete colonoscopy is performed and the patient underwent full preparation for a colonoscopy, add modifier -52 (Reduced Services) to the colonoscopy code.
- When multiple endoscopies are performed during the same operative session, report each with a separate code.
- Surgical endoscopy always includes diagnostic endoscopy. This means that when a diagnostic endoscopy is performed during the same operative session as a surgical endoscopy, report just the surgical endoscopy code.
- CMS requires screening sigmoidoscopy procedures to be reported with HCPCS level II code G0104.

Proctosigmoidoscopy and sigmoidoscopy procedures are typically performed without anesthesia. Colonoscopies usually require sedation to avoid severe patient discomfort.

EXAMPLE: Patient underwent sigmoidoscopy and colonoscopy during the same operative session. Report code 45378 for the colonoscopy only. (Do not report a code for the sigmoidoscopy because the endoscope was passed through the sigmoid colon to perform the colonoscopy. Visual examination of the sigmoid colon was performed on the way to visual examination of the rest of the colon.)

When multiple services are provided during an endoscopic procedure, report a code for each. Multiple services are reimbursed according to multiple endoscopic payment rules (e.g., discounted reimbursement for second and subsequent procedures). An exception to this rule is follow-up treatment of bleeding due to the endoscopic procedure.

Different techniques are used to remove lesions or polyps (Figure 14-16) through an endoscope. A **hot biopsy forceps** (45384) uses tweezer-like forceps connected to a monopolar electrocautery unit and a grounding pad. **Bipolar cautery** (45384) uses an electric current that flows from one tip of the forceps to the other and does not require a grounding pad. An **electrocautery snare** (45385) uses a wire loop to encircle, not grasp, the polyp. **Cold biopsy forceps** (45380 or 45385) does not use electrocoagulation; the polyp is simply pulled from the colon wall. **Laser technique** (45383) is most suitable for treatment of rectal lesions and uses a waveguide to deliver the laser beam through the endoscope to the lesion (e.g., YAG laser).

EXAMPLE: Patient underwent removal of a polyp by snare technique during a colonoscopy. During the same operative session, another area of the colon was also biopsied. Report a code for the colonoscopy with polypectomy (45385) and a different code for colonoscopy with biopsy (45380-59). (Modifier -59 is added to code 45380 because the colon biopsy was performed as a distinct and separate procedure in addition to the removal of the polyp during the colonoscopy.)

A **proctectomy** (45110–45123) is the surgical removal of the rectum. (Do not confuse this procedure with a *prostatectomy*, which is the excision of the prostate gland.) An **ileoanal anastomosis** (or **J-pouch**, **pull-through**, or **endorectal pull-through**) (45113) is a common alternative to conventional ileostomy, and it is not considered an ostomy because there is no stoma. The colon and most of the rectum are surgically removed, and an

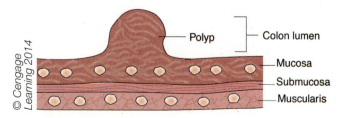

© Cengage Learning 2014

Figure 14-16   Colon polyp

internal pouch is created from the terminal portion of the ileum. An opening at the bottom of the pouch is attached (anastomosed) to the anus so that existing anal sphincter muscles can be used for continence.

EXAMPLE: Patient underwent proctopexy via abdominal approach. Report code 45540.

Anus

Codes 46020–46999 are reported for procedures performed on the anus. **Anoscopy** (46600–46615) is a diagnostic procedure during which anal mucosa and the lower rectum are visualized using an anoscope. Anoscopy is typically performed to detect hemorrhoids (Figure 14-17), polyps, anal fissures, and anal bleeding.

For hemorrhoidectomy procedures, identify what approach was used, where the hemorrhoid(s) were located (e.g., internal or external), and whether a fissurectomy was also performed. The most commonly performed procedure is a hemorrhoidectomy by simple ligature (e.g., rubber band) (46221). (Report code 46221 once regardless of the number of hemorrhoids removed.) Simple hemorrhoidectomy procedures (46255–46258) do not include plastic repair; complex and extensive hemorrhoidectomy procedures (46260–46262) do require plastic repair. When multiple methods are used to remove multiple hemorrhoids, report a code for each method.

EXAMPLE: Patient underwent hemorrhoidopexy for prolapsing internal hemorrhoids via stapling. Report code 46947.

When reporting codes for the surgical treatment of anal fistulas, apply the following definitions to codes 46270–46280:

- **Subcutaneous fistulectomy**: Removal of an anal fistula, without division of the sphincter muscle.

- **Submuscular fistulectomy**: Removal of an anal fistula, including division of the sphincter muscle.

- **Complex fistulectomy**: Excision of multiple fistulas.

- **Second stage fistulectomy or fistulotomy**: Use of a **seton**, such as a large silk suture or rubber bands, to cut through the fistula; the seton is left in place until later removal.

EXAMPLE: Patient underwent subcutaneous fistulectomy. Report code 46270.

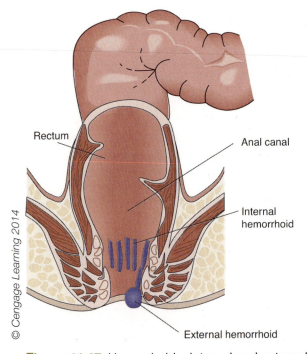

© Cengage Learning 2014

Rectum

Anal canal

Internal hemorrhoid

External hemorrhoid

Figure 14-17 Hemorrhoids: internal and external

Exercise 14.4 – Intestines (Except Rectum), Meckels Diverticulum, and the Mesentery, Appendix, Rectum, and Anus

Instructions: Assign the CPT code(s) and appropriate modifier(s) to each statement.

1. After performing an emergency cesarean section, the physician noticed that the appendix was distended, resulting in medical necessity for an appendectomy performed during the same operative session.

   _____

2. The physician freed intestinal adhesions.

   _____

3. The physician resected two segments of small intestine and performed an anastomosis between the remaining intestinal ends. An open approach was used for this surgery.

   _____

4. The physician repaired a defect in the mesentery with sutures.

   _____

5. The physician performed a laparoscopic partial colectomy with end colostomy and closure of the distal segment.

   _____

6. The physician drained a pelvic abscess through the rectum.

   _____

7. The physician removed a portion of the rectum through combined abdominal and transsacral approaches.

   _____

8. The physician performed rigid proctosigmoidoscopy and obtained brushings.

   _____

9. The physician performed a flexible sigmoidoscopy and removed a polyp. The physician inserted the sigmoidoscope through the anus and advanced the scope into the sigmoid colon. The lumen of the sigmoid colon and rectum were well visualized, and the polyp was identified and removed with hot biopsy forceps. The sigmoidoscope was withdrawn upon completion of the procedure.

   _____

10. The physician inserted a colonoscope through the anus and advanced the scope past the splenic flexure. Two polyps were identified and removed by hot biopsy forceps.

   _____

Liver

Codes 47000–47399 are reported for procedures performed to treat liver injuries and diseases, including liver transplantation. Liver injuries include gunshot wounds, stab wounds, and blunt trauma; and treatment includes various methods of hemorrhage control. The management of liver hemorrhage may require a simple suture of the liver wound, or it may require complex suturing of the liver wound or injury, with or without hepatic artery ligation (47360).

Other codes are reported to classify the exploration of a hepatic wound, extensive debridement, coagulation, and/or packing of the liver. Code 47362 is reported when re-exploration of a hepatic wound is performed for removal of packing.

A **hepatotomy** (open drainage of abscess or cyst) is performed in one or two stages, but when it is performed as a two-stage procedure, the code is not reported a second time. The percutaneous drainage of a liver abscess (47011) may also be performed in stages, and this procedure includes the initial insertion and final removal of the catheter, using radiologic guidance.

EXAMPLE 1: Patient underwent wedge biopsy of the liver. Report code 47100.

EXAMPLE 2: Patient underwent surgical laparoscopy with ablation of one liver tumor, using cryosurgery under fluoroscopic guidance. Report codes 47371 and 76940.

Biliary Tract

Codes 47400–47999 are reported for procedures performed on the organs and duct system that create, transport, store, and release bile into the duodenum (as part of the digestive process). The **biliary system** includes the following digestive accessory organs and structures (Figure 14-18):

- Gallbladder
- Bile ducts inside the liver
- Bile ducts outside the liver

- Hepatic ducts
- Common bile duct
- Cystic duct

A **cholecystectomy** (surgical removal of the gallbladder) (Figure 14-19) can be performed laparoscopically (47562–47564) or as an open procedure (47600–47620). During a cholecystectomy, common duct exploration and dilation procedures (47610) are often performed through the same incision. An operative cholangiography may also be performed (47605) during the same operative session.

Coding Tip:

When a cholecystectomy is attempted laparoscopically and converted to an open procedure, report a code for the open cholecystectomy procedure only.

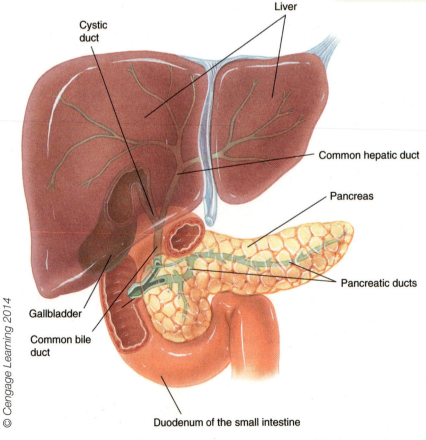

Figure 14-18 Digestive accessory organs (liver, gallbladder, and pancreas)

© Cengage Learning 2014

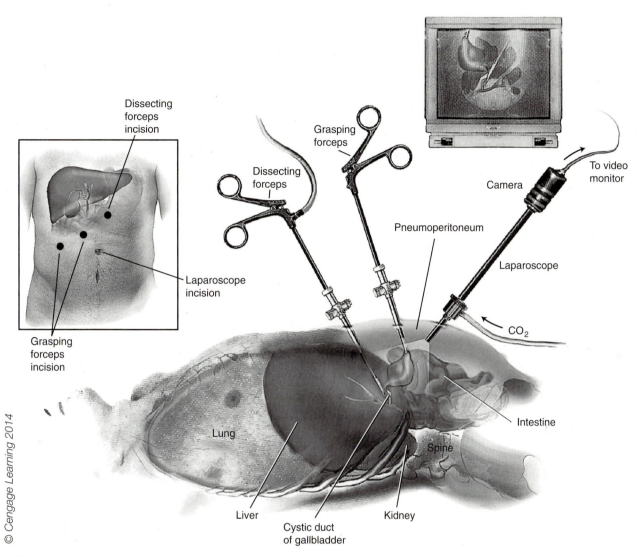

Figure 14-19 Laparoscopic cholecystectomy: lateral view

EXAMPLE: Patient underwent laparoscopic percutaneous extraction of a stone with a basket. Report code 47630.

Pancreas

Codes 48000–48999 are reported for procedures performed on the pancreas, including pancreas transplantation. The **Whipple procedure** (48150–48154) is the excision of the pancreas, duodenum, bile duct, and stomach with reconstruction; code assignment is based on the extent of the excision. The code reported for an internal anastomosis of the pancreatic duct (48520–48540) is based on the approach.

EXAMPLE: Patient underwent placement of a peripancreatic drain for pancreatitis. Report code 48000.

Abdomen, Peritoneum, and Omentum

Codes 49000–49999 are reported for procedures performed on the abdomen, peritoneum, and omentum. When reporting codes for procedures in this heading, make sure you review theoperative report to determine whether the procedure was performed via laparotomy or laparoscopy.

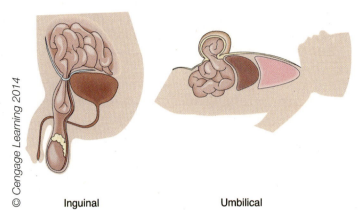

Inguinal   Umbilical

Figure 14-20 Inguinal and umbilical hernias

Hernia repair codes are classified in this heading. A **hernia** is the protrusion of internal organs (e.g., intestines) through a weakening in the musculature. To report codes correctly for hernia repair procedures, determine the:

- Hernia site (e.g., inguinal, lumbar, or femoral) (Figure 14-20)

- Patient's age

- Type of hernia (initial or recurrent)

- Clinical presentation of the hernia (e.g., reducible, incarcerated, strangulated, or recurrent)

- Use of mesh

  Hernia repairs (herniorrhaphies) include:

- Traditional/conventional (physician pushes bulging tissue back into the abdominal cavity and sutures surrounding muscle in place)

- Mesh repairs (uses mesh, such as Marlex or Prolene, instead of sutures to repair incisional or ventral hernias)

- Laparoscopic (typically performed to repair bilateral and recurrent hernias)

Coding Tip:

- Neonatal diaphragmatic and traumatic hiatal hernia repairs are not classified in the Digestive System subsection. To report codes for these repairs, refer to 39503–39541 in the Mediastinum and Diaphragm subsection.

- Implantation of mesh or other prosthesis (49568) is reported for incisional or ventral hernia repairs (49560–49566). When mesh or other prosthesis is used to repair other types of hernias, do not separately report a code. Code 49568 (Mesh) is also reported with Integumentary System codes 11004–11006.

- When strangulated organs are repaired in addition to a strangulated hernia, report a code for each procedure performed.

- When a hernia repair is performed during another open abdominal procedure, a code for the hernia repair is reported only if it was performed through a different incisional site. (Add modifier -59, Distinct Procedural Service, to the hernia repair code.) An incidental hernia repair during the course of an abdominal procedure is not coded and reported.

Exercise 14.5 – Liver, Biliary Tract, Pancreas, Abdomen, Peritoneum, and Omentum

Instructions: Assign the CPT code(s) and appropriate modifier(s) to each statement.

1. For percutaneous drainage of an abscess, the physician performed a hepatotomy in two stages.

   _____

2. Surgeons removed segments II, III, and IV (the whole left lobe) of the liver from a living donor.

   _____

3. The physician performed radiofrequency ablation of a liver tumor via an open laparotomy.

   _____

4. The physician removed the gallbladder and performed a common bile duct exploration through the laparoscope.

   _____

5. The physician performed a cholecystostomy with removal of calculus.

   _____

6. Subsequent to a previous peritoneocentesis (performed at a different operative session), the physician withdrew fluid and performed infusion and drainage of fluid from the abdominal cavity (peritoneal lavage).

   _____

7. The physician reopened a recent laparotomy incision, before the incision had fully healed, to drain a postoperative infection.

   _____

8. The physician performed laparoscopic repair of an inguinal hernia, using mesh.

   _____

9. The physician performed a ventral hernia repair and inserted mesh implantation.

   _____

10. The physician repaired an initial, reducible, inguinal hernia with hydrocelectomy in a 5-month-old infant.

    _____

Urinary System Subsection

The **urinary system** consists of the kidneys, ureters, urinary bladder, and urethra (Figure 14-21). Blood flows through the renal arteries to the kidneys, where waste materials are filtered and urine is formed. Urine is transported from the kidneys to the bladder by the ureters, and the urine ultimately passes out of the body through the urethra.

A urinary tract infection is a common disorder of the urinary system and may involve different areas of the urinary tract (e.g., urethritis, prostatitis, cystitis, and pyelonephritis). Other urinary system disorders affect the pressure within the urinary system, affect stagnation of flow (stasis), and cause the formation of stones (calculi).

> **Note:**
>
> The *ureter* is the tube that conveys urine from each kidney to the urinary bladder; there are two ureters. The *urethra* is the tube that conveys urine from the urinary bladder to the outside of the body.

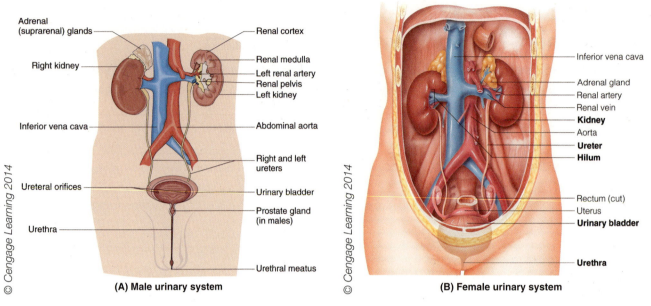

Figure 14-21 Urinary system (A) Male (B) Female

Urinary system function can also be affected by disorders such as obstruction (e.g., benign prostatic hypertrophy or strictures), which typically form in three places within the ureter:

- Ureteropelvic junction (between ureter and renal pelvis)

- Ureterovesical junction (between ureter and bladder)

- Ureter/iliac arteries

Various methods are used to treat urinary disorders, including open procedures and endoscopy or laparoscopy. Diagnostic urodynamic procedures (study of urine storage and voiding functions) include tests such as the following:

- Cystometrogram

- Urofl owmetry

- Urethral pressure profi le (UPP)

- Neuromuscular studies

- Voiding pressure (VP) studies

Urinary System subsection procedures are classified according to anatomic site and surgical approach (e.g., open, incision, percutaneous, endoscopic, or laparoscopic). The subsection also separates endoscopy procedures from open procedures.

Many procedures include the phrase *exclusive of radiologic service*, which means that an additional code from the Radiology section is assigned to report the radiologic service performed.

EXAMPLE: Codes 50551–50580 are reported for renal endoscopy through an established nephrostomy or pyelostomy. The code description states exclusive of radiologic service. If the same physician provides both services, a code from 74400–74485 or 78700–78725 is also reported.

Kidney

The **kidneys** filter and clean the blood, producing urine that carries waste. In renal (kidney) failure, filtration of blood is slowed or stopped (due to obstruction, bacterial infection, or injury). This causes waste products and other toxic substances to build up in the blood. These problems can lead to renal failure, resulting in the need for treatment such as surgery or dialysis.

In the Kidney heading, the removal of urinary calculi (stones) (Figure 14-22) is coded according to the anatomic site (e.g., renal pelvis, bladder, or urethra) and approach (e.g., open incision, percutaneous, or endoscopic).

EXAMPLE: Patient underwent nephrolithotomy to remove urinary stones. Report code 50060.

Nephrectomy (surgical removal of a kidney) requires review of the operative report to identify the:

- Type of procedure (e.g., partial or total)
- Surgical approach (e.g., laparoscopic or open)
- Other structures removed

EXAMPLE: Patient underwent partial nephrectomy. The physician made a very small periumbilical incision and inserted a fiber-optic laparoscope through a trocar. The kidney and surrounding structures were removed through an enlarged port site. Report code 50543.

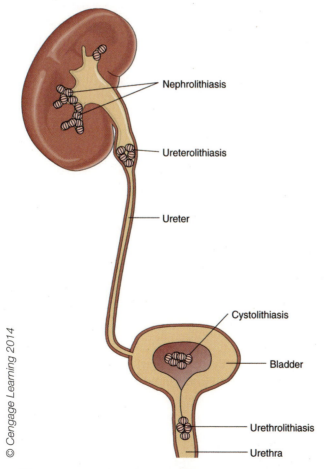

© Cengage Learning 2014

Figure 14-22 Common locations of urinary calculi (stone) formation: nephrolithiasis (kidney stone), cystolithiasis (urinary bladder stone), and urethrolithiasis (urethral stone)

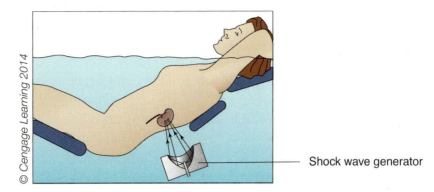

© Cengage Learning 2014

Shock wave generator

Figure 14-23 Extracorporeal shock wave lithotripsy (ESWL)

When a surgeon performs a retrograde pyelography (or retrograde ureteropyelography), one or both of the ureters are catheterized and contrast is injected slowly through the catheter.

EXAMPLE: Patient underwent injection procedure for pyelography through left nephrostomy tube. Pyelography results were negative. Report codes 50394-LT and 74425-LT.

Extracorporeal shock wave lithotripsy (ESWL) (50590) is a nonoperative procedure that uses ultrasonic shock waves to break up stones in the renal pelvis or ureter (Figure 14-23). The patient then passes the stones in urine, with minimal discomfort. **Percutaneous lithotomy** or **lithotripsy** (50080–50081) is a two-stage procedure that requires a percutaneous nephrostomy and dilation of the nephrostomy tract. Instruments (e.g., a basket or lithotripter) are inserted via nephrostomy, and the stones are removed.

Renal transplantation codes include three distinct components:

- Harvest of the kidney from a cadaver or living donor

- Physician backbench work, which includes standard preparation of a cadaver or living donor allograft prior to transplantation

- Allotransplantation (e.g., organ removal, if required, and transplantation of the allograft)

The procurement of kidneys is reported with CPT code 50300 if the organ is harvested from a cadaver or 50320 if donated by a living donor. Once the kidney is received by the hospital, backbench standard preparation is performed to prepare the kidneys for transplantation (50323–50329). The actual transplantation of the kidney (Figure 14-24) into the recipient is reported with code 50360 or 50365. (When a bilateral kidney transplant is performed, add modifier -50 to code 50360 or 50365.) (If the recipient's nonfunctioning kidney is resected, code 50340 is also reported. If both nonfunctioning kidneys are resected, modifier -50 is added to code 50340. Nonfunctioning kidneys are not always resected during a transplant procedure.)

Ureter

The **ureters** convey urine from the kidneys to the urinary bladder. The walls of the ureters contain muscle that propels urine using wavelike motions called **peristalsis**. Procedures performed on the ureters are based on two approaches:

- Open endoscopic

- Laparoscopic

To facilitate the passage of urine through the ureter(s), a physician may insert a ureteral stent. Stents used to relieve or prevent ureteral obstruction can be placed during the course of another diagnostic or therapeutic intervention. Stents may be temporary, and the physician may remove a temporary stent and insert another type of stent (e.g., indwelling).

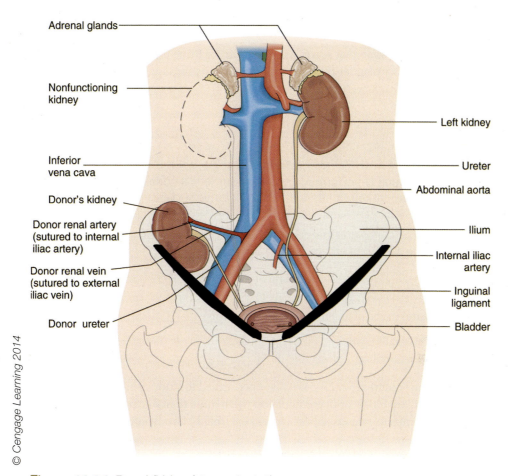

Adrenal glands

Nonfunctioning
kidney

Inferior
vena cava

Donor's kidney

Donor renal artery
(sutured to internal
iliac artery)

Donor renal vein
(sutured to external
iliac vein)

Donor ureter

Left kidney

Ureter

Abdominal aorta

Ilium

Internal iliac
artery

Inguinal
ligament

Bladder

© Cengage Learning 2014

Figure 14-24 Renal (kidney) transplantation

A **ureterolithotomy** (50610–50630) is the surgical removal of stones from the ureter. The procedure should identify the ureteral location from which the stone was removed:

- Upper one-third of ureter

- Middle one-third of ureter

- Lower one-third of ureter

(When stones are removed using the stone basket extraction technique, report code 51065 from the Bladder heading.)

Ureteral anastomosis procedures (50740–50810 and 50860) are mutually exclusive procedures, and codes for these procedures are not usually reported for the same operative session. However, if an anastomosis is performed on one ureter and a different anastomosis is performed on the other ureter, add modifier -LT and -RT to each code (to describe the service performed on the respective ureter).

Ureterostomy, transplantation of ureter to skin (50860), is mutually exclusive of codes 50800–50830 (e.g., ureterostomy, ureterocolon conduit, and urinary undiversion) unless performed on different locations. When reporting code 50860 with a code from 50800–50830, add modifier -LT and -RT to each code (to describe the service performed on the respective ureter).

Ureteral endoscopy (50951–50980) is the visualization of the ureter(s) using an endoscope. Review the operative report to locate the procedure performed through the endoscope (e.g., biopsy).

EXAMPLE: Patient underwent ureterolysis, with repositioning of ureter for retroperitoneal fibrosis. Report code 50715.

Bladder

The **urinary bladder** is a hollow organ that serves as a reservoir for urine until it passes from the body (via urination). Urine enters the urinary bladder from the ureters and exits through the urethra.

Coding Tip:

Urethral catheterization codes (51701–51702) are reported only when performed independently.

- When urethral catheterization is performed preceding surgery, a code is not separately reported. Urethral catheterization is considered integral to preoperative services provided, and represents the standard of medical practice.
- When urethral catheterization or urethral dilation is necessary to accomplish a more extensive procedure, a code for the urethral catheterization or urethral dilation is not separately reported.

Open excisional procedures of the bladder include the following:

- Excision of urachal cysts and sinuses
- Cystectomy
- Cystostomy (Figure 14-25)
- Pelvic exenteration

Diagnostic urodynamic procedures (51725–51798) are performed to study urine storage and voiding functions, and the codes may be reported separately or in combination when more than one procedure is performed. (Report as many codes as necessary to completely describe procedures performed.) Urodynamics includes the following tests:

- Cystometrogram (CMG)
- Uroflowmetry (UFR)
- Urethral pressure profile studies
- Neuromuscular studies
- Voiding pressure studies

A **cystometrogram** records urinary bladder pressure at various volumes, which is useful in diagnosing bladder outlet obstruction and other voiding dysfunctions.

- A simple cystometrogram measures the bladder's capacity, sensation, and intravesical pressure.
- A complex cystometrogram is a procedure in which the physician uses a rectal probe to differentiate abdominal pressure from bladder pressure. Components of complex cystometry include the placement of the transurethral catheter and anal probe, measurement of voiding cystometry and intra-abdominal pressure, and other provocative maneuvers (e.g., patient position changes and trials of anticholingerics or muscle depressants).

Uroflowmetry measures the amount of urine that flows from the urinary bladder per second.

- Simple uroflowmetry measures voiding time and peak flow using nonautomated equipment.
- Complex uroflowmetry measures/records mean, peak flow, and time to reach peak flow during continuous urination, and it is performed using automated equipment.

UPP studies (urethral closure pressure profile) describe tests for measuring urethral pressure. A UPP records pressures along the urethra using a special catheter. Electromyography studies measure anal or urethral sphincter muscle activity during voiding and urine flow rate. This study is usually performed on patients with voiding dysfunctions.

Voiding pressure studies involve placing a transducer into the urinary bladder to measure the patient's urine flow rate and pressure during emptying of the urinary bladder. Intra-abdominal VP (e.g., rectal, gastric, and intraperitoneal) can also be measured.

EXAMPLE 1: Patient underwent simple uroflowmetry. Report code 51736.

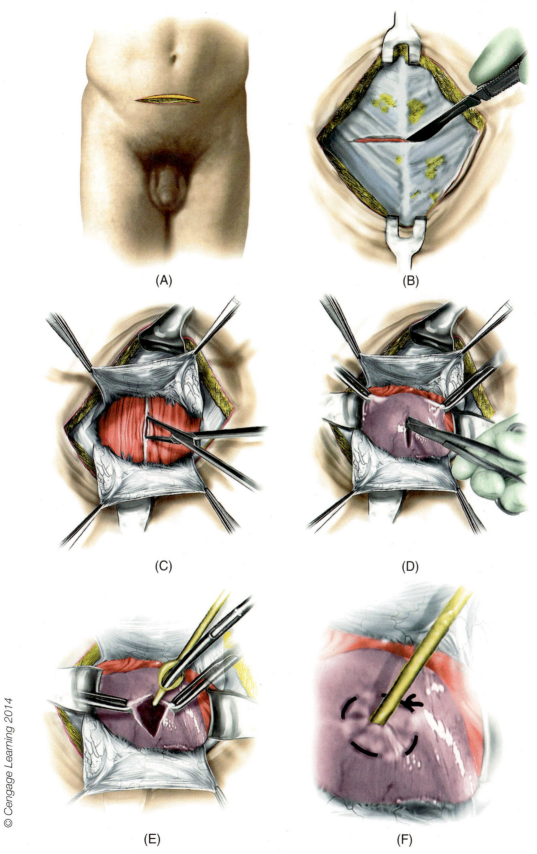

(A)

(B)

(C)

(D)

(E)

(F)

Figure 14-25 Open cystostomy (A) Incision site (B) Fascia incised (C) Muscle split (D) Bladder incised (E) Cystostomy tube inserted (F) Cystostomy tube secured with pursestring suture

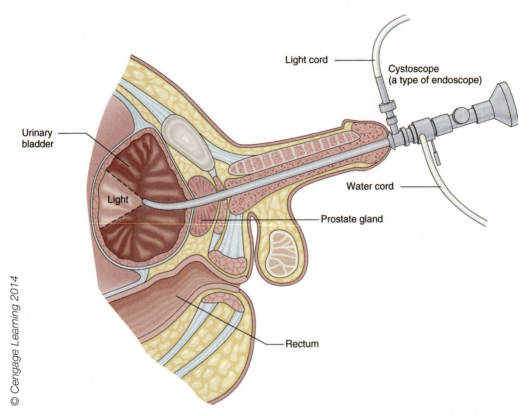

Figure 14-26 Use of a cystoscope to examine the interior of the bladder in a male

EXAMPLE 2: Patient underwent complex uroflowmetry, which required the use of calibrated electronic equipment. Report code 51741.

Urinary endoscopy procedures are classified according to:

- Anatomic area (e.g., urethra, prostate, or ureter)

- Procedure performed (e.g., cystourethroscopy with insertion of indwelling ureteral stent)

Cystoscopy, or **cystourethroscopy** (Figure 14-26), allows for the direct visual examination of the urinary bladder and urethra.

EXAMPLE: A cystourethroscope was passed through the urethra and urinary bladder to examine the urethra, bladder, and ureteral openings. No other procedure was performed. Report code 52000.

Transurethral surgery (52204–52355) is performed on the:

- Urethra and bladder

- Ureter and pelvis

In addition, a separate subheading for vesical neck and prostate procedures (52400–52700) is located under the Bladder heading. It is important to review the operative report to identify the anatomic site for the surgery performed. Diagnostic procedures (e.g., bladder biopsy) and therapeutic procedures (e.g., steroid injection into a urethral stricture) are accomplished using a transurethral approach. Trans-urethral surgeries include diagnostic cystoscopy, which is not reported separately.

When a physician performs a urethral dilation to determine the size of the cystoscope to be inserted, do not code and report the dilation procedure separately. When the physician performs a cystoscopy and later performs a transurethral dilatation for a urethral stricture during the same operative session, assign code 52281.

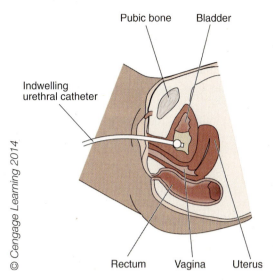

Pubic bone   Bladder

Indwelling
urethral catheter

© Cengage Learning 2014

Rectum   Vagina   Uterus

Figure 14-27 Indwelling urethral catheter
in a female patient

Cystourethroscopy with removal of foreign body, calculus, or ureteral stent from urethra or bladder is classified as either of the following:

- Simple (52310)
- Complicated (52315)

Before a transurethral therapeutic or diagnostic intervention procedure is performed, a direct visual examination is performed using a cystourethroscope. The cystoscope is passed through the male urethra to visualize the urethra, prostate, and bladder.

Notes in the Ureter and Pelvis subheading (52320–52355) clarify the reporting of temporary stents and self-retaining indwelling stents. Indwelling ureteral catheters (Figure 14-27) are inserted into the renal pelvis via the ureter to allow drainage (e.g., when a tumor is impinging on the ureters). Gibbons and double-J stents are the most common ureteral stents. The insertion and removal of a temporary ureteral stent is included in codes 52320–52355. An indwelling stent is reported with code 52332.

When a surgeon performs a **transurethral ureteroscopic lithotripsy** (52353) (instead of an ESWL), a cystoscope is inserted through the urethra into the bladder and a ureteroscope is passed into the ureters. Instruments passed through the ureteroscope into the ureters are used to manipulate and disintegrate stones (utilizing transcystoscopic electrohydraulic shock waves, ultrasound, or laser) (52353). When the ureteroscopy is not performed, report code 52325 for cystourethroscopic fragmentation of ureteral calculi (stones) (utilizing electrohydraulic or ultrasonic technique).

Transurethral resection of the prostate (TURP) is an initial resection of the prostate gland via transurethral approach using an electrosurgical device (52601). Specific codes classify laser treatment of the prostate gland (52647–52648). TURP codes include vasectomy, meatotomy, cystourethroscopy, urethral calibration, dilation, and/or internal urethrotomy. Codes for these procedures, when performed during the same operative session as a TURP, are not reported separately.

The physician may perform a prostatectomy using a number of different methods:

- Transurethral two-stage prostatectomy: Physician performs a prostatectomy in two stages, and the operative report specifies the first or second stage. (Code 52601 is reported for the first stage, and code 52601-58 is reported for the second stage.)

- Transurethral destruction of the prostate using microwave therapy: Physician uses microwave thermotherapy. (Code 53850)

- Transurethral destruction of the prostate using radiofrequency: Physician uses radiofrequency thermotherapy to destroy the prostate. (Code 53852)

Urethra

The **urethra** is a muscular tube that discharges urine from the urinary bladder. In males, the urethra also serves as a passageway for semen. Codes assigned for urethral procedures will vary depending on the sex of the patient.

> **EXAMPLE 1:** Female patient underwent total urethrectomy, including cystostomy. Report code 53210.

> **EXAMPLE 2:** Male patient underwent total urethrectomy, including cystostomy. Report code 53215.

To report codes properly for urethral excision procedures (53200–53275), locate the diagnosis in the patient's record.

> **EXAMPLE 1:** Patient underwent excision of bulbourethral gland. Report code 53250.

> **EXAMPLE 2:** Patient underwent excision of urethral polyp, distal urethra. Report code 53260.

> **EXAMPLE 3:** Patient underwent excision of urethral caruncle. Report code 53265.

For **urethroplasty** (repair of the urethra), identify:

- Whether the procedure was staged.
- Which stage of the procedure was performed (e.g., stage one or stage two).

> **EXAMPLE 1:** Patient underwent urethroplasty, first stage, to repair stricture. Report code 53400.

> **EXAMPLE 2:** Patient underwent urethroplasty, second stage, to form a urethra. Procedure included urinary diversion. Report code 53405.

> **EXAMPLE 3:** Patient underwent one-stage urethroplasty to reconstruct a male anterior urethra. Report code 53410.

For dilatation of urethral stricture, identify:

- What surgical approach was used.
- What the patient's gender was.
- Whether the dilation was initial or subsequent.

> **EXAMPLE 1:** Patient underwent initial dilation of urethral stricture by passage of sound or urethral dilator, male. Report code 53600.

> **EXAMPLE 2:** Patient underwent subsequent dilation of urethral stricture by passage of sound or urethral dilator, male. Report code 53601.

> **EXAMPLE 3:** Patient underwent initial dilation of urethral stricture by passage of filiform and follower, male. Report code 53620.

> **EXAMPLE 4:** Patient underwent initial dilation of female urethra including suppository and instillation. Report code 53660.

Coding Tip:

Urethral repair codes (53502–53515) are performed to treat urethral wounds or injuries (urethrorrhaphy). When a urethroplasty is performed, do not report a code for urethrorrhaphy because suture to repair wound or injury is included in the urethroplasty service.

Exercise 14.6 – Urinary System Subsection

Instructions: Assign the CPT code(s) and appropriate modifier(s) to each statement.

1. Physician made an open incision and inserted multiple drain tubes to drain an infection (abscess) from the kidney.

   _____

2. The physician pulverized a kidney stone (renal calculus) by directing shock waves through a water cushion that was placed against the left side of the patient's body at the location of the kidney stone.

   _____

3. The physician removed a kidney stone (calculus) by making an incision in the right kidney.

   _____

4. The interventional radiologist inserted a percutaneous nephrostomy catheter into the right renal pelvis for drainage. Fluoroscopic guidance was provided.

   _____

5. The physician performed laparoscopic ablation of a solid mass from the posterior hilum of the left kidney.

   _____

6. The physician made an incision in the left ureter through the abdominal wall for examination of the ureter and insertion of a catheter for drainage.

   _____

7. The physician examined the patient's right and left renal and ureteral structures with an endoscope, which passed through an established opening between the skin and the ureter (ureterostomy). He also inserted a catheter into the ureter.

   _____

8. The physician revised a surgical opening between the skin and the right ureter.

   _____

9. The physician injected a contrast agent through an opening between the skin and the left ureter (ureterostomy) for ureterography (study of the renal collecting system).

   _____

10. The physician made an incision in the left ureter (ureterotomy) to insert a catheter (stent) into the ureter.

    _____

11. The physician performed a transurethral resection of a bladder neck contracture using a resectoscope.

    _____

12. The physician inserted a special instrument through the cystourethroscope to fragment a calculus in the ureter using electrohydraulics.

    _____

13. The physician inserted a cystourethroscope through the urethra to drain an abscess on the prostate.

    _____

14. The physician made an incision through the abdominal wall into the urinary bladder and inserted a suprapubic catheter to withdraw urine.

    _____

15. The physician performed a cystourethroscopy with fulguration of the bladder neck and then removed a calculus from the ureter.

    _____

16. The physician performed a sling procedure using synthetic material to treat a male patient's urinary incontinence.

    _____

(continues)

Exercise 14.6 (continued)

17. The physician made an initial attempt to treat a male patient's urethral stricture using a dilator.

_____

18. The physician, in the first of two stages to reconstruct the urethra, identified the area of stricture by urethrography and marked it with ink.

_____

19. The physician performed a transurethral destruction of the prostate using microwave therapy.

_____

20. The physician excised a specimen of tissue from the urethra for biopsy.

_____

Summary

The Mediastinum and Diaphragm subsection classifies procedures performed on the mediastinum and diaphragm (also the titles of subsection headings). The Digestive System subsection includes procedures to diagnose and treat disorders of the digestive system (e.g., gastrointestinal endoscopy, laparoscopy, and gastric analysis). Similar to other Surgery subsections, procedures are classified first by anatomic area and then by type. Digestive System subsection codes are also reported for open, endoscopic, and laparoscopic procedures. The operative report must be carefully reviewed to correctly identify the surgical approach. Urinary System subsection procedures are classified according to anatomic site and surgical approach (e.g., open, incision, percutaneous, endoscopic, or laparoscopic). The subsection also separates endoscopy procedures from open procedures. Many procedures include the phrase "exclusive of radiologic service," which means that an additional code from the Radiology section is assigned to report the radiological service performed.

Internet Links

American College of Gastroenterology (ACG): Go to *www.acg.gi.org* and click on the Patients link to access information about diseases and treatments.

American Urological Association (AUA): *www.urologyhealth.org*

Society of American Gastrointestinal and Endoscopic Surgeons (SAGES): *www.sages.org*

urologyChannel®: *www.urologychannel.com*

WebSurg's World Virtual University: *www.websurg.com*

Study Checklist

❏ Read this chapter and highlight key concepts.

❏ Create an index card for each key term.

❏ Access the chapter Internet links to learn more about concepts.

❏ Complete the chapter review, verifying answers with your instructor.

❏ Complete WebTutor assignments and take online quizzes.

❏ Complete Workbook chapter, verifying answers with your instructor.

❏ Go to *www.cengagebrain.com* to access StudyWARE™ and the Premium Website. Login instructions are located in the Preface and on the Printed Access Card.

❏ Form a study group with classmates to discuss chapter concepts in preparation for an exam.

Review

Multiple Choice

Instructions: Circle the most appropriate response.

1. Which types of hernias are assigned codes from the Mediastinum and Diaphragm subsection of Surgery?
    - a. abdominal and epigastric
    - b. hiatus and diaphragmatic
    - c. incisional and inguinal
    - d. umbilicus and femoral

2. Procedures performed on the gallbladder, bile ducts, hepatic ducts, and cystic ducts are assigned codes from which heading of the Digestive System subsection of Surgery?
    - a. Abdomen, Peritoneum, and Omentum
    - b. Biliary Tract
    - c. Liver
    - d. Ureter

3. Hernia repair codes (49495–49590) are classified in which heading of the Digestive System subsection of Surgery?
    - a. Abdomen, Peritoneum, and Omentum
    - b. Anus
    - c. Appendix
    - d. Rectum

4. Which procedure(s) has/have age as a factor in determining the correct code?
    - a. colonoscopy
    - b. esophagotomy and esophagoscopy
    - c. palatopharyngoplasty
    - d. tonsillectomy and adenoidectomy

5. When assigning codes for a ureterolithotomy procedure (50610–50630), which correctly describes the location in the ureter from which the stone was removed?
    - a. right or left side of ureter
    - b. upper-left, lower-left, upper-right, or lower-right quadrant of ureter
    - c. upper, middle, or lower one-third of ureter
    - d. upper or lower half of ureter

6. Diagnostic procedures (e.g., uroflowmetry) that are performed to study urine storage and voiding functions are assigned a code from which subheading of the Bladder heading in the Urinary System subsection of Surgery?
    - a. Bladder
    - b. Endoscopy
    - c. Laparoscopy
    - d. Urodynamics

7. Codes for urethral catheterization (51701–51703) are reported when performed _____ another urinary bladder procedure.
    - a. in combination with
    - b. independently of
    - c. preceding surgery for
    - d. as a more extensive procedure than

8. Which gastrointestinal (GI) endoscopy procedure involves injecting dye through a tube in the endoscope to allow for visualization of the ducts on X-rays?
    - a. Endoscopic retrograde cholangiopancreatography (ERCP) (43260–43272)
    - b. Esophagogastroduodenoscopy (EGD) (43235–43259)
    - c. Esophagoscopy (43200–43232)
    - d. Upper GI endoscopy (esophagogastroscopy) (43234)

9. When an incomplete colonoscopy is performed and the patient underwent full preparation for a colonoscopy, which modifier is added to the colonoscopy code?
    - a. -52
    - b. -53
    - c. -58
    - d. -59

10. When a hernia repair is performed through a different incisional site during another open abdominal procedure, which modifier is added to the hernia repair code?
    - a. -51
    - b. -58
    - c. -59
    - d. -79

11. Excision of mediastinal tumor. Which CPT code is assigned?
    - a. 39200
    - b. 39220
    - c. 39400
    - d. 39499

12. Destruction of dentoalveolar lesion. Which CPT code is assigned?
    - a. 41825
    - b. 41826
    - c. 41827
    - d. 41850

13. Simple revision of colostomy. Which CPT code is assigned?
    - a. 44320
    - b. 44322
    - c. 44340
    - d. 44345

14. Incision and drainage of ischiorectal abscess. Which CPT code is assigned?
    - a. 45020
    - b. 46040
    - c. 46045
    - d. 46060

15. Proximal subtotal pancreatectomy with total duodenectomy, partial gastrectomy, choledochoenterostomy, and gastrojejunostomy with pancreatojejunostomy. Which CPT code is assigned?
    - a. 48150
    - b. 48152
    - c. 48153
    - d. 48154

16. Peritoneoscopy with partial laparoscopic colectomy and anastomosis. Which CPT code is assigned?
    - a. 44140
    - b. 44204
    - c. 49320, 44140
    - d. 49320, 44204

17. Open drainage of retroperitoneal abscess. Which CPT code is assigned?
    - a. 49020
    - b. 49041
    - c. 49060
    - d. 49061

18. Intraoral incision and drainage of hematoma of tongue, submandibular space. Which CPT code is assigned?
    - a. 41008
    - b. 41009
    - c. 41015
    - d. 41017

19. Cystourethroscopy with resection of 1.1-cm bladder tumor. Which CPT code is assigned?
    - a. 52224
    - b. 52234
    - c. 52235
    - d. 52240

20. Female patient underwent reconstructive urethroplasty. Which CPT code is assigned?
    - a. 53410
    - b. 53420
    - c. 53430
    - d. 53431

Coding Practice

Instructions: Assign the CPT code(s) and appropriate modifier(s) to each case.

Mediastinum and Diaphragm

21. A patient is found to have a cystlike lesion per MRI of the mediastinum. This is to be removed. An incision is made by the physician from the shoulder blade to the spinal column of the thoracic area. Muscles are retracted, and the rib cage is exposed. After gaining access to the thoracic cavity, the physician identified the cyst and removed it. The specimen is sent to pathology. The wound is closed in layers.

_____

22. A 45-year-old male has an acute diaphragmatic hernia. After adequate general anesthesia, an abdominal incision is made in the epigastric region. A moderate amount of abdominal tissue is protruding through the hernia into the diaphragm. These contents are moved back into proper placement. The opening of the diaphragm is closed with sutures.

_____

23. Via transabdominal approach, the physician overlaps diaphragm tissue to ensure that the diaphragm is in the correct position and the eventration or partial protrusion is corrected.

_____

24. A lacerated diaphragm tear measuring 2.5 cm is repaired with sutures.

_____

25. A patient is being seen to confirm the diagnosis of sarcoidosis. An endoscopic examination of her mediastinum is done under general anesthesia. After making an incision in the area of the sternum, the scope is inserted. The trachea, bronchi, and lymph nodes are examined. A lymph node biopsy is taken. The scope is withdrawn, and the incision is closed with sutures.

Digestive System

26. A patient had the signs and symptoms consistent with a perforated viscus. After discussion, the patient consented to suture repair of the gastric ulcer. The patient was placed in a supine position. After adequate anesthesia, attention was turned to the anterior abdominal wall. A midline incision was made. Gross contamination was visualized. This was suctioned out. The gastric ulcer was visualized, and copious irrigation with 3 liters of warm saline was performed. All gross evidence of contamination was gone. Checking was done, hemostasis was throughout, and the skin incision was closed.

27. A patient presented with a lesion of the lip; due to the patient's history of smoking, it was determined to remove the lesion and send it to analysis to rule out carcinoma. After adequate anesthesia, a wedge incision was done of the lower lip to remove the lesion. The defect was closed with a small flap and sutures.

28. A patient with the diagnosis of carcinoma of the stomach presented for a hemigastrectomy. With the patient in the supine position and after adequate level of general anesthesia, the abdomen was prepped and draped in usual sterile fashion. An upper midline incision was made to access the abdominal cavity. The abdominal ligament was retracted to the right side of the incision. The stoma was mobilized. The duodenum was divided away from the stomach. The tumor was identified. The stomach tumor was transected with cautery, and a specimen was sent for evaluation by pathology. The distal margin of the remaining stomach was cleaned. Staples were used to close the curvature area of the stomach. The abdomen was closed with running Prolene for the fascia. The skin was closed with staples.

29. An 18-year-old patient has a history of chronic tonsillitis. Under general anesthesia, the physician separated the tonsils from the tonsil bed by blunt and sharp dissection followed by the snare. No gross bleeding was found. The adenoids were extracted by the adenotome followed by the sharp curette. Again, no gross bleeding was found. The patient had minimal blood loss.

30. A 72-year-old male patient presented to the emergency department with a 14-hour history of acute right inguinal pain and obstructive symptoms. Examination found a tender nonreducible mass in the right groin. He consented to surgical intervention via exploration and correction of possible hernia. After adequate anesthesia, the patient had an oblique preperitoneal incision through the fascia. The peritoneal cavity was entered. A strangulated loop was found along with the femoral hernia. The lower edge of the inguinal ligament was grasped with clamps, and interrupted Prolenes were used to close the femoral defect using Coopers ligament repair. The defect was closed up to the edge of the external iliac vein. Once the repair was completed, the wound was irrigated with saline. The bowel was inspected and appeared to be totally revascularized, with no evidence of necrosis and no need for resection. The femoral hernia sac was reduced and resected using electrocautery. The abdominal wall was closed with interrupted polypropylene sutures for the anterior wall fascia. A Jackson-Pratt drain was brought out through a separate stab wound. The subcutaneous tissue was closed with interrupted 3-0 Vicryl, and the skin was closed with staples.

31. A patient with chronic cholelithiasis presented for a cholecystectomy. An infraumbilical incision was made, and a trocar was inserted into the abdominal cavity. After insufflation of the cavity, the laparoscope was inserted through the trocar. Two additional incisions were made to place trocars—one on the right side and one on the left. The gallbladder was identified. It was noted to be slightly enlarged and grayish in color. Multiple stones were palpable inside the gallbladder. Tissue surrounding the gallbladder was dissected. The cystic duct and artery were clipped and then cut. The gallbladder was dissected from the liver bed and removed through the umbilical trocar site. Careful irrigation of the cavity was done. The patient had minimal blood loss.

_____

32. A 19-year-old patient presented to the hospital with a history of bloody stools of three weeks duration. The patient was prepped for a sigmoidoscopy. The sigmoidoscope was passed without difficulty to about 40 cm. The entire mucosal lining was erythematous. There was no friability of the overlying mucosa and no bleeding noted anywhere. No pseudopolyps were noted. Biopsies were taken at about 30 cm; these were thought to be representative of the mucosa in general. The scope was retracted; no other abnormalities were seen.

_____

33. A patient with a history of breast cancer presented for a biopsy of her liver to confirm metastasic disease. The abdomen was exposed by an incision through the skin, fascia, and muscle. A wedge-shaped section of the liver was resected. This specimen was sent to pathology.

_____

34. A patient was found to have a sublingual abscess of the mouth. After consent and normal prep, an incision up through the supramylohyoid muscle was made. The superficial abscess was identified, an extraoral incision made, and drainage of clear liquid fluid was drained from the abscess.

_____

35. A 45-year-old patient has been diagnosed with a parotid gland mass via examination and radiograph films. The patient presented for excision of this mass. After adequate anesthesia, the initial incision was made near the midpoint of the mandible. Skin flaps were retracted to expose the parotid gland. The facial nerve was visualized. A mass was identified of the lateral lobe of the gland, and it was carefully dissected free from the space with attention not to damage the facial nerve. The mass was sent in total to pathology for analysis.

_____

Urinary System

36. A patient with the complaint of hematuria presented for an endoscopic examination under conscious sedation. A cystourethroscope was passed through the structures of the urinary system. A lesion was identified of the trigone; this was fulgurated. The cystourethroscope was removed.

_____

37. A patient was diagnosed with a urethral calculus as confirmed by X-ray. Endoscopic treatment was warranted to remove this stone. A cystourethroscope was passed through the urethra, and the stone was extracted through the endoscope. The remaining structures of the system were examined and found to be normal. The cystourethroscope was removed.

_____

38. The patient consented to cystoscopy with possible bladder tumor removal. After the endoscope was inserted through the urethra, the bladder was entered. A lesion approximately 3.0 cm in size was identified in the bladder. This was removed via excision and taken out through the scope. Minimal bleeders were cauterized. The remainder of the bladder was normal in appearance. The cystoscope was removed.

_____

39. An incision was made in the flank of the patient, between two ribs. A drainage needle was inserted and advanced to the patient's kidney. A perirenal abscess was located and drained.

_____

40. The patient was placed on a table. Water-filled bellows using coupling gel to make contact with the skin of the patient's right back were positioned at the area of the kidney stone. Shock waves were administrated and directed in short bursts toward the bellows for a total of 35 minutes. The process was overseen by the attending physician, who monitored the fragmentation of the stone. The patient was discharged with instructions to drain urine and collect stone fragments.

_____

41. An endoscope was passed through the urethra. The urethra was normal in appearance, as was the bladder upon examination. The cystourethroscope was then directed to the right ureter. Slight narrowing was seen in the distal third of this ureter. A double-J stent was placed in the right ureter. The left ureter was then examined and found to be normal. The stent will be removed at a later date.

_____

42. With the patient under general anesthesia, a midline incision was made over the abdominal cavity wall. After the bladder was accessed, a ureterocele was identified. This was removed via an incision made in the bladder. All bleeders were cauterized. Minimal blood loss was noted. The bladder was closed with absorbable sutures. A urethral Foley catheter was placed. The fascia and muscle were closed with staples. The skin was closed with sutures.

_____

43. The patient consented to a renal biopsy. The skin of the back was punctured with the biopsy needle after administration of anesthesia. The needle was advanced to the right kidney. The core of the needle was used to collect the tissue specimen. The needle core was removed to preserve the specimen for pathology. Another core was inserted in the needle, and the same method was used to collect two more specimens. The skin puncture wound was closed with two sutures.

_____

44. The patient received an incision of his back. After access was gained to the left kidney, it was incised. The kidney was examined; a stone was identified and removed. The remainder of the kidney was found to be normal in appearance. The kidney was closed with sutures. A drainage tube was inserted. The tube was allowed to drain outside the body via access through another small incision. The main incision was closed in layers.

_____

45. A patient presented for the first stage of urethroplasty. After an abdominal incision was made, the urethra was identified. The strictures were seen. An incision was made over the first stricture area. The area was opened wide and sutured to the edge of the mucosa. The second stricture area was handled in the same method. The patient will return in eight weeks for stage two of this repair.

_____

CPT Surgery V

Chapter Outline

Male Genital System Subsection
Reproductive System Procedures Subsection
Intersex Surgery Subsection
Female Genital System Subsection
Maternity Care and Delivery Subsection

Endocrine System Subsection
Nervous System Subsection
Eye and Ocular Adnexa Subsection
Auditory System Subsection
Operating Microscope Subsection

Chapter Objectives

At the conclusion of this chapter, the student should be able to:

- Define key terms.
- Explain the organization, format, and content of the CPT Male Genital System, Reproductive System Procedures, Intersex Surgery, Female Genital System, Maternity Care and Delivery, Endocrine System, Nervous System, Eye and Ocular Adnexa, Auditory System, and Operating Microscope subsections.
- Interpret CPT surgery coding notes for the Male Genital System, Reproductive System Procedures, Intersex Surgery, Female Genital System, Maternity Care and Delivery, Endocrine System, Nervous System, Eye and Ocular Adnexa, Auditory System, and Operating Microscope subsections.
- Assign CPT surgery codes from the Male Genital System, Reproductive System Procedures, Intersex Surgery, Female Genital System, Maternity Care and Delivery, Endocrine System, Nervous System, Eye and Ocular Adnexa, Auditory System, and Operating Microscope subsections.
- Add CPT and/or HCPCS level II modifiers to codes, as appropriate.

Key Terms

adhesiolysis	Auditory System	carpal tunnel	ciliary muscle
antepartum care	Bell's palsy	carpal tunnel syndrome	cochlear implant
anterior approach	burr hole	choroid	conization
anterolateral approach	carotid body	ciliary body	conjunctiva

cornea	incomplete abortion	missed abortion	sclera
corpectomy	induced abortion	myringotomy	septic abortion
costovertebral	inner ear	nervous system	somatic nerves
costovertebral approach	intersex surgery	neuroplasty	stereotaxis
delivery services	intracapsular cataract extraction (ICCE)	neurorrhaphy	strabismus
discectomy		neurostimulator	sympathetic nerves
endocrine system	iris	ocular adnexa	tear apparatus
enucleation of the eye	lacrimal apparatus	ocular implant	tenosynovitis
evisceration of ocular contents	lacrimal puncta	omentectomy	trachoma
	laminectomy		transpedicular approach
exenteration of the orbit	laminotomy	oocyte	tympanoplasty
external ear	lateral extracavitary approach (LECA)	oophorectomy	tympanostomy
extracapsular cataract extraction (ECCE)		operating microscope	uvea
	LEEP electrodissection conization	orbit	vaginal birth after cesarean (VBAC)
Eye and Ocular Adnexa		orbital implant	
eye socket	lens	osteophytectomy	varicocele
eyeball	loop electrodissection conization	postpartum care	vas deferens
female genital system		pupil	
globe	male genital system	retina	
hysteroscopy	middle ear	salpingo-oophorectomy	

Introduction

The Male Genital System subsection classifies procedures performed on the male genitalia and accessory organs. The Reproductive System Procedures classify the placement of needles into pelvic organs and/or genitalia for subsequent interstitial radioelement application. The Intersex Surgery subsection contains just two codes to classify male-to-female as well as female-to-male sex change procedures. The Female Genital System subsection classifies procedures performed on female genitalia and accessory organs. The Maternity Care and Delivery subsection classifies procedures performed and services provided for obstetrics, including antepartum, delivery, and postpartum care.

The Endocrine System subsection includes codes for procedures performed on glands. The Nervous System subsection includes codes for procedures performed on the central and peripheral nervous systems. The Eye and Ocular Adnexa subsection classifies procedures performed on the eyeball, anterior segment, posterior segment, ocular adnexa, and conjunctiva. The Auditory System subsection includes codes for procedures performed on the external ear, middle ear, internal ear, and temporal bone (middle fossa approach). The Operating Microscope subsection contains a code that is reported in addition to the primary procedure code when an operating microscope is used during a surgical procedure to perform microsurgery techniques.

CPT guidelines that apply to the subsections are located at the beginning of the Surgery section. Unique coding instructions for the Male Genital System, Intersex Surgery, Female Genital System, Maternity Care and Delivery, Endocrine System, Nervous System, Eye and Ocular Adnexa, Auditory System, and Operating Microscope subsections are located in notes below headings or codes.

Coding Tip:

Notes located beneath headings and/or subheadings apply to all codes in the heading or subheading. Parenthetical notes that are located below a specific code apply to that code only unless the note indicates otherwise.

Male Genital System Subsection

The **male genital system** (Figure 15-1) includes the prostate, seminal vesicles, penis, testicles (testes), epididymis, tunica vaginalis, vas deferens, scrotum, and spermatic cord. Codes 54000–55899

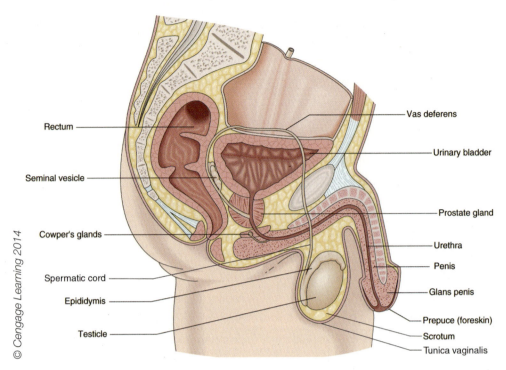

Figure 15-1 Male genital system

are reported for procedures performed on the male genital system. Code assignment is determined according to:

- Approach (e.g., incision, destruction, excision, or introduction)

- Reason for surgery

When a physician obtains a sample of testicular tissue (Figure 15-2) by needle biopsy, report code 54500. For excision of benign lesions of the male genitalia, report codes 11420–11426. For excision of malignant lesions of male genitalia, report codes 11620–11626.

When a circumcision is performed using a clamp or other device with regional dorsal penile or ring block, report code 54150. When the regional dorsal penile or ring block is not used in performing a circumcision, report code 54150 with modifier -52 (reduced services). Age of the patient is not at issue when reporting code 54150. When a surgical circumcision is performed on a neonate (28 days or age or less), report code 54160. For a surgical circumcision performed on a male older than 28 days of age (including adults), report code 54161.

When an orchiectomy procedure is performed, identify the following:

- Type of procedure (simple or radical)

- Surgical approach

- Additional procedures performed

EXAMPLE 1: Patient underwent radical orchiectomy (removal of testis) due to testicular tumor, inguinal approach. Report code 54530.

EXAMPLE 2: Patient underwent simple orchiectomy, inguinal approach, which was performed prophylactically to prevent the release of hormones that may promote tumor metastasis. Report code 54520.

When an orchiopexy for intra-abdominal testis is performed laparoscopically, report code 54692. (When performed without laparoscopy, report code 54650 for the repair of a testicle that is located intra-abdominally instead of in its usual anatomic location through the inguinal ring into the scrotum.)

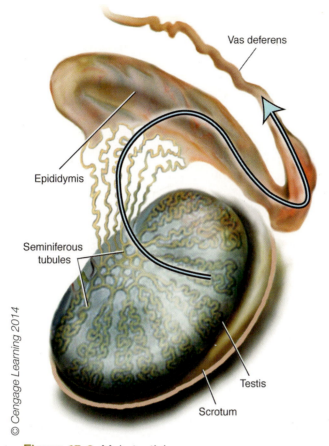

Vas deferens

Epididymis

Seminiferous
tubules

© Cengage Learning 2014

Testis

Scrotum

Figure 15-2 Male testicle

EXAMPLE 1: Patient underwent orchiopexy via abdominal approach for intra-abdominal testis. Report code 54650.

EXAMPLE 2: Patient underwent laparoscopic orchiopexy for intra-abdominal testis. Report code 54692.

The **vas deferens** is the tube that carries spermatozoa from the testis. Report code 55250 for a vasectomy procedure (Figure 15-3). Do not add modifier -50 to the code because its description includes the phrase *unilateral or bilateral.* Code 55250 also includes postoperative semen examination to determine whether the semen contains sperm.

A **varicocele** (Figure 15-4) is an abnormal dilation of the veins of the spermatic cord in the scrotum. Treatment typically involves ligation of spermatic veins or excision of the varicocele. For excision or ligation of a varicocele, review the operative report to locate the approach:

- Laparoscopic

- Abdominal

EXAMPLE: The patient underwent ligation of spermatic veins for varicocele. Report code 55530.

Benign conditions of the prostate gland include infection, inflammation, and benign prostatic hyperplasia (BPH) (also called benign prostatic hypertrophy, BPH). Men with benign prostate disease experience difficulty urinating (voiding). The degree of prostate involvement determines the therapeutic approach. For severe BPH, surgical procedures performed to restore urine flow include the following:

- Transurethral resection of the prostate (TURP) (Figure 15-5)

- Subtotal open prostatectomy (subtotal perineal prostatectomy)

- Subtotal prepubic prostatectomy

- Subtotal retropubic prostatectomy

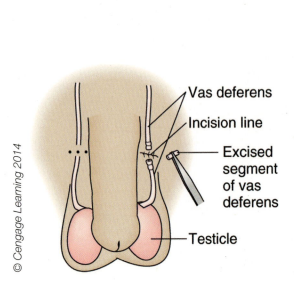

Figure 15-3 Vasectomy procedure

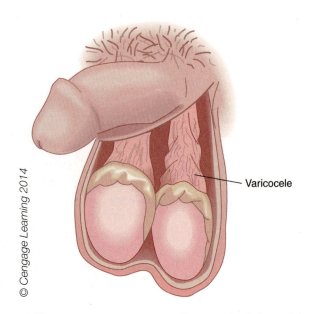

Figure 15-4 Varicocele affecting the left testicle

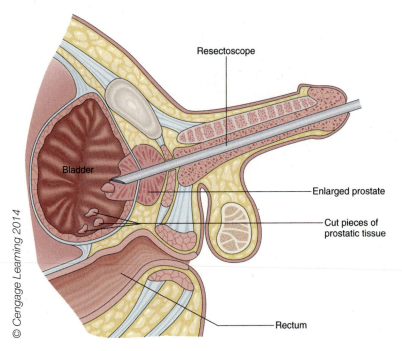

Figure 15-5 A transurethral resection of the prostate (TURP) is performed to treat benign prostatic

🔵 **EXAMPLE:** Patient underwent transurethral electrosurgical resection of the prostate, including control of postoperative bleeding. During the same operative session, complete vasectomy was performed as well as meatotomy, cystourethroscopy, urethral calibration and dilation, and internal urethrotomy. Report code 52601.

Prostate cancer treatment may involve surgery, chemical destruction, electrocautery, or radiation. Surgical procedures that are performed to treat localized prostate cancer include radical prostatectomy, laparoscopic radical prostatectomy, and cryoablation.

🔵 **Note:**

The code for transurethral electrosurgical resection of the prostate is classified in the Urinary System subsection. The procedure requires the use of an electrocautery knife to resect the prostate. (Report code 52601.)

A prostate biopsy is reported with a code from 55700–55705, depending on the type of biopsy. To report the correct CPT code, review the operative report to determine the type of biopsy performed:

- Needle

- Punch

- Incisional

The "transperineal placement of needles or catheters into prostate for interstitial radioelement application, with or without cystoscopy" describes a procedure performed for interstitial radioelement application. Code 55875 is reported for the transperineal placement of needles or catheters only.

A parenthetical note provides instruction directing the coder to radioelement application and guidance codes (77776–77787), which are reported separately.

Exercise 15.1 – Male Genital System Subsection

Instructions: Assign the CPT code(s) and appropriate modifier(s) to each statement.

1. The physician resected diseased scrotal tissue.

   _____

2. The physician removed a lesion from the left spermatic cord by dissection and excision.

   _____

3. The physician made an incision into the scrotum to search for the right testis, which failed to descend into the scrotum.

   _____

4. The physician performed a radical prostatectomy to remove the entire gland along with the seminal vesicles and the vas deferens. The incision was made between the base of the scrotum and the anus. Local lymph nodes were also removed for analysis.

   _____

5. The physician destroyed extensive condyloma of the penis using local application of a chemical.

   _____

Reproductive System Procedures Subsection

The reproductive system procedures subsection contains a code (55920) to report the placement of needles or catheters into pelvic organs and/or genitalia (Figure 15-6) for subsequent interstitial radioelement application. Code 55920 is not reported when needles or catheters are inserted into the prostate gland (for which code 55875 is reported).

> **EXAMPLE:** Patient underwent insertion of catheters into the uterus to facilitate radiation therapy. Report code 55920.

Note:

Radioactive isotopes (e.g., iodine-125) contained within tiny seeds remain inside the pelvic organs or genitalia to deliver radiation during an extended period of time (e.g., months). This method targets the prescribed body area, minimizing radiation exposure to normal tissue.

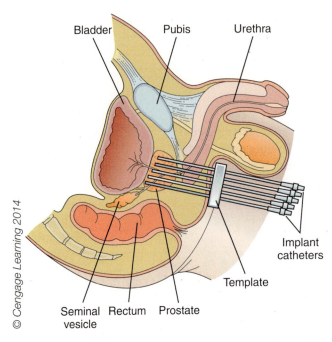

Figure 15-6 Insertion of implant catheters through perineum into prostate and seminal vesicles

Intersex Surgery Subsection

Intersex surgery (Figure 15-7) is performed as a series of staged procedures to transform the normal adult genitalia of one sex to that of the other sex (genital reconstructive surgery or sex reassignment surgery).

- For male-to-female intersex surgery, portions of the male genitalia are removed and female external genitals are formed.

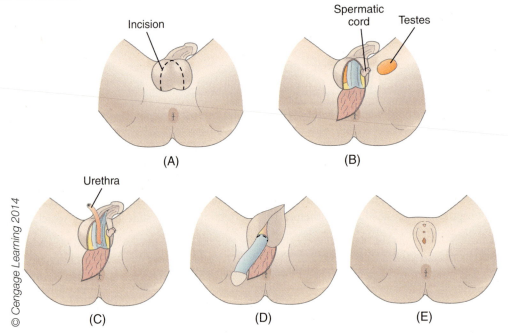

Figure 15-7 Sex reassignment surgery (A) To change male genitalia to female genitalia, an incision is made into the scrotum. (B) The flap of scrotal skin is retracted, and the testes are removed. (C) Skin is then excised from the penis but remains attached, and a shorter urethra is created. (D) All but a stump of the penis is then removed. (E) Excess skin is used to create labia (external genitalia) and the vagina.

- For female-to-male intersex surgery, a penis and scrotum are formed using pedicle flap grafts and free skin grafts and a prosthesis is inserted.

Exercise 15.2 – Reproductive System Procedures and Intersex Surgery Subsection

Instructions: Assign the CPT code(s) and appropriate modifier(s) to each statement.

1. A needle was inserted into the patient's bladder to insert a radiopharmaceutical (HCPCS level II code A9699) for the purpose of radiation therapy.

   _____

2. Surgery was performed to dissect the penis and remove portions of it to fashion a clitoris-like structure. The urethral opening was moved, and a vagina was created by dissecting and opening the perineum. Labia were created using scrotal skin and adjacent tissue.

   _____

3. In a series of staged procedures, the physician formed a penis and scrotum using pedicle flap grafts and free skin grafts. Prostheses were placed in the penis and testicles, and the vagina was closed.

   _____

Female Genital System Subsection

Codes 56405–58999 are reported for procedures performed on the **female genital system** (Figure 15-8), including the following: vulva, perineum, introitus, vagina, cervix uteri, corpus uteri, oviduct/ovary (fallopian tube), ovary, and in vitro fertilization (IVF).

When reporting codes for procedures performed on the female genital system, review the operative report to identify the following:

- Anatomy on which the procedure was performed (e.g., vulva)
- Surgical approach

Note:

Codes classified in the Female Genital System heading are reported for procedures performed on women who are *not* pregnant. To report codes for women who are pregnant, refer to the Maternity Care and Delivery heading.

Coding Tip:

- All laparoscopic procedures and nonobstetrical dilatation and curettage procedure codes are classified in the Female Genital System subsection.
- Some female genital procedures are classified in other subsection headings of the CPT coding manual, such as the open destruction of endometriomas, which is located in the Digestive System subsection, Abdomen/Peritoneum/Omentum heading, Excision/Destruction subheading.

For vulvectomy procedure codes (56620–56640), refer to the following definitions when reviewing the operative report (to select the type of procedure performed):

- *Simple procedure:* Removal of skin and superficial subcutaneous tissues.
- *Radical procedure:* Removal of skin and deep subcutaneous tissue.

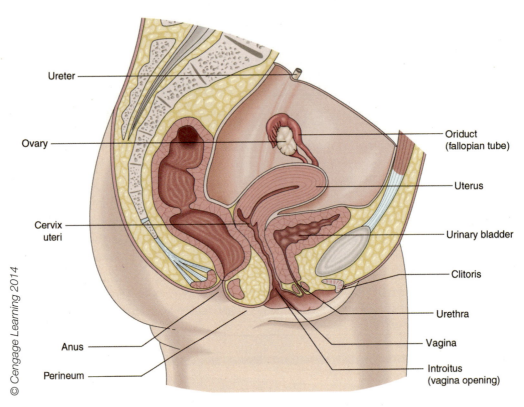

Ureter

Ovary

Cervix uteri

Anus

Perineum

Oriduct (fallopian tube)

Uterus

Urinary bladder

Clitoris

Urethra

Vagina

Introitus (vagina opening)

© Cengage Learning 2014

Figure 15-8 Female genital system

- Partial procedure: Removal of less than 80 percent of the vulvar area.

- Complete procedure: Removal of greater than 80 percent of the vulvar area.

When an open sling operation is performed for stress incontinence, report code 57288. When a laparoscopic sling operation is performed, report code 51992 from the Urinary System subsection.

Coding Tip:

Make sure you read CPT code descriptions carefully. When the code description states "with or without" another procedure, that other procedure is not reported separately if it is performed (e.g., 57240 anterior colporrhaphy, repair of cystocele with or without repair of urethrocele).

A pelvic exam under anesthesia is a routine evaluation of the surgical field, and it is reported with code 57410 *if performed separately*. This procedure is included in all major and most minor gynecological procedures, and it is *not* reported separately when performed during the same operative session as another female genital system surgical procedure.

Endoscopy codes are reported for examination and magnification, and codes distinguish among anatomic sites (e.g., vulva, vagina, cervix uteri, and oviduct/ovary). Abnormalities of the female genital system (e.g., cancer, tumors, human papilloma virus [HPV], and pruritis) are commonly diagnosed and treated with examination and magnification. For example, laparoscopy/hysteroscopy (58541–58579) is performed to visualize the corpus uteri (Figure 15-9).

When dilation of the vagina or cervix (57400 or 57800) is performed during the same operative session as another vaginal approach procedure, do not report the dilation procedure separately. When a pelvic examination under anesthesia is performed during the same operative session as a dilation and curettage (D and C) (58120) (Figure 15-10), report the code for the D and C only.

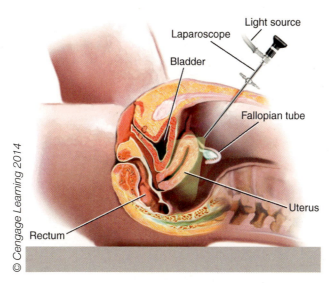

Figure 15-9 Laparoscopy

In the Cervix Uteri heading (57452–57800), **conization** of the cervix (removal of a cone-shaped piece of tissue) is reported with codes 57520–57522. Conization codes include fulguration, D and C, and repair. Conization procedures can also be performed through use of a cold knife or laser (57520) or through loop electrode excision (57522). Make sure you review the operative report carefully to assign the appropriate code.

Coding Tip:

Physicians use the terms *loop conization* and *LEEP (loop electrosurgical excision procedure) conization* interchangeably in operative reports. **Loop electrodissection conization** is a deep dissection of the cervix using a loop wire (instead of the traditional surgical scalpel). **LEEP electrodissection conization** is a more superficial dissection of the cervix using a loop wire. Report code 57522 for a loop or LEEP conization of the cervix. Report code 57460 when the loop or LEEP conization is performed via colposcopy.

Abdominal hysterectomy procedures are reported with codes 58150–58240. Make sure you review the operative report to identify whether the fallopian tubes and/or ovaries were removed during the same operative session as the hysterectomy. Then read the code descriptions carefully to select the appropriate code.

When reporting a code for vaginal hysterectomy (Figure 15-11), determine whether the surgical approach is either of the following:

- Open (58260–58294)

- Laparoscopic (58550–58554)

Coding Tip:

The code description "with or without removal of tube(s), with or without removal of ovary(s)" indicates that these procedures are bilateral. Therefore, do not report modifier -50 with codes containing such descriptions.

Hysteroscopy is the direct visualization of the cervical canal and uterine cavity using a hysteroscope. It is performed to examine the endometrium and to carry out surgical procedures (e.g., D and C or removal of a foreign body or cervical polyp). When a D and C is performed during the same operative session as a hysteroscopic biopsy or polypectomy (58558), do not report a separate code for the D and C.

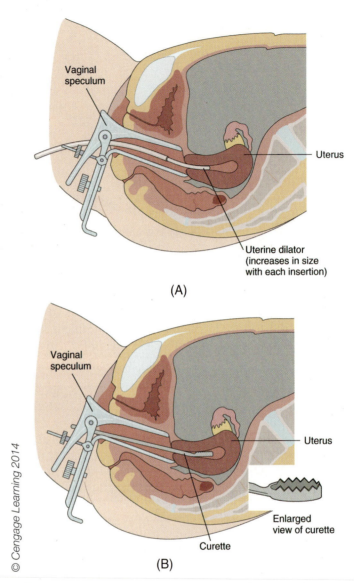

(A)

(B)

© Cengage Learning 2014

Figure 15-1O Dilation and curettage (A) Dilation is the expansion of the cervical opening. (B) Curettage is the removal of material from the endometrial lining of the uterus.

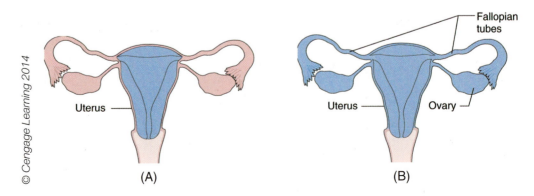

© Cengage Learning 2014

(A)   (B)

Figure 15-11 Vaginal hysterectomies (A) For a vaginal hysterectomy, just the uterus and cervix are removed. (B) For a vaginal hysterectomy with bilateral salpingo-oophorectomy, the cervix, uterus, fallopian tubes, and ovaries are removed.

The Oviduct/Ovary heading (58600–58770) includes procedures performed on the fallopian tubes. It also includes codes for endoscopic procedures performed on the ovaries. (The Ovary heading does not contain endoscopic codes.) Make sure you review the operative report to differentiate therapeutic procedures performed using surgical laparoscopy or hysteroscopy from those performed for diagnostic laparoscopy.

Review the operative report to determine the surgical approach before coding a tubal ligation procedure (e.g., ligation, transaction, or other occlusion of the fallopian tubes) (Figure 15-12):

- Abdominal or vaginal approach (58600–58605)

- Vaginal or suprapubic approach (58615)

- Laparoscopic (58670–58671)

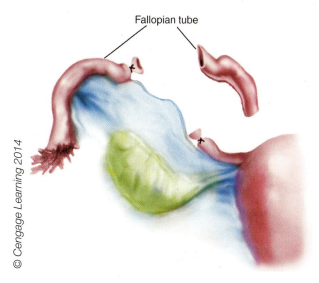

Fallopian tube

© Cengage Learning 2014

Figure 15-12 Tubal ligation

Code 58740 is reported for the open lysis of fallopian tube or ovarian adhesions. When the laparoscopic lysis of adhesions is performed as a separate procedure, report code 58660. Do not report code 58660 when the surgeon performs lysis of adhesions during the same operative session as other procedure(s) performed on the ovaries and/or fallopian tubes. However, when lysis of the adhesions are documented as dense or extensive and involve additional operating room time, increasing the risk to the patient, report code 58660 in addition to code(s) for other procedure(s) performed on the ovaries and/or fallopian tubes.

Coding Tip:

- When a postpartum tubal ligation is performed during the same hospitalization as a vaginal delivery, report code 58605.
- When a tubal ligation is performed at the time of cesarean delivery or other intra-abdominal surgery, report code 58611 in addition to the primary procedure (e.g., cesarean delivery or appendectomy).

EXAMPLE: Patient underwent a total abdominal hysterectomy during which routine lysis of adhesions was performed to access the abdomen. Report code 58150. (Do *not* report code 58660.)

Codes 58800–58960 are reported for procedures performed on the ovaries. Review the operative report to identify the surgical approach:

- Open (code 58940 is reported for oophorectomy performed via open surgery)

- Laparoscopic (code 58661 is reported for laparoscopic oophorectomy)

Code 58943 is reported for an **oophorectomy** (removal of the ovaries) due to ovarian cancer. When an ovarian malignancy is resected by performing a bilateral **salpingo-oophorectomy** (removal of both fallopian tubes and ovaries) and an **omentectomy** (removal of the omentum), report a code from 58950–58952.

 Codes 58970–58976 are reported for in vitro fertilization (IVF) procedures, which are performed during a one- to seven-day period from the time the **oocyte** (immature female reproductive cell, or egg) was aspirated from the ovary until the embryo is transferred to the uterus or is cryopreserved). IVF procedures include both male and female gametes in addition to the subsequent embryos that develop. The physician who performs the oocyte retrieval reports code 58970 (follicle puncture for oocyte retrieval, any method) to describe these services.

Coding Tip:

Any associated laboratory procedures performed during in vitro fertilization are reported separately with codes from the Pathology and Laboratory section of CPT.

Exercise 15.3 – Female Genital System Subsection

Instructions: Assign the CPT code(s) and appropriate modifier(s) to each statement.

1. The physician performed a tubal ligation immediately following vaginal delivery of a single, live newborn.

   _____

2. The physician aspirated fluid from the peritoneum through the vaginal wall.

   _____

3. The physician aspirated a mature egg from its follicle for in vitro fertilization.

   _____

4. The physician inserted an intrauterine device (IUD).

   _____

5. The physician performed laparoscopic electrical cautery destruction of an ovarian lesion with the assistance of a fiber-optic laparoscope.

   _____

Maternity Care and Delivery Subsection

In clinical terms, pregnancy is subdivided into trimesters:

- First trimester (fetal organ development)
- Second trimester (well-baby visits at the physician's office)
- Third trimester (baby maturity and delivery at 38–40 weeks)

In coding terms, the three stages of pregnancy care include services provided as part of total obstetrical care (59400, 59510, 59610, and 59618):

- Antepartum care
- Delivery of the baby
- Postpartum care

Total obstetrical care does not include diagnostic procedures (e.g., ultrasound, amniocentesis, or special screening tests), physician office visits for unrelated conditions incidental to pregnancy, and additional visits due to high-risk conditions or medical complications of pregnancy (e.g., cardiac conditions, diabetes mellitus, hyperemesis, hypertension, neurological conditions, premature rupture of membranes, preterm labor, toxemia, or hyperemesis). Codes for these services are separately reported from the Evaluation and Management and Medicine sections of CPT. For treatment of surgical complications associated with pregnancy (e.g., appendectomy, cholecystectomy, hernia repair, or removal of ovarian cyst or Bartholin cyst), codes from the Surgery section are reported separately.

Most procedures in the Maternity Care and Delivery heading (59000–59899) include just what is described in the code description. Additional procedures performed on the same day as a maternity care and delivery service are reported separately, except for the following services, which are included in the code for maternity care and delivery:

- Fetal monitoring during labor
- Episiotomy
- Delivery of the placenta

Services that are reported separately when performed during maternity care and delivery include the following:

- Amniocentesis (Figure 15-13)
- Chronic villous sampling
- Cordocentesis
- Fetal contraction stress test
- Fetal nonstress test
- Insertion of cervical dilator (e.g., laminaria and prostaglandin)

- External cephalic version with or without tocolysis
- Limited or complete obstetric ultrasound
- Fetal biophysical profile
- Fetal echocardiography
- Administration of Rh immune globulin

Antepartum Services

Antepartum care begins with conception and ends with delivery, and it includes the following:

- Initial and subsequent history
- Physical examinations
- Documentation of weight, blood pressures, and fetal heart tones
- Routine chemical urinalysis (e.g., glucose)

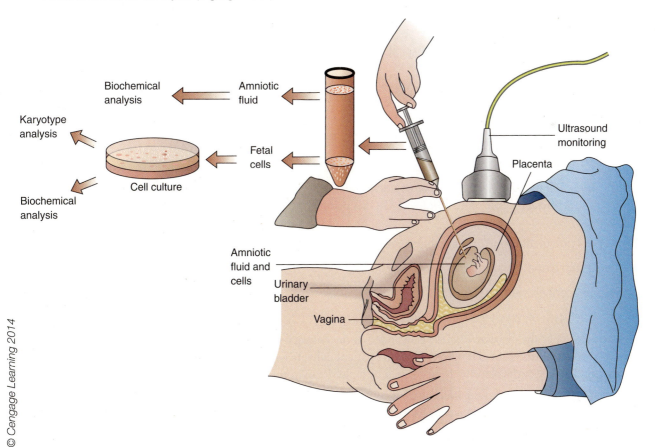

© Cengage Learning 2014

Figure 15-13 Amniocentesis and preparation of specimen for amniotic fluid analysis

- Monthly visits up to 28 weeks' gestation

- Biweekly visits to 36 weeks' gestation

- Weekly visits until delivery

The above services are included with total obstetrical care, and they are not reported separately. Services that are reported separately with a code from the Evaluation and Management or Surgery section of CPT (in addition to a code for delivery services) include the management of the following:

- Medical problems *unrelated* to pregnancy

- Complications related to pregnancy

  EXAMPLE: Patient develops gestational diabetes, which complicates her pregnancy. She requires additional office visits to monitor her blood sugar and weight. Report an appropriate evaluation and management service code for each office visit during which the patient's gestational diabetes is managed.

When a physician provides *antepartum care only* (e.g., patient's care is transferred to another physician or patient relocates out of the area), report an appropriate evaluation and management code for the first through third antepartum care visit. For the fourth and subsequent visits, report code 59425 (Antepartum care only; 4–6 visits) or 59426 (Antepartum care only; 7 or more visits).

Delivery Services

Delivery services (e.g., vaginal delivery, cesarean delivery, and delivery after previous cesarean delivery) begin with the admission of the patient to the hospital and end with delivery of the placenta (Figure 15-14). Services include the following:

- Admission of the patient to the hospital

- Admission history and physical examination

- Management of uncomplicated labor

- Vaginal delivery (with or without episiotomy and/or with or without forceps) or cesarean delivery

The induction of labor (e.g., pitocin or oxytocin) during delivery is included in the code for delivery services. The artificial rupture of membranes (AROM) prior to delivery is also included in the delivery services code.

Services provided during delivery that are reported separately include the following:

- Fetal scalp blood sampling (59030)

- External cephalic version (59412)

- Administration of regional anesthesia (e.g., epidural)

The delivery of the placenta (59414) is included in the delivery service, and it is *not* reported in addition to the delivery service. Code 59414 is reported when the patient delivers vaginally prior to admission to the hospital and subsequent delivery of the placenta is performed by a physician in the hospital.

Services that are reported separately with a code from the Evaluation and Management or Surgery section of CPT (in addition to a code for delivery services) include the following:

- Management of surgical problems that develop during the postpartum period

- Admission to the hospital for observation prior to delivery

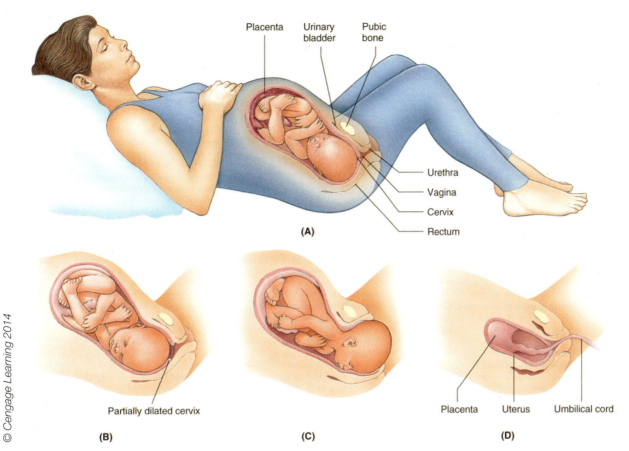

Figure 15-14 Stages of labor. (A) Position of the fetus before labor. (B) First stage of labor. (C) Second stage of labor, fetal delivery. (D) Third stage of labor, delivery of the placenta

- Medical complications of pregnancy, labor, and/or delivery that require additional resources (e.g., diabetes, hypertension, toxemia, preterm labor, or premature rupture of membranes)

- Tubal ligation (58605) performed after delivery

Coding Tip:

- Multiple births create the potential for complications during pregnancy, and they present coding challenges.

- When performing diagnostic tests on multiple fetuses (e.g., amniocentesis or biophysical profile), more work is usually required because the procedure must be performed and documented for each fetus. To indicate additional work, report the appropriate code with modifier -22 or report the code for each fetus. (Make sure you report a diagnosis code that indicates multiple gestation.)

- Codes for multiple births are reported as follows:

  o Vaginal delivery of each baby: report code 59400 for Baby A, code 59409-51 for Baby B, code 59409-51 for Baby C, and so on.

○ Vaginal delivery followed by cesarean delivery: report code 59510 for Baby B, code 59409-51 for Baby A (and subsequent vaginal delivery codes if additional babies were delivered vaginally, with modifier -51 added to each code). (Code 59510 for cesarean delivery is reported first because that procedure consumes the most resources. If multiple babies are delivered via cesarean, report code 59510 just once.)

○ Cesarean delivery of each baby: report code 59510 once (because just one cesarean section is performed). When a cesarean delivery is significantly more difficult, add modifier -22 to the code. (Submit a copy of the operative report with the claim.) Report the diagnosis code for multiple gestation.

Postpartum Care

Postpartum care begins after vaginal or cesarean section delivery and includes the recovery room visit; any uncomplicated inpatient hospital and outpatient postpartum visits; follow-up care for episiotomy; and repair of cervical, vaginal, or perineal lacerations, including follow-up care. During delivery, if a vaginal laceration occurs and the repair is minimal, it is included in the delivery services. The repair of the vaginal laceration is not coded separately.

Coding Tip:

• When a physician provides all or part of the antepartum and/or postpartum care but does not perform the delivery due to termination of pregnancy by abortion or referral to another physician for delivery, report codes from the antepartum and postpartum subheadings (59425–59426 and 59430).

• When a physician performs only the delivery, report a "delivery only" code.

EXAMPLE: The on-call obstetrician performs an emergency cesarean section on a colleague's patient. The on-call obstetrician reports code 59514. The patient's obstetrician reports codes for antepartum and postpartum care.

Delivery after Previous Cesarean Delivery

Codes 59610–59622 are reported for delivery after previous cesarean section whether an attempted vaginal birth is successful or a repeat cesarean is performed. A code from 59610–59614 is reported for **vaginal birth after cesarean (VBAC)**, which is a planned vaginal birth after previous cesarean section. When the planned VBAC fails, report a code from 59618–59622.

Abortion

Abortion treatment codes (59812–59857) are based on the method used and type of abortion:

• **Incomplete abortion**: Miscarriage in which part, but not all, of the uterine contents are expelled.

• **Missed abortion**: Miscarriage in which a dead fetus and other products of conception remain in the uterus for four or more weeks.

• **Septic abortion**: Abortion-related pelvic and uterine infection.

EXAMPLE: Patient underwent treatment for a septic abortion, which was completed surgically. Report code 59830.

- **Induced abortion**: Deliberate termination of pregnancy.

Exercise 15.4 – Maternity Care and Delivery Subsection

Instructions: Assign the CPT code(s) and appropriate modifier(s) to each statement.

1. The physician treated an ectopic pregnancy by removing the fallopian tube and ovary through an incision in the lower abdomen.

   _____

2. Using ultrasonic guidance, the physician inserted an amniocentesis needle through the abdominal wall into the interior of the pregnant uterus and directly into the amniotic sac to collect amniotic fluid for diagnostic analysis.

   _____

3. Using ultrasonic guidance, the physician inserted an amniocentesis needle through the abdominal wall into the cavity of the pregnant uterus and into the umbilical vessels to obtain fetal blood.

   _____

4. The physician used an external monitor to record fetal heart rate changes during a fetal nonstress test.

   _____

5. A physician provided all antepartum (7 visits) and postpartum care but did not perform the delivery.

   _____

Endocrine System Subsection

The **endocrine system** (Figure 15-15) includes the following glands:

- Adrenal (2)
- Gonads (ovaries in females, testes in males) (2)
- Pancreas (islets of Langerhans) (1)
- Parathyroid (divided into four lobes) (1)
- Pituitary (divided into two lobes) (1)
- Thymus (1)
- Thyroid (divided into two lobes) (1)

Coding Tip:

Codes for procedures performed on the pituitary and pineal glands are located in the Nervous System subsection.

The Endocrine System subsection includes procedures performed on the endocrine glands and the carotid body.

Thyroid Gland

Codes 60200–60240 describe increasingly complex procedures involving excision of the thyroid gland. For example, code 60210 classifies a partial thyroid lobectomy, with or without isthmusectomy, and code 60220 classifies a total thyroid lobectomy with or without isthmusectomy.

Codes 60252 and 60254 describe the total or subtotal resection of the thyroid gland for malignancy, with limited or radical neck dissection, respectively. A "total or subtotal resection" is the removal of both the left and

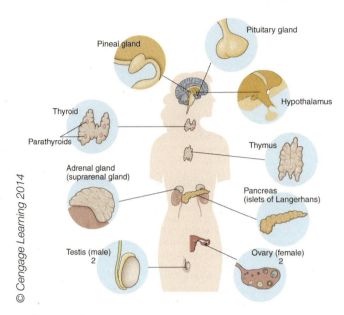

Figure 15-15 Endocrine glands

right lobes of the thyroid gland. A "limited neck dissection" is the removal of a limited number of lymph nodes. A "radical neck dissection" is the total removal of lymph nodes from one side (or both sides) of the neck.

Note:

You may recall that when a radical neck dissection is performed during the same operative session as the resection of a unilateral organ (e.g., larynx), modifier -50 is not added to the procedure codes. The thyroid gland is a unilateral organ that contains two lobes. Thus, modifiers -50, -LT, and -RT are *never* added to thyroid gland procedure codes.

EXAMPLE: A physician suspects lymphoma in a patient who has signs of diffuse neck swelling. A large core needle biopsy of the right lobe of the thyroid gland is performed. The tissue is sent for histopathology. Report code 60100.

Parathyroid, Thymus, Adrenal Glands, Pancreas, and Carotid Body

Codes 60500–60699 are reported for procedures performed on the parathyroid, thymus, -adrenal glands, and the carotid body. The **carotid body** is tissue that contains many capillaries, and it is located at the point where the carotid artery branches in the neck. It contains cells that sense oxygen and carbon dioxide blood levels so that information is sent to the brain's medulla to regulate heart rate.

Surgery performed on the adrenal glands can be performed as open or laparoscopic procedures. Make sure you review the operative report to identify the surgical approach to report the appropriate code.

The exploration of parathyroid glands is often performed using a cervical approach. In cases where further exploration is needed, the physician uses a transthoracic approach.

EXAMPLE 1: Patient underwent laparoscopic exploration with partial removal of the left adrenal gland, performed from a transabdominal approach. Report code 60650-LT.

EXAMPLE 2: Patient underwent surgical laparoscopy with complete right adrenalectomy, performed from a lumbar approach. Report code 60650-RT.

Exercise 15.5 – Endocrine System Subsection

Instructions: Assign the CPT code(s) and appropriate modifier(s) to each statement.

1. The physician determines the location of a thyroid cyst, using palpation, and aspirates it.

   _____

2. The physician performed a total thyroid lobectomy on the right and a contralateral subtotal lobectomy on the left, including isthmusectomy.

   _____

3. The physician removed remaining thyroid tissue on one side, following an earlier partial thyroidectomy.

   _____

4. Patient underwent large core needle biopsy of the thyroid gland.

   _____

5. Patient underwent incision and drainage of an infected thyroglossal cyst of the neck, which was the result of incomplete closure of the embryonic thyroglossal duct between the thyroid gland and the back of the tongue.

   _____

6. The physician performed a laparoscopic exploration of the adrenal gland through the abdomen.

   _____

7. The physician explored the parathyroid glands. During the same operative session, a parathyroid autotransplantation via sternal split was also performed.

   _____

8. Patient underwent partial adrenalectomy with biopsy, dorsal approach.

   _____

9. The physician surgically removed the parathyroid glands.

   _____

10. The physician removed a carotid body tumor, which was located just above the bifurcation of the carotid artery.

    _____

Nervous System Subsection

The **nervous system** (Figure 15-16) includes the following:

- Central nervous system (brain and spinal cord)
- Peripheral nervous system (12 pairs of cranial nerves extending from the brain and 31 pairs of spinal nerves extending from the spinal cord).

  Codes for Nervous System subsection procedures are arranged anatomically:

- Skull, meninges, and brain
- Spine and spinal cord
- Extracranial nerves, peripheral nerves, and autonomic nervous system

Nervous system procedures are performed using a variety of approaches (e.g., craniectomy, craniotomy, and laminectomy) and for specific purposes (e.g., decompression and drainage of hematomas).

EXAMPLE: Patient underwent a procedure to create subdural burr holes to drain a hematoma. Report code 61154. (The subdural burr hole is the approach, and drainage of the hematoma is the purpose.)

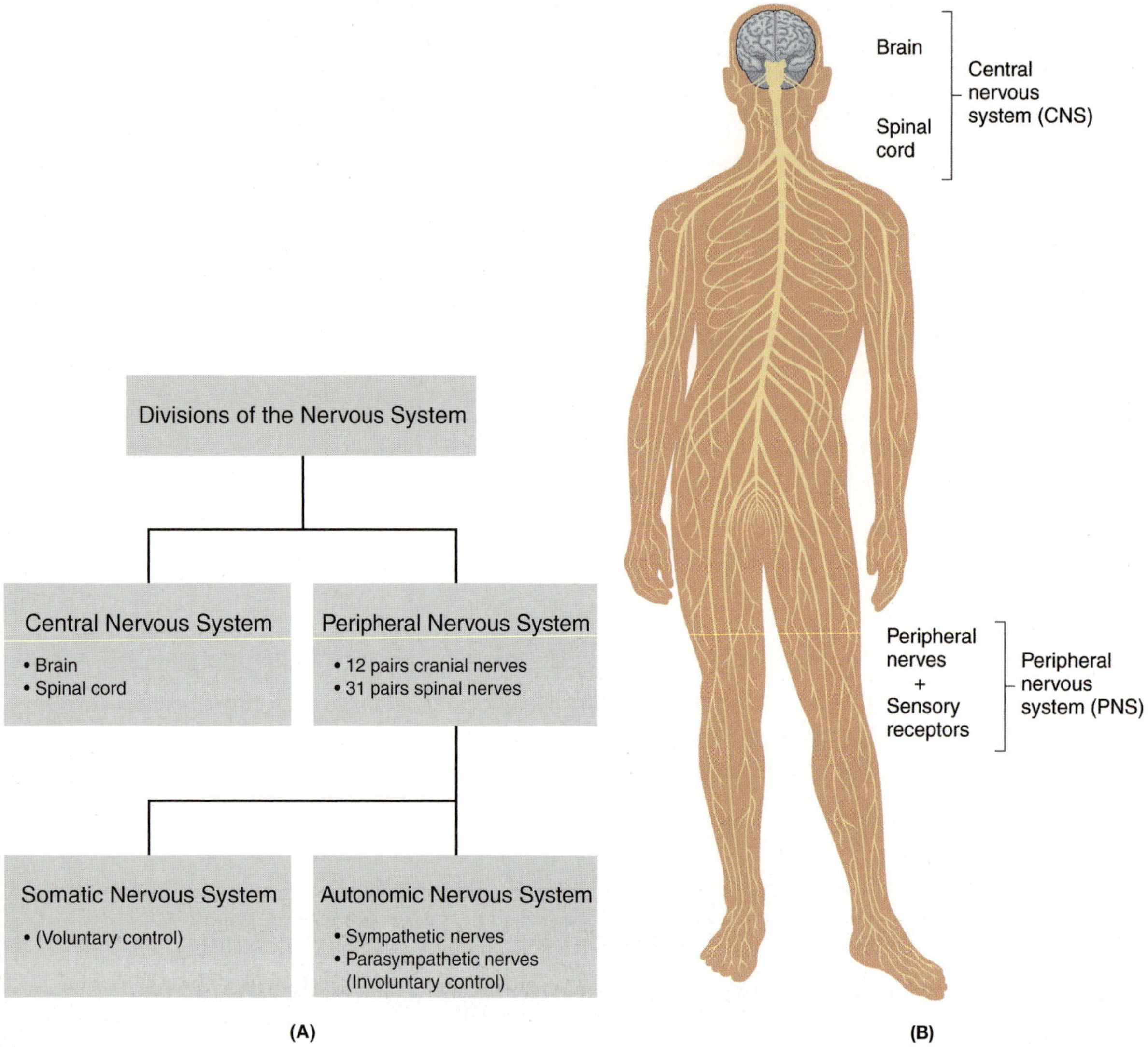

Figure 15-16 Nervous system (A) Divisions of the nervous system (B) Structure of the central nervous system and peripheral nervous system

Skull, Meninges, and Brain

The Skull, Meninges, and Brain (Figure 15-17) heading includes the following subheadings (and for "Surgery of Skull Base," further subdivisions):

- Injection, Drainage, or Aspiration

- Twist Drill, Burr Hole(s), or Trephine

- Craniectomy or Craniotomy

- Surgery of Skull Base

  ○ Approach Procedures

  ○ Definitive Procedures

  ○ Repair and/or Reconstruction of Surgical Defects of Skull Base

- Endovascular Therapy

- Surgery for Aneurysm, Arteriovenous Malformation, or Vascular Disease

- Stereotaxis

- Stereotactic Radiosurgery (Cranial)

- Neurostimulators (Intracranial)

- Repair

- Neuroendoscopy

- Cerebrospinal Fluid (CSF) Shunt

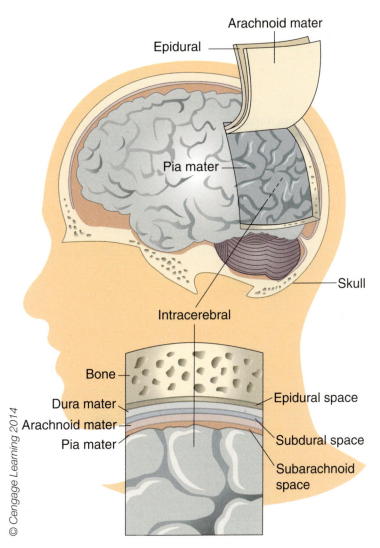

Figure 15-17 Scalp, skull, meninges, and brain

A **burr hole** is a small opening in the skull made with a surgical drill. This procedure is often necessary when intracranial surgery (e.g., craniotomy or craniectomy) is planned. The burr hole provides access to intracranial contents, it alleviates pressure in preparation of further surgery, and it allows the placement of an intracranial pressure monitoring device. (These services are integral to the performance of subsequent services, and they are not to be separately coded or reported.)

When burr holes, punctures, and/or taps are created for the purpose of performing drainage procedures (e.g., hematoma, abscess, or cyst) and additional procedures are performed, the burr hole and drainage procedure is not separately coded and reported (unless it is performed as a staged procedure). In addition, many intracranial procedures include bone grafting; such grafts are not separately coded and reported.

Injection procedures for imaging of CSF flow are reported with code 61026 in addition to codes from the Radiology section (to report the imaging procedure).

EXAMPLE 1: Patient underwent ventricular puncture through previous burr hole with injection of medication. Report code 61026. (The ventricular puncture through a previous burr hole describes the approach to access a specific area of the brain.)

EXAMPLE 2: A patient with an open head injury and a contrecoup subdural hematoma underwent a craniectomy for the open head injury and creation of a burr hole on the opposite side of the skull to drain the subdural hematoma. Report codes 61304 and 61154. (The creation of the contralateral burr hole and drainage of the subdural hematoma is considered a separate service not integral to the craniectomy. Thus, it is assigned a separate code.)

Surgery of Skull Base

Surgery of skull base codes (61580–61619) contains important notes that define anatomic areas included (e.g., skull base includes the base of the anterior, middle, and posterior cranial fossa). Notes further indicate that skull base surgery often requires the skills of several different surgical specialties that work together. Skull base surgery requires review of the operative report to identify the following variables:

- What the size of the lesion or tumor is
- What the anatomy of the individual patient is
- Whether this is an initial procedure to treat the condition or a reoperation.

Surgery of skull base codes are arranged anatomically (anterior, middle, and posterior cranial fossae), and they are further subdivided according to the following:

- Approach procedures (provide adequate exposure to the intracranial field so the definitive procedure, such as excision of lesion, can be performed).
- Definitive procedures (e.g., resection, excision, transection, ligation, and obliteration), which include primary closure of dura, mucous membranes, and skin.
- Repair and/or reconstruction of skull defects of skull base procedures (reported separately when cranioplasty, extensive dural grafting, extensive skin grafts, or local or regional myocutaneous pedicle flaps are required).

When skull base surgery is performed, a code for each procedure is reported by the surgeon who performed that aspect of the procedure: approach procedure, definitive procedure, and repair and/or reconstructive procedure. Generally, one surgeon performs the approach procedure, which exposes the area (e.g., lesion) to be treated. Another surgeon then performs the treatment (e.g., excision of lesion). A third surgeon repairs the defect created by the treatment (e.g., free tissue graft of dural defect created by excision of lesion). When one surgeon performs both the approach procedure and the definitive procedure, that surgeon reports both codes on the same claim; modifier -51 is added to the secondary procedure.

Note:

Skull base surgery procedures are not typically considered "staged" because definitive closure of the surgical field (e.g., dura, subcutaneous tissues, or skin) must be performed to avoid serious infections (e.g., osteomyelitis or meningitis).

EXAMPLE: The operative report documents a right maxillectomy with orbital exenteration, bilateral ethmoidectomies, and a sphenoidectomy. The patient underwent resection of a neoplastic lesion at the base of the anterior cranial fossa, extradural.

The approach procedure code is 61581 because a "craniofacial approach to anterior cranial fossa" includes ethmoidectomy, sphenoidectomy, maxillectomy, and orbital exenteration procedures. (Approach procedures for middle cranial fossa and posterior cranial fossa do include such procedures.) The definitive procedure code is 61600. (Do not report a code for repair and/or reconstruction of surgical defects of skull base because such procedures were not documented.)

Codes 61600 and 61601 distinguish between procedures performed extradurally (outside the dura) or intradurally (within the dura). The dura mater is the outermost, fibrous, and toughest of the three meninges (Figure 15-18) that surround the brain and spinal cord.

Some procedure codes in the Surgery of Skull Base heading (61609–61612) are add-on procedures. They are not reported alone; they must be reported with another procedure code (e.g., 61605).

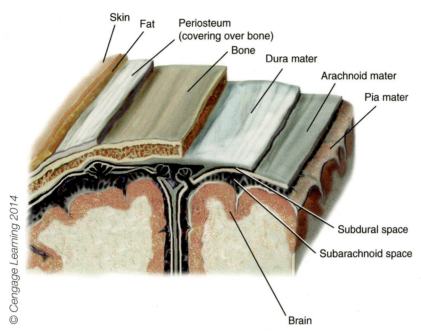

Figure 15-18 Meninges (dura mater, arachnoid mater, and pia mater) and other anatomic structures that protect the brain

EXAMPLE: A surgeon performed a resection of an infectious lesion of the parasellar area. During the same operative session, the same surgeon performed a transection of the carotid artery in a cavernous sinus, without repair. (No repair and/or reconstruction of surgical defects of the skull base was required.) Report codes 61607 and 61609. (The approach procedure was performed by a different surgeon; therefore, do not report a code for an approach procedure.)

Neurostimulators (Intracranial)

Codes describing craniotomy procedures (62100–62121) are usually bundled with craniectomy codes (61860–61875). Thus, when a craniotomy is performed during the same operative session as a craniectomy, report only the craniectomy code. Do not report the craniotomy code in addition to the craniectomy code.

EXAMPLE: When a patient undergoes "craniectomy or craniotomy for implantation of neurostimulator electrodes" during the same operative session as the creation of "twist drill or burr hole(s) for implantation of neurostimulator electrodes," only code 61860 is reported. Code 61850 is not reported in addition to code 61860.

Cerebrospinal Fluid (CSF) Shunt

A CSF shunt (Figure 15-19) is used to eliminate excess CSF in cases of hydrocephalus.

EXAMPLE: A child underwent creation of a ventriculo-peritoneal shunt. Report code 62223.

Spine and Spinal Cord

The Spine and Spinal Cord heading describes percutaneous procedures performed on the spine, as well as spinal injections and extracranial and

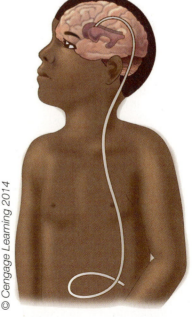

Figure 15-19 A cerebrospinal shunt allows drainage of cerebrospinal fluid (CSF) from the brain into the peritoneal cavity.

peripheral nerve injections. To report procedures codes properly, review the operative report to identify the following:

- What the anatomic site is (e.g., epidural or facet joint nerves)
- Whether the procedure is diagnostic or therapeutic
- What type of substance is injected (e.g., contrast media or neurolytic substance)
- Whether the injections are continuous

Notes located below the Injection, Drainage, or Aspiration subheading provide the following instructions:

- Injection of contrast during fluoroscopic guidance and localization is included in codes 62263–62264, 62270–62273, 62280–62282, and 62310–62319.
- Fluoroscopic guidance is reported by code 77003 except when a formal contrast study (e.g., arthrography, epidurography, or myelography) is performed; in that case, fluoroscopy is included in the supervision and interpretation code and it is *not* separately coded or reported.
- Code 72275 is reported for the radiologic supervision and interpretation of epidurography; and that code includes the epidurogram procedure, documented images, and radiologic report.
- Report code 62263 for multiple **adhesiolysis** sessions (two or more days), which includes the percutaneous lysis of epidural adhesions using solution injection (e.g., enzyme or hypertonic saline) or mechanical means (e.g., catheter). Code 62263 includes the percutaneous insertion *and removal* of an epidural catheter, which has remained in place during a period of time (e.g., several days). Code 62263 is reported just once to describe the entire series of injections and/or infusions during two or more treatment days.
- Code 62264 is reported for multiple adhesiolysis treatment sessions performed on one day.
- Codes 62263 and 62264 include the injection of contrast media for epidurography (72275) as well as fluoroscopic guidance and localization (77003) during initial or subsequent sessions. Do *not* report code 72275 or 77003 in addition to code 62263 or 62264.

EXAMPLE: Patient underwent percutaneous lysis of epidural adhesions procedure under fluoroscopic guidance on June 14. Hypertonic saline solution 3 X 2 was administered during the procedure. Report code 62264. (Do not report a separate code for fluoroscopic guidance.)

Coding Tip:

- Report code 01996 from the Anesthesia section for daily hospital management of continuous epidural or subarachnoid drug administration performed with services assigned codes 62318–62319 (injection of diagnostic or therapeutic substances).
- For a spinal puncture procedure, the administration of local anesthesia is included. Reporting a separate code for the administration of local anesthesia (e.g., nerve block or facet block) is inappropriate.
- When an anesthetic block procedure is performed and cerebrospinal fluid is withdrawn during the same operative session (to make room for the anesthetic), do not report a code for diagnostic lumbar puncture. Report a code for the nerve (or other) block only because the removal of CSF is not done for diagnostic purposes.

Catheter Implantation

The *implantation* of an epidural or intrathecal catheter placement involves penetration of the dura. A parenthetical note below the Catheter Implantation subheading provides instruction to see codes 62270–62273, 62280–62284, and 62310–62319 when reporting *percutaneous placement* of an intrathecal or epidural catheter.

EXAMPLE: Patient underwent implantation of tunneled epidural catheter for long-term medication administration via external pump. Report code 62350.

Reservoir/Pump Implantation

Programmable and nonprogrammable infusion pumps provide long-term access to the vascular or nervous system for the administration of medications. When electronic analysis and reprogramming of a programmable implanted pump is performed during the same operative session as refilling and maintenance, report code 62368.

> **EXAMPLE:** Patient underwent implantation of a subcutaneous reservoir for intrathecal drug infusion. Report code 62360.

Posterior Extradural Laminotomy or Laminectomy for Exploration/Decompression of Neural Elements or Excision of Herniated Intervertebral Disks

A **laminotomy** involves the removal of part of the lamina from one side of the vertebra. A **laminectomy** is the excision of the entire posterior arch or lamina of a vertebra. When reporting codes for a laminectomy or laminotomy (hemilaminectomy) procedure, determine the following:

- Anatomic site
- Surgical approach
- Type of procedure performed

Coding Tip:

- A laminotomy is also known as a hemilaminectomy. Therefore, review of the operative report to differentiate between laminectomy and laminotomy (or hemilaminectomy) is required.
- When a laminotomy is performed during the same operative session as a laminectomy, the laminotomy code is not reported separately.

When codes are reported for laminotomy procedures, just one vertebral interspace in a specific area of the spine is accessed. When additional interspace(s) are accessed for laminotomy during the same operative session, report appropriate add-on code(s) in addition to the primary procedure code.

When reporting codes for laminectomy procedures, if a facetectomy and foraminotomy were performed, report a code from 63045–63048. Laminectomies without facetectomy and foraminotomy are reported with codes 63001–63011 or 63015–63017.

> **EXAMPLE:** Patient underwent hemilaminectomy with decompression of nerve roots and partial facetectomy and excision of herniated intervertebral disc, C1-C2. Report code 63040. (C1-C2 is one interspace; thus, code 63040 is reported once.)

Transpedicular or Costovertebral Approach for Posterolateral Extradural Exploration/Decompression

Codes 63055–63066 describe extradural exploration/decompression procedures that are performed using a transpedicular or costovertebral approach.

- A **transpedicular approach** is performed through and inside the pedicle (segment between transverse process and vertebral body) of a thoracic vertebra to access a thoracic disc. This approach does not require retraction of the spinal cord, but it may involve removal of the lamina and facet joint.

- A **costovertebral approach** is performed where the ribs articulate (connect) with thoracic vertebrae. (**Costovertebral** refers to that area of the thoracic spine where the rib meets the vertebra.) The physician makes an incision laterally to the spine, cutting through epidermis, dermis, subcutaneous, fascia, and muscle tissue and a section of rib.

> **EXAMPLE:** Patient underwent decompression of spinal cord at T1, via costovertebral approach. Report code 63064.

Anterior or Anterolateral Approach for Extradural Exploration/Decompression

A **discectomy** is the removal of an intervertebral disk. When reporting codes 63075–63078, make sure you review the operative report to identify the *number of interspaces removed* (e.g., C1-C2 describes one interspace and C1-C2 and C2-C3 describe two interspaces) (Figure 15-20).

A **corpectomy** is the removal of a portion of the vertebra and adjacent intervertebral discs. Its purpose is for the decompression of the spinal cord and spinal nerves. A bone graft is placed to reconstruct the spine and provide stability. When reporting codes 63081–63091, make sure you review the operative report to identify the *number of segments removed* (e.g., C1 describes one segment and C1-C2 describes two segments) (Figure 15-20).

Codes 63075–63091 describe exploration/decompression procedures performed using an anterior or anterolateral approach.

- An **anterior approach** involves making an incision overlying the intervertebral disc by cutting through epidermis, dermis, subcutaneous, fascia, and muscle tissue.

Coding Tip:

- Codes 63075–63078 include **osteophytectomy**, which is the removal of bone spurs to relieve compression of the spinal cord or nerve roots.
- Codes 63075–63078 include the placement of graft material (obtained from the ilium or the removed rib) into the disk space, when performed. Grafting is performed to allow for proper spacing between vertebrae and to promote spinal fusion.
- When arthrodesis follows procedures coded with 63075–63091, report a code from 22548–22812 (in addition to the extradural exploration/decompression).
- Codes 63081–63091 include diskectomy performed above and/or below the vertebral segment involved. Do not report a separate code for diskectomy.
- For reconstruction of the spine, report the vertebral corpectomy codes (63081–63091) with bone graft codes (20930–20938), arthrodesis codes (22548–22812), and spinal instrumentation codes (22840–22855).

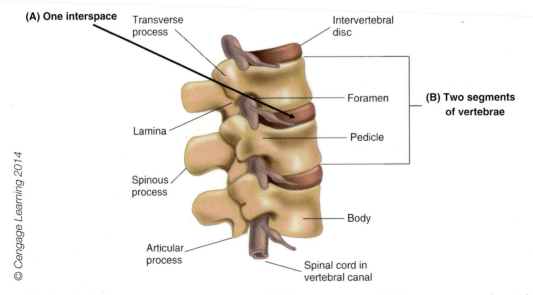

Figure 15-20 Interspaces and vertebrae (A) One interspace (B) Two segments of vertebrae

- An **anterolateral approach** involves making an incision along (and removing) the rib that corresponds to the vertebra that is located above the compressed intervertebral disc.

    EXAMPLE: Patient underwent anterior diskectomy with decompression of spinal cord, including osteophytectomy, C2-C3. Report code 63075.

Lateral Extracavitary Approach (LECA) for Extradural Exploration/Decompression

For the **lateral extracavitary approach (LECA)**, a midline incision is made in the area of the affected vertebral segment (e.g., fractured vertebra or vertebral tumor), and the incision is inferiorly curved out to the lateral plane. Paraspinous muscles are mobilized medially (denervating and devascularizing these structures). The muscles are lifted from the spinous process; and they are divided and lifted from the ribs, exposing the vertebral segment.

    EXAMPLE: Patient underwent complete vertebral corpectomy with decompression of spinal cord, T1. Report code 63101.

Incision

A laminectomy with cordotomy (63194–63199) procedure may be performed as a one-stage or two-stage procedure.

 EXAMPLE: Patient underwent one-stage cervical laminectomy procedure with cordotomy and section of one spinothalamic tract. Report code 63194.

On June 10, the patient underwent the first procedure for a two-stage cervical laminectomy procedure with cordotomy and section of both spinothalamic tracts. On June 17, the patient underwent the second of the two-stage procedure. Report code 63198. (Code 63198 is reported just once for this two-stage procedure.)

Coding Tip:

For cervical laminectomy and section of dentate ligaments, with or without dural graft, report a code from 63180–63182. Do not report code 63710.

Excision by Laminectomy of Lesion Other Than Herniated Disk

When reporting codes 63250–63290, review the operative report to identify the following:

- Anatomic site
    - Cervical
    - Thoracic
    - Lumbar
    - Sacral
- Type of procedure performed
    - Excision or occlusion of arteriovenous malformation of spinal cord (63250–63252)
    - Excision or evacuation of intraspinal lesion other than neoplasm, extradural (63265–63268)
    - Excision of intraspinal lesion other than neoplasm, intradural (63270–63273)
    - Biopsy/excision of intraspinal neoplasm, extradural or intradural (63275–63290)

Add-on code 63295 is reported for osteoplastic reconstruction of dorsal spinal elements following a primary intraspinal procedure, such as laminectomy with drainage of intramedullary cyst/syrinx to subarachnoid space (63172). (Do not add modifier -51 to code 63295.)

    EXAMPLE: Patient underwent laminectomy for excision of intraspinal neoplasm, extradural, thoracic. Report code 63276.

Excision, Anterior or Anterolateral Approach, Intraspinal Lesion

Code 63300 is reported for "vertebral corpectomy (vertebral body resection), partial or complete, for excision of intraspinal lesion, single segment; each additional segment." Add-on code 63308 is reported for each additional segment in addition to the code for the single segment. (Do *not* add modifier -51 to code 63308.)

> **EXAMPLE:** Patient underwent partial vertebral corporectomy for excision of an intraspinal lesion, extradural, C1 and C2. Report codes 63300 and 63308.

Stereotaxis

Stereotaxis uses a stereotactic guidance system to allow the physician to determine three-dimensional coordinates to:

- Create a lesion on the spinal cord (to alleviate chronic pain in a particular part of the body).
- Stimulate the spinal cord percutaneously (to create a lesion that will block pain).
- Facilitate the biopsy, aspiration, or excision of a spinal cord lesion.

> **EXAMPLE:** Patient underwent stereotactic percutaneous electrical stimulation of the spinal cord to create a lesion to block severe pain. Report code 63600.

Stereotactic Radiosurgery (Spinal)

Spinal stereotactic radiosurgery uses externally generated ionizing radiation to inactivate or eradicate spinal targets without the need to make an incision.

Neurostimulators (Spinal)

A spinal **neurostimulator** system includes an electrode and a pulse generator that are implanted along the spine to alleviate pain or control spasms. Neurostimulator codes (63650–63688) describe codes for procedures used to implant, revise, and place neurostimulators along the spine. Codes for the implantation or placement and removal or revision of the neurostimulators are reported separately.

> **EXAMPLE:** Patient underwent percutaneous implantation of neurostimulator electrode array, epidural. Report code 63650.

Coding Tip:

Initial and subsequent electronic analysis and programming of neurostimulator pulse generators are reported with medicine section codes 95970–95975.

Repair

When reporting repair codes (63700–63706), do not add modifier -63 (Procedure Performed on Infants Less Than 4 kg). (Modifier -63 is added to indicate significantly increased complexity and physician work associated with procedures performed on infants who weigh less than 4 kg.) It is not appropriate to add modifier -63 to codes 63700–63706 because the additional complexity and work is included in the procedure codes.

> **EXAMPLE:** Patient underwent repair of meningocele, 10 cm in diameter. Report code 63702.

Shunt, Spinal CSF

Procedures reported with codes 63740–63746 are reported for CSF shunt procedures, which are performed on the lumbar spine (not the brain).

> **EXAMPLE:** Patient underwent creation of percutaneous shunt, lumbar, subarachnoid-peritoneal. Report code 63741.

Coding Tip:

For CSF shunt procedures performed on the brain, report codes 62190–62192, located under the Skull, Meninges, and Brain heading.

Coding Tip:

Ophthalmologic procedures are also located in the:

- Integumentary System subsection (CPT Surgery) (e.g., Shaving of epidermal lesions from the eyelid, 11310–11313).
- Musculoskeletal System subsection (CPT Surgery) (e.g., orbital wall decompression with nasal/sinus endoscopy, 31292–31293).
- Medicine section (e.g., diagnostic/therapeutic ophthalmologic services, 92002–92499).

Note:

The following HCPCS level II modifiers are added to Eyelid heading codes when appropriate:

- E1 (upper left eyelid)
- E2 (lower left eyelid)
- E3 (upper right eyelid)
- E4 (lower right eyelid)

Eyeball

The **eyeball**, or **globe**, contains the choroid, retina, and sclera. The **sclera** is the white of the eye that comprises the eye's outer layer; it contains fibrous tissue that maintains the eye's shape and protects the eye's inner layers. The **cornea** is the transparent layer on the eye's surface; it covers the iris and pupil and provides focusing power. The **uvea** is the eye's vascular layer, which includes the choroid, ciliary body (ciliary muscle), and iris. The **choroid** is the opaque layer behind the retina that contains blood vessels. The **iris** is colored tissue that surrounds the pupil. The **pupil** is the black opening in the center of the iris that permits light to enter the eye. The **lens** is a clear, flexible, curved structure that focuses images on the retina. The **ciliary body**, or **ciliary muscle**, adjusts the shape of the lens and focuses light rays onto the retina. The **retina** contains nerve tissue.

An **evisceration of ocular contents** includes removal of the contents of the eyeball (choroid, ciliary muscles, iris, lens, retina, and vitreous); the sclera remains intact. (An implant may or may not be placed into the scleral shell.)

An **enucleation of the eye** includes severing the eyeball from extraorbital muscles and the optic nerve and removing it. (An implant may or may not be placed and attached to extraocular muscles.)

An **exenteration of the orbit** includes the removal of orbital contents and may also include removal of bone, muscle, and/or the myocutaneous flap. When a skin graft is placed, report a code from the Integumentary subsection (in addition to the exenteration of the orbit code). When the eyelid is repaired, report a code from the Reconstruction Area of the Eyelids subheading (in addition to the exenteration of the orbit code).

Codes 65125–65175 are reported for procedures performed to modify an ocular implant (e.g., alter the shape of a prosthesis to create a better fit). An **orbital implant** is inserted outside the muscular cone into the eye socket, and an intraocular lens (IOL) is placed. An **ocular implant** is inserted inside the muscular cone.

EXAMPLE: Patient underwent secondary insertion of ocular implant (after having undergone previous evisceration) into the scleral shell. Report code 65130.

CPT differentiates between the removal of a foreign body located in the eye and removal of implanted material (e.g., ocular implant). When coding the removal of a foreign body from the external eyeball, review the operative report to identify the following:

- Where the location is (e.g., intraocular)
- Whether a foreign body is embedded
- Whether a slit lamp was used

Most foreign bodies of the eye are located in the cornea and conjunctiva. Fluorescein staining with slit lamp inspection is used to visualize a corneal foreign body or abrasion.

Codes 65270–65290 are reported for laceration repairs of ocular structures. An extensive conjunctival laceration may also include a graft or flap. The repair of a laceration includes use of a conjunctival flap and restoration of anterior chamber by air or saline injection. Do *not* separately code and report these procedures.

> **EXAMPLE:** Patient underwent the removal of foreign body, external eye, superficial conjunctiva. Report code 65205.

Anterior Segment

Anterior Segment heading codes (65400–66999) are reported for procedures performed on the anterior segment of the eye, which includes the cornea, anterior chamber, anterior sclera, iris, ciliary body (ciliary muscle), and lens.

- Corneal transplant (e.g., keratoplasty) is a common procedure that includes use of fresh or preserved grafts and preparation of donor material.

- Radial keratotomy (Figure 15-23) corrects myopia; the surgeon makes numerous radial incisions (like the pattern of spokes of a wheel) extending from the pupil to the periphery of the cornea. (The procedure was accidentally discovered by Dr. Svyatoslav Fyodorov, who removed pieces of glass from a patient's eye and noted that the patient's eyesight improved after removal of the glass. The lacerations to the cornea resulted in the improved eyesight.)

- Cataract removal codes include the following procedures, which are not separately coded and reported:

  - Anterior and posterior capsulotomy
  - Iridectomy
  - Iridotomy
  - Lateral canthotomy
  - Subconjunctival or subtenon injections
  - Use of viscoelastic agents, enzymatic zonulysis, and other pharmacologic agents
  - Implantation of an IOL prosthesis *when performed during the same operative session*

The following two surgical methods are typically used to remove the lens and cataracts:

- **Intracapsular cataract extraction (ICCE):** Removal of lens and surrounding capsule.

- **Extracapsular cataract extraction (ECCE):** Removal of lens and anterior portion of capsule.

© Cengage Learning 2014

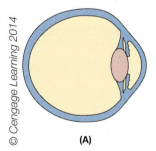  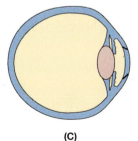

(A) (B) (C)

Figure 15-23 Radial keratotomy (A) Cross-section of eye prior to surgery (B) Small incisions are made in the cornea from the middle outward (C) Radial keratotomy causes the cornea to become flatter, improving vision

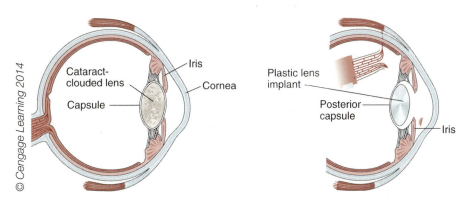

Figure 15-24 Cataract extraction with placement of intraocular lens

The extracapsular cataract removal with insertion of an IOL (Figure 15-24) is a common procedure. An iridectomy, trabeculectomy, and anterior vitrectomy may also be performed during the same operative session as the cataract removal. Codes for these procedures are *not* reported separately.

EXAMPLE: A patient presents with a cataract and evidence of glaucoma, left eye. Trabeculectomy is performed on August 15 as treatment for the glaucoma. Extracapsular cataract extraction with insertion of IOL prosthesis is performed on August 30 as treatment for the cataract. Report codes 66170-LT (August 15) and 66984-LT (August 30).

Coding Tip:

When an iridectomy is performed to accomplish the cataract extraction, it is considered an integral part of the procedure and is not reported separately.

Posterior Segment

Codes 67005–67299 are reported for procedures performed on the vitreous, retina or choroid, and sclera. Vitreous heading codes include the removal and aspiration of vitreous and other fluids. Retina or Choroid heading codes include subheadings for repair, prophylaxis, and destruction. Some retinal detachment repair procedures also include procedures performed on the vitreous.

EXAMPLE: Code 67108 is reported for the repair of a retinal detachment. The code includes the following procedures: vitrectomy, air or gas tamponade, focal endolaser photocoagulation, cryotherapy, drainage of subretinal fluid, sceral buckling, and/or removal of lens by same technique. This means that separate codes are not reported for the included procedures.

Ocular Adnexa

The **ocular adnexa** includes the orbit, eye muscles, eyelids, eyelashes, conjunctiva, and lacrimal apparatus. The **orbit**, or **eye socket**, is the bony cavity in the skull that contains and protects the eyeball (and its associated blood vessels, muscles, and nerves). The eye muscles work together to enable binocular vision. The eyelids protect the eyeball and keep its surface moist. The eyebrows and eyelashes prevent debris from getting into the eyes. The **conjunctiva** is a mucous membrane that lines the underside of each eyelid and forms a protective covering over the exposed surface of the eyeball. The **lacrimal apparatus**, or **tear apparatus**, contains structures that produce, store, and remove tears.

Codes 67311–67399 are reported for procedures performed on the eyelid that involve more than skin. Many of these codes also include surgery to correct **strabismus**, which is improperly aligned eyes, such as cross-eyes (one eye points inward) and walleye (one eye points outward). Codes 67400–67599 are reported for exploration, excision, and decompression procedures performed on the orbit, in addition to injections and orbital implants.

Strabismus surgery is performed on extraocular muscles to realign the eyes. Each strabismus surgery code reflects a procedure performed on one eye (unilateral), which means that modifier -50 is added to the appropriate code when the procedure is performed on both eyes. Two methods are used to correct the alignment of eye muscles:

- Recession: Lengthening the muscle.

- Resection: Shortening the muscle.

 For a recession procedure, the muscle is detached from the attachment site on the surface of the eyeball and reattached along the surface of the eye. For a resection procedure, a small portion of the muscle is removed and the eye muscle is reattached to the original insertion site.

When it is medically necessary to inject sclerosing agents during the same operative session as surgery to correct glaucoma, that service is included in the glaucoma surgery. CPT codes 67500, 67515, and 68200 are reported for the injection of sclerosing agents (e.g., Fluorouracil, 500 mg, which is reported with HCPCS level II code J9190); and they are *not* reported with other pressure-reducing or glaucoma procedure codes.

 Coding Tip:

Codes for the treatment of orbital bone fractures (e.g., frontal, sphenoid, zygomatic, maxilla, ethmoid, and lacrimal) are located in the Musculoskeletal System section.

> **EXAMPLE:** Patient underwent removal of an embedded foreign body, left lower eyelid. Report code 67938-E2.

Conjunctiva

Codes 68020–68899 are reported for procedures performed on the conjunctiva, including the following:

- Incision and drainage
- Excision and/or destruction
- Injection

- Conjunctivoplasty
- Other procedures
- Lacrimal system

> **EXAMPLE:** Patient underwent incision and drainage of a conjunctival cyst of the right upper eyelid. Report code 68020-E3.

The "expression of conjunctival follicles (e.g., for trachoma)" is reported with code 68040. A **trachoma** is a chronic inflammation of the conjunctiva in which granulations form. The physician uses biomicroscopic guidance to remove the conjunctival follicles with a cotton tipped swab or a curet without making an incision. Physicians often use biomicroscopic guidance (e.g., an optical instrument that looks like a microscope with two eyepieces) to treat trachoma. A slitlamp (e.g., a specialized magnifying microscope used to examine the structures of the eye) is also used with the biomicroscope.

Note:

Per the CPT note below the "Eye and Ocular Adnexa" subsection, do not report code 69990 (microsurgical techniques requiring use of operating microscope) in addition to codes 65091–68850. Use of the operating microscope is not reported separately because it is considered an essential part of eye and ocular adnexa procedures.

When a subconjunctival injection (e.g., CPT code 68200) with a local anesthetic is performed as part of a more extensive anesthetic procedure (e.g., peribulbar or retrobulbar block), do not separately code and report the injection procedure. The injection procedure is considered a routine part of the anesthetic procedure and does not represent a separate service.

Conjunctivoplasty codes (68320–68340) describe plastic surgery procedures performed on the conjunctiva. The following procedures are included in conjunctivoplasty codes, which means that they are *not* coded and reported separately: incision and drainage, excision and/or destruction, and injection of conjunctiva.

 The lacrimal system keeps the cornea and conjunctivae moist through tear production. Codes reported for procedures performed on the lacrimal system include incision, excision, repair, and probing and/or related procedures.

A common procedure is the repair of the **lacrimal puncta**, which are small openings in the inner canthus of the eyelids that channel tears. There are two puncta in each eye, an upper and lower punctum. Thus, when both puncta in one eye are treated, report the appropriate code twice. According to CPT Assistant (June 1995), when all puncta in both eyes are treated (four puncta), codes 68705 and 68760–68761 are reported four times.

Note:

There is no parenthetical note below codes 68705 and 68760–68761, unlike below code 68801, which provides instruction to add modifier -50 (Bilateral Procedure) to each code.

EXAMPLE: Patient underwent closure of the lacrimal punctum via laser surgery, both eyes. Report codes 68760, 68760, 68760, and 68760.

Exercise 15.7 – Eye and Ocular Adnexa Subsection

Instructions: Assign the CPT code(s) and appropriate modifier(s) to each statement.

1. Removal of foreign body from cornea of right eye, using a slitlamp.

   _____

2. Repair of corneal laceration with removal of foreign body, left eye.

   _____

3. A receptacle was drilled and a temporary flat-surfaced peg was inserted to enable further integration with an ocular prosthesis.

   _____

4. Nonmagnetic extraction of an intraocular foreign body from posterior segment of right eye.

   _____

5. A patient complained of sudden onset of tearing and pain in the right eye. After eversion of the upper lid, a small wood fragment was removed.

   _____

6. Cryotherapy destruction of corneal lesion, left eye.

   _____

7. Endoscopic goniotomy, right eye.

   _____

8. Insertion of intraocular lens four weeks after right cataract removal.

   _____

9. Removal of corneal lesion using scleral scissors, left eye.

   _____

10. Extracapsular cataract removal with insertion of intraocular lens prosthesis, left eye.

    _____

11. Aspiration of vitreous fluid, pars plana approach, right eye.

    _____

12. Laser photocoagulation of choroidal lesion, right eye, using fluorescein angiogram as a guide.

    _____

(continues)

Exercise 15.7 (continued)

13. Diathermy for treatment of a patient with progressive diabetic retinopathy, both eyes.

14. Scleral reinforcement with graft, left eye.

15. Prophylactic treatment of retinal detachment, left eye, using cryotherapy, four sessions.

16. Fine-needle aspiration of orbit, right eye.

17. Strabismus surgery that included a recession procedure of two horizontal muscles, both eyes.

18. Removal of chalazions from right upper eyelid and left upper eyelid.

19. Strabismus surgery was performed for the first time on one horizontal muscle of the right eye and on the superior oblique muscle of the left eye.

20. Strabismus surgery performed on two horizontal muscles during which a transposition procedure was also performed to detach and relocate two rectus muscles next to a paralyzed muscle, right eye.

21. Injection of cortical steroid into subconjunctival space, left eye.

22. Closure of a total of four lacrimal puncta using collagen plugs, both eyes.

23. Bilateral nasolacrimal duct probing with irrigation.

24. Cauterization to correct everted upper and lower lacrimal puncta, left eye.

25. Incision and drainage, conjunctival cyst, right eye.

Auditory System Subsection

The **Auditory System** (Figure 15-25) subsection is organized anatomically according to the following:

- External ear
- Middle ear
- Inner ear
- Temporal bone, middle fossa approach

Subsection notes direct the coder to otorhinolaryngologic service codes in the Medicine section (92502–92700) for diagnostic services performed on the auditory system.

> **Coding Tip:**
>
> Most procedures classified in the Auditory System subsection are unilateral. Report modifier -LT (Left side), -RT (Right side), or -50 (Bilateral Procedure) as appropriate.

External Ear

The **external ear** includes the auricle (or pinna) and the external auditory meatus (or ear canal). Codes 69000–69399 are reported for the incision, excision, removal of foreign body, repair, and other procedures performed on the external ear.

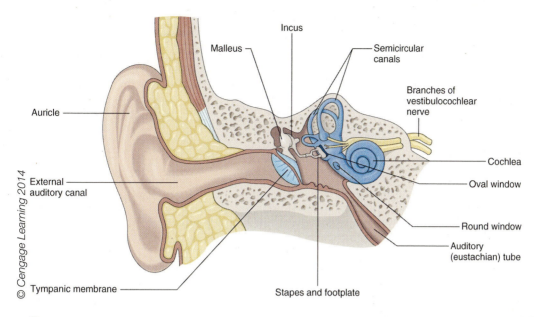

© Cengage Learning 2014

Figure 15-25 The auditory system

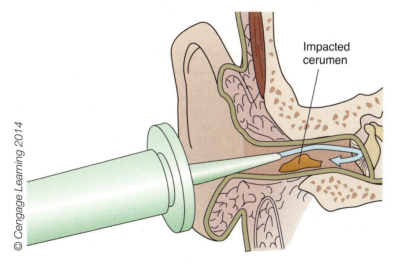

© Cengage Learning 2014

Figure 15-26 Removal of impacted cerumen

A frequently performed procedure is the "removal of impacted cerumen (separate procedure), one or both ears," which is reported with code 69210 (Figure 15-26). Report this code just once when the procedure is performed bilaterally.

EXAMPLE: Patient underwent biopsy, external ear, left. Report code 69100-LT.

Middle Ear

The **middle ear** includes the tympanic membrane, auditory ossicles, muscles, and conduction pathways. A commonly performed procedure is "tympanostomy (requiring insertion of ventilation tube), local or topical anesthesia," which is reported with code 69433. This procedure is typically performed on children who have chronic ear infections.

A **myringotomy**, or **tympanostomy**, is the surgical incision of the tympanic membrane, and it is usually performed to release pressure or fluid. A **tympanoplasty** is the repair or reconstruction of the eardrum (Figure 15-27).

EXAMPLE: Patient underwent complete mastoidectomy, left ear. Report code 69502-LT.

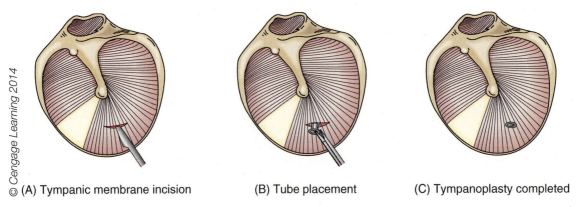

© Cengage Learning 2014

(A) Tympanic membrane incision   (B) Tube placement   (C) Tympanoplasty completed

Figure 15-27 Tympanoplasty (A) Tympanic membrane incision (B) Tube placement (C) Tympanoplasty completed

Inner Ear

The **inner ear** includes the cochlea, saccule, acoustic nerve (e.g., auditory portion), semicircular canals, utricle, and superior and inferior vestibular nerves (e.g., vestibular portion). A labyrinthotomy procedure is performed using a transcanal approach (69801). When a transcanal labyrinthotomy is performed, all required infusions performed on initial and subsequent days of treatment are included in the reported code (69801).

A **cochlear implant** is an implanted electronic device for treatment of sensory deafness. A vestibular nerve section using a transcranial approach (69950) includes the removal of the semicircular canals as well as bone over the internal auditory canal.

> **EXAMPLE:** Patient underwent cochlear device implantation with mastoidectomy, right and left ears. Report code 69930-50.

Temporal Bone, Middle Fossa Approach

Codes 69950–69970 are reported for nerve decompression or repair procedures. A common procedure performed to repair facial nerve damage is total nerve decompression, which is used to treat symptoms of **Bell's palsy** (unilateral paralysis of facial muscles resulting from dysfunction of the 7th cranial nerve, probably due to a viral infection).

> **EXAMPLE:** Patient underwent decompression of the internal auditory canal, left ear. Report code 69960-LT.

Exercise 15.8 – Auditory System Subsection

Instructions: Assign the CPT code(s) and appropriate modifier(s) to each statement.

1. Simple incision and drainage, abscess, left external ear.

2. Removal of a button from the left ear canal of a 2-year-old child.

3. Plastic surgeon reduced the size of a protruding right ear.

4. Routine cleaning of mastoidectomy cavity, right ear.

5. A family physician pierced a 1-year-old girl's ears.

_____

6. With the patient under general anesthesia, the physician removed ventilating tubes from both ears.

_____

7. With the patient under general anesthesia, tympanostomy with insertion of ventilating tubes was performed.

_____

8. Catheterization of eustachian tubes using a tympanic approach, both ears.

_____

9. Replacement of a bone conduction hearing device and removal of old device, left ear.

_____

10. Mobilization of stapes on the left.

_____

11. Decompression of intratemporal nerve, lateral to geniculate ganglion.

_____

12. Physician implanted a cochlear device bilaterally.

_____

13. A physician repaired a tympanic membrane with patch, right ear.

_____

14. Mastoidectomy and tympanoplasty with ossicular chain reconstruction, left ear.

_____

15. Neurectomy of tympanic nerve, left side.

_____

16. Removal of temporal bone tumor, left side.

_____

17. A physician treated a patient who was diagnosed with a tumor of the facial nerve by removing and grafting the nerve.

_____

18. Decompression internal auditory canal, right side.

_____

19. A physician performed an endolymphatic sac operation.

_____

20. Transcranial vestibular nerve section.

_____

Operating Microscope Subsection

When an **operating microscope** is used during a surgical procedure to perform microsurgery techniques, report add-on code 69990 in addition to the primary procedure code.

Coding Tip:

Do not report code 69990 for:

- Visualization with a magnifying loupe or corrected vision.
- Procedures for which use of an operating microscope is an inclusive component. (Refer to Operating Microscope heading notes for a list of excluded codes.)

EXAMPLE: Patient underwent vestibular nerve section, transcranial approach, with use of an operating microscope. Report codes 69950 and 69990.

Exercise 15.9 – Operating Microscope Subsection

Instructions: Assign the CPT code(s) and appropriate modifier(s) to each statement.

1. An otolaryngologist used a magnifying loupe to perform a tympanic membrane repair.

   _____

2. Diagnostic direct laryngoscopy with use of an operating microscope.

   _____

3. The physician uses an operating microscope while performing a partial mastectomy, right breast.

   _____

4. Microsurgical epididymovasostomy, bilateral.

   _____

5. The physician used an operating microscope to perform a hypophysectomy.

   _____

Summary

For procedures performed on the male genital system, code assignment is determined according to approach (e.g., incision, destruction, excision, or introduction) and reason for surgery. Reproductive System Procedures classify the placement of needles into pelvic organs and/or genitalia for subsequent interstitial radioelement application. Intersex surgery is performed as a series of staged procedures to transform the normal adult genitalia of one sex to that of the other sex (genital reconstructive surgery or sex reassignment surgery).

Codes classified in the Female Genital System heading are reported for procedures performed on women who are *not* pregnant. (Codes for women who are pregnant are reported from the Maternity Care and Delivery heading.) When reporting codes for procedures performed on the female genital system, review the operative report to identify the anatomy on which the procedure was performed (e.g., vulva, perineum, introitus, or vagina) and the surgical approach.

The three stages of pregnancy care include services provided as part of total obstetrical care (59400, 59510, 59610, and 59618): antepartum care, delivery of the baby, and postpartum care. Total obstetrical care does *not* include diagnostic procedures, physician office visits for unrelated conditions incidental to pregnancy, and additional visits due to high-risk conditions or medical complications of pregnancy. Codes for these services are separately reported from the Evaluation and Management and Medicine sections of CPT. The treatment of surgical complications associated with pregnancy are separately reported with codes from the Surgery section.

The Endocrine System subsection includes procedures performed on the endocrine glands and the carotid body. Codes for Nervous System subsection procedures are arranged anatomically (skull, meninges, and brain; spine and spinal cord; and extracranial nerves, peripheral nerves, and autonomic nervous system). Nervous system procedures are performed using a variety of approaches for specific purposes.

The Eye and Ocular Adnexa subsection describes procedures performed on the eyeball, anterior and posterior segment, ocular adnexa, and conjunctivae. When reporting codes, review the operative report to identify the anatomic site and type of procedure. The Auditory System subsection is organized anatomically according to the external ear; middle ear; inner ear; and temporal bone, middle fossa approach. When an operating microscope is used during a surgical procedure to perform microsurgery techniques, report add-on code 69990 in addition to the primary procedure code.

Internet Links

American Academy of Family Physicians: Go to *www.aafp.org* and click on the Practice Management link, then click on the Coding Resources & Assistance link and click on the Obstetrical Care Coding link.

American Academy of Otolaryngology—Health and Neck Surgery: *www.entnet.org*

American Association of Neurological Surgeons: *www.aans.org*

American College of Obstetrics: Go to *www.acog.org* and click on the CPT Coding link.and Gynecology

Carpal Tunnel Syndrome: *www.ctsplace.com*

Center for Male Reproductive Medicine (CMRM): *www.malereproduction.com*

Center for Male Reproductive Medicine and Microsurgery: *www.maleinfertility.org*

The Eye Digest: *www.agingeye.net*

familydoctor.org from the American: Go to *www.familydoctor.org* and click on any of the links below Academy of Family Physicians the Women heading.

Lacrimedics: Go to *www.lacrimedics.com* and from the Physician Information, Reference Material drop-down menu, select Billing Guide. Then click on the Billing Guide—Comprehensive Medicare & Private Insurance Guidelines link. Also select your location from the drop-down menu to view Medicare Summaries.

NeurosurgeryToday.org: *www.neurosurgerytoday.org*

Society for Endocrinology: *www.endocrinology.org*

Women's Health: *www.womenshealth.gov*

Study Checklist

- ❏ Read this chapter and highlight key concepts.
- ❏ Create an index card for each key term.
- ❏ Access the chapter Internet links to learn more about concepts.
- ❏ Complete the chapter review, verifying answers with your instructor.
- ❏ Complete WebTutor assignments and take online quizzes.
- ❏ Complete Workbook chapter, verifying answers with your instructor.
- ❏ Go to *www.cengagebrain.com* to access StudyWARE™ and the Premium Website. Login instructions are located in the Preface and on the Printed Access Card.
- ❏ Form a study group with classmates to discuss chapter concepts in preparation for an exam.

Review

Multiple Choice

Instructions: Circle the most appropriate response.

1. The tube that carries spermatozoa from the testis is the:
   - a. prostate gland.
   - b. urethra.
   - c. varicocele.
   - d. vas deferens.

2. Which procedure involves the direct visualization of the cervical canal and the uterine cavity and is performed to examine the endometrium?
   a. colposcopy
   b. hysteroscopy
   c. LEEP electrodissection conization
   d. loop electrodissection conization

3. According to the notes below the Maternity Care and Delivery subsection of Surgery, which service is included in codes reported for maternity care and delivery?
   a. cordocentesis
   b. episiotomy
   c. fetal nonstress test
   d. insertion of cervical dilator

4. How many glands are included in the endocrine system?
   a. 7
   b. 9
   c. 13
   d. 15

5. When more than one interspace is accessed for laminotomy during the same operative session, report the:
   a. appropriate add-on code(s) in addition to the primary procedure code.
   b. primary code once for each interspace accessed.
   c. primary code only.
   d. primary code with modifier -51.

6. Which surgical approach used in extradural exploration/decompression involves making an incision overlying the intervertebral disk and cutting through epidermis, dermis, subcutaneous, fascia, and muscle tissue?
   a. anterior approach
   b. anterolateral approach
   c. costovertebral approach
   d. transpedicular approach

7. Which nerves are part of the involuntary autonomic nervous system, originate in the thoracic and lumbar regions of the spinal cord, and inhibit the physiological effects of the parasympathetic nervous ystem?
   a. cranial
   b. median
   c. somatic
   d. sympathetic

8. Which is the freeing or decompression of an intact nerve from scar tissue?
   a. neuroma
   b. neuroplasty
   c. neurorrhaphy
   d. neurostimulator

9. When all puncta in both eyes are treated during the same encounter, the appropriate code is reported:
   a. once.
   b. twice.
   c. three times.
   d. four times.

10. Which includes the tympanic membrane, auditory ossicles, muscles, and conduction pathways?
    a. cochlea
    b. inner ear
    c. middle ear
    d. outer ear

11. Plastic repair of the penis due to epispadias distal to external sphincter. Patient was diagnosed with incontinence. Which CPT code is assigned?
    a. 54360
    b. 54380
    c. 54385
    d. 54390

12. Patient placed under anesthesia and an impacted foreign body removed from vagina. Which CPT code is assigned?
    a. 57110
    b. 57111
    c. 57135
    d. 57415

13. Surgical treatment of ovarian ectopic pregnancy. Vaginal salpingectomy. Which CPT code is assigned?
    a. 59120
    b. 59130
    c. 59140
    d. 59150

14. Excision of thyroglossal duct cyst. Which CPT code is assigned?
    a. 60200
    b. 60280
    c. 60281
    d. 60600

15. Burr hole with drainage of subdural hematoma. Which CPT code is assigned?
    a. 61150
    b. 61154
    c. 61156
    d. 61253

16. Replacement of cerebrospinal fluid shunt. Which CPT code is assigned?
    a. 62220
    b. 62223
    c. 62225
    d. 62230

17. Cervical laminectomy for extradural excision of intraspinal neoplasm. Which CPT code is assigned?
    a. 63250
    b. 63265
    c. 63270
    d. 63275

18. Laceration repair of conjunctiva by mobilization and rearrangement, with hospitalization. Which CPT code is assigned?

    a. 65270   b. 65272   c. 65273   d. 65285

19. Patient diagnosed as having dislocated lens in left eye. Physician performed intracapsular removal of lens. Which CPT code is assigned?

    a. 66920-LT   b. 66930-LT   c. 66940-LT   d. 66982-LT

20. Transcanal labyrinthectomy. Which CPT code is assigned?

    a. 69801   b. 69905   c. 69910   d. 69915

Coding Practice

Instructions: Assign the CPT code(s) and appropriate modifier(s) to each case.

Male Genital System

21. A biopsy needle was passed up the urethra. Using manual guidance, the surgeon identified the prostate gland and performed a punch biopsy. The needle was withdrawn.

    _____

22. The patient had been diagnosed with hydroceles, which are scheduled to be removed via excision. First, an incision was made of the patient's scrotum. The hydrocele on the right was identified and dissected free. The left side of the patient's body was treated in the same manner for the hydrocele there.

    _____

23. The patient has a papilloma of the penis. This is removed via laser surgery.

    _____

24. After being informed of the all of the risks, the parents of a newborn male patient consented to a circumcision. Regional dorsal penile block (anesthesia) was administered by the physician performing the circumcision. The foreskin of the penis was clamped, and excess skin was trimmed. The clamp was left in place, and antibiotic ointment was applied.

    _____

25. After adequate general anesthesia, the patient's scrotum was incised. The spermatic cord was identified, dissected, and cross-clamped. The right testis was carefully pushed up from the scrotum and excised. All vessels were clamped, and all bleeders were cauterized. The left testis was removed using a similar method. The spermatic cord was cross-clamped and cut.

    _____

26. Patient underwent bilateral vasectomy including postoperative semen examination. The skin over the spermatic cord was injected with a local anesthetic. The scrotum was exposed via an incision, and the tubular structures of this organ were identified. The vas deferens was identified and cut with a small section of the tube removed. The same method was performed on the opposite side.

    _____

27. A prostatectomy was being performed for prostate cancer. An incision was made at the scrotum. A urethrotomy was used to enlarge the penile urethra. The prostate was dissected via the use of an instrument. The prostate as well as supporting anatomic structures were removed. All bleeding was controlled with cauterization. Attention was then directed to pelvic lymph nodes, which were removed on both sides in total for analysis and staging.

    _____

28. Patient underwent reduction of torsion of the left testis. An incision was made in the patient's scrotum. The twisted left testis was identified. The testis was carefully detangled. Excellent blood flow was seen. Four sutures were used to anchor the testis to the wall of the scrotum to prevent further twisting.

_____

29. A patient has a spermatocele. After incising the scrotum, the physician identified the testis and the spermatocele. The spermatocele was dissected from the epididymis.

_____

30. A patient with moderate chordee presents for surgical repair of the penis to straighten the chordee for hypospadias, with mobilization of the urethra.

_____

Female Genital System

31. The patient has a diagnosis of recurrent cervical carcinoma with metastatic disease to the ovaries and bladder. After discussing with the patient and informing her of the risks, the patient consented to an abdominal hysterectomy. An incision was made at the pubic area. The fascia and muscle were retracted. The cervix and uterus were identified and excised. The bladder was found to have numerous lesions; it was also removed. The ureters were transplanted to the skin to allow for urine flow. An ileal urinary conduit, in which the ureters are implanted into a segment of small bowel, was done.

_____

32. An endoscope was inserted into the vulva and passed into the uterus. After gaining access to the cavity, a biopsy of the endometrium was done. The scope was withdrawn.

_____

33. An incision was made in the umbilical region for the insertion of laparoscope: A second incision was made on the right side of the abdomen to pass additional trocars. A Falope ring was inserted and advanced through the trocar to the area of the fallopian tubes. This ring was clamped around the fallopian tubes to provide occlusion.

_____

34. A colposcope was inserted into the patient. This allowed for visualization of the female genital organs. The vagina was found to be normal. The cervix has an area of fibrous tissue, which was biopsied. The endocervical area had an area of inflammation, which was taken away via curettage.

_____

35. After inserting a speculum into the vagina, the physician was able to visualize a vaginal cyst directly. Forceps were used to clamp the cyst. The cyst was excised and sent to pathology for analysis. The speculum was removed.

_____

36. After inserting a speculum into the vagina. The physician identified the Bartholin gland; the cyst was directly visualized. An incision was made, and the cyst was dissected free of the surrounding tissue and mucosa. The wound was closed in layers with absorbable sutures.

_____

37. After insertion of a speculum into the vagina, laser cautery was performed to remove the outer cells of the cervix.

_____

38. The physician performed a salpingostomy and identified a damaged right fallopian tube.

_____

39. After insertion of a speculum into the vagina, a catheter was passed that contained several small embryos. With the use of the catheter, the embryos were inserted into the uterus.

_____

40. After an abdominal incision was made, the left ovary was identified. The ovarian cysts were located and removed in total. The incision was closed with sutures.

_____

Intersex Surgery

41. Second-stage operation was done with the goal of constructing a penis and scrotum. This was done using multiple grafts from the patient's skin and clitoris. A penile prosthesis was implanted into the constructed organ.

_____

42. The new construction of a vagina was the goal in this staged procedure. Using tissue from the patient's penis, a clitoris structure was fashioned. The perineum of the patient was opened to form a vagina. The sides of the vagina were lined with skin grafts to add stability.

_____

Maternity Care and Delivery

43. A neonatologist attached a fetal monitoring electrode to the scalp of the fetus in utero. This was done for seven hours during the labor process. The physician read, interpreted, and made notations on the tracing coming from the electrode data.

_____

44. A patient at 39 weeks' gestation presented in labor. The patient has requested a VBAC (vaginal birth after cesarean). After 20 hours in labor, fetal distress was noted. The patient required a cesarean delivery. All antepartum and postpartum care was provided by the delivering physician.

_____

45. A woman with five fetuses presents for fetal reduction due to her severe pre-eclampsia. Using the potassium chloride method, two fetal sacs are injected. At the conclusion of the procedure, the woman has three fetal sacs intact.

_____

46. At 11 weeks' gestation, the patient had an incomplete abortion. Due to profuse vaginal bleeding, evacuating the uterus was necessary. Dilation and curettage (D and C) was done with suction of any remaining products of conception.

_____

47. A woman presents after having delivered her baby vaginally en route to the hospital in a private motor vehicle. The newborn was taken directly to the neonatal intensive care unit (NICU) for evaluation. The placenta had not been delivered on route to the hospital. Using abdominal massage, the placenta was delivered.

_____

48. An ectopic pregnancy was confirmed by ultrasound. Via a vaginal approach, the pelvic cavity was visualized and examined. All products of conception were removed using curettage. The pelvic cavity was lavaged with saline solution. The patient's right fallopian tube was affected. This tube was excised.

_____

49. After normal prenatal care, this patient presented in labor at 38 weeks. An episiotomy was done to facilitate delivery. A normal healthy newborn was born via vaginal delivery. The episiotomy was repaired.

_____

50. The patient presents for an antepartum visit. This is her fourth scheduled appointment. Her estimated gestational age is 26 weeks. The patient reports heavy vaginal bleeding overnight. After insertion of the speculum, the uterus was examined. Slight bleeding was noted. The patient has had a complete miscarriage. No products of conception are seen. There is no need for surgical intervention.

_____

51. Routine prenatal care was rendered to this patient, who presented at 41 weeks in labor. The patient was examined, and the fetus was found to be in a breech position. The fetus was turned via external abdominal approach into a cephalic position. After the turning of the fetus, an episiotomy was performed. A normal healthy 10-pound infant was born via vaginal delivery. The episiotomy was repaired. Postpartum care was delivered.

_____

Endocrine System

52. The patient's neck was palpated, and a mass was identified on the left. Local anesthesia was administered, and the position of the mass was confirmed again by palpation. A percutaneous core needle was inserted through the skin and underlying tissue into the thyroid mass. The needle was withdrawn with the sample inside the core. The sample will be sent for analysis.

_____

53. After adequate general anesthesia, a cervical incision was made. Skin, fascia, and muscle were retracted to expose the thyroid gland. A severely enlarged left lobe of the thyroid was found. The left lobe was removed in total and sent to pathology for analysis. Parathyroid glands were carefully inspected and found to be normal. These were not removed but were left intact. All bleeders were cauterized. The skin and muscle were closed in layers.

_____

54. After adequate general anesthesia, a midline abdominal incision was made. The retroperitoneal area was identified and found to be normal. The adrenal glands were directly visualized. The left adrenal gland was removed in total. A biopsy sample was taken from the right adrenal gland.

_____

55. After adequate general anesthesia, an incision was made along the thyroglossal duct cyst. A portion of the hyoid bone was removed, and recurrent thyroglossal duct cyst was excised. Wound was packed for secondary closure.

_____

56. After adequate general anesthesia, a cervical incision was made to expose the thyroid and parathyroid glands. The parathyroid glands were directly visualized. The right gland was removed.

_____

57. After several small incisions were made in the patient's back, the laparoscope was introduced. The adrenal gland on the right was identified and examined. It was normal in appearance. The left adrenal gland was found to be enlarged at the tip. This section was removed and passed through the trocar. The scope was removed and the skin incision closed with sutures.

_____

58. After a cervical incision was made, the muscles of the neck were separated to expose the thyroid and parathyroid glands. The right lobe was normal in appearance and size. The left upper thyroid gland had a goiter measuring approximately 3.0 cm. This lobe with the goiter was removed.

_____

59. Based on thyroid biopsy, this patient presented for a total thyroidectomy due to thyroid carcinoma. The neck area was cleaned and draped in the usual fashion. Under general anesthesia, the patient had a cervical incision. A radical neck dissection was performed. After the muscles of the neck were separated, the gland was exposed. Direct visualization showed the gland to be cystic and nodular in nature. The right lobe of the gland was removed first, followed by the left lobe. The parathyroid glands were inspected and appeared to be normal. The thyroid gland in total was removed and sent to pathology for analysis. All bleeders were cauterized. The incision was closed in layers with staples and sutures.

_____

60. Under general anesthesia, a cervical incision at the previous incision site was done. The neck muscles were divided and retracted. The thyroid area was exposed. The absent left lobe of the thyroid was noted. The right lobe of the thyroid was examined. It was found to be very nodular in appearance. This lobe was removed. The parathyroid glands were examined and appeared normal. The specimen of the right lobe was sent to pathology. The muscles were retracted back and closed with staples. The incision was closed in layers.

_____

61. After the patient's adrenal area was accessed through a midline abdominal incision, the retroperitoneal space was explored. A mass was identified adjacent to the left adrenal gland. This was removed. The left adrenal gland, which also appeared abnormal, was removed in total. The incision was closed.

_____

Nervous System

62. After the patient was placed in a prone position, an incision was made over the upper spinal area. The placement of the epidural drug infusion device was in the subcutaneous tissue. The incision was closed with sutures.

_____

63. The peripheral maxillary facial nerve was identified. A nerve block injection was done.

_____

64. The patient presented with a laceration of the digital nerve of the left hand. This was repaired with sutures.

_____

65. A neurostimulator electrode device is placed through the skin to the cranial nerve.

_____

66. The patient presents with a meningocele approximately 4.0 cm in diameter. This was repaired after placing the patient in a prone position and making an incision. Access was gained to the dura of the thoracic spinal region. The bulging tissue was carefully placed into normal position. The incision was closed.

_____

67. The patient was placed on his side. After local anesthesia, the biopsy needle was inserted at the lumbar region. The sheath of the needle was pulled back; cloudy fluid was seen. This fluid was collected in the hollow portion of the needle.

_____

68. This patient presented for drainage of a brain abscess. After a burr hole was drilled, the cranium was accessed to reveal the site of the abscess. The abscess was drained.

_____

69. The patient presented with an arteriovenous (AV) malformation. A craniotomy was performed to gain access to the brain and the site of the malformation. This was done without difficulty. Blood vessels leading to the malformation were identified and ligated. The malformation measured approximately 2.0 cm in size. It was carefully resected supratentorially. The bone portion from the craniotomy was replaced and secured.

_____

70. The patient presented with a nerve compression of the left leg. An incision was made overlying the compressed sciatic nerve midpoint. Scar tissue was identified and dissected free. No adhesions were seen.

_____

71. The patient presented for a replacement of his lumbosubarachnoid shunt, which was performed by first incising at the original incision site. A moderate number of adhesions were seen, which were removed. The old shunt was also removed. A new shunt was placed in the same position.

_____

Eye and Ocular Adnexa System

72. The patient presented with a foreign body sensation of the left eye. Under slitlamp examination, a small metallic-like foreign body was identified. This object was slightly embedded in the lower corneal area. It was removed via a small incision, using the slitlamp for guidance.

_____

73. The patient presented for correction of cross-eyes. The left eye was immobilized with a speculum. Incisions were made in the conjunctiva. The lateral muscle was identified and incised. The lateral muscle was sutured distally to the sclera. The medial rectus muscle was surgically incised and sutured in the same manner.

_____

74. After injection of a local anesthetic agent, the left upper eyelid was examined closely. A large chalazion was seen. The chalazion was resected in total. A moderate area of infection was noted, and this was drained. The infectious area was flushed with saline solution.

_____

75. After the injection of a local anesthetic agent, an incision was made on the patient's right side at the site of the medial canthal tendon. After careful dissection, the lacrimal sac was identified and removed.

_____

76. The patient presented with a corneal lamellar on the right side. This was excised using scleral scissors. Antibiotic ointment was applied.

_____

77. Using a laser, short bursts were administered to the patient's left eye. This iridotomy was performed to allow for the movement of fluid in the anterior chamber and to treat the patient's glaucoma.

_____

78. Using a xenon arc, spots were made on the patient's retina. This provided a good seal of the retinal tear of the right eye.

_____

79. With the patient under local anesthesia, the right lower eyelid is palpated and a foreign body is found in the upper-right quadrant near the posterior surface. The lid was everted and an incision made under the site. The foreign body was removed.

_____

80. The patient presented with a tumor of the lacrimal gland. An incision was made in the lid crease of the left upper eyelid. This had to be extended down into the lacrimal fossa. An osteotomy was necessary to gain access to the entire mass. The mass was removed in total. The incisional wound was closed.

_____

81. After making an incision in the patient's left eye at the junction of the cornea and sclera, the eye was entered. The nucleus of the eye lens was removed. The operating microscope was brought into the operating field. The soft portion of the lens was removed. This removed the entire cataract, but the capsule of the eye was left intact. An IOL was inserted. The incision was closed, and antibiotic injection was done.

_____

Auditory System

82. Impacted cerumen was removed from the left ear, using lavage and suction. After removal, the ear canal was inspected. No evidence of infection was seen. The same method was done on the right ear.

_____

83. The patient presented with a protruding left ear. The posterior auricle was incised. This allowed for the skin fold to be raised away from the ear cartilage. A new skin fold was created using several sutures. This new fold allowed for the ear to be in a more normal position.

_____

84. The patient reported a buzzing sound from her left ear. Direct examination identified an insect-like foreign object in the canal. Using a cerumen spoon, the object was removed.

_____

85. Using the punch biopsy method, a specimen was taken from the right external auditory canal.

_____

86. With the patient under general anesthesia, an incision was made at the left auricular region and tympanoplasty with mastoidectomy was performed. The outer bone of the mastoid was removed, and the mastoid antrum was entered. The tympanic membrane was identified and perforated. The eardrum was brought forward. The middle ear was examined. A cholesteatoma was found and removed. The ossicular chain was identified and examined and found to be normal.

_____

87. Through the ear canal of the patient's left ear, the aural polyp was identified under direct examination. With an ear snare, the polyp was removed. Antibiotic drops were placed in the canal. Minimal bleeding was noted.

88. After the patient's right auditory canal was examined, an abscess was noted. This required drainage. An incision was made over the location of this external abscess. The abscess was drained, with a puslike material seen. Antibiotic ointment and dressing were applied.

89. With a nasopharyngosope used for guidance, the right eustachian tube was identified. With a catheter used through the scope, air was introduced into the device to inflate the eustachian tube.

90. The patient presented with an aural glomus tumor on the left. After an incision of the skin was made posteriorly to the aural, the skin was retracted. The mastoid bone was exposed, and the tegmen was identified. The tumor was also identified. The tumor was removed in total with forceps and sent to pathology for analysis. The incision was closed.

91. The patient presented seven months postmastoidectomy for debridement of the left cavity. This was done under direct visualization using suction. Skin and debris were removed from the left side of the mastoid. No infection was observed. The skin and debris removed appeared normal in appearance.

Operating Microscope

92. The patient underwent transcanal labyrinthotomy with cryosurgery and multiple perfusion of vestibulo-active drugs. After anesthesia, an incision was made posterior to the ear canal on the right and the external ear was exposed. The operating microscope was brought into the field to facilitate the placement of temporary stapes plate. The cryolaser was used to debride tissue present in the area.

93. A patient presented with a fistula of the left salivary gland. This area was incised to expose the fistula, and the operating microscope was used to get a better view of the fistula for excision.

94. A neonatal patient presented with a diaphragmatic hernia. Under adequate anesthesia, an abdominal incision was made. The operating microscope was used to identify all vessels and small arteries. This was in part due to the size of the infant. The hernia sac was exposed and dissected free, sutures were placed to close the diaphragmatic hernia defect, and the external incision was closed in layers.

95. The patient had a malfunctioning valve of the left femoral vein. After an incision was made over the vein site, the operating microscope was used to isolate the exact site of the valve in the femoral vein. The valve was exposed and repaired with sutures.

96. The patient had an injury to his left pinkie finger. The volar plate required repair. The digit was incised at the interphalangeal joint space. The operating microscope was used to identify the area of instability. The plate was sutured to the distal bone. The wound was closed with sutures.

_____

97. An incision was made over the skin at the site of the injured blood vessel, left hand, third finger. The operating microscope was brought into the field to help identify the vessel and used to assist in the dissection. Direct repair of the vessel with sutures was performed. The surgical incision was closed with sutures.

_____

98. The infratemporal facial nerve required repair. First, an incision was made to expose the nerve. The operating microscope was then used to facilitate the repair. The surgical incision wound was closed with sutures.

_____

99. The patient presented with a lesion of the pharynx. The patient's oral cavity was assessed using the operating microscope, and the lesion was identified. After identification, the laser was brought into the field to perform the excision. Minimal bleeding was noted.

_____

100. The patient presented with several small lesions of the epiglottis. Epiglottidectomy was performed using the operating microscope.

_____

101. After an extensor tendon in the patient's left index finger was excised using the operating microscope, a synthetic rod was implanted for delayed tendon graft. The surgical incision was closed with sutures.

_____

102. The patient presented with retained ventilating ear tubes bilaterally. After general anesthesia was administered, the operating microscope was brought into the operating field. The right tympanic membrane was examined under the microscope. The tube was found and removed. The ear canal was irrigated. The left ear was handled in the same method.

_____

103. The patient presented with a cyst of the urachal. This was removed after making an abdominal incision. The urachal portion of the bladder (cord from apex of bladder to the umbilicus) was exposed. The operating microscope was used to identify several small cysts. These were removed under microscopic guidance.

_____

104. Arthrodesis of the carpometacarpal joint was performed of the right hand, second digit. After an incision was made over the joint space, the external bony structures of the carpometacarpal joint space were identified. With both the operating microscope and a small screw, the joint was repaired. The surgical incision was closed with sutures.

_____

105. A decompression fasciotomy of the right forearm was performed using the operating microscope to explore the brachial artery.

_____

CHAPTER 16

CPT Radiology

Chapter Outline

Chapter Objectives

At the conclusion of this chapter, the student should be able to:

- Define key terms.
- Explain the organization, format, and content of the CPT Radiology section.
- Interpret CPT radiology coding guidelines and notes.
- Assign CPT radiology codes.
- Add CPT and/or HCPCS level II modifiers to codes, as appropriate.

Key Terms

A-mode

amplitude modulation

angiography

anteroposterior projection

aortography

arthrography

axial plane

biometric A-scan

biomicroscopy

block (radiology)

blocking

bone density study

brightness mode

B-scan

cardiac blood pool imaging

compensator

component coding

computed axial tomography (CT) (CAT)

computed tomography angiography (CTA)

contrast agent

contrast material

contrast medium injection device

corneal pachymetry

coronal plane

cystography

cytoreduction surgery

debulking

diagnostic mammography

Doppler ultrasonography

dosimetry

dual energy X-ray absorptiometry (DEXA)

echo

epidurography

equivalent dose

external radiation

fluoroscopy

fraction (in radiation treatment management)

frontal plane

global service

gray (gy)

gray-scale ultrasound

horizontal plane

hyperthermia

internal radiation

interventional radiologic procedure

intrathecal

lateral projection

magnetic resonance angiography (MRA)

magnetic resonance imaging (MRI)

mammography

megaelectron volt

megavolt

MeV

midsagittal plane

M-mode

motion mode

nuclear imaging

nuclear medicine

oblique projection

parenterally

photons

plane of view

port

positron emission tomography (PET)

posteroanterior (PA) projection

professional component

quantitative A-scan

radiation absorbed dose (rad)

radiation oncology

radiographic projection

radiologic guidance

radiologist

radiology

radionuclide

radiopharmaceutical therapy

real-time scan

roentgen

roentgen-equivalent-man (rem)

sagittal plane

screening mammography

side view

single photon emission computerized tomography (SPECT)

slitlamp exam

supervision and interpretation

systemic radiation therapy

technical component

therapeutic port film

transverse plane

treatment volume determination

ultrasonography

ultrasound

uptake

venography

view

wedge

X-ray

X-ray beam

Introduction

The Radiology section of CPT includes subsections for diagnostic radiology (imaging); diagnostic ultrasound; radiologic guidance; breast, mammography; bone/joint studies; radiation oncology; and nuclear medicine. These subsections are further subdivided into anatomic categories. The Diagnostic Radiology (Diagnostic Imaging) subsection includes noninvasive and invasive diagnostic and therapeutic (interventional) procedures, as well as computed (or computerized) tomography and magnetic resonance imaging.

Note:

Procedures frequently performed by radiologists that are located in other CPT sections include:

- Noninvasive vascular diagnostic studies (93880–93998).
- Invasive (or interventional) radiology services (Surgery section), such as:
  - Injection procedures.
  - Transcatheter procedures.

Radiology Terminology

Radiology is a branch of medicine that uses imaging techniques to diagnose and treat disease. A **radiologist** is a physician who has undergone specialized training to interpret diagnostic X-rays, perform specialized X-ray procedures, and administer radiation for the treatment of disease (e.g., cancer). Terms unique to the radiographic procedures include the following:

- Planes of view
- Positioning and radiographic projection

EXAMPLE: Axial is a standard plane of reference for most radiology codes. For example, axial images depict the long axis of the body, from the head to foot.

Planes of View

Terminology that describes **planes of view** (Figure 16-1) used when performing radiology procedures includes the following:

- **Coronal plane** (or **frontal plane**): Divides the body into anterior or ventral and posterior or dorsal portions at a right angle to the sagittal plane, separating the body into front and back; also called ventral or dorsal plane.

- **Midsagittal plane**: Vertically divides the body through the midline into two equal left and right halves.

- **Sagittal plane**: Vertically divides the body into unequal left and right portions.

- **Transverse plane** (or **horizontal plane** or **axial plane**): Horizontally divides the body into superior and inferior portions.

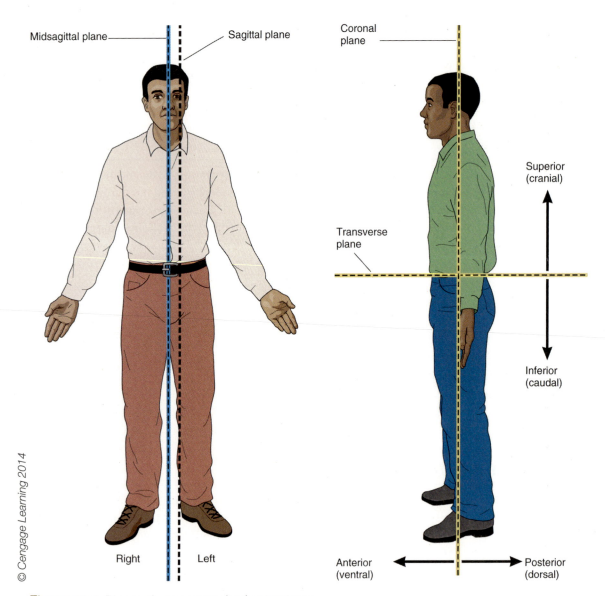

© Cengage Learning 2014

Figure 16-1 Planes that separate body structures

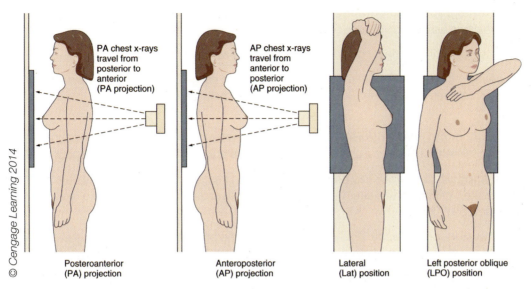

Figure 16-2 Radiographic projections

Positioning and Radiographic Projection

Patients are positioned for radiographic procedures so that a certain part of the body is placed closest to the X-ray film. The patient's position in relation to the camera is the **view** (e.g., code 71010 specifies a single frontal view of the chest). **Radiographic projection** (Figure 16-2) describes the path that the X-ray beam travels through the body, from entrance to exit. An **X-ray beam** is made up of invisible electromagnetic energy waves called **photons**, which are emitted from a radiation machine and are used to produce images (X-rays) and treat disease (e.g., cancer). Radiographic projections include the following:

- **Anteroposterior projection**: Patient is positioned with his or her back parallel to the film; the X-ray beam travels from front to back, or anterior to posterior.

- **Lateral projection**, or **side view**: Patient is positioned at a right angle to the film; the X-ray beam travels through the side of the body.

- **Oblique projection**: Patient is positioned with the body slanted sideways toward the film, halfway between a parallel and right-angle position; the X-ray beam travels through this angle of the body.

- **Posteroanterior (PA) projection**: Patient is positioned facing the film and parallel to it; the X-ray beam travels from back to front, or posterior to anterior.

Radiology Procedures

Radiology procedures include:

- **Angiography**: X-ray of a blood vessel after injection of contrast material (Figure 16-3).

- **Aortography**: X-ray of the aorta after injection of contrast material.

- **Arthrography**: X-ray of a joint after injection of contrast material.

- **Computed axial tomography (CT) (CAT)**: X-ray of horizontal and vertical cross-sectional views or "slices" of the body that are computer-processed to create three-dimensional, or 3D, images.

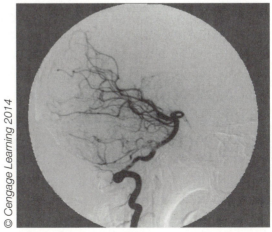

Figure 16-3 Angiography

- **Computed tomography angiography (CTA)**: X-rays of different angles create cross-sectional images of organs, bones, and tissues to visualize blood flow in arterial and venous vessels throughout the body.

- **Cystography**: X-ray of the urinary bladder after injection of contrast material.

- **Fluoroscopy**: Continuous X-ray beam generates a movielike image that is viewed on a monitor; used for invasive procedures such as intravenous/intra-arterial catheterization and extracorporeal shock wave lithotripsy.

- **Magnetic resonance imaging (MRI)**: Noninvasive X-ray procedure uses an external magnetic field to produce a two-dimensional view of an internal organ or structure such as the brain or spinal cord.

- **Nuclear imaging**: Noninvasive X-ray procedure creates an image by measuring radiation emission, or radiation "uptake," of body areas after the administration of a **radionuclide**, which is a radioactive material, such as an isotope of Iodine.

- **Positron emission tomography (PET)**: X-ray images of the body are produced after the administration of radioisotopes, which track metabolism or blood flow, not anatomy.

- **Single photon emission computerized tomography (SPECT)**: 3D X-ray images of internal organs are produced after administration of a radioactive material, which visualize anatomy *and* function.

- **Ultrasound**, or **ultrasonography**: High-frequency sound waves bounce off internal organs and create echoes; the echo pattern is displayed on the ultrasound machine monitor; an **echo** is the effect of a sound that reflects off a distant surface and returns to its source, just like the sound produced when you yell into a well and your voice "bounces back."

- **Venography**: X-ray of a vein is taken after injection of contrast material.

- **X-ray**: Radiographic visualization or imaging of internal body structures uses low-dose high-energy radiation. (High-dose high-energy radiation is used to treat diseases such as cancer.)

When a radiology procedure is performed, a device called a **block** (e.g., lead apron) made of lead or another heavy metal is placed between the radiation beam and that portion of the patient's body that requires protection from radiation.

The international unit of exposure dose for X-rays or gamma rays is called a **roentgen**, abbreviated as R or r. (Roentgen is named after Professor Wilhelm Konrad Roentgen, who discovered X-rays in 1895.) A unit of **radiation absorbed dose (rad)** is the amount of radiant energy absorbed in a tissue. Newer radiation terminology includes the term **gray**, abbreviated as **gy**, named for British physician L. Harold Gray (1905–1965) (an authority on the use of radiation for cancer treatment). (One gray equals 100 rads.) A **roentgen-equivalent-man (rem)** is the unit of measurement that includes different biological responses to different kinds of radiation. The radiation quantity measured by rem is called an **equivalent dose**. (A millirem is one-thousandth of a rem, the unit for measuring equivalent dose.)

Exercise 16.1 – Radiology Terminology

Instructions: Match each plane of view with its description.

_____ **1.** Divides body horizontally into superior and inferior portions

_____ **2.** Divides body into anterior and posterior portions

_____ **3.** Divides body vertically into unequal left and right portions

_____ **4.** Divides body vertically through midline into equal left and right halves

a. Coronal plane

b. Midsagittal plane

c. Sagittal plane

d. Transverse plane

Instructions: Match each radiographic projection with its description.

_____ 5. Patient positioned at right angle to film; X-ray beam travels through side of body.

_____ 6. Patient positioned facing film and parallel to it; X-ray beam travels back to front.

_____ 7. Patient positioned with back parallel to film; X-ray beam travels from front to back.

_____ 8. Patient positioned with body slanted sideways toward the film, halfway between parallel and right-angle position; X-ray beam travels through this angle of the body.

a. Anteroposterior
b. Lateral
c. Oblique
d. Posteroanterior

Instructions: Match each radiology procedure with its description.

_____ 9. X-ray of a vein after injection of contrast material

_____ 10. X-ray of the urinary bladder after injection of contrast material

_____ 11. Continuous X-ray beam generates a movielike image that is viewed on a monitor

_____ 12. Use of an external magnetic field to produce a two-dimensional X-ray of an internal organ

_____ 13. High-frequency sound waves bounce off internal organs, creating echoes; the echo pattern is displayed on the ultrasound machine monitor.

_____ 14. X-ray of the aorta after injection of contrast material

_____ 15. X-ray of a joint after injection of contrast material

a. Aortography
b. Arthrography
c. Cystography
d. Fluoroscopy
e. MRI
f. Ultrasound
g. Venography

Overview of Radiology Section

The Radiology section includes subsections for diagnostic radiology (diagnostic imaging); diagnostic ultrasound; radiologic guidance; breast, mammography; bone/joint studies; radiation oncology; and nuclear medicine. Procedure descriptions include the:

- Type of service (e.g., modality).
- Anatomic site.
- Use of contrast material.

Professional versus Technical Components

For radiology coding, the physician responsible for the professional and technical components of an examination must be determined. (Professional and technical components are reimbursement issues, which means that there are no CPT guidelines or notes explaining the three options.) Radiology procedures include the following three components:

- **Technical component:** Use of equipment and supplies and the employment of radiologic technologists to perform diagnostic imaging examinations and administer radiation therapy treatments.
- **Professional component**: Services provided by the physician, which include supervising the performance of a diagnostic imaging procedure, interpreting imaging films, and documenting the imaging report.
- **Global service**: Combined technical and professional components, as reported with a CPT Radiology code.

Most radiology procedures require both professional and technical components, and the following modifiers are added to radiology codes as appropriate:

- -26 (Professional Component)

- -TC (Technical Component)

Modifier -26 is added to the radiology code when a radiologist interprets the radiographic image and documents a report (but does not perform the radiologic procedure). This indicates that only the professional component was provided.

Modifier -TC is added to the radiology code when the provider performs the radiologic procedure. (A radiologist employed by another facility interprets the radiographic image and documents the report. That radiologist adds modifier -26 to the radiology code.)

When a provider owns the equipment and performs both the technical and the professional components, a global CPT code is reported. A modifier is *not* added to the radiology code. (Hospitals own radiology equipment, and they employ radiologic technicians who perform X-rays and employ or contract with radiologists who interpret radiographic images and document reports.)

 **Note:**

Some radiology codes include only a professional component, and modifier -26 is *not* added to these codes (e.g., therapeutic radiology treatment planning codes and weekly radiation therapy management codes).

EXAMPLE 1: Patient undergoes a complete chest X-ray, minimum of four views (71030), which is performed on an outpatient basis at the hospital. (The patient's primary care provider completed a requisition for the chest X-ray after having evaluated the patient in the office for shortness of breath.) The radiologic technician takes the X-ray, and the radiologist interprets the image and documents an X-ray report. A copy of the X-ray report is mailed to the patient's primary care provider. The hospital reports the X-ray code as a global service.

EXAMPLE 2: Patient undergoes a complete wrist X-ray, minimum of three views (73110), which is performed at a freestanding radiology clinic. (The patient's primary care provider had completed a requisition for the wrist X-ray after evaluating the patient in the office for severe wrist pain earlier that day.) The clinic's radiologic technician takes the X-ray, and the clinic's radiologist interprets the image and documents an X-ray report. A copy of the X-ray report is mailed to the patient's primary care provider. The clinic reports the X-ray code as a global service.

EXAMPLE 3: The patient is seen by her primary care provider, who evaluates a lump on her right pinkie finger. The office has X-ray equipment and takes a two-view X-ray of the hand (73120). The X-ray is interpreted by a hand specialist who is located in another office. The primary care provider reports the X-ray code with HCPCS level II modifier -TC (technical component). The hand specialist reports the X-ray code with CPT modifier -26 (professional component) added to it.

 Note:

Depending on the contract negotiated between radiologists and the health care facility:

- Radiologists are considered employees of the health care facility (e.g., hospital) or contractors.

- The facility submits claims to obtain reimbursement for all services provided to patients (including professional services), or the radiologists use a medical billing service to submit claims for professional services.

Use of Modifiers with Radiology Codes

Modifiers commonly added to Radiology codes include:

- -52 (Reduced Services), to indicate that a service is partially reduced at the physician's discretion.

EXAMPLE: Patient underwent ultrasound exam of swollen tonsils. Code 76536 is reported for "Ultrasound, soft tissues of head and neck (eg, thyroid, parathyroid, parotid) real time with image documentation." Because just tonsillar tissue was evaluated, code 76536-52 is reported.

- -76 (Repeat Procedure by Same Physician or Other Qualified Health Care Professional), describes a repeat procedure by the same physician on the same date of service. ("Same physician" refers to either the same physician or a physician in the same specialty or group.)

  EXAMPLE: A patient presents to the emergency department (ED) with blunt abdominal trauma. Complete acute abdomen series with supine, erect, and decubitus views and single-view chest X-ray was performed. The patient became unstable several hours later in the ED, and the X-ray was repeated. Code 74022-76 is reported for the repeat X-ray.

Coding Tip:

- Modifier -50 (Bilateral Procedure) is not added to each radiology procedure that is performed bilaterally because code descriptions may specify "bilateral." Radiology code descriptions must be carefully reviewed to determine whether modifier -50 should be added.
- Modifier -51 (Multiple Procedures) is usually not added to radiology codes. However, modifier -51 is added to nuclear medicine codes 78306, 78320, 78802, 78803, 78806, and 78807 when appropriate.
- HCPCS level II anatomic modifiers -LT (Left) and -RT (Right) are added to radiology codes when appropriate. These modifiers are reported to identify a specific side of the body.

Complete Procedure

The term *complete* as included in radiology code descriptions refers to the number of views required for the study of a designated body part. Code descriptions include language that indicates what constitutes a "complete study" for a specific type of radiologic procedure.

EXAMPLE 1: Code 70120 is reported when a mastoid X-ray of fewer than three views is performed. Code 70130 is reported when a complete mastoid X-ray is performed.

EXAMPLE 2: Code 70332 describes a radiologic diagnostic procedure that contains both radiologic and surgical components. Report code 70332 for the radiologic procedure. Report code 21116 for the injection procedure if it is performed during the same session.

Coding Tip:

Do not confuse use of the term *complete* in the code description with its use in a parenthetical note below a code.

Both components comprise a complete procedure when performed by the same physician (e.g., radiologist), and two codes are reported by that physician. However, when two physicians are involved in performing the procedure, each physician submits the code for the respective portion of the procedure performed.

Evaluation and Management (E/M) Services

When the radiologist provides E/M services as part of the radiographic procedure (e.g., invasive or interventional radiology), a CPT code is *not* reported. The services provided by the radiologist include a minimal history and examination to determine the following:

- Reason for the examination
- Presence of allergies
- Acquisition of informed consent
- Discussion of follow-up
- Review of the patient record

The complexity of medical decision making is usually limited to the following:

- Whether the invasive or interventional procedure should be performed
- Whether any comorbidities (coexisting conditions) may impact the procedure
- What discussion and education took place with the patient

However, when a significant, separately identifiable E/M service is provided by the radiologist distinct from the radiographic procedure, an appropriate E/M code is reported (e.g., initial radiation oncology consultation to determine whether to proceed with treatment).

EXAMPLE: The patient's primary care provider requests that a radiologist provide consultation services to render an opinion about the patient's candidacy for a uterine embolization procedure. The radiologist performs a comprehensive history and examination and reviews the patient's record. A pelvic MRI is performed to assist in medical decision making. The radiologist reports a code from the Office or Other Outpatient Consultations category of the CPT E/M section.

Exercise 16.2 – Overview of Radiology Section

Instructions: Complete each statement.

1. Procedure descriptions for codes in the Radiology section include _____, _____, and _____.

2. Services provided by the radiologic technologist include performing diagnostic imaging examinations and administering radiation therapy treatments. This is called the _____ component.

3. Services provided by the physician include supervising the performance of a diagnostic imaging procedure, interpreting imaging films, and documenting the imaging report. This is called the _____ component.

4. The combined technical and professional components, as reported with a CPT radiology code, is called the _____.

5. Before reporting a radiology procedure code on a claim, the responsible physician is required to have documented the X-ray _____.

Radiology Section Guidelines

Guidelines located at the beginning of the Radiology section provide instruction about the following:

- Subject listings
- Separate procedures
- Subsection information
- Unlisted service or procedure
- Special report
- Supervision and interpretation
- Administration of contrast material(s)
- Written report(s)

Instructional notes appear throughout the Radiology section to provide coding clarification and direction. The following Radiology subsections contain notes unique to the subsection:

- Diagnostic Radiology (70010–76499)
- Diagnostic Ultrasound (76506–76999)
- Radiation Oncology (77261–77799)
- Nuclear Medicine (78000–79999)

Subject Listings

When radiologic services are performed by or under the responsible supervision of a physician (e.g., radiologist) or other qualified health care professional, radiology codes are reported.

Separate Procedures

Some procedures listed in the Radiology section of CPT are considered an integral component of a total service or procedure and are identified by the descriptor *separate procedure*. These codes are *not* reported in addition to the code for the primary or total X-ray procedure unless the "separate procedure" is unrelated to or distinct from other procedures/services provided at that time.

> **EXAMPLE:** Patient undergoes laparoscopic cholecystectomy with intraoperative cholangiogram and fluoroscopy. Report codes 47563 (surgeon) and 74300. Do not report code 76000 (fluoroscopy), which is included in code 74300. The description of code 76000 includes "(separate procedure)," which means that this code is not reported unless the procedure is performed as a stand-alone procedure or is a distinct and separate procedure performed during the same session as another procedure.

Unlisted Procedures

As in other CPT sections, unlisted procedure codes describe a service or procedure that is not adequately described or listed in CPT (e.g., 76499, Unlisted diagnostic radiographic procedure).

Special Report

The radiology guidelines repeat the special report instructions found in previous sections. As in other CPT sections, when a service is new, unusual, or rarely provided, it requires a special report to validate the medical necessity and appropriateness of the service (e.g., complexity of symptoms). A special report should include all pertinent information (e.g., the time, effort, and equipment needed; diagnostic and therapeutic procedures performed; and description of the nature, extent, and need for the procedure).

Supervision and Interpretation

Imaging procedures may require a surgical procedure to access the imaged area (e.g., injection of contrast material), or a surgical procedure may require image guidance (e.g., lung biopsy with fluoroscopic guidance). In CPT, many radiological services include image guidance in their code descriptions, which means separate *radiological supervision and interpretation* codes for image guidance are *not* reported.

Interventional radiologic procedures (e.g., catheterization, injection of contrast media) are used to diagnose and treat conditions using percutaneous or minimally invasive techniques under imaging guidance. Due to the complexity of interventional radiology services, **component coding** allows for reporting a radiology procedure code *and* a surgical procedure code to completely describe the service provided. Component coding provides a mechanism for reporting interventional services whether the services are performed by a single physician or by different physicians (e.g., one physician performs the procedure and the other performs the imaging supervision and interpretation).

- When two different physicians (e.g., surgeon and radiologist) perform the surgical and radiological components, each physician reports the code(s) for his or her component of the procedure performed. The radiological portion of the procedure is designated as "radiological **supervision and interpretation**."

- When one physician performs the procedure and provides radiological supervision and interpretation, that physician reports codes for both components (from the Surgery section *and* the Radiology section).

> **EXAMPLE 1:** In a hospital outpatient setting, a radiologist performed an injection procedure and supervised and interpreted an antegrade pyelography through a previously placed nephrostomy. The hospital reports codes 50394 and 74425. (Radiologists are salaried hospital employees, and they do not submit insurance claims for reimbursement. The hospital billing department submits the claim.)
>
> **EXAMPLE 2:** Patient undergoes needle biopsy of the liver under fluoroscopic guidance. Report codes 47000 and 77002.

> **Note:**
>
> The radiological supervision and interpretation concept does *not* apply to radiation oncology procedures.

Administration of Contrast Material(s)

A **contrast agent**, or **contrast material**, (or contrast medium) is a radiopaque substance (solid or liquid) that is administered to provide better radiographic visualization of organs studied. The contrast agent is administered

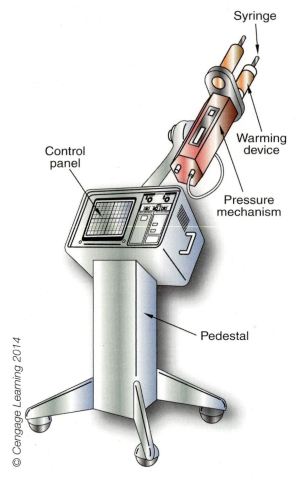

Figure 16-4 Contrast medium injection device

orally, rectally, intravenously, percutaneously, or through inhalation or urinary catheterization. A **contrast medium injection device** (Figure 16-4) is used to deliver a predetermined amount of contrast, typically for vascular imaging procedures.

Contrast agents are radiopaque (impenetrable by X-rays or other forms of radiation), and they block X-ray beams and provide excellent contrast for body structures. Common contrast agents include:

- Barium sulfate (gastrointestinal studies)
- Organic iodine (vascular and renal studies)
- Iodized oils (myelography)

Contrast materials make body structures appear white on X-rays.

> **Note:**
>
> Radiologic procedures are performed with contrast, without contrast, or with and without contrast. Separate codes are available in the Radiology section to describe all of these combinations.

 Coding Tip:

Radiology codes that contain the description "with contrast" include intravascular, intra-articular, or intrathecal administration of contrast material. When contrast material is administered orally or rectally (e.g., barium enema), the administration of the contrast material is not reported separately. It is included in the radiologic procedure performed.

Note:

The supply of contrast material is not included in radiology procedure codes. HCPCS level II codes are reported for the supply of contrast material (e.g., A4641, A4642, A9500, and A9600).

Written Report

The imaging report, documented and authenticated by the interpreting individual (e.g., radiologist), is considered an integral part of a radiologic procedure. Therefore, before reporting the radiology procedure code on an insurance claim, the documented report must be available in the patient's record.

Radiology guidelines state that the interpreting individual must sign a written report as an integral part of a radiologic procedure. However, the guidelines do *not* specify content or format.

When a teaching physician reviews a radiographic image interpreted by a resident, the teaching physician is responsible for documenting a note indicating that the image was reviewed with the resident, and the teaching physician agreed with the resident's interpretation. (If the teaching physician disagreed with the resident's interpretation, the teaching physician is responsible for documenting a corrected report.) Before a claim is submitted to Medicare for payment, the radiologic report must be authenticated by the teaching physician (and a statement of agreement with the resident's interpretation must be documented by the teaching physician).

Note:

Code of Federal Regulations, 42 CFR (Conditions of Participation for Hospitals) states, "The radiologist or other practitioner who performs radiology services must sign reports of his or her interpretations." "Authentication may include signatures, written initials or computer entry." (Electronic signatures require verification methods to ensure accuracy of the entry, such as encryption.)

Exercise 16.3 – Radiology Section Guidelines

Instructions: Complete each statement.

1. Radiological procedures that are completed as an integral component of a total service or procedure are called _____ procedures.

2. A radiological procedure that is provided to patients but that is not included in the current edition of the CPT coding manual is called a(n) _____ procedure.

3. A 5-French pigtail catheter was placed via femoral puncture in the abdominal aorta. Abdominal aortography, by serialography, with radiological supervision and interpretation was performed. Identify the surgical and radiological components.

   a. Surgical component: _____
   b. Radiological component: _____

4. Radiology codes that contain the description "with contrast" include the _____, _____, and _____ administration of contrast material.

5. When contrast material is administered orally or rectally, its administration is included in the procedure and is separately reported. TRUE or FALSE.

Radiology Subsections

The Radiology section of CPT includes seven subsections:

- Diagnostic radiology (diagnostic imaging) (70010–76499)

- Diagnostic ultrasound (76506–76999)

- Radiologic guidance (77001–77032)

- Breast, mammography (77051–77059)

- Bone/joint studies (77071–77084)

- Radiation oncology (77261–77799)

- Nuclear medicine (78012–79999)

Radiology is the medical specialty that uses X-rays (e.g., radiant energy) to diagnose and treat injuries and disease. Radiology imaging also includes MRI, magnetic resonance angiography (MRA), CT scan, ultrasound, and nuclear scans. Radiology procedure codes are found under the procedural term (e.g., transluminal atherectomy) or the anatomic site (e.g., chest).

Diagnostic Radiology (Diagnostic Imaging)

The Diagnostic Radiology (Diagnostic Imaging) subsection includes the following headings:

- Head and Neck
- Chest (Figure 16-5)
- Spine and Pelvis
- Upper Extremities
- Lower Extremities
- Abdomen

- Gastrointestinal Tract
- Urinary Tract
- Gynecological and Obstetrical
- Heart
- Vascular Procedures
- Other Procedures

The Diagnostic Radiology (Diagnostic Imaging) subsection includes diagnostic and therapeutic procedures, computed tomography (CT) (Figure 16-6), magetic resonance imaging (MRI), and magnetic resonance angiography (MRA). These diagnostic procedures can be as simple as a routine chest X-ray or as complex as a carotid angiography, which requires selective vascular catheterization.

To code diagnostic radiology procedures accurately, identify the following:

- Anatomic site
- Type of procedure
- Number of views

- Laterality of the procedure (e.g., unilateral or bilateral)
- Use of contrast media

CPT allows for various combinations of codes to address the number and type of radiographic views. For a given radiographic series, the procedure code that most accurately describes what was performed is appropriate.

A variety of combinations of views necessary to obtain medically useful information are classified in the Diagnostic Radiology subsection. A complete review of available codes for radiographic procedures ensures accurate coding so that the most comprehensive code is reported (to describe services performed). Do not report multiple codes to describe a service when a combination code is available.

Note:

A careful review of the radiology code description is required so that the most comprehensive code is reported. Codes 71010–71035 are reported for chest X-ray procedures. The radiologic report will indicate the view (e.g., single) and type of chest X-ray (e.g., frontal).
- 71010—Radiologic examination, chest, single view, frontal
- 71020—Radiologic examination, chest, two views, frontal and lateral

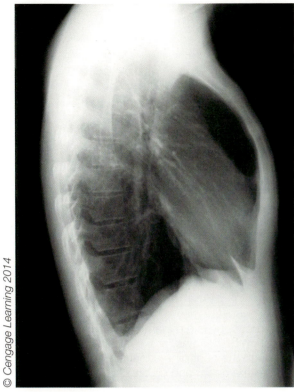

Figure 16-5 Lateral chest X-ray. Bones of the spine are white and soft tissues are shades of gray.

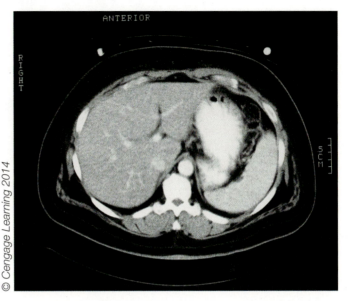

Figure 16-6 Abdominal CT scan in which the liver is predominant in the upper left and the stomach is visible in the upper right.

When radiographic procedures are repeated during the same encounter due to substandard quality, just one code is reported. However, if after reviewing initial films the radiologist elects to obtain additional views to render further interpretation, determine the third-party payer's policy regarding multiple procedures. Generally, the CPT code that describes the total service provided is reported even if the patient was released from the radiology suite and had to return for additional services.

Descriptions of many radiology codes refer to a "minimum" number of views. When more than the minimum number specified in the code description is performed and a more specific code is not available, report one code for the highest level of service. (When additional X-rays are necessary due to a change in the patient's condition, report separate radiology codes as appropriate.)

EXAMPLE 1: A three-view X-ray of the shoulder was obtained. Report code 73030. (Do *not* report codes 73020 and 73030 even though that combination of codes equals three views.)

EXAMPLE 2: The patient presented to the ED with the complaint of severe shortness of breath. A single-view, frontal, chest X-ray was obtained. A repeat chest X-ray, complete (minimum of four views), was obtained several hours later after it was noted that the patient was experiencing labored breathing unrelieved by medication. Report codes 71010 and 71030-59. (Modifier -59 indicates that the second X-ray was a separate procedure.)

Radiographic procedures are performed without contrast, with contrast, or with and without contrast. (Invasive diagnostic imaging that involves the use of contrast material is discussed later.) Separate codes are available to describe all of these combinations of contrast usage.

Preliminary scout radiographs obtained prior to contrast administration or delayed imaging -radiographs are often performed. When a CPT code is available to classify scout radiographs, it is reported. If there is no CPT code, the scout radiograph procedures are included in the reported code for the primary procedure.

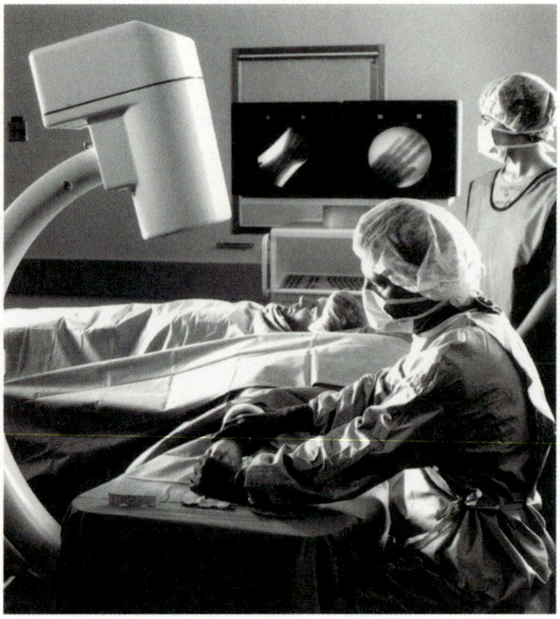

© Courtesy of GE Healthcare

Figure 16-7 Fluoroscopy unit. (Fluoroscopy is a dynamic radiographic examination that allows for visualization of flow of barium through the gastrointestinal tract, injection of a contrast agent into the heart, and so on.)

Fluoroscopy

According to *CPT Assistant*, when radiologic supervision and interpretation are performed during surgical procedures, fluoroscopy (Figure 16-7) is included in the radiologic procedure. This means that codes for fluoroscopy (76000–76001) are *not* reported in addition to the radiologic procedure code.

> **EXAMPLE:** Patient underwent a laparoscopic cholecystectomy and an intraoperative cholangiogram with fluoroscopy. Report codes 47563 (surgical component) and 74300-26 (radiologic component). Do not report code 76000 (fluoroscopy) because it is included in code 74300.

Interventional Radiologic Procedures

Interventional radiologic procedures involve the administration of contrast material orally (by mouth, such as for an upper GI), rectally (by rectum, such as for a barium enema), or **parenterally** (other than by mouth or rectum, such as implantation, infusion, or injection).

When spinal radiologic procedures are performed using CT, MRI, or magnetic resonance angiography (MRA) and the code description includes the phrase *with contrast*, do not report a code for intravenous (IV) injection. The IV injection procedure is included in the radiologic procedure code. However, when an intrathecal injection is performed, report a separate code. (**Intrathecal** refers to the fluid-filled space between layers of tissue that cover the brain and spinal cord.)

> **EXAMPLE 1:** Patient underwent CT of the cervical spine, with IV injection of contrast material. Report code 72126.

> **Coding Tip:**
>
> The administration of oral or rectal contrast material is included as part of the radiologic procedure code. (Do *not* report a separate code for the administration of oral or rectal contrast material.) However, it is acceptable to report an HCPCS level II code for the supply of the contrast material.

EXAMPLE 2: Patient underwent CT of the thoracic spine, with intrathecal injection of contrast material. Report codes 72129 and 62284.

For intra-articular injection of contrast material, report the appropriate joint injection code. When an IV line is placed for administration of contrast material, it is not coded or reported. Placement of the IV line is included in the radiologic procedure code.

EXAMPLE: Patient underwent left femoral venography, which required placement of an IV line and injection of contrast material. Report 75820 and 36005. (Do *not* report code 36000 for placement of the IV line.)

Note:

For urogenital radiography (74400-74775), the insertion of a urethral catheter (51701–51702) is included in the radiographic procedure code and not separately reported. However, a code from the CPT Surgery section for the injection procedure to administer dye or radionuclide material is reported.

EXAMPLE: Patient underwent cystography (three views), which involved insertion of a catheter through the patient's urethra into the bladder and injection of contrast material. X-rays were taken from various angles at various stages of filling to visualize the bladder. Report codes 74430 and 51600. (Do *not* report a code for catheter insertion.) (The supply of dye is reported with a code from HCPCS level II.)

Computed Tomography (CT) and Computed Tomographic Angiography (CTA)

CT (or CAT) is an X-ray of horizontal and vertical cross-sectional views or "slices" of the body (Figure 16-8), which are computer-processed to create 3D images.

Computed tomographic angiography (CTA) (Figure 16-9) (70496–70498, 71275, 72191, 73206, 73706, 74175, and 75635) is a less invasive technique that uses X-ray beams to image blood vessels. (Until the introduction of CTA, vascular evaluation was performed primarily using invasive angiography procedures, which required catheterization.)

Imaging of blood vessels is not automatically done as part of a CTA. The key distinction between CTA and CT is that CTA includes reconstruction post-processing of angiographic images and interpretation. If reconstruction post-processing is not performed, the procedure is *not* a CTA study.

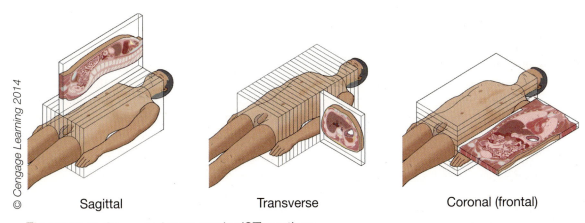

© Cengage Learning 2014

Sagittal   Transverse   Coronal (frontal)

Figure 16-8 Computed tomography (CT) sections

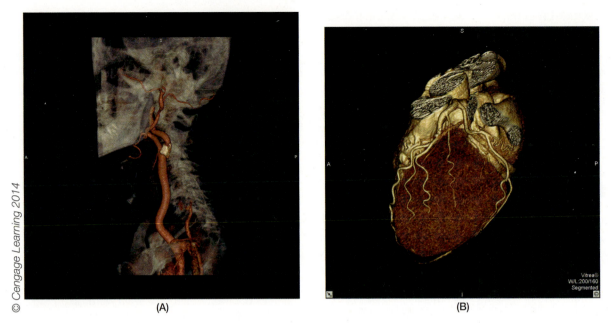

Figure 16-9   Three-dimensional computed tomography angiography (CTA) reconstructions (A) Carotid arteries (B) Coronary arteries

EXAMPLE 1: Patient underwent CT of the abdomen, with contrast material. Report code 74150.

EXAMPLE 2: Patient underwent CTA of the abdomen, first without contrast material and then followed by the injection of contrast material, and image post-processing. Report code 74175.

Do not report a code for the injection of contrast material for a "with contrast" CTA procedure. However, the supply of the contrast material is reported separately with an appropriate HCPCS level II code. (The administration of oral or rectal contrast materials does not qualify as "with contrast." Such contrast materials are not typically used in CTA because they obscure the vasculature.)

> **Coding Tip:**
>
> Make sure you review documentation carefully when reporting codes for CTA (so codes for "computed tomography" are not reported by mistake).

EXAMPLE: The patient underwent a CTA of the abdominal aorta with contrast, followed by administration of contrast material, with bilateral iliofemoral lower extremity runoff. Post-processing of the image was performed. Report code 75635.

Epidurography

Epidurography is performed to assess the structure of the spine's epidural space prior to percutaneous epidural adhesiolysis (to identify nerve construction or inflammation and the degree of fluid flow in the epidural space). Code 72275 (epidurography, radiological supervision and interpretation) is reported for a formally interpreted contrast study that involves multiplanar imaging, generating hard copy images. When epidurography is performed at *multiple* spinal levels, report code 72275 for each spinal region examined (e.g., once for the thoracic region and once for the lumbar region).

EXAMPLE: Using direct fluoroscopy, a catheter is percutaneously placed in the epidural space. Following fluoroscopic confirmation of the needle location, contrast material is injected. Permanent recording of the epidural space is performed. Report code 72275. (Do *not* report code 77003 for fluoroscopic guidance, because fluoroscopy is included as a component of epidurography.)

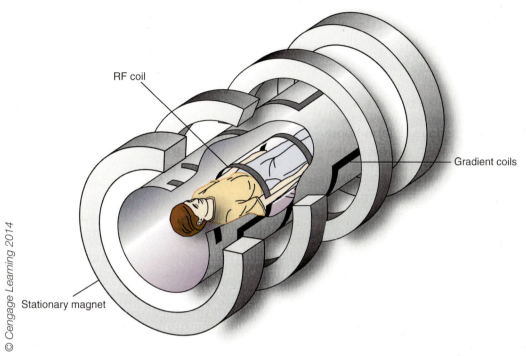

Figure 16-10 Magnetic resonance imaging (MRI) unit, which includes stationary magnet, radio frequency coil, and gradient coils

Magnetic Resonance Imaging (MRI)

Magnetic resonance imaging (MRI) (Figure 16-10) produces high-quality anatomic images. Code descriptions include studies performed without contrast materials, with contrast materials, and without contrast material followed by injection of contrast materials.

> **EXAMPLE:** A diagnostic MRI of the brain (Figure 16-11) was performed without contrast material. Report code 70551.

Magnetic Resonance Angiography (MRA)

Magnetic resonance angiography (MRA) is a noninvasive diagnostic study that is used to evaluate disorders of arterial and venous structures. MRA is performed to visualize the arteries and vessels without invasive procedures, and they are performed on MRI machines that contain hardware and software enhancements. Post-processing procedures to create the images are included in MRA codes.

> **EXAMPLE:** Patient underwent MRA of the abdomen with contrast material. Report code 74185.

Vascular Procedures

Some vascular radiographic procedures performed on the aorta and arteries are designated as selective or nonselective. The radiographic procedure codes are reported in addition to

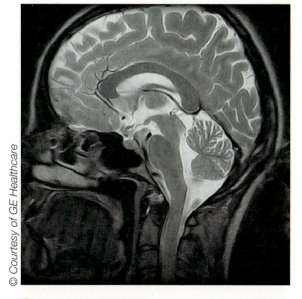

Figure 16-11 Magnetic resonance image (MRI) of the brain

appropriate catheterization codes from the Surgery section. (Chapter 13 contains content about coding of arterial catheterization procedures.)

- *Selective vascular catheterization* is the insertion and manipulation or guidance of a catheter into the branches of the arterial system (other than the aorta or the vessel punctured) for the purpose of performing diagnostic (e.g., angiography) or therapeutic (e.g., endarterectomy) procedures (e.g., 75650). Selective vascular catheterization includes introduction of the catheter and all lesser-order selective catheterizations used in the approach.

  EXAMPLE: The insertion of the catheter from the aorta into the right common and internal carotid arteries is a selective vascular catheterization procedure. (The catheter was inserted into the aorta from the brachial artery, which is a nonselective vascular catheterization procedure.)

- *Nonselective vascular catheterization* is the introduction of a catheter into a vessel and guidance of the catheter into lesser- (or first-) order vessels (e.g., 75746). (A nonselective catheterization code from the Surgery section is *not* reported with a selective radiological supervision and interpretation code.)

  EXAMPLE: The introduction of a catheter into the femoral artery and threading of the catheter into the aorta is a nonselective vascular catheterization procedure. (If the catheter is further threaded from the aorta into another vessel, such as the brachiocephalic artery, a selective vascular catheterization procedure is performed.)

For diagnostic angiography or venography (radiological supervision and interpretation) (Figure 16-12), the following interventional procedures are included in the procedure code:

- Contrast injections, angiography, roadmapping, and/or fluoroscopic guidance for the intervention

- Vessel measurement

- Post-angioplasty/stent angiography

Codes for the above procedures are not coded separately when performed during the same session as an angiography or a venography.

For diagnostic angiography or venography performed during the same session as an interventional procedure, the angiography or venography is separately coded and reported if:

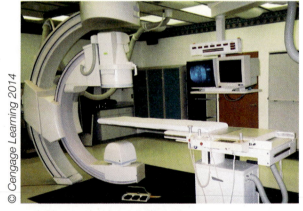

© Cengage Learning 2014

Figure 16-12 Vascular imaging (e.g., angiography, venography) equipment

- No prior catheter-based angiographic study is available and a full diagnostic study was performed *and the decision to intervene is based on the diagnostic study*.

- A prior angiographic study is available, but medical record documentation indicates the following:

  - The patient's clinical condition has changed since the prior study.

  - There was inadequate visualization of anatomy and/or pathology.

  - There was a clinical change during the procedure that requires new evaluation.

EXAMPLE: Patient underwent outpatient bilateral carotid arteriograms. Catheter was inserted into right common femoral artery, advanced to aortic arch, inserted into left carotid artery, and contrast material was injected. Catheter was withdrawn from left carotid artery, advanced to brachiocephalic artery, inserted into right carotid artery, and contrast material was injected. Bilateral carotid arteriograms were performed. Report codes 36215-LT, 36218-RT, 75680. Do not add modifier -51 to code 36218 because it is an add-on code.

Vascular Procedures—Transcatheter Procedures

Therapeutic transcatheter radiological supervision and interpretation code(s) include the following services:

- Contrast injections, angiography/venography, roadmapping, and fluoroscopic guidance for the intervention
- Vessel measurement
- Completion angiography/venography (except for those uses permitted by 75898)

Codes for the above procedures are *not* coded separately when performed during the same session as a therapeutic transcatheter procedure.

EXAMPLE: Patient underwent angiography through existing catheter for follow-up study for transcatheter therapy, via infusion. Report code 75898.

Other Procedures

Bone density studies evaluate diseases of the bone and are used to assess the response of bone disease to treatment. The studies assess bone mass (e.g., density) of the wrist, radius, hip, pelvis, spine, or heel. **Dual energy X-ray absorptiometry** (**DEXA** or DXA) is a bone density study that uses two X-ray beams with different levels of energy pulsing alternately (e.g., two-dimensional projection) to create the image. Results are scores, which are reported as standard deviations of bone density of a person the age of peak bone mass (e.g., 30 years of age). To code DEXA studies properly, determine the bone mass being measured:

- Axial skeleton (hips, pelvis, or spine)
- Appendicular skeleton (peripheral bones such as wrist or heel) (vertebra)

To differentiate bone density studies, code 77080 is specific to axial skeleton and code 77081 is reported for a peripheral study. Both codes include the examination of one or more anatomic sites.

Note: Both men and women undergo DEXA imaging.

EXAMPLE: Patient underwent DXA bone density study of the hips and pelvis. Report code 77080.

Exercise 16.4 – Diagnostic Radiology (Diagnostic Imaging)

Instructions: Assign the CPT code(s) and appropriate modifier(s) to each statement.

1. An interventional radiologist performed a percutaneous needle core, biopsy of a right breast mass using computed tomography guidance.

2. Laryngography, contrast, radiological supervision and interpretation.

3. Radiologist provided supervision and interpretation of an angiography, left brachial artery.

4. Radiological examination, sacrum and coccyx, two views.

5. Magnetic resonance spectroscopy.

Diagnostic Ultrasound

Diagnostic ultrasound uses high-frequency sound waves (e.g., mechanical oscillations) to produce an image. Radiologic ultrasound codes are organized according to anatomic site. Radiologic ultrasound procedures are often performed as follow-up studies for inconclusive diagnostic radiology procedures. They are also performed intraoperatively (e.g., during endoscopic procedures). Ultrasound is also used as guidance for the following:

- Biopsies
- Cyst localization
- Invasive procedures (e.g., ablation of renal cysts, coded as 50541)
- Paracentesis
- Pericardiocentesis
- Placement of radiation therapy fields
- Thoracentesis

Ultrasound display modes include:

- **A-mode**, or **amplitude modulation**: One-dimensional display that reflects the length of time a sound reaches a structure and is reflected back.
- **B-scan**, or **brightness mode**, or **gray-scale ultrasound**: Two-dimensional display that reflects sound waves bouncing off tissues or organs; the diagnostic ultrasound produces a two-dimensional cross-sectional view of tissues that cannot be seen directly (e.g., used to locate a lesion and determine its shape).
- **M-mode**, or **motion mode**: One-dimensional display that reflects the *movement* of structures.
- **Real-time scan**: Two-dimensional display of structures and movement that indicates the movement, shape, and size of the tissue or organ.

Ophthalmic ultrasound includes the following:

- **Biometric A-scan**: Diagnostic ultrasound that produces a one-dimensional view of normal and abnormal eye tissue and precise measurements of the eye's length (e.g., dimensions of an orbital lesion and exact depth of a foreign body).
- **Biomicroscopy**: Optical instrument that looks like a microscope, with two eyepieces.

Note:

Biomicroscopy is performed with a **slitlamp exam**, which is a high-intensity light source that can be focused to shine as a slit to look at anterior structures, including the eyelid, sclera, conjunctiva, iris, natural crystalline lens, and cornea.

- *B-scan* (see definition above).
  - **Quantitative A-scan**: Diagnostic ultrasound that produces quantitative data about the posterior eye segment and evaluates tissue consistency, mobility, and vascularity (e.g., size of an orbital lesion).
  - **Corneal pachymetry**: Noninvasive ultrasound procedure that determines thickness of the cornea (e.g., prior to performing LASIK surgery).

Complete and Limited Ultrasound Procedures

To report a code for a "complete" ultrasound, the documented report must contain a description of all elements or the reason that an element could not be visualized (e.g., organ is surgically absent). A complete study includes visualization and diagnostic evaluation of all major structures within the anatomic location.

If fewer/less than the required elements for a complete exam are documented (e.g., limited number of organs or limited portion of region evaluated), report the "limited" code for that anatomic region. A limited study could include a follow-up examination, or it might address just a single quadrant or single diagnostic problem. (A "limited" exam of an anatomic region is not reported during the same session as a "complete" exam of the same region.)

 Coding Tip:

The abdomen and retroperitoneum heading include ultrasound codes that are described as one of the following:

- Complete (e.g., entire abdomen).
- Limited (e.g., single organ or single quadrant).

A limited ultrasound of a single organ or a single quadrant is also performed as follow-up to a complete ultrasound procedure. For example, a complete abdominal ultrasound revealed an abnormality of a single organ. Patient was placed on a therapeutic regimen (e.g., medications). A limited abdominal ultrasound of that organ was performed as follow-up to determine whether abnormality still existed.

 Note:

ED physicians perform limited ultrasound procedures to evaluate a specific problem, and diagnostic ultrasound results are used to determine subsequent treatment.

 EXAMPLE 1: Patient underwent complete ultrasound of the abdominal region, B-scan and real time with image documentation. Report code 76700. (A complete ultrasound of the abdomen describes all major abdominal structures; and organ-specific findings are reported, such as the liver and spleen.)

EXAMPLE 2: Patient underwent limited ultrasound of the abdomen, B-scan and real time with image documentation. Report code 76705. (A limited ultrasound of the abdomen describes a problem-specific study, such as the presence or absence of intraperitoneal fluid.)

Coding Tip:

When there is no corresponding limited ultrasound procedure code for a complete procedure and a limited ultrasound was performed, add modifier -52 (Reduced Services) to the complete code.

EXAMPLE 3: Patient underwent a nonobstetrical transvaginal ultrasound to confirm an ectopic pregnancy. Report code 76830-52. (A complete transvaginal ultrasound procedure involves evaluation of the uterus, endometrium, adnexae, and ovaries. Because the transvaginal ultrasound was performed to confirm an ectopic pregnancy only, the procedure is limited and modifier -52 [Reduced Services] is added to the complete study code [76830]).

Doppler Ultrasound

Doppler ultrasound is effective in the evaluation of major arteries and veins, of the heart, and in obstetrics for fetal monitoring. **Doppler ultrasonography** evaluates movement by measuring changes in the frequency of echoes reflected from moving structures. It uses diagnostic ultrasound to detect moving structures (e.g., blood cells) and measures their direction and speed. Doppler ultrasound allows for real-time viewing of blood flow, which cannot be obtained by other methods.

Coding Tip:

Austrian mathematician and physicist (Johann) Christian Doppler is known for a principle called the Doppler effect (frequency of a sound wave appears to change as the source moves toward or away from you).

EXAMPLE: Patient underwent ultrasound of transplanted kidney, real time with image documentation, with duplex Doppler studies. Report code 76776.

Coding Tip:

Review Non-Invasive Vascular Diagnostic Studies subsection codes (93875–93990) located in the Medicine section to report venous Doppler studies and duplex scans.

Obstetrical Ultrasound Procedures

An ultrasound of the pregnant uterus includes fetal and maternal evaluation for single and multiple gestations, with limited and follow-up exams.

EXAMPLE: Patient underwent fetal biophysical profile with nonstress testing. Report code 76818. The fetal biophysical profile can include assessment of amniotic fluid, fetal breathing, tone, and movement.

Fetal echocardiography is performed ultrasonically according to specific criteria.

EXAMPLE: Patient underwent fetal echocardiography, cardiovascular system, real time with image documentation (2D), with M-mode recording. Report code 76825.

For female patients known to be pregnant (e.g., established diagnosis of pregnancy), it is appropriate to report an obstetrical ultrasound code from 76801–76817. However, when a female patient does not have an established diagnosis of pregnancy and undergoes an ultrasound evaluation (e.g., dysmenorrhea or pelvic pain), report a nonobstetrical ultrasound code (76856–76857). (Use of code 76856 or 76857 is not dependent upon whether the outcome of the ultrasound procedure is a diagnosis of pregnancy or a complication related to a pregnancy.)

EXAMPLE: A patient with an established diagnosis of pregnancy presents with symptoms that necessitate an ultrasound evaluation of the pelvis. Report a code from obstetrical ultrasound codes 76801–76817 even if the outcome of the procedure is that the patient is not pregnant (e.g., ultrasound confirms that miscarriage occurred).

Ultrasonic Guidance Procedures

Ultrasonic guidance procedures (76930–76965) include the use of ultrasound for the following:

- Pericardiocentesis guidance

- Central venous catheter placement

- Needle placement for other procedures

Report *either* a diagnostic ultrasound *or* a guidance ultrasound code (but not both) for the same patient during the same encounter.

EXAMPLE: Patient underwent ultrasound guidance for pericardiocentesis during the same encounter. Report codes 33010 and 76930.

Other Procedures

CPT code 76970 (Ultrasound study, follow-up) is *not* reported in addition to other echocardiograph procedures or ultrasound guidance procedures because it classifies a follow-up procedure performed on the same day.

Radiologic Guidance

Radiologic guidance is performed during a procedure to visualize access to an anatomic site. The Radiologic Guidance subsection contains four headings: fluoroscopic guidance, computed tomography guidance, magnetic resonance guidance, and other radiologic guidance (Table 16-1).

Table 16-1 Type of Radiologic Guidance and the Purpose of Each

Type of Radiologic Guidance	Purpose
Fluoroscopic Guidance	• Guidance for placement, replacement, or removal of: 　○ Catheter 　○ Central venous access device (CVAD) 　○ Needle
Computed Tomography Guidance	• Guidance for stereotactic localization • Guidance for needle placement • Guidance and monitoring of parenchymal tissue ablation • Guidance for placement of radiation therapy fields
Magnetic Resonance Guidance	• Guidance for needle placement • Guidance and monitoring of parenchymal tissue ablation
Other Radiologic Guidance	• Stereotactic localization for breast biopsy or needle placement • Mammographic guidance for needle placement, breast

EXAMPLE: A 75-year-old patient underwent fluoroscopic guidance for visualization of the subclavian vein during placement of a nontunneled central venous catheter. Report codes 36556 and 77001. (Do not report modifier -51 with add-on code 77001.)

Breast, Mammography

Mammography (Figure 16-13) is a radiological examination of the soft tissue and internal structures of the breast.

- **Screening mammography** (Figure 16-14A) is performed when a patient presents without signs and symptoms of breast disease (e.g., routine annual screening for early detection of unsuspected breast cancer) and is reported with code 77057.

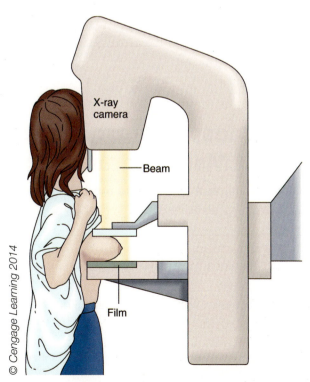

X-ray camera

Beam

Film

Figure 16-13 In mammography, the breast is flattened and then radiographed from above.

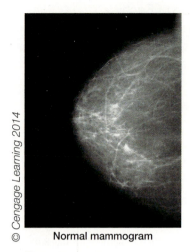
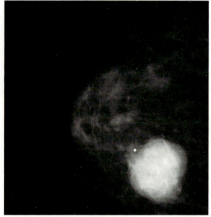

© Cengage Learning 2014

Normal mammogram   Large breast mass is visible, lower right

Figure 16-14 Mammogram images

- **Diagnostic mammography** (Figure 16-14B) includes an assessment of suspected disease (e.g., suspicious mass is palpated on physical examination) and is reported with codes 77055–77056 when an abnormality is found or suspected.

Codes 77051–77052 are add-on codes reported for computer-aided detection with further physician review for interpretation. Code 77051 is reported in addition to the diagnostic mammography code. Code 77052 is reported in addition to the screening mammography code.

EXAMPLE: Patient underwent bilateral screening mammography with computer-aided detection, which was reviewed and interpreted by the radiologist. Report codes 77057 and 77052.

Note:

Mammography code descriptions do not specify male or female, which means that the codes can be reported for either female or male patients.

Bone/Joint Studies

CPT codes 77071–77084 classify bone and joint studies.

EXAMPLE: Nine-day-old infant underwent osseous survey. Report code 77076.

Exercise 16.5 – Diagnostic Utrasound, Radiologic Guidance and Breast Mammography

Instructions: Assign the CPT code(s) and appropriate modifier(s) to each statement.

1. Radiologist performed a complete B-scan exam of the upper abdomen.

   _____

2. The patient known to have an intrauterine pregnancy based on previous physician evaluation underwent real-time ultrasound of pregnant uterus with image documentation, first trimester.

   _____

3. Patient underwent fetal biophysical profile, with nonstress testing, due to suspicion that fetus was in distress.

   _____

4. Abdominal B-scan ultrasound with real time and image documentation, stomach.

   _____

5. Ophthalmic diagnostic ultrasound for bilateral corneal pachymetry.

_____

6. Fluoroscopic guidance for needle placement during liver biopsy.

_____

7. CT guidance for stereotactic localization for treatment during removal of an intracranial lesion.

_____

8. Magnetic resonance guidance and monitoring for parenchymal tissue ablation of osteoid osteoma (bone tumor), left tibia.

_____

9. Stereotactic localization guidance for breast biopsy, left, one lesion.

_____

10. Radiologist performed bilateral mammography on a patient whose primary care noted a lump in the left breast. A lobulated nodule in the outer breast was palpated, and two additional localizing views of the left breast were performed.

_____

Radiation Oncology

Radiation oncology is the specialty of medicine that utilizes high-energy ionizing radiation in the treatment of malignant neoplasms and certain nonmalignant conditions. Distinct therapeutic modalities (methods) are directed at malignant and benign lesions. Modalities include brachytherapy, hyperthermia, stereotactic radiation, and teletherapy.

Radiation oncology codes include professional services and technical procedures that are organized according to the following types of treatment provided:

- Consultation (clinical management)
- Clinical treatment planning (external and internal sources)
- Medical radiation physics, dosimetry, treatment devices, and special services
- Stereotactic radiation treatment delivery
- Other procedures
- Radiation treatment delivery
- Neutron beam treatment delivery
- Radiation treatment management
- Proton beam treatment delivery
- Hyperthermia
- Clinical intracavitary hyperthermia
- Clinical brachytherapy

Consultation (Clinical Management)

Codes from the CPT E/M, Surgery, and/or Medicine sections are reported by the radiation oncologist who does the following:

- Provides preliminary consultation services
- Evaluates a patient prior to the decision to treat
- Delivers full medical care (in addition to treatment management)

Consultation (clinical management) services provided by the radiation oncologist include evaluation of the patient, determination of the need for radiation therapy, identification of site(s) of treatment, assessment of therapy goal(s), and the coordination and sequencing of combined modality therapy with other oncology specialists.

The radiation oncologist subsequently orders and coordinates the technical planning and execution of the treatment with ancillary staff, including radiation therapists, dosimetrists, and physicists. (The treatment is supervised by the radiation oncologist.)

Consultation services provided by radiation oncologists are the same as those provided by other physicians (e.g., a referral is required for initial consultation). The initial consultation is reported with an appropriate CPT code for outpatient consultation services (99241–99245) or inpatient consultation services (99251–99255). (The consultation code is reported just once per course of radiation therapy.)

Once the radiation oncologist has determined the appropriate radiation therapy, the best course of treatment is established. During radiation treatment, patients are monitored closely for adverse reactions that require immediate care. Thus, ongoing patient evaluation is provided as necessary. These services are reported with radiation oncology treatment management codes (77427–77499), *not* E/M service codes.

When a patient completes the course of radiation therapy, the patient continues to see the radiation oncologist during regular follow-up visits. The radiation oncologist monitors the patient's progress and reaction to treatment. This follow-up care is reported with codes from the CPT E/M section (the same as any other established patient follow-up care).

Clinical Treatment Planning (External and Internal Sources)

Clinical treatment planning is performed for each radiation therapy patient, and it includes interpretation of special testing, tumor localization, **treatment volume determination** (region within the body to which radiation therapy is directed), treatment time/dosage determination, choice of treatment modality, determination of number and size of treatment **ports** (sites on the skin where radiation beams enter the body), selection of appropriate treatment devices, and other procedures.

Radiation is administered by a machine outside the body (**external radiation**), is placed inside the body (**internal radiation**) (Figure 16-15), or uses unsealed radioactive materials that travel throughout the body (**systemic radiation therapy**). The internal radiation source is usually sealed in a small container called an implant (e.g., thin wire, catheter, ribbon, capsule, or seed) and inserted directly into the body. The type of radiation administered depends on what type of cancer it is, where it is located, how far into the body the radiation has to go, what the patient's general health and medical history are, whether the patient will have other types of cancer treatment, and other factors. Most patients receive external radiation, and some receive both external and internal or systemic radiation therapy.

 Clinical treatment planning and tumor mapping are critical to identifying the location, extent, and volume of tumor(s) to be treated and all critical and sensitive structures surrounding them. The radiation oncologist plans the appropriate course of therapy that will allow for maximum benefit while protecting surrounding tissues and structures. Clinical treatment planning may involve ordering and interpreting special tests such as CT scans, lymphangiography, MRI scans, and radionucleide scans and/or surgical exploration with biopsy. Markers may also be placed for the purpose of treatment planning and tumor localization.

Coding Tip:

Debulking (surgical removal of part of a malignant tumor; also called **cytoreduction surgery**) may be performed to enhance the effectiveness of radiation oncology treatment.

Therapeutic radiology treatment planning codes are classified according to type of planning, as follows:

- Simple
  - Single treatment area of interest
  - Single port or simple parallel opposed ports
  - Minimal (simple or no) **blocking** (device, such as lead, that shields or protects critical or sensitive organs)
  - No interpretation of special tests for localization of tumor volume

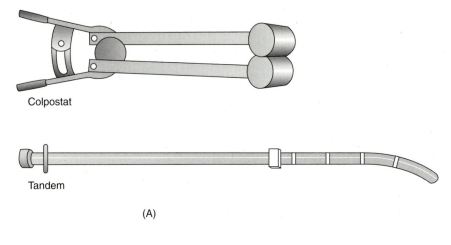

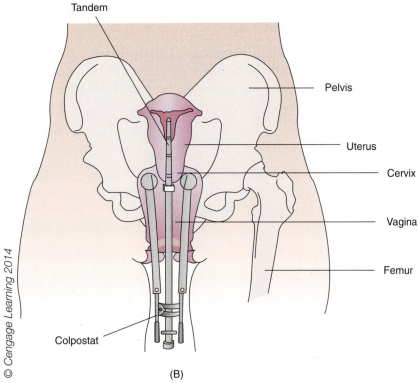

© Cengage Learning 2014

Figure 16-15 Radium implant devices (A) Colpostat and tandem
(B) Placement of colpostate and tandem within vagina and uterus

- Intermediate

  - Two separate treatment areas

  - Three or more converging ports

  - Multiple blocks to protect critical or sensitive organs

  - Special time/dose constraints

  - Interpretation of special tests for localization of tumor volume

- Complex

  - Three or more separate treatment areas

  - Highly complex blocking to protect critical or sensitive organs

- ○ Custom shielding blocks
- ○ Tangential ports
- ○ Special **wedges** (treatment beam-modifying devices that act to change the beam intensity profile)
- ○ Special **compensators** (irregularly shaped beam-modifying devices used to reconfigure beam intensity so it matches irregular tissue contour)
- ○ Rotational or special beam considerations
- ○ Combination of therapeutic modalities
- ○ Interpretation of complex testing procedures (e.g., CT and MRI localization)
- ○ Possible special laboratory testing

Simulation clinical treatment planning uses a simulator to determine various treatment ports to be used during radiation therapy. The simulator can orient a radiation beam toward a patient according to parameters that imitate the treatment proposed for actual therapy (but it does not deliver radiation therapy). Simulation may be carried out on a dedicated conventional simulator or by use of a CT scanner, radiation therapy treatment unit (e.g., linear accelerator), or other diagnostic imaging equipment (e.g., fluoroscopy, CT, or MRI). Simulation is complex because custom shielding blocks are designed, and the simulation must be coordinated with information from treatment planning CT scans and isodose plan data. Therapeutic radiology simulation-aided field setting codes are classified according to type of setting:

- • Simple
  - ○ Simulation of single treatment area
  - ○ Single port or parallel opposed ports
  - ○ Minimal (simple or no) blocking of critical or sensitive organs

- • Intermediate
  - ○ Simulation of three or more converging ports
  - ○ Two separate treatment areas
  - ○ Multiple blocking of critical or sensitive organs

- • Complex
  - ○ Simulation of tangential (peripheral) portals (or ports)
  - ○ Three or more treatment areas
  - ○ Rotation or arc therapy
  - ○ Three-dimensional (3D)
  - ○ Computer-generated 3D reconstruction of tumor volume and surrounding critical or sensitive normal tissue structures (using CT scans or MRI data in preparation for non-coplanar or coplanar therapy)
  - ○ Simulation uses documented 3D beam's eye view volume-dose displays of multiple or moving beams
  - ○ Documentation with 3D volume reconstruction and dose distribution is required

  EXAMPLE: Radiation oncologist provided therapeutic radiology treatment planning services, which required a single treatment area of interest, one port, and no blocking. Report code 77261.

Medical Radiation Physics, Dosimetry, Treatment Devices, and Special Services

"Medical radiation physics, **dosimetry** (measurement and calculation of radiation treatment doses), treatment devices, and special services" codes (77300–77399) are reported by the health care facility (e.g., hospital). There is no professional component for most of these services. (Reimbursement for the radiation oncologist's professional component is included in reimbursement for clinical treatment planning and radiation treatment management codes.)

Note:

Radiation oncologists may add modifier -26 (Professional Component) to codes 77300–77334.

A basic radiation dosimetry calculation is a photon calculation that includes central axis depth dose, time dose factor (TDF), nominal standard dose (NSD), gap calculation, off-axis and tissue inhomogeneity factors, as well as calculation of nonionizing radiation surface and depth dose. Dosimetry may be repeated during the course of treatment as required. CPT code 77300 is reported as many times as necessary during a course of radiation therapy. However, codes for teletherapy isodose planning services (77305, 77310, and 77315) are reimbursed just once per course of treatment.

Intensity modulated radiation therapy (IMRT) varies the intensity of radiation exposure depending on whether tumor is present in the beam pathway. The radiation therapy consists of multiple pencil thin beams (or beamlets) calculated to hit tumors with high-dose radiation beams and sensitive normal tissues with modulated lower-intensity beams, leaving them mostly unaffected. Planning for IMRT involves the use of computer programs that calculate the beam angle configurations and dosage intensities. CPT code 77301 is reported for an IMRT plan, which includes dose-volume histograms for target and critical structure partial tolerance specifications. CPT Category III code 0073T is reported for compensator-based beam modulation treatment delivery of inverse planned treatment using three or more high-resolution (milled or cast) compensator convergent beam modulated fields, per treatment session.

Brachytherapy isodose calculation is also reimbursed just once per course of treatment. The number of units billed for brachytherapy isodose calculation (simple, intermediate, or complex) should equal the number of brachytherapy treatments provided within the billing period. When billing is done for multiple treatment devices, there must be documentation in the clinical record to support the medical necessity of each device or set of devices.

The use of a treatment device (77332–77334) is based on the clinical judgment of the radiation oncologist and is influenced by the patient's anatomy and disease state. The selection and use of any treatment device requires medical necessity, radiation oncologist involvement, and a written and signed order for each device. The radiation oncologist must be directly involved in the design, selection, and placement of any device and must document their involvement with each device.

Treatment devices include the following:

- Beam-shaping devices are called blocks, and they are placed in an external radiation beam to modify its shape to either contour the beam around target structures or to shield normal tissues

- Immobilization devices (e.g., thermoplastic face and body masks, bite-block head holders, Styrofoam body casts, and breast boards) are used to restrict patient movement during treatment

- Beam-modifying devices include wedges, compensators, and boluses

- Shielding devices include bite blocks, eye shields, and testicular shields

Codes for treatment devices are reported at the onset of the treatment. They may be reported again later during the course of treatment if additional or new devices are required.

Codes 77336 and 77370 are reported for medical radiation physics technical procedures. Although the radiation oncologist orders these procedures, he or she generally has little involvement in the actual procedure. The medical radiation physics measurements are used to evaluate a treatment plan. After these procedures are completed, treatment management and delivery is established. Continuing medical physics consultation (CPT code 77336) is reported "per week of therapy," which means that it may be reported after every five radiation treatments *if those treatments occurred during one week of treatment. If, however, the five radiation treatments occurred over a period of five different weeks, code 77336 would be reported five times.* Code 77370 (Special medical radiation physics consultation) is reported just once during a treatment series.

> **EXAMPLE:** Radiation oncologist designed and constructed a simple block treatment device. Report code 77332.

Stereotactic Radiation Treatment Delivery

Stereotactic radiation treatment delivery includes the following types:

- *Stereotactic radiosurgery (SRS)*: Radiation therapy that focuses high-powered X-rays onto a small area, such as a brain, liver, lung, or other lesion; it is a single-session treatment that has such a dramatic effect on its target that the result is considered "surgical;" however, it is not actually considered a surgical procedure; also referred to as gamma knife or cyberknife.

- *Stereotactic body radiation therapy (SBRT)*: Radiation therapy that uses special equipment to position a patient and precisely deliver smaller doses of radiation over several days to bone, liver, and lung tumors in the body; SBRT is not administered to brain tumors; exposure to normal tissue is minimized; also called extracranial radiotherapy.

> **EXAMPLE:** Patient underwent radiation treatment delivery, which used stereotactic radiosurgery to deliver one large radiation dose to his brain tumor. Report code 77371.

Radiation Treatment Delivery

Radiation treatment delivery codes are reported for the administration of radiation therapy *per treatment*. A nonphysician may deliver radiation treatment; however, the radiation oncologist is responsible for checking and documenting the accuracy of the treatment. The radiation oncologist must also treat any adverse reactions to treatment and monitor the effects of radiation therapy on the tumor and surrounding tissues. (Radiation treatment delivery includes ongoing patient evaluation, and codes for such evaluation are not reported separately.)

- Radiation treatment delivery is measured in units of **MeV** (**megaelectron volts** or **megavolts**), which is 1 million electron volts.

- **Therapeutic port films**, are X-rays taken during delivery of radiation treatment that utilize the treatment beam of the machine. Portal films demonstrate the exact shape, size, and area covered by the treatment beam during an actual treatment.

  > **EXAMPLE 1:** Radiation therapy was directed to three separate treatment areas, and 11 MeV was administered. Report code 77416 for 20 MeV or greater (because 3 3 11 5 33 MeV). Do *not* report code 77414 (11–19 MeV) three times.

  > **EXAMPLE 2:** Patient underwent 9 MeV of radiation therapy that was directed to a single treatment area and used a single port. Report code 77403.

> **Note:**
>
> For codes 77407–77416, the MeV of radiation delivered to each treatment area is totaled, and the sum determines the code to be reported.

Coding Tip:

- The number of MeV billed should be compatible with the number of MeV in the code description.
- Codes 77401–77416 describe the areas treated, which include anatomic regions (e.g., neck, throat, bone, breast, and prostate). For example, the right and left neck are considered one area and the brain and lung are considered two areas.

Neutron Beam Treatment Delivery

Neutron beam radiation therapy is an external radiation treatment that uses higher linear energy transfer to treat certain tumors (e.g., salivary gland tumors) due to increased susceptibility, as compared with conventional radiation therapy. An interventional radiologist provides this treatment at a facility equipped with a superconducting accelerator (cyclotron). Pretreatment planning usually involves CT to locate and determine the tumor volume prior to radiation therapy.

> **EXAMPLE:** Patient underwent high-energy neutron radiation treatment delivery to a single treatment area with use of a single port. Report code 77422.

Radiation Treatment Management

Radiation treatment management is reported in units of five fractions or treatment sessions even though the service need not be performed on consecutive days. For radiation treatment management purposes, a **fraction** is a single session of radiation treatment delivered to a specific area of interest. The number of calendar days between treatment fractions is not relevant as long as the treatment is directed to the same area and is part of a single course of therapy. Thus, a claim is submitted with the treatment code for every five treatments. *Multiple fractions that represent two or more treatment sessions furnished on the same day are counted separately if there has been a distinct break in therapy sessions.*

> **EXAMPLE:** Patient received 18 daily radiation therapy fractions during a 4-week period. Report codes 77427, 77427, 77427, and 77427.

Note:

- When a patient who has completed a course of radiation therapy returns with a recurrent tumor and treatment is provided to the same area, report codes for a separate course of radiation therapy.
- HCPCS level II codes for radioactive materials, when supplied by the radiation oncologist, are reported in addition to codes for radiation therapy.

Reimbursement for weekly radiation therapy management includes payment for normal follow-up care during therapy and for three months following its completion.

> **EXAMPLE:** Radiation oncologist provided radiation therapy management for a course of treatment that consisted of two single sessions (fractions). Report code 77431.

Proton Beam Treatment Delivery

Compared to photon beams, proton beams deliver higher radiation doses to tumors, and proton beams do not exceed the radiation tolerance of normal tissue. Proton beam treatment delivery is a modality that consists of delivering smaller doses to intervening normal tissues and organs. Codes are reported according to the following types of treatment:

- *Simple*: Single treatment area utilizing a single nontangential/oblique port, custom block with or without compensation.

- *Intermediate*: One or more treatment areas utilizing two or more ports or one or more tangential/oblique ports, with custom blocks and compensators.

- *Complex*: One or more treatment areas using two or more ports per treatment area with matching or patching fields and/or multiple isocenters, with custom blocks and compensators.

> **EXAMPLE:** Patient underwent proton treatment delivery to two treatment areas using one port per treatment area and custom blocks. Report code 77523.

Hyperthermia and Clinical Intracavitary Hyperthermia

Hyperthermia involves the use of an external heat-generating source (e.g., ultrasound or microwave) to produce localized heating. Hyperthermia is usually performed immediately before or after a session of external beam radiation therapy. Typically, three to six applications of hyperthermia per course of radiation therapy are required. When hyperthermia is generated by intracavitary probe(s), report code 77620.

> **EXAMPLE:** Patient underwent hyperthermia treatment, which was generated by interstitial probe that used 10 interstitial applicators. Report code 77615.

Clinical Brachytherapy

Brachytherapy (Figure 16-16) involves the use of radioactive isotopes for internal radiation, and codes are reported according to the following applications:

- *Simple*: Application has 1 to 4 sources/ribbons.

- *Intermediate*: Application has 5 to 10 sources/ribbons.

- *Complex*: Application has greater than 10 sources/ribbons.

A *source* is an intracavitary placement or permanent interstitial placement. A *ribbon* is a temporary interstitial placement. Intracavitary brachytherapy is performed by placing applicators containing radioactive materials directly into or around a tumor area. A common use of intracavitary brachytherapy is the treatment of carcinoma of the endometrium (uterus) or cervix.

Intracavitary and interstitial applications are seldom used as the sole modality of radiation treatment. Interstitial brachytherapy is performed with needles, ribbons, or wires containing radioactive materials that are inserted directly into and around a cancerous area. The devices remain in place over a period of many days while delivering their relatively low-intensity radiation directly into the tumor. These applications are often used in conjunction with external beam radiation therapy to bring the total dose up to the desired level.

> **EXAMPLE:** Radiation oncologist supervised the handling and loading of a radiation source. Report code 77790.

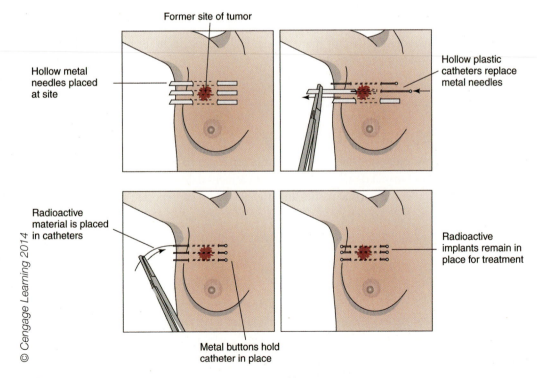

Figure 16-16 Brachytherapy for treatment of breast cancer

Exercise 16.6 – Radiation Oncology

Instructions: Assign the CPT code(s) and appropriate modifier(s) to each statement.

1. Radiation oncologist created a special teletherapy port plan for the total body.

2. Radiation oncologist provided a hyperthermia treatment that was generated by an intracavitary probe.

3. Radiation oncologist performed a therapeutic radiology simulation-aided field setting of a single treatment area with a single port.

4. Patient underwent superficial voltage radiation treatment delivery.

5. Radiation oncologist provided surface application of a radiation source.

Nuclear Medicine

Nuclear medicine involves the use of radioactive elements (e.g., radionuclides and radioisotopes) for diagnostic imaging (e.g., scan) and **radiopharmaceutical therapy** (destroys diseased tissue, such as a malignant neoplasm). The isotope emits gamma rays as it deteriorates, which enables the radiologist to visualize internal abnormalities (e.g., tumors). The images created by the contrast media (radioactive element) are detected by a gamma camera.

Nuclear medicine codes do not include the provision of radium, which means that the nuclear medicine report must be reviewed to identify the diagnostic or therapeutic radiopharmaceutical provided. Then an appropriate HCPCS level II code is reported for the radiopharmaceutical administered. (The injection of the radionuclide is included as part of the procedure, and a separate injection code is *not* reported.)

Common diagnostic nuclear medicine procedures include bone scans, cardiac scans (e.g., thallium scan and MUGA), renal scans, thyroid scans, and hepatobiliary scans (e.g., HIDA scans). Therapeutic nuclear medicine procedures are used to treat diseases such as chronic leukemia, hyperthyroidism, and thyroid cancer.

The Nuclear Medicine subsection contains two headings:

- Diagnostic
- Therapeutic

The Diagnostic heading contains the following subheadings:

- Endocrine System
- Hematopoietic, Reticuloendothelial, and Lymphatic System
- Gastrointestinal System
- Musculoskeletal System
- Cardiovascular System
- Respiratory System
- Nervous System
- Genitourinary System
- Other Procedures

The Therapeutic heading contains no subheadings.

Endocrine System

Nuclear medicine is commonly used to evaluate thyroid function (e.g., thyroid update). **Uptake** is the absorption by a tissue of a substance, material, or mineral and its permanent or temporary retention.

A thyroid uptake test measures thyroid function to determine how much iodine the thyroid absorbs (expressed as a percentage of the administered radioiodine present in the thyroid gland at a specific time after administration). Thyroid imaging (scan) is performed to assess anatomic size and physiologic function. A radioactive tracer (e.g., Iodide-123 capsule or 99m-technetium injection) is administered, which allows blood flow and vascularity of the thyroid to be monitored by imaging at different intervals.

> **EXAMPLE:** Patient underwent thyroid imaging with vascular flow for which a radioactive tracer was administered. Report code 78011.

Coding Tip:

CPT code 78020 is reported when thyroid carcinoma metastases uptake is calculated. The parenthetical note below code 78020 directs its use only with code 78018 (Thyroid carcinoma metastases imaging; whole body). Since 78020 is an add-on code, it is reported in addition to code 78018 without modifier -51.

Hematopoietic, Reticuloendothelial, and Lymphatic System

Bone marrow scans (78102–78104) evaluate bone marrow functioning and irregular marrow tissue expansion (e.g., malignancy or infection). A radiopharmaceutical radiotracer (e.g., radiolabeled sulphur colloid) is injected, and images are obtained after a two- to three-hour delay using a special camera (e.g., scintillation or gamma camera). The camera takes images by detecting gamma radiation from the radionuclide in bone marrow as it "scintillates" (e.g., emits energy in a flash of light) when coming in contact with the camera's detector.

The radiopharmaceutical volume-dilution technique (78122) evaluates plasma and red cell volume by using radiolabeled protein tracers (e.g., iodinated serum albumin) and autologous radiolabeled red blood cells. The procedure involves collecting blood and recording blood counts to calculate volumes using formulas that compare the dilution factor from a standard sample of each radiotracer.

Code 78195 (Lymphatics and lymph nodes imaging) is reported for lymphoscintigraphy. The injection of a radioactive tracer is included in the lymphoscintigraphy procedure, which means that code 38792 is not reported. Modifier -26 (Professional Component) is added to code 78195 only if the professional component was performed by the physician.

> **EXAMPLE:** Patient underwent a platelet survival study. Report code 78191.

Gastrointestinal System

Tomographic SPECT (78205–78206) is used for evaluation of the anatomy and functionality of the liver. A radiolabeled sulphur colloid is injected, and imaging of the distribution of gamma radiation emitted from the radiopharmaceutical is performed. SPECT imaging is performed by rotating a single- or multiple-head camera around the patient to provide 3D computer-reconstructed views of cross-sectional slices of the liver. For imaging done with a vascular flow test, red blood cells are labeled to enable imaging of the blood flow through the liver.

> **EXAMPLE:** Patient underwent acute gastrointestinal blood loss imaging. Report code 78278.

Musculoskeletal System

Single and dual photon absorptiometry (78350–78351) are noninvasive techniques used to measure the absorption of the photon beam (e.g., mono- or dichromatic) by bone material. The device is placed directly on the patient and uses a small amount of radionuclide to measure the bone mass absorption. This provides a measurement of the bone mineral density of cortical bone and can be used to assess an individual's response to treatment at different intervals.

> **EXAMPLE:** Patient underwent a bone density study with single photon absorptiometry, vertebral column and rib cage. Report code 78350.

Cardiovascular System

Myocardial perfusion and cardiac blood pool imaging may be performed at rest and/or during stress. When performed during exercise and/or pharmacologic stress, report an appropriate stress test code from the Medicine section (93015–93018). **Cardiac blood pool imaging** uses a gamma camera for sampling, which is performed repetitively over several hundred heartbeats during the transition of the radionuclide (e.g., technetium-99m) through the central circulation.

Nuclear imaging for noncardiac vascular flow studies (78445) is performed to evaluate arterial or venous peripheral vascular diseases or injuries. In radionuclide angiography, red blood cells are tagged with radioactivity and injected intravenously. A scintillation camera takes a series of dynamic images every two to three seconds immediately after injection, followed by static images.

For myocardial perfusion study (78491–78492), PET myocardial imaging is typically performed on patients with coronary artery disease and left ventricular dysfunction. PET scanning is also used in diagnostic and therapeutic procedures for malignant tumors. PET is a noninvasive nuclear medicine technique that produces 3D images of the distribution of radioactivity (e.g., emission of positrons) similar to a CT scan. However, PET uses radiopharmaceuticals instead of dye and X-rays. When the radiopharmaceutical agent is injected into the blood, a positron scanner detects, measures, and displays metabolism of tissues (e.g., heart and brain) and many types of tumors. PET scans are also used to diagnose dementia. (Report appropriate HCPCS level II codes for radiopharmaceutical diagnostic imaging agents or "tracers," in addition to CPT codes for PET scan procedures.)

Coding Tip:

CPT codes 78491 (Myocardial imaging, positron emission tomography (PET), perfusion, single study at rest or stress) and 78492 (Multiple studies at rest and/or stress) are reported with the following tracer codes:

- A9526: Nitrogen N-13 ammonia, diagnostic, per study dose, up to 40 millicuries
- A4641: Radiopharmaceutical, diagnostic, not otherwise classified

EXAMPLE: Patient underwent myocardial imaging, PET, metabolic evaluation. Report code 78459.

Respiratory System

A pulmonary perfusion imaging procedure is used to diagnose pulmonary emboli (Figure 16-17) and pulmonary trauma. The procedure consists of imaging a patient twice:

- Once after inhalation of a radioactive aerosol to determine pulmonary ventilation
- Once again after injection of a radioactive particulate to determine lung perfusion

  Code 78582 represents a combination code that allows accurate reporting of both components of the procedure.

  EXAMPLE: Patient underwent particulate pulmonary perfusion imaging. Report code 78580.

Nervous System

Codes 78600–78699 are reported for brain imaging, cerebral vascular flow, cerebrospinal fluid flow/leakage, and radiopharmaceutical dacryocystography radiographic procedures.

EXAMPLE: Patient underwent radiopharmaceutical dacryocystography. Report code 78660.

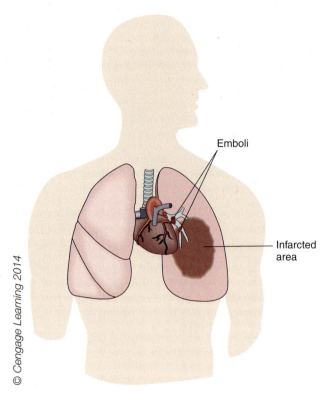

Figure 16–17 Pulmonary emboli

Genitourinary System

Codes 78700–78799 are reported for kidney imaging, kidney function study, urinary bladder residual study, ureteral reflux study, and testicular imaging radiographic procedures.

> **EXAMPLE:** Patient underwent multiple kidney imaging studies with vascular flow and function, with and without pharmacological angiotensin intervention as a converting enzyme inhibitor. Report code 78709.

Other Procedures

Tomographic SPECT imaging (78803 and 78807) allows for evaluation of complex anatomy. A radionuclide is introduced, and the distribution of gamma radiation emitted is detected with a camera that rotates around the patient. A 3D computer reconstructs views of cross-sectional slices of the body. When scanning for an inflammatory process, Gallium is the radiopharmaceutical used.

> **EXAMPLE:** Patient underwent SPECT radiopharmaceutical localization of a tumor, stomach. Report code 78803.

Therapeutic (Nuclear Medicine)

When radiopharmaceutical therapy is administered orally or intravenously, the reported code includes the mode of administration (e.g., injection or infusion). When intra-arterial, intracavitary, or intra-articular administration is the method used for radiopharmaceutical therapy, an appropriate injection and/or procedure code is reported in addition to the therapy code. When imaging guidance and radiological supervision and interpretation are provided for intra-arterial, intracavitary, or intra-articular administration, appropriate code(s) are reported in addition to the therapy and administration codes.

> **EXAMPLE:** Patient underwent radiopharmaceutical therapy for chronic leukemia, by oral administration. Report code 79005.

Exercise 16.7 – Nuclear Medicine

Instructions: Assign the CPT code(s) and appropriate modifier(s) to each statement.

1. Therapeutic radiopharmaceutical is injected directly into a vein.

   _____

2. The physician determines the location of the sentinel node(s) using scintigraphy imaging.

   _____

3. The physician administered a radiolabeled monoclonal antibody by intravenous infusion.

   _____

4. Patient underwent aerosol pulmonary ventilation and perfusion imaging.

   _____

5. Patient underwent cardiac shunt detection procedure.

   _____

Summary

Radiology is a branch of medicine that uses imaging techniques to diagnose and treat disease. A radiologist is a physician who has undergone specialized training to interpret diagnostic X-rays, perform specialized X-ray procedures, and administer radiation for the treatment of disease (e.g., cancer). The Radiology section includes subsections for diagnostic radiology (diagnostic imaging); diagnostic ultrasound; radiologic guidance; breast, mammography; bone/joint studies; radiation oncology; and nuclear medicine. Procedure descriptions include the type of service, anatomic site, and use of contrast material. Radiology guidelines are located at the beginning of the section, and they should be carefully reviewed prior to the assigning of codes.

Internet Links

Hospital for Special Surgery: Go to *www.hss.edu* and view conditions and treatments by clicking on the Select a Body Part links.

LearningRadiology.com: *www.learningradiology.com*

RadiologyInfo: *www.radiologyinfo.org*

Uniformed Services University (Radiology): *rad.usuhs.mil*

Study Checklist

❏ Read this chapter and highlight key concepts.

❏ Create an index card for each key term.

❏ Access the chapter Internet links to learn more about concepts.

❏ Complete the chapter review, and verify answers with your instructor

❏ Complete WebTutor assignments and take online quizzes.

❏ Complete Workbook chapter, verifying answers with your instructor.

❏ Go to *www.cengagebrain.com* to access StudyWARE™ and the Premium Website. Login instructions are located in the Preface and on the Printed Access Card.

❏ Form a study group with classmates to discuss chapter concepts in preparation for an exam.

Review

Multiple Choice

Instructions: Circle the most appropriate response.

1. Which are the types of radiographic projection?
   a. anteroposterior, lateral, oblique, and posteroanterior
   b. anteroposterior, posteroanterior, midsagittal, and sagittal
   c. coronal, midsagittal, sagittal, and transverse
   d. coronal, transverse, lateral, and oblique

2. Which are the three components of a radiologic procedure?
   a. coronal, transverse, and lateral
   b. posteroanterior, midsagittal, and sagittal
   c. simple, intermediate, and complex
   d. technical, professional, and global

3. Which is a common contrast agent administered to provide better radiographic visualization of organs studied?
   a. barium sulfate
   b. betadine
   c. iodized sodium
   d. sulfuric acid

4. Which is the rectal administration of contrast material?
   a. barium enema
   b. implantation
   c. infusion
   d. injection

5. A patient underwent a procedure in which a special catheter tipped with a hollow tube and rotating blades was used to cut away plaque from the arterial wall. The debris was suctioned out of the body through the tube. Which procedure was performed?
   a. dual energy X-ray absorptiometry
   b. epidurography
   c. transluminal atherectomy
   d. venography

6. Biometric A-scan, quantitative A-scan, B-scan, and corneal pachymetry are considered:
   a. types of ophthalmic ultrasound.
   b. types of X-rays.
   c. radiographic projections.
   d. ultrasound display modes.

7. Brachytherapy, hyperthermia, stereotactic radiation, and teletherapy are considered:
   a. dosimetry techniques.
   b. external heat-generating sources.
   c. therapeutic modalities for radiation oncology.
   d. treatment devices.

8. Radiation treatment management is reported on a _____ basis.
   a. daily   b. monthly   c. per session   d. weekly

9. A pulmonary perfusion imaging procedure is performed to diagnose pulmonary embolism and pulmonary trauma. The code for this procedure allows for imaging a patient:
   a. once.   b. twice.   c. three times.   d. weekly.

10. A patient underwent a nuclear medicine procedure in which radionuclides were administered to destroy a malignant neoplasm. For nuclear medicine purposes, radionuclides are an example of _____ elements and destruction of the malignant neoplasm is considered the _____ procedure.
   a. radioactive, diagnostic
   b. radioactive, radiopharmaceutical
   c. radiopharmaceutical, gamma ray
   d. therapeutic, gamma ray

11. Complete radiological exam of paranasal sinuses. Which CPT code is assigned?
   a. 70140
   b. 70160
   c. 70210
   d. 70220

12. Chest X-ray–Bucky studies. Which CPT code is assigned?
   a. 71021
   b. 71022
   c. 71030
   d. 71035

13. Computed tomography of the cervical spine without contrast on a patient, repeated the same day. Which CPT code(s) are assigned?
   a. 70450, 70450-76
   b. 72125, 72125-76
   c. 72126-76
   d. 72127-76

14. Complete hip X-ray performed on the right side of the patient. Which CPT code is assigned?
   a. 73510-RT
   b. 73510-RT-TC
   c. 73520-52-TC
   d. 73525-RT

15. Selective adrenal angiography, left side, with radiological supervision and interpretation. Which CPT code is assigned?
   a. 75726
   b. 75731
   c. 75433
   d. 75736

16. Screening mammography, bilateral breasts. Which CPT code is assigned?
   a. 77055-50
   b. 77056
   c. 77057
   d. 77057-50

17. Red cell survival study. Which CPT code is assigned?
   a. 78110
   b. 78120
   c. 78130
   d. 78140

18. Radiopharmaceutical localization of tumor, tomographic (SPECT), performed twice by the same physician during the same encounter. Which CPT code(s) are assigned?
   a. 78803
   b. 78803-51
   c. 78803-77
   d. 78803, 78803-76

19. Radiopharmaceutical therapy by intracavitary administration. Which CPT code is assigned?
   a. 79200
   b. 79403
   c. 79440
   d. 79445

20. Therapeutic radiology treatment planning, simple. Which CPT code is assigned?
   a. 77261
   b. 77262
   c. 77263
   d. 77280

Coding Practice

Instructions: Assign the CPT code(s) and appropriate modifier(s) to each case.

Radiology Subsection

21. X-RAY OF ABDOMEN: AP view of abdomen reveals no abnormal soft tissue masses, gas shadows, or calcifications. Liver and spleen not enlarged. Visualized bones appear normal.

_____

22. BARIUM ENEMA: Fluoroscopic and radiographic examination of the colon reveals normal retrograde flow of barium through all segments of the large bowel and into the terminal ileum. No diverticula or other filling defects are demonstrated. Terminal ileum is not unusual. The postevacuation response is normal, and no alteration of the mucosal pattern is demonstrated. IMPRESSION: Normal colon and terminal ileum.

_____

23. GALLBLADDER: Following administration of contrast medium, there is satisfactory concentration within the gallbladder. The outline is normal, and no calculi are detected. IMPRESSION: Normal gallbladder series.

_____

24. UPPER GASTROINTESTINAL SERIES AND ESOPHAGRAM: Radiographic examination of upper gastrointestinal tract reveals no abnormalities of the swallowing mechanism or of the entire esophagus. The stomach is readily entered, peristalsis traverses this organ in normal fashion, and a very small sliding type of hiatus hernia of the stomach is seen on one of the radiographs. No reflux of gastric contents into the esophagus or radiographic signs of esophagitis can be seen. The mucosal pattern of the stomach is not unusual. There is a suggestion of a small ulcer crater of the lesser curvature aspect of the pyloric canal of the stomach. No additional site of gastric ulceration or other abnormality is seen. The duodenal bulb fills out well, and this structure is noted to be slightly distorted in configuration; however, no ulcer crater of the duodenal bulb is appreciated. Prolapse of gastric mucosa into the base of the bulb is seen. The remainder of the duodenal loop and the upper jejunum mucosal pattern are within normal limits.

25. SMALL BOWEL SERIES: Serial films obtained show normal progression of barium through the small intestine. The jejunum and ileum show a normal caliber and position. There is no evidence of filling defect or obstruction. The mucosal pattern is normal. IMPRESSION: Normal small bowel series.

26. CHEST: Frontal and lateral projections of the chest show increased markings with some honeycomb formations, probably representing bronchiectasis associated with infiltrate. However, as compared with earlier study, there are no significant changes. Linear atelectasis is seen in the lower lung field. Otherwise, the lung fields remain clear. The heart is enlarged in its transverse diameter, and its CT ratio measures 16.0 cm/30.5 cm. Calcification is seen in the thoracic aorta.

CONCLUSION: Increased markings in both bases with honeycomb formations, most likely representing bronchiectasis probably superimposed with infiltrate. Close follow-up is recommended.

27. RIGHT RIB CAGE: AP and oblique views of the right portion of the rib cage show no evidence of fracture or other abnormality of the visualized ribs.

28. SKULL: Skull in three views shows calvarium to be intact. There is no evidence of any abnormal calcification or increased intracranial pressure. Sella turcica is normal in size and shape. There are a few teeth in the mandible, and there is poor visualization of the lamina dura.

29. LEFT HAND: Left hand in two views shows some osteoporosis of the visualized bones. There is no evidence of fracture or dislocation. Calcification is seen in the arteries around the wrist.

30. CHEST: AP upright chest radiograph at 72 inches shows the heart to be transverse in position. Significant enlargement is not apparent on this study. At both bases, there is noted air-bronchogram effect associated with pulmonary infiltration. The thoracic aorta shows atheromatous calcification, and the right acromioclavicular joint shows degenerative arthrosis, as does the thoracic spine, which also shows a scoliosis with convexity toward the right.

31. DRIP TECHNIQUE INFUSION PYELOGRAPHY: Right renal length is approximately 11.3 cm, and the left is approximately 10.8 cm. Right kidney is higher than the left. There is degenerative arthrosis of the lumbar spine. Some large and small bowel gas is present, suggesting a mild ileus. There is no definite sign of bowel obstruction. Following Renografin, there was minimal delay in excretion from the kidneys and rather poor concentration bilaterally throughout the study, particularly on the right. As far as can be seen, the renal collecting structures are grossly normal. Urinary bladder shows floor elevation

consistent with a large prostate gland; and there is at least one diverticulum present, which is noted on the right. Questionable one is suggested in the region of the fundus superiorly. Indwelling Foley catheter is present; and, therefore, a postvoiding film was not obtained. CONCLUSION: Drip infusion pyelography shows poorly functioning kidneys. For this reason, one cannot fully assess the kidneys or ureters. As far as can be seen, significant pathology is not apparent. At least one urinary bladder diverticulum is present. Urinary bladder floor shows elevation consistent with a large prostate gland.

32. SKULL: Cranial vault is intact. Sella turcica was normal in size and shape. There are no intracranial calcifications.

33. CERVICAL SPINE: Two views were done; there is no fracture or dislocation identified. Alignment is normal. There is no disc space narrowing. Neural foramina are patent bilaterally. There are no cervical ribs and no soft tissue calcifications in either side of the neck.

34. LEFT ELBOW IN FRONTAL, LATERAL, OBLIQUE, AND AXIAL PROJECTIONS: The elbow is believed to be negative for fracture or dislocation; but because of some irregularity of ossification in the distal metaphysic, conservative management and reexamination is recommended before use is allowed.

35. BOTH KNEES IN FRONTAL, OBLIQUE, AND LATERAL PROJECTIONS: There is no fracture or dislocation and no joint effusion. IMPRESSION: Negative examination of both knees.

36. LEFT WRIST RADIOGRAPHED IN FRONTAL AND LATERAL PROJECTIONS: There has been an anatomic reduction of the distal radial epiphysis.

37. ABDOMINAL SERIES: AP, oblique, and cone position abdominal films show gross distention of multiple loops of small bowel in the midabdomen with large air fluid levels. I see very little air in the colon past the hepatic flexure. The fact that this patient is only two days after abdominal surgery more or less points to a paralytic ileus, but I cannot absolutely rule out the possibility of a mechanical obstruction without a small bowel study. CONCLUSION: Multiple dilated loops of small bowel in the midabdomen. The possibility of a mechanical obstruction cannot be ruled out without a small bowel study. A repeat abdominal series would be advisable before any further studies are done.

38. NUCLEAR VENTRICULOGRAM: Following injection of 22 mCi of Tc-99m, ventriculogram was done and ejection fraction was calculated. The study was compared with prior ventricular ejection, which was 42% with a peak ejection velocity of 2.2 EDV/second. This compares with the last reported values of 31%, 33%, and 24%.

39. MASTOIDS: The left mastoid shows a surgical defect, apparently due to simple mastoidectomy. There are many small, residual cloudy areas in the periphery of the mastoidectomy defect and in the attic region and anterior to the knee of the sinus and low in the squama extending toward the root of the zygoma. No sequestrum is noted. The tegmen antri appears defective. The sinus is in good position. The internal auditory canal is of normal caliber. There are a few small cells along the sinus groove near the tip; these also appear cloudy. The malleus and incus are partly outlined. The right mastoid is highly pneumatic with cells extending into the zygoma. The malleus and incus are partly outlined. The sinus is in good position. The internal auditory canal is of normal caliber.

40. NUCLEAR LIVER-SPLEEN SCAN: The liver is of normal size with homogeneous uptake. The spleen is enlarged and is almost the same size as the liver. There is also increased activity in the spleen. I do not see any focal areas of diminished activity, and there is no significant bone marrow uptake. CONCLUSION: Splenomegaly.

---

41. ABDOMINAL ULTRASOUND: The pregnant uterus is examined via a transabdominal view. Estimated gestation is 16 weeks. A single fetus is observed. No abnormalities of the fetus or placenta are seen. Real-time imaging is provided during this ultrasound.

---

42. RADIATION TREATMENT: 4 MeV were delivered to thyroid area.

---

43. DIAGNOSTIC ULTRASOUND: The scrotum is normal in size. All tissue within appears normal. The testes are normal in appearance. The epididymis appears normal in structure.

---

44. CT SCAN: After administration of contrast dye, soft tissue structures of the neck are identified. The thyroid and parathyroid glands are seen. The right parathyroid gland shows a cyst-like structure.

---

45. CT SCAN: The lumbar spine has a right curvature of 3 mm. The vertebra at L-4 has a moderate amount of bone spur. CONCLUSION: Scoliosis.

---

46. X-RAY OF SHOULDER: AP and lateral views of the right shoulder reveal no soft tissue masses or bony abnormalities. CONCLUSION: Normal right shoulder.

---

47. PET SCAN: The chest region scan reveals no soft tissue masses or bony abnormalities. Ribs, mediastinum, and heart are normal.

---

48. X-RAY OF LEFT ANKLE: Lateral, AP, and oblique views reveal fracture of the malleolus bone on the lateral side. Soft tissue swelling is noted at the fracture site. No dislocation is seen. CONCLUSION: Fracture of left ankle.

---

49. MRI OF HEART: A complete view of the heart and cardiac structures reviewed no abnormalities. Heart valves were normal in appearance. Cardiac function was normal. CONCLUSION: Normal imaging of the heart.

---

50. NUCLEAR MEDICINE: WHOLE BODY BONE AND JOINT SCAN: Uptake was noted in the nasal area of the sphenoid sinuses. The remainder of the scan is normal. No masses, bony abnormalities, or metastatic disease are seen.

CPT Pathology and Laboratory

Chapter Outline

Overview of Pathology and Laboratory Section
Pathology and Laboratory Section Guidelines
Pathology and Laboratory Subsections

Chapter Objectives

At the conclusion of this chapter, the student should be able to:

- Define key terms.
- Explain the organization, format, and content of the CPT Pathology and Laboratory section.
- Interpret CPT pathology and laboratory coding guidelines and notes.
- Assign CPT pathology and laboratory codes.
- Add CPT and/or HCPCS level II modifiers to codes, as appropriate.

Key Terms

accession
adjuvant
aliquot
analyte
antibody
antigen
arterial puncture
assay
Bethesda System
block (tissue)
Chemstrip automated
 urine analyzer

chromatography
chromosomal breakage
 syndrome
Clinical Laboratory
 Improvement Act of
 1988 (CLIA)
cytogenetics
cytopathology
definitive identification
dipstick
evocative

fluorescence *in situ*
 hybridization (FISH)
Gram stain
gross examination
hematology
immunoglobulin
immunology
microbiology
microtechnique
necropsy
phlebotomy

presumptive
 identification
qualitative assay
quantitative assay
reagent strip automated
 urine analyzer
section
specimen
venipuncture

Introduction

The Pathology and Laboratory section of CPT includes subsections for organ or disease-oriented panels, drug testing, therapeutic drug assays, evocative/suppression testing, consultations (clinical pathology), urinalysis, chemistry, hematology and coagulation, immunology, transfusion medicine, microbiology, anatomic pathology, cytopathology, cytogenetic studies, surgical pathology, transcutaneous procedures, reproductive medicine procedures, and other procedures.

Overview of Pathology and Laboratory Section

CPT pathology and laboratory codes describe services performed on specimens (e.g., body fluids, tissue or cytological specimens) to evaluate, prevent, diagnose, or treat a disease. A **specimen** is tissue submitted for laboratory or pathological evaluation (e.g., blood, urine, tissue from an organ). Examinations are the following:

- Biophysical
- Chemical
- Cytological
- Hematological

- Immunohematological
- Microbiological
- Pathological
- Serological

> **EXAMPLE:** A wound culture is obtained from the smear of an infected area. The infective organism is identified as the result of growing the organism on a culture plate and microscopically reviewing the specimen or serologically testing the organism (e.g., antistreptolysin O titer).

Most clinical laboratory service codes include a technical component; however, some include both a technical and a professional component. In addition, because many pathology and pathology procedures can be performed using different methods, patient record documentation must be reviewed along with code descriptions and instructional notes.

Note:

Hospitals include pathology and laboratory codes on a chargemaster, which is used to report services (and supplies) for inpatients, outpatients, and emergency department patients. Coders do not assign codes to pathology and laboratory procedures that are performed on an inpatient basis because such services do not impact diagnosis-related group (DRG) assignment and facility reimbursement.

Note:

Depending on the contract negotiated between pathologists and the health care facility:

- Pathologists are considered employees of the health care facility (e.g., a hospital) or they are considered contractors.

- Facility submits claims to obtain reimbursement for all services provided to patients (including professional services) *or* the pathologists use a medical billing service to submit claims for professional services.

Specimen Collection

Laboratory codes describe the *performance* of lab tests. These codes do not include *collection of the specimen* (e.g., venipuncture, fingerstick, or lumbar puncture) used to perform the test. For safety purposes, after venipuncture, the used needle is placed in an approved *sharps container* made of hard, damage-resistant plastic (Figure 17-1).

For laboratory-testing purposes, a specimen includes tissue (e.g., blood and urine) that is submitted for individual and separate examinations and/or pathological diagnosis. Specimen collection is reported separately, in

© Cengage Learning 2014

Figure 17-1 Sharps containers

addition to the laboratory test performed. Collection methods vary from those requiring no patient preparation to invasive-type procedures, and the reason for the test typically determines the appropriate collection method. Special collection methods (e.g., urethral catheterization or suprapubic aspiration) are indicated when a specimen cannot be obtained by more common techniques.

EXAMPLE: With an indwelling urinary catheter in place, a specimen is obtained by inserting the needle into the catheter. The urine is aspirated and placed in a sterile urine container for laboratory testing.

Venipuncture, or **phlebotomy,** (36400–36425) is the puncture of a vein using a needle for the purpose of drawing blood, and it is the most common method of collecting blood specimens. **Arterial puncture** (36600) is the puncture of an artery using a needle for the purpose of drawing blood.

A code from range 36400–36410 is reported when a routine venipuncture (which is typically performed by a nurse or a phlebotomist) is unsuccessful and the skill of the physician is required to perform the procedure. It is not appropriate to report a code from range 36400–36410 when a physician performs venipuncture for patient convenience or because the nurse or phlebotomist is unavailable to perform the service. (A routine venipuncture is reported with code 36415.)

Coding Tip:

The following CPT codes are reported for routine venipuncture under the outpatient prospective payment system (OPPS):

• Collection of venous blood by venipuncture (36415)

• Collection of capillary blood specimen (e.g., finger-, heel-, or ear-stick) (36416)

The venipuncture code is reported just once per encounter for each type of specimen, regardless of the number of specimens drawn. (HCPCS level II code G0001 was deleted effective January 1, 2005.)

Professional and Technical Components

Certain laboratory procedures contain both a professional (e.g., physician) component and a technical component. The technical component of a laboratory procedure or service includes, but is not limited to, the cost of equipment, supplies, and technician salaries. (CPT guidelines do not address reporting the technical component of a pathology and laboratory procedure or service.)

Coding Tip:

When a pathology and laboratory procedure or service code description includes both the technical and the professional component, and one of the components was not performed, report the appropriate code with modifier:

- -26, to indicate that only the professional component was performed.
- -TC to indicate that only the technical component was performed.

Pathologists often oversee the clinical laboratory and assume overall responsibility for test results. When reporting codes for professional and technical components of clinical laboratory services, standard practice is for the pathologist to report the professional component of clinical laboratory services. Clinical pathology professional services include the following:

- Directing and evaluating quality assurance and control procedures (e.g., ensuring that tests and procedures are properly performed, recorded, and reported; validating test methodologies)

- Supervising laboratory technicians

- Recommending follow-up diagnostic tests, when appropriate

The hospital reports the technical component, which represents the hospital's costs (e.g., laboratory equipment, supplies, and nonphysician personnel). The hospital's technical component does *not* include the pathologist's professional services.

Pathology and laboratory services can be provided by a physician or by technologists under the supervision of a physician. Although most codes describe clinical laboratory tests, physician laboratory and pathology services are also included. Physician laboratory and pathology services include the following:

- Surgical pathology services

- Cytopathology, hematology, and blood-banking services that require a physician

- Clinical consultation services

- Clinical laboratory interpretation services

Typically, pathology and laboratory specimens are prepared by laboratory personnel with a pathologist assuming responsibility for the integrity of the results. Certain tests are personally reviewed by the pathologist. Very few CPT pathology and laboratory codes require patient contact; however, occasionally a pathologist provides evaluation and management services. Such services are reported with appropriate CPT evaluation and management codes.

Clinical Laboratory Improvement Act of 1988 (CLIA)

To perform certain pathology and laboratory tests (and to submit claims to Medicare and Medicaid), physician office labs must obtain certification under the **Clinical Laboratory Improvement Act of 1988 (CLIA)**. A waiver is available for small office labs that perform only basic testing (e.g., urine dipsticks and fingerstick glucose testing), and a special CLIA waiver number is assigned to these labs. The list of approved tests is updated periodically, which means that physician office labs must determine if they still qualify for a waiver.

Note:

Most laboratory services reported with CPT codes are paid by Medicare according to the laboratory fee schedule, which is discussed in Chapter 19.

Coding Tip:

Modifier -90, Reference (Outside) Laboratory, is reported to indicate that an outside laboratory performed the service. This modifier is often added to pathology and laboratory codes to indicate that the physician did not perform the actual test, but instead sent the specimen to an outside laboratory.

Coding Tip:

When reporting CLIA waived services to Medicare or Medicaid, add HCPCS level II modifier -QW to pathology and laboratory codes.

National Coverage Determinations (NCDs)

The Centers for Medicare and Medicaid Services (CMS) developed National Coverage -Determinations (NCDs), which define coverage for services and procedures. Medicare administrative contractors apply national coverage determinations nationwide, and local coverage decisions (LCDs, previously called LMRPs) supplement the NCDs. As of 2002, CMS had issued more than 20 national coverage decisions regarding pathology and laboratory services (e.g., complete blood counts and tumor antigens), which include lists of covered and noncovered diagnoses. Pathology and laboratory NCDs were developed to:

- Simplify administrative requirements for clinical diagnostic services.

- Promote national uniformity in processing medicare claims.

Exercise 17.1 – Overview of Pathology and Laboratory Section

Instructions: Complete each statement.

1. Although most clinical laboratory service codes include a technical component, some include both a technical and a(n) _____ component.

2. Review of patient record documentation is necessary before assigning pathology and laboratory codes because many procedures can be performed using different _____.

3. Hospital coders usually do not assign pathology and laboratory codes because they are included on a(n) _____, which is used by providers to select services provided to patients.

4. CPT laboratory codes describe the performance of lab tests, and they do not include collection of the _____, which is performed using different methods (e.g., venipuncture, fingerstick, or lumbar puncture) and is reported separately.

5. The puncture of a vein using a needle for the purpose of drawing blood as a common method of collecting blood specimens is called venipuncture, or _____.

6. A routine venipuncture (usually performed by a nurse) is assigned code _____, and it is reported in addition to the laboratory procedure code.

7. When a physician's skill is required to perform the procedure, a code from range _____ is assigned.

8. When a pathology and laboratory procedure code description includes technical and professional components, and both components were not performed, modifier _____ is added to the code to indicate that only the professional component was performed.

9. When an outside laboratory performs pathology and laboratory services, add modifier _____ to the reported code.

10. To perform certain pathology and laboratory tests (and to submit claims to Medicare and Medicaid), physician office labs must obtain certification under the _____.

Pathology and Laboratory Section Guidelines

Guidelines located at the beginning of the Pathology and Laboratory section provide instruction about the following:

- Services in pathology and laboratory
- Separate or multiple procedures
- Unlisted services or procedures
- Special reports

Services in Pathology and Laboratory

Pathology and laboratory services are provided by a physician (e.g., a pathologist) or by technologists under responsible supervision of a physician. The unit of pathology service is a *specimen,* which is tissue that is submitted for individual and separate examination and pathological diagnosis. When multiple specimens are received for pathological examination, each specimen is considered a single unit of service and each is reported with a separate code.

> **EXAMPLE 1:** Two separately identified skin lesions are submitted for individual examination and diagnosis. Report codes 88305 and 88305-59 (Skin, Other than Cyst/Tag/Debridement/Plastic Repair). (Modifier -59 is added to indicate that the second lesion was evaluated as a "distinct procedural service.")

> **EXAMPLE 2:** The uterus (with or without tubes and ovaries) is considered one specimen and is reported with code 88305 (when the uterus is removed for prolapse and shows no other abnormalities), 88309 (for neoplasia), or 88307 (for other conditions).

> **EXAMPLE 3:** A cell block prepared from cytology fluids, bone marrow aspirates, or fine-needle aspirates is coded as 88305 (Cell block, any source).

> (A **block** is a portion of tissue obtained from a specimen that is placed in a support medium, such as paraffin. A **section** is a thin slice of tissue prepared from a block that is examined.)

Separate or Multiple Procedures

It is appropriate to separately code and report multiple pathology and laboratory procedures that are provided on the same date of service. However, it is *not* appropriate to report tests that are repeated simply to confirm initial results (because of an equipment malfunction or technician error) or when a series of tests is performed (e.g., glucose tolerance tests). These services are considered part of the originally ordered test, and codes for repeated tests are not separately coded and reported.

> **EXAMPLE:** A manual platelet count (85032) was performed in addition to an automated hemogram with automated platelet count (85027). Do not report both codes 85032 and 85027 because one serves as a confirmatory test for the other. Report either code 85032 or 85027, depending on the test ordered by the physician.

Unlisted Service or Procedure

A service or procedure that is provided for which there is no CPT code is reported with an "unlisted service or procedure" code. Pathology and laboratory unlisted service and procedure codes include the following:

- Unlisted urinalysis procedure (81099)

- Unlisted chemistry procedure (84999)

- Unlisted hematology and coagulation procedure (85999)

- Unlisted antigen, each (86486)

- Unlisted immunology procedure (86849)

- Unlisted transfusion medicine procedure (86999)

- Unlisted microbiology procedure (87999)

- Unlisted necropsy (autopsy) procedure (88099)

- Unlisted cytopathology procedure (88199)

- Unlisted cytogenetic study (88299)

- Unlisted surgical pathology procedure (88399)

- Unlisted miscellaneous pathology test (89240)

- Unlisted reproductive medical laboratory procedure (89398)

Special Report

When an unlisted procedure or service code is reported on a claim, a "special report" is attached to the submitted claim to clarify the service or procedure performed. A service or procedure that is rarely performed, unusual, variable, or new may require a special report to be submitted so the third-party payer can determine the medical appropriateness of the service or procedure. The special report should include a description of the nature, extent, and need for the procedure. In addition, the following items may be included:

- Complexity of symptoms

- Final diagnosis

- Pertinent physical findings

- Diagnostic and therapeutic procedures

- Concurrent problems

- Follow-up care

Modifier -51 and Modifier -91

- Modifier -51 (Multiple Procedures) is *not* added to pathology and laboratory codes.

- Modifier -91 (Repeat Clinical Diagnostic Laboratory Test) is added to pathology and laboratory codes when procedures or services are repeated on the same date of service to obtain multiple results.

  EXAMPLE: A patient undergoes a comprehensive metabolic panel laboratory test (80053). Because of abnormal blood urea nitrogen (BUN) test results, the patient undergoes a repeat BUN test as an individual test (84520). Report codes 80053 and 84520-91.

Exercise 17.2 – Pathology and Laboratory Section Guidelines

Instructions: Complete each statement.

1. The unit of pathology service is a(n) _____, which is tissue submitted for individual and separate examination and pathological diagnosis.

2. During the same operative session, the surgeon submitted "incidental appendix" tissue and a section of fallopian tube (as the result of a sterilization procedure) for pathological evaluation. Refer to the notes located below the Surgical Pathology subsection (codes 88300–88399) to determine whether one or two codes are reported. Code 88302 is reported _____ (once/twice).

3. It is appropriate to separately code and report multiple pathology and laboratory procedures that are provided on the same _____.

4. A service or procedure that is provided for which there is no CPT code is reported with a(n) _____ code, and a(n) _____ is attached to the submitted claim.

5. When procedures or services are repeated on the same date of service to obtain multiple results, add modifier _____ to the reported pathology and laboratory code(s). It is *not* appropriate to add modifier _____ to pathology and laboratory codes.

Pathology and Laboratory Subsections

The Pathology and Laboratory section is organized according to type of procedure performed. Pathology and laboratory procedures are listed alphabetically within each subsection, which include the following:

- Organ or disease-oriented panels
- Drug testing
- Therapeutic drug assays
- Evocative/suppression testing
- Consultations (clinical pathology)
- Urinalysis
- Molecular pathology
- Chemistry
- Hematology and coagulation
- Immunology

- Transfusion medicine
- Microbiology
- Anatomic pathology
- Cytopathology
- Cytogenetic studies
- Surgical pathology
- In vivo laboratory procedures
- Other procedures
- Reproductive medicine procedures

Organ or Disease-Oriented Panels

Organ or disease-oriented panels subsection codes are reported for a defined group of tests, administered for a certain purpose. The panels were developed for coding purposes only and are not considered clinical parameters. The tests listed below each panel identify the components of that panel.

To report an organ or disease-oriented panel code, all tests listed below the panel must be performed. No substitutions can be made.

EXAMPLE: Patient underwent a general health panel (80050). A general health panel must include all of the following procedures:

- Comprehensive metabolic panel (80053)
- Blood count, complete (CBC); automated and automated differential WBC count (85025 or 85027 and 85004) *or* CBC; automated (85027) and appropriate manual differential WBC count (85007 or 85009)
- Thyroid-stimulating hormone (TSH) (84443)

These individual procedure codes are *not* reported in addition to general health panel code 80050.

When only one or several of the tests associated with a panel are performed, do not report the panel code. Instead, report codes for each individual test performed. When additional tests are performed in addition to those listed below the panel, separately code and report the additional tests (in addition to the panel code).

EXAMPLE 1: Patient underwent a glucose test and a sodium test. Report codes 82947 and 84295. (Do *not* report basic metabolic panel code 80048.)

EXAMPLE 2: Patient underwent a basic metabolic panel test and an albumin test. Report codes 80048 and 82040.

The comprehensive metabolic panel (80053) does not include the direct bilirubin test (82248) because code 80053 is reported for an incomplete survey of multiple organ systems. The total bilirubin test (82247) is included in the comprehensive metabolic panel (80053) because it indicates a wider range of pathologic conditions than a direct bilirubin test.

Drug Testing and Therapeutic Drug Assays

CPT codes reported for drug testing are located in three subsections of pathology and laboratory:

- Drug testing (80100–80104)
- Therapeutic drug assays (80150–80299)
- Chemistry (82000–84999)

An **assay** (e.g., lab test) is the measurement of the amount of a constituent in a specimen. **Qualitative assays** (which detect whether a particular substance is present) are reported with drug-testing codes. **Quantitative assays** (which detect the amount of a substance in a specimen) are reported with therapeutic drug assay or chemistry codes.

Drug testing codes distinguish between drug screens (80100, 80101) and drug confirmation (80102). Drug screen tests are further differentiated according to the method used to analyze multiple drug classes (80100) or a single drug class (80101). The codes are intended to distinguish among drug analysis methods.

EXAMPLE: Patient underwent screening for three drugs by chromatography method, which required one stationary phase and three mobile phases. Report codes 80100, 80100, 80100. (**Chromatography** is the separation of chemical substances by differential absorption into a moving, two-phase system; in gas-liquid chromatography, gaseous substances are separated by moving through a liquid.)

If the three drugs were detected using a single analysis of one stationary phase with one mobile phase, code 80100 is reported only once.

For code 80101, each single drug class method tested and reported is counted as one drug class. Immunoassays used to identify single drug classes are coded as 80101 (e.g., drug screening) regardless of whether the test is performed using a single analysis test kit or a multiple analysis test kit.

EXAMPLE: Patient underwent testing of a sample, and a rapid assay kit was used. The single kit consisted of five class-specific immunoassays, and the five classes were reported separately. Report codes 80101, 80101, 80101, 80101, 80101.

Code 80102 is reported for each drug confirmation procedure. Each combination of stationary phase and mobile phase is counted as one procedure.

EXAMPLE: Patient underwent confirmation of three drugs by chromatography, which required one stationary phase with three mobile phases. Report codes 80102, 80102, 80102.

If multiple drugs were confirmed using a single analysis method, such as one stationary phase with one mobile phase, code 80102 is reported only once.

Quantitative assays are reported with an appropriate code from the therapeutic drug assay subsection (80150–80299) or chemistry subsection (82000–84999). Quantitative drug testing specified by a method other than chromatography is reported with 80299 (Quantitation of drug, not elsewhere specified).

Evocative/Suppression Testing

Evocative/suppression test panels (80400–80440) include the administration of evocative or suppressive agents and the baseline and subsequent measurement of their effect on chemical constituents. These codes are reported for the laboratory component of the testing protocol. (**Evocative** means to cause a specific response; this term is used to describe various tests intended to cause production of hormones or other secretions.)

Coding Tip:

- To report supplies and drugs, refer to code 99070 or HCPCS level II codes.
- Report physician attendance and monitoring during evocative or suppressive agents tests with appropriate evaluation and management (E/M) codes. Prolonged physician care may also be reported separately with appropriate E/M codes, except when codes 96360 and 96361 are reported.

Consultations (Clinical Pathology)

The physician (e.g., the pathologist) review of laboratory test results is typically considered a non-face-to-face service, and the review of laboratory results is not a separately reportable service. However, when a patient's attending physician requests that a pathologist provide consultation services regarding pathology and/or laboratory test results, clinical pathology consultation codes are reported (80500–80502). The clinical pathology consultation requires:

- Additional medical interpretative judgment.
- Preparation of a written report.

Codes 80500 and 80502 are differentiated according to whether a review of the patient's history and medical records was performed as part of the clinical pathology consultation service.

> **EXAMPLE:** A surgeon orders a clinical pathology consultation to determine a patient's suitability for surgery based on the results of clinical laboratory tests. The pathologist documents a written consultation report that includes a review of patient records, including the patient's history and current laboratory results, and medical judgment about the patient's candidacy for surgery. The pathologist provided limited clinical pathology consultation services, which did not require a review of the patient's history or medical records. Report code 80500.

A pathologist who provides a clinical pathology consultation service (which includes examination of the patient) reports an appropriate evaluation and management code (e.g., outpatient, inpatient, or consultation). The pathologist is responsible for ensuring that the criteria for reporting the evaluation and management code has been met and a report has been appropriately documented in the medical record.

Clinical pathology consultation services are performed:

- At the request of another physician when test result(s) require additional medical interpretation.
- When material (e.g., tissue slides) are referred by another pathologist or facility.

Note:

A physician (e.g., a pathologist) who reports test results but who does not provide medical interpretive judgment has not provided clinical pathology consultation services.

Urinalysis

Most urine tests are performed to diagnose or monitor renal or urinary tract disease. Urine testing is easily performed and does not require an invasive skin puncture. Urine collection containers (Figure 17-2) used for routine urinalysis are made of material that is clear (translucent), and they contain lids that can be secured to prevent spills during transport. For example, protein in the urine may indicate glomerulonephritis, and urine cultures monitor the effectiveness of antibiotic treatment for urinary tract infections.

Codes 81000–81099 are reported for the analysis of one or more components of the urine. The reported code is based on method (e.g., dipstick), purpose (e.g., a pregnancy test), or element evaluated (e.g., bilirubin, bacteriuria screen).

Quantitative urine tests often require a timed collection. Timed urine collection is often performed because substances (e.g., hormones, proteins, and electrolytes) are excreted over a 24-hour period. Because exercise, hydration, and body metabolism affect excretion rates, these time periods may range anywhere from 2 to 24 hours.

A **reagent strip automated urine analyzer** (or **Chemstrip automated urine analyzer**) (Figure 17-3) is used to determine various components in the urine (including glucose, albumin,

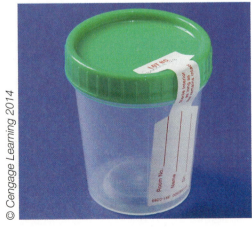

© Cengage Learning 2014

Figure 17-2 Urine collection container

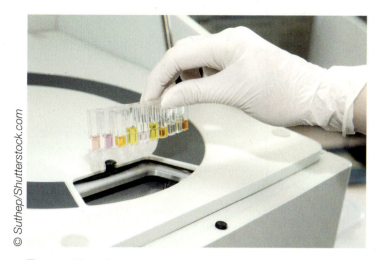

Figure 17-3 Chemstrip automated urine analyzer

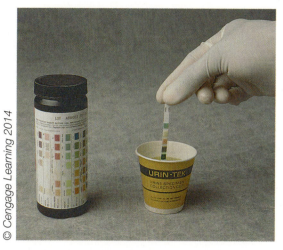

Figure 17-4 Dipstick used for routine urinalysis

hemoglobin, and bile concentrations, as well as urinary pH, specific gravity, protein, ketone bodies, nitrites, and leukocyte esterase). A **dipstick** (Figure 17-4) is a small strip of plastic that is infused with a chemical that reacts to products in urine by changing color. It is considered preliminary and may be performed for screening purposes.

The appropriate handling and storage of urine is necessary to prevent changes that adversely impact accurate results. Many **analytes** (substance or chemical compound undergoing analysis) require the use of preservatives so that they remain viable during the collection period. The choice of preservative depends on the type of collection. For example, sodium fluoride is used to preserve glucose in a 24-hour urine collection.

> **Coding Tip:**
>
> Analysis of urine is also classified in other pathology and laboratory subsections. For example, a urine chloride test is reported with code 82436 from the Chemistry subsection.

EXAMPLE: Nonautomated urinalysis by dipstick, without microscopy. Report code 81002.

Molecular Pathology

Molecular pathology laboratory procedures involve the analysis of nucleic acid to detect gene variants, which may be indicative of certain conditions (e.g., constitutional disorders, neoplasia, histocompatibility enzymes). Codes are organized as Tier 1 and Tier 2 molecular pathology laboratory procedures. CPT incorporates the Human Genome Organization–approved gene names in code descriptions along with proteins or diseases associated with the genes. Molecular pathology notes indicate that any procedures performed prior to cell lysis, such as microdissection, are to be reported separately, and an extensive list of definitions is also included.

- Tier 1 molecular pathology laboratory codes are assigned for gene-specific and genomic procedures according to the *analyte* (substance or chemical compound undergoing analysis) or the *allele* (genetic variants).

- Tier 2 codes are assigned for procedures not listed in Tier 1, and they are classified according to level of technical resources and interpretive professional work required. (Tier 2 procedures are performed less frequently than are Tier 1 procedures.)

- If a tested analyte or allele is not represented by a Tier 1 code or the technical resources/interpretive professional work is not

> **Coding Tip:**
>
> When tests require that a physician or other qualified health care professional interpret the results, and the provider performs the interpretation only, add modifier -26 (professional component) to the code.

described in a Tier 2 code, report an appropriate methodology code (codes 83890–83914 and 88384–88386).

EXAMPLE: Patient underwent the *BRCA1* and *BRCA2* gene analysis laboratory procedure to determine her risk for hereditary breast and ovarian cancer. Report code 81211.

Chemistry

Chemistry codes (82000–84999) are reported for quantitative tests unless the code description indicates otherwise (e.g., chromatography codes, 82486–82489). Qualitative tests are reported with the four drug testing codes, 80100–80103. Chemical tests performed on body materials are obtained from any source (e.g., blood or urine) unless the code description specifies otherwise. Codes in the chemistry subsection are listed in alphabetical order.

To properly assign codes from the Chemistry subsection, locate the code that describes the analyte to be tested (the specific substance to be analyzed).

- When a chemistry test is performed on multiple specimens from different sources, or on specimens that are obtained at different times, the analyte is reported separately for *each* source and for *each* specimen.

- When a code describes a method where measurement of multiple analytes may require several procedures, each procedure is coded separately (82491–82492, 82541–82544).

  ○ If two analytes are measured using a single stationary or mobile phase, report code 82492.

  ○ If the same two analytes are measured using different stationary or mobile phase conditions, report code 82491 twice.

  ○ If two analytes are measured with a single stationary and mobile phase, and two other analytes are measured using a different stationary and mobile phase, report code 82492 twice.

  ○ If two analytes are measured using a single stationary or mobile phase condition, and a third analyte is measured separately using a different stationary or mobile phase procedure, report code 82492 once for the two analytes measured under the same condition, and report code 82491 once for the third analyte measured separately.

EXAMPLE: Patient underwent two lab tests to determine total bilirubin levels. A specimen was obtained during the morning and afternoon on April 5. Report codes 82247 and 82247-91.

Stool includes waste products of digested food bile, mucus, epithelial cells, and bacteria. Stool studies are performed to evaluate bowel function (e.g., for intestinal bleeding, infections, infestations, inflammation, malabsorption, and diarrhea).

EXAMPLE: Patient underwent occult blood testing by peroxidase activity, qualitative, feces, single specimen. Report code 82272.

Body fluids can be tested for blood urea nitrogen (BUN) and creatinine to determine whether the fluid is urine. For example, code 84560 is reported for uric acid testing, other source, which is helpful in obstetrics to differentiate amniotic fluid from urine.

Hematology and Coagulation

Hematology is the study of the function and disorders of blood (Figure 17-5). *Coagulation* is the process of blood clotting. Hematology and coagulation codes (85002–85999) are reported for laboratory tests performed to evaluate blood and blood clotting, such as CBC, clotting factor tests, clotting inhibitor tests, and prothrombin and thrombin time. Bone marrow, smear interpretation (85097) is also classified in the Hematology and Coagulation subsection. However, bone marrow biopsy and cell block interpretations are reported with code 88305.

Platelet count codes are integrated into the blood count series of codes (85004–85049).

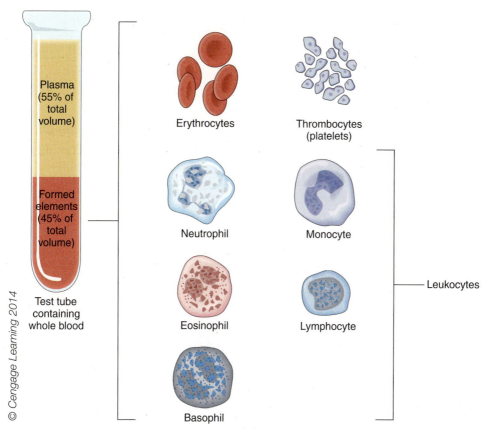

Figure 17-5 Blood components

- Platelet estimation is reported with code 85007 or 85008, depending on whether a manual differential WBC count was performed.

- Code 85041 describes an automated red blood cell count, and it is *not* reported in addition to codes 85025 or 85027 (because those codes include an automated red blood cell count).

- Code 85045 describes an automated reticulocyte count.

- Code 85048 is reported for an automated WBC count.

- Code 85049 describes an automated platelet count, and code 85032 describes a manual platelet count.

Codes 85007–85009 reflect current manual microscopic review of peripheral blood, and code 85007 also describes the microscopic examination of a blood smear with a manual differential leukocyte (WBC) count. Code 85008 describes a microscopic blood smear examination *without* a manual differential WBC count.

Code 85025 (automated CBC and automated differential WBC count) is reported when blood is tested to determine the following levels:

- Hemoglobin (Hgb)
- Hematocrit (Hct)
- Red blood cell (RBC)
- White blood cell (WBC)
- Platelet

The automated differential WBC count determines the number of basophils, eosinophils, monocytes, lymphocyte, and neutrophils. (When a manual cell count of erythrocytes, leukocytes, or platelets is performed, report code 85032 for *each*.)

EXAMPLE: Patient underwent manual CBC to determine Hct, Hgb, RBC, and WBC levels. Report codes 85014, 85018, 85032, and 85032-59. (Code 85032 is reported twice to reflect erythrocyte and leukocyte testing.)

To report an automated CBC with a manual differential WBC count, report code 85027 with either code 85007 or 85009.

EXAMPLE: Patient underwent an automated CBC and an automated differential WBC count. Report code 85025 *or* codes 85027 and 85004, depending on the laboratory's processing of the WBC differential.

Codes 85378–85380 differentiate specific methodologies for measuring D-dimer, based on the sensitivity of the analysis:

- Qualitative or semiquantitative (85378)

- Quantitative (85379)

- Ultrasensitive (85380)

A parenthetical note below code 85379 provides instruction to report that code for ultrasensitive and standard sensitivity *quantitative* D-dimer tests. CPT code 85380 is reported for ultrasensitive qualitative and semiquantitative D-dimer tests.

EXAMPLE: Patient underwent qualitative D-dimer test. Report code 85378.

Immunology

Immunology is the study of the immune system. Immunology codes classify antigen and antibody laboratory studies (86000–86804) and tissue typing (86805–86849). Antigen and antibody studies measure the reaction of:

- **Antigens** (Ag): Foreign substances that elicit the formation of antibodies.

- **Antibodies** (Ab): Proteins in the body made by the immune system that fight infection and disease.

(An **adjuvant** is a substance administered with an antigen that enhances the response to the antigen.) Figure 17-6 contains a serological centrifuge, which is used to spin test tubes of blood to test for agglutination reactions (clumping of blood cells). Hemagglutination (agglutination of red blood cells) is a method used to visualize antigen–antibody reactions.

EXAMPLE: Patient underwent HIV-1 antibody test to determine exposure to human immunodeficiency virus and subsequent antibody development. Report code 86701.

Immunoglobulins are proteins produced by plasma cells that help fight infection. Some immunoglobulins (e.g., gamma globulins) are involved in immune responses to bacteria or foreign substances (e.g., allergens or transplanted tissue). Immunoglobulins include IgA, IgD, IgE, IgG, and IgM. Two codes are reported for the quantitative and qualitative measurement of IgE:

- Quantitative or semiquantitative allergen-specific IgE (86003)

- Qualitative allergen-specific multiallergen screen (using a dipstick, paddle, or disc) (86005)

EXAMPLE: Patient underwent quantitative allergen-specific IgE testing, 5 allergens. Report code 86003 five times.

Tumor antigen codes are reported to indicate the presence of a tumor marker in the patient's blood.

EXAMPLE: Patient with previously treated stage II and stage III breast cancer underwent immunoassay for tumor antigen 125 to test for recurrence of breast cancer. Report code 86304.

Codes 86602–86804 are reported for laboratory tests performed to identify specific antibodies. Such tests are performed using a multistep method. Codes for tissue typing (86805–86849) describe procedures performed to determine compatibility between a recipient and donors for organ or bone marrow transplants.

EXAMPLE: Patient underwent HLA typing of a single antigen (A). Report code 86812. (HLA is the abbreviation for human leukocyte antigen, which determines graft acceptance.)

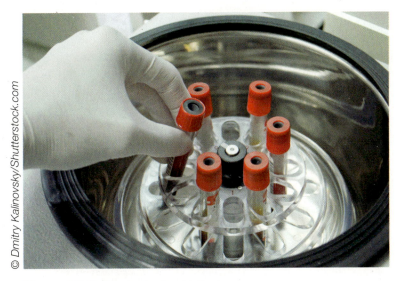

Figure 17-6 Serological centrifuge

Transfusion Medicine

Transfusion medicine codes (86850–86999) are often reported by blood banks, and they describe blood preparation services for transfusion. For transfusion services, report the appropriate CPT code as well as a HCPCS level II code for the blood product transfused. (The service code is reported with the date of service for the transfusion, not the date the blood was collected.) When autologous blood is collected but not transfused, report code 86890 or code 86891 with the number of units collected but not transfused.

Coding Tip:

Codes 86850–86870 are classified according to:

- Technique
- Elution
- Panel

Coding Tip:

- Do not assign a CPT code for freezing and/or thawing if a HCPCS level II code is available that specifies whether the type of blood product is frozen and/or thawed (e.g., P9054).
- When a HCPCS level II code is unavailable for specified types of frozen/thawed products (e.g., P9035), report a HCPCS level II code for the blood product and a CPT code for the freezing and/or thawing services (e.g., 86932). In addition, assign a CPT code for the transfusion service.

To report the collection, modification, treatment, and processing of autologous blood specimens for transplantation, report code 86890 or code 86891. When processing and storage costs are incurred for unused blood or blood products, the provider may submit charges when patient-specific preparation was done (e.g., blood typing and cross-matching).

EXAMPLE: Patient underwent transfusion of one unit of frozen blood, which included freezing (and preparation) as well as -thawing. Report code 86932. (If the type of blood product had been stated in the example, such as plasma, report more specific HCPCS level II code P9017 instead of unspecified CPT code 86932.)

Microbiology

Microbiology is the study of microbes (e.g., bacteria, parasites, and viruses). Microbiology codes (87001–87999) include bacteriology, mycology, parasitology, and virology, and the codes are intended to describe primary definitive (or final) bacterial cultures. To properly assign microbiology codes, determine the following:

- Source
- Handling method
- Stains performed
- Identification technique used

Note:

A transfusion APC (ambulatory payment classification) payment is paid just once per day regardless of the number of units or different types of products transfused when reporting codes for a health care facility (e.g., acute care hospital).

It is appropriate to separately report multiple procedures when various microbiology testing procedures are performed.

Microscopic examinations evaluate cytologic specimens to identify bacteria and other infecting organisms (e.g., determining hormone receptor assay results, chromatin identification, culture and sensitivity testing). Microbiology subsection notes provide instruction about the presumptive -identification of microorganisms and definitive identification.

- **Presumptive identification** is the identification by colony morphology, growth on selective media, Gram stains, or up to three tests (e.g., catalase, oxidase, indole, or urease).

- **Definitive identification** of microorganisms is the identification to the genus or species level that requires additional tests (e.g., biochemical panels or slide cultures). The word "definitive" refers to the final culture that identifies the organism. Reporting these codes indicates that a specific organism genus or group (e.g., *Staphylococcus, Salmonella,* or *Streptococcus*) has been identified.

When additional studies involve molecular probes, chromatography, or immunologic techniques, report the codes separately in addition to definitive identification codes (87140–87158). For multiple specimens/sites, add modifier -59 to the microbiology code. For repeat laboratory tests performed on the same day, add modifier -91 to the microbiology code.

A **Gram stain** is a method of classifying all bacteria as gram positive or gram negative. The shape of the organism (e.g., spherical or rod-shaped) may also be helpful in the identification of the infecting organism. When the Gram stain indicates Gram negative rods, the infection may be caused by *Escherichia coli*. With knowledge of Gram stain results, the physician can initiate antibiotic treatment based on the organism's identity.

EXAMPLE: A fluorescent stain for bacteria, primary source smear with interpretation, was performed. Report code 87206.

Anatomic Pathology

Anatomic pathology codes are reported for physician (pathologist) services only. Physician services involved in performing **necropsy** (autopsy) are reported with codes 88000–88099 (e.g., a postmortem examination). The codes are specific to the following:

- Portions of the body
- Gross examination
- Regional examination
- Forensic examination
- Infant/stillborn

EXAMPLE: The pathologist performed a gross and microscopic autopsy that included the brain of a stillborn infant. Report code 88029. (**Gross examination** involves visually evaluating a specimen with the naked eye.)

Cytopathology

Cytopathology is the study of diseased cells. Specimen cells are typically obtained using brushing, washing, needle biopsy, or fine-needle aspiration. Thus, the patient record must be reviewed to -determine the collection method to correctly report cytopathology codes.

- Cervical and vaginal screening codes 88174 and 88175 describe cells collected in preservative fluid using an automated thin manual layer preparation.

- Code 88106 (Cytopathology, fluids, washings or brushings, except cervical or vaginal; filter method only with interpretation) is reported when the filter method only is used.

- CPT code 88108 (Cytopathology, concentration technique, smears and interpretation; e.g., Saccomanno technique) is reported when a concentration technique is used.

Cytopathology subsection codes are reported for various cytopathology procedures, as follows:

- Cervical or vaginal cytopathology physician interpretation (88141–88155, 88164–88167, 88174–88175)

- Cytopathological smears and cytopathology of fluids, washings or brushing from sources other than cervical or vaginal (88160–88162)

- Cytohistologic studies of fine-needle aspirate (88172–88173)

- Flow cytometry tests (88182–88189)

Coding Tip:

HCPCS level II codes are also reported for cytopathology services such as:

- Screening Papanicolaou smear, cervical or vaginal, up to three smears, by technician under physician supervision [P3000]
- Screening Papanicolaou smear, cervical or vaginal, up to three smears, requiring interpretation by physician [P3001]

Pap smear (Figure 17-7) screening and physician interpretation using different methods for -preparation, screening, and reporting are reported with cytopathology codes:

- Bethesda System of reporting (88164–88167)

- Non-Bethesda reporting (88150–88154)

- Thin-layer preparations (88142–88143)

- Automated screening with any system of reporting (88147–88148)

The **Bethesda System** is a format for reporting cervical/vaginal cytology that includes a state of specimen adequacy, the general category (e.g., if the specimen is within normal limits), and a descriptive diagnosis (e.g., benign cellular changes).

Coding Tip:

Cytopathology notes provide instruction that codes 88141 and 88155 are reported in addition to the screening code when these additional services are provided:

- Cytopathology, cervical or vaginal (any reporting system), requiring interpretation by physician [88141]
- Cytopathology, slides, cervical or vaginal, definitive hormonal evaluation (e.g., maturation index, karyopyknotic index, estrogenic index) (list separately in addition to code(s) for other technical and interpretation services) [88155]

Fine-needle aspiration cytopathology services are reported with codes 88172–88173. A parenthetical note above code 88172 provides instruction to see codes 10021 and 10022 for fine-needle *aspiration* procedures.

EXAMPLE: Cytopathology evaluation of fine-needle aspirate, interpretation, and report. Report code 88173.

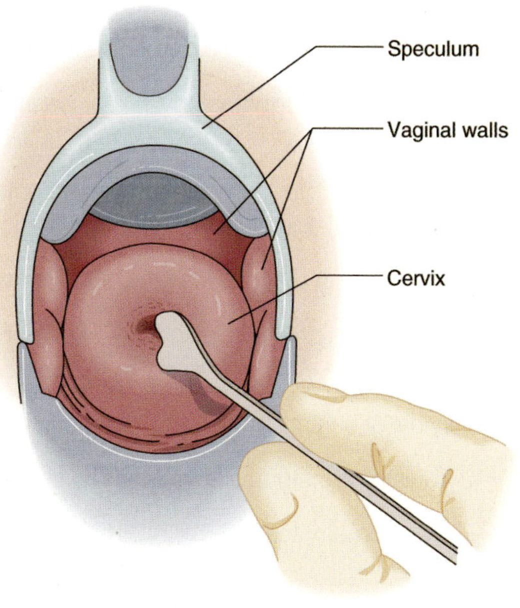
Speculum
Vaginal walls
Cervix
© Cengage Learning 2014

Figure 17-7 Performing a Pap smear

Cytogenetic Studies

Cytogenetics is the study of the cell and its heredity-related components, including chromosomes. Cytogenetic studies codes (88230–88299) are reported for tests performed to study cellular ("cyto") structure and function related to heredity ("genetics").

Cytogenetic tests are performed based on the nature of the disorder for which the patient is being tested because the cell culture and analytical standards are disease-dependent, not tissue-dependent.

EXAMPLE 1: Tissue culture for non-neoplastic disorders, lymphocyte. Report code 88230.

EXAMPLE 2: Tissue culture for neoplastic disorders, solid tumor. Report code 88239.

Cryopreservation services codes are reported for the freezing, storage, and subsequent thawing of cells, as well as the expansion of established cell lines for subsequent laboratory testing. For some testing procedures (e.g., tests for genetic disorders), the cell line is frozen to preserve the culture, and subsequent thawing must be done before an analysis can be completed. As indicated in the code descriptor, code 88240 is reported for each cell line. Code 88241 is reported separately for each aliquot because these procedures may be performed multiple times. (An **aliquot** is a portion of a specimen used for testing.)

EXAMPLE 1: Cryopreservation, freezing and storage of cells, each cell line. Report code 88240.

EXAMPLE 2: Thawing and expansion of frozen cells, each aliquot. Report code 88241.

White blood cells (e.g., T-lymphocytes) are typically used as the specimen for chromosome analysis (88245–88289).

Chromosomal breakage syndromes include genetic disorders that are usually transmitted in a genetic autosomal recessive mode. The syndromes are characterized by a defect in DNA repair mechanisms and a predisposition to cancer. Codes for chromosome analysis for breakage syndromes are classified according to the:

- Name of the specific syndrome being investigated (e.g., Fanconi anemia) (88245–88248)
- Specific technique for analysis (88249)

Codes for cytogenetic studies include a combination of codes used to describe the:

- Type of tissue cultured
- Special culture techniques or treatments of the culture
- Numbers of cells studied and analyzed
- Special analysis techniques used

Thus, submitting a claim for a single cytogenetic study typically requires reporting three or more codes.

EXAMPLE: Cytogenetic study of a standard karyotype on peripheral blood lymphocytes is reported with a code for lymphocyte culture (88230), a code for chromosome analysis counting 15 to 20 cells, two karyotypes with banding (88262), and a code to describe the physician work of interpretation and report of the cytogenetic testing performed (88291).

Molecular cytogenetics include the **fluorescence _in situ_ hybridization (FISH)** method (88271), which is performed to detect submicroscopic changes in chromosomes (e.g., genetic disorders, such as Williams syndrome) or for identification of unknown chromosomal material. Chromosomal aberrations can also be identified using FISH analyses in patients with other constitutional or acquired (e.g., neoplastic) disorders.

EXAMPLE: Molecular cytogenetics test, DNA probe (one test). Report code 88271.

Surgical Pathology

Surgical pathology codes are reported for the gross and microscopic examination of specimens submitted for pathologic evaluation (Figure 17-8). (A *specimen* is tissue submitted to the pathology department for evaluation; it is also the unit of service used to report surgical pathology codes.) Surgical pathology levels of service are determined by the following:

- Type of exam

- Type of tissue

When multiple individual tissue specimens are submitted from the same patient, a separate code is reported for each specimen.

 EXAMPLE: Two separate frozen sections of breast tissue were evaluated by the pathologist during surgery. Report codes 88331 and 88332.

Surgical pathology notes provide instruction that surgical pathology services include accession, examination, and reporting. **Accession** is the assignment of a number to record the order of tissue acquisition; an *accession number* is assigned to each pathology case (e.g., 05-00101).

Codes 88311–88365 and 88399 are reported in addition to surgical pathology codes when such services are provided.

- Codes 88311–88319 include decalcification procedures, special stains, and techniques to identify chemical components. These codes are reported in addition to codes 88300–88309.

- Code 88399 is reported for an unlisted surgical pathology procedure.

Notes also identify and define the *specimen* as the unit of service for reporting codes 88300–88309. These codes are reported according to the extent and complexity of the evaluation:

- Level I surgical pathology code 88300 is reported for any specimen the examining pathologist believes can be accurately diagnosed without microscopic examination.

Coding Tip:

Code 88291 is reported for the interpretation and report of cytogenetic and molecular cytogenetic tests. It is reported in addition to the appropriate cytogenetic testing code(s) to describe the physician work of interpretation and report of the cytogenetics and molecular cytogenetics testing performed.

Coding Tip:

Code 88300 is reported for specimens that require gross examination only.

(A)   (B)

Figure 17-8 Tissue biopsy (A) A small piece of tissue is surgically removed (B) Pathologist views tissue under microscope, looking for presence of disease

© Cengage Learning 2014

- Level II surgical pathology code 88302 is reported when gross *and* microscopic examination is performed to confirm identification of a specimen or the absence of disease.

- Level III through level VI codes 88304–88309 are reported when gross and microscopic examinations are performed, and these codes represent ascending levels of physician (pathologist) work. The codes are classified according to assigned specimens:

  ○ Uncomplicated specimen (e.g., hemorrhoids)

  ○ Single complicated specimen (e.g., kidney biopsy)

  ○ Multiple complicated specimens (e.g., breast with regional lymph nodes)

  EXAMPLE: Cervical carcinoma was diagnosed upon cervical biopsy. Patient subsequently underwent a hysterectomy. Pathologist examined the entire cervix and uterus. Code 88309 is reported whether or not residual cancer is found.

Codes 88321–88325 are reported for consultations and reports on referred slides and materials. Referred slides and materials are forwarded from an outside service (such as another facility) to the pathologist for evaluation.

Pathology consultations performed during surgery are reported with codes 88329–88334. When a section from the first block of tissue from a specimen is examined, code 88331 is reported. When sections from subsequent blocks of the same specimen are examined, report code 88332 for each section examined. When pathology consultation during surgery does not involve microscopic examination of tissue, report code 88329.

> **EXAMPLE:** A sigmoid colon biopsy is sent to the pathologist during surgery for immediate diagnosis. The pathologist examines the specimen and provides a pathological diagnosis without microscopic examination of any of the tissue. Report code 88329.

In Vivo (e.g., Transcutaneous) Laboratory Procedures

The *in vivo* (e.g., transcutaneous) procedures subsection contains codes that classify bilirubin and hemoglobin tests.

> **EXAMPLE:** Patient underwent total transcutaneous bilirubin test. Report code 88720.

Note:

A total transcutaneous bilirubin test is usually performed on newborns to diagnose jaundice, and testing is done four times a day or more to monitor the condition and determine the efficiency of therapy.

Other Procedures

The other procedures (89049–89240) subsection includes laboratory and pathology procedures that are not classified in other Pathology and Laboratory subsections.

> **EXAMPLE:** Patient underwent sweat collection via iontophoresis. Report code 89230.

Reproductive Medicine Procedures

Reproductive medicine procedures codes (89250–89398) classify new technology and evolving reproductive medical practices such as the following:

- Oocyte/embryo culture and fertilization techniques

- Oocyte/embryo biopsy techniques

- Freezing, thawing, and storage techniques

(These procedures are performed in highly specialized clinical laboratories.)

When reporting the culture and fertilization of oocytes, report the appropriate code (89250 or 89251) one time for the culture and fertilization, regardless of the number of eggs fertilized.

EXAMPLE: Patient underwent culture and fertilization of six embryos in less than four days. Report code 89250. (Code 89250 is reported just once.)

Co-culture techniques performed on tissue cultures of human embryos, oviductal, uterine, granulosa, or other cells involves the isolation of the cells, culture, plating, and the co-culture of these cells with human embryos. This procedure may involve microscopic and cytochemical examination of the culture cells to determine their viability or functionality. Code 89251 describes the work involved in culturing oocytes/embryos along with the additional work of co-culturing the embryos with feeder cells (e.g., granulosa, endometrial, and tubal). Code 89251 does *not* include the following procedures, which are reported separately when performed at the same time as culturing oocytes/embryos along with the additional work of co-culturing the embryos with feeder cells:

- Assisted embryo hatching by any method of microtechniques (89253)

- Oocyte identification from follicular fluid (89254)

- Preparation of embryo for transfer under any method (89255)

- Embryo cryopreservation (89258)

- Oocyte/embryo biopsy (89290, 89291)

The preparation of embryo for transfer, using any method, (89255) includes removing the embryo(s) from culture, preparing the embryo(s) for transfer, loading the embryo(s) into a catheter, transporting the embryo(s) to the transfer room for transfer to the patient, and examining the catheter after transfer to ensure that no embryo(s) are retained. Code 89255 does *not* include the following procedures, which are reported separately when performed at the same time as preparation of embryo for transfer, using any method:

- Intrauterine embryo transfer (58974)

- Gamete, zygote, or embryo intrafallopian transfer (58976)

- Culture of oocyte(s)/embryo(s) (89250)

- Co-culture of oocyte(s)/embryo(s) (89251)

- Extended culture (89272)

- Thawing of cryopreserved embryo(s) (89352)

- Assisted embryo hatching (89253)

However, code 89255 is reported for the preparation of either a fresh or cryopreserved embryo.

The preparation and examination of the oocyte prior to fertilization (e.g., stripping of the granulosa, cumulus oophorous, and corona radiation and verifying extrusion of the first polar body) are included in codes 89280–89281. Preparation and examination procedures are not separately coded and reported.

 Sperm identification and preparation prior to injection into the cytoplasm of the oocyte are coded and reported separately with sperm isolation and preparation codes 89260–89261, as appropriate.

Sperm identification from aspiration other than seminal fluid (89257) (e.g., from the vas deferens or epididymis) excludes identification of sperm from seminal fluid, which is described by other codes.

Code 89257 includes the work of identifying sperm and does *not* include the work of assisted oocyte fertilization by any method of microtechnique (89280–89281).

Coding Tip:

Microtechnique is one of three types of micromanipulation techniques that may be used for the preparation of an embryo for transfer. Code 89255 is reported for assisted oocyte fertilization regardless of the micromanipulation type used; there is no specific code for micromanipulation only.

Note:

Methods of assisted oocyte fertilization include the following:

- Intracytoplasmic sperm injection (ICSI)

- Subzonal insertion (SZI)

- Partial zonal dissection (PZD)

Exercise 17.3 – Pathology and Laboratory Subsections

Instructions: Assign CPT code(s) and appropriate modifier(s) to each statement.

1. Physician office lab performs a nonautomated dipstick urinalysis with microscopy.

2. Routine venipuncture. Quantitative therapeutic drugs assay to determine digoxin level.

3. Laboratory panel that includes carbon dioxide, chloride, potassium, and sodium.

4. Two separately identified basal cell carcinomas are submitted for diagnosis and evaluation of adequacy of the surgical margins. The first basal cell carcinoma specimen required frozen section from one block to confirm the adequacy of excision. The second basal cell carcinoma specimen required two frozen sections on two blocks to assure adequate excision. Surgical pathology evaluation of the two separately identified basal cell carcinomas is also performed.

5. The physician's office staff performed a urine pregnancy test using dipstick reagents that chemically react with urine. A change in color indicated positive findings and the presence of hormones found in the urine of women in early pregnancy.

6. Specimen collection via arterial puncture and blood gas determination (pH only).

7. Laboratory panel included the following tests: total calcium, carbon dioxide, chloride (blood), creatinine (blood), serum sodium, and quantitative urea nitrogen.

8. A segment of sigmoid colon with tumor was sent to the pathologist for frozen section during surgery so that immediate diagnosis could be made. The pathologist created the frozen section, examined the specimen, and rendered an intraoperative pathological diagnosis.

9. Partial thromboplastin time to measure the efficiency of plasma in forming thromboplastin. Patient has had blood clots, and this test is needed to monitor the effectiveness of anticoagulant heparin therapy. The method used was automated coagulation instrumentation.

10. Glucose screening using Dextrostix reagent strip method, capillary blood, 49-year-old patient.

11. Breast biopsy was sent to the pathologist during the operative procedure for immediate diagnosis. The pathologist examined the specimen and selected a portion to prepare as a block for frozen section, which was microscopically examined. Surgical pathology evaluation of the breast biopsy tissue was also performed, and it did not require microscopic evaluation of surgical margins.

12. Lipid panel using automated equipment was performed and included testing of HDL, total serum cholesterol, tryglycerides, and quantitative glucose.

13. General health panel and hemogram.

14. Metabolic panel using automated equipment, which included carbon dioxide, chloride, creatinine, glucose, potassium, sodium, and BUN.

   _____

15. Antibody identification test for leukocyte antibodies.

   _____

16. Pinworm exam using cellophane tape prep.

   _____

17. As the result of an appendectomy due to acute appendicitis, the appendix was sent to surgical pathology for gross and microscopic examination by the pathologist.

   _____

18. Sensitivity study using agar diffusion methodology was performed to assess whether antibiotic treatment with methicillin would be effective for a patient diagnosed with a staphylococcal B infection.

   _____

19. Collection of sweat from a patient via iontophoresis to rule out cystic fibrosis.

   _____

20. Right and left obturator lymph nodes were removed during radical prostatectomy and were submitted as separate specimens for immediate diagnosis to assess metastatic disease involvement. The pathologist examined the specimens and selected two blocks from the right specimen and three blocks from the left specimen to create frozen sections. Each frozen section was examined microscopically. Pathologist also evaluated right and left obturator lymph nodes and prostate tissue for surgical pathology.

   _____

Summary

CPT pathology and laboratory codes describe services performed on specimens (e.g., body fluids, tissue, or cytological specimens) to evaluate, prevent, diagnose, or treat a disease. Most clinical laboratory service codes include a technical component, and some include both a technical and a professional component. The Pathology and Laboratory section is organized according to type of procedure performed, and procedures are listed alphabetically within each subsection. Because many laboratory and pathology tests can be performed using different methods, patient record documentation must be reviewed along with code descriptions and instructional notes. Guidelines located at the beginning of the Pathology and Laboratory section provide instruction about services in pathology and laboratory, separate or multiple procedures, subsection information, unlisted services or procedures, and special reports.

Internet Links

Clinical Laboratory Improvement Amendments (CLIA): Go to *www.cdc.gov* and click on "C" in the A–Z index (at the top), and scroll down and click on the CLIA (Clinical Laboratory Improvement Amendments) link.

Clinical Laboratory Improvement Amendments (CLIA): Go to *www.cms.gov* and click on the Regulations and Guidance link, and then click on the Clinical Laboratory Improvement Amendments (CLIA) link.

College of American Pathologists: Go to *www.cap.org* and click on the Education Programs link to enroll (for free) and complete online pathology coding tutorials.

National Coverage Determinations for Laboratory Services: Go to *www.cms.gov* and click on the Medicare link, then scroll down and click on the Medicare Coverage—General Information link, scroll down click on the Lab NCDs link, and scroll down and click on the Index of Lab NCDs link to view all of them.

Study Checklist

- ❏ Read this chapter and highlight key concepts.
- ❏ Create an index card for each key term.
- ❏ Access the chapter Internet links to learn more about concepts.
- ❏ Complete the chapter review, verifying answers with your instructor.
- ❏ Complete WebTutor assignments and take online quizzes.
- ❏ Complete Workbook chapter, verifying answers with your instructor.
- ❏ Go to *www.cengagebrain.com* to access StudyWare™ and the Premium Website. Login instructions are located in the Preface and on the Printed Access Card.
- ❏ Form a study group with classmates to discuss chapter concepts in preparation for an exam.

Review

Multiple Choice

Instructions: Circle the most appropriate response.

1. Coders do not assign codes to pathology and laboratory procedures performed on an _____ basis because such services do not impact _____ assignment and facility reimbursement.
   - a. inpatient, diagnosis-related group (DRG)
   - b. inpatient, prospective payment system (PPS)
   - c. outpatient, diagnosis-related group (DRG)
   - d. outpatient, prospective payment system (PPS)

2. Laboratory codes (80047–87999) describe which component of lab tests?
   - a. collection
   - b. performance
   - c. performance and collection
   - d. performance, collection, and clinical consultation

3. Which modifier is added to pathology and laboratory codes when procedures or services are repeated on the same date of service to obtain multiple results?
   - a. -59
   - b. -90
   - c. -91
   - d. -QW

4. When an unlisted procedure or service code is reported on a claim, what is attached to the submitted claim to clarify the service or procedure performed?
   - a. accession code
   - b. entire patient record
   - c. special report
   - d. waiver number

5. Code(s) from the _____ subsection of Pathology and Laboratory are often reported by blood banks.
   - a. drug testing and therapeutic drug assays
   - b. hematology and coagulation
   - c. other procedures
   - d. transfusion medicine

6. Which is a substance administered with an antigen to enhance the response to the antigen?
   - a. adjuvant
   - b. aliquot
   - c. assay
   - d. specimen

7. IgA, IgD, IgE, IgG, and IgM are considered:
   - a. analytes.
   - b. antigens.
   - c. immunoglobulins.
   - d. specimens.

8. Physician attendance and monitoring during evocative or suppressive agents testing is reported with codes from the:
   a. clinical pathology consultation subsection of Pathology and Laboratory.
   b. Evaluation and Management section of CPT.
   c. Medicine section of CPT.
   d. Surgery section of CPT.

9. Which is the study of diseased cells?
   a. cytology
   b. cytopathology
   c. immunology
   d. pathology

10. Codes from the _____ subsection of Pathology and Laboratory are reported for tests performed to study cellular structure and function related to heredity.
    a. anatomic pathology
    b. cytogenetic studies
    c. cytopathology
    d. organ or disease-oriented panels

11. A patient presents with symptoms of dehydration. The physician ordered an electrolyte panel, which included carbon dioxide, chloride, potassium, and sodium. Which CPT code(s) are assigned?
    a. 80051
    b. 80051, 82374, 82435, 84132, 84295
    c. 82374, 82435, 84132, 84295
    d. 82374, 82435, 84133, 84300

12. Urinalysis. Which CPT code is assigned?
    a. 81000
    b. 81001
    c. 81002
    d. 81003

13. Qualitative fetal hemoglobin. Which CPT code is assigned?
    a. 83030
    b. 83033
    c. 83036
    d. 83045

14. Qualitative analysis of organic acids, three specimens. Which CPT code(s) are assigned?
    a. 83918, 83918, 83918
    b. 83918, 83918-91, 83918-91
    c. 83919, 83919, 83919
    d. 83919, 83919-91, 83919-91

15. Alkaline phosphatase isoenzymes. Which CPT code is assigned?
    a. 84060
    b. 84075
    c. 84078
    d. 84080

16. CBC, automated, including Hgb, Hct, RBC, WBC, and platelet count. Which CPT code(s) are assigned?
    a. 85004, 85014
    b. 85025
    c. 85027
    d. 85032

17. ABO, Rh, and MN blood typing for paternity testing. Which CPT code is assigned?
    a. 86900
    b. 86901
    c. 86905
    d. 86910

18. Thromboplastin time, partial (PTT) in plasma. Which CPT code is assigned?
    a. 85260
    b. 85347
    c. 85705
    d. 85730

19. RBC antibody screen, two different techniques. Which CPT code(s) are assigned?
    a. 86850
    b. 86850, 86850
    c. 86850, 86850-51
    d. 86850, 86850-91

20. *Chlamydia* culture. Which CPT code is assigned?
    a. 87110
    b. 87270
    c. 87487
    d. 87810

Coding Practice

Instructions: Assign CPT code(s) and appropriate modifier(s) to each case.

Pathology and Laboratory Section

21. A patient's blood is sent for the following tests: rubella antibody, Rh(D) and ABO blood typing, automated CBC and WBC, qualitative syphilis test, RBC antibody screen, and a hepatitis B surface antigen.

_____

22. A patient's blood is sent for the following tests: albumin, carbon dioxide, calcium, complete CBC, sodium, glucose, chloride, creatinine, urea nitrogen, potassium, and phosphorus inorganic.

_____

23. Urinalysis, automated with identification of sediments via microscope.

_____

24. Sperm isolation procedure including sperm wash and complete semen analysis.

_____

25. ACTH, prolactin, HGH, cortisol, TSH, LH, and FSH done using suppressive agents.

_____

26. Microorganism analysis of primary source for _Bordetella pertussis_.

_____

27. _Helicobacter pylori_ blood test.

_____

28. Blood analysis for hematocrit (Hct) level.

_____

29. Direct measurement of blood O_2 saturation level.

_____

30. Intraoperative consultation of breast tissue, single specimen; gross examination and frozen section.

_____

31. Examination of nail for the presence of fungi using KOH method.

_____

32. Testing of blood for level of TSH and T3 uptake.

_____

33. Urine sample used to perform drug screening using a chromatographic method.

_____

34. Blood test for ANA antibodies to rule out SLE.

_____

35. Gross and microscopic pathology examination of tissue taken from a patient during a radical TURP procedure.

_____

36. Shigella antibody titer testing of blood sample.

_____

37. Testing for triglyceride level.

_____

38. Blood analysis for presence of *Chlamydia* antibody.

_____

39. Gross and microscopic pathology examination of paranasal tissue taken during a biopsy.

_____

40. Prick test of skin for *candida albicans*.

_____

41. Testing of blood to determine Rh negative or Rh positive.

_____

42. Radioimmunoassay of blood for total PSA.

_____

43. T-cell count, total.

_____

44. Gross and microscopic examination of Morton's neuroma.

_____

45. CCP antibody test to rule out rheumatoid arthritis.

_____

46. Total postmortem examination of a male stillborn infant.

_____

47. Analysis of thin prep of cervical scraping specimen performed under pathologist supervision.

_____

48. Specimen of knee synovial fluid for cell count.

_____

49. Tissue culture of lymphocytes to test for Freidreich ataxia.

_____

50. Autopsy of a 45-year-old male patient's heart.

_____

CPT Medicine

Chapter Outline

Overview of Medicine Section

Medicine Section Guidelines

Medicine Subsections

Chapter Objectives

At the conclusion of this chapter, the student should be able to:

- Define key terms.
- Explain the organization, format, and content of the CPT Medicine section.
- Interpret CPT Medicine coding guidelines and notes.
- Assign CPT Medicine codes.
- Add CPT and/or HCPCS level II modifiers to codes, as appropriate.

Key Terms

adjuvant chemotherapy

allergen

allergen immunotherapy

allergy sensitivity test

autonomic function test

behavior-modifying psychotherapy

biofeedback

capitated payment method

cardiac catheterization

cardiography

central motor evoked potential study

chemotherapy

chiropractic manipulative treatment (CMT)

desensitization

determination of refractive state

dose

duplex scan

echocardiography

electrocardiography

electromyography

gamma globulin

hemodialysis

hyperventilation

immune globulin (Ig)

immune serum globulin

insight-oriented psychotherapy

interactive psychotherapy

intradermal test (intracutaneous)

intravenous push

manometry

minimally invasive procedure

multiple sleep latency

narcosynthesis

needle electromyography

noninvasive procedure

orbicularis oculi

oscilloscope

osteopathic manipulative treatment (OMT)

patch test (epicutaneous)

peritoneal dialysis

pharmacologic management

photic stimulation

physiatrist

physical medicine and rehabilitation

polysomnography

psychodynamic psychotherapy

psychosocial therapy	renal dialysis	sleep staging	talk therapy
psychotherapy	short-latency	sleep study	Tensilon test
puncture, prick, or scratch test (percutaneous)	somatosensory evoked potential study	supportive psychotherapy	visual evoked potential (VEP) test
	sleep laboratory		

Introduction

The CPT Medicine section classifies *noninvasive* or *minimally invasive* diagnostic and therapeutic procedures and services. **Noninvasive procedures** require no surgical incision or excision, and they are not open procedures. **Minimally invasive procedures** include percutaneous access. Medicine is the last section of CPT, and its codes can be reported along with those from all other sections.

Overview of Medicine Section

The Medicine section classifies procedures and services that are procedure-oriented (e.g., immunizations), that apply to various medical specialties (e.g., gastroenterology, ophthalmology, otorhinolaryngology, and psychiatry), and that apply to different types of health care providers (e.g., physical therapists and occupational therapists).

Exercise 18.1 – Overview of Medicine Section

Instructions: Complete each statement.

1. When no surgical incision or excision is required to perform a procedure, it is considered _____.
2. Percutaneous access procedures are considered _____.
3. Codes from the Medicine section _____ (can/cannot) be reported with codes from other CPT sections.
4. The Medicine section contains codes for _____ procedures and services.
5. The Medicine section classifies procedures and services that are _____, that apply to various medical specialties, and that apply to different types of health care providers.

Medicine Section Guidelines

Guidelines located at the beginning of the Medicine section provide instruction about the following:

- Add-on codes
- Separate procedures
- Unlisted service or procedure
- Special report
- Supplied materials

Instructional notes appear throughout the Medicine section to provide coding clarification and direction. Almost every Medicine subsection contains notes unique to that subsection.

Add-on Codes

Add-on codes are reported for procedures and services performed in *addition* to a *primary procedure*. They are identified in the CPT with a plus symbol (+). A parenthetical note located below an add-on code identifies the primary procedure to which an add-on code applies.

> **EXAMPLE:** A 6-year-old male patient underwent Hib booster immunization administration, which required two intramuscular injections. Report codes 90460 and 90646.

Separate Procedures

Some procedures and services classified in the Medicine section are considered an integral component of a complete procedure or service, and they are identified by the description "separate procedure." Do not report a "separate procedure" code in addition to a code for the comprehensive (or complete) procedure *unless the "separate procedure" is performed independently or is distinct from other services provided at the same time.*

When a "separate procedure" is performed independently or is distinct from other services provided at the same time, add modifier -59 (Distinct Procedural Service) to the "separate procedure" code. Modifier -59 indicates that the procedure was performed as a distinct, independent procedure.

> **EXAMPLE:** Patient underwent orthoptic training and gonioscopy. Report codes 92065 and 92020-59.

Bundled Medicine Codes

When reporting codes for outpatient hospital services and physician office services, use outpatient code editor (OCE) software or national correct coding initiative (NCCI) software to identify bundled codes for procedures and services considered necessary to accomplish the major procedure. Bundled procedure and services codes are *not* separately coded and reported with the major procedure code. Reporting the component codes in addition to the major procedure code is considered *unbundling*, which is fraud.

> **EXAMPLE:** Patient underwent a stress test. Report code 93015. (Do *not* report codes 93016, 93017, and/or 93018 with code 93015. Doing so is considered unbundling.)

Multiple Medicine Codes

When multiple procedures and/or services are performed on the same date, report a separate code for each procedure and/or service.

> **EXAMPLE:** An established patient received 60 minutes of outpatient individual psychotherapy, and after psychotherapy the psychologist prepared a mandatory progress report and submitted it to the third-party payer. Report codes 90837 and 90889.

Unlisted Service or Procedure

CPT unlisted procedure and service codes are assigned when there is no specific code that accurately describes the procedure or service performed. When reporting an unlisted procedure code to a third-party payer, submit a written report (e.g., a copy of an operative report) that describes the procedure or service performed.

Special Report

When an unlisted procedure or service code is reported to a third-party payer, a special report is submitted that describes the procedure or service performed. Special reports may also be required for procedures and services that are rarely provided or are new in order to establish that the procedure is necessary. As a minimum, documentation in a special report includes the following:

- Adequate definition or description of the nature, extent, and need for the procedure or service

- Time, effort, and equipment necessary to provide the procedure or service

The following additional items may also be documented in a special report:

- Complexity of symptoms
- Concurrent problems
- Diagnostic and therapeutic procedures
- Final diagnosis
- Follow-up care
- Pertinent physical findings

Supplied Materials

Supplies and materials provided by the physician (e.g., drugs or sterile trays) other than those typically included with a procedure or service are reported separately. Report CPT code 99070 or a specific HCPCS level II code for materials and supplies provided.

> **EXAMPLE:** Patient underwent chemotherapy administration (intramuscular) of vincristine sulfate, 1 mg. Report CPT code 96401 and HCPCS level II code J9370. (HCPCS level II code J9370 is more specific than CPT code 99070, which is a nonspecific supplies and materials code.)

Exercise 18.2 – Medicine Section Guidelines

Instructions: Complete each statement.

1. Instructional _____ appear throughout the Medicine section to provide coding clarification and direction.
2. When multiple procedures and/or services are performed on the same date, report a(n) _____ code for each procedure and/or service.
3. Add-on codes are reported for procedures and services performed in addition to a primary procedure, and they are identified in CPT with a(n) _____ symbol.
4. Some procedures and services classified in the Medicine section are considered an integral component of a complete procedure or service, and they are identified by the description _____.
5. Supplies and materials provided by the physician, other than those typically included with a procedure or service, are reported with CPT code 99070 or a specific _____ code for materials and supplies provided.

Medicine Subsections

Medicine subsections include the following:

- Immune globulins, serum or recombinant products
- Immunization administration for vaccines/toxoids
- Vaccines, toxoids
- Psychiatry
- Biofeedback
- Dialysis
- Gastroenterology
- Ophthalmology
- Special otorhinolaryngologic services
- Cardiovascular
- Noninvasive vascular diagnostic studies
- Pulmonary
- Allergy and clinical immunology
- Endocrinology
- Neurology and neuromuscular procedures
- Medical genetics and genetic counseling services
- Central nervous system assessments/tests (e.g., neurocognitive, mental status, speech testing)

- Health and behavior assessment/intervention
- Hydration, therapeutic, prophylactic, diagnostic infusions, and chemotherapy and other highly complex drug or high complex biologic agent administration
- Photodynamic therapy
- Special dermatological procedures
- Physical medicine and rehabilitation
- Medical nutrition therapy
- Acupuncture
- Osteopathic manipulative treatment
- Chiropractic manipulative treatment
- Education and training for patient self-management
- Non-face-to-face nonphysician services
- Special services, procedures, and reports
- Qualifying circumstances for anesthesia
- Moderate (conscious) sedation
- Other services and procedures
- Home health procedures/services
- Medication therapy management services

Immune Globulins, Serum or Recombinant Products

An **immune globulin (Ig)** (**gamma globulin** or **immune serum globulin**) is a sterilized solution obtained from pooled human blood plasma, which contains immunoglobulins (or antibodies) that protect against infectious agents that cause various diseases. (Antibodies are substances in blood plasma that fight infection.) Immune globulins are administered to patients who need to use someone else's antibodies to help fight off or prevent illnesses from occurring. Ig formulations produced from donors include high levels of antibodies against hepatitis B (Hepatitis B Immune Globulin-HBIG), rabies (Rabies Immune Globulin-RIG), tetanus (Tetanus Immune Globulin-TIG), and varicella (chicken pox; Varicella Zoster Immune Globulin-VZIG).

 Immune globulin codes are reported for the *supply of the immune globulin product*, which includes broad-spectrum and anti-infective immune globulins, antitoxins, and other isoantibodies. The *administration* of an immune globulin is reported separately with a code from the Therapeutic, Prophylactic, and Diagnostic Injections and Infusions subsection of the Medicine section:

Note:

The administration of an Ig provides temporary protection and is *not* considered an immunization, which provides longer-term protection.

- Intravenous infusion
- Subcutaneous infusion
- Intramuscular or subcutaneous injection
- Intravenous push

  EXAMPLE: Intramuscular injection of 250 units of human tetanus immune globulin (TIg) was administered to a patient. Report codes 90389 and 96372.

 Coding Tip:

Do not add modifier -51 (Multiple Procedures) to immune globulin codes (90281–90399).

Immunization Administration for Vaccines/Toxoids

Immunization administration for vaccines/toxoids codes are reported in addition to codes from the Medicine subsection entitled *Vaccines, Toxoids*. The immunization administration for vaccines/toxoids include the following:

- Administrative staff services (e.g., appointment scheduling, preparing a patient's record, and submitting an insurance claim to a payer)
- Clinical staff services (e.g., taking vital signs, assessing past reactions and contraindications, preparing and administering the vaccine/toxoid, monitoring reactions, and documenting in the record)

The following types of immunization administration for vaccines/toxoids are reported:

- Intradermal, intramuscular, percutaneous, and subcutaneous injections
- Intranasal and oral administration

The immunization administration of *pediatric* vaccines/toxoids are reported with codes 90460–90461 to accurately describe the work involved, which includes patient/family counseling provided by the physician during the administration of a vaccine/toxoid. (Codes 90460–90461 are reported when the physician provides face-to-face counseling for the patient/family during the immunization administration of a vaccine/toxoid. Per the CPT, when face-to-face counseling is not provided, report codes 90471–90474.)

> **EXAMPLE:** A 6-year-old female patient received immunization administration (intramuscular injection) of the rabies vaccine. Physician discussed the vaccine composition with the patient's mother, including risks and benefits. Report codes 90460 and 90675.

Coding Tip:

- Report immunization administration for vaccines/toxoids codes (90460–90474) in addition to vaccine/toxoid codes (90476–90749).
- Do not report codes 90460–90474 for the administration of allergy injections or testing, chemotherapy, placement of catheters, transfusions, or venipuncture. Refer to the appropriate Surgery or Medicine subsection for reporting such codes.

Vaccines, Toxoids

Vaccines/toxoids codes (90476–90749) identify the vaccine/toxoid product only. They are reported in addition to immunization administration for vaccines/toxoids codes (90460–90474).

> **EXAMPLE:** An 18-year-old female patient received immunization administration (subcutaneous injection) of an MMR booster. Report codes 90471 and 90707.

Coding Tip:

Do not add modifier -51 (Multiple Procedures) to vaccines/toxoids codes (90476–90749).

- When vaccines/toxoids codes are reported during a preventive medicine encounter, add modifier -25 to the evaluation and management code (e.g., 99392-25).
- New vaccines have been approved for use by the Food and Drug Administration (FDA) over recent years. CPT created a new symbol (⬀) to indicate that FDA approval is pending, which means it is anticipated that the vaccines will receive FDA approval, but that approval was pending at the time of publication. Once the vaccine is approved by the FDA, the symbol will be removed.

Reporting Evaluation and Management Service Codes with Vaccines/Toxoids Codes

There is considerable confusion regarding whether a provider should report an evaluation and management (E/M) service for an encounter for immunization administration of vaccines/toxoids. Correct coding depends on whether the provider performed a medically necessary E/M service *in addition to the immunization administration*. To assign an E/M code in addition to the immunization administration code, the E/M service must exceed services included with immunization administration codes.

When a separate E/M service is provided (e.g., performance and documentation of the "key components" of history, physical examination, and medical decision making), a separate E/M code is reported (99201–99215) in addition to the appropriate code for immunization administration and the code for the vaccine/toxoid product. Modifier -25 (Significant, separately identifiable evaluation and management service by the same physician on the same day of the procedure or other service) is added to the E/M code.

To clearly establish medical necessity of the E/M service, link an appropriate ICD-9-CM code that describes the problem treated to the E/M code. The provider should also document a separate note for provision of the E/M service (different from the immunization history and vaccine/toxoid note, which includes the product, lot number, site and method, and VIS date).

EXAMPLE: Physician provided a level 3 E/M service to a 48-year-old male patient to medically manage his hypertension. During the same encounter, the physician administered a flu shot (intramuscular injection). Report codes 99213-25, 90471, and 90658.

Note:

Reporting E/M service code 99211 does not require the presence of the physician or the documentation of key components.

Psychiatry

Psychiatrists, psychologists, and licensed clinical social workers report psychiatry codes for psychotherapy services, which include the following headings and subheadings:

- Psychiatric diagnostic or evaluative interview procedures
- Psychiatric therapeutic procedures
- Office or other outpatient facility
  - Insight-oriented, behavior-modifying, and/or supportive psychotherapy
  - Interactive psychotherapy
- Inpatient hospital, partial hospital, or residential care facility
  - Insight-oriented, behavior-modifying, and/or supportive psychotherapy
  - Interactive psychotherapy
- Other psychotherapy
- Other psychiatric services or procedures

Coding Tip:

- Psychiatric evaluation and management (E/M) services are reported by physicians, nurse practitioners, and physician assistants. Psychologists and licensed clinical social workers do not report codes from the CPT E/M section.
- Psychiatric consultation includes examination of the patient, exchange of information with the primary care physician or other pertinent individuals (e.g., family members and caretakers), and preparation of reports. Because no psychiatric treatment is provided during a psychiatric consultation, report the appropriate evaluation and management consultation code.

Psychiatric Diagnostic Procedures

Psychiatric diagnostic or evaluative interview services include the following:

- History and examination
- Mental status examination

- Patient disposition

- Communication with the family or other sources

- Ordering and medical interpretation of laboratory or other diagnostic studies

Interactive psychiatric diagnostic interview examination services are usually provided to children. They include the use of physical aids (e.g., dolls) and nonverbal communication (e.g., drawing together) to overcome barriers to the therapeutic interaction between clinician and patient.

A complete mental status examination includes the following:

- Orientation to time, place, and person

- Recent and remote memory

- Attention span and concentration

- Language (e.g., naming objects and repeating phrases)

- Fund of knowledge (e.g., awareness of current events, past history, and vocabulary)

- Mood and affect (e.g., depression, anxiety, agitation, or mania)

  EXAMPLE: Patient received interactive psychiatric diagnostic interview examination services as the result of her parents finding out that she was being routinely bullied at elementary school. Report code 90791.

Psychiatric Therapeutic Procedures

Psychiatric therapeutic services codes classify the following:

- Office or other outpatient facility's insight-oriented, behavior-modifying and/or supportive psychotherapy, and interactive psychotherapy

- Inpatient hospital, partial hospital, or residential care facility's insight-oriented, behavior-modifying and/or supportive psychotherapy, and interactive psychotherapy

- Other psychotherapy

- Other psychiatric services or procedures

Coding Tip:

- Psychiatric therapeutic procedures codes (90832–90899) include psychiatric diagnostic or evaluative interview procedures.
- When individual psychotherapy (90832–90840) and group psychotherapy (90847–90853) services are provided on the same date to the same patient, report a code for each service provided. (However, some payers reimburse just one service when both are provided on the same date.)
- Report codes for other services that are also separately provided (e.g., electroconvulsive therapy).

Psychotherapy—or **talk therapy**, *counseling*, or **psychosocial therapy**—is the treatment of mental and emotional disorders by having patients talk about their condition(s) and related issues with a mental health physician (such as a psychiatrist) or therapist (such as a psychotherapist or a licensed clinical social worker).

- **Insight-oriented psychotherapy**, or **psychodynamic psychotherapy**, is the treatment of mental illnesses and behavioral disturbances through resolution of unconscious psychological conflicts.

- **Behavior-modifying psychotherapy** is treatment that focuses on changing unhealthy or unwanted behaviors, and it typically includes a system of **desensitization** (confronting something that causes anxiety), reinforcements of positive behavior, and rewards. It can also include biofeedback and relaxation training.

Coding Tip:

- Report code 90875 or 90876 only for psychotherapy that includes biofeedback training.
- **Supportive psychotherapy** is treatment that uses supportive interactions and various activities to facilitate maintenance, restoration, and improvement of a patient's self-esteem. It is also used to prevent a patient's deterioration or relapse and to assist the patient in overcoming symptoms of mental illnesses and behavioral disorders. It does not usually result in a personality change. Treatment may include examination of relationships, real or transferential, as well as current and past patterns of emotional behavior or responses.
- **Interactive psychotherapy** involves the use of physical aids to enable interaction between the clinician and a patient who does not have the communication skills necessary to explain his or her symptoms or to understand the clinician. It is not possible to provide non-interactive services during the same session as interactive services. Each type of service is considered mutually exclusive. Therefore, do not report non-interactive psychotherapy with interactive psychotherapy.
- Patients may receive psychotherapy alone, or they may receive psychotherapy with medical evaluation and management services (e.g., evaluation of comorbid medical conditions, drug interactions, physical examinations, drug management, physician orders, and interpretation of diagnostic studies).

The psychiatric therapeutic procedures code is selected based on the following:

- Type of psychotherapy (e.g., interactive versus insight-oriented, behavior-modifying, and/or supportive)
- Place of service (e.g., office versus inpatient)
- Face-to-face time with the patient
- Whether evaluation and management services were provided with psychotherapy

Coding Tip:

- To report evaluation and management services when psychotherapy is not provided, assign an appropriate code from the Evaluation and Management Services section.
- Psychiatric therapeutic procedures codes include evaluation and management services. Thus, when evaluation and management services are provided in addition to psychiatric therapeutic procedures, do not report a separate evaluation and management code.

Psychoanalysis attempts to gain insight into a patient's motivations and conflicts to change maladaptive behavior (e.g., an inability to cope with the challenges of everyday living). The psychoanalysis code is reported on a per-day basis. Do not confuse psychoanalysis and psychotherapy codes. The psychoanalysis code refers to the practice of psychoanalysis (e.g., patient is treated by a physician who is credentialed to practice analytic therapy, and psychoanalysis is the treatment being used).

Family psychotherapy involves the patient's family in the treatment process, and the dynamics within the family are the focus of the psychotherapeutic sessions. Family psychotherapy may be performed with or without the patient present. Codes reported are based on whether the patient is present or not and whether multiple family groups are being treated.

EXAMPLE: Psychotherapy was provided on May 5 to the families of three different patients who reside in a drug treatment center. Report code 90849 on the insurance claim for *each* patient.

Other psychiatric services or procedures include the following:

- Pharmacologic management
- Narcosynthesis
- Electroconvulsive therapy
- Individual psychophysiological therapy incorporating biofeedback training
- Hypnotherapy
- Environmental intervention for medical management
- Psychiatric evaluation of hospital records
- Interpretation or explanation of psychiatric examination/procedure results
- Preparation of report of patient's psychiatric status, history, treatment, or progress for the benefit of other physicians, agencies, or third-party payers

Pharmacologic management is the evaluation of a patient's medications for affect (such as a patient's reaction to medication), proper dosage (e.g., a therapeutic dose), and renewal of prescribed medications. Pharmacologic management is provided by a physician (such as a psychiatrist) to a patient who undergoes psychotherapy from a nonphysician colleague (e.g., a psychologist or a licensed clinical social worker) or when a patient's condition is being effectively treated by psychotropic drugs alone. Generally, the patient does not receive other services from the physician during the encounter. When an evaluation and management (E/M) service is provided by the physician, the pharmacologic management is included in the E/M service. It is not coded and reported separately. (The psychotherapy provided during pharmacologic management is minimal and is also not coded or reported separately.)

Coding Tip:

Pharmacologic management is included in some psychiatric services. Therefore, do not report code 90836 (pharmacologic management) with psychiatric services codes.

Narcosynthesis is a form of psychotherapy that is provided when the patient is under the influence of a drug, such as a sedative or narcotic (e.g., a barbiturate, benzodiazepine-type drug that is administered intravenously). The administration of a medication to release inhibitions allows a patient to discuss issues that are too difficult to verbalize otherwise.

Electroconvulsive therapy is used to treat depression or life-threatening psychosis (e.g., severe affective disorders or schizophrenia) and involves the application of electric current to the brain through scalp electrodes. The term *electroconvulsive* refers to a convulsive response to an electrical stimulus. In electroconvulsive therapy, it is necessary to monitor the patient (e.g., management of the seizure, observation, and decisions regarding further treatment). If the psychiatrist also administers anesthesia for the electroconvulsive therapy, report the appropriate anesthesia code (00104), which includes cardiac and oxygen saturation monitoring.

EXAMPLE: Patient underwent narcosynthesis for psychiatric diagnostic and therapeutic purposes. Amytal (sodium amobarbital), 125 miligrams was injected prior to therapy. Report codes 90865, 96372, and J0300.

Biofeedback

Biofeedback is a technique that trains the patient to gain some control over autonomic body functions. Biofeedback services include the following:

- Reviewing the patient's history
- Preparing the biofeedback equipment
- Placing electrodes on the patient
- Reading and interpreting responses
- Monitoring the patient
- Controlling muscle responses

Code 90901 classifies the provision of biofeedback without psychophysiological therapy. Although biofeedback services may include different types of administration (e.g., electromyogram application), code 90901 is intended to identify all methods of biofeedback provided, even when more than one modality is performed during the same session. Electromyogram is a nerve-conduction study that plots the electrical activity produced by muscle contractions. **Manometry** is a diagnostic test that measures muscle function using a pressure-sensitive tube.

Coding Tip:

- Two series of biofeedback codes (90901–90911 and 90875–90876) distinguish between biofeedback training without psychophysiologic therapy and biofeedback training with psychophysiologic therapy.
- Do *not* report code 90901 or 90911 with code 90875 or 90876.

EXAMPLE: Patient underwent biofeedback of perineal muscles for bladder training to prevent urinary incontinence. Treatment included use of manometry. Report code 90911.

Dialysis

The Dialysis subsection includes the following headings:

- Hemodialysis
- Miscellaneous dialysis procedures
- End-stage renal disease services
- Other dialysis procedures

Renal dialysis artificially removes toxic waste products from the body when the patient's kidneys are unable to perform this function because of disease or deterioration. Dialysis is used for acute, temporary kidney failure (e.g., acute renal failure) or chronic renal failure (e.g., end-stage renal disease). The following types of dialysis are used, depending on the patient's condition and whether the patient is experiencing acute or chronic renal failure:

- **Hemodialysis**: Process of removing waste products, toxins, and excess fluids from the blood; patient's blood is diverted into a dialyzer, where it is treated and returned into the patient's circulation by another tube inserted into a different blood vessel (Figure 18-1).

- **Peritoneal dialysis**: Soft catheter is inserted into abdominal cavity and dialysate fluid is infused at intermittent times.

Coding Tip:

All evaluation and management (E/M) services related to end-stage renal disease (ESRD) and rendered during dialysis are included in the dialysis procedure code. An E/M service related to ESRD performed on the day of dialysis is not separately coded and reported. When the patient receives E/M services for a completely different condition that is not related to ESRD, report an appropriate E/M service code and add modifier -25 (Significant, separately identifiable E/M service by the same physician on the same day as the procedure or other service).

Hemodialysis

Hemodialysis service codes include all E/M services related to the patient's renal disease *on the day of the hemodialysis procedure*. These codes are reported when hemodialysis services are provided to ESRD and non-ESRD patients in an inpatient setting and to non-ESRD in an outpatient setting.

EXAMPLE: A 54-year-old patient was admitted as a hospital inpatient for treatment of ESRD. Admission date was August 5, and discharge date was August 10. The patient underwent hemodialysis procedures on August 5, 7, and 9, which included evaluation by his attending physician. Report codes 90935 × 3. (Attending physician should report appropriate inpatient evaluation and management service codes with modifier -25 for provision of services unrelated to ESRD and the hemodialysis procedure on those dates. For other dates, such as August 6, 8, and 10, the attending physician should report appropriate inpatient E/M service codes for daily care and discharge services.)

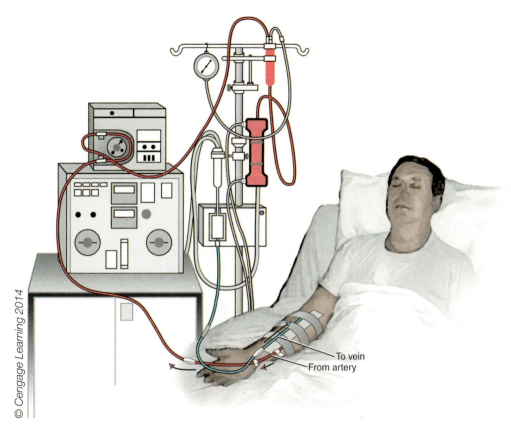

Figure 18-1   Hemodialysis filters waste from the patient's blood. Blood leaves the body via an artery, is filtered, and then is returned into a vein.

Miscellaneous Dialysis Procedures

Miscellaneous dialysis procedures codes include peritoneal dialysis, hemofiltration, and other continuous renal replacement therapies (90945–90947) (for single physician evaluation or repeated physician evaluations).

> **EXAMPLE:** Patient underwent peritoneal dialysis, which required repeated physician evaluations on the same date of treatment. Report code 90947.

End-Stage Renal Disease (ESRD) Services

ESRD services are typically performed as outpatient procedures, and reimbursement is usually made according to a monthly capitated payment method.

- ESRD services codes are reported *once per month per patient* (every 30 days). The appropriate code is reported just once, at the conclusion of a full month of ESRD services.

> **EXAMPLE:** A 48-year-old patient received ESRD related services two times each week during the entire month of June. Report code 90960.

- ESRD service codes can also be reported when less than a *full month of services* are provided to a patient. The appropriate code is reported for each day of service (e.g., when a patient requires less than a month's ESRD services after inpatient hospitalization).

> **Note:**
>
> A **capitated payment method** is the result of an agreement between a third-party payer and a health care provider in which the provider agrees to provide services to a patient in return for a fixed monthly payment.

EXAMPLE: A 54-year-old patient was hospitalized for ESRD from July 5 to July 20, and upon discharge received outpatient ESRD services on July 22, 24, 26, 28, and 30. Report codes 90970 × 5 for outpatient ESRD services.

 Coding Tip:

- For patients under 20 years of age, ESRD codes include monitoring of nutrition, assessment of growth and development, and parental counseling.
- ESRD codes include physician services related to establishing a dialyzing cycle, evaluation and management of the dialysis visits, and patient management during the dialysis, provided during a full month.

Other Dialysis Procedures

Other dialysis procedures include dialysis training (e.g., completed course of training, an individual training session), hemoperfusion (e.g., using activated charcoal or resin), and unlisted dialysis procedures (inpatient or outpatient).

EXAMPLE: Patient completed an entire course of outpatient dialysis training during the month of June. Report code 90989.

Gastroenterology

The Gastroenterology subsection includes the following headings:

- Gastric physiology
- Other procedures

Gastroenterology procedures (Table 18-1) are found in the Surgery section. Related diagnostic services are found in the Pathology and Laboratory and Radiology sections.

EXAMPLE: Patient underwent gastric motility (manometric) studies. Report code 91020.

Coding Tip:

Gastroenterology tests reported with codes 91010–91299 are frequently performed in conjunction with gastrointestinal (GI) endoscopic procedures. Do *not* report codes separately from the Gastroenterology subsection of the Medicine section with GI endoscopic procedures.

Ophthalmology

Ophthalmology services include the following headings:

- General ophthalmological services
- Special ophthalmological services
- Contact lens services
- Spectacle services (including prosthesis for aphakia)

General Ophthalmological Services

General ophthalmological services codes are reported for new or established patient examinations. A physician (such as an ophthalmologist) can report an appropriate evaluation and management (E/M) service code instead of a general ophthalmological service code. *Do not report a general ophthalmological services code (92002–92014) in addition to an E/M service code.*

Ophthalmologists have a choice when assigning codes for E/M services because they provide unique and specialized services that do not match criteria associated with E/M codes. Instead of reporting codes from the E/M section, an ophthalmologist may report codes from the Medicine section. Codes 92002–92014 describe intermediate and comprehensive levels of service, which are defined by CPT.

Table 18-1 Gastroenterology Procedures and Services

Procedure	Description
Esophageal or gastric intubation and collection of washings	• Tube is inserted through nose or mouth into esophagus or stomach. • One or more washings are obtained for *cytology* (study of cells).
Esophageal, gastric, or duodenal motility	• Tube is inserted through patient's nose or mouth into the esophagus, stomach, or duodenum. • Tube is slowly withdrawn to test muscles for weakness or abnormality (manometry).
Acid perfusion test of esophagus (or Bernstein test)	• Nasogastric tube is inserted into the esophagus. • Mild hydrochloric acid is poured through the tube in an attempt to re-create and evaluate gastric reflux symptoms. • Test is done to determine whether chest pain is due to acid reflux and not a cardiac condition.
Gastroesophageal reflux test	• Electrode is inserted through nasal catheter into esophagus to determine pH levels. • Electrode remains in esophagus over a period of time to obtain multiple levels (to determine acid reflux or non-acid reflux).
Esophageal balloon distention provocation study	• Local anesthetic is administered to numb the throat. • Balloon is inserted into esophagus and is expanded in multiple sites to increasing degrees to provoke chest pain. • This is done to rule out a cardiac source of existing chest pain.
Gastric analysis test (or Hollander test)	• Nasogastric tube is inserted through patient's nose or mouth into the stomach. • Stimulant is injected into the stomach (e.g., histamine, insulin, pentagastrin, calcium, or secretin). • Gastric contents are suctioned through the tube and are analyzed.
Gastric saline load test	• Nasogastric tube is inserted through patient's nose or mouth into the stomach. • Gastric contents are suctioned, and stomach is filled with saline. • After 30 minutes, gastric contents are resuctioned and measured to determine presence of impaired gastric emptying.
Breath hydrogen test	• Patient's exhalations are tested for hydrogen to determine whether undigested food is entering the duodenum. • Test is administered over a period of 3 to 5 hours, after patient has fasted for 12 hours and has swallowed test sugars (e.g., fructose, lactose, or lactulose).
Placement of intestinal bleeding tube	• Intestinal bleeding tube is inserted through mouth into duodenum. • Tube is monitored and used to suppress bleeding, if present.
Gastric intubation for aspiration or lavage	• Nasogastric tube is inserted through patient's nose or mouth into the stomach. • Gastric contents are suctioned to remove ingested poisons or to decompress intestinal blockage.
Gastrointestinal (GI) tract imaging	• Patient swallows a capsule that provides color imaging as it passes through the GI system. • Data is transmitted from the capsule to a data recorder.
Rectal sensation, tone, and compliance test	• Balloon is inserted into the patient's rectum and gradually inflated. • Reactions to various levels of inflation are studied.
Anorectal manometry	• This measures pressure of anal sphincter to diagnose constipation or incontinence.
Pulsed irrigation of fecal impaction (or pulsed irrigation evaluation, PCE)	• Automated enema is inserted for cases of chronic constipation when the patient has no voluntary bowel control (e.g., a paraplegic patient).
Electrogastrography (EGG)	• Electrodes are attached to the patient's abdomen. • Myoelectrical activity is detected and recorded.

When services provided are less than those described by codes 92002–92014, the ophthalmologist should report the appropriate E/M codes (99201–99215).

- Intermediate ophthalmological services include history, general medical observation, external ocular and adnexal examination, and other diagnostic procedures as indicated. This may include the use of mydriasis for ophthalmoscopy

  EXAMPLE: Established patient was seen in the office by her ophthalmologist for evaluation of glaucoma. Interval history, external examination, ophthalmoscopy, biomicroscopy, and tonometry were performed to evaluate the patient's response to glaucoma treatment. Report code 92012.

- Comprehensive ophthalmological services include a general evaluation of the complete visual system (e.g., history, general medical observation, external and ophthalmoscopic examinations, gross visual fields and basic sensorimotor examination, biomicroscopy, examination with cycloplegia or mydriasis, and tonometry). In addition, diagnostic and treatment procedures are included. Comprehensive services may be performed during multiple sessions or visits.

  EXAMPLE: An established patient previously diagnosed with glaucoma was seen in her ophthalmologist's office. The ophthalmic technician tested the patient's visual acuity, gross visual field by confrontation, ocular motility including primary gaze alignment, and intraocular pressures. The ophthalmologist examined the patient's ocular adnexae, including lids, lacrimal glands, lacrimal drainage, orbits, and preauricular lymph nodes. The pupils and irises were also examined. The ophthalmologist performed a slitlamp examination of the corneas, anterior chambers, and lenses. He also inspected the patient's bulbar and palpebral conjunctivae. The ophthalmologist prescribed medication and ordered lab work. Report code 92014.

Special Ophthalmological Services

Special ophthalmological services codes classify services that are not considered part of a general ophthalmological examination. They are considered significant, separately identifiable services, which means that their codes are reported in addition to codes for general ophthalmological examination services, when performed.

> ### Coding Tip:
>
> Routine ophthalmoscopy is included in general ophthalmological services. However, other special ophthalmological services are not included, and they should be coded and reported separately when performed (e.g., a determination of refractive state).

Determination of refractive state establishes  whether a prescription is required for vision correction. It is performed using an eye chart and refractor (a device that contains a wide range of lens strengths that can be easily and quickly changed). The fitting of glasses or contact lenses is *not* included with determination of refractive state services.

> **EXAMPLE:** Patient underwent determination of refractive state. Report code 92015.

Code 92025 is reported for computerized corneal topography (also called computer-assisted keratography or videokeratography), during which a digital camera is used to capture an image of the patient's cornea for computer analysis.

Contact Lens Services and Spectacle Services (Including Prosthesis for Aphakia)

When contact lens or spectacle services are provided, supply of the contact lenses or spectacles (glasses) is not included. Report an appropriate HCPCS level II code for the supply of materials.

> **EXAMPLE:** Patient underwent fitting of bifocal spectacles. Ophthalmologist provided "sphere, bifocal, plano to plus or minus 4.00d, per lens" glasses to the patient. Report codes 92341 and V2200.

Special Otorhinolaryngologic Services

Special Otorhinolaryngologic services include the following subheadings:

- Vestibular function tests, without electrical recording
- Vestibular function tests, with recording (e.g., ENG)
- Audiologic function tests
- Evaluative and therapeutic services
- Special diagnostic procedures
- Other procedures

When otorhinolaryngologic services are performed during an evaluation and management (E/M) service, do not code and report the component procedures separately (e.g., otoscopy, tuning fork test, whispered voice test). Special otorhinolaryngologic services that are *not* typically included in a comprehensive otorhinolaryngologic evaluation are reported separately.

 **EXAMPLE:** An otorhinolaryngologist performed a level 4 E/M service in the office, during which he reviewed the established patient's history, performed an external inspection of the ears, and conducted a rhinoscopic examination of the nose. Otoscopic examination of the external auditory canals and tympanic membranes revealed negative findings. Hearing assessment was performed with tuning forks, whispered voice, and finger-rub techniques. Report code 99214 from the E/M section. Do *not* report separate codes for the hearing assessments performed.

> **Note:**
>
> During a level 4 E/M service, such as presented in the previous example, when the physician also performs a positional nystagmus test and nasal function studies, codes 92532 and 92512 are reported in addition to E/M code 99214.

Audiologic function tests with medical diagnostic evaluation codes include testing of both ears. Do not add modifier -50 (Bilateral Procedure) to these codes. When a service is performed on one ear, add modifier -52 (Reduced Services) to the appropriate code.

EXAMPLE: Patient underwent a pure-tone screening test, air only, both ears. Report code 92551.

Codes for audiometric tests are reported separately only when calibrated electronic equipment is used. For pure-tone audiometry, earphones are used. The patient responds to different tone pitches (frequencies). Air and bone thresholds are similar to pure-tone audiometry procedures, except a bone oscillator is used instead of earphones.

EXAMPLE: Patient underwent pure-tone audiometry, air and bone, left ear. Report code 92553-52.

Cardiovascular

Cardiovascular services include the following headings:

- Therapeutic services and procedures
- Cardiography
- Cardiovascular device monitoring
- Implantable and wearable cardiac device evaluations
- Echocardiography
- Cardiac catheterization
- Intracardiac electrophysiological procedures/studies
- Peripheral arterial disease rehabilitation
- Noninvasive physiologic studies and procedure
- Other procedures

Coding Tip:

- Many therapeutic and diagnostic cardiovascular procedure codes (93451–93461, 93451–93461, 93600–93624, 93640–93650) include intravenous or intra-arterial access, electrocardiographic monitoring, and agents administered by injection or infusion. Therefore, do not separately report these codes for routine access, monitoring, injection, or infusion services.

- Cardiovascular code descriptions often state "with interpretation," or "tracing only," whereas others describe the total (global, technical, and professional) service. Be sure to carefully review code descriptions before reporting a code.

Therapeutic Services and Procedures

Therapeutic services performed during a heart catheterization, after the diagnostic images are obtained, are reported in addition to the heart catheterization codes (e.g., balloon angioplasty). Therapeutic procedures include the following:

- Cardiopulmonary resuscitation
- Transcutaneous pacing
- Cardioversion
- Circulatory assist procedures
- Thrombolysis
- Transcatheter placement of stents
- Percutaneous transluminal coronary balloon angioplasty
- Atherectomy

Percutaneous coronary artery interventions include stent placement (Figure 18-2), atherectomy, and balloon angioplasty (Figure 18-3). For a given coronary artery and its branches, report only the most complex intervention, regardless of the number of stent placements, atherectomies, or balloon angioplasties performed in that coronary artery and its branches. (Stent placement is considered more complex than an atherectomy. An atherectomy is considered more complex than a balloon angioplasty.) Do not add modifier -59 to codes reported for percutaneous coronary artery stent placement, atherectomy, or balloon angioplasty. These interventions are reported with an appropriate modifier to indicate in which coronary artery the procedure was performed. These modifiers are the following:

- -LC (left circumflex coronary artery)
- -RC (right coronary artery)
- -LD (left anterior descending coronary artery)

Coding Tip:

Medicare recognizes the following three coronary arteries for reimbursement purposes when considering first and additional vessel interventions:
- Left anterior descending
- Left circumflex
- Right coronary

   Therefore, it is possible to report up to three percutaneous interventions if an intervention is performed in each of the three coronary arteries or their branches.

- The first procedure is reported with a primary code (92980, 92982, or 92995) that describes the most complex procedure performed.

- Procedures performed in other coronary arteries are reported with the add-on codes (92981, 92984, 92996).

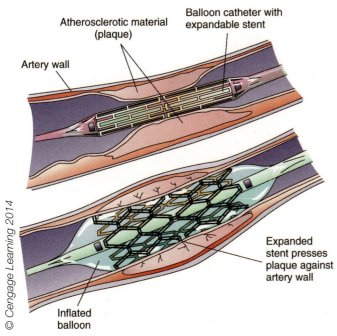

Figure 18-2 A stent is inserted after balloon angioplasty to prevent restenosis of the treated artery.

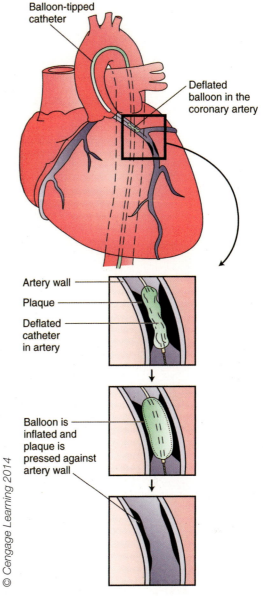

Figure 18-3 Balloon angioplasty is performed to open a blocked coronary artery.

When cardiopulmonary resuscitation (CPR) is performed *without* other evaluation and management services, report code 92950. Because critical-care services and prolonged management services are determined by time, when code 92950 is reported separately, the time required to perform CPR is not included in determining the critical care or other time-based evaluation and management services.

> **EXAMPLE:** A "code blue" is called on a hospital inpatient. The responding physician directs cardiopulmonary resuscitation. After the patient is resuscitated, the patient's attending physician resumes patient care. Report code 92950 for CPR.

Cardiography

Cardiography, or **electrocardiography**, is a diagnostic procedure that records the heart's electronic activity with a cardiograph and produces a cardiogram (or electrocardiogram, ECG, or EKG) (Figure 18-4). Cardiography codes are reported for routine electrocardiograms and other procedures (e.g., vector cardiogram, 24-hour monitoring, and patient demand recordings when ordered by the provider). Be sure to identify the total, professional, and technical components (and appropriate modifiers) before reporting cardiography codes.

The routine monitoring of EKG rhythm and hemodynamics, including cardiac outputs, is included as part of critical-care evaluation and management services. Therefore, do not separately report EKG rhythm strip and cardiac output measurement review codes with critical-care services.

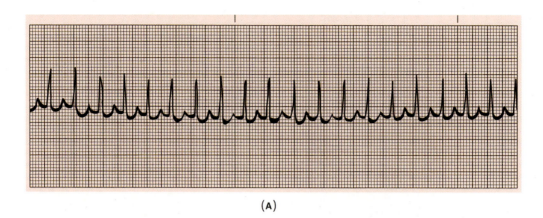

(A)

(B)

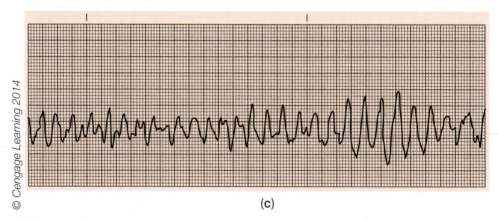

(C)

© Cengage Learning 2014

Figure 18-4   Electrocardiogram showing disruptions of heart rhythms (A) Paroxysmal atrial tachycardia (PAT) (B) Atrial fibrillation (C) Ventricular fibrillation

EXAMPLE: Patient underwent routine ECG (tracing only) in the physician's office. Report code 93005.

Cardiovascular Monitoring Services

Cardiovascular monitoring services (e.g., pacemaker programming) use in-person and remote technology to assess cardiovascular rhythm data.

EXAMPLE: Patient underwent transtelephonic rhythm strip pacement evaluation of her multiple lead pacemaker system for a period of 60 days, which included physician analysis, review, and documented report. Report code 93293 just once.

Implantable and Wearable Cardiac Device Evaluations

Cardiac device evaluation services are diagnostic medical procedures using in-person and remote technology to assess cardiac device therapy and cardiovascular physiologic data.

EXAMPLE: Patient underwent a 30-day remote interrogation device evaluation that required an implantable loop recorder system. Analysis of recorded heart rhythm data, and physician analysis, review and report were included. Report code 93298.

Echocardiography

Echocardiography (Figure 18-5) is a diagnostic procedure that uses ultrasound to obtain two-dimensional images of the heart and great arteries (aorta, vena cavae). Echocardiography codes include the total procedure. When just the professional component is performed, add modifier -26 to the code.

EXAMPLE: Patient underwent transesophageal echocardiography for congenital cardiac anomalies, which included placement of the probe, image acquisition, and interpretation and report. Report code 93315.

Cardiac Catheterization

Cardiac catheterization (Figure 18-6) is an invasive diagnostic medical procedure that includes several components. The procedure begins when the physician introduces one or more catheters into peripheral arteries and/or veins. Cardiac catheterizations include introduction, position (and repositioning) of catheter(s), recording of intracardiac and/or intravascular pressure(s), and final evaluation and preparation of a report.

Cardiac output measurement (93561–93562) is routinely performed during cardiac catheterization procedures. These codes are not reported in addition to cardiac catheterization codes.

Fluoroscopic guidance procedures are integral to invasive intravascular procedures, and codes for such procedures are not reported separately.

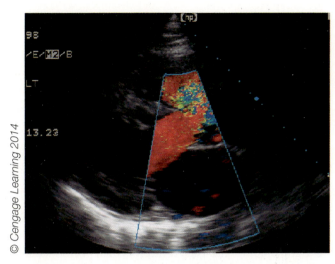

© Cengage Learning 2014

Figure 18-5 Echocardiography. The large area of red shows the flow of blood through an abnormal opening between the aorta and right atrium.

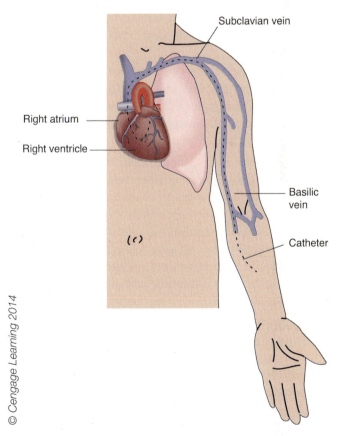

© Cengage Learning 2014

Figure 18-6 Cardiac catheterization. Once the catheter is inserted in the heart, a contrast medium is injected and an angiogram is performed to detect coronary vessel patency (openness).

When reporting codes for cardiac catheterization procedures, review patient-record documentation to determine the following:

- Catheter placement

- Injection procedure

- Supervision and interpretation of fluroscopic guidance

Coding Tip:

Do not add modifier -51 (Multiple Procedures) because of the component nature of cardiac catheterization procedures. Procedure codes are assigned once per session. Modifier -26 is added, as applicable, to cardiac catheterization procedures.

The femoral artery is the most common access point for cardiac catheterization (such as left heart catheterization, aortography, coronary angiography, internal mammary artery injection, vein bypass graft injection, and for other left heart procedures and coronary artery interventions). Right heart catheterization and pulmonary arteriography are most often performed via the right femoral vein. Each catheter is then positioned in a branch vessel or a cardiac chamber. During the catheterization procedure, recordings are made for measurement of intracardiac and intravascular pressure, oxygen saturation or blood gases, and cardiac output.

Angiography, frequently performed during a diagnostic catheterization, may require the assignment of a separate code. Angiography involves injecting a contrast medium and imaging the vessel (e.g., in order to determine the location or severity of obstructive lesions or abnormalities). Repositioning the catheter may be necessary during the procedure to perform injection of contrast for angiography. A final evaluation of all data and a report are required.

EXAMPLE: Patient underwent combined right and left heart catheterization, which included intraprocedural injection for left ventriculography with imaging supervision and interpretation. Report code 93453.

Endomyocardial biopsy (93505) provides tissue for direct pathologic evaluation of cardiac muscle using a special biopsy catheter with a bioptome tip (an open tip that closes to obtain tissue sample) to obtain myocardial tissue samples. To monitor a cardiac transplant patient for signs of rejection, the physician inserts a bioptome-tip catheter and, under fluoroscopy, advances it to the right ventricle. The instrument obtains myocardial tissue that is submitted for pathologic examination.

Insertion of a Swan-Ganz catheter (93503) is included in the cardiac catheterization codes. A Swan-Ganz catheter is a flexible, multiple-lumen, balloon-tipped flotation catheter that is introduced through a major peripheral vein (e.g., the jugular or subclavian). It is passed under pressure waveform guidance, with or without fluoroscopy, through the right atrium, right ventricle, and pulmonary artery. Then the balloon is inflated and the tip measures pressure-transmitted retrograde from the left side of the heart (left ventricular end-diastolic pressure), as well as central venous pressure. With the balloon deflated, the catheter measures pulmonary artery systolic, diastolic, and mean pressures; it then allows infusion (and some patients are fitted with pacing electrodes).

Coding Tip:

Do not separately report code 93503 for Swan-Ganz catheter insertion unless it is performed as a separate and distinct procedure from the heart catheterization.

EXAMPLE: During postoperative recovery after a heart catheterization, the patient's condition became unstable, and the physician inserted a Swan-Ganz flow-directed catheter for evaluation and monitoring. Report code 93503.

Intracardiac Electrophysiological Procedures/Studies

Intracardiac electrophysiological procedures and studies describe services that record, map, or change heart conduction (e.g., recording bundle of His, mapping tachycardia during repair surgery). Many of these codes contain instructional notes that indicate their use with other codes. Intracardiac electrophysiological procedures (EP) may be diagnostic or therapeutic, and these procedures include the insertion and repositioning of catheters.

Other Procedures

Cardiac rehabilitation is a customized program of exercise and education. Cardiac rehabilitation programs typically last about three to six months, during which the patient works with cardiologists, nurse educators, dietitians, exercise rehabilitation specialists, occupational therapists, physical therapists, psychologists, and psychiatrists. CPT codes 93797 and 93798 describe comprehensive services provided by a physician for cardiac rehabilitation. This includes all services related to cardiac rehabilitation, so it would not be appropriate to report a separate evaluation and management service code unless it is an unrelated, separately identifiable service.

> **Coding Tip:**
>
> All intracardiac electrophysiological procedures/studies codes are exempt from modifier -51.

> **EXAMPLE:** On November 15, 20, and 25, a patient received physician services for outpatient cardiac rehabilitation without continuous ECG monitoring. Report codes 93797, 93797, and 93797 for each date of service.

Noninvasive Vascular Diagnostic Studies

Noninvasive vascular diagnostic studies (e.g., a duplex scan) include ultrasound scanning to display two-dimensional structure and motion, and the codes classify arterial and venous studies. They also identify anatomic structures or areas to be evaluated. (A **duplex scan** is a noninvasive test that is performed to evaluate a vessel's blood flow.)

> **EXAMPLE:** Patient underwent a duplex scan of lower extremity arteries, bilaterally. Report code 93925.

Pulmonary

Pulmonary codes are reported for therapeutic and diagnostic pulmonary services. When pulmonary services are provided during an evaluation and management (E/M) encounter (e.g., hospital inpatient visit, emergency department service, office visit), report a code from the Pulmonary subsection of the Medicine section in addition to the appropriate E/M code.

Pulmonary services include:

- *Ventilator management* provided to patients in hospital inpatient and observation care settings, nursing facilities, and for whom home care is provided.

> **EXAMPLE:** A hospital inpatient was treated with a mechanical ventilator that was applied with a mask over his nose and mouth to assist with breathing due to emphysema. Initial ventilator management services were provided on April 5, and subsequent ventilator management services were provided on April 6 and 7. Report codes 94002, 94003, and 94003. (Do not report modifier -51, multiple services, with code 94003.)

- *Other procedures* that include laboratory procedures and interpretation of test results (e.g., spirometry, vital capacity, thoracic gas volume, and so on).

> **EXAMPLE:** During a level 3 outpatient E/M service to evaluate cystic fibrosis, the patient underwent outpatient pulmonary function testing to assess maximum breathing capacity and maximal voluntary ventilation. The physician interpreted the results of testing and adjusted the patient's medications. Report codes 99213 and 94200.

Allergy and Clinical Immunology

The Allergy and Clinical Immunology subsection includes the following headings:

- Allergy testing
- Ingestion challenge testing
- Allergen immunotherapy

Allergy Testing

Allergy sensitivity tests are performed on skin (cutaneous) and mucous membranes to identify the source of a patient's allergies (e.g., pollen as a source). Allergy skin tests include:

- **Puncture, prick, or scratch test (percutaneous)**: Tiny drops of purified allergen extracts are pricked or scratched into the skin's surface. The test is performed to identify allergies to pollen, mold, pet dander, dust mites, foods, insect venom, and penicillin (Figure 18-7).

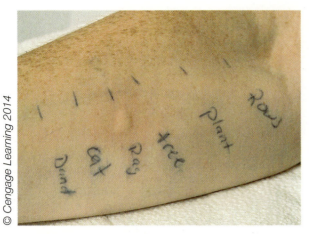

© Cengage Learning 2014

© Cengage Learning 2014

Figure 18-7 In scratch (percutaneous) tests, allergens are placed on the skin, the skin is scratched, and the allergen is labeled. Reactions usually occur within 20 minutes. Pictured is a reaction to ragweed.

Figure 18-8 Intradermal skin test

- **Intradermal test (intracutaneous)**: Purified allergen extracts are injected into the skin of patient's arm (Figure 18-8). The test is performed when an allergy to insect venom or penicillin is suspected.

- **Patch test (epicutaneous)**: An allergen is applied to a patch, which is placed on skin. The test is performed to identify substances that cause contact dermatitis, such as latex, medications, fragrances, preservatives, hair dyes, metals, and resins.

  EXAMPLE: Patient underwent two patch tests. Report codes 95044 and 95044.

Ingestion Challenge Testing

Ingestion challenge testing includes the sequential and incremental ingestion of test items. Examples of test items include drugs, foods, and other substances. Patient assessment and monitoring activities (e.g., blood pressure) that are performed during ingestion challenge testing are *not* separately reported. However, intervention therapy (e.g., injection of epinephrine), when performed, is reported separately along with appropriate evaluation and management service code(s).

  EXAMPLE: Patient underwent 120 minutes of ingestion challenge testing (strawberries). Report code 95076.

Allergen Immunotherapy

Allergen immunotherapy (also known as allergy shots, allergy vaccines, desensitization shots, or hyposensitization shots) contains small amounts of **allergens** (allergy-causing substances to which a patient reacts) to increase the patient's tolerance to allergens. Codes 95115–95117 include the administration of allergenic extract, but they do not include the supply of the allergenic extract. Codes 95120–95134 are reported for complete service, which include provision of the allergenic extract.

  EXAMPLE: A primary care provider administers a single allergy injection using allergenic extract that was previously prepared by an allergist and brought to the office by the patient. Report code 95115.

Allergen immunotherapy is administered on a schedule; patients typically receive treatment once or twice a week for about three to six months, and then once a month for three to five years. There are usually two phases of treatment:

- The buildup phase, during which patients receive shots one or two times per week for about three to six months.

- The maintenance phase, during which patients receive shots every two to four weeks for five months or longer.

Code 95144 is reported for the preparation and provision of single-dose antigens to be administered by another physician.  The number of single-dose vials prepared and provided should be specified when reporting this code. Codes 95145–95170 describe the antigen, its preparation, and the concentration/volume required for the injections. These codes are reported for the supply of antigen for prospectively planned administration. The number of doses prepared and provided must be specified when reporting these codes. Administration of injections is not included in these codes.

> **Note:**
>
> A **dose** is the amount of antigen administered in a single injection from a multiple-dose vial.

Coding Tip:

Evaluation and management services performed during the same encounter as allergy testing or allergy immunotherapy are reported only if a significant, separately identifiable service was administered.

- Code 95165 describes professional services for the supervision and provision of antigens (e.g., single or multiple) for allergy immunotherapy.

- Code 95165 does not include the injection procedure. Therefore, when a physician prepares the allergenic extract (same or different antigens) and administers the extract using single or multiple injections, report code 95165 in addition to either 95115 or 95117.

Endocrinology

Continual glucose (blood sugar) monitoring for up to 72 hours involves the subcutaneous placement of a sensor from which data is sent to a monitor. The patient calibrates the monitor on a daily basis.

> **EXAMPLE:** Dr. Jones was provided with a printout of recorded data from a subcutaneous sensor inserted into patient Mary Smith. Dr. Jones interpreted the data and prepared a report. Report code 95251.

Neurology and Neuromuscular Procedures

Neurology and neuromuscular codes classify diagnostic and therapeutic services that do not require surgical procedures. The Neurology and Neuromuscular subsection includes the following headings:

- Sleep medicine testing
- Routine electroencephalography (EEG)
- Muscle and range of motion testing
- Electromyography
- Guidance for chemodenervation and ischemic muscle testing
- Nerve conduction tests
- Intraoperative neurophysiology
- Autonomic function tests
- Evoked potentials and reflex tests
- Special EEG tests
- Neurostimulators, analysis-programming
- Other procedures
- Motion analysis
- Functional brain mapping

Sleep Medicine Testing

Sleep testing includes sleep studies and polysomnography, which are performed for the continuous monitoring and recording of various physiological parameters of sleep for six or more hours. Sleep testing is usually done in a health care facility's **sleep laboratory**, which is managed by a sleep technologist who explains and performs the sleep studies. (Sleep studies and polysomnographies are ordered, reviewed, and interpreted by physicians.) Sleeping rooms typically contain regular (not hospital) beds, an attached bathroom, and a television.

Sleep medicine testing codes include physician review and interpretation of data, and the preparation of a report.

- **Multiple sleep latency** is the observation of a patient during at least a six-hour period of sleep and includes assessment of sleep latency (dormancy) and/or wakefulness after the sleep period.

- **Sleep studies** evaluate adult and pediatric patients during sleep by monitoring brainwaves, heart rate, and eye movements. They are performed to diagnose sleep disorders, which include breathing, movement, and neurologic disorders that occur at night. Electrodes are applied to the patient's scalp, sides of the head, below the chin, chest, and legs. A sensor is placed next to the nose and mouth to measure airflow. A pulse oximetry clip is placed on the patient's finger to measure blood oxygen levels. Patients are also videotaped while asleep.

- **Polysomnography** is a sleep study that includes sleep staging with additional parameters of sleep (e.g., belts can be placed around the rib cage and abdomen to measure breathing movements). **Sleep staging** includes a 1-4 lead EEG, electro-oculogram (EOG), and submental electromyogram (EMG). Parameters that determine the polysomnography code to report include the following:

  - Airflow
  - Body positions
  - Continuous blood pressure monitoring
  - Electrocardiogram
  - End tidal gas analysis
  - Extended EEG monitoring
  - Extremity muscle activity

  - Gas exchange by oximetry
  - Gastroesophageal reflux
  - Motor activity movement
  - Penile tumescence
  - Snoring
  - Transcutaneous monitoring
  - Ventilation and respiratory effort

  EXAMPLE: A patient with a history of sleep apnea undergoes a sleep study, during which he is monitored for 6 hours. Polysomnography includes the measurement of respiration, airflow, muscle activity, continuous monitoring of blood pressure, and sleep staging with EEG, electro-oculogram, and submental electromyogram. Report code 95808.

Routine Electroencephalography (EEG)

EEG procedures include the use of the following, when appropriate:

- **Hyperventilation**: Deep or rapid breathing

- **Photic stimulation**: Reaction to light

  Extended EEG codes (95812–95813) are reported to test various stages of activity and sleep. Codes 95829–95830 are reported when an electrocortigram is performed during surgery (95829) or the physician inserts sphenoida electrodes for EEG recording (95830).

  EXAMPLE: Patient underwent a 60-minute EEG test, which included photic (pertaining to light) stimulation. Report code 95812.

Muscle and Range-of-Motion Testing

Muscle and range-of-motion testing codes are reported for muscle testing, range-of-motion measurements and reports, and Tensilon testing for myasthenia gravis. The **Tensilon test** involves injecting the drug, Tensilon (or its generic, edrophonium chloride) into a vein to block the action of the enzyme that breaks down the neurotransmitter acetylcholinesterase. The patient is then observed for rapid improvement in strength (e.g., use of eye muscles).

  EXAMPLE: Patient underwent manual muscle testing, left leg, which included physician interpretation and report. Report code 95831.

Electromyography

Electromyography (EMG) is a test that is used to detect nerve function by measuring the electrical activity generated by muscles. **Needle electromyography** testing involves inserting needle electrodes into skeletal muscles and observing electrical activity of those muscles using an **oscilloscope** (a device that displays electrical waveforms on a monitor) and a loudspeaker.

> **EXAMPLE:** Patient underwent limited needle EMG study of the left bicep muscle. Report code 95870.

Intraoperative Neurophysiology

Intraoperative neurophysiology testing codes are reported when performed during a surgical procedure. (The primary procedure code is reported as the first-listed procedure.)

> **EXAMPLE:** Patient underwent EEG needle electromyography of one extremity, during which 15 minutes of intraoperative neurophysiology testing was also performed. Report codes 95860 and 95940.

Autonomic Function Tests

Autonomic function tests evaluate autonomic nervous system functioning (e.g., heart or lungs).

> **EXAMPLE:** Patient underwent autonomic function testing, during which he was instructed to perform the Valsalva maneuver and then lie on a tilt table. The patient's blood pressure was monitored both during the maneuver and while on the tilt table. Report code 95922.

Evoked Potentials and Reflex Tests

A **short-latency somatosensory evoked potential study** involves electrically stimulating nerves to evaluate their responsiveness to the body's superficial surface and internal structures (e.g., the organs). (The appropriate code is reported according to testing site.) A **central motor evoked potential study** uses low-voltage electrodes, which are placed on the scalp and target sites to test the nervous system's pathway. A **visual evoked potential (VEP) test** of the central nervous system (CNS) involves stimulating the eye using the checkerboard or flash technique to monitor the patient's response. An **orbicularis oculi** (blink) test is monitored with sensors.

> **EXAMPLE 1:** Patient underwent a short-latency somatosensory evoked potential study, stimulation of any/all peripheral nerves or skin sites, recording from the central nervous system; in upper limbs. Report code 95925.

> **EXAMPLE 2:** Patient underwent VEP testing of the CNS using the flash technique. Report code 95930.

Special EEG Tests

Continuous electroencephalographic monitoring services codes are reported when a separately identifiable service is performed.

> **EXAMPLE:** Patient underwent 24-hour EEG monitoring and video recording; interpretation to determine localization of cerebral seizure focus by a 16-channel telemetry cable was performed. Report code 95951.

Neurostimulators, Analysis-Programming

Neurostimulators and analysis-programming codes are reported when a previously implanted neurostimulator pulse generator system is electronically analyzed to determine battery status, pulse amplitude and duration, rate, and so on.

> **EXAMPLE:** Patient underwent electronic analysis of implanted neurostimulator pulse generator system without reprogramming. Report code 95970.

Other Procedures

Other procedures codes are reported for the refill and maintenance of implantable infusion pumps or reservoirs. Code 95992 is reported for Canalith repositioning, per day. Code 95999 is reported for an unlisted neurological or neuromuscular diagnostic procedure.

> **EXAMPLE:** Medicare patient with terminal cancer undergoes a procedure to have implantable pump located in his spine refilled and maintained to ensure delivery of 100 mg of morphine sulfate, which is the loading dose prescribed for palliative care. Report codes 95990 and J2271. (Do *not* report S0093 for the morphine because that is a non-Medicare temporary code.)

Motion Analysis

Motion analysis codes are reported for services performed during major diagnostic or therapeutic decision making. During human motion analysis, patient movements are recorded, digitized, copied onto a computer, and processed.

> **EXAMPLE:** In the motion analysis lab, a patient is instructed to walk along a special walkway that includes a pressure sensor platform, which is positioned on the walkway. As the patient walks, pressure data is recorded and later analyzed for areas of the foot (e.g., halllux, heel, and metatarsal heads). The peak pressure is calculated for all areas, and the highest pressure is measured. Report code 96001. (Do not report bilateral -50 or directional -LT/-RT modifiers.)

Functional Brain Mapping

Functional brain mapping is a process by which a series of tests is administered by a physician or a psychologist to assess cognition, language, memory, movement, and sensation. The results of testing are documented in a report to identify expected versus observed locations of brain activity documented as the patient performs assigned tasks.

During functional brain mapping, the patient undergoes functional neuroimaging of the brain, which is also called functional magnetic resonance imaging (fMRI) of the brain. Report code 70555-51 in addition to code 96020 when a physician or psychologist entirely administers the functional brain mapping.

> **EXAMPLE:** Dr. Sanders performs a functional brain mapping with fMRI on a 49-year-old patient who has been experiencing memory losses and motor problems, to assess cognition, language, memory, movement, and sensation. Report codes 96020 and 70555.

> **Note:**
>
> Code 96004 is reported in addition to codes 96000–96003 when a physician reviews and interprets the results of motion analysis and documents a written report. Modifier -51 is added to code 96004 when the service is provided during the same encounter as motion analysis testing.

> **Note:**
>
> When a functional MRI (fMRI) is performed by a provider other than a physician or a psychologist, such as a psychiatric nurse, report code 70554 only. Do not report code 96020.

Medical Genetics and Genetic Counseling Services

Medical genetics and genetic counseling services are reported when a trained genetic counselor meets with an individual, couple, or family to investigate the family's genetic history and to assess risks associated with genetic defects in offspring.

> **EXAMPLE:** A married couple, who was referred to a trained genetic counselor by their fertility doctor, received 60 minutes of medical genetic counseling. Report codes 96040, 96040. (Code 96040 is reported for *each* 30-minute session of counseling.)

Central Nervous System Assessments/Tests (eg, Neuro-Cognitive, Mental Status, Speech Testing)

Central nervous system assessments/tests codes are reported when tests are performed to measure cognitive function of the central nervous system (e.g., cognitive processes, visual motor responses, and abstractive abilities). Several testing procedures are included, such as psychological testing (code 96101), which includes psychodiagnostic assessment of personality, psychopathology, emotionality, and intellectual abilities (e.g., WAI5-R, Rorschach, and MMPI tests). (Code 96101 is reported for each hour that the provider provided testing, interpreted test results, and prepared the report.)

> **EXAMPLE:** Patient underwent limited developmental testing, and the physician interpreted the results and prepared a report. Report code 96110.

Health and Behavior Assessment/Intervention

Health and behavior assessment/intervention codes are reported for tests that identify the psychological, behavioral, emotional, cognitive, and social elements involved in the prevention, treatment, or management of physical health problems. The focus of the assessment is not on mental health, but on biopsychosocial factors that are considered important to physical health problems and treatments. Health and behavior intervention procedures are used to modify factors affecting the patient. The focus of the intervention is to improve the patient's health and well-being by using cognitive, behavioral, social, and/or psychophysiological procedures.

Health and behavior assessment/intervention codes describe services associated with an acute or chronic illness that does not meet the criteria for psychiatric diagnosis, prevention of a physical disability, and maintenance of health. If the patient requires psychiatric services (90832–90899) and/or health and behavior assessment/ intervention (96150–96155), report the primary service performed. Do not report codes 96150–96155 in addition to codes 90832–90899 on the same date of service.

> **EXAMPLE:** A psychiatrist performed a 45-minute face-to-face health and behavior assessment of a child who was diagnosed with leukemia and who was suffering from severe distress and combativeness to chemotherapy administration. Report codes 96150, 96150, and 96150.

Hydration, Therapeutic, Prophylactic, Diagnostic Injections and Infusions, and Chemotherapy and Other Highly Complex Drug or Highly Complex Biologic Agent Administration

The hydration, therapeutic, prophylactic, diagnostic injections and infusions, and chemotherapy and other highly complex drug or highly complex biologic agent administration codes include the following headings:

- Hydration

- Therapeutic, prophylactic, and diagnostic injections and infusions (excludes chemotherapy and other highly complex drug or highly complex biologic agent administration)

- Chemotherapy and other highly complex drug or highly complex biologic agent administration

The following services are included in codes 96360–96549 and they are not separately coded and reported:

- Administration of local anesthesia

- Intravenous (IV) insertion

- Access to indwelling IV, subcutaneous catheter, or port

- Routine syringe, tubing, and other supplies

- Flushing performed upon completion of infusion

Note:

Patient record documentation should include physician verification of the patient's treatment plan and direction of staff who provide injection and infusion services.

Coding Tip:

- Report code 36593 for declotting a catheter or port using a fibrinolytic agent (e.g., recombinant tissue plasminogen activator, also known as tPA or alteplase).

- Code 36593 is not reported for the routine flushing of vascular access devices with saline or heparin. For example, this type of flushing is considered integral to chemotherapy administration and is not separately coded and reported.

When multiple injections or infusions or combination services are provided, report the initial code only once except *when two separate intravenous (IV) sites are required*. When the length of infusion time is included in the code description, report the code based on actual infusion time.

Hydration

Hydration codes are reported for the intravenous infusion of prepackaged fluids and electrolytes (e.g., normal saline and normal saline with potassium chloride). When reporting these codes, review the patient record for documentation that the physician supervised:

- Patient assessment (e.g., history and examination)

- Patient consent (e.g., discussion of risks and benefits)

- Patient safety (e.g., proper dose was administered; patient's response to infusion, including adverse reaction)

- Staff members who provided infusion services (e.g., the nursing staff)

   EXAMPLE: Patient received initial intravenous infusion hydration of 1,000-cc lactated Ringer's (pH–balanced electrolyte solution) for 60 minutes. Report codes 96360 and J7120.

Coding Tip:

- Do not report hydration codes for the infusion of drugs or other substances, which are reported with codes 96365–96379.

- Report HCPCS level II codes for supply of prepackaged fluids and electrolytes (e.g., J7030, normal saline solution).

Therapeutic, Prophylactic, and Diagnostic Injections and Infusions

Therapeutic, prophylactic, and diagnostic injections and infusions codes are reported for the administration of substances (other than hydration) and drugs. When reporting these codes, review the patient record for documentation that the physician supervised:

- Patient assessment

- Patient consent

- Patient safety

- Staff members who provided injection and/or infusion services

   EXAMPLE 1: Patient underwent therapeutic injection (intramuscular) of kanamycin sulfate, 500 mg. Report codes 96372 and J1840.

   EXAMPLE 2: Patient underwent routine insertion of an IV catheter for one-hour IV infusion of 1000 ml of potassium chloride and magnesium sulfate. Report codes 96365 and S5013. Do not report 36000 or 36410.

   EXAMPLE 3: Male patient required a nontunneled CVAC procedure prior to one-hour intravenous infusion of 1000 ml of potassium chloride and magnesium sulfate drug therapy. Report codes 36556, 96365, and S5013.

Staff members who administer therapeutic, prophylactic, and diagnostic injections (Figure 18-9) and infusions undergo special training to learn how to assess patients, provide informed consent, monitor patient safety, and administer injections and infusions. **Intravenous push** is an:

- Injection administered by a health care professional who is in constant attendance to administer the injection and observe the patient.

- Infusion of 15 minutes or less.

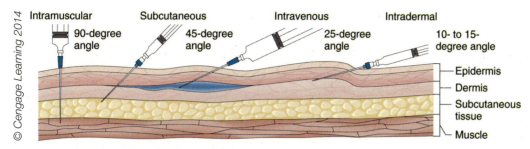

Figure 18-9   Angles of injection for administration of therapeutic, prophylactic, and diagnostic medications

Coding Tip:

- Any fluid used to administer a drug (e.g., flushing of IV with saline solution between drug therapies) is considered incidental hydration, and a separate hydration code is not reported.
- Report codes 90281–90399 for provision of immune globulin products.
- Report HCPCS level II codes for the supply of drugs (e.g., J0280, aminophylline).
- The administration of IV fluids to maintain line patency (unblocked condition) is not separately coded and reported.

Chemotherapy and Other Highly Complex Drug or Highly Complex Biologic Agent Administration

Chemotherapy is the treatment of cancer with drugs that serve to destroy cancer cells or slow the growth of cancer cells, keep cancer from spreading to other parts of the body, and prevent recurrence of the cancer. Chemotherapy administered in addition to other cancer treatments, such as surgery and/or radiation therapy, is called **adjuvant chemotherapy**.

Codes in this subheading classify the parenteral administration of chemotherapeutic agents, which means that the chemotherapy is administered by a route *other than by mouth*, such as implantation (of a catheter or port), infusion, or injection.

Coding Tip:

Do not report chemotherapy infusion with a code from range 96360–96379. To report chemotherapy infusion, select the appropriate code(s) from the chemotherapy administration series (96401–96549). These codes can be separately billed when an E/M service is rendered on the same day as the chemotherapy administration.

- The flushing of a vascular access port (e.g., saline solution) prior to the administration of chemotherapeutic agents is integral to the chemotherapy administration. It is not coded and reported separately.
- When infusion of hydrating solutions (e.g., saline solution) or drugs (e.g., heparin) other than anti-neoplastic drugs is a necessary and integral part of a procedure, a code from range 96360–96379 is *not* reported separately.

EXAMPLE: The infusion of a hydrating solution is started prior to the administration of chemotherapy. The infusion of the hydrating solution is included in the chemotherapy code, and it is not reported separately.

There are many chemotherapy drugs currently available to treat cancer, and chemotherapy is administered in a variety of ways, depending on the drugs used and the type of cancer.

Oral chemotherapy is administered by mouth in the form of a pill, capsule, or liquid, while parenteral methods of chemotherapy administration include the following:

- Implantation of a catheter or port into a central vein or body cavity

- Infusion or injection of intravenous (IV) chemotherapy into a vein

- Injection of intramuscular (IM) chemotherapy is injected into the muscle

- Injection of subcutaneous (SQ) chemotherapy under the skin

It is the parenteral methods of chemotherapy administration that are reported with codes from 96401–96549. When different techniques are used to parenterally administer chemotherapy (e.g., injection, infusion, implantation) *during the same encounter*, report a separate code for each parenteral method.

EXAMPLE 1: A patient diagnosed with malignant melanoma, skin of scalp, undergoes one hour of intravenous infusion of chemotherapy and intralesional chemotherapy administration to the scalp lesion. Report codes 96405 and 96413.

EXAMPLE 2: A patient was administered three injections of anti-neoplastic drugs and an infusion of anti-neoplastic drugs for two hours during one encounter. Report codes 96401, 96401, 96401, 96413, and 96415.

When an intravenous infusion of saline (an antiemetic) or other nonchemotherapy drug is administered at the same time as the chemotherapeutic agent(s), these infusions are not coded and reported separately. However, the supply of the drugs is reported separately with HCPCS level II codes. If the hydration or intravenous infusion is administered on the same day, but sequentially rather than at the same time as the chemotherapeutic agents, the infusions are reported with codes 96360–96368. Modifier -59 (Distinct Procedural Service) is added to these codes to indicate that the infusions were administered at different times.

> **Coding Tip:**
>
> Report code 96365 (IV infusion, for therapy, prophylaxis, or diagnosis, initial; up to 1 hour) to indicate an infusion of drugs (e.g., antihypertensive medication) *other than anti-neoplastic drugs*. Code 96366 is reported for each additional hour of infusion, up to eight hours.

EXAMPLE: Patient receives nonchemotherapy infusions for 75 minutes. Report code 96365. (A code for the remaining 15 minutes is not reported.) (Also, report level II code(s) for the drugs administered.)

Codes 96401–96549 are independent of the patient's evaluation and management (E/M) services and may occur sequentially on the same day. If performed, the appropriate E/M code should be reported as an additional code. Preparation of chemotherapy agent(s) is included in the service for administration of the agent, and it is not coded and reported separately.

Medications (e.g., antibiotics, steroidal agents, antiemetics, narcotics, analgesics, and biological agents) administered independently or sequentially as supportive management of chemotherapy administration are separately coded and reported, as appropriate. It is appropriate to report separately the appropriate HCPCS level II code(s) for the supply of chemotherapy drugs in addition to the code(s) for chemotherapy administration.

Photodynamic Therapy

Photodynamic therapy is administered by:

- External application of light to destroy malignancies.

- Endoscopic application of light that activates photosensitive drugs to destroy abnormal tissue.

Photodynamic therapy (PDT) is the application of a photosensitizing agent (e.g., 20 percent topical aminolevulinic acid HCl) directly onto a patient's lesions to treat premalignant cells (e.g., non-hyperkeratotic actinic

> **Coding Tip:**
>
> A photodynamic therapy code is reported for each exposure session, *not* for each lesion treated.

keratosis) or malignant cells.  The patient returns for a scheduled encounter during which a photodynamic therapy illuminator (light) is directed on the treated lesions. A cytotoxic reaction results when the topical agent applied to the lesions is irradiated, killing premalignant or malignant cells, preventing their spread.

Note:

Ocular photodynamic therapy consultation is reported with code 67221.

Special Dermatological Procedures

Special dermatological procedures codes describe dermatology procedures that are usually (but not always) performed in addition to an appropriate evaluation and management (E/M) service code.

> **EXAMPLE:** During a level 3 outpatient consultation encounter, the dermatologist performed a detailed history and examination; medical decision making was of low complexity. The dermatologist used ultraviolet light (actinotherapy) to treat the two areas of acne frontalis. Report codes 99243 and 96900-51.

Physical Medicine and Rehabilitation

Physical medicine and rehabilitation is a branch of medicine that focuses on the prevention, diagnosis, and treatment of disorders of the musculoskeletal, cardiovascular, and pulmonary systems that may produce temporary or permanent impairment. A **physiatrist** is a physician who specializes in physical medicine and rehabilitation and treats acute/chronic pain and musculoskeletal disorders. Physiatrists also treat disorders of the musculoskeletal system that result in severe functional limitations (e.g., a baby with a birth defect, the victim of a bad car accident, an elderly person with a broken hip). Physiatrists coordinate the long-term rehabilitation process for patients with spinal-cord injuries, cancer, stroke, brain injuries, amputations, and multiple sclerosis or other neurological disorders. The specialty focuses on the restoration of function to people with problems ranging from simple physical mobility issues to those with complex cognitive involvement.

Physiatrists offer a broad spectrum of medical services (e.g., the prescription of drugs or assistive devices such as a brace or artificial limb). However, they do not perform surgery. Physiatrists use diverse modalities (any physical agent applied to produce therapeutic changes) that include therapies such as heat and cold, electrotherapies, massage, biofeedback, traction, and therapeutic exercise.

- Physical therapy and occupational therapy reevaluations are not routinely reported during a planned course of physical or occupational therapy. However, if the patient's status changes and reevaluation is warranted, it is coded and reported with modifier -59 (Distinct Procedural Service) added.

- Physical medicine diagnostic tools include special techniques in electrodiagnostic medicine (e.g., electromyography, nerve conduction studies, and somatosensory evoked potentials) to help diagnose conditions that cause pain, weakness, and numbness.

- Therapeutic procedures are performed to effect change through the application of clinical skills in an attempt to improve function.

- Some codes for physical medicine and rehabilitation services include a length of time in their code descriptions. Because NCCI edits pair "timed" codes with other "timed" codes or non-timed codes, providers should not report more than one physical medicine and rehabilitation therapy service for the same 15-minute time period. The only exception involves a "supervised modality" defined by codes 97010–97028, which may be reported with other therapy services during the same 15-minute time period.

- Active wound management is often provided during a course of physical therapy (e.g., wound debridement or dressing change).

    EXAMPLE 1: Patient underwent diathermy. Report code 97024.

    EXAMPLE 2: A diabetic patient presents for treatment of a chronic open wound on the left foot. The wound measures 4 cm x 3 cm (or 12 sq cm), and the physician treats it by using surgical scissors to perform sharp selective debridement. Report code 97597.

Medical Nutrition Therapy

Medical nutrition therapy is classified according to:

- Type of assessment
- Individual or group therapy
- Length of time

    EXAMPLE: Patient underwent medical nutrition therapy reevaluation and assessment. The provider spent 30 minutes face to face with the patient. Report codes 97803 and 97803.

Acupuncture

Acupuncture treatment is classified as face-to-face patient contact for 15-minute increments of time and according to whether electrical stimulation was provided.

    EXAMPLE: Patient underwent acupuncture, which included five needles. The provider spent 30 minutes of one-on-one contact with the patient. Report codes 97810 and 97811.

Osteopathic Manipulative Treatment

Manipulative and body-based practices focus primarily on the structures and systems of the body, including the bones and joints, the soft tissues, and the circulatory and lymphatic systems. **Osteopathic manipulative treatment (OMT)** is a manual treatment performed by a physician, during which emphasis is placed on normal body mechanics and manipulative methods to detect and correct structure. Osteopathic practice includes diagnostic and therapeutic techniques (e.g., musculoskeletal manipulations as well as prescriptions and other therapies) and preventive measures. Combining available medical procedures with OMT provides patients the most comprehensive care. The osteopathic codes are reported according to the number of body regions treated. It is also appropriate to report codes for other restorative modalities and procedures performed on the same day when medically necessary.

 Coding Tip:

- A provider who performs OMT cannot report anesthesia services separately (e.g., nerve blocks and epidural injections) for OMT.
- According to Medicare, postoperative pain management after OMT (e.g., a nerve block or an epidural injection) is not reported separately. However, epidural or nerve block injections unrelated to the OMT may be reported with an OMT code by adding modifier -59.

    EXAMPLE: The osteopathic physician provided osteopathic manipulative treatment to four body regions. Report code 98926.

Chiropractic Manipulative Treatment

Chiropractic manipulative treatment (CMT) is a form of manual treatment to influence joint and neurophysiological function. This treatment may be accomplished using a variety of techniques.

CMT codes include a pre-manipulation patient assessment. However, additional E/M services may be reported separately by adding modifier -25 if the patient's condition requires a separate E/M service beyond the usual pre-service and post-service work associated with the CMT procedure.

For purposes of CMT, the five spinal regions include the following:

- Cervical region (e.g., atlanto-occipital joint)
- Thoracic region (e.g., costovertebral and costotransverse joints)
- Lumbar region
- Sacral region
- Pelvic region (e.g., sacroiliac joint)

The five extraspinal regions include the head (including temporomandibular joint, excluding atlanto-occipital), lower extremities, upper extremities, rib cage (excluding costotransverse and costovertebral joints), and abdomen.

EXAMPLE: A chiropractor provided chiropractic manipulative treatment to four regions of the spine. Report code 98941.

● Coding Tip:

Medicare covers CMT for five spinal regions. Physical therapy services reported with codes 97112, 97124, and 97140 are not separately reportable when performed in a spinal region undergoing CMT. If physical therapy services are performed in a different region than CMT, the physical therapy codes are reported with modifier -59.

Confusion about Medicare's chiropractic coverage resulted in publication of the CMS article entitled "Addressing Misinformation Regarding Chiropractic Services and Medicare: Information for Medicare Fee-for-Service Health Care Professionals." (Go to http://www.cms.hhs.gov, enter "SE0749" in the "Search CMS.gov" box, click the Search button, and locate the PDF file. Or, go to Google.com and enter SE0749 .pdf to locate the document.)

Education and Training for Patient Self-Management

Education and training for patient self-management is performed by a qualified, nonphysician health care professional who uses a standardized curriculum. The codes are classified according to the length of time spent face to face with one or more patients.

EXAMPLE: Patient underwent education and training for self-management of her recently diagnosed diabetes mellitus. The nonphysician health care professional spent 30 minutes providing face-to-face instruction. Report code 98960.

Non-Face-to-Face Nonphysician Services

Non-face-to-face nonphysician services that are provided by a qualified health care professional (nonphysician) include the following:

• Telephone assessment and management services

● Note:

• Codes for telephone services are not reported when they result in a patient encounter within 24 hours or at the next available urgent visit appointment. Such telephone services are considered part of the pre-service work for the subsequent face-to-face encounter.

• Telephone service codes are also not reported when the call is related to a service performed and reported by the provider within the past seven days or within the postoperative period of a previously completed procedure.

• Online medical evaluation in response to a patient's online inquiry using Internet resources

● Note:

To report codes for online medical evaluation services, the health care professional must provide a personal, timely response to the inquiry and the encounter must be permanently stored via electronic means or hard copy.

• Online medical evaluation codes are not reported when related to a service performed and reported by the same provider within the past seven days or within the postoperative period of a previously completed procedure. The online service is considered part of the previous service or procedure.

• Code 98969 is reported just once for the same episode of care during a seven-day period.

Special Services, Procedures, and Reports

Special services, procedures, and reports codes classify the completion of special reports and performance of adjunctive services. These codes describe special circumstances under which a basic procedure is performed.

EXAMPLE 1: The physician office handled and conveyed a specimen for transfer to a laboratory. Report code 99000. (If provided, report a service code for obtaining the specimen, such as venipuncture.)

EXAMPLE 2: A patient was referred to physical therapy after orthopedic surgery. The patient required a 30-day interim visit to the surgeon. Report code 99024 for the surgeon visit. (The code is not reported on a claim, and the payer does not reimburse for the service provided. However, code 99024 allows for internal tracking of postoperative care services provided by the surgeon during the global surgical period.)

Qualifying Circumstances for Anesthesia

Qualifying circumstances for anesthesia codes describe situations that complicate the administration of anesthesia services (e.g., emergencies, extreme age, hypotension, and hypothermia). Codes 99100–99140 are add-on codes, which means that they are reported in addition to the anesthesia service code reported from the Anesthesia section.

EXAMPLE: An otherwise unusually healthy 84-year-old patient underwent left hip replacement surgery, which required the administration of general anesthesia by the anesthesiologist. Report codes 01214-P1-AA (general anesthesia service) and 99100.

Moderate (Conscious) Sedation

Moderate (conscious) sedation codes classify a drug-induced depression of consciousness that requires no interventions to maintain airway patency or ventilation. CPT specifies that moderate (conscious) sedation does not include minimal sedation (e.g., anxiolysis), deep sedation, or monitored anesthesia care (MAC). Subsection notes specify services that are included in moderate (conscious) sedation codes (e.g., IV access, administration of agent, and monitoring oxygen saturation). The surgeon who performs the surgical procedure usually provides moderate (conscious) sedation services. When another physician (e.g., an anesthesiologist) provides general anesthesia, regional anesthesia, or monitored anesthesia care, that other physician reports an appropriate anesthesia code and its modifiers.

CPT's Appendix G lists procedures that include moderate (conscious) sedation as an inherent part of the procedure, identified with the bull's-eye symbol (◉).

EXAMPLE 1: A 68-year-old patient received 15 minutes of moderate sedation services, which were provided by the same physician who removed a superficial orthopedic wire. Report codes 20670 (removal of superficial implant) and 99144.

EXAMPLE 2: A 19-year-old male patient was prepped and draped for brain surgery, and he received moderate (conscious) sedation in the form of a narcotic called remifentanil (brand name Ultiva) administered in combination with propofol. It was determined that the patient could feel no pain but would be able to communicate with the operating room staff and surgeon during the procedure. Trephination craniectomy and bone flap craniotomy were performed after intraoperative brain magnetic resonance imaging (MRI) confirmed the exact location of the supratentorial tumor. It was noted that the tumor was pressing on the area of the cerebrum that controls the ability to read and speak.

During the procedure, the patient remained heavily sedated but conscious so the surgeon could talk with him while mapping the brain's sensors. The patient read a book aloud during the procedure; when the surgeon pressed on a sensitive region of the brain, the patient's reading was affected, letting the surgeon known which areas to avoid. Upon completion of brain mapping, the risky areas were marked by placing lettered pieces of paper directly onto the brain to identify the areas of risk. The surgeon then opened the brain's outer membrane and, layer by layer, removed the tumor. The patient felt no pain (because the brain has no pain receptors), and the tumor was submitted to pathology for analysis. The patient tolerated the 5-hour procedure well and was transported to the recovery room in stable condition. The patient will undergo repeat MRI in 30 days to verify total resection of the tumor. Report codes 61510, 70551, 99144 (first 30 minutes), and 99145 × 18 (subsequent 4.5 hours). (Code 99144 is reported one for the first 30 minutes of anesthesia. Then, code 99145 is assigned 18 times for the subsequent 4.5 hours of anesthesia; 4.5 hours × 60 minutes = 270 minutes divided by 15-minute increments = 18.)

Other Services and Procedures

Other services and procedures codes are reported for services and procedures that cannot be classified in another subsection of the Medicine section (e.g., anogenital examination, vision screening by nonoptical professionals, hypothermia treatment).

EXAMPLE: Patient underwent therapeutic phlebotomy. Report code 99195.

Home Health Procedures/Services

Home health procedures/services codes are reported by nonphysician health care professionals who perform procedures and provide services to the patient in the patient's residence (the patient's home, assisted living facility, or group home). Home infusion procedures are reported for the provision of home infusion services, and the codes are based on length of infusion time.

EXAMPLE 1: Patient received a home visit from a registered nurse for mechanical ventilation care. Report code 99504.

EXAMPLE 2: Patient underwent three hours of home infusion on May 14. Report codes 99601 and 99602.

Medication Therapy Management Services

Medication therapy management services (MTMS) describe face-to-face patient assessments and interventions performed by a pharmacist to:

- Optimize the patient's response to medications.
- Manage treatment-related medication interactions or complications.

Documentation of MTMS includes review of the pertinent patient history and medication profile (prescription and nonprescription), and recommendations for improving health outcomes and compliance with treatment.

Note:

MTMS codes are not reported to describe the provision of product-specific information at the point of dispensing or any other routine dispensing-related activities.

Exercise 18.3 – Medicine Subsections

Instructions: Assign CPT code(s) and appropriate modifier(s) to each statement.

1. Oral immunization administration.

2. A 60-minute individual psychotherapy session rendered during partial hospitalization, which included modifying the patient's obsessive-compulsive behavior.

(continues)

Exercise 18.3 (continued)

3. A physician performed a coronary angioplasty and percutaneous transcatheter placement of intracoronary stents in the anterior descending coronary artery and the inferior coronary artery.

_____

4. A 10-year-old patient received ESRD dialysis-related services daily from July 1 through July 10.

_____

5. A patient received a Rocephin intravenous (IV) push through an existing IV line. The IV was flushed with normal saline before and after administration of the antibiotic to check for patency and to clear the IV line.

_____

Summary

The Medicine section classifies procedures and services that are procedure-oriented, that apply to various medical specialties, and that apply to different types of health care providers. Guidelines located at the beginning of the Medicine section provide instruction about multiple procedures, add-on codes, separate procedures, subsection information, unlisted service or procedure, special reports, and materials supplied by the physician. Instructional notes appear throughout the Medicine section to provide coding clarification and direction. Almost every Medicine subsection contains notes unique to the subsection.

Internet Links

American Chiropractic Association: *www.amerchiro.org*

American Medical Association: Go to *www.ama-assn.org* and click on the Professional Resources link, click on the CPT codes and resources link, click on the CPT® Code Information and Education link, and click on the CPT® Category I Vaccine Codes link to view "early release" vaccine product codes.

American Physical Therapy Association (APTA): *www.apta.org*

Chemotherapy: Go to *www.cancer.gov* and click on the Cancer Topics link. Click on the Types of Treatment link located below the Treatment Methods heading to research chemotherapy treatments.

National Center for Complementary and Alternative Medicine: *www.nccam.nih.gov*

Study Checklist

❑ Read this chapter and highlight key concepts.

❑ Create an index card for each key term.

❑ Access the chapter Internet links to learn more about concepts.

❑ Complete the chapter review, verifying answers with your instructor.

❑ Complete WebTutor assignments and take online quizzes.

❑ Complete Workbook chapter, verifying answers with your instructor.

❑ Go to *www.cengagebrain.com* to access StudyWare™ and the Premium Website. Login instructions are located in the Preface and on the Printed Access Card.

❑ Form a study group with classmates to discuss chapter concepts in preparation for an exam.

Review

Multiple Choice

Instructions: Circle the most appropriate response.

1. Which is a manual treatment performed to influence joint and neurophysiological function?
   a. bilevel (biphasic) positive airway pressure (BiPAP)
   b. chiropractic manipulative treatment (CMT)
   c. intermittent positive pressure breathing (IPPB)
   d. osteopathic manipulative treatment

2. A physician who specializes in physical medicine and rehabilitation and who treats acute/chronic pain and musculoskeletal disorders is a(n) _____.
   a. doctor of osteopathy
   b. internist
   c. psychologist
   d. physiatrist

3. Chemotherapy administered in addition to other cancer treatments, such as surgery and/or radiation therapy, is called _____ chemotherapy.
   a. adjacent
   b. adjudicate
   c. adjunct
   d. adjuvant

4. Which uses low-voltage electrodes that are placed on the scalp and target sites to test the nervous system's pathway?
   a. central motor evoked potential study
   b. orbicularis oculi (blink) test
   c. short-latency somatosensory evoked potential study
   d. visual evoked potential (VEP) test

5. Which is a biofeedback diagnostic test that measures muscle function using a pressure-sensitive tube?
   a. electrocardiography
   b. electromyogram
   c. manometry
   d. Tensilon test

6. Which Medicine subsection classifies drug-induced depression of consciousness that requires no interventions to maintain airway patency or ventilation?
   a. Moderate (Conscious) Sedation
   b. Other Services and Procedures
   c. Photodynamic Therapy
   d. Noninvasive Vascular Diagnostic Studies

7. Which is considered an epicutaneous allergy sensitivity test?
   a. intradermal test
   b. patch test
   c. puncture test
   d. scratch test

8. End-stage renal disease (ESRD) codes include monitoring of nutrition, assessment of growth and development, and parental counseling for patients under the age of _____.
   a. 14
   b. 18
   c. 20
   d. 25

9. The Medicine section classifies procedures and services that are:
   a. diagnosis-oriented and that apply to a limited number of medical specialties.
   b. diagnosis-oriented and that apply to many medical specialties.
   c. procedure-oriented and that apply to a limited number of medical specialties.
   d. procedure-oriented and that apply to many medical specialties.

10. Codes for tests that evaluate autonomic nervous system functioning are classified in which heading in the Neurology and Neuromuscular Procedures subsection of Medicine?
    a. Autonomic Function Tests
    b. EEG Tests
    c. Electromyography and Nerve Conduction Tests
    d. Evoked Potentials and Reflex Tests

11. A 42-year-old patient received a Hepatitis A immunization injection. Which CPT code(s) are assigned?
    a. 90632, 90471   b. 90636, 90471   c. 90746, 90471   d. 90749, 90471

12. Binaural hearing aid check. Which CPT code is assigned?
    a. 92590   b. 92591   c. 92592   d. 92593

13. Cardiovascular stress test, bicycle with continuous electrocardiographic monitoring, interpretation and report only. Which CPT code is assigned?
    a. 93015   b. 93016   c. 93017   d. 93018

14. A 30-day, patient-initiated spirometric recording, including hook-up, reinforced education, data transmission and capture, trend analysis, and periodic recalibration as well as physician review and interpretation. Which CPT code is assigned?
    a. 94010   b. 94014   c. 94015   d. 94016

15. Inhalation bronchial challenge testing with histamine. Which CPT code is assigned?
    a. 95070   b. 95071   c. 95076   d. 95199

16. Comprehensive, computer-based motion analysis by videotaping and 3-D kinematics, with dynamic plantar pressure measurements during walking. Which CPT code is assigned?
    a. 96000   b. 96001   c. 96004   d. 96002

17. Physical therapy reevaluation. Which CPT code is assigned?
    a. 97001   b. 97002   c. 97004   d. 97006

18. A patient and his wife received 30 minutes of face-to-face education and training from a qualified nurse practitioner for patient self-management of diabetic testing supplies. Which CPT code(s) are assigned?
    a. 98960   c. 98961
    b. 98960, 98960-59   d. 99078

19. During a therapeutic service, a 15-year-old patient required moderate sedation in addition to the normal anesthesia. The physician administered the sedation, and an independently trained observer monitored the patient's level of consciousness and physiological status for 30 minutes. Which CPT code is assigned?
    a. 99143   b. 99144   c. 99149   d. 99150

20. A psychiatrist used dolls to communicate with a 5-year-old patient during a psychiatric interview. Which CPT code is assigned?
    a. 90791   b. 90792   c. 90845   d. 90857

Coding Practice

Instructions: Assign CPT code(s) and appropriate modifier(s) to each case.

21. The patient's prescription for bifocal lens was recorded, facial measurements were taken, and adjustment of eyeglasses was done.

_____

22. The patient had the Wisconsin Card Sorting test done on November 15. This was done on a computer. A neuropsychologist interpreted the results and documented the report.

_____

23. The patient arrived at the office for an examination. The patient has never been seen in this practice. The patient complains of redness of both eyes and a decrease in visual acuity. After reviewing the patient's medical history, including medications, the patient's eyes are examined with the ophthalmoscope. Using a slitlamp exam, several small healing ulcers of the right and left cornea are seen. The patient is given instructions for eye irrigation and a prescription for steroidal eye drops. Diagnosis: viral keratitis.

_____

24. Patient presented for a Bernstein test. After insertion of a nasogastric (NG) tube, a solution was passed through the tube to record any complaints of chest-like pain. The first solution was saline, and the patient did not report any pain. The second solution was hydrochloric acid, and this solution did elicit a pain response in the patient. The Bernstein test was positive for esophagitis.

_____

25. Patient underwent a complete transcranial Doppler study of his intracranial arteries.

_____

26. The patient, a 7-year-old female, presented for visual reinforcement audiometry (VRA) evaluation. After being placed in a sound booth, both voice and lighted toys were used for hearing assessment. An audiogram recorded the findings, which were normal.

_____

27. The patient, a 14-year-old with cystic fibrosis, was seen for chest wall cupping to help clear mucous secretion. This initial demonstration was also observed by the patient's mother as a teaching opportunity for home care by the parent.

_____

28. Patient received outpatient cardiac rehab during the sixth week of his postoperative period. He had previously undergone coronary artery bypass graft surgery of four vessels. This session included exercise and a review of diet restrictions with the patient.

_____

29. Biofeedback for perineum and urethral muscles to assist with the patient's urine incontinence. electromyogram (EMG) was used to measure contractions and muscle pressure.

_____

30. The patient presented three years' post-implantation of a dual chamber pacemaker device. Analysis was done while the patient was at rest and while on a treadmill. No pacemaker reprogramming was needed.

_____

31. After placing the patient in the supine position, ultrasound was used to record cardiac function. The patient's ventricular septal defect (VSD), which is a congenital heart condition, was identified. The size of the defect was 2.0 mm. The remainder of the cardiac structures appeared normal in size and function.

_____

32. After placing the patient on the adjustment table, chiropractic manipulation of C7, T4, and L1 were performed to reduce subluxation and increase blood flow. The patient was scheduled for another appointment in one week's time.

_____

33. A 40-year-old male patient presented for a hepatitis A and hepatitis B vaccine. This was administered by the nursing staff, IM in the left arm.

_____

34. A primary care physician provided 30 minutes of training in using adaptive utensils for eating. During the encounter, safety procedures while cooking were also discussed with this patient, who has diagnoses of arthritis and type 2 diabetes mellitus.

_____

35. Patient was awake when electrodes were placed on his head for recording. An extended electro-encephalogram (EEG) was performed during a three-hour period. The patient was awake for the entire EEG.

_____

36. Gastric electrical activity was measured by placing electrodes on the patient's skin over his abdominal cavity. The recording of gastric activity showed that the patient had decreased activity in the large intestine.

_____

37. The patient presented with facial paralysis of the left side of the lower face. An electroneuronography was done to measure nerve conduction. Electrodes were placed over the site of the paralysis. DIAGNOSIS: Bell's palsy.

_____

38. A 25-year-old patient received intramuscular tetanus and diphtheria immunization injection, which was administered by the nursing staff.

_____

39. Patient participated in a psychotherapy session for a total of 30 minutes. This session was done at a local community hospital in the mental health inpatient unit.

_____

40. After placing electrodes on the patient's chest, the heart's activity was recorded. The 12-lead strip was reviewed and a report was written by the attending physician.

_____

41. Under adequate anesthesia, incisions were made in the left leg of the patient for access of the femoral catheter. A second site allowed for insertion of the balloon-tipped catheter. After threading the balloon catheter to the heart, the blocked coronary artery was identified. The balloon was inflated, which resulted in movement of the arthrosclerosis plaque to the sides of the artery. The balloon catheter was advanced to the second blocked artery. The same inflation method was done, with good result. The balloon catheter was withdrawn. The incision sites were closed with sutures and pressure dressings.

_____

42. While the patient was exercising on a stationary bicycle, continuous ECG monitoring and recording was done. The patient's cardiologist was in attendance for the entire 45-minute stress test. At the conclusion of the test, the physician provided a written report on the findings and the interpreted electrocardiogram (ECG) recordings.

_____

43. Patient underwent gastroesophageal reflux test via esophagus, which included placement of nasal catheter pH electrodes, recording, analysis and interpretation.

_____

44. A 15-year-old patient was recently diagnosed with asthma. A home health nurse visited on May 6 to provide training in the use of bronchodilators for both the patient and mother.

_____

45. A patient is status post left side cerebrovascular accident (CVA). He presents for physical therapy evaluation to regain strength and mobility on the left side. The patient will require three visits per week, beginning next week, with a reevaluation after 60 days of treatment.

_____

46. Using allergen vials specifically kept in the office for a certain patient, a pollen and grass mix was injected into the upper-right arm. A dust mites, cat dander, and feather mixture was injected into the patient's upper-left arm. The patient was observed in the waiting room for 30 minutes post-injection, with no reaction.

_____

47. Using a laser, approximately 25 pulses were delivered to a patient's psoriasis lesions on the elbows and forearms. Total area of treatment measured approximately 10 sq cm.

_____

48. Rabies immune globulin was administered intramuscularly (IM) to the patient's upper-left arm.

_____

49. ESRD services for a 25-year-old male for the month of September. Number of visits to a physician for the month totaled 4.

_____

50. Intravenous (IV) infusion of chemotherapy drugs, two hours.

_____

PART V

Insurance and Reimbursement Overview

Insurance and Reimbursement

Chapter Outline

Third-Party Payers

Provisions of the Affordable Care Act of 2010

Health Care Reimbursement Systems

Impact of HIPAA on Reimbursement

Health Reform

Chapter Objectives

At the conclusion of this chapter, the student should be able to:

- Define key terms.
- Identify and provide examples of third-party payers.
- List and define each health care reimbursement system.
- Describe the impact of HIPAA on health care reimbursement.
- Explain the components of Health Reform, as delineated in the Affordable Care Act.

Key Terms

abuse

ambulance fee schedule

ambulatory payment classification (APC)

ambulatory surgical center (ASC) payment rate

ANSI ASC X12N 837

Balanced Budget Act of 1997

Balanced Budget Refinement Act of 1999 (BBRA)

Blue Cross and Blue Shield (BCBS)

breach of confidentiality

cafeteria plan

capitation

case mix

case-mix adjustment

charge description master (CDM)

chargemaster

chargemaster review process

check digit

Civil Monetary Penalties Act

Civilian Health and Medical Program of the Department of Veterans Affairs (CHAMPVA)

clinical laboratory fee schedule

closed-panel HMO

commercial payer

compliance guidance

confidentiality

Consolidated Omnibus Budget Reconciliation Act of 1985

consumer-directed health plan (CDHP)

conversion factor

covered benefit

covered entity

critical pathways

customized sub-capitation plan (CSCP)

decrypt

Deficit Reduction Act of 1984

Designated Standard Maintenance Organization (DSMO)

diagnosis-related groups (DRGs)

Diagnostic and Statistical Manual (DSM)

digital

direct contract model HMO

disclosed

DRG creep

durable medical equipment, prosthetics/orthotics, and supplies (DMEPOS) fee schedule

electronic data interchange (EDI)

electronic transaction standard

employer self-insurance plan

encounter form

encrypt

end-stage renal disease (ESRD) composite payment rate system

exclusion

exclusive provider organization (EPO)

explanation of benefits (EOB)

False Claims Act (FCA)

Federal Anti-kickback Statute

Federal Claims Collection Act of 1966

Federal Employee Health Benefits Program (FEHBP or FEP)

fee schedule

fee-for-service

flat file

flexible spending account (FSA)

fraud

government-sponsored programs

group model HMO

group practice without walls (GPWW)

health care reimbursement account (HCRA)

health insurance claim

health insurance policy

health maintenance organization (HMO)

health reimbursement arrangement (HRA)

health savings account (HSA)

health savings security account (HSSA)

HIPAA administrative simplification (AS)

HIPAA standards for privacy of individually identifiable health information

hold harmless clause

Home Assessment Validation and Entry (HAVEN)

home health prospective payment system (HH PPS)

indemnification

Indian Health Service (IHS)

individual practice association (IPA) HMO

inpatient prospective payment system (IPPS)

inpatient psychiatric facility prospective payment system (IPF PPS)

inpatient rehabilitation facility prospective payment system (IRF PPS)

integrated delivery system (IDS)

integrated provider organization (IPO)

IPPS 3-day payment window

IPPS 72-hour rule

IPPS transfer rule

IRF PPS 1-day payment window

IRF PPS 24-hour rule

IRF PPS transfer rule

long-term (acute) care hospital prospective payment system (LTCH PPS)

LTCH PPS 1-day payment window

LTCH PPS 24-hour rule

major diagnostic category (MDC)

managed care

management service organization (MSO)

Medicaid

medical foundation

Medicare

Medicare administrative contractor (MAC)

Medicare physician fee schedule (MPFS)

Medicare Prescription Drug, Improvement, and Modernization Act of 2003 (MMA)

Medicare severity diagnosis-related groups (MS-DRGs)

Medicare severity long-term (acute) care diagnosis-related groups (MS-LTCH-DRGs)

Medicare Summary Notice (MSN)

Military Health System (MHS)

minimum data set (MDS)

national health plan identifier (PlanID)

national individual identifier (patient identifier)

national limitation amount (NLA)

national provider identifier (NPI)

national standard employer identifier number (EIN)

network model HMO

network provider

noncovered benefits

nonparticipating provider (nonPAR)

Omnibus Budget Reconciliation Act of 1980

Omnibus Budget Reconciliation Act of 1987 (OBRA)

Omnibus Budget Reconciliation Act of 1989

Omnibus Consolidated and Emergency Supplemental Appropriations Act (OCESAA) of 1999

open-panel HMO

outlier

outpatient encounter

outpatient prospective payment system (OPPS)

outpatient visit

overpayment

overpayment recovery

participating provider (PAR)

Payment Error and Prevention Program (PEPP)

physician-hospital organization (PHO)

Physicians at Teaching Hospitals (PATH) initiative

physician self-referral law

point-of-service plan (POS)

preauthorization

preexisting medical condition

preferred provider organization (PPO)

present on admission (POA) indicator

privacy

privacy rule

privileged communication

Programs of All-inclusive Care for the Elderly (PACE)

prospective cost-based rate

prospective payment system (PPS)

prospective price-based rate

protected health information (PHI)

relative value unit (RVU)

remittance advice (remit)

Resident Assessment Validation and Entry (RAVEN)

resource-based relative value scale (RBRVS) system

resource utilization group (RUG)

revenue code

roster billing

safe harbor regulation

security

security rule

self-referral

severity of illness

skilled nursing facility prospective payment system (SNF PPS)

staff model HMO

Stark I

Stark II

State Children's Health Insurance Program (SCHIP)

status indicator (SI)

superbill

Tax Equity and Fiscal Responsibility Act of 1983 (TEFRA)

TRICARE

triple option plan

wage index

workers' compensation

Introduction

This chapter includes a discussion of third-party payers, health care reimbursement methodologies, and the impact of HIPAA on health care reimbursement. Third-party payers process health insurance claims to reimburse providers (e.g., physicians, health care facilities) for services provided to patients for covered benefits. Health care reimbursement methodologies were originally developed by Centers for Medicare and Medicaid Services (CMS) to control health care costs associated with government programs; however, most third-party payers have also adopted them. HIPAA has impacted health care reimbursement as a result of the implementation of federal regulations such as administrative simplification, privacy and security of protected health information, and more.

Third-Party Payers

A third-party payer is an insurance company or other organization (e.g., a Medicare administrative contractor) that processes health care claims for reimbursement of procedures and services. Payers serve as **Medicare administrative contractors (MACs)** by processing claims for physicians (Medicare Part B); health care facilities (Medicare Part A); suppliers of durable medical equipment, prosthetics, orthotics, and supplies (DMEPOS); and home health and hospice agencies. The CMS, an administrative agency in the Department of Health and Human Services (DHHS), selects the MACs through a competitive bidding process.

Title IX of the **Medicare Prescription Drug, Improvement, and Modernization Act of 2003 (MMA)** called for the elimination of carriers, fiscal intermediaries (FIs), and durable medical equipment regional carriers (DMERCs) and the creation of Medicare administrative contractors. The MMA limits **indemnification** (insurance against loss) for adverse judgments against MACs and associated legal costs. Providers no longer nominate carriers or FIs, and they also no longer have a right to choose who will review claims or pay benefits. MACs integrate Medicare Part A and Part B functions into one contract, and providers have a single point of contact for all claims-related activity. MACs have been established in 15 jurisdictions throughout the United States, and eight specialty MACs were also created to process durable medical equipment claims and home health care claims (four MACs for each).

Note:

By 2010, Medicare had eliminated the following to create 23 Medicare Administrative Contractors (MACs) that consolidated the administration of Medicare Part A and B benefits so that Medicare beneficiaries have claims processed by one contractor.

- *Carriers* (processed Medicare Part B claims)
- *Fiscal intermediaries* (*FIs*) (processed Medicare Part A claims)

> • *Durable medical equipment carriers (DMERCs)* (processed durable medical equipment, prosthetics, orthotics, and supplies [DMEPOS])
> Durable medical equipment, prosthetics, orthotics, and supplies (DMEPOS) claims are processed by DME MACs, and home health and hospice claims are processed by HH & H MACs.

A **health insurance policy** is an agreement between an individual and a third-party payer (or insurance company) that contains a list of reimbursable medical benefits, or **covered benefits** (which might include office visits, inpatient hospitalizations, laboratory, tests, prescription medications, treatment services, and so on). The policy also lists procedures and services that are *not* covered by the third-party payer, called **noncovered benefits**, and when an individual undergoes procedures or receives services that are not covered by the policy, the individual is responsible for reimbursing the health care provider directly (e.g., with cosmetic surgery). A health care provider is a physician or other health care practitioner (e.g., a nurse practitioner) who provides services to patients.

After patient care has been delivered, the provider submits a **health insurance claim** to an insurance plan to request reimbursement for procedures performed or services provided (e.g., CMS-1500, UB-04). The CMS-1500 (Figure 19-1) is a standard claim submitted by physician offices to third-party payers. The UB-04 (or CMS-1450) (Uniform Bill, first implemented as the UB-92 in 1992 and revised to create the UB-04 in 2004, which was implemented in 2007) (Figure 19-2) is a standard claim submitted by health care institutions to payers for inpatient and outpatient services. CMS-1500 and UB-04 claims can also be submitted as electronic data interchange (EDI) transactions using specialized software (Figure 19-3), which is discussed later in this chapter.

Effective March 1, 2007, health plans and health care clearinghouses were required to accept the new UB-04. A health care clearinghouse processes or facilitates the processing of health information (such as a claim) received from another entity (such as a provider or payer) from a nonstandard into a standard format.

Determining which claim (e.g., CMS-1500, UB-04) to submit, as well as which coding system to use to report codes on the claim, depends on the health care setting (Table 19-1). Non-institutional providers (e.g., physician offices, independent labs, ambulance companies that are not associated with a hospital, ambulatory surgery centers, and independent diagnostic testing facilities) and suppliers (for durable medical equipment, prosthetics, orthotics, and supplies dealers) submit the CMS-1500 claim to third-party payers, and they report ICD-9-CM (or ICD-10-CM) diagnosis and HCPCS/CPT procedure and service codes (and HCPCS/CPT modifiers). Institutional providers (e.g., hospitals, nursing facilities, comprehensive outpatient rehabilitation facilities, community mental health centers, outpatient physical therapy facilities, rehabilitation agencies, and end-stage renal facilities) submit the UB-04 (or CMS-1450) claim to payers. For inpatient claims, ICD-9-CM (or ICD-10-CM) diagnosis and ICD-9-CM (or ICD-10-PCS) procedure codes are reported, and for outpatient claims (e.g., emergency department and outpatient care), ICD-9-CM (or ICD-10-CM) diagnosis and HCPCS/CPT procedure and service codes (and HCPCS/CPT modifiers) are reported.

Before delivering health care services to patients, some payers require providers to obtain **preauthorization** (prior approval) of treatment (e.g., when specialists are involved) and to submit post-treatment reports. If the provider does not meet the preauthorization requirements, the claim is denied. If the patient's insurance policy contains a **hold harmless clause** (which holds that the patient is not responsible for paying what the insurance plan denies), the health care provider is prohibited from collecting payment from the patient. Claims are also denied if the medical necessity of procedures or services is not established. This means that every procedure or service reported on the claim must be linked to a condition that justifies the necessity for performing that procedure or providing that service. If the procedures or services delivered are determined to be unreasonable or unnecessary, the claim is denied.

Types of Third-Party Payers

Third-party payers include the following:

- Blue Cross and Blue Shield (BCBS)
- Government-sponsored programs (e.g., Medicaid, Medicare, TRICARE)
- Commercial insurance companies
- Managed care plans (e.g., a health maintenance organization)
- Employer self-insurance plans
- Workers' compensation

1500

HEALTH INSURANCE CLAIM FORM

APPROVED BY NATIONAL UNIFORM CLAIM COMMITTEE 08/05

PICA | PICA

1. MEDICARE (Medicare #) ☐ MEDICAID (Medicaid #) ☐ TRICARE CHAMPUS (Sponsor's SSN) ☐ CHAMPVA (Member ID#) ☐ GROUP HEALTH PLAN (SSN or ID) ☐ FECA BLK LUNG (SSN) [X] OTHER (ID)	1a. INSURED'S I.D. NUMBER (For Program in Item 1): R0001001
2. PATIENT'S NAME (Last Name, First Name, Middle Initial): PATIENT, IMA	3. PATIENT'S BIRTH DATE MM DD YY: 03 08 1934 SEX M ☐ F [X]
4. INSURED'S NAME (Last Name, First Name, Middle Initial): PATIENT, H E	
5. PATIENT'S ADDRESS (No., Street): 1 FEELBETTER STREET	6. PATIENT RELATIONSHIP TO INSURED: Self ☐ Spouse [X] Child ☐ Other ☐
7. INSURED'S ADDRESS (No., Street): 1 FEELBETTER STREET	
CITY: ANYWHERE STATE: US	8. PATIENT STATUS: Single ☐ Married [X] Other ☐
CITY: ANYWHERE STATE:	
ZIP CODE: 00001 TELEPHONE (Include Area Code): (001)555 3456	Employed ☐ Full-Time Student ☐ Part-Time Student ☐
ZIP CODE: 00001 TELEPHONE (Include Area Code): (001)555 3456	
9. OTHER INSURED'S NAME (Last Name, First Name, Middle Initial): NONE	10. IS PATIENT'S CONDITION RELATED TO:
11. INSURED'S POLICY GROUP OR FECA NUMBER:	
a. OTHER INSURED'S POLICY OR GROUP NUMBER:	a. EMPLOYMENT? (Current or Previous) ☐ YES [X] NO
a. INSURED'S DATE OF BIRTH MM DD YY: 12 30 YYYY SEX M [X] F ☐	
b. OTHER INSURED'S DATE OF BIRTH MM DD YY SEX M ☐ F ☐	b. AUTO ACCIDENT? ☐ YES [X] NO PLACE (State)
b. EMPLOYER'S NAME OR SCHOOL NAME: ANY COMPANY	
c. EMPLOYER'S NAME OR SCHOOL NAME:	c. OTHER ACCIDENT? ☐ YES [X] NO
c. INSURANCE PLAN NAME OR PROGRAM NAME: BC BS	
d. INSURANCE PLAN NAME OR PROGRAM NAME:	10d. RESERVED FOR LOCAL USE
d. IS THERE ANOTHER HEALTH BENEFIT PLAN? ☐ YES [X] NO *If yes, return to and complete item 9 a-d.*	

READ BACK OF FORM BEFORE COMPLETING & SIGNING THIS FORM.

12. PATIENT'S OR AUTHORIZED PERSON'S SIGNATURE I authorize the release of any medical or other information necessary to process this claim. I also request payment of government benefits either to myself or to the party who accepts assignment below.

SIGNED *Ima Patient* DATE *6/25/YY*

13. INSURED'S OR AUTHORIZED PERSON'S SIGNATURE I authorize payment of medical benefits to the undersigned physician or supplier for services described below.

SIGNED *H.E. Patient*

PATIENT AND INSURED INFORMATION — CARRIER

14. DATE OF CURRENT: ILLNESS (First symptom) OR INJURY (Accident) OR PREGNANCY(LMP) MM DD YY: 06 25 YY	15. IF PATIENT HAS HAD SAME OR SIMILAR ILLNESS. GIVE FIRST DATE MM DD YY
16. DATES PATIENT UNABLE TO WORK IN CURRENT OCCUPATION FROM MM DD YY TO MM DD YY	
17. NAME OF REFERRING PROVIDER OR OTHER SOURCE	17a. 17b. NPI
18. HOSPITALIZATION DATES RELATED TO CURRENT SERVICES FROM MM DD YY TO MM DD YY	
19. RESERVED FOR LOCAL USE	20. OUTSIDE LAB? ☐ YES [X] NO $ CHARGES
21. DIAGNOSIS OR NATURE OF ILLNESS OR INJURY (Relate Items 1, 2, 3 or 4 to Item 24E by Line): 1. I10. 2. E78 0 3. 4.	22. MEDICAID RESUBMISSION CODE ORIGINAL REF. NO.
23. PRIOR AUTHORIZATION NUMBER	

24. A. DATE(S) OF SERVICE From MM DD YY	To MM DD YY	B. PLACE OF SERVICE	C. EMG	D. PROCEDURES, SERVICES, OR SUPPLIES (Explain Unusual Circumstances) CPT/HCPCS	MODIFIER	E. DIAGNOSIS POINTER	F. $ CHARGES	G. DAYS OR UNITS	H. EPSDT Family Plan	I. ID. QUAL.	J. RENDERING PROVIDER ID. #
1 06 25 YY		11		99213		1	38 00	1		NPI	
2										NPI	
3										NPI	
4										NPI	
5										NPI	
6										NPI	

25. FEDERAL TAX I.D. NUMBER SSN ☐ EIN [X]: 52-1581586	26. PATIENT'S ACCOUNT NO.: 9804	27. ACCEPT ASSIGNMENT? (For govt. claims, see back) [X] YES ☐ NO	28. TOTAL CHARGE: $ 38 00	29. AMOUNT PAID: $	30. BALANCE DUE: $ 38 00
31. SIGNATURE OF PHYSICIAN OR SUPPLIER INCLUDING DEGREES OR CREDENTIALS (I certify that the statements on the reverse apply to this bill and are made a part thereof.) HEEZA FRIEND MD 0626YYYY SIGNED DATE	32. SERVICE FACILITY LOCATION INFORMATION a. NPI b.		33. BILLING PROVIDER INFO & PH # (001)555-0001 HEEZA FRIEND MD 1 INTERNATIONAL ST ANYWHERE US 12345 a. 4532085819 b.		

PHYSICIAN OR SUPPLIER INFORMATION

NUCC Instruction Manual available at: www.nucc.org

APPROVED OMB-0938-0999 FORM CMS-1500 (08/05)

Figure 19-1 Completed CMS-1500 claim

Table 19-1 Claims and Coding Systems According to Type of Health Care Setting

Claim	Codes Reported	Health Care Setting
CMS-1491	ICD-9-CM (or ICD-10-CM) diagnosis codes and HCPCS level II	Ambulance services
CMS-1500	ICD-9-CM (or ICD-10-CM) diagnosis codes, CPT, and HCPCS level II	Non-institutional providers and suppliers • Ambulatory surgery centers[1] • Anesthesiologists who administer hospital-based inpatient and outpatient anesthesia • Certified portable X-ray services • Home health agencies and hospices[2] • Independent clinical laboratories located at physician offices, group practices, hospitals, nursing facilities, end stage renal disease facilities, pharmacies, home health agencies, rural health clinics, health fairs, anatomical testing laboratories, and nuclear medicine providers • Independent diagnostic testing facilities (e.g., a certified mammography center) • Physician, chiropractor, optometrist, and podiatrist offices • Privately practicing occupational therapists and physical therapists • Roster billing[3] for flu and pneumonia vaccinations
UB-04	ICD-9-CM (or ICD-10-CM) diagnosis and ICD-9-CM (or ICD-10-PCS) procedure codes	Institutional providers (inpatient) • Acute care hospitals • Long-term care facilities • Psychiatric hospitals • Rehabilitation facilities • Short-term hospitals • Hospices (inpatient respite care)[4]
UB-04	ICD-9-CM (or ICD-10-CM) diagnosis codes, CPT, and HCPCS level II	Institutional providers (outpatient) • Hospital emergency departments • Hospital outpatient departments
UB-04	ICD-9-CM (or ICD-10-CM) diagnosis codes, CPT, HCPCS level II, and HIPPS codes	Non-institutional providers (outpatient) • Home health agencies[5] • Hospices (home care)[5]

[1]Some ASCs submit the UB-04 claim instead of the CMS-1500 claim.

[2]Some home health agencies and hospices submit the UB-04 claim instead of the CMS-1500 claim.

[3]**Roster billing** is a simplified process available to public health clinics and other non-institutional entities that offer mass immunization programs. Hospices also submit claims for the administration of pneumococcal pneumonia, influenza virus, and hepatitis B vaccines.

[4]Respite care includes services that provide primary caregivers (e.g., the spouse of a terminally ill person) with temporary relief from tasks associated with caregiving (e.g., in-home assistance, short hospital or nursing facility stays, adult day care).

[5]Physicians who are not employees of the HHA and/or hospice and who provide professional home care services for home health agencies and hospices submit claims with ICD-9-CM (or ICD-10-CM) diagnosis codes and CPT and HCPCS level II procedure/service codes.

Commercial Payers

Commercial payers include private health insurance and employer-based group health insurance. Private health insurance usually consists of an indemnity plan, which covers individuals for certain health care expenses. The insurance company reimburses the patient or the provider, depending on the contract language. Individuals pay annual premiums (with predetermined rates).

Employer-based group health insurance is often provided as an employee benefit. The employer typically pays 80 percent of insurance premiums, and the employee pays the remaining 20 percent. The employer generally contracts with a commercial health insurance plan (e.g., Aetna).

Employer Self-Insurance Plans

For **employer self-insurance plans**, an employer accepts direct responsibility (or the risk) for paying employees' health care without purchasing health insurance and creates an employer self-insurance plan. Usually, the plan contracts with a third-party administrator (TPA), which is an organization that provides the following services to employers (and insurance companies):

- Benefit design: Medical services covered by the plan

- Claims administration: Processing claims to reimburse services

- Utilization review or utilization management: Reviewing medical care for appropriateness, necessity, and quality (e.g., preadmission authorization)

Government-Sponsored Programs

 Note:

The Recovery Audit Contractor (RAC) program was implemented nationwide in 2009 as part of the Medicare Prescription Drug, Improvement, and Modernization Act of 2003 (MMA), and four regional RACs were named. Its purpose is to safeguard the Medicare Trust Fund by having RACs evaluate individual provider compliance to (1) identify overpayments (and underpayments) made by Medicare and Medicaid and (2) recover overpayments made to durable medical equipment (DME) providers, health care facilities, and physician practices. For example, RACs use proprietary software to detect errors in codes reported on CMS-1500 claims. (Go to http://www.cms.hhs.gov/rac to review results of RAC activity.) RACs also monitor Medicare's post-acute care transfer (PACT) policy that can result in reduced payments for transferring hospitals, depending on the discharge status code reported (e.g., 03-Medicare SNF with Medicare certification in anticipation of skilled care).

RACs are not the same as Medicare's Comprehensive Error Rate Testing (CERT) program, which was implemented in 2003 (and currently operates parallel to the RAC program) to evaluate Medicare administrative contractors' (MAC) program performance. For example, CERT assesses the ability of an MAC to detect errors that are considered fraudulent.

The MMA also imposed Medicare fee-for-service contracting reform, directing CMS to use competitive measures to replace the Medicare fiscal intermediaries and carriers with MACs. CMS also established Zone Program Integrity Contractors (ZPICs) to perform program integrity functions in the newly established MAC jurisdictions (or zones). ZPICs are expected to perform program integrity functions for Medicare Parts A through D, DME, home health, hospice, and Medi-Medi programs.

Government-sponsored programs include:

- CHAMPVA
- Federal Employee Health Benefits Program (FEHBP or FEP)
- Indian Health Service (IHS)
- Medicaid
- Medicare
- Military Health System (MHS)
- Programs of All-inclusive Care for the Elderly (PACE)
- TRICARE

The **Civilian Health and Medical Program of the Department of Veterans Affairs (CHAMPVA)** program provides health care benefits to dependents of veterans who:

- Are rated as 100-percent permanently and totally disabled as a result of service-connected conditions.

- Died as a result of service-connected conditions.

- Died on duty with fewer than 30 days of active service.

The **Federal Employee Health Benefits Program (FEHBP or FEP)** is a voluntary health care program that covers federal employees, retirees, and their dependents and survivors. The **Indian Health Service (IHS)** is a DHHS agency that provides federal health care services to American Indians and Alaska natives.

Medicaid (Title XIX of the Social Security Act Amendments of 1965) is a joint federal and state program that provides health care coverage to low-income populations and certain aged and disabled individuals. It is an entitlement program that is jointly financed by state and federal governments, with federal spending levels determined by the number of participants and services provided. The **State Children's Health Insurance Program (SCHIP)** was established to provide health assistance to uninsured, low-income children either through separate programs or through expanded eligibility under state Medicaid programs.

Medicare (Title XVIII of the Social Security Act Amendments of 1965) provides health care coverage to elderly and disabled persons; federal spending is funded by the Medicare Trust Fund (payroll tax). Medicare administrative contractors review local coverage determinations (LCDs) and national coverage determinations (NCDs) to specify under what clinical circumstances a service is covered, considered to be reasonable and necessary, and correctly coded. The **Programs of All-inclusive Care for the Elderly (PACE)** are community-based Medicare and Medicaid programs that provide integrated health care and long-term care services to elderly persons who require a nursing-facility level of care.

The **Military Health System (MHS)** provides and maintains readiness to provide health care services and support to members of the Uniformed Services during military operations. It also provides health care services and support to members of the Uniformed Services, their family members, and others entitled to Department of Defense health care.

TRICARE is the military health plan that covers active duty and retired members of the Uniformed Services and their dependents. It combines military health care resources (e.g., military treatment facilities) and networks of civilian health care professionals. TRICARE was formerly called CHAMPUS (Civilian Health and Medical Program of the United States).

Provisions of the Affordable Care Act of 2010

For individuals who already have health insurance, the intent of the Affordable Care Act of 2010 is to provide more stability and security by:

- Ending discrimination against people with preexisting conditions.

- Preventing insurance companies from dropping coverage when people are sick and need it most.

- Applying caps to out-of pocket expenses so people do not go broke when they get sick.

- Eliminating extra charges for preventive care like mammograms, flu shots, and diabetes tests to improve health and save money.

- Protecting Medicare for seniors and eliminating the "donut-hole" gap in coverage for prescription drugs.

    For individuals who do not have health insurance, the intent of the Act is to provide quality, affordable choices for everyone by:

- Creating a new insurance marketplace called "the Exchange," which allows people without insurance and small businesses to compare plans and buy insurance at competitive prices.

- Providing new tax credits to help people buy insurance and to help small businesses cover their employees.

- Offering a public health insurance option to provide the uninsured who cannot find affordable coverage with a real choice.

- Offering new, low-cost coverage through a national "high-risk" pool to protect people with preexisting conditions from financial ruin until the "new Exchange" is created.

The Affordable Care Act of 2010 also intends to control the costs of health care for families, businesses, and government by:

- Establishing prospective payments (so that the country's deficit is not adversely impacted).

- Creating an independent commission of physicians and medical experts to identify waste, fraud, and abuse in the health care system.

- Ordering immediate medical malpractice reform projects that could help physician focus on putting their patients first, not on practicing defensive medicine.

- Requiring large employers to cover their employees and individuals who can afford it to buy insurance so everyone shares in the responsibility.

Workers' Compensation

Workers' compensation is a state-mandated insurance program that reimburses health care costs and lost wages if an employee suffers a work-related disease or injury. Qualified employees and their dependents are eligible for reimbursement.

Managed Care

Managed care combines the financing and delivery of health care services to replace conventional fee-for-service health insurance plans with more affordable care for consumers and providers who agree to certain restrictions (e.g., patients receive care from participating providers). (Managed care plans range from structured closed-panel staff model health maintenance organizations to less structured preferred provider organizations.)

A **participating provider (PAR)** is a member of a managed care plan, while a **nonparticipating provider (nonPAR)** is not a member of the plan. (PAR and nonPAR providers are also associated with traditional health insurance plans. Patients may incur higher out-of-pocket costs when receiving care from nonPARs.)

Fee-for-service plans reimburse providers for individual health care services rendered, while managed care is financed according to a method called **capitation**. *Capitation* is the term used when providers accept preestablished payments for providing health care services to enrollees over a period of time, usually one year. If the managed care physician provides services that cost less than the capitation amount, the physician keeps any profits. If services provided cost more than the capitation amount, the physician loses money. Patients who subscribe to managed care plans receive care from *their primary care provider (PCP)*, the physician responsible for supervising and coordinating health care services, for preauthorizing referrals to specialists, and for inpatient hospital admissions, except in emergencies.

The following types of managed care plans are explained below:

- Exclusive provider organization (EPO)
- Health maintenance organization (HMO)
- Point of service plan (POS)
- Preferred provider organization (PPO)
- Triple option plan (TPO) (also called cafeteria plan)

Exclusive Provider Organization

An **exclusive provider organization (EPO)** is a managed care plan that provides benefits to subscribers if they receive services from network providers. (EPOs are regulated by state insurance departments.) A **network provider** is a physician or health care facility under contract to the managed care plan. Network providers usually sign exclusive contracts with the EPO, which means they cannot contract with other managed care plans. Subscribers are generally required to coordinate health care services through their PCP.

An **integrated delivery system (IDS)** is an organization of affiliated provider sites (e.g., hospitals, ambulatory surgical centers, or physician groups) that offer joint health care services to subscribers. Integrated delivery systems are also known as:

- Accountable health plans
- Delivery systems
- Health delivery networks
- Horizontally integrated systems

- Vertically integrated systems
- Vertically integrated plans (VIPs)
- Integrated service networks (ISNs)

Integrated delivery system models include the following:

- **Physician-hospital organization (PHO)**: Owned by hospital(s) and physician groups that obtain managed care plan contracts; physicians maintain their own practices and provide health care services to plan members.

- **Management service organization (MSO)**: Usually owned by physicians or a hospital; provides practice management and administrative and support services to individual physician practices.

- **Group practice without walls (GPWW)**: Establishes a contract that allows physicians to maintain their own offices and share services such as appointment scheduling and billing.

- **Integrated provider organization (IPO)**: Manages the delivery of health care services offered by hospitals, physicians who are employees of the IPO, and other health care organizations such as ambulatory surgery clinics and nursing facilities.

- **Medical foundation**: Nonprofit organization that contracts with and acquires the clinical and business assets of physician practices; the foundation is assigned a provider number and manages the practice's business.

Health Maintenance Organization

A **health maintenance organization (HMO)** is an alternative to traditional group health insurance coverage that provides comprehensive health care services to voluntarily enrolled members on a prepaid basis. It provides preventive care services to promote "wellness" or good health, thus reducing the overall cost of medical care. An HMO often requires patients to pay a *copayment* (or *copay*), which is a fee paid by the patient to the provider at the time health care services are rendered.

HMOs must meet requirements of the HMO Act of 1973 as well as rules and regulations of individual states. They are organized in the following way:

- **Closed-panel HMO**: Health care is provided in an HMO-owned center or satellite clinic, or by physicians who belong to a specially formed medical group that serves the HMO.

- **Open-panel HMO**: Health care is provided by individuals who are not employees of the HMO or who do not belong to a specially formed medical group that serves the HMO.

Closed-panel HMOs include the following models:

- **Group model HMO**: Contracted health care services are delivered to subscribers by participating physicians *who are members of an independent multispecialty group practice*.

- **Staff model HMO**: Health care services are provided to subscribers by *physicians employed by the HMO*.

Open-panel HMOs include the following models:

- **Direct contract model HMO**: Contracted health care services are delivered to subscribers by *individual physicians in the community*.

- **Individual practice association (IPA) HMO**: Contracted health care services are delivered to subscribers by *physicians who remain in their independent office settings*.

- **Network model HMO**: Contracted health care services are provided to subscribers by *two or more physician multispecialty group practices*.

Point of Service Plan

A **point-of-service plan (POS)** offers patients the freedom to use an HMO panel of providers or to self-refer to non-HMO providers. If the enrollee chooses to receive all medical care from the HMO network of health care providers or obtains an authorization from the POS primary care physician for specialty care outside the

HMO network, the enrollee pays only the regular copayment or a small charge for the visit, and no deductible or coinsurance responsibility applies. If the enrollee sees a non-HMO panel specialist without a referral from the PCP, this is called a **self-referral**, and the enrollee will have greater out-of-pocket expenses (e.g., a large deductible of about $250 plus 20 percent of coinsurance charges).

Preferred Provider Organization

A **preferred provider organization (PPO)** is a network of physicians and hospitals that join together to contract with insurance companies, employers, or other organizations. PPOs provide health care to subscribers for a discounted fee.

Triple Option Plan (or Cafeteria Plan)

A **triple option plan**, or **cafeteria plan**, is offered by either a single insurance plan or as a joint venture among two or more third-party payers. They provide a choice of HMO, PPO, or traditional health insurance plans.

Consumer-Directed Health Plan

Managed care is currently challenged by the growth of consumer-directed health plans, which define employer contributions and ask employees to be more responsible for health care decisions and cost-sharing.
A **consumer-directed health plan (CDHP)** is a sort of "401(k) plan" for health care. It includes many choices that provide individuals with an incentive to control the costs of health benefits and health care. Individuals have greater freedom in spending health care dollars up to a designated amount and can receive full coverage for in-network preventive care. In return, individuals assume significantly higher cost-sharing expenses after the designated amount has been expended. (The catastrophic limit is usually higher than those common in other plans.)

The CDHP has become a popular alternative to the increased costs of traditional health insurance premiums and the limitations associated with managed care plans. They include the following tiers:

- Tax-exempt account, which is used to pay for health care expenses and provides more flexibility than traditional managed care plans in terms of access to providers and services

- Out-of-pocket payments for health care expenses, which are made after the tax-exempt account is expended and before the deductible for high-deductible insurance has been met; this tier actually represents a gap in coverage

- High-deductible insurance policy, which reimburses allowable health care expenses after the high deductible has been paid

The CDHP usually provides Internet-based support so individuals can track health care expenses, improve their health by viewing useful information and learning about preventive services, obtain information about provider quality, and receive notification about provider group-rate pricing. A variety of types of consumer-directed health plans are available to individuals, all of which are subject to modification as legislation is passed and payers alter program requirements.

CDHP include the following types:

- Customized sub-capitation plan (CSCP)
- Health reimbursement arrangement (HRA)
- Flexible spending account (FSA)
- Health care reimbursement account (HCRA)

Customized Sub-Capitation Plan

A **customized sub-capitation plan (CSCP)** funds health care expenses with insurance coverage, and the individual selects one of each type of provider to create a customized network and pays the resulting customized insurance premium. Each provider is paid a fixed amount per month to provide only the care that an individual needs from that provider (*a sub-capitation payment*).

Flexible Spending Account

A **flexible spending account (FSA)** is a tax-exempt account offered by employers to any number of employees, which individuals use to pay health care bills. Employees contribute funds to the FSA through a salary reduction agreement and withdraw funds to pay medical bills. Funds in an FSA are exempt from both income tax and Social Security tax. (Employers may also contribute to FSAs.) By law, employees forfeit unspent funds remaining in the FSA at the end of the year.

> ## Note:
>
> In managed care, the primary care provider receives a *capitation payment* and is responsible for managing all of an individual's health care, which includes reimbursing health care expenses provided by other caregivers (e.g., labs and specialists).

Health Savings Account or Health Savings Security Account

A **health savings account (HSA)** or **health savings security account (HSSA)** allows participants to enroll in a relatively inexpensive, high-deductible insurance plan, and a tax-deductible savings account is opened to cover current and future medical expenses. Money deposited (and earnings) is tax-deferred, and money is withdrawn to cover qualified medical expenses tax-free. Money can be withdrawn for purposes other than health care expenses after payment of income tax, plus a 15 percent penalty. Unused balances "roll over" from year to year, and if an employee changes jobs, the HSA or HSSA can continue to be used to pay for qualified health care expenses.

Health Care Reimbursement Account

A **health care reimbursement account (HCRA)** is a tax-exempt account that is used to pay for health care expenses. The individual decides, in advance, how much money to deposit in an HCRA (and unused funds are lost).

Health Reimbursement Arrangement

A **health reimbursement arrangement (HRA)** is a tax-exempt account offered by employers with more than 50 employees, which individuals use to pay health care bills. The Internal Revenue Service (IRS) issued a tax guidance for HRAs in 2002 that stated the HRA must be used for qualified health care expenses, requires enrollment in a high-deductible insurance policy, and a provision must be in place to allow individuals to accumulate unspent money for future years. If an employee changes jobs, the HRA can continue to be used to pay for qualified health care expenses.

Exercise 19.1 – Third-Party Payers

Instructions: Complete each statement.

1. Third-party payers that process health care claims for reimbursement of Medicare Part A, Part B, and DME procedures, services, and supplies are called _____.
2. The _____ is the administrative agency in the Department of Health and Human Services (DHHS) that selects payers to process Medicare health care claims through a competitive bidding process.
3. The standard claim submitted by physician offices to third-party payers is called the _____, and the claim submitted by health care institutions is called the _____.
4. An organization that processes or facilitates the processing of health information received from another entity from a nonstandard into a standard format is called a(n) _____.

(continues)

Exercise 19.1 (continued)

5. If the patient's insurance policy contains a statement that the patient is not responsible for paying what the insurance plan denies, the health care provider is prohibited from collecting payment from the patient. This statement is called a(n) _____.

6. The government-sponsored health program that provides health care benefits to dependents of veterans rated as 100-percent permanently and totally disabled as a result of service-connected conditions, dependents of veterans who died as a result of service-connected conditions, and dependents of veterans who died on duty with fewer than 30 days of active service is called

   _____.

7. The joint federal and state program that provides health care coverage to low-income populations and certain aged and disabled individuals is called _____.

8. The government-sponsored health program that provides health care coverage to elderly and disabled persons is called _____.

9. The combined financing and delivery of health care services to replace conventional fee-for-service health insurance plans with more affordable care for consumers and providers who agree to certain restrictions is called _____.

10. The type of plan that reimburses providers for individual health care services rendered is called

    _____.

Health Care Reimbursement Systems

Prior to implementation of major government-sponsored health programs (e.g., Medicare and Medicaid) in 1965, health care services were reimbursed by the following payers:

- Blue Cross and Blue Shield (private and group health plans)

- Commercial health insurance (private)

- Employer-based group health insurance and self-insurance plans

- Government-sponsored programs, limited to the following:

  ○ Indian Health Service (limited eligibility)

  ○ Dependents' medical care program (health care for dependents of active military personnel)

- Prepaid health plans (forerunner of managed care)

- Self-pay (patients paid cash)

- Workers' compensation (limited eligibility)

Payers (except prepaid or managed care plans) typically reimbursed physicians on a fee-for-service basis, which is a retrospective payment system that billed payers after health care services were provided to the patient. Hospital reimbursement was generated on a *per diem* basis (Latin meaning "by the day"), which meant payers used a retrospective payment system to issue payment that was based on actual daily charges.

EXAMPLE: Payers typically reimbursed providers for 80 percent of charges submitted, and patients paid the remaining 20 percent (coinsurance). Thus, a provider who submitted a charge of $120 was paid $96 by the payer and $24 by the patient. (Government programs, such as Medicare, establish a physician fee schedule for services provided. The physician is reimbursed 80 percent of the fee schedule.)

Prospective Payment Systems, Fee Schedules, and Exclusions

Health care costs increased dramatically with implementation of government-sponsored health programs in 1965. This led to the creation and implementation of prospective payment systems and fee schedules (Table 19-2) for government health programs. The purpose was to control costs by reimbursing facilities with preestablished rates for inpatient care provided. Shortly after passage of Medicare and Medicaid legislation in 1965, Congress began investigating prospective payment systems. A **prospective payment system (PPS)** is a reimbursement methodology that establishes predetermined rates based on patient category or type of facility (with annual increases based on an inflation index and a geographic wage index). The CMS manage implementation of Medicare PPS, fee schedules, and exclusions according to:

- Prospective cost-based rates.

- Prospective price-based rates.

Prospective cost-based rates are based on reported health care costs (e.g., charges) from which a prospective *per diem* rate is determined. Annual rates are usually adjusted using actual costs from the prior year. This method may be based on the facility's case mix (patient acuity of types and categories of patients). Prospective payment systems based on this reimbursement methodology include resource utilization groups (RUGs) for skilled nursing care.

Prospective price-based rates are associated with a particular category of patient (e.g., inpatients), and rates are established by the payer (e.g., Medicare) prior to the provision of health care services. PPS based on this reimbursement methodology include diagnosis-related groups (DRGs) for inpatient care.

Typically, third-party payers adopt PPS, fee schedules, and exclusions after Medicare has implemented them; payers modify them to suit their needs. A **fee schedule** is cost-based, fee-for-service reimbursement methodology that includes a list of maximum fees and corresponding procedures/services, which payers use to compensate providers for health care services delivered to patients. **Exclusions** are "Medicare PPS Excluded Cancer Hospitals"

Table 19-2 Prospective Payment Systems and Fee Schedules, Year Implemented, and Prospective Rate Type

Prospective Payment System (PPS)	Year	Type
Ambulance Fee Schedule	2002	Cost-based
Ambulatory Surgical Center (ASC) Payment Rates[1]	1994	Cost-based
Clinical Laboratory Fee Schedule	1985	Cost-based
Durable Medical Equipment, Prosthetics/Orthotics, and Supplies (DMEPOS) Fee Schedule	1989	Cost-based
End-Stage Renal Disease (ESRD) Composite Payment Rate System	2005	Price-based
Home Health Prospective Payment System (HH PPS) (Home Health Resource Groups, HHRGs)	2000	Price-based
Hospital Inpatient Prospective Patient System (IPPS)	1983	Price-based
Hospital Outpatient Prospective Payment System (OPPS)	2000	Price-based
Inpatient Psychiatric Facility Prospective Payment System (IPF PPS)	2004	Cost-based
Inpatient Rehabilitation Facility Prospective Payment System (IRF PPS)	2002	Price-based
Long-Term (Acute) Care Hospital Prospective Payment System (LTC PPS)	2001	Price-based
Resource Based Relative Value Scale (RBRVS) System	1992	Cost-based
Skilled Nursing Facility Prospective Payment System (SNF PPS)	1998	Cost-based

[1]Effective January 1, 2008, the OPPS payment amount was substituted for the ASC standard overhead amount for surgical procedures performed at an ASC.

NOTE: Hospice services are not paid according to a prospective payment system or fee schedule. They are reimbursed by Medicare according to four different payment rates, which are based on the site where the patient resides at the time of service and/or number of hours of service.

(e.g., Roswell Park Memorial Institute in Buffalo, New York) that applied for and were granted waivers from mandatory participation in the hospital inpatient PPS.

> **EXAMPLE:** Prior to 1983, acute care hospitals generated invoices based on total charges for an inpatient stay. In 1982, an eight-day inpatient hospitalization at $225 per day (including ancillary service charges) would be billed $1,800. This *per diem* reimbursement rate actually discouraged hospitals from limiting inpatient lengths of stay. In 1983, a PPS rate of $950 would be reimbursed for the same inpatient hospitalization, regardless of length of stay (unless the case qualified for additional reimbursement as an outlier). The PPS rate encourages hospitals to limit inpatient lengths of stay because any reimbursement received in excess of the actual cost of providing care can be retained by the facility. (In this example, if the $950 PPS rate had been paid in 1980, the hospital would have absorbed the $850 loss.)

Inpatient Prospective Payment System (1983)

The **Tax Equity and Fiscal Responsibility Act of 1983 (TEFRA)** legislated implementation of the hospital **inpatient prospective payment system (IPPS)**, which uses diagnosis-related groups (DRGs) to reimburse short-term hospitals a predetermined rate for Medicare inpatient services. (Other payers have adopted the IPPS.)

Diagnosis-related groups (DRGs) (Figure 19-4) classify inpatient hospital cases into groups that are expected to consume similar hospital resources.

> **Note:**
>
> Certain cancer hospitals that applied and received waivers from CMS are considered excluded hospitals, which means that they do not participate in the IPPS.

- Each DRG has a payment weight assigned to it that is based on the average resources used to treat Medicare patients in that DRG.

- DRGs are organized into **major diagnostic categories (MDCs)**, which are mutually exclusive categories that are loosely based on body systems (e.g., nervous system).

- Inpatient cases that are unusually costly are called **outliers**, and the IPPS payment is increased to protect the hospital from large financial losses due to unusually expensive cases.

To determine an IPPS (DRG or MS-DRG) payment, hospitals submit a UB-04 claim for each inpatient to a *Medicare administrative contractor (MAC)*, which is a third-party payer that contracts with Medicare to carry out the operational functions of the Medicare program.

- Based on the information provided on the UB-04, the case is categorized into a DRG, which determines the reimbursement provided to the hospital.

- DRG payments are then adjusted to accommodate the wage index applicable to the area where the hospital is located, a cost-of-living adjustment factor for hospitals located in Alaska and Hawaii, a percentage add-on payment for hospitals that serve a disproportionate share of low-income patients, and/or a percentage add-on payment if the hospital is an approved teaching hospital.

- In addition, if a case is categorized as an outlier, additional payments are added to the DRG-adjusted base payment rate.

Costs not considered when calculating the Medicare DRG-adjusted base payment rates are as follows:

- *Direct costs* of medical education for interns and residents, which are based on a per resident payment amount.

- *Reasonable costs* for (1) hospital bad debts attributable to nonpayment of the Medicare deductible and coinsurance, and (2) heart, liver, lung, and kidney acquisition costs incurred by an approved transplant facility.

The **IPPS 3-day payment window** (or **IPPS 72-hour rule**) requires outpatient preadmission services provided by a hospital on the day of or during the three days prior to a patient's inpatient admission to be covered by the IPPS DRG payment and reported on the UB-04 with ICD-9-CM (or ICD-10-CM) procedure codes (*not* CPT codes) for:

- Diagnostic services (e.g., lab testing).

- Therapeutic (or nondiagnostic) services.

Medicare also requires that physicians' services clinically related to an inpatient admission and provided within 72 hours of the admission be paid at the lower facility rate (instead of the usually greater office or non-facility rate). CMS requires that HCPCS level II modifier -PD (diagnostic or related nondiagnostic item or service provided in a wholly owned or wholly operated entity to a patient who is admitted as an inpatient within three days, or 1 day) to identify claims for related services provided within 72 hours of an inpatient admission. As a result of this new requirement:

Medicare Severity Diagnosis-Related Groups (MS-DRGs)
MDC 02 – Diseases and Disorders of the Eye

CC = complication(s) and/or comorbidity(ies)
MCC = major complication(s) and/or cormorbidity(ies)

MS-DRG	Description
113	Orbital procedures w CC/MCC

MS-DRG: 113
Title: Orbital procedures w CC/MCC
Type: SURG
Major Diagnostic Category (MDC): 02 DISEASES & DISORDERS OF THE EYE
Relative Weight: 1.4141
Geometric Mean Length of Stay (days): 3.8
Arithmetic Mean Length of Stay (days): 5.5

Related Codes

MS-DRG	Title	Relative Weight	Length of Stay
113	Orbital procedures w CC/MCC	1.4141	3.8
114	Orbital procedures w/o CC/MCC	1.0292	2.0
115	Extraocular procedures except orbit	1.1185	3.3
116	Intraocular procedures w CC/MCC	0.8891	2.2
117	Intraocular procedures w/o CC/MCC	0.7094	1.5

Crosswalk of CMS-DRG to MS-DRG

CMS-DRG	MDC	MS-DRG
037 - ORBITAL PROCEDURES	02	113 - Orbital procedures w CC/MCC

MS-DRG	Description
114	Orbital procedures w/o CC/MCC
115	Extraocular procedures except orbit
116	Intraocular procedures w CC/MCC
117	Intraocular procedures w/o CC/MCC
121	Acute major eye infections w CC/MCC
122	Acute major eye infections w/o CC/MCC
123	Neurological eye disorders
124	Other disorders of the eye w MCC
125	Other disorders of the eye w/o MCC

Figure 19-4 Medicare Severity Diagnosis-Related Groups (MS-DRGs), Major Diagnostic Category 02

- Physician office claims must be held for at least three days prior to submission, and CMS requires hospitals to notify physician offices about related inpatient admissions.

- Modifier -PD must be added to CPT and HCPCS level II codes that are reported on CMS-1500 claims for any inpatients who received physician office services within 72 hours prior to admission.

In practice, physician offices need to implement a process to ensure that claims submission is delayed by three days. Also, an office staff member needs to review daily list(s) of inpatient admissions received from local hospital(s) to identify patients whose claims need to be modified by adding -PD to CPT codes.

EXAMPLE: A 79-year-old established female Medicare patient receives physician office evaluation and management (E/M) services (99214) for complaints of chest pain and shortness of breath. Her general practitioner (GP) performs a 12-lead ECG (93000), which indicates the patient is currently experiencing a myocardial infarction (MI). The patient is immediately transported by ambulance to the local hospital and admitted to the intensive care unit. Because the patient is admitted within 72 hours of the office visit, the E/M services (99214-PD) are paid to the physician at the lesser facility rate (instead of the physician office rate), and only the professional component rate of the ECG (93010-PD) is paid to the physician (instead of the higher global procedure rate). (CPT code 93010 is reported for the professional component of the ECG, not 93000 which is reported for the global service.)

According to CMS, all nondiagnostic services (other than ambulance and maintenance renal dialysis services) furnished by a hospital on the date of admission or during the three-day payment window are deemed to be related to the admission and, therefore, must be bundled with the inpatient stay if the services were provided on the day of or during the three days prior to a patient's inpatient admission. The exception to the rule is when a hospital determines, attests, and documents that the service furnished during the three-day payment window is *clinically distinct or independent from the reason for the patient's admission.* Hospitals are required to report condition code 51 with the nondiagnostic service CPT or HCPCS level II code on the outpatient UB-04.

Note:

Medicare implemented **Medicare severity diagnosis-related groups (MS-DRGs)** in 2007 to classify inpatient hospital cases into groups according to similar resource utilization. Hospitals receive a predetermined payment according to MS-DRG for treating Medicare patients. Like the original DRGs, the MS-DRGs are based on diagnoses, procedures, other demographic information, and the presence of complications or comorbidities (CCs). However, hospital inpatients are distinguished according to those with no CCs, CCs, or major CCs (MCCs). This allows Medicare to distinguish "sick patients" from "very sick patients" and to reimburse hospitals accordingly. As such, the number of MS-DRGs expands to 745 (as compared to 538 original DRGs). MS-DRGs also emphasize the importance of proper documentation of patient care, relating it to reimbursement optimization (e.g., increased diagnosis specificity to justify more severe illnesses resulting in increased reimbursement). Facilities implement clinical documentation improvement (CDI) programs to ensure thorough and accurate documentation in patient records. (*To optimize reimbursement* means to legally enhance reimbursement from payers to providers, such as assigning specific codes based on documentation in the patient record.)

Other systems developed for payment purposes (based on CMS's DRG system) include the following:

- *All Patient Refined DRGs (APR-DRGs),* which classify the non-Medicare population, such as HIV patients, neonates, and pediatric patients.

- *International Refined DRGs (IR-DRGs),* which were created by other countries that adapted DRGs for their own use, comparing resource usage across health care facilities and regions and incorporating the concept of severity of illness adjustments using multiple levels of comorbid and complication (CC) conditions.

- *New York All Patient DRGs (AP-DRGs),* which classify the nonelderly population in New York State.

- *Yale Refined Diagnosis-Related Groups (RDRGs),* which refined the original DRGs to incorporate a measure of severity, expanding the number of DRGs to 1,263 RDRGs.

An **IPPS transfer rule** states that any patient with a diagnosis associated with one to 10 CMS-determined DRGs who is discharged to a post-acute provider is treated as a transfer case.  This means that hospitals are paid a graduated *per diem* rate for each day of the patient's stay, not to exceed the prospective payment DRG rate. (Outliers are also recognized for extraordinarily high-cost cases.) CMS identified 10 high-volume DRGs that contain a disproportionate percentage of discharges to post-acute-care settings (e.g., DRG 14—Specific Cerebrovascular Disorders Except Transient Ischemic Attack). CMS defines the following as post-acute-care settings:

> **Note:**
>
> Services that are distinct from and unrelated to the inpatient admission are separately billed by the hospital *if documentation supports that the service is unrelated to the inpatient admission.*

- Hospitals or distinct units excluded from the prospective payment system

- Skilled nursing facilities

- Patient's home under a written plan of care for the provision of home health services from a home health agency if the services begin within three days of discharge

The Department of Health & Human Services, Office of Inspector General (OIG) monitors hospital readmissions that seem to focus on revenue generation rather than medical necessity when determining DRGs. When a patient is readmitted to a hospital on the day of discharge, the hospital should treat the readmission as a continuous episode of care. This means that the new admission is combined with the previous admission and that the hospital receives reimbursement for just one episode of care (according to the DRG generated). If the patient is transferred to another hospital, that admission is considered a transfer (not a new admission) and the two hospitals cost-split the DRG reimbursement rate. To convince the OIG that the hospital is properly classifying readmissions and transfers, consider implementing software that flags same-day readmissions for review, ensure that hospital discharge planners accurately assess the patient's condition upon discharge, and remind providers to document the fact that patients were discharged in a timely manner.

Hospital-Acquired Conditions and Present on Admission Reporting Guidelines

The Deficit Reduction Act of 2005 resulted in implementation of a quality adjustment in Medicare diagnosis-related group (DRG) payments for certain hospital-acquired conditions. CMS calls the program *Hospital-Acquired Conditions and Present on Admission Indicator Reporting (HAC & POA).*

All claims submitted for inpatient admissions to general acute care hospitals or other health care facilities are required to report the **present on admission (POA) indicator**, which is assigned by the coder to the principal and secondary diagnoses and external cause of injury code reported on the UB-04 or 837 Institutional (837I) electronic claim.

- The coder reviews the patient record to determine whether a condition was present on admission or not.

- Issues related to inconsistent, missing, conflicting, or unclear documentation are resolved by the provider as a result of the "physical query" process.

In this context, "present on admission" is defined as "present at the time the order for inpatient admission occurs." Thus, conditions that develop during an outpatient encounter, including emergency department, observation, or outpatient surgery, are considered as present on admission upon admission of the patient as a hospital inpatient. CMS reporting options and definitions include the following:

- Y = Yes (diagnosis was present at the time of inpatient admission)

- N = No (diagnosis was not present at the time of inpatient admission)

- U = Unknown (documentation is insufficient to determine if the condition was present at the time of inpatient admission)

- W = Clinically undetermined (provider is unable to clinically determine whether the condition was present at the time of inpatient admission)

- 1 = Unreported/not used (exempt from POA reporting; this code is equivalent to leaving a blank on the UB-04; however, because blanks are undesirable when submitting these data electronically, POA 1 is reported in the UB-04 form locator)

CODING FOR DIAGNOSIS-RELATED GROUPS (DRGS)

Diagnoses and procedures are assigned ICD-9-CM (or ICD-10-CM/PCS) codes, and they are sequenced according to CMS offi cial coding guidelines and the Uniform Hospital Discharge Data Set (UHDDS). This means that hospitals are not required to assign codes to every diagnosis and procedure documented in the patient record. However, hospitals must evaluate their institutional data needs to develop coding policies, which will determine the assignment of ICD-9-CM (or ICD-10-CM/PCS) codes to diagnoses and procedures. When assigning codes to *comorbidities* (co-existing conditions) and *complications* (conditions that develop during inpatient admission), be sure to carefully review patient record documentation to assign the most specific code possible. Revisions to the MS-DRGs comorbidities and complications (CC) list eliminated many diagnoses that were considered CCs in the past. As a result, physicians must be educated about the importance of proper documentation practices.

> **EXAMPLE** Under MS-DRGs:
>
> - Chronic obstructive pulmonary disease (COPD) is not a CC. However, acute exacerbation of COPD is a CC.
> - Congestive heart failure (CHF) is not a CC. However, chronic systolic heart failure is a CC and acute systolic heart failure is a major CC (MCC).

ICD-9-CM (or ICD-10-CM/PCS) codes are assigned for documented OR (operating room) and non-OR procedures. (Non-OR procedures are performed in the patient's room, emergency department, radiology department, and so on.) Whether ICD-9-CM (or ICD-10-CM/PCS) codes are assigned to other procedures, such as ancillary tests (e.g., EKG, laboratory tests, and so on), is dependent on the hospital's coding policy.

The present on admission (POA) indicator differentiates between patient conditions present upon inpatient admission and those that develop during the inpatient admission. Claims that do not report the POA indicator are returned to the facility for correction. Hospital-acquired conditions that are reported as not present at the time of admission are not considered when calculating the MS-DRG payment. This means that such conditions, even if included on the CC and MCC lists, are not considered a CC or MCC if diagnosed during the inpatient stay and the facility will not receive additional payment for such conditions.

Skilled Nursing Facility Prospective Payment System (1998)

 Note:

Medicare originally introduced the prospective payment system (PPS) to pay for inpatient hospital care, with other payers adopting their own PPS in subsequent years (e.g., SNF PPS). Under the IPPS, inpatients are discharged once the acute phase of illness has passed. They are often transferred to other types of health care, such as outpatient care, skilled care facilities, rehabilitation hospitals, and home health care. The transfer facilities provide an appropriate level of health care in a safe and cost-effective manner after the patient's attending physician (with the assistance of discharge planners, case managers, social workers, nurses, and others) has determined which facility is best by evaluating the patient's medical condition, special needs, and treatment goals.

The **Balanced Budget Act of 1997** legislated implementation of the **skilled nursing facility prospective payment system (SNF PPS)**, which classifies residents into **resource utilization groups (RUGs)**, version III (RUG-III), to reimburse Medicare SNF services according to a per diem prospective rate adjusted for case mix. A resident assessment instrument (RAI) completed on each SNF patient captures the **minimum data set (MDS)** according to the following schedule: 5, 14, 30, 60, and 90 days after admission. Patients are assigned to one of the RUGs categories (Table 19-3), for which a *per diem* prospective rate is established. **Resident Assessment Validation and Entry (RAVEN)** software, developed by CMS, is a data entry system that allows SNFs to capture and transmit the MDS.

Table 19-3 Resource Utilization Groups (RUGs) Categories

Rehabilitation	Residents receive physical, speech, or occupational therapy.
Extensive Services	Residents receive complex clinical care or have complex clinical needs such as IV feeding or medications, suctioning, tracheostomy care, ventilator/respirator, and comorbidities that make the resident eligible for other RUG categories.
Special Care	Residents receive complex clinical care or have serious medical conditions such as multiple sclerosis, quadriplegia, cerebral palsy, respiratory therapy, ulcers, stage III or IV pressure ulcers, radiation, surgical wounds or open lesions, tube feeding and aphasia, fever with dehydration, pneumonia, vomiting, weight loss, and tube feeding.
Clinically Complex	Residents receive complex clinical care or have conditions requiring skilled nursing management and interventions for conditions and treatments such as burns, coma, septicemia, pneumonia, foot wounds, internal bleeding, dehydration, tube feeding, oxygen, transfusions, hemiplegia, chemotherapy, dialysis, and physician visits/order changes.
Impaired Cognition	Residents have cognitive impairment in decision making, recall, and short-term memory.
Behavior Problems	Residents display behaviors such as wandering, are verbally or physically abusive or socially inappropriate, or experience hallucinations or delusions.
Reduced Physical Functions	Residents' needs are primarily for activities of daily living and general supervision.

© Cengage Learning 2014

Home Health Prospective Payment System (2000)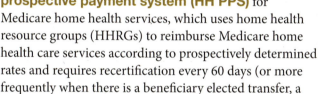

The **Omnibus Consolidated and Emergency Supplemental Appropriations Act (OCESAA) of 1999** legislated implementation of the **home health prospective payment system (HH PPS)** for Medicare home health services, which uses home health resource groups (HHRGs) to reimburse Medicare home health care services according to prospectively determined rates and requires recertification every 60 days (or more frequently when there is a beneficiary elected transfer, a

 Note:

Medicare does not reimburse durable medical equipment (DME) during the initial 60 days that a patient receives home care services. DME is reimbursed according to a fee schedule during this period.

significant change in condition resulting in a change in the case-mix assignment, or a discharge and return to the same home health agency during the 60-day episode) by the physician who reviews the plan of care.

Home health agencies (HHAs) were reimbursed under a fee-for-service system until Medicare transitioned to the HH PPS for 60-day periods of home health care. Rates for each 60-day episode of HHA care are adjusted by case-mix methodology based on entry of data elements from the outcome and assessment information set (OASIS) into **Home Assessment Validation and Entry (HAVEN)** data entry software. The HHA clinician (such as a registered nurse) conducts a comprehensive assessment and collects OASIS data elements to capture clinical severity factors, functional severity factors, and service utilization factors that influence case mix. Each data element is assigned a score value, and the scores are totaled (by HAVEN software) to determine the patient's case-mix group (and the reimbursement rate).

Outpatient Prospective Payment System (2001)

The Balanced Budget Act of 1997 legislated implementation of the hospital **outpatient prospective payment system (OPPS)**, which uses **ambulatory payment classifications (APCs)** to reimburse hospital outpatient services. Outpatient health care services are organized clinically and according to resources required. A reimbursement rate is established for each APC (Figure 19-5) and, depending on services provided, hospitals can be paid for more than one APC per encounter, with second and subsequent APCs discounted at 50 percent (if they are designated with status indicator "T").

Each CPT and HCPCS level II code is assigned a **status indicator (SI)** as a payment indicator to identify how each code is paid (or not paid) under the OPPS. For example, status indicator "S" refers to "significant procedures for

---

Outpatient Prospective Payment System (OPPS) Formula

(APC Weight x Conversion Factor x Wage Index) + Add-On Payments = Payment

NOTE: When a patient undergoes multiple procedures and services on the same day, multiple APCs are generated and payments are added together. APC software automatically discounts multiple APC payments when appropriate (e.g., bilateral procedure).

EXAMPLE: Using the sample data below, the OPPS payment for a patient who underwent cataract procedure with intraocular lens implant, chest x-ray, and ureteral reflux study in Buffalo, New York is calculated as 437.02. (NOTE: Add-on payments do not apply to this example and APC payments were not discounted.)

$$(22.98 \times \$54.561 \times 0.8192) + (0.78 \times \$54.561 \times 0.8192) + (4.29 \times \$54.561 \times 0.8192)$$

$$\$1,027.12 + \$34.86 + \$191.75 = \$1,253.73$$

Conversion Factor = \$54.561
Wage Index = 0.8192

HCPCS Code	Description	APC	APC Weight
66984	Cataract procedure with intraocular lens implant	246	22.98
71020	Chest x-ray	260	0.78
78740	Ureteral reflux study	292	4.29

© Cengage Learning 2014

Figure 19-5 Formula for determining OPPS payments

---

which the multiple procedure reduction does not apply." This means that the CPT and/or HCPCS level II code is paid the full APC reimbursement rate. OPPS status indicator "T" refers to "services to which the multiple procedure payment reduction applies." (CPT modifier -51 is not added to codes reported for OPPS payment consideration.) This means that the reported CPT and/or HCPCS level II code will be paid a discounted APC reimbursement rate when reported with other procedures on the same claim.

The unit of payment for the OPPS is an outpatient visit or encounter. An **outpatient encounter** (or **outpatient visit**) includes all outpatient procedures and services (e.g., same-day surgery, X-rays, laboratory tests, and so on) provided during one day to the same patient. Thus, a patient who undergoes multiple outpatient procedures and receives multiple services on the same day will be assigned to one or more outpatient groups (called APCs). Each APC is weighted and has a prospective payment amount associated with it; if a patient is assigned multiple APCs, the payments are totaled to provide reimbursement to the hospital for the encounter. (APC payments may be discounted when certain procedures or services are provided, such as bilateral procedures.) A **wage index** adjusts payments to account for geographic variations in hospitals' labor costs.

APC grouper software is used to assign an APC to each CPT and/or HCPCS level II code reported on an outpatient claim, as well as to ICD-9-CM (or ICD-10-CM) diagnosis codes as appropriate. Outpatient code editor (OCE) software is used in conjunction with the APC grouper to identify Medicare claims edits and assign APC groups to reported codes.

Note:

The OPPS does not cover payment of professional services, which are reported on the CMS-1500 claim and reimbursed according to a fee schedule, such as the Medicare Physician Fee Schedule (MPFS). Hospitals report outpatient encounters on the UB-04 (or CMS-1450) claim using ICD-9-CM (or ICD-10-CM) for diagnoses and HCPCS/CPT for procedures and services.

Note:

Add-ons that can increase OPPS payments include pass-through payments that provide additional reimbursement to hospitals that use innovative (new and improved) biologicals, drugs, and technical devices. During committee meetings, health care personnel routinely discuss "pass-through payments" due to new technology, such as innovative medical devices (e.g., using surgical glue instead of stitches) and new drugs and vaccines (e.g., human papillomavirus [HPV] vaccine). Other add-ons include outlier payments for high-cost services, hold harmless payments for certain hospitals, and transitional payments to limit losses under the OPPS. The hospital profits if the payment rate is higher than the cost of care provided, and the hospital loses money if the payment rate is lower than the cost of care provided.

EXAMPLE: OCE software reviews "to/from" dates of service to identify and reject claims that are submitted for reimbursement as hospital-based outpatient care when, in fact, the claim should be processed as inpatient care.

Note:

A Medicare patient's coinsurance amount is initially calculated for each APC based on 20 percent of the national median charge for services in the APC. The coinsurance amount for an APC does not change until the amount becomes 20 percent of the total APC payment, and no coinsurance amount can be greater than the hospital inpatient deductible in a given year.

Note:

New York State is phasing in ambulatory patient groups (APGs) as a new payment methodology for most Medicaid outpatient services (e.g., outpatient clinic, ambulatory surgery, and emergency department services). Implementation of APGs will result in:

- Higher payments for higher intensity services and lower payments for lower intensity services.
- The transition of funds from inpatient to outpatient services to support quality outpatient care and to address the problem of avoidable hospitalizations.

Inpatient Psychiatric Facility Prospective Payment System

The **inpatient psychiatric facility prospective payment system (IPF PPS)** was implemented as a result of Medicare, Medicaid, and SCHIP Balanced Budget Refinement Act of 1999 (BBRA) provisions that required implementation of a *per diem* patient classification system that reflects differences in patient resource use and costs. The IPF PPS replaced a reasonable cost-based payment system and affected approximately 2,000 facilities; to promote long-term cost control and utilization management. Licensed psychiatric facilities and hospital-based psychiatric units were reimbursed according to the new PPS, which was phased in over a three-year period beginning in 2004.

Health information department coders use ICD-9-CM (or ICD-10-CM) to assign codes to inpatient behavioral health diagnoses and ICD-9-CM (or ICD10-PCS) to assign codes procedures. Coders then enter data into DRG software to calculate the IPF PPS DRG. Inpatient psychiatric facilities are reimbursed according to a *per diem* payment that is calculated using DRG data, wage-adjusted rates, and facility-level adjusters. (IPPS MS-DRGs reimburse acute care hospitals a flat payment based on ICD-9-CM or ICD-10-CM/PCS codes and other data.) Providers use the **Diagnostic and Statistical Manual (DSM)**, which is published by the American Psychiatric Association. Although DSM codes do not affect IPF PPS rates, the manual contains diagnostic assessment criteria that are used as tools to identify psychiatric disorders. The DSM includes psychiatric disorders and codes, provides a mechanism for communicating and recording diagnostic information, and is used in the areas of research and statistics.

Inpatient Rehabilitation Facility Prospective Payment System (2002)

The Balanced Budget Act (BBA) of 1997 authorized implementation of the **inpatient rehabilitation facility prospective payment system (IRF PPS)**, which utilizes information from a patient assessment instrument (IRF PAI) to classify patients into distinct groups based on clinical characteristics and expected resource needs. Separate payments are calculated for each group, including the application of case- and facility-level adjustments. Each facility must demonstrate that during its most recent 12-month cost reporting period, it served an inpatient population of whom at least 75 percent required intensive rehabilitative services for the treatment of one or more of the following conditions:

- Amputation
- Brain injury
- Burns
- Congenital deformity
- Hip fracture

- Major multiple trauma
- Neurological disorders
- Polyarthritis
- Stroke
- Spinal cord injury

The **IRF PPS 1-day payment window** (or **IRF PPS 24-hour rule**) requires that outpatient preadmission services provided by an IRF up to one day prior to a patient's inpatient admission be covered by the IRF PPS payment.

The **IRF PPS transfer rule** is similar to IPPS transfer rule, except that for the IRF, the rule covers all patient diagnoses. If a patient is transferred from an IRF to another rehabilitation facility, an acute inpatient hospital, a long-term care hospital, or a nursing home that accepts payment under Medicare or Medicaid, the patient's length of stay must be reviewed. A patient who is discharged to home, outpatient therapy, home health, or a day rehabilitation program is not considered a transfer. If a patient remains in the IRF for more than three days—which is the defining length of stay for a short stay carrying its own payment classification, but fewer days than defined by the case mix group (CMG)—the transfer payment methodology is triggered. The transfer payment methodology reimburses a *per-diem*-based payment for the number of days of care in the facility prior to a transfer.

Long-Term (Acute) Care Hospital Prospective Payment System (2001)

The **Balanced Budget Refinement Act of 1999 (BBRA)** mandated implementation of the **long-term (acute) care hospital prospective payment system (LTCH PPS)**, which uses information from long-term acute care hospital patient records to classify patients into distinct **Medicare severity long-term (acute) care diagnosis-related groups (MS-LTC-DRGs)** based on clinical characteristics and expected resource needs. The LTCH PPS replaced the reasonable cost-based payment system authorized by TEFRA, which mandated DRGs (and exempted long-term acute care hospitals from participation).

The **LTCH PPS 1-day payment window** (or **LTCH PPS 24-hour rule**) requires that outpatient preadmission services provided by a long-term-acute care hospital up to one day prior to a patient's inpatient admission be covered by the MS-LTCH-DRG payment.

Clinical Laboratory Fee Schedule (1985)

The **Deficit Reduction Act of 1984** established the **clinical laboratory fee schedule** as a methodology for determining fees for existing tests, and one year later the **Consolidated Omnibus Budget Reconciliation Act of 1985** established a **national limitation amount (NLA)**, which serves as a payment ceiling or "cap" on the amount Medicare could pay for each test, originally set at 115 percent of the median of all carrier-set rates. It eventually dropped to 74 percent.

> **Note:**
>
> Do not confuse the LTCH PPS with the SNF PPS, discussed previously in this chapter. Long-term acute care hospitals are categorized as short-term hospitals, while skilled nursing facilities (SNFs) are considered long-term care facilities (LTCFs) (e.g., nursing facilities). Medicare even certifies long-term acute care hospitals as "short-term acute-care hospitals."

Durable Medical Equipment, Prosthetics/Orthotics, and Supplies Fee Schedule (1989)

The **durable medical equipment, prosthetics, orthotics, and supplies (DMEPOS) fee schedule** is a payment methodology mandated by the **Omnibus Budget Reconciliation Act of 1987 (OBRA)**. The fee schedule was implemented in 1989 (except for the surgical dressing fee schedule, which was implemented in 1994; and the parenteral and enteral nutrition (PEN) fee schedule, which was implemented in 2002). The fee schedule is released annually and updated quarterly to implement fee schedule amounts for new codes and to revise any amounts for existing codes that were calculated in error.

Resource-Based Relative Value Scale System (1992)

The **Omnibus Budget Reconciliation Act of 1989** implemented the **resource-based relative value scale (RBRVS) system**, which is used to reimburse physician services covered by Medicare Part B. The RBRVS system replaced the Medicare physician payment system of "customary, prevailing, and reasonable" (CPR) charges under which physicians were reimbursed according to the historical record of the charge for the provision of each service. This system, now called the **Medicare physician fee schedule (MPFS)**, reimburses providers according to predetermined rates assigned to services, and it is revised by CMS each year. All services are standardized to measure the value of a service as compared with other services provided. These standards, called **relative value units (RVUs)**, are payment components consisting of the following:

- *Physician work*, which reflects the physician's time and intensity in providing the service (e.g., judgment, technical skill, and physical effort).

- *Practice expense*, which reflects overhead costs involved in providing a service (e.g., rent, utilities, equipment, and staff salaries).

- *Malpractice expense*, which reflects malpractice expenses (e.g., costs of liability insurance).

Payment limits were also established by adjusting the RVUs for each locality by geographic adjustment factors (GAF), called *geographic cost practice indices (GPCIs)*, so that Medicare providers are paid differently in each state and also within each state (e.g., New York state has five separate payment localities). An annual **conversion factor** (dollar multiplier) converts RVUs into payments using a formula (Figure 19-6).

Ambulatory Surgical Centers Payments (1994)

The **Omnibus Budget Reconciliation Act of 1980** mandated that an ambulatory surgery center (ASC) could participate in Medicare if certain conditions were met (e.g., if the ASC was state-licensed) and stated that the **ambulatory surgical centers (ASCs) payment rates** are "expected to be calculated on a prospective basis . . . utilizing sample survey and similar techniques to establish reasonable estimated overhead allowances for each of the listed procedures which take account of volume (within reasonable limits)." Prior to 2008, procedures included on the ASC list were assigned to one of nine payment groups based on an estimate of the costs incurred by the facility to perform the procedure.

> **Note:**
>
> Most third-party payers, including state Medicaid programs, have adopted aspects of the MPFS. Thus, the MPFS contains fees for services not commonly provided to Medicare patients (e.g., obstetrical services).

The Medicare Prescription Drug, Improvement, and Modernization Act of 2003 (MMA) mandated implementation of a revised payment system for ASC surgical services by no later than January 1, 2008. Under the revised payment system, implemented January 1, 2008, Medicare will use the ambulatory payment classification (APC) groups and relative payment weights to reimburse ASCs for surgical procedures performed. (The payment weights are multiplied by an ASC conversion factor to calculate ASC payment rates.)

ASC relative payment weights will be updated each year using the national OPPS relative payment weights for that calendar year and, for office-based procedures, the practice expense payments under the physician fee schedule will also be updated for that calendar year. Medicare plans to make the relative payment weights budget neutral to ensure that changes in the relative payment weights from year to year do not cause the estimated amount of

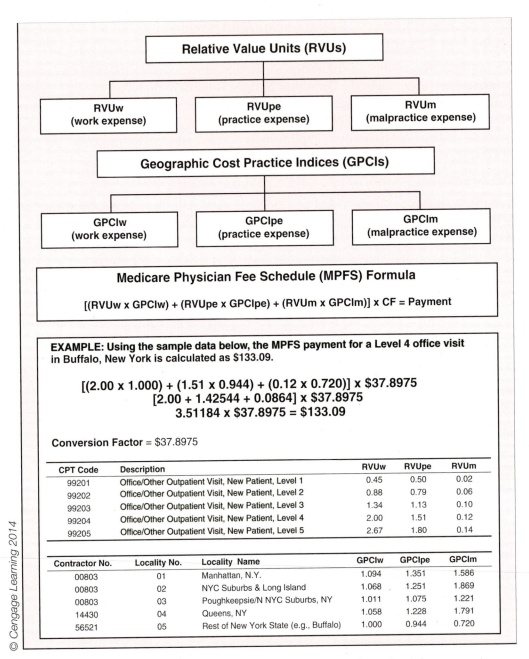

Figure 19-6 Formula for determining Medicare physician fee schedule payments

expenditures to ASCs to increase or decrease as a function of those changes. Medicare will also maintain and update an "exclusionary list of procedures" for which an ASC facility fee is not paid (because those procedures are included on the OPPS inpatient list).

Ambulance Fee Schedule (2002)

The Balanced Budget Act of 1997 legislated implementation of an **ambulance fee schedule**, which reimburses ambulance service providers a preestablished fee for each service provided. Characteristics of the fee schedule consist of the following:

- Seven categories of ground ambulance services, ranging from basic life support to specialty care transport, and two categories of air ambulance services are established.

- Payment for each category is based on the relative value assigned to the service, adjusted to reflect wage differences in different parts of the country (mileage also will affect payment levels).

- Ambulance providers will not be allowed to charge beneficiaries more than their deductible and 20 percent of Medicare's fee for the service. (Under the old payment system, providers could charge beneficiaries higher rates.)

- The fee schedule allows for increased payments when an ambulance service is provided in rural areas.

End-Stage Renal Disease Composite Payment Rate System (2005)

The **end-stage renal disease (ESRD) composite payment rate system** for dialysis services is based on a case-mix adjusted composite rate. It is a single-payment fixed rate that does not vary according to the characteristics of the beneficiary treated (and includes the cost of some drugs, laboratory tests, and other items and services provided to Medicare beneficiaries receiving dialysis). The Medicare Prescription Drug, Improvement, and Modernization Act (MMA) of 2003 established the ESRD composite payment rate system.

ESRD facilities determine the best payment rate for rendered services. They can maintain their current exception rate or be paid according to the ESRD composite payment rate system, which provides greater payments to facilities that treat more complicated and resource-intensive ESRD patients.

Case-Mix Analysis and Severity of Illness Systems

Implementation of Medicare PPS resulted in health care facilities analyzing their **case mix** (patient acuity) to:

- Forecast health care trends unique to their individual settings.

- Ensure that they continue to provide appropriate services to their patient populations.

- Recognize that different patients require different resources for care.

   EXAMPLE: Upon review of Sunnyvale Hospital's case mix, the greatest number of patients receive cardiovascular services. Wheaton Hospital's case mix indicates that the majority of its patients receive labor and delivery services. Knowing the case mix allows the hospitals to customize services required of their respective patient populations.

In addition, Medicare and other payers are interested in reviewing case-mix data because they recognize that some facilities may serve caseloads that include disproportionate shares of patients with above-average (or below-average) care needs.

Multiple possible payment rates (e.g., RUG categories) based on patients' anticipated care needs allow payment systems to decrease the average difference between the preestablished payment and each patient's actual cost to the facility (called a **case-mix adjustment**). This also results in a reduced risk to facilities and to payers, and facilities are also willing to admit high-resource cases because higher payments can be anticipated. It creates a disincentive for facilities to admit large volumes of low-need, low-cost patients, which will result in lower payments.

Health care facilities use case-mix and severity of illness software to analyze and measure standards of patient care to assess quality, including the following:

- Acute Physiological and Chronic Health Evaluation (APACHE)

- Atlas Outcomes/MediQual Systems (formerly Medical Illness Severity Grouping System, or MEDISGRPS)

- Comprehensive Severity Index (CSI)

- Patient Management Categories (PMCs)

- Severity of Illness Index (SOII)

   Severity of illness is the physiologic complexity that comprises the extent and interaction of a patient's disease(s) as presented to medical personnel. Severity of illness scores are based on physiologic measures (not just ICD-9-CM or ICD-10-CM codes) of the degree of abnormality of individual signs and symptoms of a patient's disease(s). The more abnormal the signs and symptoms, the higher the score.

   EXAMPLE: The National Institutes of Health (NIH) studied MEDISGRPS data from five hospitals that indicated severity level at admission is an important predictor of resource use, is essential for analysis of patients who deteriorate and/or respond poorly to therapy, and is useful to further specify DRGs.

Risk management tools that identify the risk of dying include the following:

- Acute Physiological and Chronic Health Evaluation (APACHE)

- Medicare Mortality Predictor System (MMPS)

  EXAMPLE: The Health Data Institute created MMPS software to capture data on Medicare patients admitted with stroke, pneumonia, myocardial infarction, and congestive heart failure. The purpose was to predict death within 30 days of hospital admission because these conditions accounted for 13 percent of discharges and 31 percent of 30-day mortality for Medicare patients over age 64 prior to 1988. The MMPS system was "calibrated on a stratified, random sample of 5,888 discharges (about 1,470 for each condition) from seven states, with stratification by hospital type to make the sample nationally representative," and predictors were abstracted from the patient record. The organization determined that "risk-adjusted predicted group mortality rates may be useful in interpreting information on unadjusted mortality rates, and patient-specific predictions may be useful in identifying unexpected deaths for clinical review."

  SOURCE: "Predicting hospital-associated mortality for Medicare patients: A method for patients with stroke, pneumonia, acute myocardial infarction, and congestive heart failure," by J. Daley, S. Jencks, D. Draper, G. Lenhart, N. Thomas, and J. Walker, Baxter Healthcare Corp., Health Data Institute, Lexington, Mass. *Journal of the American Medical Association* 260, no. 24 (December 23, 1988).

Critical Pathways

Critical pathways are interdisciplinary guidelines developed by hospitals to facilitate management and delivery of quality clinical care in a time of constrained resources. They allow for the planning of provision of clinical services that have expected time frames and resources targeted to specific diagnoses and/or procedures. The targeted clinical services are frequently those that are high in volume and resource use and, therefore, are costly. Critical pathways are usually interdisciplinary in focus, merging medical and nursing plans of care with other disciplines (e.g., physical therapy, nutrition, and mental health). Critical pathways essentially can be viewed as interdisciplinary practice guidelines with predetermined standards of care. They provide opportunities for collaborative practice and team approaches that can maximize the expertise of multiple disciplines.

> **Note:**
>
> Originally, critical pathways began with admission and ended with discharge from the hospital. Now that they are being implemented in other health care settings, there is potential for pathways to be focused more on the full range of an episode of care.

Chargemaster and Encounter Form

Hospitals use a chargemaster to record encounter data about ambulatory care provided to patients. The **chargemaster**, or **charge description master (CDM)** (Figure 19-7) is a document that contains a computer-generated list of procedures, services, and supplies, as well as corresponding revenue codes along with charges for each. A **revenue code** is a four-digit UB-04 code that is assigned to each procedure, service, or supply to indicate the location or type of service provided to an institutional patient, such as radiology or laboratory. Physician offices and clinics use an **encounter form**, or **superbill** (Figure 19-8) to record encounter data about office procedures and services provided to patients.

Chargemaster and encounter form data are entered in a patient accounting system, and charges are automatically posted to the insurance claim (UB-04 or CMS-1500, depending on the health care setting). The claim is submitted to the third-party payer to generate payment for services provided (e.g., emergency department, laboratory, physician office, or radiology). Chargemasters and encounter forms allow for accurate and efficient billing of services rendered.

Chargemaster

A chargemaster usually contains the following:

- Department code: Refers to the specific ancillary department where the service is performed.

- Service code: Internal identification of specific service rendered.

(A)

Revenue Codes and the Chargemaster

NOTE: Before 2002, revenue codes consisted of only three digits.

EXAMPLE:

-
-
-
-
-
-

(B)   EXAMPLE:

© Cengage Learning 2014

Figure 19-7 Revenue codes and chargemaster (A) Explanation of revenue codes (B) Sample portion of hospital chargemaster

- Service description: Narrative description of the service, procedure, or supply.

- Revenue code: Four-digit UB-04 code assigned to each procedure, service, or supply that indicates the location or type of service provided to a patient.

- Charge amount: Dollar amount the facility charges for each procedure, service, or supply.

- Relative value units (RVUs): Numeric value assigned to a procedure that is based on difficulty and time consumed.

A **chargemaster review process** is routinely conducted by designated hospital personnel (e.g., coding specialists) to ensure accurate reimbursement by updating CPT and HCPCS codes and linking each to appropriate UB-04 revenue codes. These designated individuals must have knowledge of proper revenue and expense matching to the Medicare cost center report (e.g., revenue codes) and must be willing to spend the time necessary on an extremely detailed and time-consuming task. Because it results in generation of gross revenue for the health care facility, all who use the chargemaster must be educated about its proper use and its impact on the facility's financial status.

Permission to reuse in accordance with http://www.cms.hhs .gov Content Reuse and Linking policy.

PATIENT INFORMATION

PATIENT'S LAST NAME	FIRST	INITIAL	BIRTHDATE		SEX ☐ MALE ☐ FEMALE	TODAY'S DATE
ADDRESS	CITY	STATE	ZIP	RELATIONSHIP TO SUBSCRIBER		INJURY DATE
SUBSCRIBER OR POLICYHOLDER				INSURANCE PAYER		
ADDRESS	CITY	STATE	ZIP	INS. I.D.	COVERAGE CODE	GROUP

ASSIGNMENT AND RELEASE: I HEREBY AUTHORIZE MY INSURANCE BENEFITS TO BE PAID DIRECTLY TO THE UNDERSIGNED PHYSICIAN. I AM FINANCIALLY RESPONSIBLE FOR NON-COVERED SERVICES. I ALSO AUTHORIZE THE PHYSICIAN TO RELEASE ANY INFORMATION REQUIRED.

OTHER HEALTH COVERAGE ☐ YES ☐ NO   IDENTIFY

DISABILITY RELATED TO: ☐ ACCIDENT ☐ INDUSTRIAL ☐ ILLNESS ☐ OTHER

SIGNED (PATIENT, OR PARENT, IF MINOR) _____ Date _____

DATE SYMPTOMS APPEARED, INCEPTION OF PREGNANCY, OR ACCIDENT OCCURRED:

✓	DESCRIPTION	CPT/MD	FEE	✓	DESCRIPTION	CPT/MD	FEE	✓	DESCRIPTION	CPT/MD	FEE
	OFFICE VISITS	NEW PT			LABORATORY (Cont'd.)				PROCEDURES		
	Level III	99203			Wet Mount	87210			EKG 93000	93005	
	Level IV	99204			Pap Smear	88141			Resp. Function Test	94010	
	Level V	99205			Handling	99000			Ear Lavage	69210	
	OFFICE VISITS	EST. PT			Hemoccult Stool	82270			Injection Inter. Jt.	20605	
	Level I	99211			Glucose	82948			Injection Major Jt.	20610	
	Level II	99212			INJECTIONS				Anoscopy	46600	
	Level III	99213			Vitamin B12/B Complex	J3420			Sigmoidoscopy	45355	
	Level IV	99214			ACTH	J0800			I & D	10060	
	Level V	99215			Depo-Estradiol	J1000			Electrocautery	17000	
	CONSULTATIONS	OFFICE			Depo Testosterone	J1070			Thromb Hemor.	46320	
	Level III	99243			Imferon	J1750			Inj. Tendon	20550	
	Level IV	99244									
	HOME	EST. PT			Influenza Vaccine - Flu	90658			MISCELLANEOUS		
	Level II	99348			Pneumococcal Vaccine	90732			Drugs, Supplies, Materials	99070	
	ER				TB Tine Test	86585			Special Reports	99080	
	Level III	99283			Aminophyllin	J0280			Services After Hrs.	99050	
	Level IV	99284			Terbutaline Sulf.	J3105			Services 10pm - 8am	99052	
	LABORATORY				Demerol HCL	J2175			Services Sun. & Holidays	99054	
	Urinalysis - Complete	81000			Compazine	J0780			Counseling	99403	
	Hemoglobin	85018			Injection Therapeutic	90782					
	Culture, Strep/Monilia	87081			Estrone Susp.	J1410					

DIAGNOSIS:

☐ Allergic Rhinitis	477.9	☐ CHF	428.0	☐ Gout	274.9	☐ Parkinsonism	332.0
☐ Anemia	280.9	☐ Cholecystitis	575.10	☐ HCVD	429.2	☐ Peripheral Vascular Dis	443.9
☐ Angina Pectoris	413.9	☐ Chronic Fatigue Synd.	300.5	☐ Headache, Vascular	784.0	☐ Pharyngitis	462
☐ Anxiety	300.00	☐ COPD	496	☐ Headache, Migraine	346.90	☐ Pneumonia, Bacterial	482.9
☐ Aortic Stenosis	424.1	☐ Costochondritis	733.99	☐ Hemorrhoids	455.6	☐ Pneumonia, Viral	480.9
☐ ASCVD	429.2	☐ CVA	431	☐ Hiatal Hernia	553.3	☐ Rectal Bleeding	569.3
☐ ASHD	414.9	☐ Cystitis	595.9	☐ Hiatal Hernia & Reflux	530.10	☐ Renal Failure, Chronic	585
☐ Asthma	493.90	☐ Deg. Disc. Disease, CX	722.4	☐ HVD	402.10	☐ Rheumatoid Arthritis	714.0
☐ Atrial Fibrillation	427.31	☐ Deg. Disc. Dis., Lumbar	722.52	☐ Hyperlipidemia	272.4	☐ Sinusitis	461.9
☐ Bigeminy	427.89	☐ Depression, Endogenous	296.20	☐ Hypothyroidism	244.9	☐ Supraventr. Tachycardia	427.0
☐ BPH	600.	☐ Dermatitis	692.9	☐ Impacted Cerumen	380.4	☐ T.I.A.	435.9
☐ Bronchitis, Acute	466.11	☐ Diabetes Mellitus, Adult	250.00	☐ Influenza, Viral	487.1	☐ Tachycardia	426.89
☐ Bronchitis, Chronic	491.9	☐ Diarrhea	558.9	☐ Irritable Bowel Syndrome	564.1	☐ Tendinitis	726.90
☐ Bursitis	726._	☐ Diverticulitis	562.11	☐ Laryngitis	464.00	☐ Tonsillitis	463
☐ Cardiomyopathy	425.4	☐ Esophagitis	530.10	☐ Menopausal Syndrome	627.2	☐ URI	465.9
☐ Carotid Artery Disease	433.10	☐ Fibrocystic Breast Disease	610.1	☐ Mitral Insufficiency	396.2	☐ UTI	599.0
☐ Cerebral Vascular Disease	437.9	☐ Fissure in Ano	565.0	☐ Neuritis	729.2	☐ Vaginitis	616.10
		☐ Gastroenteritis	558.9	☐ Otitis Media	382.9	☐ Vertigo	780.4

DIAGNOSIS: (IF NOT CHECKED ABOVE)   REF. DR. & #

DOCTOR'S SIGNATURE / DATE	NO SERVICES PURCHASED	SERVICE PERFORMED	ACCEPT ASSIGNMENT	TODAY'S FEE

INSTRUCTIONS TO PATIENT FOR FILING INSURANCE CLAIMS

MAIL THIS FORM DIRECTLY TO YOUR INSURANCE COMPANY. ATTACH YOUR OWN INSURANCE COMPANY'S FORM.

OFFICE ☐   YES ☐   AMT. REC'D TODAY

E.R. ☐   NO ☐

PLEASE REMEMBER THAT PAYMENT IS YOUR OBLIGATION, REGARDLESS OF INSURANCE OR OTHER THIRD PARTY INVOLVEMENT.

HOME ☐   TOTAL DUE

Figure 19-8 Sample encounter form (superbill)

Note:

Chargemasters (and encounter forms) are usually developed using database software that allows for the entry of thousands of items and potential charges. Each item includes an accounting code number, a CPT/HCPCS code number, and a brief narrative description.

Commercial software (e.g., Ingenix's www.ChargemasterAnalyzer.com online product) helps health care facilities maintain an accurate and complete chargemaster for billing and compliance purposes. The result is fewer claims denials and more accurate outpatient reimbursement.

Encounter Form

Encounter form data is entered in the office's practice management software to generate the CMS-1500 claim that is submitted to the payer. (Many physician offices still complete paper-based CMS-1500 claims, which are submitted to health care clearinghouses to be converted to a standardized format. The health care clearinghouse submits the standardized claims data to the payer, where it is processed to generate physician reimbursement.) Similar to the chargemaster review process, the encounter form should be assigned to one individual in the physician's office who will take responsibility for reviewing and updating it twice a year when codes (e.g., ICD, CPT, and HCPCS codes) are added, deleted, and revised. (This process used to be conducted just once each year until 2004, when federal regulations required that code changes be issued twice each year.)

Note:

Hospitals submit UB-04 claims to payers for inpatient and ambulatory care encounters, and physicians submit CMS-1500 claims for office encounters. Most health care settings participate in electronic data interchange (EDI) with-third party payers and health care clearinghouses.

REVENUE CYCLE MANAGEMENT

Revenue cycle management is the process by which health care facilities and providers ensure their financial viability by increasing revenue, improving cash flow, and enhancing the patient's experience. In a physician practice, revenue cycle management is also called *accounts receivable management*. Revenue cycle management includes the following features, typically in this order:

- *Physician order* for inpatient admission or outpatient services is documented by responsible physician.

- *Patient registration:* Patient is admitted as an inpatient or scheduled for outpatient services.

  ○ Appropriate consents for treatment and release of information are obtained

  ○ Patient demographic and insurance information is collected

  ○ Patient's insurance coverage is validated and utilization management is performed (e.g., clinical reviews) to determine medical necessity

  ○ Preadmission clearance (e.g., precertification, preauthorization, screening for medical necessity)

- *Charge capture* (or *data capture*): Providers use chargemasters or encounter forms to select

procedures or services provided (ancillary departments, such as the laboratory, use automated systems that link to the chargemaster).

- *Diagnosis and procedure coding:* Assignment of appropriate ICD-9-CM or ICD-10-CM and/or CPT/HCPCS codes, typically performed by health information management personnel, to assign APCs, DRGs, and so on.

- *Patient discharge processing:* Patient information is verified, discharge instructions are provided, patient follow-up visit is scheduled, consent forms are reviewed for signatures, and patient policies are explained to the patient.

- *Billing and claims processing:* All patient information and codes are input into the billing system, and CMS-1500 or UB-04 claims are generated and submitted to third-party payers.

- *Resubmitting claims:* Before reimbursement is received from third-party payers, late charges, lost charges, or corrections to previously processed CMS-1500 or UB-04 claims are entered, and claims are resubmitted to payers—this may result in payment delays and claims denials.

- *Third-party payer reimbursement posting:* Payment from third-party payers is posted to appropriate accounts, and rejected claims are resubmitted with appropriate documentation; this process

(continues)

REVENUE CYCLE MANAGEMENT (*continued*)

includes electronic remittance, which involves receiving reimbursement from third-party payers electronically.

- *Appeals process*: Analysis of reimbursement received from third-party payers identifies variations in expected payments or contracted rates and may result in submission of appeal letters to payers.

- *Patient billing*: Self-pay balances are billed to the patient; these include deductibles, co-payments, and non-covered charges.

- *Self-pay reimbursement posting*: Self-pay balances received from patients are posted to appropriate accounts.

- *Collections*: Payments not received from patients in a timely manner results in collections letters being mailed to patients until payment is received; if payment is still not received, the account is turned over to an outside collections agency.

- *Collections reimbursement posting*: Payments received from patients are posted to appropriate accounts.

- *Auditing process*:

  ○ *Compliance monitoring*: Level of compliance with established managed care contracts is monitored; provider performance per managed care contractual requirements is monitored; compliance risk is monitored.

  ○ *Denials management*: Claims denials are analyzed to prevent future denials; rejected claims are resubmitted with appropriate documentation.

  ○ *Tracking of resubmitted claims and appeals for denied claims*: Resubmitted claims and appealed claims are tracked to ensure payment by payers.

  ○ *Posting lost charges and late charges*: Late claims are submitted.

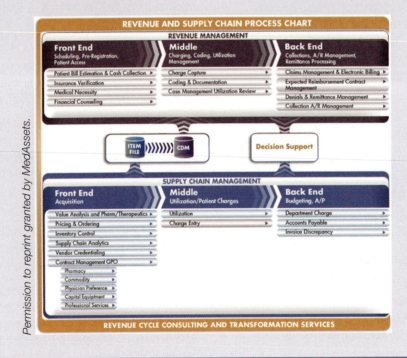

Permission to reprint granted by MedAssets.

Exercise 19.2 – Health Care Reimbursement Systems

Instructions: Complete each statement.

1. A payer reimburses a provider 80 percent of charges submitted, and the patient is responsible for paying the remaining 20-percent coinsurance amount. Mary Allen underwent an office procedure, for which the physician billed her payer $1,500. The payer reimburses the provider the amount of $ _____, and the patient reimburses the provider the amount of $ _____.

2. Two patients each undergo a four-day inpatient stay at an acute care hospital for treatment of a myocardial infarction (heart attack). The patient who has Aetna commercial insurance company can expect the hospital to be reimbursed at 80 percent of the *per diem* basis. The Medicare patient can expect the Medicare administrative contractor (MAC) to reimburse the hospital on a prospective payment basis. Daily charges incurred for the four-day stay were $1,400 per day; the DRG prospective payment rate for a myocardial infarction is $4,500. Aetna will reimburse the hospital $ _____. The MAC will reimburse the hospital $ _____.

3. Designated hospital personnel routinely conduct the _____ process to ensure accurate reimbursement by updating CPT and HCPCS codes and linking each to appropriate UB-04 revenue codes.

4. The federal legislation that resulted in the implementation of the inpatient hospital PPS is called _____.

5. The outpatient hospital PPS establishes a payment rate for outpatient care by using _____ to organize similar health care services clinically and according to resources required.

Matching: Match the payment system with the type of prospective rate. Answers may be used more than once.

_____ 6. Ambulance fee schedule	**a.** Cost-based
_____ 7. Ambulatory surgical center rates	**b.** Price-based
_____ 8. Home health prospective payment system	
_____ 9. Long-term (acute) care hospital prospective payment system	
_____ 10. Resource-based relative value scale system	

Matching: Match the present on admission (POA) indicator with each case scenario.

a. Y = Yes (diagnosis present at the time of inpatient admission)

b. N = No (diagnosis was not present at the time of inpatient admission)

c. U = Unknown (documentation is insufficient to determine if the condition was present at the time of inpatient admission)

d. W = Clinically undetermined (provider is unable to clinically determine whether the condition was present at the time of inpatient admission)

e. 1 = Unreported/not used (exempt from POA reporting; this code is equivalent to a blank on the UB-04; however, because blanks are undesirable when submitting these data electronically, POA 1 is reported in the UB-04 form locator)

_____ 11. A patient is admitted to the hospital for open cholecystectomy due to acute cholecystitis with cholelithiasis. After 24 hours of intravenous antibiotic therapy, the surgery is successfully performed. What is the POA indicator for the acute cholecystitis with cholelithiasis?

(continues)

Exercise 19.2 *(continued)*

_____ **12.** A patient was admitted for inpatient hospitalization due to weakness and unsteady gait, and a diagnosis of cerebrovascular accident was established. What is the POA indicator for the cerebrovascular accident?

_____ **13.** A hospital inpatient falls out of bed on day 2 of his stay and fractures his left hip. What is the POA indicator for the left hip fracture?

_____ **14.** An 84-year-old patient is admitted for inpatient hospitalization due to fever with a temperature of 104 degrees, severe weakness, dehydration, and productive cough. The diagnosis is established as viral pneumonia. During admission, her condition rapidly deteriorates and she is admitted to the intensive care unit. The physician documents severe sepsis as a secondary diagnosis. When queried as to whether the sepsis was present on admission, the physician replies by stating that the patient went downhill so fast that he does not know if the sepsis was present on admission. What is the POA indicator for the severe sepsis?

_____ **15.** Twin liveborn infants are delivered via Cesarean section in the hospital. The physician documents that Twin A has neonatal bradycardia. What is the POA indicator for the Twin A's neonatal bradycardia?

Impact of HIPAA on Reimbursement

The Health Insurance Portability and Accountability Act of 1996 (HIPAA) amended the Internal Revenue Code of 1986 to improve portability and continuity of health insurance coverage in the group and individual markets; to combat waste, fraud, and abuse in health insurance and health care delivery; to promote the use of medical savings accounts; to improve access to long-term care services and coverage; to simplify the administration of health insurance by creating unique identifiers for providers, health plans, employers, and individuals; to create standards for electronic health information transactions; and to create privacy and security standards for health information.

HIPAA legislation is organized according to five titles:

- Title I—Health Care Access, Portability and Renewability

- Title II—Preventing Health Care Fraud and Abuse, Administrative Simplification, and Medical Liability Reform

- Title III—Tax-Related Health Provisions

- Title IV—Application and Enforcement of Group Health Plan Requirements

- Title V—Revenue Offsets

> **Note:**
>
> The Federal False Claims Act provides CMS with regulatory authority to enforce fraud and abuse statutes for the Medicare program, and HIPAA extends that authority to all federal and state health care programs.

> **Note:**
>
> This section will cover health care access, portability and renewability, prevention of health care fraud and abuse, administrative simplification, and medical liability reform issues.

Health Care Access, Portability, and Renewability

HIPAA provisions were designed to improve the portability and continuity of health coverage by limiting exclusions for **preexisting medical conditions**, which are illnesses or injuries that required treatment during a prescribed period of time (e.g., six months) prior to the insured's effective date of coverage under a new insurance policy. HIPAA provisions require that individuals be granted credit for prior health coverage and that a process be implemented to transmit certificates and other information concerning prior coverage to a new group health plan or issuer. Individuals will also be allowed to enroll in health coverage when they lose other health coverage, change from group to individual coverage, or gain a new dependent. HIPAA prohibits discrimination practices associated with health coverage enrollment eligibility and the establishment of premiums (for employees and their dependents) based on health status. The availability of health insurance coverage is also guaranteed to employees of small companies, and both small and large group markets are guaranteed renewability of health insurance coverage. HIPAA preserves the traditional role of individual states in regulating health insurance, and states are provided with flexibility to require greater protection.

Preventing Health Care Fraud and Abuse

HIPAA defines **fraud** as "an intentional deception or misrepresentation that someone makes, knowing it is false, that could result in an unauthorized payment." The attempt itself is considered fraud, regardless of whether it is successful. Fraud is an act that represents a crime against payers or other health care programs (e.g., Medicare), or attempts or conspires to commit those crimes. **Abuse** "involves actions that are inconsistent with accepted, sound, medical, business, or fiscal practices." Abuse includes actions that result in unnecessary costs to payers and government programs (e.g., Medicare), reimbursement for services not medically necessary, or that fails to meet professionally recognized standards for health care services. The difference between fraud and abuse is the individual's intent; however, both have the same impact in that they steal valuable resources from the health care industry.

Examples of fraud include the following:

- Billing Medicare for services or supplies not provided
- Entering another person's Medicare number on a claim to obtain reimbursement for a patient not eligible for Medicare
- Unbundling codes reported on claims (reporting multiple codes to increase reimbursement, when a single combination code should be reported)
- Upcoding claims submitted to payers (reporting codes not supported by documentation in the patient record to increase reimbursement)
- Misrepresenting the diagnosis to justify payment
- Soliciting, offering, or receiving a kickback
- Falsifying certificates of medical necessity, plans of treatment, and medical records to justify payment.

Note:

According to the Department of Health and Human Services, Office of Inspector General, providers are not subject to criminal, civil, or administrative penalties for innocent or negligent errors. The False Claims Act covers offenses committed with actual knowledge of the falsity of the claim, reckless disregard, or deliberate ignorance of the falsity of the claim. The False Claims Act does not cover mistakes, errors, or negligence. The Civil Monetary Penalties Law is an administrative remedy that is similar in scope and effect to the False Claims Act, and it also has exactly the same standard of proof.

EXAMPLE: The medical review of claims submitted to Medicare by a physician group practice that contains mental health providers identified a pattern of psychiatric services billed on behalf of nursing facility patients with a medical history of dementia. Review of patient record documentation at the nursing facility revealed no mental health care physician orders or plans of treatment. This is considered billing for services not furnished, and it is an example of fraud.

Examples of abuse include the following:

- Billing a Medicare patient using a higher fee schedule rate than used for non-Medicare patients
- Submitting claims to Medicare when Medicare is not the beneficiary's primary payer
- Submitting excessive charges for services or supplies

- Submitting claims for services that aren't medically necessary
- Violating Medicare's participating provider agreements with payers
- Improper billing practices that result in payment by a government program when the claim is the legal responsibility of another payer.

Note:

Medical necessity requires the documentation of services or supplies that are proper and are needed for the diagnosis or treatment of a medical condition; are provided for the diagnosis, direct care, and treatment of a medical condition; meet the standards of good medical practice in the local area; and are not mainly for the convenience of the physician.

EXAMPLE: During her first 30 days on the job, Sally Adams mistakenly submitted CMS-1500 claims to Medicare instead of the patients' workers' compensation payers. When she noticed the error, she informed her supervisor, who immediately contacted the Medicare administrative contractors to cancel processing of the submitted claims. Sally then correctly submitted the CMS-1500 claims to the workers' compensation payers. This is considered submitting claims to Medicare when Medicare is not the beneficiary's primary payer, and it is an example of abuse if not corrected.

DRG CREEP

Health Care Fraud and Abuse: Diagnosis Related Group (DRG) Creep, by W. McKay Henderson, Partner, Price Waterhouse Coopers, Health Care Fraud and Abuse Practice. (Permission to reuse granted by W. McKay Henderson, Price Waterhouse, Inc.)

What is it? **DRG creep** is an initiative by the Department of Justice (DOJ) that focuses on the medical necessity and billing patterns of DRG coding to determine whether the claims that hospitals submit accurately reflect the care required or given to the patient. The government believes that hospitals are maximizing their Medicare reimbursements by choosing diagnosis codes that result in higher payments.

In 1993, the Agency for Health Care Policy and Research examined more than 17,000 documented cases of pneumonia to determine the incidences of low-risk versus high-risk pneumonia. The survey found that the diagnosis code for low-risk pneumonia was used in only 3.3 percent of the cases in the study group. While this is significantly lower than you'd expect to find in the general population, it is not surprising since the Medicare reimbursement for a diagnosis of low-risk pneumonia is $2,000 less than a diagnosis of high-risk pneumonia. But what separates a simple miscoding error from a false claim? The Office of Inspector General (OIG) contends that upcoding has become a game hospitals play to maximize their revenue, often hiring consultants or investing in sophisticated computer packages to help them win.

And the DOJ and OIG put a stop to it. (*To maximize revenue* means to fraudulently increase reimbursement from payers to providers, such as reporting codes not supported by documentation that increase the DRG payment rate.)

Which DRG codes is the government focusing on? Prior to 2013, the government reported that the ICD-9-CM Principal Diagnosis Code, 482.89 (Other Specific Bacteria) was being overused. DRG 79 (Respiratory Infections and Inflammations) and DRG 89 (Simple Pneumonia and Pleurisy) were investigated. It is anticipated that the DOJ will continue to use administrative database information to screen for unusual billing patterns. Future reviews may include DRG 127 and 475 (Respiratory Failure with Mechanical Ventriculation) and DRG 415 and 320 (Septicemia and Urinary Tract Infection).

How does upcoding happen? It is speculated that the government believes the upcoding trend is due to either computer software packages that assign the link between ICD codes and DRGs, and/or to consultants who have trained the hospital staff who assign DRG codes. As part of its investigation, the DOJ requested hospitals to provide not only medical records and hospital documentation but also audit results, analyses of computer programs, and all consultants' reports. Those hospitals and medical centers that voluntarily disclose overpayments related to DRG miscoding may receive a reduction in fines and penalties levied against them.

Deterring Fraud and Abuse

CMS employs a four-part strategy to deter fraud and abuse, which focuses on prevention, early detection, coordination, and enforcement.

- Prevention involves paying the claim correctly the first time, and it is the most desirable approach. It is also the best way to guarantee initial accuracy of claims and payments, and it avoids the requirement to "pay and chase" providers, which is a lengthy, uncertain, and expensive process.

- Early detection identifies patterns of fraudulent activity by using data to monitor unusual billing patterns and other indicators of the integrity and financial status of providers, promptly identifying and collecting overpayments, and making appropriate referrals to law enforcement. If CMS finds errors, repayment is pursued and further action may be warranted depending on the facts and circumstances of each case.

- Coordination with partners is another important way by which CMS maximizes its success in preventing fraud; information and tactics for fighting fraud and abuse are shared with individual states, the DOJ, and the private sector.

- When fraudulent providers are discovered, enforcement action is taken against them (e.g., suspension of payment, referral to OIG for potential exclusion from Medicare program, disenrollment, collection of overpayments, and imposition of civil monetary penalties). Investing in prevention, early detection, and enforcement has a proven record of returns to the Medicare Trust Fund; the Medicare Integrity Program saved an estimated $7.5 billion in fiscal year 1997, mostly by preventing inappropriate payments through audits, medical reviews, and ensuring that Medicare does not pay for claims owed by private insurers. The Correct Coding Initiative (CCI) was implemented to reduce Medicare program expenditures by detecting inappropriate coding on claims and denying payment for them.

The Health Insurance Association of America (HIAA) conducted a survey in 1997, which revealed the following health care fraud activities:

- Billing for services not rendered (34 percent)
- Misrepresented diagnoses (43 percent)
- Waivers of patient deductibles (21 percent)
- Other (2 percent)

In 2000, the American Medical Association found that "one in three physicians stated patients have asked them to deceive third-party payers to help obtain coverage for health care services," and "one of ten physicians have reported signs or symptoms a patient did not have in order to secure coverage for services provided."

Regulating Fraudulent Practices

When a Medicare provider commits fraud, an investigation is conducted by the Department of Health and Human Services (DHHS). The Office of Inspector General (OIG) prepares the case for referral to the DOJ for criminal and/or civil prosecution. A person found guilty of Medicare fraud faces criminal, civil, and/or administrative sanction penalties, including the following:

- Civil penalties ranging from $5,000 to $10,000 per false claim *plus* triple damages

- Criminal fines and/or imprisonment for up to 10 years if convicted of health care fraud or, for violations of the Medicare/Medicaid Anti-kickback Statute, imprisonment of up to five years and/or a criminal fine of up to $25,000

- Administrative sanctions, which include up to a $10,000 civil monetary penalty per line item on a false claim, assessments of up to triple the amount false claimed, and/or exclusion from participation in Medicare and state health care programs.

In addition to these penalties, those who commit health care fraud can be tried for mail and wire fraud.

Medicare fraudulent practices are regulated by the following:

- Civil Monetary Penalties Act
- Compliance guidelines
- Federal Claims Collection Act of 1966
- Health Insurance Portability and Accountability Act (HIPAA)

- Correct Coding Initiative (CCI)
- False Claims Act (FCA)
- Federal Anti-kickback Statute

- Physician self-referral laws (Stark I and Stark II)
- Physicians at Teaching Hospitals (PATH) initiative
- Payment Error and Prevention Program (PEPP)

The **Civil Monetary Penalties Act** imposes a maximum penalty of up to $10,000 plus a maximum assessment of up to three times the amount claimed by providers who knew that a procedure/service was not rendered as submitted on the claim. Violators can also be excluded from participation in government programs (e.g., Medicaid or Medicare).

> **EXAMPLE:** A provider bills Medicare for services provided to a patient that are not documented in the patient record. The charges submitted on the claim total $95. If found guilty of fraud, the provider would be required to pay a fine in the amount of $10,285.

The DHHS Office of the Inspector General (OIG) developed a series of provider-specific **compliance guidances**, which identify risk areas and offer concrete suggestions to improve and enhance an organization's internal controls so that billing practices and other business arrangements are in compliance with Medicare's rules and regulations. Voluntary compliance guidelines have been established for the following:

Note:

By law, providers are not subject to civil, criminal, or administrative sanction penalties for innocent errors, or even for negligence.

- Ambulance industry
- Ambulance suppliers
- Clinical laboratories
- Durable medical equipment prosthetics, orthotics, and supply industry
- Home health agencies
- Hospices

- Hospital industry
- Hospitals
- Individual and small-group physician practices
- Nursing facilities
- Medicare Advantage organizations
- Pharmaceutical manufacturers
- Third-party medical billing companies

A voluntary compliance program helps providers avoid generating erroneous and fraudulent claims by ensuring that submitted claims are true and accurate, expediting and optimizing proper payment of claims, minimizing billing mistakes, and preventing conflicts with self-referral and anti-kickback statutes.

> **EXAMPLE** If a coder determines that a physician's documentation is unclear or conflicting, the coder should ask the physician for clarification. In some facilities, the policy is to have the coder contact the physician directly. In others, the coder completes a preprinted form, entering pertinent information about the need for clarification, and this form is forwarded to the physician.

The National Correct Coding Initiative (NCCI) was developed by CMS to promote national correct coding methodologies, eliminate improper coding, and reduce Medicare program expenditures by detecting inappropriate codes on claims and denying payment for them. The principles for the CCI are to ensure that the service:

- Represents the standard of care in accomplishing the overall procedure.
- Is necessary to successfully accomplish the comprehensive procedure (and that failure to perform the service may compromise the success of the procedure).
- Does not represent a separately identifiable procedure unrelated to the comprehensive procedure planned.

(The HCPCS Level II and CPT coding systems are used by physicians and others to describe services rendered.) CCI edits are based on HCPCS/CPT coding principles along with current standards of medical and surgical coding practice, input from specialty societies, and analysis of current coding practice. Table 19-4 contains a list of CCI terms, definitions, and examples.

The federal **False Claims Act (FCA)** was enacted in 1863 in response to widespread abuses by government contractors during the Civil War, and it was amended in 1986 to strengthen the law and increase monetary awards

Table 19-4 National Correct Coding Initiative (NCCI) Terms and Definitions

Term	Definition	Example	
CCI Edits	Pairs of HCPCS level II and/or CPT codes, which are not separately payable except under certain circumstances (e.g., reporting appropriate modifier). The edits are applied to services billed by the same provider for the same beneficiary on the same date of service.	A surgeon intends to perform laparoscopic cholecystectomy; upon visualization of the gallbladder, it is determined that an open cholecystectomy is required. If the surgeon reports CPT codes for removal of an organ through an open incision, as well as with laparoscopy, the CCI edit results in claims denial.	NOTE: if a laparoscopic procedure becomes an open procedure, report only the open procedure code.
Comprehensive Code	The major procedure or service when reported with another code. The comprehensive code represents greater work, effort, and time as compared to the other code reported (also called *Column 1* codes). Higher payments are associated with comprehensive codes.	A patient undergoes deep biopsy aswell as superficial biopsy of the samesite. If the surgeon reports CPT codesfor the deep and superficial biopsies, the CCI edit results in claims denial.	NOTE: Report only the deep biopsy when both deep and superficial biopsies are performed at the same location.
Component Code	The lesser procedure or service when reported with another code. The component code is part of a major procedure or service and is often represented by a lower work relative value unit (RVU) under the Medicare Physician Fee Schedule as compared to the other code reported (also called *Column 2* codes). Lower payments are associated with component codes.	If the surgeon determines that the superficial biopsy code should be reported in addition to the deep biopsy code, supporting documentation in the patient's record must be evident.	NOTE: To have component code(s) considered for possible reimbursement, attach a modifier to the code(s). A modifier is a two-digit code added to a code to indicate a procedure or service has been altered (e.g., bilateral procedure).
Column1/ Column 2 Edit Table	Code combinations (or edit pairs), where comprehensive code and only the comprehensive code is paid. (If clinical circumstances justify appending a CCI-associated modifier to either code of a code pair edit, payment of both codes may be allowed.)	Figure 19-9 contains a partial listing of the table of Column 1/Column 2 codes. Refer to Column 1, code 10140. If code 10140 is reported on a CMS-1500 claim, none of the codes from Column 2 can be reported on the same claim (unless a modifier is attached and supporting documentation is found in the patient's record).	NOTE: Column 2 codes are components of column 1 codes, which means a column 1 code includes all procedures/services described by column 2 codes. Thus, column 2 codes cannot be reported with column 1 codes because overpayments would result.
Mutually Exclusive Codes	Procedures or services that could not reasonably be performed at the same session by the same provider on the same beneficiary.	A claim that contains codes for cystourethroscopy, with internal urethrotomy of a female (CPT code 52270) with that of a male (CPT code 52275) will result in denial as a result of this CCI edit.	NOTE: To have mutually exclusive code(s) considered for possible reimbursement, attach a modifier to the code(s).
Mutually Exclusive Edit Table	Code combinations (or edit pairs), where one of the procedures/ services would not reasonably be performed with the other. (If clinical circumstances justify adding a CCI modifier to either code of a code pair edit, payment of both codes may be allowed.)	Figure 19-10 contains a partial listing of the table of mutually exclusive codes. Refer to Column 1, code 10060. If code 10060 is reported on a CMS-1500 claim, none of the codes from Column 2 can be reported on the same claim (unless a modifier is attached and supporting documentation is found in the patient's record).	NOTE: When mutually exclusive codes are reported on the same claim (for the same date of service), reimbursement is based on the lower-paying code.

National Correct Coding Initiative Column 1/Column 2 Edits					
Column 1	**Column 2**	* = In existence prior to 1996	**Effective Date**	**Deletion Date** * = no data	**Modifier** 0 = not allowed 1 = allowed 9 = not applicable
10021	J2001		20040701	*	1
10021	19290		20020101	*	1
10021	36000		20021001	*	1
10021	36410		20021001	*	1
10021	37202		20021001	*	1
10021	62318		20021001	*	1
10021	62319		20021001	*	1
10021	64415		20021001	*	1
10021	64416		20030101	*	1
10021	64417		20021001	*	1

© Cengage Learning 2014

Figure 19-9 Sample of NCCI column 1/Column 2 edits

National Correct Coding Initiative Mutually Exclusive Edits					
Column 1	**Column 2**	* = In existence prior to 1996	**Effective Date**	**Deletion Date** * = no data	**Modifier** 0 = not allowed 1 = allowed 9 = not applicable
10060	11401		19960101	*	1
10060	11402		19960101	*	1
10060	11403		19960101	*	1
10060	11404		19960101	*	1
10060	11406		19960101	*	1

© Cengage Learning 2014

Figure 19-10 Sample of NCCI mutually exclusive edits

(e.g., up to $10,000 per false claim, plus three times the amount of damages that the government sustains). It imposes civil liability on those who submit false/fraudulent claims to the government for payment and can exclude violators from participation in government programs (e.g., Medicaid and Medicare).

Note:

Qui tam provisions of the FCA encourage and reward private individuals (sometimes called whistle-blowers) who are aware of fraud being committed against the government to report that information. In addition, the FCA only covers offenses that are committed with actual knowledge of the falsity of the claim, or reckless disregard or deliberate ignorance of the truth or falsity of a claim. The FSA does not penalize mistakes, error, or negligence. The OIG has stated that it is mindful of the difference between innocent errors (e.g., erroneous claims) and reckless or intentional conduct (e.g., fraudulent claims).

The **Federal Anti-kickback Statute** prohibits the offer, payment, receipt, or solicitation of compensation for referring Medicaid/Medicare patients and imposes a $25,000 fine per violation, plus imprisonment for up to 10 years. Civil penalties may also be imposed, and violators can be excluded from participation in government programs (e.g., Medicaid and Medicare). **Safe harbor regulations** were also implemented, which specify various payment and business practices that, although potentially capable of inducing referrals of business reimbursable under federal health care programs, would not be treated as criminal offenses under the Anti-kickback Statute.

EXAMPLE The DHHS implemented a safe harbor for the waiver or reduction of coinsurance or deductible amounts (cost-sharing amounts) for inpatient hospital services reimbursed under the PPS. For full or partial waivers to be protected, three standards had to be met: (1) the hospital could not claim waived amounts as bad debt or otherwise shift the cost of the waivers; (2) the hospital could not discriminate in offering waivers or reductions based on the patient's reason for admission; and (3) the waivers or reductions could not result from an agreement between the hospital and a third-party payer. The DHHS concluded that waivers of cost-sharing amounts for inpatient hospital services that complied with these standards would not increase costs to the Medicare program, shift costs to other payers, or increase patient demand for inpatient hospital services.

Subtitle A of the Health Insurance Portability and Accountability Act of 1997 (HIPAA) authorized implementation of a fraud and abuse control program, which coordinates federal, state, and local law enforcement programs to control fraud and abuse with respect to health plans; conducts investigations, audits, evaluations, and inspections relating to delivery of and payment for health care in the United States; facilitates enforcement of health care fraud and abuse provisions; provides for modification and establishment of safe harbors; and issues advisory opinions and special fraud alerts to provide for reporting and disclosure of certain final adverse actions against health care providers, suppliers, or practitioners.

The **Federal Claims Collection Act of 1966** established uniform procedures for government agencies to follow in the collection, compromise, suspension, termination, or referral for litigation of debts owed to the government.  This means that MACs (as agents of the federal government) are responsible for attempting to collect **overpayments**, which are funds that a provider or beneficiary receives in excess of amounts due and payable under Medicare and Medicare statutes and regulations. Any review conducted by the MAC for overpayment recovery must

Note:

The act does not apply where there is an indication of fraud, for which such cases are submitted to the OIG for review and referral to the DOJ.

be done within three calendar years after the year in which the overpayment was made. Once a determination of overpayment has been made, the amount so determined is a debt owed to the U.S. government.

Examples of overpayments include the following:

- Payment based on a charge that exceeds the reasonable charge
- Duplicate processing of charges and/or claims
- Payment made to the wrong payee (e.g., payment made to a provider on a nonassigned claim, or payment made to a beneficiary on an assigned claim)
- Payment for noncovered items and services, including medically unnecessary services
- Incorrect application of the deductible, coinsurance, or copayment
- Payment for items or services rendered during a period of nonentitlement
- Primary payment for items or services for which another entity is the primary payer
- Payment for items or services rendered after the beneficiary's date of death (postpayment reviews are conducted to identify and recover payments with a billed date of service that is after the beneficiary's date of death).

Once a Medicare administrative contractor determines that an overpayment was made, it proceeds with recovery by issuing an overpayment demand letter (Figure 19-11) to the provider. The letter contains information about the review and statistical sampling methodology used, as well as corrective actions to be taken. Corrective actions include payment suspension, imposition of civil monetary penalties, institution of pre- or postpayment review, and additional edits.

 Note:

A provider is not liable for overpayments received if found to be without fault as determined by the MAC, such as when reasonable care was exercised in billing and accepting payment and the provider had a reasonable basis for assuming that payment was correct. In addition, if the provider had a reason to question the payment and promptly brought the question to the attention of the MAC, the provider may be found without liability.

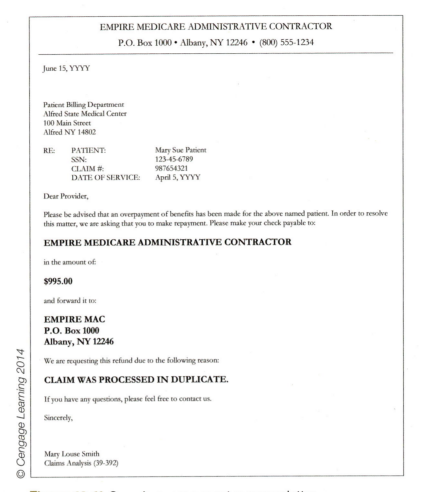

EMPIRE MEDICARE ADMINISTRATIVE CONTRACTOR
P.O. Box 1000 • Albany, NY 12246 • (800) 555-1234

June 15, YYYY

Patient Billing Department
Alfred State Medical Center
100 Main Street
Alfred NY 14802

RE: PATIENT: Mary Sue Patient
       SSN: 123-45-6789
       CLAIM #:   987654321
       DATE OF SERVICE: April 5, YYYY

Dear Provider,

Please be advised that an overpayment of benefits has been made for the above named patient. In order to resolve this matter, we are asking that you to make repayment. Please make your check payable to:

EMPIRE MEDICARE ADMINISTRATIVE CONTRACTOR

in the amount of:

$995.00

and forward it to:

EMPIRE MAC
P.O. Box 1000
Albany, NY 12246

We are requesting this refund due to the following reason:

CLAIM WAS PROCESSED IN DUPLICATE.

If you have any questions, please feel free to contact us.

Sincerely,

Mary Louse Smith
Claims Analysis (39-392)

© Cengage Learning 2014

Figure 19-11 Sample overpayment recovery letter

The **Payment Error and Prevention Program (PEPP)** identifies and reduces improper Medicare payments, resulting in a reduction in the Medicare payment error rate. It also participates in **overpayment recovery** by collecting overpayments made by Medicare, Medicaid, and other payers.

A **physician self-referral law**, **Stark I**, enacted as part of the Omnibus Budget Reconciliation Act of 1989, prohibits a physician from referring Medicare patients to clinical laboratory services where they or a member of their family have a financial interest. (The financial interest includes both ownership/investment interests and compensation arrangements.) By 1994, because some providers routinely waived coinsurance and copayments, the DHHSOIG issued the following fraud alert:

Routine waiver of deductibles and copayments by charge-based providers, practitioners or suppliers is unlawful because it results in (1) false claims, (2) violations of the anti-kickback statute, and (3) excessive utilization of items and services paid for by Medicare.

(The only exception to the alert is waiving deductibles and copayments for financial hardship cases, but this *cannot be done on a routine* basis.)

In 1995, the **Stark II** physician self-referral law expanded the Stark I law by including referrals of Medicare *and* Medicaid patients for the following designated health care services (DHCS):

- Clinical laboratory services
- Durable medical equipment and supplies
- Home health services
- Inpatient and outpatient hospitalization services

- Occupational therapy services
- Outpatient prescription drugs
- Parenteral and enteral nutrients, equipment, and supplies
- Physical therapy services
- Prosthetics, orthotics, and prosthetic devices and supplies
- Radiation therapy services and supplies
- Radiology services, including MRIs, CAT scans, and ultrasound services

Medicare Part A reimburses health care facilities for costs associated with training residents. The **Physicians at Teaching Hospitals (PATH) initiative** resulted from the discovery that some health care organizations were billing Medicare Part B for services that were already paid under Part A. The PATH initiative requires a national review of teaching hospitals' compliance with reimbursement rules and training of physicians who provide services at teaching facilities.

Administrative Simplification

The purpose of **HIPAA administrative simplification (AS)** provisions is to develop standards for the maintenance and transmission of health information required to identify individual patients. These standards are designed to improve efficiency and effectiveness of the health care system by standardizing the interchange of electronic data for specified administrative and financial transactions. In addition, the intent is to protect the security and confidentiality of electronic health information. HIPAA provisions require compliance by all health care organizations that maintain or transmit electronic health information. The law also establishes significant penalties for violations (e.g., $100 for each violation, a $25,000 maximum penalty for violations of an identical requirement, a $50,000 wrongful disclosure penalty and/or imprisonment of not more than one year, a $100,000 penalty for offenses under false pretenses and/or imprisonment of not more than 5 years, and a $250,000 penalty for offense with intent to sell information and/or imprisonment of not more than 10 years).

> **Note:**
>
> HIPAA established the **Designated Standard Maintenance Organization (DSMO)**, which is made up of organizations that agree to maintain the electronic transactions standards adopted by the Secretary of DHHS and to develop or modify adopted standards. Approved DSMOs include the Accredited Standards Committee X12, Dental Content Committee of the American Dental Association, Health Level Seven (HL7), National Council for Prescription Drug Programs, National Uniform Billing Committee, and National Uniform Claim Committee.

Unique Identifiers

HIPAA administrative simplification provisions require the following national identifiers to be established:

- **National standard employer identifier number (EIN)**. The IRS's federal tax identification number was adopted as the national employer identifier, retaining the hyphen after the first two numbers (e.g., 12-3456789). The EIN is assigned to employers who, as sponsors of health insurance for their employers, must be identified in health care transactions.

- **National provider identifier (NPI)**. HIPAA provisions require hospitals, doctors, nursing homes, and other health care providers to obtain a unique identifier consisting of 10 numeric digits (e.g., 1234567890) for filing electronic claims with public and private insurance programs. Providers apply for the NPI once and keep it if they relocate or change specialties. Currently, health care providers are assigned different ID numbers by each health plan, which results in slower payments, increased costs, and a lack of coordination.

> **Note:**
>
> A **check digit** is a one-digit character, alphabetic or numeric, that is used to verify the validity of a unique identifier.

- **National health plan identifier (PlanID)**. The PlanID is assigned to third-party payers, and it contains 10 numeric positions including a check digit in the tenth position (e.g., 1234567890). (The PlanID was formerly called the PAYERID.)

- **National individual identifier (patient identifier)**. The HIPAA provision for a national individual identifier (or patient identifier) has been withdrawn. Although HIPAA included a requirement for the assignment of a unique personal health care identifier to each person in the United States, Congress is proposing legislation that would eliminate the requirement to establish a national individual identifier.

Electronic Health Care Transactions

HIPAA requires payers to implement **electronic transaction standards**, a uniform language for electronic data interchange. **Electronic data interchange (EDI)** is the computer-to-computer transfer of data between provider and third-party payer (or provider and health care clearinghouse) in a data format agreed upon by the sending and receiving parties. HIPAA's administrative simplification provisions directed the federal government to adopt national electronic standards for the automated transfer of certain health care data among health care payers (e.g., Medicare administrative contractors), payers (e.g., BCBS), and providers (e.g., hospitals and physicians). The provisions enable the entire health care industry to communicate electronic data using a single set of standards, eliminating all nonstandard formats currently in use. The standards allow a health care provider to submit a standard transaction for eligibility, authorization, referrals, claims, or attachments containing the same standard data content to any payer. This "simplifies" clinical, billing, and other financial applications, and it reduces costs.

Computer-generated paper claims are not considered EDI. Providers that generate paper-based claims submit them to health care clearinghouses, which convert them to a standardized electronic format for submission to payers. A health care clearinghouse performs centralized claims processing for providers and health care plans; it receives claims from providers, transmits claims to payers, receives remittance advice and payment instructions from payers, and transmits that information to providers (all in a HIPAA-compliant format). A health care clearinghouse also conducts eligibility and claim status queries in the format prescribed by HIPAA.

A **remittance advice (remit)** (Figure 19-12) is a statement sent by the payer to the provider, which details how submitted claims were processed and contains reimbursement amounts. If a claim is denied, an explanation of denial is included on the remittance advice. Providers may receive an electronic remittance advice (ERA) or a paper-based statement, called a standard paper remittance (SPR). The remittance advice includes the following information: patient name, health insurance claim number (HICN), provider's name, date(s) of service, type of service, procedure codes and modifiers, charges (both submitted and allowed), reimbursement amount including any deductions (e.g., copayments), reason and/or remark codes (e.g., explanation of denial), and an indication that the claim has been forwarded to a supplemental carrier for processing, if applicable.

EXAMPLE Health care providers submit electronic claims data to payers on computer tape, diskette, or by computer modem or fax. The payer receives the claim, processes the data, and sends the provider the results of processing electronic claims (an electronic remittance advice).

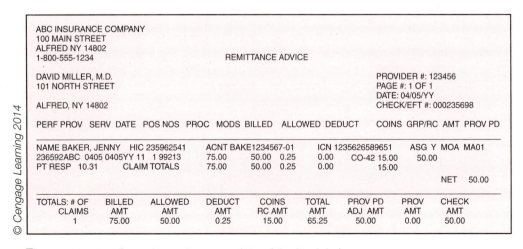

Figure 19-12   Sample remittance advice (single claim)

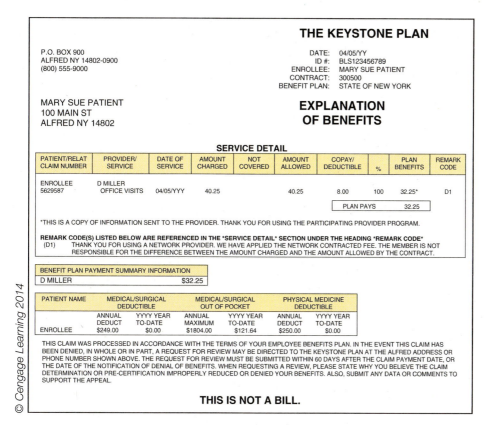

Figure 19-13A Sample explanation of benefits (EOB)

An **explanation of benefits (EOB)** (Figure 19-13A) is sent to the patient by the payer, and it contains the same information as the remittance advice but it is in an easy-to-read format.  Medicare patients receive a **Medicare Summary Notice (MSN)** (Figure 19-13B) (instead of an EOB), which is an easy-to-read monthly statement that clearly lists health insurance claims information.

Effective 2003, electronic claims will not be processed by Medicare administrative contractors if they are not in an electronic format. Advantages of EDI include the following:

- Claim status and eligibility information in 24 hours or less
- Cost effectiveness and reduction in opportunity for error
- Electronic funds transfer of accounts receivable into the provider's bank
- Electronic remittances sent to a provider-preferred location
- Faster payment of electronic claims
- Lower administrative, postage, and handling costs
- Online receipt or acknowledgement
- Standardized electronic claims submission, coordination of benefits exchange, and remittance receipt reduce system costs.

Three electronic formats are supported for health care claims transactions, including the UB-04 flat-file format (Figure 19-14), the National Standard Format (NSF) (Figure 19-15), and the **ANSI ASC X12N 837** format (American National Standards Institute, Accredited Standards Committee, Insurance Subcommittee X12N, claims validation table 837) (Figure 19-16).

Note:

The MSN replaced the Explanation of Medical Benefits (EOMB), the Medicare Benefits Notice (Part A), and benefit denial letter.

Medicare Summary Notice
for Part B (Medical Insurance)

Page 1 of 5

The Official Summary of Your Medicare Claims from the Centers for Medicare & Medicaid Services

Facility Name
Your Name Here
Street Address
City, State 12345-6789

THIS IS NOT A BILL

Notice for Your Name

Medicare Number	XXX-XX-1234A
Date of This Notice	September 16, 2011
Claims Processed Between	June 15 – September 15, 2011

Your Deductible Status

Your deductible is what you must pay for most health services before Medicare begins to pay.

Part B Deductible: You have now met **$85** of your **$162** deductible for 2011.

Be Informed!

Register at www.MyMedicare.gov for direct access to your Original Medicare claims, track your preventive services and print an "On the Go" report to share with your provider. Visit the Web site to sign up and access your personal Medicare information.

Your Claims & Costs This Period

Did Medicare Approve All Services?	**NO**
Number of Services Medicare Denied	**2**

See claims starting on page 3. Look for **NO** in the "Service Approved?" column. See the last page for how to handle a denied claim.

Total You May Be Billed	**$150.86**

Providers with Claims This Period

June 18, 2011
Jane Doe, M.D.

June 28, 2011
John Doe, M.D.

June 29 – June 30, 2011
Any Doctor, M.D.

¿Sabía que puede recibir este aviso y otro tipo de ayuda de Medicare en español? Llame y hable con un agente en española.
如果需要国语帮助，请致电联邦医疗保险，请先说 "agent"，然后说 "Mandarin"．   **1-800-MEDICARE (1-800-633-4227)**

© Cengage Learning 2014

Figure 19-13B Sample explanation of benefits (EOB)

Note:

A **flat file** consists of a series of fixed-length records (e.g., eight spaces for the patient's date of birth). The UB-04 flat file is used to bill institutional services (e.g., hospitals), and the National Standard Format (NSF) flat file is used to bill physician and noninstitutional services (e.g., the physician's office). ANSI ASC X12N 837 is a variable-length file format that is used to bill institutional, professional, dental, and drug claims. The flat-file formats were developed for use in claims processing software application programs because the ANSI ASC X12N 837 format is not suitable for use in an application program, and it must be translated into a flat-file format prior to claims processing.

Medicare administrative contractors do not accept flat-file format transactions for claims submission. Medicare administrative contractors also do not send electronic remittance advices in the flat-file format or exchange electronic eligibility queries/responses in any version not adopted as a national standard in the final rules for the HIPAA Administrative Simplification transaction standards. However, providers can use health care clearinghouses to translate outgoing and/or incoming electronic transactions, which will convert flat-file formats to the ANSI ASC X12N 837 format. Providers who do not use a health care clearinghouse must install software that can send and receive files in the ANSI ASC X12N 837 format.

```
MSG_HDR BCBS ECM_Y06 SndApp SndFac RcApp RcFac 20060105 2369 56941
INS_CLM 562697 20060105 20060110 ADLO5691 125.00
PRV_DT1 M_P Smith DKSL23659
PRV_DT1 M_H Jones DLEP65915
PAT_IDF DCB5432 Green 19941205
CRD_STS Y Y N
SRV_CMN GM 20060105 50.00
SRV_FEE CP 45.00
SRV_FEE CK 12.00
SRV_CMN GM 20060106 55.00
SRV_FEE CO 10.00
SRV_FEE RK
```

Figure 19-14 Sample UB-04 electronic flat-file format

```
ELECTRONIC MEDIA CLAIMS NATIONAL STANDARD FORMAT
RECORD NAME: CLAIM HEADER RECORD "PATIENT DATA"              RECORD TYPE:   CA0
```

FIELD NUMBER	FIELD NAME	FIELD LENGTH	FIELD TYPE	FIELD POSITIONS FROM	TO
01.0	RECORD ID "CA0"	3	X	01	03
02.0	RESERVED (CA0-02.0)	2	X	04	05
03.0	PATIENT CONTROL NUMBER	17	X	06	22
04.0	PATIENT LAST NAME	20	X	23	42
05.0	PATIENT FIRST NAME	12	X	43	54
06.0	PATIENT MIDDLE INITIAL	1	X	55	55
07.0	PATIENT GENERATION	3	X	56	58
08.0	PATIENT DATE OF BIRTH	8	X	59	66
09.0	PATIENT GENDER	1	X	67	67
10.0	PATIENT TYPE OF RESIDENCE	1	X	68	68

Figure 19-15 Portion of electronic medical claims National Standard Format (NSF)

UB-04 data elements in ANSI ASC X12N 837 format	Description of data elements
ST*837*123456~ BHT*0019*00*A98765*YYYY0504*0830~	Header
NM1*41*2*GOODMEDICINE HOSPITAL*****54*888229999~	Submitter name
NM1*40*2*CAPITAL BLUE CROSS*****54*16000~	Receiver name
HL*1**20*1~	Service provider hierarchical level for submitter
NM1*85*2*GOODMEDICINE HOSPITAL*****54*888229999~ REF*1J*898989~	Service provider name
HL*2*1*22*1~ SBR*P*******BL~	Subscriber (patient) hierarchical level
NM1*IL*1*PUBLIC*JOHN*Q**MI*GRNESSC1234~ N3*1247 HILL STREET~ N4*ANYWHERE*US*12345~ DMG*D8*19820805*M**::RET:3::RET:2~ REF*SY*150259874~	Subscriber (patient) name
NM1*PR*2*CAPITAL BLUE CROSS*****PI*00303~	Payer name
CLM*ABH123456*5015***11:A:1~ DTP*096*TM*1200~ DTP*434*RD8*YYYY0504-YYYY0510~ DTP*435*DT*YYYY05101100~ CL1*2*1*01~ HI*BK:66411*BJ:66411~ HI*BF:66331:::::::Y*BF:66111:::::::N*BF:V270:::::::N~ HI*BR:7569:D8:YYYY0510~	Claim information
SE*91*123456~	Trailer

Figure 19-16 Portion of UB-04 data submitted in ANSI ASC X12N 837 electronic format

HIPAA administrative simplification provisions also require the following code sets to be used:

- *Current Dental Terminology (CDT)*: Dental services
- *International Classification of Diseases, 9th Revision, Clinical Modification (ICD-9-CM)*: All diagnoses and inpatient hospital procedures and services
- *Current Procedural Terminology (CPT)*: Outpatient hospital and physician procedures and services
- *Health Care Common Procedure Coding System, Level II (National)*: Outpatient hospital and physician procedures and services, and institutional/professional pharmacy transactions
- *National Drug Code (NDC)*: Retail pharmacy transactions

ICD-10 Alert!

ICD-9-CM will be replaced by ICD-10-CM and ICD-10-PCS when adopted for implementation.

Note:

No standard code set was adopted for nonretail pharmacy drug claims.

Privacy and Security Rules

Any information communicated by a patient to a health care provider is considered **privileged communication**, which means that it is private. Patients have the right to **confidentiality**, which is the process of keeping privileged communication secret and means that information cannot be disclosed without the patient's authorization. (Exceptions include information released via *subpoena duces tecum*, court order, and according to statutory reporting requirements.) A **breach of confidentiality** occurs when patient information is **disclosed** (or released) to other(s) who do not have a right to access the information. In this situation, the disclosing provider failed to obtain patient authorization to release privileged communication; this results in violation of federal law (HIPAA). According to HIPAA privacy and security provisions, patients have the right to an expectation of **privacy** regarding their privileged communication, which means information cannot be disclosed without their authorization. **Security** safeguards also must be implemented to ensure that facilities, equipment, and patient information are safe from damage, loss, tampering, theft, or unauthorized access.

The **HIPAA standards for privacy of individually identifiable health information**, or **privacy rule**, include provisions that protect the security and confidentiality of health information. Because the use and disclosure of health information is inconsistently protected by state laws, patients' privacy and confidentiality is also inconsistently protected. The HIPAA privacy rule establishes standards to protect the confidentiality of individually identifiable health information maintained or transmitted electronically in connection with certain administrative and financial transactions (e.g., electronic transfer of health insurance claims). The rule provides new rights for individuals with respect to protected health information (PHI) and mandates compliance by **covered entities**, which are private and public sector organizations that must follow HIPAA provisions. For the privacy rule, covered entities include health care providers that conduct certain transactions in electronic forms, health plans, and health care clearinghouses.

Protected health information (PHI) is information that is identifiable to an individual (or individual identifiers) such as name, address, telephone number, date of birth, Medicaid ID number and other medical record numbers, Social Security number (SSN), and name of employer. In most instances, covered entities are required to obtain an individual's authorization prior to disclosing the individual's health information, and HIPAA has established specific requirements for an authorization form. All medical records and other individually identifiable health information used or disclosed by a covered entity in any form, whether electronically, paper-based, or verbally, are covered by the privacy rule.

The HIPAA **security rule** contains standards and safeguards for PHI that is collected, maintained, used, or transmitted electronically. Covered entities impacted by this rule include health plans, health care clearinghouses,

Note:

HIPAA is the first federal law that governs the privacy of health information nationwide. If security policies and procedures are not established and enforced, concerns might be raised about the security of patient information during legal proceedings. This could result in questioning the integrity of the medical record.

and certain health care providers. CMS is responsible for overseeing compliance with and complaints about security rules.

The standard for electronic signature is **digital**, which applies a mathematical function to the electronic document resulting in a unique bit string (computer code) called a message digest, which is encrypted and appended to the electronic document. (**Encrypt** means to encode a computer file, making it safe for electronic transmission so unauthorized parties cannot read it.) The recipient of the transmitted electronic document **decrypts** (decodes) the message digest and compares the decoded digest to the transmitted version. If they are identical, the message is unaltered and the identity of the signer is proven.

The DHHS Medicare Program, other federal agencies operating health plans or providing health care, state Medicaid agencies, private health plans, health care providers, and health care clearinghouses must assure their customers (e.g., patients, insured individuals, providers, and health plans) that the integrity, confidentiality, and availability of electronic PHI they collect, maintain, use, or transmit is protected. The confidentiality of health information is threatened not only by the risk of improper access to stored information, but also by the risk of interception during electronic transmission of the information. The purpose of the *security rule* is to adopt national standards for safeguards to protect the confidentiality, integrity, and availability of electronic PHI. Prior to publication of the *security rule*, no standard measures existed in the health care industry to address all aspects of the security of electronic health information while being stored or during the exchange of that information between entities. In general, security provisions should include the following procedures:

- Define authorized users of patient information to control access

- Implement a tracking procedure to sign out records to authorized personnel

- Limit record storage access to authorized users

- Lock record storage areas at all times

- Require the original medical record to remain in the facility at all times (except when a court order requires the original medical record to be submitted to the court clerk)

Although security and privacy are linked, be sure you do not confuse the purpose of each rule. The *security rule* defines administrative, physical, and technical safeguards to protect the availability, confidentiality, and integrity of PHI. The standards require covered entities to implement basic safeguards to protect electronic PHI from unauthorized access, alteration, deletion, and transmission. In contrast, the *privacy rule* establishes standards for how PHI should be controlled; it also establishes what uses (e.g., continuity of care) and disclosures (e.g., third-party reimbursement) are authorized or required, as well as what rights patients have with respect to their health information (e.g., patient access).

Medical Liability Reform

The threat of excessive awards in medical liability cases has increased providers' liability insurance premiums, which has resulted in increases in health care costs. Because of this, some providers have stopped practicing medicine in areas of the country where liability insurance costs are highest, and the direct impact on individuals and communities across the country has been reduced access to quality medical care. Although medical liability reform was included in HIPAA legislation, no final rule was published. Although individual states, such as Ohio, have passed medical liability reform, the U.S. Congress is also formulating separate federal medical liability reform legislation. The Senate introduced legislation that will implement reasonable, comprehensive, and effective health care liability reforms designed to improve the availability of health care services in cases in which health care liability actions have been shown to be a factor in the decreased availability of services; reduce the incidence of "defensive medicine" and lower the cost of health care liability insurance, all of which contribute to the escalation of health care costs; ensure that persons with meritorious health care injury claims receive fair and adequate compensation, including reasonable noneconomic damages; improve the fairness and cost-effectiveness of our current health care liability system to resolve disputes over, and provide compensation for, health care liability by reducing uncertainty in the amount of compensation provided to injured individuals; and provide increased sharing of information in the health care system, which will reduce unintended injury and improve patient care. (Go to http://thomas.loc.gov and enter medical liability reform in the "Search Bill Text" box to view the list of proposed legislation.)

Exercise 19.3 – Impact of HIPAA on Reimbursement

Instructions: Match the term in Column 2 with the example in Column 1.

_____   **1.** Submitting excessive charges for services or supplies   **a.** Abuse

_____   **2.** Unbundling codes reported on claims   **b.** Fraud

_____   **3.** Billing Medicare for services or supplies not provided

_____   **4.** Submitting claims for services that aren't medically necessary

_____   **5.** Violating Medicare participating provider agreements with payers

Instructions: Complete each statement.

6. Formerly called the PAYERID, the _____ is assigned to third-party payers, and it contains 10 numeric positions including a check digit in the tenth position.

7. The IRS's federal tax identification number was adopted as the _____, which is assigned to employers who, as sponsors of health insurance for their employers, must be identified in health care transactions.

8. Health care providers must obtain a(n) _____, which consists of nine alphanumeric characters plus a check digit, and is used for filing electronic claims with public and private insurance programs.

9. The computerized exchange of health information between provider and payer in a format agreed upon by the sending and receiving parties is called _____.

10. HIPAA requires the implementation of standards and safeguards to protect health information that is collected, maintained, used, or transmitted electronically, which is called the _____ rule.

Health Reform

In 2010, two significant federal laws were implemented that resulted in health reform. The Patient Protection and Affordable Care Act (PPACA):

- Allows young adults to remain on a parent's plan until the age of 26.

- Assists employers that provide retiree health benefits.

- Creates health insurance exchanges.

- Ends insurance company abuses.

- Establishes a competitive health insurance market.

- Expands Medicaid eligibility.

- Immediately establishes a plan for the uninsured.

- Maintains employer-sponsored coverage for most Americans who currently have it.

- Prohibits the denial of coverage/claims based on pre-existing conditions.

- Provides 32 million uninsured children and families with access to coverage.

- Provides incentives for businesses to provide health care benefits.

- Reduces the maximum time period for submitting Medicare fee-for-service claims to one calendar year after the date of service.

- Subsidizes insurance premiums.

- Supports medical research.

The Health Care and Education Reconciliation Act (HCERA) amended the PPACA to:

- Close the Medicare Part D "donut hole" by 2011, and give seniors a rebate of $250.

- Delay implementation on taxing "Cadillac health care plans" until 2018.

- Eliminate several special deals given to senators.

- Establish a Medicare tax on unearned incomes of families who earn more than $250,000 annually.

- Extend the ban on lifetime limits and rescission of coverage to all existing health plans within six months.

- Increase Medicaid payment rates to primary care physicians to match Medicare payment rates and provide states that already insure childless adults under Medicaid with more federal money for covering that group through 2018.

- Increase tax credits to buy insurance.

- Lower the penalty for not buying insurance from $750 to $695.

- Offer more generous subsidies to lower income groups.

- Provide a 50 percent discount to Medicare patients on brand-name drugs effective 2011 (and by 2020, provide up to a 75 percent discount on brand-name and generic drugs, eventually closing the coverage gap).

- Require doctors who treat Medicare patients to be reimbursed at the full rate.

The costs of the above provisions are offset by a variety of taxes, fees, and cost-saving measures, such as new Medicare taxes for high-income brackets, taxes on indoor tanning, cuts to the Medicare Advantage program in favor of traditional Medicare, and fees on medical devices and pharmaceutical companies. Also included is a tax penalty for citizens who do not obtain health insurance (unless they are exempt due to low income or other reasons).

Summary

A third-party payer is an insurance company or other organization (e.g., a Medicare administrative contractor) that processes health care claims for reimbursement of procedures and services. Third-party payers include Blue Cross and Blue Shield (BCBS), commercial insurance companies, employer self-insurance plans, government-sponsored programs (e.g., Medicaid, Medicare, and TRICARE), managed care plans (e.g., a health maintenance organization), and workers' compensation. A health insurance policy is an agreement between an individual and a third-party payer (or insurance company) that contains a list of reimbursable medical benefits (or covered benefits) (e.g., office visits, inpatient hospitalizations, laboratory, tests, prescription medications, and treatment services).

Government programs reimburse providers according to prospective cost-based rates and prospective payment systems. Typically, third-party payers adopt prospective payment systems, fee schedules, and exclusions after Medicare has implemented them; payers modify them to suit their needs.

The Health Insurance Portability and Accountability Act of 1996 (HIPAA) amended the Internal Revenue Code of 1986 to improve portability and continuity of health insurance coverage in the group and individual markets; combat waste, fraud, and abuse in health insurance and health care delivery; promote the use of medical savings accounts; improve access to long-term care services and coverage; simplify the administration of health insurance by creating unique identifiers for providers, health plans, employers, and individuals; create standards for electronic health information transactions; and create privacy and security standards for health information.

Internet Links

Accredited Standards Committee X12N (ASC X12N): *www.x12.org*

Centers for Medicare and Medicaid Services: *www.cms.gov*

CMS Quarterly Provider Update: Go to *www.cms.gov* and click on the Regulations & Guidance link, then click on the Quarterly Provider Updates - Regulations link

Designated Standard Maintenance Organization (DSMO): *www.hipaa-dsmo.org*

EDI Healthcare: *www.iplexus.net*

Health Care Compliance Association (HCCA): Go to *www.hcca-info.org* and click on the Compliance Info. link.

Health Level Seven (HL7): *www.hl7.org*

Health Reform: Go to *www.healthreform.gov* to learn more about the Patient Protection and Affordable Care Act (PPACA) and the Health Care and Education Reconciliation Act (HCERA).

HIPAA: *www.hipaa.org*

Innovative Resources for Payors: Go to *www.irp.com* and click on the Medicare DRG Calculator link or the IRP Refined DRG Calculator link.

MedAssets: Go to *www.MedAssets.com* to learn more about revenue cycle management services and solutions.

Medicare *Conditions for Coverage* and *Conditions of Participation*: Go to *www.cms.gov* and click on the Regulations & Guidance link, then click on the Conditions for Coverage (CfCs) & Conditions of Participation (CoPs) link.

Medicare National Heritage Insurance Company: Go to *www.medicarenhic.com* and click on the Part B link to join the mailing list.

Medicare Payment Systems: Go to *www.cms.gov* and click on the Medicare link, then click on one or more of the topics below the Medicare Fee-for-Service Payment heading.

Medicare Preventive Services (coverage issues): Go to *www.cms.gov* and click on the Medicare link, then click on one or more of the topics below the Prevention heading.

MEDPAR: Go to *www.cms.gov* and click on the Research, Statistics, Data, & Systems link, then click on the Medicare Fee-for-Service Statistics link and click on the MEDPAR link.

National Uniform Billing Committee: *www.nubc.org*

National Uniform Claim Committee: *www.nucc.org*

Office of Inspector General of the Department of Health and Human Services: *www.oig.hhs.gov*

Quality Improvement Organizations: Go to *www.cms.gov* and click on the Medicare link, then scroll down and click on the Quality Improvement Organizations link.

Workgroup for Electronic Data Interchange (WEDI): *www.wedi.org*

Study Checklist

- ❏ Read this chapter and highlight key concepts.
- ❏ Create an index card for each key term.
- ❏ Access the chapter Internet links to learn more about concepts.
- ❏ Complete the chapter review, verifying your answers with your instructor.
- ❏ Complete WebTutor assignments and take online quizzes.
- ❏ Complete Workbook chapter, verifying answers with your instructor.

❑ Go to www.cengagebrain.com to access StudyWARE™ and the Premium Website. Login instructions are located in the Preface and on the Printed Access Card.

❑ Form a study group with classmates to discuss chapter concepts in preparation for an exam.

Review

Multiple Choice

Instructions: Circle the most appropriate response.

1. An insurance policy is an agreement between a third-party payer and a(n):
   a. health care facility.
   b. health care provider.
   c. individual.
   d. insurance company.

2. Which of the following prohibits the health care provider from collecting payment from the patient for claims that the insurance plan has denied?
   a. hold harmless clausec
   b. indemnification
   c. medical necessity
   d. preauthorization

3. Under an employer self-insurance plan, who would be responsible for payment of the employees' health care?
   a. employee
   b. employer
   c. third-party payer
   d. workers' compensation

4. Which third-party payer is state-mandated rather than government-sponsored?
   a. Indian Health Service (IHS)
   b. Programs of All-inclusive Care for the Elderly (PACE)
   c. State Children's Health Insurance Program (SCHIP)
   d. workers' compensation

5. A patient who has the option to be seen by a non-HMO provider without obtaining a referral from the primary care physician (PCP), thus incurring a greater out-of-pocket expense, would be using which type of managed care plan?
   a. exclusive provider organization (EPO)
   b. health maintenance organization (HMO)
   c. point-of-service plan (POS)
   d. preferred provider organization (PPO)

6. In the customized sub-capitation type of consumer-directed health plan (CDHP), each provider is paid:
   a. a fixed amount per month to manage all of an individual's health care, which includes reimbursing for services provided by labs and specialists.
   b. a fixed amount per month to provide only the care that an individual needs from that provider.
   c. a variable amount per month to manage all of an individual's health care from a tax-exempt account established by an employee.
   d. both a fixed and a variable amount each month to manage an individual's health care when the employee uses the provider's services.

7. A cancer hospital that has been granted a waiver from mandatory participation in the hospital inpatient prospective payment system is called a(n) _____ by CMS.
   a. exception
   b. exclusion
   c. pardon
   d. release

8. Which prospective payment system uses information from the patient assessment instrument to classify patients into groups based on clinical characteristics and expected resource needs?
   a. HH PPS
   b. IRF PPS
   c. LTC PPS
   d. OPPS

9. The DRG payment window for outpatient preadmission services provided by a long-term (acute) care hospital is _____ hours.
   a. 24   b. 36   c. 48   d. 72

10. The resource-based relative value scale (RBRVS) system is now commonly called the _____.
    a. Ambulance Fee Schedule
    c. Diagnosis Related Group (DRG)
    b. Clinical Laboratory Fee Schedule
    d. Medicare Physician Fee Schedule (MPFS)

11. Case-mix adjustments:
    a. allow payment systems to increase preestablished payments.
    b. create an incentive for facilities to admit large volumes of low-cost patients.
    c. result in fewer possible payment rates based on anticipated care needs.
    d. result in higher anticipated payments for high-resource cases.

12. Severity of illness scores are based on _____.
    a. DRG assignment
    b. ICD-9-CM (or ICD-10-CM) codes
    c. physiologic measures, signs, and symptoms
    d. the admission diagnosis

13. Monitoring unusual billing patterns and other indicators is an example of which of the strategies used by CMS to deter fraud and abuse?
    a. coordination   b. early detection   c. enforcement   d. prevention

14. A person found guilty of Medicare fraud faces _____.
    a. administrative sanction penalties
    b. civil penalties
    c. criminal, civil, and/or administrative sanction penalties
    d. criminal penalties

15. When a modifier is be added to a code to indicate that the procedure or service is part of a major procedure or service, the code is known as a _____.
    a. code combination
    b. component code
    c. comprehensive code
    d. mutually exclusive code

16. Under the Federal Claims Collection Act of 1966, any review conducted by a Medicare administrative contractor for recovery of overpaid funds must be done within how many calendar years after the year in which the overpayment was made?
    a. two   b. three   c. five   d. seven

17. HIPAA administrative simplification provisions require that national identifiers be established. Which identifier has been withdrawn and is awaiting legislation by Congress to eliminate the requirement?
    a. national health plan identifier (PlanID)
    b. national individual identifier (patient identifier)
    c. national provider identifier (NPI)
    d. national standard employer identifier number (EIN)

18. Which was published by HIPAA to adopt standards and safeguards to protect health information that is collected, maintained, used, or transmitted electronically?
    a. confidentiality rule
    b. disclosure rule
    c. privacy rule
    d. security rule

19. Which is a statement sent by the payer to the provider that contains reimbursement amounts and details how submitted claims were processed?
    a. electronic data interchange (EDI)
    b. explanation of benefits (EOB)
    c. remittance advice
    d. transaction for eligibility

20. The threat of excessive awards in medical liability cases has resulted in:
    a. decreased health care costs.
    b. increased access to quality medical care.
    c. increased liability insurance premiums for providers.
    d. increased numbers of practicing providers.

21. The Recovery Audit Contract (RAC) program was implemented as part of _____ legislation.
    a. HIPAA
    b. MMA
    c. SSA amendments
    d. TEFRA

22. Medicare's Comprehensive Error Rate Testing (CERT) program was implemented to evaluate:
    a. individual provider compliance with Medicare regulations.
    b. Medicare administrative contractor (MAC) program performance.
    c. reimbursement made to hospitals serving more acutely ill patients.
    d. the transition from CMS-DRGs to MS-DRGs throughout the country.

23. Under the MS-DRG PPS, the abbreviation MCC refers to _____ comorbid and complication conditions.
    a. major
    b. Medicare
    c. MedPAC
    d. major diagnostic categories

24. All claims submitted for inpatient admissions to general acute care hospitals or other health care facilities are required to report the _____ indicator, which is assigned by the coder to the principal and secondary diagnoses and external cause of injury code (E code) reported on the UB-04 or 837 Institutional (electronic) claim.
    a. CMS
    b. DRG
    c. MDC
    d. POA

25. Which did Medicare implement October 1, 2007, to classify inpatient hospital cases into groups according to similar resource utilization?
    a. AP-DRGs
    b. APR-DRGs
    c. MS-DRGs
    d. RDRGs

Appendix I: *E/M Codebuilder*

(For use with CMS *1997 Documentation Guidelines for Evaluation & Management Coding*), which are located on the Premium Website at www.cengagebrain.com.

CMS also published the *1995 Documentation Guidelines for Evaluation & Management Coding*, which providers can opt to use. It is your author's opinion that because the 1997 guidelines are more specific and require documentation of specific elements, they are easier for student to use when learning how to select CPT E/M codes. (Providers must select one set of guidelines to be consistently used for CPT E/M code selection.)

Note:

Make copies of this *E/M CodeBuilder* (or print the document at the Premium Website at www.cengagebrain.com) to use when assigning E/M codes. Use of this document will reinforce the process required to assign E/M codes, and eventually selecting criteria will make using the form unnecessary.

Introduction

The evaluation and management (E/M) code reported to a third-party payer must be supported by documentation in the patient's record (e.g., SOAP or clinic note, diagnostic test results, operative findings). Although providers are responsible for selecting the E/M code from the encounter form, superbill, or chargemaster at the time patient care is rendered, insurance specialists audit records to make sure that the appropriate level of E/M code was reported to the third-party payer.

This *E/M CodeBuilder* form can be used for that purpose, and it can also be used as a tool to teach appropriate assignment of E/M level codes. To assign a code, just review the documentation in the patient's record, record your findings (based on the directions provided), and refer to the CPT coding manual to select the E/M code to be reported.

E/M code selection is based on three key components: *history, examination*, and *medical decision making*. This *E/M CodeBuilder* form emphasizes those components. It is important to be aware that contributory components (*counseling* and *coordination of care*) also play an important role in selecting the E/M code when documentation in the patient record indicates that counseling or coordination of care dominated the visit. In this situation, the contributory component of *time* can be considered a key or controlling factor in selecting a level of E/M service (code).

Note:

Time and *nature of presenting problem* are listed in some E/M code descriptions to assist in determining which code number to report.

Selecting the Level of History

To select the level of history, review the following elements in the patient record. If an element is not documented, it cannot be considered when selecting the level of E/M service code.

- History of present illness (HPI)
- Review of systems (ROS)
- Past, family, and/or social history (PFSH)

History of Present Illness (HPI)

Review the clinic or SOAP note in the patient's record, and for each documented HPI element (below), enter an X in the box in front of the element on this form. Then, total the Xs and enter that number on the line in front of the Total

Score (below). Finally, select the level of HPI based on the total number of elements documented, and enter an X in the appropriate box.

- ☐ **Location:** Of pain/discomfort (e.g., is pain diffused/localized or unilateral/bilateral; does it radiate or refer?).
- ☐ **Duration:** Of pain/discomfort; length of time condition has persisted (e.g., pain began three days ago).
- ☐ **Quality:** A description of the quality of the symptom (e.g., is pain described as sharp, dull, throbbing, stabbing, constant, intermittent, acute or chronic, stable, improving, or worsening?).
- ☐ **Severity:** Use of self-assessment scale to measure subjective levels (e.g., on a scale of 1–10, how severe is the pain?), or comparison of pain quantitatively with previously experienced pain.
- ☐ **Timing:** Establishing onset of pain and chronology of pain development (e.g., migraine in the morning).
- ☐ **Context:** Where was the patient and what was he or she doing when pain began (e.g., was patient at rest or involved in an activity; was pain aggravated or relieved, or does it recur, with a specific activity; did situational stress or some other factor precede or accompany the pain)?
- ☐ **Modifying factors:** What has patient attempted to do to relieve pain (e.g., heat vs. cold; does it relieve or exacerbate pain; what makes the pain worse; have over-the-counter drugs been attempted—with what results)?
- ☐ **Associated signs/symptoms:** Clinician's impressions formulated during the interview may lead to questioning about additional sensations or feelings (e.g., diaphoresis associated with indigestion or chest pain, blurred vision accompanying a headache, etc.).
- _____ **Total Score:** Enter the score for number of Xs entered above (representing number of HPI elements), and enter an X in front of the HPI type below:
- ☐ Brief HPI (1–3 elements)
- ☐ Extended HPI (4 or more elements)

Review of Systems (ROS)

Review the clinic or SOAP note in the patient's record, and for each documented ROS elements, enter an X in the box in front of the element on this form. Then, total the Xs and enter that number on the line in front of the Total Score. Finally, select the level of ROS based on the total number of elements documented, and enter an X in the appropriate box.

 Note:

To properly assess review of systems documentation, have *CMS Documentation Guidelines for Evaluation & Management Coding* available as you review the patient's record. (Go to www.cms.hhs.gov and click on Outreach & Education, MLN Educational Web Guides, and Documentation Guidelines for E & M services to print the guidelines and use with this section of the *E/M Code Builder*.)

- ☐ Constitutional symptoms
    - ☐ Allergic/Immunologic
    - ☐ Cardiovascular
    - ☐ Ears, nose, mouth, throat
    - ☐ Endocrine
    - ☐ Eyes
    - ☐ Gastrointestinal
    - ☐ Genitourinary
    - ☐ Hematologic/Lymphatic
    - ☐ Integumentary (including skin and breast)
    - ☐ Musculoskeletal
    - ☐ Neurologic
    - ☐ Psychiatric
    - ☐ Respiratory
    - _____ **Total Score:** Enter the score for number of Xs entered above (representing number of ROS elements), and enter an X in front of the ROS type below:
- ☐ None
- ☐ Problem pertinent ROS (1 body system documented)

☐ Extended ROS (2–9 body systems documented)

☐ Complete ROS (all body systems documented)

Past, Family, and/or Social History (PFSH)

Review the clinic or SOAP note in the patient's record, and for each documented PFSH elements, enter an X in the box in front of the element on this form. Then, total the Xs and enter that number on the line in front of the Total Score. Finally, select the level of PFSH based on the total number of elements documented, and enter an X in the appropriate box.

☐ Past history (patient's past experience with illnesses, operations, injuries, and treatments)

☐ Family history (review of medical events in the patient's family, including diseases that may be hereditary or place the patient at risk)

☐ Social history (an age-appropriate review of past and current activities, such as alcohol use, occupation, and so on)

_____ **Total Score:** Enter the score for number of Xs entered above (representing number of PFSH elements), and enter an X in front of the PFSH type below:

☐ None

☐ Pertinent PFSH (1 history area documented)

☐ Complete PFSH (2 or 3 history areas documented)

Level of History

Circle the type of HPI, ROS, and PFSH in the table below (as determined from the entries selected above); then, circle the appropriate Extent of History determined in the table below.

HPI	Brief	Brief	Extended	Extended
ROS	None	Problem Pertinent	Extended	Complete
PFSH	None	None	Pertinent	Complete
EXTENT OF HISTORY	PROBLEM FOCUSED	EXPANDED PROBLEM FOCUSED	DETAILED	COMPREHENSIVE

Current Procedural Terminology © 2010 American Medical Association. All rights reserved.

Selecting the Level of Examination

To select the level of examination, first determine whether a *single organ examination* (specialist exam such as ophthalmologist) or a *general multisystem examination* (e.g., family practitioner) was completed.

Single Organ System Examination

The single organ system examinations recognized by CPT are described in detail beginning on page 18 of the CMS *1997 Documentation Guidelines for Evaluation & Management Services* (located on the Premium Website at www.cengagebrain.com). Single organ system examinations are usually performed by specialists (e.g., ophthalmologist, psychiatrist). You will notice variations among types of single organ examinations, which reflect differing emphases among specialties. Enter an X in front of the appropriate exam type below, after determining which content and documentation requirements of a single organ system examination have been met.

☐ PROBLEM FOCUSED EXAMINATION (1–5 elements identified by a bullet)

☐ EXPANDED PROBLEM FOCUSED EXAMINATION (at least 6 elements identified by a bullet)

☐ DETAILED EXAMINATION (at least 12 elements identified by a bullet)

☐ COMPREHENSIVE EXAMINATION (all elements identified by a bullet; document every element in each box with a shaded border and at least one element in each box with an unshaded box)

Note:

For eye and psychiatric examinations, at least nine elements in each box with a shaded border and at least one element in each box with a shaded or unshaded border is documented.

General Multisystem Exam

General multi-system examinations are described in detail beginning on page 13 of the CMS *1997 Documentation Guidelines for Evaluation & Management Services* (located on the Premium Website at www.cengagebrain.com). General multi-system examinations are performed by both general practitioners and specialists. Enter an X in front of the organ system or body area when the maximum number of allowed elements has been documented. For example, when two or more Neck exam are documented, you can enter an X in front of that body area. *If less than the number of elements located in parentheses is documented, do not enter an X in front of that organ system or body area.*

- ☐ Constitutional (2)
- ☐ Cardiovascular (7)
- ☐ Chest (breasts) (2)
- ☐ Ears, nose, mouth, throat (6)
- ☐ Eyes (3)
- ☐ Gastrointestinal (abdomen) (5)
- ☐ Genitourinary (male–3; female–6)
- ☐ Lymphatic (2)
- ☐ Musculoskeletal (6)
- ☐ Neck (2)
- ☐ Neurologic (3)
- ☐ Psychiatric (4)
- ☐ Respiratory (4)
- ☐ Skin (2)

_____ **Total Score:** Enter the score for number of Xs entered (representing number of exam elements), and enter an X in front of the exam type below:

- ☐ PROBLEM FOCUSED EXAMINATION (1–5 elements identified by a bullet on *CMS Documentation Guidelines for Evaluation & Management Services*)
- ☐ EXPANDED PROBLEM FOCUSED EXAMINATION (at least 6 elements identified by a bullet on *CMS Documentation Guidelines for Evaluation & Management Services*)
- ☐ DETAILED EXAMINATION (at least 2 elements identified by a bullet from each of 6 organ systems or body areas, or at least 12 elements identified by a bullet in two or more systems or areas, on *CMS Documentation Guidelines for Evaluation & Management Services*)
- ☐ COMPREHENSIVE EXAMINATION (documentation of all elements identified by a bullet in at least 9 organ systems or body areas, and documentation of at least 2 elements identified by a bullet from each of 9 organ systems or body areas, on *CMS Documentation Guidelines for Evaluation & Management Services*)

Medical Decision Making

Select the appropriate level of medical decision making based upon the following criteria:

Number of Diagnoses or Management Options	Amount/Complexity of Data to be Reviewed	Risk of Complications and/or Morbidity/Mortality	Medical Decision Making
Minimal	Minimal or none	Minimal	Straightforward
Limited	Limited	Low	Low complexity
Multiple	Moderate	Moderate	Moderate complexity
Extensive	Extensive	High	High complexity

Current Procedural Terminology © 2010 American Medical Association. All rights reserved.

E/M Code Selection

Select the E/M code based on selection of level of history, examination, and medical decision making:

History	Problem focused	Expanded problem focused	Expanded problem focused	Detailed	Comprehensive
Examination	Problem focused	Expanded problem focused	Expanded problem focused	Detailed	Comprehensive
Medical Decision Making	Straightforward	Low complexity	Moderate complexity	Moderate complexity	High complexity

Current Procedural Terminology © 2010 American Medical Association. All rights reserved.

Go to the appropriate E/M category/subcategory, and select the code based upon the previously selected information.

Appendix II: ICD-10-CM Draft Official Guidelines for Coding and Reporting 2013

Appendix II: ICD-10-CM Draft Official Guidelines for Coding and Reporting 2013 are located on the Premium Website to accompany *3-2-1 Code It!*, Fourth Edition.

To access Appendix II and the other free resources for this textbook, go to www.cengagebrain.com and follow the instructions on the printed access card that is bound into this textbook.

Appendix III: Coding Practice Using www.EncoderPro.com Encoder Software

The purpose of this assignment is allow students to become familiar with the use of encoder software to assign ICD-9-CM, CPT, and HCPCS Level II codes to diagnoses and procedures/services. Students should review the *How to Use www.EncoderPro.com* content in this textbook's preface and log in to the website **when instructed to do so by their instructor.**

Overview

Carefully review each case study below, determine diagnoses and procedures/services to be coded, and use the www.EncoderPro.com to assign ICD-9-CM, CPT, and HCPCS Level II codes. (The website can also be used to assign ICD-10-CM/PCS codes using its crosswalk feature.) Refer to coding guidelines in Chapters 2 through 18 of this textbook as you assign codes to each diagnosis and procedure/service, and explore the use of special features at www.EncoderPro.com that facilitate accurate coding. Be sure to sequence codes properly according to coding conventions and guidelines, including the definition of principal diagnosis and procedure (inpatient cases) and first-listed diagnosis (outpatient cases).

Assignment III-1: Inpatient Coding

Instructions: Assign ICD-9-CM diagnosis and procedure codes (and ICD-10-CM diagnosis and ICD-10-PCS procedure codes) to each statement.

1. Acute lymphocytic leukemia patient who is in remission was admitted with septicemia due to -*Streptococcus A*. Patient developed oral ulcerative stomatitis about two weeks ago that became infected with *Streptococci*, leading to septicemia. Excisional debridement of the oral mucosa was performed. The patient was placed on a regimen of intravenous antibiotics, supplemented with penicillin G, and high-dose steroids were administered.

2. Nodular pulmonary tuberculosis, confirmed by histology. During inpatient hospitalization, an initial course of intravenous isoniazid, rifampin, pyrazinamide, and ethambutol medications was administered. The patient was discharged and scheduled to return to the outpatient clinic to continue medication treatment.

3. Tuberculous osteomyelitis, right lower leg (confirmed by histology). Patient underwent radical open excisional debridement of right tibial and right fibular osseous tissue. Patient was treated with intravenous antitubercular multidrug therapy consisting of isoniazid, vitamin B6, rifampin, ethambutol, and pyrazinamide. Patient also received consultation with an orthopedic surgeon about possible total joint arthropathy; patient decided to consult with another physician to obtain a second opinion.

4. Glioma of the parietal lobe of the brain (neoplasm, brain, malignant, primary). Fractionalized stereotactic radiotherapy was administered.

5. Paget's disease with infiltrating duct carcinoma of breast nipple, left. Unilateral radical mastectomy, left.

6. Toxic diffuse goiter with thyrotoxic crisis. Patient underwent subtotal open thyroidectomy.

7. Sickle cell disease with crisis. Intravenous fluids, pain medications, and hydroxyurea (medication) were administered.

8. Acute exacerbation of chronic undifferentiated schizophrenia. Crisis intervention treatment consisted of clinical psychiatric mental status determination, psychiatric visits, and oral antipsychotic and antidepressant medications.

9. *Neisseria* meningitis. Culture and sensitivity of spinal fluid specimen. Intravenous administration of antibiotics.

10. Retinal detachment with single retinal defect, left eye. Repair of retinal detachment with diathermy, left eye.

11. Malignant hypertensive nephropathy with stage 5 renal failure. Patient underwent single hemodialysis treatment.

12. Arteriosclerotic heart disease (native coronary arteries) with angina pectoris. Patient underwent aortocoronary bypass surgery of three coronary arteries, which was accomplished by grafting the greater saphenous vein that was extracted from the right leg using an open approach. Continuous extracorporeal circulation was provided to the heart using pulsatile compression.

13. Aspiration pneumonia due to regurgitated food. Patient was placed on cardiac monitoring (telemetry) and was treated with intravenous antibiotics and corticosteroids.

14. Acute respiratory failure due to acute exacerbation of myasthenia gravis. Temporary open tracheostomy with insertion of atracheostomy device was performed for the purpose of continuous invasive mechanical ventilation (respirator) for 72 consecutive hours. Patient began breathing spontaneously and was removed from the respirator. Temporary tracheostomy was sutured and bandaged.

15. Acute perforated peptic ulcer. Endoscopy (closed) stomach biopsy.

16. Subserosal uterine leiomyoma, cervical polyp, and endometriosis of uterus. Hysteroscopy.

17. Moderate preeclampsia complicating third-trimester pregnancy, delivered this admission. Vaginal assisted spontaneous delivery of single liveborn infant.

18. Cellulitis of the left foot. Culture revealed *Staphylococci*. Intravenous antibiotics administered.

19. Displacement of lumbar intervertebral disc. Open discectomy resection procedure, L1 and L2, with open spinal fusion using autologous bone graft (posterior technique/approach, posterior column).

20. Complete unilateral cleft lip (upper). Surgical repair of complete unilateral cleft lip.

Assignment III-2: Outpatient Coding

Instructions: Assign ICD-9-CM, ICD-10-CM, CPT, and HCPCS Level II codes to each statement.

1. Chronic hypertension. Level 2 established patient E/M service.

2. Kaposi's sarcoma. Excision of 2-cm malignant lesion (Kaposi's sarcoma), skin of chest.

3. Carcinoma *in situ* of the skin, left cheek. Excision of 4-cm malignant lesion, skin of left cheek.

4. Simple cyst on left ovary. Incision and drainage, left ovarian cyst, vaginal approach.

5. Ganglion right wrist. Excision of recurrent ganglion cyst, dorsum of right wrist.

6. Early yaws, frambeside. Level 4 new patient office E/M service.

7. RUQ abdominal mass. Single posteroanterior view abdominal X-ray.

8. Adverse reaction to vaccine 15 minutes after administration of intramuscular DT vaccine during well-baby E/M service (age 2).

9. High blood pressure due to prescription albuterol. Level 3 established patient office E/M service.

10. Premarital physical examination of white male, age 38 (new patient).

11. Open LeFort I fracture, maxilla. LeFort I repair of open maxillary fracture. (Procedure performed during inpatient hospitalization. Surgeon's coding staff assigns and reports codes on CMS-1500 claim.)

12. First-degree burn, 8 percent of anterior chest wall. Initial local treatment of first-degree burn (performed in the physician's office).

13. Hodgkin's granuloma of intra-abdominal lymph nodes and spleen. Radiopharmaceutical therapy, by intravenous administration of therapeutic iodine I-131 tositumomab radiopharmaceutical therapy, one treatment dose.

Note:

For a 24-hour urinary cortical (free) laboratory test, the patient's urine is collected several times during a 24-hour period and cortical levels are tested. Cortical levels higher than 50 to 100 micrograms per day (for an adult) indicate Cushing's syndrome.

14. Cushing's syndrome. 24-hour urinary cortisol (free) level laboratory test.

15. Fanconi anemia. Chromosome analysis laboratory test was performed to detect breakage syndromes, such as Fanconi anemia.

16. Malignant neutropenia. Complete blood count laboratory test (automated).

17. Anxiety reaction manifested by fainting. Insight-oriented and supportive individual psychotherapy administered in a psychologist's office, 60 minutes (face-to-face with patient).

18. Congestive heart failure. Benign hypertension. Level 3 established patient E/M service.

19. Esophageal reflux with esophagitis. Diagnostic esophagoscopy.

20. Abnormal cervical Pap smear. Cervical Pap smear performed, requiring interpretation by physician.

Answer Key to Assignment III-1 (Inpatient Coding)

1. 038.0, 204.01, 528.09, 88.22, 99.29 (A40.0, C91.01, K12.39, 0CB4XZZ, 3E03329, 3E0333Z)
2. 011.15, 99.29 (A15.0, 3E033GC)
3. 015.55, 730.86, 77.67, 99.29 (A18.03, M90.861, 0QBG0ZZ, 0QBJ0ZZ, 3E033GC)
4. 191.3, 93.39 (C71.3, 3E033GC)
5. 174.0, 85.45 (C50.012, 0HTU0ZZ)
6. 242.01, 06.39 (E05.01, 0GTK0ZZ)
7. 282.62, 99.29 (D57.00, 3E033GC)
8. 295.64, 94.35 (F20.5, GZ2ZZZZ, 3E0D7GC)
9. 036.0, 90.03, 99.29 (A39.0, 8E01XY7, 3E033GC)
10. 361.01, 14.51 (H33.012, 08QF3ZZ)
11. 403.01, 39.95 (I12.0, N18.5, 5A1D00Z)
12. 414.01, 413.9, 36.13, 39.61 (I25.119, 021209W, 06DP0ZZ, 5A02215)
13. 507.0, 89.54, 99.29 (J69.0, 4A12X4Z, 3E03329, 3E0333Z)
14. 518.81, 358.01, 31.1, 96.71, 31.72 (J96.00, G70.01, 5A1945Z, 0B110F4, 0BQ10ZZ)
15. 533.10, 44.14 (K27.1, 0DB68ZX)
16. 218.2, 622.7, 617.0, 68.12 (D25.2, N84.1, N80.0, 0UJD8ZZ)
17. 642.41, V27.0, 73.59 (O14.03, Z37.0, 10E0XZZ)
18. 682.7, 041.10, 99.29 (L03.116, B95.8, 3E03329)
19. 722.10, 80.51, 81.07, 81.62 (M51.26, 0ST20ZZ, 0ST20ZZ, 0SG0071)
20. 749.11, 27.54 (Q36.9, 0CQ0XZZ)

Answer Key to Assignment III-2 (Outpatient Coding)

1. 401.9 (I10), 99212
2. 176.0 (C46.0), 11602
3. 232.3 (D04.39), 11644
4. 620.2 (N83.29), 58800-LT
5. 727.41 (M67.431), 25112-RT
6. 102.2 (A66.2), 99204
7. 789.31 (R19.01), 74000
8. V20.2, V06.5, 995.29, E948.6 (Z00.129, Z23, T50.A15A), 90471, 90702, 99392
9. 401.9, E945.7 (T48.6x5A, I10), 99213
10. V70.3 (Z02.89), 99385
11. 802.5 (S02.411B), 21422
12. 942.12 (T21.11xA, T31.0), 948.00, 16000
13. 201.18 (C81.98), 79101, A9545
14. 255.0 (E24.9), 82530
15. 284.09 (D61.09), 88248
16. 288.09 (D70.8), 85027
17. 300.00 (F41.9), 90837
18. 428.0, 401.1 (I50.9, I10), 99213
19. 530.11 (K21.0), 43200
20. 795.00 (R87.619), 88141

Bibliography

Books and Manuals

Abraham, P. R. (2001). *Documentation and reimbursement for home care and hospice programs.* Chicago, IL: American Health Information Management Association.

American College of Radiology & Society of Interventional Radiology. *Interventional radiology coding user's guide.* (2011). Restin, VA: American College of Radiology.

American Medical Association. (2012). *CPT.* Chicago, IL: Author.

American Medical Association. (2012). *CPT changes: An insider's view.* Chicago, IL: Author.

American Medical Association. (2012). *Medicare RBRVS: The physicians' guide.* Chicago, IL: Author.

American Medical Association. (2012). *Principles of CPT coding.* Chicago, IL: Author.

Arroyave, E. (2006). *Understanding cosmetic procedures: Surgical and nonsurgical.* Clifton Park, NY: Delmar Cengage Learning.

Bowie, M. J., & Schaffer, R. M. (2012). *Understanding ICD-9-CM coding.* Clifton Park, NY: Delmar Cengage Learning.

Bowie, M. J., & Schaffer, R. M. (2012). *Understanding ICD-10-CM and ICD-10-PCS: A Worktext.* Clifton Park, NY: Delmar Cengage Learning.

Carlton, R. R., & Adler, A. M. (2006). *Principles of radiographic imaging: An art and a science* (4th ed.). Clifton Park, NY: Delmar Cengage Learning.

Centers for Medicare & Medicaid Services. (2013). *Internet-only manuals.* Washington, DC: Department of Health and Human Services.

College of American Pathologists. (2003). *College of American Pathologists professional relations manual.* Northfield, IL: Author.

Diamond, M. S. (2007). *Understanding hospital coding and billing: A worktext.* Clifton Park, NY: Delmar Cengage Learning.

Ehrlich, A., & Schroeder, C. L. (2013). *Medical terminology for health professionals.* Clifton Park, NY: Delmar Cengage Learning.

Frank, Eugene D., B. W. Long, & B. J. Smith. (2012). *Merrill's atlas of radiographic positioning & radiologic procedures.* Philadelphia, PA: Elsevier, Inc.

Funk, D. L., & Beebe, R. (2010). *Fundamentals of basic emergency care.* Clifton Park, NY: Delmar Cengage Learning.

Green, M. A., & Bowie, M. J. (2011). *Essentials of health information management: Principles and practices.* Clifton Park, NY: Delmar Cengage Learning.

Green, M. A., & Rowell, J. (2013). *Understanding health insurance: A guide to billing and reimbursement.* Clifton Park, NY: Delmar Cengage Learning.

Grider, Deborah J. (2009). *Preparing for ICD-10-CM: Make the Transition Manageable.* Chicago, IL: American Medical Association.

Grider, Deborah J. (2012). *Coding with modifiers: A guide to correct CPT and HCPCS modifier usage.* Chicago, IL: American Medical Association.

Grider, Deborah J. (2012). *Principles of ICD-10-CM Coding.* Chicago, IL: American Medical Association.

James, E. (2008). *Documentation and reimbursement for long-term care.* Chicago, IL: American Health Information Management Association.

Jones, B. D. (2011). *Comprehensive medical terminology.* Clifton Park, NY: Delmar Cengage Learning.

Lazo, D. L. (2005). *Fundamentals of sectional anatomy: An imaging approach.* Clifton Park, NY: Delmar Cengage Learning.

Marrelli, T. M. (2005). *Hospice and palliative care handbook: Quality, compliance, and reimbursement.* Philadelphia, PA: Elsevier, Inc.

Marrelli, T. M. (2009). *Handbook of home health standards: quality, documentation and reimbursement.* Philadelphia, PA: Elsevier, Inc.

Merriam-Webster. (2006). *Merriam-Webster's medical desk dictionary.* Clifton Park, NY: Delmar Cengage Learning.

Neighbors, M., & Tannehill-Jones, R. (2010). *Human diseases*. Clifton Park, NY: Delmar Cengage Learning.

OptumInsight. (2011). *Ingenix coding lab: Implementing ICD-10*. Salt Lake City, UT: Author.

OptumInsight. (2011). *Ingenix coding lab: Understanding modifiers 2011*. Salt Lake City, UT: Author.

OptumInsight. (2012). *Coder's desk reference for diagnoses*. Salt Lake City, UT: Author.

OptumInsight. (2012). *Coder's desk reference for HCPCS*. Salt Lake City, UT: Author.

OptumInsight. (2012). *Coder's desk reference for ICD-9-CM procedures*. Salt Lake City, UT: Author.

OptumInsight. (2012). *Coding and payment guide: Anesthesia services*. Salt Lake City, UT: Author.

OptumInsight. (2012). *Coding and payment guide: Behavioral health services*. Salt Lake City, UT: Author.

OptumInsight. (2012). *Coding and payment guide: For the physical therapist*. Salt Lake City, UT: Author.

OptumInsight. (2012). *Coding guide: Chiropractic services*. Salt Lake City, UT: Author.

OptumInsight. (2012). *Coding guide: Dental services*. Salt Lake City, UT: Author.

OptumInsight. (2012). *Complete guide for interventional radiology*. Salt Lake City, UT: Author.

OptumInsight. (2012). *DRG desk reference*. Salt Lake City, UT: Author.

OptumInsight. (2012). *DRG expert*. Salt Lake City, UT: Author.

OptumInsight. (2013). *HCPCS level II*. Salt Lake City, UT: Author.

OptumInsight. (2013). *ICD-9-CM, Volumes 1, 2, & 3*. Salt Lake City, UT: Author.

OptumInsight. (2013). *ICD-10-CM*. Salt Lake City, UT: Author.

OptumInsight. (2013). *ICD-10-PCS*. Salt Lake City, UT: Author.

Rizzo, D. C. (2010). *Delmar's fundamentals of anatomy and physiology*. Clifton Park, NY: Delmar Cengage Learning.

Scott, A., & Fong, E. (2009). *Body structures & functions*. Clifton Park, NY: Delmar Cengage Learning.

Smith, G. I. *Basic CPT/HCPCS coding*. (2012). Chicago, IL: American Health Information Management Association.

Smith, G. I. *Coding Surgical Procedures: Beyond the Basics*. (2011). Clifton Park, NY: Delmar Cengage Learning.

Smith, M. A., & Runge, D. *Lab billing and coding: Effective strategies for compliance*. Marblehead, MA: HCPro, Inc.

Waters, Joann M. (2007). *Mastering the reimbursement process*. Chicago, IL: American Medical Association.

Woodrow, R. (2011). *Essentials of pharmacology for health occupations*. Clifton Park, NY: Delmar Cengage Learning.

Journals and Newsletters

Advance for health information professionals. King of Prussia, PA: Merion Publications.

Coding clinic for HCPCS. Chicago, IL: American Hospital Association.

Coding clinic for ICD-9-CM. Chicago, IL: American Hospital Association.

Coding edge. Salt Lake City, UT: AAPC.

Coding educator. Marblehead, MA: HCPro, Inc.

CPT assistant. Chicago, IL: American Medical Association.

EdgeBlast. Salt Lake City, UT: AAPC.

Family practice management. Leawood, KS: American Academy of Family Physicians.

For the record. Spring City, PA: Great Valley Publishing Co., Inc.

Home healthcare nurse. Philadelphia, PA: Lippincott Williams & Wilkins.

Journal of the American health information management association. Chicago, IL: American Health Information Management Association.

Just coding news: inpatient. Marblehead, MA: HCPro, Inc.

Just coding news: outpatient. Marblehead, MA: HCPro, Inc.

Medicare part A newsletter. Denison, TX: Trailblazer Health Enterprises, LLC.

Medicare part B newsletter. Denison, TX: Trailblazer Health Enterprises, LLC.

Medicare update for physician services. Marblehead, MA: HCPro, Inc.

Medicare weekly update. Marblehead, MA: HCPro, Inc.

Physician billing and reimbursement e-zine. Gaithersburg, MD: DecisionHealth.

Internet-Based References and Listservs

AAPC ICD-10 Code Translator
http://www.aapc.com

American Society for Therapeutic Radiology and Oncology
http://www.astro.org

American Society of Anesthesiologists
http://www.asahq.org

Anesthesia Nursing & Medicine
http://www.anesthesia-nursing.com

CMS Medicare Manuals
http://www.cms.gov

Coding educational resources
http://www.justcoding.com

Coding Pro-L listserv
http://www.decisionhealth.com

Comprehensive guide to Hodgkin's and non-Hodgkin's lymphoma
http://www.lymphomainfo.net

E&M Coder **software by Spring Management Systems**
http://www.emcoder.com

Free ICD-9-CM encoder
http://www.icd9coding.com

HomeCareCoding-L listserv
http://www.decisionhealth.com

ICD-10 Code Lookup **by North Carolina State Center for Health Statistics**
http://www.schs.state.nc.us/SCHS/data/icd10/icd10lookup.cfm

Medical Newswire
http://medicalnewswire.com

Medicare Parts A and B newsletters and manuals
http://www.trailblazerhealth.com

Medline Plus Encyclopedia
http://www.nlm.nih.gov/medlineplus

Meta ICD-10 Learning Tools
http://www.metahealth.com

OptumInsight's online ICD-9-CM, CPT, and HCPCS level II encoders with ICD-10 crosswalks
http://www.encoderpro.com

The radiology information resource for patients
http://www.radiologyinfo.org

World Health Organization
http://www.who.int

Software

Delmar Cengage Learning. (2013). *SimCLAIM*. Clifton Park, NY: Author.

OptumInsight. (2012). *Encoder Pro Expert*. Salt Lake City, UT: Author.

Glossary

NOTE: The chapter in which each term appears as a key term is indicated in parentheses.

A

ablation (11) removal.

abuse (19) actions that are inconsistent with accepted, sound medical, business, or fiscal practices; includes actions that result in unnecessary costs to payers and government programs, that result in reimbursement for services not medically necessary, or that fail to meet professionally recognized standards for health care services.

accession (17) assignment of a number to record the order of tissue acquisition.

acellular dermal replacement (11) bioengineered artificial skin.

actinic keratosis (AK) (11) common sun-induced skin lesion of the epidermis that has the potential to become skin cancer.

acute care facility (ACF) (5) hospital that provides health care services to patients who have serious, sudden, or acute illnesses or injuries and/or who need certain surgeries.

acute care hospital (5) *see* short-term hospital.

add-on code (8) reported when another procedure is performed in addition to the primary procedure during the same operative session; modifier -51 (multiple procedures) is *not* used with add-on codes.

adenoids (13) located at the rear of the nose; contain lymphoid tissue that helps fight infections.

adhesiolysis (15) percutaneous lysis of epidural adhesions using solution injection or mechanical means.

adjacent tissue transfer/rearrangement (11) closure of defects by relocating a flap of adjacent normal, healthy tissue to a defect.

adjuvant (17) substance administered with an antigen that enhances the response to the antigen.

adjuvant chemotherapy (18) chemotherapy administered in addition to other cancer treatments, such as surgery and/or radiation therapy.

adjuvant technique (13) additional procedure or technique that may be required during a lower extremity bypass graft procedure.

admitting diagnosis (5) provisional or tentative diagnosis entered in a field on the inpatient face sheet by admissions office staff; it is often a sign or symptom.

advance beneficiary notice (ABN) (7) waiver signed by the patient acknowledging that because medical necessity for a procedure, service, or supply cannot be established, the patient accepts responsibility for reimbursing the provider or DMEPOS dealer for costs associated with the procedure, service, or supply.

advancement flap (11) movement of tissue in a straight line from donor to defect site using a sliding process; once movement is achieved, the flap is sutured in place.

aircraft (4) any device used for transporting passengers or goods in the air and includes airplanes, balloons, bombers, dirigibles, gliders (hang), military aircraft, and parachutes.

airway management (10) ensuring an open airway to the patient's lungs.

A-line (10) *see* intra-arterial line.

aliquot (17) portion of a specimen used for testing.

allergen (18) allergy-causing substances to which a patient reacts.

allergen immunotherapy (18) small amounts of allergens administered to increase a patient's tolerance to allergens.

allergy sensitivity test (18) performed on skin (cutaneous) and mucous membranes to identify the source of a patient's allergies.

allogenous (12) graft that involves tissue organ transplanted from one person to another.

allograft (11) transplantation of tissue from someone of the same species.

ambulance fee schedule (19) reimburses ambulance service providers a preestablished fee for each service provided.

ambulatory care (6) *see* outpatient care.

ambulatory patient (6) patient who is treated and released the same day and who does not stay overnight in the hospital.

ambulatory surgery patient (6) patient who undergoes procedures that can be performed on an outpatient basis, with the patient treated and released the same day.

ambulatory surgical center (ASC) payment rate (19) reimbursement rate calculated on a prospective basis; rate is based on sample survey data and use of similar surgical techniques to establish reasonable estimated overhead allowances for each listed procedure.

A-mode (16) one-dimensional display that reflects the length of time a sound reaches a structure and is reflected back.

amplitude modulation (16) *see* A-mode.

analgesia (10) loss of pain sensation without loss of consciousness.

analgesic (10) drug that reduces pain, resulting in analgesia.

analyte (17) substance or chemical compound undergoing analysis.

ancillary service (5) diagnostic and/or therapeutic service provided to inpatients and outpatients.

anesthesia (10) process of inducing a loss of sensitivity to pain in all or part of the body, resulting from the administration of an anesthetic.

anesthesia conversion factor (10) dollar amount assigned to a geographic location.

anesthesia time unit (10) based on total anesthesia time and reported as one unit for each 15 minutes (or fraction thereof) of anesthesia time.

anesthesiologist (10)   physician who, after medical school, completes a one-year internship and three-year residency in anesthesia.

anesthetic (10)   drug or agent that causes a loss of feeling, awareness, and/or consciousness.

aneurysm (13)   bulge in an artery that can weaken the arterial wall and eventually burst, resulting in hemorrhage.

angiogenesis (13)   growth of new capillaries.

angiography (16)   X-ray of a blood vessel after injection of contrast material.

angioscopy (13)   microscopic visualization of substances as they pass through capillaries.

anoscopy (14)   diagnostic procedure during which anal mucosa and the lower rectum are visualized using an anoscope.

ANSI ASC X12N 837(19)   variable-length file format that is used to bill institutional, professional, dental, and drug claims.

antepartum care (15)   begins with conception and ends with delivery, including initial and subsequent history; physical examinations; documentation of weight, blood pressures, and fetal heart tones; routine chemical urinalysis (glucose); monthly visits up to 28 weeks' gestation; biweekly visits to 36 weeks' gestation; and weekly visits until delivery.

anterior approach (15)   making an incision overlying the intervertebral disc by cutting through epidermis, dermis, subcutaneous, fascia, and muscle tissue.

anterolateral approach (15)   making an incision along (and removing) the rib that corresponds to the vertebra that is located above the compressed intervertebral disk.

anteroposterior projection (16)   patient is positioned with his or her back parallel to the film; the X-ray beam travels from front to back, or anterior to posterior.

antibody (17)   proteins in the body made by the immune system that fight infection and disease.

antigen (17)   foreign substances that elicit the formation of antibodies.

aortic anomaly (13)   results from unusual patterns of aortic development and includes conditions such as tracheal decompression (or tracheomalacia), aberrant vessels (or vascular ring formation), aortopulmonary septal defect (APSD), patent ductus arteriosus, coarctation of aorta, and hypoplastic aortic arch (or interrupted aortic arch).

aortic sinus (13)   *see* sinus of Valsalva.

aortography (16)   X-ray of the aorta after injection of contrast material.

Appendix A of CPT (8)   contains a list of CPT modifiers and detailed descriptions.

Appendix B of CPT (8)   contains annual CPT coding changes that include added, deleted, and revised CPT codes; it serves as the basis for updating interoffice documents and billing tools.

Appendix C of CPT (8)   contains clinical examples for codes found in the Evaluation and Management section.

Appendix D of CPT (8)   contains a list of add-on codes that are identified throughout CPT with a plus (+) symbol.

Appendix E of CPT (8)   contains a list of codes that are exempt from modifier -51 reporting rules and that are identified throughout CPT with a forbidden (∅) symbol.

Appendix F of CPT (8)   contains a list of codes that are exempt from modifier -63.

Appendix G of CPT (8)   contains a summary of CPT codes that include conscious sedation and that are identified throughout CPT with a bull's-eye (⊙) symbol.

Appendix H of CPT (8)   contains an alphabetic index of performance measures by clinical condition or topic.

Appendix I of CPT (8)   contains genetic testing modifiers.

Appendix J of CPT (8)   contains an electrodiagnostic medicine listing of sensory, motor, and mixed nerves that are reported for motor and nerve studies codes 95900, 95903, and 95904, respectively.

Appendix K of CPT (8)   contains a list of codes that are pending FDA approval but that have been assigned CPT codes; in the CPT manual, these codes are preceded by the flash (⚡) symbol.

Appendix L of CPT (8)   contains a list of vascular families that is intended to assist in the selection of first-, second-, third-, and beyond third-order branch arteries.

Appendix M of CPT (8)   contains a list of deleted CPT codes and descriptions with a crosswalk to new CPT codes.

Appendix N of CPT (8)   contains a list of CPT codes that do not appear in numeric order. CPT codes are resequenced (instead of deleted and renumbered) so that existing codes can be relocated to a more appropriate location; out-of-sequence codes are preceded by the number symbol (#).

application service provider (ASP) (1)   third-party entity that manages and distributes software-based services and solutions to customers across a wide area network (WAN) from a central data center.

arterial puncture (17)   puncture of an artery with a needle for the purpose of drawing blood.

arteriography (10)   visualization of an artery via X-ray after injection of a radiopaque.

arteriovenous fistula (13)   abnormal passageway between an artery and a vein, which allows blood to flow directly into a vein.

arthrocentesis (12)   procedure done to puncture a joint for fluid removal or medication injection.

arthrodesis (12)   surgical fixation of a joint.

arthrography (16)   X-ray of a joint after injection of contrast material.

arthroscopy (12)   visual examination of the inside of a joint.

artificial ankylosis (12)   *see* arthrodesis.

arytenoidectomy (12)   excision of an arytenoid cartilage, which is located in the bilateral vocal fold.

arytenoidopexy (12)   surgical fixation of arytenoidal cartilage and/or surrounding muscles.

assay (17)   measurement of the amount of a constituent in a specimen, such as via laboratory test.

Assessment (A) (1)   judgment, opinion, or evaluation made by the health care provider; considered part of the problem-oriented record (POR) SOAP note.

assumption coding (1)   inappropriate assignment of codes based on assuming, from a review of clinical evidence in the patient's record, that the patient has certain diagnoses or received certain procedures/services even though the provider did not specifically document those diagnoses or procedures/services.

Auditory System (15)   organized anatomically according to the external ear; middle ear; inner ear; and temporal bone, middle fossa approach.

augmentation (12) process of enlarging or increasing.

autogenous (12) originating in the patient's body.

autograft (11) transplantation of tissue from the same individual.

automated case abstracting software (1) software program that is used to collect and report inpatient and outpatient data for statistical analysis and reimbursement purposes.

automated record (1) type of record that is created using computer technology.

autonomic function test (18) evaluates autonomic nervous system functioning.

axial plane (16) *see* transverse plane.

axis of classification (ICD-10-PCS) (5) the sections, body parts, root operations, and so on that comprise the 7-character ICD-10-PCS code; each axis specifies information about the procedure performed, and within a defined code range, a character specifies the same type of information for that axis of classification.

B

backbench work (12) preparing the cadaver donor heart and/or lung allograft prior to lung transplantation and dissecting allograft from surrounding soft tissues to prepare the aorta, superior vena cava, inferior vena cava, pulmonary artery, left atrium, trachea, pulmonary venous/atrial cuff, and/or bronchus for implantation.

Balanced Budget Act of 1997 (19) legislated implementation of the skilled nursing facility prospective payment system, which uses resource utilization groups, version III (RUG-III), to reimburse Medicare SNF services according to a *per diem* prospective rate adjusted for case mix; also legislated implementation of an ambulance fee schedule, which reimburses ambulance service providers a preestablished fee for each service provided.

Balanced Budget Refinement Act of 1999 (BBRA) (19) mandated implementation of the long-term (acute) care hospital prospective payment system, which uses information from long-term acute care hospital patient records to classify patients into distinct long-term (acute) care hospital diagnosis-related groups based on clinical characteristics and expected resource needs.

base unit value (10) represents the degree of difficulty associated with providing anesthesia for a surgical procedure.

bed count (5) *see* bed size.

bed size (5) total number of inpatient beds for which a facility is licensed by the state; facility must be equipped and staffed to care for these patient admissions.

bedsore (11) *see* pressure ulcer.

behavior-modifying psychotherapy (18) treatment that focuses on changing unhealthy or unwanted behaviors; typically includes a system of desensitization, reinforcements of positive behavior, and rewards; can also include biofeedback and relaxation training.

behavioral health care hospital (5) health care facility that specializes in treating individuals with mental health diagnoses.

Bell's palsy (15) unilateral paralysis of facial muscles resulting from dysfunction of the 7th cranial nerve, probably due to a viral infection.

benign (2) not cancerous.

benign hypertension (4) hypertension of prolonged or chronic duration; this type of hypertension is usually controlled by medication.

Bethesda system (17) format for reporting cervical/vaginal cytology that includes a state of specimen adequacy, the general category, and a descriptive diagnosis.

Bier block (10) *see* intravenous regional anesthesia.

biliary system (14) organs and duct system that create, transport, store, and release bile into the duodenum (as part of the digestive process); includes the gallbladder, bile ducts inside the liver, bile ducts outside the liver, hepatic ducts, common bile duct, and cystic duct.

biofeedback (18) technique that trains the patient to gain some control over autonomic body functions.

biometric A-scan (16) diagnostic ultrasound that produces a one-dimensional view of normal and abnormal eye tissue and precise measurements of the eye's length.

biomicroscopy (16) optical instrument that looks like a microscope with two eyepieces.

biopsy (11) removal and examination of tissue to establish a diagnosis, confirm a diagnosis, or determine the extent of a disease.

bipolar cautery (14) technique that uses an electric current that flows from one tip of the forceps to the other and does not require a grounding pad.

blepharoplasty (11) any surgical repair of an eyelid.

block (radiology) (16) device used when a radiology procedure is performed; made of lead or another heavy metal, it is placed between the radiation beam and that portion of the patient's body that requires protection from radiation.

block (tissue) (17) portion of tissue obtained from a specimen that is placed in support medium, such as paraffin.

blocking (16) device, such as lead, that shields or protects critical or sensitive organs during radiology treatment.

blood (13) tissue that consists of plasma, red blood cells, white blood cells, and platelets (or thrombocytes).

Blue Cross and Blue Shield (BCBS) (19) cover the costs of hospital care and physician services; Blue Cross initially covered just hospital care and Blue Shield covered just physicians' services; today each offers a full range of health care coverage.

bone density study (16) evaluates diseases of the bone; used to assess the response of bone disease to treatment.

bone marrow (13) spongy material that fills large bones' cavities; consists of red marrow (produces red blood cells, white blood cells, and platelets) and yellow marrow (replaces red marrow with fatty tissue that does not produce blood cells).

bone marrow aspiration (13) use of a needle to remove a sample of the liquid bone marrow for examination under a microscope.

bone marrow biopsy (13) boring a small hole into a long bone and using a large, hollow needle to remove bone marrow for examination under a microscope.

breach of confidentiality (19) occurs when patient information is disclosed to other(s) who do not have a right to access the information.

brightness mode (16) *see* B-scan.

bronchoscopy (12) visual examination of the interior of the bronchus.

brushing (12) combing the mucous lining of the trachea or bronchus with a bronchial brush to collect cells.

B-scan (16) diagnostic ultrasound that produces a two-dimensional cross-sectional view of tissues that cannot be seen directly; it reflects sound waves bouncing off tissues or organs; e.g., used to locate a lesion and determine its shape; also called brightness mode (B-mod).

bullet symbol (8) symbol (●) located to the left of CPT codes that identifies new procedures and services added to CPT.

bull's-eye symbol (8) symbol (◉) located to the left of CPT codes that identifies procedures that include conscious sedation.

bunion (12) caused by bone inflammation and swelling and results in medial deviation and axial rotation of the first metatarsophalangeal (MTP) joint.

burr hole (15) small opening in the skull made with a surgical drill.

C

cadaver donor cardiectomy with or without pneumonectomy (13) harvesting the allograft (heart with or without lung tissue) and preserving the allograft with cold preservation solution and cold maintenance.

cadaver donor pneumonectomy (12) harvesting the allograft (lung tissue) and preserving the allograft with cold preservation solution and cold maintenance.

cafeteria plan (19) *see* triple option plan.

cancer staging (13) determination that cancer has or has not spread anatomically from its point of origin.

cannula (10) hollow needle.

capitated payment method (18) agreement between a third-party payer and a health care provider in which the provider agrees to provide services to a patient in return for a fixed monthly payment.

capitation (19) provider accepts preestablished payments for providing health care services to enrollees over a period of time, usually one year.

capnography (10) monitoring carbon dioxide levels.

carcinoma (Ca) *in situ* (4) malignant tumor that is localized, circumscribed, encapsulated, and noninvasive, but has not spread to deeper or adjacent tissues or organs.

cardiac ablation (13) stops atrial or ventricular fibrillation by using radiofrequency waves (modified electrical energy) to create small scars on the heart's surface.

cardiac blood pool imaging (16) use of a gamma camera for sampling, which is performed repetitively over several hundred heartbeats during the transition of the radionuclide through the central circulation.

cardiac catheterization (18) invasive diagnostic medical procedure that includes several components, beginning when the physician introduces one or more catheters into peripheral arteries and/or veins.

cardiac tumor (13) growth that develops in the heart's endocardium, myocardium, or pericardium.

cardiac valves (13) flap of tissue that keeps blood flowing in one direction to allow for the efficient one-way flow of blood through the heart's chambers.

cardiography (18) diagnostic procedure that records the heart's electronic activity with a cardiograph and produces a cardiogram (or electrocardiogram, ECG or EKG).

cardiopulmonary bypass (13) procedure to divert blood from the heart to the aorta, using a pump oxygenator.

care plan oversight services (9) cover the physician's time supervising a complex and multidisciplinary care treatment program for a specific patient who is under the care of a home health agency, hospice, or nursing facility.

carotid body (15) tissue that contains many capillaries; located at the point where the carotid artery branches in the neck.

carpal tunnel (15) eight bones in the wrist (carpals) that form a tunnel-like structure; the tunnel is filled with flexor tendons that control finger movement and provide a pathway for the median nerve to reach sensory cells in the hand.

carpal tunnel syndrome (15) painful progressive condition caused by compression of the median nerve at the wrist.

case-mix (19) types and categories of patients cared for by a health care facility.

case-mix adjustment (19) decrease of average difference between preestablished payment and each patient's actual cost to a facility.

category code (2) three-digit ICD-9-CM disease code or two-digit ICD-9-CM procedure code within a section.

Category I code (8) procedures/services identified by a five-digit CPT code and descriptor nomenclature; this type of code is traditionally associated with CPT and organized within six sections.

Category II code (8) optional CPT "performance measurements" tracking code that is assigned an alphanumeric identifier with a letter in the last field; this type of code is located after the CPT Medicine section.

Category III code (8) "emerging technology" temporary CTP code assigned for data collection purposes that are assigned an alphanumeric identifier with a letter in the last field; this type of code is located after the Medicine section, and it will be archived after five years if it is not accepted for placement within Category I sections of CPT.

caudal anesthesia (10) local anesthetic injected into the caudal canal, which is the sacral portion of the spinal canal.

cell washing (12) flushing fluid into an area and removing the fluid, using aspiration technique to collect cells.

Centers for Medicare & Medicaid Services (CMS) (1) administrative agency in the federal Department of Health & Human Services.

central motor evoked potential study (18) testing a patient's nervous system's pathway by placing low-voltage electrodes on the scalp and target sites.

central nervous system (CNS) (10) brain and spinal cord.

central venous access device (CVAD) (10) thin plastic tube that is inserted into a vein and connected to a monitor.

central venous pressure (CVP) catheter (10) *see* central venous pressure (CVP) line.

central venous pressure (CVP) line (10) catheter that is inserted through a vein in the neck or a vein in the upper chest under the collarbone and then into a large central vein in the chest.

certificate of medical necessity (CMN) (7) prescription for durable medical equipment, services, and supplies.

certified registered nurse anesthetist (CRNA) (10) licensed registered nurse who has earned a bachelor's degree in science or nursing, has at least one year of acute care nursing experience, has completed a 24- to 36-month nurse anesthesia program leading to a master's degree, and has passed the national certification exam.

charge description master (CDM) (19) *see* chargemaster.

chargemaster (19) document that contains a computer-generated list of procedures, services, and supplies and corresponding revenue codes along with charges for each.

chargemaster review process (19) routinely conducted by designated hospital personnel to ensure accurate reimbursement by updating CPT and HCPCS codes and linking each to appropriate UB-04 revenue codes.

check digit (19) one-digit character, alphabetic or numeric, that is used to verify the validity of a unique identifier.

cheiloplasty (14) plastic surgery of the lips.

chemical peel (11) use of chemical agents to remove wrinkles and abnormal pigmentation.

chemosurgery (11) use of chemicals to destroy diseased tissue, such as for skin cancer.

chemotherapy (18) treatment of cancer with drugs that serve to destroy cancer cells or slow the growth of cancer cells and keep cancer from spreading to other parts of the body, preventing recurrence of the cancer.

Chemstrip automated urine analyzer (17) *see* reagent strip automated urine analyzer.

chief complaint (CC) (9) patient's description of medical condition stated in the patient's own words.

chiropractic manipulative treatment (CMT) (18) manual treatment performed to influence joint and neurophysiological function.

cholecystectomy (14) surgical removal of the gallbladder.

choroid (15) opaque layer behind the retina that contains blood vessels.

chromatography (17) separation of chemical substances by differential absorption into a moving two-phase system; in gas-liquid chromatography, gaseous substances are separated by moving through a liquid.

chromosomal breakage syndrome (17) genetic disorder that is usually transmitted in a genetic autosomal recessive mode.

chyle (13) digestive fluid that contains proteins and fats.

ciliary body (15) adjusts the shape of the lens and focuses light rays onto the retina.

ciliary muscle (15) *see* ciliary body.

Civil Monetary Penalties Act (19) imposes a maximum penalty of up to $10,000 plus a maximum assessment of up to three times the amount claimed by providers who knew that a procedure/service was not rendered as submitted on the claim.

Civilian Health and Medical Program of the Department of Veterans Affairs (CHAMPVA) (19) program that provides health care benefits to dependents of veterans rated as 100 percent permanently and totally disabled as a result of service-connected conditions, veterans who died as a result of service-connected conditions, and veterans who died on duty with less than 30 days of active service.

claims examiner (1) *see* health insurance specialist.

Classification of Drugs by AHFS List (2) located in ICD-9-CM Appendix C; contains the American Hospital Formulary Services (AHFS) List number and its ICD-9-CM equivalent code number.

Classification of Industrial Accidents According to Agency (2) located in ICD-9-CM Appendix D; based on employment injury statistics adopted by the Tenth International Conference of Labor Statisticians.

classification system (1) *see* coding system.

clearinghouse (1) public or private entity that processes or facilitates the processing of health information and claims from a nonstandard to a standard format.

cleft lip (10) congenital deformity of the upper lip that failed to close during development; types include unilateral, bilateral, and median (harelip) and may be accompanied by defects of the maxilla and hard palate.

clinic outpatient (6) patient who receives scheduled diagnostic and therapeutic care.

clinical examples (9) contained in Appendix C of the CPT coding manual; assist providers in selecting the appropriate code for documented E/M services.

clinical laboratory fee schedule (19) methodology for determining fees for laboratory tests as a result of enacted legislation called the Deficit Reduction Act of 1984; the Consolidated Omnibus Budget Reconciliation Act of 1985 later established a national limitation amount (NLA) on the clinical laboratory fee schedule.

Clinical Laboratory Improvement Act of 1988 (CLIA) (17) certification that is required to perform certain pathology and laboratory tests (and to submit claims to Medicare and Medicaid).

closed fracture (4) type of fracture that is contained beneath the skin and has intact ligaments and skin.

closed fracture treatment (12) fracture site that is not surgically opened or exposed.

closed laparoscopy (14) insufflation of the abdominal cavity using a percutaneously placed needle; performed to examine peritoneal contents using a laparoscope.

closed-panel HMO (19) HMO-owned center or satellite clinic that provides health care services.

CMS-1450 (1) *see* UB-04.

CMS-1500 (1) standard claim submitted by physicians' offices to third-party payers.

cochlear implant (15) implanted electronic device for treatment of sensory deafness.

code (1) numeric and alphanumeric characters that are reported to health plans for health care reimbursement and to external agencies (e.g., state departments of health) for data collection, in addition to being reported internally (e.g., acute care hospital) for education and research.

coder (1) acquires a working knowledge of coding systems (e.g., CPT, HCPCS level II, and ICD-9-CM), coding principles and rules, government regulations, and third-party payer requirements to ensure that all diagnoses (conditions), services (e.g., office visit), and procedures (e.g., surgery and X-ray) documented in patient records are coded accurately for reimbursement, research, and statistical purposes.

coding (1) assignment of codes to diagnoses, services, and procedures based on patient record documentation.

coding conventions (ICD-9-CM) (3) general rules used in the ICD-9-CM classification systems that are independent of coding guidelines.

abbreviations (3) use of NEC (not elsewhere classifiable) and NOS (not otherwise specified). (NEC and NOS abbreviations do *not* appear in ICD-10-PCS.)

> **NEC (not elsewhere classifiable) (3)** equivalent of "other specified"; identifies codes that are to be assigned when information needed to assign a more specific code cannot be located in the coding manual.

> **NOS (not otherwise specified) (3)** the equivalent of "unspecified"; identifies codes that are to be assigned when information needed to assign a more specific code cannot be obtained from the provider.

and (3) interpreted as meaning "and/or."

boxed note (3) defines terms, provides coding instruction, and lists fifth-digit subclassifications for categories that use the same fifth digits; Index to Procedures boxed notes also provide coding instruction and list fourth-digit subclassifications for categories that use the same fourth digits. (Boxed notes do not appear in ICD-10-CM or ICD-10-PCS.)

cross-references (3) instructions to refer to another entry in the index (e.g., *see*, *see also*, *see* condition) or tabular list (e.g., *see* category) to assign the correct code.

> ***see* (3)** instructional term in the index that directs the coder to refer to another term.

> ***see also* (3)** instructional term in the index that is located after a main term or subterm and directs the coder to another main term (or subterm) that may provide additional useful index entries.

> ***see* category (3)** instructional term in the index that directs the coder to the tabular list, where a code can be selected from the options provided.

> ***see* condition (3)** instructional term in the index that directs the coder to the main term for a condition.

due to (3) index subterm (in alphabetical order) that indicates the presence of a cause-and-effect (or causal) relationship between two conditions.

eponym (3) disease, syndrome, or procedure named for a person.

etiology and manifestation rules (3) include the following in the tabular list: code first underlying disease; code, if applicable, any causal condition first; use additional code; and in diseases classified elsewhere.

> **code first underlying disease (3)** tabular list instructional note that assists with proper sequencing of codes.

> **code, if applicable, any causal condition first (3)** tabular list instructional note requires causal conditions to be sequenced first, if present.

> **in diseases classified elsewhere (3)** phrase that indicates that manifestation codes are a component of the etiology/manifestation coding convention.

> **use additional code (3)** instructional note that assists in proper sequencing of the codes.

excludes note (3) appears below codes in the tabular list to direct the coder to another location in the tabular list to classify conditions (or procedures) that are excluded from the code.

format (3) index subterms are indented two spaces below a main term; second, third, and fourth qualifiers are indented two, four, and six spaces, respectively, below the subterm.

in (3) Index to Diseases subterm (in alphabetical order) that indicates the presence of a cause-and-effect (or causal) relationship between two conditions.

includes note (3) appears immediately below tabular list codes to further define terms or provide examples.

inclusion term (3) listed below certain codes in the tabular list; includes conditions or procedures for which that code number is to be assigned; can be synonyms of the code title or, for "other" codes, a list of conditions or procedures assigned to that code.

other and other specified (3) assigned when patient record documentation provides detail for which a specific code does not exist in the coding manual.

punctuation (3) slanted brackets, square brackets, parentheses, and colons.

> **colon (3)** used after an incomplete term in the tabular list when one or more additional terms (called modifiers) after the colon must be documented in the diagnostic statement to classify a condition.

> **parentheses (3)** used in the indexes and tabular lists to enclose nonessential modifiers, which are supplementary words that may be present in or absent from the physician's statement of a disease or procedure without affecting the code number to which it is assigned.

> **slanted brackets (3)** used in the index to identify manifestation codes. (Square brackets are used in ICD-10-CM for this purpose.)

> **square brackets (3)** used in the tabular lists to enclose synonyms, alternative wording, or explanatory phrases. (Used in ICD-10-CM index to enclose manifestation codes, which are always sequenced second.)

tables (3) index feature that organizes subterms, second qualifiers, and third qualifiers and their codes in columns and rows to make it easier to select the proper code. (Tables also appear in ICD-10-PCS, instead of a tabular list, to facilitate assignment of values to create the seven-character code.)

unspecified code (3) assigned when patient record documentation is insufficient to assign a more specific code.

with (3) located immediately below the main term in the indexes, *not in alphabetical order*.

coding conventions (ICD-10-CM) (3) general rules used in the ICD-10-CM classification system that are independent of coding guidelines.

abbreviations (3) use of NEC (not elsewhere classifiable) and NOS (not otherwise specified). (NEC and NOS abbreviations do *not* appear in ICD-10-PCS.)

> **NEC (not elsewhere classifiable) (3)** equivalent of "other specified"; identifies codes that are to be assigned when information needed to assign a more specific code cannot be located in the coding manual.

> **NOS (not otherwise specified) (3)** equivalent of "unspecified"; identifies codes that are to be assigned when information needed to assign a more specific code cannot be obtained from the provider.

and (3) interpreted as meaning "and/or."

cross-references (3) instruction to refer to another entry in the index (e.g., *see*, *see also*, *see* condition) or tabular list (e.g., *see* category) to assign the correct code.

> ***see* (3)** instructional term that directs the coder to refer to another term in the indexes the code.

> ***see also* (3)** instructional term that is located after a main term or subterm in the index and directs the coder

to another main term (or subterm) that may provide additional useful index entries.

see category (3) instructional term that directs the coder to the tabular list, where a code can be selected from the options provided there.

see condition (3) instructional term that directs the coder to the main term in the index for a condition.

due to (3) index subterm (in alphabetical order) that indicates the presence of a cause-and-effect (or causal) relationship between two conditions.

eponym (3) disease, syndrome, or procedure named for a person.

etiology and manifestation rules (3) include the following in the tabular list: code first underlying disease; code, if applicable, any causal condition first; use additional code; and in diseases classified elsewhere.

code first underlying disease (3) tabular list instructional note that assists with proper sequencing of codes.

code, if applicable, any causal condition first (3) tabular list instructional note that requires causal conditions to be sequenced first, if present.

in diseases classified elsewhere (3) indicates that manifestation codes are a component of the etiology/manifestation coding convention.

use additional code (3) instructional note that assists in proper sequencing of the codes.

excludes1 note (3) appears below codes in the ICD-10-CM tabular list to direct the coder to another location in the tabular list to classify conditions that are excluded from the code—code either the original code or the code to which the excludes1 note directs you.

excludes2 note (3) appears below codes in the ICD-10-CM tabular list to direct the coder to another location in the tabular list to classify conditions that are excluded from the code; both the original code and the code to which the excludes2 note directs you can be reported if documentation supports both conditions.

format (3) index subterms are indented two spaces below a main term; second, third, and fourth qualifiers are indented two, four, and six spaces, respectively, below the subterm.

in (due to) (3) index subterm (in alphabetical order) that indicates the presence of a cause-and-effect (or causal) relationship between two conditions.

includes note (3) appears immediately below tabular list codes to further define terms or provide examples.

inclusion term (3) listed below certain codes in the tabular lists; includes conditions or procedures for which that code number is to be assigned; can be synonyms of the code title or, for "other" codes, a list of conditions or procedures assigned to that code.

other and other specified (3) codes that are assigned when patient record documentation provides detail for which a specific code does not exist in the coding manual.

punctuation (3) slanted brackets, square brackets, parentheses, and colons.

colon (3) used after an incomplete term in the tabular list when one or more additional terms (called modifiers) after the colon must be documented in the diagnostic or procedural statement to classify a condition or procedure.

parentheses (3) used in the index and tabular list to enclose nonessential modifiers, which are supplementary

words that may be present in or absent from the physician's statement of a disease or procedure without affecting the code number to which it is assigned.

square brackets (3) used in the tabular lists to enclose synonyms, alternative wording, explanatory phrases, and manifestation codes.

tables (3) index feature that organizes subterms, second qualifiers, and third qualifiers and their codes in columns and rows to make it easier to select the proper code. (Tables also appear in ICD-10-PCS, which facilitate assignment of values to create the seven-character code.)

unspecified code (3) assigned when patient record documentation is insufficient to assign a more specific code.

with (3) index term that is located immediately below the main term, *not in alphabetical order*.

coding conventions (ICD-10-PCS) (3) general rules used in the ICD-10-PCS classification systems that are independent of coding guidelines.

abbreviations (3) use of NEC (not elsewhere classifiable) and NOS (not otherwise specified). (NEC and NOS abbreviations do not appear in ICD-10-PCS.

NEC (not elsewhere classifiable) (3) equivalent of "other specified"; identifies codes that are to be assigned when information needed to assign a more specific code cannot be located in the coding manual.

NOS (not otherwise specified) (3) the equivalent of "unspecified"; identifies codes that are to be assigned when information needed to assign a more specific code cannot be obtained from the provider.

and (3) interpreted as meaning "and/or."

cross-reference (3) instruction to refer to another entry in the index (e.g., *see*).

see (3) instructional term in ICD-9-CM and ICD-10-CM/PCS that directs the coder to refer to another term in the indexes the code.

format (3) subterms in the index are indented two spaces below a main term; qualifiers are indented two spaces below the subterm.

punctuation (3) parentheses.

parentheses (3) used in the index to enclose nonessential modifiers, which are supplementary words that may be present in or absent from the physician's statement of a procedure without affecting the code number to which it is assigned.

tables (3) facilitate assignment of values to create the 7-character code.

with (3) located below an index main term or subterm *in alphabetical order*.

Coding Guidelines for Outpatient Diagnostic Tests (6) instructions and examples that are to be used when assigning ICD-9-CM (or ICD-10-CM) codes for diagnostic test results.

coding system (1) organizes a medical nomenclature according to similar conditions, diseases, procedures, and services; it contains codes for each.

cold biopsy forceps (14) technique that does not use electrocoagulation; the polyp is simply pulled from the colon wall.

colectomy (14) removal of part or all of the large intestine.

colonoscopy (14) visual examination of the entire colon, from the rectum to the cecum, and may include the terminal ileum.

colostomy (14)   removal of a portion of the colon or rectum; the remaining colon is brought to the abdominal wall.

column 1/column 2 edits (8)   code pairs that should not be billed together because one service inherently includes the other; previously called comprehensive/component edits.

combination code (4)   single code used to classify two diagnoses (or procedures), a diagnosis with an associated secondary process (manifestation), or a diagnosis with an associated complication.

commercial payer (19)   private health insurance company or employer-based group health insurance company.

commercial transport aircraft (4)   any device used for collective passenger or freight transportation by air, whether run on commercial lines for profit or by government authorities, with the exception of military craft.

commissurotomy (13)   narrowed valve leaflets are widened by carefully opening the fused leaflets with a scalpel.

comorbidity (5)   coexisting condition (e.g., diabetes mellitus) that is treated during the same encounter as or impacts the medical management of another condition (e.g., myocardial infarction).

compensator (16)   irregularly shaped beam-modifying device used to reconfigure beam intensity so it matches irregular tissue contour.

complex fistulectomy (14)   excision of multiple fistulas.

compliance guidance (19)   document that identifies risk areas and offers concrete suggestions to improve and enhance an organization's internal controls so that billing practices and other business arrangements are in compliance with Medicare's rules and regulations.

complication (5)   condition that occurs during the course of an inpatient hospital episode.

component coding (16)   reporting a radiology procedure code and a surgical procedure code to completely describe the service provided.

composite graft (13)   vein and synthetic graft material or segments of veins from two or more locations.

compound fracture (4)   *see* open fracture.

comprehensive examination (9)   general multisystem examination or complete examination of a single organ system.

comprehensive history (9)   chief complaint, extended history of present illness, review of systems directly related to the problem(s) identified in the history of present illness in addition to a review of all additional body systems, and complete past/family/social history.

computed axial tomography (CT) (CAT) (16)   X-ray of horizontal and vertical cross-sectional views or "slices" of the body that are computer-processed to create three-dimensional, or 3D, images.

computed tomography angiography (CTA) (16)   X-rays of different angles to create cross-sectional images of organs, bones, and tissues that visualize blood flow in arterial and venous vessels throughout the body.

computer-assisted coding (CAC) (1)   uses computer software to automatically generate medical codes by "reading" transcribed clinical documentation; uses "natural language processing" theories to generate codes that are reviewed and validated by coders for reporting on third-party payer claims.

concha (12)   *see* turbinates.

concurrent care (9)   provision of similar services, such as hospital inpatient visits, to the same patient by more than one provider on the same day.

concurrent coding (1)   review of records and/or use of encounter forms and chargemasters to assign codes during an inpatient stay or an outpatient encounter; typically performed for outpatient encounters because encounter forms and chargemasters are completed in "real time" by health care providers as part of the charge-capture process.

concurrent medically directed anesthesia procedures (10)   maximum number of procedures an anesthesiologist or a CRNA medically directs within the context of a single procedure when the procedures overlap.

confidentiality (19)   process of keeping privileged communication secret; means that information cannot be disclosed without the patient's authorization.

conization (15)   removal of a cone-shaped piece of tissue.

conjunctiva (15)   mucous membrane that lines the underside of each eyelid and forms a protective covering over the exposed surface of the eyeball.

Consolidated Omnibus Budget Reconciliation Act of 1985 (19)   federal legislation that established a national limitation amount, which serves as a payment ceiling, or cap, on the amount Medicare could pay for each test.

consultation (9)   examination of a patient by a health care provider, usually a specialist, for the purpose of advising the referring or attending physician in the evaluation and/or management of a specific problem with a known diagnosis.

consumer-directed health plan (CDHP) (19)   a sort of "401(k) plan for health care"; includes many choices that provide individuals with an incentive to control the costs of health benefits and health care.

contiguous sites (4)   adjacent locations as in cancer of multiple sites that overlap or border each other (e.g., nasopharynx and oropharynx cancer).

continent ileostomy (14)   surgical variation of an ileostomy in which a reservoir pouch is created inside the abdomen using a portion of the terminal ileum, a valve is constructed in the pouch, and a stoma is brought through the abdominal wall.

continuity of care (1)   documenting patient care services so that others who treat the patient have a source of information on which to base additional care and treatment.

contrast agent (16)   radiopaque substances (solid or liquid) that obstruct the passage of X-rays, making the structure containing the agent appear white on radiographic film; administered to provide better radiographic visualization of organs studied.

contrast material (16)   *see* contrast agent.

contrast medium (10)   *see* contrast agent; plural is *contrast media*.

contrast medium injection device (16)   instrument used to deliver a predetermined amount of contrast, typically for vascular imaging procedures.

contributory components (9)   include counseling, coordination of care, nature of presenting problem, and time; they are used to select the appropriate E/M service code when patient record documentation indicates that they were the focus of the visit.

conversion factor (19)   dollar multiplier that converts relative value units into payments using a formula.

cooperating parties for the ICD-9-CM (2)   AHIMA, AMA, CMS, and NCHS.

cooperating parties for the ICD-10-CM/PCS (2)   AHIMA, AMA, CMS, and NCHS.

coordination of care (9) component in which physician makes arrangements with other providers or agencies for services to be provided to a patient.

cornea (15) transparent layer on the eye's surface; covers the iris and pupil; provides focusing power.

corneal pachymetry (16) noninvasive ultrasound procedure that determines thickness of the cornea.

coronal plane (16) divides the body into anterior or ventral and posterior or dorsal portions at a right angle to the sagittal plane, separating the body into front and back; also called ventral or dorsal plane.

coronary artery bypass graft (CABG) (13) procedure performed to improve flow of blood to the heart.

coronary endarterectomy (13) removal of the inner layer of coronary arteries that contain cholesterol plaques.

corpectomy (15) removal of a portion of the vertebra and adjacent intervertebral disks.

costovertebral (15) area of the thoracic spine where the rib meets the vertebra.

costovertebral approach (15) procedure performed where the ribs articulate with thoracic vertebrae.

covered benefit (19) reimbursable medical benefit.

covered entity (19) private or public sector organization that must follow HIPAA provisions.

critical access hospital (CAH) (5) located more than 35 miles from any hospital or another CAH; state certified as being a necessary provider of health care to area residents.

critical care (9) delivery of medical care services to critically ill or injured patients who require the full, exclusive attention of the physician.

critical illness or injury (9) one that acutely impairs one or more vital organ systems, jeopardizing the patient's survival.

critical pathways (19) interdisciplinary guidelines developed by health care facilities to facilitate management and delivery of quality clinical care in a time of constrained resources; allows for the planning of provision of clinical services that have expected time frames and resources targeted to specific diagnoses and/or procedures.

cross-over vein graft (13) making an incision to expose the vein's incompetent valve, dividing that section of the vein, and connecting it to a nearby vein that has functioning valves.

cryosurgery (11) application of extreme cold, such as liquid nitrogen, to destroy abnormal tissue cells, such as warts or small skin tumors.

***Current Procedural Terminology* (CPT) (1)** coding system used by physicians and outpatient health care settings to assign CPT codes for reporting procedures and services on health insurance claims; considered level I of the Healthcare Common Procedure Coding System (HCPCS); published and updated by the American Medical Association (AMA) to classify procedures and services; listing of descriptive terms and identifying codes for reporting medical services and procedures; provides a uniform language that describes medical, surgical, and diagnostic services to facilitate communication among providers, patients, and third-party payers.

customized sub-capitation plan (CSCP) (19) funds health care expenses with insurance coverage; individual selects one of each type of provider to create a customized network and pays the resulting customized insurance premium.

cutdown (13) a procedure whereby a catheter is inserted directly into a vein through an incision.

cystography (16) X-ray of the urinary bladder after injection of contrast material.

cystometrogram (14) records urinary bladder pressure at various volumes; useful in diagnosing bladder outlet obstruction and other voiding dysfunctions.

cystoscopy (14) allows for direct visual examination of urinary bladder and urethra.

cystourethroscopy (14) *see* cystoscopy.

cytogenetics (17) study of the cell and its heredity-related components, including chromosomes.

cytopathology (17) study of diseased cells.

cytoreduction surgery (16) *see* debulking.

D

database (1) contains a minimum data set of patient information collected on each patient, including chief complaint; present conditions and diagnoses; social data; past, personal, medical, and social history; review of systems; physical examination; and baseline laboratory data; considered part of the problem-oriented record (POR).

debulking (16) surgical removal of part of a malignant tumor to enhance the effectiveness of radiation oncology treatment.

decrypt (19) decode.

decubitus ulcer (11) *see* pressure ulcer.

defect (11) wound that is the result of surgical intervention or trauma.

Deficit Reduction Act of 1984 (19) established the clinical laboratory fee schedule as a methodology for determining fees for existing tests.

definitive identification (17) specialized testing performed for identification at the genus or species level.

delivery services (15) services from patient admission to the hospital through delivery of the placenta.

demographic data (1) patient identification information that is collected according to facility policy (e.g., patient's name, date of birth, mother's maiden name, and Social Security number).

dermabrasion (11) use of a rotary device to sand down raised lesions or thickened tissue, regenerating smoother skin; performed for conditions such as acne scarring, wrinkles, rhytids, and general keratosis.

descriptive qualifiers (8) clarify assignment of a CPT code; occur in the middle of a main clause or after the semicolon; may or may not be enclosed in parentheses.

desensitization (18) confronting something that causes anxiety.

Designated Standard Maintenance Organization (DSMO) (19) to maintain, electronic transactions standards adopted by the Secretary of DHHS and develops or modifies adopted standards.

destruction (11) ablation of benign, premalignant, or malignant tissues by any method.

detailed examination (9) extended examination of the affected body area(s) and other symptomatic or related organ system(s).

detailed history (9) includes chief complaint, extended history of present illness, problem pertinent system review extended to include a limited number of additional systems, and pertinent past/family/social history directly related to patient's problem.

determination of refractive state (18) establishes whether a prescription is required for vision correction.

diagnosis-related groups (DRGs) (19) classifies inpatient hospital cases into groups that are expected to consume similar hospital resources; each DRG has a payment weight assigned to it that is based on the average resources used to treat Medicare patients in that DRG.

Diagnostic and Statistical Manual (DSM) (19) manual published by the American Psychiatric Association that contains diagnostic assessment criteria used as tools to identify psychiatric disorders; DSM includes psychiatric disorders and codes, provides a mechanism for communicating and recording diagnostic information, and is used in the areas of research and statistics.

Diagnostic Coding and Reporting Guidelines for Outpatient Services: Hospital-Based and Physician Office **(6)** developed by the federal government and approved for use by hospitals and providers for coding and reporting hospital-based outpatient services and provider-based office visits.

diagnostic endoscopy (14) use of instrumentation for surgical visualization to determine extent of disease.

diagnostic mammography (16) assessment of suspected disease of breasts?

diagnostic/management plan (1) information about the patient's condition and the planned management of conditions; considered part of the problem-oriented record (POR).

diagnostic procedure (11) laboratory, radiographic, and other tests performed to evaluate the patient's complaints or symptoms and to establish the diagnosis.

diaphragm (14) thin muscle below the heart and lungs; separates the chest from the abdomen.

digestive system (14) bodily system that begins at the mouth and extends to the anus.

digital (19) applies a mathematical function to an electronic document, resulting in a unique bit string (computer code) called a message digest that is encrypted and appended to the electronic document.

dipstick (17) small strip of plastic that is infused with a chemical; reacts to products in urine by changing color.

direct contract model HMO (19) contracted health care services delivered to subscribers by individual physicians in the community.

direct laryngoscopy (12) insertion of a flexible (fiberoptic) or rigid laryngoscope to visualize throat structures.

discharge note (1) documented in the progress note section of the problem-oriented record (POR) to summarize the patient's care, treatment, response to care, and condition on discharge.

discectomy (15) removal of an intervertebral disc.

disclosed (19) released.

dislocation (12) total displacement of bone from its joint.

diverticula (14) small pouches (herniations) in the colon that bulge outward through weak spots.

diverticulosis (14) presence of diverticula in the mucosa and submucosal, through or between fibers of the colon's major muscle layer.

DME MAC medical review policies (7) local coverage determinations and national coverage determinations.

document imaging (1) *see* optical disk imaging.

documentation (1) includes dictated and transcribed, typed or handwritten, and computer-generated notes and reports recorded in the patient's records by a health care professional.

Documentation Guidelines for Evaluation and Management Services (9) explain how E/M codes are assigned according to elements associated with comprehensive multi-system and single-system examinations.

donor site (11) Anatomic site from which healthy skin is removed.

Doppler ultrasonography (16) evaluates movement by measuring changes in the frequency of echoes reflected from moving structures.

dose (18) amount of antigen administered in a single injection from a multiple-dose vial.

dosimetry (16) measurement and calculation of radiation treatment doses.

double pedicle flap (11) maintains blood supply is from both ends of a flap incision that was made to create a curvilinear flap contiguous with the defect; flap is pivoted and sutured in place over the defect.

downcoding (1) routinely assigning lower-level CPT codes as a convenience instead of reviewing patient record documentation and the coding manual to determine the proper code to be reported.

DRG creep (19) federal Department of Justice (DOJ) initiative that focuses on medical necessity and billing patterns of DRG coding to determine whether claims hospitals submit accurately reflect care required or provided to the patient; DOJ investigates claims for which facilities receive higher reimbursement as a result of reporting higher paying ICD codes.

driver (4) occupant of a motor vehicle, whether operating it or intending to operate it.

dual chamber (13) contains two electrodes; one placed in the right atrium and the other is in the right ventricle.

dual energy X-ray absorptiometry (DEXA) (16) bone density study that uses two X-ray beams with different levels of energy pulsing alternately to create the image.

duplex scan (18) noninvasive test that is performed to evaluate a vessel's blood flow.

dura mater (10) membrane that forms the outer covering of the central nervous system.

durable medical equipment, prosthetics, orthotics, and supplies (DMEPOS) (7) includes items such as artificial limbs, braces, medications, surgical dressings, and wheelchairs.

durable medical equipment, prosthetics, orthotics, and supplies (DMEPOS) dealers (7) supply patients with durable medical equipment.

durable medical equipment, prosthetics, orthotics, and supplies (DMEPOS) fee schedule (19) payment methodology mandated by the Omnibus Budget Reconciliation Act of 1987 (OBRA); the fee schedule is released annually and updated on a quarterly basis to implement fee schedule amounts for new codes and to revise any amounts for existing codes that were calculated in error.

E

E code (ICD-9-CM) (2) describes external causes of injury, poisoning, or other adverse reactions affecting a patient's health; E codes are located in a supplementary classification in the ICD-9-CM Tabular List of Diseases.

echo (16) effect of a sound that reflects off a distant surface and returns to its source.

echocardiography (18) diagnostic procedure that uses ultrasound to obtain two-dimensional images of the heart and/or great arteries (aorta and vena cavae).

electrocardiography (18) *see* cardiography.

electrocautery snare (14) technique that uses a wire loop to encircle, not grasp, a polyp.

electroconvulsive therapy (ECT) (10) briefly applying an electric current to the brain to produce a seizure; its purpose is to relieve depression, schizophrenia, and severe affective disorders.

electromyogram (EMG) (10) nerve conduction study that plots the electrical activity produced by muscle contractions; results in a graphic tracing of a muscle's electrical activity at rest or during contraction; used to diagnose nerve and muscle disorders.

electromyography (18) test used to detect nerve function by measuring the electrical activity generated by muscles.

electronic data interchange (EDI) (19) computer-to-computer transfer of data between provider and third-party payer (or provider and health care clearing house) in a data format agreed upon by the sending and receiving parties.

electronic health record (EHR) (1) collection of patient information documented by a number of providers at one or more facilities regarding one patient; multidisciplinary and multienterprise approach to record keeping because it has the ability to link patient information created at different locations according to a unique patient identifier; provides access to complete and accurate health problems, status, and treatment data; contains alerts and reminders for health care providers.

electronic medical record (EMR) (1) created on a computer, using a keyboard, a mouse, an optical pen device, a voice recognition system, a scanner, or a touch screen; records are created using vendor software, which also assists in provider decision making regarding patient care and treatment.

electronic transaction standard (19) uniform language for electronic data interchange.

electrophysiology (13) study of heart arrhythmias.

electrosurgery (11) use of an electrical device to destroy abnormal tissue.

embolectomy (13) surgical removal of an embolus.

embolus (13) blood clot that circulates throughout the bloodstream.

emergency care patient (6) patient treated for urgent problems and either released the same day or admitted to the hospital as an inpatient.

emergency condition (10) results when a delay in treatment of the patient would lead to a significant increase in threat to life or body part.

emergency department service (9) provided in a hospital, and open 24 hours a day for the purpose of providing unscheduled episodic services to patients who require immediate medical attention.

employer self-insurance plan (19) employer accepts direct responsibility for (or the risk of) paying employees' health care without purchasing health insurance.

en bloc (13) as a whole.

encoder (2) software that automates the coding process.

encoding (1) process of standardizing data by assigning numeric values (codes or numbers) to text or other information.

encounter (2) face-to-face contact between a patient and a health care provider who assesses and treats the patient's condition; Medicare uses the term *encounter* in the guidelines for coding and reporting using ICD-9-CM to indicate all health care settings, including inpatient hospital admissions.

encounter form (19) document used to record encounter data about office procedures and services provided to patients.

encrypt (19) to encode a computer file, making it safe for electronic transmission so that unauthorized parties cannot read it.

endocardium (13) inner lining of the heart.

endocrine system (15) composed of glands including the adrenal, gonads, pancreas, parathyroid, pituitary, thymus, and thyroid.

endorectal pull-through (14) *see* ileoanal anastomosis.

endoscopic retrograde cholangiopancreatography (ERCP) (14) passing an endoscope through the esophagus, stomach, and duodenum to the ducts of the biliary tree and pancreas.

endoscopy (11) procedure performed to visualize a body cavity, using a medical instrument that consists of a long tube that can be inserted into the body, either through a small incision or a natural opening.

endotracheal tube (ET) (10) artificial airway used for short-term airway management or mechanical ventilation due to potential or actual respiratory system insufficiency.

end-stage renal disease (ESRD) composite payment rate system (19) single-payment fixed rate that does not vary according to the characteristics of the beneficiary treated (and includes the cost of some drugs, laboratory tests, and other items and services provided to Medicare beneficiaries receiving dialysis).

enterectomy (14) resection of small bowel segments.

enterolysis (14) freeing of intestinal adhesions.

enucleation of the eye (15) severing of the eyeball from extraorbital muscles and optic nerve and its removal.

epidural anesthesia (10) local anesthetic injected into the epidural space, where it acts primarily on spinal nerve roots; anesthetized area includes the abdomen or chest to large regions of the body.

epidurography (16) performed to assess the structure of the spine's epidural space prior to percutaneous epidural adhesiolysis (to identify nerve construction or inflammation and the degree of fluid flow in the epidural space).

equivalent dose (16) radiation quantity measured by rem.

esophageal varices (14) uneven, enlarged, tortuous veins of the esophagus.

esophagogastroduodenoscopy (EGD) (14) use of a fiberoptic endoscope to visualize the esophagus, stomach, and proximal duodenum.

esophagogastroscopy (14) *see* upper GI endoscopy.

esophagoscopy (14) visualization of the esophagus, using an endoscope.

essential modifier (2) *see* subterm.

established patient (9) one who *has* received professional services within the past three years from the physician or from another physician of the same exact specialty or subspecialty who belongs to the same group practice.

etiology (2) cause of disease.

evisceration of ocular contents (15) removal of the contents of the eyeball; the sclera remains intact.

evocative (17) causing a specific response; this term is used to describe various tests intended to cause production of hormones or other secretions.

excision (11) removal of a portion or all of an organ or another tissue, using a scalpel or another surgical instrument.

excisional biopsy (11) removal of a lump or suspicious area in its entirety.

exclusion (19) "Medicare PPS Excluded Cancer Hospital" that applies for and is granted a waiver from mandatory participation in the hospital inpatient PPS.

exclusive provider organization (EPO) (19) managed care plan that provides benefits to subscribers if they receive services from network providers.

exenteration of the orbit (15) removal of orbital contents; may also include removal of bone, muscle, and/or the myocutaneous flap.

expanded problem focused examination (9) limited examination of the affected body area or organ system and other symptomatic or related organ system(s).

expanded problem focused history (9) chief complaint, brief history of present illness, and problem pertinent system review.

explanation of benefits (EOB) (19) statement sent by the payer to the patient that contains the same information as a remittance advice but in an easy-to-read format.

extensive cellulitis (11) acute inflammation of skin's connective tissue, caused by infection with bacteria.

extensor tendons (12) tendons that serve to straighten the fingers.

extent of examination (9) categorized according to problem focused examination, expanded problem focused examination, detailed examination, and comprehensive examination.

extent of history (9) categorized according to problem focused history, expanded problem focused history, detailed history, or comprehensive history.

external catheter (10) catheter that is not implanted under the patient's skin and does not require a needle to be inserted into the skin to deliver medications.

external ear (15) auricle and external auditory meatus.

external fixation device (12) hardware inserted through bone and skin that is held rigid with cross-braces outside of the body; external fixation is always removed after the fracture has healed

external radiation (16) radiation administered by a machine outside the body.

extracapsular cataract extraction (ECCE) (15) removal of lens and anterior portion of capsule.

extracorporeal shock wave lithotripsy (ESWL) (10) use of ultrasound shock waves to crush calculi (stones) located in the bladder, renal pelvis, or ureter.

extradural procedure (10) performed on the outer side of the dura mater.

Eye and Ocular Adnexa (15) describes procedures performed on the eyeball, anterior and posterior segment, ocular adnexa, and conjunctivae.

eye socket (15) *see* orbit.

eyeball (15) consists of the choroid, retina, and sclera.

F

face-to-face time (9) amount of time the office or outpatient care provider spends with the patient and/or family.

False Claims Act (FCA) (19) law enacted in 1863 in response to widespread abuses by government contractors during the Civil War; amended in 1986 to strengthen the law and increase monetary awards.

family history (9) review of medical events in the patient's family, including diseases that may be hereditary or that may present a risk to the patient.

federal anti-kickback statute (19) prohibits the offer, payment, receipt, or solicitation of compensation for referring Medicaid/Medicare patients and imposes a $25,000 fine per violation, plus imprisonment for up to ten years.

Federal Claims Collection Act of 1966 (19) law that established uniform procedures for government agencies to follow in the collection, compromise, suspension, termination, or referral for litigation of debts owed to the government.

Federal Employee Health Benefits Program (FEHBP or FEP) (19) voluntary health care program that covers federal employees, retirees, and their dependents and survivors.

fee schedule (19) cost-based fee-for-service reimbursement methodology that includes a list of maximum fees and corresponding procedures/services; payers use fee schedules to compensate providers for health care services delivered to patients.

fee-for-service (19) method of reimbursing providers for individual health care services rendered.

female genital system (15) includes the vulva, perineum, and introitus; vagina; cervix uteri; and uterus, oviduct (fallopian tube), and ovary.

femur (12) long bone of the thigh; articulates with the hip bone, tibia, and patella.

field block (10) subcutaneous injection of local anesthetic in area bordering the field to be anesthetized.

fine-needle aspiration (FNA) (11) procedure in which a thin needle is inserted through a mass several times to remove fluid from a cyst or cells from a solid mass; suction is applied as the needle is withdrawn to obtain strands of single cells for cytologic diagnosis.

first-order vessels (13) blood vessels that extend as primary arterial branches from the aorta.

first-listed diagnosis (6) diagnosis, condition, problem, or other reason for encounter/visit documented in the patient record to be chiefly responsible for the services provided.

flail chest (12) condition in which a segment of the thoracic wall becomes detached from the remainder of the chest wall.

flap (11) relocation of a mass of tissue (usually skin) that has been partially removed from one part of the body so it retains its own blood supply.

flash symbol (8) symbol (𝗡) located to the left of CPT codes that identifies products pending FDA approval but that have been assigned a CPT code.

flat file (19) fixed-length file format that was developed for use in claims processing (because the ANSI ASC X12 837 variable-length file format is not suitable for use in an application program and must be translated into a flat file format prior to claims processing).

flexible spending account (FSA) (19) tax-exempt account offered by employers with any number of employees that individuals use to pay health care bills; participants enroll in a relatively inexpensive high-deductible insurance plan, and a tax-deductible savings account is opened to cover current and future medical expenses.

flexor tendons (12) tendons that serve to bend the fingers.

fluid management (10) administering IV fluids to avoid dehydration, maintain an effective circulating volume, and prevent inadequate tissue perfusion.

fluorescence *in situ* hybridization (FISH) (17) test performed to detect submicroscopic changes in chromosomes (e.g., genetic disorders such as Williams syndrome) or to identify unknown chromosomal material.

fluoroscopy (16) procedure in which a continuous X-ray beam generates a movielike image that is viewed on a monitor; used for invasive procedures such as intravenous/intra-arterial catheterization and extracorporeal shockwave lithotripsy.

forbidden symbol (8) symbol (⊘) located to the left of CPT codes that identifies codes exempt from modifier -51.

fraction (In radiation treatment management) (16) single session of radiation treatment delivered to a specific area of interest.

fracture (4) break in a bone resulting from injury or a disease process.

fraud (19) intentional deception or misrepresentation that someone makes, knowing it is false, that could result in an unauthorized payment.

free flap (11) flap consisting of skin and subcutaneous tissue with a pedicle composed only of nutrient vessels, which is detached from donor site and reattached at recipient site via microvascular anastomosis.

free skin graft (11) complete separation of skin from the donor site before being transferred to the recipient site.

frontal plane (16) *see* coronal plane.

full-thickness skin graft (11) removal (harvesting) of epidermis and dermis for grafting.

functional modifier (8) pricing modifier that a third-party payer considers when determining reimbursement.

G

gamma globulin (18) *see* immune globulin.

gastrectomy (14) removal of all or a portion of the stomach.

general anesthesia (10) administration of anesthetic agents that are inhaled or administered intravenously.

general equivalence mapping (GEM) (2) published crosswalks of codes that facilitate the location of corresponding diagnosis and procedure codes between two code sets, such as ICD-9-CM and ICD-10-CM.

general hospital (5) acute care facility that provides emergency care, general surgery, and inpatient admission services based on licensing by the state.

glabellar frown lines (11) vertical furrows located in the forehead area between the eyebrows.

global period (11) time established (0, 10, or 90 days) for each surgical procedure.

global service (16) combined technical and professional components.

global surgical package (11) ensures that payments are made consistently for the same services across all Medicare administrative contractor jurisdictions and prevents Medicare payments for services that are more or less comprehensive than intended.

globe (15) *see* eyeball.

government-sponsored programs (19) include CHAMPVA, Federal Employee Health Benefits Program, Indian Health Service, Medicaid, Medicare, Military Health System, Programs of All-inclusive Care for the Elderly, and TRICARE.

graft (11) procedures that involve moving healthy tissue from one site to another to replace diseased or defective tissue.

Gram stain (17) method of classifying all bacteria as gram-positive or gramnegative.

gray (gy) (16) newer radiation terminology for the amount of radiant energy absorbed in a tissue; one gray equals 100 rads.

gray-scale ultrasound (16) *see* B-scan.

green reference symbol (8) symbol (⤶) located below a code description to indicate that the coder should refer to the *CPT Assistant* monthly newsletter and/or the *CPT Changes: An Insider's View* annual publication that contains all coding changes for the current year.

gross examination (17) evaluating a specimen visually, with the naked eye.

group model HMO (19) contracted health care services delivered to subscribers by participating physicians who are members of an independent multispecialty group practice.

group practice without walls (GPWW) (19) contract that allows physicians to maintain their own offices and share services such as appointment scheduling and billing.

guidelines (8) define terms and explain the assignment of codes for procedures and services located in a particular section of CPT.

H

harvesting (12) removing tissue for transplantation.

HCPCS level I (7) five-digit Current Procedural Terminology (CPT) codes developed and published by the American Medical Association (AMA).

HCPCS level II (1) coding system managed by the Centers for Medicare & Medicaid Services (CMS) that classifies medical equipment, injectable drugs, transportation services, and other services not classified in the CPT.

HCPCS level II miscellaneous codes (7) include *miscellaneous/not otherwise classified* codes that are reported when a DMEPOS dealer submits a claim for a product or service for which there is no existing HCPCS level II code.

HCPCS level II modifiers (7)   two-digit alpha or alphanumeric codes added to any HCPCS level I (CPT) or II (national) code to provide additional information regarding the product or service reported.

HCPCS level II permanent national codes (7)   maintained by the HCPCS National Panel, which unanimously makes decisions about additions, revisions, and deletions.

HCPCS level II temporary codes (7)   maintained by the CMS and other members of the HCPCS National Panel, independent of permanent level II codes, and allow payers the flexibility to establish codes that are needed before the next January 1 annual update.

HCPCS national codes (1)   *see* HCPCS level II.

health care clearinghouse (1)   *see* clearinghouse.

health care provider (1)   *see* provider.

health care reimbursement account (HCRA) (19)   tax-exempt account that is used to pay for health care expenses.

health data collection (1)   performed by health care facilities to do administrative planning, to submit statistics to state and federal government agencies (and other organizations), and to report health claims data to third-party payers for reimbursement purposes.

health insurance claim (19)   electronic transmission or paper-based document submitted by the provider to an insurance plan to request reimbursement for procedures performed or services provided.

health insurance policy (19)   agreement between an individual and a third-party payer (or insurance company) that contains a list of reimbursable medical benefits.

Health Insurance Portability and Accountability Act of 1996 (HIPAA) (1)   federal legislation that amended the Internal Revenue Code of 1986 to improve portability and continuity of health insurance coverage in the group and individual markets, combat waste/fraud/abuse in health insurance and health care delivery, promote the use of medical savings accounts, improve access to long-term care services and coverage, simplify the administration of health insurance by creating unique identifiers for providers/health plans/employers, create standards for electronic health information transactions, and create privacy/security standards for health information.

health insurance specialist (1)   employed by third-party payers to review health-related claims to determine whether the costs are reasonable and medically necessary based on the patient's diagnosis.

health maintenance organization (HMO) (19)   alternative to traditional group health insurance coverage that provides comprehensive health care services to voluntarily enrolled members on a prepaid basis.

health plan (1)   contract established by an insurance company to reimburse health care facilities and patients for procedures and services provided.

health reimbursement arrangement (HRA) (19)   tax-exempt account offered by employers with more than 50 employees, which individuals use to pay health care bills.

health savings account (HSA) (19)   *see* flexible spending account.

health savings security account (HSSA) (19)   *see* flexible spending account.

Healthcare Common Procedure Coding System (HCPCS) (1)   includes level I codes (CPT) and level II codes (HCPCS level II national codes).

heart murmur (13)   extra heart sound.

hematology (17)   study of the function and disorders of blood.

hemic system (13)   blood-producing system.

hemodialysis (18)   process of removing waste products, toxins, and excess fluids from the blood; patient's blood is diverted into a dialyzer, where it is treated and returned to the patient's circulation by another tube inserted into a different blood vessel.

heparin (10)   anticoagulant that prevents blood clots from developing in a catheter.

hepatotomy (14)   open drainage of abscess or cyst.

hernia (14)   protrusion of internal organs through a weakening in the musculature.

HIPAA administrative simplification (AS) (19)   developed standards for the maintenance and transmission of health information required to identify individual patients; designed to improve efficiency and effectiveness of the health care system by standardizing the interchange of electronic data for specified administrative and financial transactions.

HIPAA standards for privacy of individually identifiable health information (19)   provisions that protect the security and confidentiality of health information.

history (9)   interview of the patient that includes the following elements: history of the present illness (including the patient's chief complaint), a review of systems, and a past/family/social history.

history of present illness (HPI) (9)   chronological description of patient's present condition from time of onset to present.

hold harmless clause (19)   statement that the patient is not responsible for paying what the insurance plan denies.

hollow circle symbol (8)   symbol (○) located to the left of a Category III code to indicate a reinstated or recycled code.

Home Assessment Validation and Entry (HAVEN) (19)   software that allows for entry of data elements from the outcome and assessment information set (OASIS), which is used to determine reimbursement rate for home health agency care based on a case mix methodology.

home health prospective payment system (HH PPS) (19)   uses home health resource groups (HHRGs) to reimburse Medicare home health care services according to prospectively determined rates.

home services (9)   provided to individuals and families in their place of residence to promote, maintain, or restore health and/or to minimize the effects of disability and illness, including terminal illness.

horizontal plane (16)   *see* transverse plane.

horizontal triangle symbols (8)   symbols (►◄) that surround revised guidelines and notes; these symbols are *not* used for revised code descriptions.

hospital discharge service (9)   include the final examination of the patient; discussion of the hospital stay with the patient and/or caregiver; instructions for continuing care provided to the patient and/or caregiver; and preparation of discharge records, prescriptions, and referral forms.

hospital inpatient service (9)   provided to hospital inpatients, including partial hospitalization services, and indicated when the patient's condition requires services and/or procedures that cannot be performed in any other place of service without putting the patient at risk.

hospitalist (1)   physician whose practice emphasizes providing care for hospital inpatients.

hot biopsy forceps (14)   technique that uses tweezerlike forceps connected to a monopolar electrocautery unit and a grounding pad to remove lesions or polyps.

hybrid record (1)   combined paper-based and computer-generated documents.

hyperthermia (16)   use of an external heat-generating source to produce localized heating.

hyperventilation (18)   deep or rapid breathing.

hypopharynx (14)   organ that extends from the upper edge of the epiglottis to the larynx/esophagus juncture.

hypovolemia (10)   abnormally decreased blood volume.

hysteroscopy (15)   visualization of the cervical canal and uterine cavity using a hysteroscope.

I

ICD-9-CM Coordination and Maintenance Committee (2)   NCHS and CMS Department of HHS federal agencies that are responsible for overseeing all changes and modifications to ICD-9-CM diagnosis (NCHS) and procedure (CMS) codes.

ICD-10-CM/PCS Coordination and Maintenance Committee (2)   NCHS and CMS Department of HHS federal agencies that are responsible for overseeing all changes and modifications to ICD-10-CM (NCHS) and ICD-10-PCS (CMS).

ileoanal anastomosis (14)   common alternative to conventional ileostomy, and it is not considered an ostomy because there is no stoma.

ileostomy (14)   removal of the colon and rectum with the small intestine brought to the abdominal wall.

immobilize (12)   *see* stabilize.

immune globulin (Ig) (18)   sterilized solution obtained from pooled human blood plasma, which contains immunoglobulins (or antibodies) that protect against infectious agents that cause various diseases.

immune serum globulin (18)   *see* immune globulin.

immunoglobulin (17)   protein produced by plasma cells that help fight infection; antibody that protects against infectious agents that cause various diseases.

immunology (17)   study of the immune system.

implanted port (10)   small reservoir that has a rubber plug attached to the catheter and is inserted into the patient's vein below the collarbone and threaded into the superior vena cava.

incision (11)   a cut made with a knife, electrosurgical unit, or laser especially for surgical purposes (e.g., on body tissue).

incision and drainage (I&D) (11)   cutting open a lesion and draining its contents.

incisional biopsy (11)   removal of a portion of a lesion by slicing into it or incising it.

incomplete abortion (15)   miscarriage in which part, but not all, of the uterine contents are expelled.

indemnification (19)   insurance against loss.

Index (ICD-10-PCS) (5)   organizes ICD-10-PCS main terms in alphabetic order, providing the first 3-4 characters (and sometimes all 7 characters) of a code as well as direction to a specific location in the Tables.

Index to Diseases (2)   alphabetical listing of ICD-9-CM main terms and their codes; sections include Index to Diseases, Table of Drugs and Chemicals, and Index to External Causes of Injury and Poisoning; main terms are boldfaced, and subterms and qualifiers are indented below main terms.

Index to Diseases and Injuries (2)   alphabetical listing of ICD-10-CM main terms and their codes; subdivided into Index to Diseases and Injuries (includes a Neoplasm Table and a Table of Drugs and Chemicals) and Index to External Causes of Injury; main terms are boldfaced, and subterms and qualifiers are indented below main terms.

Index to Procedures and Tabular List of Procedures (2)   included in the hospital version of commercial ICD-9-CM coding manuals as a combined alphabetical index and tabular list of inpatient procedures and services.

indexed (1)   identified according to a unique identification number.

Indian Health Service (IHS) (19)   DHHS agency that provides federal health care services to American Indians and Alaska Natives.

indirect laryngoscopy (12)   insertion of a small hand mirror in the patient's mouth at the back of the throat while the physician wears headgear that contains a mirror and light source; the mirror worn by the physician reflects light into the patient's mouth, allowing the physician to visualize the patient's throat.

individual practice association (IPA) HMO (19)   contracted services enables to be delivered to subscribers by physicians who remain in their independent office settings.

induced abortion (15)   deliberate termination of pregnancy.

infant (9)   very young child, up to one year old.

inferred words (8)   used to save space in the CPT index when referencing subterms.

infiltration anesthesia (10)   topical injection of local anesthetic into tissue.

informational modifiers (8)   clarify aspects of the procedure or service provided for the payer.

initial plan (1)   documentation of the strategy for managing patient care and actions taken to investigate the patient's condition and to treat/educate the patient; the initial plan consists of three categories: diagnostic/management plans, therapeutic plans, and patient education plans; considered part of the problem-oriented record (POR).

inner ear (15)   includes the cochlea, saccule, acoustic nerve, semicircular canals, utricle, and superior and inferior vestibular nerves.

inpatient (5)   patient who remains overnight in a facility for 24 or more hours and who is provided with room and board and nursing services.

inpatient neonatal and pediatric critical care and intensive service (9)   provided to critically ill neonates and infants by a physician.

inpatient psychiatric facility prospective payment system (IPF PPS) (19)   *per diem* patient classification system that reflects differences in patient resource use and costs; IPF PPS replaced a reasonable cost-based payment system; promotes long-term cost control and utilization management.

inpatient prospective payment system (IPPS) (19) implemented as part of the Tax Equity and Fiscal Responsibility Act of 1982 (TEFRA); uses diagnosis-related groups (DRGs) to classify inpatient hospital cases into groups that are expected to consume similar hospital resources.

inpatient rehabilitation facility prospective payment system (IRF PPS) (19) use of information from a patient assessment instrument (PAI) to classify patients into distinct groups based on clinical characteristics and expected resource needs.

insight-oriented psychotherapy (18) treatment of mental illnesses and behavioral disturbances through resolution of unconscious psychological conflicts.

integrated delivery system (IDS) (19) organization of affiliated provider sites that offer joint health care services to subscribers.

integrated provider organization (IPO) (19) manages the delivery of health care services offered by hospitals, physicians who are employees of the IPO, and other health care organizations such as ambulatory surgery clinics and nursing facilities.

integrated record (1) arranged in strict chronological date order (or in reverse date order), which allows for observation of how the patient is progressing according to test results and how the patient responds to treatment based on test results.

intensivist (9) physician who has received extensive training and experience in critical care and who specializes in the care of critically ill patients, usually in an intensive care unit (ICU).

interactive psychotherapy (18) use of physical aids to enable interaction between the clinician and a patient who does not have the communication skills necessary to explain his or her symptoms or to understand the clinician.

interfacility transport (9) transfer of a patient from one health care facility to another; usually involves use of an ambulance or a helicopter.

internal catheter (10) catheter implanted completely under the skin.

internal fixation device (12) pins, screws, and/or plates inserted through or within a fracture area to stabilize and immobilize the injury; often called open reduction with internal fixation, or ORIF.

internal radiation (16) radiation placed inside the body.

International Classification of Disease (ICD) (2) published by the World Health Organization and used to classify mortality data from death certificates.

International Classification of Diseases, Ninth Revision, Clinical Modification (ICD-9-CM) (1) adopted in 1979 to classify diagnoses (Volumes 1 and 2) and procedures (Volume 3); all health care facilities assign ICD-9-CM codes to report diagnoses, and hospitals report ICD-9-CM procedure codes for inpatient procedures and services.

International Classification of Diseases, Tenth Revision, Clinical Modification (ICD-10-CM) (1) will replace ICD-9-CM as diagnosis classification system; implementation date has not yet been established.

International Classification of Diseases, 10th Revision, Clinical Modification/Procedure Coding System,

(ICD-10-CM/PCS) (1) shortened name the Centers for Medicare and Medicaid Services uses to identify the classification systems.

International Classification of Diseases, Tenth Revision, Procedure Coding System (ICD-10-PCS) (1) developed by the National Center for Health Statistics (NCHS) to replace Volume 3 of ICD-9-CM; when implemented, it will be used to classify inpatient procedures and services.

internship (1) student placement in a health care facility to provide on-the-job experience prior to graduation.

internship supervisor (1) person to whom a student reports at an internship site.

intersex surgery (15) performed as a series of staged procedures to transform the normal adult genitalia of one sex to that of the other sex; also called genital reconstructive surgery or sex reassignment surgery.

interventional radiologic procedure (16) use of percutaneous or minimally invasive techniques under imaging guidance to diagnose and treat conditions.

intra-arterial cannula (10) *see* intra-arterial line.

intra-arterial catheter (10) *see* intra-arterial line.

intra-arterial line (10) thin plastic tube, cannula, or catheter that is inserted into an artery and connected to a monitor to measure immediate changes in intra-arterial blood pressure and concentrations of oxygen and carbon dioxide; also used to collect frequent blood samples for lab tests.

intracapsular cataract extraction (ICCE) (15) removal of lens and surrounding capsule.

intracranial (10) introduced into or within the skull.

intradermal test (intracutaneous) (18) injection of purified allergen extracts into skin to test for allergy to suspected insect venom or penicillin.

intraservice time (9) a variable that is predictive of the "work" of E/M services, which includes **face-to-face time** for office and other outpatient visits or **unit/floor time** for hospital and other inpatient visits.

intrathecal (16) fluid-filled space between layers of tissue that cover the brain and spinal cord.

intravenous push (18) injection administered by a health care professional who is in constant attendance to administer the injection and observe the patient.

intravenous regional anesthesia (10) insertion of IV cannula into the extremity on which the procedure is to be performed and a tourniquet applied to interrupt blood circulation; then a large volume of local anesthetic injected into a peripheral vein, anesthetizing the extremity.

introduction (11) procedures that inject, insert, puncture, or scope.

IPPS 3-day payment window (19) requires outpatient preadmission services provided by a hospital up to three days prior to a patient's inpatient admission to be covered by the IPPS DRG payment for diagnostic services or therapeutic services for which the inpatient principal diagnosis code (ICD-9-CM) exactly matches that for preadmission services.

IPPS 72-hour rule (19) *see* IPPS 3-day payment window.

IPPS transfer rule (19) states that any patient with a diagnosis from one of ten CMS-determined diagnosis-related groups who is discharged to a post acute provider is treated as a transfer case.

IRF PPS 1-day payment window (19)   requires that outpatient preadmission services provided by an IRF up to one day prior to a patient's inpatient admission be covered by the IRF PPS payment.

IRF PPS 24-hour rule (19)   see IRF PPS 1-day payment window.

IRF PPS transfer rule (19)   states that any patient who is discharged to an inpatient rehabilitation facility is treated as a transfer case.

iris (15)   colored tissue that surrounds the pupil of the eye.

island flap (11)   flap consisting of skin and subcutaneous tissue with a pedicle comprised only of nutrient vessels; also called island pedicle flap.

island pedicle flap (11)   see island flap.

J

jamming (1)   routinely assigning an unspecified ICD-9-CM or ICD-10-CM disease code instead of reviewing the coding manual to select the appropriate code number.

J-pouch (14)   see ileoanal anastomosis.

jukebox (1)   equipment that stores large numbers of optical disks, resulting in huge storage capabilities.

K

key components (9)   history, examination, and medical decision making; required when selecting an E/M level of service code.

kidney (14)   filters and cleans blood, producing urine that carries waste.

knee (12)   "hinge" joint composed of bones, cartilage, ligaments, and tendons.

Kock pouch (14)   see continent ileostomy.

L

lacrimal apparatus (15)   contains structures that produce, store, and remove tears.

lacrimal puncta (15)   small openings in the inner canthus of the eyelids that channel tears.

laminectomy (15)   excision of the entire posterior arch or lamina of a vertebra.

laminotomy (15)   removal of part of the lamina from one side of the vertebra.

laparoscopy (14)   examination of the peritoneal contents using a laparoscope that is inserted through the abdominal wall.

laryngoscopy (12)   visualization of the back of the throat, including the larynx and vocal cords.

larynx (12)   voice box.

LASER (light amplification by stimulated emission of radiation) (11)   device filled with a gas, liquid, or solid substance that is stimulated to emit light to a specific wavelength for the purpose of burning, cutting, or dissolving tissue.

laser technique (14)   technique that is most suitable for treatment of rectal lesions and uses a waveguide to deliver the laser beam through the endoscope to the lesion.

laser-assisted uvulopalatoplasty (14)   procedure that uses a laser technique to remove tissue from the uvula, soft palate, and pharynx.

late effect (4)   residual (long-term condition produced, called the sequela) that develops after the acute phase of an illness or injury has ended.

lateral extracavitary approach (LECA) (15)   making a midline incision in the area of the affected vertebral segment, is inferiorly curved out to the lateral plane.

lateral projection (16)   positioning patient at a right angle to the film, so the X-ray beam travels through the side of the body.

LEEP electrodissection conization (15)   superficial dissection of the cervix.

LeFort I (12)   procedure that brings the lower midface forward (from the level of the upper teeth) to just above the nostrils.

LeFort II (12)   surgical fracture of the midfacial skeleton at an apex near the superior aspect of the nasal bones.

LeFort III (12)   procedure that brings the entire midface forward, from the upper teeth to just above the cheekbones.

legacy classification system (2)   see legacy coding system.

legacy coding system (2)   classification system that is used as archive data; it is no longer supported or updated; for example, when ICD-10-CM and ICD-10-PCS are implemented, ICD-9-CM will become a legacy coding system.

lens (15)   clear, flexible, curved structure that focuses images on the retina of the eye.

lesion (10)   abnormal tissue resulting from autoimmune or metabolic disorders, infection, neoplasm, or trauma.

lexicon (4)   glossary of terms.

ligament (12)   tissue that connects bone to bone.

Limberg flap (11)   see rhomboid flap.

List of 3-Digit Categories (2)   located in ICD-9-CM Appendix E; contains a list of three-digit category diseases codes organized beneath section headings.

listserv (1)   see online discussion board.

lithotripsy (14)   see percutaneous lithotomy.

lithotripter (10)   device that administers a high-voltage electrical discharge through a spark gap under water, which produces a compressive force and breaks apart the stones so they can pass in urine.

lobectomy (12)   removal of a single lobe of the lung.

local anesthesia (10)   applying a topical agent on the body's surface or injecting a local anesthetic agent for the purpose of numbing a small part of the body; appropriate for minor surgeries.

local coverage determinations (LCDs) (7)   define coverage criteria, payment rules, and documentation required as applied to DMEPOS claims processed by DME MACs for frequently ordered DMEPOS equipment, services, and supplies; formerly called local medical review policies (LMRPs).

long-term acute care hospital (LTACH) (5)   health care facility designed specifically for patients who need functional restoration and/or rehabilitation and medical management for an average of three to six weeks; LTAC hospitals have an average inpatient length of stay of more than 25 days and provide extended medical and rehabilitative care for patients who are clinically complex and may suffer from multiple acute or chronic conditions.

long-term (acute) care hospital prospective payment system (LTCH PPS) (19)   uses information from long-term care hospital patient records to classify patients into distinct long-term (acute) care diagnosis-related groups based on clinical characteristics and expected resource needs.

long-term hospital (5)   *see* long-term acute care (LTAC) hospital.

loop electrodissection conization (15)   deep dissection of the cervix.

low birth weight (9)   less than 1500 grams.

LTCH PPS 1-day payment window (19)   requires that outpatient preadmission services provided by a long-term acute care hospital up to one day prior to a patient's inpatient admission be covered by the LTC PPS diagnosis-related group payment.

LTCH PPS 24-hour rule (19)   *see* LTC PPS 1-day payment window.

lumbar puncture (LP) (10)   inserting a cannula at the L3-4 or L4-5 (lumbar vertebrae) to remove cerebrospinal fluid for diagnostic or therapeutic purposes.

lumen (10)   opening.

lumpectomy (11)   partial mastectomy.

luxation (12)   *see* dislocation.

lymph (13)   clear fluid that contains chyle, some red blood cells, and lymphocytes, which help fight infection and disease.

lymph nodes (13)   clusters of bean-shaped nodules that act as the body's filtration system, removing cell waste and excess fluid and helping to fight infection.

lymphatic system (13)   consists of the spleen, thymus, tonsils, adenoids, vessels that carry lymph, and lymph nodes.

M

M code (2)   *see* Morphology of Neoplasms.

magnetic resonance angiography (MRA) (16)   noninvasive diagnostic study that is used to evaluate disorders of arterial and venous structures.

magnetic resonance imaging (MRI) (16)   noninvasive X-ray procedure that uses an external magnetic field to produce a two-dimensional view of an internal organ or structure such as the brain or spinal cord.

main term (2)   printed in boldfaced type and followed by the ICD-9-CM code number.

major diagnostic category (MDC) (19)   refers to mutually exclusive categories that are loosely based on body systems (e.g., nervous system); diagnosis-related groups (DRGs) are organized into MDCs.

male genital system (15)   includes the prostate, seminal vesicles, penis, testicles (testes), epididymis, tunica vaginalis, vas deferens, scrotum, spermatic cord, seminal vesicles, and prostate.

malignant (2)   cancerous.

malignant hypertension (4)   accelerated, severe hypertensive disorder with progressive cardiovascular damage and a poor prognosis; characterized by rapidly rising blood pressure greater than 140 diastolic.

malunion (4)   failure of the ends of a fractured bone to heal (unite).

mammography (16)   radiological examination of the soft tissue and internal structures of the breast.

managed care (19)   combines financing and delivery of health care services; replaces conventional fee-for-service health insurance plans with more affordable care for consumers and providers who agree to certain restrictions.

management service organization (MSO) (19)   physician- or hospital-owned organization that provides practice management, administrative, and support services to individual physician practices.

manifestation (3)   condition that occurs as the result of another condition; a manifestation code is always reported as a secondary code.

manipulation (12)   realignment of bones.

manometry (18)   diagnostic test that measures muscle function using a pressure-sensitive tube.

manual record (1)   paper-based record that includes handwritten progress notes and physician orders, graphic charts, and so on.

mass spectrometry (10)   monitors proper levels of the anesthetic.

maximizing reimbursement (5)   reimbursement that is not permitted because it involves selecting and reporting as principal diagnosis the ICD-9-CM code that results in the highest level of reimbursement for the facility whether that diagnosis meets the criteria for selection or not; it also includes assigning a higher-paying ICD-9-CM code to a diagnosis (or ICD-9-CM or CPT/HCPCS code to a procedure) even if patient record documentation does not support that code selection.

Maze procedure (13)   stops atrial fibrillation or atrial flutter by using incisions in heart tissue to stop abnormal heart rhythm.

Meckel's diverticulum (14)   common congenital abnormality of the gastrointestinal tract that results in a pouch in the wall of the small bowel that contains remnants of fetal gastrointestinal tissue.

mediastinum (14)   space in the thoracic cavity between the lungs that contains the aorta, the esophagus, the heart, and other structures.

Medicaid (19)   joint federal and state program that provides health care coverage to low-income populations and certain aged and disabled individuals.

medical assistant (1)   health care professional employed by a provider to perform administrative and clinical tasks.

medical coding process (1)   requires the review of patient record documentation to identify diagnoses, procedures, and services for the purpose of assigning ICD-9-CM (or ICD-10-CM/PCS), HCPCS level II, and/or CPT codes.

medical decision making (MDM) (9)   refers to the complexity of establishing a diagnosis and/or selecting a management option as measured by the number of diagnoses or management options, the amount and/or complexity of data to be reviewed, and the risk of complications and/or morbidity or mortality.

medical foundation (19)   nonprofit organization that contracts with and acquires the clinical and business assets of physician practices; the foundation is assigned a provider number and manages the practice's business.

medical management software (1)   combination practice management and medical billing software that automates the daily workflow and procedures of a physician's office or clinic.

medical necessity (1)   determination that a service or procedure rendered is reasonable and necessary for the diagnosis or treatment of an illness or injury.

medical nomenclature (1)   vocabulary of clinical and medical terms (e.g., arthritis, gastritis, and pneumonia) used by health care providers to document patient care.

medical record (1) *see* patient record.

Medicare (19) provides health care coverage to elderly and disabled persons; federal spending is funded by the Medicare Trust Fund (payroll tax).

Medicare administrative contractor (MAC) (19) processes claims for physicians, health care facilities, and suppliers of durable medical equipment, prosthetics, orthotics, and supplies.

Medicare Carriers Manual (MCM) **(7)** provides direction about services and procedures to be reimbursed by the Medicare administrative contractor.

Medicare National Coverage Determinations Manual **(7)** indicates whether a service is covered or excluded under the Medicare program.

Medicare physician fee schedule (MPFS) (19) common name for resource-based relative value scale system, which is used to reimburse physician services covered by Medicare Part B.

Medicare Prescription Drug, Improvement, and Modernization Act (MMA) (2) federal legislation that requires all code sets to be valid at the time services are provided.

Medicare Prescription Drug, Improvement, and Modernization Act of 2003 (MMA) (19) eliminated carriers, fiscal intermediaries, and durable medical equipment regional carriers and created Medicare administrative contractors.

Medicare Pricing, Data Analysis, and Coding (PDAC) contractor (7) Assists suppliers and manufacturers in determining HCPCS codes to be used; previously called the Statistical Analysis Durable Medical Equipment Regional Carrier (SADMERC).

Medicare severity diagnosis-related groups (MS-DRGs) (19) classifies inpatient hospital cases into groups according to similar resource utilization, which results in hospitals receiving a predetermined payment according to MS-DRG for treating Medicare patients; like the original DRGs, MS-DRGs are based on diagnoses, procedures, other demographic information, and the presence of complications or comorbidities (CCs); however, hospital inpatients are distinguished according to those with no CCs, CCs, or major CCs (MCCs), which allows Medicare to distinguish "sick patients" from "very sick patients" and reimburse hospitals accordingly; the number of MS-DRGs expands to 745 (as compared to 538 original DRGs).

Medicare severity long-term (acute) care diagnosis-related groups (MS-LTC-DRGs) (19) based on clinical characteristics and expected resource needs; replaced the reasonable cost-based LCT PPS authorized by TEFRA that had mandated the implementation of DRGs (and originally exempted long-term acute care hospitals from participation).

Medicare Summary Notice (MSN) (19) an easy-to-read monthly statement sent to Medicare beneficiaries, which clearly lists health insurance claims information.

megaelectron volt (16) *see* MeV.

megavolt (16) *see* MeV.

metastatic cancer (4) *see* secondary malignancy.

MeV (16) 1 million electron volts.

microbiology (17) study of microbes.

microdermabrasion (11) skin-freshening technique used to repair facial skin that is damaged by the sun and the effects of aging.

microtechnique (17) one of three types of micromanipulation techniques that may be used for the preparation of an embryo for transfer.

middle ear (15) includes the tympanic membrane, auditory ossicles, muscles, and conduction pathways.

midsagittal plane (16) vertically divides the body through the midline into two equal left and right halves.

Military Health System (MHS) (19) provides and maintains readiness to provide health care services and support to members of the Uniformed Services during military operations; also provides health care services and support to members of the Uniformed Services, their family members, and others entitled to Department of Defense health care.

minimally invasive procedure (18) includes percutaneous access.

missed abortion (15) miscarriage in which a dead fetus and other products of conception remain in the uterus for four or more weeks.

M-mode (16) one-dimensional display that reflects the movement of structures.

moderate (conscious) sedation (11) moderate sedation or analgesia that results in a drug-induced depression of consciousness.

modified Maze procedure (13) *see* cardiac ablation.

modified radical mastectomy (11) total mastectomy that includes removal of the breast and nipple, axillary lymph nodes, and pectoralis minor muscle.

modifier (3) additional term included after the colon in the ICD-9-CM tabular lists that is to be included in the statement to classify a condition or procedure.

modifying unit (10) part of anesthesia formula that recognizes added complexities associated with the administration of anesthesia, including physical factors and difficult circumstances.

Mohs microsurgery (11) technique of excising skin tumors by removing tumor tissue layer by layer, examining the removed portion microscopically for malignant cells, and repeating the procedure until the entire tumor is removed.

monitored anesthesia care (MAC) (10) administration of varying amounts of local, regional, and certain mind-altering drugs by an anesthesiologist or a CRNA during a patient's diagnostic or therapeutic procedure.

morbidity (2) disease

morphology (2) indicates the tissue type of a neoplasm.

Morphology of Neoplasms (M codes) (2) located in ICD-9-CM Appendix A; contains a reference to the World Health Organization publication *International Classification of Diseases for Oncology* (ICD-O); also called M codes.

mortality (2) death.

motion mode (16) *see* M-mode.

motor vehicle (4) any mechanically or electrically powered device not operated on rails upon which any person or property may be transported or drawn upon a highway.

motor vehicle accident (4) transport accident involving a motor vehicle.

motor vehicle nontraffic accident (4) any motor vehicle accident that occurs entirely in any place other than a public highway.

motor vehicle traffic accident (4) any motor vehicle accident occurring on a public highway (i.e., originating, terminating, or involving a vehicle partially on the highway).

motorcycle (4) two-wheeled motor vehicle having one or two riding saddles and sometimes having a third wheel for the support of a sidecar.

motorcyclist (4) driver of a motorcycle.

mucocutaneous margin (14) consists of mucous membrane and skin.

multiaxial approach (ICD-10-PCS (5) a value from each of seven hierarchies (positions) is assigned to construct an ICD-10-PCS code.

multihospital system (5) two or more hospitals owned, managed, or leased by a single organization; these may include acute, long-term, pediatric, rehabilitation, or psychiatric care facilities.

multiple codes (4) more than one ICD-9-CM code that is assigned to completely classify the elements of a complex diagnosis (or procedure) statement.

multiple sleep latency (18) observation of a patient during at least a six-hour period of sleep and includes assessment of sleep latency (dormancy) and/or wakefulness after the sleep period.

mutually exclusive edit (8) code pairs that, for clinical reasons, are unlikely to be performed on the same patient on the same day.

mycocutaneous flap (11) autologous graft consisting of both skin and muscle tissue from the donor site.

myocardium (13) muscle layer of the heart.

myringotomy (15) surgical incision of the tympanic membrane; usually performed to release pressure or fluid.

N

narcosynthesis (18) form of psychotherapy that is provided when the patient is under the influence of a drug, such as a sedative or narcotic.

nasal vestibule (12) entrance to the nose.

nasopharynx (14) located above the soft palate.

National Correct Coding Initiative (NCCI) (8) implemented by the Centers for Medicare & Medicaid Services (CMS) to promote national correct coding methodologies and to control the improper assignment of codes that results in inappropriate reimbursement of Medicare Part B claims.

national coverage determinations (NCDs) (7) define coverage criteria, payment rules, and documentation required as applied to DMEPOS claims processed by DME MACs for frequently ordered DMEPOS equipment, services, and supplies.

national health plan identifier (PlanID) (19) assigned to third-party payers, contains 10 numeric positions including a check digit in the tenth position (e.g., 1234567890); formerly called the PAYERID.

national individual identifier (patient identifier) (19) HIPAA provision for a national individual identifier (or patient identifier) has been withdrawn.

national limitation amount (NLA) (19) serves as a payment ceiling, or cap, on the amount Medicare could pay for each test.

national provider identifier (NPI) (19) assigned to hospitals, doctors, nursing homes, and other health care providers contains 10 numeric digits (e.g., 1234567890).

national standard employer identifier number (EIN) (19) IRS's federal tax identification number (EIN) adopted as the national employer identifier, retaining the hyphen after the first two numbers (e.g., 12-3456789); the EIN is assigned to employers who, as sponsors of health insurance for their employers, must be identified in health care transactions.

nature of the presenting problem (9) disease, condition, illness, injury, symptom, sign, finding, complaint, or other reason for the encounter, with or without a diagnosis being established at the time of the encounter.

necropsy (17) autopsy.

needle core biopsy (11) tissue sample obtained using a hand-operated needle or stereotactic localization.

needle electromyography (18) inserting needle electrodes into skeletal muscles and observing electrical activity of those muscles using an oscilloscope and a loudspeaker.

neonate (9) newborn, up to 28 days old.

neoplasm (2) new growth, or tumor, in which cell reproduction is out of control.

nephrectomy (14) surgical removal of a kidney.

nerve plexus (10) network of intersecting nerves.

nervous system (15) includes the central nervous system and the peripheral nervous system.

network model HMO (19) contracted health care services provided to subscribers by two or more physician multispecialty group practices.

network provider (19) physician or health care facility under contract to the managed care plan.

neuroplasty (15) freeing or decompression of an intact nerve from scar tissue.

neurorrhaphy (15) repair of nerves.

neurostimulator (15) electrode and pulse generator that are implanted along the spine to alleviate pain or control spasms.

new patient (9) one who has *not* received any professional services within the past three years from the physician or from another physician of the same exact specialty or subspecialty who belongs to the same group practice.

newborn care services (9) includes services provided to newborns in a variety of health care settings.

newborn patient (5) patient who receives infant care upon birth and, if necessary, receives neonatal intensive care (either within a hospital or as the result of transfer to another hospital).

Nissen fundoplasty (14) mobilizing the lower end of the esophagus by suturing the fundus of the stomach around the circumference of the lower esophagus at the esophagogastric junction.

noncovered benefits (19) procedures and services that are not covered by the third-party payer.

nonessential modifier (2) qualifying word contained in parentheses after the main term in the ICD-9-CM Index to Diseases that does not have to be included in the diagnostic or procedural statement for the code number listed after the parentheses to be assigned.

noninvasive procedure (18) requires no surgical incision or excision; not an open procedure.

nonparticipating provider (nonPAR) (19) health care provider (e.g., physician) who is not a member of a health care plan; nonPAR providers do not receive reimbursement directly from a payer; the reimbursement is sent to the patient, and the nonPAR provider must collect payment for services rendered from the patient.

nonselective vascular catheterization (13)   introduction of a catheter into a vessel without further advancement past the punctured vessel *or* introduction of a catheter into any portion of the aorta or vena cava from any approach (e.g., axillary, brachial, femoral, jugular).

nontunneled catheter (10)   *see* external catheter.

nonunion (4)   *see* malunion.

notes (8)   appear throughout CPT sections to clarify the assignment of codes.

Notice of Exclusions from Medicare Benefits (NEMB) (8) form completed and signed by a Medicare beneficiary before items, procedures, and services excluded from Medicare benefits are provided.

nuclear imaging (16)   noninvasive X-ray procedure that creates an image by measuring radiation emission, or radiation "uptake," of body areas after the administration of a radionuclide.

nuclear medicine (16)   use of radioactive elements for diagnostic imaging and radiopharmaceutical therapy.

number symbol (8)   symbol (#) located to the left of CPT codes to indicate out-of-numerical sequence codes.

O

Objective (O) (1)   observations about the patient, such as physical findings or lab or X-ray results; considered part of the problem-oriented record (POR) SOAP note.

oblique projection (16)   positioning the patient with the body slanted sideways toward the film, halfway between a parallel and right-angle position; the X-ray beam travels through this angle of the body.

observation patient (6)   patient who receives services furnished on a hospital's premises that are ordered by a physician (or another authorized individual), including use of a bed and periodic monitoring by nursing or other staff, and that are reasonable and necessary to evaluate the outpatient's condition or determine the need for possible admission as an inpatient.

observation service (9)   provided in a hospital outpatient setting; the patient is considered an outpatient.

obturator (12)   object used to close a gap.

ocular adnexa (15)   includes the orbit, eye muscles, eyelids, eyelashes, conjunctiva, and lacrimal apparatus.

ocular implant (15)   inserted inside the muscular cone.

office or other outpatient services (9)   provided in a physician's office, a hospital outpatient department, or another ambulatory care facility.

Official ICD-9-CM Guidelines for Coding and Reporting (2) rules developed to accompany and complement official conventions and instructions provided in ICD-9-CM.

Official ICD-10-CM Guidelines for Coding and Reporting (2) rules developed to accompany and complement official conventions and instructions provided in ICD-10-CM.

Official ICD-10-PCS Guidelines for Coding and Reporting (2)   rules developed to accompany and complement official conventions and instructions provided in ICD-10-PCS.

off-road motor vehicle (4)   motor vehicle of special design that enables it to negotiate rough terrain, soft terrain, or snow.

omentectomy (15)   surgical removal of the omentum.

Omnibus Budget Reconciliation Act of 1980 (19)   federal legislation mandating that an ambulatory surgery center could participate in Medicare if certain conditions were met and stated that the ambulatory surgical centers payments are "expected to be calculated on a prospective basis...utilizing sample survey and similar techniques to establish reasonable estimated overhead allowances for each of the listed procedures which take account of volume (within reasonable limits)."

Omnibus Budget Reconciliation Act of 1987 (OBRA) (19) federal legislation that mandated the payment methodology for durable medical equipment, prosthetics, orthotics, and supplies fee schedule.

Omnibus Budget Reconciliation Act of 1989 (19)   federal legislation that implemented the resource-based relative value scale (RBRVS) system, which is used to reimburse physician services covered by Medicare Part B.

Omnibus Consolidated and Emergency Supplemental Appropriations Act (OCESAA) of 1999 (19)   federal legislation that implemented the home health prospective payment system for Medicare home health services.

one-lung ventilation (OLV) (10)   isolation of the right or left lung so that one lung is ventilated and the other is allowed to collapse.

online discussion board (1)   Internet-based or e-mail discussion forum that covers a variety of topics and issues.

oocyte (15)   immature female reproductive cell, or egg.

oophorectomy (15)   surgical removal of an ovary or ovaries.

open biopsy (11)   incisional or excisional removal of a lesion.

open fracture (4)   type of fracture that has an associated open wound.

open fracture treatment (12)   surgically opening fracture site or exposing it so treatment can be provided.

open laparoscopy (14)   insufflation of the abdomen using a trocar, which is placed under direct vision (using a laparoscope) after making a small celiotomy incision.

open transluminal angioplasty (13)   making an incision in the skin overlying the artery and carrying it down to free the artery from surrounding structures.

open transluminal atherectomy (13)   making an incision in the skin overlying the artery, and puncturing the artery with a large needle.

open-panel HMO (19)   health care provided by individuals who are not employees of the HMO or who do not belong to a specially formed medical group that serves the HMO.

operating microscope (15)   used during a surgical procedure to perform microsurgery techniques.

opportunistic infection (4)   one that takes advantage of the body's weakened defenses, such as in an HIV-positive patient.

optical disk imaging (1)   alternative to traditional microfilm or remote storage systems because patient records are converted to an electronic image and saved on storage media.

optimizing reimbursement (5)   determining which of several diagnoses to report as the principal diagnosis when multiple diagnoses equally meet the criteria for selection as the principal diagnosis.

orbicularis oculi (18)   blink test that is monitored with sensors.

orbit (15) bony cavity in the skull that contains and protects the eyeball and its associated blood vessels, muscles, and nerves.

orbital implant (15) inserting an implant outside the muscular cone into the eye socket, and placing an intraocular lens (IOL).

organ harvest (10) surgical removal of an organ for transplantation.

oropharynx (14) area between the soft palate and the upper portion of the epiglottis, including the tonsils.

orthotics (7) branch of medicine that deals with the design and fitting of orthopedic (relating to bone disorders) devices.

oscilloscope (18) device that displays electrical waveforms on a monitor.

osteogenesis (12) bone growth.

osteopathic manipulative treatment (OMT) (18) manual treatment performed by a physician during which emphasis is placed on normal body mechanics and manipulative methods to detect and correct structure.

osteophytectomy (15) removal of bone spurs to relieve compression of the spinal cord or nerve roots.

osteotomy (12) surgical incision into bone.

ostomy (14) surgically creating an opening in the body for the discharge of body wastes.

other (additional) diagnosis (5) any condition that coexists at the time of admission, that develops subsequently, or that affects the treatment received and/or the length of stay.

other road vehicle (4) any device (except a motor vehicle and pedestrian conveyance) in, on, or by which any person or property may be transported on a highway.

other significant procedure (5) carries an operative or anesthetic risk, requires highly trained personnel, or requires special facilities or equipment; also called secondary procedures.

outlier (19) inpatient case that is unusually costly.

outpatient (6) see ambulatory patient.

outpatient care (6) any health care service provided to a patient who is not admitted to a facility.

outpatient encounter (19) all outpatient procedures and services (e.g., same-day surgery, X-rays, laboratory tests, and so on) provided during one day to the same patient; also called outpatient visit.

outpatient prospective payment system (OPPS) (19) uses ambulatory payment classifications (APCs) to reimburse hospital outpatient services.

outpatient visit (19) see outpatient encounter.

overcoding (1) reporting codes for signs and symptoms associated, in addition to an established diagnosis code.

overlapping sites (4) see contiguous sites.

overpayment (19) reimbursement a provider or beneficiary receives in excess of amount due.

overpayment recovery (19) collecting excess payments made by Medicare, Medicaid, and other payers.

P

pacemaker (13) device that regulates the patient's heartbeat to prevent arrhythmias; includes a pulse generator and electrodes.

pacing cardioverter-defibrillator (PCD) (13) similar to a pacemaker in that it includes a pulse generator and electrodes, but it uses a combination of antitachycardia pacing and low-energy cardioversion or defibrillating shocks to regulate the patient's heartbeat and prevent arrhythmias.

palatopharyngoplasty (14) surgical resection of excess tissue from the uvula, soft palate, and pharynx to open the airway.

panniculectomy (10) surgical removal of excess abdominal panniculus.

panniculus adiposus (10) layer of subcutaneous adipose tissue, or fat, below the dermis that contains fat deposits, blood vessels, and nerves.

pannus (10) see panniculus adiposus.

parenterally (16) other than by mouth or rectum, such as implantation, infusion, or injection.

paring and curettement (11) removal of growths or other material from the wall of a cavity or another surface.

partial hospitalization (9) short-term, intensive treatment program in which individuals who are experiencing an acute episode of an illness can receive medically supervised treatment during a significant number of daytime or nighttime hours.

partial mastectomy (11) involves making an incision through skin and fascia over the breast tumor and clamping lymphatic and blood vessels; the physician then excises the tumor mass along with a section of breast tissue.

participating provider (PAR) (19) health care provider (e.g., physician) who is a member of a health care plan; PAR providers receive reimbursement directly from the payer.

passenger (4) authorized occupant of a motor vehicle.

past medical history (9) summary of past illnesses, operations, injuries, treatments, and known allergies.

patch test (epicutaneous) (18) applying an allergen to a patch, which is placed on skin; the test is performed to identify substances that cause contact dermatitis, such as latex, medications, fragrances, preservatives, hair dyes, metals, and resins.

patency (13) open and unblocked status of a blood vessel or another tube in the body.

patient education plan (1) program to educate the patient about conditions for which the patient is being treated; considered part of the problem-oriented record (POR).

patient record (1) business record for an inpatient or outpatient encounter that documents health care services provided to a patient; stores patient demographic data and documentation that supports diagnoses and justifies treatment; and contains results of treatment provided.

Payment Error and Prevention Program (PEPP) (19) identifies and reduces improper Medicare payments, resulting in a reduction in the Medicare payment error rate.

pedal cycle (4) any road transport vehicle operated solely by pedals that includes bicycles, pedal cycles, and tricycles.

pedal cyclist (4) any person riding on a pedal cycle or in a sidecar attached to such a vehicle.

pedestrian (4) any person involved in an accident who was not at the time of the accident riding in or on a motor vehicle, railroad train, streetcar, animal-drawn or other vehicle, or on a bicycle or animal.

pedestrian conveyance (4) any human-powered device by which a pedestrian may move other than by walking or by which a walking person may move another pedestrian.

pediatric critical care patient transport (9) includes the physical attendance and direct face-to-face care provided by a physician during the interfacility transport of a critically ill or critically injured patient aged 24 months or younger.

pedicle skin graft (11) transferring a portion of skin graft to the recipient area, and attaching a remaining portion (the base) to the donor site so there is a vasculature and nerve supply for the recipient area.

percutaneous lithotomy (14) two-stage procedure that requires a percutaneous nephrostomy and dilation of the nephrostomy tract.

percutaneous myocardial revascularization (PMR) (13) insertion of a catheter with a laser inside through an artery into the left ventricle of the heart.

percutaneous needle biopsy (12) insertion of a long needle through the skin and into other tissue (e.g., chest wall, lung, or mediastinum) to obtain tissue for diagnostic evaluation.

percutaneous skeletal fixation (12) use of an external or internal fixation device to stabilize and immobilize a fracture; types include external fixation and internal fixation.

percutaneous transluminal angioplasty (PTA) (13) puncturing an artery and inserting a sheath, guidewire, and guiding catheter (after removing the guidewire).

percutaneous transluminal atherectomy (13) puncturing an artery with a large needle, inserting a guidewire and introducer sheath into the artery, and inserting an atherectomy device for the purpose of removing plaque from inside a blood vessel.

percutaneous transmyocardial laser revascularization (PTMR) (13) *see* percutaneous myocardial revascularization (PMR).

percutaneous vertebroplasty (12) injection of bone cement (that hardens in about 10 minutes) under pressure directly into a fractured vertebra; cement causes fragments of fractured vertebra to congeal, providing stability.

pericardial sac (13) *see* pericardium.

pericardiectomy (13) removal of part of the pericardium (to treat chronic pericarditis).

pericardiocentesis (13) insertion of a needle to withdraw fluid from the pericardial sac.

pericardiotomy (13) requires thoracotomy as incision for pericardial drainage, fluid collection, or foreign body removal.

pericardium (13) membrane that surrounds the heart; also called pericardial sac.

perinatal period (4) interval of time occurring before, during, and up to 28 days following birth.

peripheral nerve block (10) injection of local anesthetic in the vicinity of a peripheral nerve to anesthetize that nerve's area of innervation.

peripherally (13) access via a peripheral vein.

peristalsis (14) wavelike motions that propel urine.

peritoneal dialysis (18) insertion of soft catheter into abdominal cavity and infusion of dialysate fluid at intermittent times.

peritoneoscopy (14) *see* laparoscopy.

personal care and support services (6) assistance in performing daily living activities such as bathing, dressing, grooming, going to the toilet, and fixing meals; instruction in how to travel and how to access recreational services is also provided.

pharmacologic management (18) evaluation of a patient's medications for effect, proper dosage, and renewal of prescribed medications.

phlebotomy (17) *see* venipuncture.

photic simulation (18) reaction to light.

photons (16) invisible electromagnetic energy waves.

physiatrist (18) physician who specializes in physical medicine and rehabilitation and treats acute/chronic pain and musculoskeletal disorders.

physical examination (9) assessment of the patient's organ and body systems.

physical medicine and rehabilitation (18) branch of medicine that focuses on the prevention, diagnosis, and treatment of disorders of the musculoskeletal, cardiovascular, and pulmonary systems that may produce temporary or permanent impairment.

physical status modifier (10) added to each reported anesthesia code to indicate the patient's condition at the time anesthesia was administered.

physician case management (9) process in which a physician is responsible for direct care of a patient and for the coordination and control of access to or initiation and/or supervision of other health care services needed by the patient.

physician query process (1) contacting the responsible physician to request clarification about documentation and codes to be assigned; the process is activated when the coder notices a problem with documentation quality.

physician self-referral law (19) prohibits a physician from referring Medicare patients to clinical laboratory services where they or a member of their family have a financial interest; enacted as part of the Omnibus Budget Reconciliation Act of 1989.

physician-hospital organization (PHO) (19) owned by hospital(s) and physician groups that obtain managed care plan contracts; physicians maintain their own practices and provide health care services to plan members.

Physicians at Teaching Hospitals (PATH) initiative (19) federal program that resulted from the discovery that some health care organizations were billing Medicare Part B for services that were already paid under Part A.

pilonidal cyst (11) entrapped epithelial tissue and hair located in the sacral area at the top of the crease between the buttocks, which can become infected.

place of service (POS) (9) the physical location where health care is provided to patients.

Plan (P) (1) diagnostic, therapeutic, and education plans to resolve the problems; considered part of the problem-oriented record (POR) SOAP note.

plane of view (16) terminology used when performing a radiology procedure.

pleura (12) membrane that envelopes the lungs and lines the walls of the pleural cavity.

pleural effusion (12) fluid in the pleural cavity preventing the lung from fully expanding, making it difficult for the patient to breathe.

plexus anesthesia (10) injection of local anesthetic in the vicinity of a nerve plexus.

plus symbol (8) symbol (+) located to the left of CPT codes that identifies add-on codes (also located in Appendix D of CPT) for procedures that are commonly, but not always, performed at the same time and by the same surgeon as the primary procedure.

pneumocentesis (12) puncture of the pleural space with a transthoracic needle to drain fluid or to obtain material for diagnostic study.

point-of-service plan (POS) (19) offers patients the freedom to use an HMO panel of providers or to self-refer to non-HMO providers.

polysomnography (18) sleep study that includes sleep staging with additional parameters of sleep.

port (16) skin site where radiation beams enter the body.

positron emission tomography (PET) (16) producing X-ray images of the body after administering radioisotopes, which tracks metabolism or blood flow, not anatomy.

post-anesthesia evaluation (10) evaluation of the patient during recovery from anesthesia, as well as evaluation, treatment, and follow-up of possible anesthesia-related complications.

posteroanterior (PA) projection (16) positioning the patient is facing the film and parallel to it; the X-ray beam travels from back to front, or posterior to anterior.

postoperative pain management (10) administration of epidural or subarachnoid medications on the date(s) of service after the date of surgery.

postpartum care (15) begins after vaginal or cesarean section delivery and includes the recovery room visit; any uncomplicated inpatient hospital and outpatient postpartum visits; episiotomy; and repair of cervical, vaginal, or perineal lacerations.

preadmission testing (PAT) (6) occurs after a surgical patient registers with a facility's admitting department, when the patient undergoes preoperative nursing assessment and receives preanesthesia evaluation by an anesthesiologist.

pre-anesthesia evaluation (10) assessing information from the patient's record, interviewing the patient, conducting a physical examination, evaluating preoperative test results, and ensuring that informed anesthetic consent has been obtained.

preauthorization (19) prior approval.

preexisting medical condition (19) illness or injury that required treatment during a prescribed period of time prior to the insured's effective date of coverage under a new insurance policy.

preferred provider organization (PPO) (19) network of physicians and hospitals that join together to contract with insurance companies, employers, or other organizations.

preoperative clearance (9) occurs when a surgeon requests that a specialist or another physician examine a patient and indicate whether the patient can withstand the expected risks of a specific surgery.

present on admission (POA) indicator (19) assigned to each diagnosis and external cause of injury code that is coded and reported on inpatient UB-04 or 837 Institutional (electronic) claims.

pressure ulcer (11) ulceration of the skin and underlying tissue that occurs over a bony prominence.

presumptive identification (17) identification by colony morphology, growth on selective media, or Gram stains.

preventive medicine services (9) include routine examinations or risk management counseling for children and adults who exhibit no overt signs or symptoms of a disorder while presenting to the medical office for a preventive medical physical.

pricing modifier (8) *see* functional modifier.

primary care (6) acute care and preventive services provided as outpatient care and referred to as the *point of first contact*.

primary care provider (6) manages and coordinates the patient's care, including referring the patient to a medical specialist for consultation and a second opinion; physician responsible for supervising and coordinating health care services and preauthorizing referrals to specialists and for overseeing inpatient hospital admissions, except in emergencies.

primary defect (11) wound resulting from initial surgical intervention (e.g., excision of lesion) or trauma (e.g., deep abrasions).

primary malignancy (4) original tumor site.

principal diagnosis (5) condition established after study to be chiefly responsible for occasioning the admission of the patient to the hospital for care.

principal procedure (5) performed for definitive treatment rather than for diagnostic or exploratory purposes; necessary to treat a complication, or is most closely related to the principal diagnosis.

privacy (19) patient's right to prohibit disclosure of information without his or her authorization.

privacy rule (19) *see* HIPAA standards for privacy of individually identifiable health information.

privileged communication (19) any information communicated by a patient to a health care provider.

problem focused examination (9) limited examination of the affected body area or organ system.

problem focused history (9) consists of chief complaint and brief history of present illness or problem.

problem list (1) serves as a table of contents for the patient record because it is filed at the beginning of the record and contains a numbered list of the patient's problems, which helps to index documentation throughout the record; considered part of the problem-oriented record (POR).

problem-oriented record (POR) (1) systematic method of documentation that consists of four components: database, problem list, initial plan, and progress notes.

proctectomy (14) surgical removal of the rectum.

proctosigmoidoscopy (14) visual examination of the rectum and sigmoid colon.

professional component (16) services provided by the physician, which include supervising the performance of a diagnostic imaging procedure, interpreting imaging films, and documenting the imaging report.

professional services (9) face-to-face services provided by a physician or nonphysician practitioner (e.g., nurse practitioner, physician assistant) and reported by assigning an E/M code.

Programs of All-inclusive Care for the Elderly (PACE) (19) community-based Medicare and Medicaid programs that provide integrated health care and long-term care services to elderly persons who require a nursing-facility level of care.

progress notes (1) narrative notes documented by the provider to demonstrate continuity of care and the patient's response to treatment; when using the SOAP format, a narrative is documented for each problem assigned to the patient according to subjective (S), objective (O), assessment (A), and plan (P).

prohibitory symbol (8)   *see* forbidden symbol.

prolonged services (9)   physicians' services involving patient contact that are considered beyond the usual service in either an inpatient or an outpatient setting.

prospective cost-based rate (19)   based on reported health care costs from which a prospective *per diem* rate is determined; annual rate is usually adjusted using actual costs from the prior year; may be based on the facility's case mix (patient acuity of types and categories of patients).

prospective payment system (PPS) (19)   reimbursement methodology that establishes predetermined rates based on patient category or type of facility, with annual increases based on an inflation index and a geographic wage index.

prospective price-based rate (19)   associated with a particular category of patient; rate is established by the payer prior to the provision of health care services.

prosthetics (7)   branch of medicine that deals with the design, production, and use of artificial body parts.

protected health information (PHI) (19)   information that is identifiable to an individual, such as name, address, telephone numbers, date of birth, and Medicaid ID number.

provider (1)   physician or other health care professional who performs procedures or provides services to patients.

psychodynamic psychotherapy (18)   *see* insight-oriented psychotherapy.

psychosocial therapy (18)   *see* psychotherapy.

psychotherapy (18)   treatment of mental and emotional disorders by having patients talk about their condition(s) and related issues with a mental health physician or therapist.

public highway (4)   entire width between property lines (or other boundary lines) of every way or place of which any part is open to the use of the public for purposes of vehicular traffic as a matter of right or custom.

pull-through (14)   *see* ileoanal anastomosis.

pulmonary wedge pressure (10)   indirect measurement of left atrial pressure that is useful in the diagnosis of left ventricular failure and mitral valve disease.

pulse oximetry (10)   arterial oxyhemoglobin saturation.

pump oxygenator (10)   device that substitutes for the heart (pump) and lungs (oxygenator) during open heart surgery.

puncture, prick, or scratch test (percutaneous) (18)   procedure in which tiny drops of purified allergen extracts are pricked or scratched into the skin's surface; performed to identify allergies to pollen, mold, pet dander, dust mites, foods, insect venom, and penicillin.

pupil (15)   black opening in the center of the iris that permits light to enter the eye.

pyramidal fracture (12)   *see* LeFort II.

Q

qualified diagnosis (6)   diagnosis documented as probable, suspected, questionable, rule out, or working diagnosis.

qualifying circumstance (10)   coded when anesthesia services are provided during situations or circumstances that make anesthesia administration more difficult.

qualitative assay (17)   detects whether a particular substance is present.

quantitative A-scan (16)   diagnostic ultrasound that produces quantitative data about the posterior eye segment and evaluates tissue consistency, mobility, and vascularity.

quantitative assay (17)   detects the amount of a substance in a specimen.

R

radiation absorbed dose (rad) (16)   amount of radiant energy absorbed in a tissue.

radiation oncology (16)   specialty of medicine that utilizes high-energy ionizing radiation in the treatment of malignant neoplasms and certain nonmalignant conditions.

radical mastectomy (11)   total mastectomy, which includes removal of the breast and nipple, pectoralis muscles (major and/or minor), axillary lymph nodes, and internal mammary lymph nodes.

radiographic projection (16)   describes the path that the X-ray beam travels through the body, from entrance to exit.

radiologic guidance (16)   performed during a procedure to visualize access to an anatomic site fluoroscopic guidance to guide the placement, replacement, or removal of a catheter, central venous access device (CVAD), or needle.

radiologist (16)   physician who has undergone specialized training to interpret diagnostic X-rays, perform specialized X-ray procedures, and administer radiation for the treatment of disease.

radiology (16)   branch of medicine that uses imaging techniques to diagnose and treat disease.

radionuclide (16)   radioactive material, such as an isotope of iodine.

radiopaque (10)   cannot be penetrated by electromagnetic radiation.

radiopharmaceutical therapy (16)   destroys diseased tissue, such as a malignant neoplasm.

railroad (4)   *see* railway.

railway (4)   right-of-way designed for traffic on rails that is used by carriages or wagons transporting passengers or freight and by other rolling stock and that is not open to other public vehicular traffic.

railway accident (4)   transport accident involving a railway train or another railway vehicle operated on rails, whether in motion or not.

railway train (4)   any device with or without cars coupled to it that is designed for traffic on a railway.

railway vehicle (4)   *see* railway train.

random pattern flap (11)   mycocutaneous flap with a random pattern of arteries.

range of codes (8)   code numbers separated by a dash or a series of codes separated by commas in the CPT index.

reagent strip automated urine analyzer (17)   instrumentation used to determine various components in the urine.

real-time scan (16)   two-dimensional display of structures and movement that indicates the movement, shape, and size of the tissue or organ.

recipient heart with or without lung allotransplantation (13)   removal (harvesting) of heart with or without lung tissue; includes transplantation of the allograft and care of the recipient.

recipient lung allotransplantation (12)   transplantation of a single or double lung allograft and care of the recipient.

recipient site (11) anatomic site to which healthy skin is attached.

reconstruction (11) surgical rebuilding of a body part, such as the breast or the knee joint.

reconstruction of the vena cava (13) surgical procedure performed to correct a congenital defect or to repair the vena cava when the patient sustains trauma or the vena cava is damaged due to long-term drug therapy.

red reference symbol (8) symbol (⊖) located below a code description to indicate that the coder should refer to the *Clinical Examples in Radiology* quarterly newsletter.

reduction (12) *see* manipulation.

referral (9) recommendation to transfer a patient's care from one provider to another.

referred outpatient (6) patient who receives diagnostic or therapeutic care because such care is unavailable in the primary care provider's office.

regional anesthesia (10) anesthesia agents injected into or near the spinal fluid and around a nerve or network of nerves to block the nerve supply to a specific part of the body.

rehabilitation hospital (5) health care facility that admits patients who are diagnosed with trauma or disease and who need to learn how to function.

relative value unit (RVU) (19) payment component that consists of physician work, practice expense, and malpractice expense.

remittance advice (remit) (19) statement sent by the payer to the provider that details how submitted claims were processed and contains reimbursement amounts.

removal (11) procedures performed to eliminate tissue (e.g., amputations) or take something out (e.g., removal of implants, such as buried wire, pins, or screws).

renal dialysis (18) artificial removal of toxic waste products from the body when the patient's kidneys are unable to perform this function due to disease or deterioration.

repair (11) procedure performed to surgically improve improperly functioning parts of the body.

replantation (12) surgical reattachment of a finger, a hand, a toe, a foot, a leg, or an arm that has been completely severed from a person's body.

Resident Assessment Validation and Entry (RAVEN) (19) data entry system that allows a skilled nursing facility (SNF) to capture and transmit the minimum data set (MDS).

resident physician (1) individual who participates in an approved graduate medical education (GME) program.

residual condition (4) long-term condition produced after the acute phase of an illness or injury has terminated, which is called the sequela.

resource utilization group (RUG) (19) prospective payment system implemented by the federal government to control costs in nursing facilities.

retina (15) part of eye that contains nerve tissue.

revenue code (19) four-digit UB-04 code that is assigned to each procedure, service, or supply to indicate the location or type of service provided to an institutional patient, such as radiology or laboratory.

review of systems (ROS) (9) *see* system review.

revision (11) surgical modification of a previous procedure or a device.

rhinoplasty (14) repair of skin defect of the nose using harvested tissue or plastic surgery to change the nose's shape or size.

rhomboid flap (11) random pattern flap that can be raised on any or all corners of a parallelogram configuration, typically 120 and 60 degrees; also called Limberg flap.

rhytidectomy (11) excision of a section of skin to eliminate wrinkles.

rhytides (12) wrinkles.

roadway (4) that part of the public highway designed, improved, and ordinarily used for vehicular travel.

roentgen (16) international unit of exposure dose for X-rays or gamma rays.

roentgen-equivalent-man (rem) (16) unit of measurement that includes different biological responses to different kinds of radiation.

roster billing (19) simplified claims submission process available to public health clinics and other noninstitutional entities that offer mass immunization programs.

rotation flap (11) incision made to create a curvilinear flap contiguous with the defect; flap is dissected, freed, and pivoted and sutured in place over the defect.

rule of nines (11) divides total body surface area (BSA) into nine segments by percentage.

S

saddle block anesthesia (10) *see* caudal anesthesia.

safe harbor regulation (19) specifies various payment and business practices that, although potentially capable of inducing referrals of business reimbursable under the federal health care programs, would not be treated as criminal offenses under the anti-kickback statute.

sagittal plane (16) vertically divides the body into unequal left and right portions.

salpingo-oophorectomy (15) surgical removal of both fallopian tubes and ovaries.

saphenopopliteal vein anastomosis (13) surgical incision to expose the saphenous vein and connect it to the popliteal vein using end-to-end anastomosis.

scanner (1) equipment that captures paper record images onto the storage media.

sclera (15) white of the eye that comprises the eye's outer layer; contains fibrous tissue that maintains the eye's shape and protects the eye's inner layers.

screening mammography (16) radiographic (X-ray) of the breast that is performed when a patient presents without signs and symptoms of breast disease.

secondary defect (11) wound resulting from removal of tissue to create flap(s) or graft(s).

secondary malignancy (4) tumor that has metastasized, or spread, to a secondary site either adjacent to the primary site or to a remote region of the body.

secondary procedure (5) *see* other significant procedure.

second-order vessels (13) branch from first-order vessel.

second-stage fistulectomy/fistulotomy (14) in treatment of anal fistulas, use of a seton to cut through the fistula; the seton is left in place until later removal.

section (2) group of ICD-9-CM three-digit disease categories within a chapter.

sectionalized record (1) *see* source-oriented record.

security (19) ensures that facilities, equipment, and patient information are safe from damage, loss, tampering, theft, or unauthorized access.

security rule (19) HIPAA regulation that requires covered entities to adopt standards and safeguards to protect health information that is collected, maintained, used, or transmitted electronically.

sedation (10) administration of medication into a vein to relieve pain and anxiety, making the patient feel calm.

segmentectomy (12) removal of one segment of a lobe.

selective vascular catheterization (13) insertion and manipulation or guidance of a catheter into the branches of the arterial system (other than the aorta or the vessel punctured) for the purpose of performing diagnostic or therapeutic procedures.

self-referral (19) an enrollee seeing a non-HMO panel specialist without a referral from the primary care physician.

semicolon (8) symbol (;) used to save space in CPT code descriptions.

separate procedure (11) performed as an integral component of a total service or procedure.

septal defects (13) occurs when the tissue doesn't completely close between the heart's chambers.

septic abortion (15) abortion-related pelvic and uterine infection.

septum (13) tissue that separates the heart's left and right sides.

seton (14) large silk suture or rubber bands.

severity of illness (19) physiologic complexity that comprises the extent and interactions of a patient's disease(s) as presented to medical personnel.

shaving (11) horizontal slicing to remove epidermal and dermal lesions; removal includes scissoring or any sharp method.

shock therapy (10) *see* electroconvulsive therapy.

short-latency somatosensory evoked potential study (18) electrical stimulation of nerves to evaluate their responsiveness to the body's superficial surface and internal structures.

short-term hospital (5) average length of stay (LOS) of 4–5 days and a total LOS of fewer than 25 days.

shunting procedure (13) performed to move blood from one area to another for conditions such as atrial septal defect (ASD), coarctation of the aorta, patent ductus arteriosus (PDA), tricuspid atresia, and ventricular septal defect (VSD).

side view (16) *see* lateral projection.

sigmoidoscopy (14) visual examination of the entire rectum and sigmoid colon and may include a portion of the descending colon.

simple closure (11) *see* simple repair.

simple fracture (4) *see* closed fracture.

simple repair (11) involves the use of staples, sutures, and/or tissue adhesives to repair superficial wounds involving epidermis, dermis, and/or subcutaneous tissues; also called one-layer closure, nonlayered closure, and single-layer closure.

single chamber (13) contains a single electrode that is positioned in the heart's right atrium *or* right ventricle.

single code (8) single code number listed in the CPT index.

single hospital (5) hospital that is self-contained and not part of a larger organization.

single photon emission computerized tomography (SPECT) (16) three-dimensional X-ray images of internal organs produced after administration of a radioactive material, which visualize anatomy and function.

sinus of Valsalva (13) anatomic dilation of ascending aorta that occurs just above aortic valve (e.g., left anterior aortic sinus that gives rise to the left coronary artery); defects include aneurysms and fistulas for which repair and closure procedures are performed.

skeletal traction (12) exerts a pulling force on the affected limb to realign bone or joint.

skilled nursing facility prospective payment system (SNF PPS) (19) classifies residents into resource utilization groups.

sleep laboratory (18) area in a hospital facility that is managed by a sleep technologist who explains and performs the sleep studies.

sleep staging (18) during a sleep study (polysomnography), involves the use of a 1-4 lead electroencephalogram (EEG), electro-oculogram (EOG), and submental electromyogram (EMG).

sleep study (18) evaluation of adult and pediatric patients during sleep by monitoring brain waves, heart rate, and eye movements; performed to diagnose sleep disorders, which include breathing, movement, and neurologic disorders that occur at night.

slitlamp exam (16) high-intensity light source that can be focused to shine as a slit to visualize anterior structures, including the eyelid, sclera, conjunctiva, iris, natural crystalline lens, and cornea.

small boat (4) any watercraft propelled by paddle, oars, or small motor, with a passenger capacity of fewer than 10.

social history (9) age-appropriate review of past and current activities such as daily routine, dietary habits, exercise routine, marital status, occupation, sleeping patterns, smoking, use of alcohol and other drugs, and sexual activities.

somatic nerves (15) control voluntary movements and conscious sensation; include voluntary motor and sensory nerves.

source-oriented record (SOR) (1) reports organized according to documentation source, each of which is located in a labeled section of the record.

special evaluation and management services (9) provided for establishment of baseline information prior to life or disability insurance certificates being issued and for examination of a patient with a work-related or medical disability problem.

special report (8) document that must accompany the claim to describe the nature, extent, and need for the procedure or service when an unlisted procedure or service code is reported.

specialty coders (1) individuals who has obtained advanced training in medical specialties (e.g., anesthesia, obstetrics) and who is skilled in that medical specialty's compliance and reimbursement areas. In addition to maintaining core credential(s), completes rigorous, in-depth exam, and earns additional continuing education units biannually. Specialty coders typically analyze provider documentation for accuracy, completeness, and timeliness; maintain and update chargemasters and/or encounter forms; meet with coding staff to educate them about revised rules and regulations; review patient charges to accuracy in reported codes and modifiers and enter billing edits; and write letters of appeals to address third-party payer reimbursement denials.

specialty hospital (5) health care facility that delivers care to a particular population of patients or type of disease.

specimen (17) tissue submitted for laboratory or pathologic evaluation; also the unit of service used to report surgical pathology codes.

spinal anesthesia (10) local anesthetic injected into cerebrospinal fluid at the lumbar spine, where it acts on spinal nerve roots and part of the spinal cord; anesthetized area extends from the legs to the abdomen or chest.

spinal tap (10) *see* lumbar puncture.

spleen (13) organ that produces mature lymphocytes, destroys worn-out red blood cells, and serves as a reservoir for blood.

splenoportography (13) radiographic visualization of the splenic and portal veins.

split-thickness skin graft (11) graft of entire epidermis and a portion of the dermis; typically used to repair edematous, infected, or large wounds (e.g., result of burns).

stab phlebectomy (13) multiple tiny incisions made over varicose vein sites; at each stab site the varicosity is extracted and then the varicose segment is removed.

stabilize (12) to secure bone in a fixed position.

staff model HMO (19) health care services provided to subscribers by physicians employed by an HMO.

standby service (9) physician, or other qualified health care professional, spending a prolonged period of time *without patient contact* waiting for an event to occur that will require the physician's or professional's service.

Stark I (19) *see* physician self-referral law.

Stark II (19) expanded the Stark I physician self-referral law by including referrals of Medicare and Medicaid patients for designated health care services.

State Children's Health Insurance Program (SCHIP) (19) federal health program established to provide health assistance to uninsured, low-income children either through separate programs or through expanded eligibility under state Medicaid programs.

status indicator (SI) (19) payment indicator that identifies how each code is paid (or not paid) under the Outpatient Prospective Payment System (OPPS).

stem cells (13) cells contained in bone marrow.

stented valve (13) includes framework on which the replacement heart valve is mounted to provide support for the valve's leaflets.

stentless valve (13) an actual heart valve obtained from either a human donor (homograft) or a pig; it does not contain framework.

stereotactic localization (11) use of specialized three-dimensional imaging to target a nonpalpable lesion.

stereotaxis (15) use of a stereotactic guidance system to allow the physician to determine three-dimensional coordinates in order to create a lesion on the spinal cord (to alleviate chronic pain in a particular part of the body); to stimulate the spinal cord percutaneously (to create a lesion that will block pain); or to facilitate the biopsy, aspiration, or excision of a spinal cord lesion.

stoma (14) surgically created opening between ureter, small intestine, or large intestine, through to abdominal wall.

strabismus (15) improperly aligned eyes.

streetcar (4) device that is designed and used primarily for transporting people within a municipality, that runs on rails, that is usually subject to normal traffic control signals, and that operates principally on a right-of-way that forms part of the traffic way.

stroma (11) supporting tissue (matrix) of an organ.

subacute care patient (5) receives specialized services such as chemotherapy, injury rehabilitation, ventilator support, wound care, and other types of health care services provided to seriously ill patients.

subcategory code (2) four-digit ICD-9-CM disease code or three-digit ICD-9-CM procedure code within a category; each subcategory code contains a decimal followed by one number.

subclassification code (2) five-digit ICD-9-CM disease code or four-digit ICD-9-CM code within a subcategory; each subclassification code contains a decimal followed by two numbers.

subcutaneous fistulectomy (14) removal of an anal fistula, without division of the sphincter muscle.

subglottic stenosis (12) narrowing of the airway below the vocal cords, adjacent to the cricoid cartilage.

Subjective (S) (1) patient's statement about how he or she feels, including symptomatic information; considered part of the problem-oriented record (POR) SOAP note.

subluxation (12) partial displacement of a bone from its joint.

submuscular fistulectomy (14) removal of an anal fistula, including division of the sphincter muscle.

subterm (2) qualifying word listed below the main term in the ICD-9-CM Index to Diseases; list alternate sites, etiology, or clinical status.

superbill (19) *see* encounter form.

supervision and interpretation (16) term for the radiological portion of a procedure when two different physicians perform the surgical and radiological components of a procedure.

supportive psychotherapy (18) treatment that uses supportive interactions and various activities to facilitate maintenance, restoration, and improvement of a patient's self-esteem.

surface anesthesia (10) topical application of local anesthetic cream, solution, or spray to skin or mucous membranes.

surgical curettement (11) scraping tissue to remove abnormal tissue.

surgical endoscopy (14) performed when anything in addition to visualization is done, such as the removal of a foreign body.

surgical package (11) services performed that are integral to the standard of medical/surgical services, such as the cleansing, shaving, and prepping of skin and the insertion of intravenous access for medication.

suture (11) surgical closure of a wound, using catgut, glue, silk thread, wire, or other materials.

Swan-Ganz catheter (10) thin, flexible, flow-directed multilumen plastic tube (or catheter) that is advanced from a peripheral vein into the right atrium and then positioned in a branch of the pulmonary artery.

swing bed (5) allows a rural hospital to admit a nonacute care patient.

sympathectomy (13) excision of a segment of the sympathetic nerve.

sympathetic nerves (15) part of the involuntary autonomic nervous system; originate in the thoracic and lumbar regions of the spinal cord; inhibit the physiological effects of the parasympathetic nervous system.

system review (9) inventory by systems to document subjective symptoms stated by the patient; also provides an opportunity to gather information that the patient may have forgotten to mention or that may have seemed unimportant.

systemic radiation therapy (16) unsealed radioactive materials that travel throughout the body.

T

Tables (ICD-10-PCS) (5) used to construct a complete and valid ICD-10-PCS code; contain terms (and definitions) and rows that contain values (characters) needed to construct a valid code.

Tabular List of Diseases (2) ICD-9-CM tabular list of diseases arranges codes and descriptions in numerical order and contains 17 chapters, 2 supplemental classifications, and 4 appendices; ICD-10-CM tabular list of diseases is chronological list of codes, divided into 21 chapters based on body system or condition.

talk therapy (18) see psychotherapy.

Tax Equity and Fiscal Responsibility Act of 1983 (TEFRA) (19) federal legislation that resulted in implementation of the inpatient prospective payment system, which uses diagnosis related groups to reimburse short-term hospitals a predetermined rate for Medicare inpatient services.

teaching hospital (1) hospital engaged in an approved graduate medical education (GME) residency program in medicine, osteopathy, dentistry, or podiatry.

teaching physician (1) physician (other than another resident physician) who supervises residents during patient care.

tear apparatus (15) see lacrimal apparatus.

technical component (16) use of equipment and supplies as well as the employment of radiologic technologists to perform diagnostic imaging examinations and administer radiation therapy treatments.

tenosynovitis (15) swollen tendon sheaths.

Tensilon test (18) involves injecting the drug Tensilon (or its generic form edrophonium chloride) into a vein to block the action of the enzyme that breaks down the neurotransmitter acetylcholinesterase.

tetralogy of Fallot (13) congenital heart condition that includes ventral septal defect, stenosis of the infundibulum, hypertrophy of the right ventricle, and an abnormally positioned aorta.

therapeutic apheresis (13) removal of blood components, cells, or plasma solute and retransfusion of the remaining components into the patient.

therapeutic plan (1) specific medications, goals, procedures, therapies, and treatments used to treat the patient; considered part of the problem oriented record (POR).

therapeutic port film (16) X-rays taken during delivery of radiation treatment that utilize the treatment beam of the machine.

therapeutic surgical procedure (11) performed to treat specific conditions or injuries; includes the procedure itself and normal, uncomplicated follow-up care.

third-order vessels (13) blood vessels that branch from second-order vessels.

third-party administrator (TPA) (1) entity that processes health care claims and performs related business functions for a health plan; the TPA might contract with a health care clearinghouse to standardize data for claims processing.

third-party payer (1) see health plan.

thoracentesis (12) surgical puncture of the chest wall with a needle to obtain fluid from the pleural cavity.

thoracoscopy (12) visual examination of the pleural cavity; provides an alternative to open lung or thoracotomy procedures to treat pleural disorders surgically.

thrombectomy (13) surgical removal of a thrombus.

thromboendarterectomy (13) surgical excision of a thrombus and atherosclerotic inner lining from an obstructed artery.

thymus (13) produces T lymphocytes, which are important to the body's immune function.

tibia (12) larger of the two lower leg bones.

tibial plateau (12) lower portion of the femur, which articulates with the tibia.

tissue approximation (11) method of replacing sutures with material or substance (e.g., surgical glue), which facilitates enhanced cosmetic results and faster healing of defects.

tissue rearrangement (11) defined by anatomic site and size of defect; includes excision of the defect or lesion.

tissue section (17) thin slice of tissue prepared from a block that is examined.

tissue-cultured autograft (11) graft material supplied by laboratories; such grafting is often performed as part of a staged procedure.

tonsils (13) located at the back of the throat; contain lymphoid tissue that helps fight infections.

total mastectomy (11) surgical removal of the entire breast, including the pectoral fascia and a sampling of axillary lymph nodes.

total pneumonectomy (12) removal of the entire lung.

trachea (12) windpipe.

tracheobronchoscopy (12) visual examination of the interior of the trachea and bronchus.

trachoma (15) chronic inflammation of the conjunctiva in which granulations form.

trafficway (4) see public highway.

transfer note (1) documentation when a patient is transferred to another facility; summarizes the reason for admission, current diagnoses and medical information, and reason for transfer.

transitional pass-through payment (7) temporary additional payment (over and above the OPPS payment) made for certain innovative medical devices, drugs, and biologicals provided to Medicare beneficiaries.

transluminal angioplasty (13) surgical repair of a blood vessel through its lumen (opening).

transluminal atherectomy (13) excision of plaque from inside a blood vessel.

transmyocardial revascularization (TMR) (13) procedure that uses a high-powered laser to create small channels in the heart muscle to increase blood supply to the myocardium.

transpedicular approach (15) performed through and inside the pedicle (segment between transverse process and vertebral body) of a thoracic vertebra to access a thoracic disk.

transport accident (4) any accident involving a device designed primarily for, or being used at the time primarily for, conveying people or goods from one place to another.

transposition of great vessels (13) congenital reversal of the aorta and pulmonary artery.

transurethral resection of the prostate (TURP) (14) resection of the prostate gland via transurethral approach using an electrosurgical device.

transurethral ureteroscopic lithotripsy (14) procedure in which a cystoscope is inserted through the urethra into the bladder and a ureteroscope is passed into the ureters.

transverse plane (16) horizontally divides the body into superior and inferior portions.

treatment volume determination (16) region within the body to which radiation therapy is directed.

triage (6) organized method of identifying and treating patients according to urgency of care required.

triangle symbol (8) symbol (▲) located to the left of CPT codes that identifies revised code descriptions.

TRICARE (19) military health plan that covers active duty and retired members of the uniformed services and their dependents.

triple option plan (19) health plan that is offered as a single insurance plan or as a joint venture among two or more third-party payers.

truncus arteriosus (13) congenital malformation in which just one artery arises from the heart to form the aorta and pulmonary artery.

trust the index (3) concept that inclusion terms listed in the Tabular List of Diseases are not meant to be exhaustive and that additional terms found *only* in the Index to Diseases (but not in the Tabular List of Diseases) may also be assigned to a code.

tube pericardiostomy (13) insertion of a tube for drainage or specimen collection.

tunneled (13) implanted.

tunneled catheter (10) *see* internal catheter.

turbinates (12) bony plates covered by spongy mucosa with curved margins; there are three turbinates on each side of the nasal vestibule: inferior, middle, and superior.

tympanoplasty (15) repair or reconstruction of the eardrum.

tympanostomy (15) *see* myringotomy.

type 1 diabetes mellitus (4) a condition in which patient's body is unable to produce insulin.

type 2 diabetes mellitus (4) a condition in which patient's body is unable to properly use insulin produced.

type of service (TOS) (9) refers to the kind of health care services provided to patients, including critical care, consultation, initial hospital care, subsequent hospital care, and confirmatory consultation.

U

UB-04 (1) standard claim submitted by health care institutions to payers for inpatient and outpatient services.

ultrasonography (16) *see* ultrasound.

ultrasound (16) high-frequency sound waves that bounce off internal organs and create echoes; the echo pattern is displayed on the ultrasound machine monitor.

unbundling (1) reporting multiple codes to increase reimbursement when a single combination code should be reported.

uncertain behavior (4) subsequent morphology or behavior that cannot be predicted based on the submitted specimen; the tissue appears to be in transition, and the pathologist cannot establish a definitive diagnosis.

undermining (11) process of using a surgical instrument to separate skin and mucosa from its underlying stroma so that the tissue can be stretched and moved to overlay a defect.

Uniform Ambulatory Care Data Set (UACDS) (6) established by the federal government as a standard data set for ambulatory care facility records.

Uniform Hospital Discharge Data Set (UHDDS) (5) established by the federal government to define data collected for inpatient hospitalizations.

unit/floor time (9) amount of time the provider spends at the patient's bedside and at management of the patient's care on the unit or floor.

unlisted procedure (8) code assigned when the provider performs a procedure or service for which there is no CPT code.

unlisted service (8) *see* unlisted procedure.

unspecified hypertension (4) ICD-9-CM subcategory assigned when the provider does not document benign or malignant type hypertension, likely because the provider has the mistaken impression that a "benign" condition is limited or minor in nature.

unspecified nature (4) neoplasm is identified, but the results of pathology examination are not available; thus, there is no indication as to histology or nature of the tumor.

upcoding (1) reporting codes that are not supported by documentation in the patient record for the purpose of increasing reimbursement.

upper GI endoscopy (14) direct visualization of the esophagus and the stomach.

uptake (16) absorption by a tissue of a substance, material, or mineral and its permanent or temporary retention.

ureter (14) tube that conveys urine from each kidney to the urinary bladder; there are two ureters.

ureterolithotomy (14) surgical removal of stones from the ureter.

urethra (14) muscular tube that discharges urine from the urinary bladder to the outside of the body.

urethrocystoscopy (10) visualization of urethra and urinary bladder.

urethroplasty (14) surgical repair of the urethra.

urinary bladder (14) hollow organ that serves as a reservoir for urine until it passes from the body (via urination).

urinary system (14) consists of the kidneys, ureters, urinary bladder, and urethra.

uroflowmetry (14) measures the amount of urine that flows from the urinary bladder per second.

uvea (15) eye's vascular layer, which includes the choroid, ciliary body, and iris.

V

V code (ICD-9-CM) (2) reported for patient encounters when a circumstance other than disease or injury is documented; V codes are located in a supplementary classification in the ICD-9-CM Tabular List of Diseases.

vaginal birth after cesarean (VBAC) (15) planned vaginal birth after previous cesarean section.

value (ICD-10-PCS) (5) characters (individual letters and numbers) assigned to each of seven unique hierarchies (positions), which construct a valid ICD-10-PCS code.

valvular atresia (13) valve failure to develop properly; completely closed at birth.

valvular heart disease (13) abnormality or dysfunction of one or more of the heart's four valves (aortic, mitral, pulmonary, and tricuspid).

valvular prolapse (13) condition in which two valvular flaps do not close properly, resulting in backflow of blood.

valvular regurgitation (13) backflow of blood because one or more cardiac valves closes improperly.

valvular stenosis (13) narrowing of one or more cardiac valves.

valvuloplasty (13) open-heart surgery during which the surgeon removes the damaged valve and replaces it with a prosthetic, homograft or allograft, stented, or stentless valve.

valvulotomy (13) open heart surgery in which an incision is made into a valve to repair valvular damage.

varicocele (15) abnormal dilation of the veins of the spermatic cord in the scrotum.

vas deferens (15) tube that carries spermatozoa from the testis.

vascular family (13) group of vessels that is accessed by the same first-order vessel and is supplied by the same primary branch from the aorta.

venipuncture (17) puncture of a vein with a needle for the purpose of drawing blood; most common method of collecting blood specimens.

venography (16) X-ray of a vein after injection of contrast material.

venous anomaly (13) associated with systemic veins and pulmonary veins, and includes conditions such as cor triatriatum, pulmonary vein stenosis, Scimitar syndrome, supravalvar mitral ring, and total anomalous pulmonary venous return (TAPVR).

venous valve transposition (13) surgical procedure performed to treat chronic deep venous insufficiency.

ventricular assist device (VAD) (13) provides temporary support for the heart by substituting for left or right heart function.

very low birth weight (9) 1500–2500 grams.

view (16) patient's position in relation to the camera during radiographic procedures.

visceral arteries (13) supply blood to the intestines, liver, and spleen.

visual evoked potential (VEP) test (18) stimulation of the eye using the checkerboard or flash technique to monitor the patient's response.

volvulus (14) twisting or displacement of the intestines, causing obstruction.

V-Y-plasty (11) procedure whereby, after surgical creation of a V-shaped incision, the edges of the incision are drawn together and sutured, converting the incision to a Y shape.

W

wage index (19) adjusts payments to account for geographic variations in hospitals' labor costs.

watercraft (4) any device for transporting passengers or goods on the water.

wedge (16) treatment beam-modifying device that acts to change the beam intensity profile.

wedge resection (12) surgical removal of a portion of lung that is less than a segment.

Whipple procedure (14) surgical removal of the pancreas, duodenum, bile duct, and stomach with reconstruction.

workers' compensation (19) state-mandated insurance program that reimburses health care costs and lost wages if an employee suffers a work-related disease or injury.

W-plasty (11) surgical trimming of both edges of a wound or defect into the shape of a W or multiple Ws.

X

xenograft (11) surgical transplantation of tissue from a different species.

X-ray (16) radiographic visualization or imaging of internal body structures using low-dose high-energy radiation.

X-ray beam (16) consists of invisible electromagnetic energy waves that are emitted from a radiation machine and used to produce images and treat disease.

Z

Z code (ICD-10-CM) (2) reported for patient encounters when a circumstance other than disease or injury is documented; Z codes are located in Chapter 21 of the ICD-10-CM Tabular List of Diseases and Injuries.

Z-plasty (11) making a surgical incision along with two additional incisions, one above and another below, creating a Z formation.

Index

Inpatient ICD-9-CM (or ICD-10-CM/PCS) Coding

Uniform Hospital Discharge Data Set (UHDDS) Definitions

Assign ICD-9-CM (or ICD-10-CM/PCS) codes in accordance with UHDDS definitions and CMS' *Official Guidelines for Coding and Reporting, Official ICD-10-CM Guidelines for Coding and Reporting,* and/or *Official ICD-10-PCS Guidelines for Coding and Reporting.*

Principal Diagnosis	<ul><li>That condition established after study to be chiefly responsible for occasioning the admission of the patient to the hospital for care.</li><li>The phrase *after study* requires review of the entire inpatient record to determine the clinical reason for admission.</li><li>The circumstances of admission that impact selection of the principal diagnosis include the patient's:<ul><li>chief complaint.</li><li>signs and symptoms on admission. (The above are documented on the history and physical examination.)</li></ul></li><li>If selection of the principal diagnosis is unclear, query the physician and make sure the results of the query are corroborated by supporting documentation in the patient record.</li><li>ICD-9-CM (or ICD-10-CM) coding conventions take precedence over official coding guidelines when determining the principal diagnosis.</li><li>Codes for symptoms, signs, and ill-defined conditions from ICD-9-CM Chapter 16 (or ICD-10-CM Chapter 18) are not reported as the principal diagnosis when a related definitive diagnosis has been established.</li><li>When two or more interrelated conditions (e.g., diseases located in the same ICD-9-CM or ICD-10-CM chapter and manifestations associated with a certain disease) potentially meet the definition of principal diagnosis, either condition may be sequenced first unless the circumstances of the admission, the therapy provided, or the ICD-9-CM (or ICD-10-CM) index or tabular list indicates otherwise.</li><li>When two or more diagnoses *equally* meet the criteria for principal diagnosis as determined by one or more of the following, any one of the diagnoses may be reported as the principal diagnosis:<ul><li>Circumstances of admission</li><li>Diagnostic workup and/or therapy provided</li><li>Alphabetic index, tabular list, or other coding guidelines do not provide sequencing direction</li></ul></li><li>When two or more contrasting or comparative diagnoses are documented as *either/or* (or similar terminology), they are coded as if the diagnoses were confirmed. The diagnoses are sequenced according to the circumstances of the admission. If no determination can be made as to which diagnosis should be principal, either diagnosis may be sequenced first.</li><li>When a symptom or symptoms are followed by contrasting/comparative diagnoses, the symptom code is sequenced first. The contrasting/comparative diagnoses are coded as other (additional) diagnoses, defined below.</li><li>When inpatient treatment was not carried out due to unforeseen circumstances, the principal diagnosis is that condition established after study to be chiefly responsible for occasioning the admission of the patient to the hospital for care.</li><li>When inpatient admission is for treatment of a complication resulting from surgery or other medical care, sequence the complication code as principal diagnosis. (In ICD-9-CM, when the complication is classified to the 996–999 code series and the code lacks the necessary specificity in describing the complication, an additional code for the specific complication is assigned.)</li></ul>

(continues)

	• If the principal diagnosis documented at the time of discharge is qualified as probable, suspected, likely, questionable, possible, or still to be ruled out, code the condition as if it existed or was established. The basis for this guideline is the diagnostic work-up, arrangements for further work-up or observation, and initial therapeutic approach that correspond most closely with the established diagnosis.
Other (Additional)	• **All conditions that coexist at the time of admission, that develop subsequently, or that affect the treatment received and/or the length of stay.** • Diagnoses related to an earlier episode that have no bearing on the current hospital stay are not coded. • A comorbidity is a condition that coexists at the time of admission (e.g., diabetes mellitus, hypertension, or asthma). • A complication is a condition that occurs during the course of the inpatient hospital episode (e.g., fractured hip resulting from fall while gait training, postoperative infection, or hospital-acquired staphylococcus infection). • Diagnoses included in the list documented on the discharge summary or the face sheet in the patient record are ordinarily coded. However, some providers document diagnoses for resolved conditions or chronic diagnoses and status post procedures from previous admissions that have no bearing on the current inpatient stay. Such conditions are not coded. However, family and personal history codes are reported as secondary codes *if* the historical condition or family history impacts current care or influences the patient's treatment. • Abnormal findings (e.g., ancillary tests such as laboratory, X-ray, pathologic, and other diagnostic results) are not coded unless the provider documents their clinical significance. If the ancillary test findings are outside the normal range and the attending provider has ordered other tests to evaluate the condition or prescribed treatment, it is appropriate to ask the provider whether the abnormal finding should be added.
Principal Procedure (*not* required for Medicare coding)	• The principal procedure is (1) performed for definitive treatment rather than for diagnostic or exploratory purposes (2) necessary to treat a complication (3) most closely related to the principal diagnosis.
Other Significant Procedure(s)	• Carry an operative or anesthetic risk, require highly trained personnel, or require special facilities or equipment.
Long-Term Care Coding (e.g., Nursing Facility)	• The UHDDS definition of principal diagnosis for long-term care (e.g., nursing home) is **that condition established after study to be chiefly responsible for occasioning the admission of the patient to the hospital for care or continued residence in the nursing facility.** • Do not assign codes to qualified (uncertain) diagnoses (e.g., probable, possible, and rule out). (These diagnoses are coded for inpatient stays at short-term, acute, long-term care, and psychiatric *hospitals* only.) • Do not assign codes to signs and/or symptoms *except when* a definitive diagnosis has not been established or documented in the patient record.

 Note:

Do not confuse a long-term care facility with a long-term (acute) care hospital. A long-term care facility is a nursing facility, such as a skilled nursing facility, an intermediate care facility, or a nursing home. The definitions and guidelines located at left apply. A long-term (acute) care hospital provides acute care, and acute care hospital definitions and guidelines (located in previous sections) apply.

Outpatient ICD-9-CM (or ICD-10-CM) Coding

Diagnostic Coding and Reporting Guidelines for Outpatient Services—Hospital-Based and Physician Office

First-Listed Condition	• The diagnosis, condition, problem, or other reason for encounter/visit documented in the patient record to be chiefly responsible for the services provided. • The first-listed condition is determined in accordance with ICD-9-CM coding conventions (or rules) as well as general and disease-specific coding guidelines.
ICD-9-CM (or ICD-10-CM) Tabular List	• The appropriate code or codes from the ICD-9-CM (or ICD-10-CM) tabular list must be assigned to identify diagnoses, symptoms, conditions, problems, complaints, or other reason(s) for the encounter/visit.
Accurate Reporting of ICD-9-CM (or ICD-10-CM) Diagnosis Codes	• For accurate reporting of ICD-9-CM (or ICD-10-CM) diagnosis codes, the documentation should describe the patient's condition, using terminology that includes specific diagnoses as well as symptoms, problems, or reasons for the encounter. There are ICD-9-CM (or ICD-10-CM) codes to describe all of these.
Reason for Encounter	• In ICD-9-CM, codes 001.0 through 999.9 will frequently be used to describe the reason for the encounter. In ICD-10-CM, codes A00.0 through T88.9, Z00–Z99.8 are used to identify diagnoses, symptoms, conditions, problems, complaints or other reason(s) for the encounter/visit. • These codes classify diseases and injuries (e.g., infectious and parasitic diseases; neoplasms; and symptoms, signs, and ill-defined conditions).
Signs and Symptoms	• Codes that describe symptoms and signs, as opposed to definitive diagnoses, are acceptable for reporting purposes when the physician has not documented an established diagnosis or confirmed diagnosis. • ICD-9-CM Chapter 16 (Symptoms, Signs, and Ill-defined Conditions, 780.0–799.9) (or ICD-10-CM, Symptoms, Signs and Abnormal Clinical and Laboratory Findings, Not Elsewhere Classified, R00–R99) contains many, but not all, codes for symptoms. Some symptom codes are located in other ICD-9-CM or ICD-10-CM chapters, which can be found by properly using the ICD-9-CM or ICD-10-CM indexes.
Factors Influencing Health Status and Contact with Health Services (ICD-9-CM V Codes) (or ICD-10-CM Z codes)	• ICD-9-CM (or ICD-10-CM) provides codes to deal with encounters for circumstances other than a disease or an injury. The ICD-9-CM Supplementary Classification of Factors Influencing Health Status and Contact with Health Services (V01.0–V89) contains codes for occasions when circumstances other than a disease or an injury are recorded as diagnosis or problems. (In ICD-10-CM, Chapter 21 contains codes for Factors Influencing Health Status and Contact with Health Services.) • Coding guidelines require the assignment of an additional code that identifies the underlying condition (e.g., abnormality of gait) when rehabilitation ICD-9-CM codes V57.1–V57.9 (or ICD-10-CM code Z51.89) are reported as the first-listed code on an insurance claim. • Certain ICD-9-CM V codes (or ICD-10-CM Z codes) can be reported as a first-listed or additional diagnosis for outpatient care. • If a third-party payer or Medicare administrative contractor denies a claim that contains a ICD-9-CM V code, contact your regional CMS office or the HIPAA enforcement office (which is located at CMS) for resolution.
Level of Detail in Coding	• ICD-9-CM diagnosis codes contain three, four, or five digits. (ICD-10-CM codes contain three, four, five, or six characters. Some codes require a seventh character, and for codes that do not contain 6 characters, a placeholder "x" is used to fill in the empty characters.) • Codes with three digits are included in ICD-9-CM as the heading of a category of codes that may be further subdivided by the assignment of fourth and/or fifth digits, which provide greater specificity. In ICD-10-CM, codes with three characters as the heading of a category of codes may be further subdivided by assigning fourth, fifth, sixth, and seventh characters to provide greater specificity. • In ICD-9-CM, a three-digit code is to be assigned only if it is not further subdivided. (In ICD-10-CM, a three-character code is assigned only if it is not further subdivided.) • In ICD-9-CM, where fourth-digit subcategories and/or fifth-digit subclassifications are provided, they must be assigned. (In ICD-10-CM, where fourth-, fifth-, and sixth-character subcategories and/or seventh-character codes are provided, they must be assigned.) • A code is invalid if it has not been coded to the full number of digits (or characters) required for that code.

(continues)

Diagnostic Coding and Reporting Guidelines for Outpatient Services—Hospital-Based and Physician Office (continued)

Sequencing ICD-9-CM (or ICD-10-CM) Diagnosis Codes	• Report first the ICD-9-CM (or ICD-10-CM) code for the diagnosis, condition, problem, or other reason for encounter/visit shown in the medical record to be chiefly responsible for the services provided. • Then report additional codes that describe any coexisting conditions that were treated or medically managed or that influenced the treatment of the patient during the encounter. • In some cases, the first-listed diagnosis may be a symptom when a diagnosis has not been established (confirmed) by the physician.
Qualified Diagnoses	• Do not code diagnoses documented as probable, suspected, questionable, rule out, or working diagnosis, which are considered qualified diagnoses. Instead, code condition(s) to the highest degree of certainty for that encounter/visit, such as symptoms, signs, abnormal test results, or other reasons for the visit. • Qualified diagnoses are a necessary part of the hospital and office chart until a specific diagnosis can be determined. Although qualified diagnoses are routinely coded for hospital inpatient admissions and reported on the UB-04 claim, CMS specifically prohibits the reporting of qualified diagnoses on the CMS-1500 claim submitted for outpatient care. CMS regulations permit the reporting of patient's signs and/or symptoms instead of the qualified diagnoses.
Chronic Diseases	• Chronic diseases treated on an ongoing basis may be coded and reported as many times as the patient receives treatment and care for the condition(s).
Code All Documented Conditions That Coexist	• Code all documented conditions that coexist at the time of the encounter/visit and that require or affect patient care treatment or management. • Do not code conditions that were previously treated and that no longer exist. • History codes may be reported as secondary codes if the historical condition or family history has an impact on current care or influences treatment.
Encounter for Diagnostic Services	• For patients receiving diagnostic services only during an encounter/visit, report first the diagnosis, condition, problem, or other reason for encounter/visit that is documented in the medical record as being chiefly responsible for the outpatient services provided during the encounter/visit (the first-listed diagnosis). • Codes for other diagnoses (e.g., chronic conditions) may be reported as additional diagnoses. • For outpatient encounters for diagnostic tests that have been interpreted by a physician and for which the final report is available at the time of coding, code any confirmed or definitive diagnoses documented in the interpretation. Do not code related signs and symptoms as additional diagnoses.
Encounter for Therapeutic Services	• For patients receiving therapeutic services only during an encounter/visit, sequence first the diagnosis, condition, problem, or other reason for encounter/visit shown in the medical record to be chiefly responsible for the outpatient services provided during the encounter/visit. • Assign codes to other diagnoses (e.g., chronic conditions) that are treated or medically managed or that would affect the patient's receipt of therapeutic services during this encounter/visit. (The only exception to this rule is when the reason for admission/encounter is for chemotherapy, radiation therapy, or rehabilitation. For these services, the appropriate V code (ICD-9-CM) or Z code (ICD-10-CM) for the service is listed first and the diagnosis or problem for which the service is being performed is reported second.)
Encounter for Preoperative Evaluations	• For patients receiving preoperative evaluations only, assign and report first the appropriate subclassification ICD-9-CM code located under subcategory V72.8, Other Specified Examinations, to describe the pre-op consultations. (In ICD-10-CM, report first the appropriate code from subcategory Z01.8, Encounter for other specified special examinations, Z01.810–Z01.818). • Assign an additional code for the condition that describes the reason for the surgery. • Also assign additional code(s) to any findings discovered during the preoperative evaluation.
Ambulatory Surgery (or Outpatient Surgery)	• For ambulatory surgery (or outpatient surgery), assign a code to the diagnosis for which the surgery was performed. If the postoperative diagnosis is different from the preoperative diagnosis when the diagnosis is confirmed, assign a code to the postoperative diagnosis instead (because it is more definitive).
Routine Outpatient Prenatal Visits	• For routine outpatient prenatal visits when no complications are present, report ICD-9-CM code V22.0 (Supervision of normal first pregnancy) or ICD-9-CM V22.1 (Supervision of other normal pregnancy) as the first-listed diagnosis. In ICD-10-CM, report an appropriate code from category Z34 (Encounter for supervision of normal pregnancy). • Do not report the ICD-9-CM codes V22.0 or V22.1 in combination with ICD-9-CM Chapter 11 codes.

CPT Coding

CPT Index	
Organization of CPT Index	• Organized by alphabetical main terms printed in boldface.
	• The main terms represent procedures or services, organs, anatomic sites, conditions, eponyms, or abbreviations. The main term may be followed by indented terms that modify the main term; these are called *subterms*.
	• The CPT index organizes procedures and services according to the following:
	○ Procedure or service (e.g., arthroscopy)
	○ Organ or other anatomic site (e.g., ankle)
	○ Condition (e.g., wound)
	○ Synonyms (e.g., finger joint or intercarpal joint)
	○ Eponyms (e.g., Billroth I or II)
	○ Abbreviations (e.g., EKG)
	• To locate a CPT code, review patient record documentation to locate the service and/or procedure performed and then the main term in the index (located in the back of the coding manual).
Boldfaced Type	• Main terms in the CPT index are printed in boldfaced type, along with CPT categories, subcategories, and code numbers.
Cross-Reference Term See	• *See* is a cross-reference that directs coders to an index entry under which codes are listed.
	• No codes are listed under the original *See* cross-reference entry.
Single Codes and Code Ranges	• Index code numbers for specific procedures may be represented as a single code number, a range of codes separated by a dash, a series of codes separated by commas, or a combination of single codes and ranges of codes.
	• All listed codes should be investigated before a code is assigned for the procedure or service.
Inferred Words	• To save space in the CPT Index when subterms are referenced, inferred words (e.g., *of*) *are* used.
CPT Appendices	
Appendix A	• Contains a list of CPT modifiers and detailed descriptions.
	• Place a marker at the beginning of Appendix A because you will refer to it often.
Appendix B	• Contains annual CPT coding changes, which include added, deleted, and revised CPT codes.
	• Carefully review Appendix B of your current CPT manual because it will serve as the basis for updating interoffice documents and billing tools.
Appendix C	• Contains clinical examples for codes found in the E/M section of CPT.
Appendix D	• Contains a list of add-on codes that are identified throughout CPT with a ✚ symbol.
	• An add-on code is reported when another procedure is performed in addition to the primary procedure during the same operative session.
	• Modifier -51 (multiple procedures) is *not* added to add-on codes.
Appendix E	• Contains a list of codes that are exempt from modifier -51 reporting rules.
	• These codes are identified throughout CPT with the forbidden (⊘) symbol.
Appendix F	• Contains a list of codes that are exempt from modifier -63.
Appendix G	• Contains a summary of CPT codes that include moderate (conscious) sedation and that are identified throughout CPT with a bull's-eye (⊙) symbol.
	• This means that providers who report moderate (conscious) sedation codes should not report a code from 99143–99150 for that encounter.
Appendix H	• Contains an alphabetical index of performance measures by clinical condition or topic.
Appendix I	• Contains genetic testing modifiers.
Appendix J	• Contains an electrodiagnostic medicine listing of sensory, motor, and mixed nerves that are reported for motor and nerve studies codes 95900, 95903, and 95904, respectively.
	• There is also a table that indicates the "type of study and maximum number of studies" generally performed for needle electromyogram (EMG), nerve conduction studies, and other EMG studies. (The AMA's *CPT Changes 2008: An Insider's View* calls this table a "... tool to detect outliers.")
Appendix K	• Contains a list of codes that are pending FDA approval but that have been assigned a CPT code. In the CPT manual, these codes are preceded by the flash symbol (↗).
Appendix L	• Contains a list of vascular families that is intended to assist in the selection of first-, second-, third-, and beyond third-order branch arteries.
Appendix M	• Summary of deleted CPT codes and descriptions that are crosswalked to current CPT codes.
	• Contains a list of CPT codes that do not appear in numeric order.

(*continues*)

CPT Appendices (*continued*)	
Appendix N	• 99391
	• 90473
	• 90712

CPT Symbols	
Bullet (•)	• Identifies new procedures and services added to CPT.
Triangle (▲)	• Identifies a code description that has been revised.
Horizontal Triangles (► ◄)	• Surrounds revised guidelines and notes. (This symbol is *not* used for revised code descriptions.)
Semicolon (;)	• To save space in CPT, some code descriptions are not printed in their entirety next to a code number. Instead, the entry is indented and the coder must refer back to the common portion of the code description that is located before the semicolon.
	• The common portion begins with a capital letter, and the abbreviated (or subordinate) descriptions are indented and begin with lowercase letters.
Plus (✚)	• Identifies add-on codes (Appendix D of CPT) for procedures that are commonly, but not always, performed at the same time and by the same surgeon as the primary procedure.
	• Parenthetical notes, located below add-on codes, often identify the primary procedure to which add-on codes apply.
Forbidden (Prohibitory) (⊘)	• Identifies codes that are exempt from modifier -51.
	• They are **reported** in addition to other codes, but they are not classified as add-on codes.
Bull's-Eye (⊙)	• Indicates a procedure that includes moderate (conscious) sedation.
	• CPT Appendix G includes a list of CPT codes that include moderate (conscious) sedation.
Flash (↗)	• Indicates codes that classify products that are pending FDA approval but have been assigned a CPT code.
Hollow circle (○)	• Indicates a reinstated or recycled code in Category III of CPT.
Number (#)	• Indicates out-of-numerical sequence codes.
Green reference symbol (⟳)	• Indicates coder should refer to *CPT Assistant* and/or *CPT Changes: An Insider's View*.
Red reference symbol (⟳)	• Indicates coder should refer to *Clinical Examples in Radiology* quarterly newsletter.

Coding with CPT	
Subsections, Categories, and Subcategories	• CPT Category I codes are organized according to six sections that are subdivided into subsections, categories, and subcategories.
	• CPT Evaluation & Management Section uses categories and subcategories language (instead of subsections and categories).
Guidelines	• Guidelines are located at the beginning of each CPT section.
	• Guidelines define terms and explain the assignment of codes for procedures and services located in a particular section.
	• Guidelines in one section do not apply to another section in CPT.
Notes and Descriptive Qualifiers	• Codes located in CPT subsections, headings or categories, or subheadings or subcategories are clarified by notes and descriptive qualifiers.
CPT Modifiers	• Modifiers clarify services and procedures performed by providers.
	• Although the CPT code and description remain unchanged, modifiers indicate that the description of the service or procedure performed has been altered.
	• CPT modifiers are reported as two-digit numeric codes added to the five-digit category I or five-character category II and III CPT code.
	• HCPCS level II modifiers are reported as two-digit alphanumeric characters added to the five-digit CPT code. (CPT and HCPCS level II modifiers are also added to the five-character HCPCS level II code.)
National Correct Coding Initiative (NCCI)	• The Centers for Medicare & Medicaid Services (CMS) created NCCI edits to promote national correct coding methodologies and to control the improper assignment of codes that result in inappropriate reimbursement of Medicare Part B claims.
	• NCCI edits are used to process Medicare Part B claims.
	• NCCI coding policies are based on the:
	○ Analysis of standard medical and surgical practice.
	○ Coding conventions included in CPT.
	○ Coding guidelines developed by national medical specialty societies (e.g., CPT Advisory Committee, which contains representatives of major medical societies).
	○ Local and national coverage determinations.
	○ Review of current coding practices.